JOHN BROWN

JOHN BROWN
1800—1859;

𝔄 𝔅iography 𝔉ifty 𝔜ears 𝔄fter

BY

OSWALD GARRISON VILLARD
A.M., Litt.D.

WITH ILLUSTRATIONS

GLOUCESTER, MASS.
PETER SMITH
1965

Copyright, 1910, by Oswald Garrison Villard
Reprinted 1966 by Permission of
Henry H. Villard

TO THE MEMORY OF
MY BELOVED AND HIGH-MINDED FATHER
HENRY VILLARD

PREFACE

"THERE never was more need for a good life of any man than there was for one of John Brown," wrote Charles Eliot Norton in March, 1860, in expressing in the *Atlantic Monthly* his dissatisfaction with the first biography of the leader of the attack upon Harper's Ferry. Twenty-six years later, in the same publication, Mr. John T. Morse, Jr., wrote that "so grand a subject cannot fail to inspire a writer able to do justice to the theme; and when such an one draws Brown, he will produce one of the most attractive books in the language. But meantime the ill-starred 'martyr' suffers a prolongation of martyrdom, standing like another St. Sebastian to be riddled with the odious arrows of fulsome panegyrists." Since 1886 there have appeared five other lives of Brown, the most important being that of Richard J. Hinton, who in his preface gloried in holding a brief for Brown and his men.

The present volume is inspired by no such purpose, but is due to a belief that fifty years after the Harper's Ferry tragedy, the time is ripe for a study of John Brown, free from bias, from the errors in taste and fact of the mere panegyrist, and from the blind prejudice of those who can see in John Brown nothing but a criminal. The pages that follow were written to detract from or champion no man or set of men, but to put forth the essential truths of history as far as ascertainable, and to judge Brown, his followers and associates in the light thereof. How successful this attempt has been is for the reader to judge. That this volume in no wise approaches the attractiveness which Mr. Morse looked for, the author fully understands. On the other hand, no stone has been left unturned to make accurate the smallest detail; the original documents, contemporary letters and living witnesses have been examined in every quarter of the United States. Materials never before utilized have been drawn upon, and others discovered whose existence has heretofore been unknown. Wherever sources have been quoted, they have been cited *verbatim et literatim*, the effort being to reproduce exactly spelling, capitalization and punctuation, particularly in John Brown's own letters, which have suffered hitherto from free-hand editing. If at times, particularly in dealing with the Kansas period of John Brown's life, it may seem as if there were a superfluity of detail, the explanation is that already a hundred myths have attached themselves to John Brown's name which often hinge upon a date, or the possibility of his presence at a given place at a given hour. Over some of them have raged long and bitter controversies which give little evidence of the softening effects of time.

So complex a character as John Brown's is not to be dismissed by merely likening him to the Hebrew prophets or to a Cromwellian Roundhead, though both parallels are not inapt; and the historian's task is made heavier since nearly all characterizations of the man have been at one extreme or another. But there is, after all, no personality so complex that it cannot be tested by accepted ethical standards. To do this sincerely, to pass a deliberate and accurate historical judgment, to bestow praise and blame without favor or sectional partisanship, has been the author's endeavor.

His efforts have been generously aided by the friends, relatives and associates of John Brown, whenever approached, and by many others who pay tribute, by their deep interest, to the vital force of John Brown's story. It would be impossible to mention all here. But to Salmon Brown and Henry Thompson is due the writer's ability to record for the first time the exact facts as to the happenings on the Pottawatomie, and the author is also particularly indebted to Jason Brown, Miss Sarah Brown, Mrs. Annie Brown Adams, and Mrs. John Brown, Jr. Thomas Wentworth Higginson, F. B. Sanborn, Horace White, George B. Gill, Luke F. Parsons, Mrs. Emma Wattles Morse, Mrs. Rebecca Spring, Jennie Dunbar (Mrs. Lee Garcelon) and R. G. Elliott, of Lawrence, are a few of the survivors of John Brown's time who have aided by counsel or reminiscence. Special thanks are due to George W. Martin, Miss Adams and Miss Clara Francis, of the Kansas Historical Society, for valuable assistance, as well as to the Historical Department of Iowa, the Western Reserve Historical Society, the Department of Archives and History of the Virginia State Library, the Pennsylvania and Massachusetts Historical Societies, and to Louis A. Reese, lately of Brown University, who generously placed at the author's disposal the manuscript of his admirable work on "The Admission of Kansas as a State." Mrs. S. L. Clark, of Berea, Kentucky, Mrs. S. C. Davis, of Kalamazoo, Miss Leah Taliaferro, of Gloucester County, Virginia, Miss Mary E. Thompson, Mrs. Ellen Brown Fablinger, Mrs. J. B. Remington, of Osawatomie, Kansas, Dr. Thaddeus Hyatt, the family of the late Joshua R. Giddings, Dr. Frederick C. Waite, of Western Reserve University, Dr. Henry A. Stevens, of Boston, Cleon Moore, of Charlestown, West Virginia, William E. Connelley, of Topeka, Kansas, and Edwin Tatham, of New York, have placed the author under special obligations here gratefully acknowledged.

Dr. Thomas Featherstonhaugh, of Washington, has been most generous in giving the author free access to his rich collections of books, pamphlets and photographs, and they have been largely drawn upon. The author also gladly records his lasting indebtedness to Miss Katherine Mayo, whose journeys in search of material for his use have covered a period of more than two years and many thousands of miles. But for her judgment, her tact and skill, and her enthusiasm for the work, it could hardly have approached its present comprehensiveness. Finally, without the approval, generous aid and encouragement of his uncle, Francis Jackson Garrison, of Boston, the author could not have undertaken or completed this book.

NEW YORK, August 1, 1910.

CONTENTS

I. THE MOULDING OF THE MAN 1
II. "HIS GREATEST OR PRINCIPAL OBJECT" 42
III. IN THE WAKE OF THE WAR CLOUD 79
IV. THE CAPTAIN OF THE LIBERTY GUARDS 112
V. MURDER ON THE POTTAWATOMIE 148
VI. CLOSE QUARTERS AT BLACK JACK 189
VII. THE FOE IN THE FIELD 225
VIII. NEW FRIENDS FOR OLD VISIONS 267
IX. A CONVENTION AND A POSTPONEMENT 310
X. SHUBEL MORGAN, WARDEN OF THE MARCHES . . . 346
XI. THE EVE OF THE TRAGEDY 391
XII. HIGH TREASON IN VIRGINIA 426
XIII. GUILTY BEFORE THE LAW 467
XIV. BY MAN SHALL HIS BLOOD BE SHED 511
XV. YET SHALL HE LIVE 558
NOTES 591
APPENDIX
    A. "Sambo's Mistakes," by John Brown 659
    B. John Brown's Covenant for the Enlistment of his Volunteer-Regular Company, August, 1856 661
    C. John Brown's Requisition upon the National Kansas Committee, for an outfit for his proposed Company, January, 1857 664
    D. John Brown's Peace Agreement 665
    E. Shubel Morgan's Company 666
    F. John Brown's Wills 667
    G. John Avis's Affidavit as to his Association with John Brown 670
    H. A Chronology of John Brown's Movements from his departure for Kansas, August 13, 1855, to his death, December 2, 1859 672
    I. John Brown's Men at Arms 678

CONTENTS

BIBLIOGRAPHY
  I. Manuscript Collections 689
  II. Biographies 689
  III. Magazine and Other Articles 690
  IV. Authorities on the Kansas Period 694
  V. Books, Pamphlets and Periodicals relating particularly to the Harper's Ferry Raid 697
  VI. Reports of Important Meetings dealing with the Raid and Execution 700
  VII. Important Speeches and Addresses on John Brown, as separately published 701
  VIII. Some Typical Sermons 702
  IX. Biographies, Autobiographies and Reminiscences of Correlated or Important Persons 703
  X. Local and General Histories with Special References to John Brown and his Men 707
INDEX 711

ILLUSTRATIONS

JOHN BROWN . . . . *Frontispiece*
    From a painting by Nahum B. Onthank in the Boston Athenæum. This was based on a photograph from life by J. W. Black, of Boston, in May, 1859, and the artist had the benefit of the criticisms and suggestions of Mrs. Brown, John Brown, Jr., and other members of the family. Onthank made two paintings, one of which was purchased by Thaddeus Hyatt and presented by him to the People of Hayti, through President Geffrard. The second was purchased by subscription and given to the Athenæum.

OWEN BROWN, FATHER OF JOHN BROWN 14
    From a photograph

FOUR OF JOHN BROWN'S SONS IN LATER YEARS: JOHN BROWN, JR., JASON, SALMON AND OWEN BROWN 166
    From photographs.

THE OSAWATOMIE BATTLEFIELD, LOOKING TOWARD THE RIVER 244
    From a photograph.

PART OF THE BLACK JACK BATTLEFIELD 244
    From a photograph.

MAIN STREET OF TABOR, IOWA 268
    From a photograph.

THE PUBLIC SQUARE AT TABOR 268
    From a photograph.

JOHN BROWN 282
    Photogravure from a daguerreotype (1857?) kindly loaned by Mrs. Charles Fairchild, Cambridge, Mass.

HOUSE OF REV. JOHN TODD, TABOR, IOWA 316
    Where John Brown stored his guns and ammunition.
    From a photograph.

THE SCHOOL-HOUSE AT SPRINGDALE 316
    Where the Mock Legislature met.
    From a photograph.

JOHN BROWN 338
    Photogravure from a photograph taken (probably in June, 1858) by J. J. Hawes, of Boston

JOHN BROWN'S NORTHERN SUPPORTERS: GEORGE L. STEARNS, GERRIT SMITH, FRANK B. SANBORN, THOMAS WENTWORTH HIGGINSON, THEODORE PARKER, SAMUEL G. HOWE . . . 396
    From photographs.

xiv   ILLUSTRATIONS

THE HOUSE AT KENNEDY FARM, MARYLAND 404
   From a woodcut.

THE CABIN ACROSS THE ROAD FROM THE FARMHOUSE . . . 404
   From a woodcut.

SCHOOL-HOUSE GUARDED BY JOHN E. COOK 404
   From a woodcut.

MAP OF THE HARPER'S FERRY REGION 414

GENERAL VIEW OF HARPER'S FERRY, WEST VIRGINIA . . . 428
   From a photograph kindly furnished by the Baltimore & Ohio Railroad.

HARPER'S FERRY: THE FIGHTING AT THE ENGINE-HOUSE . 444
   From a woodcut.

VICTIMS OF HARPER'S FERRY: JOHN H. KAGI, AARON D. STEVENS, OLIVER BROWN AND WATSON BROWN 448
   From photographs.

THE STORMING OF THE ENGINE-HOUSE 452
   From a woodcut.

THE PRISON, GUARD-HOUSE, AND COURT-HOUSE, CHARLESTOWN, WEST VIRGINIA 486
   From a woodcut.

ONE OF JOHN BROWN'S LETTERS FROM PRISON 542
   Fac-simile from the original in possession of Mr. Theodore P. Adams, of Plymouth, Mass.

JOHN BROWN'S LAST PROPHECY 554
   Fac-simile from the original in possession of Mr. Frank G. Logan, of Chicago.

THE NORTH ELBA FARMHOUSE 562
   From a photograph.

JOHN BROWN'S GRAVE 562
   From a photograph.

NOTE. — The Osawatomie and Black Jack battlefields, the Todd house at Tabor, and school-house at Springdale, were photographed by the author in 1908; the views of Kennedy Farm, of the fighting at Harper's Ferry, and of the Charlestown Court-House and Prison are reproduced from woodcuts in *Frank Leslie's Illustrated Paper* (New York) for October and November, 1859; the portraits of Owen Brown (father of John Brown), Kagi, Stevens, Oliver and Watson Brown, and the views of the Farmhouse and Grave at North Elba, are from photographs kindly lent by Dr. Thomas Featherstonhaugh, of Washington, D. C.; the portraits of John Brown, Jr., and of Salmon and Owen Brown are from photographs belonging to Mrs. John Brown, Jr., Put-in Bay, Ohio; that of Jason Brown, from a photograph made in 1908, for Mr. Earl E. Martin, editor of the Cleveland *Press*.

JOHN BROWN

*All through the conflict, up and down
Marched Uncle Tom and Old John Brown,
 One ghost, one form ideal;
And which was false and which was true,
And which was mightier of the two,
The wisest sibyl never knew,
 For both alike were real.*

O. W. HOLMES.

JOHN BROWN

CHAPTER I

THE MOULDING OF THE MAN

RED ROCK, IOWA 15th July, 1857

MR. HENRY L. STEARNS.

MY DEAR YOUNG FRIEND I have not forgotten my promise to write you; but my constant care, & anxiety: have obliged me to put it off a long time. I do not flatter myself that I *can* write anything that will very much interest you: but have concluded to send you a short story of a certain boy of my acquaintance: & for convenience & shortness of name, I will call him John. This story will be mainly a naration of follies and errors; which it is to be hoped *you may avoid;* but there is one thing connected with it, which will be calculated to encourage any young person to persevereing effort; & that is the degree of success *in accomplishing his objects* which to a great extent marked the course of this boy throughout my entire acquaintance with him; notwithstanding his moderate capacity; & still more moderate acquirements.

John was born May 9th, 1800, at Torrington, Litchfield Co. Connecticut; of poor but respectable parents: a decendant on the side of his Father of one of the company of the Mayflower who landed at Plymouth 1620. His mother was decended from a man who came at an early period to New England from Amsterdam, in Holland. Both his Fathers and his Mothers Fathers served in the war of the revolution: His Father's Father; died in a barn at New York while in the service, in 1776.

I cannot tell you of anything in the first Four years of John's life worth mentioning save that at that *early age* he was tempted by Three large Brass Pins belonging to a girl who lived in the family & *stole them.* In this he was detected by his Mother; & after having a full day to think of the wrong;

received from her a thorough whipping. When he was Five years old his Father moved to Ohio; then a wilderness filled with wild beasts, & Indians. During the long journey which was performed in part or mostly with an *Oxteam;* he was called on by turns to assist a boy Five years older (who had been adopted by his Father & Mother) & learned to think he could accomplish *smart things* in driving the Cows; & riding the horses. Sometimes he met with Rattle Snakes which were very large; & which some of the company generally managed to kill. After getting to Ohio in 1805 he was for some time rather afraid of the Indians, & of their Rifles; but this soon wore off: & he used to hang about them quite as much as was consistent with good manners; & learned a trifle of their talk. His father learned to dress Deer Skins, & at 6 years old John was installed a young Buck Skin. He was perhaps rather observing as he ever after remembered the entire process of Deer Skin *dressing;* so that he could at any time dress his own leather such as Squirel, Raccoon, Cat, Wolf or Dog Skins; and also learned to make Whip Lashes: which brought him some change at times; & was of considerable service in many ways. At Six years old John began to be quite a rambler in the wild new country finding birds and Squirrels and sometimes a wild Turkeys nest. But about this period he was placed in the School of *adversity;* which my young friend was a most necessary part of his early training. You may *laugh* when you come to read about it; but these were *sore trials* to John: whose earthly treasures were very *few, & small*. These were the beginning of a severe but *much needed course* of dicipline which he afterwards was to pass through; & which it is to be hoped has learned him before this time that the Heavenly Father sees it best to take all the little things out of his hands which he has ever placed in them. When John was in his Sixth year a poor *Indian boy* gave him a Yellow Marble the first he had ever seen. This he thought a great deal of; & kept it a good while; but at last *he lost it* beyond recovery. *It took years to heal the wound* & I *think* he cried at times about it. About Five months after this he caught a young Squirrel tearing off his tail in doing it; & getting severely bitten at the same time himself. He however held on *to the little bob tail Squirrel;* & finally got him perfectly tamed, so that he almost idolized his pet. *This too he lost;* by its wandering away; or by getting killed; & for a year or two John was *in mourning;* and looking at all the Squirrels he could see to try & discover Bobtail, *if possible.* I must not neglect to tell you of a verry *bad & foolish* habbit to which John was somewhat addicted. I mean *telling lies;* generally to screen himself from blame; or from punishment. He could not well endure to be reproached; & I now think had he been oftener encouraged to be entirely frank; *by making frankness a kind of atonement* for some of his faults; he would not have been so often guilty in after life of this fault; nor have been obliged to struggle *so long* with *so mean* a habit.

John was *never quarrelsome;* but was *excessively* fond of the *hardest & roughest* kind of plays; & could *never get enough* [of] them. Indeed when for a short time he was sometimes sent to School the opportunity it afforded to wrestle, & Snow ball & run & jump & knock off old seedy Wool hats; offered to him almost the only compensation for the confinement, & restraints of school. I need not tell you that with such a feeling & but little chance of going to school *at all:* he did not become much of a schollar. He would always choose to stay at home & work hard rather than be sent to school; & during the Warm season might generally be seen *barefooted & bareheaded:* with Buck skin Breeches suspended often with one leather strap over his shoulder but sometimes with Two. To be sent off through the wilderness alone to very considerable distances was particularly his delight; & in this he was often indulged so that by the time he was Twelve years old he was sent off more than a Hundred Miles with companies of cattle; & he would have thought his character much injured had he been obliged to be helped in any such job. This was a boyish kind of feeling but characteristic however. At Eight years old, John was left a Motherless boy which loss was complete & permanent for notwithstanding his Father again married to a sensible, inteligent, and on many accounts a very estimable woman; yet he never *adopted her in feeling;* but continued to pine after his own Mother for years. This opperated very unfavorably uppon him; as he was both naturally fond of females; &, withall, extremely diffident; & deprived him of a suitable connecting link between the different sexes; the want of which might under some circumstances, have proved his ruin. When the war broke out *with England:* his Father soon commenced furnishing the troops with beef cattle, the collecting & driving of which afforded him some opportunity for the chase (on foot) of wild steers & other cattle through the woods. During this war he had some chance to form his own boyish judgment of *men & measures:* & to become somewhat familiarly acquainted with some who have figured before the country since that time. The effect of what he saw during the war was to so far disgust him with Military affairs that he would neither train, *or drill;* but paid fines; & got along like a Quaker untill his age finally has cleared him of Military duty. During the war with England a circumstance occurred that in the end made him a most *determined Abolitionist:* & led him to declare, *or Swear: Eternal war* with Slavery. He was staying for a short time with a very gentlemanly landlord since a United States Marshall who held a slave boy near his own age very active, inteligent, and good feeling; & to whom John was under considerable obligation for numerous little acts of kindness. *The Master* made a great pet of John: brought him to table with his first company; & friends; called their attention to every little smart thing he *said or did:* & to the fact of his being more than a hundred miles from home with a company of cattle alone; while the *negro boy* (who was fully if not more than his equal) was badly clothed, poorly fed; *& lodged in cold weather;* & beaten before his eyes with Iron Shovels or any other thing that came first to hand. This brought John to reflect on the wretched, hopeless condition, of *Fatherless & Motherless* slave *children:* for such children have neither Fathers or Mothers to protect & provide for them. He sometimes would raise the question *is God their Father?* At the age of Ten years, an old friend induced him to read a little history, & offered him the free use of a good library; by; which he acquired some taste for reading: which formed the principle part of his early education: & diverted him in a great measure from bad company. He by this means grew to be verry fond of the company & conversation of old & inteligent persons. He never attempted to dance in his life; nor did he ever learn to know *one* of a pack of *Cards* from *another*. He learned nothing of Grammer; nor did he get at school so much knowledge of comm[on] Arithmetic as the Four ground rules. This will give you some general idea of the first Fifteen years of his life; during which time he became very strong & large of his age & ambitious to perform the full labour of a man; at almost any kind of hard work. By reading the lives of great, wise & good men their sayings, and writings; he grew to a dislike of vain & frivolous *conversation & persons;* & was often greatly obliged by the kind manner in which older & more inteligent persons treated him at their houses: & in conversation; which was a great relief on account of his extreme bashfulness. He very early in life became ambitious to excel in doing anything he undertook to perform. This kind of feeling I would recommend to all young persons both *Male & female:* as it will certainly tend to secure admission to the company of the more inteligent; & better portion of every community. By all means endeavour to excel in some laudable pursuit. I had like to have forgotten to tell you of one of John's misfortunes which set rather hard on him while a young boy. He had by some means *perhaps* by gift of his Father become the owner of a little Ewe Lamb which did finely till it was about Two Thirds grown; & then sickened and died. This brought another protracted *mourning season:* not that he felt the pecuniary loss so heavily: for that was never his disposition; but so strong & earnest were his attachments. John had been taught from earliest childhood to "fear God & keep his commandments;" & though quite skeptical he had always by turns felt much serious doubt as to his future well being; & about this time became to some extent a convert to Christianity & ever after a firm believer in the divine authenticity of the Bible. With this book he became very familiar, & possessed a most unusual memory of its entire contents.

Now some of the things I have been *telling of;* were just such as I would recommend to you: & I would like to know that you had selected these out; & adopted them as part of your own plan of life; & I wish you to have *some deffinite plan.* Many seem to have none; & others never to stick to any that they do form. This was not the case with John. He followed up with *tenacity* whatever he set about so long as it answered his general purpose: & hence he rarely failed in some good degree to effect the things he undertook. This was so much the case that he *habitually expected to succeed* in his undertakings. With this feeling *should be coupled;* the consciousness that our plans are right in themselves.

During the period I have named, John had acquired a kind of ownership to certain animals of some little value but as he had come to understand that the *title of minors* might be a little imperfect: he had recourse to various means in order to secure a more *independent;* & perfect right of property. One of these means was to exchange with his Father for something of far less value. Another was by trading with other persons for something his Father had never owned. Older persons have sometimes found difficulty with *titles*.

From Fifteen to Twenty years old, he spent most of his time working at the Tanner & Currier's trade keeping Bachelors hall; & he officiating as Cook; & for most of the time as foreman of the establishment under his Father. During this period he found much trouble with some of the bad habits I have mentioned & with some that I have not told you of: his conscience urging him forward with great power in this matter: but his close attention to *business;* & success in its management; together with the way he got along with a company of men, & boys; made him quite a favorite with the serious & more inteligent portion of older persons. This was so much the case; & secured for him so many little notices from those he esteemed; that his vanity was very much fed by it: & he came forward to manhood quite full of self-conceit; & self-confident; notwithstanding his *extreme* bashfulness. A younger brother used sometimes to remind him of this: & to repeat to him *this expression* which you may somewhere find, "A King against whom there is no rising up." The habit so early formed of being obeyed rendered him in after life too much disposed to speak in an imperious or dictating way. From Fifteen years & upward he felt a good deal of anxiety to learn; but could only read & studdy a little; both for want of time; & on account of inflammation of the eyes. He however managed by the help of books to make himself tolerably well acquainted with common Arithmetic; & Surveying; which he practiced more or less after he was Twenty years old. At a little past Twenty years led by his own inclination & *prompted also* by his Father, he married a *remarkably plain;*

THE MOULDING OF THE MAN

but neat industrious & economical girl; of excellent character; earnest piety; & good practical common sense; about one year younger than himself. This woman by her mild, frank, *& more than all else;* by her very consistent conduct; acquired & ever while she lived maintained a most powerful; & good influence over him. Her plain but kind admonitions generally had the right effect; without arousing his haughty obstinate temper. John began early in life to discover a great liking to fine Cattle, Horses, Sheep, & Swine; & as soon as circumstances would enable him he began to be a practical *Shepherd: it being* a calling for which *in early life* he had a kind of *enthusiastic longing:* together with the idea that as a business it bid fair to afford him the means of carrying out his greatest or principal object. I have now given you a kind of general idea of the early life of this boy; & if I believed it would be worth the trouble; or afford much interest to any good feeling person; I might be tempted to tell you something of his course in after life; or manhood. I do not say that I *will do it.*

You will discover that in using up my *half sheets to save paper;* I have written Two pages, so that one does not follow the other as it should. I have no time to write it over; & but for unavoidable hindrances in traveling I can hardly say when I should have written what I have. With an honest desire for your best good, I subscribe myself,

Your Friend,
J. BROWN.

P. S. I had like to have forgotten to acknowledge your contribution in aid of the cause in which I serve. God Allmighty *bless you;* my son.

J. B.

In this simple, straightforward, yet remarkable narrative [1] John Brown of Osawatomie and Harper's Ferry outlined his youth to the thirteen-year-old son of his benefactor, George Luther Stearns. It remains the chief source of knowledge as to the formative period of one who for a brief day challenged the attention of a great nation, compelled it to heart searchings most beneficent in their results, and through his death of apparent ignominy achieved not only an historical immortality, but a far-reaching victory over forces of evil against which he had dared and lost his life. John Brown, a Puritan in the austerity of his manner of living, the narrowness of his vision and the hardships he underwent, came of a family of pioneers. But he was not of those adventurers into the wilderness who are content, after carving out with the axe a little kingdom for themselves, to rule peacefully to the end of their days. His early adventures, his contact with the American aborigines, his boyish experiences with the flotsam and jetsam of armies in the field, all bred up in him a restlessness not characteristic of the original Puritans, but with him a dominant feature of his whole career. To John Brown life from the outset meant incessant strife, first against unconquered nature, then in the struggle for a living, and finally in that effort to be a Samson to the pro-slavery Philistines in which his existence culminated. "I expect nothing but to endure hardness," he wrote to a friend in an attempt to enlist him in the Harper's Ferry enterprise. It would have been surprising, indeed, had he expected anything else, for to nothing else was he accustomed. From the "school of adversity" in which he was placed, as he wrote, at the age of six years, he graduated only at his death.

The picture which John Brown drew of his experiences in the early settlement of Ohio, just a century ago, was by no means over-colored. The American public is apt to think that pioneering was difficult only in New England in the seventeenth century, in Kentucky and Tennessee in the eighteenth, and in the far West in the nineteenth. But the story of the settlement of the Middle West reads in no essential differently, if perhaps less dramatically, than the better known extensions of the ever-expanding frontier. There were the same hardships, the same facing of death by disease or, at times, in ambush, the same exhausting toil, the same terrifying loneliness, the same never-ending battling against relentless elements. This struggle for existence Brown's family shared with those fellow emigrants who ventured with them into the Ohio forest primeval, destroying it with great labor, driving the wolves, panthers and bears from their rude cabin doors, and subsisting, penuriously enough, on the wild game of the woods and such scanty crops as the squirrels, blackbirds, raccoons and porcupines permitted to grow to maturity among

THE MOULDING OF THE MAN

the stumps of the cleared tracts. As late as 1817 there were bears who helped themselves in this district of Ohio to the settlers' pigs, and in 1819, in a great hunt, no less than one hundred deer and a dozen and a half bears and wolves were corralled and shot down by the hunters of four townships [2] around Hudson. These wild animals of the forest not only supplied meat for the scantily furnished larders, but skins wherewith to make clothing and caps for others besides John Brown. Farms were bought and paid for in hard and bitter experiences. The roads were but a pretence, rough log bridges led across the swamps, and the only means of transportation which could survive long were the roughest sleds, ox-carts and stone-boats. In the summer of 1806, the year after John Brown arrived, there were, according to an old settler,[3] frosts every month, "no corn got ripe, and the next spring we had to send to the Ohio river for seed corn to plant." This was the beginning of the "school of adversity" for John Brown, and the next summer's session was one of the hardest that the pioneers ever stored away in their recollections. But not the worst; that John Brown thought the summer of 1817, which he described as a period " of *extreme scarcity* of not *only money*, but of the greatest distress for want of provisions known during the nineteenth century."[4] He and three others were destitute "between the seaside and Ohio," but they had learned not to be afraid of "spoiling themselves by hard work," and they managed to keep body and soul together. Even in times of plenty, provisions were hard to get, and were best purchased by labor of those fortunate enough to have an abundance, the rate being three and a half pounds of pork for a day's service. Fortunately, the neighboring Indians, Senecas, Ottawas and Chippewas, were well behaved and friendly, rarely sinning, but often sinned against. It was in this atmosphere so friendly to the steeling of muscles, the training of eyes and hands, the enduring of arduous labor and the cultivation of the primal virtues, that John Brown grew up to self-reliant manhood. Under these conditions was his character moulded and forged, until there emerged a man of singular natural force, direct of speech, earnest of purpose, and usually resolute, with the frontiersman's ability to shift readily from one occupation to another and an incurable readiness to wander.

"Although the time when a man comes into the world and the place where he appears are in certain ways important and may well begin his story," declared Professor N. S. Shaler in his all too brief autobiography, "the really weighty question concerns his inheritances and the conditions in which they were developed. That he brings with him something that is in a measure independent of all his progenitors, a certain individuality which makes him distinct in essentials from like beings he succeeds, is true — vastly true; but the way he is to go is, to a great extent, shaped by those who sent him his life."[5] The conditions of early life in Ohio were precisely those for which John Brown's inheritances should best have fitted him. He came of simple, frugal, hard-working folk, deeply interested in religion and the church into which they sent some of their best, and, above all, imbued with a strong love of liberty. His father's father, who died "in a barn in New York" while a captain of the Ninth Company, or Train-band 9, in the Eighteenth Regiment of the Connecticut Colony, likewise bore the name of John Brown, and on the other side the tradition of arms came down to him from his maternal grandfather. The Revolutionary Captain John Brown was the son and grandson of men of the same name, likewise citizens of Connecticut, the senior of whom, born February 4, 1694, was the son of Peter Brown, of Windsor, Connecticut. Through this Peter Brown, John Brown of Osawatomie, like many another of his patronymic, believed himself descended from Peter Brown of the goodly Mayflower company, — erroneously, for modern genealogical research has proved that the Mayflower Peter Brown left no male issue.[6] But the possession of an actual Mayflower progenitor is not indispensable to the establishment of a long line of ancestry, and so Peter Brown of Windsor, born in 1632, can surely lay claim to being among the earliest white colonists on this continent, — early enough at least to make it plain that in John Brown of Osawatomie's veins ran the blood of solid middle-class citizens, the bone and sinew of the early colonies, as of the infant American republic.

It is not related of any of the colonial John Browns that they were especially distinguished. When Captain John Brown, of the Eighteenth Connecticut, gave his life for the independence of his country, he left a wife and ten children at West Simsbury, now Canton, Connecticut, and a posthumous son came into the world soon after his father perished, the oldest child, a daughter, being then about seventeen. "The care and support of this family," wrote his son Owen many years later, "fell mostly on my mother. The laboring men were mostly in the army. She was one of the best mothers; active and sensible. She did all that could be expected of a mother; yet for the want of help we lost our crops, then our cattle, and so became poor." In the "dreadful hard winter" of 1778-79 they were deprived of nearly all their sheep, cattle and hogs, and the spring found them in the greatest distress. This was the "school of adversity" in which John Brown's father was trained, he also beginning at the age of six the lessons in hardship which made of him a sturdy, vigorous, honest pioneer, and hardened his body for its long existence of eighty-five years. In the autobiography [7] which he wrote at his children's request, when nearly eighty years of age, Owen Brown summed up his career in this sentence: "My life has been of little worth, mostly filled up with vanity." In this harsh judgment his neighbors would not have concurred. Owen Brown stood well with everybody, even with those who had no liking for his militant son. Yet this sentence gives a key to the piety which filled Owen's life, and explains, too, whence the son received his own strong religious tendency. In Owen Brown's last letter to his son, penned only six weeks before his death, occurs this wish: " I ask all of you to pray more earnestly for the salvation of my soul than for the life of my body, and that I may give myself and all I have up to Christ and honer him by a sacrifise of all we have." [8]

Similar pious expressions are to be found in almost every one of John Brown's letters to the members of his family. Their salvation, their clinging to the orthodox Congregational faith to which he held so tenaciously, their devotion to the Scriptures, — these are things which ever concerned him. Indeed, the resemblance of John Brown to his father appears in many ways, not the least in their respective biographies. Owen's is as characteristic a document as the one which begins this volume. In it he relates his wanderings as an apprentice and later as a full-fledged shoemaker and tanner.

But if he moved about a good deal in the struggle to support himself, learn a trade and relieve the heavily burdened mother of his support, when he finally reached Ohio, in 1805, Owen Brown remained in one locality for fifty-one years, until his death, May 8, 1856. Owen received, he narrates, considerable instruction from the Rev. Jeremiah Hallock, the minister of Canton, who was a connection of many of the Browns, hiring out to this worthy pastor for six months in 1790. In the spring of 1791 the family fortunes were again in the ascendant. One brother, John by name, was for many years an honored citizen of New Hartford, Connecticut; another, Frederick, after serving in the Connecticut Legislature during the War of 1812, moved to Wadsworth, Medina County, Ohio, where he was long a highly respected county judge. Of this Frederick's sons, two became successful physicians and one a minister.

In the fall of 1790, Owen Brown became acquainted with his future wife, Ruth Mills, "who was the choice of my affections ever after, although we were not married for more than two years." He was, at this time, it appears, "under some conviction of sin but whether I was pardoned or not God only knows — this I know I have not lived like a Christian." The beginning of his married life Owen Brown described thus:

"Feb 13th 1793 I was married to Ruth Mills in March begun to keep House and here I will say was the begining of days with me. I think our good Minister felt all the anxiety of Parent that we should begin wright, he gave us good counsel and I have no doubts with a praying spiret, here I will say never had any Person such an assendence over my conduct as my wife, this she had without the lest appearence of userpation, and if I have been respected in the World I must ascribe it more to her than to any other Person. We begun with but very little property but with industry and frugality, which gave us a very comfortable seport and a small increas. We took in children to live with us very soon after we began to keep House.* Our first Child was born at Canton June 29th 1794 a son we called Salmon he was a very thrifty forward Child, we lived in Canton about two years, I worked at Shoemaking, Tanning and Farming we made Butter and Chees on a small scale and all our labours turned to good account. we had great calls [cause] for thanksgiven, we were at peace with all our Neighbours, we lived in a rented House and I seamed

---

* Levi Blakeslee, early adopted by Owen and Ruth Brown, became the head of a highly respected Ohio family.

THE MOULDING OF THE MAN 13

to be called to build or moove. I thought of the latter and went directly to Norfolk as I was there acquainted and my wife had kept a school there one summer. the People of Norfolk incoureged me and I bought a small Farm with House and Barn, I then sold what little I had, and made a very suddon move to Norfolk, we found Friends in deed and in kneed. I there set up Shoemaking and tanning, hired a journaman did a small good business and gave good sattisfaction. . . . In Feb, 1799 I had an oppertunity to sell my place of Norfolk which I did without any consultation of our Neighbours who thought they had some clame on my future servises as they had been very kind and helpfull and questioned weather I had not been hasty but I went as hastely to Torrington and bought a place, all though I had but very little acquantence there. I was very quick on the moove we found very good Neighbours I was somewhat prosperus in my business. In 1800, May 9th John was born one hundred years after his Great Grand Father nothing very uncommon. . . . my determination to come to Ohio was so strong that I started with my Family in Comp[any] [with] B Whedan Esq and his Family all though out of health on the 9th of June 1805 with an Ox teem through Pennsylvania here I will say I found Mr. Whedan a very kind and helpfull Companion on the Road. we arived at Hudson on the 27 of July and was received with many tokens of kindness we did not come to a land of idleness neither did I expect it. Our ways were as prosperious as we could expect. I came with a determination to help to build up and be a help in the seport of religion and civil Order. We had some hardships to undergo but they appear greater in history than they were in reality. I was often calld to go into woods to make devisians of lands sometimes 60 or 70 Miles [from] home and be gone some times two week and sleep on the ground and that without injery. When we came to Ohio the Indians were more numorous than the white People but were very friendly and I beleave were a benifet rather than injery there [were] some Persons that seamed disposed to quarel with the Indians but I never had, they brought us Venson Turkeys Fish and the like sometimes wanted bread or meal more than they could pay for, but were faithfull to pay there debts. . . . My business went on very well and was somewhat prosperious in most of our conceirns friendly feelings were manfest the company that called on us was of the best kind the Missionarus of the Gospel and leading men traviling through the Cuntry call on us and I become acquaint with the business People and Ministers of the Gospel in all parts of the Reserve and some in Pennsilvany 1807 Feb 13th Fredrick my 6th Son was born I do not think of anything to notice but the common blessings of health peace and prosperity for which I would ever acknowledge with thanksgiven I had a very pleasent and orderly family untill December 9th 1808 when all my earthly prospects appeared to be blasted My beloved Wife gave birth to an Infent Daughter that died in a few ours as my wife expresed [it] had a short pasage through time My wife followed in a few ours after these were days of affliction I was left with five (or six, including Levi Blakesley, my adopted son) small Children the oldes but a little one 10 years old this sean all most makes my heart blead now these were the first that were ever buried in ground now ocupide at the Centre of Hudson."

Owen Brown was subsequently married twice, his second wife being Sallie Root, and his third Mrs. Lucy Hinsdale. He was the father of ten sons and six daughters, the most distinguished of them, next to John Brown, being Salmon Brown, who died in New Orleans September 6, 1833, a lawyer of standing, the editor of the New Orleans *Bee*, and a politician bitterly opposed to President Jackson and his methods. Owen Brown was early in life an Abolitionist, and in a quaint manuscript left the story of his becoming one. A Mr. Thomson, a Presbyterian or Congregational minister of Virginia, brought his slaves to New Canaan, Connecticut, for safety during the Revolution. In 1797 or 1798 he returned to move them back to Virginia, at which they rebelled, one married slave running away. The owner declared that he would carry the wife and children back to bondage without him. The situation was complicated by Mr. Thomson's having been asked to preach. He was finally requested not to appear in the pulpit; the matter then came before the assembled church, and there was a vigorous debate in Mr. Thomson's presence. What happened is thus told by Owen Brown:[9]

"An old man asked him if he could part man and wife contrary to their minds. Mr. T. said he married them himself, and did not enjoin obedience on the woman. He was asked if he did not consider marriage to be an institution of God; he said he did. He was again asked why he did not do it in conformity of God's word. He appeared checked, and only said it was the custom. He was told that the blacks were free by the act of the Legislature of Connecticut; he said he belonged to another State, and that Connecticut had no controle over his property. I think he did not get his property as he call[ed] it. Ever since, I have been an Abolitionist; I am so near the end of life I think I shall die an Abolitionist."

And this he did, as consistently as he had lived a voluntary agent of the Underground Railroad, never failing to aid a fugitive slave who appealed to him for food and forwarding toward the North Star.[10] Thus his son John had every incentive to follow in his footsteps. How deeply Owen Brown felt

OWEN BROWN
Father of John Brown

THE MOULDING OF THE MAN

appears from his withdrawal of his long-sustained and active interest in Western Reserve College, when that institution refused admission to a colored man.[11] He then became a supporter of Oberlin College, of which he was a trustee from November 24, 1835, until August 28, 1844.[12]

Of Ruth Mills, John Brown's mother, it is to be noted, besides her premature death when her famous son was but eight years old, that her ancestry goes as far back in the colonial records as does her husband's. The Mills family is descended from Peter Wouter van der Meulen, of Amsterdam, whose son Peter settled in Windsor, Connecticut. He refused to Anglicize his name, but his son Peter, born 1666, became plain Peter Mills. Of the next generation, the Rev. Gideon Mills graduated from Yale College, but died before the Revolution, in which his son, Lieutenant Gideon Mills, served well. When fifty-one years of age, in 1800, the latter removed to Ohio, five years before his daughter Ruth and her husband, Owen Brown, followed him into that wild territory. Through his maternal grandmother, Ruth Humphrey, John Brown of Osawatomie was connected with a well-known divine, the Rev. Luther Humphrey, and was cousin also to the Rev. Dr. Heman Humphrey, sometime president of Amherst College, as well as to the Rev. Nathan Brown, long a missionary in India and Japan. There was thus on both sides a family connection of which John Brown might well be proud, that warranted, in later Kansas days, his introduction to a committee of the Massachusetts Legislature as a representative of the best type of old New England citizenship. It is undeniable, too, that the influence of his ancestry was a powerful one throughout Brown's entire life. In some respects, as has been often suggested, he seems to have belonged to the eighteenth rather than to the nineteenth century, if not to a still earlier one. It can hardly be doubted that, had he been brought face to face with his ancestors, there would have been discovered a marked resemblance in character, if not in looks; for the main traits which marked the frugal, sober-minded, religious, soil-tilling farmer-folk of New England were all in that descendant who, so far as history records, was the first member of the family to go to what is usually considered an infamous death, as he was the first American to be hanged for treason.

Of John Brown's boyhood but few incidents remain to be told; his early maturity is, perhaps, partly a reason for this. For boys who at twelve assume such duties and responsibilities as were his, there is but a brief childhood. He seems to have had to his credit or discredit the usual number of rough pranks. There is a story that he tried to explode some powder under his step-mother, and that, when his father attempted to punish him for this offence, a sheepskin carefully tucked away in his clothes protected him from the force of the blows. Again, it is variously said that he precipitated his father, or his step-mother, from the hay-mow of the barn to the floor beneath, by placing loose planks over an opening and then enticing the victim across it. But these and even less authenticated stories emanate often from prejudiced sources,[13] and if John Brown was guilty of unduly rough or dangerous horse-play, it is a fact that he was always on the best of terms with his father, as their letters show, and with his step-mother. It is said of him that he was early one of the best Bible teachers available, and therefore in demand in the Sunday Schools of the communities in which he lived. To his steadfast perusal of the Bible is undoubtedly due most of the directness, the clearness and the force of his written English. It was, declared in after years his daughter, Ruth Brown Thompson,[14] his favorite volume, "and he had such a perfect knowledge of it that when any person was reading it, he would correct the least mistake." His range of reading was, however, at no time wide; his taste was for historical works. Franklin's writings, Rollin's Ancient History, Æsop's Fables, Plutarch's Lives, a life of Oliver Cromwell, and one of Napoleon and his Marshals, all had their influence upon him. His Pilgrim's Progress he naturally knew well, and Baxter's Saints' Rest was to him a safe and sure guide to devout Christianity, while the works of Edwards and Witherspoon were always on his shelves. In all his letters, there is hardly a reference to any book save the Bible.

As for John Brown's schooling, as his autobiography records, it was fitful and scanty. The public schools of a newly occupied region are not often of the best. The first one in Hudson was established in 1801, in a log-house near the centre of the Hudson township, and it is probable that John Brown attended this school, as Owen Brown's home was in this vicinity. The Rev. Dr. Leonard Bacon, of New Haven, was a schoolmate of Brown's at Tallmadge, Ohio, in 1808, in a school founded by Bacon's father. An old lady, years afterwards, when Bacon shortly before his death revisited Tallmadge, reminded him of a curious dialogue at a school exhibition between himself as William Penn and John Brown as Pizarro.[15] When a tall stripling, either in 1816 or 1819, Brown revisited Connecticut with his brother Salmon and another settler's son, Orson M. Oviatt, with the idea of going to Amherst College and entering the ministry. During his brief stay in the East, he attended the well-known school of the Rev. Moses Hallock at Plainfield, Massachusetts, and Morris Academy in Connecticut.[16] A son of Mr. Hallock, in 1859, remembered him as a "tall, sedate and dignified young man. He had been a tanner, and relinquished a prosperous business for the purpose of intellectual improvement. He brought with him a piece of sole leather about a foot square, which he himself had tanned for seven years, to resole his boots. He had also a piece of sheepskin which he had tanned, and of which he cut some strips, about an eighth of an inch wide, for other students to pull upon." The schoolmaster confidently tried to snap one of these straps, but in vain, and his son long remembered "the very marked, yet kind, immovableness of the young man's [Brown's] face on seeing his father's defeat." [17] But an attack of inflammation of the eyes put an end to Brown's dream of a higher education, and he returned to Hudson and the tanning business, living in a cabin near the tan-yard, at first keeping bachelor's hall with Levi Blakeslee, his adopted brother. John Brown was early a remarkably good cook, with a strong liking for this part of housekeeping which lasted throughout his life.[18] The neatness of his kitchen was surpassed by that of no housewife, and the pains he took to sweep and sand the floor are still remembered.

It was while he was living thus that there occurred another incident to confirm his opposition to slavery. To John Brown and Levi Blakeslee came a runaway slave begging for aid. He was at once taken into the cabin, where John Brown stood guard over him while Blakeslee, when evening had come, went up to the town for supplies. Suddenly the slave and his Samaritan heard the noise of approaching horses. John Brown motioned to the slave to go out of the window and hide in the brush. This he did. Soon the alarm proved to have been occasioned only by neighbors returning from town, and Brown went out into the dark to look for the negro. "I found him behind a log," he said in telling the story, "and I heard his heart thumping before I reached him. At that I vowed eternal enmity to slavery." [19] Another story of John Brown's kindness of heart probably belongs to this period. His uncle, Frederick Brown, then judge of Wadsworth County, obtained a requisition from Governor Trimble, of Ohio, on the Governor of New York for the arrest of a young horse thief, and gave it to his nephew in Hudson to serve. John Brown found the boy and arrested him. Then Brown managed, because it was a first offence and the boy was repentant, and because the penitentiary would ruin his character, to save him from that fate, and to have him, instead, indentured till his twenty-first year to the man whose horse he stole. He got the neighbors to go bond for the boy's good behavior during the period. This was done, the boy reformed, and died a respected citizen in old age.[20] These and other incidents would seem to show that when John Brown professed religion in 1816 and joined the Congregational Church, to which he was ever after so devoted, he had made up his mind to try to practise as well as to profess the doctrines of Christianity.

Good cook that John Brown was, he had been having his bread baked by Mrs. Amos Lusk, a widow living near by. Soon he decided that it would be better if she moved into his log-cabin with her daughter and took charge of the entire housekeeping, now become serious by reason of the growth of his tanning business and the increase in the number of journeymen and apprentices. The propinquity of the young home-maker and of the "remarkably plain" daughter of Mrs. Lusk led promptly to matrimony. They were married June 21, 1820, when the husband lacked nearly eleven months of being of age. If Dianthe Lusk was plain and rather short in stature, she attracted by her quiet, amiable disposition. As deeply religious as her husband, she was given to singing well, generally hymns and religious songs, was neat and cheerful, and without a marked sense of humor. In the twelve years of

THE MOULDING OF THE MAN 19

their married life, Dianthe gave birth to seven children, dying August 10, 1832, three days after the coming of a son. Of her other six children, five grew to manhood and womanhood, all of marked character and vigorous personality: John Brown, Jr., Jason, Owen, Ruth and Frederick, the last named meeting a cruel death in Kansas in his twenty-sixth year. Of these, Jason alone survives at this writing, at the age of eighty-six. Dianthe Lusk, too, could boast of an old colonial lineage, for her ancestry traced back to the famous Adams family of Massachusetts. There was, however, a mental weakness in the Lusk family which manifested itself early in her married life, as it did in her two sisters.[21] In two of her sons, John Brown, Jr., and Frederick, there was also a disposition to insanity. Devoted as he was to his wife, John Brown ruled his home with a strong hand, in a way that seemed to some akin to cruelty; but his children and an overwhelming mass of evidence prove the contrary. He did not get on well with his brother-in-law, Milton Lusk, who refused to attend the wedding because John Brown the Puritan had asked him to visit his mother and sister on some other day than the Sabbath.[22] They were at no time congenial, though in later years Milton Lusk bore no ill-will to his brother-in-law; yet he always disliked the rigor imposed upon his sister's household. But the Brown children were devoted to both parents, and revered always the memory of their mother. They remembered, too, when symptoms of mental illness appeared, the kindliness and tenderness with which the husband shielded and tended and watched over his wife.

As to his children, John Brown at first believed in the use of the rod, and he was particularly anxious that they should not yield to the "habit of lying" which had worried him so much in his own boyhood. "Terribly severe" is the way his punishments were described, and he made no allowance for childish imaginings. Once when Jason, then not yet four years old, told of a dream he had had and insisted that it was the reality, his father thrashed him severely, albeit with tears in his eyes.[23] But in later years, it is pleasant to record, John Brown, after travelling about the world, came to realize that there were other methods of dealing with children, and softened considerably, even expressing regret for his early theory and practice of punishments. There are instances in number of touching devotion to this or that child; of his sitting up night after night with an ailing infant. Once he hurried to North Elba from Troy on the rumor that smallpox had broken out in a near-by village, in order that he might be on hand to nurse if the scourge entered his family. He nursed several of his children through scarlet fever without medical aid, and in consequence became in demand in other stricken homes in the neighborhood. "Whenever any of the family were sick, he did not often trust watchers to care for the sick ones, but sat up himself and was like a tender mother. At one time he sat up every night for two weeks, while mother was sick, for fear he would oversleep if he went to bed, and the fire would go out, and she take cold. No one outside of his own family can ever know the strength and tenderness of his character," wrote Mrs. Ruth Brown Thompson in her reminiscences of her father. His character was not an unusual one in this respect; the combination of iron discipline with extreme tenderness of heart is often the mark of deep affection and high purpose in men of power and rigid self-control, and so it was with him. Not unnaturally, his children reacted from "the very strict control and Sunday School rules" under which they lived, and used, as Salmon puts it, "to carry on pretty high," as some of the neighbors who still live can tell the tale.

Sabbath in the Brown family had all the horrors of the New England rest day of several generations ago. There were strict religious observances, and there was no playing and no pretence at playing. Visiting was discouraged, as well as receiving visits. The head of the family was not without humor, but as Fowler, the phrenologist, correctly said of him, his jokes were "more cutting than cute." He inclined to sarcasm, and "his words were as sharp as his eyes to those who did not please him." In the final drama at Harper's Ferry, Watson Brown said to his father: "The trouble is, you want your boys to be brave as tigers, and still afraid of you." "And that was perfectly true" is Salmon Brown's confirmation of the remark. Similarly, John Brown wanted his children to be as true as steel, as honest as men and women possibly can be and as truthful, and yet afraid of him. As was often the case, the intense religious training given to his children in the broadening period of the first half of the nineteenth century resulted in a reaction. All his sons were strangers to church-ties. In this their strong feeling in regard to slavery, to which they came naturally from grandfather and father, played a great part. Yet this dislike of slavery was never beaten into them; nor is it true that John Brown ever forced a son into one of his campaigns. It is doubtful if he could often have commanded such strong natures. Dislike of human bondage, as the children grew up, became as much a factor in the family's life as the natural desire for food and clothing and shelter. It was no more assumed than inculcated; they hated it with a hatred greater in some cases than their wish to live. Whatever else may be said of the Brown family life, or of the father as a disciplinarian, it is a fact that the children grew up into honorable men and women, not successful in accumulating worldly goods in any degree, but as illustrative of the homely virtues as their father and their grandfather. Temperate they all of them were, like their father, yet not all or always total abstainers. John Brown himself, though an abstainer after 1829, firmly believed that "a free use of pure wines in the country would do away with a great deal of intemperance, and that it was a good temperance work to make pure wine and use it." [24] For a time two of his sons devoted themselves to grape-growing for wine purposes, until they finally came to have scruples against it.

Of John Brown's early life after his marriage there is, fortunately, a reliable record. James Foreman, one of his journeymen in 1820, wrote down his recollections of his employer shortly after the latter's death in 1859,[25] for the benefit of Brown's first biographer, who did not, however, utilize them.

"It was John Brown's fixed rule," wrote Mr. Foreman, "that his apprentices and journeymen must always attend church every Sunday, and family worship every morning. In the summer of 1824 a journeyman of his stole from him a very fine calfskin. Brown discovered the deed, made the man confess, lectured him at length and then told him he would not prosecute him unless he left his place; but, that, if he did leave, he should be prosecuted to the end of the law.

"The journeyman staid about two months, through fear of prosecution; and in the meantime all hands about the tannery and in the house were strictly forbidden speaking to him, not even to ask a question; and I think a worse punishment could not have been set upon a poor human being than this was to him: But it reformed him and he afterward became a useful man.

"In the fall of the same year his wife was taken sick under peculiar circumstances, and Brown started for the Dr. and some lady friends, from his residence 1½ miles to the centre of Hudson. On his way he espied two men tying up two bags of apples and making ready to put them on their horses. Brown immediately tied his own horse, went to the men and made them empty their apples, own up to the theft, and settle up the matter before he attended to the case of his wife. Such was his strict integrity for honesty and justice."

Once, Mr. Foreman remembered, Brown fell into a discussion with a Methodist minister, who, being flippant and fluent, seemed to talk the tanner down.

"[Brown] afterward commented on the man's manners and said he should like a public debate with him. Soon after the preacher came to enquire whether Brown desired, as was reported, a public debate, and whether, also, if he had said the speaker was 'no gentleman, let alone a clergyman.' Brown replied: 'I did say you were no gentleman. I said more than that, sir.' 'What did you say, sir?' enquired the preacher. 'I said, sir,' replied Brown, 'that it would take as many men like you to make a gentleman as it would take wrens to make a cock turkey!' The public debate, however, came off, conducted in questions and answers, Brown first to ask all his questions, which the other should answer and then the reverse. But John Brown's questions so exhausted and confused his opponent, that the latter retired without opening his side of the debate. . . . So strict was he that his leather should be perfectly dry before sold, that a man might come ten miles for five pounds of sole leather and if the least particle of moisture could be detected in it he must go home without it. No compromise as to amount of dampness could be effected. . . . He was jocose and mirthful, when the conversation did not turn on anything profane or vulgar, and the Bible was almost at his tongue's end. . . . He considered it as much his duty to help a negro escape as it was to help catch a horse thief, and of a new settler . . . [his] first enquiry . . . was whether he was an observer of the Sabbath, opposed to slavery and a supporter of the gospel and common schools; if so, all was right with him; if not, he was looked upon by Brown with suspicion. In politics he was originally an Adams man and afterwards a Whig and I believe a strong one. Yet I do not believe the time ever was that he would have voted for Henry Clay, for the reason that he had fought a duel and owned slaves. . . . His food was always plain and simple, all luxuries being dispensed with and not allowed in his family, and in the year 1830 he rigidly adopted the teetotal temperance principle.

"Hunting, gunning and fishing he had an abhorrence of as learn-

THE MOULDING OF THE MAN 23

ing men and boys to idle away their time and learn them lazy habits, and it was with the greatest reluctance that he would trust a man with a piece of leather who came after it with a gun on his shoulder. . . . He took great pains to inculcate general information among the people, good moral books and papers, and to establish a reading community."

In May, 1825, despite the success of his Hudson tannery and his having built himself a substantial house the year before, John Brown moved his family to Richmond, Crawford County, Pennsylvania, near Meadville, where with noteworthy energy he had cleared twenty-five acres of timber lands, built a fine tannery, sunk vats, and had leather tanning in them all by the 1st of October.[26] The virgin forests and cheap cost of transportation lured him to his new home. Here, like his father at Hudson, John Brown was of marked value to the new settlement at Richmond by his devotion to the cause of religion and civil order. He surveyed new roads, was instrumental in erecting school-houses, procuring preachers and "encouraging everything that would have a moral tendency." It became almost a proverb in Richmond, so Mr. Foreman records, to say of an aggressive man that he was "as enterprising and honest as John Brown, and as useful to the county." This removal of his family gave its young members just such a taste of pioneering as their father had had at Hudson, and was the first of ten migrations under the leadership of their restless head, prior to the emigration to Kansas of the eldest sons in 1854–55. In Richmond the family dwelt nearly ten years, until for business reasons the bread-winner felt himself compelled to return to Ohio.[27]

In the year 1828 John Brown brought into Crawford County the first blooded stock its settlers had ever seen. Being instrumental in obtaining the first post-office in that region, he received this same year the appointment of postmaster from President John Quincy Adams, January 7, serving until May 27, 1835, when he left the State; and there are letters extant bearing his franks as postmaster of Randolph, as the new post-office was called. The first school was held alternately in John Brown's home and that of a Delamater family, connections of Dianthe Lusk, the Delamater children boarding for the winter terms in Brown's home, and the Brown children spending the summer terms at the Delamaters', for a period of four years, only a few other children attending. George B. Delamater, one of the scholars, retained a vivid impression of the early winter breakfasts in the Brown family, "immediately after which Bibles were distributed, Brown requiring each one to read a given number of verses, himself leading; then he would stand up and pray, grasping the back of the chair at the top and inclining slightly forward," which solemn moment, so Salmon Brown remembers, the elder children frequently utilized for playing tricks on one another. Sunday religious exercises were at first held in Brown's barn. Of them Mr. Delamater says, "everything seemed fixed as fate by the inspiring presence of him whose every movement, however spontaneous, seemed to enforce conformity to his ideas of what must or must not be done. . . . He was no scold, did nothing petulantly; but seemed to be simply an inspired paternal ruler; controlling and providing for the circle of which he was the head," — testimony of value as showing that even at this early age Brown had the compelling power of masterful leadership.

Here in Richmond the first great grief came into John Brown's life in the death of a four-year-old son, Frederick, on March 31, 1831, and the demise in August, 1832, of Dianthe Brown and her unnamed infant son who also had such a "short passage through time."[28] Their graves are still to be found near the old, now rebuilt, tannery, and are cared for and protected out of regard for John Brown. Nearly a year later he was married for the second time, to Mary Anne Day,[29] daughter of Charles Day, of Whitehall, New York, who was then a resident of Troy township, Pennsylvania. Her father was a blacksmith, who had been fairly well-to-do, but had lost his property by endorsing notes, so that Mary Day grew up with narrow means and almost no schooling. For a time after the death of Dianthe Brown, Mary's elder sister went to John Brown's as housekeeper, and Mary, presently, was engaged to come there to spin. She was then a large, silent girl, only sixteen years of age. John Brown quickly grew fond of her, perhaps saw the staying powers in her, and one day gave her a letter offering marriage. She was so overcome that she dared not read it. Next morning she found courage to do so, and when she went down to the spring for water for the house, he followed her and she gave him her answer there. A woman of rugged physical health and even greater ruggedness of nature, she bore for her husband thirteen children within twenty-one years, of whom seven died in childhood, and two were killed in early manhood at Harper's Ferry. Besides the lives of the latter, Oliver and Watson, Mary Day Brown made cheerfully and willingly many other sacrifices for the cause to which her husband also gave his life, as will appear later. No one but a strong character could have borne uncomplainingly the hardships which fell to her lot, particularly in her bleak Adirondack home in the later years. But she was as truly of the stuff of which martyrs are made as was her husband — even if she had had less advantages and opportunities for learning and culture than he. If there ever was a family in which the mother did her full share and more of arduous labor, it was this one. Nothing but the complete faith he had in her ability to be both mother and guardian of his flock made possible for John Brown his long absences from home year after year, both when in business and when warring against slavery in Kansas and Virginia. And Mary Day Brown was a woman of few words, even after the catastrophe at Harper's Ferry.

During part of the interval between Dianthe Brown's death and her husband's remarriage, John Brown boarded with Mr. Foreman, who had just married. Even in his first grief, Mr. Foreman remembers, John Brown had a deep interest in the welfare of his neighbors. Others remember Brown as the organizer of an Independent Congregational Society, which came into being on January 11, 1832, its articles of faith being written out in his hand as clerk of the society. It is recalled, too, that besides being postmaster he had for some years the carrying of the mails between Meadville and Riceville, a distance of twenty miles. Politically, he was at this time an Adams man, and he was still as interested in the fugitive slave as he had been in Hudson. There was in the haymow of his barn a roughly boarded room, entered by a trap-door, and ventilated and equipped for the use of escaping slaves. The whole was always so cleverly concealed by hay that a man might stand on the trap-door and yet see no signs of the hiding-place. In striking contrast to John

Brown's later development into a man of disguises, assumed names and many plots, was his dislike of the Masonic orders. He became a member of a lodge while residing either in Hudson or in Richmond, and for a while was an ardent disciple. Then, however, he rebelled and withdrew. "Somewhere," so John Brown, Jr., told the story in after years, "in an historical museum, I think, is the first firearm that father ever possessed. The way he came to get it was this: Father had been a Free Mason for years. You have read about the great excitement over the disappearance of Morgan, who had threatened to expose the secrets of Masonry? Well, father denounced the murder of Morgan in the hottest kind of terms. This was when we lived over in Pennsylvania. Father had occasion to go to Meadville. A mob bent on lynching him surrounded the hotel, but Landlord Smith enabled him to escape through a back entrance. Father then got a sort of pistol that was about half rifle, and he became very adept in its use, killing deer with it on several occasions." [30] It was in September, 1826, that the country was so excited over the anti-Masonic revelations of William Morgan which resulted in his murder.

After just ten years of residence in Richmond, John Brown removed to Franklin Mills, Portage County, Ohio, to go into the tanning business with Zenas Kent, a well-to-do business man of that town. In a letter written to him on April 24, 1835, John Brown thus details the financial distress he found himself in, which no doubt accentuated his desire for a new field of activity: [31]

"Yours of the 14th was received by last Mail. I was disappointed in the extreme not to obtain the money I expected; & I know of no possible way to get along without it. I had borrowed it for a few days to settle up a number of honorary debts which I could not leave unpaid and come away. It is utterly impossible to sell anything for ready cash or to collect debts. I expect Father to come out for cattle about the first of May and I wish you without fail to send it by him. It is now to late to think of sending it by mail. I was intending to turn everything I could into shingles as one way to realize cash in Ohio, before you wrote me about them. 25, dollars of the money I want is to enable me to carry that object into effect...."*

---

* In spelling and punctuation these earlier letters are superior to the later epistles; the handwriting is by this time the familiar one, full of character and strength.

THE MOULDING OF THE MAN 27

The partnership of Kent & Brown was not destined to be of long duration, for the latter had no sooner completed the tannery at Franklin than it was rented by Marvin Kent, a son of the senior partner, even before the departments were ready for operation and the vats in place, so that the business of tanning hides was never actually carried on by the firm.[32] John Brown then secured a contract for the construction of part of the Ohio and Pennsylvania Canal, from Franklin Mills to Akron, during which time he dealt chiefly with the Kents. It was a year later that John Brown began some land speculations which proved quite disastrous and did much to injure his standing and business credit. With a Mr. Thompson he purchased a farm of more than a hundred acres owned by a Mr. Haymaker, which then adjoined Franklin village (now the prosperous town of Kent), believing that the coming of the canal and other changes would make Franklin a great manufacturing town. For this farm there was paid $7000, mostly money borrowed of Heman Oviatt, who had acquired large means as a trader with the Indians, and of Frederick Wadsworth. The farm was quickly plotted by Brown as "Brown and Thompson's addition to Franklin Village." But he was far ahead of his time in this scheme, and within a couple of years the land was foreclosed by Oviatt and Wadsworth. This tract, crossed by three trunk-line railroads, is now of great value, containing as it does an island park, the shops of the Erie Railroad and some large manufactories. The Haymaker house in which Brown lived is still standing. About the same time, John Brown, with twenty-one other prominent men of Franklin, Ravenna and Akron, formed the Franklin Land company, and purchased of Zenas Kent and others the water-power, mills, lands, etc., in both the upper and lower Franklin villages. Through the coöperation of the canal company, the two water-powers were combined midway between the two villages. A new settlement was then laid out between both places, and would undoubtedly have been a successful enterprise, had the canal company lived up to its agreement. Instead, it drew off largely the waters of the Cuyahoga River, ostensibly for canal purposes, but in reality, in the opinion of John Brown and his partners, for the purpose of pushing Akron ahead at the expense of the new village, to which the Brown and Thompson addition was planned before the town itself was well under way.

In these and other schemes John Brown became so deeply involved that he failed during the bad times of 1837, lost nearly all his property by assignment to his creditors, and was then not able to pay all his debts, some of which were never liquidated. His father also lost heavily through him. While he says in his autobiography that he "rarely failed in some good degree to effect the things he undertook," this cannot apply to his business affairs in the 1835 to 1845 period of his life, or even later, but must be taken as referring to those philanthropic or public-spirited undertakings in which he had won a name for himself a short time previous to that story of his life. In 1842 he was even compelled to go through bankruptcy. Naturally, all this greatly damaged Brown's business standing, and created with some people who had lost money through him that doubt of his integrity which so often follows the loss of money through another. But the final verdict in the vicinity of Franklin was summed up recently by the late Marvin Kent. To him Brown was at this early period a man of "fast, stubborn and strenuous convictions that nothing short of a mental rebirth could ever have altered;" a "man of ordinary calibre with a propensity to business failure in whatever he attempted." * There is no allegation of dishonesty, despite the unpaid accounts and protested notes still on the books of Marvin Kent and his father. Heman Oviatt, of Richfield, Ohio, who lent John Brown money and became involved in lawsuits in consequence, testified to his integrity, and so do many others. But there can be no question that after leaving Richmond, Pennsylvania, he was anything but successful in business, and his affairs became so involved as to make it a matter of regret that he could not have devoted himself exclusively to tanning and farming in Richmond. To his son, John Brown, Jr., he in after years explained his misfortunes by saying that these grew out of one root — doing business on credit.[33] "Instead of being thoroughly imbued with the doctrine of pay as you go, I started out in life with

---

* "It is a Brown trait to be migratory, sanguine about what they think they can do, to speculate, to go into debt, and to make a good many failures." — Jason Brown, December 28, 1908.

THE MOULDING OF THE MAN   29

the idea that nothing could be done without capital, and that a poor man must use his credit and borrow; and this pernicious notion has been the rock on which I, as well as many others, have split. The practical effect of this false doctrine has been to keep me like a toad under a harrow most of my business life. Running into debt includes so much evil that I hope all my children will shun it as they would a pestilence." The purchase of four farms on credit seems to have been a chief cause of Brown's collapse.[34] Three of these Franklin farms were said to be worth twenty thousand dollars before the financial crash of 1837.

Brown quitted Franklin Mills in 1837, returning with his family to Hudson, but only for a brief period. He seems to have alternated between the two places until 1841. One of his ventures at this period was breeding race-horses. In 1838 began his long years of travelling about the country. His first recorded visit to New York, after reaching manhood, was on December 5, 1838, when he drove some cattle from Ohio to Connecticut. "My unceasing & anxious care for the present and everlasting welfare of every one of my family seems to be threefold as I get seperated farther and farther from them," he wrote home from the metropolis.[35] On this trip he negotiated for the agency of a New York steel scythes house, and on the 18th of January, at West Hartford, Connecticut, made a purchase of ten Saxony sheep for one hundred and thirty dollars, — this being the beginning of his long career as John Brown the Shepherd.[36] Other purchases of Saxony sheep follow in quick succession, according to the entries in the first of a series of notebooks which often did duty as rough diaries. The sheep he seems to have taken by boat to Albany and driven thence to Ohio; his notebook teems at this time with hints for the care of sheep and such quaint entries as the following: "Deacon Abel Hinsdale left off entirely the use of Tobacco at the age of 66 now 73 & has used none since that time. No ba[d] consequnses have followed. Qery When will a man become to old to leave off any bad habit."

In June, 1839, when his family was again in Franklin Mills, he made another trip to the East on cattle business, the following being a typical home letter of this, for him, so trying and disastrous period: [37]

NEWHARTFORD 12th June 1839

MY DEAR WIFE & CHILDREN

I write to let you know that I am in comfortable health & that I expect to be on my way home in the course of a week should nothing befall me If I am longer detained I will write you again. The cattle business has succeeded about as I expected, but I am now some what in fear that I shall fail of getting the money I expected on the loan. Should that be the will of Providence I know of no other way but we must consider ourselves verry poor for our debts must be paid, if paid at a sacrifise. Should that happen (though it may not) I hope God who is rich in mercy will grant us all grace to conform to our circumstances with cheerfulness & true resignation. I want to see each of my dear family verry much but must wait Gods time. Try all of you to do the best you can, and do not one of you be discouraged, tomorrow may be a much brighter day. Cease not to ask Gods blessing on yourselves and me. Keep this letter wholly to yourselves, excepting that I expect to start for home soon, and that I did not write confidently about my success should anyone enquire Edward is well, & Owen Mills. You may shew this to my Father, but to no one else.

I am not without great hopes of getting relief I would not have you understand, but things have looked more unfavourable for a few days. I think I shall write you again before I start. Earnestly commending you every one to God, and to his mercy, which endureth forever, I remain your affectionate husband and father

JOHN BROWN

The friends here I believe are all well.

J. B.

Three days after writing this letter, John Brown received from the New England Woolen Company, at Rockville, Connecticut, the sum of twenty-eight hundred dollars through its agent, George Kellogg, for the purchase of wool, which money, regrettably enough, he pledged for his own benefit and was then unable to redeem.[38] Fortunately for him, the Company exercised leniency toward him, in return for which Brown promised, in 1842, after having passed through bankruptcy, to pay the money from time to time, with interest, as Divine Providence might enable him to do. This moral obligation he freely recognized, as will appear from the following letter to Mr. Kellogg, written in 1840, when Brown was temporarily in Hudson again, and in such distressing circumstances that he had not the means to pay the postage for forwarding two letters from Mr. Kellogg which had been sent to him at Franklin Mills:[39]

THE MOULDING OF THE MAN 31

"That means are so very limited is in consequence of my being left penyless for the time being, by the assignment and disposal of my property with no less than a family of ten children to provide for, the sickness of my wife and three of my oldest children since that time, and the most severe pressure generally for want of money ever known in this Country. Specie is almost out of the question and nothing but specie will pay our postage. . . . I learned a good while after the delivery of the Flour and Wool, to my further mortification and sorrow that they had not been forwarded when I expected, but was assured they should be immediately. I hope they have been received safe, and I most earnestly hope that the Devine Providence will yet enable me to make you full amends for all the wrong I have done, and to give you and my abused friend Whitman (whose name I feel ashamed to mention) some evidence that the injury I have occasioned was not premeditated and intentional at least."

In pledging himself to pay, John Brown promised to prove "the sincerity of my past professions, when legally free to act as I choose." [40] At his death in 1859, this debt like many another was still unpaid, and John Brown bequeathed fifty dollars toward its payment by his last will and testament. It was not only that he was visionary as a business man, but that he developed the fatal tendency to speculate, doubtless an outgrowth of his restlessness and the usual desire of the bankrupt for a sudden coup to restore his fortunes.

In the intervals of sheep and cattle trading, he and his father conceived the idea in 1840 of taking up some of the Virginia (now in Doddridge and Tyler counties of West Virginia) land belonging to Oberlin College. He appeared April 1, 1840, before a committee of Oberlin trustees and opened negotiations with it for the survey and purchase of some of the Virginia possessions.[41] Two days later, the full board considered a letter from John Brown in which he offered "to visit, survey and make the necessary investigation respecting boundaries, etc, of those lands, for one dollar per day, and a modest allowance for necessary expenses." This communication also stated frankly that this was to be a preliminary step towards locating his family upon the lands, "should the opening prove a favorable one." The trustees promptly voted to accept the offer, and the treasurer was ordered to furnish John Brown with "a commission & needful outfit." This was promptly done the same day, and by the 27th of April, Brown thus wrote from Ripley, Virginia, to his wife and children: "I have seen the spot where, if it be the will of Providence, I hope one day to live with my family." He liked the country as well as he had expected to, "and its inhabitants rather better." Were they, he believed, "as resolute and industrious as the Northern people, and did they understand how to manage as well, they would become rich; but they are not generally so." That John Brown did not subsequently settle on these Virginia lands is not, however, to be charged to the will of Providence, but to himself. His surveys and reports were duly received by the Oberlin trustees on July 14, 1840, and on August 11 they voted to address a letter to him on the subject. Through his own fault, however, negotiations dragged so that the whole plan fell through. This appears from John Brown's letters to Levi Burnell, the treasurer of Oberlin, who had duly notified him that the Prudential Committee of the trustees had been authorized by the board to perfect negotiations and convey to "Brother John Brown of Hudson One Thousand acres of our Virginia Land on conditions suggested in the correspondence . . . between him and the Committee." On October 20, Mr. Burnell wrote to Owen Brown asking for the status of the negotiations. He received no answer from John Brown until January 2, 1841. This reply shows that the latter had been vacillating throughout the fall as to whether he should or should not move to Virginia, and runs in part thus:

"I should have written you before but my time has been completely taken up, and owing to a variety of circumstances I have sometimes allmost given up the idea of going to the south at all; but after long reflection, and consultation about it, I feel prepared to say definitely that I expect Providence willing to accept the proposal of your Board, and that I shall want every thing understood, and aranged as nearly as may be, for my removal in the next Spring. I would here say that I shall expect to receive a thousand acres of land in a body that will includ a living spring of water dischargeing itself at a heighth sufficient to accommodate a tanery as I shall expect to pursue that business on the small scale if I go. It is my regular occupation. I mentioned several such springs in my report, but found them very scarce."

Meanwhile, the college had experienced a change of heart, apparently, because of Brown's procrastination, as appears from his letter of February 5, 1841, to Mr. Burnell:

THE MOULDING OF THE MAN 33

HUDSON 5th Feby 1841

LEVI BURNELL ESQR

DR SR: I have just returned from a journey to Pa, and have read yours of 20th Jany, & must say that I am somewhat disappointed in the information which it brings; & considering all that has passed, that on the part of the Institution I had not been called upon to decide positively nor even advised of any hurry for a more definite answer; & that on my part I had never intimated any other than an intention to accept the offer made; nor called for my pay, I should think your Committee would have done nearer the thing that is right had they at least signified their wish to know my determination, before putting it out of their power to perform what they had engaged. Probably I was not so prompt in makeing up my mind fully, & in communicating my determination as I had ought to be, & if Providence intends to defeat my plans there is no doubt the best of reasons for it, & we will rejoice that he who directs the steps of men knows perfectly well how to direct them; & will most assuredly make his counsel to stand. A failure of the consideration I do not so much regard as the derangement of my plan of future opperations. If the Virginia lands are, or are not disposed of, I wish you would give me the earliest information, & in the event of their still remaining on hand I suppose it not unreasonable for me still to expect a fulfillment of the offer on the part of the Institution. Should the land be conveyed away perhaps your Committee or some of the friends might still be instrumental in getting me an employment at the south. Please write me as soon as you have any information to give

Respectfully your friend

JOHN BROWN.

To this letter no answer was returned. On March 26, Brown again wrote from Hudson asking whether the lands had been sold. If the committee no longer wished to negotiate with him, they need only say so frankly and send him thirty dollars (for which he had waited nearly a year), upon receipt of which he would "consider the institution discharged from all further obligation." Thus ended the first plan for an exodus of the John Brown family.

As a result of this disappointment, Brown was compelled to turn to sheep-herding, taking charge in the spring of 1841 of the flocks of Captain Oviatt at Richfield, Ohio, and speedily becoming known as a remarkable shepherd, able to tell at a glance the presence within his flock of a strange animal. This partnership arrangement proving satisfactory, Brown again moved his family, in 1842, to Richfield, where he had the great misfortune to lose, in 1843, four of his children, aged respectively, nine, six, three and one years, three of them being buried at one time, — a crushing family calamity. The beginning of the family's stay in Richfield was marked, too, by Brown's discharge as a bankrupt, stripped of everything but a few articles which the court had decided on September 28, 1842, were absolutely necessary to the maintenance of the family, — among them eleven Bibles and Testaments, one volume entitled 'Beauties of the Bible,' one 'Church Member's Guide,' besides two mares, two cows, two hogs, three lambs, nineteen hens, seven sheep, and, last of all, three pocket knives valued at 37½ cents.[42] Gradually, Brown became well known as a winner of prizes for sheep and cattle at the annual fairs of Summit County, and before his removal from Richfield to Akron, April 10, 1844, he had established a tannery which, at the beginning of that year, was unable to keep up with the business offered to it. This change of residence was due to the establishment of a new business partnership, the longest and the final one of John Brown's career. It was, to quote him:[43]

"a copartnership with Simon Perkins, Jr., of Akron, with a view to carry on the sheep business extensively. He is to furnish all the feed and shelter for wintering, as a set-off against our taking all the care of the flock. All other expenses we are to share equally, and to divide the profits equally. This arrangement will reduce our cash rents at least $250 yearly, and save our hiring help in haying. We expect to keep the Captain Oviatt farm for pasturing, but my family will go into a very good house belonging to Mr. Perkins, — say from a half a mile to a mile out of Akron. I think this is the most comfortable and most favorable arrangement of my worldly concerns that I ever had, and calculated to afford us more leisure for improvement, by day and by night, than any other. I do hope that God has enabled us to make it in mercy to us, and not that he should send leanness into our souls. . . . This, I think, will be considered no mean alliance for our family, and I most earnestly hope they will have wisdom given to make the most of it. It is certainly indorsing the poor bankrupt and his family, three of whom were but recently in Akron jail, in a manner quite unexpected, and proves that notwithstanding we have been a company of 'Belted Knights,' our industrious and steady endeavors to maintain our integrity and our character have not been wholly overlooked. Mr. Perkins is perfectly advised of our poverty, and the times that have passed over us."

THE MOULDING OF THE MAN

John Brown was within bounds in thus exulting; the most trying financial periods of his life were now behind him, even though the Perkins partnership resulted eventually in severe losses and dissolution. At least it was a connection with a high-minded and prosperous man, and it lasted ten years. When it was over, the partners were still friends, but Mr. Perkins did not retain a high opinion of John Brown's ability or sagacity as a business man.

It was a lovely neighborhood, this about Akron, to which Brown now removed his family. They occupied a cottage on what is still known as Perkins Hill, near Simon Perkins's own home, with an extended and charming view over hill and dale, — an ideal sheep country, and a location which must have attracted any one save a predisposed wanderer. Here the family life went on smoothly, though not without its tragedies, notably the death of his daughter Amelia, accidentally scalded to death through the carelessness of an elder sister. This brought forth from the afflicted father, who was absent in Springfield, the following letter:[44]

Sabbath evening   SPRINGFIELD 8th Nov 1846
MY DEAR AFFLICTED WIFE & CHILDREN
I yesterday at night returned after an absence of several days from this place & am uterly unable to give any expression of my feelings on hearing of the dreadful news contained in Owens letter of the 30th & Mr. Perkins of the 31st Oct. I seem to be struck almost dumb.
One more dear little feeble child I am to meet no more till the dead small & great shall stand before God. This is a bitter cup indeed, but blessed be God: a brighter day shall dawn; & let us not sorrow as those that have no hope. Oh that we that remain, had wisdom wisely to consider; & to keep in view our latter end. Divine Providence seems to lay a heavy burden; & responsibility on you *my dear Mary;* but I trust you will be enabled to bear it in some measure as you ought. I exceedingly regret that I am unable to return, & be *present* to share your trials with you: but anxious as I am to be once more at home I do not feel at liberty to return yet. I hope to be able to get away before verry long; but cannot say when. I trust that none of you will feel disposed to cast an unreasonable blame on my dear Ruth on account of the dreadful trial we are called [to] suffer; for if the want of proper care in each, & all of us has not been attended with fatal consequenses it is no thanks to us. If I had a right sence of my habitual neglect of my familys

Eternal interests; I should probably go crazy. I humbly hope this dreadful afflictive Providence will lead us all more properly to appreciate the amazeing, unforseen, untold, consequences; that hang upon the right or wrong doing of things seemingly of trifling account. Who can tell or comprehend the vast results for good, or for evil; that are to follow the saying of one little word. Evrything worthy of being done *at all;* is worthy of being done in *good earnest,* & in the best possible manner. We are in midling health & expect to write some of you again soon. Our warmest thanks to our kind friends Mr. & Mrs. Perkins & family. From your affectionate husband, & father

JOHN BROWN

While Brown's self-accusation of "habitual neglect" is no more to be borne out than his father's charging himself with a wasted life, it is true that some of his neighbors wondered that he did not give more time to his family. That Akron home he ruled, as he did the later one at Springfield, with iron firmness and complete mastery, and as long as the children were with him they were under strict discipline, although the cane figured now but little. This was a relief to him as well as to his sons, for it is related of him that after he had given only a certain part of some blows he meant to bestow, he gave his whip to his son and bade him strike his father.[45] Yet he exacted loyalty of his children as he did fealty from his animals. It is a widely believed story in Akron to this day that John Brown once shot — to the horror of the children — a valuable shepherd dog, because it was so fond of the Perkins children as to be unwilling to stay at home. It is similarly narrated that he compelled his wife to ride to church with him on a pillion on a young and unbroken horse he wished to tame, with the result that she was twice thrown.[46] One thing is beyond doubt: but little reference to his children's schooling appears in his letters, if we except those written to his daughter Ruth while she was away at school. Only John Brown, Jr., obtained special educational advantages.

While the family life flowed on in this wise, the aftermath of its head's business failure remained to plague him in the shape of many lawsuits. On the records of the Portage County Court of Common Pleas at Ravenna, Ohio, are no less than twenty-one lawsuits in which John Brown figured

THE MOULDING OF THE MAN 37

as defendant during the years from 1820 to 1845.[47] Of these, thirteen were actions brought to recover money loaned on promissory notes either to Brown singly or in company with others. The remaining suits were mostly for claims for wages or payments due, or for non-fulfilment of contracts. Judgment against Brown was once entered by his consent for a nominal sum, and another case was an amicable suit in debt. In ten other cases he was successfully sued and judgments were obtained against him individually or jointly with others. In three cases those who sued him were "non-suited" as being without real cause for action, and two other cases were settled out of court. Four cases Brown won, among them being a suit for damages for false arrest and assault and battery, brought by an alleged horse-thief because Brown and other citizens had aided a constable in arresting him. A number of these suits grew out of Brown's failure and his real estate speculations. A serious litigation was an action brought by the Bank of Wooster to recover on a bill of exchange drawn by Brown and others on the Leather Manufacturers Bank of New York, and repudiated by that institution on the ground that Brown and his associates had no money in the bank. During the suit the original amount claimed was rapidly reduced, and when the judgment against Brown and his associates was rendered, it was for $917.65. In June, 1842, Brown was sued by Tertius Wadsworth and Joseph Wells, in partnership with whom he had been buying and driving cattle to Connecticut. In 1845, Daniel C. Gaylord, who several times had sued Brown, succeeded in compelling Brown and his associates to convey to him certain Franklin lands which they had contracted to sell, but the title for which they refused to convey. The court upheld Gaylord's claim. The only case in which Brown figured as plaintiff was settled out of court in his favor.

But the most important suit of Brown's business life, and the one which has been oftenest cited to injure his business reputation, was a complicated one which grew out of one of these Ravenna cases.[48] On July 11, 1836, he applied to Heman Oviatt, Frederick Brown, Joshua Stow and three brothers of the name of Wetmore, to become security for him on a note to the Western Reserve Bank for $6000. The note not being paid, the bank sued and obtained judgment against all of them in May, 1837, and on August 2, 1837, they all gave their joint judgment bond to the bank, payable in sixty days. This not being paid, the bank again sued, and, an execution being issued, Heman Oviatt was compelled to pay the bank in full. He then in turn sued John Brown and his fellow endorsers. The litigation which followed was greatly complicated by Brown's actions in connection with a piece of property known as Westlands, for which he had at first not the title, but a penal bond of conveyance. Brown gave this bond to Oviatt as collateral for Oviatt's having endorsed the judgment bond to the bank. When the deed for the Westlands property was duly given to Brown, he recorded it without notifying Oviatt of this action. Later, he mortgaged this property to two men, again without the knowledge of Heman Oviatt. Meanwhile Daniel C. Gaylord had recovered judgment against Brown in another transaction, and to satisfy it, caused the sale of Westlands by the sheriff. At John Brown's request, Amos P. Chamberlain, heretofore a warm friend and business associate of Brown's, bought in the property at the sheriff's sale, doubtless with the idea that Brown would presently find the money to buy it back for himself. But as soon as Oviatt was compelled to pay off the judgment bond at the Western Reserve Bank, he naturally wished to reimburse himself by the penal bond of conveyance of Westlands, which, he felt, gave him the title to the property. Finding that, through the land transactions already related, the penal bond had become valueless, he brought suit to have the sale of Westlands to Chamberlain set aside as fraudulent. The Supreme Court of Ohio held that Chamberlain had a rightful title and dismissed the suit. John Brown himself was not directly sued by Oviatt, being, to use a lawyer's term, "legally safe" throughout the entire transaction. From the point of view of probity and fair play he does not, however, escape criticism. He was morally bound to reimburse those who had aided him to obtain the money from the bank and had suffered thereby. Even after this lapse of years, his action in secretly recording the transfer of the land and then mortgaging it bears an unpleasant aspect. It is quite probable that this complication was due to the great confusion of Brown's affairs, and his own poor business head. Moreover, it may well be that in due course Oviatt and the other securities were repaid in full by Brown during his period of prosperity with Mr. Perkins. Certainly, as already stated, Heman Oviatt bore Brown no grudge in after years. On the other hand, Brown may have taken advantage of the bankruptcy proceedings to escape liability for these debts.

The story of this case does not, however, end here. John Brown refused for a time to give up Westlands to Amos Chamberlain, believing that he had the right to pasture his cattle there temporarily, and still, apparently, thinking that Chamberlain had purchased the farm not for occupancy but for the purpose of turning it back to him. After having repeatedly summoned Chamberlain for trespass on the land which Chamberlain had actually purchased, John Brown and his sons held a shanty on the place by force of arms until compelled to desist by the arrival of the sheriff summoned by Chamberlain. According to the Chamberlain family, John Brown ordered his sons to shoot Chamberlain if he set foot on the farm, — a statement vigorously denied by John Brown, Jr. Jason Brown recollects that "father put us all in the cabin on the farm with some old-fashioned muskets and we stayed in it night and day. Then Mr. Chamberlain sued father and sent a constable and his posse to drive us out. We showed them our guns. Then he got the sheriff of Portage County to come out and arrest us. Of course we could not resist the sheriff." Finally the sheriff arrested John Brown and two sons, John and Owen, who were thereupon placed in the Akron jail. Chamberlain, having destroyed the shanty which Brown had occupied and obtained possession of the land, allowed the case to drop, and Brown and his sons were released.[49]

Fortunately for John Brown's side of the case, there has just come to light a letter he wrote to Mr. Chamberlain in order to prevent, if possible, the carrying on of a long litigation. It records the spirit in which John Brown acted, and proves him to have been sincerely of the opinion that he had been gravely wronged, and that, in holding his farm as he did, Mr. Chamberlain not only injured Brown, but also the latter's innocent creditors. No one can maintain, after the perusal of this communication, that Brown was unreasoning in the matter, or that he was deliberately trying to defraud a neighbor of land righteously purchased. It is altogether likely that if similar documents in regard to the other cases cited, which appear, on the surface, to make against John Brown's probity, could be found, these other entanglements would also be susceptible of a far better interpretation. The letter to Mr. Chamberlain, offering peace or arbitration before war, reads as follows:[50]

HUDSON 27th April 1841

MR. AMOS CHAMBERLAIN
DEAR SIR

I was yesterday makeing preparation for the commencement and vigorous prosecution of a tedious, distressing, wasteing, and long protracted war, but after hearing by my son of some remarks you made to him I am induced before I proceed any further in the way of hostile preparation: to stop and make one more earnest effort for Peace And let me begin by assureing you that notwithstanding I feel myself to be deeply and sorely injured by you, (without even the shadow of a provocation on my part to tempt you to begin as you did last October;) I have no conciousness of wish to injure either yourself or any of your family nor to interfere with your happiness, no not even to value of one hair of your head. I perfectly well remember the uniform good understanding and good feeling which had ever (previous to last fall) existed between us from our youth. I have not forgotten the days of cheerful labour which we have performed together, nor the acts of mutual kindness and accomodation which have passed between us. I can assure you that I ever have been and still am your honest, hearty friend. I have looked with sincere gratification uppon your steady growing prosperity, and flattering prospects of your young family. I have made your happiness and prosperity my own instead of feeling envious at your success. When I antisipated a return to Hudson with my family I expected great satisfaction from again haveing you for a neighbour. This is true whatever you may think of me, or whatever representation you may make of me to others. And now I ask you why will you trample on the rights of your friend and of his numerous family? Is it because he is poor? Why will you kneedlessly make yourself the means of depriveing all my honest creditors of their Just due? Ought not my property if it must be sacrifised to fall into the hands of honest and some of them poor and suffering Creditors? Will God smile on the gains which you may acquire at the expence of suffering families deprived of their honest dues? And let me here ask Have you since you bid off that farm felt the same inward peace and conciousness of right you had before felt? I do not believe you have, and for this plain reason that you have been industrious in circulateing evil reports of me (as I believe) in order to prevent the community from enquiring into your motives and conduct. This is perfectly natural, and no new thing under the sun. If it could be made to appear that Naboth the Jezreelite had blasphemed God and the King, then it would be perfectly right for Ahab to possess his vineyard. So reasoned wicked men thousands of years ago. I ask my old friend again is your path a path of peace? does it promise peace? I have two definite things to offer you once and for all. One is that you take ample security of Seth Thompson for what you have paid and for what you may have to pay (which D. C. Gaylord has ever wickedly refused) and release my farm and thereby provide for yourself an honorable and secure retreat out of the strife and perplexity and restore you to peace with your friends and with yourself. The other is that if you do not like that offer, that you submit the matter to disinterested, discreet, and good men to say what is just and honest between us.

You may ask why do not you go to Thompson for your relief. I answer that I should do so at once, but I cannot recover anything of Thompson but the face of the note and interest, nothing for all the costs, and expences, and penalties and sacrifise of my property. All Thompson is either morally or legally bound to pay is the note and interest. He is an innocent and honest debtor and when in his low state of health, and the extreme pressure he could not pay the money promptly came forward [and] offered his land as security. That security is still kept for the purpose, as I positively know any statements to the contrary notwithstanding.

I now ask you to read this letter calmly, and patiently, and often, and show it to your neighbours, and friends, such as Mr. Zina Post and many other worthy men and advise with them before you attempt to force your way any further. I ask you to make it your first business and give me without delay your final determination in regard to it.

Respectfully your friend

John Brown.

This appeal to reason and friendliness ought to have softened Mr. Chamberlain's heart. No one now knows just what the result was; but since there is no evidence of a "tedious, distressing, wasteing, and long protracted war" between the neighbors, it is likely that it had its effect. At any rate, it closes a chapter of John Brown's business life which, besides occasioning him deep and poignant distress, left its marks upon him. Had he not, however, been withal a strong, serious and fundamentally honest character, he must have been completely wrecked upon the shoals out of which, with Mr. Perkins's aid, he was now to find his way.

CHAPTER II

"HIS GREATEST OR PRINCIPAL OBJECT"

WHEN was it that John Brown, practical shepherd, tanner, farmer, surveyor, cattle expert, real estate speculator and wool-merchant, first conceived what he calls in his autobiography "his greatest or principal object" in life — the forcible overthrow of slavery in his native land? The question is not an idle one, since the object adopted as the magnetic needle to guide his destiny eventually resulted in the rousing of a nation to its smallest hamlet, and beyond doubt precipitated the bloody civil war which others besides John Brown clearly foresaw. The mystery of individuality does not lose anything of its spell with the passage of time; in the case of this strongly marked character, there is nothing concerning it of greater interest than the transformation of the simple guardian of flocks and tiller of the soil, Spartan in his rugged simplicity of living, into an arch-plotter, a man of many disguises, a belligerent pioneer, a fugitive before the law at one moment and an assailant of a sovereign government in the next. Psychologists must find in such an evolution of spirit a field for inquiry and speculation without end. Why should one who so hated the profession of arms be the first to take it up in order to free the slave from his chains? What was there in the humdrum life of an Ohio farmer to cause him to espouse the rôle of a border-chieftain in the middle of the nineteenth century? From what midnight star did this shepherd draw his inspiration to go forth and kill? What was there in the process of tanning to make a man who had never seen blood spilt in anger ready to blot out the lives of other beings whose chief crime was that they differed with him as to the righteousness of human bondage? Why should the restless iron spirit of the Roundhead suddenly have manifested itself in this prosaic seller of town lots when he had spent more than five decades in peace and quiet? Doubtless the answer to some of these questions must be left to the new science which would plot and chart the soul, and measure to

HIS GREATEST OR PRINCIPAL OBJECT

the hundredth of a degree each quivering emotion. But the historian may properly inquire when it was that the "greatest or principal object" of this militant reformer's life first began to manifest itself in his acts and deeds.

John Brown's horror of the South's "peculiar institution," as it affected individuals, we know to have come to him, as the autobiography again testifies, at the age of twelve, when, he says, he declared, or swore, "eternal war with slavery." But the oaths of a lad of such tender years do not often become the guiding force of maturity; in John Brown's case, not even his constant friendliness to fugitive slaves permits the assumption that early in his manhood he had definitely resolved upon the plan of overthrowing slavery by men and arms which he finally chose. Not until his thirty-fifth year is there direct documentary evidence that his mind was especially concerning itself with the welfare of the black man in bondage, — that is, to any greater extent than were the minds and consciences of hundreds, if not thousands, of Ohio farmers who were later among the strongest enemies of human bondage, and even then were dauntless station-masters and conductors on the rapidly expanding Underground Railroad. In November, 1834, when John Brown's stay in Pennsylvania was actually within six months of its close, when he was, however, apparently to remain in Richmond as a successful tanner and farmer, he first expressed on paper a wish to aid his fellow-Americans in chains. It is in the following epistle to his brother Frederick, unstamped because it bears the frank of John Brown, then still postmaster at Randolph, of which Richmond was a part:[1]

RANDOLPH, Nov. 21, 1834.

DEAR BROTHER, — As I have had only one letter from Hudson since you left here, and that some weeks since, I begin to get uneasy and apprehensive that all is not well. I had satisfied my mind about it for some time, in expectation of seeing father here, but I begin to give that up for the present. Since you left here I have been trying to devise some means whereby I might do something in a practical way for my poor fellow-men who are in bondage, and having fully consulted the feelings of my wife and my three boys, we have agreed to get at least one negro boy or youth, and bring him up as we do our own, — viz., give him a good English education, learn him what we can about the history of the world, about business, about general subjects, and, above all, try to teach him the fear of God. We think of three ways to obtain one: First, to try to get some Christian slave-holder to release one to us. Second, to get a free one if no one will let us have one that is a slave. Third, if that does not succeed, we have all agreed to submit to considerable privation in order to buy one. This we are now using means in order to effect, in the confident expectation that God is about to bring them all out of the house of bondage.

I will just mention that when this subject was first introduced, Jason had gone to bed; but no sooner did he hear the thing hinted, than his warm heart kindled, and he turned out to have a part in the discussion of a subject of such exceeding interest. I have for years been trying to devise some way to get a school a-going here for blacks, and I think that on many accounts it would be a most favorable location. Children here would have no intercourse with vicious people of their own kind, nor with openly vicious persons of any kind. There would be no powerful opposition influence against such a thing; and should there be any, I believe the settlement might be so effected in future as to have almost the whole influence of the place in favor of such a school. Write me how you would like to join me, and try to get on from Hudson and thereabouts some firstrate abolitionist families with you. I do honestly believe that our united exertions alone might soon, with the good hand of our God upon us, effect it all.

This has been with me a favorite theme of reflection for years. I think that a place which might be in some measure settled with a view to such an object would be much more favorable to such an undertaking than would any such place as Hudson, with all its conflicting interests and feelings; and I do think such advantages ought to be afforded the young blacks, whether they are all to be immediately set free or not. Perhaps we might, under God, in that way do more towards breaking their yoke effectually than in any other. If the young blacks of our country could once become enlightened, it would most assuredly operate on slavery like firing powder confined in rock, and all slaveholders know it well. Witness their heaven-daring laws against teaching blacks. If once the Christians in the free States would set to work in earnest in teaching the blacks, the people of the slaveholding States would find themselves constitutionally driven to set about the work of emancipation immediately. The laws of this State are now such that the inhabitants of any township may raise by a tax in aid of the State school-fund any amount of money they may choose by a vote, for the purpose of common schools, which any child may have access to by application. If you will join me in this undertaking, I will make with you any arrangement of our temporal concerns that shall be fair. Our health is good, and our prospects about business rather brightening.

Affectionately yours,   JOHN BROWN.

HIS GREATEST OR PRINCIPAL OBJECT

It will be noticed, as has heretofore been pointed out,[2] that there is here a total absence of any belligerent intention on the writer's part; he who afterwards became disgusted with the Abolitionists because their propaganda involved talk alone, and no violent physical action against slavery, was planning, when nearly thirty-five, nothing more startling than a school for blacks, confident in the belief that their education in the North would shatter the whole system of slavery in the South, and turning for aid exclusively to friends in his former Ohio home. Again, he shows no knowledge of the prejudice in the North against teaching blacks which had resulted in his native State in the suppression of schools for them in New Haven in 1831, and in Canterbury in 1834. Throughout his correspondence of these years, and later, there is little to indicate that Brown was in touch with much of what was going on in the nation. Indeed, as late as June 22, 1844, he wrote to his family, "I am extremely ignorant at present of miscellaneous subjects."[3] It is the recollection of the family, however, that before this time they were called upon by their father to take a solemn oath to do all in their power to abolish slavery, after hearing from him of his purpose of attacking the institution. Jason Brown fixes the date of this event at 1839, the place as Franklin, and those who were party to it as Mrs. Brown, a colored preacher, Fayette by name, and the three sons, John, Jr., Jason and Owen. He specifies merely that they were sworn "to do all in their power to abolish slavery," and does not use the word "force." John Brown, Jr., writing to F. B. Sanborn in December, 1890, thus expressed his opinion:[4]

"It is, of course, impossible for me to say when such idea and plan first entered his [John Brown's] mind and became a purpose; but I can say with certainty that he first informed his family that he entertained such purpose while we were yet living in Franklin, O. (now called Kent), and before he went to Virginia, in 1840, to survey the lands which had been donated by Arthur Tappan to Oberlin College; and this was certainly as early as 1839. The place and the circumstances where he first informed us of that purpose are as perfectly in my memory as any other event in my life. Father, mother, Jason, Owen and I were, late in the evening, seated around the fire in the open fire-place of the kitchen, in the old Haymaker house where we then lived; and there he first informed us of his determination to make war on slavery—not such war as Mr. Garrison* informs us 'was equally the purpose of the non-resistant abolitionists,' but war by force and arms. He said that he had long entertained such a purpose — that he believed it his duty to devote his life, if need be, to this object, which he made us fully to understand. After spending considerable time in setting forth in most impressive language the hopeless condition of the slave, he asked who of us were willing to make common cause with him in doing all in our power to 'break the jaws of the wicked and pluck the spoil out of his teeth,' naming each of us in succession, Are you, Mary, John, Jason, and Owen? Receiving an affirmative answer from each, he kneeled in prayer, and all did the same. This posture in prayer impressed me greatly as it was the first time I had ever known him to assume it. After prayer he asked us to raise our right hands, and he then administered to us an oath, the exact terms of which I cannot recall, but in substance it bound us to secrecy and devotion to the purpose of fighting slavery by force and arms to the extent of our ability. According to Jason's recollections, Mr. Fayette, a colored theological student at Western Reserve College, Hudson, Ohio, was with us at the time but of this I am not certain."

It must be noted here that in this letter John Brown, Jr., gives the date of the oath as 1839; in his lengthy affidavit in the case of Gerrit Smith against the Chicago *Tribune*, he gave the date as 1836, three years earlier, and in an account given in Mr. Sanborn's book he placed it at 1837; three distinct times for the same event. It can, therefore, best be stated as occurring before 1840.[5] At this time, John Brown, Jr., was in his nineteenth year, Jason about sixteen years old, and Owen between fourteen and fifteen. The only testimony as to an early project akin to that of the final raid, available from any one else outside the family, is that of George B. Delamater,[6] who says, "Having spent several days and nights with Old John Brown at various times between 1840 and 1844, I enjoyed his society and was made acquainted with his views in regard to American slavery and its relations at that time from various standpoints, and also with the scheme which he had under consideration for freeing persons held in bondage." Mr. Delamater at this period was a mere stripling; it is an interesting contrast to his recollections that Mr. Foreman, in his long account of John Brown's

* Wendell Phillips Garrison, in *The Preludes of Harper's Ferry.*

HIS GREATEST OR PRINCIPAL OBJECT

stay at Richmond from 1825 to 1835, makes no mention of having heard of any deliberate project; yet he was much older and more intimate with Brown than was Mr. Delamater, who, in this earlier Richmond period, was only a school-boy.

That the subject was undoubtedly much in his mind prior to this appears again from an anecdote related by General Henry B. Carrington, and placed by him in the year 1836, although probably occurring in 1838, when there is the first definite record of John Brown's having been in Connecticut after his school days. General Carrington thus tells this incident of his boyhood:[7]

"When I was a boy and went to school in Torrington, there came into the school room one day a tall man, rather slender, with grayish hair, who said to the boys: 'I want to ask you some questions in geography. Where is Africa?' 'It is on the other side of the ocean, of course,' said a boy. 'Why "of course,"' asked the man. The boy could n't say why 'of course.' Then the man proceeded to tell them something about Africa and the negroes, and the evil of the slave trade, and the wrongs and sufferings of the slaves, and then said, 'How many of you boys will agree to use your influence, whatever it may be, against this great curse, when you grow up?' They held up their hands. He then said that he was afraid that some of them might forget it, and added, 'Now I want those who are *quite sure* that they will not forget it, who will promise to use their time and influence toward resisting this evil, to rise.' Another boy and I stood up. Then this man put his hands on our heads and said, 'Now may my Father in Heaven, who is your Father, and who is the Father of the African; and Christ, who is my Master and Saviour, and your Master and Saviour, and the Master and Saviour of the African; and the Holy Spirit, which gives me strength and comfort, when I need it, and will give you strength and comfort when you need it, and which gives strength and comfort to the African, enable you to keep this resolution which you have now taken.' And that man was John Brown."

Most important after that of the Brown family is the testimony of Frederick Douglass, the colored leader, who states in his autobiography [8] that Brown confided the Virginia plan to him, without specifying Harper's Ferry or speaking of the arsenal, "about the time" he began his newspaper enterprise in Rochester in 1847, and among other details added that Brown explained his frugal manner of living by his wish to lay by money for this abolition project. Frederick Douglass

visited Brown in his home in Springfield on this occasion.
"From this night spent with John Brown," said Mr. Douglass,
". . . while I continued to write and speak against slavery,
I became all the same less hopeful of its peaceful abolition.
My utterances became more and more tinged by the color
of this man's strong impressions. Speaking at an anti-slavery
convention in Salem, Ohio, I expressed the apprehension that
slavery could only be destroyed by blood-shed, when I was
suddenly and sharply interrupted by my good old friend
Sojourner Truth with the question, 'Frederick, is God dead?'
'No,' I answered, 'and because God is not dead, slavery can
only end in blood.'"

If this testimony seems to show that the plan of using force
was then, in 1847, taking shape in Brown's mind, — it may
have been delayed in coming to earlier maturity by his bankruptcy and financial distress, — there is nothing in John
Brown's letters or diary to indicate so early an all-ruling
plan of applying force to slavery as John Brown, Jr., records.
It is said that his father first conceived the idea of using the
Allegheny Mountains as the scene for an armed attack on
slavery, and a means of running off freed slaves to the North,
when he surveyed the Oberlin lands.[9] But his letter to his
family from Ripley, Virginia, April 27, 1840,[10] already cited,
is peaceable enough, and his hope of settling his family there
is hardly consistent with his anti-slavery policy of later years.
Indeed, while recording his pleasure that the residents of the
vicinity were more attractive people than he had thought,
he had nothing to say about the institution of slavery which
he then, for the first time, really beheld at close range. So
far as the evidence of contemporary documents goes, until
1840, at least, there is nothing to show that there was anything more than a family agreement to oppose slavery, without specification as to the precise method of assault.

The transformation of the peaceful tanner and shepherd
into a man burning to use arms upon an institution which
refused to yield to peaceful agitation would seem to have
taken place in the latter part of his fourth decade, as Mr.
Douglass testified. Gradually his plan took final shape. There
was nothing in the surroundings of pastoral Richfield or
Akron to suggest narrow defiles and mountainous passes

HIS GREATEST OR PRINCIPAL OBJECT   49

teeming with sharpshooters. But, little by little, visions of this kind came into Brown's brain more and more as the years passed, until in the early fifties his plan was clear to him in its outlines, much as actually put into execution. The salient idea was that mountains had throughout history been the means of enabling a few brave souls, whether gladiators, or slaves, or free men, Swiss, Italians, or Spaniards, or Circassians, to defy and sometimes to defeat armies of their oppressors. Into the mountain fastnesses regular troops penetrated, it was thought, with difficulty, and the ranges themselves afforded an easy line of communication even through a wholly hostile country. Moreover, mountains were just the place to assemble bondmen and to give them arms with which to fight for liberty. For the project was now far different from that John Brown described to his brother in 1834; slavery, it appeared, was, after all, not to be undone by educating the negroes already freed, but by the sword of Gideon and a band as carefully chosen as was his. Gradually the practical shepherd felt his blood stirring within him, but not until after removal to Springfield, Massachusetts, in 1846, when he had the opportunity to come into closer knowledge of the militant Boston Abolitionists, is there written evidence of this. He had seen the *Liberator* in his father's home, for Owen Brown early became a subscriber to this and other vigorous anti-slavery journals. John Brown's children also remember to have received the *Liberator* in Ohio, when it was still a youthful publication,[11] and later in North Elba. The *Tribune*, too, as it attained fame under Greeley, was as welcome a visitor to this home as to so many thousands of others. Its approval of the doctrine of opposing slavery with Sharp's rifles commended it particularly in the Kansas days to John Brown, who was by nature unable to sympathize with the Garrisonian doctrine of non-resistance to force, although there are some who would believe Brown to have been a non-resistant as late as 1830. They cite in support of their contention a garbled anecdote, according to which he permitted himself to be cowhided without resisting his assailant's fury.[12] Brown's residence in Springfield gave him the opportunity not only to attend anti-slavery meetings, but also to meet many colored people; in the first written evidence of his growing aggressiveness towards slavery there is reference to enlightenment at the hands of Abby Kelley Foster,* Garrison "and other really benevolent persons." This curious production of Brown's bespeaks the influence upon him of Franklin's writings; throughout, it is an admonition to the negroes to avoid their besetting sins, an incentive to thrift, frugality and solidarity, and it is written as if from the pen of a black man, Sambo. Contributed in 1848 or 1849 to a little-known Abolition newspaper, *The Ram's Horn*, published and edited by colored men in New York, this essay denounces the negroes for their supineness in the face of wrong, instead of their "nobly resisting" brutal aggressions.†

But for all its denunciation of the negro's "tamely submitting to every species of indignity, contempt and wrong," it cannot be maintained that this satirical article indicated that Brown had gone very far along the path toward an armed attack on slavery, although started in that direction. Nor does it appear from this that he had as yet reached the conclusion that the New England Abolitionists were to be shunned because they were all talk. In 1851, however, the policy of armed resistance becomes much more clearly developed; the man of war is now emerging from the chrysalis of peace. On January 15 of that year there was organized in Springfield a branch of the United States League of Gileadites — the first and apparently the only one. It was Brown's idea; he chose the title, and it was his first effort to organize the colored people to defend themselves and advance their interests. It was a practical application of the teachings of Sambo, and was inspired by the passage of the Fugitive Slave Law, which made legal in the North the rendition of negroes who had found their way to free States. The "Words of Advice" for the Gileadites, "as written and recommended by John Brown" and adopted as the principles of the new organization, begin with the motto "Union is Strength,"

---

* "John Brown was strong for women's rights and women's suffrage. He always went to hear Lucretia Mott and Abby Kelley Foster, even though it cost him considerable effort to reach the place where they spoke." — Annie Brown Adams.

† See Appendix.

and declare in the first sentence that "Nothing so charms the American people as personal bravery."[13] The object of the Gileadites was not, however, to attack slavery on its own territory, but to band the colored people together to resist slave-catchers and make impossible the returning to the South of a fugitive who had reached Northern soil. Brown wrote:

> "No jury can be found in the Northern States, that would convict a man for defending his rights to the last extremity. This is well understood by Southern Congressmen, who insisted that the right of trial by jury should not be granted to the fugitive. Colored people have more fast friends amongst the whites than they suppose. . . . Just think of the money expended by individuals in your behalf in the past twenty years! Think of the number who have been mobbed and imprisoned on your account. Have any of you seen the Branded Hand? Do you remember the names of Lovejoy and Torrey? Should one of your number be arrested, you must collect together as quickly as possible so as to outnumber your adversaries who are taking an active part against you. Let no able-bodied man appear on the ground unequipped, or with his weapons exposed to view; let that be understood beforehand. Your plans must be known only to yourself, and with the understanding that all traitors must die, wherever caught and proven to be guilty. 'Whosoever is fearful or afraid, let him return and depart early from Mount Gilead.' (Judges, VII chap., 3 verse; Deut. XX Chap. 8 verse.) Give all cowards an opportunity to show it on condition of holding their peace. Do not delay one moment after you are ready; you will lose all your resolution if you do. Let the first blow be the signal for all to engage; and when engaged do not do your work by halves; but make clean work with your enemies, and be sure you meddle not with any others . . . Your enemies will be slow to attack you after you have once done up the work nicely. . . ."

All this has the characteristic ring of John Brown the Kansas fighter, particularly the admonition to make "clean work with your enemies." Here is the stern Puritan parent, intolerant of childish fault, developed into a man urging not only shedding the blood of one's enemies, but the making of "clean work" of it, much as pirate captains advocated the walking of the plank as a sanitarily satisfactory way of disposing of one's captives. This advice, as will be seen later in this narrative, recurs frequently in the days when the Roundhead was in the field at work. Certainly, when engaged, he always lived up to his doctrine of going at once to close quarters with his enemy, after the manner of John Paul Jones. The transformation of the practical shepherd was thus coming on apace.

Characteristic, too, is Brown's suggestion in the "Words of Advice," that a lasso might be "applied to a slave-catcher for once with good effect." "Stand by one another, and by your friends, while a drop of blood remains; and be hanged, if you must, but tell no tales out of school," — this is another solemn admonition which smacks of the Spanish Main, yet accurately foreshadows his own conduct when overcome by his enemies. Original is the hint to the colored people to embroil their white friends in the event of trouble: "After effecting a rescue, if you are assailed, go into the houses of your most prominent and influential white friends with your wives, and that will effectually fasten upon them the suspicion of being connected with you, and will compel them to make a common cause with you, whether they would otherwise live up to their profession or not. This would leave them no choice in the matter." These "Words of Advice" were followed by an agreement and nine resolutions which practically restate the agreement. This was signed by forty-four colored men and women of Springfield. It is typical of other documents John Brown drew up on, to him, serious occasions, and is in his best style:[14]

AGREEMENT

As citizens of the United States of America, trusting in a just and merciful God, whose spirit and all-powerful aid we humbly implore, we will ever be true to the flag of our beloved country, always acting under it. We, whose names are hereunto affixed, do constitute ourselves a branch of the United States League of Gileadites. We will provide ourselves at once with suitable implements, and will aid those who do not possess the means, if any such are disposed to join us. We invite every colored person whose heart is engaged for the performance of our business, whether male or female, old or young. The duty of the aged, infirm, and young members of the League shall be to give instant notice to all members in case of an attack upon any of our people. We agree to have no officers except a Treasurer and Secretary *pro tem.*, until after some trial of courage and talent of able-bodied members shall

HIS GREATEST OR PRINCIPAL OBJECT 53

enable us to elect officers from those who shall have rendered the most important services. Nothing but wisdom and undaunted courage, efficiency, and general good conduct shall in anyway influence us in electing our officers.

It is not of record that any members of the Gileadites actually took a hand in a slave-rescue "with suitable implements." There is, on the other hand, no doubt that the determined Springfield wool-merchant, in drafting these resolutions in his fifty-first year, meant them to contain advice which may briefly be summed up as forcible resistance to the officers of the law, and an admonition to shoot to kill on all such occasions. As long as he was in Springfield, John Brown continued to concern himself with these colored friends. On November 28, 1850, just before he organized the Gileadites, he wrote to his wife:[15] "I of course keep encouraging my colored friends to 'trust in God and keep their powder dry.' I did so today, at Thanksgiving meeting, publicly."

From the Gileadites to plans for guerrilla warfare was an easy step. In his second memorandum-book, preserved in the Boston Public Library, there is an entry which was probably recorded early in 1855. It reads thus:

"Circassia has about 550,000
Switzerland 2,037,030
Guerilla warfare see Life of Lord Wellington Page 71 to Page 75 (Mina). See also Page 102 some *valuable hints* in same Book. See also Page 196 some most important instructions to officers. See also same Book Page 235 these words Deep and narrow defiles where 300 men would suffice to check an *army*. See also Page 236 on top of Page."

The book in question is Joachim Hayward Stocqueler's two-volume 'Life of Field Marshal the Duke of Wellington,' published in London in 1852, and the activity of the Spanish guerrillas under their able leader Mina was what attracted Brown's attention. The "most important instructions to officers" related to discipline and cooking, and page 235 furnished a description of the mountainous and broken topography of Spain. Directly opposite the entry quoted above is a list of Southern towns, with four Pennsylvania cities mixed in, as if Brown were considering such strategic points as Little Rock, Arkansas; Charleston, South Carolina; San Antonio,

Texas; St. Louis, Missouri; Augusta, Georgia, and others, in an elaborate plan for assailing the slave-power and running off its much cherished property. Some Ohio friends of Brown, Colonel Daniel Woodruff, an officer of the War of 1812, his son-in-law, Mr. Henry Myers and his daughter, according to the recollections of the two latter (Colonel Woodruff having died soon after), learned from John Brown the details of his Virginia plan as early as the late fall of 1854 or the beginning of 1855.[16] According to Mr. Myers, who heard the discussion between John Brown and his father-in-law, the former's object in visiting Colonel Woodruff was to persuade him to join in a raid on Harper's Ferry, to take place at that time, if it could be organized. He had seen active military service, and Brown wanted the aid of his practical experience. During his stay, which he spent in urgent endeavor to persuade Colonel Woodruff, Brown detailed his whole scheme, so that all the Woodruff household came to understand it. He spoke of the evil days in Kansas, then existing, and he wished to relieve Kansas and to retaliate by striking at another point. He wanted to attack the arsenal at Harper's Ferry: first, to frighten Virginia and detach it from the slave interest; second, to capture the rifles to arm the slaves; and third, to destroy the arsenal machinery, so that it could not be used to turn out more arms for the perhaps long guerrilla war that might follow; and to destroy whatever guns were already stored there that he could not carry away.

That this revelation of his plan is not improbable appears from other testimony. In August, 1854, John Brown wrote to his sons, who were then planning to combat slavery by settling in Kansas as Free State men, that he could not join them because he felt a call to duty in another section of the country.[17] Evidently, the practical shepherd now clearly realized what was his greatest object in life and was devoting himself to it. His daughter, Annie Brown Adams, says that she first learned the plan of the raid the winter she was eleven years old (in 1854); and then she heard of it as to take place at Harper's Ferry.[18] Later, in hearing other people's stories, she found other places mentioned. Salmon explained this to her by saying that their father several times changed his plans, and that he had spoken of them to various other people

HIS GREATEST OR PRINCIPAL OBJECT 55

at these different times. "I think I may say," writes Mrs. Adams, "without any intention of boasting, that I knew more about his plans than anyone else, or at least anyone else who 'survived to tell the tale.' He always talked freely to me of his plans, from the time he first explained them to me, the winter before he went to Kansas, when I was eleven years old. He would say as if for a sort of apology to himself, perhaps, 'I know I can *trust* you. You never tell anything you are told not to,' after talking with me of his affairs."

During all the North Elba period from 1849 to 1851, so Miss Sarah Brown thinks, she and all the children knew that a blow was to be struck at Harper's Ferry. She clearly remembers how, when Harper's Ferry came into the lesson at school, her heart hammered and she shivered as with cold. Yet she cannot recall that any of them were ever cautioned to keep silence as to this. She thinks they all understood the necessity of secrecy as to all their father's plans so well, that warnings were known to be superfluous. She clearly recalls standing behind her father's chair and watching him draw diagrams of log forts, explaining how the logs were to be laid, how the roofs were to be made, and how trees were to be felled without, and laid as obstacles to attacking parties. This was to be in the mountains near Harper's Ferry, and her father was making the pictures and explaining his plans to one Epps, a negro neighbor, who was looking on, and whom her father was endeavoring — vainly — to induce to join the raiders. Her father was so ready to trust others with his plans, with sublime faith in their ability to keep a secret, that his visit to Colonel Woodruff would have been entirely in keeping. It is related, too, that he confided in Thomas Thomas, a negro porter in the employ of Perkins & Brown in Springfield, soon after his arrival there in 1846,[19] but there is no direct confirmatory evidence of his having laid his plan before some of the Gileadites. Thomas Thomas took no active interest in Brown's plans, being neither conspicuous in the League, nor a member of his employer's Chatham convention in 1858, preceding the raid on Harper's Ferry.

As to the purposes behind the plan and the objects to be obtained, it is probable that they may have varied as the years passed, precisely as did the details of the programme and the actual place of starting his revolt. Thus, while he first thought of Harper's Ferry, as Mrs. Annie Brown Adams testifies,[20] other places were at times discussed; even up to the raid, it was thought by some of the Boston backers of Brown that the place of striking the first blow would be some other locality than Harper's Ferry,[21] which, by its nearness to the capital of the nation and its being on a railroad, was rendered much less desirable for the purpose in hand than some place nearer the Ohio boundary. So, too, the prime object was at one time the terrorizing of the slaveholders and the making of slaveholding less profitable, by reducing the value of slaves along the border. Not until later was there thought out a plan for capturing, controlling and governing a whole section of the United States. Again, in the Kansas years, a prime motive was to relieve the pro-slavery pressure upon Kansas by attacking slavery elsewhere. At one time, as his son Salmon points out, John Brown hoped to force a settlement of the slavery question by embroiling both sections. This was in line with his whole Kansas policy of inducing a settlement by bringing armed pro-slavery and Free State forces to close quarters, and letting them fight it out. After the Kansas episode, John Brown planned agitation for the purpose of setting the South afire. The Southern leaders in Congress having continually threatened secession, John Brown hoped to help them carry out their threat or force them into it, saying that the "North would then whip the South back into the Union without slavery." Salmon Brown declares that he heard his father and John Brown, Jr., discuss this by the hour, and insists that "the Harper's Ferry raid had that idea behind it far more than any other," the biographers of his father having failed heretofore to bring out this central far-reaching idea to the extent it merits.[22] But the main motive was, after all, to come to close quarters with slavery, and to try force where argument and peaceful agitation had theretofore failed to break the slaves' chains. And so, shortly before he reached the age of fifty, this unknown and inconspicuous wool-merchant and cattle-raiser had fully resolved to be the David to the Goliath of slavery. He entertained no doubt that he could accomplish that end, if he could but command the funds necessary for the purchase of arms.

HIS GREATEST OR PRINCIPAL OBJECT 57

While all this metamorphosis of the man was going on, John Brown's new business venture had really brought him into smoother waters, even though it was not destined to be lasting or a financial success. After tending the Perkins flocks for two years, it was decided to establish a headquarters in Massachusetts for the sale of the wool, and there followed the residence in Springfield which meant so much for Brown's development. It was in 1846 that he opened the office, and the next year his family joined him there. Frederick Douglass, after seeing the fine store of Perkins & Brown, was prepared to find Brown's residence in Springfield similarly impressive. "In fact," he wrote,[23] "the house was neither commodious nor elegant, nor its situation desirable. It was a small wooden building, on a back street, in a neighborhood chiefly occupied by laboring men and mechanics; respectable enough to be sure, but not quite the place, I thought, where one would look for the residence of a flourishing and successful merchant. Plain as was the outside of this man's house, the inside was plainer. Its furniture would have satisfied a Spartan. . . . There was an air of plainness about it [the house] which almost suggested destitution." The meal was "such as a man might relish after following the plow all day, or performing a forced march of a dozen miles over a rough road in frosty weather." Everything in the home implied to Mr. Douglass "stern truth, solid purpose, and rigid economy." "I was not long," he added, "in company with the master of this house before I discovered that he was, indeed, the master of it, and was likely to become mine too if I stayed long enough with him. He fulfilled St. Paul's idea of the head of the family. His wife believed in him, and his children observed him with reverence. Whenever he spoke his words commanded earnest attention. . . . Certainly I never felt myself in the presence of a stronger religious influence than while in this man's house."

As for John Brown the man, he was then in his forty-eighth year, without the stoop that a few years later made him seem prematurely old. His attire, however simple, was always neat and of good materials; in Ohio, the testimony is, he dressed like a substantial farmer in the woolen suits of the time and wore cowhide boots. Physically strong and sinewy, he was not five feet eleven in height, with a disproportionately small head, an inflexible and stern mouth and a prominent chin. His hair, already tinged with gray, was closely trimmed and grew well over his forehead. But his bluish gray eyes were what held and won people; they fairly shone when he talked. Mr. Douglass remembers that they were "full of light and fire."[24] His nose was somewhat prominent and of what is known as the Roman type. With all, the face was vigorous, shrewd and impressive. Once a visitor to the North Elba homestead remarked to a family group: "I think your father looks like an eagle." "Yes," replied Watson Brown, "or some other carnivorous bird."[25] But the comparison was not meant to be unflattering; it was the keenness of the eagle's looks, the sharp watchfulness of his glance, even with half-shut eyes, that suggested the comparison. On the prairies, those who rode with John Brown were struck with the range and the alertness of his vision, from which nothing escaped, while those who saw him in the cities noticed the long springing step and apparent deep absorption in his own reflections. Yet all agreed upon the impressiveness of John Brown's bearing; even in later years, when his appearance was so rural as to attract attention on the streets of Boston, the earnestness of his face and the vigor of his form prevented any disposition to ridicule.

The object of the establishment of Perkins & Brown's office in Springfield was to classify wools for wool-growers, in order that they might thus obtain a better value for their product than had been the case up to that time, and to sell it on a commission of two cents per pound.[26] Having warehouses, Perkins & Brown received large shipments of wool from farmers known to them, and then by carefully sorting the fleeces were able to approach manufacturers of cashmere, broadcloth, jeans or satinette, with the wools of the grade they desired. In the first Springfield letter-book of the firm, into which were laboriously copied in long-hand all its letters,[27] the first epistle bears the date of June 23, 1846, and is a tribute to John Brown's probity in that it notifies Mr. Marvin Kent that, if he should send wool to the firm to sell, the amount of the commissions earned would be used to liquidate John Brown's old debts to himself and his father. The times were not, however, propitious for the new enter-

HIS GREATEST OR PRINCIPAL OBJECT 59

prise. The Walker tariff was just being passed by Congress, and the war with Mexico was on. The legislative uncertainty made the wool market dull and unstable, and when the Walker bill was signed, the price of Saxony wool, in which Perkins & Brown were especially interested, dropped from seventy-five to twenty-five cents. Perkins & Brown were, however, able to start off by selling the splendid wool of their own flocks for the good price of sixty-nine cents, and early in July, in a letter in Brown's handwriting, they asserted that "we receive at this place more of the first class of American wools than any other house in the country." [28] Many of the firm's letters are in the handwriting of John Brown, Jr., who, having finished an excellent schooling and being ready for business life, became a clerk in the Springfield office, in which Jason Brown also served. By August 26, John Brown was able to report, cheerfully, to the senior partner in Ohio, as follows: [29] "We are getting in wool rapidly, generally from 50 to 80 bales per day. We are selling a little and have very frequent calls from manufacturers. Musgrave paid up our note at the Agawam [bank] yesterday so that I now have our name clear of any paper in this country. . . . We have had a big wool-growers meeting at Springfield; Bishop Campbell presiding, in reference to sending wool hereafter to Europe."

This project of exporting wool to England and the Continent deeply interested Brown from the beginning of his Springfield residence, particularly as he found himself, in the fall of 1846, loaded up with other people's wool, unable to sell it for them at fair figures, and quite unwilling to sacrifice it at forced sales. On November 27, 1846, he wrote to a client [30] that he would have gone across the Atlantic with a quantity of wool save for unforeseen hindrances. He had sent to England in 1845, from Ohio, some fleeces "which received unqualified praise both for condition and quality," and, as he said in this letter, the firm was bent on encouraging exportation "and in giving character to American wools in Europe." Indeed, the sale of their higher grades of wool to an Englishman for export on December 21, 1846, was all that saved Perkins & Brown from a disastrous ending to their first season's business. They were being hard pushed by those who had sent the wool and were in need of money, and who could not understand why the firm had not been able to sell a single pound of fine wool from July to December. Moreover, some customers had just grievances, for the letter-book contains far too many apologies for failure to acknowledge letters and shipments and to make out accurate accounts, for so young a firm. To one of the protestants, John Brown explained the situation thus:[31]

"We have at last found out that some of the principal manufacturers are leagued together to break us down, as we have offered them wool at their own price & they refuse to buy. . . . We hope every wool-grower in the country will be at Steubenville [Ohio] 2d Wednesday of Feb'y next, to hear statements about the wool trade of a most interesting character. There is no difficulty in the matter as we shall be abundantly able to show, if the farmers will only be true to themselves. . . . Matters of more importance to farmers will then be laid open, than what kind of Tarriff we are to have. No sacrifise kneed be made, the only thing wanted is to get the broad shouldered, & hard handed farmers to understand how they have been imposed upon, & the whole matter will be cured effectually."

At this convention Brown made his peace with the Ohio wool-growers who had shipped to him, but he did not find a means of checkmating the cloth manufacturers. He read to the convention a report on the best mode of making wools ready for market and kindred subjects. It was resolved that better care should be taken in preparing and washing the wools, that commission-house depots be appointed, East and West, for the sale of wools, Perkins & Brown to be the Eastern house, and a committee of five, of which John Brown was one, was appointed to obtain a foreign market for American wools.[32] The wicked manufacturers continued, however, to make trouble for the wool-growers and the commission house of Perkins & Brown, whose eventual retirement from the wool business is still laid at their doors. They did not wish the wool-growers to organize and unite; but in all fairness to the manufacturers, the final failure should as well be shared by Perkins & Brown themselves.[33] For, though the Springfield business continued in 1848 and 1849, as time passed it was evident that John Brown, wholly lacking as he was in a merchant's training, was not fitted for the work. He did not

HIS GREATEST OR PRINCIPAL OBJECT 61

know how to trade, being far too rigid in his prices. He waited to make them until he had all his wool sorted; then, when the prices were finally fixed, the manufacturers had bought elsewhere. It is related [34] that John Brown once declined sixty cents a pound for the firm's own splendid Saxony fleeces and insisted on shipping them to England for sale. The Northampton, Massachusetts, manufacturer who made the offer bought this shipment in England, had it returned to Springfield, and showed it in triumph to John Brown as having cost him in freight and all only fifty-two cents a pound, eight cents less than he had first offered for it. Brown had apparently put no restriction of price upon his London agent.

The idea of checkmating the manufacturers by sales abroad continued to engross Brown, and he was finally able to carry out his idea of a trip to Europe in 1849. He sailed August 15, 1849, by the steamer Cambria, arriving in London on the 27th, on a journey which afterwards played a great part in his discussions of his military plans, for, aside from his business venture, he was by this time particularly anxious to study some European fortifications. Finding on his arrival in London that no sales could be effected until the middle of September, he left for Paris on the 29th of August. Some of his first impressions of England are thus set down in a letter to his son: [35]

"England is a fine country, so far as I have seen; but nothing so very wonderful has yet appeared to me. Their farming and stone-masonry are very good; cattle, generally more than middling good. Horses, as seen at Liverpool and London, and through the fine country betwixt these places, will bear no comparison with those of our Northern states, as they average. I am here told that I must go to the Park to see the fine horses of England, and I suppose I must; for the streets of London and Liverpool do not exhibit half the display of fine horses as do those of our cities. But what I judge from more than anything is the numerous breeding mares and colts among the growers. Their hogs are generally good, and mutton-sheep are almost everywhere as fat as pork."

Of the people and their institutions John Brown recorded no impressions in the letters of this period now extant. Nor is his entire Continental itinerary known. According to carefully saved hotel bills,[36] he was in Calais on August 29 and 30, and in Hamburg on September 5. Between these two dates he was in Paris, going thence to Brussels, where he visited the battlefield of Waterloo on his way eastward. Various surmises have been made as to where the other eleven or twelve days between his visit to Hamburg and his return to London were spent, but there is no documentary evidence to prove the number of battlefields he visited, or that he actually penetrated in so brief a time into Switzerland and Northern Italy, as is sometimes alleged. As already stated, this short trip to the Continent played a great part in his later conversations, when he was called upon to defend the peculiar features, from the military point of view, of his Harper's Ferry plans. But obviously, no thorough military studies were possible in so scant a time as John Brown had in Europe.

He was in London again not later than September 17, when an auction sale of some of his wool took place that set the seal of disaster upon his business venture. The story was thus related to his son by the traveller:[37]

LONDON [Friday] 21st Sept 1849

DEAR SON JOHN

I have nothing new to write excepting that I [am] still well & that on Monday last a lot of No. 2 wool was sold at the auction sale at $^s_1$ $^d_1$ to $^s_1$ $^d_{2\frac{1}{4}}$ or in other words at from .26 to .29 cents pr lb. This is a bad sale, & I have withdrawn all other wools from the public sales. Since the other wools have been withdrawn I have discovered a much greater interest amongst the buyers, & I am in hopes to succeed better with the other wools but cannot say yet how it will prove on the whole. I have a great deal of stupid, obstinate, prejudice, to contend with as well as conflicting interests; both in this country, & from the United States. I can only say that I have exerted myself to the utmost; & that if I cannot effect a better sale of the other wools privately; I shall start them back. I believe that not a pound of the No 2 wool was bought for the United States, & I learn that the general feeling is now; that it was quite undersold. About 150 Bales were sold. I regret that so many were put up; but it cannot be helped now, for after wool has been subjected to a London examination for a public sale it is very much injured for selling again. The agent of Thirion Maillard & Co has been looking at them today, & seemed highly pleased, said he had never seen superior wools; & that he would see me again. We have not yet talked about price. I now think I shall begin to think of home quite in earnest at least in another fortnight possibly sooner. I do not think the sale made a full test of the opperation.

   Farewell   Your Affectionate Father

              JOHN BROWN

On October 5, Brown had again returned to London, after visiting "Leeds, Wortley, Branley, Bradford & other places," and wrote thus to his son John, Jr.:[38] "I expect to close up the sale of wool here today, & to be on my way home One week from today. . . . It is impossible to sell the wool for near its value compared with other wools, but I expect to do better some than in the first sale. I have at any rate done my utmost, & can do no more. I do not expect to write again before I leave. . . . My health is good but I have been in the midst of sickness and death." During this interval, too, John Brown visited in London the first of the long series of world's fairs, and took advantage of it to exhibit some of the beautiful Saxony wool he had brought with him. Long after his return to his home, he received a bronze medal which the wool judges awarded him for his exhibit. Here, too, must be recorded the story early recorded by Redpath, of the attempt of some English wool-merchants to play a trick on the rustic Yankee farmer who came to them with wool to sell, by handing him a sample and asking him what he would do with it: "His eyes and fingers were so good that he had only to touch it to know that it had not the minute hooks by which fibres of wool are attached to each other. 'Gentlemen,' said he, 'if you have any machinery that will work up dogs' hair, I would advise you to put this into it.' The jocose Briton had sheared a poodle and brought the hair in his pocket, but the laugh went against him; and Captain Brown, in spite of some peculiarities of dress and manner, soon won the respect of all he met." It is also said that if given samples of Ohio and Vermont wool, he could readily distinguish them when blindfolded or in the dark.

Apparently he was able to despatch his business about as he had hoped to, for he was in New York by the end of October, bringing back the wool that he was unable to sell. The loss on this venture was probably as high as forty thousand dollars.[39] Not unnaturally this added neither to the standing nor the progress of the firm, and the skies were much darkened for the partners. Even before the trip to Europe, they had talked of giving up the business. Nearly a year later, John Brown thus described an interview with his financial backer and partner:[40]

BURGETTSTOWN PA 12th April 1850

DEAR SON JOHN, & WIFE

When at New York on my way here I called at Mess Fowlers & Wells office, but you were absent. Mr. Perkins has made me a visit here, & left for home yesterday. All well in Essex when I left. All well at Akron when he left one week since. Our meeting together was one of the most cordial, & pleasant, I ever experienced. He met a full history of our difficulties, & *probable losses* without a frown on his countenance, or one sylable of reflection, but on the contrary with words of comfort, & encouragement. He is wholly averse to any seperation of our business or interests, & gave me the fullest assurance of his undiminished confidence, & personal regard. He expressed a strong desire to have our flock of sheep remain undivided to become the joint possession of our families when we have gone off the stage. Such a meeting I had not dared to expect, & I most heartily wish each of my family could have shared in the comfort of it. Mr. Perkins has in this whole business from first to last set an example worthy of a Philosopher, or of a *Christian*. I am meeting with a good deal of trouble from those to whom we have *over advanced* but feel nerved to face any difficulty while God continues me such a partner. Expect to be in New York within 3 or 4 weeks.*

By November the firm's situation was much worse. "We have trouble," wrote John Brown to his son on the 4th of that month,[41] "with Pickersgills, McDonald, Jones, Warren, Burlington & Patterson & Ewing. These different claims amount to $40 M; [$40,000] & if lost will leave me *nice & flat*. (This is in confidence.) Mr. Perkins bears the trouble a great deal better than I had feared. I have been trying to collect & am still trying." Just a month later, he informed his sons that the prospect for the fine-wool business was improving. "What burdens me most of all is the apprehension that Mr. Perkins expects of me in the way of bringing matters to a close what no living man can possibly bring about in a short time, and that he is getting out of patience and becoming distrustful. . . . He is a most noble-spirited man, to whom I feel most deeply indebted; and no amount of money would atone to my feelings for the loss of confidence and cordiality on his part." That this loss did not come to pass is attested by a letter from Mr. Perkins's son, George T. Perkins, who writes:† "My father, Simon Perkins, was associated with Mr.

---

* Signature missing.
† To the author, from Akron, Ohio, December 26, 1908.

HIS GREATEST OR PRINCIPAL OBJECT

Brown in business for a number of years, and always regarded him as thoroughly honest and honorable in all his relations with him. Mr. Brown was, however, so thoroughly impractical in his business management, as he was in almost everything else, that the business was not a success and was discontinued. Their relations were afterwards friendly." On the other side, the Browns felt that too much responsibility had been put upon their father. While most successful as a railroad man, Mr. Perkins was not as well fitted by experience and aptitude for the wool business. But despite John Brown's failures, he gave him one chance after another. "John Brown was, however, entirely obstinate, insisted always on having his own way, and at last Mr. Perkins broke the connection." [42] The senior partner did not, moreover, share the junior's antipathy to slavery.

The final winding up of the firm's affairs lasted for some years, because of prolonged litigation growing out of the trouble with some of the houses and customers John Brown mentioned. Against one of them, Warren, his indignation was never checked. As late as April 16, 1858, he warned his family, when purchasing land from his daughter and son-in-law, against the possibility of trouble from creditors of Perkins & Brown: [43]

"Since I wrote you, I have thought it possible; though not probable; that some persons might be disposed to hunt for any property I may be supposed to possess, on account of liabilities I incurred while concerned with Mr. Perkins. Such claims I ought not to pay if I had *ever so much given me;* for my service in Kansas. Most of you know that I gave up all I then had to Mr. Perkins while with him. . . . I also think that . . . *all the family* had better decline saying anything about their land matters. Should any disturbance *ever be made* it will most likely come *directly or indirectly* through a scoundrel by the name of Warren who defrauded Mr. Perkins and I out of several thousand dollars."

The trial of the Perkins & Brown suit against Warren took place in Troy, New York, late in January, 1852; from a report of John Brown to Mr. Perkins on the 26th of January, [44] it looked as if the suit were going in the firm's favor. He did obtain a verdict in this lower court, only to have it appealed to a higher court, with the result, according to John Brown, that Warren was successful in his attempt to defraud the firm. A more serious suit was one brought against Perkins & Brown for no less than sixty thousand dollars damages, for breach of contract in supplying wool of certain grades to the Burlington Mills Company of Burlington, Vermont. It finally came to trial January 14, 1853, and after progressing somewhat it was settled out of court, his counsel deeming it wiser to compromise than to face a jury.[45] There were still other suits brought by or against the firm to vex John Brown during these years 1850 to 1854, and to add by their costliness and tedious delays to the financial losses. This was the unfortunate wind-up to John Brown's career as a wool-merchant. Thereafter he lived first on the products of his farming in Ohio or in the Adirondacks, and then on gifts made to maintain him as a guerrilla leader in Kansas, or as a prospective invader of Virginia. From August, 1856, when he first returned from Kansas, until October, 1859, he was thus maintained, without a regular business or regular labor of any kind, while part of his family obtained a penurious living in the Adirondacks, and the grown sons shared their father's poverty and hardships in Kansas or worked and farmed at intervals in Ohio, until the final disaster at Harper's Ferry. Although unable to impress others with his fitness as a business man, when he finally abandoned the career of a merchant for that of a warrior against slavery, he had so little difficulty in convincing friends and acquaintances of his ability, usefulness and sagacity as a guerrilla chief and leader of a slave revolt, that he readily obtained thousands of dollars to maintain him and his followers during at least three years of their warring upon the South's cherished ownership of human property.

It is only just to add that, while the financial losses of Perkins & Brown's mercantile business were heavy, Mr. Perkins was not only willing to continue in the farming and sheep-raising part of it with Brown, but insisted on it until well into the spring of 1854. The last year of this phase of their joint enterprise was "quite successful." "We have great reason to be thankful," wrote John Brown in February, "that we have had so prosperous a year, and have terminated our connection with Mr. Perkins so comfortably and on such

HIS GREATEST OR PRINCIPAL OBJECT 67

friendly terms."[46] Early in April, 1854, he again wrote: "I had a most comfortable time settling last year's business and dividing with Mr. Perkins and have to say of his dealings with me that he has shown himself to be every inch a gentleman."[47] The only drawback, in John Brown's mind, was his inability to move his family back to North Elba. This he had to put off for another year, during which he rented and worked three farms near Akron, meanwhile turning everything into cash that he could in preparation for the final settlement in his new home in the Adirondacks.

For John Brown was content to stay neither in Akron nor anywhere else in Ohio. The residence of his family in Springfield had lasted, all told, but two years, from 1847 to 1849; then the restlessness of his nature dictated another move. While in Springfield he occupied the house at number 31 Franklin Street, where Frederick Douglass found him, and in which his daughter Ellen was born on May 20, 1848, only to die a year later in her sorely tried father's arms. Still another child, an infant son, he was yet to lose, — the seventh of the thirteen children of his second marriage to die in childhood, while two more were destined to perish at Harper's Ferry before his eyes. It is still remembered that the parlor of this Springfield house was not furnished, that the money it would cost might be given to fugitive slaves.[48] Indeed, Springfield still abounds in anecdotes of the wool-dealer in whom, at the time of his residence there, no one saw any signs of greatness. The best known one concerns his attempt to prove that the hypnotism practised by La Roy Sunderland, a well-known hypnotist of this period, 1848 or 1849, was a fraud. So many garbled versions of this story have appeared from time to time that it is best to give it in Mr. Sunderland's own words, as he described it on December 9, 1859:[49]

"His conduct in one of my lectures on Pathetism, in Springfield, Mass., some twelve years since, has been referred to in the papers, lately. That occasion offered a grand opportunity for the exhibition of his real character, as, at that time, he had not engaged in the defence of Kansas, and he had had no personal encounters with Slavery. He had witnessed the surgical operation performed on a lady whom I had rendered insensible to pain, as she alleged, by Pathetism. This, with the other phenomena which he witnessed in my lectures, was beyond his comprehension; and so he arose one evening, and pronounced my lectures a humbug, and he offered to prove it, if I would only allow *him* to come upon my platform, and *test* the consciousness of one of my patients. To this proposal I consented, on two conditions, namely, that his tests should not endanger the health of my patient; and this to be determined by the physicians of the town; and secondly, that Brown himself should submit to the same processes which he should inflict upon the entranced lady. To this he readily agreed, although it was quite evident that when he at first proposed his test he had no idea of going through with it himself. He had consulted a physician for a process which should, beyond all doubt, demonstrate the consciousness of pain, if any such consciousness existed in the lady who was entranced. And so the next night, Brown and his physicians were on hand, with a vial of concentrated ammonia and a quantity (*q. s.*) of *dolichos pruriens* (cowhage). This 'cow itch,' as it is sometimes called, is the sharp hair of a plant, and when applied to the skin, it acts mechanically for a long time, tormenting the sufferer like so many thistles or needles being constantly thrust into the nerves. No one, I am sure, would willingly consent to suffer the application of cowhage to his body more than once. Brown bore it like a hero. But, then, he had the advantage of the entranced lady — the skin of his neck looking like sole leather; it was tanned by the sun, and looked as if it was impervious. Not so, however, when the ammonia was held to his nose; for then, by a sudden *jerk* of his head, it became manifest that he could not, by his own volition, screw up his nervous system to endure what I had rendered a timid lady able to bear without any manifestation of pain. The infliction upon Brown was a terrible one, for he confessed, three days afterwards, that he had not been able to sleep at all since the cowhage was rubbed into his neck. In submitting himself to that test, the audience declared him 'foolhardy,' as it proved nothing against the genuineness of my experiments. It would not follow, that because he could endure an extraordinary amount of physical pain, therefore another person could do the same. The degree of COURAGE manifested by John Brown made him the extraordinary man he was. . . ."

The church Brown attended while in Springfield was naturally the Zion Methodist, for it was formed by dissenters from an older church because of their anti-slavery views. John Brown found also a congenial friend in a Mr. Conkling, a clergyman, who later became estranged from his congregation by reason of his Abolition opinions.[50] While John Brown himself never faltered in his religious faith, the backsliding of his sons disturbed him not a little, so that he wrote to them a number of pathetically earnest letters, endeavoring to recall them to the ways of godliness. It was characteristic of him

HIS GREATEST OR PRINCIPAL OBJECT

that, strong as was his nature and intense as was his belief in the orthodox Congregational faith, this difference of religious conviction never interfered with the affection which existed between father and sons. To some of his children he addressed the following letter on this subject while in Troy, New York:[51]

TROY, N. Y., 23 Jan. 1852]

DEAR CHILDREN:

I returned here on the evening of the 12th inst. and left Akron on the 14th, the date of your letter to John. I was very glad to hear from you again in that way, not having received anything from you while at home. I left all in usual health and as comfortable as could be expected; but am afflicted *with you* on account of your little Boy. Hope to hear by return mail that you are all well. As in this trouble you are only tasteing of a cup I have had to drink of deeply, and very often; I need not tell how fully I can sympathize with you in your anxiety. My attachments to this world have been very strong, and Divine Providence has been cutting me loose one bond after another, up to the present time, but notwithstanding I have so much to remind me that all ties must soon be severed; I am still clinging like those who have hardly taken a single lesson. I really hope some of my family may understand that this world is not the *home* of man; and act in accordance. *Why* may I not hope this of you? When I look forward as regards the religious prospects of my numerous family (the most of them) I am forced to say, and to feel too; that I have *little, very little* to cheer. That this should be so, is I perfectly well understand, the legitimate fruit of my own planting; and that only increases my punishment. Some ten or twelve years ago I was cheered with the belief that my elder children had chosen the *Lord* to be their *God;* and I valued much on their influence and example in attoning for my deficiency and bad example with the younger children. But, *where are we now?* Several have gone to where neither a good or a bad example from me will better their condition or prospects, or make them the worse. The younger part of my children seem to be far less thoughtful and disposed to reflection than were my older children at their age. I will not dwell longer on this distressing subject but only say that so far as I have gone; it is from no disposition to reflect on anyone but myself. I think I can clearly discover where I wandered from the Road. How to now get on it with my family is beyond my ability to see; or my courage to hope. God grant you *thorough* conversion from sin, and full purpose of heart to continue steadfast in his ways through the *very short* season of trial you will have to pass.

How long we shall continue here is beyond our ability to foresee, but think it very probable that if you write us by return mail we shall get your letter. Something may possibly happen that may enable us, or one of us, to go and see you but do not look for us. I should feel it a great privilege if I could. We seem to be getting along well with our business, *so far;* but progress miserably slow. My journeys back and forth this winter have been very tedious. If you find it difficult for you to pay for Douglas paper, I wish you would let me know *as I know I took* some *liberty* in ordering it continued. You have been very kind in helping me and I do not mean to make myself a burden.

Your Affectionate Father
JOHN BROWN.

On the 6th of August of the same year he again took up the religious question with his son John in this fashion:[52]

AKRON, Ohio 6th Aug 1852

DEAR SON JOHN

. . . .

One word in regard to the religious belief of yourself, & the ideas of several of my children. My affections are too deep rooted to be alienated from them, but 'my Grey Hairs must go down to the grave in sorrow,' unless the 'true God' forgive their denyal, & rejection of him, & open their Eyes. I am perfectly conscious that their 'Eyes are blinded' to the real Truth, & minds prejudiced by Hearts unreconciled to their maker & judge; & that they have no right appreciation of his true character, nor of their Own. 'A deceived *Heart* hath turned them aside.' That God in infinite mercy for Christs sake may grant to you & Wealthy, & to my other Children 'Eyes to see' is the most earnest and constant prayer of your Affectionate Father

JOHN BROWN.

Just a year later, John Brown returned to the charge and spent a month writing a letter of pamphlet length, mostly composed of Scriptural quotations strung together.[53] "I do not feel 'estranged from my children,'" he wrote, "but I cannot flatter them, nor cry peace when there is no peace." He was particularly pained because, as he said of his younger sons: "After *thorough and candid* investigation they have discovered the Bible to be *all* a fiction! Shall I add that a letter received from *you* sometime since gave me little else than pain and sorrow? 'The righteous shall hold on his way:' 'By and by he is offended.'"

It was his all-impelling desire to help the colored people that led him early to plan for the removal of his family to the Adirondacks. Gerrit Smith, of Peterboro, had offered to give,

HIS GREATEST OR PRINCIPAL OBJECT 71

on August 1, 1846, no less than one hundred and twenty thousand acres of land of his vast patrimony in northern New York to worthy colored people, whom he aided in many other ways as well.[54] By April 8, 1848, John Brown had fully decided to settle his family in the midst of the negro colonists, in order to aid them by example and precept. He later visited his brother-in-law, Orson Day, who was then living in Whitehall, New York, and from Mr. Day's home went on into the Adirondack wilderness as far as the little negro settlement of North Elba, where he became convinced that this was the place for him to settle. He was at once charmed with the superb scenery which has made this region of late such a highly prized summer resort. The great mountains appealed irresistibly to him, and the negro colony offered an opportunity for training men in the armed warfare against slavery which was now taking shape in his mind. Gerrit Smith, whom Brown had visited on April 8, 1848, before seeing North Elba, was greatly pleased at the prospect of having so sturdy and experienced a farmer settle on his land, and became forthwith a warm friend of his visitor from Springfield.[55] Thus began a relationship of enormous value to John Brown as the years passed, without which it is by no means certain that he could have obtained the "greatest or principal object" of his life to the extent he did. No one in the North was more earnest in his opposition to slavery than Gerrit Smith, and none could reinforce their opinions with such princely generosity, or gave as readily and as unselfishly. Chosen a member of Congress in 1852, as an independent candidate, Gerrit Smith had long been no mean figure in State politics. Indeed, in commenting on his going to Congress, Horace Greeley thus described Mr. Smith to his readers:[56] "We are heartily glad that Gerrit Smith is going to Washington. He is an honest, brave, kindhearted Christian philanthropist, whose religion is not put aside with his Sunday cloak, but lasts him clear through the week. We think him very wrong in some of his notions of political economy, and quite mistaken in his ideas that the Constitution is inimical to slavery, and that injustice cannot be legalized; but we heartily wish more such great, pure, loving souls could find their way into Congress. He will find his seat there anything but comfortable, but his presence there will do good, and the country will know him better and esteem him more highly than it has yet done." Of this philanthropist Brown purchased several farms, paying for them as rapidly as his circumstances permitted. The first removal of his family to North Elba or Timbucto, as it was called in its early days, occurred in the spring of 1849, the year of his European trip. As there was no home on his land and he could not himself reside much in North Elba, because of the necessity of carrying on the business in Springfield, John Brown hired for two years the farm of a Mr. Flanders, on the road from Keene to Lake Placid.[57] It had a good barn on it, but only a tiny one-story house. "It is small," said Brown to his family, "but the main thing is *all* keep good natured." Some fine Devon cattle bought in Connecticut were driven to the new home by three sons, Owen, Watson and Salmon, and with these animals Brown won, in September, 1850, a prize at the Essex County Fair by an exhibition of cattle which, according to the annual report of the exhibition society in control, "attracted great attention and added much to the interest of the fair."[58] He was able, also, to buy an excellent pair of horses; the driver, Thomas Jefferson, a colored man, who at the same time moved his family from Troy to North Elba, was in Brown's employ until the first stay in this bleak mountain home came to an end. That Brown felt deeply his responsibility towards his negro neighbors appears from the following extract from a letter, one of many written to Willis A. Hodges, who was likewise active in settling negroes on the Smith lands:[59]

SPRINGFIELD, MASS. January 22, 1849.

FRIEND HODGES — DEAR SIR: Yours of the 11th January reached me a day or two since. We are all glad to hear from you again and that you were getting along well with the exception of your own ill health. We hope to hear better news from you in regard to that the next we get from you. . . .

Say to my colored friends with you that they will be no losers by keeping their patience a little about building lots. They can busy themselves in cutting plenty of hard wood and in getting any work they can find until spring, and they need not fear getting too much wood provided. Do not let anyone forget the vast importance of sustaining the very best character for honesty, truth, industry and faithfulness. I hope every one will be determined to not merely

HIS GREATEST OR PRINCIPAL OBJECT 73

conduct as well as the whites, but to set them an example in all things. I am much pleased that your nephew has concluded to hang on like a man.

With my best wishes for every one, I remain,
Yours in truth
JOHN BROWN

P. S. I hear that all are getting through the winter middling well at Timbucto, for which I would praise the Lord.   J. B.

The original settlers were not particularly pleased at the arrival of so many colored people, and were reluctant at first to supply them with provisions, charging, when they did so, exorbitant prices. So rapidly were the new arrivals' means exhausted that there was some danger of famine. When John Brown came on the scene, he at once defended them against those who sought to injure them, saving to one colored man the farm of which he was being cheated. Seeing their destitution, he sought in every way to provide work for them, and on each Sabbath when he was there, he called the negroes together for instruction in the Scriptures. On October 25, 1848, before he had moved to North Elba, he bought five barrels of pork and five of flour, and shipped them to Mr. Hodges; the contents of at least four of these barrels were distributed among the needy colored at Timbucto.[60] But even with all of the supervision and aid John Brown and Hodges gave, these settlements were not a success. Beautiful as the region was and is, it is not a farming country. To live required the most arduous labor in the brief summer season. There were few tourists to help out the settlers' income, and the cold, desolate and bleak winters bore heavily upon all, but particularly upon the negroes, many of whom were there by virtue of their having fled from slavery in the warm Southern States, where they had known hitherto no stimulus to labor save the lash. There were good common schools, and a church at which, in summer, visiting ministers of note preached.[61] But with all that, North Elba was a dreary and an inaccessible place, particularly in winter. On one occasion, strong as he was, John Brown nearly lost his life in the deep snow in endeavoring to walk in from Keene. "Before he came within several miles of home," so his daughter Ruth remembered the story,[62] "he got so tired and lame that he had to sit down in the road. The snow was very deep and the road but little trodden. He got up again after a little while, went on as far as he could, and sat down once more. He walked a long distance in that way, and at last lay down with fatigue, in the deep snow beside the path, and thought he should get chilled there and die. While lying so, a man passed him on foot, but did not notice him. Father guessed the man thought he was drunk, or else did not see him. He lay there and rested a while and then started on again, though in great pain, and made out to reach the first house, Robert Scott's. . . ."

Shortly after the Brown family moved into the Flanders house at North Elba, Richard Henry Dana, Jr., of Boston, and two friends came to their home, June 27, 1849, in a state of utter exhaustion, having lost their way in the woods and been for twenty-four hours without food. They were kindly received and cared for. Fortunately, Mr. Dana kept an extensive diary, which enabled him in after years to publish the following account from it of his impressions of the Brown family in the Adirondacks:[63]

"The place belonged to a man named Brown, originally from Berkshire in Massachusetts, a thin, sinewy, hard-favored, clear-headed, honest-minded man, who had spent all his days as a frontier farmer. On conversing with him, we found him well informed on most subjects, especially in the natural sciences. He had books, and had evidently made a diligent use of them. Having acquired some property, he was able to keep a good farm, and had confessedly the best cattle and best farming utensils for miles around. His wife looked superior to the poor place they lived in, which was a cabin, with only four rooms. She appeared to be out of health. He seemed to have an unlimited family of children, from a cheerful, nice healthy woman of twenty or so, and a full sized red-haired son, who seemed to be foreman of the farm, through every grade of boy and girl to a couple that could hardly speak plain. . . . June 29, Friday — After breakfast, started for home. . . . We stopped at the Browns' cabin on our way, and took affectionate leave of the family that had shown us so much kindness. We found them at breakfast, in the patriarchal style. Mr. and Mrs. Brown and their large family of children with the hired men and women, including three negroes, all at the table together. Their meal was neat, substantial, and wholesome."

John Brown was at North Elba in January, 1851, soon after the passage of the Fugitive Slave Law, which stirred him to

HIS GREATEST OR PRINCIPAL OBJECT 75

the depths and had just led him to organize his Springfield Gileadites. He at once went around among his colored friends who were fugitives and urged them to resist the law at all costs. Men and women, he declared, should arm themselves and refuse to be taken alive. He told his children of this wicked bill, and commanded them to join in resisting any attempt that might be made to drag back into Southern chains their neighbors who had been slaves, and to give no thought to possible fines and imprisonment. "Our faithful boy, Cyrus," wrote Mrs. Ruth Brown Thompson afterwards, "was one of that class and it aroused our feelings so that we would *all* have defended him, if the women folks had had to resort to *hot water*. Father said 'Their cup of iniquity is almost full.'"

The reasons for John Brown's abandonment of North Elba in 1851, after only two years there, were the burden of the lawsuits of Perkins & Brown, which kept him travelling about from one place to another, and the necessity of continuing in partnership with Mr. Perkins in the farming and sheep-raising side of their business. It was in March, 1851, that he again moved his family, now so accustomed to shifting its domicile, back to Akron, the sons driving overland the prize Devon cattle.[64] As we have seen, the partnership with Mr. Perkins could not be terminated as quickly thereafter as John Brown had hoped, and when it was, he was compelled to work the three hired farms for another year before he had accumulated sufficient money to move back to North Elba and to make possible his venture to Kansas. Throughout 1854 he was busily planning for his removal to North Elba and for the purchase of another small farm there. The record-breaking drought of 1854 ruined many farmers in Ohio, but he fared much better, according to a letter to his children of August 24, 1854, than most people. His two sons, Jason and Owen, were living on a large farm belonging to Mr. Perkins near Tallmadge; they with John Brown, Jr., had, as already stated, made up their minds to seek new homes in Kansas, in order to help stem the slave-power which, with the opening of that Territory by the Kansas and Nebraska act of May 30, 1854, was now seeking to make Kansas its own. On February 13, 1855, John Brown felt certain that he could get off to North Elba with his immediate family in March; to accomplish this purpose he was willing, if necessary, to sacrifice some of his Devon cattle.[65] Not until June, 1855, however, was he able to make the move:

ROCKFORD ILL 4th June 1855

DEAR CHILDREN

I write just to say that I have finally sold my cattle without making much sacrifise; & expect to be on the way home Tomorrow. Oliver expects to remain behind & go to Kansas. After I get home I expect to set out with the family for North Elba as soon as we can get ready: & we may possibly get off this Week; but hardly think we can. I have heard nothing further as yet from the Boys at Kansas All were well at home a few days since.

Your Affectionate Father
JOHN BROWN[66]

When he and his charges finally arrived at North Elba, they moved into an unplastered four-room house, the rudest kind of a pioneer home, built for him by his son-in-law, Henry Thompson, who had married his daughter Ruth. Here the family still lived when the disaster at Harper's Ferry deprived it of its head and two of his most promising sons. But though John Brown was so attracted by North Elba as to buy three farms there,[67] and though the very pioneering aspect of the new life appealed to him, his restlessness left him no peace. He was now ready to abandon the field to which in the year before he had felt himself committed to operate, and to follow his sons to Kansas. So strong was the call to duty there that he was impelled to leave everything at North Elba,— the uncompleted house, the newly arrived family with no fixed means of support and the severest of winter climates to contend with, his activity among his colored neighbors, and his still unpaid debts in Ohio and elsewhere. Besides his sons, Owen, Oliver, Salmon, Frederick, Jason and John Brown, Jr., Henry Thompson, too, yielded to the desire to aid in carving out with axe and rifle Kansas's destiny. There remained at North Elba of the grown sons only Watson, then in his twentieth year, to aid their brave mother and home-keeper. But she was quite ready to fight cold and privation, if thereby her husband and sons could live up to what they as truly considered the call of duty as did their Revolutionary ancestor, who gave up his life in New York City, the appeal to arms in 1777.

HIS GREATEST OR PRINCIPAL OBJECT

Thenceforth John Brown could give free rein to his *Wanderlust;* the shackles of business life dropped from him. He was now bowed and rapidly turning gray; to everyone's lips the adjective "old" leaped as they saw him. But his was not the age of senility, nor of weariness with life; nor were the lines of care due solely to family and business anxieties, or the hard labor of the fields. They were rather the marks of the fires consuming within; of the indomitable purpose that was the mainspring of every action; of a life devoted, a spirit inspired. Emancipation from the counter and the harrow came joyfully to him at the time of life when most men begin to long for rest and the repose of a quiet, well-ordered home. Thenceforth he was free to move where he pleased, to devote every thought to his battle with the slave-power he staggered, which then knew nothing of his existence.

The metamorphosis was now complete. The staid, sombre merchant and patriarchal family-head was ready to become Captain John Brown of Osawatomie, at the mere mention of whose name Border Ruffians and swashbuckling adherents of the institution of slavery trembled and often fled. Kansas gave John Brown the opportunity to test himself as a guerrilla-leader for which he had longed; for no other purpose did he proceed to the Territory; to become a settler there, as he had hoped to in Virginia in 1840, was furthest from his thoughts. Leadership came readily to him; to those who fell under his sway, it seemed as natural that he should become the commander as that there should be a President in Washington. Even those who walked not in his ways respected him as a captain of grim determination, of iron will. Of no particular distinction as an executive in his business enterprises, he had somehow or other acquired in the home circle, in the marts of trade, in the quiet fields and woods, that something which makes some men as inevitably leaders as others are predestined to become satellites or lieutenants of those of stronger will, greater imagination and clearer prevision. Imagination our wool-merchant had, even if its range was not great; for when the hour came to act, he was on hand with his nerves under control, his head clear, his courage unbounded, ready to meet emergencies. Indeed, one may ask if he really had nerves, so complete was their subordination to the ego, to the will that forced its own way, either when it was a matter of convincing rebellious followers of the wisdom of the plan they revolted against, or of standing steadily on the scaffold trap-door to eternity. Yet this man was the product of piping times of peace; of the counting-room and the petty life of the rural follower of a trade, which are so widely supposed to weaken the fibre, attenuate the blood and develop the craven. The secret of this riddle lies not merely in the Puritan inheritances of John Brown, nor in his iron will, nor in his ability to visualize himself and his men in a mountain stronghold of the Alleghenies. To all these powers of an intense nature were added the driving force of a mighty and unselfish purpose, and the readiness to devote life itself to the welfare of others. However one may dislike the methods he adopted or the views he held, here is, after all, the explanation of the forging of this rough, natural leader of men. "Why," said one of his abolition co-workers, who believed in very different means of attacking slavery, "it is the best investment for the soul's welfare possible to take hold of something that is righteous but unpopular. . . . It teaches us to know ourselves, to know what we are relying on, whether we love the praise of men, or the praise of God." The essentially ennobling feature of John Brown's career, that which enabled him to draw men to him as if by a magnet, was his willingness to suffer for others,—in short, the straightforward unselfishness of the man.

As John Brown left for Kansas, he turned once more to the members of his family and said: "If it is so painful for us to part with the hope of meeting again, how of poor slaves?"[68]

CHAPTER III

IN THE WAKE OF THE WAR CLOUD

"IF you or any of my family are disposed to go to Kansas or Nebraska, with a view to help defeat *Satan* and his legions in that direction, I have not a word to say; *but I feel committed to operate in another part of the field.* If I were not so committed, I would be on my way this fall,"— thus it was that John Brown wrote to his son John on August 21, 1854.[1] The latter and his brothers had, as we have seen, grown restless in Ohio, where they then resided with but indifferent prospects for material success, particularly because of the great damage done by the drought of 1854;[2] and the emigration of their uncle, the Rev. Samuel Lyle Adair, to Osawatomie, Kansas, had determined their settling in that locality.[3] To Kansas they would, however, have gone had he not preceded them, for their inherited antipathy to slavery made them earnest observers of the exciting political conditions resulting from the Kansas-Nebraska bill, which left to the settlers themselves the decision whether slavery should or should not exist within those Territories. This abrogation of the Missouri Compromise of 1820, which had prohibited slavery north of 36° 30′ north latitude, roused its enemies in the North to unwonted efforts. If, they reasoned, the South could thus abrogate a sacred agreement which had for thirty-four years prevented the growth of slavery toward the North, it might within a few years permit the extension of its favorite institution to still other portions of the original Louisiana purchase acquired from France in 1803. Only seven years had then elapsed since the unholy war with Mexico had made possible the annexation of the great State of Texas and the other Territories acquired by the peace treaty of 1848. That tremendous expansion to the south and southwest would, it was thought, satisfy the slaveholders for years to come. But the wastefulness and short-sightedness of their methods of cotton-culture, the uneconomic and shiftless character of slave labor itself, made the appetite for virgin lands insatiable.

Moreover, Southern leaders were blind neither to the danger to their political supremacy involved in the carving of new free States out of the great West, whose possibilities were now beginning to be understood because of the rush to California, nor to the peculiarly dangerous position of their outpost State, Missouri.[4] With Illinois on the east and Iowa on the north, if Kansas and Nebraska should become free territory, Missouri would be surrounded on three sides by Abolitionists, and the safety of her unpaid labor system would be gravely menaced. Since the popular indignation in the North had failed to prevent the passage of the Kansas-Nebraska bill, for which forty-four Northern Democrats voted in the House and fourteen in the Senate, under the lead of Stephen A. Douglas, the North could revenge itself only by preventing the return to Washington of thirty-seven out of the forty-four Congressmen,[5] and by throwing itself heartily into the work of beating the South at its own game of colonization. By emigrant aid societies, by widespread appeals to the liberty-loving citizens of the North to settle Kansas, by mass meetings and public subscriptions to the funds raised to forward settlers in large parties to the new Territories, — in a hundred different ways, some of the necessary thousands were induced to become a living bulwark to the extension of slavery. Fortunately for them, the propagandists were aided enormously by the rich character of the Kansas soil, the beauty of its prairies, the charm of its climate, and the promise of its streams. Had there been no question of slavery or freedom involved, there must have been the same prompt taking up of the public lands which has inevitably followed the throwing open of new territory to settlement. The sons of John Brown were no more unmoved by the "glowing accounts of the extraordinary fertility, healthfulness and beauty of the territory of Kansas," than were thousands of others who sold off their homes in New York, Ohio and Illinois to better their fortunes beyond the Missouri River. To many of them, as to the Browns, the opportunity to help save Kansas from the curse of slavery was heartily welcome; to multitudes of others this was a subsidiary issue, which interested them but little until they suddenly found themselves in the maelstrom of Kansas political passions and compelled to take sides, whatever their original opinions or desires.

Owen, Frederick and Salmon Brown left Ohio for Kansas, all unsuspicious of the tragedies before them, in October, 1854, taking eleven head of cattle and three horses, their joint property, to Chicago by water, and driving them thence to Meridosia, Illinois. Here men and animals wintered until the arrival of spring made it possible for them to cross the Missouri.[6] On April 20, 1855, they entered Kansas, and on May 7, Jason and John were also at Osawatomie,[7] having left Ohio with their families at the opening of navigation.* Theirs was a typical Kansas settler's journey; to hundreds of other Kansas home-seekers would John Brown, Jr.'s narrative of this migration read almost as if written of their own experiences after leaving St. Louis:

"At this period there were no railroads west of St. Louis; our journey must be continued by boat on the Missouri at a time of extremely low water, or by stage at great expense. We chose the river route, taking passage on the steamer 'New Lucy,' which too late we found crowded with passengers, mostly men from the South bound for Kansas. That they were from the South was plainly indicated by their language and dress; while their drinking, profanity, and display of revolvers and bowie-knives, openly wearing them as an essential part of their make-up, clearly showed the class to which they belonged and that their mission was to aid in establishing slavery in Kansas.

"A box of fruit-trees and grape-vines which my brother Jason had brought from Ohio, our plow and the few agricultural implements we had on the deck of that steamer, looked lonesome, for these were all we could see which were adapted to the occupations of peace. Then for the first time arose in our mind the query: Must the fertile prairies of Kansas, through a struggle at arms, be first secured to freedom before free men can sow and reap? If so, how poorly were we prepared for such work will be seen when I say that for arms for five of us brothers we had only two small squirrel rifles and one revolver. But before we reached our destination other matters claimed our attention. Cholera, which then prevailed to some extent at St. Louis, broke out among our passengers, a number of whom died. Among these, Brother Jason's son, Austin, aged four years, the elder of his two children, fell a victim to this scourge, and while our boat lay by for repair of a broken rudder at Waverley, Mo., we buried him at night near that panic-stricken town, our

---

* Mrs. Annie Brown Adams states that Salmon and Oliver Brown, as well as their father and Henry Thompson, went to Kansas only to fight, not to settle; the others were home-seekers. (See her letter of September 5, 1886, to the Kansas Historical Society.)

lonely way illumined only by the lightning of a furious thunderstorm.

"True to his spirit of hatred of Northern people, our captain, without warning to us on shore, cast off his lines and left us to make our way by stage to Kansas City, to which place we had already paid our fare by boat. Before we reached there, however, we became very hungry, and endeavored to buy food at various farmhouses on the way; but the occupants, judging from our speech that we were not from the South, always denied us, saying, 'We have nothing for you.' The only exception to this answer was at the stage-house at Independence, Mo.

"Arrived in Kansas, her lovely prairies and wooded streams seemed to us indeed like a haven of rest. Here in prospect we saw our cattle increased to hundreds and possibly to thousands, fields of corn, orchards, and vineyards. At once we set about the work through which only our visions of prosperity could be realized. Our tents would suffice for shelter until we could plow our land, plant corn and other crops, fruit-trees, and vines, cut and secure us hay enough of the waving grass to supply our stock the coming winter."[8]

But if they were thus apparently bent on the occupations of peace, they were from the beginning keeping an eye out for the clash of arms. In his very first letter from the Territory to his father, dated "Brownsville," May 21, 1855, Salmon, while mentioning his "very pleasant trip through Missouri," added:

"We saw some of the curses of slavery and they are many. . . . The boys have their feelings well worked up so that I think that they will fight. there is a great lack of arms here in Brownsville. I feel more like fight now than I ever did before and would be glad to go to Alabama."

He reported further that he had no doubt of the success of their emigration, for they had as many as five good claims, had planted considerably and could already behold the first tender shoots pushing their way into the air. Their claims were eight miles from Osawatomie, on the very outskirts of which stood and yet stands the picturesque log-cabin which for nearly fifty years served as the homestead of the Adair family, and is still prized by them beyond all other earthly possessions. Here the Browns were certain of a hearty welcome from their father's half-sister Florilla and her husband, the Rev. Mr. Adair.

On May 20 and 24, John Brown, Jr., wrote a long,

IN THE WAKE OF THE WAR CLOUD 83

minutely detailed letter to his father, in which appear clearly the mixed motives that had led to the emigration. The character of the country, the weather encountered, the planting operations and the implements in use are all set forth, as well as the low financial condition to which their frontier venture had already brought them, and their almost general satisfaction with the change:[9]

". . . Salmon Fredk and Owen say that they never was in a country that begun to please them as well. And I will say, that the present prospect for health, wealth, and usefulness much exceeds even my most sanguine anticipations. I know of no country where a poor man endowed with a share of common sense & with health, can get a start so easy. If we can succeed in making this a free State, a great work will be accomplished for mankind."

But the really important part of the letter deals with the political impressions already acquired by the new settlers of four weeks' standing:

"And now I come to the matter, that more than all else I intended should be the principal subject of this letter. I tell you the truth, when I say that while the interest of despotism has secured to its cause hundreds and thousands of the meanest and most desperate of men, armed to the teeth with Revolvers, Bowie Knives, Rifles & Cannon, — while they are not only thoroughly organized, but under pay from Slave-holders — the friends of freedom are *not one fourth* of them *half armed*, and as to *Military Organization* among them it *no where exists in this territory* unless they have recently done something in Lawrence. The result of this is that the people here exhibit the most abject and cowardly spirit, whenever their dearest rights are invaded and trampled down by the lawless bands of Miscreants which Missouri has ready at a moment's call to pour in upon them. This is the *general* effect upon the people here so far as I have noticed, there are a few, and but a few exceptions. Of course these foreign Scoundrels know what kind of '*Allies*' they have to meet. They boast that they can obtain possession of the polls in any of our election precincts without having to fire a gun. I enclose a piece which I cut from a St. Louis paper named the St. Louis '*Republican;*' it shows the spirit which moves them. Now Missouri is not alone in the undertaking to make this a Slave State. Every Slaveholding State from Virginia to Texas is furnishing men and money to fasten Slavery upon this glorious land, by means no matter how foul. . . .

"Now the remedy we propose is, that the Anti slavery portion of the inhabitants should *immediately, thoroughly arm* and *organize themselves* in *military companies.* In order to effect this, some persons must begin and lead in the matter. Here are 5 men of us who are not only anxious to fully prepare, but are thoroughly determined to fight. We can see no other way to meet the case. As in the language of the memorial lately signed by the people here and sent to Congress petitioning help, 'it is no longer a question of negro slavery, but it is the enslavement of ourselves.'

"The General Government may be petitioned until the people here are grey, and no redress will be had so long as it makes slavery its paramount interest. — We have among us 5, 1 Revolver, 1 Bowie Knife, 1 middling good Rifle 1 poor Rifle, 1 small pocket pistol and 2 slung shot. What we need in order to be thoroughly armed for each man, is 1 Colts large sized Revolver, 1 *Allen & Thurbers*' large sized Revolver manufactured at Worcester, Mass, 1 *Minnie Rifle* — they are manufactured somewhere in Mass or Connecticut (Mr. Paine of Springfield would probably know) and 1 heavy Bowie Knife — I think the Minnie Rifles are made so that a sword bayonet may be attached. With these we could compete with men who even possessed Cannon. The real Minnie Rifle has a killing range almost equal to Cannon and of course is more easily handled, perhaps enough so to make up the difference. Now we want you to get for us these arms. We need them more than we do bread. Would not Gerrit Smith or someone, furnish the money and loan it to us for one, two or three years, for the purpose, until we can raise enough to refund it from the *Free* soil of Kanzas? . . ."

This appeal for arms John Brown could not have resisted had he desired to. He subsequently recorded that on the receipt of this letter he was "fully resolved to proceed at once to Kansas; and join his children." [10] The wish to "operate elsewhere" had disappeared early in 1855. Indeed, before the second detachment of his sons had started, he had begun to arrange his affairs so that he too might emigrate. On February 13 he notified John W. Cook, of Wolcottville, Conn., of his intentions:

"Since I saw you I have undertaken to direct the opperations of a Surveying, & exploring party, to be employed in Kansas for a considerable time perhaps for some Two or Three years; & I lack for time to make all my arrangements, & get on to the ground in season." [11]

Labor as he might, he was not able to dispose of his cattle, wind up odds and ends of his business in Illinois, Ohio and New England, collect arms for his sons, take leave of his family at North Elba and start for the West, until the middle

IN THE WAKE OF THE WAR CLOUD 85

of August. On June 28 he was at Syracuse, attending a convention of anti-slavery men who called themselves Radical Political Abolitionists. Frederick Douglass, Gerrit Smith, Lewis Tappan and Samuel J. May were among the speakers, as well as John Brown, and the convention unanimously resolved that its members should do what they could to prevent the return of fugitives. There was, however, considerable difference of opinion in consequence of the proposal to raise money for John Brown, that he might collect arms for his sons. Douglass, of course, spoke earnestly in Brown's behalf. Others were unwilling to encourage violence, but, as Douglass afterwards reported: "The collection was taken up with much spirit, nevertheless; for Capt. Brown was present and spoke for himself; and when he spoke men believed in the man."[12] He received in all about sixty dollars in cash, twenty dollars being from Gerrit Smith, and five dollars from an old British Army officer, Charles Stuart. By April 24 he was able to ship from Springfield to Cleveland a box of firearms and flasks, which he subsequently picked up in Cleveland on his way West.[13]

Ex-Sheriff S. A. Lane, of Akron, testified, in an interview printed in the Akron *Beacon-Journal* of February 1, 1898, that during his visit to Akron, on his way West in August, Brown held open meetings in one of the public halls of the village. Because of their interest in the Kansas crisis, and in the Browns, their former neighbors, the people were quickly roused by Brown's graphic words, and liberally contributed arms of all sorts, ammunition and clothing. Committees of aid were appointed, and Lane was deputed to accompany Brown in a canvass of the village shops and offices for contributions. Several cases of guns belonging to the State of Ohio, then being collected from the disbanded militia companies of Akron and Tallmadge, were "spirited away" to the same end. General Lucius V. Bierce later testified to his own gift of broadswords, the property of a defunct filibustering company. On the 15th of August, Brown reported to those remaining at North Elba that he was leaving Cleveland via Hudson, and would have been off before had he not met with such success in obtaining "Guns Revolvers, Swords, Powder, Caps, & money," that he thought it best to "detain a day or Two longer on that account." He had raised nearly two hundred dollars in that way in the two previous days, principally in arms and ammunition.[14] But the harvest being gathered, he and his son-in-law, Henry Thompson, arrived in Chicago August 18, after stopping at Cleveland and Detroit, where they met Oliver Brown and at once prepared for the overland journey by buying a "nice young horse for which we paid here $120, but have so much load that we shall have to walk a good deal; enough probably, to give opportunity to supply ourselves with game. We have provided the most of what we need on our outward march " — so Brown wrote to his "Dear Wife and Children; every one" on August 23, the day of leaving Chicago, with solemn injunctions to write often and to direct the letters to Oliver, since Oliver's name was "not so common as either Henry's or mine."[15] The heavily loaded one-horse wagon was in obedience to advice from John Brown, Jr., who opined that his father would find it just what he wanted in Kansas to carry on the business of surveying. Moreover, this method of reaching Osawatomie was, if the slowest, the best and cheapest way of travelling, particularly because the navigation of the Missouri River was, as the son put it, "a horrid business in a low stage of water which is a considerable portion of the year."[16]

Not that roughing it could discourage John Brown, as we know. There was found, after his capture in Virginia, in his papers, the beginnings of an autobiographical volume entitled: ' A brief history of John Brown, otherwise (old B) and his family: *as connected With Kansas;* By one who knows.'[17] This was composed early in August, 1858, for on the 9th of that month he wrote to his son John from Moneka, Kansas, asking that certain letters and other material be sent him for this book, which, had it been completed, would have been sold for "the benefit of the *whole* of my family, or to promote the cause of Freedom as may hereafter appear best for both objects."*[18] In this all too brief fragment, written in the third person, appears the story of his trip to Kansas, including

---

* "I am *certain*," he added, "from the manner in which I have been pressed to narrate, and the greedy swallowing everywhere of what I have told, and complaints in the newspapers voluntarily made of my backwardness to gratify the public, that the book would find a ready sale."

IN THE WAKE OF THE WAR CLOUD 87

fresh assurance from his own pen that "with the exposures, privations, hardships, and wants, of pioneer life he was familiar; & thought he could benefit his Children and the new beginners from the older parts of the country and help them to shift."

The nice, stout young horse had all he could do, so Brown records, to drag the load when he and his son and son-in-law left Chicago behind them. Hence, continues his own narrative, just cited:

"Their progress was extremely slow; & just before getting into Missouri their horse got the distemper: after which for most of the journey they could only gain some Six to Eight miles in a day. This however gave them great opportunity for seeing & hearing in Missouri. Companies of armed men, and individuals were constantly passing and repassing Kansaswise continually boasting of what deeds of patriotism; & chivalry they had performed in Kansas; & of the still more mighty deeds they were yet to do. No man of them would blush when telling of their cruel treading down & terrifying of defenceless Free State men; they seemed to take peculiar satisfaction in telling of the fine horses, & mules they had many of them killed in their numerous expeditions against the d—d Abolitionists. The coarse, vulgar, profane, jests, & the bloodthirsty brutal feelings to which they were giving vent continually would have been a most exquisite treat to Ears; and their general appearance to the Eys of the past and the present Administration. Of this there cannot be the slightest doubt or of the similiarly refined feeling amongst their truly Democratic supporters and the dough faces. Witness the rewards of such men as Clark and others.

" On the way at Waverly Missouri he took up the body of his little grandson who had died of cholera . . . thinking it would afford some relief to the broken hearted Father and Mother they having been obliged to leave him amidst the ruffian-like people by whom (for the most part) they were themselves so inhumanly treated in their distress. The parents were almost frenzied with joy on being told that the body of their dear child was again with them. On his arrival at the place where his sons had located he found all the company completely prostrate with sickness (Chill fever, and Fever and Ague) except the wife of John Jr and her little boy of some three years old. The strongest of all the five men scarcely able to bring in their Cows, cut their fuel, bring the water, and grind the little corn which with a little dried fruit they had left; a very few Potatoes they had raised and a small supply of milk. . . ."

One picturesque and characteristic incident of the crossing of the enemy's territory John Brown himself did not record, since fate intervened here and prevented the addition of another word to what was to have been his first venture into literature. His son-in-law, Henry Thompson, relates that when they reached the Missouri River at Brunswick, Missouri, they set themselves down to await the ferry. There came to them an old man, frankly Missourian, frankly inquisitive after the manner of the frontier. "Where," said he, "are you going?" "To Kansas," replied John Brown. "Where from?" asked the old man. "From New York," answered John Brown. "You won't live to get there." "We are prepared," said John Brown, "*not to die alone.*" Before that spirit and that eagle eye, the old man quailed; he turned and left.[19]

It was on October 6 that the advance guard of the caravan reached the family settlement at Osawatomie. Brown himself, being very tired, did not cover the last mile or two until the next day. They arrived in an all but destitute condition, with but sixty cents between them, to find the little family settlement in great distress, not only because of the sickness already noted, but because of the absence of any shelter save tents. The bitterly cold and cutting winds, which did much to disillusionize so many of the emigrants, kept the Browns shivering over their little fires, and the exposure added to their ill-health. The crops that had been raised were not cared for; there was no meat, little sugar, and nothing to make bread with, save corn ground by great labor in a hand mill two miles off.[20] The men, enfeebled by the chills and ague which racked, sooner or later, all the new arrivals in Kansas, had lost their initiative and vigor, and needed the resolute sternness of the head of the family to stimulate them to new efforts. By postponing the building of cabins, they had been able to devote themselves to the crops; and the abundance of excellent corn, potatoes, pumpkins, squashes, melons, beans, etc., which had earlier constituted their fare, compensated them for most of the inconveniences they had been compelled to put up with, so wrote Mrs. John Brown, Jr., to her mother-in-law at North Elba.[21]

But the time had more than arrived when they should devote themselves to home-building. On October 25 there was the "hardest freezing" John Brown had ever witnessed south of North Elba at that season of the year, as he reported

IN THE WAKE OF THE WAR CLOUD

to his wife, in order that she should know, "in that miserable Frosty region" of North Elba, that "those here are not altogether in Paradise."[22] Indeed, nobody in Kansas that unusually cold winter of 1855–56 knew what comforts were. Had there been no political anxieties to vex them, the frightful hardships of pioneering and the acclimating sicknesses would have made that period truly dreadful to look back upon. While the Browns paid the penalty for living on low ground in a ravine and in tents, that first summer, their bitter experience was yet vastly better than that of many another family. Starvation and death looked in at many a door where parents lay helpless, while famished children crawled the unboarded floors crying for food, shrieking with fear if any footstep approached, lest the comer be a Border Ruffian instead of a friend. For pure misery and heart-breaking suffering, these pioneer tales of Kansas in 1855–58 are not surpassed by any in the whole history of the winning of the West.*

By November 2, Jason's and John's "shanties" were well advanced; by the 23d, their father reported these two families so well sheltered that they would not suffer any more, and that he had made some progress in preparing another house, in the face of icy rains and freezing nights. "Still," wrote the indomitable directing spirit, "God has not 'forsaken us;' & we get 'day by day our dayly Bread;' & I wish we had a great deal more gratitude to mingle with our undeserved blessings."[23] One dread that had worried them prior to their departure from home proved unnecessary. "You recollect we used to talk a great deal about the Indians," wrote Mrs. John Brown, Jr., "and how much I feared them — they are the least of my troubles — there is scarcely a day but they go along in sight of us in droves of from 30 to 40, sometimes more and sometimes less, and frequently four or five of them will come galloping up to see us; they have always treated us perfectly civil and I believe if we treat them the

---

* See, for instance, Mrs. M. D. Colt, *Went to Kansas*, Watertown, New York, 1862; Mrs. Sara T. L. Robinson's *Kansas, its Interior and Exterior Life*, Boston, 1858; Thaddeus Hyatt's MS. *Journal of Investigations in Kansas*, 1856–57, Kansas Historical Society; *Six Months in Kansas*, by a Lady (Hannah Anderson Ropes), Boston, 1856; 'Memoir of Samuel Walker,' in *Kansas Historical Society Collections*, vol. 6, pp. 249–274; *Three Years on the Kansas Border*, by a Clergyman of the Episcopal Church, New York, 1856.

same they will do us no harm." [24] Her prophecy was a correct one. It was not the red but the white men of the border they had to fear. Terrified as they were when the first big band of Sacs and Foxes in war-paint surrounded their tents, whooping and yelling, the Browns had the good sense to ground their arms, and the Indians did likewise. Thereafter both sides were great friends. John, Jr., went often to visit their old chief; once, when, in the following summer, the Indians came to call in numbers, they were "fought" with gifts of melons and green corn. "That," says Jason Brown, "was the nicest party I ever saw."

John Brown, Jr., used to ask the old chief questions, as: "Why do you Sacs and Foxes not build houses and barns like the Ottawas and Chippewas? Why do you not have schools and churches like the Delawares and Shawnees? Why do you have no preachers and teachers?" And the chief replied in a staccato which summed up wonderfully the bitter, century-long frontier experience of his people: "We want no houses and barns. We want no schools and churches. We want no preachers and teachers. We bad enough now." [25]

The men really to be feared were not long in putting in appearance. A few days after the arrival of the Brown advance guard in April, six or eight heavily armed Missourians rode up and inquired if any stray cattle had been seen in that neighborhood. On receiving a prompt negative, in the vernacular of the border they inquired how the newcomers were "on the goose." "We are Free State," was the answer, "and more than that, we are Abolitionists." The visitors rode away at once and, says Jason Brown, "from that moment we were marked for destruction. Before we had been in the Territory a month, we found we had to go armed and to be prepared to defend our lives." The leader of that band of Missourians might not have been allowed to ride away, had the outspoken Northerners before them realized the sinister part the Rev. Martin White was to play in their lives, — if they could have dreamed that he was to shoot down one of their number in cold blood within a twelvemonth. [26]

It must be said, however, that the Browns were aggressive from the beginning. They not only nailed their colors to the mast and let all who would behold them, but they gave play

IN THE WAKE OF THE WAR CLOUD 91

to those feelings which, as Salmon reported, had been so well worked up in crossing Missouri. John Brown, Jr., Jason, Frederick and Owen eagerly attended Free State settlers' meetings,[27] and the first-named figured soon in the political history of the Territory. On the afternoon of Monday, June 25, 1855, he was elected a vice-president of the Free State convention which, then in session at Lawrence, solemnly urged all the people of Kansas to throw away their differences and make the freedom of Kansas the sole issue. Its members called upon Free State representatives to resign from the bogus Shawnee Legislature chosen by Missouri votes, declared that the convention did not feel that its members should obey any laws of the Legislature's exacting, and finally resolved, with a spirit that must have gratified every Brown, "That in reply to the threats of war so frequently made in our neighbor state, our answer is, 'WE ARE READY.'"[28] Naturally, John Brown, Jr.'s participation in this expression of feeling — he was a member of the committee on resolutions — did not improve his standing with his Southern neighbors, of whom a good many were soon to be free with their threats and boasts that they would drive off every Yankee.[29] But this did not deter him in the least from attending the radical Lawrence gathering of August 15, in which, according to the *Herald of Freedom*, he was a member of the steering, or business committee, nor from becoming a member of the first Territorial Executive Committee, an outgrowth of the Big Springs convention of September 5.[30]

When the fraudulent Pawnee Legislature convened, July 2, 1855, it enacted, true to its lawless inception, a code of punishments for Free State men that must always rank as one of the foremost monuments of legislative tyranny and malevolence in the history of this country. Under that code no one conscientiously opposed to slavery, or who failed to admit the right of everybody to hold slaves, could serve as a juror; and the right to hold office was restricted to pro-slavery men. Five years at hard labor was to be the fate of any one introducing literature calculated to make a slave disorderly or dangerous or disaffected. Death itself was the penalty for raising a rebellion among slaves or supplying them with literature which advised them to rise or conspire against any citizen. The mere voicing of a belief that slavery was illegal in Kansas was made a grave crime, in the following words:

"Sec. 12: If any free person, by speaking or writing, assert or maintain that persons have not the right to hold slaves in this Territory, print, publish, write, circulate, or cause to be introduced into the Territory, any book, paper, magazine, pamphlet or circular, containing any denial of the right of persons to hold slaves in this Territory, such persons shall be deemed guilty of felony, and punished by imprisonment at hard labor for a term of not less than five years." [31]

This clause was obviously aimed at the New York *Tribune* and other anti-slavery journals, and was meant to be an effective padlock upon free speech. General J. H. Stringfellow, a resident of Atchison and the Speaker of the House that passed this gag-law, boasted that it and other legislation "will be enforced to the very letter." [32] This challenge John Brown, Jr., promptly accepted. The code from which we have quoted became operative on September 15, 1855. What he did on that day, John Brown, Jr., recorded on the next in a letter to his mother:

"Yesterday I told a man who I since learn has a slave here that no man had a right to hold a slave in Kansas, that I called on him to witness that I had broken this law and that I still intended to do so at all times and at all places, and further that if any officer should attempt to arrest me for a violation of this law and should put his vilainous hands on me, I would surely kill him so help me God. He made no reply but rode off. — Nothing is now wanting but an attempt to enforce this Law with others of like import, which Gov. Shannon has declared he will do, and we shall have war here to the knife." [33]

"Perhaps," wrote Mrs. John Brown, Jr., to her brother-in-law, Watson, then at North Elba, "we shall all get shot for disobeying their beautiful laws, but you might as well die here in a good cause as freeze to death there." [34] The belligerent attitude of the men of her party might well have given her anxiety. It was as if they had intended from the first to make Osawatomie the storm centre of southeastern Kansas, and to bring down upon them the special attentions of the most radical men on the other side of the border, men of the type of General Stringfellow, a brother of B. F. Stringfellow, who declared on August 28, 1855, in his newspaper, the *Squatter Sovereign*, published at Atchison, Kansas, on the Missouri line:

"We can tell the impertinent scoundrels of the [New York] *Tribune* that they may exhaust an ocean of ink, their Emigrant Aid Societies spend their millions and billions, their representatives in Congress spout their heretical theories till doomsday, and his excellency Franklin Pierce appoint abolitionist after free-soiler as governor, yet we will continue to tar and feather, drown, lynch and hang every white-livered abolitionist who dares to pollute our soil."[35]

With those and other threats ringing in their ears, the sons of John Brown unloaded the arms donated by friends of free Kansas in the East and hauled by that stout young horse across Illinois and Missouri, while John Brown himself surveyed the settlement of Osawatomie, whose name was henceforth to be linked with his and thus obtain an imperishable place in American history, although his own stay in the simple frontier settlement was to be brief indeed, — not eleven months in all.

To Kansas John Brown came with no thought of settling. Surveying was to give him a livelihood while he remained, but he came to fight, prepared to battle along that Kansas-Missouri line for two or three years, by which time he felt the victory should be won, and he be free to assail slavery at another point.[36] The Kansas country delighted him. Indeed, he told his children that, if a younger man, he would certainly stay with them, but that so long as he had a good farm at North Elba, he felt that by common industry he could maintain his wife and daughters there while his sons settled where fancy led them.[37] He went so far, on his arrival, as to think of taking a claim near his sons' settlement, but the battles and tragedies of the immediate future prevented his considering the matter further.[38] In March, 1859, he wrote to John Teesdale that "it has been my deliberate judgment since 1855 that the most ready and effectual way to retrieve Kansas would be to meddle directly with the peculiar institution." He arrived ready to grapple with it, to meet violence with violence, to do to the Border Ruffians what they were doing to Free Soilers. To accomplish this, he was ready to take from the pro-slavery men their chattels, whether living or immobile, and even their lives.

Until well into the spring of 1855 the drift of affairs in Kansas had been wholly against the Free Soilers, despite the emigration from New England.[39] Bona fide Missouri settlers were naturally first in the field, by reason of their proximity to the newly opened lands, and were quicker in organizing, under the leadership of Atchison and of the Stringfellow brothers and their allies. They were on hand at the first election held in the Territory, November 29, 1854, for a delegate to Congress, and to their aid came hundreds of residents of Missouri, on horseback and in wagons, with guns, bowie-knives, revolvers and plenty of whiskey. Encamping near the polling places,[40] on election day, these visitors cast 1729 fraudulent votes[41] to the satisfaction of their leaders, thus electing the pro-slavery candidate, General J. W. Whitfield. Atchison, on November 6, had pointed out in a speech at Weston, Missouri, how easily the trick could be turned: "When you reside in one day's journey of the Territory, and when your peace, your quiet and your property depend upon your action, you can without an exertion send five hundred of your young men who will vote in favor of your institutions. Should each county in the State of Missouri only do its duty, the question will be decided quietly and peaceably at the ballot-box. If we are defeated, then Missouri and the other Southern States will have shown themselves recreant to their interests and will deserve their fate."[42] As it happened, "some of the leading men of Missouri, comprising merchants, doctors and lawyers, were recognized among the ballot-box stuffers." Judges, too, were there, and the city attorney of St. Joseph. There was nothing concealed about the transaction. The coming of the Missourians was foretold by Free Soil correspondents.[43] When the visitors had closed the polls, they gayly shouted, "All aboard for Kansas City and Westport," and drove or rode away.[44] In one district, the seventh, seventy-five miles from the Missouri line, — which had three months afterward only 53 voters according to the official census, — there were cast 604 votes. The Howard Committee* reported that fully 584 of these were illegal.[45]

---

* Authorized by the House of Representatives, March 19, 1856, to investigate the Kansas situation. It consisted of William A. Howard, of Michigan, John Sherman, of Ohio, and Mordecai Oliver, of Missouri.

This invasion, curiously enough, was quite unnecessary to carry the day for Missouri, for the Free Soilers were then in a numerical minority to the bona fide Missouri settlers, as also when the official census was taken three months later, in February, 1855.[46] Indeed, for fully eight months after the opening of the Territory on July 1, 1854, the Missourians bade fair to overrun Kansas. Moreover, at the time of the election, the Free Soilers were divided in their counsels, without recognized leaders or a definite policy, and took little interest in the voting, not one-half of them going to the polls.[47] But the appetite for illegal interference in a sister State grew with its indulgence. The victory of November 29 was proclaimed as a great and lasting triumph for the slavery forces. The *Kansas Herald* of Leavenworth announced that "the triumph of the pro-slavery party is complete and overwhelming, . . . Kansas is saved,"[48] and its jubilation was echoed throughout Missouri. The *St. Louis Pilot* rejoiced "at this decisive result, — as well on account of the success of General Whitfield, as that it will tend to quiet the fear and anxiety pervading the Western frontier, that this State would be flanked on the west with an unprincipled set of fanatics and negro-thieves, imported expressly to create annoyance, and disturb the social relations of the people of the frontier counties."[49] The friends of liberty in the East were correspondingly depressed. "We believe that there are at this hour four chances that Kansas will be a Slave State to one that she will be Free," wrote Horace Greeley in the *Tribune* of December 7. In Washington it was generally thought that the South had possessed itself of Kansas,[50] even though the February, 1855, census showed that only 192 slaves had been taken into the Territory, in which there were also 151 free negroes. "Some of the Southern men coolly say they have taken Kansas so easily that they think it may be worth while to take Nebraska also," reported Greeley's Washington correspondent on February 13, 1855.

Naturally, in the East the November invasion was used by the *Tribune* and other backers of the Emigrant Aid Societies to stimulate recruiting for the Kansas holy war.[51] On the other hand, the arrival of bands of New Englanders sent out by the Emigrant Aid Societies, the first of which reached Lawrence August 1, 1854,[52] had intensely inflamed the Missourians, and continued to do so for the next two years. "Shall we allow such cut-throats and murderers, as the people of Massachusetts are, to settle in the territory adjoining our own state?" asked the *Liberty Platform*, a Missouri border newspaper, in June, 1854; and it answered its own question thus: "No! If popular opinion will not keep them back, we should see what virtue there is in the force of arms."[53] In August, on hearing of the arrival of the first Emigrant Aid party, the *Platte County Argus* declared that: "It is now time to sound the alarm. We know we speak the sentiments of some of the most distinguished statesmen of Missouri when we advise that counter-organizations be made both in Kansas and Missouri to thwart the reckless course of the Abolitionists. We must meet them at their own threshold and scourge them back to their covers of darkness. They have made the issue, and it is for us to meet and repel them."[54] To the Missourians in 1854 and later, their fellow countrymen from the historic Bay State appeared the scum of Northern cities, hired to vote, and not intending to settle Kansas in a normal way; "the lowest class of rowdies;" "the most unmitigated looking set of blackguards;" "hellish emigrants and paupers whose bellies are filled with beggars' food;" men of "black and poisonous hearts,"[55] — thus had one section of Americans been set against their brothers by the divine institution of slavery. "Riff-raff," "scoundrels" and "criminals" were mild adjectives applied to Eastern settlers, in whose eyes the Border Ruffians were an equally low and degraded set of beings, drunken bandits "armed to the teeth" and revelling in cruelty, — in brief, fiends incarnate. "Rough, coarse, sneering, swaggering, dare-devil looking rascals as ever swung upon a gallows," was the way Dr. J. V. S. Smith, of Boston, characterized them.[56]

"Reader," asked William A. Phillips, the Kansas correspondent of the *Tribune*, "did you ever see a Border Ruffian? . . . Imagine a fellow, tall, slim, but athletic, with yellow complexion, hairy-faced, with a dirty flannel shirt, or red or blue, or green, a pair of common-place, but dark-colored pants, tucked into an uncertain altitude by a leather belt, in which a dirty-handled bowie-knife is stuck rather ostentatiously, an eye slightly whiskey-red, and teeth the color of a

IN THE WAKE OF THE WAR CLOUD

walnut. Such is your Border Ruffian of the lowest type." "In a representation," he added, "of the 'Forty Thieves,' they would have been invaluable, with their grim visages, their tipsy expression, and, above all, their oaths and unapproachable swagger."[57] To Thomas H. Gladstone, a relative of the great statesman of that name, the Border Ruffians seemed to be "wearing the most savage looks and giving utterance to the most horrible imprecations and blasphemies. . . . Looking around at these groups of drunken, bellowing, blood-thirsty demons, who crowded around the bar of the house shouting for drink, or vented their furious noise on the levee without, I felt that all my former experiences of border men and Missourians bore faint comparison with the spectacle presented by the wretched crew, who appeared only the more terrifying from the darkness of the surrounding night."[58] This of the men he met in Kansas City after they returned from the sacking of Lawrence in 1856. The earlier invaders of Kansas Mrs. Charles Robinson described as "rough, brutal-looking men, of most nondescript appearance;" "bands of whiskey-drinking, degraded, foul-mouthed marauders."[59]

Undoubtedly their ranks did include the scum of the border; that was inevitable. But, aside from their desire to foster slavery in Kansas, they had been easily convinced by their leaders that the coming by droves of New England Yankees actually menaced their homes, their wives and children, their property, human or otherwise. As soon as Kansas was submerged by the incoming tide of Abolition, the anti-slavery attack was to be directed against Missouri and Texas, and then the fall of slavery would be certain. Senator Atchison, in his speech at Weston which has already been cited, declared that "if we cannot do this [take Kansas], it is an omen that the institution of Slavery is to fail in this and the other Southern States." As late as July, 1856, the Charleston, S. C., *Courier* affirmed that: "Now, upon the proposition that the safety of the institution of Slavery in South Carolina is dependent upon its establishment in Kansas, there can be no rational doubt." "The touchstone of our political existence is Kansas — that is the question," wrote the Washington correspondent of the Charleston *Mercury*, January 5, 1856, six months earlier.[60] For what other purpose could the Yankees be carrying arms, was asked after the election in 1855, when Charles Robinson succeeded, through his agent, George W. Deitzler, in obtaining Sharp's rifles from the officers of the Emigrant Aid Society in Boston, they being shipped to him labelled "Revised Statutes" and "Books."[61]

Elated as they were by their triumph at the polls in the first election, the Missourians were disposed to take no chances of defeat when the second one took place. This was called by the first Territorial Governor, Andrew H. Reeder, for March 30, 1855,[62] and in preparing for it the Missouri pro-slavery men displayed that talent for rapid military organization which was so evident in the South in 1861. Since this election was for the choice of the first Territorial Legislature, its importance was far greater than the mere selection of a delegate to Congress. Both sides felt that whoever chose the Legislature settled the destiny both of the Territory and of the future State of Kansas as well. No one could accuse the Free Soilers of lacking interest this time. But they were still too young upon the soil, and had not suffered enough indignities, to make them united for a common cause. Moreover, the winter of 1854–55 had been not only unusually mild, but politically quiet as well.[63] Hence the Missourians again carried everything before them when they invaded Kansas for the second time to deny to its citizens of Northern and Eastern origin the votes to which they were rightfully entitled. They came by companies, each assigned to its special field of activity, and overawed every election district save one.[64] One thousand men devoted their attention to Lawrence as the home of the most Abolitionists.[65] Some of these had belonged to the then disbanded Platte County, Missouri, "Self-Defensive Association," which by formal vote of its members was pledged to "bring to immediate punishment all Abolitionists," and to remove from Kansas Territory on demand of any citizen of that Territory, "any and all emigrants who go there under the auspices of the Northern Emigrant Associations."[66] The Blue Lodges, similar organizations for the protection of Missouri by making Kansas impossible to all save emigrants from the South, were well in evidence. Each wagon of the raiders bore the designation of an order or lodge.[67] What happened on March 30 was merely a repetition of November 29 on a larger and bolder and more flagrant scale. The violations of law and order, the stuffing of the ballot-boxes, the terrorizing of the Free Soilers, the expelling of Northern election officials, — in brief, the subversion of the most precious of our free institutions was complete. The sacredness of the ballot was nowhere respected. Of the 6307 votes cast, nearly five-sixths were those of the invaders.[68] The thirty-nine men who were elected were all representatives of the South, with one exception. Seven of the pro-slavery men Governor Reeder unseated, not because of the frauds, but because of technical flaws in their election. He later explained his not declaring more seats vacant, although he knew that the whole election was a fraud, by stating that no other complaints had been filed, and that he thus lacked official information, — a valid technical excuse. Complaints were not readily made because the Missourians threatened with death any who might venture to file them. Indeed, the Governor deserves some credit for unseating those legislators he did. He rendered his decision in a room crowded by fourteen of his friends, all armed, and by the thirty-nine successful candidates, veritable walking arsenals![69] But no shooting occurred. The Missourians were well content with the disqualification of only seven of their number. Subsequently, they summarily ousted the seven Free Soilers legally elected to fill these vacancies, and the remaining Free Soil member promptly resigned.[70] The Legislature was thus pro-slavery throughout.

It must not be thought that this high-handed outrage, which fairly set the North aflame with indignation, went without reprobation from the soberer elements in Missouri. The exultant Stringfellows and Atchisons represented the blood and thunder pro-slaveryites; but there were other voices. To their credit be it recorded that the Parkville *Luminary*, Boonville *Observer*, Independence *Messenger*, Jefferson City *Inquirer*, *Missouri Democrat*, St. Louis *Intelligencer*, Columbia *Statesman*, *Western Reporter*, Glasgow *Times*, Fulton *Telegraph*, Paris *Mercury* and Hannibal *Messenger* spoke out bravely against the invasion of Kansas by mobs and the frauds at the polls.[71] For its conscientious scruples the Parkville *Luminary* promptly met an unmerited fate. It was completely destroyed on April 14, its plant being thrown into the river and its editors warned that, if found in town three weeks later, they would follow their type into the Missouri. If they moved to Kansas, the mob assured them, they would be followed and hanged wherever found.[72] If a citizens' meeting at Webster, Missouri, highly approved of this action and asserted that they had "no arguments against abolition papers but Missouri River, bonfire and hemp rope,"[73] there were plenty of more conservative citizens. Unfortunately, they remained in the minority; but to them appealed the argument that if the entire border population of Missouri were to move into Kansas, the injury to Missouri's progress and prosperity would be great. They felt, all the more as they were attached to their own homes, that upon the States farther South rested the duty of colonizing Kansas.[74]

The first Territorial Legislature, which so thoroughly misrepresented Kansas, met at Pawnee on July 2. After unseating the Free Soil delegates and organizing, it adjourned to meet again at Shawnee on July 16. This change of location gave Governor Reeder the opportunity which he had been seeking. He had vetoed the removal bill, only to have it passed over his veto.[75] He then declared that the Legislature was no longer a legal body. In this contention he was not upheld by the Chief Justice of the Territory, S. D. Lecompte, the Associate Justice, Rush Elmore, and the United States District Attorney, A. J. Isacks,[76] and the Legislature thereafter went its own way and had little to do with the Executive. It did, however, petition President Pierce for Reeder's removal. Its messenger learned on his way that Reeder had been dismissed from office on July 28, ostensibly not because of the quarrel with the Legislature, but because of his speculations in Indian lands near Pawnee.[77] The underlying reason was, none the less, the pro-slavery party's hatred of him.[78] As for his land speculations, he openly stated to the Howard Committee the circumstances connected therewith, and they have not been held to reflect on his character.[79] Governor Reeder at once became a valuable leader of the Kansas Free Soilers, being thus forcibly converted into an Abolitionist from a sympathizer with the Squatter Sovereignty policy, and was regarded in the East as a martyr to the Abolition cause, particularly after he was compelled to flee from Kansas in disguise, in May, 1856, never to return to that State. As for the Legislature, it spent July and August in authorizing a militia, appointing a full staff of pro-slavery military and civil officers, in establishing a complete code of laws for the government of the Territory, based on the Missouri code, and in passing those extreme Black Laws which John Brown, Jr., was so quick to violate. On the last day of its session, the Speaker, General J. H. Stringfellow, offered a characteristic resolution, which was readily adopted: "It is the duty of the Proslavery Party, the Union men of Kansas Territory, to know but one issue, Slavery; and that any party making or attempting to make any other, is, and should be, held, as an ally of abolitionism and disunion."[80] For all this, no genuine attempt was made to enforce the Black Laws; they were dead letters from the time of enactment. If they were intended to frighten off further emigration from free States, they failed miserably; if they were intended to terrorize those already in the Territory, they were an even more dismal failure. On the other hand, reprinted in pamphlet form and widely circulated throughout the North and East, the Black Laws added fuel to the already intense flame of Northern indignation, and became an unanswerable demonstration of the intolerance of the pro-slavery domination of Kansas and the lengths to which it would go.

The Free State men, especially those in Lawrence, among whom Charles Robinson, the agent of the New England Emigration Society, and Martin F. Conway were beginning to stand out as leaders, as soon as they could calmly consider the situation, decided that the bogus Legislature and its laws must be repudiated.[81] It soon became their policy to call a Constitutional convention, frame a Constitution and then apply to Congress for admittance as a free State. As has already been pointed out, they were not united among themselves. If there were ardent Abolitionists among them, there were also many who were unfriendly to the free negro, even when they wished slavery excluded from the Territory. The men who had settled Kansas represented every state of political belief, for the magnet of free land was all that had drawn many of them there. In the summer of 1855 they might roughly have been classed as moderates and radicals; there existed, too, considerable jealousy on the part of the other emigrants toward those New Englanders who came out under the auspices of the Emigrant Aid Societies.[82] The first of six conventions to meet in Lawrence on or before August 15, in order to repudiate the Legislature, was composed of citizens of that settlement. It assembled June 8 and decided to issue a call for a State convention, to be made up of five delegates from each of the eighteen election districts in Kansas. This convention was to have as its purpose the taking "into consideration the relation the people of this Territory bear to the Legislature about to convene at Pawnee."[83] It was to this gathering that John Brown, Jr., came on June 25, to help to draft the announcement that the Free State men answered "Ready" to the threats of war from Missouri. This convention further resolved that it was in favor of making Kansas a free Territory and in consequence a free State. Finally, since the Pawnee Legislature "owed its existence to a combined system of fraud and force," the members of the convention resolved that they were bound by no laws whatsoever of its creation.[84]

Two days later, June 27, James H. Lane made his first appearance in Kansas history as chairman of the abortive attempt to organize the National Democratic party in the Territory, this failure soon bringing Lane into the ranks of the Free Soilers. Unlike all the other conventions of this period, it in no wise attempted to repudiate the Legislature.[85] The next gathering, that of July 11, was attended by the expelled Free State members of the Legislature and other citizens. In it the conflict of opinion between radicals and moderates was very marked, the repudiation of the Legislature and the call for a mass meeting in Lawrence on August 14, to consider the government of the Territory, alone being unanimous.[86] The August 14 convention, in which Lane participated, turned out to be ready for a fairly radical stand. Dr. Charles Robinson was chairman of the committee on resolutions, which roundly denounced the bogus Legislature, repudiated its authority, and committed the Free State party to the forming of a State Constitution of their own with a view to admission to the Union, but provided no machinery by which this should be done. If the resolutions were radical, the net result was conservative. On the second day there was also adopted a call for a convention at Big Springs, to be held on September 5. Delegates to it were to be appointed at a meeting on August 25, and the purpose of these gatherings was to be left largely to what the hour might demand.

Curiously, as if the specific relationship and purpose of these gatherings were not puzzling enough, a second convention also met in Lawrence on August 15, while the first was still in session. This second body was presided over by Dr. A. Hunting, and comprised the radicals of the Free State party, some of whom, like Charles Robinson and M. F. Conway, were actually members of both conventions. John Brown, Jr., was one of the committee on "business," which turned out to be a call for a constitutional gathering at Topeka on October 19, for the "speedy formation of a State constitution, with an intention of immediate application to be admitted as a State into the Union of the United States of America." The distinction between these two simultaneous conventions of August 15 may be stated thus: The first and larger one, of six hundred members, had as its aim the organization of the Free State political party by means of the Big Springs convention; the second and radical one looked to the immediate establishment of a Free State government, to be set up in opposition to the pro-slavery Legislature still sitting at the Shawnee Mission, and now presided over by the second Territorial Governor, Wilson Shannon, of Ohio, — a Governor, in truth, to please the most violent Border Ruffian or pro-slavery agitator.[87]

Out of these numerous meetings came the Big Springs convention on September 5, which adopted a platform — the first one — for the Free State party, and nominated ex-Governor Reeder as delegate to Congress. The platform was a great disappointment to the radical Abolitionists of the John Brown type, both in Kansas and New England, for while it resolved that slavery was a curse and that Kansas should be free, it announced that it would consent "to any fair and reasonable provision in regard to the slaves already in the Territory." More than that, it specifically voted that Kansas should be a free white State, and recorded itself as being in favor of "stringent laws excluding all negroes, bond and free, from the Territory." Indeed, as if to answer the Southern charge that the Free Soil citizens of Kansas were radical, no-union-with-slaveholders, anti-slavery men, the convention denounced attempts to interfere with slavery and slaves, and declared "that the stale and ridiculous charge of Abolitionism so industriously imputed to the Free State party . . . is without a shadow of truth to support it."[88] It is hardly surprising that to those men who, like the Browns, had come to Kansas to wage war with slavery, this policy of compromise—a last attempt to head off a violent conflict between the two forces contending for control of the Territory —should have smacked of the cowardly. Nor did the vigorous denunciation of the Shawnee Legislature in the resolutions passed by the convention mollify men of this type. Charles Stearns, the only Lawrence representative of the *Liberator* school of Abolitionists, denounced the proceedings with the vigor of language characteristic of that school, and was in turn reprobated as an impossible Garrisonian of the deepest dye. "All sterling anti-slavery men, here and elsewhere, cannot keep from spitting upon it [the platform]," wrote Stearns to the *Kansas Free State* of September 24, 1855, "and all pro-slavery people must, in their hearts, perfectly despise the base sycophants who originated and adopted it."[89] In the East, Horace Greeley reluctantly accepted the platform in the following words: "Why free blacks should be excluded it is difficult to understand; but if Slavery can be kept out by a compromise of that sort, we shall not complain. An error of this character may be corrected; but let Slavery obtain a foothold there and it is not so easily removed."[90]

Doubtless when Lawrence was threatened with destruction less than three months later, by the pro-slavery forces encamped on the Wakarusa River, Mr. Stearns cited their presence as proof that the Big Springs platform had utterly failed to mollify the hostile Missourians or to lessen their contempt for the Free Soilers, whom they still despised as arrant cowards. Certain it is that the trend of events speedily forced the Free State party itself into an entirely different attitude from that it sought to maintain at Big Springs. The anti-negro attitude of the party was, however, upheld at the

IN THE WAKE OF THE WAR CLOUD 105

Topeka convention, which met at Topeka on October 23 to form a Constitution in obedience to the decision of the earlier delegate convention of September 19 (ordered by the radical Lawrence convention of August 15). The Topeka Constitutional convention of thirty-four members, presided over by James H. Lane, consisted of four physicians, twelve lawyers, thirteen farmers, two merchants, two clergymen and one saddler; a majority favored the exclusion of free negroes, but finally decided to submit this question to the people.[91] By 1287 ballots to 453, the voters of the Territory upheld the negro exclusion policy on December 15, and made it clear to the rest of the country that, if slavery in Kansas itself was opposed by the Free Soil party, it was not in the least due to any liking for negroes, or any desire to extend to those who were free the opportunities afforded by the opening of the Territory, or to any belief that the continuance of human bondage was inconsistent with American institutions. Three-fourths of the Free State settlers were in favor of a free white State, and the heaviest voting against the free negro was in Lawrence and Topeka.[92] Obviously, those who had come to Kansas with the purpose of opposing the extension of slavery were in a small minority, just as the scanty slave population shows either that few of the Missouri settlers came solely for slavery's sake, or else that, if they had such a purpose, they feared to bring their slaves with them.[93]

On the credit side of the record of the Big Springs convention must be noted its denunciation of the bogus pro-slavery Legislature, its demand for the sacredness of the "great 'American Birthright' — the elective franchise," and its endorsement of the coming Topeka convention to consider the adoption of a Constitution. There was, moreover, a serious threat in one of its resolutions that there would be submission to the Legislature's laws no longer than the Territory's best interests required, when there would follow opposition "to a bloody issue as soon as we ascertain that peaceable remedies shall fail, and forcible resistance shall furnish any reasonable measure of success."[94] All of this threatening of fire and slaughter was placed not in the platform, but in the resolutions; it was obviously an attempt at facing both ways, and as such is justified by men who subsequently became radical antagonists of all who favored slavery.* The convention also ignored the Legislature's action in appointing October 1 as the day for the election of a Territorial delegate to the Thirty-fourth Congress, and fixed upon October 9 as the proper day for this election; the returns from this voting were subsequently ordered turned over to the "Territorial Executive Committee," instead of to the Legislature. This "Executive Committee," also a creation of the Big Springs Convention, and the first Free State steering committee appointed by a delegate convention to take charge of Free State affairs, was headed by Charles Robinson as chairman, with Joel K. Goodin as secretary, and had among its twenty-one other members Martin F. Conway and John Brown, Jr.[95] Finally, it was at this Big Springs meeting that James H. Lane first made his mark as a Kansas political leader; to his eloquence is attributed the saving of the convention from a dangerous split, in that he brought about its approval of the preliminary Constitutional convention at Topeka.[96] As to Lane's attitude on the negro, John Brown, Jr., has testified to Lane's saying in Lawrence, about this time: "So far as the rights of property are concerned I know no difference between the negro and a mule."[97] Later, however, Lane switched about on this as on other issues.

The two elections for Territorial delegate took place as scheduled. At the pro-slavery one on October 1, General J. W. Whitfield, who had represented Kansas in the national Legislature during the three months of the Thirty-third Congress remaining after his election on November 30, 1854, received 2721 out of 2738 votes cast, the Free State men abstaining from the polls. The Howard Committee pronounced 857 of these votes illegal after only a partial examination of the returns.[98] Eight days later, with conditions reversed, Reeder received 2849 Free Soil votes.[99] His election was, of course, ignored by the Territorial Governor, Shannon. When Reeder and Whitfield both presented themselves at Washington, the latter was given his seat on February 4, 1856, only to be igno-

---

* For instance, R. G. Elliott, who played an important part in the Big Springs Convention, declares that it faced "an important condition that had to be dealt with practically and with conciliatory discrimination." — *Kansas Historical Society Collections*, vol. 8, p. 373.

miniously ousted on August 4,[100] after the report of the Howard Committee had been received by the House of Representatives.* The House could not, however, then bring itself to seating Reeder. But his appearance at Washington and his vigorous urging of his claims were the reason for the appointment of the Howard Committee. This was in itself a splendid triumph for the new policy of the Free State leaders and their plan of an organized political demand upon Congress for recognition. Not only are the majority and minority reports of the Howard Committee, with their voluminous sworn testimony, an invaluable record for the historian and the best source of information as to the period in Kansas history covered by its inquiry, but the publication of the results thereof made a profound impression upon the country at large, at a critical period in the Territory's history.

From the double election for delegates in October, 1855, dates that duality in the political life of the strife-torn Territory which lasted for two years thereafter, and adds so much to the perplexity of the cursory student of Kansas history prior to its statehood. It is not only that there were henceforth two governments, but that they were supported by factions bitterly hostile even to the extent of bloodshed. There were always separate elections for the same offices at separate places, with the double machinery of counting and proclaiming the returns, and there was even a duality of management on the Free Soil side. The supplemental Topeka Constitutional convention met, as determined by the preliminary one of September 19, on October 23, and remained in session until November 11. The Constitution it adopted followed closely those of the other free States, providing that there should be no slavery, and that no indenture of any negro or mulatto made elsewhere should be valid within the State. It fixed March 4, 1856, as the day for the meeting of the General Assembly called for by the document.[101] This was submitted to the people on December 15 and ratified by a vote of 1731 for, to 46 against. The poll-books at Leavenworth having been destroyed by a pro-slavery mob, its vote is

* The Howard Committee reported that both Whitfield's and Reeder's elections were illegal, but that Reeder had received more votes of resident citizens than Whitfield. See Howard Report, p. 67.

not recorded in the above total.[102] Thereafter the Free Soil forces insisted that Kansas was an organized free State, when demanding its admission into the Union. The convention, before adjourning, appointed another Free State Executive Committee, with the same secretary as had the Robinson Committee, Joel K. Goodin, but with Lane, already a serious rival of Charles Robinson, as its chairman, and five other members. Lane, therefore, emerged from the Topeka convention with additional prestige and thoroughly committed to the Free State policies.

Out of all the meetings and conventions of the nine months after the stolen March 30 election, there had come, then, great gains to the Free State movement. The liberty party had been organized, leaders had been developed, and a regular policy of resistance by legal and constitutional measures adopted. If counsels of compromise were still entirely too apparent and too potent, the train of events which resulted in Kansas's admission as a free State was well under way. Not unnaturally, the pro-slavery leaders at first regarded this growing opposition with amusement or contempt. They were still convinced in October, 1855, that Kansas was theirs by right of their larger battalions and by right of conquest. Moreover, Governor Shannon, with all his authority, was on their side, and behind him the Federal Government. The adoption of the Topeka constitution did, however, arouse their anger; to this their answer was the organization in November of their own party, which, with unconscious irony, they dubbed the "Law-and-Order Party," at a meeting over which Governor Shannon presided.[103] Indeed, as their hitherto triumphal overriding of Kansas began to meet a more and more compact resistance, their mood began to change. The leaders were quick to feel their power slipping from their hands, particularly when, the first rush from Missouri being over, the steady stream of emigration from the East made it evident that they were being outnumbered. Their followers, also, began to get out of hand; from overawing by a show of force, it was easy to proceed to actual physical violence in the hope of terrifying the hated Free Soiler or of driving him from the Territory. The temptation to crime was all the greater since there was no non-partisan judicial machin-

IN THE WAKE OF THE WAR CLOUD 109

ery, and often no machinery at all outside of the Federal judiciary.[104]

The Howard Committee found that, of all the crimes testified to during its sessions, an indictment had been found in but one case.[105] In that, the man charged with murder was a Free Soiler, Cole McCrea by name, who had killed a pro-slavery man, Malcolm Clark, at Leavenworth, on April 30, 1855, in a quarrel over certain trust lands and McCrea's right to participate in and vote in a squatter's meeting. The first of the long series of homicides which was to make of the Territory in very truth a "bleeding Kansas," was not a political one. It occurred near Lawrence on the first election day, November 30, 1854, Henry Davis, a Border Ruffian from Kentucky, being killed by Lucius Kibbey, of Iowa. Davis, in an intoxicated condition, had assailed Kibbey with a knife.[106] Such an election-day crime might easily have occurred anywhere. The killing of Clark,[107] in the following spring, became, on the other hand, of marked political significance, because of the treatment of his slayer, McCrea. The latter was imprisoned at Leavenworth until late in November. The injustice of his case lay in the court's denying to McCrea his counsel, James H. Lane, because the latter would not take the oath of allegiance to the pro-slavery Legislature, and in McCrea's subsequent treatment, on September 17, when he was brought before the grand jury of nineteen men summoned by Chief Justice Lecompte and picked by him. Sixteen were openly selected and three in private; one of the nineteen had been engaged with Clark in the attack on McCrea. For a whole week Justice Lecompte endeavored to induce the jury to indict McCrea, but in vain; the evidence was too strongly in favor of McCrea for even this picked jury to find a true bill against him. As the foreman refused to bring in a verdict of "not found," Justice Lecompte adjourned the court until the second Monday of November, when McCrea was finally indicted, after having been illegally deprived of liberty during the intervening period. When, in November, he was able to make his escape from jail and leave the Territory by way of Lawrence, the inability of its citizens to offer him protection added greatly to their stress of mind. The whole episode of McCrea's confinement had roused the indignation of the Free

Soilers everywhere, convinced as they were that McCrea had shot in self-defence.[108]

Even more stirring to the friends of liberty was the ill-treatment of William Phillips, an active Free State lawyer of Leavenworth, and a friend of Cole McCrea's, who was present when Clark was killed. Phillips received notice on April 30, from the pro-slavery vigilance committee appointed on that date, to leave the Territory. On his refusal to go or to sign a written agreement that he would leave Kansas, a majority of the committee, so one of its members testified, "voted to tar and feather him. The committee could get no tar and feathers this side of Rialto; and we took him up there and feathered him a little above Rialto, Missouri."[109] This witness forgot to add that one side of Phillips's head was shaved; that after his clothes were stripped from him and the tar applied, he was ridden on a rail for a mile and a half, and then sold for one dollar by a negro auctioneer at the behest of his tormentors. A public meeting at Leavenworth on May 19 heartily endorsed this treatment of "William Phillips, the moral perjurer."[110] The next day the Leavenworth *Herald* said of the mob's work: "The joy, exultation and glorification produced by it in our community are unparalleled." This outrage failed to daunt Phillips's courage; he stayed in Kansas, only to die later at the hands of his pro-slavery enemies. As John Brown was leaving Ohio for Kansas, a similar experience befell the Rev. Pardee Butler at Atchison. His pro-slavery fellow citizens, on August 16, placed him on a raft and shipped him down the Missouri, throwing stones at him and his queer craft as the current bore him away. His forehead was ornamented with the letter R; and the flags on his raft bore the inscriptions, "Greeley to the rescue, I have a nigger;" "Eastern Aid Express;" and "'Rev. Mr. Butler,' agent to the Underground Railroad."[111] The *Squatter Sovereign*, the Stringfellow newspaper, notified all the world that "the same punishment we will award to all free-soilers, abolitionists and their emissaries." In fact, one J. W. B. Kelly had already encountered the hatred of the pro-slavery leaders, for in the first week of August he was severely thrashed and ordered out of town for holding Abolition views.[112] Yet Butler returned to Atchison, as Phillips did to Leavenworth, only to

IN THE WAKE OF THE WAR CLOUD

meet a graver fate. Another clergyman, the Rev. William C. Clark, was assaulted on a Missouri river steamer in September, for avowing Free State beliefs that seemed to his assailants to call for physical punishment.[113]

As John Brown crossed the boundary between Missouri and Kansas, on October 4, these outrages were still agitating the Territory and causing men everywhere to arm. That the pro-slavery election of October 1 had passed off peacefully, although fraudulently, had reassured no one; within five days the Free Soilers were to hold their own election and thus begin a Free Kansas governmental structure. Would their lawless Border Ruffian neighbors permit this without additional bloodshed and violence? Many a Free Soil settler who had found his way into Kansas only in the face of outspoken Missouri hostility, enduring privation if not starvation on the way, because of his being a Yankee,* envied the little Brown colony their rich supply of arms and ammunition. Upon John Brown, the apostle of the sword of Gideon, and his militant sons, outspoken in their defiance of slavery and its laws, each separate crime by a Missourian made a deep and lasting impression. Without loss of time their settlement was to become known on both sides of the border as a centre of violent resistance to all who wished to see human slavery introduced into the Territory. Indeed, three days after his arrival at his destination, October 9, he and his sons went to the election for a Free State delegate "most thoroughly armed (except Jason, who was too feeble) but no enemy appeared," so John Brown wrote his wife on October 14, adding, "nor have I heard of any disturbance in any part of the Territory."[114] The spirit of the Massachusetts minute-men was alive in Kansas.

---

* For instance, Samuel Walker, later a leading citizen of Lawrence, was not allowed, in April 1855, to take his little girl, who was suffering from a broken leg, into the house of a Baptist minister living on the Missouri border, because he came from the North. Not until he reached the Shawnee nation could he, a Yankee, get shelter at night for his injured child; food was obtained only at night and from slaves.—*Kansas Historical Collections*, vol. 6, p. 253.

CHAPTER IV

THE CAPTAIN OF THE LIBERTY GUARDS

FORTUNATELY, the Brown minute-men were not called upon for active service for a few weeks after the arrival of their arms, so that home-building could progress with some rapidity, if one can really give the name of home to a shed open in front, its roof of poles covered by long shingles, and its three sides formed of bundles of long prairie grass pressed close between upright stakes. Such a shanty sheltered John Brown, Jr., his wife and some of the others, until late in February, 1856; while Jason's mansion during that period consisted only of log walls and a roof of cotton sheeting. It had some advantages, however, for Mrs. Jason Brown wrote, on November 25, 1855, that "the little house we live in now has no floor in it, but has quite a good chimney in so that I can cook a meal without smoking my eyes almost out of my head." [1] The permanent house-building was rendered slow and difficult by the enfeeblement of two of the new arrivals, for Henry Thompson and Oliver Brown succumbed to the prevailing ague in November, and had not recovered by the end of the month.[2] Nor had Jason when, late in November, there came the first real call to arms of the Brown settlement, to which its poverty-stricken owners had given at various times three names, Brown's Station, Brownsville and Fairfield. Not one of them has survived, and the last, from the beginning a misnomer, was particularly so in November, 1855, not only because of the exceptionally cold and bleak Kansas winter, but also because of the reports of new and alarming crimes of which Free State men were the victims.

The killings began in earnest on October 25, at Doniphan, a town near Atchison, when Samuel Collins, owner of a saw-mill at Doniphan, was shot by a pro-slavery man, Patrick Laughlin by name, for political reasons. Laughlin, having betrayed a secret Free Soil society known as the "Kansas Legion," of which he had for a time been a member, was denounced by Collins for his action. Like Montagues and Capulets, they met armed the next morning, with friends or relations about them. When the fight was over, Collins lay dead; Laughlin, seriously wounded, recovered and lived on in Atchison, no effort being made to indict or punish him.[3] If there was possibly room for doubt as to whether Collins or Laughlin assumed the offensive, there was none whatever in the case of Charles Dow, a young Free State man from Ohio, who was shot from behind and cruelly murdered near Hickory Point, Douglas County, by Franklin N. Coleman, of Virginia, a pro-slavery settler. This killing was due to a quarrel over Coleman's cutting timber on Dow's claim, and was, therefore, in its origin non-political. Yet out of it, too, came alarming political consequences. After attending a Free Soil settlers' meeting, called November 26 to protest against the crime and to bring the murderer to justice, Jacob Branson, the Free State man with whom Dow had been living, was arrested that same night by the pro-slavery sheriff, Samuel J. Jones, who resided at Westport, Missouri. Jones was postmaster of Westport while also sheriff of Douglas County, Kansas, and as will be seen, the gravest menace to the peace of the little Lawrence community. The pro-slavery warrants upon which Jones arrested Branson charged him with making threats and with breaches of the peace. As Sheriff Jones and his posse, which had then shrunk to fifteen men, neared Blanton's Bridge with their prisoner, after having spent two hours carousing at a house on the road, a party of fifteen Free State men headed by Samuel N. Wood, of Lawrence, stopped them with levelled guns. In the parley which followed, Branson went over to his rescuers, who absolutely refused to recognize the authority of Sheriff Jones, and told him that the only Jones they knew was the postmaster at Westport. The rescuing party reached Lawrence with Branson before dawn;[4] there it was at once recognized that the rescue would give the pro-slavery men precisely the excuse they needed for an attack upon the town. To an excited meeting of citizens held that evening, Branson related his story. His auditors were, however, calm enough to decline all responsibility for the affair in the name of Lawrence. Realizing that this action would probably avail them but little, a Committee of Safety was organized to form the citizens into guards and to put the town into a position of defence.[5]

Meanwhile, Sheriff Jones, after first despatching a messenger to his own State, Missouri, for aid, appealed on advice of others to the Governor of Kansas, who might naturally be expected to have a greater interest in the affair than any one in Missouri.[6] Governor Shannon's interest was soon sufficiently aroused for him to issue to the murderer, three days after the crime, a commission as justice of the peace.[7] Being also of a confiding nature, he was thus doubly prepared to believe the exaggerated statements made to him by Sheriff Jones, who declared that he must have no less than three thousand men forthwith in order to carry out the laws,[8] as the Governor might consider an "open rebellion" as having already commenced,—this as a result of the rescue of a single prisoner, in which not a shot was fired. But the Free State men having destroyed three cabins, those of Coleman and two settlers named Hargus and Buckley, and thereby frightened some pro-slavery families into returning to Missouri, Jones was easily able to make Governor Shannon think that an armed band had burnt a number of homes, destroyed personal property, and turned whole families out of doors.[9] The Governor at once ordered Major-General William P. Richardson and Adjutant-General H. J. Strickler, of the newly organized pro-slavery militia, to repair to Lecompton with as large forces as they could raise, and report to Sheriff Jones to aid him in the execution of any legal process in his hands.[10] This was the beginning of the so-called "Wakarusa War."

Thus the Branson rescue gave the extreme pro-slavery men the opportunity they had been looking for to mass their forces against Lawrence. But it is also probably true that, as Sheriff Jones declared later in an affidavit, he would have met with violence had he attempted to serve any warrant in that town where the citizens, armed with the much dreaded Sharp's rifles, were daily drilling, and were outspoken in their refusal to obey any of the laws enacted by the Pawnee Legislature. Governor Shannon, being sworn to enforce the laws of the Territory, had no other course open to him than to give aid to Jones. But his pro-slavery feelings led him to swallow every statement made to him by Jones. In the number of men he

THE CAPTAIN OF THE LIBERTY GUARDS 115

called together, his willingness to have Missourians figure as Kansas militia, and his readiness to assume that there was a serious "rebellion" in Lawrence despite the assertions of its citizens, he again showed his bias. Moreover, he cannot altogether escape the charge of duplicity, for, while he never modified his orders of November 27 to his generals, he wrote to President Pierce the next day that the sheriff had called on him for more troops than were really needed, that "five to eight hundred men" would be enough. If his excuse for this inconsistency is his belief that his generals could not raise more than five or six hundred men, instead of the three thousand Jones asked for, he certainly did not make it plain to the citizens of Kansas that he wanted the smaller number. Again, while he subsequently testified that he had never dreamed that any one would go to Missouri for men to reinforce Jones, he made not the slightest effort to reprove any one for having done so, or to send back those citizens of Missouri who were there in the belief that he had summoned them. True, he wrote to Pierce that the reinforcing of Jones by sufficient citizens of the Territory to enable him to execute his processes "is the great object to be accomplished, to avoid the dreadful evils of civil war."[11] But he lifted no finger to prevent when there swarmed into Kansas the same men who had already invaded Kansas three times in order to stuff or steal the ballot-boxes, and were now only too happy to encamp near Lawrence with guns in their hands under the sanction of the government. His subsequent defence that after the arrival of the Missourians he deemed it best "to mitigate an evil which it was impossible to suppress, by bringing under military control these irregular and excited forces,"[12] reads oddly enough. He did beg help of Pierce, and did try his best to call out the United States troops under Colonel E. V. Sumner at Fort Leavenworth, to aid him in preventing an attack on the citizens of Lawrence, who he had at the same time declared could best be subdued by citizens of Kansas reinforcing Sheriff Jones! In other words, he now asked Colonel Sumner to protect Lawrence from Jones and his men. But Sumner refused.

Altogether, Governor Shannon claimed, two hundred and fifty Kansas militia rendezvoused near Franklin on the Wakarusa, a small tributary of the Kansas River, south of Lawrence. But this statement rests on his assertion alone; most students of this period agree that not many more than fifty Kansans joined Major-General Richardson and Adjutant-General Strickler.[13] Of the Missourians, the first company to appear at Franklin and go into camp as Kansas militia was one of fifty men from Westport, Missouri. At Liberty and Lexington, Missouri, two hundred men with three pieces of artillery and one thousand stand of arms were quickly brought together and sent into Kansas.[14] Brigadier-General Lucien J. Eastin, commander of the Second Brigade of Kansas Militia, was also editor of the Leavenworth *Herald*, and with the aid of his presses not only ordered his own "brigade" to assemble at Leavenworth on December 1, but circulated the following appeal throughout the Missouri border counties:

TO ARMS! TO ARMS!!

It is expected that every lover of *Law and Order* will rally at Leavenworth, on Saturday Dec. 1, 1855, prepared to march at once to the *scene of the rebellion*, to put down the outlaws of Douglas County, who are committing depredations upon persons and property, burning down houses and declaring open hostility to the laws, and have forcibly rescued a prisoner from the Sheriff. Come one, come all! The laws must be executed. The outlaws, it is said, are armed to the teeth and number 1000 men. Every man should bring his rifle and ammunition and it would be well to bring two or three days' provisions. Every man to his post, and do his duty.[15]

Many Citizens.

A letter purporting to come from Daniel Woodson, the Secretary of the Territory, urging Eastin to call out the Platte County, Missouri, Rifle Company, "as our neighbors are always ready to help us," and adding "do not implicate the Governor whatever you do," was subsequently denounced to the Howard Committee as a forgery by Mr. Woodson when under oath.[16] It did much, however, to infuriate the Kansans, and was effectively used in the East as proof of Shannon's and Woodson's betrayal of Kansas. The highest estimate of those who assembled to besiege Lawrence is one by Sheriff Jones of eighteen hundred; it is generally believed that twelve hundred is the more accurate figure.[17] Atchison was, of course, conspicuous in urging on the invasion. Speaking at Platte City on December 1, in his usual bombastic style, he said: [18]

"Fellow Citizens: We have done our duty. We have done nothing but our duty. Not you — not me — but those that have gone into Kansas to aid Governor Shannon to sustain the law and put down rebellion and insurrection. 250 men are now on the march and probably 500 more will go from the County of Platte. Why are you not with them — you and you? I wish that I was with them at their head. . . ."

In St. Louis, on the other hand, the *Intelligencer*, on December 1, took a very different view of Missouri's duty from that of Atchison:

". . . The people of Missouri are not the ones to be called on to back up the miserable political puppets that Frank Pierce shall send out from the Eastern States to play the fool and introduce bloodshed and anarchy in Kansas. Now, let Pierce reap the fruits of his imbecility. Let not the people of Missouri, by any urgent appeal or cunning device, be drawn into the internal feuds of Kansas. It looks very much as if there were a preconcerted effort to do this very thing. . . . It does seem to us that one of the devil's own choicest humbugs is exploding in the call on Missouri for 'help.'"

Naturally, this hastily gathered together "army" lacked cohesion and discipline; according to anti-slavery descriptions, its members were far gone in drink and supported themselves by pillaging the neighborhood. Andreas, the most reliable of Kansas historians, states that they were in the "delirium coming from exposure, lack of food, and plentiful supplies of strong drink," and this is the tenor of all contemporary Free Soil accounts.[19] In the Lexington, Mo., *Express* of December 7, on the other hand, two citizens of that town reported, after having visited the pro-slavery forces, that all the men were "comfortably fixed, with plenty of provisions and all were in high spirits and anxious for a fray. . . . The arrangements were good, and the most perfect order and decorum were preserved at all times. The sale of liquor was prohibited." Some of the weapons of this "noble and gallant set of fellows" were proved before the Howard Committee to have been stolen from the United States Arsenal at Liberty, Mo., which arms the Border Ruffians, with surprising carelessness, failed to return when the Wakarusa "war" was over.[20]

The citizens of Lawrence, on hearing of the coming of the Missourians, were content neither with sending away Branson and his rescuers, nor with organizing their citizens as guards, nor with fortifying the town and smuggling a howitzer from the North through the enemy's lines. A general call was sent out in all directions to Free State men in Kansas to come to the rescue of Lawrence.[21] The settlers rallied in response, arriving alone and in squads, on foot, on horseback and in wagons, regularly armed companies coming from Bloomington, Palmyra, Ottawa Creek and Topeka. Naturally, it was the opportunity for which the Brown minute-men had been longing. It was not until December 6, however, that authentic news reached them of what was going on, and that their aid was asked. John Brown, Jr., was on the way to Lawrence on horseback to ascertain the facts, when the runner who was summoning the countryside met him. What happened then, John Brown himself described to his wife and children at North Elba in a long letter dated December 16, 1855:

"On getting this last news it was at once agreed to break up at Johns Camp & take Wealthy, & Jonny to Jason's camp (some Two Miles off); & that all the men but Henry, Jason & Oliver should at once set off for Lawrence under Arms; those Three being wholly unfit for duty. We then set about providing a little Corn-Bread; & Meat, Blankets, Cooking utensils, running Bullets & loading all our Guns, Pistols etc. The Five set off in the Afternoon, & after a short rest in the Night (which was quite dark), continued our march untill after daylight next Morning when we got our Breakfast, started again; & reached Lawrence in the Forenoon, all of us more or less lamed by our tramp. On reaching the place we found that negotiations had commenced between Gov. Shannon (haveing a force of some Fifteen or Sixteen Hundred men) & the principal leaders of the Free-State men; they having a force of some Five Hundred men at that time. These were busy Night & day fortifying the Town with Embankments; & circular Earthworks up to the time of the Treaty with the Gov, as an attack was constantly looked for; notwithstanding the negotiations then pending. This state of things continued from Friday until Sunday Evening. On the Evening we left a company of the invaders of from Fifteen to Twenty-five attacked some Three or Four Free-State men, mostly unarmed, killing a Mr. Barber from Ohio wholly unarmed. His boddy was afterward brought in; & lay for some days in the room afterward

THE CAPTAIN OF THE LIBERTY GUARDS 119

occupied by a part of the company to wh we belong; (it being organized after we reached Lawrence.) The building was a large unfinished Stone Hotel; in which a great part of the Volunteers were quartered; & who witnessed the scene of bringing in the Wife & other friends of the murdered man. I will only say of this scene that it was Heart-rending; & calculated to exasperate the men exceedingly; & one of the sure results of Civil War. After frequently calling on the leaders of the Free-State men to come & have an interview *with him*, by Gov. Shannon; & after *as often* getting for an answer that if he had any business to transact with anyone in Lawrence, to come & attend to it; he signified *his wish* to come into the Town; & an escort was sent to the Invaders' Camp to conduct him in. When there the leading Free-State men finding out his weakness, frailty & consciousness of the awkward circumstances into which he had really *got himself;* took advantage of his Cowardice, & Folly; & by means of that & the free use of Whiskey; & some Trickery; succeeded in getting a written arangement with him much to their own liking. He stipulated with them to order the pro-slavery men of Kansas home; & to proclaim to the Missouri invaders that they must quit the Territory without delay; and also to give up Gen. Pomeroy a prisoner in their camp; which was all done; he also recognizing the Volunteers as the Militia of Kansas, & empowering their Officers to call them out whenever in their discretion the safety of Lawrence or other portions of the territory might require it to be done. He Gov. Shannon gave up all pretension of further attemp to enforce the enactments of the Bogus Legislature, & retired subject to the derision & scoffs of the Free-State men (into whose hands he had committed the welfare & protection of Kansas); & to the pity of some; & the curses of others of the invading force. So ended this last Kansas invasion the Missourians returning with *flying Colors*, after incuring heavy expences; suffering great exposure, hardships, & privations, not having fought any Battles, Burned or destroyed any infant towns or Abolition Presses; leaving the Free-State men *organized* & *armed*, & in *full possession* of the Territory; not having fulfilled any of all their dreadful threatenings, except to murder One *unarmed* man; & to commit some Roberies & waste of proppery upon defenceless families, unfortunately in their power. We learn by their papers they boast of a great victory over the *Abolitionists;* & well they may. Free-State men have only hereafter to retain the footing they have gained; *and Kansas is free.* Yesterday the people passed uppon the Free-State constitution. The result, though not yet known, no one doubts. One little circumstance connected with our own number showing a little of the true character of those invaders: On our way about Three Miles from Lawrence we had to pass a bridge (with our Arms & Amunition) of which the invaders held possession; but as the Five had each a Gun, with Two large Revolvers in a Belt (exposed to view) with a Third in his Pocket; & as we moved directly on to the

Bridge without making any halt, they for some reason suffered us to pass without interruption; notwithstanding there were some Fifteen to Twenty-five (as variously reported) stationed in a Log-House at one end of the Bridge. We could not count them. A Boy on our approach ran & gave them notice. Five others of our Company, *well armed;* who followed us some Miles behind, met with equally civil treatment the same day. After we left to go to Lawrence until we returned when disbanded; I did not see the least sign of cowardice or want of self-possession exhibited by any volunteer of the Eleven companies who constituted the Free-State force & I never expect again to see an equal number of such well-behaved, cool, determined men; fully as I believe sustaining the high character of the Revolutionary Fathers; but enough of this as we intend to send you a paper giving a more full account of the affair. We have cause for gratitude in that we all returned safe, & well, with the exception of hard Colds; and found those left behind rather improving." [22]

It would be hard to add anything to this admirable summary of the close of the Wakarusa "war." That it was temperate and did not overemphasize the part played by the Missourians appears from the opinion of John Sherman and William A. Howard, of the Howard Committee, who affirmed that:

"Among the many acts of lawless violence which it has been the duty of your Committee to investigate, this invasion of Lawrence is the most defenceless. A comparison of the facts proven with the official statements of the officers of the government will show how groundless were the pretexts which gave rise to it. A community in which no crime had been committed by any of its members, against none of whom had a warrant been issued or a complaint made, who had resisted no process in the hands of a real or pretended officer, was threatened with destruction in the name of 'law and order,' and that, too, by men who marched from a neighboring State with arms obtained by force and who at every stage of their progress violated many laws, and among others the Constitution of the United States.

"The chief guilt must rest on Samuel J. Jones. His character is illustrated by his language at Lecompton, when peace was made. He said Major Clark and Burns both claimed the credit of killing that damned abolitionist, (Barber) and he did n't know which ought to have it. If Shannon hadn't been a damned old fool, peace would never have been declared. He would have wiped Lawrence out. He had men and means enough to do it." [23]

John Brown's company comprised others than himself and his four sons, Frederick, Owen, Salmon and John, Jr., and was

THE CAPTAIN OF THE LIBERTY GUARDS 121

well named the "Liberty Guards." He himself received here for the first time the historic title of Captain, and the original muster roll of his company, still preserved, gives the facts as to its composition and service:[24]

"Muster Roll of Capt. John Brown's Company in the Fifth Regiment, First Brigade of Kansas Volunteers, commanded by Col. Geo. W. Smith, called into the service of the people of Kansas to defend the City of Lawrence, in the Territory of Kansas from threatened demolition by foreign invaders. Enrolled at Osawatomie K. T. Called into the service from the 27th day of November, A. D. 1855, when mustered, to the 12th day of December, when discharged. Service, 16 days. Miles travelled each way, 50. Allowance to each for use of horse $24.

"Remark — One keg of powder and eight pounds of lead were furnished by William Partridge and were used in the service."

			Age
John Brown sen. Capt.			55
Wm. W. Up De Graff	1st	Lieut.	34
Henry H. Williams	2nd	"	27
Jas. J. Holbrook	3rd	"	23
Ephraim Reynolds	1st	Sergt.	25
R. W. Wood	2nd	"	20
Frederic Brown	3rd	"	25
John Yelton	4th	"	26
Henry Alderman	1st	Corp	55
H. Harrison Up De Graff	2nd	Corp	23
Dan'l W. Collis	3rd	Corp	27
Wm. Partridge	4th	"	32
Amos D Alderman			20
Owen Brown			31
Salmon Brown			19
John Brown, jr.			34
Francis Brennen			29
Wm. W. Coine			19
Benj. L. Cochren			24
Jeremiah Harrison			22

This muster roll was certified to as correct "on honor" by George W. Smith, Colonel commanding the Fifth Regiment Kansas Volunteers, but it will be noted that it gives the Liberty Guards credit for at least nine days more service than they were entitled to according to John Brown's own story. So does the honorable discharge of John Brown, Jr., which was countersigned not only by Colonel Smith, but also by J. H. Lane as General, First Brigade, Kansas Volunteers, and

"C. Robinson, Maj. Gen'l.," in that it dates his service from November 27. This apparently was the date of entry into service fixed for all the volunteers of this quaint "army," with its elaborate organization and high titles.[25] As a matter of fact, the active service of the Liberty Guards comprised only Friday the 7th and Saturday the 8th of December, during which time the peace negotiations were under way. They remained in Lawrence until the 12th or later, when the other companies also left for their homes.

In his narrative of what happened during his brief participation in the siege of Lawrence, Brown slurs over his own part in the proceedings, which was sufficiently conspicuous to make him well known to all who were in the threatened town. "I did not see Brown's entry into Lawrence," writes R. G. Elliott, at the time an editor of the *Kansas Free State*, "which was the first introduction of the mysterious stranger into the Kansas drama, but I do know that his grim visage, his bold announcements, with the patriarchal organization of his company, gave him at once welcome entrance into the military counsels of the defenders, and lightened up the gloom of the besieged in their darkest hour."[26] Here in Kansas, too, John Brown made upon every one the impression of age, owing to the stoop of his shoulders, the measured step, the earnestness and impressiveness of his manner, and other signs of seniority and natural leadership, even though there was in his endurance, the resoluteness of his movements, and the promptness of his speech, nothing approaching senility.* The title of captain fitted him readily; where he was, he led. And so at Lawrence, — hardly arrived, he was at the fortifications. "There," reports an eye-witness, James F. Legate, he "walked quietly from fort to fort and talked to the men stationed there, saying to each that it was nothing to die if their lives had served some good purpose, and that no purpose could be higher or better than that which called us to surrender life, if need be, to repel such an invasion."[27] Even though the discussion of peace was on, he suggested the gathering of pitchforks for use in repelling a possible charge.[28] The peace itself produced in him only anger, when first he heard of it.

---

* The Lawrence *Herald of Freedom* reported the arrival on December 7 of "Mr. John Brown, an *aged* gentleman from Essex County, N. Y."

THE CAPTAIN OF THE LIBERTY GUARDS 123

It was not only, as he wrote to Orson Day on reaching home, that there was "a good deal of trickery on the one side and of cowardice, folly, & drunkenness on the other;" [29] there was suppression of facts as well. For the actual terms of peace, involving as they did a compromise, were at first concealed by the leaders in expectation of dissatisfaction. As a matter of fact, the agreement pledged the Free State men to "aid in the execution of the laws when called upon by proper authority;" its equivocal concluding sentence read: "We wish it understood, that we do not herein express any opinion as to the validity of the enactments of the Territorial Legislature." This was signed on December 8.

An open-air meeting was held on Saturday afternoon about the still unfinished Free State Hotel, where a box outside the door served as a platform and door-sill, there being no steps but planks leading to the ground. Shannon, Robinson and Lane, fresh from signing the treaty, harangued the crowd. What the terms of the treaty were, they would tell no one that day. Shannon expressed his satisfaction at the discovery that he had misunderstood the people of Lawrence, that they were really estimable and orderly persons. He hoped now to preserve order and get out of the Territory the Missourians, who, he remarked, were there of their own accord. Lane's eloquence evoked cheers; he declared that "any man who would desert Lawrence until the invaders below had left the Territory, was a coward." Governor Robinson was pacific, discreet and brief. He stated, according to William Phillips, the *Tribune's* correspondent, that "they had taken an honorable position." [30] But the crowd was not so sure of that. A rumor had been circulating that the treaty was in reality a complete surrender on the part of Robinson and Lane, and an acceptance of the hated pro-slavery laws. John Brown, boiling over with anger, mounted the shaky platform and addressed the audience when Robinson had finished. He declared that Lawrence had been betrayed, and told his hearers that they should make a night attack upon the pro-slavery forces and drive them out of the Territory. "I am an Abolitionist," he said, "dyed in the wool," and then he offered to be one of ten men to make a night attack upon the Border Ruffian camp. Armed and with lanterns, his plan was to string his men along the camp far apart. At a given signal in the early morning hours, they were to shout and fire on the slumbering enemy. "And I do believe," declared John Brown in telling of it, "that the whole lot would have run." [31] Lane, too, had been secretly in favor of an attack, but peace councils prevailed.[32] John Brown was pulled down by friends and foes from the improvised rostrum, and, according to one responsible witness, it was Robinson who stamped out the incipient mutiny by calmly assuring the crowd that the unpublished treaty was a triumph of diplomacy.[33]

That same evening, Shannon, Lane and Robinson spoke to thirteen pro-slavery captains at Franklin, who grumblingly accepted the treaty and gave their word that they would endeavor to induce the Missourians to return quietly to their homes.[34] But the Missouri leaders were not all pleased at the outcome. General Stringfellow declared, in a speech in the camp near Lecompton, that "Shannon has played us false; the Yankees have tricked us." Sheriff Jones's regret that Shannon did not wipe out Lawrence has already been recorded. Atchison was for peace, — there are doubts if he really was a fighting man when it came to the point. "If you attack Lawrence now," he declared, "you attack it as a mob, and what would be the result? You would cause the election of an Abolition President and the ruin of the Democratic party." [35] If there was some grumbling among the rank and file at Shannon's ordering them to return to their homes, the cold storm of that Saturday night helped on the dissolution of the pro-slavery forces. Many left on Monday morning, worn, sleepless and frozen. Moreover, the whiskey had given out, and this, with the fear of a possible Free State attack, sent more and more home, until on Tuesday only a few parties remained. Finally, these few gave in to the inevitable and departed, says Phillips, "cursing Shannon and the 'cunning Abolitionists.'" [36]

As for Shannon, the tricky Robinson had again taken advantage of his weakness by inviting him and Sheriff Jones to a peace gathering in the Free State Hotel on Sunday evening, December 9, despite protests from Lane and others that no such enemy of Lawrence as Jones should be given the right hand of fellowship. In the course of the evening, when

THE CAPTAIN OF THE LIBERTY GUARDS 125

the Governor was thoroughly enjoying himself, Robinson rushed up to him and informed him that the Missourians had left the Wakarusa and were marching on Lawrence. He insisted that the Governor should at once sign a paper authorizing him and Lane to defend the town. The Governor, after a little urging, put his name to the following document:

To C. Robinson and J. H. Lane, commanders of the Enrolled Citizens of Lawrence:
You are hereby authorized and directed to take such measures and use the enrolled forces under your command in such manner, for the preservation of the peace and the protection of the persons and property of the people of Lawrence and its vicinity, as in your judgment shall best secure that end.

WILSON SHANNON.
LAWRENCE, Dec. 9, 1855.

His Excellency thereupon returned to the delights of the reception and, says Phillips, "on that eventful Sunday, if Governors ever get drunk, his supreme highness, Wilson the First, got superlatively tipsy." [37]

When he came to his senses and discovered that he had given legal authority to arm and fight to the leaders of that very mob to suppress which he had called out the Territorial militia, he was properly chagrined. The force which he had denounced for assembling to upset the laws was now duly empowered by him to act at its own discretion without limit of time. Naturally, the Governor was indignant. In a long letter to the Kansas correspondent of the New York *Herald*, dated December 25, 1855, he sought to justify himself and explain his predicament, saying: [38]

". . . amid an excited throng, in a small and crowded apartment, and without any critical examination of the paper which Dr. Robinson had just written, I signed it; but it was distinctly understood that it had no application to anything but the threatened attack on Lawrence that night. . . . It did not for a moment occur to me that this pretended attack upon the town was but a device to obtain from me a paper which might be used to my prejudice. I supposed at the time that I was surrounded by gentlemen and by grateful hearts, and not by tricksters, who, with fraudulent representations, were seeking to obtain an advantage over me. I was the last man on the globe who deserved such treatment from the citizens of Lawrence."

It is evident that the Governor had reason for his anger. Dr. Robinson's successful stratagem can best be justified by that familiar theory that everything is permissible in war. This has excused many a more heinous crime; but Shannon could properly have urged that, as peace had been signed, this trick was indefensible even as a war measure.

The treaty was, from the beginning, an ill-fated document, and met the destiny double-dealing compromises deserve. As events turned out, the Missourians had their revenge on Lawrence and Robinson within seven months. Though he afterwards became a respected citizen of Lawrence, Shannon was, until his removal in 1856, despised by its residents and berated by the pro-slavery men in and out of the Territory, who sought to saddle upon him the blame for their undeniable defeat. "The discomfited and lop-eared invaders," wrote Horace Greeley in the *Tribune* of December 25, in characteristic style, "pretend that against their wish they were kept from fighting by the pusillanimity of Gov. Shannon." Thus ended the Wakarusa "war." It had cost but one life, that of Barber, the unexpected sight of whose dead body in the Free State Hotel had done much to make Shannon see some justice in the Free Soil cause. Barber had been shot from behind, probably by the United States Indian agent, Major George E. Clarke, for the sole reason that he had been visiting Lawrence. " I have sent another of those damned Abolitionists to his winter quarters," boasted Clarke. But Colonel James N. Burns, of Missouri, disputed his right to this honor, and, since both fired at the same moment, no one has ever been able to decide to whom Barber owed his death wound.[39]

The night after his abruptly ended speech John Brown passed with James F. Legate. He asked Legate for minute particulars of the latter's ten years of experience in the South, so far as it related to the slaves, asking especially if they had any attachment for their masters and would fight for liberty. Then they had an argument as to the nature of prayer; it ended by Brown's praying for power to repel the slaveholders, the enemies of God, and for freedom all over the earth.[40]

On December 14, Brown, his four sons and their half-starved horse, which dragged the heavily laden wagon, were

THE CAPTAIN OF THE LIBERTY GUARDS 127

back and settled at Brown's Station, apparently reconciled to the treaty, for on that date he wrote to Orson Day of his over-sanguine belief that "the Territory is now entirely in the power of the Free State men," and of his confident expectation that the "Missourians will give up all further hope of making Kansas a Slave State." [41]

The result of the vote on the Free State Constitution, on December 15, further helped to make John Brown contented with the Shannon compromise. Apparently there was a peaceful winter before them, and this proved to be the case. Its very inclemency made further hostile operations impossible, and left the Kansans free to keep body and soul together as best they could. John Brown himself utilized the opportunity to go a number of times into the enemy's country in January in search of supplies, without meeting with any unpleasant experiences. On January 1, 1856, he wrote from West Point, Missouri, "In this part of the State there seems to be but little feeling on the slave question." [42] As the temperature had ranged from ten to twenty-eight degrees below zero in the week previous to his writing, and there were in places ten inches of snow on the ground, it is obvious that the need of pork and flour which made Brown venture forth must have been pressing. By the 4th he was back in Osawatomie again, for on the 5th he was appointed chairman of a convention in Osawatomie, called for the purpose of nominating State officers. His son, John Brown, Jr., was duly nominated for the Legislature, and, so Henry Thompson reported the next day, "the meeting went off without any excitement and to our satisfaction." [43] This was but an index of the place the Browns had already made for themselves, a recognition of their dominating characters. Further proof of this is to be found in a letter from Mrs. John Brown, Jr., to her mother-in-law. Writing on January 6, 1856, she says: "You need not in the least feel uneasy about your husband, he seems to enjoy life well, and I believe he is now situated so as to do a great deal of good; he certainly seems to be a man here who exhibits a great amount of influence and is considered one of the most leading and influential minds about here. . . . Our men have so much *war* and *elections* to attend to that it seems as though we were a great while getting into a house." [44]

On the 8th of January, John Brown went back to Missouri for more provisions, accompanied by Salmon and driving the faithful horse for the last time, since that hard-worked animal must needs be sold to a pro-slavery master, that the provisions might be obtained for the oxen to bring home, and to replace moneys belonging to S. L. Adair used by John Brown on the road to Kansas. "By means of the sale of our Horse and Waggon: our present wants are tolerably well met; so that if health is continued to us we shall not probably suffer much," wrote Brown to his wife on February 1, on his return from a third trip to Missouri. He reported also that the weather continued very severe: "It is now nearly Six Weeks that the Snow has been almost constantly driven (like dry sand) by the fierce Winds of Kansas." There were also serious alarms of war: "We have just learned of some *new;* and shocking outrages at Leavenworth: and that the Free-State people there have fled to Lawrence: which place is again threatend with an attack. *Should* that take place we may soon again be called upon to 'buckle on our armor;' which by the help of God we will do: when I suppose Henry, & Oliver will have a chance."[45] He added, however, that in his judgment there would be no general disturbance until warmer weather. In this view he was as correct as he had previously been wrong in estimating the results of the Wakarusa "war."

The Leavenworth troubles, to which he referred, were so serious as to be taken on both sides as ending the truce signed by Shannon. They grew out of the election, on January 15, of members of the Free Soil Legislature and the State officers under the Topeka Constitution. Just as the Missourians had refrained from interfering with the Free State voting in the adoption of the Constitution, they now permitted the January 15 election to pass off in peace, except at Leavenworth, where the pro-slavery mayor forbade the holding of the election. It took place clandestinely and was then adjourned to Easton, twelve miles away, where it was again held on the 17th, despite the disarming and driving away of some of the Free State voters. That night there was severe fighting between the two sides, in which the pro-slavery men lost one killed and two wounded, while two of the Free Soilers were injured. Later, the pro-slavery forces, which had been reinforced by a militia

THE CAPTAIN OF THE LIBERTY GUARDS 129

company, the Kickapoo Rangers, captured Captain Reese P. Brown, the leader of the Free State men, as he was returning to Leavenworth. Him the Rangers mortally wounded the next day, when he was unarmed and defenceless.[46] "These men, or rather demons," reported Phillips to the *Tribune*, "rushed around Brown and literally hacked him to death with their hatchets." Not an effort was made to punish the murderers, though they were well known to the Territorial authorities. Some of the pro-slavery newspapers, like Stringfellow's *Squatter Sovereign*, upheld the deed, that journal calling for "War! War!!"[47] The Leavenworth *Herald* justified the murder and gave notice to the Free State men that: "These higher-law men will not be permitted longer to carry on their illegal and high-handed proceedings. The good sense of the people is frowning it down. And if it cannot be in one way it will in another."[48] The *Kansas Pioneer* of Kickapoo was an accessory to Brown's murder before the fact, for on the morning of the crime it had published this appeal: "Sound the bugle of war over the length and breadth of the land and leave not an Abolitionist in the Territory to relate their treacherous and contaminating deeds. Strike your piercing rifle balls and your glittering steel to their black and poisonous hearts."[49]

But the black-hearted Free Soilers voted nevertheless, casting, in the entire Territory, 1628 ballots for Mark W. Delahay, the candidate for delegate to Congress who had just previously, on December 22, 1855, had a taste of Missouri intolerance, when the printing-presses of his Leavenworth newspaper, the *Territorial Register*, were thrown into the Missouri River because of the Free Soil sentiments of its editor.[50] For Charles Robinson as Governor there were cast 1296 votes. This result increased the anger of the pro-slavery men. On that day of balloting, Sheriff Jones wrote to Robinson and Lane, asking whether they had or had not pledged themselves to aid him with a posse in serving a writ. Their answer was only that they would make no "further resistance to the arrest by you of one of the rescuers of Branson, . . . as we desire to test the validity of the enactments of the body that met at the Mission, calling themselves the Kansas Legislature, by an appeal to the Supreme Court of the United States."[51]

Jones and the Border Ruffians thereupon insisted that the Free State men had violated the truce of Lawrence, and deemed themselves no longer bound by it. By February 4, ex-Senator Atchison was again threatening the sword of extermination, or rather the bowie-knife: "Send your young men . . . drive them [the Abolitionists] out. . . . Get ready, arm yourselves; for if they abolitionize Kansas you lose $100,000,000 of your property. I am satisfied I can justify every act of yours before God and a jury," [52] — words that could not have gone unread at Brown's Station, where they received and pored over "Douglas newspapers" as well as Free Soil ones. The election had passed off quietly enough at Osawatomie, John Brown, Jr., being duly elected to the Legislature, but shortly afterwards the minute-men led in the expulsion of a claim-jumper, as a result of a settlers' meeting held on January 24 to consider the case. Henry Thompson, John Brown, Jr., and his brothers Oliver and Frederick were the committee which, well armed, knocked the man's door in and threw his belongings out. Henry Thompson's part was watching, with a loaded revolver in his hand, every action of the claim-jumper until he disappeared in the distance, vowing vengeance on each and every Brown.[53]

It was also on January 24, that President Pierce sent a special message to Congress which aroused the ire of every Free State settler, and of every anti-slavery man the country over. In it, yielding to the influence of Jefferson Davis, and of Governor Shannon, who was then in Washington, he squarely took the side of the South, proclaiming the pro-slavery Shawnee Legislature legal, whatever election frauds might have been committed, and denouncing the acts of the Free State men as without law and revolutionary in character, "avowedly so in motive," which would become "treasonable insurrection" if they went to the "length of organized resistance by force to the fundamental or any other Federal law, and to the authority of the general government." On February 11 the President went even further, and issued a proclamation which deprived the Free State forces of all hope of any aid from the Federal Government. It placed the entire authority and power of the United States on the side of pro-slavery men, and of all those persons who opposed the Topeka movement. While

THE CAPTAIN OF THE LIBERTY GUARDS 131

condemning the lawless acts of both sides, he placed the Fort Riley and Fort Leavenworth troops at Shannon's behest, except that he was cautioned not to call upon them unless it was absolutely necessary to do so to enforce the laws and keep peace; even then this proclamation must be read aloud before the soldiers acted. Naturally, the South rejoiced and the hearts of the defenders of Lawrence were downcast. The *Squatter Sovereign* was emboldened on February 20 to say: "In our opinion the only effectual way to correct the evils that now exist is to hang up to the nearest tree the very last traitor who was instrumental in getting up, or participating in, the celebrated Topeka Convention."

John Brown had anticipated this action of Pierce's, and his feelings sought relief on the same day in the following letter to Joshua R. Giddings, the well-known anti-slavery Congressman from Ohio:

OSAWATOMIE KANSAS TERRITORY 20th Feby 1856
HON. JOSHUA R. GIDDINGS
WASHINGTON, D. C.
DEAR SIR,

I write to say that a number of the United States Soldiers are quartered in this vicinity for the ostensible purpose of removing *intruders* from certain Indian Lands. It is, however, *believed* that the Administration has no thought of removing the Missourians from the Indian Lands; but that the real object is to have these men in readiness to act in the enforcement of those *Hellish enactments* of the (so called) Kansas Legislature; absolutely abominated by a great majority of the inhabitants of the Territory; and spurned by them up to this time. I confidently believe that the next movement on the part of the Administration and its Proslavery masters will be to drive the people here, either to submit to those Infernal enactments; or to assume what will be termed *treasonable grounds* by shooting down the poor soldiers of the country with whom they have no quarrel whatever. I ask in the name of Almighty God; I ask in the name of our venerated fore-fathers; I ask in the name of all that good or true men ever held dear; will Congress suffer us to be driven to such "dire extremities"? *Will anything be done?* Please send me a few lines at this place. Long acquaintance with your public life, and a slight personal acquaintance incline and embolden me to make this appeal to yourself.

"Everything is still on the surface here just now. Circumstances, however, are of a most suspicious character.

Very Respectfully yours,
JOHN BROWN.[54]

Before this earnest letter was far on its way there came an important answer to its appeal, and to the proclamation of the President, in the organization of the "National Republican Party" at Pittsburgh, February 22, 1856, the name of Charles Robinson being placed on its National Committee as representative of Kansas, on the motion of S. N. Wood, leader of the Branson rescuers, who was present as a delegate. On account of the terrible weather [55] — the snow was often eighteen inches deep, and the thermometer as low as twenty-seven degrees below zero — the mails were slow in leaving Kansas,[56] and it was not until March 17 that Mr. Giddings assured his Osawatomie correspondent:

" . . . you need have no fear of the troops. The President will never *dare* employ the troops of the United States to shoot the citizens of Kansas. The death of the first man by the troops will involve every free State in your own fate. It will light up the fires of civil war throughout the North, and we shall stand or fall with you. Such an act will also bring the President so deep in infamy that the hand of political resurrection will never reach him. . . ."[57]

Governor Shannon returned to Kansas on March 5, exulting in his having the regular troops commanded by Colonel Sumner under him, especially as that excellent officer had refused to come to his aid during the Wakarusa "war" without express authority from Washington.[58] The day before, on March 4, the Free State Legislature had duly assembled as required by the Topeka Constitution, without the slightest regard for Pierce's message or proclamation.[59] It remained in session only eleven days, receiving Governor Robinson's inaugural address, electing Governor Lane and ex-Governor Reeder Senators of the United States in the event of the State's being admitted to the Union, preparing a memorial to Congress begging that admission, and receiving the report of the Territorial Executive Committee, headed by Lane, which then went out of existence. Adjournment was on March 15 until July 4, when it met again, only to be dispersed by Colonel Sumner's troopers. John Brown, Jr., was in attendance at the session in March; his father recorded this in a letter to North Elba on March 6, in which he also complained of the lack of any letters or news because of deep snows and high water, so that, he wrote, "we

THE CAPTAIN OF THE LIBERTY GUARDS 133

have no idea what Congress has done since early in Jany:"[60] John Brown, Jr., did not, however, arrive in Topeka, with Henry H. Williams, a fellow Representative, until the morning of the 5th, so Mr. Williams wrote on the 7th to a friend. His letter shows that there was considerable trepidation among the arriving delegates in view of Pierce's position. "Shannon," he wrote, "is at the Big Springs on a bender I learn. . . . Mr. Brown has been put on a committee to select six candidates from which three are to be elected Commissioners to revise and codify the laws and rules of practise. . . ."[61]

Only fifteen of the Topeka legislators signed the memorial to Congress asking for the admission of Kansas as a Free State under the Topeka Constitution, a copy of which was attached to their petition. John Brown, Jr., was of course one of the fifteen.[62] He was also one of the committee of three to draft resolutions in regard to the murder of Captain R. P. Brown. He figured also as a member of the standing committee on vice and immorality, and presented a petition from fifty-six ladies of Topeka praying for the enactment of a law prohibiting the manufacture and sale of liquor,[63] for all of which legislative service, and for his subsequent partaking in the meetings of the committee to select the commissioners to codify the laws,[64] this unfortunate man paid a terrible price within the next three months. Soon after John Brown, Jr., returned, his father, Frederick and Oliver Brown, and Henry Thompson went on a surveying tour to the west of their settlement, fixing the boundaries of their lands for the Indian neighbors they had learned to respect and like. The Ottawas, having found that many whites were settling on their lands, held a council and asked the Browns to trace their southern boundary. "There is a good many settlers on their lands," wrote Henry Thompson to his wife, "that will probably have to leave — mostly proslavery."[65] This prospect could hardly have raised the Browns in the esteem of these neighbors and their sympathizers. This surveying party was, however, one of those experiences in Kansas which made Henry Thompson write to his wife a month later, April 16, when the outlook for the Free State had grown gloomy enough: "It is a great trial to me to stay away from you, but

I am here, and feel I have a sacrifice to make, a duty to perform. Can I leave that undone and feel easy, and have a conscience void of offence? Should I ever feel that I had not put my hand to the plough and looked back?"[66] It was not only the cause which held Mr. Thompson in Kansas, but his very great regard for John Brown. Upon Brown's plans he later wrote to his wife, would depend his own, "until School is out."[67]

April 16 was also the date of a settlers' meeting of momentous importance to Osawatomie. It attracted widespread attention elsewhere in the Territory, since it was the first open defiance, after the President's proclamation, by any body of men, of the Shawnee Legislature's laws. The call for the gathering was signed by twenty-three citizens, who wished to confer as to the proper attitude to be taken toward the officials appointed by the Shawnee Legislature to assess property and collect taxes. Richard Mendenhall presided, and there was full discussion of the situation.[68] No less ominous a figure than the Rev. Martin White presented the Border Ruffian side. The Rev. S. L. Adair, brother-in-law of John Brown, recorded many years later that "Martin White stood up for the laws, and charged rebellion and treason on all who declined to obey them. Captain John Brown was for regarding the Legislature as a fraud and their laws as a farce and their slave code as wicked, and if an attempt was made to enforce them to resist it." Martin White put it differently. "I went," he declared in a speech to the Kansas Legislature in February, 1857, when telling of his experiences with the Free State men, "to one of their meetings and tried to reason with them for peace, but in so doing I insulted the hero [John Brown] of the murder of the three Doyles, Wilkinson and Sherman, and he replied to me and said that he was an 'Abolitionist of the old stock — was dyed in the wool and that negroes were his brothers and equals — that he would rather see this Union dissolved and the country drenched with blood than to pay taxes to the amount of one-hundredth part of a mill.'" As to his own position, Mr. Adair testified: "I had said but little. But the question was put directly: was I ready to obey the laws or to take up arms against them? I replied I should not regard the authority of those laws, yet was not ready

THE CAPTAIN OF THE LIBERTY GUARDS 135

to take up arms against them but was ready if necessary to suffer penalties." This was the spirit in which the Free Soil pioneers were meeting the situation created by Pierce's siding with the pro-slavery forces. They were willing to "suffer penalties" for their beliefs in the good old New England fashion, and were in no wise to be swerved from their sense of duty by the thundering of the highest authority in the land.

As a result of the discussion and the appointment of a committee of five to prepare them, the following resolutions were adopted by the meeting:

Resolved, That we utterly repudiate the authority of that Legislature as a body, emanating not from the people of Kansas, but elected and forced upon us by a foreign vote, and that the officers appointed by the same, have therefore no legal power to act.

Resolved, That we pledge to one another mutual support and *aid* in a forcible resistance to any attempt to compel us with obedience to those enactments, let that attempt come from whatever source it may, and that if men appointed by that legislature to the office of Assessor or Sheriff, shall hereafter attempt to assess or collect taxes of us, they will do so at the peril of such consequences as shall be necessary to prevent same.

Resolved, That a committee of three be appointed to inform such officers of the action of this meeting by placing in their hands a copy of these resolutions.

Resolved, That a copy of these resolutions with the proceedings of this meeting be furnished to the several papers of Kansas with a request to publish the same.

RICHARD MENDENHALL, *Pres't*.[69]
OSCAR V. DAYTON, *Sec'ry*.

One cannot but admire the courage which prompted this spreading abroad of the decision of the meeting. It was, however, soon to have dire results for the little settlement itself.

About this same time there had come to a neighboring pro-slavery settlement of the Shermans, one of whom was known as "Dutch Henry," a Judge, Sterling G. Cato, to hold court in the name of the bogus Territorial Legislature. The Browns soon heard that he had issued warrants for their arrest, either because of their participation in the meeting of April 16, or because of prior dislike of them as Abolitionists. John Brown sent to the court his son Salmon and Henry Thompson, "to see," so Salmon Brown affirms, "if Cato would arrest us. We went over ten miles afoot and stood around to see if they would carry out their threat. I did not like it. I did not want to be in the middle of a rescue. That's a risky situation. I thought father was wild to send us, but he wanted to *hurry up the fight*—always." [70] This ruse having failed, Brown himself went with his armed company to see what was going on. The result of this he described to his brother-in-law, Adair:

Brown's Station, 22d April, 1856.

Dear Brother Adair:—
. . . Yesterday we went to Dutch Henrys to see how things were going at Court, my boys turned out to train at a house near by. Many of the volunteer Co. went in without show of arms to hear the charge to Grand Jury. The Court is *thoroughly Bogus* but the Judge had not the nerve to avow it openly. He was questioned on the bench in writing civilly but plainly whether he intended to enforce the Bogus Laws or not; but would give no answer. He did not even mention the so called Kansas *Legislature or name their acts* but talked of *our* laws; it was easy for any one conversant with law matters to discover what code he was charging the jury under. He evidently felt much agitated but talked a good deal about having criminals punished, &c. After hearing the charge and witnessing the refusal of the Judge to answer, the volunteers met under arms passed the Osawatomie Preamble & Resolutions, every man voting aye. They also appointed a committee of Three to wait on the Judge at once with a coppy in full; which was immediately done. The effect of that I have not yet learned. You will see that matters are in a fair way of comeing to a head.
Yours sincerely in haste,
John Brown [71]

James Hanway, a leading Free State settler, has recorded the following additional details of this occurrence:

"John Brown, Jr. left the court room, and in the yard he called out in a loud voice: 'The Pottawattomie Rifle Company will meet at the parade ground,' and the company consisting of some thirty men, marched off to meet as ordered. There was not a disrespectful word uttered, nor were there deadly weapons displayed on the occasion — there were doubtless a few pocket pistols, but they were hid from sight. Between dark and daylight, Judge Cato and his officials had left; they journeyed toward Lecompton in Douglas County, which was the Bastile of the proslavery party. This was the first and the last of the proslavery court holding their sessions in this section of the country." [72]

This incident, Mr. Hanway added, got into the pro-slavery newspapers in a magnified and distorted form, and became a standing charge against the Free State party of Kansas as one of their heinous crimes, for Judge Cato portrayed himself thereafter as a court compelled to flee for safety.

About the time that Judge Cato's court was in session at Dutch Henry's, there arrived in the neighborhood a company of Southerners who had come to the Territory from Georgia, Alabama and South Carolina, in order to make it a slave State. John Brown lost no time in discovering their objects, and he did it in a manner which has become famous in Kansas. "Father," says Salmon Brown, "had taken advantage of his knowledge of surveying, and, as a surveyor, ran a line through their camp. He had been surveying the old Indian lands, previously, for the Indians. The Border Ruffians never suspected us to be anything but friends, for only pro-slavery men got government jobs then, and surveyors were supposed to be government officers. So they talked freely about their plans and one big fellow said: 'We came up here for self first and the South next. But one thing we will do before we leave, we'll clear out the damned Brown crowd.'" [73] This last was an empty boast, as time showed. But the arrival of these men in the neighborhood of Osawatomie was but another sign of the impending crisis. They were part of the force raised by Major Jefferson Buford at Eufaula, Silver Run and Columbus, Georgia, and Montgomery, Alabama, as the result of an appeal for Southern emigrants to settle in Kansas.[74] The organization was military, but the men went unarmed as far as Kansas City, where they arrived between four and five hundred strong, late in April. On May 2 they passed into Kansas with weapons in plenty, scattering for a time in search of homes, only to be called upon in short order as a military force. But before this came to pass, they had added greatly to the terror of the Free Soil settlers by their swashbuckling marches through the Territory. Just as they left Montgomery, Buford's men had been marched to the bookstore of the Messrs. McIlvaine in that city, where each man received a Bible. "But," says a correspondent of the *Tribune*, "on the trip up the river [from St. Louis] the Bibles were thrown promiscuously into a large bucket on the hurricane deck, and the company were below handling an article known among gamblers as a 'pocket testament.'" [75] "The people of Westport were glad to see Buford's men come; they were doubly glad when they went away finally," reported an old citizen of Westport, and there is little doubt that they got out of hand soon after entering Kansas, for as settlers they were a dismal failure. When their service in the sack of Lawrence was over, after pillaging and roaming for a while, they gradually began to return to the South.

Here those who returned afforded fresh proof of the inability of that section to colonize its favorite institution as far North and West as Kansas. A number enlisted in the United States troops in Kansas, while others went over to the Free State men and thus became traitors to the cause of human bondage. Still others stayed for months near Westport, a veritable plague to their friends.[76] In short, the expedition was a disastrous failure politically, economically and financially; it served no other purpose than to aid in the wanton destruction of part of the city of Lawrence and the throwing into chains of the Free State leaders.

Beyond doubt the arrival of Buford's men raised high the spirits of the Southern leaders, who fondly believed that there would now be sufficient emigration of their own people to offset the continuing stream of arrivals from New England, notably a remarkable colony from New Haven, one hundred strong, who settled sixty-five miles above Lawrence on the Kansas River and, unlike Buford's men, knew how to plough and plant. "Our town," wrote a correspondent of the *Tribune* from Lawrence on April 19, "is crowded with immigrants from all parts. A number of companies are camping here, anxiously awaiting their exploring committees, who have gone out to look at different localities. There is a large company from Ohio — one from Connecticut — one from New Hampshire, and others are daily arriving. . . . The emigrants of this season are much superior to those of last year. They come in the face of difficulties and are prepared to meet them." [77] But fears of a similar tide of Southerners impelled Horace Greeley to impassioned editorials urging the youth of the Northeast to save Kansas, by force of arms and devotion to principle.[78] A correspondent of the Albany *Journal*, writing on March 16 from a steamboat on the Mississippi, gave this picture of the outlook:

THE CAPTAIN OF THE LIBERTY GUARDS 139

"I have just come up from Tennessee and let me assure you that the South are now moving in earnest in sending settlers to Kansas. I heard a letter from Kansas . . . read at a Kansas meeting, in which the South were (sic) urged to send their men immediately. 'The only hope,' the writer stated, was in sending on enough to whip the d——d Abolitionists before the 1st of July, or the Territory would be lost. The writer says: 'There are now at least three Abolitionists to one friend of the South, and if anything is done it must be done quickly.'"

A *Tribune* correspondent in Kansas City wrote late in April that: "It is unquestionable that the South has gone into the 'actual settlement' business to a great extent this Spring."[79] Horace Greeley himself wrote to his newspaper from Washington on March 1:

"The Free-State men of Kansas now in this city have letters from various points in that embryo State down to the 18th and 19th ult. Their general tone implies apprehension that a bloody collision is imminent. The Border Ruffians have been raised entirely off their feet by Pierce's extraordinary Messages, which they regard as a complete endorsement of all their past outrages and an incitement to persevere in their diabolical work. It is believed by our friends that the organization of the State Government at Topeka the coming week will be made the pretext for a raid, and if possible a butchery, at the hands of the Slavery party. . . ."[80]

It was only in the time set that this prognostication was wrong. But meanwhile, as James Redpath has recorded, the acts of the Washington allies of Atchison, Stringfellow and Jones were daily making of the Free State pioneers more and more ardent advocates of freedom, and unifying them in their determination to resist to the last the pro-slavery aggressions:

"I have heard men who were semi-Southerners before, declare with Garrison:
"'I am an Abolitionist!
 I glory in the name!' —
since Kansas was invaded. I have heard others hint that even Garrison himself was rather an old fogy, *because he does not go far enough in opposition to Slavery*. 'The world *does* move.'"[81]

In April the pro-slavery net began to tighten around Lawrence. Sheriff Jones had reappeared there on April 19, 1856, to vex anew its citizens. He had decided that it was time for him to attempt again the arrest of those persons who five months previously had taken from him his prisoner Branson. Jones's thumbs had begun to itch for S. N. Wood, the leader of the rescuers; he was, therefore, quite willing to take Robinson and Lane at their word, that they would not resist the enforcement of a writ by proper authority, and quite ready to take a chance — if he did not court it — of again embroiling the citizens of Lawrence with the Territorial authorities. Jones easily found Wood and arrested him, but in the crowd which speedily gathered he lost his prisoner.[82] Jones reappeared the next day and called on the citizens to help him serve the four warrants he had in his hands. The crowd refused, saying, 'Take the muster roll, Jones, we all resist.'[83] Jones then personally laid hands on Samuel F. Tappan, who thereupon struck the sheriff in the face. This was sufficient resistance to satisfy the sheriff, who forthwith left, returning three days later, on April 23, with First Lieutenant James McIntosh, of the First Cavalry, and ten troopers. With the aid of these regulars he arrested six citizens on the extraordinary charge of contempt of court, in that they had declined to aid him in serving his warrants, — an unheard-of form of the crime of disrespect to the judiciary. His prisoners were put in a tent to await the pleasure of their captor. That evening, while Jones was sitting in his tent, with his shadow outlined against it by the light within, he was shot from without and gravely wounded by James N. Filer,[84] a young New Yorker, though the blame long rested on Charles Lenhart, a printer, subsequently prominent in the attempt to rescue Brown from his Virginia prison. Lenhart was undoubtedly outside the tent when Jones was shot, and as he was a reckless fellow, suspicion not unnaturally fell upon him.

Nothing more unfortunate could have happened for the citizens of Lawrence than the shooting of Jones, even though his life was spared, for the pro-slavery newspapers at once announced his death, and called upon their readers to avenge his murder. None of the regrets that the citizens of Lawrence expressed could undo the injury inflicted by Filer's shot. They held a mass meeting on April 24, addressed by Reeder, Robinson, Grosvenor P. Lowry and others, who condemned the crime in proper terms as cowardly and dastardly.[85]

THE CAPTAIN OF THE LIBERTY GUARDS

But their expressions went for naught. It was precisely the overt act needed to give Jones and his men the appearance of being hindered in the performance of their duty, and assaulted because of their devotion to it. The scene of the shooting — Lawrence — was particularly satisfactory to the pro-slavery party, since it enabled them to concentrate anew their enmity upon that hated town. "We are now in favor of levelling Lawrence and chastising the Traitors there congregated, should it result in total destruction of the Union," declared the *Squatter Sovereign* on April 29, 1856. A week later, May 6, still keeping alive the falsehood of Jones's death, it thus incited to murder:

"When a proslavery man gets into a difficulty with an Abolitionist let him think of the murdered Jones and Clark, and govern himself accordingly. In a fight, let our motto be, 'War to the knife, and knife to the hilt;' asking no quarters from them and granting none. *Jones' Murder Must Be Revenged!!*"

Appeals like this speedily bore fruit. On the next day, J. N. Mace, a Free State settler, who had testified before the Howard Committee then sitting at Lawrence, was shot in the leg by two men, who, thinking him dead, went off, rejoicing in his hearing that there was "more abolition bait for the wolves."[86] At an indignation meeting held in Lawrence on May 2 to consider Mace's case, Governor Robinson again soothed the perturbed feelings of the multitude, urged his listeners to go on making laws of their own, but not to give way to any spirit of revenge, and deprecated the attack upon Sheriff Jones as cowardly and base.[87] April 30 had been a fateful day for the Rev. Pardee Butler, who, undeterred by his being sent down the Missouri on a raft by his neighbors, returned then to Atchison. He was immediately stripped and cottoned (for lack of feathers), turned loose on the prairie, and a committee of three was appointed to hang him the next time he came to Atchison. His sole offence, according to his own testimony, was his telling the *Squatter Sovereign* that he was a Free Soiler and meant to vote accordingly.[88] On May 19 there fell, shot in the back near Blanton's Bridge, John Jones, who, according to the existing evidence, gave up his life merely because he, a boy of twenty, was accused of being an Abolitionist.[89] Three young men, Charles Lenhart, John Stewart and John E. Cook (who subsequently died on a Virginia gibbet, after John Brown), rode out toward the scene of this crime as soon as it was reported. On their way to Blanton's Bridge they fell in with several Missourians, who subsequently testified that they were fired upon first and one of them wounded; that in self-defence they shot and killed Stewart. Lenhart and Cook stated that Stewart hailed the Missourians by asking them where they were going. Their reply was a shot and Stewart fell dead. The Free State men with him were convinced that Coleman, the murderer of Dow, had in this case also fired the fatal shot.[90]

Judge Lecompte next stirred up the Territory in behalf of the pro-slavery cause by charging the grand jury in session at Lecompton during the second week in May that all the laws passed by the Shawnee Legislature were of United States authority and making; that, therefore, all who "resist these laws, resist the power and authority of the United States; and are therefore, guilty of high treason." * "If," he continued, laying down a principle new in American judicial procedure, "you find that no such resistance has been made, but that combinations have been formed for the purpose of resisting them, and that individuals of influence and notoriety have been aiding and abetting in such combinations, then must you find bills for *constructive treason.*" At once, without hearing any witnesses, the grand jury indicted Reeder, Robinson, Lane, George W. Brown, George W. Deitzler, Samuel N. Wood, Gaius Jenkins and George W. Smith on the charge of treason.[91] It is in keeping with this performance that Governor Robinson, who, with his wife, had left Lawrence at its most critical moment, in order to lay the true situation before the friends of Free Kansas in the East, should have been taken from the steamer Star of the West at Lexington, Missouri, on May 10, on the charge of fleeing from an indictment, when that indictment was not reported by the jury until

---

* "Section 3, Article 3, of the Constitution of the United States says: "Treason against the United States shall consist only in levying War against them, or in adhering to their Enemies, giving them Aid and Comfort. No person shall be convicted of Treason unless on the Testimony of two witnesses to the same overt act, or on Confession in open Court."

THE CAPTAIN OF THE LIBERTY GUARDS 143

a week after his detention.[92] Better evidence of the way the whole machinery of justice was being prostituted to pro-slavery ends could hardly be produced; it resulted in Robinson's being taken to Leavenworth, where he remained until his release on bail of five thousand dollars, on September 10, after four months' confinement. Ex-Governor Reeder escaped from Kansas in disguise, after having claimed protection in vain as a witness before the Howard Committee, and having told the United States deputy marshal that any attempt to take him prisoner would be attended with serious results.[93] Lane escaped Robinson's fate only by happening to be in Indiana on a visit. The Free Soil movement was thus deprived of its leaders. But the complaisant Lecompton grand jury was not content with indictment for treason; it took the still more extraordinary course of recommending the abatement as nuisances of the Lawrence Free Soil newspapers, *The Herald of Freedom* and *The Kansas Free State*. Charging that the Free State Hotel in Lawrence had been built for use as a fortress as well as a caravansary, the jurors expressed their opinion that its demolition was desirable.

Ex-Governor Reeder's refusal to submit to arrest was a greatly desired opportunity to another Jones, the United States marshal for Kansas Territory, I. B. Donaldson. He at once issued (on May 11) the following proclamation:

To The People of Kansas Territory:

Whereas, certain judicial writs of arrest have been directed to me by the First District Court of the United States, etc., to be executed within the county of Douglas; and, whereas, an attempt to execute them by the United States Deputy Marshal was violently resisted by a large number of citizens of Lawrence; and as there is every reason to believe that any attempt to execute these writs will be resisted by a large body of armed men:

Now, therefore, the law-abiding citizens of the Territory are commanded to be and appear at Lecompton as soon as practicable, and in numbers sufficient for the proper execution of the law.[94]

Like Sheriff Jones, Donaldson believed most of the law-abiding citizens of Kansas lived in Missouri, for his proclamation went first to the border towns and to Leavenworth and Atchison, the strongest pro-slavery settlements in Kansas.[95] Before the proclamation was known to the Free Soil settlers, the Border Ruffians had begun to assemble in the neighborhood of Lawrence, stopping travellers, patrolling the roads, even pillaging, as if they were a conquering army, and generally in high feather, for this time they felt certain of their prey, since it had been officially delivered over to them. The United States Court had issued the warrants; the United States marshal had called out them instead of the United States troops, who, after their visit in numbers to Lawrence under Colonel Sumner upon the shooting of Jones, had been allowed to return to their garrisons. In the Wakarusa " war," Shannon, not having power over the regulars, called eagerly for their aid; now that they were at his disposal, he refused to send them to Lawrence for the protection of its citizens, as the latter implored him to, or to urge Donaldson to use them as his posse.* Whereas in the previous December Governor Shannon had been willing to keep the peace, and eager to arrive at a compromise, he was ready now to have the tables turned upon those who had tricked him when in his cups, well knowing what the outcome would be. "But so long," he wrote to the Lawrence committee which begged protection of him, "as they [the citizens of Lawrence] keep up a military or armed organization to resist Territorial laws and the officers charged with their execution, I shall not interpose to save them from the legitimate consequences of their illegal acts."[96]

It was the van of Donaldson's forces which killed Stewart and Jones. His band comprised, first, Buford's newly arrived men, whom their leader hastily called together from their easy-going search for home-sites, four hundred in all responding. They represented in Donaldson's eyes, after being nineteen days in Kansas, the "law-abiding citizens of the Territory." General David R. Atchison, of Missouri, headed a Missouri company, the Platte County Riflemen, with two pieces of artillery; while the Kickapoo Rangers, who had hacked Captain R. P. Brown to death, and other Kansas pro-slavery companies eagerly joined the forces.[97] Both the Stringfellows

---

* When President Pierce heard of Donaldson's plans, he was much worried, and telegraphed to Shannon suggesting that the United States troops be used, and then only after the marshal had met with actual resistance. The telegram came too late to be of avail. See *Kansas Historical Collections*, vol. 4, p. 414.

THE CAPTAIN OF THE LIBERTY GUARDS 145

were there, ready to be in at the death, and hoping that this meant the extermination of the hated Abolitionists. About seven hundred and fifty in all, this "swearing, whiskey-drinking, ruffianly horde,"[98] who were there to uphold the majesty of the law, appeared near Lawrence on May 21, after a committee from there had vainly tried to induce Marshal Donaldson to agree to a compromise by which the town should be surrendered to Colonel Sumner and his cavalry regiment, to be held until the writs were served.[99] But the serving of the warrants was not Donaldson's real purpose, nor that of the men associated with him. The deputy marshal, Fain, made two arrests in Lawrence without difficulty or resistance, on the evening of May 20.[100] Accompanied by ten unarmed men, he returned at eleven o'clock the next morning and summoned five citizens of Lawrence to join his posse; they did so, and he then arrested George W. Deitzler, George W. Smith and Gaius Jenkins on the charge of treason. They submitted cheerfully. While Fain was at the Free State Hotel, he received a communication from the eight citizens of Lawrence who were acting as a committee of public safety. This committee, speaking for the entire town, acknowledged the "constituted authorities of the Government," and stated that they would "make no resistance to the execution of the law National or Territorial." This submission was in vain. Fain, having his prisoners in hand, announced to the Border Ruffians that he had peacefully accomplished his purpose, but added that Sheriff Jones had writs yet to be served, and that they could act as his posse if they desired.

With the utmost alacrity the invitation was accepted, but no pretence of serving any writs was made. The Southerners were stimulated by the oratory of Atchison, but recently presiding officer of the United States Senate, who declared among other things: "And now we will go in with our highly honorable Jones, and test the strength of that damned Free State Hotel. Be brave, be orderly, and if any man or woman stand in your way, blow them to hell with a chunk of cold lead." But they did not go in until the Free State men had surrendered their arms to Jones, as further evidence of good faith. Once in, there was no John Brown to counsel resistance to them, no Lane to lead, and no Robinson to temporize. There was no real leader. The military company, the Stubbs, was not in evidence. There were only two hundred rifles and ten kegs of powder in all Lawrence. Many of the citizens were either in arrest or in hiding to escape capture. Many others had left town to save their families. So no defence was attempted when the two newspaper offices were destroyed and the types, papers, presses and books thrown into the river. The Free State Hotel remained, however, and the order of the court that it be "abated" was not yet enforced. Here Major Buford again protested that he had not come to Kansas to destroy property, and Atchison seems to have been sobered some. But Jones wanted his triumph complete, and the Free State Hotel was soon in flames, after the pro-slavery cannon had sent thirty-two shot into it, Atchison firing the first shot.[101] "This," said Jones, "is the happiest moment of my life." As the walls of the hotel fell, he cried out in glee, "I have done it, by God, I have done it,"[102] and it in no wise troubled him that, when he dismissed his drunken posse, as the hotel lay in ruins, it promptly robbed the town, winding up by the burning of Governor Robinson's house. The majesty of the law was upheld; its flouting by Free Soilers avenged.

The pro-slavery leaders and their disbanded followers left the Territory exulting in their victory, and wholly unable to realize that it was not only to be their defeat, but that they had let loose a veritable Pandora's box of evil passions, and finally inaugurated a reign of bloodshed, midnight assassination and guerrilla warfare. Besides, they had aroused the whole North to fresh anger by the destruction of Lawrence, at first reported to have been accompanied by heavy loss of life. The inscriptions on their banners, "Southern Rights" and "South Carolina" and

> "Let Yankees tremble, abolitionists fall,
> Our Motto is, Give Southern rights to all,"[103]

alone brought dozens of recruits to the Free State cause. "From this time no further effort was required to raise colonies. They raised themselves," records Eli Thayer, the Worcester, Massachusetts, organizer of the Emigrant Aid Societies.[104] The raiding of Lawrence put an arsenal of arguments into the hands of the new-born Republican party, and fastened the nation's attention on the Territory. On the day of the raid, Horace Greeley declared that the "bloody collision in Kansas," which seemed to him "almost inevitable," would "hardly fail to shake the Union to its center." [105]

CHAPTER V

MURDER ON THE POTTAWATOMIE

To his "Dear Wife and Children Every One," wrote John Brown, "near Brown's Station, K. T., June, 1856," as follows: [1]

"It is now about five weeks since I have seen a line from North Elba, or had any chance of writing you. During that period we here have passed through an almost constant series of very trying events. We were called to go to the relief of Lawrence, May 22, and every man (eight in all) except Orson [Day], turned out; he staying with the women and children, and to take care of the cattle. John was captain of a company to which Jason belonged; the other six were a little company by ourselves. On our way to Lawrence we learned that it had been already destroyed, and we encamped with John's company over night. Next day our little company left, and during the day we stopped and searched three men. . . . On the second day and evening after we left John's men we encountered quite a number of proslavery men, and took quite a number of prisoners. Our prisoners we let go; but we kept some four or five horses. We were immediately after this accused of murdering five men at Pottawatomie, and great efforts have since been made by the Missourians and their ruffian allies to capture us. John's company soon afterward disbanded, and also the Osawatomie men."

In this brief, equivocal fashion John Brown reported to the absent members of his family that event in his life which made him most famous in Kansas and has caused more discussion than any other single event in the history of Kansas Territory. Upon the degree of criminality, if any, which should attach to John Brown for his part in the proceedings, the debate in Kansas to-day is almost as bitter as at the time of the crime, or when Brown's tragic end kindled the Kansas interest in it anew. As one views Brown's conduct in the killing of the five pro-slavery men on Pottawatomie Creek depends to a large degree the place which may be assigned to him in history. Certainly, without a clear appreciation of what happened on the night of the 24th to the 25th of May, 1856, a true understanding of Brown, the man, cannot be reached. The actual

MURDER ON THE POTTAWATOMIE

details have been veiled for nearly half a century in a mystery which the confessions of one of the party only partially dispelled. Fortunately for the truth of history, there are two other participants, Henry Thompson and Salmon Brown, still surviving after this long stretch of time, who have now set forth what happened. There are also many narratives of contemporary witnesses available which, when weighed together, make possible not only a real knowledge of the conditions precedent to the Pottawatomie massacre, but of its effects upon the Free Soil cause.

John Brown, Jr., was engaged in planting corn when the messenger from Lawrence arrived. "Without delay," he recorded in a defence of his father,[2] "I rode to Osawatomie with the word and then rallied the men of my company whose homes were mostly on Pottawatomie and Middle Creeks." His first lieutenant, Henry H. Williams, assisted him in this work, and by six o'clock in the evening thirty-four armed men met at the rendezvous, the junction of the Osawatomie and California roads. "The 'Marion Rifles' and 'Pomeroy Guards' from Osawatomie," narrated Williams,[3] in what is truly most valuable contemporary testimony, since it was written only two months after the event, while Williams was still a prisoner at Leavenworth, "had promised to meet us here by agreement, but only two men came, who reported that another messenger from Lawrence had arrived and contradicted the former report, and that, therefore, the Osawatomie companies would await further orders. The Pottawatomies, however, agreed to push on to Lawrence and ascertain the facts for themselves. Accordingly we moved on, and two miles from the Meridezene [Marais des Cygnes] we met a messenger from near Lawrence who reported that the Border Ruffians had taken the town without any resistance and were razing it to the ground. This startling news was received in silence by the company. Then the word 'onward' was passed along the line and although scarcely a word was spoken the thoughts of every one could be read in his countenance. We pushed on, and a messenger was dispatched to arouse the settlers at Osawatomie. At Prairie City we learned that there was no organized Free State force in Lawrence and that the 'Border Ruffians' were in possession of Blanton's Bridge, and had assembled in force at Lecompton. We concluded to encamp at Prairie City and await reinforcements."

At this camp the company of John Brown, Jr., and Lieutenant H. H. Williams remained until the next day, the 23d. Captain Shore and his Osawatomie company, together with the "Pomeroy Guards," joined the camp, bringing details of the sack of Lawrence and also the news that a force of four hundred men under Buford was in camp a few miles to the east.[4] That evening, hearing that Governor Robinson was being taken, a prisoner, from Westport to Lecompton, guarded by Border Ruffians, the three companies moved to Palmyra (now the prosperous town of Baldwin), then a little near-by settlement, twelve miles from Lawrence, in order that they might rescue the Free State leader if he were brought that way over the Santa Fé trail.[5] In their new camp they were joined by the Marion Rifles, Captain Updegraff. On the 24th, Captain John Brown, Jr., went with a scouting party into Lawrence to view the ruins.[6] His report and that of his men, that the citizens of that ill-fated town had not united in defending themselves against the common enemy, made the four companies at Palmyra decide they could not fight Lawrence's battles alone. "Accordingly," wrote Mr. Williams, "we broke up our camp, each company returning to its respective locality, the men dispersing to their homes." This homeward movement was hastened by the arrival of thirteen soldiers of the First Cavalry under Second Lieutenant John R. Church, a young West Pointer, whose official report of the meeting, dated May 26, 1856, has fortunately been preserved. Lieutenant Church, after a long talk with John Brown, Jr., ordered him to disband the camp in compliance with his (Church's) orders to disperse all armed bodies he encountered, whether pro-slavery or Free Soil.[7]

Curiously enough, the Pottawatomies returned to their homes the next day under the command of a new captain, Henry H. Williams, having deposed John Brown, Jr., on his way back from Lawrence, because he had freed two slaves.[8] "The arrival of those slaves in camp next morning caused a commotion," so their liberator has recorded. "The act of freeing them, though attended by no violence or bloodshed, was freely denounced, and in accordance with a vote given by a

MURDER ON THE POTTAWATOMIE 151

large majority of the men, those freed persons, in opposition to my expressed will, were returned to their master. The driver of the team which carried them overtaking him on his way to Westport, received a side-saddle as his reward." There was still another reason why the men of John Brown, Jr.'s company chose a new captain. On this same day, when the company was near Ottawa Creek on its return, a rider came tearing into camp — his horse panting and lathered with foam — and without dismounting yelled out: "Five men have been killed on Pottawatomie Creek, butchered and most brutally mangled, and old John Brown has done it!" — thus Jason Brown records it. "This information," he states, "caused great excitement and fear among the men of our company and a feeling arose against John and myself which led the men all to desert us." [9]

As John Brown himself wrote to his family, he and a small party left his son's company the morning after their long night tramp to Prairie City, on Friday, May 23. The circumstances leading up to his departure are thus set forth by Jason Brown:

"Father cooked for our company. While he was cooking breakfast, I heard him, Townsley and Weiner talking together. I heard Townsley say: 'We expect to be butchered, every Free State settler in our region,' and Townsley pleaded that help should be sent. I heard their talk only in fragments. Then I heard father say to Weiner: 'Now something *must* be done. We have got to defend our families and our neighbors as best we can. Something *is going to be done now*. We must show by actual work that there are two sides to this thing and that they cannot go on with impunity.'" [10]

Weiner also told Martin Van Buren Jackson, in the camp, "that he, his man Benjamin and also Bondi, had been insulted, abused and ordered to leave the county within three days, by the Shermans and other pro-slavery parties living in the neighborhood of Dutch Henry's Crossing; and that Dutch Bill (Sherman), as he was called, was drunk and very abusive. He said this was the second time they had been to his place in the past few days, and he did not propose to stand such treatment much longer." [11]

Moved by this and other provocations, John Brown acted at once. "Pottawatomie," says Salmon Brown, "was resolved upon by father, supported by the leading men in John's company — maybe a dozen — and by his own crowd. The plan was thoroughly discussed there in camp, not before the whole company, but in the council thus selected." [12] August Bondi, a faithful follower of John Brown, remembers the council well, for Brown used to him practically the same words — "Something must be done to show these barbarians that we, too, have rights," [13] — which he had previously spoken to Weiner and Townsley. It is clear that John Brown did reveal to the council the general outline of his plan. [14] "It was now and here resolved that they, their aiders and abettors, who sought to kill our suffering people, should themselves be killed, and in such manner as should be likely to cause a restraining fear," declares John Brown, Jr., and Salmon Brown testifies:

"The general purport of our intentions — some radical retaliatory measure — some killing — was well understood by the whole camp. You never heard such cheering as they gave us when we started out.[15] They were wild with excitement and enthusiasm. The principal man — the leader — in the council that resolved on the necessity of Pottawatomie, — was H. H. Williams: I do not know that I ought to tell this since he himself has not; but it is the fact. He was wholly determined that the thing must be done. He knew all those men on the Pottawatomie, better than any of us. He lived among them — was familiar with all their characters. He was now the most active of us all in urging this step. And not fifteen minutes before we left to go to Pottawatomie I saw him, myself, write out a list of the men who were to be killed and hand it to father. This was on the crest of the wave of enthusiasm. Williams was a little cautious, I always thought, even then. He was a first-rate fellow; but he was too smart, even in enthusiasm, to go into a thing like that, personally, when he could get some one else to do it for him. Then, when it was all over, and he found how the people down at home took it, he got scared. He had n't the backbone to stand by his own mind, against popular opinion, — he went back on his own radical measures, weakened, did not confess to his own share in their origin, and counselled peace. In fact, he got scared. Benjamin told me about this afterward. Williams wrote down the names of the men whom, he said, it was necessary to pick off to prevent the utter destruction of the whole community and handed the paper to father. We started back, thereupon, for the Pottawatomie country, which was the headquarters for the pro-slavery men, under Judge Cato, for that region, to pick off the designated men prominent in enforcing Border Ruffian laws." [16]

MURDER ON THE POTTAWATOMIE

About noon, John Brown selected for his party Henry Thompson, Theodore Weiner, and four sons, Owen, Frederick, Salmon and Oliver. In order to secure the use of his wagon, John Brown went to James Townsley, of the Pottawatomie Rifles, saying he had just heard trouble was expected on the Pottawatomie. He asked Townsley whether he could not take his team of grays and convey him with his sons back to Pottawatomie. Townsley consented, and the departure was fixed for two o'clock.[17] The interim was devoted to the sharpening of some of the odd-shaped cutlasses, the gift of General Lucius V. Bierce, of Akron, Ohio, that John Brown had brought West with him, for use in border warfare.[18] John Brown, Jr., and Jason devoted themselves to the cutlasses, while a boy, Bain Fuller, turned the grindstone; but Jason insists that he had no idea of the real purpose of the expedition.[19] Seeing the grinding operation, George Grant remarked to Frederick Brown: "That looks like business." "Yes," was the reply, "it does." When Grant asked whether he might not also ride back in Townsley's wagon, Frederick Brown consulted his father, only to return and report: "Father says you had better not come."[20] Bain Fuller, whose father had received John Brown's word that the boy should not get into trouble, was told to go home and to be sure to have witnesses as to his whereabouts for that night.[21] Before Townsley's horses were ready and the cutlasses had received their edge, a feeling came over some of the men in the camp that the radical leader of the returning party might not act with sufficient discretion. One of them went to John Brown, so relates Judge James Hanway, and urged "caution." At this, Brown, who was packing up his camp fixtures, instantly stood erect and said: "Caution, caution, sir. I am eternally tired of hearing that word caution. It is nothing but the word of cowardice."[22] In the *Kansas Monthly*, for January, 1880, Judge Hanway wrote: "I ventured to approach one of the eight, and from him learned the program contemplated. In fact, I received an invitation to be one of the party, and being unwilling to consent before I learned the object, I was made acquainted with the object of the expedition; it shocked me."

With the shouts of their comrades in their ears, the party

set off in Townsley's wagon, except Weiner, who, riding his pony, gave them mounted escort as they retraced their way over the road they had traversed in such haste and excitement the night before. "As we turned back with the evil news [the fate of Lawrence] and had just got to the top of the hill south of the Wakarusa — the high ridge," says Salmon Brown, "a man named Gardner came to us with the news of the assault upon Senator Sumner of Bully Brooks,* — carrying the message hidden in his boot. At that blow the men went crazy — *crazy*. It seemed to be the finishing, decisive touch." Two men have affirmed that they met the expedition as it took its way toward what is now the little hamlet called Lane. Captain J. M. Anthony and a squad of Free State men encountered it near the residence of Ottawa Jones, and in their surprise at seeing fighting men returning when Lawrence was in distress, asked eagerly whither the men in the lumber wagon were bound. "They gave us," says Captain Anthony, "no answer except that they were going to attend to very urgent business and would be right back to join us on the march to Lawrence." [23] Near sundown, between Pottawatomie and Middle Creek, James Blood descried a wagon with a mounted man alongside, going toward Pottawatomie Creek. As he neared the wagon, John Brown rose in it and cried "Halt!" Blood remembered afterwards that the men in the wagon were armed with rifles, revolvers, knives and General Bierce's short heavy broadswords, for John Brown had given him one of these cutlasses when in Lawrence during the Wakarusa excitement. Brown, Blood found to be very indignant that Lawrence had been sacked without a shot being fired in its behalf. He denounced the leading Free State men as cowards or worse. "His manner," wrote Colonel Blood twenty-three years later, "was wild and frenzied, and the whole party watched with excited eagerness every word or motion of the old man. Finally, as I left them, he requested me not to mention the fact that I had met them, as they were on a secret expedition and did not want anyone to know that they were in the neighborhood." [24]

That night, says Townsley, they "drove down to the edge

* Congressman Brooks, of South Carolina, assaulted Senator Sumner in the Senate on May 22, 1856, striking him on the head with a heavy cane.

MURDER ON THE POTTAWATOMIE   155

of the timber between two deep ravines, and camped about one mile above Dutch Henry's Crossing."[25] And there, Townsley asserts, John Brown told him for the first time of his bloodthirsty intentions, and refused to let him go when he, Townsley, asked to be allowed to take his team and return home. All the next day, Saturday, the 24th, the little company literally lay on their arms in their open-air camp. For it was in the night that John Brown proposed to strike his blow, in order, Salmon Brown declares, that they might be sure to catch their quarry in their lairs. "Maybe," he adds, "Father took into consideration the terrifying effect of such a means." Certainly, the hour suited the deed. The chase was trapped; save in one instance. Henry Sherman, whose absence in pursuit of wandering cattle saved his life for another year, was one of three brothers, German in origin, and therefore known in the community as Dutch Bill, Dutch Henry and Dutch Pete. Border Ruffians by their sympathies and their instincts, their character is painted black enough by their Free Soil neighbors, who credited them with no honest ways of life, generally thought of them as ignorant and drunken, living at the crossing which bore the name of Dutch Henry, and subsisting by making money out of the emigrants or "lifting" a horse or a cow or two from the caravans as they came by. For this well-known ford was the point where the much-used road from Fort Scott to the Santa Fé trail and the old California road, or road to Oregon, used by emigrants going still further west, crossed the Pottawatomie. Weiner's store near-by also drew patronage from these emigrant parties, and to it the Shermans and their pro-slavery neighbors had carried their drunken threats of extermination of the Abolitionists that had so stirred Weiner, Townsley and Bondi. Indeed, the two diverse elements had even come to blows, as Henry Thompson testifies. For several midwinter months he had helped Weiner to keep his store. Returning to it on Christmas Day, he found Weiner with an axe handle beating "Dutch Bill" Sherman, who fled on the approach of Thompson. "He attacked me in my own store," said Weiner by way of explanation.[26] "They were brutes and bullies," declares one woman who resided at Osawatomie at this time, in speaking of the murdered men, and this seems to sum up their character accurately, if the adjective "ignorant" be added.[27]

The men of the Doyle family, father and two sons, were low "poor whites" from Tennessee, who, while sympathizing with the pro-slavery element, went to Kansas because, according to Mrs. Doyle, they had found that slavery was "ruinous to white labor."[28] Mrs. Doyle herself was illiterate, and it is altogether likely that the men were. The family seems to have been very intimate with "Dutch Bill," who was one of the oldest settlers in the region, and considerably under his influence. Allen Wilkinson, on the other hand, was a man of some education; he was a member of the pro-slavery Legislature, and returned from its meetings at the Shawnee Mission more than ever a pro-slavery man. George W. Grant and his brother, Henry Grant, have testified that Wilkinson was a dangerous man, whom everybody feared; "the most evil looking man" they ever saw, "who fearfully abused a nice wife, well liked by the neighbors."[29] Wilkinson, too, was free with his threats to the Free Soil settlers, urging them to "clear out" and avoid trouble. All of them were friendly with the Missourians who passed by, acting as their guides and advisers. There is also no doubt that when the Browns entered the camp of Buford's men as surveyors, they found these obnoxious pro-slavery neighbors on good terms with the invaders.[30]

Not unnaturally, a different character was assigned after their murders to these men by the pro-slavery leaders. Thus, Henry Clay Pate, correspondent of the St. Louis *Republican* and leader of a pro-slavery company, testified that "they had no fault as quiet citizens but being in favor of slavery. That was the crime for which they forfeited their lives."[31] The Rev. Martin White insisted to the pro-slavery Legislature that Wilkinson was a noble man, whose "greatest crime" was that "he was a member of the first legislature in this territory," which crime, White added, was the reason for his death.[32] Congressman Oliver, the Democratic member of the Howard Committee, was satisfied, after taking testimony in the case of the murders, that Wilkinson was a quiet, inoffensive man. "My husband was a quiet man, and was not engaged in arresting or disturbing anybody. He took no

MURDER ON THE POTTAWATOMIE 157

active part in the pro-slavery cause, so as to aggravate the Abolitionists, but he was a pro-slavery man," was Mrs. Wilkinson's characterization of her husband.[33] The *Kansas Weekly Herald* of Leavenworth affirmed on June 7, 1856, that Wilkinson was a member of the Legislature, and that the other victims were "plain, honest, peaceable farming settlers." But the weight of evidence is too strong on the other side to make it possible to accept this characterization as correct. Excepting perhaps Wilkinson, the others were of the rough, brutal, disorderly element to be found in every frontier outpost, whether it be mining camp or farmers' settlement.

During the morning of Saturday, the 24th, when John Brown's party of avengers lay in the timber between two deep ravines a mile above Dutch Henry's Crossing, Townsley, so he asserts, did his best to dissuade the leader and his sons from carrying out their plans, and to this end "talked a good deal." But Brown insisted always that it had become necessary "to strike terror into the hearts of the pro-slavery people." Townsley even avers that the day's delay was due to his protests and his refusal to guide the company up to the forks of Mosquito Creek, some five or six miles above, and point out where pro-slavery men resided, so that Brown's men might sweep the creek of them as they came down. This Salmon Brown declares to be nonsense, a plan that "never was dreamed of." Moreover, Weiner, the storekeeper, might well have been as efficient a guide as Townsley, since he had been in Kansas longer and naturally had a wider acquaintance. The delay, too, is not hard to explain. The men must have been fairly exhausted when they encamped in the timber, since they had marched all the previous night and, after working all the morning, had driven back over rough roads between two o'clock and sundown. To postpone the raid in order to obtain necessary sleep was most natural. Then, since night-time was deemed necessary to trap the prey sought, the day in camp was inevitable. But on this fateful day the sun finally sank into the prairies, and long before it disappeared, Townsley had resigned himself to his situation sufficiently to decide that he would go along, albeit unwillingly, as he declares.

As for the rest, aside from Weiner, whom Salmon Brown

describes as a "big, savage, bloodthirsty Austrian" who "could not be kept out of any accessible fight,"[34] they needed no persuasion. Whether it was the compelling personality of their father, whose dominating manner and will-power later led men willingly to their death under circumstances against which their common sense revolted, or whether there was in the sons a sufficient touch of an inherited mental disturbance to make them less than rational in their reasoning, there was no attempt at a filial revolt against a parental decision, even when they went unwillingly. Two sons, at least, Frederick and Oliver, kept their hands unstained,[35] and probably protested, only to submit and accompany their father and imperious commander as witnesses of the horrors of that night, sharing the guilt of all in the eyes of the law. The other brothers, then unaccustomed to the sight of blood, who had hitherto led the untroubled lives of plain American citizens, were exalted or nerved now to deeds at which a trained professional soldier might easily and creditably shrink. The sword of Gideon was unsheathed. About the hour of ten o'clock the party, armed with swords, revolvers and rifles, proceeded in a northerly direction, "crossing Mosquito Creek above the residence of the Doyles." Soon after crossing the creek, some one of the party knocked at the door of a cabin. There was no reply, but from within came the sound of a gun rammed through the chinks of the cabin walls. It saved the owner's life, for, relates Salmon Brown, "at that we all scattered. We did not disturb that man. With some candle wicking soaked in coal oil to light and throw inside, so that we could see within while he could not see outside, we would have managed it. But we had none. It was a method much used later."

Thence it was but a short distance to the ill-fated Doyles'. To add to the natural terrors of the night and of the dark design, there came to meet them, at the very threshold of the house, two dogs — "very savage bull dogs." One of these sentinels Townsley claims to have helped despatch, for though, according to his own story, an unwilling abettor under compulsion, he carried one of the deadly Bierce swords and was thus an *armed* prisoner. It was about eleven o'clock, Mrs. Doyle testified, that her family heard a knock.[36]

"My husband got up and went to the door. Those outside inquired for Mr. Wilkson [Wilkinson] and where he lived. My husband told them that he would tell them. Mr. Doyle, my husband, opened the door, and several came into the house, and said that they were from the army. My husband was a pro-slavery man. They told my husband that he and the boys must surrender, they were their prisoners. These men were armed with pistols and large knives. They first took my husband out of the house, then they took two of my sons — the two oldest ones, William and Drury — out, and then took my husband and these two boys, William and Drury, away. My son John was spared, because I asked them in tears to spare him. In a short time afterward I heard the report of pistols."

Thus, without warning or notice, her husband and two sons were torn from her and despatched. "When we entered the Doyle cabin," says Salmon Brown, "Mrs. Doyle stormed, raved at her men, after we had taken them prisoners. 'Haven't I told you what you were going to get for the course you have been taking?' she screamed. 'Hush, mother, hush,' replied her husband." Her two boys, twenty-two and twenty years of age, were granted, like her husband, no time to make their peace, no time to ask forgiveness of their sins. Townsley affirms that he, Frederick Brown and Weiner were at some distance from the house, but near enough to cry out in protest if he had wished to, and near enough to see that John Brown "drew his revolver and shot old man Doyle in the forehead, and Brown's two younger sons immediately fell upon the younger Doyles with their short two-edged swords." But in this, according to Salmon Brown, Townsley was mistaken, just as he erred in insisting that Watson Brown, then at North Elba, was present and playing the part of executioner. "Not one of the Doyles ran a single step," is Salmon's positive statement. "They fell where they stood. I think that the father Doyle was not the first of the three to be killed."

As for John Brown's own part, he killed none of them with his own hand; to this both Henry Thompson and Salmon Brown bear positive witness, as did John Brown himself. But Mrs. Doyle did hear one shot at least. Salmon Brown will not positively state that his father fired it, but admits that no one else in the party pulled a trigger. He is at a loss to explain why the shot was fired. "It did no possible good, as a bullet, for Doyle had long been stone dead." And his father could therefore truthfully say that he had raised his hand against no living man. "I was three hundred yards away when the shot was fired," is Henry Thompson's statement. "Those who were on the spot told me that it was done after Doyle was dead." Even with Oliver and Frederick, a younger and older son, taking no part, the killings lasted but a moment. Doyle and his two sons in an instant lay lifeless, —a Free State warning to the pro-slavery forces that it was to be a tooth for a tooth, an eye for an eye, henceforth, so far as one wing of the Free State party was concerned. If pro-slavery men had not been made to die when Lawrence fell, here were three to even up the score. "My husband, and two boys, my sons," testified the simple, untutored, pitiful Mahala Doyle, "did not come back any more. I went out next morning in search of them, and found my husband and William, my son, lying dead in the road near together, about two hundred yards from the house. My other son I did not see any more until the day he was buried. I was so much overcome that I went into the house. They were buried the next day. On the day of the burying I saw the dead body of Drury. Fear of myself and the remaining children induced me to leave the home where we had been living. We had improved our claim a little. I left all and went to the State of Missouri."

"I found my father and one brother, William, lying dead in the road, about two hundred yards from the house," testified John Doyle.[37] "I saw my other brother lying dead on the ground, about one hundred and fifty yards from the house, in the grass, near a ravine; his fingers were cut off, and his arms were cut off; his head was cut open; there was a hole in his breast. William's head was cut open, and a hole was in his jaw, as though it was made by a knife, and a hole was also in his side. My father was shot in the forehead and stabbed in the breast." "Owen and another killed the Doyles," says Salmon Brown, and by a process of elimination it is apparent that the other could only have been himself. "It is not true," Townsley testifies, "that there was any intentional mutilation of the bodies after they were killed. They were slain as quickly as possible and left, and whatever gashes they received were inflicted in the process of cutting them

MURDER ON THE POTTAWATOMIE

down with swords. I understand that the killing was done with these swords so as to avoid alarming the neighborhood by the discharge of firearms."

The next man to meet his fate at the hands of John Brown's merciless party was Wilkinson. The same procedure was adopted. Somewhere between the hours of midnight and daybreak, "we were disturbed by the barking of the dog," Mrs. Wilkinson informed Congressman Oliver, under oath.[38] She continued:

"I was sick with the measles, and woke up Mr. Wilkinson, and asked if he heard the noise and what it meant? He said it was only someone passing about, and soon after was again asleep. It was not long before the dog raged and barked furiously, awakening me once more; pretty soon I heard footsteps as of men approaching; saw one pass by the window, and some one knocked at the door. I asked, who is that? No one answered. I awoke my husband, who asked, who is that? Someone replied, 'I want you to tell me the way to Dutch Henry's.' He commenced to tell them, and they said to him, 'Come out and show us.' He wanted to go, but I would not let him; he then told them it was difficult to find his clothes, and could tell them as well without going out of doors. The men out of doors, after that, stepped back, and I thought I could hear them whispering; but they immediately returned, and, as they approached, one of them asked of my husband, 'Are you a northern armist?' He said, 'I am!' I understood the answer to mean that my husband was opposed to the northern or freesoil party. I cannot say that I understood the question. My husband was a pro-slavery man, and was a member of the territorial legislature held at Shawnee Mission. When my husband said 'I am,' one of them said, 'You are our prisoner. Do you surrender?' He said, 'Gentlemen, I do.' They said, 'open the door.' Mr. Wilkinson told them to wait till he made a light; and they replied, 'if you don't open it, we will open it for you.' He opened the door against my wishes, and four men came in, and my husband was told to put on his clothes, and they asked him if there were not more men about; they searched for arms, and took a gun and powder flask, all the weapon that was about the house. I begged them to let Mr. Wilkinson stay with me, saying that I was sick and helpless, and could not stay by myself. My husband also asked them to let him stay with me until he could get someone to wait on me; told them that he would not run off, but would be there the next day, or whenever called for. The old man, who seemed to be in command, looked at me and then around at the children, and replied, 'You have neighbors.' I said, 'So I have, but they are not here, and I cannot go for them.' The old man replied, 'it matters not.' I [he?] told him to get ready. My husband wanted to put on his boots and get ready, so as to be protected from the damp and night air, but they would n't let him. They then took my husband away. One of them came back and took two saddles; I asked him what they were going to do with him, and he said, 'take him a prisoner to the camp.' I wanted one of them to stay with me. He said he would, but 'they would not let him.' After they were gone, I thought I heard my husband's voice, in complaint, but do not know; went to the door, and all was still. Next morning Mr. Wilkinson was found about one hundred and fifty yards from the house in some dead brush. A lady who saw my husband's body, said that there was a gash in his head and in his side; others said that he was cut in the throat twice."

"We divided our forces at Wilkinson's, I think, into two parties to go on separate errands," is Salmon Brown's testimony. "Henry Thompson and Weiner killed Wilkinson and Sherman. My party was not present when Wilkinson and Sherman were killed. Townsley could not have been present at each crisis, as he implies. No one else was." Yet Townsley attributes Wilkinson's murder to "one of the younger Browns" and adds: "After he was killed his body was dragged to one side and left." Henry Thompson states that he was not present when the Doyles were killed, but is silent as to the fate of Wilkinson and Sherman.

The "old man" to whom Mrs. Wilkinson's pleading for her husband's life had "mattered not" was still unplacated when Wilkinson's dead body lay in the brush. The next and last man to die was William Sherman. "We then crossed the Pottawatomie and came to the house of Henry Sherman," is Townsley's tale. "Here John Brown and the party, excepting Frederick Brown, Weiner and myself, who were left outside a short distance from the door, went into the house and brought out one or two persons, talked with them some, and then took them in again. They afterward brought out William Sherman, Dutch Henry's brother, marched him down into the Pottawatomie Creek, where he was slain with swords by Brown's two youngest sons and left lying in the creek." But Townsley was again wrong as to his details, for the house was not Sherman's, but that of James Harris, who promptly made affidavit thereto and thus related what befell: [39]

"On last Sunday morning, about two o'clock, (the 25th of May last,) whilst my wife and child and myself were in bed in the house

MURDER ON THE POTTAWATOMIE 163

where we lived, we were aroused by a company of men who said they belonged to the northern army, and who were each armed with a sabre and two revolvers, two of whom I recognized, namely, a Mr. Brown, whose given name I do not remember, commonly known by the appellation of 'old man Brown,' and his son, Owen Brown. They came in the house and approached the bedside where we were lying, and ordered us, together with three other men who were in the same house with me, to surrender; that the northern army was upon us, and it would be no use for us to resist. The names of these other three men who were then in my house with me are, William Sherman, John S. Whiteman, the other man I did not know. They were stopping with me that night. They had bought a cow from Henry Sherman, and intended to go home the next morning. When they [the Browns] came up to the bed, some had drawn sabres in their hands, and some revolvers. They then took into their possession two rifles and a Bowie knife, which I had there in the room — there was but one room in my house — and afterward ransacked the whole establishment in search of ammunition. They then took one of these three men, who were staying in my house, out. (This was the man whose name I did not know.) He came back. They then took me out, and asked me if there were any more men about the place. I told them there were not. They searched the place, but found none others but we four. They asked me where Henry Sherman was. Henry Sherman was a brother to William Sherman. I told them that he was out on the plains in search of some cattle which he had lost. They asked if I had ever taken any hand in aiding pro-slavery men in coming to the Territory of Kansas, or had ever taken any hand in the last troubles at Lawrence, and asked me whether I had ever done the free State party any harm or ever intended to do that party any harm; they asked me what made me live at such a place. I then answered that I could get higher wages there than anywhere else. They asked me if there were any bridles or saddles about the premises. I told them there was one saddle, which they took, and they also took possession of Henry Sherman's horse, which I had at my place, and made me saddle him. They then said if I would answer no to all questions which they had asked me, they would let [me?] loose. Old Mr. Brown and his son then went into the house with me. The other three men, Mr. William Sherman, Mr. Whiteman, and the stranger were in the house all this time. After old man Brown and his son went into the house with me, old man Brown asked Mr. Sherman to go out with him, and Mr. Sherman then went out with old Mr. Brown, and another man came into the house in Brown's place. I heard nothing more for about fifteen minutes. Two of the northern army, as they styled themselves, stayed on with us until we heard a cap burst, and then these two men left. That morning about ten o'clock I found William Sherman dead in the creek near my house. I was looking for Mr. Sherman, as he had not come back, I thought he had been murdered. I took Mr. William Sherman out of the creek and examined him. Mr. Whiteman was with me. Sherman's skull was split open in two places and some of his brains was washed out by the water. A large hole was cut in his breast, and his left hand was cut off except a little piece of skin on one side. We buried him."

Here Thompson and Weiner were again the executioners, according to Salmon Brown. "Neither of the younger sons, nor Owen, was present when William Sherman was killed." Then, at last, John Brown was satisfied. He had told Townsley that he must take matters into his own hands "for the protection of the Free State settlers; that it was better that a score of bad men should die than that one man who came here to make Kansas a Free State should be driven out." The rising Sabbath sun shone on five mutilated bodies, their very starkness, in their executioner's eyes, a protection to the Free State settlers for many miles around. The bloody night's work was over. Confusion now had made his masterpiece.

Three and one half years later, when in jail and under sentence of death, John Brown received the following letter purporting to come from Mahala Doyle. Mrs. Doyle could not write, and the letter is obviously, in its style, beyond her homely powers of expression, though she may have signed it, and there is nothing in it she might not have said in her own way:

CHATTANOOGA, TENNESSEE Nov. 20th, 1859.[40]

JOHN BROWN: — SIR, — Altho' vengence is not mine I confess that I do feel gratified, to hear that you were stopped in your fiendish career at Harper's Ferry, with the loss of your two sons, you can now appreciate my distress in Kansas, when you then & there entered my house at midnight and arrested my Husband and two boys, and took them out of the yard and in cold blood shot them dead in my hearing, you cant say you done it to free slaves, we had none and never expected to own one, but has only made me a poor disconsolate widow with helpless children, while I feel for your folly I do hope & trust that you will meet your just reward. O how it pained my heart to hear the dying groans of my Husband & children, if this scrawl gives you any consolation you are welcome to it

MAHALA DOYLE.

N. B. My son John Doyle whose life I beged of you is now grown up and is very desirous to be at Charlestown on the day of your execution, would certainly be there if his means would permit it that he might adjust the rope around your neck if Gov. Wise would permit it.
M. DOYLE.

MURDER ON THE POTTAWATOMIE 165

Townsley asserts that Brown was intent upon killing George Wilson, Probate Judge of Anderson County, whom he hoped to find at Sherman's, for the reason that he had been warning Free State men to leave the Territory. Townsley claimed to have received such a notice himself. But Salmon Brown and Henry Thompson deny positively that Wilson was on the proscribed list. Be this as it may, there was no further search for any one, and the blood-stained party went back to the camping-place in the timber between the two deep ravines, their swords, "unmannerly breached with gore," being first washed in Pottawatomie Creek. Just before daylight, Townsley avers, Owen Brown came to him and said, "There shall be no more such work as that." In the afternoon the eight men started back to rejoin the Pottawatomie company under John Brown, Jr. They found it about midnight, encamped near Ottawa Jones's farm, where, as we have seen, the news of their awful deed had already preceded them, and where John Brown, Jr., had resigned the captaincy of the company. As soon as Jason Brown, whose hatred of blood-letting had deprived him of his father's confidence when violent deeds were under way, met his father face to face, he encountered him tremblingly, — for this was the "worst shock" that ever came to him in his life.[41] "Did you," he demanded of his father, "have anything to do with the killing of those men on the Pottawatomie?" "I did not do it," the father replied, "but I approved of it." "I spoke to him as I then felt about it," continues Jason; "I did not fully understand the cause of it then, and told him I was very sorry the act had been done. I said to him: 'I think it was an uncalled for, wicked act.' He said: 'God is my judge. It was absolutely necessary as a measure of self-defence, and for the defence of others.' I cannot give his exact language, but this was the purport of it. It seemed to hurt his feelings that I felt so about it. He soon after left us, and John and I returned to Osawatomie." Not, however, until he had sought additional information. He inquired of his brother Frederick if he knew who the murderers were. "Yes I do, but I can't tell you." "Did you kill any of them with your own hands?" "No; when I came to see what manner of work it was, I *could not* do it." The tears rolled down Frederick's face as he spoke, Jason reports; and this eye-witness of the tragedy seems never to have learned to approve of it. In this he was in marked contrast to Townsley, for, unwilling participant as he was, he stated that after the event he became convinced that it resulted in good to the Free State settlers on Pottawatomie Creek.

Jason and John Brown, Jr., felt too badly to join forces with their father. The Pottawatomie Company started for home under H. H. Williams in a very different frame of mind toward the men they had so gayly cheered out of camp but three days before, either because of a sudden repentance, or of their having expected a stand-up fight instead of a slaughter, or because the deed in its reality seemed so much worse than in anticipation that those in the secret joined the others in their detestation of it. John Brown and his fellow executioners fell behind the company, after crossing Middle Creek, and struck off by themselves in the direction of Jason's and the younger John's homes. Jason and John headed not for their cabins but for Osawatomie. Already the roads were lined with men, so Jason narrates,[42] from Palmyra to Osawatomie, looking for the Browns. The brothers got to the Adair cabin, where both their wives had taken refuge during their absence, at about 9 P. M. Adair came to the door with his gun. "Who's there?" said he. "John and I." "Can't keep you here. Our lives are threatened. Every moment we expect to have our house burned over our heads." To their entreaties, he only repeated: "I cannot keep you." "Here are we two alone," pleaded Jason. "We have eaten nothing all day. Let us lie on your floor until morning — in your out-house — anywhere." Then Mrs. Adair came and asked, "Did you have anything to do with the murders on the Pottawatomie?" "I did not," said Jason. "And John had no action in it." "Then," said Mrs. Adair, "you may stay. But we risk our lives in keeping you." They gave the two a mattress on the floor beside the Adairs' bed, and the four talked till midnight, Jason telling all he knew of the affair. John lay groaning. In the middle of the night John spoke to his Aunt Florilla. "I feel that I am going insane," said he, and in the morning he was insane. Jason had slept after a while, but John could not. His mind was gone, yet not so far gone but that he was able to understand and to acquiesce when

SALMON BROWN

JOHN BROWN, JR.

JASON BROWN

OWEN BROWN

FOUR OF JOHN BROWN'S SONS
In later years

MURDER ON THE POTTAWATOMIE 167

Jason advised him to hide, and to act upon it. About two or three o'clock that same night, a knock had been heard at the door. "Who's there?" called out Adair. "Owen." "Get away, get away as quick as you can! You endanger our lives." Adair would not parley or let him in. "You are a vile murderer, a marked man!" said he.[43] "I intend to *be* a marked man!" shouted Owen, and rode away — on one of the murdered men's horses.

The Rev. Mr. Adair was not the only one to feel outraged at first by the murders committed by his relatives. John T. Grant and Judge Hanway, two of the best Free State settlers in that region, talked the matter over, so J. G. Grant, a son of the former, recollects,[44] and agreed that John Brown's action was inexcusable. He had taken, they said, the moment when the families of all the men who had gone to the rescue of Lawrence were helpless, to commit a crime which invited and provoked a vengeful attack upon the settlement. Was that sane or decent, they asked? And was it excusable for him, after the murder, to march away from the seat of danger and rejoin the company at Ottawa Jones's, thus leaving the women and children more than ever helpless? Not until some time afterwards did Adair and Hanway, like Townsley, come around to an approval of the deed as they saw it in retrospect. "Last Sunday or Monday," wrote on May 31, 1856, James H. Carruth, another Osawatomie Free State settler of character, to the Watertown, New York, *Reformer*,[45] "five pro-slavery men were killed seven or eight miles from here. It is said that they had threatened to hang another pro-slavery man who had sold provisions to the free state men unless he left the territory in a few hours, and that one of them had been around the neighborhood brandishing his bowie-knife and threatening to kill people. It was murder, nevertheless, and the free-state men here coöperate with the pro-slavery men in endeavoring to arrest the murderers." "Threatened and ordered to leave in given time under penalty of death, some few persons committed the horrid murders at Pottawatomie 10 miles above," was the way O. C. Brown described the crime on June 24, 1856, in a letter to a friend.[46] The writer was no relative of the murderers, but a staunch Free State man and a leader at Osawatomie. H. L. Jones, another settler, declares that the act was generally believed by Free State men to be warranted at the time, but that "policy dictated that the deed should be disavowed as having general disapproval." [47] George Thompson, a settler who lived four miles northeast of the Brown claims, testified, in 1894, that "at the time of the executions of the Doyles, Wilkinson and Sherman, with many of my neighbors I did not approve the act, but since, on more fully understanding the circumstances, I believe the act to have been wise and justifiable." [48]

Three days after the murders, a public meeting was held in Osawatomie, of which C. H. Price was chairman and H. H. Williams secretary. It adopted unanimously the following emphatic resolutions:

"Whereas, An outrage of the darkest and foulest nature has been committed in our midst by some midnight assassins unknown, who have taken five of our citizens at the hour of midnight from their homes and families, and murdered and mangled them in the most awful manner; to prevent a repetition of these deeds, we deem it necessary to adopt some measures for our mutual protection and to aid and assist in bringing these desperadoes to justice. Under these circumstances we propose to act up to the following resolutions:

"Resolved, That we will from this time lay aside all sectional and political feelings and act together as men of reason and common sense, determined to oppose all men who are so ultra in their views as to denounce men of opposite opinion.

"Resolved, That we will repudiate and discountenance all organized bands of men who leave their homes for the avowed purpose of exciting others to acts of violence, believing it to be the duty of all good disposed citizens to stay at home during these exciting times and protect and if possible restore the peace and harmony of the neighborhood; furthermore we will discountenance all armed bodies of men who may come amongst us from any other part of the Territory or from the States unless said parties shall come under the authority of the United States.

"Resolved, That we pledge ourselves, individually and collectively, to prevent a recurrence of a similar tragedy and to ferret out and hand over to the criminal authorities the perpetrators for punishment.

"H. H. Williams *
   Secretary

C. H. Price, President
R. Golding, Chairman
R. Gilpatrick
W. C. McDow
S. V. Vandaman
A. Castele
John Blunt

Committee"

* If Salmon Brown's memory of H. H. Williams's instigation of the murders

MURDER ON THE POTTAWATOMIE

The *Kansas Weekly Herald* of Leavenworth, on June 14, in printing these resolutions,[49] says: "The outlaws that are now prowling about over the country and murdering harmless and innocent men, it will be seen, have been denounced publicly by persons of their own political opinions. The President of the meeting is a Pro-slavery man, and the Secretary, Free State." "The respectability of the parties and the cruelties attending these murders have produced an extraordinary state of excitement in that portion of the territory, which has, heretofore, remained comparatively quiet," Governor Shannon reported on May 31, 1856, to President Pierce.[50] "The effect of this massacre on the inhabitants of the creeks was greatly to alarm both parties. The pro-slavery settlers almost entirely left at once and the Free State people were constantly fearful," was the statement of George W. and H. C. Grant, also sons of J. T. Grant.[51] "No one can defend the action of the marshal's posse at Lawrence, in burning the hotel, destroying the printing-press and other outrages," wrote Major John Sedgwick, First Cavalry, from Fort Leavenworth, on June 11, 1856, seventeen days after the Pottawatomie massacre, and just eight years before he gave his life for the Union as a distinguished major-general of volunteers in the battle of Spottsylvania, "but no life was lost, no one was threatened or felt himself in danger. In retaliation for this act, inoffensive citizens have been plundered, their houses robbed and burned, and five men were taken out of their beds, their throats cut, their ears cut off, their persons gashed more horribly than our savages have ever done. I sincerely think that most of the atrocities have been committed by the free-soil party, but I cannot think that they countenance such acts — that is, the respectable class." [52]

If Major Sedgwick was correct in his estimate of the attitude of the Free State men toward midnight assassination, at the hour he wrote, it is undeniable that as time passed, opinions about Brown's actions began to change. "I never had much doubt that Capt. Brown was the author of the blow at Pottawatomie, for the reason that he was the only man who comprehended the situation, and saw the absolute neces-

is correct, his serving at this settler's meeting convicts Williams of almost incredible hypocrisy and cowardice.

sity of some such blow and had the nerve to strike it," wrote Governor Charles Robinson, February 5, 1878, nearly two years before Townsley's confession was published.[53] Judge Hanway, as we have already seen, altered his position radically, and in the following statement of February 1, 1878, accurately summarizes the progress of public opinion in the neighborhood of the crime:

". . . So far as public opinion in the neighborhood, where the affair took place, is concerned, I believe I may state that the *first* news of the event produced such a shock that public opinion was considerably divided; but after the whole circumstances became known, there was a reaction in public opinion and the Free State settlers who had claims on the creek considered that Capt. Brown and his party of eight had performed a justifiable act, which saved their homes and dwellings from threatened raids of the proslavery party."[54]

Thomas Wentworth Higginson, in his 'Cheerful Yesterdays,' states:

"In regard to the most extreme act of John Brown's Kansas career, the so-called 'Pottawatomie massacre' of May 24, 1856, I can testify that in September of that year, there appeared to be but one way of thinking among the Kansas Free State men. . . . I heard of no one who did not approve of the act, and its beneficial effects were universally asserted — Governor Robinson himself fully endorsing it to me. . . ."[55]

How may the killings on the Pottawatomie, this terrible violation of the statute and the moral laws, be justified? This is the question which has confronted every student of John Brown's life since it was definitely established that Brown was, if not actually a principal in the crime, an accessory and an instigator. There have been advanced many excuses for the killings, and a number of them deserve careful scrutiny. That there may be times in a newly settled country when it becomes necessary for the conservative elements to take the law into their own hands, in the absence of proper judicial machinery, lest the community fall into a state of utter lawlessness and anarchy, has been admitted ever since lynch law brought order out of chaos in San Francisco in 1849. But it has similarly been recognized that even this wild justice, when set afoot, must follow a certain procedure; that committees of safety or vigilance should be formed and a kind of drum-head trial be instituted for the purpose of giving the accused men some opportunity to be heard in their own defence. History shows, moreover, that lynch law should only be proclaimed and obeyed for the briefest of periods, lest the second state be worse than the first; and that, even when instituted, public proceedings on the part of the self-appointed regulators are essential, both in order to make the punishments as deterrent as possible, and to persuade the community that it is *justice*, however rude, that is being dispensed.

In Kansas in 1856 the situation was different from that of California in 1849–50, in that most of the existing lawlessness had its origin largely in the national politics of the day. That there were the same rude and dangerous characters to be found on every frontier is proved by the recital of the crimes committed in Kansas prior to the Pottawatomie murders. In the case of Kansas, the high character of part of the emigration was offset by the lawless character of the Border Ruffians. Slavery itself tended to that overbearing lawlessness which is inevitable wherever the fate of a dark-colored people is placed unreservedly in the hands of whites. It was the spirit of intolerance and lawlessness bred by slavery which dictated the destruction of Lawrence and made the abuse of the ballot-boxes seem proper and justifiable. But, granting that there was friction full of grave possibilities between a handful of the pro-slavery settlers on the Pottawatomie and their Free Soil neighbors, it is by no means clear either that the conditions prior to the killings were so grave as to demand the establishment of martial law, or that they called for the installation of vigilance committees to inflict extreme penalties upon the desperadoes. Not a single person had been killed in the region around Osawatomie, either by the lawless characters or by armed representatives of the pro-slavery cause. The instances of brutality or murder narrated in the preceding chapters all took place miles to the north, in the vicinity of Lawrence or Leavenworth. Beyond doubt the publication of these atrocities inflamed not only the Browns, but kindled the anger and curdled the blood of every Free Soil settler who read of them. Yet the companies that set forth from Osawatomie to Lawrence deemed it quite safe to leave the settlements to themselves, despite the character of the Shermans and the Doyles and certain occurrences that might well have given ground for uneasiness.

What those occurrences were becomes of great importance, because many loose statements about them have been brought forward from time to time as affording ample justification for the Pottawatomie blood-letting. The most careful search for and weighing of many testimonies, contemporary and reminiscent, establishes in the neighborhood of Osawatomie only five definite pro-slavery offences, after hearsay recollections and wholly unsubstantiated stories are eliminated. It seems to be established beyond doubt that Poindexter Manes, a Free Soil settler, was knocked down and beaten for having a New York *Tribune* in his pocket.[56] Less well substantiated is the case of one Baker, a Vermonter, living on the Pottawatomie, who was taken from his cabin and strung up to a tree, but who was cut down in time to save his life. There is no record of his assailants, nor can the time be accurately fixed beyond that it was in the month of April.[57] To the Doyles and Shermans is attributed the frightening of a woman named Holmes, who was nearing confinement, by the brandishing of a knife and the demand that she reveal the whereabouts of the men of her family. It is variously stated that she died and that she "came near dying," in consequence.[58] Along the same line and more important is the statement that "Dutch Bill," in the absence of the men on their trip to Lawrence, entered the cabin of John T. Grant and attempted an assault upon the person of Mary Grant, his daughter. This story is the basis for the allegation that a messenger reached John Brown in the first night's camp, near Prairie City, and reported the attack upon Mary Grant, and that the persons of the women of his own family had been threatened. Fortunately, Mary Grant, as well as Mrs. John Brown, Jr., is still alive.* The latter states positively that the women of the settlement were never harmed.[59] In this she is emphatically borne out by a contemporary declaration of Jason Brown in a letter to North Elba on June 28, 1856, a month after the killings: "No women have been injured yet; so far as I know. Some of the five pro-slavery men who were killed had threat-

---

* Since the above was written, Mary Grant Brown has died.

ened the lives of Free State men near them; and also to cut the throat of a young woman, a neighbor."[60] As Jason Brown's wife was with him in Kansas, it is only natural to suppose that if her safety and that of his sister-in-law had been in danger, he would have reported it. Salmon Brown affirms that: "The statement that women were in any way molested is entirely without foundation." Mary Grant, the young woman neighbor, whose throat was threatened at the time, a remarkably pretty and attractive young woman, who had never feared to go freely to Wilkinson's post-office and to meet there the Doyles and Shermans, told recently this story of her experience with "Dutch Bill," which experience is the sole basis for the fabrication that John Brown was recalled because Free State women were in danger:[61]

"Dutch Bill arrived at our house, one day, horribly drunk, with a whiskey bottle with a corncob stopper, and an immense butcher knife in his belt. Mr. Grant, my father, was sick in bed, but when they told him that Bill Sherman was coming, in that state, he said: 'Put my shot gun beside the bed.' There was also a neighbor present, who was armed. 'Old woman,' said Bill Sherman to my mother, 'you and I are pretty good friends, but damn your daughter. I'll drink her heart's blood.' Yet my little brother Charley, a mere boy of twelve or fourteen, succeeded in cajoling him away without violence."

This story, says Mary Grant (Mrs. Mary E. Brown, of San José, California), Frederick Brown asked her for again and again, *before* the men marched to Lawrence. It is thus clear that the episode was in itself precisely what might happen in any isolated settlement which contained a drunken, worthless settler, and that it was known to at least one Brown long before the sudden start for Lawrence. Jason Brown relates it in his letter in its proper proportions. Mrs. B. F. Jackson, a resident of Osawatomie at the time, also testifies[62] that she never heard of any of the women of Osawatomie or Pottawatomie being troubled; yet news of attacks on them, had such occurred, must have travelled faster and made a more lasting impression upon the women of the frontier than anything else. In this connection it is interesting to note that although Gihon makes wholesale charges of rape against the Border Ruffians,[63] Mrs. Charles Robinson, than whom the

Ruffians have never had a severer critic, states that she knows of only a single case of criminal assault upon women during Kansas's troubled times. This case she records in her book as having occurred in August, 1856, or months after the Pottawatomie massacre.[64] Similar favorable testimony is given by many other women, who were early settlers, when asked this specific question. In all the mass of material accumulated by the Kansas Historical Society, there is not a proved instance of Border Ruffian misconduct of this kind, unless we except that cited by Mrs. Robinson and the case of two sisters who lived five miles northwest of Lawrence, which is reported in the *Tribune* of June 9, 1856, on the not always reliable authority of James Redpath. What frontier settlement in a time of great excitement and unrest can show a better record? It must be noted, too, that whereas elsewhere there might have been a natural desire to suppress such facts, there were plenty of correspondents besides Redpath eager for such terrible happenings with which to blacken the case against the Border Ruffians and stir more Northerners to coming to the rescue of Free Kansas.

A fifth Missouri outrage is directly brought home by the Grant family to Wilkinson, the Shermans and Doyles. This was the case of an old man named Morse, from Michigan, who had sold lead for bullets to the Browns. As George Grant narrates the story,

"The next morning, after the company had started to go to Lawrence, a number of these proslavery men, Wilkinson, Doyle, his two sons, and William Sherman, known as 'Dutch Bill' — took a rope and were going to hang him [Morse] for selling the lead to the Free State men. They frightened the old man terribly; and finally told him he must leave the country before eleven o'clock, or they would hang him. They then left and went to the Shermans and went to drinking. About eleven o'clock a portion of them, half drunk, went back to Mr. Morse's and were going to kill him with an axe. His little boys — one was only nine years old — set up a violent crying, and begged for their father's life. They finally gave him until sundown to leave. He left everything and came at once to our house. He was nearly frightened to death. He came to our house carrying a blanket and leading his little boy by the hand. When night came he was so afraid that he would not stay in the house, but went out doors and slept on the prairie in the grass. For a few days he lay about in the brush, most of the time getting his meals at our house. He was then taken violently ill and died in a very short time. Dr. Gilpatrick attended him during his brief illness, and said that his death was directly caused by the fright and excitement of that terrible day when he was driven from his store." [65]

It will be noticed that the threats to Morse were made the day after the company had gone, or on Friday. It is perfectly plain, therefore, that no news of this could have reached John Brown in camp near Prairie City before two o'clock of the same day, when he started back in Townsley's wagon, bent on the killings. Furthermore, there was no communication between his party, as it lay in the timber between the ravines on the day of the killing, and the settlements. Whatever else may have actuated John Brown, it was not the attack upon the old man, Morse, of which he knew nothing, not even if a messenger bearing stories of threatened outrage on the Pottawatomie reached Brown on that one morning in camp when the cutlasses were being ground.

This question of the alleged messenger bringing news of the threats against the Free Soil settlers is one that has deeply agitated the apologists for and critics of John Brown. The identity of this Mercury has never been established. He is variously thought to have been "Bondi or some one sent by him" — according to George Grant; or Weiner, according to O. C. Brown and John Hutchings. Townsley and Judge Hanway were sure that George Grant himself was the messenger, but as George Grant denies this and points out that he marched out with the Pottawatomie Rifles, this guess must be eliminated. H. H. Williams, on January 20, 1883, wrote to R. J. Hinton that he was the messenger. Unfortunately for this theory, his own contemporary letter to the *Tribune*, written within two months of the killings, proves that he went up toward Lawrence not as a messenger but as first lieutenant of the Pottawatomie Rifles, for he relates various incidents of the night march. Among others who affirm that there was a messenger are John Brown, Jr., August Bondi, J. F. Legate, Samuel Anderson, Mary Grant, J. G. Grant and C. S. Adair; but none of them has a clue to his identity. Salmon Brown, on the other hand, is positive that there was no messenger. So is Colonel James Blood. If there was a messenger who reached camp on Friday morning, he could only have had later news by two or three hours than the men of the Pottawatomie Rifles themselves brought, for they marched from the cross-roads near Osawatomie at six P. M., and were not much over six hours in camp the next day before John Brown left on his way back. If the company had received tidings revealing grave danger to their women and children at home, it is incredible that they would not have returned at once with John Brown, to protect their families. Instead, they were content to remain idly in camp for two days. If Colonel Blood's narrative of meeting Townsley's wagon-load is true, it is again astonishing that John Brown never inquired of him what had happened during their twenty-four hours' absence. Had they done so, Blood could have told Brown that when he himself rode through the Pottawatomie settlement that afternoon, he found the place perfectly quiet, the only excitement relating to Lawrence; that a few men were in the fields and the women and children were about the cabins.[66] But the height of absurdity is the supposition that eight able-bodied men, heavily armed, would spend all of one night and the whole of the next day, Saturday, in the timber between two ravines near Pottawatomie Creek without stirring to inquire how the Brown kinsmen and kinswomen, the Adairs, the Days, Mrs. John Brown, Jr., and Mrs. Jason Brown, were faring during the twenty-four hours between the return and the murders, if these relatives were known to be in danger. If the killings were due to any sudden alarm that the creek was to be cleared of all Free State settlers, then the eight men were craven, indeed, to spend this day without scouting the neighborhood. This supposition is incredible in view of John Brown's known bravery. His men hid because they did not wish their connection with the murders known, and after the crime they returned stealthily to Ottawa Jones's without having troubled any one with a question as to the fate of the unguarded women and children of their comrades of the Pottawatomie Rifles.

The truth must be that John Brown decided on the murders because of some general reason or previous conviction that it was necessary to remove the victims, and not because of any sudden news. As to the messenger, there was none;

MURDER ON THE POTTAWATOMIE 177

the reports of threats to Free State settlers made by the Shermans and Doyles, which were undoubtedly talked of in the camp and hastened John Brown's action, were brought in not by any one man or any two men, but by Bondi, Weiner, Townsley and others of the Rifles. H. H. Williams, in his contemporary letter, records that he rode ten miles up and down the creek to call his company together, and that thirty-four men had come from various distances by six P. M. to the rendezvous. As they marched that night, they doubtless exchanged news and gossip; the story about "Dutch Bill" and Mary Grant may have been magnified in the telling and re-telling and reached many ears for the first time as the little column stumbled forward over the dark roads, while the excitement of the hour probably led some of the men to think that "Dutch Bill's" drunken threat had just been uttered.

To find the reason and the excuse for the cold-blooded murder of the Doyles, Sherman and Wilkinson, we must, therefore, look elsewhere. The Grants[67] and others tell of a meeting at "Dutch Henry's," immediately after the departure of the Rifles, at which the subsequently murdered men swore to drive out all the Free State settlers within a given time and reduce their houses to ashes. On the other hand, Salmon Brown declares positively that "it was not the report of any such meeting specifically that started us off to Pottawatomie." Nor, as we have seen, could the news of this meeting have reached the camp near Prairie City before John Brown started for home. That the meeting occurred, the Grants are positive, but it, too, must be discarded as a motive for the bloody deed on the Pottawatomie.

There remains, then, the question how far the threats against the Browns, heard in the Buford camp, and those made against the Free State settlers on the Pottawatomie as a whole, were the controlling reason for the crime. It is impossible to avoid the belief that they were a most important factor in moving John Brown to adopt Border Ruffian tactics. Salmon Brown declares that his father and the others were well aware that the pro-slavery men of the Doyle-Sherman type had decided on extreme measures against them. The stories of Bondi, Weiner, Benjamin and Townsley all had their effect upon the Browns. According to Horace Haskell

Day, son of Orson Day, when his father went to Weiner's store, which was just one and a half miles from the Doyles' cabin, he found a notice up that all Free State men must get off the creek within thirty days, or have their throats cut. Weiner said to Mr. Day: "We ought to cut their throats." Mr. Day not consenting, Weiner said: "That is the way we serve them in Texas," — from which place he had come.[68] Orson Day being a brother-in-law of John Brown and residing directly opposite John Brown, Jr., it would have been easy for him to repeat this happening to his relatives. There are witnesses like Mr. M. V. B. Jackson, who heard from Weiner, Bondi and Townsley direct the threats made against them. Mr. Jackson testifies that three days was the time of grace allowed to Weiner, Benjamin and Bondi, at the expiration of which they were to leave under pain of lynch law.[69] John B. Manes is another witness to Benjamin's being warned. "I know," he has affirmed,[70] "that there was a reign of terror, of which the men who were killed were the authors; and I am surprised that any one should believe that the killing of these men was without reasonable excuse." He asks whether the Free State men were to abandon Kansas, or to fold their arms and await martyrdom when their days of grace expired. Or were they to slay the would-be murderers, to save themselves? Here again the question recurs: If John Brown knew of the notice posted in Weiner's store, and was also aware that the pro-slavery men had given the Free Soil settlers but three or five days in which to leave, why did he march off to Lawrence leaving the women and children defenceless and the Doyles and Shermans free to do their worst? He could not know that he would be free to return within twenty-four hours, for the fate of Lawrence was not learned until the company had marched twenty-five miles. For all any of the men could foresee, they might be going off on a campaign that would last for some days — perhaps even weeks.

It must not be forgotten, too, that threats of slicing a man's throat, or cutting his heart out, or driving him away, were the cheapest and most conspicuous product of Border Ruffian activity. Every drunken pro-slavery man had a quiver-full of them. The *Squatter Sovereign* has them on every page; the blasphemy and promises of extermination that marked the

MURDER ON THE POTTAWATOMIE

harangues of Atchison, Jones and men of that stamp are to be found broadcast in the files of the *Tribune* and the volumes of Gladstone, Redpath, Phillips, Sara Robinson and the other contemporary Free Soil writers. The threats uttered on the Pottawatomie must have been convincing, indeed, to incite John Brown to do what the Border Ruffians only talked of doing. But this merely adds to the mystery why the appeal of Lawrence should have taken precedence over the safety of Pottawatomie, as does the affirmation of Jason Brown that a friendly pro-slavery man had given to the Rev. Mr. Adair a list of those whose deaths had been agreed upon by his pro-slavery friends, — a story of which Mr. Adair has left no written record to aid his kinsman's reputation.[71]

What did John Brown himself ever assign as the reason? According to E. A. Coleman, Brown, by means of his surveying disguise, obtained the views of the murdered men and found that they "had each one committed murder in his heart and according to the Scriptures they were guilty of murder and I felt justified in having them killed." These words Coleman places in John Brown's mouth;[72] they are confirmed by Colonel Edward Anderson's report of Brown's statement to him that the murdered men were planning to "wipe out the Free Soil settlers."[73] According to Coleman's story, therefore, Brown, assuming the powers of judge or military autocrat, adjudged the Doyles, Shermans and Wilkinson deserving of death because they had had murder in their hearts. If this version be accepted, we must decide that John Brown believed planning murder to be worse than murder itself. We have here a most extraordinary confusion of ethics and morals. Granting that persecution, and even murders, had followed similar threats in other portions of Kansas, and that the terrible happenings in the Territory were ever present in John Brown's brain, one cannot but wonder that he assumed to himself the functions of chief executioner and deemed himself the one to say just when and how the Sixth Commandment, "Thou shalt not kill," should be violated. He was not content merely to defend Free State homes and patrol the roads; it did not occur to him to form a vigilance committee and warn the pro-slavery rascals to cease from troubling and remove from the neighborhood, as did in another year James Montgomery, in Linn County; he was not even content to leave to the Almighty, to whom he nightly prayed, that vengeance which the Lord has reserved as His.

But there are plenty of other excuses offered for the crime, after the various motives we have examined are discarded. It is pointed out that there was no law for Free Soil men in the Territory, — only Catos and Lecomptes on the bench to dispense injustice. There was no legal road to safety. It is averred that the Free Soil settlers were few, half starved, sick and intimidated, grown so spiritless, the lack of resistance at Lawrence indicated, as to call for some deed of violence to rouse them from their helpless inertia. To prove to the Border Ruffians that they could no longer destroy and murder with impunity, such a terrible warning as that given at Pottawatomie was, therefore, absolutely necessary. Again, it is insisted that John Brown's foresight, his consecrated sagacity and devotion to the cause, made him strike the blow in order to force men to take sides, in order to bring on the righteous and necessary war which, to John Brown, was the sole solution of the issue in Kansas. If this conflicts with the widely held theory that the Pottawatomie killings, by ending the outrages in the neighborhood of Osawatomie and stopping the aggressiveness of the Border Ruffians, was a peace measure, it does not deter many from excusing the crime as an act of war executed in war time. The dogs of war, it is argued, had been let slip by Jones and Donaldson, and as the Doyles, Shermans and Wilkinson were spies and informers in league with the enemy, they richly merited their fate, which came only just in time to save the Osawatomie settlers from general expulsion, if not murder. Then, too, it was said to be but a just act of retaliation for the sack of Lawrence and retribution for the killing of R. P. Brown, Dow, Barber, Stewart, Jones and Collins; it is even alleged, by miscounting these six victims of Border Ruffian violence, that John Brown was not eager to kill Dutch Henry, but chose his five victims as a deliberate offset to the five Free Soilers killed up to that time. Next, it is asserted that John Brown was merely carrying out the orders of Free Soil leaders who, for motives of policy, did not admit at the time that this killing was done with their connivance and consent. Finally, it is averred by at least one

MURDER ON THE POTTAWATOMIE   181

biographer that John Brown was divinely inspired, — God-driven to this dire act, because the Deity "makes His will known in advance to certain chosen men and women who perform it consciously or unconsciously."

Into this field of theological speculation the historian unfortunately cannot enter; he is limited to judging or recording human motives, particularly as this theory of divine inspiration has for centuries been the excuse for many of the most terrible crimes in history. More capable of critical examination is the argument that there existed no law and no courts for Free State men; but if the absence of law and just courts sanctions midnight assassination, the world is far behindhand with its canonizations. The road to legal safety under such conditions does not lead by the way of private vengeance; the sole substitute is, as has already been pointed out, lynch law openly proclaimed and openly administered. That the Pottawatomie murders cannot be both a peace and a war measure is obvious. Unfortunately, as will be set forth when the consequences of the crime are examined, the evidence shows that it neither ended the attacks upon individuals nor stopped the raids of large armed bodies, as has been alleged by many writers, including John Speer. He declared, January 30, 1886, that "the spirit of murder was checked," [74] while F. G. Adams, Secretary of the Kansas Historical Society, on October 25, 1883, averred of Brown's killings that they "put an end to the assassination of Free State men for all time," [75] — as if, for example, Frederick Brown and David Garrison were not shot down like dogs on August 30, 1856, to say nothing of the cold-blooded murders after Pottawatomie of Hoppe, Cantrall, Hoyt, Gay and William Phillips, and almost numberless assaults upon persons and attacks upon private property. These might, it is true, have continued had John Brown struck no blow at Pottawatomie, for the Border Ruffians were drunk with their success in looting Lawrence; but it certainly cannot be true that they were "stopped" by the assassinations. But as a war measure, John Brown's murders were beyond doubt successful; they were actually followed by more killings of Free State men than had taken place previously in the Territory; they led to the burning of Osawatomie and other settlements, to attacks upon the Border

Ruffian "forts," and to the stand-up fighting at Black Jack and Osawatomie. If John Brown intended to set men at each others' throats, to make every man take sides, to bring matters in Kansas to a head, he was wholly successful when he lived up to the Biblical doctrine he often quoted, that "without the shedding of blood there is no remission of sin."

As to the theory that John Brown was directed by higher authorities in the Free State ranks, the best evidence is a recently discovered letter from Samuel C. Pomeroy to Rebecca B. Spring, written in Georgetown, D. C., January 16, 1860, just after Brown's execution, when the events of 1856 should have been fresh in his memory, and here first printed:

"I am waiting here quietly to see the progress of Mason's 'Investigating Committee.' They have *declined* to *summon* me — or any other man, who *dare under oath, defend* John Brown!! I dont care what are the consequences to me *politically*, I will, upon the first occasion, at the Capitol of this country — *defend* that old man, who offered up himself *gloriously* — from the *charge* or *crime* of *murder!* No blow had been struck by any one of us — up to May 21st, 1856. I was in command as Chairman of the 'Committee of Public Safety,' at Lawrence, upon that *memorable occasion.*

"I insisted — though our Town was threatened with destruction — and the invading army was then within *12 miles* of Town! and numbered over 1200 men — well armed — That we should give the *Government* a *fair opportunity* to *protect us,* And to this end I applied to those in authority. But in the course of that day I found that the Government was yielded to the 'border Ruffians.' — I still insisted (though against the earnest appeal of John Brown & his men) that the *government should commit* the *first overt* act. And I told *them, then* and *there,* that so soon as I could demonstrate before this Country that the Government was powerless for *protection,* Then I *was with them,* for taking care of *ourselves!* So *we stood still,* upon *that day* and saw our Presses & buildings *madly destroyed.* The few monuments of our civilization, which had been hastily erected, were strewn to the winds, or consumed in the *flames!*

"Upon the morning of the 22nd of May we called a little meeting — of *sad* but *earnest* men. Taking each other by the hand we convenanted, each with the other, that what there was *left* to *us in this life,* and if *need be,* all we hoped for in the life to come, should now be *offered up,* to the FREEDOM of KANSAS, and the country.

"A poorly written badly spelled note, passed round that meeting that Doyl, Wilkinson, Sherman, and others upon the Pottawatomie Creek, had insulted the females of *one family,* whose *head was then present,* and warned others under pain of death to leave the Territory by the 25th Inst., *that very week!* What could I say? Or do? I had withheld our impatient men, until before us lay the smoking ruins of the *home* we loved the *best*, of any spot upon earth.

"You know what was *said* and '*did*.' As the Government afforded no protection to us, even when we placed ourselves under its *special protection*, it was *then* and *there* Resolved — that every man be [we?] met that *invaded* or *threatened* our lives, or homes, or our families & *friends, should without delay* of *law* or *courts*, or *officers*, be *driven* to Missouri or to *death!!*

"We separated that morning, *each* to the *great work* of *life*, viz. *to do his duty* — to himself — to *his country* & to *his God*. John Brown did not personly go the whole distance with the party that went down upon Pottawatomy creek. But he *approved* of the course *decided* upon for action, — and SO DID I! And I am not now going to *repudiate* old *Brown*, or to shrink from the responsibility!

"He did not *commit* the 'murders' as they are called, but we all then *endorsed them*, — and from *that hour* the *invaders fled*. That *one act* struck terror into the hearts of our enemies, and gave us the dawning of success! Those deaths I have no doubt saved a *multitude* of lives, and was the cheapest sacrifice that could be offered!"[76]

Unfortunately for the accuracy of this statement, we know now that neither the Brown women nor those of the Grant family were insulted. The testimonies of fifty-two witnesses of value in connection with the Pottawatomie murders have been examined for light on this subject. Pomeroy is the only one to suggest that John Brown was in Lawrence on May 21 and 22, with the exception of Daniel W. Wilder, who even adds that he was there with six sons and his son-in-law.[77] It is not conceivable that John Brown could have been there and have fired no shot to defend the town. Moreover, his surviving sons and son-in-law know nothing about it — Salmon Brown denying it positively. If this is not enough, the character of John Brown's own statements should suffice; he would never have suppressed the fact that he saw Lawrence destroyed; and finally, the dates he gives for his movements prior to the murders, corroborated by many witnesses, render it physically impossible for him to have been in Lawrence at the time specified.

The belief that John Brown was inspired by Robinson, Pomeroy and Lane was, however, held by others. Congressman Oliver made the general charge, in his minority report to the Howard Committee Report, that Brown's victims "were deprived of their lives . . . in consequence of the insurrectionary movements . . . set on foot by the reckless leaders of the Tokepa Convention,"[78]—an allegation not specific enough to call for refutation in this connection. In a letter written on February 8, 1875, Captain Samuel Walker alleges that Brown complained to him in the summer of 1856 that Lane and Robinson were instigators of the crime, but would not sustain him in it.[79] Captain Walker also informed Frank B. Sanborn that Lane and Robinson asked him to commit the same murders, but that he indignantly refused to do so.[80] John Brown, Jr., once charged Robinson in great detail with asking his father in the following September to dispose of the leading pro-slavery men by killing, which request, he said, was indignantly spurned.[81] Henry Thompson testifies similarly.[82] But Robinson positively denied the charge, as he most emphatically denied any complicity in the Pottawatomie murders. One cannot have entire respect for Governor Robinson's character; in this instance he at one time likened John Brown to Jesus Christ, and hailed him as a saviour of Kansas, only to turn around a couple of years later and denounce him,— even to speak of the "punishment due John Brown for his crimes in Kansas."[83] On the other hand, John Brown, Jr.'s mind was, unfortunately, not always clear. It is important to remember here that John Brown at no time during the rest of his life made any positive statement which would indicate that he was acting under orders in doing his bloody work at Pottawatomie,— not even when, in jail and facing death, he was asked by Judge Russell, of Boston, for a definite statement as to his responsibility for the crime.[84] If he cherished the feeling of anger against Robinson and Lane which Walker declared he voiced in 1856, he does not appear to have expressed it again.

To mitigate the abruptness and cruelty of the tragedy, it is often loosely asserted that the victims were duly tried by a jury. John Sherman stated that he had this from John Brown's own lips shortly after the crime.[85] But no one else avers this, while the survivors of the massacre, Henry Thompson and Salmon Brown, deny it. No member of the Brown family has advanced this theory. The testimony of Townsley and the families of the murdered men as to the speed of the

MURDER ON THE POTTAWATOMIE

executions and their taking place consecutively is also conclusive, as is the fact that no juryman has ever been discovered.

In the light of all the evidence now accumulated, the truth would seem to be that John Brown came to Kansas bringing arms and ammunition, eager to fight, and convinced that force alone would save Kansas. He was under arms at the polls within three days of his arrival in Kansas, to shed blood to defend the voters, if need be, and he was bitterly disappointed that the Wakarusa "war" ended without a single conflict. Thereafter he believed that a collision was inevitable in the spring, and Jones and Donaldson proved him to be correct. Fired with indignation at the wrongs he witnessed on every hand, impelled by the Covenanter's spirit that made him so strange a figure in the nineteenth century, and believing fully that there should be an eye for an eye and a tooth for a tooth, he killed his men in the conscientious belief that he was a faithful servant of Kansas and of the Lord. He killed not to kill, but to free; not to make wives widows and children fatherless, but to attack on its own ground the hideous institution of human slavery, against which his whole life was a protest. He pictured himself a modern crusader as much empowered to remove the unbeliever as any armored searcher after the Grail. It was to his mind a righteous and necessary act; if he concealed his part in it and always took refuge in the half-truth that his own hands were not stained, that was as near to a compromise for the sake of policy as this rigid, self-denying Roundhead ever came. Naturally a tender-hearted man, he directed a particularly shocking crime without remorse, because the men killed typified to him the slave-drivers who counted their victims by the hundreds. It was to him a necessary carrying into Africa of the war in which he firmly desired himself engaged. And always it must not be forgotten that his motives were wholly unselfish, and that his aims were none other than the freeing of a race. With his ardent, masterful temperament, he needed no counsel from a Lane or a Robinson to make him ready to strike a blow, or to tell him that the time for it had come. The smoke of burning Lawrence was more than sufficient.

If this interpretation of the man and his motives lifts him

far above the scale of that Border Ruffian who boasted that he would have the scalp of an Abolitionist within two hours and actually killed and scalped the very first one he met, it cannot be denied that the Border Ruffians who sacked Lawrence believed as thoroughly in the justice of their cause, and their right to establish in Kansas what was to them a sacred institution, as John Brown did in his. Their leaders had told them of an agreement in Congress that Kansas should be a slave State and Nebraska free.[86] Hence their belief that the North had broken this compact rendered them particularly bitter against the Free Soilers. It was to them also a holy war in which they were engaged, — even with its admixture of whiskey and lawlessness, characteristics of the Southern "poor white" civilization of the period. If one grants to John Brown absolution for the Pottawatomie murders because he struck in what was to him a moral crusade, one must come near granting it to the Border Ruffian Hamilton, who made eleven men, most of whom he had never seen before, stand up in line on May 19, 1858, that he might shoot them down.[87] In his behalf it could much more truthfully be said that there was war in Linn County in 1858 than that there was war about Osawatomie in 1856. Hamilton doubtless intended also to send terror to the hearts of his enemies, to drive them from the Territory. That the five men he killed were of blameless reputation, while John Brown's five victims were weak or bad characters, does not alter the case from the moral or the legal point of view. Murder is murder, whatever the character of the victims; it remains, in its essence, unchanged in these two cases, even though the leader of one set of self-appointed executioners has been excused by his friends, and the other universally execrated. Might not Hamilton, too, have been portrayed as the tool of a vengeful Deity? Might he not, to use James Freeman Clarke's characterization of John Brown, have maintained that he believed in "fighting fire with fire," that "there was no malice or desire for vengeance in his constitution"?[88] Certainly, Hamilton's catholic choice of victims — he seized them in the fields and on the roads as he met them — would prove that he also killed without personal enmity. It may be that Hamilton thought that by so blood-curdling an assassination he could stop the hostile operations of armed

MURDER ON THE POTTAWATOMIE 187

Free Soil bands led by Montgomery, Jennison — admittedly a bad character — and others. If this theory is wrong, Hamilton's Marais des Cygnes massacre ought at least to have estopped James Freeman Clarke and other defenders of Brown from saying that after Brown's victims were killed, "the country had peace." It should have prevented any likening of John Brown to Grant, Sherman and Sheridan, whose orders killed thousands in "another war," — as if war could exist save under those rules of war which as peremptorily forbid midnight assassination as they do the violation of women and the poisoning of wells. Finally, a real war-commander always assumes the responsibility for his acts, while John Brown was ever disingenuous about the Pottawatomie massacres.

From the point of view of ethics, John Brown's crime on the Pottawatomie cannot be successfully palliated or excused. It must ever remain a complete indictment of his judgment and wisdom; a dark blot upon his memory; a proof that, however self-controlled, he had neither true respect for the laws nor for human life, nor a knowledge that two wrongs never make a right. Call him a Cromwellian trooper with the Old Testament view of the way of treating one's enemies, as did James Freeman Clarke, if you please; it is nevertheless true that Brown lived in the nineteenth century and was properly called upon to conform to its standard of morals and right living. What would become of society if it permitted all whose spirits would hark back to the modes of life of other times and other morals to have their way? Describing Brown as a misplaced Crusader cannot, moreover, conceal the regrettable fact that the Pottawatomie murders deprived the Free Soil cause of an enormous moral advantage. Up to May, 1856, its adherents had suffered, bled and died, without any blood-guilt attaching to them. This gave them, as unoffending victims of pro-slavery fury, an unsurpassed standing in the court of public opinion. Their hands were clean; they had been attending to their own affairs and were crying out against wrong and injustice by the time-honored methods of protest, — through the press, the ballot-box, the right of assembly, the setting up a government of their own to be passed upon by the highest tribunals of the land, that is, the courts and the Congress of the United States. The Free State leaders had hitherto counselled peaceful submission to wrong as the surest way to the sympathies of the nation, and to that eventual justice which no believer in American institutions could despair of, even in 1856, when the whole weight of the Federal Government and its troops had been thrown against the Free Soilers. For the court of last resort, the conscience of the American people, had not yet been heard from as it was but a few years later. Of a sudden, all this great moral superiority was flung away;[89] the sack of Lawrence, the Pottawatomie murders, brought about a complete change of policy. The militant Abolitionists of the John Brown, Horace Greeley, Henry Ward Beecher type reaped their harvest. The Sharp's rifles, "Beecher's Bibles," now came into play. But the South at last had its *tu-quoque*. "You sacked Lawrence," said the North. "But you resorted to the vilest of midnight assassinations of unarmed men and boys," replied the South. Sumner could not have delivered unaltered his wonderful philippic, the "Crime Against Kansas," after the crimes against Missouri had begun. There was now blood upon both sides.

For John Brown no pleas can be made that will enable him to escape coming before the bar of historical judgment. There his wealth of self-sacrifice, and the nobility of his aims, do not avail to prevent a complete condemnation of his bloody crime at Pottawatomie, or a just penalty for his taking human life without warrant or authority. If he deserves to live in history, it is not because of his cruel, gruesome, reprehensible acts on the Pottawatomie, but despite them.[90]

CHAPTER VI

CLOSE QUARTERS AT BLACK JACK

WAR! WAR!

Eight Pro-Slavery men murdered by the Abolitionists in Franklin County, K. T.

LET SLIP THE DOGS OF WAR!

We learn from a despatch just received by Col. A. G. Boone, dated at Paola, K. T., May 26, 1856, and signed by Gens. Heiskell and Barbee, that the reported murder of eight pro-slavery men in Franklin County, K. T., is but too true.

It was thus that the Westport, Missouri, *Border Times* gave to its readers, on May 27, 1856, the news that was intended to strike terror to their hearts. The only reason for the crime the despatch assigned was that "the abolitionists (the court being in session) were afraid that these men [their victims] would be called upon to give evidence against them, as many of them were charged with treason." The *Border Times* supplemented this news with an appeal to the South for men and money, because civil war with all its horrors now reigned in Kansas. The Jefferson, Missouri, *Inquirer* of the 29th, and the Lexington, Missouri, *Express* of the 26th reprinted the *Western Despatch's* account of the crime and also its editorial assertion that "for every Southern man thus butchered a decade [dozen?] of these poltroons should bite the dust." Henry Clay Pate, correspondent of the St. Louis *Missouri Republican*, wrote on May 30 that no personal grudges existed between the murdered and the murderers, "in fact no cause whatever can be or is attempted to be assigned for their savage barbarity but that the deceased were proslavery in their sentiments." Thirteen persons supposed to be connected with the crime were under arrest, and if ever lynch laws were justifiable, in Pate's opinion this was the time. The pro-slavery *Kansas Weekly Herald* of Leavenworth, in its issue of June 7, reprinted a column and a half of news from the Lecompton *Union*, in the course of which that newspaper sarcastically said:

"These are the 'Free State men' who have been so deeply outraged by the law and order party, but have, like martyrs, passed through the fire, without the stain of blood upon their skirts or the mark of pillage upon their consciences. This is the party so pure and untarnished with dishonor that their very natures revolt at and recoil from the countenancing of even a minor disgrace, *much less the foul assassination* of Sheriff Jones. This is the party that held an indignation meeting in Lawrence, headed by Charles Robinson and A. H. Reeder, passed resolutions and even offered a reward for the apprehension of him who shot Jones. . . . These are the men who are cursing the Marshal and posse for blowing up this 'Northern Army's' fortress and destroying their mouthpieces and are denominating them plunderers and committers of arson, and this news is taken up by their agents in the North, heralded forth from one extreme to the other as truth, asking protection for these innocent free state creatures."

Another correspondent of the *Missouri Republican*, one J. Bernard, reporting from Westport the arrival there of Mrs. Doyle, added that "a more cruel murder has scarcely been committed;" it was a "foul and inhuman act." The fighting *Squatter Sovereign*, of Atchison, was distinctly sobered by the news from Kansas, but still ready to fight, for on June 10 it thus freed its ever surcharged mind:

"Midnight murders, assassinations, burglaries, and arson seem now to be the watchwords of the so-called Free State party. Whilst those rebellious subjects confined themselves to the resistance of the law, in their attempts to make arrests, and execute processes in their hands, the pro-slavery party in the territory was determined to stand by the law, and aid the officers in executing process and the courts in administering justice. And that we have no doubt is still the determination of every pro-slavery man, but there is a time for all things. Self-protection — defence of one's life, family and property, are rights guaranteed to all law-abiding citizens; and the manner and mode of keeping off murderers, assassins, &c., are not confined to any very strict rules of law. . . . Hundreds of the Free State men, who have committed no overt acts, but have only given countenance to those reckless murderers, assassins and thieves, will of necessity share the same fate of their brethren. If civil war is to be the result in such a conflict, there cannot be, and will not be, any neutrals recognized."

CLOSE QUARTERS AT BLACK JACK

The St. Louis *Morning Herald* on June 13 informed its readers, on the authority of a Lecompton correspondent, that: "The Abolitionists are continuing their assassinations and plunder. Robinson has given orders for a guerrilla war. Besides the murders at Ossawatomie, by the noted Brown, others have been attempted in the neighborhood." Six days later, hearing from Lawrence that the Pottawatomie massacre was done for the deliberate purpose of impressing the Border Ruffians, it said: "Here is the avowal of a man who ought to know; he tells you that midnight assassination, which revives in all their atrocity the most fiendish barbarities of the darkest ages and which, we repeat, is without parallel in Christendom since the Revolution in France, is *deliberately* planned to strike terror into the hearts of political opponents! Whether such will be the effect of the lesson remains to be seen." Editorially, the *Morning Herald* had already expressed the hope that the pro-slavery party would not retaliate in kind and would refrain from lynching the assassins, while its rival, the *Missouri Republican*, was quick to see the advantage which lay in declaring that this bloody outcome of civil war was the "legitimate result of the counsels of such preachers as Beecher." Curiously enough, as James Ford Rhodes points out,[1] the Democratic press of the country as a whole, except that on the border, made comparatively little use of the killings. One Northern newspaper, the Burlington, Iowa, *Gazette*, denounced them on June 25; the *Liberator*, whose editor, William·Lloyd Garrison, strongly protested against the Sharp's rifle teachings of Beecher and the militant Abolitionists,[2] wholly failed to record Brown's crime. Senator Toombs, of Georgia, and Congressman Oliver cited the murders in the course of speeches in the Senate and House. But the Republican newspapers, intentionally or unintentionally, deceived their readers by garbled reports of the crime. It was generally represented that five of a pro-slavery gang, caught hanging a Free State settler, were shot by the latter's friends as they came to his rescue, and the Republican press took extremely good care not to give much space to the affair. As Mr. Rhodes explains, the hitherto excellent character of the Free State settlers rendered it impossible for the East to credit the story, or for the Democrats to bring it home to them as they should have.

Only in Missouri did the Southern press make of it all that was possible. The address of the Law and Order Party to their friends of the South, signed by Atchison, B. F. Stringfellow, Major Buford and others on June 21,[3] naturally used the massacre to the utmost, declaring, among other things, that Wilkinson had been "flayed alive," and that besides the "six victims," the bodies of four others were still missing.

Governor Shannon promptly reported the murders to President Pierce. From Lecompton, May 31, he wrote: [4]

". . . Comment is unnecessary. The respectability of the parties and the cruelties attending the murders have produced an extraordinary state of excitement in that portion of the Territory, which has heretofore remained comparatively quiet. . . . I hope the offenders may be brought to Justice; if so, it may allay to a great extent the excitement, otherwise I fear the consequences."

Governor Shannon's anxiety was justified. On the 27th of May the news of the Pottawatomie crimes was posted all over Leavenworth. The leading Free State business men were arrested, and, according to an eye-witness, William H. Coffin, only the urgent solicitation of such men as General Richardson and other leading pro-slavery officials prevented their meeting with violence.[5] Other influential Free State men were banished. Four days later, the 31st, when Governor Shannon was writing his report, a meeting of the Law and Order Party was held in Leavenworth to protest against the Pottawatomie murders. At this gathering, so the *Tribune* reported,[6] "leading pro-slavery citizens — some of them heretofore moderate men — were the officers and speechmakers. Violent speeches were made, and resolutions of the same character were passed, condemning all Free State men without distinction, and appointing a Vigilance Committee of fifty to watch their movements, and to warn offenders from the Territory." [7]

At Fort Scott, the Southeastern rendezvous of Border Ruffians, the news that Lawrence was burned was received with a general feeling of joy, but it was followed by the rumor that at Osawatomie five, and some said nine, pro-slavery men had been called up in the night and, as soon as they made their appearance, had been shot by the Abolitionists. This caused a general feeling of alarm and indignation, and the young men of Fort Scott, on their own responsibility, organized them-

CLOSE QUARTERS AT BLACK JACK 193

selves into a "watch guard" to protect the Fort from invasion by the Abolitionists, for, to add to the excitement, it had been currently reported that Fort Scott was to be burned as a retaliation for the destruction of Lawrence.[8] Some of the Missourians at once took the offensive. Although Mrs. Robinson was of the opinion that "the news of the horrible massacre fell upon the ears of the Border Ruffians like a thunderbolt out of a clear sky, and carried fear and trembling into many Missouri homes," and that "his [Brown's] name became one of terror, like that of hobgoblins to silly children, or that of Lafitte upon the sea,"[9] Captain Henry Clay Pate, the fighting correspondent of the *Missouri Republican*, went at once with his company to Paola, eight miles from Osawatomie, to assist the United States Marshal in arresting the Pottawatomie Creek murderers. On June 2, General J. W. Whitfield, the delegate to Congress, wrote from Westport to the editor of the *Border Times* that news had reached there of disaster to Captain Pate's company. This was his statement of the situation:

> There can scarcely be a doubt that this small force has been annihilated. This town, where the congressional committee are now taking evidence, has been thronged during the day with men with their families, fleeing from the territory to avoid assassination and butchery. I am constantly in receipt of letters and appeals for protection. The cowardly and fiendish manner in which the assassinations have been perpetrated, particularly those on Pottawatomie creek (which I am informed by Judge Cato just in from that place have not been exaggerated in the public accounts, indeed do not equal the reality,) leaves but little hope that these abolition monsters can be actuated by any other consideration than that of fear. I have, therefore, determined to start in an hour or two, with as many men as can be raised, in the hope, if not too late, of relieving the little band, under Capt. Pate, and afford what protection I can to the peaceful citizens of the territory, and restore in it order and peace. . . .
>
> JNO. W. WHITFIELD.[10]

Two of John Brown's sons fell readily into the hands of the Missourians, — John Brown, Jr., and Jason Brown. They had spent but one night in the Adair cabin, — the one in which, as we have seen, John Brown, Jr., became insane. Leaving their wives the next morning, in fear lest their presence attract the Border Ruffians, they set off, Jason with the idea of surrendering to the United States troops and demanding protection. Jason shortly thereafter encountered a body of Border Ruffians headed by the notorious "Rev." Martin White. He has thus told the story of the encounter: [11]

"I did not recognize in the leader the man who had led the squad of 'steer hunters' to our camp when we first reached the Territory. But he was that same Martin White. I walked straight up to him. 'Can you tell me the way to Taway Jones's?' 'You are one of the very men we are looking for! Your name is Brown. I knew your father. I knew your brother!' shouted White. Up came all the guns clicking. 'Down with him!' the squad yelled. 'You are our prisoner,' said White. 'Got any arms?' 'A revolver.' 'Hand it out.' 'Now go ahead of the horses.' I was weak with ague, excitement, fatigue. But I was terribly afraid of torture. I knew what these men had done to others, and all my habitual stammering left me. 'My name is Jason Brown,' I said, standing facing them. 'I am a Free State man, and what you call an Abolitionist. I have never knowingly injured a human being. Now if you want my blood for that, there is a mark for you.' And I pulled open the bosom of my shirt. I expected to be shot to pieces. And they took *that* for courage! Three-fourths of them laid their guns across their saddles and began to talk friendly. Martin White said: 'We won't kill you now. But you are our prisoner and we hold every man a scoundrel till he is proven honest.' One man, a villainous face, kept his gun up. I dared not turn my back, until I had backed thirty rods or so. I wanted to be killed quickly, not to be tortured. They drove me four miles at a fast walk. Then we came to a cabin and store. I was having chills every day, then, and at that moment my chill came on. They gave me a sack of coffee for a pillow. The man who had kept his gun levelled came and looked at me, with his bowie knife raised. 'Do you see anything bad about me?' I asked. 'I don't see anything good about ye!' he snarled, but went away. As the fever came on they put me on a horse, tied my feet beneath him and my arms behind me and took me, with a guard of twenty men, to Paola, where were about three hundred armed pro-slavery men. One flourished a coil of new hemp rope over his head as we rode up. 'Swing him up! Swing him up!' he shouted. They hustled me over to a tree and that man flung his rope end over a limb and stood ready. I sat down on the grass by the tree. I did n't suppose I had a friend in that crowd. Then came what changed my whole mind and life as to my feeling toward slave-holders. I can't see a Southerner or a Southern soldier, now, whatever he thinks of *me*, without wanting to grasp his two hands.

"As I sat there waiting under the dangling rope, I saw three men aside from the yelling crowd, differently dressed from the rest. One of them came quietly, tapped me on the shoulder and showed me a scrap of paper in the palm of his hand. 'Whose writing is that?' asked he. 'My father's.' 'Is old John Brown your father?' 'Yes.' Never another word did he say, but went around and spoke to the crowd, who made so much noise that I could not hear what he said. Then he came back, (he was Judge Jacobs, of Lexington, Kentucky, and one of his companions was Judge Cato,) and quietly said to me: 'Come with me to my house and I will treat you like my own son, but we must hold you prisoner.' Mrs. Doyle was also staying in that house and we all sat at the same table for meals. She said nothing. There I was, one lone coward, and about forty proslavery men in the house that night. . . . On the third night John was brought in. We lay together and I slept soundly on the front side of the bed. In the night there was a sudden commotion and a crowd of men rushed in. One brandished a bowie knife over me as if to drive it into my right side. I slept on. John bared my heart, and, pointing to it, said, 'Strike there.' They took me away, two men holding my tied arms, in the middle of the night, leaving John, up to the Shawnee Mission. But they were afraid to keep me there and the same night brought me back again. . . ."

Jason did not see John again for about two weeks. Then the latter was becoming sane. But presently a squad arrived to escort Jason and John to Osawatomie.

"Capt. Wood himself came into the room where we two were sleeping, seized John by the collar with, — 'Come out here, sir,' and jerked him out of bed. Wood himself bound John's wrists behind him, and then his upper arms, using small, hard hemp rope, and he set his teeth and pulled with all his force, tightening the turns. Later another rope some forty feet long was passed between these two, to drive him by. Outside the leader of the squad which was to take us to Osawatomie (I think this was Pate) was calling orders to his men. 'Oyez, Oyez, Oyez,' he shouted. 'Form a line of battle.'

"They drove John afoot all the way from Paola to Osawatomie. Me, on the other hand, they carried in a wagon. When I saw John in the new camp, (they had to change camp as the horses grazed the grass off,) John was a maniac and in a terrible condition. They had never loosened the cords around his upper arms and the flesh was swollen so that the cords were covered. They had driven him through the water of Bull Creek and the yellow flints at the bottom had cut through his boots and terribly lacerated his feet. I found him chained by each ankle, with an ox-cart chain, to the center pole of the guard tent. John, who then fancied himself commander of the camp, was shrieking military orders, jumping up and down and casting himself about. Capt. Wood said to me: 'Keep that man still.' 'I can't keep an insane man still,' said I. 'He is no more insane than you are. If you don't keep him still, we'll do it for you.'

I tried my best, but John had not a glimmer of reason and could not understand anything. He went on yelling. Three troopers came in. One struck him a terrible blow on the jaw with his fist, throwing him on his side. A second knelt on him and pounded him with his fist. The third stood off and kicked him with all his force in the back of the neck. 'Don't kill a crazy man!' cried I. 'No more crazy than you are, but we'll fetch it out of him.' After that John lay unconscious for three or four hours. We camped about one and a half miles southeast of the Adairs. There we stayed about two weeks. Then we were ordered to move again. They drove us on foot, chained two and two. I was chained to George Partridge. In a gang they drove us up right up in front of Adair's house. Aunt Florilla came out and talked to Lieut. Iverson, (he was a cruel man!) 'What does this mean in this Land of the Free? What does this mean that you drive these men like cattle and slaves!' and she went on, giving him a terrible cutting. Iverson made no reply. Aunt gave us all some little food. At Ottawa ford young Kilbourne dropped in a sun-stroke. . . . We camped near 'Taway Jones's. All the time these troops were looking for Old Brown. And father would show himself from time to time, at daylight, at different places, at a distance from his real camp. Then word would come to Wood that Old Brown and his men had been seen at such a time, here or there on Marais des Cygnes. Wood would order out his men to look for him, forty miles off, the men would spend themselves hunting along the river-bottoms, through dense, prickly tangles, and come back at night worn out and furious, their horses done. I heard one say, one night, out of his officer's hearing: 'D—d if I'm going after Old Brown any more. If I'm ordered out any more, I'll go into the bushes and hide.' This kept up three or four days, and all the time John Brown was camped so close that he heard the bugle calls, and got his water at the same spring where they got theirs. He was hoping for a chance to effect a rescue. One day word came to Wood that John Brown was near and would attempt a rescue. Thereupon he repeated the message to me, commenting: 'If such a rescue be attempted and you try to escape, you will be the first ones that we will shoot.'"

A correspondent of the New York *Times* thus described the torture of the prisoners: [12]

"*A scene then followed which has no parallel in a republican government. They were chained two and two by taking a common trace-chain and using a padlock at each end*, which was so fixed as to make a close clasp around the ankle. Like a gang of slaves they were thus driven on foot the whole distance at the rate of twenty-five miles per day, dragging their chains after them. They were unaccustomed to travelling — their chains had worn upon their ankles until one of them became quite exhausted and was put in a wagon.

CLOSE QUARTERS AT BLACK JACK 197

What a humiliating, disgusting sight in a free government — to see a chained gang of men who had committed no crime whatever, driven sixty-five miles by their merciless prosecutors to attend a trial, then have granted them an unconditional release and no provision for redress!"

This shocking ill-treatment of John Brown, Jr., which is confirmed by much contemporary testimony, aroused indignation in the North, and to its effect upon John Brown was attributed, though erroneously, much of the father's bitterness toward the slaveholders. According to a special correspondent of the New York *Tribune*, First Lieutenant James McIntosh, First Cavalry, stated to him in June that the reason for the arrest of John Brown, Jr., and Jason Brown, and the severity of their treatment, was the soldiers' belief that they were two of the Pottawatomie murderers.[13] As for Captain Thomas J. Wood, it was pointed out at the time that he was a native of Kentucky, and it was, therefore, taken for granted that his sympathies were with the South, and his cruelties due to friendliness for the Border Ruffians. It is an interesting fact that this officer later became, like Major Sedgwick, a distinguished Northern general, one of the very best division commanders in the Army of the Cumberland, in which he was conspicuous for his wounds, his ability and his gallantry. After spending two weeks on Ottawa Creek with his prisoners, Captain Wood marched them to Lecompton via Palmyra and Lawrence. Here, after an examination, Jason was released, but John Brown, Jr., was held on the charge of high treason because of his political activity, and was not released until September 10. Jason returned to his own claim only to find his house burned by the Border Ruffians and his cattle driven off, though his oxen later returned to him, of themselves, from Missouri. He built himself a shelter of fence rails, but soon joined his father's company as the only place where he could find safety. His wife and the other women went into the Osawatomie block-house for security, for by this time almost all the Free State men were out under arms.[14]

John Brown and those who had participated with him in the Pottawatomie murders arrived at Jason Brown's claim and went into hiding on May 26, sending his son Owen to Osawatomie a day or two later for provisions. Meeting his brother, John Brown, Jr., wandering in the brush, Owen endeavored to persuade him to join his father, but he admitted frankly that they were now hunted outlaws, likely to be separated for months from all of their families. John then declined, only to meet the worse fate already recorded.[15] On Owen's return there came to the camp O. A. Carpenter, a Free Soiler from the neighborhood of Prairie City, who offered to pilot Brown to the headwaters of Ottawa Creek, as there were two companies, one of cavalry and one of Missourians, then in search of the murderers. The Brown party broke camp at once and started at nightfall in the direction of Lawrence; it comprised then, besides the leader, John Brown, his sons Frederick, Salmon, Owen and Oliver, Henry Thompson, Weiner, Townsley, August Bondi and the guide, Carpenter, "Dutch Henry's" horses furnishing some of the mounts. In the course of the first few hours of the march, they rode straight into the bivouac of a detachment of United States troops presumably in pursuit of them. It was near the crossing of the Marais des Cygnes River, according to Owen Brown, and the troops ordered them to halt. "It was dark," he narrates, "and father called for the captain. In the meantime we placed our horses one beyond the other and close together so as to look like a small company. After some time the captain came out in front of his tent and asked: 'Who are you?' I think father replied, 'There are a few of us going towards Lawrence.' The captain answered: 'All right, pass on.'" This these modern successors of Robin Hood lost no time in doing, and in bivouacking for the night some distance away, but not far from the farm of Howard Carpenter, a brother of their guide.

The next day they entered some virgin woods on Ottawa Creek and camped near a fine spring. Bondi, an able Austrian Jew, who had put himself under Brown's leadership after hearing of the Pottawatomie murders, has left the following picture of their *al fresco* life in the forest primeval:[16]

"We stayed here up to the morning of Sunday, the 1st of June, and during these few days I fully succeeded in understanding the exalted character of my old friend [John Brown]. He exhibited at all times the most affectionate care for each of us. He also attended to cooking. We had two meals daily, consisting of bread, baked in skillets; this was washed down with creek water, mixed with a little ginger and a spoon of molasses to each pint. Nevertheless we kept in excellent spirits; we considered ourselves as one family, allied to one another by the consciousness that it was our duty to undergo all these privations to further the good cause; had determined to share any danger with one another, that victory or death might find us together. We were united as a band of brothers by the love and affection towards the man who with tender words and wise counsel, in the depth of the wilderness of Ottawa creek, prepared a handful of young men for the work of laying the foundation of a free commonwealth. His words have ever remained firmly engraved on my mind. Many and various were the instructions he gave during the days of our compulsory leisure in this camp. He expressed himself to us that we should never allow ourselves to be tempted by any consideration to acknowledge laws and institutions to exist as of right if our conscience and reason condemned them.

"He admonished us not to care whether a majority, no matter how large, opposed our principles and opinions. The largest majorities were sometimes only organized mobs, whose howlings never changed black into white, or night into day. A minority conscious of its rights, based on moral principles, would, under a republican government, sooner or later become the majority."

On May 30 James Redpath, the correspondent of the St. Louis *Democrat* and the *Tribune*, rode by accident into this gathering. His description, too, is worth reprinting, since the scene he portrays beyond doubt represents many similar ones in John Brown's life:[17]

"I shall not soon forget the scene that here opened to my view. Near the edge of the creek a dozen horses were tied, all ready saddled for a ride for life, or a hunt after Southern invaders. A dozen rifles and sabres were stacked around the trees. In an open space, amid the shady and lofty woods, there was a great blazing fire with a pot on it; a woman, bareheaded, with an honest, sun-burnt face, was picking blackberries from the bushes; three or four armed men were lying on red and blue blankets on the grass; and two fine-looking youths were standing, leaning on their arms, on guard near by. One of them was the youngest son of Old Brown, and the other was 'Charley,' the brave Hungarian, who was subsequently murdered at Ossawatomie. Old Brown himself stood near the fire, with his shirt-sleeves rolled up, and a large piece of pork in his hand. He was cooking a pig. He was poorly clad, and his toes protruded from his boots. The old man received me with great cordiality, and the little band gathered about me. But it was for a moment only; for the Captain ordered them to renew their work. He respectfully but firmly forbade conversation on the Pottawatomie affair; and said that, if I desired any information from the company in relation to their conduct or intentions, he, as their Captain, would answer for them whatever it was proper to communicate.

"In this camp no manner of profane language was permitted; no man of immoral character was allowed to stay, excepting as a prisoner of war. He made prayers in which all the company united, every morning and evening; and no food was ever tasted by his men until the Divine blessing had been asked on it. After every meal, thanks were returned to the Bountiful Giver. Often, I was told, the old man would retire to the densest solitudes, to wrestle with his God in secret prayer. One of his company subsequently informed me that, after these retirings, he would say that the Lord had directed him in visions what to do; that, for himself, he did not love warfare, but peace, — only acting in obedience to the will of the Lord, and fighting God's battles for His children's sake.

"It was at this time that the old man said to me: 'I would rather have the small-pox, yellow fever, and cholera all together in my camp, than a man without principles. It's a mistake, sir,' he continued, 'that our people make, when they think that bullies are the best fighters, or that they are the men fit to oppose these Southerners. Give me men of good principles; God-fearing men; men who respect themselves; and, with a dozen of them, I will oppose any hundred such men as these Buford ruffians!'"

Besides Charles Kaiser, subsequently murdered in cold blood by the Border Ruffians, as Redpath records, Benjamin Cochrane, a settler on the Pottawatomie, had joined Brown's band, the latter bringing the news that Bondi's cabin had been burned, his cattle stolen and Weiner's store plundered, in plain view, he alleged, of United States troops. Captain Samuel T. Shore, of the Prairie City Rifles, and a Dr. Westfall also visited the camp, bringing news of Border Ruffian outrages and asking for aid.[18] Captain Shore brought provisions, and on May 31 reported that a large force of Missourians had gone into camp near Black Jack, a spring on the Santa Fé trail, named for a group of "black jack" oaks. It was agreed that Brown's party and as many men as Shore could get together should meet at Prairie City at ten o'clock in the forenoon of the next day. This took place, Brown's men attending a service held by an itinerant preacher, with part of the congregation in a building, part outside. The services were interrupted by the passing of three strangers in the direction of Black Jack. Two of them were captured, and, when questioned by John Brown, admitted that they were from the camp of Henry Clay Pate, the correspondent of the St. Louis

CLOSE QUARTERS AT BLACK JACK 201

Missouri Republican, a captain in the Missouri militia and a deputy United States Marshal, who, as already related, on the news of the Pottawatomie murders, had marched at once to Paola and, after assisting in the round-up there of Free State men, including John Brown, Jr., and Jason Brown, had pushed on into the Territory in search of the other Browns.

At that time twenty-four years of age, a native of Kanawha County, Virginia, and a former student of the University of Virginia, Pate had in him the making of a fine soldier, for he died, well spoken of, as Colonel of the Fifth Virginia Cavalry, in command of a brigade of cavalry, on the same day and, it is said, within a hundred yards of where the brilliant Confederate General, J. E. B. Stuart, was mortally wounded. This was near Yellow Tavern, Virginia, May 11, 1864.[19] Pate's, John Brown's and Stuart's careers were thus strangely interwoven; Pate and Brown first met each other in battle at Black Jack, and encountered Lieutenant J. E. B. Stuart three days later, when Pate's men were set free. Stuart and Brown met again in the Harper's Ferry raid, and Pate visited his old captor in jail shortly thereafter. They could not have foreseen that there would be three acts in all to their public appearance; or that all were to perish violently within eight years, two of them after having won for themselves imperishable renown, the one by reason of his death on the scaffold, the other because of military achievements which have placed him in the front rank of American cavalry leaders. There could be no clearer illustration than the meeting of these men of the direct relation of "Bleeding Kansas" to Harper's Ferry and to the national convulsion of 1861 to 1865. Kansas was but the prelude; what more natural than that some of the actors who appeared in the prologue should hold the centre of the stage in the later acts of the greatest drama of the nineteenth century?

Members of the startled Prairie City congregation were eager to leave at once in search of Pate, particularly because the sons of a preacher named Moore, who had been captured near Westport the day before and taken off, learned now that their father was in Pate's camp. Brown counselled, more wisely, that the night be awaited and the enemy assailed at sunrise. About forty men volunteered to go as the Prairie

City Rifles, but their numbers dwindled rapidly as the distance to the enemy decreased. At daylight on June 2 Brown's men were fed, and at sunrise they were dismounted at the Black Jack oaks, Frederick Brown being left in charge of the horses.[20] A half mile distant was Pate's camp, the covered wagons in front, then the tents, and then, on higher ground to the rear, the picketed horses and mules. A Missouri sentinel fired the first shot. As to what happened thereafter, there is a mass of testimony. Henry Clay Pate, in a rare pamphlet published in New York in 1859,[21] has given his side of the story. John Brown described the whole "battle" in a letter to his family dated "near Brown's Station, June, 1856." Both Pate and Brown discussed the fight at length in the *Tribune* of June 13 and July 11 respectively, and Brown's *Tribune* letter, hitherto entirely overlooked by his various biographers, must be taken as the final word in settling several long-disputed points. Besides the principal actors, Lieutenant Brockett, Bondi, Owen Brown, Henry Thompson, Salmon Brown and the preacher Moore, who was Pate's prisoner, have recorded their recollections of the conflict.

In his letter to his family John Brown thus outlines the skirmish:

"As I was much older than Captain Shore, the principal direction of the fight devolved on me. We got to within about a mile of their camp before being discovered by their scouts, and then moved at a brisk pace, Captain Shore and men forming our left, and my company the right. When within about sixty rods of the enemy, Captain Shore's men halted by mistake in a very exposed situation, and continued the fire, both his men and the enemy being armed with Sharpe's rifles. My company had no long-shooters. We (my company) did not fire a gun until we gained the rear of a bank, about fifteen or twenty rods to the right of the enemy, where we commenced, and soon compelled them to hide in a ravine. Captain Shore, after getting one man wounded, and exhausting his ammunition, came with part of his men to the right of my position, much discouraged. The balance of his men, including the one wounded, had left the ground. Five of Captain Shore's men came boldly down and joined my company, and all but one man, wounded, helped to maintain the fight until it was over. I was obliged to give my consent that he should go after more help, when all his men left but eight, four of whom I persuaded to remain in a secure position, and there busied one of them in shooting the

CLOSE QUARTERS AT BLACK JACK 203

horses and mules of the enemy, which served for a show of fight. After the firing had continued for some two or three hours, Captain Pate with twenty-three men, two badly wounded, laid down their arms to nine men, myself included, — four of Captain Shore's men and four of my own. One of my men (Henry Thompson) was badly wounded, and after continuing his fire for an hour longer was obliged to quit the ground. Three others of my company (but not of my family) had gone off. Salmon was dreadfully wounded by accident, soon after the fight; but both he and Henry are fast recovering." [22]

Captain Pate always alleged that he had been taken prisoner by John Brown by trickery and treachery, when under a flag of truce, "a barbarity unlooked for in this country, and unheard of in the annals of honorable warfare." But Pate admits on the same page that his object in using the flag of truce was "to gain time, and if possible have hostilities suspended for a while."

"With this view," he says, "a flag of truce was sent out and an interview with the captain requested. Captain Brown advanced and sent for me. I approached him and made known the fact that I was acting under the orders of the U. S. Marshal and was only in search of persons for whom writs of arrest had been issued, and that I wished to make a proposition. He replied that he would hear no proposals, and that he wanted an unconditional surrender. I asked for fifteen minutes to answer. He refused. . . . Had I known whom I was fighting I would not have trusted to a flag of truce. The enemy's men were then marched up to within fifty paces of mine and I placed before them. Captain Brown commanded me to order my company to lay down their arms. Putting a revolver to my breast he repeated the command, giving me one or two minutes to make the order. He might have shot me; his men might have riddled me, but I would not have given the order for a world, much less my poor life." [23]

His company, he explains, saved his life by voluntarily laying down their arms. There is more braggadocio, and also the admission that "there is another consolation for me, if I showed the white feather at Black Jack, namely: they who fight and run away shall live to fight another day," — which was surely a correct prophecy. But he admits that at Black Jack he resorted to the flag of truce because he saw — what no one else did — that "reinforcements for the Abolitionists were near and that the fight would be desperate, and if they persisted not one would be left to tell the tale of carnage that must follow."

To Pate's allegations John Brown replied thus in the *Tribune* of July 11, 1856:

LAWRENCE, K. T., Tuesday, July 1, 1856.

I have just read in the *Tribune* of June 13, an article from the pen of Capt. H. C. Pate, headed "The Battle of Black Jack Point," (in other words the battle of Palmyra), and take the liberty of correcting a very few of Capt. Pate's statements in reference to that affair, having had personal cognizance of what then occurred. The first statement I would notice is in these words: "At first the enemy squatted down in open prairie and fired at a distance from 300 to 400 yards from us. Their lines were soon broken and they hastily ran to a ravine for shelter." This is wrong, as my company formed a distinct line from Capt. Shore and his men, and without stopping to fire a gun passed at once into a ravine on the enemy's right, where we commenced our fire on them, and where we remained till the enemy hoisted the white flag. I expected Capt. Shore to form his men and occupy a similar position on the left of the enemy, but was disappointed, he halting on the eastern slope above the ravine, in front of the enemy's camp. This I consider as the principal mistake in our part of the action, as Capt. Shore was unable to retain this unfortunate position: and when he, with part of his men left it and joined my company, the balance of his company quit the field entirely. One of them was wounded and disabled. Capt. Shore and all his men, I believe, had for a considerable time kept that position, and received the fire of the enemy like the best regular troops (to their praise I would say it) and until they had to a considerable extent exhausted their ammunition. Capt. Pate says: "When the fight commenced our forces were nearly equal." I here say most distinctly, that twenty-six officers and men all told, was the entire force on the Free State side who were on the ground at all during the fight or in any way whatever participated in it. Of these Capt. Shore and his company numbered sixteen all told. My company, ten only, including myself. Six of these were of my own family. He says further, "but I saw reënforcements for the Abolitionists were near," &c. Capt. Pate, it seems, could see much better than we; for we neither saw nor received any possible reënforcements until some minutes after the surrender, nor did we understand that any help was near us, and at the time of the surrender our entire force, officers and men, all told, had dwindled down to but fifteen men, who were either on or about the field. Capt. Shore and his men had all left the field but eight. One of his men who had left was wounded and was obliged to leave. Of the eight who remained four, whose names I love to repeat, stood nobly by four of

CLOSE QUARTERS AT BLACK JACK

my men until the fight was over. The other four had, with two of my company, become disheartened and gone to a point out of reach of the enemy's fire, where, by the utmost exertion, I had kept them to make a little show, and busied one of them in shooting mules and horses to divert the others and keep them from running off. One of my men had been terribly wounded and left, after holding on for an hour afterward. Fifteen Free State men, all told, were all that remained on and near the ground at the time the surrender was made; and it was made to nine men only, myself included in that number. Twenty-five of the enemy, including two men terribly wounded, were made prisoners. Capt. Pate reproaches me with the most dishonorable violation of the rights secured under a flag of truce, but says: "My object was to gain time, and if possible have hostilities suspended for a while." So much, in his own language, for good faith, of which he found me so destitute. Now for my own dishonorable violation of the flag of truce: When I first saw it I had just been to the six discouraged men above named, and started at once to meet it, being at that moment from sixty to eighty rods from the enemy's camp, and met it about half way carried by two men, one a Free State man, a prisoner of theirs; the other was young Turner, of whom Capt. Pate speaks in such high terms. I think him as brave as Capt. Pate represents. Of his disposition and character in other respects I say nothing now. The country and the world may probably know more hereafter. I at once learned from those bearing the flag of truce that in reality they had no other design than to divert me and consume time by getting me to go to their camp to hear explanations. I then told young James to stand by me with his arms, saying, "We are both equally exposed to the fire of both parties," and sent their prisoner back to tell the Captain that, if he had any proposal to make, to come at once and make it. He also came armed to where I and young James were — some forty or fifty rods from either party and I alone. He immediately began to tell about his authority from the General Government, by way of explanation, as he said. I replied that I should listen to nothing of that kind, and that, if he had any proposal to make, I would hear it at once, and that, if he had none for me, I had one for him, and that was immediate and unconditional surrender. I then said to him and young James, (both well armed,) "You must go down to your camp, and there all of you lay down your arms," when the three started, they continuing armed until the full surrender was made. I, an old man, of nearly sixty years, and fully exposed to the weapons of two young men at my side, as well as the fire of their men in their camp, so far, and no further, took them prisoners under their flag of truce. On our way to their camp, as we passed within hailing distance of the eight men, who had kept their position firm, I directed them to pass down the ravine in front of the enemy's camp, about twenty rods off, to receive the surrender. Such was my violation of the flag of truce. Let others judge. I had not during the time of the above transactions with Capt. Pate and his flag of truce a single man secreted near me who could have possibly have pointed a rifle at Capt. Pate, nor a man nearer than forty rods till we came near their camp. Capt. Pate complains of our treatment in regard to cooking, &c, but forgets to say that, after the fight was over, when I and some of my men had eaten only once in nearly forty-eight hours, we first of all gave Capt. Pate and his men as good a dinner as we could obtain for them, I being the last man to take a morsel. During the time we kept them it was with difficulty I could keep enough men in camp away from their business and their families to guard our prisoners; I being myself obliged to stand guard six hours — between four in the afternoon and six in the morning. We were so poorly supplied with provisions that the best we could possibly do was to let our prisoners use their own provisions; and as for tents, we, for the most part, had none, while we sent a team and brought in theirs, which they occupied exclusively. Capt. Pate and his men had burned or carried off my own tent, where one of my sons lived, with all its contents, provisions &c, some four or five days before the fight. We did not search our prisoners, nor take from them one cent of their money, a watch, or anything but arms, horses, and military stores. I would ask Capt. Pate and his men how our people fared at their hands at Lawrence, Osawattamie, Brown's Station, and elsewhere, my two sons, John, jr., and Jason Brown, being of the number? We never had, at any time, near Capt. Pate, or where his men were, to exceed half the number he states. We had only three men wounded in the fight, and all of those have nearly recovered, and not one killed or since dead. See his statement. I am sorry that a young man of good acquirements and fair abilities should, by his own statement, knowingly and wilfully made, do himself much greater injury than he even accuses "Old Brown" of doing him. He is most welcome to all the satisfaction which his treatment of myself and family before the fight, his polite and gentlemanly return for my own treatment of himself and his men have called forth since he was a prisoner, and released by Col. Sumner, can possibly afford to his honorable and ingenuous mind. I have also seen a brief notice of this affair by Lieutenant Brockett, and it affords me real satisfaction to say that I do not see a single sentence in it that is in the least degree characterized by either direct or indirect untruthfulness. I will add that when Capt. Pate's sword and pistols were taken from him at his camp, he particularly requested me to take them into my own care, which I did, and returned them to him when Col. Sumner took him and his men from us. I subjoin a copy of an agreement made with Capt. Shore and myself by Capt. Pate and his Lieutenant Brocket, in regard to exchange of prisoners taken by both parties, which agreement Col. Sumner did not require the Pro-Slavery party to comply with. A good illustration of governmental protection to the people of Kansas from the first:

CLOSE QUARTERS AT BLACK JACK

(*Copy*)

This is an article of agreement between Captains John Brown, sen., and Samuel T. Shore of the first part, and Capt. H. C. Pate and Lieut. W. B. Brocket of the second part, and witnesses, that in consideration of the fact that the parties of the first part have a number of Capt. Pate's company prisoners that they agree to give up and fully liberate one of their prisoners for one of those lately arrested near Stanton, Osawattamie, and Potawatamie and so on, one of the former for one of the latter alternately until all are liberated. It is understood and agreed by the parties that the sons of Capt. John Brown, sen, Capt. John Brown, jr., and Jason Brown, are to be among the liberated parties (if not already liberated), and are to be exchanged for Capt. Pate and Lieut. Brocket respectively. The prisoners are to be brought on neutral ground and exchanged. It is agreed that the neutral ground shall be at or near the house of John T. or Ottawa Jones of this Territory, and that those who have been arrested, and have been liberated, will be considered in the same light as those not liberated, but they must appear in person or answer in writing that they are at liberty. The arms, particularly the side arms, of each one exchanged, are to be returned with the prisoners, also the horses so far as practicable.

(Signed)

JOHN BROWN,
S. T. SHORE,
H. C. PATE,
W. B. BROCKET.

PRAIRIE CITY, KANSAS TER'Y. June 2, A. D., 1856.

Captain Pate, after his interview with Brown in jail at Charlestown, to which he had three witnesses, obtained their signatures to an account of the Black Jack fight which in some respects is obviously erroneous; in it he endeavors to represent that John Brown admitted that the flag of truce was violated. Unfortunately for Pate's reputation as a chronicler, his pamphlet is frankly partisan. Moreover, there were several witnesses who testified that Pate ordered his men to lay down their arms, instead of risking death by silence, as he avers.

The crux of the "battle" of Black Jack came when John Brown ordered Shore's men to shoot Pate's horses and mules. As soon as he noticed this going on, Frederick Brown, who had been left behind with the horses, could no longer contain himself in inactivity, but, mounting one of the animals and brandishing his sword, rode around Pate's camp with his horse at a run, crying out, "Father, we have got them surrounded and have cut off their communications!" Frederick Brown was a large man, and on this occasion he acted in such a wild manner as to give rise to the charge that he was not of sound mind. His extraordinary appearance undoubtedly frightened Pate's men, who naturally believed that he had other men behind him and that they were really surrounded. They fired a number of shots at him in vain, and it was only a few minutes after this that they raised the flag of truce and the firing ceased. It is interesting to note that among those who ran away with Shore's men was James Townsley, the first to tell the story of the Pottawatomie murders. Pate's Free Soil prisoners were of course at once released by John Brown, after having been under fire throughout the engagement, which ended between one and two o'clock. Among them, besides the preacher Moore, was a Dr. Graham, who had been shot through the leg in endeavoring to escape. He was not sufficiently hurt, however, to prevent his attending to the wounded, of whom Henry Thompson was the most seriously injured. After the battle, Shore's men returned, and with them the company known as the Lawrence "Stubbs," under Captain J. B. Abbott, a well-known Lawrence fighter, who had marched as rapidly as possible in order to succor Brown. Owen Brown estimates that this reinforcement amounted to one hundred and fifty men, and in this he is probably not far wrong. As John Brown himself put it:

"After the fight, numerous Free State men who could not be got out before were on hand; and some of them I am ashamed to add, were very busy not only with the plunder of our enemies, but with our private effects, leaving us, while guarding our prisoners and providing in regard to them, much poorer than before the battle." [24]

"We were taken," records Pate, "to a camp on Middle Ottawa Creek and closely guarded. We had to cook for ourselves, furnish provisions, and sleep on the ground, but we were not treated unkindly. Here we remained for three days and nights, until Colonel Sumner at the head of a company of Dragoons released us from our imprisonment." [25]

Colonel Sumner officially reported from Leavenworth, on June 5, his rescue of Pate's command, and his heading off about two hundred and fifty men under General Whitfield

CLOSE QUARTERS AT BLACK JACK

and General Coffee, of the militia, who, as we have already seen from Whitfield's letter, were bent on rescuing Captain Pate. Colonel Sumner's force was only fifty men. With him were Major Sedgwick and Lieutenant Stuart, who thus met Pate and Brown. Colonel Sumner records the prompt dispersal of Brown's men, and his surprise at finding General Whitfield, a Member of Congress, and General Coffee, of the Militia, at the head of the advancing Border Ruffians. He informed them that he was there,

"by order of the President, and the proclamation of the Governor, to disperse all armed bodies assembled without authority; and further, that my duty was perfectly plain, and would certainly be done. I then requested General Coffee to assemble his people, and I read to them the President's despatch and the governor's proclamation. The general then said that he should not resist the authority of the general government, and that his party would disperse, and shortly afterwards they moved off. Whether this is a final dispersion of these lawless armed bodies, is very doubtful. If the proclamation of the Governor had been issued six months earlier, and had been rightly maintained, these difficulties would have been avoided. As the matter now stands, there is great danger of a serious commotion."[26]

Major Sedgwick recorded the dispersal of Brown's band in the following words:

"Things are getting worse every day, and it is hard to foresee the result. One of these things must happen: either it will terminate in civil war or the vicious will band themselves together to plunder and murder all whom they meet. The day after writing my last letter I started with a squadron of cavalry to go about forty miles to break up an encampment of free-soilers who had been robbing and taking prisoners any pro-slavery man they could meet. I proceeded to the place, and when within a short distance two of their principal men came out and wanted to make terms. They were told that no terms would be made with lawless and armed men, but that they must give up their prisoners and disperse at once. We marched into their camp, situated on a small island and entrenched, and found about one hundred and fifty men and twenty prisoners, who were released and the men dispersed."[27]

It was John Brown himself who came out and endeavored to negotiate with the forces of the United States as if he were in control of a coördinate body. It was he, too, who had insisted on the camp's being so heavily entrenched. On June 3 he had directed the pillaging of the store of one J. M.

Bernard at Centropolis, he being a pro-slavery sympathizer, in order, Brown's devoted follower Bondi declared:

"to improve our exterior, the Brown outfit being altogether in rags. Frederick and Oliver Brown and three members of the Stubbs were the raiding party. They returned with some palm-leaf hats, check shirts, linen coats, a few linen pants, and bandanna handkerchiefs."[28]

To the victors belonged the spoils. Since it was now "war" in deadly earnest, the raiding of the country for supplies was, in John Brown's opinion, wholly justified, as had already been the "impressing" of pro-slavery horses. Within one hour subsequent to the interview between Sumner and Brown, reported Bondi, Camp Brown had ceased to exist, and this hasty movement was not delayed by Salmon Brown's accidentally shooting himself in the right shoulder. Subsequently, Colonel Sumner was severely criticised by the pro-slavery men for not having arrested Brown. He had, however, no warrants for anybody's arrest, and there was with his command a deputy United States marshal, William J. Preston by name. The latter seems to have been afraid, even in the presence of troops, to serve the warrants he had with him.[29] Salmon Brown and Henry Thompson testify that Colonel Sumner told John Brown that Preston had warrants and that they would be served in his presence. Then he ordered Preston to proceed. "I do not recognize any one for whom I have warrants," replied the deputy marshal. "Then what are you here for?" asked Colonel Sumner indignantly.[30]

The Brown family did not move far after being ordered to disperse. The wounded Salmon was taken to Carpenter's near-by cabin and nursed by Bondi; the others, with Weiner, camped in a thicket about half a mile from the abandoned Camp Brown. On June 8 Bondi rejoined them, Salmon being no longer in need of his services, and was at once asked to visit John Brown, Jr., and Jason Brown, then prisoners in Captain Wood's near-by camp. At their request Bondi visited the Adairs and found the Brown women safe at the residence of David Garrison, a neighbor. On Thursday, June 10, Bondi had returned to John Brown, and at a council held that day it was agreed to separate. Weiner had business in Louisiana; Henry Thompson was also taken to Carpenter's cabin, and

CLOSE QUARTERS AT BLACK JACK 211

Bondi accompanied Weiner as far as Leavenworth on the latter's way to St. Louis. He then returned to the seat of war. John Brown and his unwounded sons remained hidden in the thickets.

Governor Shannon, on hearing of the Black Jack episode, reported it to President Pierce as a sign of the unrest of the Territory, with a comment that could hardly have gratified Captain Pate, for it charged him with being "at the head of an unauthorized company." [31] This weak Governor was not having a particularly easy time of it. The Territory was seething with lawlessness. The administration at Washington was getting restless in view of the outburst of anger in the North over the sacking of Lawrence. Indeed, on May 23, before the news of this raid had reached Washington, President Pierce sent two despatches [32] to Governor Shannon which betray his extreme nervousness. He wished to know if it was true that Marshal Donaldson was near Lawrence, if it had been necessary to use troops to enforce writs, and, if so, whether other forces besides those of Sumner and Lieut.-Col. Cooke, of the Dragoons, had been called in. In his second despatch he urged Governor Shannon to "repress lawless violence in whatever form it may manifest itself," and it was this despatch which Colonel Sumner read to General Whitfield, together with Shannon's proclamation commanding "all persons belonging to military organizations within this Territory, not authorized by the laws thereof, to disperse and retire peaceably to their respective abodes," under penalty of being dispersed by the United States troops. Shannon further ordered [33] that all law-abiding citizens, without regard to party names and distinctions, should be protected in their persons and property, and that "all aggressing parties from without the Territory must be repelled." It is only fair to Shannon to add that he made requisitions for sufficient United States troops, and urged upon their commanders that the country to the south of Lawrence be properly protected. When Shannon's proclamation was two days old, President Pierce again telegraphed to the Governor: "Maintain the laws firmly and impartially, and take care that no good citizen has just ground to complain of the want of protection." [34]

Despite these admonitions and the activity of the troops,

the disorders continued. Early in the morning of the 5th of June, Major Abbott, with his Wakarusa company of Free State men and a body of Lawrence youths, assailed Franklin, four and a half miles from Lawrence, where were some Missourians charged with being members of the Law and Order party and with having amassed considerable plunder.[35] It was, in the eyes of the Free State men, a "mischievous camp." The pro-slavery men, who had one man killed and several wounded, defended themselves with a cannon, but inflicted no loss on their assailants. The Wakarusa company arrived too late to take part in the fighting, and busied itself in levying on the stores of the pro-slavery men, loading a wagon with all the rifles, powder, caps, flour, bacon, coffee, sugar, etc., that could be found. They made Franklin, says Andreas, "too hot for the enemy, and compelled them to evacuate." It is interesting to note that this and similar robberies by Free State men were treated in the Northern press and by subsequent historians as absolutely proper and legitimate acts of war, while similar outrages on the part of the pro-slavery forces were pictured as too terrible to be borne. Thus Bondi relates that the final pro-slavery wrongdoing, which led John Brown to leave his camp and march after Pate, was the entering of a Free State house by three of Pate's men and their stealing the guns of the seven Free Soilers who occupied it. "It was impossible," says Bondi, "to put up with such a shameful outrage,"[36] — especially so for the men who bore the guilt of the Pottawatomie murders. Later on in his reminiscences, Bondi relates with great gusto how he and his companions, when in need of fresh meat, sought out "Dutch Henry" Sherman's herd of cattle and killed what they needed without asking any one's permission. This was, of course, a justifiable act of war, in his opinion. The dispersal of Free State forces by Federal troops was always an outrage; similar treatment of the pro-slavery bands, just and proper.

Two days after the Free State attack on Franklin, Whitfield's men, returning to Missouri, reached Osawatomie just after Major Sedgwick, with a company of dragoons, had left it on his return to Fort Leavenworth. They seized the opportunity to take revenge for the Pottawatomie murders. Every house was entered and pillaged, women being robbed even of earrings, and fourteen horses were stolen,[37] thus justifying

CLOSE QUARTERS AT BLACK JACK

Colonel Sumner's fears as to the genuineness of Whitfield's promise to disperse his men. That anything was left standing was due to fear that United States troops might appear. After an hour and a half of terrorizing women and children and the few men left at home, Whitfield's forces moved on, laden with booty, and finally disbanded on reaching Westport. As this town lies to the northeast of Prairie City, and Osawatomie far to the southeast, it is obvious that Whitfield deliberately disobeyed Sumner's instructions to leave the Territory, and went out of his way to revenge upon the Free State settlement at Osawatomie the Pottawatomie murders that were the original reason for his and Pate's entry into Kansas. Sumner was naturally indignant, so the *Tribune* reported on June 23, when he heard of Whitfield's breach of faith; but the mischief was then done, and Whitfield doubled on his tracks and returned safely to Westport. This Whitfield raid, while unaccompanied by loss of life, by itself wholly disposes of the contention of James Freeman Clarke and others that after John Brown's murders "the country had peace." Certainly it is plain proof that the killings of the Doyles, Sherman and Wilkinson, far from stopping the aggressiveness of the Border Ruffians, brought down their especial vengeance upon Brown's Free State neighbors.

Even before they plundered Osawatomie, Whitfield's men were credited with one of the worst crimes of this bloody period. They had tried one Cantrall, a Missourian, on the charge of "treason to Missouri," for sympathizing with and aiding the Free State forces at Black Jack, although he was not an actual participant in the engagement. After a mock courtmartial, Cantrall was taken into a near-by ravine. Other prisoners of Whitfield reported afterwards that there was a "shot, followed by the cry, 'O God! I am shot! I am murdered.' Then there was another shot followed by a long scream; then another shot and all was silent." One of the prisoners escaped and told this story, and the body was found in the ravine with three bullet-holes in the breast.[38] Lieut.-Col. Philip St. George Cooke, commanding the Second Dragoons, the other Federal regiment in Kansas, reported officially on June 18 that "the disorders in the Territory have, in fact, changed their character, and consist now of robberies and assassinations, by a set of bandits whom the excitement of the times has attracted hither."[39] W. A. Phillips, one of the best of the contemporary chroniclers, wrote that during the period between the Pottawatomie murders and June 18,

"proslavery parties stealthily prowled through the territory or hung upon the Missouri borders. Outrages were so common that it would be impossible to enumerate them. Mu :ders were frequent, many of them passing secretly and unrecorded; some of them only revealed by the discovery of some mouldering remains of mortality. Two men, found hanging on a tree near Westport, ill-fated free-state settlers, were taken down and buried by the troops; but so shallow was the grave that the prairie wolves dug them up and partly devoured them, before they were again found and buried."[40]

Lieutenant James McIntosh, First Cavalry, reported on June 13, from Palmyra, that a great many robberies were being committed on the various roads, and one detachment of his men reported to him that at Cedar Creek, twenty-five miles away,

"several men were lying murdered. They saw the body of one who they knew from his dress to be a Mr. Carter, who was taken prisoner from this place a few nights ago. This body was shown to them by a member of one of the companies who was under the influence of liquor, and who told my men that he could point out the other abolitionists if they wished to see them."[41]

O. C. Brown, the founder of Osawatomie, wrote on June 24, 1856, that for thirty days (since Pottawatomie) there had been a "reign of terror."

"Hundreds of men," he declared, "have come from Missouri, and the Southern and pauper crowd that live by plunder are hunting down the supposed murderers at Pottawatomie. But almost daily murders are committed near Westport and nothing done." He added: "Keep us in flour and bacon and we can stand it a good pull longer. . . . Remember that *now, now, now,* is the time to render us aid."[42]

There is other contemporary testimony to the straits to which John Brown's act reduced Osawatomie.

Free Soilers in numbers were stopped and turned out of the Territory when caught near the border. One John A. Baillie was shot and badly injured, besides being robbed of his possessions.[43] A young man named Hill was similarly robbed, and then bound and barbarously gagged.[44] Another victim of Border Ruffian fury was strung up to a tree only to be let down again. The list of murders runs all through the summer. A young Free Soil Kentuckian named Hopkins was deliberately killed in Lawrence on June 16 by a deputy sheriff named Haine, or Haynau, a notorious bully.[45] William Gay, an Indian Agent, was murdered two miles from Westport, on June 21, by three strangers, who blazed away at him as soon as they discovered, after drinking with him, that he was from Michigan.[46] Laben Parker was shot, stabbed and hanged, his dangling body being found July 24, eleven miles from Tecumseh, with this placard upon it: "Let all those who are going to vote against slavery take warning!"[47] Major David S. Hoyt, formerly of Deerfield, Massachusetts, was killed August 11, on his return to Lawrence from the Georgian camp on Washington Creek, which he had entered on a mission of peace. A corrosive acid was thrown upon his face, and his body, half-buried, was torn by wild beasts. His object had been to ask that the Georgians join the people of Lawrence in stopping just such crimes.[48]

But the worst of all this terrible list of inhuman outrages, the one that infuriated the Free State men beyond all else, was the killing, on August 17, of William Hoppe, a brother-in-law of the Rev. Ephraim Nute, the Unitarian minister of Lawrence. Hoppe was shot in his buggy, when within two miles of Leavenworth, by a follower of General Atchison, named Fugit or Fugert.[49] This wretch had made a bet of six dollars to a pair of boots that he would go out and return with the scalp of an Abolitionist within two hours. He asked but one question of his victim. When Hoppe replied that he was from Lawrence, Fugit shot him and scalped him, with an Indian's dexterity, without waiting even to ascertain if Hoppe was dead. Brandishing the bloody scalp, Fugit rode back and received his boots. In May, 1857, he was arrested at Leavenworth and acquitted of the charge of murder! For downright atrocities committed on individuals, the pro-slavery men were infinitely worse than the Free State, even remembering the Pottawatomie killings.

There were, however, plenty of Free State guerrillas at work. Charles Lenhart and John E. Cook (who later perished on the scaffold at Charlestown) were members of a well-mounted body of "cavalry scouts" of about twenty young men who ranged about the country.[50] The stealing of cattle and horses went on fearlessly on both sides.[51] "The substance of the Territory is devoured by the roving, roystering bands of guerrilla fighters who, under the plea that war prevails, perpetrate deeds of robbery, rapine, slaughter and pillage that nothing can justify," reported the St. Louis *Evening News* early in June. It added that the "body of good citizens, once numerous in the Territory, who sided with neither party, but attended to their own affairs, regardless of the issue of the dispute, is not now to be found. Every man has been compelled to join one party or the other, and to become active in its behalf." This referred, of course, both to the Free Soilers and to the non-slaveholding pro-slavery men who wished to mind their own business. "All over the Territory," the *Evening News* truthfully said, "along the roadside, houses are deserted and farms abandoned, and nowhere are there visible evidences of industry."[52] The Boonsville, Missouri, *Observer* was of the opinion that "unless the United States Government rigorously interposes its authority in behalf of peace and order, the horrors of civil war will rage on, and we fear accumulate to such an extent as to imperil the Union."[53]

The pro-slavery circular of June 21, signed by Atchison, Buford and Stringfellow, presented the Southern view of the situation thus:

"The [Pottawatomie] outrages above specified were preceded, and up to the present time have been followed by others of a like character, and dictated by a like settled policy on the part of our enemies to harrass and frighten by their deeds of horror, our friends from their homes in the Territory. Undoubtedly this policy (a well settled party system) has dictated the notices lately given in all the disturbed districts, by armed marauding bands of abolitionists, to the law and order men of their respective neighborhoods, immediately to leave the country on peril of death. Under such notices, our friends about Hickory Point and on Pottowatomie and Rock Creeks, have all been driven out of the Territory, their stores have been robbed, their cattle driven off, their houses burned, their horses stolen, and in some cases they have been assassinated for daring to return. Some, too, of these outrages, have been perpetrated under the very nose of the United States troops, who all the

CLOSE QUARTERS AT BLACK JACK 217

while assure us that all is peace and quietness, and that they will afford ample protection, without the necessity of our banding together in armed bodies for mutual defence."[54]

This pro-slavery criticism of the United States troops is the more interesting because the Free Soil writers of the period also assail the regulars and accuse them of sympathizing with and abetting Border Ruffian outrages, while admitting that Colonel Sumner's and Major Sedgwick's leanings were toward the North. The latter fact probably had something to do with Colonel Sumner's going on leave on July 15, in the midst of the troubles, and his turning over the command to Brigadier-General Persifor F. Smith, who did not, however, take the field in person. Colonel Sumner's disrepute with the pro-slavery Pierce administration is very plain. In his annual report for 1856, Jefferson Davis pointedly praised Lieut.-Col. Cooke and avoided all mention of Colonel Sumner, beyond printing his (Davis's) censures of Colonel Sumner for having dispersed by force the Topeka Free State Legislature, in harmony with the proclamation of acting Governor Woodson,[55] and positive instructions from Governor Shannon to use force if necessary.[56] Colonel Sumner did not again figure prominently in the Kansas troubles. If Pierce desired a scapegoat for the Kansas lawlessness, Colonel Sumner was the natural victim. It must be pointed out, however, that Colonel Sumner's and Lieut.-Col. Cooke's regiments would not have been large enough to patrol successfully all of eastern Kansas, had they been of full strength. General Smith reported officially on August 22, that "Colonel Sumner's regiment cannot now muster four hundred men, including Captain Stewart's company, on its way to Fort Laramie, and a detachment under Lieutenant Wharton, *en route* for Fort Kearney with the Sioux prisoners. Lieut.-Col. Cooke's six companies have a little more than one hundred horses."[57]

The breaking up of the Topeka or Free State Legislature Colonel Sumner declared to be the most trying episode of his long military career.[58] Governor Shannon wrote to Colonel Sumner on June 23,[59] that he was compelled to leave the Territory for ten days, and that he wished him to use his command in the most effective way for preserving peace, and to be sure to have two companies at Topeka on July 4. Shannon wrote also of his belief that if the Free State Legislature assembled on that date, it

"would produce an outbreak more fearful by far in its consequences than any which we have heretofore witnessed. . . . Two governments cannot exist at one and the same time in this Territory in practical operation; one or the other must be overthrown; and the struggle between the legal government established by Congress and that by the Topeka Constitution would result in a civil war, the fearful consequences of which no one can foresee. Should this body reassemble and enact laws (and they can have no other object in meeting), they will be an illegal body, threatening the peace of the whole country and therefore *should be dispersed*."

This view Colonel Sumner shared, for he wrote to acting Governor Woodson on June 28, "I am decidedly of the opinion that that body of men ought not to be permitted to assemble. It is not too much to say that the peace of the country depends upon it." Mr. Woodson then issued his proclamation of July 4, forbidding all persons "claiming legislative powers and authorities . . . from assembling, organizing or attempting to organize or act in any legislative capacity whatever. . . ." To this Colonel Sumner added over his own name these words: "The proclamation of the President and the order under it require me to sustain the Executive of the Territory in executing the laws and preserving the peace. I therefore hereby announce that I shall maintain the proclamation at all hazards."

Colonel Sumner had been so completely under the orders of Governor Shannon that he believed himself wholly justified in carrying out Shannon's and Woodson's instructions, the latter being with him on July 4, and directing him by word of mouth. Moreover, Jefferson Davis, who had praised Colonel Sumner on May 23, for his zeal, had assured him in the same letter that it was his duty to maintain "the duly authorized government of the Territory," and added that "for the great purpose which justifies the employment of military force, it matters not whether the subversion of the law arises from a *denial of the existence of the government*" or from lawless disregard of the rights of persons or property. The Topeka Legislature was surely in itself a "denial of the existence of the government," but after the dispersal of the Topeka

CLOSE QUARTERS AT BLACK JACK 219

Legislature, Secretary Davis took, on August 27, the view that Colonel Sumner had exceeded his instructions, and disavowed the dispersal of the Legislature. To this rebuke Colonel Sumner respectfully replied that he felt bound to consider the Topeka Legislature insurrectionary, under the President's proclamation of February 11, and, therefore, was compelled to suppress it, particularly because, as he pointed out, the principal officers of the Topeka government were at that moment actually under arrest for high treason.

But if the logic was on Colonel Sumner's side, the authority was on Jefferson Davis's; a scapegoat was wanted, and the veteran of thirty-seven years' service was at hand. Not unnaturally it was believed by the Free Soil men that Colonel Sumner's expressions of regret in disbanding the Legislature, and his friendliness for the North, were the real reasons for his being given leave, and for the censure passed upon him. A year later, a new Secretary of War was glad to entrust to Sumner the command of an important and successful campaign against the Cheyenne Indians.

The actual dispersal of the Legislature was dramatic. In the absence of the Speaker and the Chief Clerk, Samuel F. Tappan, the Assistant Clerk, called the roll in the House of Representatives on July 4, to which date the Legislature had adjourned on March 4. Seventeen members answered to their names. As Tappan knew there were others in the town, he ordered the sergeant-at-arms to summon the rest. Colonel Sumner then rose and said:

"Gentlemen: This is the most disagreeable duty of my whole life. My orders are to disperse the Legislature, and I am here to tell you that it must not meet, and to see it dispersed. God knows I have no partisan feelings in the matter, and I will have none so long as I hold my present position in Kansas. I have just returned from the border, where I have been driving out bands of Missourians, and now I am ordered here to disperse you. You must disperse. This body cannot be permitted to meet — Disperse. Let me again assure you that this is the most disagreeable duty of my whole life." [60]

He had taken ample military precautions, for he had concentrated at Topeka, on July 3, five companies of his regiment and two pieces of artillery. The proclamation of the acting

Governor was first read to the crowd of about five hundred men, but Colonel Sumner's hope that this would suffice to prevent the meeting of the Legislature was vain; he was forced to march his command into town, draw it up before the building in which the Legislature was meeting, and array it in the face of several Free State volunteer companies. These military manœuvres deeply impressed the crowd, for Colonel Sumner's bearing, like that of his men, was eminently businesslike and soldierly.

As Colonel Sumner rode away, so the Philadelphia *North American's* correspondent reported,

"some one gave 'three cheers for Col. Sumner,' which was responded to. Then there were three hearty cheers for John C. Fremont, three cheers for the Constitution and State Legislature, and just as the dragoons got the word of command, 'march,' three groans were given for Franklin Pierce, and the retreating squadron of dragoons moved off amid the deep groaning for the President."

During all these exciting Topeka happenings, John Brown was not far away. He had remained in hiding on Ottawa Creek, near Palmyra, throughout June, awaiting the recovery of his sick and wounded sons, and gradually recruiting his band.[61] Henry Thompson, in addition to his wound, suffered from bilious fever, and Owen Brown was also a fever victim. The invalid's chief nurse was Lucius Mills, a cousin, and John Brown looked in upon them from time to time, and aided when the country was clear of Border Ruffians and troops. Food they gathered where possible, the Carpenters, Ottawa Jones and other neighbors helping. Not until the beginning of July did John Brown terminate this life in the bush and again become active. On July 2 he boldly entered Lawrence and called upon the *Tribune's* correspondent, William A. Phillips. To him Brown stated that he was on his way to Topeka with his followers, to be on hand at whatever crisis might arise at the opening of the Legislature. "He was not in the habit," Colonel Phillips records, "of subjecting himself to the orders of anybody. He intended to aid the general result, but to do it in his own way." That evening Phillips started with John Brown's company, toward Topeka. They camped in the open, a mile southwest of Big Springs. At two o'clock A. M.

CLOSE QUARTERS AT BLACK JACK

on the 3d, they resumed the march, straight across country, regardless of streams and rough going. At sunrise they reached the Shunga-nung, heard Colonel Sumner's camp bugles, and John Brown halted in the timber by the creek, one of the men going with Phillips into town to bring back word when the company should be needed. "He [Brown] sent messages to one or two of the gentlemen in town, and, as he wrung my hand at parting, urged that we should have the Legislature meet and resist all who should interfere with it, and fight, if necessary, even the United States troops."

Colonel Phillips has left, in the *Atlantic Monthly* for December, 1879, a charming picture of that night ride and the conversation he had with Brown as they lay "bivouacking in the open beneath the stars:"

"He seemed to be as little disposed to sleep as I was, and we talked; or rather he did, for I said little. I found that he was a thorough astronomer; he pointed out the different constellations and their movements. 'Now,' he said, 'it is midnight,' as he pointed to the finger marks of his great clock in the sky. The whispering of the wind on the prairie was full of voices to him, and the stars as they shone in the firmament of God seemed to inspire him. 'How admirable is the symmetry of the heavens; how grand and beautiful! Everything moves in sublime harmony in the government of God. Not so with us poor creatures. If one star is more brilliant than others, it is continually shooting in some erratic way into space.'

"He criticized both parties in Kansas. Of the proslavery men he said that slavery besotted everything, and made men more brutal and coarse; nor did the Free-State men escape his sharp censure. He said that we had many noble and true men, but too many broken-down politicians from the older States, who would rather pass resolutions than act, and who criticized all who did real work. A professional politician, he went on, you never could trust; for even if he had convictions, he was always ready to sacrifice his principles for his advantage. One of the most interesting things in his conversation that night, and one that marked him as a theorist, was his treatment of our forms of social and political life. He thought society ought to be organized on a less selfish basis; for while material interests gained something by the deification of pure selfishness, men and women lost much by it. He said that all great reforms, like the Christian religion, were based on broad, generous, self-sacrificing principles. He condemned the sale of land as a chattel, and thought that there was an infinite number of wrongs to right before society would be what it should be, but that in our country slavery was the 'sum of all villainies,' and its abolition the first essential work. If the American people did not take courage and end it speedily, human freedom and republican liberty would soon be empty names in these United States."

How long John Brown remained at the Willets farm near Topeka, to which he now proceeded, and where he spent the next two or three weeks, is not known. He neither entered Topeka on the fateful July 4, nor immediately thereafter. It is probable that he returned promptly to the neighborhood of his sick sons, more than ever disgusted with Free State leaders and their inability to adopt his view that the way to fight was to "press to close quarters."[62] On July 26, John Brown, Jr., wrote from his Leavenworth prison to his father:

"Am very glad that you have started as all things considered I am convinced you can be of more use where you contemplate going than here. My anxiety for your safe journey is very great. Hope that I shall yet see you all again. Where I shall go, if I get through this is more than I can tell, of one thing I feel sure now, and that is that I shall leave Kansas. I must get away from exciting scenes to some secluded region, or my life will be a failure. . . . The treatment I have received from the Free State party has wearied me of any further desire to coöperate with them. They, as a party, are guided by no principle but *selfishness*, and are withal most arrant *cowards* — they deserve their fate. . . ."[63]

Four days later, John Brown, Jr., wrote to Jason Brown that his father and his party were at Topeka "a few days ago on their way to the States. They were supplied at Topeka with provisions for the trip and by this time I hope they have passed without the limits of the Territory."[64] The party comprised Owen, Oliver, Frederick and Salmon Brown, and their father, Henry Thompson, and Lucius Mills, for whom John Brown had little regard because he had no desire to fight and was content to play the nurse and doctor. Salmon Brown states that they left because Lucius Mills insisted on the invalids' being moved, and because they were a drag on the fighting men. In their hot, primitive quarters, in which the flies were a scourge, Owen had been reduced "almost to a skeleton," and Henry Thompson was not much better off, while Salmon himself was still a cripple. Henry Thompson affirms that he, Oliver, Owen and Salmon had had enough of Kansas. They did not wish to

CLOSE QUARTERS AT BLACK JACK

fight any more. They felt that they had suffered enough, that the service they had been called upon to perform at Pottawatomie squared them with Duty. They were, they thought, entitled to leave further work to other hands. They were sick of fighting and trouble. The burden of Pottawatomie did not, however, weigh upon Salmon; it was as an invalided soldier that he consented to leave. Jason Brown stayed at Osawatomie with his wife. John Brown himself never expressed an opinion as to his sons' resolution or their leaving Kansas.

A heretofore unrelated incident of this journey is now set forth by Salmon Brown. Oliver Brown, a great, stout, strapping fellow, was forbidden by his father to give to Lucius Mills a fine revolver. Says Salmon Brown:

"Oliver wanted to make him a present of a revolver that he [Oliver] had captured at Black Jack. Father objected; forbade Oliver to give Mills the pistol, saying that Mills would never use it. Oliver persisting, Father set out to take the pistol away from him by force. In the scuffle that ensued, I, alarmed lest the weapon might be accidentally discharged, took it out of Oliver's belt, saying: '*Now you fellows fight it out!*' It looked *foolish*, to me. The pistol was Oliver's pistol. And the match was not an equal one. Father had been a strong man in his day, but his prime was past. Oliver was a splendid wrestler. Up in North Elba, he had thrown thirty lumbermen one day, one after the other, in a big 'wrastle.' Father was like a child in his hands. And Oliver was determined. He grabbed Father by the arms and jammed him against the wagon. 'Let go of me!' said Father. 'Not till you agree to behave yourself,' said Oliver. And Father had to let him have his way."[65]

On August 3 and 4, John Brown and those with him were overtaken by a party of Free State men who were marching north to the Nebraska line, to meet James H. Lane's Free State caravan and to protect it from the merciless Kickapoo Rangers, the murderers of Captain R. P. Brown. One of these volunteer guards, Samuel J. Reader, still a resident of Kansas, has transcribed from his journal the following impressions of his meeting with John Brown:[66]

"Between three and four o'clock we formed in marching column, and started forward at a swinging pace. We were all well rested, and a little tired of staying in camp. We had been on the road perhaps an hour or more when someone in front shouted, 'There he is!' Sure enough, it was Brown. Just ahead of us we saw the dingy old wagon-cover, and the two men, and the oxen, plodding slowly onward. Our step was increased to 'quick time;' and as we passed the old man, on either side of the road, we rent the air with cheers. If John Brown ever delighted in the praises of men, his pleasure must have been gratified, as he walked along, enveloped in our shouting column. But I fear he looked upon such things as vainglorious, for if he responded by word or act, I failed to hear it or see it. In passing I looked at him closely. He was rather tall, and lean, with a tanned, weather-beaten aspect in general. He looked like a rough, hard-working old farmer; and I had known several such who pretty closely resembled Brown in many respects. He appeared to be unarmed; but very likely had shooting irons inside the wagon. His face was shaven, and he wore a cotton shirt, partly covered by a vest. His hat was well worn, and his general appearance, dilapidated, dusty and soiled. He turned from his ox team and glanced at our party from time to time as we were passing him. No doubt it was a pleasing sight to him to see men in armed opposition to the Slave Power."

Mr. Reader, on this expedition, on August 7, was an eye-witness of the first meeting between John Brown and a remarkable man who subsequently became one of Brown's most trusted lieutenants, Aaron Dwight Stevens, who at that time went by the name of Captain Whipple, for the good reason that he had escaped from the military prison at Fort Leavenworth while serving a three years' sentence for taking part in a soldiers' mutiny at Don Fernandez de Taos, New Mexico, and resisting the authority of an officer of his regiment, Major G. A. H. Blake, of the First Dragoons.[67]*

John Brown himself did not set foot in Iowa, but turned back at Nebraska City, on the Nebraska boundary, his invalids then being quite safe.[68] "Frederick turned and went back with his father," Henry Thompson testifies. "Frederick felt that Pottawatomie bound him to Kansas. He did not wish to leave. He felt that a great crime had been committed, and that he should go back into Kansas and live it out." It was a decision that cost him his life.

* A myth that this officer was Captain James Longstreet, later the famous Confederate Lieutenant-General, persists in lives of Brown and sketches of A. D. Stevens. Captain Longstreet, at the time of Stevens's trial, was on duty with his regiment, the Eighth Infantry, in Texas, and does not figure in the court-martial

CHAPTER VII

THE FOE IN THE FIELD

AT Nebraska City, John Brown found a notable caravan. Under the erratic James Henry Lane, there had arrived at that point a body of several hundred Free State emigrants, many of whom had attempted to reach Kansas by the usual route of the Missouri River, only to learn that the chivalric Missourians had barred that means of entrance. As early as June 20, 1856, a party of seventy-five men from Chicago, understood to be the vanguard of the "army of the North" which Lane had been raising in Chicago and elsewhere, was forced to give up its arms on the steamer Star of the West, at Lecompton, Missouri, by a mob of Missourians headed by Colonel Joseph Shelby, later a prominent Confederate brigadier. At Kansas City, General Atchison, with another armed force, compelled the Northerners to stay on their boat and return to Illinois, an achievement about which the Border Ruffian press boasted loudly and long.[1] Thereafter parties of Northerners, on the steamers Sultan and Arabia and other river-craft, were similarly driven back, some even being robbed of their possessions.[2] By the 4th of July, the blockade of the river was complete; thereafter the Free State reinforcements were compelled to take the tedious and expensive overland trip from Iowa City, which was in railroad communication with Chicago, to Nebraska City, and thence southward through Nebraska to Kansas. This route was opened by Lane, whose party finally comprised one hundred and twenty-five well-armed single men, and is said by most writers to have numbered, all told, six hundred men, women and children when he reached the Kansas line. There General Lane found it desirable to assume the name of "General Joe Cook." While in the East, General Lane had made a sensation by a most eloquent speech in behalf of Kansas, delivered at Chicago on the 31st of May, 1856.[3] He made full use of the sacking of Lawrence and of the pro-slavery outrages in the Territory, and it was in large part to his eloquence that much of the heavy emigration to Kansas in the summer and fall of 1856 was due. How great his oratorical powers were may be seen from a letter of Thomas Wentworth Higginson, of September 18, 1856, now preserved in the collections of the Kansas Historical Society:

"Last night he [Lane] spoke in a school house; never did I hear such a speech; every sentence like a pistol bullet; such delicacy and lightness of touch; such natural art; such perfect adaptation; not a word, not a gesture, could have been altered; he had every nerve in his audience at the end of his muscles; not a man in the United States could have done it; and the perfect ease of it all, not a glimpse of premeditation or effort; and yet he has slept in his boots every night but two for five weeks."

The opening of the presidential campaign between Frémont and Buchanan, as well as the events in the Territory, kept Kansas in the forefront of national politics. The first Republican National Convention resolved, on June 17, that "Kansas should be immediately admitted as a state of the Union with her present free constitution." [4] The majority of the Howard Committee submitted its report on July 1, with much resultant Congressional discussion of the Kansas situation, and Oliver, the minority of the committee, followed suit on July 11 with his report containing the evidence in regard to the Pottawatomie massacre. Even then, curiously enough, the Pottawatomie affair did not in any degree injure the Free State cause in the North.[5] Oliver himself used it in a speech on July 31,[6] and Toombs, of Georgia, also made a passing reference to it;[7] but no one else in Congress. The Democrats continued to base most of their criticisms upon the general policy of the Free State settlers in taking Sharp's rifles with them to Kansas. The Elections Committee of the House reported against the admission of Whitfield as a delegate and in favor of Reeder; the House on August 1 voted against Whitfield by 110 to 92, and against Reeder by 113 to 88, and thus neither was given a seat.[8] There were various attempts to legislate during the summer. On June 25, Congressman Grow, of Pennsylvania, presented a bill in the House for the admission of Kansas under the Tokepa Constitution, and the House passed it by 99 to 97 on the day before Colonel Sumner dispersed the Topeka Legislature.[9] On July 2 the Senate had passed by 33 to 12 votes the Toombs bill, which had been reported by Senator Douglas from the Committee on Territories, in a form which betrayed clearly the alarm of the slave-power over the injury done its cause by the excesses of its agents in Kansas. The Toombs bill provided for a census of all white males over twenty-one years of age, bona fide residents of the Territory. Those who were thus counted were to be allowed to vote on November 1 for delegates to a Constitutional convention, and due precautions were taken in the bill to guard against fraud, intimidation and election irregularities.

But neither house of Congress would agree to the other's bills, and the final adjournment came without any definite legislation for the relief of Kansas. The House endeavored to embarrass the President by attaching to two appropriation bills riders in the interest of the Free State settlers. One of these was soon dropped, but the other, attached to the Army Appropriation bill by John Sherman, practically forbade the President to use the troops for the purpose of sustaining the bogus Kansas Legislature. As a result, the Army Appropriation bill failed. When Congress adjourned on August 18, a special session was called by the President. It met on August 21, and on August 30 the Army Appropriation bill was passed without the Kansas amendment by a majority of three votes.[10]

More important for Kansas, during this period, was the organization at Buffalo of the National Kansas Committee, with Thaddeus Hyatt, of New York city, as president, in the second week in July. In the six months of its existence this National Kansas Committee forwarded two thousand emigrants by way of the land route of Iowa and Nebraska, and received more than eighty-five thousand dollars in cash, besides gifts of clothing aggregating more than one hundred and ten thousand dollars.[11] By January 25, 1857, the conditions in Kansas had so improved, from the Free State point of view, as to make further activity on the part of the National Committee unnecessary. This record of its Chicago headquarters is, of course, wholly distinct from the even more remarkable record of the New England Emigration Society and the Massachusetts State Kansas Committee.

John Brown made but a short stay at Nebraska City. He took leave of his invalids, obtained horses for himself and his son, and joined a party of thirty men headed by Captain Samuel Walker, and General Lane, upon whose shoulders from now on rested the practical direction of the Free State cause in Kansas, until the release, in September, of the leaders in prison at Leavenworth. As Captain Walker had received a message urging him to return to Lawrence at once, Lane decided that they should push on to that town, one hundred and fifty miles distant, as fast as humanly possible. He rode into Lawrence alone, thirty hours later, arriving at three A. M. of the morning of August 11, all of his companions having dropped by the wayside.[12] Captain Walker rode nearly to Lawrence, but John Brown stopped off at Topeka with about one hundred and twenty miles to his credit.

As to his intercourse with John Brown during their two or three days' journey to Nebraska City and their rapid return, Captain Walker, one of the stoutest of the Free State fighters, has left an interesting record in the shape of a curiously illiterate letter of February 8, 1875, addressed to Judge Hanway, of Lane.[13] In this epistle Walker declares his belief that John Brown was insane during the summer of 1856. Brown would always go off and camp by himself. One morning, when Walker went to wake him, he was asleep, leaning against a tree, with his rifle across his knees. "I put my hand on his shoulder; that moment he was on his feet, his rifle at my breast. I pushed the muzzle up and the ball grazed my shoulder. Thereafter, I never approached Brown when he was sleeping, as it seemed to be his most wakeful time." As they were riding together on the day of this incident, Walker referred to the Pottawatomie murders and frankly told Brown that he would not have them on his conscience for the world. Brown admitted that he was in charge of the murder party and ordered the executions, but averred that he had not raised his hand against any one man. It was on this occasion, Captain Walker states, that Brown charged that the responsibility of the crime rested upon Robinson and Lane as instigators, as already related.* Walker also says that to oblige Brown he took a message to John Brown, Jr., in which

* See page 184.

the father promised to effect his son's rescue on a certain night; and that John Brown, Jr., replied that he wished the senior to stay away, as he was the cause of the son's arrest. The latter did not, Walker averred, then approve of his father's acts, and wished to have nothing to do with him at that time, — a statement absolutely contradicted by the son's letters from prison.*

The arrival of Lane and Brown at Lawrence, to which place the latter soon returned from Topeka, despite his son's earnest protest that he should not expose himself on any account to the danger of arrest, was followed by aggressive warfare on the part of Free State men. On August 5 the Lawrence military companies, together with a few volunteers from Osawatomie, among them August Bondi, had driven out the pro-slavery settlement at New Georgia, on the Marais des Cygnes, not far from Osawatomie.[14] Word of their coming had preceded them, and the Southern colony of from sixty to seventy-five persons fled as the Free State men, at whose head rumor placed the dread John Brown, approached. The victors burned the block-house and such of the abandoned provisions as they could not carry away. To them the settlement was a nuisance; its inhabitants were charged with stealing horses, killing cows, injuring fences and being drunk in the streets of Osawatomie.[15] To the Southerners this was a wicked attack, announcing the beginning of civil war upon unarmed men and women, whose property was wantonly destroyed or stolen, even to the clothes of the children. To the arrival of Lane's army the outrage was attributed in a bellicose proclamation issued at Westport on August 16 by Atchison and B. F. Stringfellow.[16] It is an interesting fact that, if drunkenness was a sin in Missourians, it did not prevent the Captain, Austin, of the Osawatomie company from completely intoxicating himself on the road to this bloodless battle.[17]

"Old Capt. Brown can now be raised from every prairie and thicket," wrote Jason Brown to his sister Ruth on August 13, 1856,[18] after hearing the pro-slavery story that his

* "You and those with you have done nobly and bravely," wrote the son to his father on August 13, 1856. — Original letter in possession of Mrs. John Brown, Jr.

father was in command at New Georgia. Atchison and Stringfellow placed John Brown at the head of the Free Soil men in every skirmish and raid of this month.[19] The New York *Times's* correspondent called him the "terror of all Missouri" and the "old terrifier."[20] O. C. Brown, of Osawatomie, says, "Old John Brown's name was equal to an army with banners."[21] At Paola, seven miles from Osawatomie, a proslavery meeting broke up in the greatest haste on hearing that John Brown was coming to "take out" some men; and the creek over which the invader would have to come was heavily guarded all night by the frightened citizens of Paola.[22] Mary Grant records that once, when a large party of Missourians was returning to its State, the rear ranks called out, by way of joke, "John Brown is coming!" whereupon the van cut the mules from their traces and rode for their lives.[23] It is the opinion of R. G. Elliott, of Lawrence, that:

"Brown was a presence in Kansas and an active presence all through '56. Yet it was his presence more than his activities, that made him a power, — the *idea* of his *being*. He was a ghostly influence. No man in Kansas was more respected. Yet after Pottawatomie he moved much in secret."[24]

"War! War!! War!!! The Bloody Issue Begun! Up Sovereigns! and to your duty! Patience has ceased to be a virtue" — these were the headlines of the Leavenworth *Journal's* extra on August 14, in which it described the next aggressive movement of the Free State forces, the second attack upon Franklin.[25] Despite the lesson taught to the Southerners by the successful raid of June 5, they persisted in living in their Franklin homes. The original motive for this new raid was the desire of Captain Thomas Bickerton's artillery company for a six-pounder known to be at Franklin, which had been originally captured at Lawrence, for which town it had been purchased by Horace Greeley, Charles King, David Dudley Field and other prominent New Yorkers.[26] Part of Captain Bickerton's report of the operations of August 12 is as follows:[27]

"The Franklin affair was kept secret from the people. They thought when they saw us going that we were going out by the church to drill by moonlight. When we got up near to Franklin who

THE FOE IN THE FIELD 231

should come along but this 'Jo Cook,' on horseback, and make himself known to the boys. They were very much elated with seeing Lane. . . . After the taking of the place, our men, I am ashamed to say, were so crazy over the way, in gutting Crane's store, that I could hardly get any of them to help me in taking the cannon out of the blockhouse. . . . The postoffice was not disturbed. . . . I went in only to see if any arms or powder were there. Found no cartridges and only five balls. Got the cannon on the carriage and brought it to Lawrence. . . . I then went to work and made a pattern for a ball; as there was no lead in the place, and we had no way of making them of iron, we had to take [G. W.] Brown's type of the *Herald of Freedom*."

The firing lasted, as usual, for several hours, and the town was not surrendered until a wagon of burning hay was backed up to the block-house. The Free State loss was one killed and six wounded, while three pro-slavery men were severely and one mortally wounded. The sack of Osawatomie was avenged now by the securing of a rare amount of plunder, composed of provisions, guns and ammunition.[28] Major Buford, of the Georgia colonizers, complained in a letter to the Mobile *Tribune* that:

"Our money, books, papers, clothing, surveying instruments, and many precious memorials of kindred and friends far away, were all consumed by the incendiary villains who hold the sway. . . . We are now destitute of everything except our muskets and an unyielding determination to be avenged. . . . Southerners come and help us. Bring each of you a double barrel gun, a brace of Colt's repeaters, and a trusty knife." [29]

The news of the atrocious murder of Major Hoyt on the same day undoubtedly inflamed the Franklin raiders. It made the Free State men everywhere determined to drive out the pro-slavery camps. They assailed, on August 15, "Fort" Saunders, a strong log-house on Washington Creek, about twelve miles southwest of Lawrence. After the customary fusillade, the pro-slavery men retreated without bloodshed on either side.[30] Next on the list was "Fort" Titus, the stronghold of Colonel H. T. Titus, an active pro-slavery leader. It was in order to assault Titus's fort that Captain Bickerton's men desired to recapture the Franklin cannon. There was real fighting at Fort Titus, which Captain Samuel Walker, Captain Joel Grover and a Captain Shombre attacked at sunrise of

August 16 with fifty determined men.* Captain Shombre was killed and nine out of ten men with him wounded in a rush on the block-house.[31] In a short time eighteen out of the remaining forty attackers were wounded, including Captain Walker. After several hours of fighting, Free State reinforcements appeared, including Captain Bickerton with the six-pounder and its slugs made of molten type. It was run to within three hundred yards of the fort and fired nine or ten times. At its first shot its cannoneer cried, "This is the second edition of the *Herald of Freedom!*" As Titus still showed no white flag, a load of hay was again resorted to, and with the same success as at Franklin. As the wagon was backed up to the log-fort, and before the match was applied, the party surrendered. Colonel Titus was discovered badly wounded by a shot fired by Luke F. Parsons, later a devoted follower of John Brown.[32] Walker captured thirteen horses, four hundred guns, a large number of knives and pistols, a "fair stock of provisions" and thirty-four prisoners, six of whom were badly wounded. One dead man was found in the block-house before it was burned to the ground. A Free State man stole a satchel containing fifteen thousand dollars belonging to Titus, but, says Walker, "it did him little good. He died a miserable death in the far West." Everything not burned was appropriated by the Free State men. Colonel Titus himself narrowly escaped with his life. But for Captain Walker he would have been summarily killed on being taken, and but for that same brave, vigorous character he would have been executed at Lawrence, to which place the prisoners were at once removed.

The testimony as to whether John Brown was at Saunders and Titus is conflicting. He himself left no statement bearing upon it, and Luke Parsons, James Blood, O. E. Leonard and others are positive that he was not at either place. The weight of evidence would seem to be on that side. John Brown, after the Wakarusa "war," left Lawrence, saying, "I offered to help you and you would not listen. I will still work with you, but under no commander but old John Brown."[33] Thereafter his

* "Within sight and hearing of the United States camp, where were guarded the treason prisoners." The fight was witnessed by Major Sedgwick's troopers, who failed, however, to interfere. — C. Robinson, *The Kansas Conflict*, p. 307.

THE FOE IN THE FIELD

disposition was to fight only when he was in sole command. Moreover, his remaining at Lawrence during those crowded days after his and Lane's arrival there might easily be explained by his desire to be near his imprisoned son, whose rescue, if possible and advisable, was perhaps the strongest motive for his return to Kansas from Nebraska City.[34] But that John Brown was at Lawrence when Walker arrived with his prisoners admits of no doubt. Again his voice was raised for the extreme penalty; again he asked a sacrifice of blood. As Captain Walker portrays it:

"At a little way out of Lawrence I met a delegation sent by the committee of safety with an order for the immediate delivery of Titus into their hands. Knowing the character of the men I refused to give him up. Our arrival at Lawrence created intense excitement. The citizens swarmed around us, clamoring for the blood of our prisoner. The committee of safety held a meeting and decided that Titus should be hanged, John Brown and other distinguished men urging the measure strongly. At four o'clock in the evening I went before the committee, and said that Titus had surrendered to me; that I had promised him his life, and that I would defend it with my own. I then left the room. Babcock followed me out and asked me if I was fully determined. Being assured that I was, he went back, and the committee by a new vote decided to postpone the hanging indefinitely. I was sure of the support of some 300 good men, and among them Captain Tucker, Captain Harvey, and Captain Stulz. Getting this determined band into line, I approached the house where Titus was confined and entered. Just as I opened the door I heard pistol shots in Titus's room, and rushing in I found a desperado named 'Buckskin' firing over the guard's shoulders at the wounded man as he lay on his cot. It took but one blow from my heavy dragoon pistol to send the villain heels-over-head to the bottom of the stairs. Captain Brown and Doctor Avery were outside haranguing the mob to hang Titus despite my objections. They said I had resisted the committee of safety, and was myself, therefore, a public enemy. The crowd was terribly excited, but the sight of my 300 solid bayonets held them in check."

Colonel Titus was finally saved by Governor Shannon. In his official Executive Minutes of August 18, Governor Shannon has thus recorded the final act of his governorship:[35]

"Governor Shannon this day resigned the office of Governor of the Territory of Kansas, and forwarded his resignation by mail to the President of the United States, having previously visited the town of Lawrence, at the imminent hazard of his life, and effected the release of Col. H. T. Titus and others, who had been forcibly taken there by the armed organization of outlaws whose headquarters are at that place, and who had on the day before battered down with artillery the house of said Col. Titus, robbed his premises of everything valuable, and then burned his house to the ground, killing one of his companions, and taking the remainder, with Col. Titus and their plunder, to their fortified headquarters — Lawrence — at which place said Titus was put on trial for his life, and *sentenced to die;* which sentence would doubtless have been executed, but for the timely interposition of Governor Shannon, who, in consideration of the release of said Titus and his companions, consented to release *five men* held in custody in Lecompton under legal process, charged with being engaged in the late midnight attack and sacking of the town of Franklin — the outlaws having *peremptorily refused* to release said Titus and others, upon his demand as the executive officer of the Territory."

In the course of his farewell speech to the citizens of Lawrence, Governor Shannon promised to deliver over to Major Sedgwick the cannon taken from Lawrence on the 21st of May, and added: "Fellow-citizens of Lawrence, before leaving you I desire to express my earnest desire for your health, happiness and prosperity. Farewell." [36] Governor Shannon in later years returned to Lawrence and settled there, winning the regard and respect of his neighbors and former opponents. Even his old enemy, Dr. Charles Robinson, whose opinions about his former associates were subject to radical changes with the lapse of years, paid him a high tribute after his death. But his record as Governor was not one in which he could righteously take pride.[37] His resignation was not accepted by President Pierce and he was removed from his office,[38] his successor being John W. Geary, who arrived in the Territory on September 9, and remained only six months in this position, resigning on March 20, 1857.

Besides the larger raids already recounted, August was a month of minor warfare. Thus on August 13 the home of the Rev. Martin White was raided by Free State men, among them James H. Holmes, and ten pro-slavery horses were weaned from their allegiance to a wicked and failing cause. White, a prejudiced witness, asserted that the horses were laden with plunder, but on this point the memories of Holmes and Bondi, both participants, failed them.[39] A reprisal was reported by the *Tribune* on August 28, in these words:

THE FOE IN THE FIELD

"On the 22nd the Quaker Mission, on the road from Westport to Lawrence, was attacked by an armed band of Georgians who plundered the place, taking all the horses they could find, and committing all manner of wanton outrages upon persons and property. . . . The inoffensive people were compelled to flee for their lives, their property all stolen or destroyed."

The loss of horses seemed especially grievous to the *Tribune's* Lawrence correspondent, who doubtless had not heard of the exploit at Martin White's.

John Brown's brief period of inactivity in Lawrence came to an end immediately after the exchange of prisoners with Shannon.* According to Bondi, he arrived in Osawatomie, for the first time after the Pottawatomie murders, about August 20, "with a spick and span four-mule team, the wagon loaded with provisions; besides, he was well supplied with money and all contributed by the Northern friends of the Free State Kansas, men like Thaddeus Hyatt." Brown's avowed object was to give the pro-slavery settlements of Linn and Bourbon counties "a taste of the treatment which their Missouri friends would not cease to extend to the Free State settlements of the Marais des Cygnes and Pottawatomie," — a statement by Bondi which again refutes the allegation that the Pottawatomie murders freed that vicinity from interference by the Border Ruffians.

Naturally, as a good general, John Brown's first concern was for the mounts of his men. Bondi avers that some of Brown's men received prompt orders to capture all of "Dutch Henry" Sherman's horses. He himself obtained, when these orders were executed, "a four year old fine bay horse for my mount," and "old John Brown rode a fine blooded bay," while "Dutch Henry" fell back, it is to be presumed, upon Shanks' mare, and, between meditations upon his just punishment for sympathizing with Missouri, doubtless gave thanks that he was still alive. He was shot down in the road —

* The following appeal from Lane was sent to John Brown from Topeka on August 12: "Mr. Brown — *Gen. Joe Cook* wants you to come to Lawrence this night, for we expect to have a fight on Washington Creek. Come to Topeka as soon as possible, and I will pilot you to the place. Yours in Haste, H. Stratton." This Mr. Stratton is one of those who are certain that John Brown commanded the "right wing of cavalry" in the attack on Fort Saunders on August 15. The original of Stratton's message is in the Kansas Historical Society.

as had been many an innocent Free Soiler — by Archie Cransdell, a Free State man, in the presence of James H. Holmes, on March 2, 1857.[40] With Brown came between thirty and forty men, whom he forthwith began to organize into what he called a "regular volunteer force," for the purpose of serving throughout the war under his command. The "Covenant"* drawn up by him under which the men enlisted, together with the first enlistments and the by-laws which were intended to be the articles of war, still exists, and shows that his company organized as if the authority of a State were behind its commander.[41]

Associated with Brown's company was one comprising in part some recently arrived Iowans, "every one mounted on captured pro-slavery horses." John Brown now gave considerable thought to the best way of defending Osawatomie. According to C. G. Allen, one of the men encamped there, Brown desired to meet the enemy at the Marais des Cygnes crossing, to the east of the town, and then to fall back on the twin block-houses. He was certain that the Missourians, rumors of whose approach were already in the air, would come in considerable force if at all, a prognostication eminently correct.[42]

On August 24 the Brown and Cline companies set out for the South, marching eight miles and camping on Sugar Creek, Linn County. That evening John Brown made a speech to his company, in which, according to Bondi, he made these prescriptions for the conduct of his men when on the warpath:

"He wished all of us to understand that we must not molest women or children, nor to take or capture anything useless to use for Free State people; further, never destroy any kind of property wantonly, nor burn any buildings, as Free State people could use them after the Pro-slavery people were driven out; never consider that any captured horses or cattle were anything else but the common property of the Free State army, the horses for military use and the cattle for food for the Free State soldiers and Free State settlers. He ordered, also, that we, his company, should always keep some distance in camp from the Cline Company, as they were too riotous."

* See Appendix.

THE FOE IN THE FIELD

While in camp here, news reached the captains that a large pro-slavery force was in the immediate neighborhood. The Cline company took the lead the next morning, going in one direction, Brown's in another. The luck of running down the enemy came to Captain Cline. He captured some spies and finally reached and charged the camp, taking twelve prisoners and the camp equipage, one of the Missourians being terribly wounded in one leg. In the course of this fight at South Middle Creek, the Free State men released George W. Partridge, of Osawatomie, who had been taken prisoner by the Missouri men the day before. But this rescue was of doubtful value, since he met a violent end but five days later. The Border Ruffians fled in all directions for dear life, shouting that John Brown was pursuing.[43] As part of the Border Ruffians had gone toward Pottawatomie, John Brown and his men went in that direction for a while and then circled back. The next morning, August 26, at daybreak, the two Free State bodies met, Brown charging at the head of his determined company in accordance with his characteristic tactics of seeking close quarters. Fortunately, before an actual collision took place, the friends recognized each other. An eye-witness in Cline's company, Dr. J. W. Winkley, has thus described this incident:

"They came swiftly up over the brow of the hill, in full view, with Brown at their head, and, without halting or even slackening their speed, swung into line of battle. Only thirty men! Yet they presented a truly formidable array. The line was formed two deep, and was stretched out to give the men full room for action. Brown sprang his horse in front of the ranks, waving his long broadsword, and on they came, sweeping down upon us with irresistible fury. . . ."[44]

After exchanging mutual congratulations, both bodies parted again, not, however, until the prisoners had been duly exhorted by John Brown and made to promise that they would not take up arms again, and then set adrift. Dr. Winkley thus recalls some of Brown's earnest and stirring words:[45]

"You are fighting for slavery. You want to make or keep other people slaves. Do you not know that your wicked efforts will end in making slaves of yourselves? You come here to make this a slave

State. You are fighting against liberty, which our Revolutionary fathers fought to establish in this Republic, where all men should be free and equal, with the inalienable rights of life, liberty, and the pursuit of happiness. Therefore, you are traitors to liberty and to your country, of the worst kind, and deserve to be hung to the nearest tree. . . . You we forgive. For, as you yourselves have confessed, we believe it can be said of you that, as was said of them of old, you being without knowledge, 'you know not what you do.' But hereafter you will be without excuse.

"Go in peace. Go home and tell your neighbors and friends of your mistake. We deprive you only of your arms, and do that only lest some of you are not yet converted to the right. We let you go free of punishment this time; but, do we catch you over the border again committing depredations, you must not expect, nor will you receive, any mercy."

John Brown then rode off to raid the pro-slavery settlements on Sugar Creek. By a coincidence, the leader of the Border Ruffian force was named Captain John E. Brown. To his house the anti-slavery Brown paid an early visit, taking as his toll fifty pro-slavery cattle and all the men's clothes the house contained. Captain Brown assured the badly frightened mistress of the house that there was no reason for alarm, — that he never hurt women and children as did her husband, for whom he left his compliments and the message that he had an old score to settle with him.[46] Other houses were similarly searched, and their cattle taken, on the ground that they had originally been Free State before being purloined by the pro-slavery settlers.

On Thursday evening, August 28, Brown reached Osawatomie, travelling slowly because of the one hundred and fifty head of cattle he drove before him. Both his company and Cline's bivouacked in the town that night. The next morning early they divided their plunder and cattle, and Brown moved his camp to the high ground north of Osawatomie, where now stands the State Insane Asylum.[47] It was then known as Crane's ranch. An ordinary commander would have allowed all his men to rest. But not John Brown. He was in the saddle all day, riding with James H. Holmes and others of his men miles along Pottawatomie Creek, whence he crossed to Sugar Creek, returning to Osawatomie with more captured cattle by way of the Fort Scott trail. The locality they rode through bore many evidences of the irregular warfare going on;

THE FOE IN THE FIELD

they passed near the homes of the murdered pro-slavery men and the deserted cabins of Free State settlers. One of Brown's companions, George W. Partridge, passed his own claim, and there saw his aged parents for the last time, all unconscious of the impending and, for him, fatal conflict of the next day. To Holmes, John Brown appeared on that afternoon more than ever the natural leader. He rode a tall and strong chestnut horse; his spare form was more impressive when he was mounted than when he was afoot. Alert and clear-sighted, he ceaselessly watched the landscape for evidences of the enemy.[48]

It was as he was returning thus, in a cloud of dust, and driving the motley herd before him, that he met a party of men galloping toward him. The newcomers turned out to be his son Frederick, Alexander G. Hawes, John Still, George Cutter and a Mr. Adamson, who had been sent down from Lawrence by General Lane with the earnest request that John Brown and the other leading Free State men go at once to Lawrence, to take part in the reorganization of the Free State forces, and also to oppose Atchison, who was then reported about to invade Kansas once more and with a large body of men.[49] After consultation it was decided that the call should be heeded on the next day. As both parties reached Osawatomie, about sundown, John Brown and his son Frederick parted for the last time. The son went on toward Lawrence, but, according to George Cutter, he felt indisposed and decided to spend the night at the house of a settler named Carr, on the Lawrence road, only a couple of hundred yards from the cabin of his uncle, the Rev. Mr. Adair. With Frederick Brown stayed Mr. Hawes. Either at Carr's or in the neighboring Cronkhite house were Still, Cutter and Adamson as lodgers for the night.

John Brown and his party, with the exception of Holmes, who spent the night in town, crossed the Marais des Cygnes to their camp on the Crane claim, taking their cattle with them. Captain Cline and about fifteen men remained in the town, at the juncture of the Marais des Cygnes and the Pottawatomie; here stood the hamlet and its block-house, the latter facing toward the east, from which direction it was feared the Missourians might come. The cry of wolf had, however, been heard in Osawatomie so often, that on the 29th of August no especial apprehension was felt.

Captain Shore and a small company of Chicago men left about three o'clock in the afternoon, bound northward toward Lawrence, and no sentinels were put on guard save by John Brown, in accordance with the articles of enlistment of his company. Two of his men, Bondi and Benjamin, were on guard from two A. M. on the morning of the 30th until the firing began,[50] but they were at a considerable distance from Osawatomie, facing toward Paola to the northeast, from which direction John Brown himself expected that the advance, if any, would be made. Early in the night the long-expected warning came, after nearly every one had gone to bed. John Yelton, a mail-carrier, arrived fresh from a ten days' captivity in the town of New Santa Fé, Missouri, and warned the Greer family that the citizens must prepare either to fight at once or flee. Both Holmes and Dr. Updegraff were sleeping in the house, but were too tired fully to comprehend the warning. Action was therefore deferred until daylight.

Yelton's information was wholly correct. The plan to raid Osawatomie and finally destroy it had carefully matured in the minds of the pro-slavery leaders, but Osawatomie was only one objective of the formidable expedition which left Westport on August 23, and marched on the same day to New Santa Fé. There four hundred and eighty pro-slavery men were found in camp. By the 25th, the number of the Ruffians then being eleven hundred and fifty, they were regularly organized as two regiments, with Atchison as major-general, John W. Reid, a Mexican War veteran, as brigadier-general, and Colonel P. H. Rosser, of Virginia, as colonel of the second regiment, while the first was entrusted to a Colonel Brown. Camp was broken on the 26th. On the 29th, at Bull Creek, forty miles from Osawatomie, General Reid, with two hundred and fifty mounted men and one six-pounder, was detached to proceed to the Abolition settlement. According to a pro-slavery officer, W. Limerick, who wrote to General Shields, of Lexington, Missouri, on the 29th from Bull Creek, the plan was to attack Osawatomie at once:

"It will all be destroyed; we then go to Hickory Point, all the houses in the settlement will be burned; Topeka will share the same fate. We will wait at this place for some 200 or 300 men expected

THE FOE IN THE FIELD

to arrive to-morrow. We are confident of success and expect to clear the whole territory of Abolitionists before our return. . . . I am just informed that Lawrence will be attacked on Sunday next."

General Reid made an all-night march, on leaving Bull Creek, and, taking a leaf out of John Brown's tactics, reached Osawatomie in the early morning. He was too experienced a soldier to enter from the direction from which he would be expected, but passed the town to the south and, after getting well beyond it, went northward until he struck the Lawrence road. He then turned his army again, and just as the light began to glimmer in the east, on the morning of the 30th, reached the high ground above the town, near the Adair, Carr and Cronkhite houses. He thus not only entered from the west, but had the opportunity to charge downhill into the settlement, if he wished to utilize it.

On his way, Reid's men were joined by the Rev. Martin White, as malignant as ever in his hatred of all Free Soil men, and particularly eager to enter Osawatomie in order to recapture some of his stolen horses. Because of his knowledge of the country, White joined the "point" of the advance guard, composed of two or three men. As they came over the crest of the hill, with the Adair cabin to the left of the road and the Carr house to their right, a tall and vigorous man approached them, all unsuspicious of their purpose. It was Frederick Brown, who had risen early to feed the horses, which had been left overnight on the Adair place, preparatory to a prompt start for Lawrence. It is the tradition in Osawatomie that Frederick Brown greeted White in a friendly way. White himself thus told the story to the Kansas (pro-slavery) House of Representatives on February 13 of the next year:

"Whilst I was acting as one of the advance guard coming in contact with their picket guard, Frederick Brown, one of their guard, advanced toward us. We halted and I recognized him and ordered him to 'halt,' but he replied, 'I know you!' and continued to advance towards me. I ordered him a second time to 'halt.' By this time he was getting very close to me, and threw his hand to his revolver; to save my own life I shot him down."[51]

White's first bullet went straight through his victim's heart and Brown tumbled to the ground, — probably without having any thought of violence before consciousness fled forever.

If it was the spell of the Pottawatomie murders which had brought him back to the neighborhood of the dread crimes upon which he had gazed helpless, between a sense of wrong and fidelity to his dominating father, he had now paid in full for his participation as an accessory. Certain it is that Frederick Brown was no more prepared for his sudden end than were the men whose blood had been shed by John Brown's orders, that there might be remission of sin for the Border Ruffians. White pretended to recognize the boots on Brown as a pair stolen from his son in the raid upon White; but there is no evidence to show that Frederick Brown was at that time elsewhere than in Lawrence. On January 1, 1860, White wrote to the Bates County, Missouri, *Standard:* "The same day I shot Fred, I would have shot the last devil of the gang that was in the attack on my house, if I had known them and got the chance," — a truly Christian sentiment for a minister of the gospel.

The pretence that he saw in Frederick Brown a picket of the enemy was obviously an afterthought of White's. There was no sign of any stirring as the two men met, and the next few developments certainly dispel the theory that the laws of war were being followed. The shot that killed Brown was heard both at the Adair and Carr houses, as well as the noise of horses' feet as the advance guard passed on toward the town. As the Rev. Mr. Adair came hurriedly out of his house, he met David Garrison, a relative and a settler in that vicinity, who had slept in a shed in the rear of the Adair cabin. They hurried to the road, and, looking down it, Garrison asked: "What is that lying on the road?" Adair thought it a blanket — only to find it was the body of his nephew Frederick. As they stood over the corpse, some of the others, Cutter and Hawes among them, arrived from the Carr house. Adair hurried westward to see if any one else was coming, and quickly perceived the head of the main column of Reid's forces, now steadily approaching. He hurried back, shouting to the others to save themselves. Adair safely reached his own cabin, gave a warning, and then hid in the bushes unharmed until his children found him and notified him that he might return. No such good fortune attended the others. Garrison, Hawes and Cutter made the mistake of returning to Carr's, where they were

THE FOE IN THE FIELD

speedily seen and pursued into the brush. Hawes miraculously escaped without injury, the Border Ruffians almost riding over him. Cutter, being overtaken after exchanging shots with his pursuers, received in his head and body four charges of buckshot. Leaving him for a moment, the Ruffians followed the unarmed Garrison, and overhauled and summarily despatched him. Returning to Cutter, one of the Ruffians dismounted, kicked him, turned him over and said: "He breathes; if I only had another charge in my gun, I would put it in his head. I guess that would fix him." Fortunately for Cutter, the Missourian could not make his revolver work, and so rode off saying: "Let him rip, he will die fast enough!" — Such was humanity in Kansas on the 30th of August, 1856! Despite thirty distinct wounds, Cutter survived his terrible experience, Hawes bringing him aid and food as soon as the Ruffians disappeared.

Had Reid's men now galloped directly into the village, which was but a mile and a half away, they would have been in complete control before any one could have slipped away. Instead, his men delayed on the ridge, perhaps for breakfast, and the news of their coming and of the death of Frederick Brown was carried into the town by Charles Adair, a mere boy, who galloped in. A messenger at once crossed the river to alarm John Brown. The first to take the aggressive were Dr. Updegraff and Holmes. The latter, who was saddling up when the news came, rode up toward the Adairs' until he sighted the Border Ruffians, upon whom he fired three times from his Sharp's rifle. This incident again checked the advance and gave the Free State men time to rally to the defence. Brown himself was preparing breakfast as the news of his son's death reached him. He seized his arms, cried, "Men, come on!" and with Luke F. Parsons hurried downhill to the crossing nearest the town. The others delayed to finish their coffee, but most of them overtook their leader as he reached the town. On their way John Brown asked: "Parsons, were you ever under fire?" "I replied, 'No,'" relates Parsons, "'no, but I will obey orders. Tell me what you want me to do.'" To which Brown answered with the well-known sentence, "Take more care to end life well than to live long." With this sentiment on his lips, the grim chieftain of the "volunteer regulars" entered the engagement which gave him more renown than anything save the climax of his career; from this time forward it was as "Old Osawatomie Brown" that he was most generally known.

As they reached the block-house, Brown said: "Parsons, take ten men and go into that block-house and hold your positions as long as you can. I'll take the rest of the men, go into the timber and annoy them from the flank." This Parsons did, finding in the block-house Spencer Kellogg Brown, son of O. C. Brown, the founder of the town, a lad fourteen years old, of rare pluck and daring disposition, who, being allowed to go and get a rifle, returned with it in a few minutes. From the second story, Parsons's men saw the Border Ruffians coming in two long lines with their brass cannon. One of them cried, "We cannot stay here, they will drive us out." When Parsons and Austin took their places in the second story to study the situation, their men all decamped to join Brown. Following them, Parsons met Captain Cline and his company of fifteen well-mounted men retiring through the town, abandoning their cattle and other plunder. Only four days previously, this little band, then considerably larger, had gallantly charged the Border Ruffians on South Middle Creek. On this particular morning, Captain Cline could not be induced to stay very long on the line of battle; one of his men, Theodore Parker Powers, was killed in the few minutes they were at the front. Captain Cline explained to the *Tribune* [52] that his men did not retire until they ran out of ammunition. In any event, their disappearance weakened the Free State force not a little. Parsons and Austin found that Brown had skilfully hidden his men behind the trees and brush in the fringe of timber along the Marais des Cygnes, which ran nearly parallel to the road down which the Missourians were coming. There is to-day still a fringe of timber along the river, and still the open space across which the opposing forces fired at each other.

The Border Ruffians were mounted and in the open. When the shots from the Free State men struck among them, the agitation caused by wounded men or horses threw the companies into confusion, which they at first tried to correct by re-forming under fire. As the firing grew hotter, more men

THE OSAWATOMIE BATTLEFIELD
Looking toward the river

PART OF THE BLACK JACK BATTLEFIELD

THE FOE IN THE FIELD

joined John Brown, among them Alexander Hawes, undeterred by his narrow escape when Garrison and Cutter were shot. As each man came under his eye, Brown placed him behind a tree or a rock, but the leader himself walked up and down, encouraging the others and bidding them make their fire effective. His son Jason was near him most of the time. Once Brown stopped and asked Parsons if he could see anything torn or bloody upon his back. "No, Captain, I cannot," replied Parsons. "Well, something hit me a terrible rap on the back," said Brown; "I don't intend to be shot in the back if I can help it."

It is not probable that, all told, John Brown had more than thirty-eight or forty men in line, aside from Cline's force. He himself said about thirty. They held their ground well, even after Reid brought his cannon into play. His grape-shot went too high into the trees, bringing down branches and adding to the discomfort of the Free Soil men, but not actually injuring anybody. Next, the Border Ruffians dismounted, and, urged by General Reid, who waved his sword and shouted loudly, advanced toward the woods. At once Brown's men began to retreat, following the stream and keeping in the protection of the timber until they had gone some distance down toward the saw-mill. When they were on the bank, all suddenly turned as if an order had been given and jumped into the river. It was the Border Ruffians' opportunity. In a skirmish or in real warfare, to have an unfordable river at one's back is the worst of tactics. For this John Brown must not be censured, since it was the only place where he could have made a stand, unless he had chosen to fight in the settlement itself and risked the lives of the women and children there.

But if Brown was not to blame for this strategy, the consequences of it were serious, in that George Partridge was killed in the river. Holmes saved his life miraculously by diving when under heavy fire. Parsons and Austin narrowly escaped Partridge's fate, Austin by hiding between some logs near the saw-mill, and shooting a Border Ruffian out of his saddle. Dr. Updegraff, who had been badly wounded in the thigh, managed to escape. George Grant had time to notice that John Brown, as he waded the river, cut a "queer figure, in a broad straw hat and a white linen duster, his old coat-tails floating outspread upon the water and a revolver held high in each hand, over his head." Jason Brown, too, remembers the generalissimo's linen duster; he, like his father, got safely across. The fourteen-year-old soldier, Spencer K. Brown, fell into the enemy's hands, as did Robert Reynolds, H. K. Thomas and Charles Kaiser. The latter, a veteran of a European revolution, fought to the last on the edge of the river before yielding to a relentless enemy. William B. Fuller, a settler, was captured before the fight began, and Joseph H. Morey later in the day.

In later years, General Reid insisted that there was no battle at Osawatomie, — "merely the driving out of a flock of quail."[53] But after the quail had crossed the river, there was still mischief for Reid to do. He fired a round or two at the blockhouse before all of Brown's men were out of range and hearing, and then, when there was no reply, his Ruffians began the work of reducing Osawatomie to ashes. This was done despite General Reid's protest. If he had held his men bravely to their work in the hour's fighting with Brown, he was unequal now to saving the twenty-five to thirty houses and stores, that were plundered and then burned. O. C. Brown's safe was robbed of one hundred and twenty-five dollars, after which the torch was applied to his house. Three bags full of mail, which the warning mail-carrier, John Yelton, had brought, were cut open and their contents examined and flung to the winds. The horses and cattle at hand were gathered up and carried off, including Cline's booty from South Middle Creek. The saw-mill of the Emigrant Aid Society was not harmed, because, it is said, a single man, Freeman Austin, opened such a brisk fire on the Border Ruffians as they approached, that they retired in haste.

By ten o'clock of that evening, General Reid's command was back at the Bull Creek camp. On the next day he made the following official report of his enterprise:

CAMP BULL CREEK, Aug. 31.

GENTLEMEN: — I moved with 250 men on the Abolition fort and town of Osawattomie — the headquarters of Old Brown — on night before last; marched 40 miles and attacked the town without dismounting the men about sunrise on yesterday. We had a brisk fight for an hour or more and had five men wounded — none dan-

THE FOE IN THE FIELD

gerously — Capt. Boice, William Gordon and three others. We killed about thirty of them, among the number, *certain*, a son of Old Brown, and almost certain Brown himself; destroyed all their ammunition and provisions, and the boys would burn the town to the ground. *I could not help it.*

We must be supported by our friends. We still want more men and ammunition, ammunition of all sorts. Powder, muskets, balls and caps is the constant cry.

I write in great haste, as I have been in saddle, rode 100 miles, and fought a battle without rest.

Your friend,

REID.[54]

A joint letter of Congrave Jackson and G. B. M. Maughas, "Capt. of Company B," dated at Bull Creek, September 1, gives another pro-slavery view of the fight:

"The enemy commenced firing on us at half a mile, which is point blank range for Sharp's Rifles. They had taken cover under a thick growth of underwood and numbered about 150. We charged upon them, having to march 800 yards across an open prairie, against an unseen foe, through a hail-storm of rifle bullets. This was done with a coolness and ability unsurpassed, until we got within 50 yards of them when we commenced a galling fire, which together with some telling rounds of grape from our cannon, soon drove them from their hiding place with a loss of some 20 or 30 men killed. We had lost not a single man, and had only five or six wounded."[55]

The report of the death of John Brown persisted for only a few days. That it was believed, or hoped for, in St. Louis a week later, appears from the following editorial in the St. Louis *Morning Herald* of September 6, 1856, which declared that because of Pottawatomie, "by far the most atrocious and inexcusable outrage yet perpetrated in that distracted Territory, . . . his death and the destruction of his family would, for that reason, be less a matter of regret even with men of the humanest feeling."

Brown made no attempt to rally his force after it was driven across the Marais des Cygnes. It was too scattered to make that possible. Indeed, Bondi, Benjamin and Hawes set off at once for Lawrence, and so, by himself, did Holmes. John Brown and Jason spent a good part of the day searching for a ford above the town by which they might cross to the Adair house. But before they set out to reach their relatives and find the dead body of their son and brother, Frederick, they stood on the bank above the river and watched the smoke and flames of burning Osawatomie. "God sees it," said John Brown, according to Jason, as he watched this spectacle, the tears rolling down his face. "I have only a short time to live — only one death to die, and I will die fighting for this cause. There will be no more peace in this land until slavery is done for. I will give them something else to do than to extend slave territory. I will carry the war into Africa."

If the Border Ruffians were at sea in their estimate of the loss of life they had inflicted, John Brown was still further from the mark in his report of General Reid's casualties. This appears from his letter of September 7 to his family:

LAWRENCE K T 7th Sept 1856

DEAR WIFE & CHILDREN EVERY ONE I have one moment to write to you to say that I am yet alive that Jason, & family were well yesterday John; & family I hear are well; he being yet a prisoner. On the morning of the 30th Aug an attack was made by the ruffians on Osawatomie numbering some 400 by whose scouts our dear Fredk was shot dead without warning he supposing them to be Free State men as near as we can learn. One other man a Cousin of Mr. Adair was murdered by them about the same time that Fredk was killed & one badly wounded at the same time. At this time I was about 3 miles off where I had some 14 or 15 men over night that I had just enlisted to serve under me as regulars. These I collected as well as I could with some 12 or 15 more & in about $\frac{3}{4}$ of an Hour attacked them from a wood with thick undergrowth. with this force we threw them into confusion for about 15 or 20 minuets during which time we killed & wounded from 70 to 80 of the enemy *as they say* & then we escaped as well as we could with one killed while escaping; Two or Three wounded; & as many more missing. Four or Five Free-State men were butchered during the day in all. Jason fought bravely by my side during the fight & escaped with me he being unhurt. I was struck by a partly spent Grape, Canister, or Rifle shot which bruised me some, but did not injure me seriously. "Hitherto the Lord hath helped me" notwithstanding my afflictions. Things seem rather quiet just now; but what another Hour will bring I cannot say. I have seen Three or Four letters from Ruth & one from Watson, of July or Aug which are all I have seen since in June. I was very glad to hear once more from you & hope that you will continue to write to some of the friends so that I may hear from you. I am utterly unable to write you for most of the time. May the God of our fathers bless & save you all

Your Affectionate Husband & Father,

JOHN BROWN.

THE FOE IN THE FIELD

MONDAY MORNING, 8th Sept. 56

Jason has just come in Left all well as usual. Johns trial is to come off or commence today. Yours ever

JOHN BROWN.[56]

Subsequently, John Brown thus summarized the results of the fight for Lydia Maria Child:

Border Ruffian force at Osawatomie Aug. 30th 400 men.
Free State force 30 men.
Ruffians (as by their private account 31 or 32) killed, & from 45 to 50 wounded.
Loss of Free State men in the fight one killed & 2 wounded Free Statemen murdered Four; & one left for dead with twenty shot & bullet holes. One proslavery man murdered by themselves.
Your friend

JOHN BROWN.[57]

The pro-slavery man reported murdered was named William Williams, said to have been a "Free State Missourian," whom neither party claimed; his name is not on the Osawatomie monument. He was killed in the town before the Border Ruffians left. As to the loss of the latter, there is no evidence to show in contemporary accounts or newspapers that it was as heavy as Brown himself thought. He prepared for the press, on the same day that he wrote the above letter, a more elaborate story of the battle, which in no wise differed from the letter in any of its facts. It is a concise and excellently written narrative, one of the best products of his pen. In it he thus explains his plan in taking his men into the timber:

"As I had no means of learning correctly the force of the enemy, I placed twelve of the recruits in a log-house hoping we might be able to defend the town. I then gathered some fifteen more men together, whom we armed with guns, and we started in the direction of the enemy. After going a few rods we could see them approaching the town in line of battle, about half a mile off, upon a hill west of the village. I then gave up all idea of doing more than to annoy, from the timber near the town, into which we were all retreated, and which was filled with a thick growth of underbrush; but I had no time to recall the twelve men in the log-house, and so lost their assistance in the fight. At the point above named I met with Captain Cline, a very active young man, who had with him some twelve or fifteen mounted men, and persuaded him to go with us into the timber, on the southern shore of the Osage, or Marais des Cygnes, a little to the northwest from the village."[58]

It would seem from the above that John Brown was not aware that the men from the block-house joined his line. Yet he must have known that Parsons and Austin joined him. This confusion may account for his underestimate of the men who, from their own narratives and those of others, are known to have fought with him in the timber. As for the prisoners, Charles Kaiser met the same cruel fate as did Dow, Major Hoyt, Hoppe and the long list of those murdered in cold blood by the Border Ruffians. Two days after his capture, on September 1, after the army of Atchison had retreated to Cedar Creek, he was taken out and shot to death, — first having been told, it is said, to run for his life. This cowardly murder is assigned by one of the prisoners as a reason why the Border Ruffian force, the command of which was resigned by General Atchison to General Reid on the same day, began to melt away.[59] Spencer Kellogg Brown, the boy prisoner, was set free by the Border Ruffians, only to die, if anything, more tragically than Kaiser. After having been a useful Federal spy, he was caught by the Confederates and hanged in Richmond on September 25, 1863, when but twenty-one years old.[60] The other four prisoners were sent down the Missouri River on the Polar Star, under pain of death if they returned to Kansas. At St. Louis they were permitted to go their way.

The news of Brown's defeat and the burning of Osawatomie intensified an altogether critical situation in Kansas. The acting Governor, Woodson, was openly pro-slavery; it was his proclamation of August 25, declaring Kansas to be "in a state of open insurrection and rebellion," and calling on all good citizens to put down the "large bodies of armed men, many of whom have just arrived from the States," which gave Atchison and Reid's army the excuse to masquerade once more as Kansas militia, or assistants to the legally constituted authorities. That they were a large body of armed men, all of whom had just arrived from another State, did not in the least excite Mr. Woodson's distrust. Three days after the battle of Osawatomie, on September 5, he even went so far as to order Lieut.-Col. Cooke, of the United States Dragoons, to proceed at once to Topeka, to invest the town and disarm and arrest "all the insurrectionists or aggressive invaders against the organized government" to be found at or near Topeka, and to retain them as prisoners. He was especially ordered to level all their breastworks, forts or fortifications, to the ground, and to intercept all armed persons coming over "Lane's trail" from the Nebraska line to Topeka.[61] Naturally, Lieut.-Col. Cooke declined to obey so extraordinary and partisan an order, for which decision he was subsequently highly commended by the Secretary of War. Jefferson Davis, however, was so greatly wrought up over the situation in the Territory on September 3, that "the position of the insurgents" seemed to him "open rebellion against the laws and constitutional authorities, with such manifestation of a purpose to spread devastation over the land, as no longer justifies further hesitation or indulgence." In thus expressing himself to General Smith, he added that "patriotism and humanity alike require that rebellion should be promptly crushed. . . ." To this end, General Smith was notified that the President had ordered the organization of the Kansas militia; that the general was to ask for as much of this force as he needed for the work of pacification, and, if he could not get sufficient aid from this source, he was authorized to call upon the Governors of Kentucky and Illinois for the two regiments of foot militia requisitioned that same day by President Pierce from each State, in accordance with his constitutional rights.[62] An excellent regiment of regular infantry, the Sixth, had already been sent to the Territory as a reinforcement to the First Cavalry and Second Dragoons. As it turned out, the Territory could raise only a few companies of bona fide militia for General Smith, but a sudden change in events made it unnecessary for him to ask for more troops, or to call on the Illinois and Kentucky executives.

General Smith himself, in explaining, under date of September 10, to the War Department how it was that Osawatomie was sacked when there were regulars in the vicinity, reported that Brown had had thirteen men killed, and bluntly added, "though there is nothing to regret as to those who suffered, yet the act was a grossly unlawful act, and deprives those who took part in it of all consideration for the future." Their consideration in the near future was already the problem of Lieut.-Col. Cooke; for Reid's force, after retiring to Missouri, was again being recruited for a fresh and final attack on Lawrence. Meanwhile, the Free State men were Cooke's immediate care. Lane, still pretending to be "Joe Cook," had made a weak effort to pursue Reid, but had fallen back just as he arrived within striking distance. Then, on learning that Marshal Donaldson and two deputies, supported by bands of bogus militia, were raiding Free State homes with warrants for the owners, and burning their houses if the owners were absent, Lane and Colonel Harvey decided to march upon Lecompton, make an armed demonstration, and demand the release of the newest prisoners and of those who had been arrested in August for complicity in the raid on Franklin.

After some marching and counter-marching, a force from Lawrence under Lane — who had concealed himself in the ranks — and Captain Samuel Walker arrived at Lecompton on September 5, late in the afternoon. Lieut.-Col. Cooke instantly ordered out his regiment, took up a position between Walker's men and the town, and notified Walker that he could fight that day only with United States troops.[63] For this privilege the Free State men were not thirsting; but, with the aid of the veteran dragoon colonel, they accomplished the release of the prisoners. Woodson had already decided to let them go, but his order, not yet executed, was now put into force. As the Missouri militia had been dismissed by Woodson that morning and had almost all left, Lieut.-Col. Cooke greatly regretted the appearance of Lane's men; he assured them that "everything was going in their favor, and that it apparently would be so if they would refrain entirely from reprisals, or any outrages, return to their occupations, and show moderation." [64]

This good advice the Free State men refused to take. On returning to Lawrence, they found it full of refugees from Leavenworth, where William Phillips, the Free State lawyer who was tarred and feathered in May, 1855, had been deliberately murdered on September 2, as a result of the election for mayor. From elsewhere in the Territory the law-abiding and the lawless were also moving into Lawrence, and to all of them the refugees from Leavenworth, with their stories of the shooting of Phillips in his own house, of murders and other out-

THE FOE IN THE FIELD

rages along the roads, and the driving out of hundreds of defenceless women and children, made a strong appeal. At a council of war on September 7, Lane, Harvey and other officers and men of the Free State forces decided to march on Leavenworth. This council was interrupted by the cheering on the streets with which John Brown's arrival in Lawrence was greeted. Henry Reisner, of Topeka, an eye-witness, remembers distinctly Brown's impassive demeanor and his bent figure on his gray horse, with his gun across the saddle before him. The uproar of cheering was, he says, "as great as if the President had come to town, but John Brown seemed not to hear it and paid not the slightest attention." [65] Brown brought with him his sick adherent, Luke F. Parsons, and was followed the next day by his son Jason. When asked where he had been since his retreat under Reid's fire across the Marais des Cygnes at Osawatomie, he related that he had encamped on the Hauser farm, two and a half miles from Osawatomie, for about a week, at first attempting to fortify it. But the lack of men and the illness of Parsons and others prevented.[66]

From there Jason Brown and his father both went to their friend Ottawa Jones, on Ottawa Creek, where they saw the ruins of his home. Jones, who was an educated Indian, with a New England woman for his wife, had befriended and helped to feed John Brown and his party while they were in the brush before and after Black Jack. No other charge could have been brought against him than friendliness for Free State people; but a part of Atchison's army, guided by Henry Sherman,* not only destroyed the house the evening of the battle at Osawatomie, but robbed Mrs. Jones of everything valuable. Not content with that, they partially cut the throat of a helpless man, Nathaniel Parker, who was ill in an upstairs room, and threw him over the bank of the creek.

It is easy to imagine John Brown's indignation at this outrage; but there was nothing to be accomplished now south of Lawrence, and so, placing Parsons in a wagon, he had driven

---

* "Henry Sherman led the mob that burnt Ottawa Jones's house last summer and tried to kill Jones." — Rev. S. L. Adair to Mr. and Mrs. S. C. Davis, Osawatomie, March 4, 1857. — Original in possession of Mrs. S. C. Davis.

with him to Lawrence. After Brown's arrival, the Sunday morning council reassembled and decided on the movement against Leavenworth. Most of the men thereupon offered the command to John Brown,— a responsibility he declined out of deference to the other leaders; and it was then entrusted to Colonel James A. Harvey. With two companies, Harvey marched on Easton and Alexandria, in Leavenworth County, helped himself to pro-slavery provisions in the now approved fashion, and then captured a small company of pro-slavery men on Slough Creek, near what is now Oskaloosa. John Brown did not accompany the command, which never reached Leavenworth; it was recalled by a message from Lane, advising the abandonment of the object because of the arrival of the new Governor, John W. Geary. Almost simultaneously with Harvey's movements, Charles Whipple, better known as Aaron D. Stevens, raided Osawkee, a pro-slavery settlement, taking eighty horses and nearly as many arms. Stevens was now colonel of the "Second Regiment Kansas Volunteers." "We in Kansas," he wrote to his brother about this time, "have struggled against every species of oppression that the wickedness of man invented or the power of the Devil ever enforced."[67] Carrying off eighty pro-slavery horses was in his eyes no wrong; the United States marshal, Donaldson, thought differently, and seven days after the raid, on September 17, he arrested twelve of Whipple's men.[68] Four of them, including John H. Kagi, who met his end at Harper's Ferry under Brown, were committed by Judge Cato for highway robbery, — an action they doubtless described as another Border Ruffian outrage. "What in thunder," wrote Charles F. Gilman, a Council Grove, Kansas, leader, on hearing of some of these Free State raids, "is Missouri doing; is she going to let these miserable, thieving, lying Nigger-Stealers and horsewhipping scamps take this fine Territory without striking a blow for its deliverance?"[69]

September 10 witnessed the reunion of John Brown with his long imprisoned son and namesake, the political prisoners being then freed. John Brown, Jr., who had never even been indicted, was released on one thousand dollars bail, and hurried at once to Lawrence. "This evening," wrote the correspondent of the New York *Times*, "large numbers assembled in front of General Lane's headquarters, where they were addressed by Judge Smith, the Rev. Dr. Nute, E. B. Whitman, Governor Robinson, General Lane and John Brown. The meeting was one of the most enthusiastic and heart-cheering of any that has ever been held in Kansas." [70] John Brown, Jr., brought his chains, worn bright by long use, with him; they were subsequently forwarded to Henry Ward Beecher as a souvenir of Bleeding Kansas. But a better era than the Territory had yet known was now ushered in with the arrival of John W. Geary, the new Governor. He reached Lecompton from Leavenworth at about the same time that the Lawrence jubilation over the release of the prisoners was at an end. The next day he issued a reassuring address to the people, and two excellent proclamations, which, like his first report of September 9 to Secretary Marcy, show how clearly he grasped the actual situation.[71] In his address he urged that Kansas begin anew; that the past be buried in oblivion.

"Men of the North — men of the South — of the East and of the West *in Kansas* — you, and you alone," he said, "have the remedies in your own hands. Will you not suspend fratricidal strife? Will you not cease to regard each other as enemies, and look upon one another as the children of a common mother, and come and reason together?"

The blame for the situation he placed upon "men outside of the Territory, who . . . have endeavored to stir up internal strife, and to array brother against brother." In his first proclamation he ordered the complete disbandment of the pro-slavery militia; in the other he ordered the formation of a new body, which he intended should be composed of bona fide settlers, and be mustered by his order into the service of the United States. His policy was, first of all, to stop all lawlessness and guerrilla warfare, and in this he was soon successful. He was as bitter against the pro-slavery murderers of Leavenworth as against the Abolition marauders of the Whipple type, and became, as time went on, more and more favorable to the Free State side, with the result that he finally resigned office for the reason that the Buchanan administration, alienated by his friendliness to the Northern side, withdrew from him its support.

One of the immediate blessings of Governor Geary's arrival was the prompt disappearance from the scene of General Lane. He left for Nebraska at once, with a small band, stopping on the way, however, to attack some pro-slavery raiders. Finding them well barricaded in log-cabins at Hickory Point, Lane sent back to Topeka for reinforcements. Whipple and fifty men responded, but on their arrival, Lane wanted Captain Bickerton's cannon and sent to Lawrence for them. Colonel Harvey, just in from Slough Creek, and about two hundred men responded, and arrived at Hickory Point on Sunday morning, September 14. Meanwhile, General Lane abandoned the siege on hearing of Governor Geary's proclamations. As Harvey's men came straight across country, contrary to orders, they missed both Lane and Whipple. Nevertheless, they at once attacked the pro-slavery force, and after several hours of fighting captured it, killing one and wounding four, and having five wounded on their side.[72] Both sides fraternized, agreed to retire without plunder, and then separated. But Harvey's Nemesis was at hand in the person of the Captain T. J. Wood already referred to, who appeared on the scene that night with two troops of the First Cavalry and a deputy marshal, with whom he had been searching for Whipple's band. Harvey escaped, but Captain Wood returned to Lecompton with one hundred and one prisoners and such of their arms as he could find, including the cannon. The prisoners were shown no favors, were all kept in confinement for some time, and, after enduring genuine hardships, were tried at the October term. The majority were acquitted; a number received sentences at hard labor, with ball and chain, for periods of from five to ten years. With the men of Whipple's force and others, there were now one hundred and eighteen Free State men awaiting trial at one time, — quite enough to serve as a vigorous deterrent to the other Free Soilers. John Brown might easily have shared their fate. Those sentenced did not, however, remain in jail long; they had all escaped or been pardoned by the following March. But Captain Wood's great haul was a stunning blow to Free State lawlessness.

Governor Geary made his first visit to Lawrence on September 13. News having been received by him that pro-slavery

THE FOE IN THE FIELD

forces were threatening the town, he routed out Lieut.-Col. Cooke's troops in the early morning of September 13.[73] Four hundred soldiers left at 2.20 A. M., the governor going with them, and they arrived at Lawrence at sunrise to find everything quiet. Three hundred Missourians had, however, been seen the day before, and Governor Geary had received a communication from General Heiskell, announcing that in response to acting Governor Woodson he was on Mission Creek with eight hundred men, "ready for duty and impatient to act." Governor Geary found between two and three hundred men in Lawrence and, being well received, addressed them earnestly and then conversed at length with Governor Robinson and other leaders, upon whom he made a favorable impression. John Brown was not at these gatherings. By nine o'clock the Governor and the troops left on their return to Lecompton, the citizens giving three hearty cheers for Governor Geary and Lieut.-Col. Cooke as they rode away. The very next evening, on September 14, Geary again ordered all of Lieut.-Col. Cooke's troops to Lawrence in hot haste, to prevent an impending collision.[74] They left at once under Lieut.-Col. Joseph E. Johnston, First Cavalry, later the distinguished Confederate general. The next morning Lieut.-Col. Cooke and Governor Geary followed. This time it had been no cry of wolf. Atchison, Reid, Heiskell, Stringfellow, Whitfield and the other Missouri leaders had arrived at Franklin, determined on a final attempt to conquer Kansas by force of arms. They had with them no less than twenty-seven hundred men, some of them completely uniformed and well equipped. Besides infantry and cavalry there was a six-pounder battery, — in all a remarkably strong force. Its advance guard had come in sight of the men on guard at Lawrence on the afternoon of the 14th, and after an hour's shooting at long range, the Missourians had retired on Franklin. Naturally, the people of Lawrence were in great alarm; few were able to sleep that night, remembering as they did Atchison's last visit to their town. There was, therefore, general rejoicing when, on the next morning, Lieut.-Col. Johnston's troops were found to be encamped on Mount Oread, the hill overlooking Lawrence, where they had arrived during the night.

The town of Lawrence was at this time a strange mixture of "stone houses, log cabins, frame buildings, shake shanties and other nondescript erections," so wrote Colonel Richard J. Hinton in his journal on September 3.[75] He added:

"Lawrence presents a sad picture of the evils this partizan warfare is bringing over us. Buildings half finished or deserted are now occupied as quarters for the small army of devoted men who are fighting the battle of Freedom. Trade is at a standstill. Work is not thought of, and the street is full of the eager, anxious citizens who cluster eagerly around every new-comer, drinking in greedily the news, which generally is exaggerated by the fears or imagination of those who tell it. To a stranger, it seems a wild confusion, and however much they may desire, the incidents come in so fast that it is morally impossible to form a just estimate of the true condition of things."

The defenders of this straggling town had erected some fortifications, of which they were very proud, a stone "fort" of the remains of the Free State Hotel, and four earthworks which excited the risibles of Lieut.-Col. Cooke and his officers, — "ridiculous attempts at defences," Cooke officially called them, "which I could ride over." But the day before Lieut.-Col. Johnston's arrival, these amateur fortifications were filled with very earnest Free Soil men, ready to defend Lawrence at any cost. In the absence of Lane, the command was as much in the hands of Major J. B. Abbott and Captain Joseph Cracklin, of the "Stubbs," as of any one else. Some partisans of John Brown have attempted to prove that he was in command, but the evidence is conclusive that he declined Major Abbott's offer of the command of a company, and then, at his request, went from one of the "forts" to another, encouraging the men, urging them to fire low, and giving them such military information as was his, everywhere, according to Major Abbott, with excellent results.[76] Other men who were in the forts that day, when Captain Cracklin and his "Stubbs" returned the long range fire of the Border Ruffians, have testified to the value of Brown's presence, and the inspiration he gave them. To a group of citizens in the main street he made the following address, standing on a dry-goods box:

"Gentlemen — It is said there are twenty-five hundred Missourians down at Franklin, and that they will be here in two hours.

THE FOE IN THE FIELD 259

You can see for yourselves the smoke they are making by setting fire to the houses in that town. This is probably the last opportunity you will have of seeing a fight, so that you had better do your best. If they should come up and attack us, don't yell and make a great noise, but remain perfectly silent and still. Wait till they get within twenty-five yards of you, get a good object, be sure you see the hind sight of your gun, then fire. A great deal of powder and lead and very precious time is wasted by shooting too high. You had better aim at their legs than at their heads. In either case, be sure of the hind sight of your gun. It is for this reason that I myself have so many times escaped, for, if all the bullets which have ever been aimed at me had hit me I would have been as full of holes as a riddle." [77]

Fortunately for all concerned, the worth of the forts and the mettle of their defenders were never tested. The aggressive and active Governor rode into town with Lieut.-Col. Cooke at ten on the morning of the 15th. They found that Lieut.-Col. Johnston had distributed his men in strong positions on the outskirts of the town. Scarcely stopping to confer with that officer, Cooke and Geary pushed right on to meet a Missourian mounted company then in plain sight, not two miles away. This company at once constituted itself a guard of honor for the colonel and the Governor. At Franklin the pro-slavery generals and chief officers were called together in a large room "and very ably and effectively addressed by Governor Geary" — so Cooke reported. After some inflammatory speeches from the other side, the veteran dragoon himself addressed the assembly, urging them,

"as an old resident of Kansas and friend to the Missourians to submit to the patriotic demand that they should return, assuring them of my perfect confidence in the inflexible justice of the Governor, and that it would become my painful duty to sustain him at the cannon's mouth. Authority prevailed, and the militia honorably submitted to march off, to be disbanded at their place of rendezvous."

It would have been well, however, if some of Cooke's men had supervised this withdrawal. He himself went back to Lawrence with the Governor and calmed the greatly excited town, while Governor Geary again addressed the principal men. They bivouacked with the troops, who slept under arms after two night marches with scant provisions. The next day, Cooke and the Governor returned to Lecompton, following the trail of the notorious Kickapoo Rangers. Some of these men had burned the saw-mill near Franklin, "lifted" horses and cattle, and mortally wounded David C. Buffum, for refusing to give up the horse with which he was ploughing. Governor Geary insisted on Judge Cato's taking the dying man's deposition, and, to his credit be it said, made every effort, though with little success, to have the murderer punished, the pro-slavery judges giving no assistance.[78]

Thus ended the last organized Missourian invasion of Kansas, and for a time thereafter the Territory was at peace, particularly as Lieut.-Cols. Cooke and Johnston were active in capturing armed Free Soil men coming in from Iowa. They took prisoners on October 9, for instance, two hundred and twenty-three armed immigrants, headed by S. C. Pomeroy, Colonel Eldredge and others.[79] By November 12 the Governor of Kansas announced to General Smith, commanding the Department of the West, that peace prevailed throughout the Territory, for which fact Governor Geary deserves great credit. In consideration of these conditions and of the approach of winter, all the regular troops, with the exception of two companies, returned to their regular stations.[80]

The disbandment of Atchison's army was a fatal blow to the hopes of the Missourians, and in the South generally it was now beginning to be understood that the battle for Kansas was rapidly being lost. Even before Atchison's disbandment, an intelligent South Carolinian, member of the Territorial militia, writing home in a moment of anger at the release of the Free State prisoners in the presence of Lane's and Harvey's men at Lecompton, blurted out the truth about the uselessness of those Southerners remaining who had come merely to battle:

"And why should we remain? We cannot *fight*, and of course cannot prevent our enemy from voting. The object of our mission will then, of course, be defeated, and we had as well return. Whichever way the Kansas question be decided, 't is my opinion, and the opinion with all with whom I have conversed, that a dissolution of the Union will be effected by it. The Abolitionists themselves say they 'will have Kansas if it splits the Union into a thousand pieces.'"[81]

THE FOE IN THE FIELD

Not even the abstention of the Free State men from the election of October 6 for delegate to Congress, for members of the Legislature, and on the question of a Constitutional convention, and the consequent election of Whitfield and other pro-slavery men, raised any genuine hopes in the hearts of the slavery leaders.

The restoration of peace, the release of his son and the approach of winter were the reasons why John Brown decided to leave Kansas for the East in search of rest and additional funds to carry on the war for freedom. He had never meant to be a settler, and there was nothing left to take him or his sons back to Osawatomie. Their cabins, such as they were, had been destroyed, and with them all their personal property, and the books of John Brown, Jr., upon which he placed a value of three hundred dollars. This son thought that to preserve his reason he must return to a placid life and quiet scenes.[82] John Brown himself, suffering from the prevailing dysentery and chills and fever, was compelled to leave in a wagon. He wrote to his family, however, that he would return to Kansas if the troubles continued.[83] With him into Iowa went his three sons, John, Jason and Owen, while his two daughters-in-law and their little sons took the river route, now open to Free Soil traffic of this kind.

On departing from the Territory, Brown left the remainder of his Osawatomie "volunteer-regular" company under the command of James H. Holmes, with instructions to "carry the war into Africa." This Holmes did by raiding into Missouri and appropriating some horses and arms and other property, for which he was promptly and properly indicted and long pursued by the Kansas and Missouri authorities.[84] By October 10, John Brown and his sons were safely at Tabor, after a very narrow escape from the vigilant Lieut.-Col. Cooke, who, reporting on October 7 from a "camp near Nebraska boundary," wrote: "I arrived here yesterday, at noon. I just missed the arrest of the notorious Osawatomie outlaw, Brown. The night before, having ascertained that after dark he had stopped for the night at a house six miles from the camp, I sent a party who found at 12 o'clock that he had gone."[85] Evidently, Lieut.-Col. Cooke was not aware of Osawatomie Brown's presence at Lawrence when he was there; nor did he know of the "outlaw's" other narrow escapes from capture. One of these incidents of the return from Kansas is thus related by Jason Brown:

"We crossed the river at Topeka. We had a four-mule team, and a one-horse covered wagon. The mule team was full of arms and ammunition that father was taking out to Tabor. I cannot remember just now the name of the driver, but he was a man who was always faithful to us and had stuck to us right through. In the covered, one-horse team was a fugitive slave, covered over with hay, father, lying sick, Owen, John and I. Owen, John and I walked all we could to save the horse. At New Holton we came out on a high prairie and saw the U. S. troops — a large body — encamped on the stream below. When John and I saw that, we thought we had fallen into a trap. 'We'll go right down there,' said father. 'If we do,' said John, 'we'll be captured. I for one won't go.' 'I, for another, won't go,' said I. So father drove right on down, and camped *just outside* their pickets, that night. But before he got within two miles of that camp of troops, John and I left him, — it was dark — and walked about six or eight miles — I am not sure of the distance — around — and met father next morning, about sunrise on the Nebraska road. Owen, as always, stuck with father. For a time we and father travelled different roads and did not meet. We finally got both wagons together at the ferry at Nebraska City and camped. Next morning we crossed the river, by rope ferry, into the southwest corner of Iowa. When we landed we let the contraband out from the hay, fixed him up the best we could, and travelled on to Tabor. There Owen stopped, and the negro there found work. John and I had the horse to go to Iowa City with. We rode and tied, to that point, where the railway began."[86]

Before leaving Lawrence, John Brown received two letters from Charles Robinson, both of them of special interest because of the Governor's subsequent attacks upon Brown in the never-ending and extremely bitter controversy as to whether Brown or Lane or Robinson was the real saviour of Kansas:

LAWRENCE, Sept. 15, 1856.

CAPT. JOHN BROWN: MY DEAR SIR:— I take this opportunity to express to you my sincere gratification that the late report that you were among the killed at the battle of Osawatomie is incorrect.

Your course, so far as I have been informed, has been such as to merit the highest praise from every patriot, and I cheerfully accord to you my heartfelt thanks for your prompt, efficient and timely action against the invaders of our rights and the murderers of our citizens. History will give your name a proud place on her pages, and posterity will pay homage to your heroism in the cause of God and Humanity.

Trusting that you will conclude to remain in Kansas and serve during the war the cause you have done so much to sustain, and with earnest prayers for your health and protection from the shafts of Death that so thickly beset your path, I subscribe myself,

Very respectfully
Your Ob't Servant
C. ROBINSON.[87]

The other letter, dated earlier, reads as follows:

LAWRENCE, Sept 13, '56

CAPT. BROWN
DEAR SIR

Gov Geary has been here and *talks very well*. He promises to protect us, etc., etc. There will be no attempt to arrest anyone for a few days, and I think no attempt to arrest you is contemplated by him. He talks of letting the past be forgotten so far as may be and of commencing anew.

If convenient can you not come into town and see us. I will then tell you all that the Gov. said and talk of some other matters.

Very respectfully
C. ROBINSON [88]

On the back of this note is a pencilled memorandum of John Brown, Jr., to his father, which includes among other advice these words: "Don't go into that secret military refugee plan talked of by Robinson, I beg of you." Over this letter and sentence there was a vitriolic controversy between John Brown, Jr., and Governor Robinson in 1883 and 1884, the former insisting that at the private meeting requested, the Governor asked Brown to undertake the kidnapping of the leading pro-slavery generals, and the doing away of others in Pottawatomie fashion, and that his father replied: "If you know of any job of that sort that needs to be done, I advise you to do it yourself." [89] No one else has publicly accused Governor Robinson of sinking quite to the depths of urging deliberate assassination, and it is needless to say that he indignantly denied the charge. Those who would decide where the truth lies must make up their minds which man's word was the weightier.

Free from any other blood-stain, John Brown quitted the ravaged Territory. If he had deliberately committed the

Pottawatomie murders in order to embroil Kansans and Missourians, he had every reason to view with satisfaction the results of his bloody deed. The carnival of crime and the civil war inaugurated by the sacking of Lawrence and the midnight assassinations in the hitherto peaceful region of Osawatomie, had brought eastern Kansas to the lowest state of her fortunes. Governor Geary accurately portrayed it in his farewell to the people of Kansas on March 12 of the next year:

"I reached Kansas and entered upon the discharge of my official duties in the most gloomy hour of her history. Desolation and ruin reigned on every hand; homes and firesides were deserted; the smoke of burning dwellings darkened the atmosphere; women and children, driven from their habitations, wandered over the prairies and among the woodland, or sought refuge and protection even among the Indian tribes; the highways were infested with numerous predatory bands, and the towns were fortified and garrisoned by armies of conflicting partisans, each excited almost to frenzy, and determined upon mutual extermination. Such was, without exaggeration, the condition of the Territory at the period of my arrival." [90]

Between November 1, 1855, and December 1, 1856, about two hundred people are known to have lost their lives in the anarchical conditions that prevailed, and the property loss in this period is officially set down at not less than two millions of dollars, one half of which was sustained by bona fide settlers, the larger portion falling on the Free State emigrants.[91] However superior in character and intelligence and industry the latter indubitably were in the beginning, there was but little to choose between the Border Ruffians and the Kansas Ruffians in midsummer of 1856. The Whipples and Harveys and Browns plundered and robbed as freely on one side as did the Martin Whites, the Reids and the Tituses on the other, and there was not the slightest difference in their methods. Both sides respected women; but in remorseless killing of individuals, the Border Ruffians were guilty of a savagery that would place them far below the scale of the Free Soil men, were it not for the massacre on the Pottawatomie. If the Eastern press discreetly refused to believe a single Free State outrage, or to portray raids like those on Franklin in their true colors, the pro-slavery partisans met every charge with the allegation that it was an "Abolition lie." In the eyes of New England,

Reid's taking the lives of Free Soil men at Osawatomie was "butchery," while the exterminating of Border Ruffians was merely "killing," — as John Brown phrased these incidents in his story of that fight. Probably no one in the East in October, 1856, realized the utter demoralization of the Free State men, or the violence and lawlessness of their methods. For this ignorance the excitement of the Presidential campaign, which resulted in Frémont's defeat, may have been in part responsible. To many of the radical Abolitionists in the East, the bloodshed in Kansas was a plain indication that slavery could hereafter be ended only by the bayonet.[92]

It is, of course, undeniable that the Border Ruffian outrages in Kansas enormously aroused the North on the slavery question and prepared the way for the tremendous outburst of excitement or anger over the Harper's Ferry raid. But it is idle to assert that Kansas would never have been free, had it not weltered in blood in 1856; if the Sharp's rifle policy had not been followed. Climate and soil fought in Kansas on the side of the Free State men. The Southerners themselves complained that their settlers who did reach Kansas were inoculated with the virus of liberty, became Free Soilers and often freed their slaves.[93] The familiar slave crops never could have been raised in Kansas with its bleak winters. Moreover, the South was never a colonizing section; the history of the settlement of our Western communities proves this, if the fate of Buford's band and its inability to settle down anywhere did not. The final failure of the slave-power to hold the great advantage it had in Kansas in 1855 was not due to fear of weapons, but to inability to place farmers and pioneers on the battle-ground. The wave of emigrants from the East was from the beginning certain to roll over the Kansas plains, even if it had not been expedited by the Emigrant Aid Societies, to whom due credit for hastening the turning of the tide must be given.

Equally certain is it that no one man decided the fate of Kansas. In this narrative no effort has been made to estimate the relative values to Kansas of Eli Thayer, the founder of the Emigrant Aid movement, or of Charles Robinson, or of James H. Lane, or of Brown. It would be an invidious undertaking; to enter into the bitter disputes of the partisan followers of

Robinson, Lane and Brown is a task which no historian would attempt unless compelled by his theme to do so. Their adulators have forgotten that properly to understand and estimate the forces brought into play in Kansas, one must fairly go back to the foundation of our government. The irrepressible conflict between freedom and slavery would have gone on and come to a head had Kansas never been thrown open to settlement, and that Territory must have been free had there been no Lane and no Robinson and no John Brown. The great nation-stirring movement of which they were a part can best be likened to a glacier; for decades it moved imperceptibly; suddenly the people it overshadowed awoke to the fact that their very existence was threatened by this monstrous mass of prejudice and wrong and crime.

Of John Brown, as he left Kansas after just a year of activity, with the most important period of his service to the Territory behind him, it may truthfully be said that his deeds, good and evil, had appealed strongly to the imagination of all who read of him sympathetically. Like a relentless Highland chieftain of old, he appeared to personify indomitable, unswerving resistance to the forces of slavery. To those Free Soilers who believed in the argumentative methods of the Old Testament, his name was henceforth one to conjure with. Not in his methods, however, but in his uncompromising hostility to that human bondage for which he was ready to sacrifice his life, lies his undoubted claim to a place in the history of Kansas and of the Nation.

CHAPTER VIII

NEW FRIENDS FOR OLD VISIONS

At Tabor, Iowa, John Brown, weak and ill, met with a hearty reception at the hands of that colony of Ohioans. Under the leadership of George B. Gaston, for four years a missionary among the Pawnee Indians, and the Rev. John Todd, there had been founded at Tabor, in 1848, a community which was intended to be another Oberlin.[1] Most of its settlers came from that earnestly religious and bravely anti-slavery town. They were steeped in its Abolition views and in sympathy with its protests against hyper-Calvinism, — in short, brought with them the Oberlin devotion to truth and liberty. It was the most congenial soil upon which John Brown had set foot since his departure from Ohio. Here all men and women thought his own thoughts and spoke his own words. Though it was then but a straggling prairie town of twenty-five houses, with little of the present beauty of its wide and richly shaded streets, Tabor was ever an attractive haven for John Brown and his sons. On the overland route into Kansas, it was far enough from the Territory to be free from disorder, and the arriving and departing emigrant trains gave it an especial interest and kept it in touch with the storm-centre of the nation. News from Kansas came regularly, while the scattered pro-slavery sympathizers in the neighborhood, who acted as spies for the Missourians, or those who passed through *en route* to the Territory, added zest to the town's life, particularly when the Southern visitors were in search of the slaves who passed on to safety and freedom by the underground route. This long counted Tabor one of its important far Western stations.

Mrs. Gaston has left the following account of conditions in Tabor during the time of John Brown's visit:

"That summer and autumn our houses, before too full, were much overfilled, and our comforts shared with those passing to and from Kansas to secure it to *Freedom*. When houses would hold no more, woodsheds were temporized for bedrooms, where the sick and dying were cared for. Barns also were fixed for sleeping rooms. Every place where a bed could be put or a blanket thrown down was at once so occupied. There were comers and goers all times of day or night — meals at all hours —many free hotels, perhaps entertaining angels unawares. *After* battles they were here for rest —*before* for preparation. General Lane once stayed three weeks secretly while it was reported abroad that he was back in Indiana for recruits and supplies, which came ere long, consisting of all kinds of provisions, Sharps rifles, powder and lead. A cannon packed in corn made its way through the enemy's lines, and ammunition of all kinds in clothing and kitchen furniture, etc., etc. Our cellars contained barrels of powder and boxes of rifles. Often our chairs, tables, beds and such places were covered with what weapons every one carried about him, so that if one *needed* and got time to rest a little in the day time, we had to remove the Kansas furniture, or rest with loaded revolvers, cartridge boxes and bowie knives piled around them, and boxes of swords under the bed."[2]

Here John Brown stayed about a week after his arrival from Kansas. Here he stored the arms he had brought with him, and this place he chose as the coming headquarters of the band of one hundred "volunteer-regulars" for whom he now planned to raise funds in the East to the amount of twenty thousand dollars, and here actual training for war-service against the forces of slavery was soon to begin. For this was the plan which John Brown's brain had now formulated. The peace of Geary he did not value; indeed, he unjustly denounced the Governor at this period as having been unpardonably slow in reaching Lawrence with the Federal troops, when that town was menaced by Atchison and Reid. He wanted a secret unpaid force that would subsist as best it might between periods of activity, but be ready with rifle, pistol and sword to come together to repel invasion, or even to undertake a counter-invasion. If he rightly judged that hostilities between the two contending parties in Kansas were not yet over, he overestimated the likelihood of a fresh outbreak when the spring should come again. By then he hoped to return to Kansas with plenty of arms and ammunition, and recruit the men he wanted.

After his brief stay for recuperation, John Brown set out over the overland route to Chicago by way of Iowa City and Springdale, arriving there about the 22d or 23d of October

MAIN STREET OF TABOR, IOWA

THE PUBLIC SQUARE AT TABOR

NEW FRIENDS FOR OLD VISIONS

with his sons, Jason and John Brown, Jr., who had preceded him from Tabor. The father reported at once at the offices of the National Kansas Committee, where his presence aroused great interest. He was soon asked to accompany the train of "freight" for the Free State cause then being conducted through Iowa to Kansas by Dr. J. P. Root, in order to advise that leader.

"Capt. Brown," wrote General J. D. Webster to Dr. Root on October 25, "says the immediate introduction of the supplies is not of much consequence compared to the danger of *losing* them." On the next day, Horace White, then assistant secretary of the National Kansas Committee, later editor of the Chicago *Tribune* and New York *Evening Post*, wrote to him this note:[3]

OFFICE NATIONAL KANSAS COMMITTEE,
CHICAGO, Oct. 26, 1856.

CAPTAIN BROWN, — We expect Mr. Arny, our General Agent just from Kansas to be in tomorrow morning. He has been in the territory particularly to ascertain the condition of certain affairs for our information. I know he will very much regret not having seen you. If it is not absolutely essential for you to go on tonight, I would recommend you to wait & see him. I shall confer with Col. Dickey on this point.

Rev. Theodore Parker of Boston is at the Briggs House, & wishes very much to see you.
Yours truly,
HORACE WHITE, *Assist. Sec., etc.*

If you wish one or two of those rifles, please call at our office between 3 & 5 this afternoon, or between 7 & 8 this evening.
W.

It is the testimony of Salmon Brown that his father did turn back and return to Tabor in the wake of the Root train. This had a special interest for him, because with it went his two sons Salmon and Watson, who had received, when digging potatoes at North Elba, the news of the battle of Osawatomie, and of a speech by Martin White boasting of his having killed Frederick Brown. The next morning they were on their way back to Kansas for the avowed purpose of killing White, Salmon going to the Territory for the second time, Watson for the first.[4] Assisted by Gerrit Smith, Frederick Douglass and other friends (to whom naturally they did not reveal their exact errand), they reached Chicago, where Mr. White gave them each a Sharp's rifle, and then joined Dr. Root's party. With it they unwittingly passed their father in Iowa, as he was bound to Chicago. At St. Charles, Iowa, Watson wrote on October 30 to North Elba that the train travelled very slowly, and that he had heard a report that his father had gone East.[5] John Brown, on learning in Chicago of their whereabouts, at once communicated with his son Owen, who had remained at Tabor, urging him to stop the younger sons there until he could arrive. Owen delivered the message, and Watson awaited his father's arrival, Salmon pushing on to carry out his plan. When he reached Topeka, he heard and credited a false story of Martin White's death, and returned to his Uncle Jeremiah Brown's at Hudson, Ohio, by the aid of a cavalry horse bought from the hanger-on of a camp of the natural enemies of the Brown family, — some regular cavalry, — without, however, a perfect title to the mount.

At Tabor, Dr. Root's train deposited its arms and gave up the attempt to enter Kansas. Curiously enough, there were in its wagons the two hundred rifles which John Brown and his men subsequently took to Harper's Ferry. The Rev. John Todd's cellar was filled with boxes of clothing, ammunition, these two hundred rifles, sabres and a brass cannon, for the whole of that winter of 1856–57. With his son Watson, John Brown soon left Tabor. They "rode and tied across Iowa on a big mule and got to Ohio two weeks after I did," writes Salmon Brown, whose cavalry steed had carried him eastward in phenomenally short time. John Brown stopped again in Chicago, early in December, arriving in Ohio after an absence of over fifteen months.* He was not content, however, to linger with his relatives in Hudson; he pushed on to Albany, Rochester and Peterboro.

---

* It was probably at this time that John Brown, visiting his half-sister, Mrs. S. C. Davis, in Grafton, Ohio, made a characteristic reply to Mrs. Davis's question: "John, is n't it dreadful that Frémont should have been defeated and such a man as Buchanan put into office!"

"Well, truly," answered Brown, "as I look at it now, I see that it was the right thing. If Frémont had been elected, the people would have settled right down and made no further effort. Now they know they must work if they want to save a free State." — Statement of Mrs. S. C. Davis, Kalamazoo, Mich., November 24, 1909, to K. Mayo.

NEW FRIENDS FOR OLD VISIONS 271

But his overweening desire to obtain men, weapons and supplies for Kansas left him no time for his Adirondack home. Just after the New Year he arrived in Boston, and there began a series of friendships which became of the greatest value to him during the remainder of his life. Here he met for the first time Frank B. Sanborn, ever afterward his most ardent Massachusetts friend and defender, who was then acting as a secretary of the Massachusetts State Kansas Committee. Sanborn, then but a year and a half out of Harvard, was on fire for the anti-slavery cause, and ready to worship any of its militant leaders. John Brown, fresh from the Kansas battlefields, made a deep impression upon this young Concord school-master, who had turned over his scholars to a Harvard student while he worked for Kansas. On January 5, Sanborn thus recorded his first impressions of his life's hero to Mr. Thomas Wentworth Higginson, the fighting young Unitarian parson of Worcester:

"'Old Brown' of Kansas is now in Boston, with one of his sons, working for an object in which you will heartily sympathize—raising and arming a company of men for the future protection of Kansas. He wishes to raise $30,000 to arm and equip a company such as he thinks he can raise this present winter, but he will, as I understand him, take what money he can raise and use it as far as it will go. Can you not come to Boston tomorrow or next day and see Capt. Brown? If not, please indicate when you will be in Worcester, so he can see you. I like the man from what I have seen — and his deeds ought to bear witness for him."[6]

To Mr. Sanborn, John Brown brought a personal letter of introduction from a relative in Springfield, Massachusetts, and a general one from Governor Salmon P. Chase, of Ohio, based on Charles Robinson's letter of commendation, and dated December 20, 1856.* At once Mr. Sanborn took him to Dr. Samuel G. Howe and Theodore Parker. Patrick Tracy Jackson, the treasurer of the Massachusetts State Kansas Committee, George L. Stearns, Amos A. Lawrence, Dr. Samuel Cabot, Jr., Judge Thomas Russell, Wendell Phillips and William Lloyd Garrison were some of the other friends Brown made. Mr. Garrison he met one Sunday evening in January at Theodore Parker's. They were at oppo-

* Governor Chase gave Brown twenty-five dollars on this occasion.

site poles of thought in their methods of dealing with slavery. Mr. Garrison, a non-resistant, could conceive no situation in which it was right to take up arms, — "carnal weapons," as he often called them, — while Brown was all impatience with men who only talked and would not shoot. The debate lasted until late in the evening. Mr. Garrison, it has been recorded,

"saw in the famous Kansas chieftain a tall, spare, farmer-like man, with head disproportionately small, and that inflexible mouth which as yet no beard concealed. They discussed peace and nonresistance together, Brown quoting the Old Testament against Garrison's citations from the New, and Parker from time to time injecting a bit of Lexington into the controversy, which attracted a small group of interested listeners."[7]

Mr. Parker soon became one of five men who grouped themselves as an informal committee to aid Brown in whatever attacks he might make on slavery, though Mr. Parker was not certain that Brown's general plan for attacking the hated institution would be successful. "I doubt," he said, "whether things of this kind will succeed. But we shall make a great many failures before we discover the right way of getting at it. This may as well be one of them."[8] When the final blow was struck, no one wrote more vigorously in Brown's support than did Theodore Parker.

George Luther Stearns, a successful merchant of Boston and an exceptionally public-spirited man, became, as he himself put it, "strongly impressed" with Brown's "sagacity, courage, and strong integrity," and thereafter practically put his purse at Brown's disposal.[9] He and Gerrit Smith gave to him more liberally than any one else, as will hereafter appear, and their homes were always open to him. It was on Sunday, January 11, 1857, that Brown first entered the hospitable Stearns mansion, entertaining the family at table with an account of Black Jack, grimly humorous.[10] To Mr. Stearns he gave his views of the Kansas chieftains, Pomeroy, Robinson, etc., exalting Martin F. Conway as the best of the political leaders, but characterizing him as lacking in force. The memory of that dinner is still kept green in the Stearns family; its immediate effect was a determination on Mr. Stearns's part to do everything in his power to get Brown the arms and money he desired.

NEW FRIENDS FOR OLD VISIONS 273

Amos A. Lawrence, who had known Brown when he was in Springfield in the wool business, records in his diary on January 7: "Captain Brown, the old partisan hero of Kansas warfare, came to see me. I had a long talk with him. He is a calm, temperate and pious man, but when roused he is a dreadful foe. He appears about sixty years old."[11] In view of Mr. Lawrence's complete change of opinion in regard to Brown in later years, it is interesting to note that he about this time characterized Brown as the "Miles Standish of Kansas."

"His severe simplicity of habits," Mr. Lawrence continued, "his determined energy, his heroic courage in the time of trial, all based on a deep religious faith, make him a true representative of the Puritanic warrior. I knew him before he went to Kansas and have known more of him since, and should esteem the loss of his service, from poverty, or any other cause, almost irreparable."[12]

This opinion Mr. Lawrence was also willing to back with his money. He offered to be

"one of ten, or a smaller number, to pay a thousand dollars per annum till the admission of Kansas into the Union, for the purpose of supporting John Brown's family and keeping the proposed company in the field."

This record of the impression made by John Brown upon those whom he met about this time would not be complete without a quotation from Henry D. Thoreau, in whose house at Concord Brown saw, in March, Ralph Waldo Emerson. It was eminently characteristic of the strength of Brown's personality, and of the vigor of his mentality, that he should have made both of these men his devoted adherents. Like Theodore Parker's, their support of him became of enormous value in 1859, in shaping the judgment of the time upon John Brown. In his eloquent 'Plea for Captain John Brown,' Thoreau thus describes Brown as he found him in 1857:[13]

"A man of rare common-sense and directness of speech, as of action; a transcendentalist above all, a man of ideas and principles, — that was what distinguished him. Not yielding to a whim or transient impulse, but carrying out the purpose of a life. I noticed that he did not overstate anything, but spoke within bounds. I remember, particularly, how, in his speech here, he referred to what his family had suffered in Kansas, without ever giving the least vent to his pent-up fire. It was a volcano with an ordinary chimney-flue. Also, referring to the deeds of certain Border Ruffians, he said, rapidly paring away his speech, like an experienced soldier, keeping a reserve of force and meaning, 'They had a perfect right to be hung.' He was not in the least a rhetorician, was not talking to Buncombe or his constituents anywhere, had no need to invent anything, but to tell the simple truth, and communicate his own resolution; therefore he appeared incomparably strong, and eloquence in Congress and elsewhere seemed to me at a discount. It was like the speeches of Cromwell compared with those of an ordinary king."

It must not be forgotten, in this connection, that very little was known in Boston at this time about the Pottawatomie murders, and still less about John Brown's connection with them. Frank Preston Stearns, the biographer of his father, states that the latter never knew of John Brown's connection with the crime,[14] and it may well be that Theodore Parker and others passed off the scene without a full realization of the connection between the Harper's Ferry leader and the tragedy of May 24, 1856. To none of these new-found friends did Brown at this period communicate his Virginia plan. He kept it to himself a year longer; but he did not conceal from some of them his desire to defend Kansas by raiding in Missouri, or by attacking slavery at some other vulnerable point. With the general idea they were, like Theodore Parker, in accord, but not sufficiently interested to ask for details, so abounding was the faith in himself which the mere appearance of the man created.

John Brown's first practical encouragement came on January 7, when the Massachusetts State Kansas Committee, of which Stearns was chairman, voluntarily voted to give him the two hundred Sharp's rifles, together with four thousand ball cartridges and thirty-one thousand percussion caps, then in the Rev. John Todd's cellar at Tabor.[15] These arms Brown was glad to obtain, because of their nearness to the scene of action; he was to take possession of them as the agent of the committee, and, more than that, was authorized to draw on the treasurer, Mr. P. T. Jackson, for not less than five hundred dollars for expenses. The only conditions were that these rifles were to be held subject to the order of the committee, and that Brown was to report from time

NEW FRIENDS FOR OLD VISIONS

to time the condition of the property and the disposition made of it, "so far as it is proper to do so." Subsequently (April 15, 1857), Brown was authorized to sell one hundred of these rifles to Free State settlers in Kansas for not less than fifteen dollars each, and to apply the proceeds to relieve the suffering inhabitants of the Territory.[16] These weapons, originally purchased by Dr. Cabot, under instructions voted on September 10, were first intended to be "loaned to actual settlers for defence against unlawful aggressions upon their rights and liberties."[17] Afterwards, there arose a misunderstanding as to the ownership of these arms between the State Committee, the National Committee and the Central Committee for Kansas at Lawrence, which was finally straightened out by the National Committee's relinquishment of all claim to the rifles, just as the Massachusetts Committee was about to proceed legally for their recovery.

It was at the Astor House in New York that the National Kansas Committee met on Saturday, January 24, for the session at which the rifles were returned to the original donors. John Brown applied for them, but, as Horace White subsequently testified, there was a good deal of opposition to the policy of granting him arms.[18] Twelve boxes of selected clothing, sufficient for sixty persons, were given to him, but the question of the rifles was settled by transferring them to the Massachusetts Committee, on motion of Mr. Sanborn. A resolution appropriating five thousand dollars for John Brown was violently opposed by those who were against giving him the rifles; they felt that he was too radical and violent to be trusted with such a sum, and that he would, if given it, disburse it in ways the Committee might not sanction.[19] The Secretary of the National Committee, H. B. Hurd, recorded in 1860 that he asked Brown before the Committee: "If you get the arms and money you desire, will you invade Missouri or any slave territory?" To which he [Brown] replied:

"I am no adventurer. You all know me. You are acquainted with my history. You know what I have done in Kansas. I do not expose my plans. No one knows them but myself, except perhaps one. I will not be interrogated; if you wish to give me anything I want you to give it freely. I have no other purpose but to serve the cause of liberty."[20]

While the reply was not satisfactory so far as the rifles in question were concerned, the Committee did vote five thousand dollars "in aid of Capt. John Brown in any *defensive* measures that may become necessary." He was authorized to draw five hundred dollars whenever he wished it, but it is interesting to note that he never obtained more than one hundred and fifty dollars, and that not until the summer of 1857, the Committee having no more to give. How this failure rankled in Brown's mind appears in his letter of April 3, 1857, to William Barnes, of Albany, who yet preserves the original: "*I am prepared to expect nothing but bad faith from the National Kansas Committee at Chicago, as I will show you hereafter. This is for the present confidential.*" In notifying Brown officially, after the action of the Committee, Mr. Hurd stated that "such *arms* and supplies as the Committee may have and which may be needed by Capt. Brown" were appropriated to his use, "provided that the arms & supplies be not more than enough for one hundred men."[21] But this obviously did not apply to the rifles previously returned to Massachusetts. Under this provision, twenty-five Colt's navy revolvers were subsequently sent to Brown at Lawrence through Mr. W. F. M. Arny, agent of the Committee, but they never reached Brown himself. As he did not appear to claim them, they were loaned to the Stubbs military company. John Brown, in explanation of his attitude, told Horace White that he "had had so much trouble and fuss and difficulty with the people of Lawrence, that he would never go there again to claim anything."[22]

Immediately after the adjournment of the National Committee, Brown placed in Horace White's hands a substantial list of articles he needed for the equipment of fifty volunteers, and the cost thereof delivered in Lawrence or Topeka.[23]* Jonas Jones, of Tabor, who was in official charge of the Free State supplies there, was ordered to retain everything in his hands until John Brown had made his choice. By February 18, Mr. White wrote that the articles Brown had requisitioned would be shipped the following week, and on March 21 he notified Brown that he would shortly go to Kansas and work there to fit Brown out with all the supplies he was entitled to

* See Appendix for this requisition.

under the New York resolution;[24] while in the same month, W. F. M. Arny wrote that he had packed and sent to Jonas Jones fourteen boxes of clothing for Brown's use.[25] While his interests were thus considerately being cared for, after the New York meeting, Brown again went to Peterboro, by way of Vergennes, Vermont and Rochester, to visit Gerrit Smith, who, although contributing a thousand dollars a month to the National Kansas Committee, was quite ready to help Brown from time to time, and never kept account of the sums he gave to the Kansas fighter. From Peterboro, Brown made, with John Brown, Jr., a flying trip to his wife and family at North Elba, whom he had not seen for a year and a half.[26] But he was in Boston again on February 16, where he wrote to Augustus Wattles, asking for the latest Kansas news and for Wattles's honest conviction in regard to Governor Geary.[27] Indeed, from now on until he finally went to Tabor, *en route* to Kansas, the story of his movements is one of incessant and restless wandering throughout New England and New York.

On the 18th of February he made what was his most notable public appearance in New England — before the Joint Committee on Federal Relations of the Massachusetts Legislature. The friends of Kansas were urging upon the Legislature an appropriation of one hundred thousand dollars, on the ground that, as Mr. Sanborn assured the Legislature, "the rights and interests of Massachusetts have suffered gross outrage in Kansas." No labored argument seemed to him necessary, but there were witnesses to testify to what had occurred in Kansas, among them E. B. Whitman, Martin F. Conway and John Brown. Whitman and Brown were introduced as having the best blood of the Mayflower in their veins and being descendants of soldiers of the Revolution. Brown's lengthy speech was, in substance, a story of his own experiences (Pottawatomie omitted) and a review of the Border Ruffian outrages upon individuals and towns, without mentioning any of the Free State reprisals. In it he paid a tribute to Ottawa Jones and his wife for their care of himself and his sons.

"I," he said, "with Five sick, & wounded sons, & son in law; were obliged for some time to lie on the ground without shelter, our Boots & clothes worn out, destitute of money, & at times almost in a state of starvation; & dependent on the charities of the Christian Indian, & his wife whom I before named."

In the manuscript of this address, still preserved in the Kansas Historical Society, there is the following conclusion:

"It cost the *U S* more than half a Million for a year past to harrass poor Free State settlers, in Kansas, & to violate *all Law*, & *all right, Moral,* & *Constitutional*, for the *sole & only* purpose, *of forceing Slavery* uppon that Territory. I chalenge this whole nation to prove before *God or mankind to contrary*. Who paid this money to enslave the settlers of Kansas; & worry them out? I say nothing in this estimate of the money wasted by Congress in the management of this *horribly tyranical, & Damnable affair*."

In answer to the chairman's question as to what sort of emigrants Kansas needed, Brown replied: "We want good men, industrious men, men who respect themselves; who act only from the dictates of conscience; men who fear God too much to fear anything human," — an interesting statement in view of the omission of all reference to slavery.[28]

Despite Brown's emphatic words and the moving story of his own sufferings, the Massachusetts Legislature decided not to vote anything for the Kansas cause, and so Brown turned again to raising the money he needed for his own company. Besides his trip to Concord, with his two nights in the Thoreau and Emerson homes, he visited, in March, Canton, Collinsville, Hartford and New Haven, in Connecticut, and was several times at the Massasoit House in Springfield, where he was a particularly welcome visitor by reason of the interest in him of its proprietors, the Messrs. Chapin, who had notified him in the previous September of their readiness to send him fifty or one hundred dollars "as a testimonial of their admiration of your brave conduct during the war."[29] At New Haven, on March 18, he received a promise of one thousand dollars. In and about Hartford six hundred dollars were raised for him; and from Springfield, Brown was able to send four hundred dollars to William H. D. Callender, of Hartford, who for some time acted as his agent and treasurer.[30] At Canton, where both his father and mother had grown up, Brown was gratified by a promise to send to his family at North Elba, "Grand-Father John Brown's old Granite Monument, about 80 years old; to be faced and inscribed in memory *of our poor* Fredk

NEW FRIENDS FOR OLD VISIONS 279

who sleeps in Kansas," — which stone marks to-day Brown's own grave.[31] He also received in Canton and Collinsville the sum of eighty dollars, after lecturing for three evenings on Kansas affairs. About this time he obtained seventy dollars sent through Amos A. Lawrence, as he did one hundred dollars in April contributed by a friend of Mr. Stearns through that generous patron.[32] The five hundred dollars voted to him by the Massachusetts Kansas State Committee on January 7, and a second five hundred voted on April 11, Brown did not obtain until the 19th or 20th of April, when, at Mr. G. L. Stearns's suggestion, he drew upon the Committee through Henry Sterns, of Springfield.[33] To aid him in his quest, Brown wrote and published in the *Tribune* and other newspapers the following appeal for aid:

TO THE FRIENDS OF FREEDOM

The undersigned, whose individual means were exceedingly limited when he first engaged in the struggle for Liberty in Kansas, being now still more destitute and no less anxious than in time past to continue his efforts to sustain that cause, is induced to make this earnest appeal to the friends of Freedom throughout the United States, in the firm belief that his call will not go unheeded. I ask all honest lovers of *Liberty and Human Rights, both male and female*, to hold up my hands by contributions of pecuniary aid, either as counties, cities, towns, villages, societies, churches or individuals.

I will endeavor to make a judicious and faithful application of all such means as I may be supplied with. Contributions may be sent in drafts to W. H. D. Callender, Cashier State Bank, Hartford, Ct. It is my intention to visit as many places *as I can* during my stay in the States, provided I am first informed of the disposition of the inhabitants to aid me *in my efforts*, as well as to receive my visit. Information may be communicated to me (care Massasoit House) at Springfield, Mass. Will editors of newspapers friendly to the cause kindly second the measure, and also give this some half dozen insertions? Will either gentlemen or ladies, or both, who love the cause, volunteer to take up the business? It is with *no little sacrifice of personal feeling* that I appear in this manner before the public.

JOHN BROWN.[34]

On March 19, while in New Haven, John Brown thus turned to Amos A. Lawrence for aid in his private affairs:

The offer you so kindly made through the Telegraph some time since emboldens me to propose the following for your consideration.

For One Thousand Dollars cash I am offered an improved piece of land which with a little improvement I now have might enable my family consisting of a Wife & Five minor children (the youngest not yet Three years old) to procure a Subsistence should I never return to them; my Wife being a good economist, & a real old fashioned business woman. She has gone through the Two past winters in our open cold house: unfinished outside; & not plastered. I have no other income or means for their support. I have never hinted to anyone else that I had a thought of asking for any help to provide in any such way for my family; & *should not to you:* but for your own suggestion. I fully believe I shall get the help I need to opperate with West. Last Night a private meeting of some gentlemen here; voted to raise me One Thousand Dollars in New Haven, for that purpose. If you feel at all inclined to encourage me in the measure I have proposed I shall be grateful to get a line from you; Care of Massasoit House, Springfield, Mass; & will call when I come again to Boston. I do not feel disposed to weary you with my oft repeated *visitations.* I believe I am indebted to *you* as the *unknown giver* of One Share of Emigrant aid stock; as I can think of no other so likely to have done it. *Is my appeal right?*

       Very Respectfully Your Friend
          JOHN BROWN.[35]

Mr. Lawrence at once replied that he had just sent fourteen thousand dollars to Kansas to found the best possible school system, and therefore was short of cash.

"But," he added, "in case anything should occur while you are in a great and good cause to shorten your life, you may be assured that your wife and children shall be cared for more liberally than you now propose. The family of Captain Brown of Osawatomie will not be turned out to starve in this country, untill Liberty herself is driven out."[36]

Later, Mr. Lawrence and Mr. Stearns both agreed to this proposal, but this thousand dollars was as slow to appear as that promised at New Haven. It was, however, finally raised (unlike the New Haven sum) and applied to the purchase of the land. The list of contributors to this fund and their gifts runs as follows:

Wm. R. Lawrence,	Boston	$50
Amos A. Lawrence,	"	310
Geo. L. Stearns,	"	260
John E. Lodge,	"	25
J. Carter Brown,	Providence, R. I.	100
J. M. S. Williams,	Boston	50

NEW FRIENDS FOR OLD VISIONS 281

W. D. Pickman,	Salem	50
R. P. Waters,	"	10
S. E. Peabody,	"	10
John H. Silsbee,	"	10
B. H. Silsbee,	"	5
Cash,		10
Wendell Phillips,	Boston	25
W. I. Rotch,	New Bedford	10
John Bertram,	Salem	75
		$1000 [37]

This was not brought together until Brown had found it necessary to write, on May 13, the day he left for the West: "I must ask to have the $1000 made up *at once;* & forwarded to Gerrit Smith. *I did not* start the measure of getting up *any subscription for me;* (although I was sufficiently needy as God knows); nor had I thought of *further burdening* either of my dear friends *Stearns,* or *Lawrence.* . . ."[38] The reason for this urgency was that he had committed himself for the purchase of the land to the brothers Thompson. Even then the transaction dragged on until late in August, when Mr. Sanborn visited North Elba and put it through.[39]

From the 21st to the 26th of March, except for a hasty trip to Springfield, Brown was in Worcester, part of the time as a guest of Eli Thayer. On the 23d he spoke at an anti-slavery meeting, and on the 25th he lectured in the City Hall, on Kansas. On these and other occasions he relied largely upon the address he had given before the Committee of the Massachusetts Legislature, to which he had appended the following statement of his own plans when in Connecticut:[40]

"I am trying to raise from $20, to 25,000 Dollars in the Free States to enable me to continue my efforts in the cause of Freedom. Will the people of Connecticut *my native State* afford me some aid in this undertaking? . . . I was told that the newspapers in a certain City were dressed in mourning on hearing that I was killed & scalped in Kansas. . . . Much good it did me. In the same place I met a more cool reception than in any other place where I have stoped. If my friends will hold up my hands while I live: I will freely absolve them from any expence over me when I am dead. . . ."

Dr. Francis Wayland, who heard him at Worcester, was not inspired by his oratorical powers. "It is one of the curious facts," he wrote, "that many men who *do* it are utterly unable to *tell* about it. John Brown, a flame of fire in action, was dull in speech." [41] Emerson, on the other hand, in recording in his diary Brown's speech at Concord, said he gave,

"a good account of himself in the Town Hall last night to a meeting of citizens. One of his good points was the folly of the peace party in Kansas, who believed that their strength lay in the greatness of their wrongs, and so discountenanced resistance. He wished to know if their wrong was greater than the negro's, and what kind of strength that gave to the negro." [42]

Later, Emerson wrote this tribute to Brown's powers as a speaker:

"For himself, he is so transparent that all men see him through. He is a man to make friends wherever on earth courage and integrity are esteemed, the rarest of heroes, a pure idealist, with no by-ends of his own. Many of you have seen him, and everyone who has heard him speak has been impressed alike by his simple, artless goodness joined with his sublime courage." [43]

The financial results of the Worcester meetings were slim. But Eli Thayer gave him five hundred dollars' worth of weapons — a cannon and a rifle — while Ethan Allen and Company also contributed a rifle. [44] March ended for Brown with a flying trip to Easton, Pennsylvania, in company with Frank Sanborn and Martin Conway, as representatives of the Massachusetts Kansas Committee, in a fruitless effort to induce ex-Governor Reeder to return to Kansas and assume the leadership of the Free State party. [45] But Mr. Reeder was too happily situated at Easton; he was, however, so heartily in sympathy with Brown's plan that the latter wrote to him for aid on his return to Springfield, explaining that the only difference between them was as to the number of men needed, and hoping that Mr. Reeder would soon discern the necessity of "going out to Kansas this spring." [46] It was on this visit to the Massasoit House that Brown found a letter from his wife telling him of his sons' decision to fight no more. To this he replied on March 31:

"I have only to say as regards the resolution of the boys to 'learn and practice war no more,' that it was not at my solicitation that they engaged in it at the first — that while I may perhaps feel no

NEW FRIENDS FOR OLD VISIONS

more love of the business than they do, still I think there may be possibly in their day that which is more to be dreaded, if such things *do not now exist*."[47]

His financial progress to the end of March by no means satisfied Brown. On the 3d of April he wrote thus despondently to William Barnes, of Albany:

"I expect soon to return West; & to go back without securing even an outfit. I go with a *sad heart* having failed to secure even the means of equiping; to say nothing of feeding men. I had when I returned no more that I could peril; & could make no further sacrifice, except to go about in the attitude of a beggar: & that I have done, humiliating as it is."

The winter was slipping away rapidly; spring was at hand. He was impatient to return to Kansas, and his benefactors expected him to be there in the spring in time for any fresh aggression by the Border Ruffians. But his travelling expenses were not light, and there were two matters that rapidly reduced his cash resources, especially during the month of April. On the occasion of Brown's first visit to Collinsville, about the beginning of March, he met, among others, Charles Blair, a blacksmith and forge-master, who attended Brown's lecture on Kansas and heard his appeal for funds. The next morning he saw Brown in the village drug-store, where, to a group of interested citizens, the Captain was exhibiting some weapons which were part of the property taken from Pate and not returned to him. Mr. Blair testified in 1859:[48]

"Among them was a two-edged dirk, with a blade about eight inches long, and he [Brown] remarked that if he had a lot of those things to attach to poles about six feet long, they would be a capital weapon of defense for the settlers of Kansas to keep in their log cabins to defend themselves against any sudden attack that might be made on them. He turned to me, knowing, I suppose, that I was engaged in edge-tool making, and asked me what I would make them for; what it would cost to make five hundred or one thousand of those things, as he described them. I replied, without much consideration, that I would make him five hundred of them for a dollar and a quarter apiece; or if he wanted a thousand of them, I thought they might be made for a dollar apiece. I did not wish to commit myself then and there without further investigation. . . . He simply remarked that he would want them made. I thought no more about it until a few days afterwards. . . . The result was that I made a contract with him."

This document was not signed until March 30, ten days after Blair had shipped one dozen spears as samples to the Massasoit House. This was the genesis of the Harper's Ferry pikes, for the weapons Brown contracted for were never delivered until 1859, — long after any Kansas need for them had disappeared.

The reason for this delay is not to be explained, as some have thought, by the theory that Brown from the first intended to use the spears elsewhere than in Kansas. There is evidence, besides his statements and letters to Blair, that he really thought these weapons would be of value even to the Free State women of the embattled Territory. Undoubtedly, Brown looked forward to a further attack upon slavery after the Kansas battle was won. The fate of Kansas appealed to him only in so far as it involved an aggressive attack upon slavery. He did not, so Mr. Sanborn testifies, reveal his Virginia plans, which were always in the back of his head, to any of his new Massachusetts friends until 1858. But in view of his long-cherished scheme for a direct assault upon slavery, and his confidences at this time to Hugh Forbes, there can be no question that, in asking for far more arms than could be used by a hundred or even two hundred men, his mind was fixed upon further use for them after the Border Ruffians had ceased from troubling. Kansas was to be a prologue to the real drama; the properties of the one were to serve in the other. Had Brown obtained the money he needed to pay for the pikes, he would surely have received them in July, 1857, on the 1st of which the delivery was to be made. But Brown was not able to make the first payment of five hundred dollars within ten days, as required by the contract. Instead, he sent only three hundred and fifty dollars, and did not make his next payment of two hundred dollars until April 25.

Blair was a canny Yankee. While he bought all the material needed — the handles were of ash and the spearheads strong malleable iron, two inches wide and about eight inches long, with a screw and ferrules to connect the blade to the

NEW FRIENDS FOR OLD VISIONS

handle or shank — and did some work on the contract, he stopped when he had done enough work to have earned the five hundred and fifty dollars. The handles were laid aside in bundles to season, and the iron work carefully preserved until such time as Brown should give further orders and supply additional funds. It was not until he received a letter dated February 10, 1858, that Blair again heard from his Kansas friend, and, with the exception of another letter, written on March 11, 1858, nothing further happened until Brown unexpectedly appeared at Blair's door on June 3, 1859, and took the necessary steps to have the pikes completed without loss of time. Then, certainly, it was Brown's idea to place these weapons in the hands of slaves, in order that, unaccustomed as they were to firearms, they might with them fight their way to liberty.

Brown's second investment at this period cost him still more money than the pikes, and resulted in little or no benefit and some very considerable injury to his long-cherished plan of carrying the "war into Africa," of making the institution of slavery insecure by a direct attack upon it. On one of his trips to New York he met, late in March, through the Rev. Joshua Leavitt, of the New York *Independent,* one Hugh Forbes, a suave adventurer of considerable ability, who habitually called himself colonel, because of military service in Italy under Garibaldi, in the unsuccessful revolution of 1848-49.[49] Forbes was typical of the human flotsam and jetsam washed up by every revolutionary movement. A silk merchant for a time in Sienna, he was perpetually needy after his arrival in New York, about 1855, living by his talents as a teacher of fencing, and by doing odd jobs on the *Tribune* as translator or reporter. About forty-five years of age, he was a good linguist and had acquired in Italy some knowledge of military campaigning, — quite enough to impress John Brown, who believed he had found in Forbes precisely the expert lieutenant he needed, not only for the coming Kansas undertaking, but for the more distant raid upon Virginia. Vain, obstinate, unstable and greatly lacking funds, as Forbes was, Brown's projects appealed mightily to him; he speedily saw himself in fancy the Garibaldi of a revolution against slavery. John Brown, the reticent and self-contained, unbosomed himself to this man as he had not to the Massachusetts friends who were advancing the money upon which he lived and plotted. The result was Forbes's engagement as instructor, at one hundred dollars a month, of the proposed "volunteer-regular" company, to operate first in Kansas and later in Virginia, into which undertaking Forbes entered the more willingly as he learned of the wealthy New England men who were backing Brown.

For Brown this was an unhappy alliance; dissimilar in character, training and antecedents, and alike only in their insistence on leadership, mutual disappointment and dissatisfaction were the only possible outcome of the association of the two men. Forbes, as will be seen later, became the evil genius of the Brown enterprise. First of all, he absorbed money, when Brown had none too much for his own immediate needs and the first payments to Blair for the pikes. Forbes was authorized by Brown, early in April, to draw upon Mr. Callender, of Hartford, for six hundred dollars, and he did so within the month. But he showed so little inclination to follow Brown westward that the latter soon became suspicious.

Forbes had several excuses for delaying. It had been agreed that he should translate and condense a foreign manual of guerrilla warfare; this he did under the title of 'Manual of the Patriotic Volunteer.' This work dragged interminably; on June 1, Joseph Bryant, a New York friend of Brown's, who acted for him, reported, after a call on Forbes, that the latter was content with his progress and certain that he was losing no time. On June 16, Forbes assured Bryant that the book would be ready in ten days; that he was not ready to join Brown; indeed, he now had doubts whether any help would be needed in Kansas until winter. This report so alarmed Brown that on June 22 he sent to Forbes, through Bryant, a demand for the immediate repayment of the six hundred dollars, or as much of it as he might have drawn through Callender. Bryant at once took the order to Forbes, but becoming convinced that "the colonel" was acting in good faith, and that much of the money had already been spent, did not show it to the budding author, who was now certain of finishing his book "in about a week."

NEW FRIENDS FOR OLD VISIONS 287

To that volume, however, Forbes had not devoted all his energies, for he had spent considerable time in endeavoring to raise more money with which to bring his family over from Paris, where they were eking out a precarious existence. Of Brown's six hundred dollars the family had received one hundred and twenty dollars; sums amounting to seven hundred dollars Forbes obtained from Horace Greeley and other friends of Free Kansas, according to a statement of Mr. Greeley in the *Tribune* for October 24, 1859. What became of these funds is not known, but by June 25 Forbes had given up his idea of bringing his family over, and had decided to send to Paris the daughter who was in New York, that she might be with her mother. Finally, Forbes drifted westward, arriving at Tabor on August 9, two days after Brown's appearance at the same place. He had stopped at Gerrit Smith's at Peterboro on his way out, and successfully appealed to the purse of that ever generous man, who had "helped" John Brown to a "considerable sum" ($350) when they parted in Chicago on June 22. Nevertheless, Forbes obtained one hundred and fifty dollars, of which he sent all but twenty dollars back to New York toward the cost of printing his book. Gerrit Smith "trusted," so he wrote to Thaddeus Hyatt, that Forbes would "prove very useful to our sacred work in Kansas." "We must," he added, "not shrink from fighting for Liberty — & if Federal troops fight against her, we must fight against them."[50]

Aside from his negotiations with Forbes, and with Mr. Blair for the pikes, April was for Brown another month of active solicitation of funds, but with even more disappointing results, complicated by the news, received from his son Jason, that a deputy United States marshal had passed through Cleveland, bound East to arrest him for some of his Kansas transactions.[51] He wrote on the 16th, from Springfield, to Eli Thayer that:

"One of U S Hounds is on my track; & I have kept myself hid for a few days to let my track get cold. I have no idea of being taken; & *intend* (*if* '*God will*';) to go back with Irons *in* rather than *uppon* my hands. ... I got *a fine lift* in Boston the other day; & hope Worcester will not be *entirely behind*. I do not mean *you;* or Mr. Allen, & Co."[52]

This keeping himself hid had reference to his stay with Judge and Mrs. Russell in Boston for a week, during which time Mrs. Russell allowed no one but herself to open the front door, lest the "U S Hounds" appear. The Russell house was chosen because it was in a retired street, and Judge Russell himself was never conspicuous in the Abolitionist ranks, in order that he might be the more serviceable to the cause in quiet ways. Mrs. Russell remembers to this day Brown's sense of humor and his keen appreciation of the negro use of long words and their grandiloquence. She recalls, too, that he frequently barricaded his bedroom, told her of his determination not to be taken alive, and added, "I should hate to spoil your carpet."[53]

It was while staying with the Russells that he came downstairs one day with a written document which voiced his bitter disappointment at his non-success in obtaining the funds he needed. He read it aloud, as follows:

"Old Browns *Farewell:* to the Plymouth Rocks; Bunker Hill, Monuments; Charter Oaks; and Uncle Toms, Cabbins.

"Has left for Kansas. Was trying since he came out of the territory to secure an outfit; or in other words *the means of arming and equipping thoroughly;* his regular minuet men: who are mixed up *with the people of Kansas:* and *he leaves the States;* with a DEEP FEELING OF SADNESS: that after having exhausted *his own small means:* and with his *family and his* BRAVE MEN: suffered hunger, nakedness, cold, sickness, (and some [of] them) imprisonment, with most barbarous, and cruel treatment: *wounds, and death:* that after lying on the ground for Months; in the most unwholesome *and* sickly; as well as uncomfortable *places:* with sick and wounded destitute of any shelter a part of the time; dependent (*in part*) on the care, and hospitality of the Indians: and hunted like Wolves: that after all this; in order to sustain a cause, which *every Citizen* of this '*Glorious Republic*,' is under equal Moral obligation to do: (*and for the neglect of which* HE WILL *be held accountable* TO GOD:) in which *every Man, Woman, and Child of the entire human family;* has a *deep and awful interest:* that when *no wages* are *asked, or expected:* he canot secure (amidst all the wealth, luxury, and extravagance of this '*Heaven exalted*' people;) even the necessary supplies, for a common soldier. 'HOW ARE THE MIGHTY FALLEN?'

JOHN BROWN.[54]

"BOSTON, April, 1857."

For one encouraging happening about this time, John Brown was again indebted to the generosity of Mr. Stearns.

NEW FRIENDS FOR OLD VISIONS 289

He had set his heart on receiving two hundred revolvers, in addition to the twenty-five donated by the National Kansas Committee, and through Mr. Thayer he had made inquiry as to the prices of several manufacturers. Finally, he received a low bid of thirteen hundred dollars for two hundred revolvers from the Massachusetts Arms Company, through its agent, T. W. Carter, at Chicopee Falls, who stated that the low price — fifty per cent of the usual charge — was due solely to the company's generous purpose "of aiding in your project of protecting the free state settlers of Kansas and securing their rights to the institutions of *free America*." [55] John Brown at once reported this offer to Mr. Stearns, saying: "Now if Rev T Parker, & other good people of Boston, would make up that amount; I might *at least be well armed*." [56] Mr. Stearns immediately notified Mr. Carter that he would purchase the revolvers and pay for them by his note at four months from date of delivery, as this would give him time to raise the money by subscription if he desired to. The company accepted the proposition, and shipped the revolvers on May 25 to "J. B. care Dr. Jesse Bowen, Iowa City, Iowa," with the company's hope "that there may be no occasion for their service in securing rights which ought to be guaranteed by the principles of justice and equity." As if he had a little doubt about their ultimate use, Mr. Carter added: "We have no fear that they will be put to service in your hands for other purposes." In notifying Brown that his offer had been accepted, Mr. Stearns significantly remarked, "I think you ought to go to Kansas as soon as possible and give Robinson and the rest some Backbone." For himself, Mr. Stearns asked only that, if he paid for these revolvers, all the arms, ammunition, rifles, as well as the revolvers not used for the defence of Kansas, be held as pledged to him for the payment of the thirteen hundred dollars. The Massachusetts Kansas Committee by formal vote assented to this suggestion.

By April 23, Brown's hopes of further aid had vanished. On that day he wrote to his family from New Haven, asking that they have "some of the friends" drive at once to Westport and Elizabethtown to meet him.[57] But he was in Springfield on the 25th, and on the 28th, owing to an attack of fever and ague, he had only just reached Albany on his way to North

Elba, where he remained about two weeks with his family, before leaving for Iowa by way of Vergennes, Vermont. From this place he wrote on May 13 to George L. Stearns, "I leave here for the West today," [58] without the slightest idea that it would take him three months to reach the rendezvous in Tabor. He had not, however, during the months before his departure, lost his interest in Kansas or failed to keep in direct touch with the situation there. Augustus Wattles and James H. Holmes had corresponded with him, and to the former Brown had written, on April 8, the following letter, which not only records clearly the spirit in which he again set his face toward Kansas, but is of special interest because it appears to be the first one to which he signed the *nom-de-plume* "Nelson Hawkins," that later appears so frequently in his correspondence:

BOSTON, MASSACHUSETTS April 8, 1857.

MY DEAR SIR: Your favor of the 15th March, and that of friend H. of the 16th, I have just received. I cannot express my gratitude *for them both*. They give me just the kind of news I was *most of all things* anxious to hear. *I bless God* that he has not left the free-State men of Kansas to *pollute themselves* by the *foul and loathesome* embrace of the *old rotten whore*. I have been trembling *all along* lest they might *back down* from the *high and holy ground* they *had* taken. I say, in view of the *wisdom, firmness, and patience* of my friends and *fellow-sufferers*, (in the cause of humanity,) *let God's name be eternally praised!* I would most gladly give my hand to all whose "garments are not defiled;" and I humbly trust that I shall *soon again* have opportunity to rejoice (or suffer *further* if need be) *with you*, in the strife between Heaven and Hell. I wish to send my most cordial and earnest salutation to *every one of the chosen*. My efforts this way have not been altogether fruitless. I wish you and friend H. both to accept this for the moment; may write soon again, and hope to hear from you both at Tabor, Frémont County, Iowa — Care of Jonas Jones, Esq.

Your sincere friend,
NELSON HAWKINS.[59]

AUGUSTUS WATTLES, ESQ.
LAWRENCE, KANSAS TERRITORY.

At least one member of Brown's family was disturbed at the father's return to Kansas. John Brown, Jr., wrote to him thus: "It seems as though if you return to Kansas this Spring I should never see you again. But I will not look on the dark

NEW FRIENDS FOR OLD VISIONS

side. You have gone safely through a thousand perils and hairbreadth escapes." [60] It was more than a mere undefined dread that worried the son. His views as to the political situation in Kansas are set forth in this letter with noteworthy ability. The just announced return of James H. Lane to the Territory would give an opportunity to see if the United States authorities there were still bent on arresting the Free Soil leaders, and whether the Free Soilers would unresistingly submit to such a happening. He also felt that, in view of the renewed hostilities which he believed were at hand, it would be well for his father to delay his entrance into Kansas, and thus,

"place it out of the power of Croakers to say that the 'peace' had been broken only in consequence of the advent there of such disturbers as 'Jim Lane' and 'Old Brown.' And further, when war begins, if the people there take the right ground, you could raise and take in with you a force which might in truth become a 'liberating army,' when they most stood in need of help."

John Brown, Jr., then admitted that he feared that the Kansans, for whom his father was ready to peril his life, would, out of their slavish regard for Federal authority, be ready to "hand you over to the tormentor." The extent to which he was in his father's confidence, and the way in which both their minds were working upon the great post-Kansas project, appears clearly from a question in this same letter: "Do you not intend to visit Canada before long? That school can be established there, if not elsewhere."

However much he may have taken his son's warnings to heart, John Brown left for Kansas master of considerable supplies. On May 18, Mr. Stearns estimated that the contributions of arms, clothing, etc., of which Brown had entire control, were worth $13,000.[61] A careful count of the sums he is known to have received after January 1 shows that they aggregated $2363, exclusive of the $1000 raised by Lawrence and Stearns for the purchase of the North Elba land. Out of this sum had come travelling expenses, some provision for his family, the $550 paid for the pikes, and the $600 absorbed by Forbes. To it must be added the $350 given to him in Chicago on June 22 by Gerrit Smith. The total sum he raised was, of course, larger than this; he obtained, for instance, some small gifts in Chicago. One large credit he did not use. In his enthusiasm for the cause, his admiration of the man and his complete confidence in Brown's "courage, prudence and good judgment," Stearns gave his Kansas friend authority to draw upon him for $7000, as it was needed, to subsist the one hundred "volunteer-regulars," provided that it became necessary to call that number into active service in Kansas in 1857.[62] This emergency not occurring, Brown returned the credit untouched. Mr. Stearns, be it noted, testified in 1859 that, in addition to everything else, he had from time to time given Brown money of which he never kept any record. Counting the credit of $7000, the supplies worth $13,000, and estimating the other cash contributions at only $3000, it appears that Brown was successful in raising $23,000 toward his project of putting a company into the field. But his inability to use the $7000 *en route*, and his long delay in reaching Tabor, together with necessary expenditures for horses and wagons and wages, reduced him soon to distress. When he arrived at his base of action, Tabor, he had only twenty-five dollars left.[63]

Various causes contributed to Brown's delay. He was at Canastota on May 14, at Peterboro on May 18, reached Cleveland on May 22, and Akron the next day. On May 27 he wrote from Hudson that he was "still troubled with the ague" and was "much confused in mind." If he should never return, he wished that "no other monument be used to keep me in remembrance than the *same plain old one* that records the death of my Grandfather & Son & that *a short story* like those already on it be told of John Brown the 5th under that of Grandfather."[64] He added that he was already very short of expense money, and that he did not expect to leave for four or five days. On June 3, while still at Hudson, he wrote thus to Augustus Wattles, over the name of "James Smith:"

MY DEAR SIR: I write to say that I started for Kansas some three weeks or more since, but have been obliged to stop for the fever and ague. I am now righting up, and expect to be on my way again soon. Free-State men need have no fear of my *desertion*. There are some half dozen men I want a visit from at Tabor, Iowa, to come off in the most QUIET WAY, viz: *Daniel Foster*, late of Boston Massachusetts; *Holmes*, *Frazee*, a Mr. *Hill* and *William David*,

NEW FRIENDS FOR OLD VISIONS 293

on Little Ottawa creek; a Mr. Cochran, on Pottawatomie creek; or I would like *equally* well to see *Dr. Updegraff* and *S. H. Wright*, of Ossawatomie; or *William Phillips*, or CONWAY, or *your honor*. I have some very important matters to confer with some of you about. Let there be *no words* about it. Should any of you come out to see me *wait* at Tabor if you get there *first*. Mr. Adair, at Ossawatomie, may supply ($50,) fifty dollars, (if need be), for expenses on my account on *presentation of this*. Write me at Tabor, Iowa, *Fremont County*.[65]

On the 9th of June, Brown wrote to William A. Phillips in a similar strain, to which Phillips replied from Lawrence on June 24,[66] saying that neither he nor Holmes nor others whom he had seen could go to Tabor, that there was then no necessity for military measures, and that the arms were safer with Brown than with any one else. If he came into Kansas, he would be protected. Wattles's reply was similarly discouraging, bringing the oracular advice: "Come as quickly as possible, or not come at present, as you choose."[67] Frazee (the teamster who had taken Brown out of Kansas in the previous fall) had not returned; Foster, Mr. Wattles did not know; Holmes was ploughing at Emporia, and Conway and Phillips were talking politics. Meanwhile, Brown had visited Milwaukee on June 16, for what specific purpose is not known; he had tried to induce Forbes to meet him in Cleveland on June 17,[68] and then went to Chicago to meet Gerrit Smith. On June 24 he attended at Tallmadge, Ohio, the semi-centennial of the founding of that town. The address was delivered by the Rev. Leonard Bacon. At its close, a message came to the speaker that John Brown was present and would like to speak about Kansas. Mr. Bacon sent back word to Brown that any such address would be "entirely inconsistent with the character of the occasion," — a happening which inspired Mr. Bacon to write to Governor Wise, after Brown's capture, that it was to many at Tallmadge proof of Brown's evident derangement on the slavery question.[69] Brown's pocket memorandum-book, a rough diary from January 12, 1857, on, contains this entry on June 29, also showing that he had returned to Ohio from Chicago: "June 29th Wrote Joseph Bryant Col Forbes, and D Lee Child; all that I leave here Cleveland this day for Tabor, Iowa; & advise Forbes, & Child, to call on Jonas Jones."

By July 6 the memorandum-book records Brown's presence in Iowa City. Here he received word from Richard Realf, for some time to come one of his followers, and afterwards well known as a poet of no mean ability, that he was awaiting him at Tabor with one hundred and ten dollars — the hundred and fifty of National Kansas Committee money, minus Realf's expenses. This money had been sent to Brown on June 30 by Edmund B. Whitman, the Committee's agent in Lawrence, in response to an urgent appeal from Brown, to whom Realf wrote also the good news that, as the government had entered a *nolle prosequi* in the case of the Free State prisoners, Brown need be under "no apprehension of insecurity to yourself or the munitions you may bring with you."[70] By July 17, Brown had only reached Wassonville, Iowa. He had had to obtain two teams and two wagons at a cost of seven hundred and eighty-six dollars, and to hire a teamster (his third son, Owen, who had been at Tabor for a time). He had had to "rig up and load" the teams, and in consequence of an injury to a horse, he had lost ten days on the road. In order to make their scant funds hold out, "and to avoid notice," he and his son "lived exclusively on herring, soda crackers, and sweetened water for more than three weeks (sleeping every night in our wagons), except that twice we got a little milk and a few times some boiled eggs."[71] At last, on August 7, he and his son reached their old quarters in Tabor, the home of Jonas Jones.

By this time it was perfectly apparent that there was to be no bloodshed in Kansas that summer. There was another new Governor in the Territory, Robert J. Walker, of Mississippi, who had succeeded Governor Geary after that official's resignation in March, because of the failure of the pro-slavery Pierce administration to give him proper support. So fair an historian as Mr. Rhodes has declared that Geary was an ideal Governor,[72] and a study of his brief administration of Kansas inevitably leads to the conclusion that, whatever his faults, he strove earnestly to be judicial and honorable, and to bring peace and justice to Kansas. Like Reeder, Geary was a firm Democrat, and like him he left Kansas convinced of the righteousness of the Free State cause. Walker, his successor, had been Senator from Mississippi, Secretary of the Treasury, had practically framed the tariff act of 1846, and was, therefore,

NEW FRIENDS FOR OLD VISIONS

well known to the country as a politician of more than usual ability and standing. He was reluctant to go to Kansas, where he arrived on May 26, having obtained before his departure the consent of the new President, Buchanan, that any Constitution for the State of Kansas which might be framed should be submitted to the people. His appointment in itself helped to avert any outbreaks, since the Southerners felt sure — too sure — that he was one of their own. As soon as it was apparent that he and his able secretary of state, Frederick P. Stanton, were bent on seeing justice done, the pro-slavery forces, and President Buchanan as well, turned against them, with the result that Secretary Stanton was removed from office, and Governor Walker resigned, in the following December. Walker, the fourth governor since October 6, 1854, exceeded by only thirty days Governor Geary's brief stay of six months.[73]

As a whole, however, the outlook for freedom in Kansas was comparatively favorable when John Brown reached Tabor. The Lecompton conspiracy, by which a pro-slavery Constitution was to be forced on Kansas by a trick, had not yet developed; and while there had been sporadic cases of lawlessness in certain counties, and James T. Lyle, a pro-slavery city recorder of Leavenworth, had been killed by William Haller, a Free State man, in an affray at the polls, the year 1857 was, on the whole, one of quiet and progress for the bona fide settlers of Kansas. Free Soilers were pouring into the State in large force, and the number of slaves remained so small that both sides realized the growing ascendency of the Free Soil cause. The Topeka, or Free State, Legislature had met on January 6, 7 and 8, when a dozen of its members had been arrested and taken to Tecumseh; it met again in Topeka on June 13, without interference from Governor Walker, and adjourned four days later after passing some excellent measures. About this time, there was a Free State convention in Topeka, presided over by General Lane, which endorsed the Topeka movement, urged Free State men not to participate in the 15th of June election of delegates to the Lecompton Constitutional convention, and declared the Territorial laws to be without force. A similar Free State convention met in Topeka on July 15 and 16, with James H. Lane again presiding and Governor Robinson as one of the speakers. It called a mass convention for August 26, at Grasshopper Falls, urged upon the Governor the propriety of submitting the Topeka Constitution to the people, and made nominations for the offices to be filled at the coming Free State election on August 9. Meanwhile, in accordance with what afterwards seemed a gravely mistaken decision of the Topeka convention of June 9, the Free State men had declined to participate in the election of June 15 for delegates to the Constitutional convention. Only twenty-two hundred pro-slavery votes were cast in all, which showed that the Free State men could easily have outvoted their enemies, as was clearly proved when more than seventy-two hundred anti-slavery votes were cast at the Free State election of August 9. It was then too late; the Lecompton Constitutional convention was in the hands of the pro-slavery men, headed by the Surveyor-General, John Calhoun, a bitter and unscrupulous slavery champion. They agreed upon a Constitution which had been carefully prepared by the Southern leaders in Washington, and lent themselves readily to the plan to get slavery into Kansas without the consent of the majority of its bona fide inhabitants.

The Free State election of August 9 was held two days after Brown's arrival at Tabor. The heavy vote cast was fresh proof of the ascendency of the party of peace among the Free State men. The Grasshopper Falls convention also showed, by its decision to participate in the election of October 5 for Territorial delegate, that the drift was toward working out a Kansas victory by resort to the time-honored American method of correcting abuses — the ballot-box. Governor Walker guaranteed a fair election, and lived up to his promise by setting aside fraudulent returns. Robinson and Lane favored taking part in the election, Conway, Phillips and Redpath, three of Brown's staunchest friends, opposing. Altogether, Brown found that nothing had been lost by the long delay in his arrival near the scene of action; there was not the slightest need for his "volunteer-regulars;" the only time Governor Walker had ordered out the United States troops was when dissatisfied with the holding of an independent city election at Lawrence on July 13. This course the Governor denounced as certain

NEW FRIENDS FOR OLD VISIONS 297

to mean treason and bring on "all the horrors of civil war," if persisted in. His prompt action discouraged the radicals under Lane, who thereupon was the more ready for a different course. Rifles the Free State men had at this moment no need of or desire for. As to becoming a political leader and putting the stiffening into Robinson's backbone, for which Mr. Stearns and others hoped, that was a line of action not to Brown's taste, and the defeat of his friends in the Grasshopper Falls convention must have added to his dissatisfaction with Kansas conditions. It is not, therefore, surprising if his mind turned more and more to the coming raid against slavery along a more timid and more vulnerable frontier than that of Missouri.

The day after his arrival at Tabor, John Brown wrote to Mr. Stearns of his various disappointments, hindrances and lack of means; these and ill-health had depressed him greatly. Two days later he wrote again and in better spirits.[74] He was "in *immediate* want of from Five Hundred to One Thousand Dollars for *secret service & no questions asked.*" "Rather interesting times" were expected in Kansas, he wrote, "but no great excitement is reported." "Our next advices," he continued, "may entirely change the aspect of things. *I hope* the friends of Freedom will respond to my call: & 'prove me now herewith.'" He had "learned with gratitude" what had been done to render his wife and children comfortable by the purchase of the Thompson farm. Then, as the result of Forbes's arrival, he forwarded to Mr. Stearns "the first number of a series of Tracts lately gotten up here," of which Forbes, and not Brown, was the author. It is entitled 'The Duty of the Soldier,' and is headed, in small type, "Presented with respectful and kind feelings to the Officers and Soldiers of the United States Army in Kansas," the object being to win them from their allegiance to their colors and induce them to support the Free State cause. This it does indirectly by asking whether the "soldiery of a Republic" should be "vile living machines and thus sustain Wrong against Right." There are but three printed pages of rambling and discursive discussion of the soldiery of the ancient republics, and of the princes of antiquity, and a consideration of authority, legitimate and illegitimate — as ill-fitted as possible an appeal to the regular soldier of 1857. To the copy which he sent to Augustus Wattles, Brown appended the following in his own handwriting, as a "closing remark:"

It is as much the duty of the common soldier of the U S Army according to his ability and opportunity, to be informed *upon all subjects* in any way affecting the political or general welfare of his country: & to watch with jealous vigilance, the course, & management of all public functionaries both civil and military: *and to govern his actions as a citizen Soldier accordingly: as though he were President of the United States*.

Respectfully yours,   A Soldier.[75]

Other copies John Brown sent to Sanborn, Theodore Parker and Governor Chase, of Ohio,[76] asking each for his frank opinion of the tract and also for aid in raising the five hundred to one thousand dollars he needed so sorely. Sanborn, and probably Parker, wrote his disapproval of Forbes's attempt to seduce the soldiery of the Union; and only Gerrit Smith, to whom Forbes himself sent a copy with an appeal for help for his family in Paris, seems to have been pleased with it. He thought it "very well written," and added, "Forbes will make himself very useful to our Kansas work." For the Forbes family he subscribed twenty-five dollars, and urged Thaddeus Hyatt to raise some money in New York for this purpose and forward it to Sanborn "as soon as you can."[77]

But Forbes's usefulness to Brown was not of long duration; by November 2 he was on his way back to the East from Nebraska City.[78] He had found no one at Tabor to drill save his employer and one son, Owen; and no funds save sixty dollars, which Brown gave to him (doubtless out of the National Kansas Committee's one hundred and ten) toward his expenses.[79] Rifle-shooting at a target on the outskirts of Tabor was their out-door drill, while in-doors they studied Forbes's 'Manual of the Patriotic Volunteer,' and discussed military tactics and their respective plans in regard to the raid into Virginia.[80]

One of those who met John Brown at this time, the Rev. H. D. King, now of Kinsman, Ohio, records thus his recollections of some of their table talk:[81]

NEW FRIENDS FOR OLD VISIONS

"I tried to get at his theology. It was a subject naturally suggested by my daily work. But I never could force him down to dry sober talk on what he thought of the moral features of things in general. He would not express himself on little diversions from the common right for the accomplishment of a greater good. For him there was only one wrong, and that was slavery. He was rather skeptical, I think. Not an infidel, but not bound by creeds. He was somewhat cranky on the subject of the Bible, as he was on that of killing people. He believed in God and Humanity, but his attitude seemed to be: 'We don't know anything about some things. We do not know about the humanity matter. If any great obstacle stand in the way, you may properly break all the Decalogue to get rid of it.'"

"We are beginning *to take lessons* & have (we think) a very capable Teacher. Should no *disturbance occour:* we may *possibly* think best *to work back eastward*. Cannot *determine yet*," wrote Brown to his wife and children on August 17.[82] But this life at Tabor soon palled on Forbes, particularly as there was a sharp disagreement between Brown and himself as to the future campaign, and increasing evidence that there was to be no active service in Kansas that year. The needs of his family weighed heavily upon him, and a growing sense of wrong done him by the Massachusetts friends of Brown, whom Forbes dubbed "The Humanitarians," in not supplying the salary Brown had promised, led to bitter denunciations of them soon after Forbes arrived in the East.

Jonas Jones and the Rev. John Todd having promptly turned over to Brown the arms stored in the clergyman's cellar, he was able to write on August 13 to Sanborn that he had overhauled and cleaned up those that were most rusted. All were in "middling good order."[83] The question then was how to get them to Kansas, and this involved also a decision as to Brown's own policy. Although apparently anxious to return to Kansas at once, he did not leave Tabor for the Territory until the day he saw Forbes off for the East at Nebraska City, November 2. Various reasons are apparently responsible for the delay: the failure of Kansas friends to come to him; the desire to await the outcome of the fall elections; an injury to his back, and a recurrence of his fever and ague. The arms were finally left behind; when Brown started for Lawrence, he went in a wagon drawn by two horses and driven by his son Owen.

As to Brown's return to Kansas, James H. Holmes wrote, on August 16,[84] that there might be a very good opening for the "business," for which Brown had bought his "stock of materials, ... about the first Monday in October next. ... I am sorry," he continued,

"that you have not been here, in the territory, before. I think that the sooner you come the better so that the people & the Territorial authorities may become familiarized with your presence. This is also the opinion of all other friends with whom I have conversed on this subject. You could thus exert more influence. Several times we have needed you very much."

But Augustus Wattles, a wise counsellor, wrote on August 21 without enthusiasm as to Brown's final arrival, that "those who had entertained the idea of resistance [to outside authority] have entirely abandoned the idea."[85] Only the erratic Lane, who was then the sole person trying to stir up strife in Kansas, and is accused by reputable witnesses of planning schemes of wholesale massacre of pro-slavery men through a secret order, was on fire for Brown's presence in the Territory, but it was the Tabor arms rather than their owner he really desired. His first letter to Brown ran thus:

(*Private*)

LAWRENCE Sept. 7, 57.

SIR

We are earnestly engaged in perfecting an organization for the protection of the ballot box at the October election (first Monday.) Whitman & Abbott have been east after money & arms for a month past, they write encouragingly, & will be back in a few days. We want you with *all* the *materials* you have. I see no objection to your coming into Kansas publicly. I can furnish you just such a force as you may deem necessary for your protection here & after you arrive. I went up to see you but failed.

Now what is wanted is this — write me concisely what transportation you require, how much money & the number of men to escort you into the Territory safely & if you desire it I will come up with them.

     Yours respectfully
      J. H. LANE.[86]

To this Brown replied, on the 16th of September,[87] that he had previously written to Lane of his "strong desire" to

NEW FRIENDS FOR OLD VISIONS 301

see him; "as to the job of work you enquire about I suppose that three good teams with *well covered* waggons, & ten really ingenious, industrious men (not gassy) with about $150. in cash, could bring it about in the course of eight or ten days." Before an answer to this could arrive, Brown learned from Redpath, who also hoped to see him in the Territory soon, that Lane had appointed him "Brigadier-General 2nd Brigade 1st Division,"[88] rather an empty honor, for Lane was as generous with brigadier-generalcies as a profligate European potentate with decorations for his creditors, even casual visitors to the Territory receiving these commissions.[89] Certain it is that this distinction did not cause Brown to exert himself additionally to enter Kansas, not even when there appeared a Mr. Jamison, who bore the high-sounding title of "Quartermaster-General of the Second Division." "General" Jamison brought a letter from Lane, dated Falls City, September 29,[90] declaring that "it is *all important* to Kansas that your things should be in at the *earliest possible moment* & that you should be much nearer at hand than you are." He enclosed fifty dollars, added that "Gen'l" Jamison had more, and insisted that "every gun and all the ammunition" be sent in. "I do not know that we will have to use them, but I do know we should be prepared." All of this made not the slightest impression on Brown, as Jamison came alone, having left the ten staunch men Brown had asked for "about thirty miles back." The names of these men were all unknown to him, and on inquiring about Jamison, Brown found that "Tabor folks (some of them) speak slightingly of him, notwithstanding that he too is a general."[91] Moreover, Jamison brought no teams with him. Brown thereupon returned the fifty dollars to Lane with the following letter:[92]

TABOR IOWA 30 Sept. 57.

MY DEAR SIR

Your favor from Falls City by Mr. Jamison is just received also $50. (fifty dollars) sent by him, which I also return by same hand as I find it will be *next to impossible in my poor state of health* to go through in such very short notice, four days only remaining to get ready load up & go through. I think, considering all the uncertainties of the case *want of teams* &c, that I should *do wrong to set out. I am disappointed in the extreme.*

Very respectfully your friend

JOHN BROWN.

The next day, Brown wrote at length to Mr. Sanborn, enclosing copies of his correspondence with Lane.[93] He outlined his immediate future as follows: "I intend at once to put the supplies I have in a secure place, and then to put myself and such as may go with me where we may get more speedy communications, and can wait until we know better how to act than we do now." He also wrote: "I am now so far recovered from my hurt as to be able to do a little; and foggy as it is, 'we do not give up the ship.' I will not say that Kansas, watered by the tears and blood of my children, shall yet be free or I fall." Brave as this sentiment is, it only increases the mystery of Brown's delaying at Tabor. In this same letter to Sanborn, he wrote in high praise of Lane's speech at the Grasshopper Falls convention, and throughout, Lane had been more sympathetic to Brown than any of the other Kansas leaders. There is nothing to show that the injury of which he wrote twice to Lane was a serious one. Brown did not report it to Mr. Sanborn in his long letter of August 13, after his arrival in Tabor, nor is there any mention of it in his family letters of this period, so far as they have been preserved. True, his financial conditions had not improved, because he had apparently received from the East only $72.68, which came from James Hunnewell, Treasurer of the Middlesex County Massachusetts Kansas Aid Committee.[94] Besides having Owen Brown and Hugh Forbes to aid him, he was in a community not only intensely Abolition, but at this time extremely loyal to him personally, and ready to help. Yet there was none of the determination to reach Kansas at any cost, to be expected from the iron-nerved man who captured Harper's Ferry. An excuse given by Brown to Mr. Sanborn was the lack of news: "I had not been able to learn by papers or otherwise distinctly what course had been taken in Kansas until within a few days; and probably the less I have to say the better." Still, he had received a number of letters from friends in Kansas, and Tabor was always obtaining news from there. Why did he not despatch Owen Brown or Forbes, or go himself quietly, if he was in doubt?

Four days after writing as above to Mr. Sanborn, Brown's state of mind appears from a letter of October 5 to the Adairs at Osawatomie,[95] in which he said:

NEW FRIENDS FOR OLD VISIONS 303

"I have been trying all season to get to Kansas; but have failed as yet through ill health, want of means to pay Freights, travelling expenses &c. *How to act now;* I do not know. If you have not already sent me the $95 sent for me; to my family last season; I would be most glad to have it come by Mr. Charles P. Tidd; if you can do it without distressing yourself, or family."

In addition, he asked for all that Mr. Adair could tell him about conditions in Kansas, and for "reliable Kansas late papers." Obviously, Brown, grim, self-willed, resolute chieftain that he generally was, appears baffled here and lacking wholly in a determination to reach the scene of action at any cost. Whether it was because of physical disability; or fear of arrest and punishment for the Pottawatomie crimes; or mere uncertainty as to the drift of affairs in Kansas; or whether his mind was now so bent on Virginia that he had lost interest in all else, and did not wish to lose his arms; or whether the physical and financial difficulties were insurmountable, or because of all these reasons, that he lingered so long in Tabor, is not likely ever to become known. It will be seen that, when he finally reached Kansas, he stayed but a few days, was practically in hiding, and gave more time and thought to securing recruits for Harper's Ferry than to anything else.

At least one of the Massachusetts backers was impatient and angry at the delay, — Thomas Wentworth Higginson, then, as always in the Abolition days, flaming for quick and vigorous action. To soothe his discontent, Mr. Sanborn wrote to him thus on September 11, in defence of Brown:[96]

". . . You do not understand Brown's circumstances. . . . He is as ready for a revolution as any other man, and is now on the borders of Kansas safe from arrest but prepared for action, but he needs money for his present expenses, and *active* support. I believe he is the best Disunion champion you can find, and with his hundred men, when he is put where he can raise them, and drill them (for he has an expert drill officer with him) will do more to split the Union than a list of 50,000 names for your Convention, good as that is.

"What I am trying to hint at is that the friends of Kansas are looking with strange apathy at a movement which has all the elements of fitness and success — a good plan, a tried leader, and a radical purpose. If you can do anything for it *now*, in God's name do it — and the ill result of the new policy in Kansas may be prevented."

This letter is of special value in view of subsequent efforts to make Brown appear as one who had no sympathy with the disunion doctrines of the radical wing of the Abolitionists.[97] The fact remains that at this time Brown himself was not willing to do and dare at any cost, and was unable to triumph over the obstacles that confronted him at Tabor, until financial aid finally came from E. B. Whitman in Lawrence. The latter reported to Mr. Stearns, under date of October 25,[98] that he had borrowed one hundred and fifty dollars to send to Brown, who would be at Lawrence "a week from Tuesday [November 3] at a very important council, Free State Central Com., Ter. Executive Com., Vigilance Committee of 52, Generals and Capts of the entire organization." "By great sacrifice," wrote Lane to Brown on October 30,[99] "we have raised, & send by Mr. Tidd, $150. I trust the money will be used to get the guns to Kansas, or as near as possible. . . . One thing is certain: if they are to do her any good, it will be in the next few days. Let nothing interfere in bringing them on." This time Brown accepted the money, — he also received one hundred dollars from the Adairs at this juncture, — and entered Kansas, without, however, gratifying Lane by bringing in the arms. He set out on November 2, parting from Forbes at Nebraska City, and drove straight to the vicinity of Lawrence, where he stopped at the home of E. B. Whitman, arriving after the council at which Mr. Whitman had hoped for his presence — probably on November 5.

He stayed but two days with Mr. Whitman,* obtaining tents and bedding and some more money, five hundred dollars, from that able agent of the Massachusetts Kansas Committee, who, in the following February, could not conceal his vexation at Brown's disappearance from Kansas. After receiving the supplies, wrote Mr. Whitman,[100]

"he then left, declining to tell me or anyone where he was going or where he could be found, pledging himself, however, that if difficulties should occur he would be on hand and pledging his life to redeem Kansas from slavery. Since then nothing has been heard of him and I know of no one, not even his most intimate friends,

* Among those he saw at this time was William A. Phillips, who recorded in the *Atlantic Monthly* for December, 1879, the outlines of their conversation, which he erroneously placed in February, 1857, instead of November of that year.

NEW FRIENDS FOR OLD VISIONS 305

who know where he is. In the meantime he has been much wanted, and very great dissatisfaction has been expressed at his course and now I do not know as even his services would be demanded in any emergency."

It is interesting to note in this connection that, in November, 1857, a Free State "Squatters' Court" was organized in the southern Kansas counties of Linn, Anderson and Bourbon, for the trial of contested land claims and similar cases. In order to inspire terror, the judge of the court was called "Old Brown," although John Brown was distant from the Territory. Dr. Rufus Gilpatrick was elected judge of the court.[101] If John Brown was absent, his reputation was on hand and in service.

Within a week, Brown was in Topeka, from which place he reported as follows to Mr. Stearns:[102]

TOPEKA KANSAS T. 16th Nov 1857

DEAR FRIEND

I have now been in Kansas for more than a Week: & for about Two days with Mr. Whitman, & other friends at Lawrence. I find matters quite *unsettled;* but am decidedly of the opinion that there will be no use for the Arms or ammunition here before another Spring. I have them all safe, *& together unbroken: & mean to keep them so:* until I can see how the matter will be finally terminated. I have many calls uppon me for their *distribution;* but shall do no such thing until I am satisfyed that they are *really needed.* I mean to be busily; but *very quietly* engaged in perfecting my arangements during the Winter. Whether the troubles in Kansas *will continue* or not; will probably depend on the action of Congress the coming Winter. Mr. Whitman has paid me $500 for you which will meet present wants as I am keeping only a *small* family. Before getting your letter saying to me not to draw on you for the $7000 (by Mr. Whitman) I had fully determined not to do it unless driven to the last extremity. *I did not mean that* the secret service money I asked for; should come out of you; & hope it may not. Please make this hasty line answer for friend Sanborn; & for other friends for this time. May God bless you all; is the earnest wish of your greatly obliged Friend

JOHN BROWN

P S If I do not use the Arms & Ammunition in *actual service;* I intend to restore them unharmed; but you *must not* flatter yourself on that score *too soon.*

Yours in Truth
J B

To the Adairs he wrote on November 17:[103] "I have been for some days in the territory but keeping very quiet, & looking about to see how the land lies. We left Tabor at once on the return of Mr. Tidd who brought us your letter; & $100 cash. . . . I do not wish to have any noise about me at present; as *I do not mean* to 'trouble Israel.'" Kansas at that time was quiet enough, despite Lane's feeling that the arms might be needed. The election of October 5 for the new Territorial Legislature and for delegate to Congress had resulted in a great Free State victory. The Free State men elected their delegate by 4089 votes and chose thirty-three out of fifty-two members of the Legislature. Governor Walker set aside the fraudulent returns from several precincts in which there had been scandalous frauds; but there was no allegation of interference from outside the State. It is hard to understand what vague fears or wild schemes led Lane to think on October 30 that there might be some important happenings within the next few days. Marcus J. Parrott, the Free State delegate to Congress, had received his certificate of election, and the utmost tranquillity reigned. The Lecompton Constitutional convention did not, it is true, adjourn until November 3, and the product of its deliberation, or rather of the deliberations of the Southern leaders in Washington, was not yet on its way to the Capitol, where the debate over it, with Stephen A. Douglas opposed, was to absorb the nation for a period of three months, February, March and April of 1858. But Lane was not justified, even then, in anticipating any fraud or outrage calling for forcible intervention; his own opportunity, in which he was at his best, came later in November, when, by stumping the Territory, he largely induced the acting Governor, Stanton, to call a special session of the Legislature to order the submission of the Lecompton Constitution to the people for approval.

In brief, the party of peace was in the ascendant; even in the East there was beginning to be a realization that successes at the polls were more effective than "Beecher's Bibles." Thus Mr. Stearns wrote on November 14 to E. B. Whitman:[104] "I believe your true policy is, to meet the enemy at the polls, and vote them down. You can do it and should do it, only being prepared to defend yourselves if attacked but

NEW FRIENDS FOR OLD VISIONS

by no means to attack them." This was treachery to Brown's blood-and-iron policy in the home of his friends. The decision of the Free State leaders to make the best of the situation and work under the existing Territorial government, instead of refusing to have anything to do with it, involved, of course, a complete change of policy. It touched no responsive chord in Brown's breast. One of his biographers remarks that there was no fighting for him to do in 1857 because he had done his work so thoroughly in 1856. Nothing could be further from the fact. The progress to freedom and prosperity of Kansas was due to several causes, but especially to an abandonment of the policy of carrying on an unauthorized war, and of meeting assassination with assassination.

There is only one allegation that Brown came in touch with the Free State leaders during his brief stay in Kansas in 1857. There was then in existence a Free State secret society, called into being by fear of the Lecompton Constitutional convention, and determined to prevent the success of the conspiracy to force slavery upon Kansas through its acts. Mr. R. G. Elliott, of Lawrence, states [105] that the society was pledged to

"'*unman*' the convention soon after its adjournment, a term of elastic definition, meaning anything from obtaining resignations of officials by persuasion, to removing them by capital excision. Abduction was the method indicated at that juncture. . . . John Brown had recently come from Tabor, Iowa, and was in the neighborhood in seclusion, was communicated with by William Hutchinson and expressed his readiness to execute the plans of the order but with the men exclusively of his own selection. To the fear expressed by Robinson that Brown would resort to bloodshed, Hutchinson gave assurance that Brown pledged his faith to be governed strictly by the expressed wishes of the order, and furthermore that he had surveyed the situation at Lecompton and that he could seize Calhoun [the head of the Constitutional convention] and carry him to a place within one hundred miles where he could hold him safely for three months."

But the scheme was blocked by Calhoun's removing to St. Joseph.

The most important result of this visit of Brown to Kansas was his recruiting his first men for the Harper's Ferry raid. No sooner had he reached Mr. Whitman's than he sent for John E. Cook, whom he had met after the battle of Black Jack, before the dispersal of his forces by Colonel Sumner.[106] When Cook came, Brown informed him simply that he was engaged in organizing a company for the purpose of putting a stop to the aggressions of the pro-slavery forces. Cook agreed to join him, and recommended Richard Realf, Luke F. Parsons and R. J. Hinton. On Sunday, November 8, Cook and Parsons had a long talk with Brown in the vicinity of Lawrence, and a few days later, Cook received a note asking him to join Brown, with Parsons if possible, on Monday, November 16, at a Mrs. Sheridan's, two miles south of Topeka. They were to bring their arms, ammunition and clothing. Cook made all his preparations to meet Brown at the time appointed, but had to go alone. He stayed with Brown a day and a half at Mrs. Sheridan's, and then went to Topeka, where they were joined by Aaron D. Stevens (Charles Whipple), Charles W. Moffet and John H. Kagi. They at once left Topeka for Nebraska City, and camped at night on the prairie northeast of Topeka. What followed, Cook stated in his Harper's Ferry confession:

"Here, for the first, I learned that we were to leave Kansas, to attend a military school during the winter. It was the intention of the party to go to Ashtabula County, Ohio. Next morning [November 18] I was sent back to Lawrence to get a draft of $80. cashed [$82.50 according to Brown's memorandum-book], and to get Parsons, Realf and Hinton to go back with me. I got the draft cashed. Capt. Brown had given me orders to take boat to St. Joseph, Mo., and stage from there to Tabor, Iowa, where he would remain for a few days. I had to wait for Realf for three or four days; Hinton could not leave at that time. I started with Realf and Parsons on a stage for Leavenworth. The boats had stopped running on account of the ice. Stayed one day at Leavenworth, and then left for Weston where we took stage for St. Joseph, and from thence to Tabor. I found C. P. Tidd and Leeman at Tabor. Our party now consisted of Capt. John Brown, Owen Brown, A. D. Stephens, Chas Moffett, C. P. Tidd, Richard Robertson [Richardson], Col. Richard Realf, L. F. Parsons, W. M. Leeman and myself.* We stopped some days at Tabor, making preparations to start. *Here we found that Capt Brown's ultimate destination was the State of Virginia.*"

The very day that Brown wrote to the Adairs, "I may find it best to go back to Iowa," he set off for Tabor. The vacilla-

* Cook overlooked here John H. Kagi, who was also present.

NEW FRIENDS FOR OLD VISIONS

tion of the last three months was over. His whole soul was now wrapped up in his Harper's Ferry plan; Kansas was thenceforth forgotten. Upon her further struggles for freedom, her soil watered by his children's "tears and blood," he turned his back; his readiness to die for her if necessary was put aside. He would never have returned to the Territory, had not untoward and unexpected circumstances compelled him to resume the rôle of border chieftain in 1858. Henceforth his whole energies were concentrated on "troubling Israel" in Virginia.

CHAPTER IX

A CONVENTION AND A POSTPONEMENT

JOHN BROWN'S newest recruits, Cook, Realf and Parsons, did not take kindly to the announcement, at Tabor, that Virginia was to be the scene of their armed operations against slavery. Warm words passed between Cook and their leader, for Cook, like Realf and Parsons, had supposed that they were to be trained to operate against Border Ruffians only.[1] After a good deal of wrangling, Cook stated, they agreed to continue, as they had not the means to return to Kansas, and the rest of the party were so anxious that they should go on with them. Like their associates, these three men were adventurous spirits, spoiled, like thousands of others, by the Kansas troubles for leading a quiet and settled life. Anything that smacked of excitement irresistibly appealed to them. Most of them were very young;[2] some had seen their names in the newspapers because of their warfare in Kansas, and were not averse to further notoriety and the chance to make reputations for themselves. All of them were steadfast opponents of slavery and ready to go to any lengths to undermine it. But beyond all this, in the dominating spirit of John Brown himself must be found the true reason for their readiness to join so desperate a venture as Brown outlined to them. There was, Mr. Parsons testifies, a magnetism about Brown as difficult for these simpler men to resist as for the philosophers at Concord.[3] He walked now more than ever like an old man, and made the impression of one well on toward threescore and ten, when not yet fifty-eight years old, with hair that was not white but gray. Yet there was as little doubt about his vigor and strength as there was of the intensity of his hatred of slavery. To his new followers Brown declared that "God had created him to be the deliverer of slaves the same as Moses had delivered the children of Israel; "[4] and they found nothing in this statement to make them doubt his sanity, or that seemed inherently improbable. A fanatic they recognized him to be; but fanatics have at all

A CONVENTION AND A POSTPONEMENT 311

times drawn satellites to them, even when the alliance meant certain death. And so Parsons, Realf and Cook, like Leeman, Tidd and Kagi — the latter a man of unusual parts — were content to go onward across Iowa. During their brief stay in Tabor, Brown offered to take his men, go to Nebraska City, and rescue from jail a slave who had run away and had lost his arm when captured, if the Tabor people would pay the actual expenses. He promised to put the slave into their hands, but they were afraid of the consequences and did not give him the means.[5]

It was on the long wintry journey to Springdale, Iowa, with two wagons laden with the Sharp's rifles and ammunition, that the details of the Virginia venture were gradually discussed. The caravan left the friendly hamlet of Tabor on December 4, according to the diary of Owen Brown, valuable fragments of which survived the Harper's Ferry raid.[6] "Took leave of Tabor folks perhaps for the last time," and "started for Iowa City, Springdale and Ohio," are the entries which record the departure. Progress was slow, for all of the men walked and the weather was bitter cold; sometimes it is recorded that "Father used harsh words" in keeping the party, and particularly the son, in hand. They camped by the wayside, avoiding towns as much as possible, and made up in warmth of debate for the heat they lacked otherwise. On December 8 the entry reads:

" Cold, wet and snowy; hot discussion upon the Bible and war ... warm argument upon the effects of the abolition of slavery upon the Southern States, Northern States, commerce and manufactures, also upon the British provinces and the civilized world; whence came our civilization and origin? Talk about prejudices against color; question proposed for debate, — greatest general, Washington or Napoleon."

This is an excellent sample of the wide range of the daily talks through the five months these strongly marked characters were leagued together. The diary concludes on this day: "Very cold night; prairie wolves howl nobly; bought and carried hay on our backs two and a half miles; some of the men a little down in the mouth — distance travelled 20 miles." Fortunately, these travellers were inured to hardships. Their skill with the rifle aided in eking out their limited commissary.

Sundays they stayed in camp. Evenings were frequently spent in singing, by Brown's request; he always joined with a hearty good-will and named the pieces that he wanted sung, such as "The Slave has seen the Northern Star," "From Greenland's Icy Mountains," etc. In this amusement Stevens led; for he had an exquisite voice, with clear, bugle notes. On Christmas Day they passed Marengo, a town about thirty miles from Iowa City; and presumably reached their immediate destination, Springdale, fifteen miles beyond Iowa City, on the third day thereafter.

On December 29, according to John Brown's own diary, Realf began to board with James Townsend, mine host of the tavern at West Branch, known as the Traveller's Rest. Of this Quaker Boniface unsupported tradition has it that when Brown, dismounting from a mule at his door on the trip through Iowa in October, 1856, asked Townsend whether he had heard of John Brown, the tavern-keeper, "without replying, took from his vest pocket a piece of chalk and, removing Brown's hat, marked it with a large X; he then replaced the hat and solemnly decorated the back of Brown's coat with two large X marks; lastly he placed an X on the back of the mule." All of which pantomime was an indication that Brown and his animals were on the free list of the hotel.[7]

On the 29th, at noon, the other ten members of Brown's party began to board with John H. Painter, a friendly Quaker at Springdale, with whom they remained until January 11, when they moved to the farmhouse of William Maxson, some distance from the village, which still stands, albeit in a condition of growing ill-repair.[8] One dollar and a half a week was the moderate price asked for each man's board, "not including Washing nor extra lights." Here Brown speedily found it necessary to abandon his plan to continue on to Ashtabula in his adopted State. He was unable to sell his teams and wagons for cash; the financial panic of 1857 was now in full swing; board was cheap at Springdale, and the village itself was as remote a place, and as little likely to be thought the scene of plottings against the peace of a sovereign American state, as any hamlet in the country. Moreover, Mr. Maxson was ready to take the teams and wagons off Brown's hands and pay for them by boarding his men. It was a fortunate arrange-

A CONVENTION AND A POSTPONEMENT 313

ment all around, and it left the leader free to go eastward and unfold to his New England friends the precise nature of the assault on Israel upon which he was now embarked.

On January 15, 1858, before he left for the East, Brown did, however, go with some of his men into even greater details of his Virginia plan than on the winter's trip across Iowa. To Parsons, for instance, he here mentioned Harper's Ferry for the first time, but without speaking of an attack upon the arsenal. John Henrie Kagi knew this Virginia district well, and Brown's plan, as it was at this time, commended itself to his mind, which was severely analytical and not given to enthusiasms.

Just what the plan for the raid then was, appears from a long letter of Hugh Forbes, of May 14, 1858, to Dr. S. G. Howe, detailing his differences of opinion with Brown and demanding that he and his men be disarmed.[9] As soon as he reached Tabor, in August, 1857, Forbes says, they compared notes as to the coming attack on slavery in Virginia and brought out their respective schemes. Brown proposed, with from twenty-five to fifty colored and white men, well armed and taking with them a quantity of spare arms, "to beat up a slave quarter in Virginia." Forbes objected to this that:

"No preparatory notice having been given to the slaves (no notice could go or with prudence be given them) the invitation to rise might, unless they were already in a state of agitation, meet with no response, or a feeble one. To this Brown replied that he was sure of a response. He calculated that he could get on the first night from 200 to 500. Half, or thereabouts, of this first lot he proposed to keep with him, mounting 100 or so of them, and make a dash at Harper's Ferry manufactory destroying what he could not carry off. The other men not of this party were to be sub-divided into three, four or five distinct parties, each under two or three of the original band and would beat up other slave quarters whence more men would be sent to join him.

"He argued that were he pressed by the U. S. troops, which after a few weeks might concentrate, he could easily maintain himself in the Alleghenies and that his New England partisans would in the meantime call a Northern Convention, restore tranquility and overthrow the pro-slavery administration. This, I contended, could at most be a mere local explosion. A slave insurrection, being from the very nature of things deficient in men of education and experience would under such a system as B. proposed be either a flash in the pan or would leap beyond his control, or any control, when it would become a scene of mere anarchy and would assuredly be suppressed. On the other hand, B. considered foreign intervention as not impossible. As to the dream of a Northern Convention, I considered it as a settled fallacy. Brown's New England friends would not have courage to show themselves, so long as the issue was doubtful, see my letter to J. B. dated 23 February."

After weeks of discussion, Brown, Forbes declared, "acquiesced or feigned to acquiesce" in a mixed project styled "The Well-Matured Plan," to which Forbes assented to secure mutual coöperation. Forbes's own plan, it must be admitted, sounds much more reasonable and practical than Brown's, and deserves, therefore, to be made a matter of record, particularly as it had without doubt its influence on Brown. It was as follows:

"With carefully selected white persons to organize along the Northern slave frontier (Virginia and Maryland especially) a series of stampedes of slaves, each one of which operations would carry off in one night and from the same place some twenty to fifty slaves; this to be effected once or twice a month, and eventually once or twice a week along the non-contiguous parts of the line; if possible without conflict, only resorting to force if attacked. Slave women accustomed to field labor, would be nearly as useful as men. Everything being in readiness to pass on the fugitives, they could be sent with such speed to Canada that pursuit would be hopeless. In Canada preparations were to be made for their instruction and employment. Any disaster which might befall a stampede would at the utmost compromise those only who might be engaged in that single one; therefore we were not bound in good faith to the Abolitionists (as we did not jeopardize them) to consult more than those engaged in this very project. Against the chance of loss by occasional accidents should be weighed the advantages of a series of successful 'runs.' Slave property would thus become untenable near the frontier; that frontier would be pushed more and more Southward, and it might reasonably be expected that the excitement and irritation would impel the proslaveryites to commit some stupid blunders."

As he stated his plan to Parsons at Springdale, Brown laid stress upon his determination not to fight or molest any one, except to help the escaping slaves to defend themselves or to flee to Canada. This satisfied Parsons for the moment, but it is to be noted that the men left at Springdale did not much discuss the details of their project with one another. Owen

A CONVENTION AND A POSTPONEMENT 315

Brown's diary for February tells that on the 12th there was "talk about our adventures and plans." In the main, discussion ranged from theology and spiritualism to caloric engines, and covered every imaginable subject between them. Much talk of war and fighting there was, and drilling with wooden swords. Stevens, by reason of his service in the Mexican War, and subsequently in the United States Dragoons, was drillmaster in default of Forbes. Sometimes they went into the woods to look for natural fortifications; again they discussed dislodging the enemy on a hill-top by means of "zigzag trenches." Forbes's 'Manual' was diligently perused. Sometimes the men quarrelled with one another; sometimes their boisterousness during their long stay irritated their peaceful Quaker neighbors, many of whom were but recent settlers in that vicinity. Some of them, Owen Brown records, suspected Mr. Maxson's boarders of being Mormon spies in disguise, and others declared that they were "no better than runaways" and ought to be driven out of the community, — a thought suggested, perhaps, by the rapidity with which they won for themselves sweethearts in the neighborhood by Othello-like tales of their adventures and daring in their Kansas wanderings. But some of these affairs of the heart resulted seriously and unfavorably to two or three of the raiders, who carried the scars thereof to their end. "One of the diversions at their home was the trial by jury of any member violating certain proprieties or rules. I see that I have made a note of a trial given Owen for writing down in his pocket-book the name of a lady in the vicinity. [Miss Laura Wascott.] Owen pleaded guilty," [10] — thus Parsons recalled an incident of the winter. But in the main their discipline was rigid; there were black marks given for misconduct, and Cook was once seriously and severely censured "for hugging girls in Springdale Legislature."

This was the mock body with which they beguiled the long winter evenings, drafting laws for an ideal "State of Topeka;" in it Cook, Kagi and Realf displayed their unusual powers as debaters. Sometimes this legislature met at Mr. Maxson's, more often in the village school, a mile or so away, and it followed the regulation procedure with its bills and its debates. Soon Realf was in demand as a speaker and lecturer.[11] But when at Springdale he was not the poorest of the band in the manœuvres and gymnastics practised in the field behind the Maxson house for three hours every fair day, with a view to developing the men physically to the utmost advantage. Only a few of the neighbors suspected or knew that these exercises were not intended to fit the men for service in behalf of Kansas. Townsend of the Traveller's Rest; Maxson and Painter, Dr. H. C. Gill and Moses Varney were more or less in John Brown's confidence in 1858, and most of them tried to dissuade him from his project.[12] But, as the Eastern friends found out, there was no possibility of success along that line of argument. Brown had made up his mind to realize the plan of his lifetime, even though it sorely troubled the peace-loving Quaker friends at Springdale. One of them, Painter, gave twenty dollars to Brown, saying: "Friend, I cannot give thee money to buy powder and lead, but here's twenty dollars toward thy expenses."[13]

In short, the Springdale settlement as a whole wished him well, despite the fact that he was emphatically a man of war, and that his men, as Owen Brown at this time recorded, believed with Jay that "he that is guilty of such oppression [as slavery], making it perpetual upon the posterity of the oppressed, might justly be killed outright." To them slavery was the sum of all oppression, and one of their debates was an inquiry into the reason why the spirit of 1776 was so lacking in the face of the wrongs of 1858. But this little group of young men, among whom was Richard Richardson, a runaway slave from Lexington, Missouri, who had attached himself to Brown at Tabor, found their stay in Springdale as care-free as if they had not agreed to challenge with their lives the most powerful of American institutions. As has been set forth at length in Irving B. Richman's charming and valuable essay, 'John Brown Among the Quakers,' "the time spent in Springdale was a time of genuine pleasure to Brown's men. They enjoyed its quiet, as also the rural beauty of the village and the gentle society of the people."[14] Brown's men have all gone; hardly any one remains in Springdale to tell the tale of their stay; the Maxson and other houses of '58 are falling into decay; but the quiet beauty of Springdale remains. It still consists of one broad street with modest frame houses surrounded

THE SCHOOL-HOUSE AT SPRINGDALE, IOWA
Where the Mock Legislature met

HOUSE OF REV. JOHN TODD, TABOR, IOWA
Where John Brown stored his guns and ammunition

A CONVENTION AND A POSTPONEMENT 317

by green and rolling fields; but the Quaker element is little noticeable, and there are fewer people residing there to-day than fifty years ago.

Thirteen days after leaving Tabor, John Brown was in the Rochester house of Frederick Douglass,[15] who had so long been the confidant of his plan as to Virginia, and in numerous talks informed him that the time was ripe for the long-cherished undertaking. On the way East he had stopped in Lindenville, Ohio,[16] to visit his son John and talk over with him the unpleasant developments in regard to Hugh Forbes, about which Brown had written to his son on January 15, at Springdale. He had decided, on receiving a violent and abusive letter, to correspond with Forbes through a third person; the malevolent spirit displayed by that adventurer making it necessary for his safety, if for no other reason. Forbes had not waited long after his return to the East — he had stopped at Rochester on his way to New York and obtained financial aid from Frederick Douglass [17] — to begin, in December, 1857, a long series of abusive letters to all of Brown's Eastern friends and to the leading anti-slavery statesmen in Washington. Having now firmly convinced himself that he had been outrageously treated, he took somewhat of the blackmailer's position and demanded money on pain of publishing to the world the facts about Brown and his plans. The needs of his family, whether genuine or exaggerated, became an obsession with him; of Brown he demanded another six months' pay, on the ground that his engagement was for a year. His begging was endless and persistent; had he devoted but a tithe of the energy he put into his letters to earning a livelihood, he must have supported easily those dependent upon him. To most of those he addressed he was utterly unknown or at most a name; he had not, of course, any document to prove that he had been employed either by the Massachusetts Kansas Committee or the National Kansas Committee. Yet he insisted that he had been, — misled, perhaps, into believing that the Kansas Committees were similar to the European revolutionary bodies of which he had had experience or cognizance. He even forced his way, in the spring of 1858, to Senator Henry Wilson, on the floor of the Senate, during a recess of that body, and retailed to him in great excitement the story of his wrongs, renewing to Senator Wilson the demand he had then for some time been making, that Brown and his men be disarmed.[18] To William H. Seward he portrayed Brown as a "very bad man who would not keep his word;" "a reckless man, an unreliable man, a vicious man."[19]

As a sample of his utterances, the following will suffice to show either that the man was unbalanced, or that he was deliberately trying to use Brown's inability to pay him more than six months' salary as a club to get means — whether earned or not — from the New England friends:[20]

"Capt. B. came to me with a letter from the Rev. Joshua Leavitt of the New York *Independent*. Upon my making inquiries of him he stated that Capt. B. had no means of his own to meet any obligations but that he believed him to be backed by good and responsible men, and that at any rate I might repose faith in his word. Brown on his part trusted to the New England promises made to him, which promises being subsequently broken (because it was imagined that the border ruffians had abandoned Kansas) he of course could not fulfill his compact with me, and when I remonstrated, the humanitarians replied 'We do not know you — We made no engagement with you;' while Brown said 'Be quiet do not weaken my hand;' and when I refused to be quiet, since my children were being killed by slow torture through the culpability of the humanitarians, then B. denies his obligation to me rather than displease the men of money. The humanitarians and Brown are guilty of perfidy and barbarity, to which may be added stupidity. . . . You do not take into consideration that you are perpetrating an atrocious wrong, while I am struggling to save my family. I am the natural protector of my children, nothing but death shall prevent my defending them against the barbarity of the New England speculators."

He was by this time charging that the whole Virginia proposal was a scheme of A. A. Lawrence and others interested in New England mills, to make money by temporarily causing an increase in the price of cotton through the panic bound to follow Brown's attack.

On February 9, Brown wrote to his son John, directing him to reply to a letter from Forbes in the following disingenuous terms:[21]

"Your letter to my father, of 27th January, after mature reflection, I have decided to return *to you*, as I am unwilling he should, with all his other cares, difficulties and trials, be vexed with what I am apprehensive he will accept as *highly offensive and insulting*,

A CONVENTION AND A POSTPONEMENT

while I know that he is disposed to do all he consistently can for you, and will do so unless you are yourself the cause of his disgust. I was trying to send you a little assistance myself,—say about forty dollars; but I must hold up till I feel different from what I do now. I understood from my father that he had *advanced* you already six hundred dollars, or six months' pay (disappointed as he has been) to enable you to provide for your family; and that he was to give you one hundred dollars per month for just as much time as you continued in his service. Now, you in your letter undertake to *instruct* him to say that he had positively engaged you for one year. I fear he will not accept it well to be asked or told to state what he considers an *untruth*. Again, I suspect you have greatly mistaken the man, if you suppose he will take it kindly in you, or any living man, to assume to instruct him how he should conduct his own business and correspondence. And I suspect that the seemingly spiteful letters you say you have written to some of his particular friends have not only done you great injury, but also weakened his hands with them. While I have, in my poverty, deeply sympathized with you and your family, *who*, I ask, is likely to be moved by any exhibition of a wicked and spiteful temper on your part, or is likely to be dictated to by you as to their duties?"

To this son, Brown explained that he wished to see how a sharp and well-merited rebuke would affect Forbes; if it had the desired effect, they would send forty dollars. "I am anxious," Brown added, "to understand him fully before we go any further. . . ."

While the Forbes matter was doubtless much on his mind during his stay of three weeks with Frederick Douglass, his chief concern was to bring about a meeting of his warmest and most generous supporters at Gerrit Smith's, in Peterboro, in the latter half of February. He declined a call from Mr. Stearns and Mr. Sanborn to visit Boston because: [22]

"It would be almost impossible for me to pass through Albany, Springfield, or any of those points, on my way to Boston; & not have it known; & my reasons for keeping quiet were such that when I left Kansas; I kept it from *every friend there;* & I suppose it is still understood that I am hiding somewhere in the territory; & such will be the idea; untill it comes to be generally known that I am in these parts. I want to continue that impression as long as I can; *or for the present.* . . . My reasons for keeping still are sufficient to keep me from seeing *my Wife; &* Children: *much as I long to do so.*"

To them Brown had written at length, on January 30,[23] of his relief of mind at being again so near them, of his hope of devising a way of meeting some one of the deserted North Elba homestead:

"The anxiety I feel to see my *Wife;* & Children once more; I am unable to describe. . . . The *cries* of my poor *sorrowstricken despairing Children* whoose '*tears on their cheeks*' are *ever* in my *Eye;* & whose *sighs* are *ever* in my Ears; may however prevent my enjoying the happiness I so much desire. But *courage, courage, Courage* the great work of my life (the unseen Hand that 'girded me; & who has *indeed* holden *my right* hand may hold it still;) *though* I have not known Him;' at all *as I ought:*) I may yet see accomplished; (*God helping;*) & be permitted to return, *& rest* at Evening."

To Thomas Wentworth Higginson he thus appealed:[24]

"I now want to get for the *perfecting* of BY FAR the most *important* undertaking of my whole life; from $500, to $800, within the next Sixty days. I have written Rev Theodore Parker, George L. Stearns, and F. B. Sanborn Esqur, on the subject; but do not know as either Mr Stearns, or Mr Sanborn, are abolitionists I suppose they are. Can you be induced to opperate at Worcester, & elsewhere during that time to raise from *Anti-*slavery *men & women* (or any other parties) some part of that amount? . . . Hope this is my last effort in the begging line."

Higginson could not go to Peterboro, neither could Mr. Stearns; moreover, Brown's letters failed to interest them because of their indefiniteness. To Mr. Sanborn the invitation was particularly attractive because of the presence at Gerrit Smith's of a classmate, Edwin Morton, then a tutor in Mr. Smith's family. "Our old and noble friend, Captain John Brown of Kansas arrives this evening," is the entry in Gerrit Smith's diary on February 18, 1858,[25] and his welcome was in keeping with these words. For Brown this worthy philanthropist conceived a genuine affection, which appears in the later letters to the raider, and not even in the Stearns or Russell homes was he a more welcome guest. On this, the most important of all visits, he lost no time in unfolding his plans to his generous patron, and on the 24th he was able to write to his family:[26] "Mr. Smith & family go *all* lengths with me,"— a significant phrase in view of Mr. Smith's subsequent efforts to make it appear that he was not really cognizant of the lengths to which Brown's plan was to carry them. The final and most important exchange of views was held when Mr.

A CONVENTION AND A POSTPONEMENT

Sanborn arrived, on Washington's Birthday. What took place then has been set forth in detail by Mr. Sanborn at various times.[27] In an upper room of the Smith mansion, Brown "unfolded his plans" for a campaign somewhere in slave territory east of the Alleghanies, and read to them, so Mr. Sanborn records,

"the singular constitution drawn up by him [in the Frederick Douglass house in Rochester] for the government of the territory, small or large, which he might rescue by force from slavery, and for the control of his own little band. It was an amazing proposition — desperate in its character, wholly inadequate in its provision of means, and of most uncertain result. Such as it was, Brown had set his heart on it as the shortest way to restore our slave-cursed republic to the principles of the Declaration of Independence; and he was ready to die in its execution — as he did."

Amazing proposition that it was, Brown's auditors gave him respectful attention until after midnight, "proposing objections and raising difficulties; but nothing could shake the purpose of the old Puritan." He was able in some fashion to meet every criticism of his plans, to suggest a plausible way out of every difficulty, while to the chief objection, the slender means for undertaking a war upon the dominating American institution, he opposed merely a Scriptural text: "If God be for us, who can be against us?" He wanted to open his campaign in the spring; all he needed was five hundred or eight hundred dollars, for he now had the arms and sufficient men. "No argument could prevail against his fixed purpose." The discussion went over until the next day; and despite the foolhardiness of the venture, despite the strange Constitution, which to many minds remains the strongest indictment of Brown's sanity, his will prevailed. He did not at this time, Mr. Sanborn testifies, speak specifically of starting at Harper's Ferry or taking the arsenal; the point of departure was left vague, but the general outlines were about as he had described them to Forbes. Back of it all, in his head, was the purpose of setting the South afire and precipitating a conflict. Finally, says Mr. Sanborn:[28]

"We saw we must either stand by him or leave him to dash himself alone against the fortress he was determined to assault. To withhold aid would only delay, not prevent him. As the sun was setting over the snowy hills of the region where we met, I walked for an hour with Gerrit Smith among woods and fields (then included in his broad manor) which his father purchased of the Indians and bequeathed to him. Brown was left at home by the fire, discussing points of theology with Charles Stewart [Stuart]. Mr. Smith restated in his eloquent way the daring propositions of Brown, whose import he understood fully, and then said in substance: 'You see how it is; our dear old friend has made up his mind to this course, and cannot be turned from it. We cannot give him up to die alone; we must support him. I will raise so many hundred dollars for him; you must lay the case before your friends in Massachusetts, and ask them to do as much. I see no other way.' I had come to the same conclusion, and by the same process of reasoning. It was done far more from our regard for the man than from hopes of immediate success."

Well might Brown rejoice. With Mr. Smith's wealth and influence behind him, it could now be only a short while before he would have in hand the small sum he asked, and be actually in battle with the forces of slavery.

Mr. Sanborn left on February 24 for Boston, ready to work for the plan there and summon a gathering of a trusted few who could be counted on to put their shoulders to the wheel. He had scarcely left when Brown, in his exaltation and exultation of spirit, sent him these characteristic lines: [29]

My Dear Friend

Mr Morton has taken the liberty of saying to me that you felt ½ inclined to make a common cause with me. I *greatly rejoice at this;* for I believe when you come to look at the *ample field* I labour in: & the rich harvest which (not only this entire country, but) the whole world during the present & future generations *may reap* from its successful cultivation: you will feel that you are out of your element until you find you are in it; an entire Unit. What an inconceivable amount of good you might so effect; by your *counsel,* your *example, your encouragement, your natural, & acquired ability;* for active service. And then how *very little* we can possibly loose? Certainly the cause is enough *to live for;* if not to ——* for. I have only had *this one* opportunity in a life of nearly Sixty years, & could I be continued Ten times as long again, I might not again have another equal opportunity. God has honored but comparatively *a very small* part of mankind with any possible chance for such mighty & soul satisfying rewards. But my dear friend if you should make up your mind to do so I trust it will be wholly from the promptings of

* Word omitted.

A CONVENTION AND A POSTPONEMENT

your own spirit; after having *thoroughly counted* the cost. I would *flatter no man* into such a measure if I could do it ever so easily. *I expect nothing* but to "endure *hardness*": but I expect to effect a mighty conquest even though it be like the last victory of Samson. I felt for a number of years *in earlier life:* a steady, strong, desire; *to die:* but since I saw any prospect of becoming a "reaper" in the *great* harvest I have not only felt quite willing to *live:* but have enjoyed life much; & am now rather anxious to live for *a few* years more.

On the same day, Brown left Peterboro for the home of Dr. and Mrs. J. N. Gloucester, a well-to-do colored couple of Brooklyn, who by wise investments and steady industry had accumulated a fortune.[30] To them he revealed his plan, with full confidence in their ability to keep a secret, just as he got into frank communication with J. W. Loguen, a negro of Syracuse. These and other colored people assisted him with counsel and funds, came to believe whole-heartedly in the success of his project, and remained faithful to the end. On the 11th of March, Brown was in Philadelphia, where he met on the 15th, at the residence of the Rev. Stephen Smith in Lombard Street, a little group of colored men, among them Frederick Douglass, the Rev. Henry H. Garnett and William Still.[31] To them, too, with surprising but justified faith in the ability of numbers to keep so important a conspiracy to themselves, Brown stated his project and appealed for men and money, and John Brown, Jr., seconded him, for he had met his father in Philadelphia to discuss his own part in the great undertaking. His father wished him to take a trip to "Bedford, Chambersburg, Gettysburg, and Uniontown, in Pennsylvania, travelling slowly along, and inquiring of every one on the way or every family of the right stripe." He also urged his son to go "even to Harper's Ferry."[32] William Still, long an active Underground Railroad worker in Philadelphia, was especially valuable in this time, because of his knowledge of the Pennsylvania routes and stations.

All through this period Brown was endeavoring to enlist new recruits. He counted on Frederick Douglass, and the survivors of his family still feel that the great colored orator failed, when the real test came, to live up to his obligations.[33] A particular disappointment at this period in 1858 was his inability to reënlist his son-in-law, Henry Thompson, whose services and bravery in Kansas had so commended themselves to him. Of his daughter Ruth he asked whether any plan could

"be devised whereby you could let Henry go 'to school' (as you expressed it in your letter to him while in Kansas:) I would rather NOW have *him* 'for another term': than to have a Hundred average schollars. I have a PARTICULAR & VERY IMPORTANT; (*but not dangerous*) place for HIM *to fill;* in the 'school'; & I know of NO MAN *living;* so well adapted to fill it. I am quite confident some way can be devised; so that *you; & your children* could be *with* him; & be quite happy *even:* & safe but '*God forbid*' me to flatter you into trouble. I *did not do it before*." [34]

The daughter replied in doubt, asking what the post of his duty was to be, and saying that her husband felt that too high an estimate had been placed on his "qualifications as a scholar." Ruth's desire to preserve her husband's life conquered in the end her wish to be of service to her father and the great cause of the Brown family.[35] To this Mr. Thompson probably owes the fact that he is still, at this writing, in the land of the living.

Before his Philadelphia conference, Brown had made a hasty trip to Boston, where he met Higginson, Parker, Howe, Sanborn and Stearns, at the American House during his four days' stay from March 5 to 8. To Mr. Parker he wrote, on March 7, asking his aid in "composing a substitute for an address you saw last season, directed to the officers and soldiers of the United States Army." He had never been able to clothe his ideas in language to satisfy himself, but he tried to tell the great pulpit orator what he wanted, in these words:[36]

"In the first place, it must be short, or it will not be generally read. It must be in the simplest or plainest language; without the least affectation of the scholar about it, and yet be worded with great clearness and power. The anonymous writer must (in the language of the Paddy) be 'after others,' and not 'after himself, at all, at all.' If the spirit that 'communicated' Franklin's Poor Richard (or some other good spirit) would dictate, I think it would be quite as well employed as the 'dear sister spirits' have been for some years past. The address should be appropriate, and particularly adapted to the peculiar circumstances we anticipate, and should look to the actual change of service from that of Satan to the service of God. It should be, in short, a most earnest and powerful appeal to man's sense of right, and to their feelings of humanity."

A CONVENTION AND A POSTPONEMENT 325

Brown also asked for a similar short address,

"appropriate to the peculiar circumstances, intended for all persons, old and young, male and female, slaveholding and non-slaveholding, to be sent out broadcast over the entire nation. So by every male and female prisoner on being set at liberty, and to be read by them during confinement."

Particularly striking is this passage, since it foreshadows exactly his treatment of his prisoners at Harper's Ferry:

"The impressions made on prisoners by kindness and plain dealing, instead of barbarous and cruel treatment, such as they might give, and instead of being slaughtered like vile reptiles, as they might very naturally expect, are not only powerful, but lasting. Females are susceptible of being carried away entirely by the kindness of an intrepid and magnanimous soldier, even when his bare name was but a terror the day previous."

By this appeal Mr. Parker was not moved, his only reply being to send to Brown Captain George B. McClellan's recently issued report on the armies of Europe.[37] That Brown was much concerned with the reading of his followers appears from his asking Mr. Sanborn, in February, for copies of Plutarch's 'Lives,' Irving's 'Life of Washington,' the best written 'Life of Napoleon' and other similar books, for use at Springdale.[38]

Some idea of the method of raising the funds for Brown appears from Mr. Sanborn's letters of this period to Mr. Higginson. On March 8 he reported:[39]

"Hawkins* has gone to Philadelphia today, leaving his friends to work for him. $1000 is the sum set to be raised here — of which yourself, Mr. Parker, Dr. Howe, Mr. Stearns and myself each are assessed to raise $100 — Some may do more — perhaps you cannot come up to that — nor I, possibly — But of $500 we are sure — and the $1000 in all probability. . . . Hawkins goes to prepare agencies for his business near where he will begin operations. Dr. Cabot knows something of the speculation, but not the whole, not being quite prepared to take stock. No others have been admitted to a share in the business, though G. R. Russell has been consulted."

A meeting was called for March 20, at Dr. Howe's rooms, to discuss raising funds, in Mr. Stearns's name. The next day Mr. Sanborn stated that:

* Brown.

"Mr. Stearns is Treasurer of the enterprise for N. E. — and has now on hand $150 having paid H—— $100. . . . Mr. Stearns has given $100 & promises $200 more, but holds it back for a future emergency. Mr. Parker has raised his $100 & will do something more. Dr. H. has paid in $50 and will raise $100 more. . . . I paid Brown $25 — my own subscription — but have as yet been able to get nothing else — though I shall do so." [40]

By April 1 there were three hundred and seventy-five dollars in hand, but three weeks later, Brown had received only four hundred and ten dollars and was calling urgently for the remainder of the one thousand dollars promised. In all he received at this time only about six hundred dollars, together with other sums raised in New York and Philadelphia — a pittance, indeed, with which to begin his crusade. Mr. Higginson early did his share. His interview with Brown in March had made so deep an impression upon him that he was thereafter ready to do and dare with Brown with unflinching courage. As it is often said that Brown's chief success lay in influencing weaker minds, it is worth noting the impression a single talk with him made upon this able and virile Worcester clergyman:

"I met him in his room at the American House [No. 126] in March, 1858. I saw before me a man whose mere appearance and bearing refuted in advance some of the strange perversions which have found their way into many books, and which often wholly missed the type to which he belonged. In his thin, worn, resolute face there were the signs of a fire which might wear him out, and practically did so, but nothing of pettiness or baseness; and his talk was calm, persuasive, and coherent. He was simply a high-minded, unselfish, belated Covenanter; a man whom Sir Walter Scott might have drawn, but whom such writers as Nicolay and Hay, for instance, have utterly failed to delineate. To describe him in their words as 'clean but coarse' is curiously wide of the mark; he had no more of coarseness than was to be found in Habakkuk Mucklewrath or in George Eliot's Adam Bede; he *had*, on the contrary, that religious elevation which is itself a kind of refinement; the quality one may see expressed in many a venerable Quaker face at yearly meeting. Coarseness absolutely repelled him; he was so strict as to the demeanor of his men that his band was always kept small, while that of Lane was large; he had little humor, and none of the humorist's temptation toward questionable conversation." [41]

On one of his Boston visits, Brown also met the Rev. James Freeman Clarke at Senator Sumner's residence, according

A CONVENTION AND A POSTPONEMENT 327

to Mr. Clarke,[42] where Brown begged to see the coat worn by the Senator when he was attacked, and "looked at it as a devotee would contemplate the relic of a saint." This was his only recorded meeting with the victim of Preston Brooks's assault, the news of which had so stirred Brown and his men prior to the Pottawatomie murders.

From Philadelphia, John Brown and John, Jr., made a brief visit to New Haven and New York; at the latter place the well-known Gibbons and Hopper families, prominent among the anti-slavery Quakers, were now assisting him. Thence they went direct to North Elba, on what was to have been a farewell visit prior to the risking of their lives, arriving on March 23.[43] By April 2 they were at Gerrit Smith's, again under way, and found Mr. Smith as encouraging as usual. After a day spent in discussing the Virginia plan, they left for Rochester, where they separated on April 5, Brown heading for St. Catherine's, Canada, where he arrived on the 7th in company with his colored helper, J. W. Loguen.[44] Here he met by appointment a remarkable negro woman, Harriet Tubman, known as the "Moses of her People," whom he now relied upon to work for him among the escaped slaves then living in large numbers in Canada West, as he later hoped that she would be a chief guide to the North of the slaves he wished to free in the neighborhood of Harper's Ferry. Of her Brown wrote that she was "the most of a man, naturally, that I ever met with." Well might she win his admiration, for her exploits in leading runaway slaves to freedom, at the risk of her own life, form one of the most moving and thrilling stories of the entire struggle against slavery.

At this time there were some thirty to forty thousand colored people in Upper Canada, and about twelve hundred in Toronto, some of them free-born and in good circumstances; a great majority, "freight" of the Underground Railroad.[45] At Buxton, near the shore of Lake Erie, was the "Elgin Association," a model colony for escaped slaves; and not far from this was Chatham, chief town of the County of Kent, also a favorite place for the colored men who had found under the British flag the personal liberty denied them under the stars and stripes. Here were some well-to-do colored farmers and mechanics, who had established a good school, Wilberforce

Institute, for the education of their children, several churches and a newspaper of their own.[46] Brown soon made up his mind that this would be the best place for the convention of his followers upon which he had now set his heart. He was not willing to commence his raid upon slavery without some formality. Just as he had drawn up regular by-laws for his Kansas company to sign, so he now wished to inaugurate his movement only with a certain ceremonial. It would have been cheaper and easier to have gone direct to the scene of action in Virginia, but his mind was set on his convention, upon which he also counted to draw to his enterprise some, if not many, of the escaped slaves in Canada West.

His visit to St. Catherine's with J. W. Loguen was, therefore, in the nature of a reconnoissance. It lasted a trifle less than three weeks, and included a trip to Ingersoll, Chatham, and probably to other near-by points. Neither the letters now available nor Brown's memorandum-book of 1858 have recorded any details of his movements. But his pen was ever busy, and the recruits for his convention were gradually enlisted, among them a colored physician, Dr. Martin R. Delany, who subsequently served in the colored volunteers, with the rank of major, during the Civil War. To see this able man, Brown went three times to Chatham [47] before finding him, refusing on the first two occasions to leave his name or address. To him Brown stated that it was men he wanted, not money, and Dr. Delany promised to be on hand at the Chatham convention and to bring others as well. Finally, Brown was ready to lead to Canada the "flock of sheep" he had wintered at Springdale, to which place he journeyed by way of Chicago. He arrived at Mr. Maxson's home the 25th of April, and two days later was ready to start, as he wrote on that day to his family.

He found the band of conspirators reinforced by George B. Gill, a native of Iowa, and Stewart Taylor, a young Canadian, who responded to his name at the final roll-call in Harper's Ferry and there lost his life. Gill, a man of education and some literary ability, had known Brown in previous enterprises, had been in Kansas and introduced Taylor to John Brown. Two other notable accessions were the brothers Coppoc, Barclay and Edwin, who also participated in the final raid, much to

A CONVENTION AND A POSTPONEMENT 329

the grief of their Quaker mother, whose quaint and fast-decaying house may still be seen in Springdale. A woman of marked intelligence, a strong Abolitionist, she had herself instilled into the minds of her sons that hatred of slavery which had led Barclay to Kansas in 1857, to aid in making it a free State, and resulted in Edwin's giving up his life on the scaffold with that pure faith and calm resignation naturally associated with the Quaker training.[48] The Coppocs were not ready to go to Chatham, and so did not figure in the convention, as did the men who had boarded at Mr. Maxson's. These John Brown found still harmonious, despite some occasional friction, to be expected, perhaps, among vigorous men of strong, restless character, cooped up in one small farmhouse. Leeman had given Owen Brown the greatest concern of all,[49] and Tidd had laid himself open to a grave charge by the father of a Quaker maiden resident not far away.[50] But aside from this, there seems to have been genuine regret at the leaving of this body of vigorous young men who had done so much to enliven and entertain the neighborhood; several of them kept up a lengthy correspondence with friends in Springdale up to the hour of the tragedy which gave them a place in history. Certainly, Brown could not complain of the spirit of his followers, when he rejoined them. Stevens wrote to his sister on April 8: "I am ready to give up my life for the oppressed if need be. I hope I shall have your good will and sympathy in this glorious cause." [51] Leeman rejoiced that he was "warring with slavery the greatest *Curse* that ever infested America." Richard Realf's and John E. Cook's letters are in a similar strain.

Leaving Springdale with nine of the men, shortly before noon on the 27th, Brown and his followers took a three o'clock train for West Liberty, and arrived at Chicago at five the next morning. For breakfast they went to the Massasoit House, only to be told that one of their number, the negro, Richard Richardson, could not be served with them. True to their belief that all men were created free and equal, and to their comradeship, they marched out of the hotel, Brown at their head, and soon found another hostelry, the Adams House, at which the color-line was not drawn.[52] Leaving Chicago at four-thirty, the ten were in Detroit at six o'clock on the morning of Thursday, April 29, and were breakfasting at the Villa

Tavern, Chatham, by nine o'clock. "Ten persons begin to board with Mr. Barber 29th April at Dinner. Three others began May 1st at Breakfast," Brown's memorandum-book records. He himself made his headquarters with James M. Bell, a colored man. "Here," wrote Richard Realf to Dr. H. C. Gill at Springdale,[53]

"we intend to remain till we have perfected our plans, which will be in about ten days or two weeks, after which we start for *China*. Yesterday and this morning we have been very busy in writing to Gerrit Smith and Wendell Phillips and others of like kin to meet us in this place on Saturday, the 8th of May, to adopt our Constitution, decide a few matters and bid us goodbye. Then we start. . . . The signals and mode of writing are (the old man informs me) all arranged. . . . Remember me to all who know our business, but to all others be as dumb as death."

Despite Brown's admonition to his men to write no letters while here, John E. Cook was another who corresponded freely with friends in Springdale; to two young women he observed[54] that only one thing kept him

"from being absolutely unhappy, and that is the consciousness that I am in the path of duty. I long for the 10th of May to come. I am anxious to leave this place, to have my mind occupied with the great work of our mission. . . . Through the dark gloom of the future I fancy I can almost see the dawning light of Freedom; . . . that I can almost hear the swelling anthem of Liberty rising from the millions who have but just cast aside the fetters and the shackles that bound them. But ere that day arrives, I fear that we shall hear the crash of the battle shock and see the red gleaming of the cannon's lightning."

Not only were compromising letters of this kind written freely to friends and relations, but similar ones received were carried about by all the men and kept intact up to the raid itself.

Finally, the 8th of May, the day for the opening of the convention, arrived. None of the Eastern backers were present, neither Wendell Phillips, nor Gerrit Smith, nor F. B. Sanborn, and no white men save Brown's own party. This was now composed, besides himself, of Leeman, Stevens, Tidd, Gill, Taylor, Parsons, Kagi, Moffet, Cook, Realf and Owen Brown, — twelve in all. The colored men were thirty-four in number, among them Richard Richardson, Osborn P.

A CONVENTION AND A POSTPONEMENT

Anderson, James H. Harris, afterwards Congressman from North Carolina and Dr. Delany. Only one of these thirty-four, O. P. Anderson, actually reached the firing-line. The presiding officer was William Charles Munroe, pastor of a Detroit colored church, and the secretary was John H. Kagi.[55] There were really two distinct conventions. The first, a "Provisional Constitutional Convention," met on Saturday, May 8, at ten in the morning, in a frame school-building on Princess Street, the remaining sessions being held in the First Baptist Church and in "No. 3 Engine House," which had been erected by some colored men, who also formed the fire-company. In order to mislead any one who might inquire the meaning of these assemblages, it was stated that they were for the purpose of organizing a Masonic lodge among the colored people. After the election of officers, on motion of Dr. Delany, John Brown arose to state at length the object of the permanent convention and the plan of action to follow it. Dr. Delany and others spoke in favor of both projects, and they were agreed to by general assent.

In his testimony before the Mason Committee, early in 1860, Richard Realf thus set forth the substance of the leader's speech:[56]

"John Brown, on rising, stated that for twenty or thirty years the idea had possessed him like a passion of giving liberty to the slaves. He stated immediately thereafter, that he made a journey to England in 1851, in which year he took to the international exhibition at London, samples of wool from Ohio, during which period he made a tour upon the European continent, inspecting all fortifications, and especially all earth-work forts which he could find, with a view, as he stated, of applying the knowledge thus gained, with modifications and inventions of his own, to such a mountain warfare as he thereafter spoke upon in the United States. John Brown stated, moreover, that he had not been indebted to anybody for the suggestion of that plan; that it arose spontaneously in his own mind; that through a series of from twenty to thirty years it had gradually formed and developed itself into shape and plan."

After telling of his studies of Roman warfare, of the successful opposition to the Romans of the Spanish chieftains, of the successes of Schamyl, the Circassian chief, and of Toussaint L'Ouverture in Hayti, and of his own familiarity with Haytian conditions, Brown spoke of his belief that, "upon the first intimation of a plan formed for the liberation of the slaves, they would immediately rise all over the Southern States. He supposed that they would come into the mountains to join him, where he proposed to work, and that by flocking to his standard they would enable him (by making the line of mountains which cuts diagonally through Maryland and Virginia down through the Southern States into Tennessee and Alabama, the base of his operations) to act upon the plantations on the plains lying on each side of that range of mountains, and that we should be able to establish ourselves in the fastnesses, and if any hostile action (as would be) were taken against us, either by the militia of the separate States or by the armies of the United States, we purposed to defeat first the militia, and next, if it were possible, the troops of the United States, and then organize the freed blacks under this provisional constitution, which would carve out for the locality of its jurisdiction all that mountainous region in which the blacks were to be established and in which they were to be taught the useful and mechanical arts, and to be instructed in all the business of life. Schools were also to be established, and so on. That was it. . . . The negroes were to constitute the soldiers. John Brown expected that all the free negroes in the Northern States would immediately flock to his standard. He expected that all the slaves in the Southern States would do the same. He believed, too, that as many of the free negroes in Canada as could accompany him, would do so. . . . The slaveholders were to be taken as hostages, if they refused to let their slaves go. It is a mistake to suppose that they were to be killed; they were not to be. They were to be held as hostages for the safe treatment of any prisoners of John Brown's who might fall into the hands of hostile parties. . . . All the non-slaveholders were to be protected. Those who would not join the organization of John Brown, but who would not oppose it, were to be protected; but those who did oppose it, were to be treated as the slaveholders themselves. . . . Thus, John Brown said that he believed, a successful incursion could be made; that it could be successfully maintained; that the several slave States could be forced (from the position in which they found themselves) to recognize the freedom of those who had been slaves within the respective limits of those States; that immediately such recognitions were made, then the places of all the officers elected under this provisional constitution became vacant, and new elections were to be made. Moreover, no salaries were to be paid to the office-holders under this constitution. It was purely out of that which we supposed to be philanthropy — love for the slave."

After this address, John Brown presented a plan of organization, entitled "Provisional Constitution and Ordinances for the People of the United States," and moved the read-

A CONVENTION AND A POSTPONEMENT

ing of it. To this there was objection until an oath of secrecy was taken by each member of the convention. An oath being moved, John Brown arose and informed the convention that he had conscientious scruples about taking any oath; that all he desired was a promise that any person who thereafter divulged any of the proceedings "agreed to forfeit the protection which that organization could extend over him." Nevertheless, the oath was voted and the president administered the obligation. Thereupon the proposed Constitution was read, and after debate on one article, the forty-sixth, it was unanimously adopted. The afternoon session was brief, being occupied solely with signing the Constitution, "congratulatory remarks" by Dr. Delany and Thomas M. Kinnard and final adjournment. At the evening session the convention was a new body, — that called by the Constitution adopted by the "Provisional Convention," "for the purpose of electing officers to fill the offices specially established and named by said Constitution." With the same officers, the new convention appointed a committee to make nominations. Upon its failing to do so promptly, the convention itself elected John Brown Commander-in-Chief, and John H. Kagi, Secretary of War. On Monday, May 10, the balloting was resumed. Realf was made Secretary of State, George B. Gill, Secretary of the Treasury, Owen Brown, Treasurer, and Osborn P. Anderson and Alfred M. Ellsworth, members of Congress. After the position of President had been declined by or for two colored men, the filling of this and other vacancies was left to a committee of fifteen, headed by John Brown. It is not of record, however, that the vacancies were ever filled.

If, after a lapse of fifty years, it seems at first as if the Constitution and the entire proceeding belonged to the domain of the mock Springdale legislature, the earnestness and seriousness of the Chatham proceedings cannot be denied, so far as the moving spirits were concerned. Some of the men doubtless signed without much consideration; but to the colored men, at least, it seemed as if freedom from bondage were really in sight for their enslaved brethren. Since Brown was able to overrule the objections of practical men like Gerrit Smith and George L. Stearns, it is, of course, not to be wondered at if the little gathering in Chatham accepted at its face value the extraordinary document which John Brown laid before them. They could but applaud the admirably written preamble:[57]

"Whereas, Slavery, throughout its entire existence in the United States is none other than a most barbarous, unprovoked, and unjustifiable War of one portion of its citizens upon another portion; the only conditions of which are perpetual imprisonment, and hopeless servitude or absolute extermination; in utter disregard and violation of those eternal and self-evident truths set forth in our Declaration of Independence: *Therefore*, we *CITIZENS* of the *UNITED STATES*, and the *OPPRESSED PEOPLE*, who, by a *RECENT DECISION* of the *SUPREME COURT ARE DECLARED* to have *NO RIGHTS WHICH* the *WHITE MAN* is *BOUND* to *RESPECT; TOGETHER WITH ALL OTHER PEOPLE DEGRADED* by the *LAWS THEREOF*, *DO*, for the *TIME BEING ORDAIN* and *ESTABLISH* for *OURSELVES* the *FOLLOWING PROVISIONAL CONSTITUTION* and *ORDINANCES*, the *BETTER* to *PROTECT* our *PERSONS, PROPERTY, LIVES*, and *LIBERTIES:* and to *GOVERN* our *ACTIONS*."

This statement, in its definition of slavery as *war*, is the keynote to Brown's philosophy, and explains better than anything else why it was consistent with his devout religious character for him to kill, and to plunder for supplies in Kansas, and to take up arms against slavery itself. There was for him no such thing as peace so long as there were chains upon a single slave; and he was, therefore, at liberty to plot and intrigue, to prepare for hostilities, without regard to public order or the civil laws. Passing beyond the preamble, the Constitution * suggests the word "insane," which the historian Von Holst applies to certain of its provisions. It actually contemplates not merely the government of forces in armed insurrection against sovereign States and opposed to the armies of the United States, but actually goes so far as to establish courts, a regular judiciary and a Congress. As if that were not enough, it provides for schools for that same training of the freed slaves in manual labor which is to-day so widely hailed as the readiest solution of the negro problem. Churches, too, were to be "established as soon as may be," — as if anything

* See Appendix.

A CONVENTION AND A POSTPONEMENT 335

could be more inconsistent with the fundamental plan of breaking the forces up into small bands hidden in mountain fastnesses, subsisting as well as possible off the land, and probably unable to communicate with one another. At this and at other points the whole scheme forbids discussion as a practical plan of government for such an uprising as was to be carried out by a handful of whites and droves of utterly illiterate and ignorant blacks. As has already been said, it is still a chief indictment of Brown's saneness of judgment and his reasoning powers. Von Holst, one of his greatest admirers, describes it as a "piece of insanity, in the literal sense of the word," and a "confused medley of absurd, because absolutely inapplicable, forms." [58] Yet no one can deny that in many of its articles the Brown Constitution is admirable in spirit, as, for instance, in the provisions for the enforcement of morality and for the humanitarian treatment of prisoners, as well as in other measures well adapted to the undertaking. As a chart for the course of a State about to secede from the Union and to maintain itself during a regular revolution, the document was also not without its admirable features. It is impossible, however, as regards this extraordinary Constitution, to forget that it was drawn for the use of possibly fifty white men and hordes of escaping slaves fighting for their lives, not on the open prairies of Kansas, or among its scattered hamlets, but in well-populated and well-settled portions of the South.

The Constitution simply emphasizes anew Brown's belief that he really could engage in warfare against slavery, and could keep at bay the United States army while doing so; that with a handful of men and a few hundred guns and mediæval pikes, he could grapple and shake to its foundations an institution the actual uprooting of which nearly cost the United States Government its existence, and necessitated the sacrificing of vast treasure and an enormous number of human lives. Brown was careful even to provide that no treaty of peace — presumably either with the United States or the several Southern States — could be ratified save by his President, his Vice-President, a majority of his Congress and of his Supreme Court, and of the general officers of the army; that is, his half-company of officers was to be considered equal as a treaty-making power with a great nation and its coördinate parts! It is best, therefore, not to attempt to analyze the Chatham Constitution, but to admire its wording and its composition, and lay it aside as a temporary aberration of a mind that in its other manifestations defies successful classification as unhinged or altogether unbalanced. Fanatical, Brown's mind was; concentrated on one idea to the danger-point, most alienists would probably agree; but still it remained a mind capable of expressing itself with rare clearness and force, focussing itself with intense vigor on the business in hand, and going straight to the end in view.

One point of the Constitution remains to be considered. Brown maintained at his trial that he had not sought to overthrow the United States Government or that of Virginia; the Chatham Constitution was cited against him. A biographer, R. J. Hinton, insisted [59] that Brown was justified in his position by Article XLVI of the Constitution, which reads: "The foregoing Articles shall not be construed so as in any way to encourage the overthrow of any State Government or of the General Government of the United States: and look to no dissolution of the Union but simply to Amendment and Repeal. And our flag shall be the same that our Fathers fought under in the Revolution." This was the only article challenged at Chatham, and one vote was cast for the motion to strike it out. Accepting it as a disclaimer of hostility to the various governments only increases the difficulty. It then appears that he was ready to oppose, and if necessary to kill, troops of the United States, and to create a civil government over certain portions of its territory, as the best way of inducing the United States Government to adopt his view of the slavery question. The radical Abolitionists openly worked for division by peaceful means and refused to make use of their rights as citizens; John Brown sought to oppose the authority of the Union by force of arms, while denying that any one could construe his actions as treason or disloyalty.

A definite and immediate result of the Chatham convention was the complete exhaustion of Brown's treasury. His Boston friends were expecting him to "turn loose his flock" about May 15, but the day before that he was still at Chatham, and wrote to Mr. Sanborn asking for three or four hundred dollars, "without delay."[60] On the 25th he wrote to

A CONVENTION AND A POSTPONEMENT 337

his family that "we are completely nailed down at present for want of funds, and we may be obliged to remain inactive for months yet, for the same reason. You must all learn to be patient—or, at least I hope you will." [61] Brown's chagrin at this condition of affairs was intensified by the needs of his men. They had left Chatham on May 11 and gone to Cleveland and near-by Ohio towns, in search of work to maintain them temporarily until they got the signal to reassemble. Now, obtaining work even in the most humble capacity was not easy in the spring of 1858, when the country had not yet begun to recover from the great financial depression of the previous fall. To Gill, who had written at once of the poor outlook,— there were two thousand men out of work in Cleveland,— Brown replied: [62]

"I will only inquire if you, any of you, think the difficulties you have experienced, so far, are sufficient to discourage a *man?* ... *I* and three others were in exactly *such a fix* in the spring of 1817: between the seaside and Ohio, in a time of *extreme scarcity* of not *only money*, but of the greatest distress for want of provisions, known during the nineteenth century. ... We are here [Realf, Kagi, Richardson and Leeman had remained in Canada] busy getting information and making other preparations. I believe no time has yet been lost. Owing to the panic on the part of *some* of our Eastern friends, we may be compelled to hold on for months yet. *But what of that?*"

Three days later, Brown expressed his satisfaction that all but three of the men had then obtained work "to stop their board bills." [63] He had received only fifteen dollars from the East, but was in "hourly expectation of help sufficient to pay off our bills here, and to take us on to Cleveland to see and advise with you." He was compelled to say in this letter that:

"such has been the effect of the course taken by F. [Forbes] that I have some fears that we shall be compelled to delay further action for the present. ... It is in such times that men mark themselves. 'He that endureth unto the end,' the same shall get his reward. Are our difficulties sufficient to make us give up one of the noblest enterprises in which men were ever engaged?"

The difficulties were not great enough to make any of the men abandon the project then, though some were indubitably in straits at times. Indeed, some of them actually plotted to go South and raid by themselves, if help did not soon come.[64] Cook was the leader in this; during his stay in Cleveland he was highly indiscreet, boasting that he was on a secret expedition; that he had killed five men in Kansas; swaggering openly in his boarding-house, and revealing much to a woman acquaintance, so that Realf feared that if the expedition were to be postponed, the greatest danger would not be from Forbes, but from Cook's "rage for talking." Richard Richardson and John A. Thomas, another colored man, who had gone to Cleveland with Brown and Realf, soon returned to Canada in fear of arrest, and are not thereafter heard from in connection with Brown.[65] Realf later went to New York to watch Forbes, and to plan his trip to England to raise funds for the cause.

John Brown himself left Chatham on May 29, and went direct to Boston, after having been there just a month.[66] He had been urged by Mr. Stearns to meet him in New York, to discuss the question of the arms in his possession, during the week beginning May 16, but he was unable to do so, and did not see any of the Boston friends until he arrived at the American House on May 31. As Brown had stated to his men, renewed activity on the part of Forbes had filled the Boston backers with consternation. Before and during the Chatham convention, Brown was writing almost daily to some one about "F.," as he referred to him in his memorandum-book. Mr. Higginson wrote on May 7 to John Brown, from Brattleboro, protesting against the postponement already talked of: [67]

DEAR FRIEND
Sanborn wrote an alarming letter of a certain H. F. who wishes to veto our veteran friend's project entirely. Who the man is I hv. no conception — but I utterly protest against any postponement. *If the thing is postponed, it is postponed for ever* — for H. F. can do as much harm next year as this. His malice must be in some way put down or *outwitted* — & after the move is *once begun*, his plots will be of little importance. I believe that we have gone too far to go back without certain failure — & I believe our friend the veteran will think so too.

This was Brown's own belief. But before he reached Boston the die was cast against him, as is seen from this note of Mr. Sanborn to Mr. Higginson: [68]

A CONVENTION AND A POSTPONEMENT

Concord May 18th '58.

The enclosed from our friend explains itself. The Dr. [Howe] has written to —— an adroit and stinging letter, intended to baffle him. Wilson as well as Hale and Seward, and God knows how many more have heard about the plot from F. To go on in the face of this is mere madness and I place myself fully on the side of P. [Parker] S. [Stearns] and Dr. H. [Howe] with G. S. [Gerrit Smith] who *does* count. What Dana says of F's character seems probable. Mr. S. [Stearns] and the Dr. will see Hawkins in New York this week and settle matters finally.

The letter from Senator Henry Wilson to Dr. Howe which had particularly alarmed the conspirators was a reflection of Forbes's sudden appearance before him on the floor of the Senate. It bore date of May 9 and read thus:[69]

"I write to you to say that you had better talk with some few of our friends who contributed money to aid old Brown to organize and arm some force in Kansas for defence, about the policy of getting those arms out of his hands & putting them in the hands of some reliable men in that Territory. *If they should be used for other purposes, as rumor says they may be, it might be of disadvantage to the men who were induced to contribute to that very foolish movement.* If it can be done, get the arms out of his control and keep clear of him at least for the present. This is in confidence."

On May 14, Mr. Stearns sent to Brown, at Chatham, a copy of this letter and, writing officially as chairman of the Massachusetts State Kansas Committee, thus admonished him:[70]

"You will recollect that you have the custody of the arms alluded to, to be used for the defence of Kansas, as agent of the Massachusetts State Kansas Committee. In consequence of the information thus communicated to me [by Dr. Howe and Senator Wilson], it becomes my duty to warn you not to use them for any other purpose, and to hold them subject to my order as chairman of said committee."

It was in regard to the arms that Mr. Stearns had sought the interview with Brown in New York. The latter agent of the Committee besought his Boston friends not to move hastily, and pledged himself not to act other than to obtain a perfect knowledge of the facts in regard to Forbes, if the two or three hundred dollars he needed were sent to him.

The outcome of Brown's conferences in Boston, which resulted in the temporary abandonment of the Virginia plan and

Brown's departure for Kansas, together with the attitude of the various conspirators, is thus succinctly set forth in a carefully preserved memorandum of Mr. Higginson's:[71]

"Saw [J. B.] in Boston. He showed me F's letter also one fr. S. announcing the result of a meeting between himself, G. S., G L S., T. P. & Dr H. It was to postpone till next winter or spring when they wd. raise $2000 or $3000; he meantime to blind F. by going to K. [Kansas] & to transfer the property so as to relieve them of responsibility — & they in future not to know his plans.

"On probing B. I gradually found that he agreed entirely with me, considered delay very discouraging to his 13 men & to those in Canada, — impossible to begin in the autumn & he wd. not lose a day (he finally said) if he had $300 — it wd. not cost $25 apiece to get his men fr. Ohio & that was all he needed. The knowledge that F. cd. give of his plan wd. be injurious, for he wished his opponents to underrate him: but still (as I suggested) the increased terror produced wd. perhaps counterbalance this & it wd. not make much difference. If he had the means, he wd. not lose a day.

"On my wondering that the others did not agree with us, he said the reason was *they were not men of action*, they were intimidated by Wilson's letter &c. & overrated the obstacles. G. S. he knew to be a timid man. G. L. S. & T. P. he did not think abounded in courage. H. had more & had till recently agreed with us.

"But the —— * old veteran added, he had not said this to them, & had appeared to acquiesce far more than he really did; it was essential that they shld. not think him reckless, & as they held the purse he was powerless without them, having spent nearly every thing received thus far (some $650 fr. them by his book wh. he showed — they having promised $1000) — on account of the delay — a month at Chatham &c But he wished me not to tell them what he had said to me.

"On Saturday, June 6, I went to see Dr. H. & found that things had ended far better than I supposed. The Kansas Com. had put some $500 in gold into his [Brown's] hands & all the arms — with only the understanding that he shld. go to K. & then be left to his own discretion. H. went off in good spirits. H. still claimed to agree with me, bt said the others 'wd. not hear of it — even P.' & he had to acquiesce & even write a letter urging H to go to Kansas."

This memorandum is erroneous in that it speaks of the Kansas Committee having given the $500 and the arms. The plain fact is that the money came from the same unofficial group of friends, and that the arms were given to Brown by the simple expedient of having Mr. Stearns foreclose on them. Mr.

* Word illegible.

Stearns had advanced large sums to the Kansas Committee, which had never been repaid, asking at the time that the arms if unused should come back to him, that he might reimburse himself for his outlay. It will be remembered that the Kansas Committee had agreed to this by formal vote, just after Mr. Stearns had paid for the two hundred pistols he had purchased of the Massachusetts Arms Company for Brown out of his own pocket, but in the name of the Kansas Committee. Mr. Stearns now simply exercised this option, and so notified the immediate conspirators verbally, and then presented all the arms, whose possession he had that minute assumed, to Brown. As soon as possible thereafter, says Mr. Sanborn, "the business of the Kansas Committee was put in such shape that its responsibility for the arms in Brown's possession should no longer fetter his friends in aiding his main design." [72] When the dénouement finally came, however, the public and press did not take a very favorable view of the transaction; it was too difficult to distinguish between George L. Stearns, the benefactor of the Kansas Committee, and George L. Stearns, the Chairman of that Committee. Again, there appear to have been some dissatisfied members of the Kansas Committee who remained uninformed of the transfer of the arms until the whole thing came out, and they resented the charge of having aided Brown in his Virginia foray. Mr. Sanborn admits that "it is still a little difficult to explain this transaction concerning the arms without leaving a suspicion that there was somewhere a breach of trust." [73]

To a recent historian, Rear-Admiral F. E. Chadwick, this incident is "not a pleasant story;" [74] he accuses the Kansas Committee and Dr. Howe of "duplicity" and "gross prevarication," the latter for writing to Senator Wilson on May 12:

"I understand perfectly your meaning. No countenance has been given to Brown for any operation outside of Kansas *by the Kansas Committee;*" and three days later: "Prompt measures have been taken and will resolutely be followed up to prevent any such monstrous perversion of a trust as would be the application of means raised for the defence of Kansas to a purpose which the subscribers of the fund would disapprove and vehemently condemn."

Technically, the Committee has a valid defence. Doubtless in the business world, and especially according to the standards of certain large industrial concerns of late years, the Committee's stratagem is quite defensible as a simple way out of a trying difficulty, and an easy method of obtaining for Brown the desired arms. It cannot be denied that frankness and straightforwardness would have dictated the notifying of Senator Wilson that the arms had passed into the possession of individual members of the Committee, which would not thereafter be responsible for them or the uses made of them. As it is, there was no actual recall of the arms from Brown whatever, as Senator Wilson was permitted to believe, save a purely nominal one. No one, says Mr. Sanborn, suggested that they should pass out of Brown's actual possession.[75] It is one of those unpleasant episodes which so often happen when the business of individuals and of organizations to which they belong becomes intertwined. Had Mr. Stearns not been Chairman of the Kansas Committee, but a mere outsider, no allegation of breach of trust could have lain in the premises. But even this admirable man sometimes split delicate hairs in discussing what actually happened at this period. Thus he later appeared before the Mason Committee and testified that John Brown had not asked for the two hundred Sharp's rifles in January, 1857, — the time that Brown was beseeching the National Kansas Committee and the Boston members of the Massachusetts State Committee to fit out his proposed "volunteer regular company" with arms! It must be pointed out, too, that the decision of the little Boston group, after giving Brown the five hundred dollars and arms, in 1858, to know no more of his plans, is the first sign of the effort to evade responsibility which became so apparent after the raid. They had encouraged him to attack slavery in the mountains of the South, giving him money and arms to do it with, and sanctioned his going ahead, — only they said: "Do not tell us the details of it." This attitude inevitably suggests that of those modern corporation directors who are perfectly aware that their agents, the executives of the company, are using the funds of the stockholders illegally, but salve their consciences by never broaching the matter in or out of the board-room, or examining the accounts. It further lays them open to the criticism of being ready to help others to assail a wrong, but of being themselves unwilling to take the full consequences of their acts.

As for the arms themselves, they were at this time in Ohio.[76] After Brown had brought them to Springdale, they were shipped from West Liberty, with the two hundred revolvers bought by Mr. Stearns, by freight to John Brown, Jr., at Conneaut, Ashtabula County, Ohio. By him they had been transported to, and concealed in, the village of Cherry Valley, where they were stored in the furniture ware-rooms of King Brothers. Here, for safety's sake, they were covered by a lot of ready-made coffins awaiting sale. The visit of a tax assessor made John Brown, Jr., nervous about them, but the arms remained here until early in May, when, by his father's directions, they were moved by night to the barn of a farmer named William Coleman, in the adjoining township of Wayne, who helped him to build by night a little store-room in his haymow. Some of the arms and the powder were for a time in the sugar-house of E. Alexander Fobes, a brother-in-law of John Brown, Jr. From here they were moved in 1859 to the scene of action. On May 1, 1858, John Brown, Jr., wrote to his father that he had been examining the arms, and that he had them "nearly all packed and ready to start on Monday next should nothing happen." He had examined the smaller "articles of freight," and found that the oil on the locks and elsewhere had become "so gummy" as to render the arms useless until thoroughly overhauled and cleaned.[77]

Rejoicing in his ownership of the arms and his fresh money-supply, Brown swallowed his disappointment over the postponement of the raid and went straight to North Elba, where he was on June 9. This time there was no indecision about his movements or hesitancy about returning to Kansas. He was in Cleveland by June 20, for on the next day he called his scattered followers together and, notifying them of the decision of the Boston friends, gave them what money he could and bade them be true to the cause.[78] A general break-up ensued. Realf, as already related, was to go to New York and watch Forbes; Owen went to his brother Jason's at Akron, Ohio, while Kagi and Tidd left that same day with Brown for Kansas by way of Chicago. Leeman and Taylor first went with Owen, and then drifted about in Ohio and Illinois, while Parsons spent the summer on Fobes's farm, where the arms were concealed, and then returned to his home at Byron, Illinois.[79] Moffet worked his way home to Iowa, after staying for some time in Cleveland, while Gill and Stevens went back to Springdale on their way to Kansas, where they later joined John Brown's little company. To Cook was assigned the difficult and responsible task of going to Harper's Ferry to live as a spy in the enemy's country, an outpost stealthily to reconnoitre the vicinity. This he did successfully, arriving there on June 5, 1858.[80]

By this delay and change of plan, Brown lost five of his twelve followers who took part in the Chatham convention. Parsons had lost his zeal for the venture on learning of the plan to attack the arsenal at Harper's Ferry.[81] He had not calculated on a direct assault on the United States Government, and so when the call to rejoin Brown reached him at Council Bluffs in 1859, where he was, *en route* to Pike's Peak, he heeded the admonition of his mother which came with it. "They are bad men," she wrote him. "You have got away from them, now keep away from them." Mr. Parsons has an excellent war service to his credit as a commissioned officer, and is still living at Salina, Kansas. Moffet, too, was probably disaffected, though it was claimed for him by his sister, in 1860, that "obligations from which he could not be released" prevented his rejoining Brown. Of his own failure to reach Harper's Ferry, George B. Gill, who also survives, says:[82]

"I was on my way to Harper's Ferry at the time of the premature blow and apparent failure. I had been in correspondence with Kagi and knew the exact time to be on hand and was on my way to the cars when the thrilling news came that the blow had been struck. Of course I went no further. I had been sick much of the spring and summer previous and in my last interview with the old man I would not promise to follow him farther, being worn out physically and not feeling any more sanguine of the necessary funds being raised, and having been east the previous year on a wild goose chase I could not see the necessity of going further at present."

Realf, on his trip to England, underwent a sea-change, and after the raid was charged with treachery. Richardson, the colored man, did not reappear from Canada. But Cook, Leeman, Tidd, Owen Brown, Stevens, Taylor and Kagi followed their leader to Harper's Ferry, whence only Tidd and Owen Brown returned.

In company, then, with two of the faithful ones, Brown reached Chicago on June 22; on June 25 two of his later biographers met him under these conditions in Lawrence: "We were at supper, on the 25th of June, 1858, at a hotel in Lawence, Kansas. A stately old man, with a flowing white beard, entered the room and took a seat at the public table. I immediately recognized in the stranger, John Brown. Yet many persons who had previously known him did not penetrate his patriarchal disguise." Thus wrote Redpath.[83] The whole aspect of Brown was now changed; the long gray beard familiar to all the world at the time of his execution concealed the sharpness of his chin, the thin lips and the resolute, sharp line of the mouth. But there was no change in the man. On Monday, June 28, he was off for southern Kansas, where he reappeared disguised not only as to his physiognomy but as to his name. Thereafter there was a new border chief in southeastern Kansas, — Shubel Morgan.

CHAPTER X

SHUBEL MORGAN, WARDEN OF THE MARCHES

THE Kansas to which John Brown returned in June, 1858, had made distinct progress toward the realization of the hopes of the Free State party. In October, 1857, it had captured the Territorial Legislature, which met on January 4, 1858, but it had abstained from voting at the election of December 21 on the Lecompton Constitution, because the only alternative was to vote "for the Constitution with slavery" or "for the Constitution with no slavery." But the Constitution without slavery made that institution perpetual within the State, by providing for the maintenance of the slaves then in the Territory, and their offspring, and specifically declaring that slaves were property. The "Constitution-with-slavery" provision was carried by 6266 votes to 569, owing to the abstention of the Free State men; 2720 of the affirmative votes were proved to be fraudulent. Since the election did not turn upon the Constitution itself, but upon the issue whether the Constitution with or without slavery should be adopted, the Free State men, Lane in particular, had, as already pointed out, induced the Acting Governor, Stanton, to call a special session of the Legislature for December 7, which promptly ordered the submission of the entire Lecompton Constitution to the people. When this was done, on January 4, the pro-slavery men abstained from the polls. No less than 10,226 votes were cast against the Constitution, 138 for it with slavery, and 24 for it without slavery. Both parties joined in the election for officers under the Lecompton Constitution, the Free State men winning. Of the 6875 pro-slavery votes, 2458 subsequently proved to be illegal;[1] the Free State men chose 42 out of 53 members of the Legislature. George W. Smith, Free State, was elected Governor. On January 5, the old Topeka Legislature met again to receive a message from *its* Governor, Robinson, asking that the old rump State organization be kept up, although the Territorial Legislature was now safely Free State. In his message to this body, the new Acting Governor, Denver, who had succeeded Stanton, recommended that all legislation of importance be deferred until Congress should act upon the Lecompton Constitution.

When that document was submitted to Congress by the President, on February 2, that body had received a petition from all the State officers chosen under this Constitution, asking that it be defeated. While Brown was collecting his funds in the East, revealing his Virginia plan to his Boston friends, and preparing for the Chatham convention, Congress was struggling with this Lecompton issue, which was not decided until April 30. During all that period the debate had aroused the country, and wrought Congress itself up to a pitch of great excitement. Even Stephen A. Douglas, author of the Squatter Sovereignty theory to which all of Kansas's misfortunes were due, opposed the Lecompton Constitution. Finally, Congress passed a compromise measure known as the English bill, which provided that Kansas should be admitted to the Union if, on resubmission, a majority of its voters approved the Lecompton Constitution. This was emphatically a pro-slavery victory. In order to bribe the voters of the State into accepting the Constitution that had once been rejected by them, Congress offered to give to the new State two sections of land in each township for school purposes, seventy-two sections for a State university, and ten sections for public buildings, in all five and a half million acres; also all the salt springs, not exceeding twelve in number, and six sections of land with each spring; and, finally, five per cent of all the public lands for State roads. No such bribe had ever been offered to any other State; if it should not be accepted, the bill required that no new delegates to frame a Constitution should be chosen until Kansas had a population equalling the ratio of representation required for a member of the House of Representatives — then 93,560 people. Kansas was in the throes of a discussion of this measure when John Brown arrived, for the date set for the vote on the resubmitted Constitution was August 2. He had, therefore, the satisfaction of being in the Territory at this final defeat of the pro-slavery forces, when 13,088 votes were cast, 11,300 of them against the odious Constitution. Thereafter Kansas was safe. No other Constitution was framed until the next year; but the defeat of the slavery forces was beyond all dispute and final.[2]

But if the political outlook in the Territory was favorable to the Free State men, there had been in southeastern Kansas, particularly in Linn and Bourbon counties, a recrudescence of the lawlessness of 1856. Indeed, the whole Territory, as Brown entered it, was still ringing with one of the most atrocious crimes in the annals of the border warfare, to which reference has already been made. Charles A. Hamilton, a graduate of the University of Georgia, later a colonel in the Confederate army, and a member of an excellent family, had boasted that if pro-slavery men could not make headway in the Territory, Abolitionists should not live there. Crossing the Missouri boundary on May 19, near the Trading Post in Linn County, he captured Free State men wherever he found them, on their wagons, in the fields, or in their homes, until he had eleven reputable citizens,—the Rev. B. L. Reed, W. E. Stilwell, Asa Hairgrove, William Hairgrove, Amos Hall, William Colpetzer, Michael Robinson, John F. Campbell, Charles Snyder, Patrick Ross and Austin Hall. An effort was made to capture Eli Snyder, a blacksmith, his brother and a young son, Elias Snyder, but they fought too vigorously. Lining up his eleven prisoners in a little ravine, Hamilton placed his thirty-odd men on the bank above them, and ordered them to aim at the prisoners. One of the men, Brockett, who had been Pate's lieutenant at the battle of Black Jack, declined to obey Hamilton's order and withdrew. At the word of command, the others fired at the unflinching Free State men. To make sure of their work, the brazen and brutal murderers then kicked the prostrate men and finished two of the dying, Ross and Amos Hall, by shooting them again. Then they made off. The Snyders, lying in the bushes near-by, hearing the shooting and groans, were afraid to move lest it might all be a ruse. They were finally summoned by Austin Hall, who, unwounded, had had presence of mind to fall with the others and remain rigid when kicked by a ruffian who wished to ascertain if he still breathed. It was found that five men, Campbell, Colpetzer, Ross, Stilwell, and Robinson, had been killed. The remaining five survived their serious wounds.

Nothing can be said in defence of this crime. None of the

eleven had given special reason for Border Ruffian dislike. Hamilton thought, perhaps, that by imitating the Pottawatomie murders of John Brown he could at one blow intimidate southeastern Kansas; perhaps he believed himself the agent of the Almighty to exterminate these men. At any rate, he, too, killed five, as had Brown, and with as little warning; the consequences — the stirring up of the worst kind of bushwhacking strife — were in both cases the same.[3]

Soon after the massacre, two hundred Kansans, led by Sheriff McDaniel, Colonel R. B. Mitchell and James Montgomery, marched to West Point, Missouri, from which place Hamilton had started. The murderers, however, had timely warning of their coming and escaped, Montgomery's advice to surround the town before entering it being disregarded.[4] Although occurring some distance from the river of that name, this killing has always been known as the Marais des Cygnes Massacre; it inspired Whittier's commemorative poem, "Le Marais du Cygne," published in the *Atlantic Monthly* for September, 1858. In justice to Hamilton it must be stated that he and a large number of other pro-slavery settlers, who were in Free State eyes inimical to the peace and progress of the communities in which they had resided, had been ordered by James Montgomery, the Free State leader, to leave their homes post-haste and flee to Missouri. The Marais des Cygnes Massacre was the revenge for this expulsion, which the majority of the Free State settlers considered wholly warranted by the careers of those expelled. Hamilton originally headed a band of five hundred Missourians. All but Hamilton and his ignoble thirty were dissuaded from entering Kansas, or lost courage when they reached the Territorial line. There ensued after the massacre a week of extreme lawlessness, although Federal troops had already been ordered out into Bourbon County. Montgomery tried to burn the pro-slavery town of Fort Scott, and there were grave conditions, indeed, until Governor Denver personally arrived on the scene in June and induced both sides to agree to a treaty of peace. Bygones were to be bygones. He promised to remove the Federal troops from Fort Scott at once; to order a new election for county officials; to station militia along the border in order to prevent invasion from Missouri; and to suspend the operation of old writs, if

Montgomery's men and all other armed bodies would withdraw from the field. This compact was religiously adhered to through the summer and fall.

James Montgomery was one of the most interesting figures of the border warfare. He was thus described in a letter to the New York *Evening Post* in 1858:[5]

"In conversation he talks mildly in a calm, even voice, using the language of a cultivated, educated gentleman. His antecedents are unexceptionable; he was always a Free State man, although coming from a Slave State, where he was noted as a good citizen and for his mild, even temperament. In his daily conduct he maintains the same character now; but when in action and under fire, he displays a daring fearlessness, untiring perseverance, and an indomitable energy that has given him the leadership in this border warfare."

His own cabin was often attacked in days when nobody who had caution unbarred his door to a visitor's hail without being assured as to the ownership of the voice.[6] His wife was a fit companion for a border chieftain. It is related of her that she had the indomitable spirit, if not the culture, of her husband, and that she once said: "I do get plumb tired of being shot at, but I won't be druv out."[7] It must not be thought, however, that all of Montgomery's neighbors were unanimous as to his usefulness; but they always agreed as to his honesty. A leader of "jayhawkers," he had but little respect for man-made laws; he met violence with violence, and often could not control the excesses of his men.

The original incentive for Montgomery's taking to the brush was the pro-slavery outrages of 1856 in Linn County; thereafter his own actions led to frequent efforts to retaliate by the pro-slavery men, who feared and hated him more than any one else. "His operations," says Andreas,[8] "may be classed as defensive, preventive and retaliatory, and it is doubtless true that he did many things which, when judged outside of their immediate and remote causes and connections, would not stand the test of the moral code." Yet after it was all over, and the Civil War at hand, he was made Colonel of the Third Kansas Volunteer Infantry, later Colonel of the Second South Carolina (Negro) Regiment, with which he fought in Florida; and during the Price raid into Missouri, he was Colonel of the Sixth Kansas Militia Regiment. Both in

Kansas and in the South, as a regimental commander, he aroused criticism by his ruthless destruction and plundering of captured towns and villages, partly in obedience to orders.[9] In Kansas, in 1858, one of the deeds which made him conspicuous was an attack on part of Captain G. T. Anderson's company of the First United States Cavalry, April 21, when he and seven other men were overtaken by it. Taking to the timber, Montgomery opened fire, killing one soldier and injuring Captain Anderson and two soldiers, whereupon the company fled, to their and their commander's disgrace, Captain Anderson being forced to resign from the service in consequence.[10] Another exploit was Montgomery's destruction of the ballot-boxes, in imitation of similar Missouri outrages, at the election for Governor under the Lecompton Constitution, January 4, 1858, because he did not sympathize with the decision of a part of the Free State party to vote under the Constitution.[11] That his neighbors might not vote, he broke the ballot-box and scattered the ballots, for which he was indicted but never tried. Many other acts of violence were rightly or wrongly laid at his door, chief among the former being the attempt to burn Fort Scott, early in June, 1858. Governor Denver officially charged him with this, and with firing indiscriminately into the houses of the town, and expressed his astonishment at meeting men fully aware of this "most outrageous attempt at arson and murder," who yet "uphold and justify Montgomery and his band in their conduct." Of the ravaged district in which Montgomery operated, Governor Denver, after his personal tour of inspection, thus wrote to Lewis Cass, Secretary of State:

"From Fort Scott to the crossing of the Osage river, or Marais des Cygnes as it is there called, a distance of about 30 miles, we passed through a country almost depopulated by the depredations of the predatory bands under Montgomery, presenting a scene of desolation such as I never expected to have witnessed in any country inhabited by American citizens. . . . The accounts given of the flight of the people were heart-rending in the extreme."

Governor Denver, throughout his official correspondence, was extremely hostile to Montgomery, while not failing to say that, however great the outrages he committed, there was no excuse for taking revenge on innocent persons, as Hamilton had done on the Marais des Cygnes.[12]

To this guerrilla Montgomery, to the scene of his operations and the crimes of Hamilton, Brown's mind turned as soon as he arrived in Lawrence. The numerous outrages upon individuals were a close parallel to conditions as he found them around Lawrence when he first entered the Territory in 1855. Montgomery was obviously a border chieftain after his own heart, and, besides, in his district was the only possible opportunity for active service. "Fort Scott," wrote the Lawrence correspondent of the Chicago *Tribune* on April 4, 1858,[13] "is the only place within the Territory where the Border Ruffians now show their teeth." Their worst specimens, he reported, were in refuge there. Fugit, the murderer of Hoppe, lived in the neighborhood. Clarke, who killed Barber in 1855, was then Register of the Land Office at Fort Scott. Eli Moore, one of W. A. Phillips's murderers, and one of those who shot R. P. Brown at Easton, "has his rendezvous in the same vicinity." Brockett was clerk in the Land Office. Most of such of Titus's ruffians as had not gone to Nicaragua with Walker were also there. These became the leaders of immigrants from southwestern Missouri. The land was rich and desirable. The Free State men persisted in coming in, being then two to one, and located chiefly in the northern half of the county. Ever since the preceding fall, the correspondent reported, they had been harassed and plundered by the proslavery men, to worry them out, by burning cabins, stealing cattle and horses, and making false arrests,—all so that they should not dominate the region. It was to end this that Hamilton and his followers had been ordered by Montgomery to leave the Territory immediately, with the result that Hamilton later conceived and carried out his horrible plan of revenge.

Redpath and Hinton stated that on Sunday, June 27, when they again met Brown in the hotel in Lawrence, he asked them about the movements and character of Montgomery, as well as of the trend of political developments,[14] and informed them that he would start south the next day to see his relatives and Montgomery. To Mr. Sanborn, Brown sent, on Monday, the 28th, the following unsigned letter:[15]

LAWRENCE, KANSAS TER. 28th June 1858.

F. B. SANBORN ESQ; and *Dear Friends* at *Boston, Worcester* and *Peterboro*.

I reached Kansas with friends on the 26th inst; came here last night, and leave *here today;* for the neighborhood of late troubles. It seem the troubles are not *over* yet. Can write you but few words now. Hope to write you more fully after a while. I do hope you will be in earnest now to carry out *as soon as possible* the measure proposed in Mr. Sanborn's letter inviting me to Boston *this last Spring*. I hope there will be *no delay* of that matter. Can you send me by Express; Care E. B. Whitman Esqr half a Doz; or a full Doz whistles such as I described? at once?

Write me till further advised, under sealed envelope directing stamped ones to Rev. S. L. Adair, Osawatomie Kansas Ter.

Yours in Truth

On July 9, John Brown, or Shubel Morgan, as he now called himself, wrote to his son [16] from the "log-cabin of the notorious Captain James Montgomery, whom I deem a very brave and talented officer, and, what is infinitely more, a very intelligent, kind gentlemanly and most excellent man and lover of freedom." While Brown visited Montgomery on other occasions, he was oftenest at the house of Augustus Wattles, near Moneka, to which locality the latter had removed with his family from the neighborhood of Lawrence. But the headquarters of Shubel Morgan's company were on the claim of Eli Snyder, the brave blacksmith, and not many hundred yards from the very scene of the Hamilton Massacre. Half a mile from the Missouri line, this hill, now densely wooded, offered in 1858 a beautiful view of the surrounding country. Brown arrived there about the 1st of July, with Eli Snyder, coming directly from the home of Augustus Wattles. Elias, the boy, drove back with Brown to Wattles's for his belongings,[17]— blankets, provisions, cooking utensils, clothing and a good supply of arms and ammunition. Kagi and Tidd were with Brown throughout his stay, Gill and Stevens arriving later in the summer, by way of Iowa. The first camp, in which they lived for four weeks, was located between Snyder's house and his blacksmith-shop, near a fine spring, which still wells up under the farmhouse now standing on the site of the camp. Here, true to his custom, John Brown drew up "Articles of Agreement for Shubel Morgan's Company." *

* See Appendix.

On July 20, Shubel Morgan began a long letter to Mr. Sanborn and the other Boston friends, which he could not finish until August 6. In it he gave this description of conditions in the vicinity of the claim:[18]

"Deserted farms: & dwellings lie in all directions for some miles along the line; & the remaining inhabitants watch every appearance of persons moveing about with anxious jealousy; & vigilance. Four of the persons wounded or attacked on that occasion* are staying WITH me. The Blacksmith *Snyder* who fought the murderers with his brother; & son are *of* the number. Old Mr. Hargrove who was teribly wounded at the same time is another. The blacksmith returned *here* with me; & intends to bring back his family on to his claim within Two or Three days. A constant fear of new troubles seems to prevail on both sides the line; & on both sides are companies of armed men. Any little affair may open the quarrel afresh. Two *murders;* & cases of robery are reported of late I have also a man with me who fled from his family; & farm; in Missouri but a day or Two since; his life being threatened on account of being accused of informing Kansas men of the whereabouts of one of the murderers who was lately taken; & brought to this side. I have concealed the fact of my *presence pretty* much; lest it should tend to create excitement; but it is getting leaked out; & will soon be known to all. As I am not *here* to *seek* or to *secure revenge;* I do not mean to be the first to *reopen* the quarrel. How soon it may be raised against me I cannot say; nor am I *over* anxious. A portion of my men are in other neighborhoods We shall soon be in *great want* of a small amount in a Draft or Drafts on New York, *to feed us*. We cannot work *for wages;* & provisions *are not easily* obtained on the frontier. . . . I may continue here for some time."

A significant passage of this letter is the following comment on a man who ever since, unless we except Charles Robinson, has been Brown's bitterest critic,—and still is: "I believe all *honest, sensible* Free State men *in* Kansas consider *George Washington* Brown's '*Herald of Freedom*' one of the most mischievous, traitorous publications in the whole country." On August 6 he added that he had been down with the ague since July 23, and had no safe way of getting his letter off. Under date of Moneka, August 9, 1858, Brown wrote to his son, John Brown, Jr., this valuable review of the situation, here printed for the first time:[19]

"Your letter with enclosures, exactly those I wanted, of the 23rd of July is received. I have been spending some weeks on the Mis-

* The Hamilton Massacre.

souri line on the same quarter section where the horrible murders of May 19th were committed. Confidence seems to be greatly restored amongst the Free State men in consequence, several of whom returned to their deserted claims. The Election of the 2nd Inst. passed off quietly on this part of the Line. Its general result in the Territory you are probably advised of. Our going onto the line was done with the utmost quiet & so far as I am concerned under an assumed name to avoid creating any excitement. But the matter was in some measure leaked out and over into Missouri. Some believed the report of O. B.'s [Old Brown's] being directly on the Line and in the immediate vicinity of West Point, but the greater part on the Kansas side did not believe it. In Missouri the fact was pretty generally understood, & the idea of having such a neighbour improving a Claim (as was the case) right on a conspicuous place and in full view for miles, around in Missouri, produced a ferment there which you can better imagine than I can describe. Which of the passions most predominated, fear or rage, I do not pretend to say. We had a number of visitors from there, some of whom we believed at the time and still believe were spies. One avowed himself a pro-slavery man after I had told him my suspicions of himself & of those who came before him, but at the same time assured him that notwithstanding he was in a perfect *nest* of the most *ultra Abolitionists*, not a hair of his head should fall so long as we knew of no active mischief he had been engaged in. When I told him my suspicions of him he seemed to be much agitated, though to all appearance a man of great self-possession and courage — I recited to him briefly the story of the Missouri invasions, threatenings, bullyings, boastings, driving off, beating, robbing, burning out and murdering of Kansas people, telling him pro-slavery men of Missouri had begun and carried steadily forward in this manner with most miserably rotten and corrupt pro-slavery Administrations to back them up, shield and assist them while carrying on their Devilish work. I told him Missouri people along the Line might have perfect quiet if they honestly desired it, and further, that if they chose *War* they would soon have all they might *any of them* care for. I gave him the most powerful Abolition lecture of which I am capable, having an unusual gift of utterance for me; gave him some dinner and told him to go back and make a full report and then sent him off. Got no such visits afterwards. I presume he will not soon forget the old Abolitionist 'mit de' white beard on. I gave him also a full description of my views of a Full Blooded Abolitionist and told him who were the *real nigger-stealers* &c. . . ."

The postscript to this letter, longer than the missive itself, begins thus:

"P. S. Our family interest in Kansas affairs is so often misstated by those who do not know and oftener do not care to tell the truth that Mr. Wattles had determined for some time past to bring out our history from time [to time] in a kind of series as he could collect facts, and instantly called on me for them. I have consented to supply them, & have commenced."

He then directs his son to collect material for that sketch of his career: "A brief history of John Brown, otherwise (old B) and his family: *as connected With Kansas;* By one who knows," to which reference was made in an earlier chapter.* Brown began this never finished autobiographical sketch at Wattles's house,[20] from which he wrote as above.

As soon as he reached the Snyder claim, Brown began to build a small fortification of stone and wood for defence against the Missourians,[21] which speedily became magnified by popular report into a "Fort Snyder." There is no doubt, too, that he commenced negotiations for the purchase of the claim, and this has given rise to a long controversy in Kansas as to whether he was or was not the owner or an owner of this land at one time. The facts seem to be that Snyder never perfected his claim to the land; that when Brown arrived there, he did begin negotiations with Snyder, which must have been not for the land, but for the squatter's claim to it; that subsequently Snyder changed his mind and Brown's effort to purchase came to an end, giving rise to charges of bad faith against Snyder. When the land was disposed of by the government, the name of neither Brown nor Snyder figured in the transaction, the government selling 180.84 acres for $225.80 to C. C. Scadsall (generally called Hadsall).[22] Snyder appears to have offered the place to Hadsall, after accepting money from Brown in part payment. Hadsall, it is reported, declared that when he told Brown of Snyder's offer,

"Brown showed the only anger that Hadsall had ever witnessed, but walked away without saying much. Shortly after he told Hadsall that he was content for him to have the place, but he, Brown, wanted to reserve all privileges of military occupation at his pleasure. It seemed that Brown had not made all his payments to Snyder, who in a way not unusual to him was trying to get some money from Hadsall. That day Brown wrote out and signed a bill of sale to Hadsall and signed it in his own name, and Snyder, after turning over to Hadsall his three yoke of oxen, cows, wagons, and plows,

* See ante, page 86.

received six hundred dollars from Hadsall and added his quit-claim to the bill of sale. Hadsall lost this precious bit of paper during the war." [23]

John Brown made, early in August, an attempt to get the revolvers sent to him in 1856 by the National Kansas Committee, which had been in Lawrence ever since that time; for them, as he had told Horace White, he himself was not willing to ask, when in Lawrence. On August 3 he wrote from Moneka to William Hutchinson, asking for the names of those to whom the revolvers had been loaned subject to his recalling them. This information Mr. Hutchinson cheerfully gave, but it does not appear that Brown ever obtained any of these weapons.[24] For an interesting incident of the stay with Snyder, we have the doughty blacksmith's own narrative:[25]

"During the time that Brown was at my place (1858), he wished me to take a short trip into Missouri and I agreeing, Brown took an old surveyor's compass and chain and he and I followed down along the river, while Kagi and Tidd took the road to Butler. They pretended to be looking for situations to teach a school. We were all to meet at Pattenville, but not to appear to know each other. Brown and I were ostensibly surveying. On meeting at Pattenville we had an opportunity to come to an understanding to meet again at a clump of trees on a certain hill. Brown and I took the river and when we met again Martin White's house was half a mile east of us. Brown had a small field glass which I asked him to loan me, as I had seen some one near the house that I took to be Martin White, whom I knew; having heard him address a meeting at West Point a few days after the burning of Osawatomie, when Clarke was raising a force to drive and burn out Free State men between there and Fort Scott. At that time White had just returned from accompanying Reid and I heard him describe how he killed Frederick Brown, — making the motion of lowering a gun. Brown adjusted the glass and looking I could recognize Martin White reading a book as he sat in a chair in the shade of a tree. I handed the glass to Brown and asked him to look and he said he also recognized him saying: — 'I declare that is Martin White.' For a few minutes nothing was said when I remarked 'Suppose you and I go down and see the old man and have a talk with him.' 'No, no, I can't do that,' said Brown. Kagi said, 'let Snyder and me go.' Capt. Brown said: 'Go if you wish to but don't you hurt a hair of his head; but if he has any slaves take the last one of them.' Kagi said: 'Snyder and I want to go without instructions, or not at all.' Therefore as Brown was unwilling that Martin White, who had murdered his son, should receive any harm we did not go near him. It was thus shown that John Brown had no revenge to gratify."

There is other evidence to this effect; Brown never permitted any attack to be made on White, tried to head off his sons when they were on White's trail, and repeatedly stated that he did not wish for White's death, — an attitude which cannot be too highly commended. To James Hanway he once said:[26]

"People mistake my objects. I would not hurt one hair of his [White's] head. I would not go one inch to take his life; I do not harbour the feelings of revenge. *I act from a principle.* My aim and object is to restore human rights."

Brown's obstinate ague or malarial fever, to which he referred in his letter of August 9 to his family, did not yield because of his sojourn with Augustus Wattles. About the middle of August, he was taken by William Partridge to the Rev. Mr. Adair's hospitable cabin at Osawatomie,[27] and there, in a corner of the living-room, he lay for fully four weeks, nursed with the greatest fidelity by the devoted Kagi and the Adair family. On September 9 he wrote to John Brown, Jr.,[28] that since August 9, the date of his last letter, he had been "entirely laid up with Ague and Chill fever. Was never more sick." As the Adairs look back upon it, the disease appears to them now to have been a malarial or typhoid fever; they were often asked by visitors who the sick man in the sitting-room was, but they knew always how to describe him by other than his right name.[29] Dr. Gilpatrick, of Osawatomie, was called in to aid the patient. Finally, on September 23, Kagi was able to report to his sister his arrival in Lawrence, after being

"compelled to lay off at Osawatomie for a month, during which time by my taking care of him, [Brown], I was down but only for a week. . . . B. has not quite recovered. . . . Things are now quiet. I am collecting arms, etc. belonging to J. B. so that he may command them at any time."[30]

On September 13, Brown notified his wife that he was still very weak and wrote only with great labor; even on the 11th of October, he had to tell her that he had been "very feeble," but had improved a great deal during the last week. "I can now see," he added, "no good reason why I should not be located nearer home as soon as I can collect the means for defraying expenses." [31]

John Brown probably reached Lawrence with Kagi late in September, and was there again on October 14, 15 and 16. Martin F. Conway testified before the Mason Committee [32] that he saw Brown there twice in the summer and fall, and discussed with him his relations to the National Kansas Committee, after Brown's illness in southern Kansas, but he erroneously places the date of the first visit as late in July or early in August, when Brown was on Snyder's claim. A receipt given by Mr. Conway to John Brown for documents put in his possession is still in existence, and fixes the date for the second interview as October 15, 1858.[33] As to the first interview, Conway testified that it took place at Mrs. Killan's hotel, and that Brown declared that he was greatly in need and had received an order from the National Kansas Executive Committee for a large sum of money which he had never been able to obtain. By "order" Brown meant, if he used that word, the resolution of the National Kansas Committee of January 24, 1857, giving him the five thousand dollars, of which he had received only so small a part, and also "such arms and supplies as the Committee may have" up to an amount sufficient to provide for one hundred men, besides a "letter of approbation." In the summer of 1858, John Brown received from George L. Stearns a package of promissory notes which had been given by Kansas farmers to the National Kansas Committee in exchange for food-supplies or aid of one kind or another. Mr. Stearns, as in the case of the Brown rifles and revolvers, had advanced large sums for this purpose to the Massachusetts State Committee, and was given these notes as security for his advances.[34] Some of these he now sent to Brown, who proceeded to collect on them for his immediate needs. He told Mr. Conway that,

"the National Kansas Committee had passed a resolution sometime before upon which he based a right to act himself as agent for that Committee in the Territory in the collection of debts due it, and as Mr. Whitman did not seem to satisfy him in that business he had taken it upon himself to make collections. . . . He claimed to have received a commission, and, as a result of his labors he produced a package of papers, which he said were promissory notes from parties in the Territory, who had received provisions and clothing from this Committee during the troubles in 1856. They had engaged to pay for them and they had given these notes, and he had got them, and he came to me to ask a favor that I would take these documents and put them in my safe and keep them subject to his order." [35]

To this Mr. Conway added that he had signed the receipt written for him by Kagi, which fixes the date of this transaction. Apparently, Brown collected on these notes several hundred dollars. He also receipted on October 16, at Lawrence, for goods received from the National Kansas Committee, signing as its agent. [36]

In the use of this signature John Brown undoubtedly went too far, and his authority to do so was sharply denied by H. B. Hurd, the Secretary of the National Kansas Committee, on October 26, 1858, when Mr. Hurd wrote to Colonel E. B. Whitman:

"Capt. John Brown has no authority to take, receive, collect or transfer any notes or accounts belonging to the National Kansas Committee nor has he ever had. Nor will any such dealing be recognized or sanctioned by our Committee. We wish you to hold all persons responsible who undertake to retain or deal with such notes and accounts. You will recollect that you were given full authority to act in reference to said notes & accounts including authority to transfer the same by assignment. This authority has never been revoked or given to any other person. All the papers that Mr. Brown has from us are a copy of the Resolutions passed in the New York Meeting certified by me, and an order for some small arms & tents that were at Lawrence I think about the time B. returned to Kansas after you met him at our office in Chicago. He has never been to our office since that time nor have we had any communication with him since then. I have seen him once since then but only for a few minutes & then nothing was said or done about the matter above referred to." [37]

But there are strong reasons why this error of judgment should not be charged up against Brown as a moral delinquency. The relations of the National Committee and the Massachusetts Committee were inextricably mixed in Kansas, where E. B. Whitman acted at this time as agent for both Committees; Brown had received the notes from Mr. Stearns with directions to collect on them; Mr. Whitman was not to be found when Brown tried to get at him, and finally he doubtless conscientiously believed that the resolution in his favor of the National Committee gave him sufficient authority. This latter point appears from the following letter written about this time: [38]

Mr. J. T. Cox;

Sir:— You are hereby notified that I hold claims against the National Kansas Committee which are good against them and all persons whatever; and that I have authority from said committee to take possession, as their Agent, of any supplies belonging to said Committee, wherever found.

You will therefore retain in your hands any monies or accounts you may now have in your custody, by direction of said Committee or any of its Agents, and hold them subject to my call or order, as I shall hold you responsible for them, to me as Agent of said Committee

Ottumwa, Oct. 7, 1858

John Brown
Agt. Nat. Kan. Com."

In this, again, Brown quite exceeded the actual wording of the New York resolution, which limited the supplies to the needs of one hundred men, of which he had received a considerable portion in 1857 after the vote. Nevertheless, as Mr. Sanborn records,[39] "the Massachusetts Committee . . . stood firmly by Brown" in the "lively dispute in Kansas" excited by his action.

"They had collected much money, had expended it judiciously, and had allowed a generous individual, their chairman, to place in their hands more money, for which he was willing to wait without payment until the property of the Committee could be turned into cash; then, to give him all the security in its power, the Committee had made over this property to him, with no restriction as to what he should do with it; and Mr. Stearns had chosen to give it to Brown."

William F. M. Arny, another agent of the National Kansas Committee, testified to seeing Brown in Lawrence several times during the summer and fall of 1858,[40] and Brown on one of these occasions spent a day or two at his home, when they discussed, in general terms, Brown's plan for attacking slavery elsewhere than in Kansas. It must have been on one of these visits, too, that Colonel William A. Phillips had the third of those interviews with Brown which he described at length in the *Atlantic Monthly* for December, 1879, and apparently erroneously placed in the year 1859. To him, on this occasion, Brown set forth his views on the slavery question at great length, first sketching the history of American slavery from its beginnings. He said to Phillips:

"And now we have reached a point where nothing but war can settle the question. Had they [the slavery men] succeeded in Kansas, they would have gained a power that would have given them permanently the upper hand, and it would have been the death knell of republicanism in America. They are checked, but not beaten. They never intend to relinquish the machinery of this government into the hands of the opponents of slavery. It has taken them more than half a century to get it and they know its significance too well to give it up. If the Republican party elect its president next year, there will be war. The moment they are unable to control, they will go out, and as a rival nation along-side they will get the countenance and aid of the European nations, until American republicanism and freedom are overthrown."

To Phillips, Brown spoke of the opportunity and achievements of Spartacus, and suggested that something similar might happen. To this Phillips objected that the American negroes were a "peaceful, domestic, inoffensive race; in all their sufferings they seemed to be incapable of resentment or reprisal." Brown's reply was quick and sharp: "You have not studied them right, and you have not studied them long enough. Human nature is the same everywhere."

In connection with the National Kansas Committee's notes, Brown visited other places besides Ottumwa, where his letter to Mr. Cox shows him to have been on October 7. It is established that he visited Emporia on this same business, and this is as far west as he is known to have gone during his stay in the Territory.[41] On October 11 he was again in Osawatomie, as already recorded, and on October 15 and 16 in Lawrence, when he returned for a day or two to the South; for Kagi records in the *Tribune* his and Brown's being at Osawatomie on October 25. According to this letter, Brown went up from Linn County on Friday, October 22, bringing news that Montgomery had forcibly entered the court-house at Fort Scott on the 21st and taken possession of the court and of the papers of the grand jury, compelled the former to adjourn, and destroyed the latter. "He is now in the field" wrote

Kagi, "ready to meet the worst." Of Brown, Kagi wrote, "The Captain has shown that he *can* be in the Territory without making war. He will now, if necessary, take the field in aid of Montgomery."[42] The Captain soon returned to the disturbed districts. There, on the 30th of October, an attempt was made to assassinate Montgomery, his wife and children, by pro-slavery men, who attacked his cabin at night and fired a volley into it.[43] Brown himself was at Augustus Wattles's, that night. The occurrence led his men to fortify strongly the cabin of Montgomery's mother-in-law, near Montgomery's own. Gill, Tidd and Stevens did most of the work, for Brown was not yet himself; he aided by indulging in his favorite occupation of cooking.[44] On November 1, while at Mr. Wattles's, he wrote two letters to members of his family, describing himself as much better in health, "but not very strong yet." In both of them he stated, doubtless with the Montgomery incident in mind, that "things at this moment look quite threatening along the line."[45]

The Wattles family preserves some interesting recollections of these ever-welcome visits of Brown.[46] There was nothing of the swashbuckler about him; as quiet in his manner as any Quaker, he was ready to do his share of the household drudgery as soon as he arrived. Reading to the Wattles family a newspaper article which excused his bitterness against slavery on the ground of his personal injuries, he commented indignantly: "It seems strange in a Christian country that a man should be called a monomaniac for following the plain dictates of our Saviour." To Mrs. Wattles he then said: "I can put up with the abuse of my enemies, but the excuses of my friends are more than I like to bear."

November was, in the main, a quiet month for Brown and his men. Besides building the Montgomery fort, theirs was the frontiersman's life. "Sometimes," records Mr. Gill,[47] of his own and Kagi's activities, "one had the ague, sometimes both. Sometimes we fished, sometimes we had our supper and beds; at other times we went supperless and took the prairie for our bed with the blue arch for our covering." One or the other of these men was generally Brown's companion at this time. He was not drawn to Tidd, and Stevens worried him because the ex-soldier would not take Brown's orders except in situations in which it was a captain's right to command. It was not in Stevens's nature to be uniformly submissive. Once, it is related by Mr. Gill, Stevens said to Brown: "If God controls all things, and dislikes the institution of slavery, why does He allow it to exist?" "Well," replied Brown, floored for once, "that is one question I cannot answer."

On the 13th of November there was a touch of active service for Shubel Morgan, — the only incident in this month which bore out Kagi's statement of his readiness to take the field to aid Montgomery. The latter, learning that he had been indicted at Paris, Kansas, by a pro-slavery jury, for his destruction of the ballot-box in the January previous, marched with Brown and his followers upon the town, in search of the indictments and warrants, Brown remaining upon the outskirts while Montgomery searched unsuccessfully.[48] This raid did not improve their standing with the Territorial authorities. The bias of the acting Governor, Hugh S. Walsh (who filled the Governor's chair in the interim between Governor Denver's resignation and the arrival of his successor, Samuel Medary, the last Territorial Governor), against the Free State men was perfectly apparent. He wrote on November 19 to Secretary Cass,[49] urging that "a reward of $300 for Montgomery and $500 for old John Brown, and their delivery at the fort, would secure their persons and break up their organization or drive them from the Territory." A Captain A. J. Weaver, who saw everything through pro-slavery eyes, was the chief medium of Walsh's and Medary's information, until he accidentally killed himself while bringing into the State some Federal arms loaned to Kansas for a militia company he had been authorized to raise.[50] On November 30, Captain Weaver and the sheriff, McDaniel, plotted to capture Brown and Montgomery; for Weaver was sure, as he wrote to the acting Governor, they were preparing "for some infernal diabolical act."[51] Brown, not knowing of this impending visitation, left with Gill for Osawatomie on the morning of Wednesday, December 1. What happened in his absence was thus described by Kagi in the columns of the Lawrence *Republican:*[52]

"When the intended attack became known, the people came in from all quarters, for the defence of the little garrison. They came unobserved, that the great posse might not become frightened, and run before an opportunity was given to whip them handsomely. Montgomery heard the news while on the Little Osage, and returned with a small force on Thursday morning [December 2]. A portion of the Free State men were placed in 'the fort;' Montgomery with the remainder placed himself in a good position nearby."

When the posse took up their march and had approached within a few rods of the fort, Whipple notified them that the Free State men were prepared to "resist the whole universe, with the devil thrown in." The next day, the posse having disintegrated, the sheriff had but a handful of men left. These commenced stopping and harassing single Free State men on the highways. Immediately on hearing of this, Montgomery's men moved. Their first act was to send four men to capture the sheriff and one R. B. Mitchell, as a checkmate. The latter was deprived of his rifle and brace of revolvers. "After a wholesome lecture they were released." The sheriff's pathetic account of this humiliating experience, properly garbled, is still preserved.[53] It fully bears out a statement of Captain Weaver's that "many of the people of the county are intimidated and afraid — some of old Brown and others of Montgomery."[54] Thus ended ingloriously one of a number of attempts to capture Shubel Morgan.

That energetic citizen wrote to his family on December 2, from Osawatomie:[55] "I have just this moment returned from the South where the prospect of quiet was probably never so poor," little dreaming that his own camp was at that moment being menaced. "Other parts of the Territory are undisturbed and may very likely remain so; unless drawn into the quarrel of the border counties. I expect to go South again immediately. . . ." His health was improving, but "I still get a shake pretty often." As to his plans, he said: "When I wrote you last I thought the prospect was that I should soon shift my quarters somewhat. I still have the same prospect, but am wholly at a loss as to the exact time." As soon as he returned South, he took the unexpected step of drafting a peace agreement. This was presented to a joint meeting of pro-slavery and Free Soil men, which had been called for December 6 at Sugar Mound, as a direct result of the humiliation put upon the sheriff after the failure of his attack upon Brown.[56] Montgomery himself was present at the meeting, and presented Brown's draft of the treaty. Shubel Morgan had urged that this should be signed by a number of the prominent men of both parties, but Montgomery found it unwise to insist upon this. With slight verbal alterations, the draft was adopted. It was in effect a renewal of the Denver agreement.* This had been adhered to until the action of the Paris court, together with the attempt to assassinate him and the visit of the sheriff to Brown's camp, had convinced Montgomery that it was abrogated.[57] Not that his men were altogether blameless during this period; sporadic "jayhawking" doubtless went on, despite Montgomery's efforts to control. But the new Sugar Mound convention was hardly agreed to before it was violated. On Thursday, December 16, Montgomery again attacked Fort Scott,[58] in order to release Benjamin Rice, a Free State settler, who had been arrested on November 16, in violation, Montgomery claimed, of the Denver treaty of June 15. When Rice was not promptly released after the Sugar Mound treaty, Montgomery organized, on December 14, a force of nearly one hundred men and invited John Brown to join it. This he did, together with Kagi and Stevens. The night before the attack, there was a conclave near Fort Scott as to the command. After much discussion it was decided that Montgomery should lead,[59] whereupon Brown, with his customary dislike of serving under another, took but a small part in the subsequent proceedings, going only to the rendezvous.

It was well that he did not lead. While Rice was being freed from his chains in the Free State Hotel, J. H. Little, the owner of a store across the way, fired a load of buckshot at Kagi, whose heavy overcoat alone saved him from severe injury. In the mêlée which followed, Little was killed and his store plundered, some seven thousand dollars' worth of goods being stolen. Charles Jennison, subsequently Colonel of the Seventh Kansas Cavalry, is credited with being specially active among the plunderers, and in some accounts Little's death is laid to Stevens, but unjustly. The whole affair reflects credit upon no one; it at once gave the pro-slavery men the incentive to reprisal, and enabled them to obtain from Governor Medary the authority to organize militia for the defence of their

* See Appendix.

town,[60] besides prejudicing the new Governor more than ever against the Free State leaders. Brown was subsequently wrongly charged by Governor Robinson and others with the leadership and instigation of the Fort Scott outrage, both of which questionable honors belong clearly to Montgomery. It must be stated, in the interest of historical accuracy, that Montgomery subsequently averred on a number of occasions that it was absolutely necessary for him to assume the leadership, because John Brown was determined to burn the entire town of Fort Scott to the ground, whereas Montgomery was opposed to violence and bloodshed and was exceedingly vexed at the killing of Little.[61] Governor Medary was so alarmed by the attack on Fort Scott that he at once applied for four companies of Federal cavalry, and for 600 arms and 10,000 rounds of ammunition with which to equip some militia.[62]

There was in store for him, and for the Governor of Missouri, an even greater shock. On the 19th of December began one of the most picturesque incidents in John Brown's life, without which its warfare against slavery would hardly have seemed complete. Certainly, nothing could have wound up his final visit to Kansas in a more dramatic way. This was his incursion into Missouri and the liberation of eleven slaves by force of arms. While, as already recorded, Brown had taken two slaves out of Kansas to freedom before this wholesale liberation, and was throughout his life an ever-ready agent of the Underground Railroad, he was at no time especially interested in this piecemeal method of weakening slavery. It was to his mind wasting time, when a bold attack might liberate five hundred or a thousand slaves. Yet, when on December 19, 1858, a slave crossed the Missouri line and told to George Gill the story of his impending fate, John Brown promptly and heartily closed with his follower's suggestion that here was just the right opportunity to "carry the war into Africa." [63]

"As I was scouting down the line," relates Mr. Gill, "I ran across a colored man, whose ostensible purpose was the selling of brooms. . . . I found that his name was Jim Daniels; that his wife, self, and babies belonged to an estate and were to be sold at an administrator's sale in the immediate future. His present business was not the selling of brooms particularly, but to find help to get himself, family, and a few friends in the vicinity away from these threatened conditions. Daniels was a fine-looking mulatto. I immediately hunted up Brown, and it was soon arranged to go the following night and give what assistance we could. I am sure that Brown, in his mind, was just waiting for something to turn up; or, in his way of thinking, was expecting or hoping that 'God would provide him a basis of action.' When this came he hailed it as heaven-sent."

Shubel Morgan decided to lead a party of ten or more to the home of Harvey G. Hicklan, or Hicklin, Daniels's temporary master, while Stevens, Tidd, Hazlett and others, to the number of eight, were to visit other plantations and rescue one or two more slaves who desired to drink of the cup of liberty. On the night of the 20th the two bands slowly took their way into Missouri. With Brown were a well-known horse-thief, "Pickles" by designation, Charles Jennison, Jeremiah Anderson, Gill, Kagi and two young men by the name of Ayres, in addition to one or two others. At midnight Hicklan's door was quickly forced, and then, with pointed revolvers, he was informed of the mission of the raiders. Brown had decided to take some of the personal property of the estate to which the slaves belonged, in order to maintain them. It was not easy to differentiate between Hicklan's property and that of the Lawrence estate, and Gill, who was told off to prevent plundering, confessed that he found his task a difficult one. "I soon discovered," he says, "that watches and other articles were being taken; some of our number proved to be mere adventurers, ready to take from friend or foe as opportunity offered." In this they were not different from some other Free State marauders, who were often willing to line their pockets while helping the cause of liberty. Mr. Hicklan always insisted that:

"Nothing that was taken was ever recovered. I learn that it was stated by John Brown that he made his men return all the property they had taken from me. This is not true. They did not give anything back. Brown said to me that we might get our property back if we could; that he defied us and the whole United States to follow him. He and his men seemed anxious to take more from me than they did, for they ransacked the house in search of money, and I suppose they would have taken it if they had found it. . . . What I have stated is the truth, and I am willing to swear to it. I do not hold any particular malice or prejudice on account of these old transactions. Old things have passed away, but the truth can never pass away." [64]

From Hicklan's, it was but three-quarters of a mile to the residence of John Larue, where five more slaves were liberated; thence, taking with them John B. Larue and a Dr. Ervin, a guest of the family, as prisoners, Brown and his men returned to Kansas. According to pro-slavery accounts:

"Besides the negroes, Brown took from the Lawrence estate two good horses, a yoke of oxen, a good wagon, harness, saddles, a considerable quantity of provisions, bacon, flour, meal, coffee, sugar, etc., all of the bedding and clothing of the negroes, Hicklin's shotgun, over-coat, boots, and many other articles belonging to the whites. From Larue were taken five negroes, six head of horses, harness, a wagon, a lot of bedding and clothing, provisions, and, in short, all the 'loot' available and portable." [65]

Meanwhile, Stevens's expedition had released but one slave, and that at the cost of the owner's life. David Cruise, a wealthy settler, had a woman slave whom the Daniels party wished to take along on their journey toward the North Star. Stevens had hardly entered the house when he thought that Mr. Cruise was reaching for a weapon. He fired instantly and the old man dropped dead. A thirteen-year-old son, who had recognized Hazlett, afterwards charged him with the crime. But Stevens freely admitted the killing, though it weighed heavily upon him. Once, while at the Kennedy Farm, just before the raid on Harper's Ferry, he was asked to tell of it, and consented to if not urged again, for, he said, "I dislike to talk of it." He went, he declared,[66] to the cabin and demanded the girl. The old man asked him in. Thoughtlessly he entered, when the old man slipped behind him, locked the door and "pulled a gun." It became instantly a case of shoot first. "You might call it a case of self-defence," asserted Stevens, "or you might also say that I had no business in there, and that the old man was right." Subsequently the Cruise family also charged wholesale looting of the house, the taking of two yoke of oxen, a wagon-load of provisions, eleven mules and two horses. It was also declared that a valuable mule was taken from another neighbor, Hugh Martin.[67]

Naturally, the death of Mr. Cruise created great excitement in Missouri, for, Stevens's narrative to the contrary notwithstanding, he ranked as a peaceful, law-abiding citizen, accustomed to minding his own business. This murder instantly imperilled the safety of all the Kansas settlements near the border line, for it was wholly unprovoked and without a shadow of the usual apology, that Cruise had been guilty of outrages upon the people of Kansas. In 1856 such an event would have been excuse enough for a wholesale military invasion of the Territory. As it was, Montgomery found it wise to be more than ever vigilant in the protection of the border. Stevens himself was not naturally bloodthirsty, but was the bravest of all Brown's men. Gill says of him, that he "was one of nature's noblemen if there ever was one. Generous and brave, impulsive and loving, one cannot speak too well or too kindly of him." [68]

But the result of the killing was bad enough. The Harrisonville, Missouri, *Democrat* called the raiders robbers and assassins, and urged the Governor to do "something to protect our people." [69] The Wyandotte City *Western Argus* declared that Montgomery, who was first charged with being one of the raiders, and Brown "will have a heavy account to settle some day — for surely a terrible retribution will come to them sooner or later." It added that their "infamous deeds destroy the prospects of Territorial advancement," and would prevent the coming of emigrants next spring. [70] The Lawrence newspapers were also hostile to the Missouri adventure, even the *Republican* criticising it, after having been urged to do so by George A. Crawford at Governor Medary's request. The editor of the Leavenworth *Herald* wrote from Jefferson City, Missouri, January 21, 1859, that "in the present state of affairs, the people of Kansas owe it to themselves, to the country, and to justice and right to put down these outlaws and preserve the peace. There is no earthly excuse for their invasion of Missouri." [71] General Lane, seeing his opportunity for another piece of bravado, wrote on January 9 to Governor Medary, offering, if given proper authority by him, to produce both Brown and Montgomery, after having procured their disbandment, "before the Kansas Legislature, now in session, or before any tribunal you may name." This offer elicited only a diplomatic letter of thanks from Governor Medary, and led the vicious *Herald of Freedom* to affirm [72] that, however Lane's offer might appear to others, it was to its editors "conclusive evidence of the complicity of Lane in those disturbances," — a ridiculous assertion. The St. Louis *Missouri-Democrat* printed, early in January, a letter from an Osawatomie correspondent, who thus portrayed the effect of Brown's raid, before describing it in detail: [73]

"Hardly has the mind cooled down from the fever heat into which it was thrown by the Ft. Scott tragedy, before it is wrought up to a frenzied condition by the enactment of new scenes in the present exciting drama. Hardly is the ear saluted by one piece of startling intelligence before it is stunned by additional news, of a nature so revolting that the mind grows dizzy with horror, and involuntarily inquires whether we are not relapsing into the barbarism of the middle ages. It is not probable that the killing of Cruise was premeditated, but finding himself attacked by robbers, he resisted, as was natural, and as he had a right to do, and he was shot down remorselessly by the fiend who had attacked him. I have yet to see the first free State man of position in or around Osawatomie, who does not condemn in the strongest terms, any going into Missouri or committing depredations."

Finally, the President of the United States offered a reward of $250 for the arrest of Brown and Montgomery, and the Governor of Missouri $3000 for the capture of Brown.[74]

With his two white prisoners and the slaves, Brown had moved slowly back to Kansas, meeting Stevens's party with its unhappy report of Cruise's death. As soon as the sun was well up, the whole party drew aside into a deep-wooded ravine, some distance from the road. Remaining in camp throughout the day, they resumed their journey after dark, and at midnight on Wednesday reached the home of Augustus Wattles, two miles north of Mound City. Montgomery and a few of his men were sleeping, as Mrs. Emma Wattles Morse has related the story,[75] in Wattles's loft, and were awakened

"by the chattering and laughing of the darkies as they warmed around the stove while Mrs. Wattles was getting supper. Montgomery put his head down the stairway, exclaiming: 'How is this, Capt. Brown? Whom have you here?' Brown replied, waving his hat around the circle, 'Allow me to introduce to you *a part* of my family. Observe I have carried the war into Africa.' After supper the women and children were taken to the house of J. O. Wattles, only a few steps away, the men went to their wagons, while Brown and two of his men lay on the floor for the two or three hours remaining of the night."

At dawn on Thursday the caravan started again, and this time without Brown. Two of his men accompanied the one ox-team, which was sent forward, one going ahead to act as pilot. But the latter turned back to "see the fun," believing that Brown was going to have some fighting with the pursuers hourly expected. Thus the man driving the team went on alone with his valuable living freight. It was near sunset and quite cold when they arrived at Osawatomie, Mr. Adair stated, and it was Christmas Eve as well. Mr. Adair wrote,[76] in recalling the arrival of this pathetic band of dusky fugitives, that:

"The fugitive slave law was still in force. I realized in some measure the responsibility of receiving them, consulted my wife, calling her attention to our responsibility, but would do as she said. She considered the subject for a few moments, then said: 'I cannot turn them away.' By this time the team was in the road in front of the house. All were taken round to the backyard, and the colored people were brought into the back kitchen and kept there that night. . . ."

It was at two A. M. of the morning after Christmas that the fugitives were finally placed in the old abandoned preëmption cabin on the south fork of the Pottawatomie, south of Osawatomie, belonging to a young Vermonter, Charles Severns.[77] Of unhewn hickory poles, neither chinked nor daubed, without door, floor, or windows, it must nevertheless have seemed a haven of rest and safety to the negroes escaping from the evil fate which would have been theirs, had they gone on the auction-block in Missouri. If they were not beyond danger of recapture, there were kind neighbors to bring them food, give them encouragement and stand guard over them. There were friendly armed men constantly watching the cabin, which could be seen for a long distance from several sides. The slaves were armed and told on no account to surrender. They quickly made the cabin habitable, building a chimney of prairie sod, and the naturally gay spirits of the race bubbled over so that frequently they had to be cautioned to be quiet. Several times they were on the verge of discovery, but the danger was always staved off. Pottawatomie Creek for twenty-five miles southwest of Osawatomie, with all its tributaries, was in vain searched by armed Missourians, who gave special attention to the timber along the streams. The open prairie was after all the safest place.

Meanwhile, Shubel Morgan, whose raid into Missouri was the eighth undertaken by Kansas Free State men, was in readiness to repel a counter-invasion. William Hutchinson, the Kansas correspondent of the New York *Times*, who had come South to see for himself how things stood, met John Brown at noon on Thursday, December 30, and went with him to Wattles's home.[78] He wrote to his wife a few days later:

"Have heard the full history of Brown's going into Missouri and shall justify him. I met with Brown and his boys about noon that day, Thursday. We went to Wattles that night together, and we were together all night and next day, talking much with him and Wattles and others who called on us. They took special pains to have a war council on my account, and appeared to have great confidence in the opinion of 'the man from Lawrence,' as some termed me. I am so vain as to think my advice did have some good effect. I recommended *one more* trial for a settlement before resorting to rash measures, and they accepted my plans, and we drew up a paper for signatures and Wattles started to circulate it among both parties."

This was undoubtedly a second draft of the John Brown plan referred to above. Mr. Hutchinson in later years had a vivid recollection of that night with John Brown.

"Our bed was a mattress made of hay, laid upon the floor of the second story. Sleep seemed to be a secondary matter with him. I am sure he talked on that night till the small hours, and his all absorbing theme was 'my work,' 'my great duty,' 'my mission,' etc., meaning of course, the liberation of the slaves. He seemed to have no other object in life, no other hope or ambition. The utmost sincerity pervaded his every thought and word."

From Wattles's home Brown went into camp on Turkey Creek, not far from Fort Scott, where he witnessed the beginning of the last calendar year of his life. On January 2 he formally wrote to Montgomery,[79] asking him to hold himself in readiness to call out reinforcements at a moment's notice, to prevent a possible invasion because of a raid into Missouri. Montgomery, meanwhile, was eagerly at work for peace, and attended with Mr. Hutchinson a peace meeting three miles from Mapleton. Mr. Hutchinson wrote the resolutions that were adopted.

"Montgomery," he says, "made a good speech, and every man on the ground seemed fully to endorse him. . . . The whole country along the border is in arms and I fear the end is distant. . . . The blood is up on this side and they won't stop now for trifles, from late reports. To-day, Jan. 3rd, some 500 men from Fort Scott crossed the river (Little Osage) near the State line going North, and we all expect warm work is near."

Fortunately for all concerned, there was no great bloodshed, — merely skirmishes, in one of which three Free State men were wounded. In these engagements Kagi commanded, for Brown had already gone North, — he reached Osawatomie on January 11. The pro-slavery forces were a posse bent on capturing the Free State invaders of Missouri.[80]

Early in January, Shubel Morgan was visited by George A. Crawford, a Free State Democrat, who went South at Governor Medary's request, and reported both to him and to President Buchanan. Writing to Eli Thayer, of Worcester, on August 4, 1879, Mr. Crawford thus described in part this interview near the Trading Post:

"I protested to the Captain against this violence [the killing of Cruise]. We were settlers — he was not. He could strike a blow and leave. The retaliatory blow would fall on us. Being a free-state man, I myself was held personally responsible by pro-slavery ruffians in Ft. Scott for the acts of Capt. Brown. One of these ruffians — Brockett — when they gave me notice to leave the town, said, 'When a snake bites me I don't go hunting for that particular snake. I kill the first snake I come to.' I called Capt. Brown's attention to the fact that we were at peace with Missouri — that our Legislature was then in the hands of Free State men to make the laws — that even in our disturbed counties of Bourbon and Linn they were in a majority and had elected officers both to make and execute the laws — that without peace we could have no immigration — that no Southern immigration was coming — that agitation such as his was only keeping our Northern friends away, etc., etc. The old man replied that it was no pleasure to him, an old man, to be living in the saddle, away from home and family, exposing his life, and if the Free State men of Kansas felt that they no longer needed him he would be glad to go. . . . I think the conversation made an impression on him, for he soon after went to his self-sacrifice at Harper's Ferry."[81]

To Brown's final visit to his staunch friend Wattles especial interest attaches, for it was at this time that he produced the 'Parallels' published in the New York *Tribune* and elsewhere, which attracted great attention and are more often quoted in connection with Brown than anything else except his final address to the Virginia jury. Mr. Wattles had severely censured his old friend "for going into Missouri contrary to our agreement and getting these slaves." He replied, Mr. Wattles testified in 1860: [82] "I considered the matter well; you will have no more attacks from Missouri; I shall now leave Kansas; probably you will never see me again; I consider it my duty to draw the scene of the excitement to some other part of the country." Montgomery and Kagi were parties to this discussion as to the storm his raid had created. Brown had been writing letters as they talked.[83] Finally, turning to the others with a manuscript in his hand, he said: "Gentlemen, I would like to have your attention for a few minutes. I usually leave the newspaper work to Kagi, but this time I have something to say *myself*." He then read the 'Parallels,' which he had dated at the Trading Post, lest the usual date line, Moneka, prove a cause of trouble to the staunch Wattles household. They are as follows:

TRADING POST, KANSAS, Jany. 1859.

Gents: You will greatly oblige a humble friend by allowing the use of your colums while I briefly state two parallels, in my poor way. Not One year ago Eleven quiet citizens of this neighborhood (viz) Wm Robertson, Wm Colpetzer, Amos Hall, Austin Hall, John Campbell, Asa Snyder, Thos Stilwell, Wm Hairgrove, Asa Hairgrove, Patrick Ross, and B. L. Reed, — were gathered up from their work, & their homes by an armed force (under One *Hamilton*) & without trial; or opportunity to speak in own defence were formed into a line & all but one shot, Five killed & Five wounded. One fell unharmed, pretending to be dead. All were left for dead. The only crime charged against them was that of being Free-State men. Now, I inquire what action has ever, since the occurrence in May last, been taken by either the President of the United States; the Governor of Missouri, or the Governor of Kansas, or any of their tools; or by any proslavery or *administration man?* to ferret out and punish the perpetrators of this crime?

Now for the other parallel. On Sunday the 19th of December a negro called Jim came over to the Osage settlement from Missouri & stated that he together with his Wife, Two Children, & another Negro man were to be sold within a day or Two & beged for help to get away. On Monday (the following) night, Two small companies were made up to go to Missouri & forcibly liberate the Five slaves *together with other slaves*. One of these companies I assumed to direct. We proceeded to the place surrounded the buildings liberated the slaves & also took certain property supposed to belong to the estate. We however learned before leaveing that a portion of the articles we had taken belonged to a man living on the plantation as a tenant, & who was supposed to have no interest in the estate. We promptly returned to him *all we had taken* so far I believe. We then went to another plantation, where we freed Five more slaves, took some property; & Two *white* men. We moved all slowly away into the Territory for some distance, & then sent the White men back, telling them to follow us as soon as they chose to do so. The other company freed One female slave, took some property; &, as I am informed, killed One White man (the master), who fought against the liberation. Now for a comparison. Eleven persons are forcibly restored to their *natural; & inalienable rights*, with but one man killed; & all "Hell is stirred from beneath." It is currently reported that the Governor of Missouri has made a requisition upon the Governor of Kansas for the delivery of all such as were concerned in the last-named "dreadful outrage." The Marshal of Kansas is said to be collecting a *possee* of Missouri (not Kansas) men at West Point in Missouri a little town about Ten miles distant, to "enforce the laws," & all proslavery conservative Free-State, and dough-faced men & Administration tools are filled with holy horror.

Consider the two cases, and the action of the Administration party.

Respectfully yours,

JOHN BROWN.[84]

Indubitably, the parallel was an effective one. The theft of black human property was always the most heinous offence known in the South during slavery days; and, although he had expressed due horror at the Hamilton massacre, Governor Denver had neither requisitioned the Governor of Missouri for the delivery of Hamilton's criminals, nor offered a reward for their apprehension. Now, however, the case was different.[85] Governor Medary sent a message to the Legislature on January 11, denouncing both Brown and Montgomery, refusing to give the names of his informants as to their movements in Linn and Bourbon counties, and asking the Legislature to act at once, besides repeating his offer of $250 reward each for the arrest of Brown and Montgomery.[86] To this a committee of the Legislature made a remarkably spirited and able reply. While censuring Brown and Montgomery, and attributing to them the "ruin and desolation" that had "settled down on two of the most beautiful counties in Kansas," the committee was "clearly of the opinion that all armed bands should be dispersed, and the law should be sustained. Kansas has too long suffered in her good name from the acts of lawless men and from the corruption of Federal officers." As to the Federal Government's offer of a reward, the committee was emphatic in its statement that this policy would not succeed. "The man of Kansas," it said, "that would, for a reward, deliver up a man to the General Government, would sink into the grave of an Arnold or a Judas. . . . Such have been the acts of the General Government in this Territory, that public sentiment will not permit any person to receive the gold of the General Government as a bribe to do a duty."[87] There being a minority report of a different character, the Legislature referred the whole matter to a select committee, which brought in a harmless report that the Legislature should uphold the Governor in enforcing the law.

Montgomery promptly wrote, on January 15, a long letter to the Lawrence *Republican*,[88] setting forth actual conditions and saying among other things: "For Brown's doings in Missouri I am not responsible. I know nothing of either his plans or intentions. Brown keeps his own counsels, and acts on his own responsibility. I hear much said about Montgomery and his company. I have no company. We have had no organization since the 5th day of July." Montgomery, with splendid courage, followed this letter up in person, arriving in Lawrence on January 18, and, boldly walking into court in the afternoon, surrendered himself to Judge Elmore, by whom he was turned over to the sheriff. As the only indictment pending against him was one for robbing a post-office, this border leader was promptly released on four thousand dollars' bail. Two days later, he spoke for nearly three hours before a large audience in the Lawrence Congregational Church, detailing the whole history of the border troubles.[89] Frequently interrupting him with applause, the audience, at the conclusion of his story, gave three cheers for him, and three more for

"Old John Brown." The next day, Montgomery went back to the South, where he continued his efforts in behalf of peace. On February 2 he returned to Lawrence with six of his men, who likewise surrendered to Judge Elmore, to Governor Medary's great satisfaction.[90]

As for John Brown, he was now ready to leave the Territory for the last time. Of constructive work there was no more to his credit than when he left the Territory in 1856. The terror of his name undoubtedly acted as a deterrent while he was on the Missouri line. But there had been peace in Linn and Bourbon counties, and would have been, had he not appeared, until Montgomery rightly or wrongly assumed the offensive in November, — except for the usual lawlessness of a frontier where the courts are not respected. As Montgomery said, Shubel Morgan kept his own counsels and went his own way, and the sole act of any significance to be credited to him during this six months in southern Kansas is the capture of the slaves. On the other hand, his presence in Linn, after deducting properly the numerous acts wrongfully attributed to him and his men, was in itself the cause of excitement and strife. It was an incentive to men of the Weaver type to spread stories of impending trouble for their own ends. Certain it is that the Missouri raid, in violation of his agreement, caused many peaceful Free State settlers to flee their homes for fear of violence, and might have resulted seriously but for the efforts of certain Missourians to keep the peace, and for the pusillanimity of those who wished to retaliate but feared the consequences. In Missouri, however, that raid had caused sufficient alarm to convince Brown again of the telling effect upon the crumbling foundations of slavery of a similar undertaking on a larger scale. "All the slaves in the thickest slave settlements in Missouri for twenty or thirty miles have been carried into Texas or Arkansas, or are closely guarded by a large force every night," reported, on January 15, a *Tribune* correspondent from Lawrence.[91]

It is not to be believed that if the Massachusetts friends of John Brown had been fully informed as to what little good he had achieved, after they sent him back to Kansas, or of the results of his surrounding himself with armed followers, they would have been wholly content with the outlay they had made to send him there. Gerrit Smith and others rejoiced in the Missouri liberations,[92] but it does not appear that they were aware that quiet was restored as soon as Brown left the Territory and Montgomery decided to work for peace. This was finally assured by the Legislature's passage of an act granting amnesty to all who had committed crimes in Linn and Bourbon and four other counties. This act was approved by Governor Medary on February 11,[93] when Brown was on his way out of the Territory. Thereafter there was peace and quiet in Kansas until the Civil War came with its renewal of strife, of anarchy and border lawlessness, with the Quantrell massacre at Lawrence and the other episodes of the long war between brothers.

Brown parted about January 20 from his kinspeople at Osawatomie, and, with a disregard and contempt akin to Montgomery's for the rewards offered for his arrest, set out with the liberated slaves for the long journey to Canada, with Gill as his sole helper on the road to Lawrence. On the 11th of January he had written to his family [94] of his middling health and his regret that he had been unable to finish up his business as rapidly as he had hoped to, when he wrote previously (December 2). He was still unable to give an address for them to write to, and he made no reference to his rescue of the slaves, or to his impending departure for the East. This was delayed by the arrival of a twelfth fugitive, a baby born to one of the slave women; to it was given the name of John Brown. "A day or two before starting," records Mr. Gill:

"I had learned of a span of horses held by a Missourian stopping temporarily a few miles from Osawatomie, and the suspicion was well grounded that he had appropriated them from free state owners. At Garnett I acquainted Stevens and Tidd with the fact, who set out the same evening that we did, to replevin these horses. After doing so they proceeded to Topeka to await us; Kagi also scouted ahead for some purpose, most probably to arrange stopping places for us, and then went on ahead also for Topeka, leaving Brown and myself alone with the colored folks."

With this reconversion of pro-slavery horses into loyal Free State animals, Brown's men wound up their career in southeastern Kansas.

Shubel Morgan's trip from the cabin near Garnett to Major

J. B. Abbott's house near Lawrence was as trying as it was daring. Through mud, and then over frozen ground, without a dollar of money in their pockets, their shoes all but falling apart, Gill and Brown resolutely drove the slow-going ox-team, with its load of women and children.[95] These two staunch men demonstrated here, if ever, their willingness to suffer for others; Gill's feet were frozen when they reached Major Abbott's, on January 24, and "the old man," Gill relates, "had fingers, nose and ears frozen." From this haven of rest they sent the ox-team and wagon into Lawrence to be sold, and in its place obtained horses and wagons. Samuel F. Tappan, who, like Major Abbott, had been one of Branson's rescuers in 1855, loaned a two-horse wagon, with Eben Archibald as driver.[96] It was while he was staying with Major Abbott or a near-by neighbor, Mr. Grover, that Brown received a visit from Dr. John Doy, whose subsequent misfortune aroused indignation throughout the North. Dr. Doy had been asked to pilot a number of negroes from Lawrence to safety, and it was first agreed that he should join forces with Brown. Circumstances altered, however, and it was decided that they should move separately. Dr. Doy spent one evening endeavoring to induce Brown to change his mind, or at least to give him part of his small escort.[97] But Brown had, besides Archibald, only Gill and possibly one other. The next day both Doy and Brown were on their way. The resoluteness and intrepidity of the latter carried him safely through to Nebraska. But where he escaped posses and United States troops, Dr. Doy was easily taken, his negroes — two of them free-born — sent back to a hateful bondage, while Dr. Doy himself was sentenced to five years in the Missouri penitentiary, to which he would have gone, had not the brave and ever ready Major Abbott and other friends rescued him from jail, in St. Joseph, in the nick of time.

Somehow or other, Brown recruited his finances while near Lawrence,[98] and his wagons, when he drove away, were creaking with the weight of provisions contributed by Major Abbott and Mr. Grover. He narrowly escaped capture on the road by men who were expecting him to come by in an ox-cart. Leaving Lawrence on the evening of the 25th for Topeka, he stopped at the residence of a Mr. Owen, two miles north of the town.[99] There Gill dropped out to rest and recuperate, the indomitable Stevens taking his place. But there was no rest for Brown. On the 28th his little train reached Holton amid all the discomfort of a driving prairie snow-storm.[100] Here fugitives and conductors alike were compelled to seek refuge from the elements in the tavern, with the result that news of their presence spread quickly. The following day the fates were clearly against them, for when they reached their next Underground Railroad station, six miles away, the cabin of Abram Fuller on Straight, or Spring, Creek, that stream was too high to ford.

All day Sunday the adventurers rested in cabins near the creek, while a messenger sent to Topeka called a congregation out of church to go to Brown's aid; for on Saturday Brown had discovered the presence in his immediate neighborhood of a posse from Atchison, headed by Mr. A. P. Wood, which barred the way to liberty on the other side of the creek, — a fact at once triumphantly announced to President Buchanan by Governor Medary.[101] The latter hastily sent a special deputy marshal, Colby by name, to Colonel Sumner, who was now commandant of Fort Leavenworth, with a request for troops to capture Brown.[102] But long before Colby and the cavalry given him could reach Holton, that elusive bird for whom the net was spread had flown, — precisely as he had when Lieut.-Col. Cooke's dragoons so nearly captured him, — leaving Medary and Buchanan to swallow their chagrin as best they might. Their *bête noir* had leisurely traversed Kansas, his presence being known to many, yet the Territorial authorities had failed to lay hands upon him.

How Brown thus escaped from Kansas is both an amusing and a characteristic story. His policy of going to close quarters when in the presence of the enemy again demonstrated its value on this occasion, which has been dubbed the "Battle of the Spurs." When the reinforcements from Topeka, headed by Colonel John Ritchie, arrived, the creek was still high and the crossing bad. What happened is told by an eye-witness, Llewellyn L. Kiene:[103]

"'What do you propose to do, Captain?' asked one of the body guard.

"'Cross the creek and move north,' he responded, and his lips closed in that familiar, firm expression which left no doubt as to his purpose.

"'But captain, the water is high, and the Fuller crossing is very bad. I doubt if we can get through. There is a much better ford 5 miles up the creek,' said one of the men who had joined the rescuers at Holton.

"The old man faced the guard and his eyes flashed. 'I have set out on the Jim Lane road,' he said, 'and I intend to travel it straight through, and there is no use to talk of turning aside. Those who are afraid may go back, but I will cross at the Fuller crossing. The Lord has marked out a path for me, and I intend to follow it. We are ready to move.'"

It is needless to say that no one faltered. Gill, who had come with the rescuers from Topeka, thus relates the story of the fray as he saw it:

"At noon the next day [Monday] we reached McClain's cabins, where we found our company. I believe that they were glad to see us. Stevens had, awhile previous to our coming, gone out alone and demanded a surrender from four armed men. Three ran. One had to drop, as a 'bead' was drawn upon him. We now learned that there were about 80 ruffians waiting for us at the ford. We numbered 22 — all told, of men, black and white. We marched down upon them. They had as good a position as eighty men could wish, to defeat a thousand, but the closer we got to the ford the farther they got from it. We found some of their horses. Our boys mounted and gave chase to them; succeeded in taking three or four prisoners. The last that was seen of the marshal was in the direction of Lecompton, and appearances suggested the idea that his mind was fixed upon the fate of Lot's wife."

In such haste was the posse to escape that two men mounted one horse, and others clung to the tails of the horses of their comrades without taking time to mount their own. Such was the terror of John Brown's name. "There is a great deal of the old fighting spirit up," reported the *Missouri Democrat*,[104] in giving its account of the "Battle of the Spurs." "The chase," said the Leavenworth *Times*,

"was a merry one and closed by Brown's taking off three of his pursuers as prisoners; with four horses, pistols, guns, &c., as legitimate plunder. The prisoners were carried some twenty miles, and then sent back to Atchison both wiser and sadder men. They feel rather chop-fallen, and vent their wrath on their captain, whom they denounce as a blusterer and coward. The terms might be applied to the whole party as well, for aught we know. Old Captain Brown is not to be taken by 'boys' and he cordially invites all proslavery men to try their hands at arresting him."[105]

From Holton, Brown's day's journey carried him to Sabetha, at the head of Pony Creek, six miles from the Nebraska line, where he again found helpful and earnest friends. The men were divided among three houses in the neighborhood for the night. The next day, February 1, was his last in Kansas. Mr. Graham, of Sabetha, writes:

"The morning Brown left Kansas he wanted me to go along and help them over the Nemaha river, and I did. When we came to the river it was so high we could not ford it, and the weather was very cold. We hoped it would freeze that night so that the ice would bear; and we stayed at the log-house of a half-breed Indian, named Tessaun, on the Sac and Fox Reservation [in Nebraska]. He had a double log-house, and gave us a large room with a bed in it. As I had no blankets, I was assigned to the bed with John Brown. In the morning the ice was strong enough to bear a man, but not a team; so they took the wagons to pieces and pushed them across; then laid poles across, with rails and bushes and boards on them, and over this bridge they led the horses. Then I bade them good bye, and returned to Sabetha."

On the 4th, Brown crossed the Missouri at Nebraska City and stood on Iowa soil, eluding another posse of fifty, just before entering Nebraska City, which Gill met and avoided by a stratagem. One day more and he was in the familiar town of Tabor.[106] The exodus from Kansas was over; the flight from the Egyptians had passed its most dangerous stage. Five days after his arrival there, on February 10, Brown wrote to his "Dear Wife and Children All:"

"I am once more in Iowa through the great mercy of God. Those with me & *other* friends are well. I hope soon to be at a point where I can learn of *your welfare* & perhaps send you something besides my good wishes. I suppose you get the common news. May the God of my *fathers* be *your* God."[107]

It was the same, yet for John Brown a changed, Tabor which he entered with the rescued slaves, elated over standing on free soil. The news of his coming had preceded him, and with it the details of the Missouri exploit, the killing of Cruise, the taking of oxen, horses and wagons. Strongly anti-slavery as the town was, this seemed to it transgression of the bounds. Throughout the North public sentiment was then practically unanimous on the side of the fugitive slave. In Massachusetts the Federal Government itself was now powerless to take back the slave who had fled from his chains, so bitter was the anger of the citizens of the State after the rendition of Anthony Burns in 1854. The moral sentiment of the time perceived, moreover, no wrong in the slave's taking such things as he needed for his flight. Were they not but a small part of the wage he had earned which had been wickedly withheld from him? And would not flight in most cases have been impossible if they did not take at least the clothes they wore, which belonged not to them but to the master? To Ellen Craft, who, wearing her owner's suit and high hat, impersonated a white man travelling North, with her husband as an attendant slave, no stigma of theft attached. Slavery to the Abolitionists was the sum of human wickedness, and nearly all measures taken to escape from it were justifiable. Not, however, the taking of human life. It was this that stuck in the crops of the Tabor community, which also had the frontier town's horror of the horse-thief. So that when John Brown's train of wagons arrived, there was a curious but a cold crowd to greet him. The slaves were put into a little school-house which yet stands, and the teams unloaded on the public common that is still the particular attraction of Tabor. For a week, at least, Brown desired to rest and recuperate for the long overland trip across Iowa to Springdale.

The next day being the Sabbath, as the Rev. John Todd, whose hospitable home had sheltered many an armed emigrant ready to take human life in defence of Kansas, entered his church, there was handed to him the following note in John Brown's handwriting, which is still preserved in the Historical Department of Iowa at Des Moines:

"John Brown respectfully requests the church at Tabor to offer public thanksgiving to Almighty God in behalf of himself, & company: *& of their rescued captives, in particular* for his gracious preseveration of their lives, & health; & his signal deliverance of all out of the hand of the wicked, hitherto. 'Oh give thanks unto the Lord; for he is good: for his mercy endureth forever.'"

The Rev. Dr. H. D. King was in the pulpit with Parson Todd, and to him the perplexed preacher turned for advice.

"Brother Todd," said Mr. King,[108] "this is your church, but if I were you I would not make a prayer for them. Inasmuch as it is said they have destroyed life and stolen horses, I should want to take the charge under examination before I made a public prayer." So, when the congregation was seated, Todd announced: "A petition is before us. But perhaps under the circumstances it is better not to take public action. If any persons wish to help privately, it is their privilege to do so." There was also announced a meeting of the citizens for the next day.

When this was called to order, John Brown was asked to speak in his own behalf. Just as he began his story, a Dr. Brown, of St. Joseph, Missouri, a well-known medical specialist and a slaveholder, entered the church. Recognizing him, John Brown very quietly said that "one had just entered whom he preferred not to have hear what he had to say and would therefore respectfully request him to withdraw." Instantly a prominent citizen sprang to his feet and said he "hoped nothing would be heard that all might not hear." John Brown very quietly remarked that if that man remained he had nothing more to say, and soon afterward silently withdrew from the meeting. It was understood that he said to one of his men without: "We had best look to our arms. We are not yet among friends."[109] George Gill relates that after Brown had declined to go on, Stevens arose and in his superb bass voice declared that "'So help him God he never would sit in council with one who bought and sold human flesh,' and left the hall as did the rest of our party."[110] After a long discussion, lasting it is said several hours, the meeting adopted the following resolutions, to John Brown's disgust:

Resolved, That while we sympathize with the oppressed, & will do all that we conscientiously can to help them in their efforts for freedom, nevertheless, we have no Sympathy with those who go to Slave States, to entice away Slaves, & take property or life when necessary to attain that end.
TABOR Feb 7th 1859
J. SMITH
Secretary of said meating.[111]

It cannot be denied that the element of fear entered into the conclusion reached.[112] There were those in Tabor who thought that too great hospitality to Brown at this juncture might lead to pro-slavery attacks upon the town. Certain it is that, had "Jim" Daniels come to Parson Todd, or almost any other inhabitant of Tabor, and asked for aid for his family, providing it were near by, he would not have been turned away unaided; for this belief the town's record as an Underground Railroad station is reason enough.[113]

John Brown finally turned his back on Tabor on February 11, and began his journey across Iowa. It was not without danger, for all the pro-slavery influences in the State were at work to prevent his reaching Canada, and many venturesome persons were attracted by the heavy reward for his head. Nevertheless, Brown took a well-beaten road, and did not shun the towns as he had in the previous winter, when moving the arms overland to Springdale. They stopped at Toole's, presumably an Underground Railroad station, on the night of the 12th, at Lewis's Mills on the next day, and at Grove City on the 14th.[114] Dalmanutha was their resting-place on the 15th, Aurora on the next day, and "Jordan's" on the 17th. The next day they boldly entered Des Moines, stopping, Mr. Gill says, "quite a while in the streets, Kagi hunting up Editor [John] Teesdale of the *Register*, an acquaintance of his; he also proved to be an old acquaintance of Brown's. Mr. Teesdale paid our ferriage across the Des Moines River." It was to Mr. Teesdale that Brown wrote in the next month, March, 1859,[115] in reply to a request for his reasons for entering Missouri, that:

"First it has been my deliberate judgment since 1855 that the most ready and effectual way to retrieve Kansas would be to meddle directly with the peculiar institution. Next, we had no means of moving the rescued captives without taking a portion of their lawfully acquired earnings. All we took has been held sacred to that object and will be."[116]

After the parting from Mr. Teesdale, the night was spent at a Mr. Hawley's; on the next day, the 19th, the stop was at Dickerson's, and on the 25th, the caravan was enthusiastically welcomed at Grinnell, the home of Josiah Busnell Grinnell, the most prominent Abolitionist in the State, whose life record, it has been said, would be a history of Iowa. To his house Brown went on arrival, and no welcome could have been more cordial. Mr. Grinnell himself has left a record of it,[117] and Brown was so touched by it as to be moved to send the following summary of it to the backsliders in Tabor as coals of fire for their unworthy heads:

RECEPTION OF BROWN & PARTY AT GRINNELL, IOWA

1st. Whole party & teams kept for Two days free of cost.
2^d Sundry articles of clothing given to captives.
3^d. Bread, Meat, Cakes, Pies, etc. prepared for our journey.
4th Full houses for Two Nights in succession at which meetings Brown and Kagi spoke and were loudly cheered; & fully indorsed. Three Congregational Clergymen attended the meeting on Sabbath evening (notice of which was given out from the Pulpit). All of them took part in justifying our course & in urging contributions in our behalf & there was no dissenting speaker present at either meeting. Mr. Grinnell spoke at length & has since laboured to procure us a free and safe conveyance to Chicago: & effected it.
5th Contributions in cash amounting to $26.50 Twenty Six Dollars & Fifty cents.
6th Last but not least Public thanksgiving to Allmighty God offered up by Mr. Grinnell in the behalf of the whole company for His great mercy; & protecting care, with prayers for a continuance of those blessings.
As the action of Tabor friends has been published in the newspapers by some of her people (as I suppose), would not friend Gaston or some other friend give publicity to all the above.
Respectfully your friend
JOHN BROWN
SPRINGDALE, IOWA 26th Feby 1859
P. S.
our reception among the Quaker friends here has been most cordial.
Yours truly,
J. B.[118]

From Grinnell on, the party, moving slowly, reached Iowa City on the morning of the 25th, and the familiar Springdale on the same afternoon. Here the slaves and Brown remained until March 10, when they departed from West Liberty for Chicago, because of persistent rumors that the pro-slavery element in Iowa City, headed by Samuel Workman, the Buchanan postmaster, would endeavor to recapture the slaves. Indeed, an effort was made to arrest Brown and Kagi when they spent a night in Iowa City, after reaching Springdale.[119] While Brown and Kagi were in the back of a restaurant, two men appeared at the front door and demanded the "damned nigger-thief of Kansas," whom they were going to hang with the rope in their hands. The restaurant-keeper, Baumer by name, sent them away and notified Brown. There was at that time a street-meeting going on, and to it Baumer went, and returning, reported that there was an excited discussion going on as to how Brown could be taken without risking the captors' skins. Finally, a picked force was sent to Dr. Jesse Bowen's stable to watch it, for Brown's team was correctly thought to be there. Dr. Jesse Bowen, William Penn Clarke, L. A. Duncan and a Colonel Trowbridge, Abolitionist friends, rallied to Brown's support, and spirited him and Kagi out of town early in the morning. Colonel Trowbridge led them safely by unfrequented roads,

"to a Quaker's house not far from Pedee, and there left them to their own resources, while he made his way back to Iowa City. There was then a post-office called Carthage, six miles east of the city, in Scott township, and a man named Gruilich was the postmaster. At this place there was a party of men shooting at a target, drinking liquor, and waiting for old John Brown to come along."

It was while staying in Springdale, on this last visit, that Brown wrote a letter to Dr. Bowen at Iowa City, which is of value as showing clearly that he still felt himself morally and legally entitled to some of the arms remaining in Tabor, under the National Committee vote of January 24, 1857 (not January 2 as below):

SPRINGDALE, CEDAR CO, IOWA, 3rd March 1859

DR JESSE BOWEN
  DEAR SIR
  I was lately at Tabor in this State where there is lying in the care of Jonas Jones Esqr. one brass field piece fully mounted; & carriage good. Also a quantity of grape and round shot: together with part of another carriage of some value. Also some twenty or over U. S. rifles with flint locks. The rifles are good and in good order, I have held a claim on these articles since Jan 2 1857 that is both morally and legally good against any and all other parties: but I informed Mr. Jones that I would most cheerfully; and even gladly waive it entirely in your favor: knowing the treatment you have received. I should think these articles might be so disposed of as

to save you from ultimate loss: but I need not say to you how important is perfect and secure possession in such cases: & you are doubtless informed of the disordered condition of the National Kansas Committee matters. I left with you a little cannon & carriage. Could you, or any one induce the inhabitants of your city to make me up something for it; & buy it either to keep as an old relic; or for the sake of helping me a little? I am certainly quite needy; and have moreover quite a family to look after. There are those who would sooner see me supplied with a good halter than anything else for my services. Will you please write me frankly to John H. Painter Esqr or by bearer whether you think anything can be done for me with the gun; or otherwise? My best wishes for yourself & family.

Respectfully your friend
JOHN BROWN [120]

Whether through Dr. Bowen's efforts or those of some one else, this little cannon now ornaments the library of the University of Iowa, at Iowa City.

The kindly Quakers of Springdale were quite relieved when Brown finally disbanded his escort and moved on, for they were well aware that he and his men would fight before they would give up the slaves. Stevens, Gill related, on hearing that there might be a rescue attempted, said: "Just give me a house and I'll defend them against forty." "A bystander," continued Mr. Gill, "has since told me that he had often heard of the eyes flashing fire, but that he never believed it until then. It was in the dusk of evening, and he declared that he did actually see the sparks flying from his [Stevens's] eyes." [121] It is said that a posse did leave Iowa City for Springdale, but thought better of it on hearing that Brown was in readiness for them; on at least one occasion the young Quakers of the vicinity stood guard with Brown's men most of the night, to protect the fugitives.[122] On March 9, with a strong guard of white men, the slaves were moved to Keith's steam mill at West Liberty, the nearest railroad station. Here they were kept overnight, and in the morning, when the first train from Iowa City passed, it conveniently left a box-car near the mill. "Acting no doubt," says an eye-witness,[123] "upon the supposition it was intended for use, it was at once made ready, the colored people and property placed within." At eleven o'clock the Chicago train came along, only to leave with the innocent-looking box-car safely between the engine and the express car.

The use of the box-car had finally been obtained by William Penn Clarke, by making the agent at West Liberty believe that the railroad officials knew and connived.[124] This he did by showing him a draft of fifty dollars for Brown from John F. Tracy, the superintendent of the road, and a friendly letter from Hiram Price, the secretary of the road, to a deputy superintendent. Mr. Grinnell, by engaging the car in Chicago, aided, and Mr. Tracy refused to accept payment for the car on the ground that "we might be held for the value of every one of those niggers." [125]

At Chicago, Brown, with Kagi and Stevens * and his dusky followers, awakened Allan Pinkerton, of detective fame, at 4.30 the next morning, March 11. Pinkerton at once distributed them and got them under cover, sending John Brown to his friend John Jones, a negro, and taking others into his own house. He got some breakfast, and then hurried to Jones's to see Brown, who explained that he was on the way to Canada. After some talk they decided to wait until after a lawyers' meeting that day, at which Pinkerton hoped to get some money. He actually did raise between five and six hundred dollars, and obtained a car from Colonel C. G. Hammond, the General Superintendent of the Michigan Central Railway, who personally saw to it that the car was stocked with provisions and water.[126] At 4.45 that same afternoon, the party left Chicago for Detroit in charge of Kagi, arriving at ten o'clock on March 12, Brown going by an earlier train to make sure of meeting Frederick Douglass, then in Detroit. He was on hand to have the happiness of seeing his black charges on the ferry-boat for Windsor, where they were soon rejoicing in their freedom under the Union Jack. One of the slave women had had six masters, and four of the party had served sixteen owners in all.[127] Henceforth they were to be in control of their own persons and profit by their own labor. As for their benefactor, John Brown, he had brought them safely eleven hundred miles in eighty-two days from the date of their liberation, six hundred miles of which had been covered in wagons in the dead of winter. The hegira was at an end.

* Gill had parted at Springdale from Brown finally, because of inflammatory rheumatism.

CHAPTER XI

THE EVE OF THE TRAGEDY

THERE was no period of rest and jubilation for John Brown, however it might be with the rescued slaves in their new Canadian surroundings. He and Kagi arrived in Cleveland on March 15, from Detroit, and spent about a week with Mrs. Charles M. Sturtevant, a sister of Charles W. Moffet, before going on to Ashtabula County to visit his sons there domiciled.[1] While in Cleveland, Brown sought to raise money by two methods, lecturing and the sale of two of his captured horses and a "liberated" mule. The Cleveland *Leader* of March 18, 1859, announced the lecture in this manner:

"'Old Brown' of Kansas, the terror of all Border Ruffiandom, with a number of his men, will be in Cleveland tonight, when he, and J. H. Kagi, Kansas correspondent of the N. Y. *Tribune*, will give a true account of the recent troubles in Kansas, and of the late 'Invasion of Missouri,' and what it was done for, together with other highly interesting matters that have never yet appeared in the papers. The meeting will be held in Chapin's Hall 7½ o'clock. These men have fought and suffered bravely for Free Kansas, and with good effect. Go and hear them and you will not grudge your quarter, necessary to defray the expenses to which they have been subjected by the persecutions of their enemies, aided and abetted by the faithless Democratic administration."

On account of a violent storm, few people attended the lecture, which was therefore postponed. The *Leader* next announced it for March 21, promising an evening of "thrilling interest."[2] But even this announcement failed to attract; it was a "slim attendance" which the newspapers recorded the next day. The reporters were there, however, and to them we owe full accounts of the meeting. One of these, that of the *Plain Dealer*,[3] is very "journalistic," as may be judged from the following description of Brown from the pen of "Artemus Ward," then the *Plain Dealer*'s city editor:

"He is a medium-sized, compactly-built and wiry man, and as quick as a cat in his movements. His hair is of a salt and pepper hue and as stiff as bristles, he has a long, waving, milk-white goatee, which gives him a somewhat patriarchal appearance, his eyes are gray and sharp. A man of pluck is Brown. You may bet on that. He shows it in his walk, talk, and actions. He must be rising sixty, and yet we believe he could lick a yard full of wild cats before breakfast and without taking off his coat. Turn him into a ring with nine Border Ruffians, four bears, six Injuns and a brace of bull pups, and we opine that 'the eagles of victory would perch on his banner.' We don't mean by this that he looks like a professional bruiser, who hits from the shoulder, but he looks like a man of iron and one that few men would like to 'sail into.'"

To "Artemus Ward," Kagi appeared but a "melancholy brigand;" some of his statements were to "Ward" "no doubt false and some shamefully true. It was 'Bleeding Kansas' once more."

On Brown's statements the friendly and unfriendly reporters agreed pretty well. The *Plain Dealer's* representative thus summarized the salient points of the address:

"He [Brown] had never, during his connection with Kansas matters, killed anybody. He had never destroyed or injured the property of any individual unless he knew him to be a violent enemy of the free-state men. All newspaper statements to the contrary were false. The Border Ruffians had created the war and he had looked upon it as right that they should defray the expenses of the war. He had told the young men that some things might be done as well as others, and they had done 'em. He had regarded the enemy's arms, horses, etc., as legitimate booty. He had never seen but one pro-slavery house on fire, but had seen free state villages on fire and in ashes. He had seen the ashes of his own children's homes, and one of his sons had been murdered — shot down like a dog — by Border Ruffians, the only provocation being that said son was a free state man."

As to the raid into Missouri, this is the impression Brown's narration of it made upon the humorist, who was obviously sent to ridicule or run down the whole proceeding:

"Brown's description of his trip to Westport and capture of eleven niggers was refreshingly cool, and it struck us, while he was giving it, that he would make his jolly fortune by letting himself out as an Ice Cream Freezer. He meant this invasion as a direct blow at slavery. He did n't disguise it — he wanted the audience to distinctly understand it. With a few picked men he visited Westport in the night and liberated eleven slaves. He also 'liberated' a large number of horses, oxen, mules and furniture at the same time. . . .

THE EVE OF THE TRAGEDY 393

A man lately from the Missouri Border was present and stated that there was 'a great antipathy against him (Brown) down there,' and the old gentleman cheerfully said he thought it 'highly probable.' On being asked if he should return to Kansas, he said it 'depended on circumstances.' He had never driven men out of the Territory. He did not believe in that kind of warfare. He believed in settling the matter on the spot, and using the enemy as he would fence stakes — drive them into the ground where they would become permanent settlers. A resolution approving of Brown's course in Kansas was introduced and adopted by the audience. He thanked the audience very sincerely, although he was perfectly sure his course was right before."

Brown's statement in regard to the "fence stakes" was thus reported in the more sober account of the *Leader* of March 22. He "had never by his own action driven out pro-slavery men from the territory, but if occasion demanded it he would drive them into the ground like a fence-stake where they would remain permanent settlers." Of great significance in connection with Pottawatomie is the friendly *Leader's* record of his saying that "he had never killed anybody, although on some occasions he had *shown his young men with him*, how some things might be done as well as others, and they had done the business." Financially, the lecture was a great failure: only about fifty persons were present to pay a quarter apiece for admission;[4] and the hall had to be paid for, as well as the advertising. As for the horses, Brown described one of them as a "beautiful racker, of very decided wind," while the other horse had "many excellent points;" but like the mule, both were somewhat thin. "They brought an excellent price," Brown afterwards said.[5] Probably these animals were shipped from Springdale to Cleveland. Brown, in selling them, freely announced that they were of Missouri origin, and that he could give no sound title thereto.[6] "They are Abolition horses," he told the purchaser, and when asked how he knew, he responded, "I converted them." This action, like his advertising and holding his lectures, well illustrated his contempt for the United States authorities. For, as they walked the streets of Cleveland, Brown and Kagi saw numerous posters announcing in large type the President's offer of $250, and that of $3000 of the Governor of Missouri, to any one who would arrest and detain Brown where he might be given into the hands of the Missouri authorities. One of these posters was conspicuously placed less than two blocks from the City Hotel in which Brown and Kagi stayed, the hotel itself being but four blocks from the office of the United States marshal who had put up the posters.[7] The explanation of Brown's immunity is probably that public sentiment in Cleveland was too strongly against the South to encourage the marshal to claim the $3250 reward.

On March 25, Brown was able to send from Ashtabula $150, part of the proceeds of the horse-sale, to his family at North Elba,[8] with the request that they purchase with it a team of young oxen, and that the balance be saved unless they were actually in debt. While at West Andover, he received from Joshua R. Giddings, the brave anti-slavery Congressman from Ohio, an invitation to come to Jefferson and speak in the Congregational church at that place. Mr. Giddings had seen the Cleveland accounts of Brown's lecture and, as he afterwards stated,[9] "our people had felt a great desire to see him, and we were a little surprised that he did not call at our village, which is the seat of justice for the county, as it was said he had visited a son who was living in that vicinity." Brown went to Jefferson on March 26, to arrange for his lecture, and spoke on the following day, after the regular church service. "Republicans and Democrats," said Mr. Giddings, "all listened to his story with attention. . . . He gave us clearly to understand that he held to the doctrines of the Christian religion as they were enunciated by the Saviour." After Brown finished, Mr. Giddings made an appeal for contributions, and "every Democrat as well as Republican present gave something." At the close of the meeting, Brown went to Mr. Giddings's house to take tea, and had a long talk with the Congressman and his wife. Neither then, nor in his lecture, did Brown give the slightest hint as to the Harper's Ferry plan, or refer to his associates or arms. Mr. Giddings, whose purse always had something in it for the fugitive slave, gave a modest three dollars to Brown for his work, which sum was swelled to three hundred dollars by reports from Harper's Ferry after the raid, in the effort to connect Mr. Giddings and other Republican politicians with Brown's attack. Kagi soon returned to Cleveland, where he busied himself particularly

THE EVE OF THE TRAGEDY

with the Oberlin-Wellington rescuers then in jail for taking an escaped slave away from slave-catchers armed with United States warrants. Kagi also carried on considerable correspondence with the men enlisted for the raid.[10]

To his family Brown wrote on April 7, from Kingsville, Ohio, that he had had a severe recurrence of his malarial trouble, "with a terrible gathering" in his head which had entirely prostrated him for a week.[11] He was, however, mending and hoped to be on his way home soon. In conclusion he added: "My best wish for you all is that you may truly love God; & his commandments." By April 10 he was well enough to leave for Peterboro, where he arrived on April 11, with Jeremiah Anderson, after a brief visit, *en route*, to Rochester. On this last visit, so Mr. Smith's biographer narrates:[12]

"Brown held a public meeting, at which he told the story of his exploit in carrying a number of slaves from Missouri to Canada and asked help to prosecute the work on a larger scale. Mr. Smith was moved to tears by the veteran's eloquence — headed the subscription paper with four hundred dollars, and made an impressive speech, in which he said — 'If I were asked to point out — I will say it in his presence — to point out the man in all this world I think most truly a Christian, I would point out John Brown. I was once doubtful in my own mind as to Captain Brown's course. I now approve of it heartily, having given my mind to it more of late'" —

a very different attitude from that assumed by Mr. Smith six months later. Encouraged by his stay there, Brown was at Westport on the 16th,[13] awaiting a conveyance to take him to his home at North Elba, which he reached on the 19th. Even the splendid Adirondack air did not break up the recurring ague with which he was still paying for his exposure to the Kansas elements. The trouble with his head also returned, so that he wrote on April 25 to Kagi that he had not yet been able to attend to any business, and would not be able to for another week or longer.[14] On May 2 he was still at North Elba, as his memorandum-book shows, and four days later was at Troy,[15] buying provisions and supplies for his family before the final parting. On May 7 he spent his last birthday at Concord with Mr. Sanborn.[16]

Even before Brown's arrival, Mr. Sanborn had been faithfully laboring for him. To raise more money for his venture was no easy task, but thanks to the two benefactors, Stearns and Smith, the two thousand dollars Brown now needed before finally embarking on his enterprise were in hand by the end of the month of May. Indeed, the skies had cleared greatly when he reached Boston. Forbes had subsided, or at least had shot his bolt. He had revealed Brown's plot to many who should not have heard of it; but the truth itself carried no conviction, it seemed so fantastic. Moreover, the ruse of Brown's returning to Kansas had worked successfully. His raid on Missouri had been widely advertised; he was still, in the public mind, associated with Kansas. There was, therefore, no reason why the great blow should not be struck, for which the leader was so eager. It was only a question of funds. As early as March 14, Mr. Sanborn was writing to Mr. Higginson and asking if admiration of Brown's exploits in the raid on Missouri would not loosen the strings of some Worcester purses.[17] Gerrit Smith then proposed to raise one thousand dollars and Judge Hoar perhaps fifty dollars. On May 30, Mr. Sanborn wrote: "Capt. B. has been here for three weeks, and is soon to leave — having got his $2000 secured. He is at the U. S. Hotel; and you ought to see him before he goes, for now he is to begin." But Mr. Higginson was unable to go to Boston, so Mr. Sanborn reported to him on June 4:

"Brown has set out on his expedition, having got some $800 from all sources except from Mr. Stearns, and from him the balance of $2000; Mr. Stearns being a man who 'having put his hand to the plough turneth not back.' B. left Boston for Springfield and New York on Wednesday morning at 8½ and Mr. Stearns has probably gone to N. Y. today to make final arrangements for him. He means to be on the ground as soon as he can — perhaps so as to begin by the 4th July. He could not say where he shall be for a few weeks — but a letter addressed to him under cover to his son John Jr. West Andover, Ashtabula Co. Ohio, [would reach him.] This point is not far from where B. will begin, and his son will communicate with him. Two of his sons will go with him. He is desirous of getting someone to go to Canada and collect recruits for him among the fugitives, with H. Tubman, or alone, as the case may be, & urged me to go, — but my school will not let me. Last year he engaged some persons & heard of others, but he does not want to lose time by going there himself now. I suggested you to him. . . . Now is the time to help in the movement, if ever, for within the next two months the experiment will be made."

GEORGE L. STEARNS GERRIT SMITH

FRANK B. SANBORN T. W. HIGGINSON

THEODORE PARKER SAMUEL G. HOWE

JOHN BROWN'S NORTHERN SUPPORTERS

THE EVE OF THE TRAGEDY

Mr. Higginson did not feel that he could do much this time. As he wrote to Brown, he had drawn so largely on his Worcester friends for similar purposes, that he found it hard to raise additional sums, particularly as so many of Worcester's best men were facing business difficulties.[18] Then Mr. Higginson had not gotten over his disappointment of the previous year. "My own loss of confidence," he wrote, "is also in the way — loss of confidence not in you, but in the others who are concerned in the measure. Those who were so easily disheartened last spring, may be again deterred now." "It had all begun to seem to me rather chimerical," Mr. Higginson subsequently stated.[19] He heard occasionally from Mr. Sanborn during the summer. When he got the news of the raid on Harper's Ferry, it came as a surprise, so far as the locality was concerned. "Naturally," he declared, "my first feeling was one of remorse, that the men who had given him money and arms should not actually have been by his side."

The other conspirators besides Mr. Higginson were still ignorant of the precise locality Brown had chosen for his attack; but were perfectly aware of its general outlines. Mr. Sanborn positively states that out of a little over four thousand dollars which passed through the hands of the secret committee, or was known to them to have been contributed, "at least $3800 were given with a clear knowledge of the use to which it would be put."[20] During Brown's last stay in Boston he met the members of the secret committee frequently. From his memorandum-book it would seem that their first conference was on May 10, at three o'clock, at Dr. Howe's office. Theodore Parker, having gone to Europe in a vain effort to improve his failing health, was not present. The burden of the undertaking rested, therefore, upon Dr. Howe, Mr. Sanborn and George L. Stearns. On May 16, Brown was able to write encouragingly to Kagi, to John, Jr., Owen and Jason. To Kagi he said that he was "very weak," but that "there is *scarce a doubt* but that all will set right in a few days more, so that I can be on my way back."[21] Indeed, his correspondence at this time was very voluminous, although little of it has survived. To his small daughter Ellen, in North Elba, then not five years old, he sent on May 13, from Boston, the following note:[22]

My Dear Daughter Ellen,
    I will send you a short letter.
    I want very much to have you *grow* good every day. To have you learn to mind your mother very quick; & sit very still at the table; & to mind what all older persons say to you that is right. I hope to see you soon again; & if I should bring some little thing that will please you; it would not be very strange. I want you to be uncommon *good natured*. God bless you my child.
                            Your Affectionate Father
                                        JOHN BROWN.

In the letter to his wife of the same date, in which this note was enclosed, Brown wrote:[23] "I feel now very confident of *ultimate success;* but have to be patient. . . ." To Augustus Wattles, to the Rev. Mr. Adair, Congressman Giddings, Frederick Douglass, and others, went missives at this period.[24]

Despite his recurrent ague, he was able to make some new friends and to meet the old. At Concord, the day after his arrival at Sanborn's, he addressed another meeting in the Town Hall, where Bronson Alcott heard him for the first and only time. Mr. Alcott recorded later:[25]

"Our people heard him with favor. He impressed me as a person of surpassing sense, courage, and religious earnestness. A man of reserves, yet he inspired confidence in his integrity and good judgment. He seemed superior to any legal traditions, able to do his own thinking; was an idealist, at least in matters of State, if not on all points of his religious faith. He did not conceal his hatred of Slavery, and less his readiness to strike a blow for freedom at the fitting moment. I thought him equal to anything he should dare: the man to do the deed necessary to be done with the patriot's zeal, the martyr's temper and purpose. . . . I am accustomed to divine men's tempers by their voices; — his was vaulting and metallic, suggesting repressed force and indomitable will. . . . Not far from sixty, then, he seemed alert and agile, resolute and ready for any crisis. I thought him the manliest of men and the type and synonym of the just."

An acquaintance made in this month of May was that of John M. Forbes, a public-spirited and broad-minded business man of Boston. Mr. Forbes noted that there was a "little touch of insanity" about Brown's "glittering gray-blue eyes;" "he repelled, almost with scorn, my suggestion that firmness at the ballot-box by the North and West might avert the storm; and said that it had passed the stage of ballots, and

THE EVE OF THE TRAGEDY

nothing but bayonets and bullets could settle it now."[26] Mr. Forbes had invited several friends in to hear the talk, besides Mr. Sanborn, who came with Brown, and, when the hour for retiring came, bade Brown good-by, as the latter was to take the earliest train for Boston in the morning. Mr. Forbes relates an interesting incident which closed Brown's stay in his home:

"When our parlor girl got up early, to open the house, she was startled by finding the grim old soldier sitting bolt upright in the front entry, fast asleep; and when her light awoke him, he sprang up and put his hand into his breast pocket, where I have no doubt his habit of danger led him to carry a revolver. . . . By an odd chance, the very next day Governor Stewart, the pro-slavery Governor of Missouri (who had set the price of $3000 on John Brown's head), appeared on railroad business, and he too passed the night at Milton, little dreaming who had preceded him in my guest room."

Another distinguished man whom John Brown met was Senator Henry Wilson. They were introduced at a dinner of the Bird Club, at which Stearns and Howe were also present, but there seems to have been a marked lack of cordiality in the greeting. At least, Senator Wilson gave the following account of it to the Mason Committee:[27]

"I was introduced to him and he, I think, did not recollect my name, and I stepped aside. In a moment, after speaking to somebody else, he came up again and, I think, he said to me that he did not understand my name when it was mentioned, and he then said, in a very calm but firm tone, to me: 'I understand you do not approve of my course;' referring, as I supposed, to his going into Missouri and getting slaves and running them off. It was said with a great deal of firmness of manner, and it was the first salutation after speaking to me. I said I did not. He said, in substance, I understand from some of my friends here you have spoken in condemnation of it. I said, I had; I believed it to be a very great injury to the anti-slavery cause; that I regarded every illegal act, and every imprudent act, as being against it. I said that if this action had been a year or two before, it might have been followed by the invasion of Kansas by a large number of excited people on the border, and a great many lives might have been lost. He said he thought differently, and he believed he had acted right, and that it would have a good influence, or words to that effect."

It was on the same day of his conversation with Senator Wilson that he visited his benefactor, A. A. Lawrence, who, as his diary shows,[28] had cooled off considerably in his admiration for "the Miles Standish of Kansas." This is the entry relating to the call:

"Captain John Brown of Osawatomie came to see me with one of his rangers [Jeremiah Anderson]. He has been stealing negroes and running them off from Missouri. He has a monomania on that subject, I think, and would be hanged if he were taken in a slave State. He has allowed his beard to grow since I saw him last, which changes his appearance entirely, as it is almost white and very long. He and his companion both have the fever and ague, somewhat, probably a righteous visitation for their fanaticism."

While calling at a friend's house during this stay in Boston, on a Sunday evening, John Brown also met John A. Andrew, then a prominent lawyer of Boston and soon to be the able War Governor of Massachusetts. Mr. Andrew was so impressed with Brown, whom he described as a "very magnetic person," that he sent him twenty-five dollars.[29] "I did it," he testified the next year, "because I felt ashamed, after I had seen the old man and talked with him . . . that I had never contributed anything directly towards his assistance, as one whom I thought had sacrificed and suffered so much for the cause of freedom." This chance meeting stood Brown in good stead later, when it came to providing the Virginia State prisoner with counsel. His last public appearance, as a speaker, in the North, was at a meeting of the Church Anti-Slavery Society, at Tremont Temple, in the last week in May. He sat on the stage, and was called upon to speak, but the large audience manifesting an eagerness to hear rather the orator of the day, Dr. Cheever, Brown broke off abruptly after saying a sentence or two, remarking, as he sat down, that he was more accustomed to action than to speaking.[30]

On June 3, 1859, this pleasant interlude in Brown's life drew to its close. Thereafter every energy was bent upon "troubling Israel" at Harper's Ferry, and there was much to be endured, in the sense of hardships and anxiety, during the period of preparation of four months now before him. From Boston he went to Collinsville, to put through the purchase of the pikes. He appeared at Mr. Blair's door as soon as he could get there from the train and said to him: "I have been unable, sir, to fulfill my contract with you up to this time;

THE EVE OF THE TRAGEDY 401

I have met with various disappointments; now I am able to do so."[31] Blair was disinclined to go on with the job. "What good," he asked, "can they be if they are finished; Kansas matters are all settled, and of what earthly use can they be to you now?" Brown answered that if they were finished up, he could dispose of them in some way, but as they were, they were good for nothing. Finally, Blair agreed for four hundred and fifty dollars to finish the weapons, if he could find a skilled man to do the work, as he was now himself too busy with other orders. Brown came again early on June 4, and gave him a check for one hundred dollars, and fifty dollars in cash. Three days later, writing from Troy, Brown sent three hundred dollars more to Mr. Blair, who found the workman he needed, with the result that the pikes were in Brown's hands in Chambersburg early in the following September, their receipt being acknowledged to Blair in a letter dated September 15.

From Troy, Brown went to Keene, New York, after making some purchases for his family, where he wrote to Kagi on June 9 that he was on his way to Ohio, after being "midling successful."[32] The next day he was at Westport,[33] on his way in to North Elba, where he remained less than a week. He brought in with him many things for his family which he had purchased on going to Massachusetts and on his way back; and in the brief interval of this, his final stay in his mountain home, he did everything possible for the comfort of his family. There is no record of their parting, a last earthly one for several. Nor is it probable that there was much emotion displayed; the Browns were neither emotional nor demonstrative, and their iron-willed and stern father had before this returned from venturesome undertakings in which his life was at stake. More than that, they were, as a family, ready for the sacrifice for which they had been trained and prepared these many years. It was probably on Thursday, June 16, that the parting occurred, for two days later, June 18, Brown's diary shows that he was at West Andover, Ohio.[34] "Borrowed John's old compass, and left my own, together with Gurley's book, with him at West Andover; also borrowed his small Jacob staff; also gave him for expenses $15, write him, under cover to Horace Lindsley, West Andover." On the 23d of June he sent to his family, from Akron, his first report since leaving them.[35] Hudson and Cherry Valley were other places visited by Brown in Ohio, and in nearly every one he seems to have discussed with one or more friends the active service he now contemplated — usually in general terms. He did not hesitate to say that he had arms and men, and was contemplating an attack upon Virginia; but those who remember those conversations are certain that there was no mention of Harper's Ferry, or of an attack upon United States property.[36]

He had, of course, long talks with his sons, Owen and John, Jr. The latter was engaged in drumming-up men and calling together the faithful of the previous year's band. This process went on during the summer. A surprisingly large number of persons knew or suspected what was going on, yet no inkling of it leaked out from this staunch anti-slavery neighborhood. From Ohio Brown went into Pennsylvania. He reached Pittsburg the same day he wrote to his family from Akron, for there is a letter to Kagi in his handwriting dated in Pittsburg on that date, and signed "S. Monroe."[37] He was at Bedford Springs with his son Oliver, who had accompanied him from North Elba, on June 26, and at Bedford on June 27, going thence to Chambersburg for a two or three days' stay there in the rôle of "I. Smith & Sons," Owen being the other son with him.[38] On the 30th he left for the future seat of war, with both sons and the ever-faithful Jeremiah Anderson, who in his rustic garb had attracted much attention when walking the streets of Boston with his equally rustic leader. To Kagi, Brown thus announced his departure:[39]

CHAMBERSBURG, PA, 30th June, 1859.

JOHN HENRIE ESQR
 DEAR SIR
 We leave here to day for Harpers Ferry; (via) Hagerstown. When you get there you had best look on the Hotel register for I. Smith & Sons without making much enquiry. We shall be looking for cheap lands near the Rail Road in all probability. You can write I Smith & Sons at Harpers Ferry should you *need* to do so.
Yours in truth
I SMITH

At Hagerstown the four men spent the night at the Hagerstown tavern,[40] not dreaming that a little more than three

THE EVE OF THE TRAGEDY

years later this small hotel would be filled with the Northern men wounded at Antietam in that war against slavery which the "old man" was so resolutely predicting. From Hagerstown their route led them to Harper's Ferry, perhaps partly on foot, for it was apparently not until July 3 that they reached their destination by train and were able to obtain cheap board at Sandy Hook, a small village one mile beyond Harper's Ferry on the Maryland side.[41] Then the Commander-in-Chief of the Army established under the Provisional Government was on his battlefield; the contest between one dauntless spirit and the institution of slavery which had so long dominated American social and political life was on in earnest.

The 1859 anniversary of the Independence of the United States, John Brown and his three companions spent reconnoitring in Maryland. It was about two-thirds of a mile beyond Harper's Ferry that John C. Unseld,[42] a resident in that neighborhood, met them between eight and nine o'clock in the morning and asked them if they were prospecting for gold and silver. "No," replied Brown, "we are not, we are out looking for land; we want to buy land; we have a little money, but we want to make it go as far as we can." After asking the price of land in that vicinity and expressing surprise at its costliness, and other desultory conversation, they parted, Unseld going on into Harper's Ferry. On returning from the town he again met them, and Brown expressed his satisfaction with what he had seen and asked whether there was any farm for sale in the neighborhood. Unseld informed him that the heirs of a Dr. Kennedy had one for sale, four miles from where they were talking. Brown then expressed the opinion that it would be better for him to rent rather than to buy, and, after declining an invitation to dinner at Mr. Unseld's, went on toward the farm. He was not long in making up his mind to take it, went to Sharpsburg, saw those in charge of the property, and rented for only thirty-five dollars the two houses, pasture for a cow and a horse, and firewood, all until the first day of March, 1860. To Unseld he stated also that his real business was buying fat cattle and driving them on to the State of New York for disposal there. Others in the neighborhood retained the impression that the newcomers were really mineral prospectors, particularly as Brown sometimes appeared with surveying instruments and carried a sensitive magnetic needle in a small bucket.[43] Naturally, there was at first much curiosity in the neighborhood, but it gradually waned until, later in the fall, it waxed again.

As for the Kennedy Farm, it is about five miles from Harper's Ferry. The main house, since altered and enlarged, was by no means commodious. There was a basement kitchen and storeroom, a living-room and bedrooms on the second story, and an attic in which some of the men slept. The house stands three hundred yards from the road, on the left as one approaches from Harper's Ferry, and was about six hundred yards from the simple cabin across the road, the second house leased, since destroyed. This stood about three hundred yards from the road, on the right-hand side, facing the main house. The place suited Brown exactly, and, as soon as the lease was signed, he moved his men up from Sandy Hook to dwell in it. After the occupation it became apparent that the farm was, after all, too near the highway, and that the neighbors were too inquisitive for comfort. They were constantly "dropping in," after the friendly Southern fashion, and could not understand why they were not asked into the house.[44] Mr. Unseld was once urged to come in, but as Brown had steadfastly refused to enter his home, Mr. Unseld declined to enter Brown's, or Smith's, as the Northerner was everywhere known.

Even before he was settled on the farm, Brown came to the conclusion that he must have women with him at Harper's Ferry, in order to avert suspicion while the arms were being moved in and the company assembled. He therefore soon sent Oliver Brown back to North Elba with the following letter to his wife, with the misleading date-line of Chambersburg, July 5:[45]

Dear Wife

I would be most glad to have you & Anne come on with Oliver, & make me a visit of a few weeks while I am prepareing to build. I find it will be indispensable to have some women of our own family with us for [a] short time. I dont see how we can get along without, & on that account have sent Oliver at a good deal of expence to come back with you; & if you cannot come, I would be glad to have

THE CABIN ACROSS THE ROAD
FROM THE FARMHOUSE

SCHOOL HOUSE GUARDED BY
JOHN E. COOK

THE HOUSE AT KENNEDY FARM, MARYLAND

THE EVE OF THE TRAGEDY

Martha & Anne come on. You will have no more exposure here than at North Elba; & can return after a short visit. I would not have you fail to come on by any means. I do not think you need hesitate to leave Ellen; with Martha, & Sarah; & I think you would not find it an unpleasant visit. You need not bring anything but your *plain* clothes, & a few Sheets, & Pillow-cases. What you could pack in a single Trunk, & a clean bag; would be (I should think) quite sufficient. A few Towels, & something for milk strainers might come. Have your bag; or bags marked, *I, S; plain.* I want you to come right off. It will be *likely to prove* the most valuable service you can ever render to the world. *Do not* consult your neighbors at all about it. Oliver can explain to you the reasons why we want you now. Should Oliver be too unwell; I want Salmon, or Watson to come on with you; if they go right back; at once. One might come & go in a little more than a Week.

Your Affectionat Husband
I. SMITH

Mrs. "Smith" was not ready to leave her home and her young children, although she wished for her husband "health and success in the great and good cause you are engaged in;"[46] but Martha, Oliver's wife, and Annie promptly responded to the call. Both were very young, seventeen and sixteen years old respectively. Oliver accompanied them, and Watson soon followed. Martha was cook and housekeeper, all unsuspecting of the tragic end so soon to come to her boy-husband — he was not twenty — and herself, and, until the raid, certain that Watson would shortly rejoin her at North Elba. By Saturday, July 16, the two young girls were at or near the Kennedy Farm, boarding with a farmer named Nicholls from their arrival until they moved in and began housekeeping on the 19th.[47] Young as they were, their services were indeed as valuable as John Brown had foreseen they would be. Mere girls, they had old heads upon their shoulders. They filled their arduous posts well and bravely, and fully won the respect of the hardy men as the long summer wore slowly on.

Pass it did before anything happened, — much to the disappointment of some in the enterprise. To live in the open in the Virginia mountains in the fall, to say nothing of the dead of winter, requires a venturesome man; the prospect was enough to daunt the toughest campaigner of Kansas plains, to say nothing of slaves with the negro dislike of the intense cold. There was every reason, therefore, why the blow should have been struck in midsummer. But one thing after another delayed it. The pikes did not reach the Kennedy Farm until well on in September. The men dropped in slowly, and meanwhile the two thousand dollars with which Brown had set out from Boston melted away so that he was compelled in August to appeal once more for money — three hundred dollars — to the ever-helpful Boston friends.[48] His own uneasiness was manifest on July 10 in the following letter to Kagi, then in Chambersburg:[49]

"I wish you to give such explanations to our friends as to our situation here; as after advising with Owen you will be able to do. We can of course do nothing to purpose till our freight is mostly received. You know also that it takes a great deal longer to start some folks than it does others. It will be distressing *in many ways* to have a lot of hands for many days out of employ. We must have time to get on our freight; & also to get on some who are at a distance; before calling on those who are ready & waiting. We *must* make up our lot of hands as nearly *at one, & the same time;* as possible. *Do not* use much paper to put names of persons & plans uppon. Send back word about the price of board with you."

Kagi had intended to be at Kennedy Farm, but he had hardly stepped off of the train at Harper's Ferry before he was recognized by some one who had known him during his residence in the vicinity.[50] Hence it was decided to station him at Chambersburg as the forwarding agent for the supplies, which were all sent there, Owen Brown acting at first as teamster on the night trips between the two places, and as pilot for some of the recruits as they joined. By July 12, Brown instructed Kagi to order Moffet and Tidd to go to Chambersburg.[51] Tidd answered the call, but Moffet had already written on June 20 that he could not come.[52]

John Brown, Jr., was unfortunately trusted with the forwarding of the arms, as he was not relied upon for active service. In May, 1858,[53] he had written that he had been "subject to a period of the most depressing melancholy," and that he was "almost disqualified for anything which is engrossing in its nature." His terrible experience in Kansas was still hanging over him, so that he was little fitted for the position of Ohio agent for the expedition. As such he reported on July

THE EVE OF THE TRAGEDY

23, 1859,[54] to Kagi, that he had the day before forwarded to the canal at Hartstown, Pennsylvania, just across the Ohio line, "11 Boxes Hardware & Castings from King & Brothers. They are numbered and marked thus #1 to 11– By R. Rd. Via Pittsburg & Harrisburg; I. Smith & Sons, Chambersburg, Pa; Shall send balance Hardware, &c., on Monday next — #8 and #9 are those which were on store with E. A. F.[obes] at Lindenville; Mr. Smith will remember." On the following Wednesday, John Brown, Jr., reported the despatch of the other four boxes of arms, and a little later six boxes and a chest of household supplies were sent on their way.[55] On August 11, Kagi reported [56] the arrival of the fifteen boxes of arms at Chambersburg, with freight charges of eighty-five dollars attached, so "very high" in Brown's opinion as to make him write at once to his son: [57]

"I begin to be apprehensive of getting into a tight spot for want of a little more funds, notwithstanding my anxiety to make my money hold out. As it will cost no more expense for you to solicit for me a little more assistance while attending to your other business, say two or three hundred dollars in New York, — drafts payable to the order of I. Smith & Sons, — will you not sound my Eastern or Western friends in regard to it? . . . It is terribly humiliating to me to begin soliciting of friends again; but as the harvest opens before me with increasing encouragements, I may not allow a feeling of delicacy to deter me from asking the little further aid I expect to need."

From Chambersburg the arms were laboriously transported to the Kennedy Farm by a young "Pennsylvania Dutchman" with a large freight wagon.[58] For the ordinary supplies and the household belongings, the small covered wagon purchased from a neighbor was the means of transportation. After Owen was compelled to give up being teamster, either John Brown himself, Watson Brown or Jeremiah Anderson made the trips to and from Chambersburg. "They had a horse and a mule, which they hitched to the wagon alternately, one riding in the wagon and the other on horseback, a short distance either before or behind, to keep a look out for danger." People along the road gradually grew suspicious of this little wagon and its mounted escort, and often stopped them to ask questions about their business.[59]

The conspirators were soon face to face with another danger besides the inquisitiveness of their neighbors, — their own loquaciousness and freedom of expression in their letters home. John E. Cook was the man Brown most dreaded, so far as looseness of tongue was concerned. He had married on April 18, 1859, Mary V. Kennedy, a resident of Harper's Ferry, and had secured a position as lock-tender on the old canal across the Potomac from the town.[60] Cook from the beginning favored the plan of taking the town and arsenal, and obtained a good deal of information of value while his comrades were at the Kennedy Farm. He even wished to go about among the plantation negroes and give them vague hints of what was coming. "This," says Mrs. Annie Brown Adams, now the sole survivor of those who gathered at the Kennedy Farm, "father positively forbade his doing. Father lived in constant fear that Cook would make a confidant of someone who would betray us, all that summer. He never doubted his bravery, his honesty, or good intentions, but considered him very impulsive and indiscreet." But while the others were in no danger of talking too much, their pens were by no means always well controlled. William H. Leeman, for instance, wrote to his mother, two weeks before the raid:[61]

"I am now in a Southern *Slave State* and before I leave it, it will be a *free State*, Mother. . . . Yes, mother, I am waring with Slavery the greatest Curse that ever infested America; In Explanation of my Absence from you for so long a time I would tell you that for three years I have been Engaged in a Secret Association of as gallant fellows as ever puled a trigger with the sole purpose of the *Extermination of Slavery*."

Letters similar in tenor passed from the members of the expedition throughout the summer, until finally John Brown wrote the only wrathy letter to be found in all his voluminous correspondence. It was dated at the Kennedy Farm, August 11, 1859, and addressed to J. Henrie [Kagi] at Chambersburg:[62]

"I got along Tuesday evening all right; with letters &c. I do hope all corresponding except on business *of the Co: will be droped for the present.* If everyone must write some *girl;* or some other *extra* friend telling, or shoing our location; & telling (*as some have done*) all about

THE EVE OF THE TRAGEDY

our matters; we might as well get the whole published *at once*, in the New York Herald. Any person is a *stupid Fool* who expects his *friends* to keep *for him;* that which he cannot keep himself. All our friends have each got *their special friends;* and they *again have theirs;* and it would not be right to lay the burden of keeping a secret on any one; at the end of a long string. I coul[d] tell you of some reasons I have for feeling rather keenly on this point. I do not say this on account of any tale bearing that I accuse any of you of. Three more hands came on from North E. on Saturday last. Be sure to let me know of anything of interest."

A special reason for vexation and anxiety Brown had expressed in a letter to his son on August 6. To the defection of Parsons and Moffet was then added the news of that of George Gill, Secretary of State of the Provisional Government, who had been so near to Brown during the long trip with the slaves. Then, a man named Henry Carpenter, of Medina County, Ohio, who had promised to join, lost heart after starting and turned back. "I hope," wrote the leader,[63] "George G. will so far *redeem himself* as to try: & do his duty after all. I shall rejoice over '*one* that repenteth.' . . . I was sorry about the mistake by which Mr. C. was parted from O. on the way back. He has not come on; & we suppose he found his way to you again. Every thing seems exactly right; & will be so, I have no doubt; if our own imprudence & folly do not secure a failure." Brown's own circumspection appears from the following letter, quite characteristic of this Kennedy Farm period:

CHAMBERSBURG, PA, 27th July, 1859.
DEAR WIFE & CHILDREN ALL.
I write to say that we are all well; & that I think Watson, & D. had *not* best set out until we write again; & not until sufficient hay has been secured to winter all the stock *well*. To be buying hay in the Spring; or last of the winter is ruinous: & there is *no prospect* of our getting our freight *on;* so as to be ready to go to work under some little time *yet*. We will give you timely notice. When you write enclose *first* in a small envelope *put a stamp on it; seal it, &* direct it to *I. Smith & Sons Harpers ferry, Va;* then enclose it *under a Stamped* Envelope; *which direct* to *John Henrie Chambersburg, Pa.* I need not say *do all* your *directing & enclosing* at home; & *not* at the Post Office.
Your Affectionate Husband & Father
I. SMITH [64]

But with at least eighty persons in the secret of the raid, it was inevitable that something should leak out. A disclosure of the plans actually took place on August 25, when so high an official as the Secretary of War, John B. Floyd, received this letter:[65]

CINCINNATI, August 20.

SIR: I have lately received information of a movement of so great importance that I feel it my duty to impart it to you without delay.

I have discovered the existence of a secret association, having for its object the liberation of the slaves at the South by a general insurrection. The leader of the movement is "*Old John Brown*," late of Kansas. He has been in Canada during the winter, drilling the negroes there, and they are only waiting his word to start for the South to assist the slaves. They have one of their leading men (a white man) in an armory in Maryland — where it is situated I have not been able to learn. As soon as everything is ready, those of their number who are in the Northern States and Canada are to come in small companies to their rendezvous, which is in the mountains in Virginia. They will pass down through Pennsylvania and Maryland, and enter Virginia at Harper's Ferry. Brown left the North about three or four weeks ago, and will arm the negroes and strike the blow in a few weeks; so that whatever is done must be done at once. They have a large quantity of arms at their rendezvous, and are probably distributing them already.

As I am not fully in their confidence, this is all the information I can give you. I dare not sign my name to this, but trust you will not disregard the warnings on that account.

So explicit a warning and so well written a letter might, it would seem, have roused the interest of the Secretary of War to the extent of a careful investigation. Mr. Floyd was at the Red Sweet Springs in Virginia when he received the letter. He was constantly receiving anonymous communications and destroying them. This one received more than the usual consideration, in that he preserved it. But one error in the letter, the reference to the arsenal in Maryland, Mr. Floyd afterwards said to the Mason Committee, "confused me a little." There being no armory in Maryland, he jumped to the conclusion that there was nothing of truth in the entire epistle. "Besides," he declared, "I was satisfied in my own mind that a scheme of such wickedness and outrage could not be entertained by any citizens of the United States." After the raid, Mr. Floyd recalled the friendly warning and, feeling that John

THE EVE OF THE TRAGEDY

Brown's attack had more than local significance, had it published, "that the country might be put on their guard against anything like a concerted movement." Again John Brown had encountered good fortune. Had the easy-going Floyd connected the John Brown of the letter with the John Brown for whose apprehension the President of the United States was offering a reward of $250, he might at least have made some investigation at Harper's Ferry, and perhaps have prevented the attack by increasing the guards.

For a long time the authorship of the so-called "Floyd letter" was in doubt. The survivors of the attack on Harper's Ferry and their friends were naturally eager to find out who had played the traitor. Both Moffet and Realf were suspected, and also a Cincinnati editor, Edmund Babb by name. Not until comparatively recent years was the mystery explained, when it appeared that the motive behind it was not one of hostility to Brown or friendliness to the South, but a desire to preserve Brown's life from his own folly by giving an alarm which would cause him to abandon his rash enterprise. "Our only thought," says the author of the letter, David J. Gue, "was to protect Brown from the consequences of his own rashness and devotion, without injuring him, or letting him fall into the hands of his enemies." [66] In August, 1859, Mr. Gue with a brother, Benjamin F. Gue, and a cousin, A. L. Smith, of Buffalo, were residing in a log-cabin in Scott County, Iowa, twenty miles from Springdale, to which place they drove on August 13, in order to visit Moses Varney and other friends of their own Quaker persuasion. To Smith, on August 14, Varney revealed the details of Brown's plans, exclaiming: "Something must be done to save their lives. I cannot betray their confidence in me. Consult your friends. But do something!" That day, on their return, Smith informed the Gues, and they discussed at length plans of intervention, determined not to let Brown and his men rush into death if they could help it. They could not betray Varney. They felt themselves young and inexperienced, yet dared not consult their elders. At last they determined to write two letters, from different localities, to the Secretary of War, giving facts enough to alarm him. This, they thought, would occasion an increase of the guard at the Harper's Ferry arsenal.

This Cook would see, would understand to mean that the authorities were informed, and would warn Brown, who would then lead his men away to safety. It was not easy to word a letter so as to command attention, while anonymous. Yet they wished to conceal their identity, in order not to be called on to testify further. So they gave Brown's name, thinking that his past record would gain credence for their story. Smith dated his letter Philadelphia, and enclosed it in a sealed, stamped envelope addressed to Mr. Floyd. This he enclosed to the Postmaster of Philadelphia and mailed it at Wheatland, Clinton County, Iowa. David J. Gue addressed his to "J. B. Floyd, Sec'y of War," marked it "Private," enclosed it to the Postmaster of Cincinnati, and mailed it at Big Rock. This was the letter that became historic. They hoped to convey the idea of two persons, non-sympathizers with John Brown, who, at widely different places, had accidentally learned of the affair, and felt it a duty to warn the Government. The postmaster at Cincinnati forwarded the letter to Mr. Floyd, but the missive sent to Philadelphia never reached its destination.

Fortunately for his peace of mind, John Brown received no inkling of this well-meant effort to frustrate his life's ambition. He had other worries in sufficiency to occupy him. The last financial question was, however, easily solved for him in August and September,[67] and on the eve of the raid there arrived a well-to-do recruit, — the final one, — Francis J. Meriam, of Boston, who placed six hundred dollars in gold in the joint treasury. The faithful colored friend in Brooklyn, Mrs. Gloucester, forwarded another contribution of ten dollars through Frederick Douglass,[68] and some other small gifts were probably received. Douglass brought Mrs. Gloucester's contribution to Chambersburg, when, at Brown's request, he met him there for a final conference on August 19, 20 and 21. Through Harry Watson, a colored Chambersburg agent of the Underground Railroad, of great service to Brown at this time, Douglass soon found the appointed rendezvous, in an old stone-quarry, and here Douglass, Shields Green, Kagi and Brown sat down to talk over the enterprise. The colored orator vehemently opposed the taking of the arsenal, when that plan was unfolded to him, and, according to his own story, characterized it as assuredly fatal to all engaged.[69] "It would be

THE EVE OF THE TRAGEDY

an attack upon the federal government, and would array the whole country against us. . . . I told him . . . that all his arguments, and all his descriptions of the place, convinced me that he was going into a perfect steel-trap, and that once in he would never get out alive." Finally, Douglass said that, as the plan was so completely changed, he should return home, and turning to Shields Green, a negro he had brought from Rochester with him, asked him what he should do. Shields Green promptly answered, "I b'lieve I'll go wid de ole man." Brown could not conceal his disappointment at Douglass's defection. "I will defend you with my life," he said. "I want you for a special purpose. When I strike, the bees will begin to swarm, and I shall want you to help me hive them." Douglass's withdrawal, as has already been stated, subjected him to considerable criticism, not only for his change of mind, but because of the way he withdrew, and of what he afterward said and wrote about the raid.

Other men, colored and white, disappointed Brown. J. H. Harris, later the colored Congressman from North Carolina, and a member of the Chatham convention, wrote from Cleveland, August 22, that he was disgusted with himself "and the whole negro set, ———— ———— 'em."[70] Alexis Hinckley, a family connection of Brown's at North Elba, who had been ready the year before, was not on hand now because of domestic troubles;[71] Realf had quite disappeared; George B. Gill did not "repent" until too late; and R. J. Hinton, also, started too late. Henry Thompson and Jason and Salmon Brown were averse to joining, and Richard Richardson could not be induced to leave Canada, — indeed, the Canadian negro reinforcement that Brown had counted upon wholly failed to materialize, except in the case of Osborn P. Anderson, who paid his own way. Perhaps it was too much to expect that many men who had, at the risk of torture, escaped from lifelong bondage, should now be willing to place their necks in the noose again; perhaps they were not properly informed as to the hour for the revolt.

For John Brown, Jr., seems to have been the victim of a curious mental aberration. Although he had shipped the arms to Chambersburg and apologized for the delay in getting them off, he suddenly wrote on September 8 to Kagi:[72] "From what

I even, had understood, I had supposed you would not think it best to commence opening the coal banks before spring, unless circumstances should make it important. However, I suppose the reasons are satisfactory to you and if so, those who own similar shares, ought not to object." Kagi was constantly urging John Brown, Jr., to send forward men, but without much avail. The latter's trip to New York, Boston and Canada, in August, also seems to have been of little use; it is obvious that a stronger forwarding agent — Kagi, for instance — would have obtained many more recruits. Certainly, the "associations" which John Brown, Jr., formed in Canada for recruiting purposes were never heard from; but it would be wrong to attribute this to any lack of valor on the part of the negroes, — as some have tried to, — in the absence of definite information as to John Brown, Jr.'s statements and directions. There were a number of white men who claimed later an intention to join, and alleged misinformation as to the exact date, besides Hinton and Gill. Charles W. Lenhart, of Kansas fame, is not of this number. He had settled down to the study of the law in Cincinnati, and decided to stick to it.

Gradually, however, the officers and men of the tiny army of the Provisional Government did assemble at the Kennedy Farm, until there were in all twenty-one men besides the commander-in-chief. Watson Brown and the brothers Thompson, William and Dauphin, arrived on August 6.[73] Next came Tidd, then Stevens, followed shortly thereafter by Hazlett, Taylor and the two Coppocs. Leeman was on hand toward the end of August, being preceded, after the Douglass conference, by Shields Green, who, in company with Owen Brown, narrowly escaped being taken by some men who pursued them when coming down from Chambersburg. As they lay concealed in a thicket, in a corn-field near Hagerstown, three passers-by caught sight of Owen's coat and, suspicious that there might be a runaway slave episode at hand, returned twice to catechize Owen and Green. Finally, Owen was compelled to frighten them off with his revolver. Instantly, he and Green set out for the mountains and travelled all night, pursued by parties of searchers, often heard and sometimes seen, finally reaching Kennedy Farm in a nearly exhausted condition. "Oh, what a poor fool I am!" said Green to his

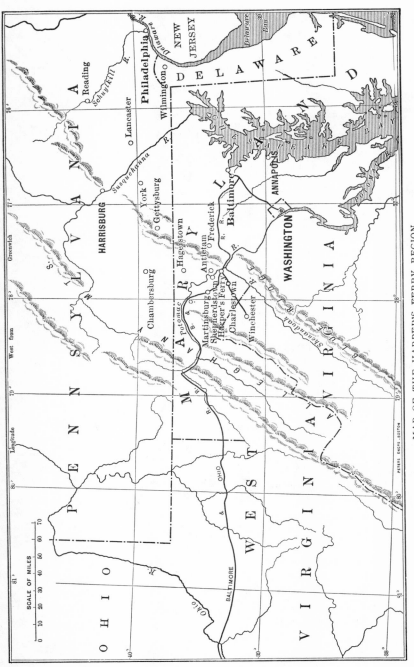

MAP OF THE HARPER'S FERRY REGION

THE EVE OF THE TRAGEDY

companion on the way. "I had got away out of slavery, and here I have got back into the eagle's claw again!"[74] Thereafter, Owen Brown abandoned his wagon trips to Chambersburg. When Osborn P. Anderson arrived, on September 25,[75] all the men were on hand except John Copeland, Lewis S. Leary and Francis J. Meriam. The others who had joined were Cook, from Harper's Ferry, and Dangerfield Newby, a negro who had been given his freedom, and was now hoping to achieve with the rifle the release of his wife and seven children who remained in bondage. As late as August 16,[76] this wife and mother begged her husband to buy her and the baby that had just "commenced to crawl," "as soon as possible, for if you do not get me somebody else will." "Oh, Dear Dangerfield," wrote this poor slave woman, "come this fall without fail, money or no money I want to see you so much: that is one bright hope I have before me." But fate decreed that Newby should neither save his wife from sale South, nor ever see the baby which had just "commenced to crawl," but whose body belonged to some one else than its parents.

It was a strangely mixed company which had now assembled to undergo close confinement in the cabin or the house, prior to a brief day or two of activity and disaster. All day long they lay in their garrets for fear of detection. But, ill-educated as most of them were, rough, unvarnished, some with soiled lives behind them, their hearts throbbed with a mighty purpose; the tie that bound them together was the outcry of their natures against the monstrous wrong they now beheld at close quarters. They were willing to give their lives for the sake of others, that others might live and be free; and "a greater love than this hath no man." They had willingly turned their backs upon their homes and upon the women and little children some of these harbored. There is extant a most touching series of letters between Watson Brown and his young wife, which no one can read unmoved, even fifty years after, for the Browns have all had the gift of earnest and moving English. There had been born to them, just before Watson left for the front, a boy baby, to whom was given the name of Frederick, the Kansas victim. "Oh, Bell," wrote Watson to the wife who was so soon to lose at one fell stroke her husband, her two brothers (the Thompsons), and her brother-in-law:

"I do want to see you and the little fellow very much but must wait. There was a slave near where we live whose wife was sold to go South the other day and he was found hanging in Thomas Kennedy's orchard, dead, the next morning. I cannot come home as long as such things are done here. . . . I sometimes think perhaps we shall not meet again." Later, he wrote: "If we should not [meet] you have an object to live for, — to be a mother to our little Fred. He is not quite a reality to me yet." And again, on October 14: "We are all eager for the work and confident of success. There was another slave murdered near our place the other day, making in all five slaves murdered and one committed suicide near our place since we lived here. . . . I can but commend you to yourself and our friends if I should never see you again." [77]

And the brave wife wrote, in reply, of her infant's pranks, and then added: "Now Watson keep up good courage and do not worry about me and come back as soon as possible. I think of you all night in my dreams." [78]

When men feel as did Watson Brown, it is easy to go to certain death; this the Harper's Ferry plan seemed to many of those assembled at the Kennedy Farm. Twice at least there was almost a revolt against the armory plan. Tidd, on one occasion, felt so outraged and angered at it that he left the farm and went, says Mrs. Adams, for three days to Cook's house, near the Ferry, "to cool off." Once John Brown tendered his resignation as commander-in-chief; but it was not accepted. He was their leader and they would follow him. On the 18th of August, Owen Brown gave his father the following letter on behalf of those on hand: [79]

HARPERS FERRY, Aug. 18th, '59.

DEAR SIR,

We have all agreed to sustain your decisions, until you have *proved incompetent*, & many of us will adhere to your decisions as long as you will.

    Your Friend,

        OWEN SMITH.

They were ready to do or die. But, meanwhile, the weary weeks of waiting — the raid was finally set for October — were trying indeed. Of their daily life, Mrs. Annie Brown Adams has kindly furnished the following recollections:

"My father encouraged debating and discussions on all subjects among the men, often taking a lively part in the debate himself.

THE EVE OF THE TRAGEDY

Sometimes it would commence between two in the dining room, then others would join, those who were upstairs coming down into the room to listen or take a part, some sitting on the stairs ready to jump and run back out of sight, if the danger signal was given that someone was approaching. Although he did not always agree with them, he encouraged them to discuss religious questions with him, and to express themselves freely on the subject. It is claimed by many that they were a wild, ignorant, fanatical or adventurous lot of rough men. *This is not so*, they were sons from good families well trained by orthodox religious parents, too young to have settled views on many subjects, impulsive, generous, too good themselves to believe that God could possibly be the harsh unforgiving being He was at that day usually represented to be. Judging them by the rules laid down by Christ, I think they were uncommonly good and sincere Christians if the term Christian means follower of Christ's example, and too great lovers of freedom to endure to be trammeled by church or creed. Self interest or self aggrandizement was the farthest thing from their thoughts or intentions. It was a clear case of an effort to help those who were oppressed and could not help themselves, a practical application of the Golden Rule. I heard them ask father one day if the money to pay the expenses was furnished by orthodox church members or liberal Christians. He said he must confess that it came from the liberal ones. Tidd spoke up and said 'I thought so, the orthodox ones do not often do such things.'

"After breakfast Father usually read a chapter in the Bible and made a plain, short, sensible prayer, standing while praying. (I have seen him kneel, but not often.) This was his custom both at home and at Kennedy Farm. Evenings he usually sat on a stool in the kitchen because it was warm there, and he once told me he did not wish to disturb the 'boys,' or spoil their enjoyment and fun by his presence in the living room. He thought they did not feel quite so free when he was there.

"As the table was not large enough for all to sit down at one time and the supply of dishes quite limited, Martha and I usually ate alone after all the rest were done. She 'dished up' the victuals and washed dishes while I carried things into the room and waited on the table. There was no door between the kitchen and dining room then, both rooms opened on to the porch, making a great deal of walking back and forth. After the meals I cleared off the table and washed the dishes and swept the floors of the room and porch, constantly on the look out for Mrs. Huffmaster, our nearest neighbor. She was a worse plague than the fleas. Of our supplies of food a few things were occasionally bought at Harper's Ferry when the men went to the post office after *The Baltimore Sun*, which father subscribed for. Most of the mail was sent to Kagi at Chambersburg — merely for appearance sake. The rest of our food supplies was purchased at the towns and all along the road from Chambersburg down, a few things at a time or place so as not to arouse suspicion. Owen brought a barrel of eggs at one time because they were cheaper than meat. We had potatoes, onions and bacon. Then Martha was an extra good 'light bread' maker. . . . We had a cookstove in the small kitchen off the porch upstairs, where we did our cooking. We used the basement kitchen and other cemented room on the ground floor only for storing purposes.

"The middle room in the second story was used for dining and general living room as the stairway from above came down into that room. The men came down and took their meals at the table, except on special occasions when some stranger or neighbor was calling there. If he or she stayed too long something was carried up the ladder at the back end of the house and passed into the window to the men. Sometimes Mrs. Huffmaster with her brood of little ones would be seen coming while the men were at the table eating. They would then gather up all the things, table-cloth and all, and go so quietly upstairs that no one would believe they existed, finish their meal up there and come back down bringing the things, when the visitor had gone. We did not have any stove or way of warming any of the rooms except the kitchen. The white men most of them, would watch their chance, when no one was in sight and skulk into the kitchen and stay and visit Martha awhile to relieve the monotony. If any one came they would climb the ladder into the loft over the kitchen and stay there until Mrs. Huffmaster (usually) was gone. The colored men were never allowed to be seen by daylight outside of the dining room. After Mrs. Huffmaster saw Shields Green in that room, they stayed upstairs closely.

"I was there to keep the outside world from discovering that John Brown and his men were in their neighborhood. I used to help Martha with the cooking all she would let me. Father would often tell me that I *must* not let any work interfere with my *constant watchfulness*. That others could help do the housework, but he *depended* on me to watch. When I sat on the porch or just inside the door, in the day time, I either read or sewed, to appear occupied if any one came near. When I washed the dishes I stood at the end of the table, where I could see out of the window and open door if any one was approaching the house. I was constantly on the look-out while carrying the victuals across the porch, from the kitchen, and while I was sweeping and tidying the rooms, and always at my post on the porch while the men ate their meals, when not passing in and out from the kitchen with food, or waiting on them in other ways at the table. My evenings were spent on the porch or sitting on the stairs, watching, and listening.

"The men did nearly all the washing; we spread the clothes on the fence and on the ground to dry. Martha and I would bring them in as fast as they dried, but Mrs. Huffmaster would have some excuse to come to the garden, which she had rented before we went there, and then she would notice the clothes and tell us 'Your men folks

THE EVE OF THE TRAGEDY

has a right smart lot of shirts.' No one can ever imagine the pestering torment that little barefooted woman and her four little children were to us. Martha called them the little hen and chickens. We were in constant fear that people would become suspicious enough to attempt an investigation and try to arrest the men. The rifles were in boxes called 'furniture' and were used to sit on and kept standing against the walls in the dining room, one box of pistols being in one bedroom near Martha's bed. She used it for a stand, table or dressing case, whatever name you wish to call it by. I had to tell people who called that: 'My mother was coming soon and that she was very particular and had requested us to not unpack her furniture until she arrived,' to account for the boxes in the room.

"At Kennedy Farm, my father wore a short beard, an inch or an inch and a half long. He had made this change as a disguise, on his return from Kansas, thinking it more likely to disguise him than a clean face or than the long beard.

"Hazlett and Leeman were the hardest ones to keep caged of all of 'my invisibles,' as I called them. They would get out and wander off in the woods and even go down to Harper's Ferry, going to Cook's home and back in daylight. We were so self-conscious that we feared danger when no man pursued or even thought of it. Watson, Oliver, Leeman and Kagi were all a little more than six feet in height, J. G. Anderson and Dauphin Thompson were next them in height but a little less than six feet; William Thompson and Stewart Taylor were above or about medium height but not quite as tall as the two last. Dangerfield Newby was I think above medium size, spare and showed the Scotch blood plainly in his looks and ways. His father was a Scotchman, who took his family of mulatto children into Ohio and gave them their freedom. Newby was quiet, sensible and very unobtrusive. Stevens and Stewart Taylor were the only ones who believed in 'spiritualism' and their belief was more theoretical than otherwise. The latter was nearer to a 'born crank' than any other man in the company. He believed in dreams and all sorts of 'isms,' and predicted his own death, which really came true. He talked as coolly about it as if he were going into another room. He considered it his duty to go to Harper's Ferry and go he did, although he knew he was going to his end. He was all the time studying and 'improving his mind' as he called it. He had learned to write shorthand. O. P. Anderson was accustomed to being confined in the house, being a printer by trade, so that he was not so restive as some of the others.

"William Thompson was an easy-going, good-natured person who enjoyed telling funny stories, mimicking old people for the amusement of any company he was in. But for all his nonsense he possessed an abundance of good common sense. When the occasion seemed to demand it, he knew how to use it to advantage. He was kind hearted and generous to a fault. Dauphin Thompson was the youngest one of a family of eighteen children. He was a quiet person, read a good deal, said little. He was a perfect blond, with yellow, curly hair and blue eyes, innocent as a baby, nearly six feet high, good size, well proportioned — a handsome young man. I heard Hazlett and Leeman, one day, saying that 'Barclay Coppoc and Dauphin Thompson were too nearly like good girls to make soldiers;' that they ought to have gone to Kansas and 'roughed it' awhile to toughen them, before coming down there. To while away the time the men read magazines, sang, told stories, argued questions, played cards and checkers, studied military tactics, and drilled under Stevens. When there was a thunderstorm they would jump about and play, making all kinds of noise to rest themselves, as they thought no one could hear them then."

At the end of September orders came for the women guardians of the conspirators to leave for North Elba. The exact date for the attack was not yet fixed, but Oliver Brown, who escorted his wife and sister as far as Troy, was ordered to hurry back, as the party might be obliged to commence operations before he returned.[80] The girls left Kennedy Farm on September 29, and with them went the gay spirits of the garrison. "The men then sobered down," said O. P. Anderson afterwards, "and acted like earnest men working hard preparing for the coming raid."[81] Among their other occupations they then busied themselves with overhauling revolvers and rifles, browning the barrels, and affixing the nearly one thousand pike-heads to the shafts of wood. On the 30th of September, Annie and Martha parted forever from John Brown in the station at Harrisburg,[82] where he had just returned from a hasty trip to Philadelphia with Kagi on some final important business, and whence the girls went on to New York. John Brown's trips from the Kennedy Farm were quite frequent during the summer, but this is the only recorded journey beyond Chambersburg. There is a fable that he made a hasty trip to Iowa and Kansas in the summer of 1859, but that is wholly without foundation. Between July 5 and October 16 there is a record of eight trips to Chambersburg, in addition to his passing through and returning on the visit to Philadelphia.

Francis Jackson Meriam, the grandson of the Abolitionist leader, Francis Jackson, of Boston, arrived at Chambersburg the day after Brown's final departure for Harper's Ferry. Just before Meriam appeared with his six hundred dollars

THE EVE OF THE TRAGEDY

in gold, John Brown had been compelled to borrow forty dollars from Barclay Coppoc,[83] — to such straits was the Commander-in-Chief of the Provisional Government reduced. "The good Father in Heaven who furnishes daily bread sent Francis J. Meriam down there with his money to help them just at the moment it was needed," says Mrs. Adams. His money was Mr. Meriam's only contribution of value to the cause. Erratic and unbalanced, frail in his physique, his joining Brown had been strongly opposed by both Higginson and Sanborn, on the ground that he was a "very unfit person" for Brown's enterprise.[84] "The only very positive thing about Meriam was his hatred of slavery," was Owen Brown's judgment of him.[85] In 1858, Meriam had taken a trip to Hayti with James Redpath; in that year he had made up his mind to give a large portion of his inheritance to the anti-slavery cause as soon as he obtained it. He had tried to join John Brown in 1858, and was seriously planning devoting his life to aiding slaves to escape, for he wrote to a boyhood friend asking what the consequences of detection would be, death or imprisonment.[86] It was Lewis Hayden, a Boston negro, who, on meeting Meriam on the street, told him of Brown's being at Chambersburg and in dire financial distress. Meriam set off almost at once, after seeing Higginson in Worcester, and as soon as he arrived in Chambersburg, had his will drawn by Alexander K. McClure (later the famous Philadelphia editor), and duly attested.[87] He next went to Philadelphia and Baltimore, to buy military supplies, and then to the Wager House at Harper's Ferry, on the day before the raid, being brought up to the farm by one of Brown's sons. Here, on Sunday morning, he, the brothers Coppoc, Leary, Copeland and Green were told of the plan of attack, heard the Provisional Constitution read by Stevens, and took the oath of fidelity and secrecy administered by John Brown himself.[88] The latter promptly took Meriam's measure and assigned to him the duty of guarding the arms left at Kennedy Farm, to which fact he owed his escape to Canada. He was then twenty-two years of age, and had lost the sight of one eye.

On October 8, Brown sent his last letter to his family prior to the raid:[89]

CHAMBERSBURG, PA. 8th Oct, 1859.

DEAR WIFE; & CHILDREN ALL

Oliver returned safe on Wednesday of this week. I want Bell, & Martha both to feel that they have a home with you untill *we* return. *We* shall do all in our power to provide for the wants *of the whole* as *one family;* till that time. If Martha; & Anne, had any money left after getting home: I wish it to be used to make *all* as comfortable as may be; for the present. All are in usualy good health. I expect John will send you some assistance soon. Write him *all* you want to say to us. God bless you all

YOUR AFFECTIONATE HUSBAND & FATHER

Two days later, October 10, Kagi sent from Chambersburg his last report to John Brown, Jr., in Ohio, who was still writing of the recruits he was going to forward in the immediate future, but never got off. This letter of Kagi's is particularly important, since it is a clear reflection of Brown's own ideas as to the prospects for success in the venture before them:[90]

Your father was here yesterday but had not time to write before returning. I shall leave here this afternoon "for good." This is the last of our stay here, for we have not $5 left, and the men must be given work or they will find it themselves. We shall not be able to receive *any thing* from you after to-day. It will not do for any one to try to find us now. You must by all means keep back the men you talked of sending and furnish them work to live upon until you receive further instructions. Any one arriving here after to-day and trying to join us, would be trying a very hazardous and foolish experiment. They must keep off the border until we open the way clear up to the line (M. & D's) from the South. Until then, it will be just as dangerous here as on the other side, in fact more so: for, *there* there will be protection also, but not here. It will not do to write to Harper's Ferry. It will never get there — would do no good if it did. *You* can communicate with us thus ——————— * (This must be a profound secret) Be sure no one gets into trouble in trying to get to us. We will try to communicate with you as soon as possible after we strike, but it may not be possible for us to do so soon. If we succeed in getting news from the outside our own district it will be quite satisfactory, but we have not the most distant hope that it will be possible for us to receive *recruits* for *weeks*, or quite likely *months* to come. We must first make a complete and undisputably open road to the free states. That will require both labor and time.

This is just the right time. The year's crops have been good, and they are now perfectly housed, and in the best condition for use. The moon is just right. Slaves are discontented at this season more

* This space not filled out.

THE EVE OF THE TRAGEDY 423

than at any other, the reasons for which reflection will show you. We can't live longer without money,—we could n't get along much longer without being exposed. A great religious revival is going on, and has its advantages. Under its influence, people who are commonly barely *unfavorable* to Slavery under religious excitement in meetings speak boldly against it. In addition to this and as a stimulant to the religious feeling, a fine slave man near our headquarters, hung himself a few days ago because his master sold his wife away from him. This also arouses the slaves. There are more reasons which I could give, but I have not time.

I will not close without saying that John E. Cook's wife & children are here, (at Mrs. R's) and will board here probably until *the end*. She came on Friday, has lived at the "Ferry." Her board is paid until the 1st of November, but after that we shall expect to see you or some one under your direction, have it paid *monthly* in advance, from $10 to $15 besides the necessary etceteras, clothing &c. — This must be our last for a time.

Yours
J. H.

John Brown's last letter to his son was dated October 1, and read as follows:[91]

DEAR FRIEND:—

I wrote you yesterday at Cleveland in which I forgot to say that any *person or thing* that reaches this place on Thursday the 6th Octo. inst. will *in all probability* find the *Road open*, but beyond that day we cannot be at all certain for some time at least. If you were here, I could fully *explain* all but cannot do so now. From Harrisburg by Rail Road remember.

"Associations" to *hinder*, *delay* and *prevent* our *Adversaries*, might perhaps effect much. Our *active enemies*, should be spotted to a man, and some shrewd person should be on the border to look after that matter somewhat *extensively*. Can you dig up a *good and true* man, to communicate with us on the border, *or close to it* where we may name places from time to time?

Yours ever
I. S.

Yet, in the face of these two letters, John Brown, Jr., frequently stated that the news of the raid took him completely by surprise,—which reveals a condition of mind hardly helpful to the grave venture upon which his father was embarked.

Francis Jackson Meriam's arrival seems to have removed the last obstacle to Brown's delivering the attack. Up to that time, waiting for men and money had steadily postponed the issue. Perhaps, too, there was in the delay something of that curious indecision that was so fatal to the original project when the raid was undertaken, and which also occasioned the delay in his entering Kansas from Tabor in 1857. Salmon Brown asserts that the reason for his not joining the expedition was his belief that his father would hesitate and delay until he was trapped, precisely as happened, waiting for circumstances to be exactly as he wished them to be. "I said," he declares,[92] "to the boys before they left, 'you know father. You know he will *dally* till he is trapped!' Father had a peculiarity of insisting on *order*. I felt that at Harper's Ferry this very thing would be likely to trap him. He would insist on getting everything arranged just to suit him before he would consent to make a move." There has been a vast amount of discussion as to whether the raid was hastened or delayed. John Brown, Jr.'s position has given color to the theory that it was hastened; so, too, has the fact that Gill and Hinton were left behind. Again, there are frequent stories that Brown learned of a betrayal of his plans, and so hurried to strike the blow; that a posse was being formed near by to investigate the goings on at Kennedy Farm, which had to be anticipated; that news that twelve thousand arms were to be taken away from the Harper's Ferry armory had reached Brown's ears; and finally that criticism by some of the Boston friends, who were impatient at the expense and delay, had precipitated the attack. The truth is that there was danger of discovery from the Huffmasters and other neighbors, and that the men could no longer stand the inaction and close confinement; some were already getting out of hand. When Meriam's money came, it was the last impetus needed to an attack which had been delayed much longer than any one dreamed of when Brown set out from Boston for the last time. So far as climatic conditions were concerned, it had been postponed far too long.

"One day, while we were alone in the yard," writes Mrs. Adams, "Owen remarked as he looked up at the house: 'If we succeed, some day there will be a United States flag over this house. If we do not, it will be considered a den of land pirates and thieves.'" It was with this conviction that the majority of the men went to their doom. All save Taylor

THE EVE OF THE TRAGEDY

hoped by some stroke of fortune to come out alive; but only a few believed in the plan of campaign, or looked upon the arsenal venture as anything else but a death-trap. Yet it was in an exalted frame of mind that they spent their last Sabbath and came together for their last meal. For them the hour had struck; their sacrifice was ready for the altar of liberty.

CHAPTER XII

HIGH TREASON IN VIRGINIA

"MEN, get on your arms; we will proceed to the Ferry." With these words, John Brown, Commander-in-Chief of the Provisional Army, set in motion his troop of liberators on that peaceful Sabbath, the 16th of October, 1859. It took but a minute to bring the horse and wagon to the door, to place in it some pikes, fagots, a sledge-hammer and a crow-bar. His men themselves had been in readiness for hours; they had but to buckle on their arms and throw over their shoulders, like army blankets, the long gray shawls which served some for a few brief hours in lieu of overcoats, and then became their winding-sheets. In a moment more, the commander-in-chief donned his old battle-worn Kansas cap, mounted the wagon, and began the solemn march through the chill fall night to the bridge into Harper's Ferry, nearly six miles away. Tremendous as the relief of action was, there was no thought of any cheering or demonstration. As the eighteen men with John Brown swung down the little lane to the road from the farmhouse that had been their prison for so many weary weeks, they bade farewell to Captain Owen Brown and Privates Barclay Coppoc and F. J. Meriam, who remained as rear-guard in charge of the arms and supplies. The brothers Coppoc read the future correctly, for they embraced and parted as do men who know they are to meet no more on earth. The damp, lonely night, too, added to the solemnity of it all, as they pressed forward through its gloom. As if to intensify the sombreness, they met not a living soul on the road to question their purpose, or start with fright at the sight of eighteen soldierly men coming two by two through the darkness as though risen from the grave. There was not a sound but the tramping of the men and the creaking of the wagon, before which, in accordance with a general order, drawn up and carefully read to all, walked Captains Cook and Tidd, their Sharp's rifles hung from their shoulders, their commissions, duly signed and officially sealed, in their pockets. They were detailed to destroy the telegraph wires on the Maryland side and then on the Virginian, while Captains John H. Kagi and A. D. Stevens, bravest of the brave, were to take the bridge watchman and so strike the first blow for liberty.[1] But as they and their comrades marched rapidly over the rough road, Death himself moved by their side.

As for their general, he not only was the sole member of the attacking force to believe in the assault on the property of the United States at Harper's Ferry, but he was, as they neared the all-unsuspecting town, without any clear and definite plan of campaign. The general order detailed the men who were to garrison various parts of the town and hold the bridges, but beyond that, little had been mapped out. It was all to depend upon the orders of the commander-in-chief, who seemed bent on violating every military principle. Thus, he had appointed no definite place for the men to retreat to, and fixed no hour for the withdrawal from the town. He, moreover, proceeded at once to defy the canons by placing a river between himself and his base of supplies, — the Kennedy Farm, — and then left no adequate force on the river-bank to insure his being able to fall back to that base. Hardly had he entered the town when, by dispersing his men here and there, he made his defeat as easy as possible. Moreover, he had in mind no well-defined purpose in attacking Harper's Ferry, save to begin his revolution in a spectacular way, capture a few slaveholders and release some slaves. So far as he had thought anything out, he expected to alarm the town and then, with the slaves that had rallied to him, to march back to the school-house near the Kennedy Farm, arm his recruits and take to the hills. Another general, with the same purpose in view, would have established his mountain camp first, swooped down upon the town in order to spread terror throughout the State, and in an hour or two, at most, have started back to his hill-top fastness.

Aside from the opportunity to assail directly the Federal Government, Harper's Ferry would, moreover, seem to have been the last place for an attack upon the institution against which John Brown was in arms. It was by no means a typical Southern town, for a large majority of its three thousand residents were mechanics brought there from Springfield, Massachusetts, and elsewhere, — "foreigners" in the eyes of the real Southerners.[2] The very slave-owners of the vicinity lived, not at the Ferry, but on their neighboring farms, driving in occasionally to the bright little town, prosperous and happy because the United States paid regularly and well the bulk of the citizenship, and set every householder a good example by the neatness and beauty of its grounds, adorned as they were by smiling flowers and by handsome buildings. As for the gentlemen farmers of the Virginia vicinity, they were content to raise only what produce they actually needed; they lived too far north to cultivate great crops of cotton. Hence their bondmen were largely well-kept house-servants, of the kind upon whom the ills of slavery rested most lightly, and among whom the desire for freedom was least keen.

The arsenal to which John Brown's little "army" took its way had been established as far back as 1794, in the Presidency of George Washington, on the peninsula formed by the juncture of the Potomac and Shenandoah rivers. The natural beauty of its surroundings is greatly enhanced by the Maryland Heights, thirteen hundred feet high, on the opposite bank of the Potomac, and the Loudon Heights, but little lower, on the other side of the Shenandoah, the two forming, as it were, a gateway to the Valley of Virginia of veritable grandeur. Thomas Jefferson said of it:[3] "The passage of the Potomac through the Blue Ridge is perhaps one of the most stupendous scenes in nature; . . . worth a voyage across the Atlantic" to witness; the heights he called "monuments of war between rivers and mountains which must have shaken the earth itself to its centre." Harper's Ferry has but a narrow, level space along each river; then there rises a hill involving a steep ascent before one reaches the plateau of Bolivar Heights. The town climbs the hill after the manner of European mountain villages, and is far below the Heights. "You may climb to the graveyard," wrote a traveller in 1856, "by the lightning rod of the Episcopal church, or you may slide down the rain-spout of the hotel to the ladies' car of the Wheeling train — only you must take care not to fling yourself, an unpremeditated soap-and-candle Curtius, down the paymaster's kitchen chimney, or put your foot in the soup

A   B   C   D

GENERAL VIEW OF HAR
A. Loudon Heights. B. Shenandoah River. C. Site of Old Bridge by which Brown and his men en
with the road over v
(Kennedy Farm, the rendezvous of Brown's party prior to the raid, lies between the hills on the ex

M MARYLAND HEIGHTS
). New Railroad Bridge. E. Bolivar Heights. F. Potomac River. G. Chesapeake and Ohio Canal
om Kennedy Farm.
re, in Maryland. Charlestown is on the high ground beyond the curve of the Shenandoah River.)

tureen of the master armorer who is taking dinner in the basement, which is a sort of antipodean attic." [4]

While nature has thus distinguished the town, its desirability as a military position is not enhanced by its surroundings, for, as was shown later, in the Civil War, it lies at the mercy of any force which scales the Loudon or Maryland Heights; from them it is easy for sharpshooters to pick off any one in the Ferry. In the rear, to defend it successfully, the enemy must be prevented from reaching Bolivar Heights. In 1859, the chief approaches to Harper's Ferry were by way of a bridge over the Shenandoah, and by a covered bridge from Maryland across the Potomac which was used both by the railroad and by vehicular traffic. The danger to any raiding force would come from losing possession of these bridges, in which case the sole means of escape would be by swimming the rivers or climbing up through the town toward Bolivar Heights, in the direction of Charlestown,* eight miles away by road, then, as now, the county seat of Jefferson County, and an important place.

It was half-past ten when Kagi and Stevens, as advance guard, entered the Maryland bridge and made William Williams, the watchman, their prisoner. He thought it a good joke, for he recognized Brown and Cook in the group that followed; but he was soon made to realize that here was grim earnest, and, like the others captured early in the raid, was utterly dumfounded.[5] On crossing the bridge, the raiders next came to the combined railroad station and hotel of Harper's Ferry, known as the Wager House. On the left side, on the bank of the Shenandoah, was a low saloon known as the Galt House, and straight ahead were the buildings of the arsenal in which the completed guns were stored. To the right, running along the Potomac for six hundred yards or more, extended the shops of the armory, protected on the river-side by the railroad track, but always in danger from freshets at high water. Of the armory proper, the first building was the watch-room and fire-engine house, in which Brown and his men were finally penned up; it was but sixty yards or so from the ends of both bridges. Indeed, the whole tragedy which ensued was within an extraordinarily small space.

* The modern spelling is Charles Town.

Beyond the fire-engine house were the forging shop, the machine shop, the stocking shop, the "component department" and the rolling-mills of the arsenal. About half a mile distant, on the Shenandoah, were what is known as the rifle works, separate shops in which sixty expert gunsmiths turned out weapons for the regular army.[6] Contrary to the custom of the present day, the arsenals of the government in 1859 were cared for by civilians, not by regularly enlisted soldiers of the Ordnance Corps; there were, in fact, but a few watchmen on duty at night at Harper's Ferry. John Brown, therefore, had nothing to fear from any armed guard on the spot. Hence, he confidently hoped to retire to the mountains before catching sight of a soldier of the regular army or of the militia, — by no means an unjustifiable expectation. For Harper's Ferry and the surrounding country knew nothing of war or its alarums. It had never seen belligerent men with guns in their hands since Revolutionary days, and in October, 1859, it no more feared an armed invasion than does the quietest and sleepiest New England village to-day. Its citizens would as soon have expected a cataclysm of nature as bloodshed in their streets.

After crossing the bridge, the second prisoner was taken. He was another watchman, Daniel Whelan, who held the armory gate. Not even when the raiders clapped their guns to his breast and told him to give up the key, would he be unfaithful to his trust. Here the crow-bar in the wagon found its first usefulness; it was but a minute before entrance was forced. "One fellow," said Whelan, "took me; they all gathered about me and looked in my face; I was nearly scared to death for so many guns about; I did not know the minute or the hour I should drop; they told me to be very quiet and still and make no noise or else they would put me to eternity." John Brown with two men held the big gate. To Whelan and Williams the leader said: "I came here from Kansas, and this is a slave State; I want to free all the negroes in this State; I have possession now of the United States armory, and if the citizens interfere with me I must only burn the town and have blood."[7] Then he crossed the street and, unopposed, took possession of the arsenal buildings, Albert Hazlett and Edwin Coppoc being made the arsenal's temporary garrison. Grad-

HIGH TREASON IN VIRGINIA

ually, other prisoners came in; there were two or three young fellows captured on the street, and others on the Shenandoah bridge. Thence Brown, A. D. Stevens, and a group of the raiders proceeded to the rifle works, captured a watchman there and put John H. Kagi and John A. Copeland in possession, Lewis Sheridan Leary reinforcing them later.[8]

Meanwhile, the commander-in-chief had despatched a raiding expedition up to and beyond Bolivar Heights. John Brown knew well the value of the dramatic in all his undertakings, and understood what would appeal to the popular imagination. There lived, five miles from Harper's Ferry, a Colonel Lewis W. Washington, a great-grandnephew of the first President, and like him a gentleman-farmer and slave-owner. In Colonel Washington's possession was a pistol presented to General Washington by Lafayette, as well as a sword, now in possession of the State of New York, which, according to unverified legend, was the gift of Frederick the Great to George Washington. John E. Cook had seen these weapons in Colonel Washington's home, and John Brown, beginner of a new American revolution, wished to strike his first blow for the freedom of a race with them in his hands. It was at midnight that Colonel Washington was awakened by four armed men, who stood at his chamber door with a burning flambeau and notified him that he was their prisoner.[9] Had the Heavens fallen, he could not have been more astonished than by the appearance of Osborn P. Anderson, who with Stevens, Tidd, Cook, Leary and Shields Green, formed this raiding party. One act of his captors in particular must have rankled with him. By John Brown's specific instructions, Stevens compelled Colonel Washington to hand over the illustrious Frederick's sword to the negro Anderson,—another bit of that symbolism by which Brown set such store.[10] Then Colonel Washington was led forth to his own carriage; behind it stood his four-horse farm-wagon, into which climbed the raiders and Washington's slaves, who were told to come and fight for their liberty, and the caravan set off for Harper's Ferry. On its way there was a stop at a neighbor's, Mr. John H. Allstadt's, where much the same scene was enacted. The crash of a fence-rail against the front door woke the house to cries of murder from the women of the family.

"Presently," recalls Mr. John Thomas Allstadt, then a boy of eighteen,

"they led my father and me outside. There we saw Colonel Washington, sitting in his own team. They put us, my father and me, on the seat of Colonel Washington's four-horse wagon. In the body, behind us, our six negroes and Colonel Washington's quota stood close packed. As we drove inside the Armory yard, there stood an old man. 'This,' said Stevens, by way of introduction, 'is John Brown.' 'Osawatomie Brown of Kansas,' added Brown. Then he handed out pikes to our negroes, telling them to guard us carefully, to prevent our escape. 'Keep these white men inside,' said he. There were no other local negroes within the enclosure, save Colonel Washington's and ours. We arrived at the Armory just about daybreak. We were not taken inside the building until several men had fallen. In the interval we were permitted to walk up and down before the engine house, east and west, but not on the east side, on which were the gates."[11]

Said John Brown to Lewis Washington, as he greeted him at the engine-house at the armory:

"I think, after a while, possibly, I shall be enabled to release you, but only on the condition of getting your friends to send in a negro man as a ransom. I shall be very attentive to you, sir, for I may get the worst of it in my first encounter, and if so, your life is worth as much as mine. I shall be very particular to pay attention to you. My particular reason for taking you first was that, as the aid to the Governor of Virginia, I knew you would endeavor to perform your duty, and perhaps you would have been a troublesome customer to me; and, apart from that, I wanted you particularly for the moral effect it would give our cause having one of your name, as a prisoner."[12]

Meanwhile, as the night had worn on, the town had become aroused. Patrick Higgins, the night watchman of the Maryland bridge, who came to relieve William Williams, was shot at for striking Oliver Brown and refusing to surrender. The bullet ploughed a furrow in his scalp, but did not prevent his seeking safety in the Wager House and helping to give the alarm. At 1.25 in the morning, the Baltimore and Ohio train bound from the West to Baltimore arrived in Harper's Ferry and attempted to cross the bridge. As it was in the act of starting on, Patrick Higgins came up to Conductor Phelps and told his story of being attacked by men carrying rifles.

The engineer and baggage-master went forward to investigate, but returned immediately on being fired at and seeing the muzzles of four rifles resting on a railing; at once the train backed away.[13] It was at this moment that Shephard Hayward, a free negro who acted as baggage-master of the station, went around the corner of the hotel and on toward the bridge, to look for the missing watchman. He, too, received a command to halt, but it probably meant as little to him as it had to Patrick Higgins,* and as he turned to retrace his steps to the station, a bullet passed through his body a little below his heart. He lay in agony in the railroad station until his death, nearly twelve hours later, attended at times by a doctor and Patrick Higgins, who brought him water.

This was, indeed, an ill omen for the army of liberation. The first man to fall at their hands was neither a slave-owner, nor a defender of slavery, nor one who suffered by it, but a highly respected, well-to-do colored man, in full possession of his liberty and favored with the respect of the white community. He had not even offered to resist.[14] And so at the very first moment was violated a final charge which John Brown gave to his men before he ordered them to take the road. "And now, gentlemen," he said, "let me impress this one thing on your minds; you all know how dear life is to you, and how dear your lives are to your friends; and in remembering that, consider that the lives of others are as dear to them as yours are to you: do not, therefore, take the life of anyone if you can possibly avoid it; but if it is necessary to take life in order to save your own, then make sure work of it." [15]

As for the train, it remained there until daylight, although Conductor Phelps received word at three o'clock from Brown through a prisoner that he might proceed; he would not trust his train across the bridge until daylight.[16] Then John Brown let him go — to spread abroad the tidings of what had happened. At 7.05 A. M., Phelps arrived at Monocacy and telegraphed to W. P. Smith, the master of transportation at Baltimore, the story of the night: that he and his baggage-

---

* "Now," says Patrick Higgins, "I did n't know what 'Halt' mint then any more than a hog knows about a holiday." He still lives at Sandy Hook.

master had been fired at, that Hayward had been shot, and that the insurrectionists were one hundred and fifty strong.

"They say," his despatch went on, "they have come to free the slaves and intend to do it at all hazards. The leader of those men requested me to say to you that this is the last train that shall pass the bridge either East or West. If it is attempted it will be at the peril of the lives of those having them in charge. . . . It has been suggested you had better notify the Secretary of War at once. The telegraph wires are cut East and West of Harper's Ferry and this is the first station that I could send a dispatch from." [17]

But so extraordinary a message did not find credence in those piping times of peace. The master of transportation telegraphed dubiously at nine o'clock: "Your dispatch is evidently exaggerated and written under excitement. Why should our trains be stopped by Abolitionists, and how do you know they are such and that they numbered one hundred or more? What is their object? Let me know at once before we proceed to extremities." "My dispatch was not exaggerated," replied Conductor Phelps from Ellicott's Mills at eleven o'clock, "neither was it written under excitement as you suppose. I have not made it half as bad as it is. . . . I will call at your office immediately on my arrival and tell you all." Before this reply was received, the president of the railroad, John W. Garrett, had seen the conductor's despatch, and lost no time in acting upon it. At half-past ten he had telegraphed to the President of the United States, to Governor Wise, of Virginia, and to Major-General George H. Stewart, commanding the First Light Division, Maryland Volunteers, in Baltimore, that an insurrection was in progress in Harper's Ferry, in which free negroes and whites were engaged. Thus the first alarm was given hours before it should have been. Moreover, from Monocacy word had reached Frederick, a short distance away, and by ten o'clock the military company of that place was under arms.

Unfortunately for John Brown's belief that he had hours of immunity before he need think of beginning his retreat, Harper's Ferry had its Paul Revere. He was John D. Starry, a physician of the town, who lived but a stone's throw from the Wager House. The shot which mortally wounded Hayward aroused him, as did the injured man's cry of distress.[18]

He went at once to Hayward's side, only to find that he was beyond help. He heard the firing on the street which made the conductor of the train beat a retreat, but Dr. Starry himself was not to be frightened. He stood at the corner of the station and watched three of the raiders approaching; then he notified the alarmed passengers who had crowded into the waiting-room that he would follow the strangers into the armory and find out what it was all about. He did so, was challenged, and returned to the station without the information he desired. Later, he exchanged words with the raiders who held the bridge, quite unmolested, although other citizens were arrested on sight. This was characteristic of the haphazard character of the raid and the lack of specific instructions. Dr. Starry devoted the rest of the night to watching; saw Colonel Washington's four-horse wagon arrive, and then, at five minutes after five o'clock, saw it drive over the Maryland bridge in charge of John E. Cook and disappear on the other bank; three men with pikes in their hands were in the wagon and two with rifles marched alongside. At daylight he could stand it no longer; he saddled his horse, rode first to the residence of A. M. Kitzmiller, who was in charge of the arsenal in the absence of the superintendent, Mr. Barbour, and aroused him and a number of other officials and workmen with the story of the night. He then put spurs to his horse and climbed the hill to Bolivar Heights, where he again awoke some sleepers. Without dismounting, he rode back into the town, going straight to the rifle works, where he found three armed men. With admirable courage he rode to within twenty-five or thirty paces of them. As they did not molest him, he decided to take charge of matters and drive the invaders out.

He lost not a minute's time, for, in his own words:

"I went back to the hillside then, and tried to get the citizens together, to see what we could do to get rid of these fellows. They seemed to be very troublesome. When I got on the hill I learned that they had shot Boerley. That was probably about 7 o'clock. Boerley was an Irishman living there, a citizen of the town. He died very soon afterwards. . . . I had ordered the Lutheran church bell to be rung to get the citizens together to see what sort of arms they had; I found one or two squirrel rifles and a few shot guns; I had sent a messenger to Charlestown in the meantime for Captain Rowan, commander of a volunteer company there: I also sent messengers to the Baltimore and Ohio Railroad to stop the trains coming east and not let them approach the Ferry, and also a messenger to Shepherdstown. When I could find no guns fit for use, and learned from the operatives and foreman at the armory that all the guns that they knew of were in the arsenal and in possession of these men, I thought I had better go to Charlestown myself, perhaps; I did so and hurried Captain Rowan off. When I returned to the Ferry, I found that the citizens had gotten some guns out of one of the workshops — guns which had been placed there to keep them out of the high water — and were pretty well armed. I assisted, from that time until some time in the night, in various ways, organizing the citizens and getting them to the best place of attack, and sometimes acting professionally."

Charlestown, as already stated, was eight miles away. When Dr. Starry reached there on his foam-flecked horse, the alarm bells were being rung, and from bed or breakfast men hurried to the court-house, the centre of the town, to learn that Abolitionists and slave-stealers were murdering innocent men in the streets of Harper's Ferry. What the South had been dreading ever since the Nat Turner insurrection of 1831 had come to pass: there was another servile uprising in the land. For years patrols had ridden the roads and men had watched of night lest the negroes turn upon their masters. It was an ever-present fear; that the Abolitionists wished the slaves to rise and kill their masters in their beds was a belief widely held in the South and often publicly expressed, and no happening that could be imagined contained a greater possibility of horror and bloodshed. But the men of Charlestown faltered not at all, now that the long-dreaded hour had come. The militia, called the Jefferson Guards, fell into line ununiformed; and then boys and men, "accoutred as they were" with muskets or rifles or squirrel-guns, their scant ammunition in their pockets, formed still another company, also with no sign of a uniform. On the moment, the new company chose officers, and at ten o'clock both companies were off by train for their first active service.[19] But not their last, for in this column were brave men who fought from 1861 to 1865 with the indomitable courage of the Confederacy, even when their homes were in ruins or in the enemy's hands, their clothes in tatters, their feet bare.

Uniforms were needless in 1859 or 1865, when the martial spirit was so high and the sense of duty so keen. It was something that John Brown had not counted on, nor would any one else in his place have thought it possible; not now, fifty years later, would it be possible to get men as quickly on the spot again. An example of the natural military talent of the South, it should by itself have silenced, a year and a half later, those who thought to march from Washington to Richmond as if on an afternoon's promenade. And the Jefferson Guards, besides their speed of assembly, were well led, for with excellent military judgment they left the citizens' company on Bolivar Heights, and, crossing the Potomac by boat, a mile or more above the arsenal, and then the Chesapeake and Ohio Canal, re-formed upon its bank, on Maryland soil, and marched down to the bridge over the same road over which the raiders had come from Kennedy Farm the preceding night.[20]

While the Charlestown military was hurrying to the scene with such astonishing promptitude, there had been, after the departure of the train and the killing of the unfortunate Mr. Boerly, for a time a cessation of hostilities in Harper's Ferry. During this interval, John Brown ordered and had served from the Wager House, breakfast for forty-five persons, which, however, neither he nor Mr. Allstadt nor Colonel Washington would touch, — all three fearing that the employees of the Wager House had poisoned the food.[21] Throughout this long day, John Brown and most of his men fought without a morsel to eat. The prisoners had rapidly increased in number, for, as the master mechanics and workmen approached the gates, they were quickly bagged, until such time as the town was thoroughly alarmed. Estimates of the number of prisoners finally confined in the watch-house have gone as high as a hundred and as low as thirty; the latter number is more nearly correct. Between nine and ten o'clock, Leeman, who had gone with John E. Cook and Colonel Washington's wagon toward the Kennedy Farm, had arrived with a prisoner, Terence Byrne, a farmer and slave-owner who lived in Maryland, about three miles from Harper's Ferry. With them returned William Thompson, whom Brown had sent to notify Owen Brown, at the school-house near the Kennedy Farm, that all was going well, — a message soon to be singularly misleading.[22]

Throughout the early morning, John Brown received urgent messages from his able lieutenant, Kagi, at the rifle works, begging him to leave the town at once. For him the indecision of Brown was shortly to be fatal. Just why it was that the commander-in-chief let slip the golden hours when escape was possible will never be wholly explained. He himself averred that his thought for his prisoners had much to do with it. There is no doubt, too, that he still expected the negroes to rise in numbers and swell his force to irresistible proportions. The lack of a carefully thought out programme told as well. Though he kept perfectly cool and clear-headed, he proved incapable of attempting anything aggressive, and the citizens were speedily aware that the raiders were on the defensive. Between nine and ten o'clock, Brown had actually discussed with his prisoners negotiations with the citizens looking to a cessation of firing, and to leaving him in possession of the armory. A brave prisoner named Joseph A. Brua went backward and forward begging the citizens not to shoot, as they endangered the lives of Colonel Washington and the other prisoners.[23] But soon after ten o'clock general firing began.

It was about noon that the Jefferson Guards reached the Maryland end of the Potomac bridge. They quickly drove from it Oliver Brown and the rest of the guard, and, crossing, entered the Wager House; but not until they had had a sharp exchange of volleys with such of the raiders as John Brown could hastily assemble. In this rush of the Jefferson Guards, one of its members was severely wounded in the left arm and crippled for life.[24] But the purpose of the movement was achieved: one door of the Harper's Ferry trap was closed, and as it was sprung, communication with the Kennedy Farm was cut off. The strategy of Colonel John T. Gibson, of Charlestown, who, as Colonel of the Fifty-fifth Virginia Infantry, commanded both companies, or of Captain Rowan, the Mexican War veteran, who led the Jefferson Guards, had accomplished far more than its originator could at the moment have imagined.

But with their arrival at the Wager House, the initiative

of the Charlestown militia ceased. The newly formed company of their townsmen had, meanwhile, come down from Bolivar Heights under Captain Botts and occupied the Galt House and the Shenandoah bridge, while a detachment under Captain John Avis and Richard B. Washington took possession of some houses between the hill and the arsenal, from which they could fire readily into the yard.[25] They had hardly taken their places, when Mr. Washington shot and instantly killed Dangerfield Newby, who, with William Thompson and Oliver Brown, had been driven off the bridge by the Jefferson Guards and was fleeing back to the armory.[26] Newby was thus the first to die of John Brown's men, and with him perished the hope of liberty of his poor slave wife, who so ardently longed for her "dear Dangerfield" to release her and her brood of seven slave children. John Brown was now entirely cut off from his three men in the rifle works, and from Hazlett and Anderson, the guard in the arsenal. He had left at this hour but a single way of retreat, — through the armory buildings under the hill, — with no means of crossing the Potomac to the Maryland shore.

After the loss of the Potomac bridge and the killing of Newby, whose body was subjected to shocking indignities, — his ears were sliced off for souvenirs,[27] — at Brown's request, a prisoner named Cross went out with William Thompson to stop the firing, with the sole result that Thompson fell into the hands of the enemy.[28] A little later, Brown despatched another flag of truce by Stevens and Watson Brown, with whom went Mr. Kitzmiller, the acting superintendent of the armory. If the citizens understood what the flag meant, they did not respect it. Stevens fell, shot twice by George W. Chambers, a saloon-keeper, from a window in the Galt House, the slugs used inflicting terrible wounds.[29] Watson Brown, mortally wounded a moment earlier than Stevens, dragged himself back to the fire-engine house, where his father had now assembled the remnants of his band, the slaves he had armed, and eleven of the most important prisoners: Washington; the Allstadts; Brua; Byrne; Benjamin Mills, the master armorer; A. M. Ball, the master machinist; J. E. P. Daingerfield, the paymaster's clerk, and others, nearly all of whom testified later in detail to the scenes of which they were such unwilling witnesses.

The remainder of the prisoners were left in the watch-room, which comprised a third of the fire-engine house, but was without a communicating door. Unguarded as they were, these watch-room prisoners were too terrified to venture out until the arrival of the Martinsburg company in the middle of the afternoon. In sharp contrast to their inactivity was the conduct of Mr. Brua, whose humanitarian spirit made him volunteer to go to the aid of Stevens as he lay bleeding in a gutter. Thanks to him, Stevens was carried into the Wager House and given medical attention.[30]

Mr. Brua's deed, the more striking because he again returned to take his place as a prisoner, has unfortunately been overlooked, because of the barbarities attending the killing of some of the raiders. For instance, the death, about one o'clock in the afternoon, of William H. Leeman, the youngest of Brown's men, has frequently been cited to prove the "savagery" which the raiders encountered. About the time that Stevens and Watson Brown were wounded, Leeman made an attempt from the upper end of the yard to escape across the Potomac, a little above the bridge. He soon found himself under such a heavy fire that he stopped on a tiny islet. According to a generally accepted story, he was here killed, after he had surrendered, by a citizen, G. A. Schoppert, who, it was alleged, deliberately placed his weapon at the unarmed eighteen-year-old boy's head before shooting. In 1900, Mr. Schoppert made an affidavit that Leeman had a pistol and a knife when killed, and that he refused to surrender when called on to do so. In his assertion that this was a justifiable killing, Mr. Schoppert had the support of Colonel J. T. Gibson, an eyewitness. It remains, however, a melancholy fact that the lad's body, lying for hours in plain sight on the rock, was riddled and mutilated repeatedly by whole companies, as well as by individuals who found the dead Abolitionist an attractive target, particularly from the bridge.[31] Unfortunately for the troops, the bars at the Wager House and the Galt House were not affected by the street-fighting that went on, and continued to dispense liquor, with disastrous results to the *morale* of the troops as the hours passed.[32]

About two o'clock the death of George W. Turner, a slaveholder, a farmer of means and prominence in the vicinity of

Harper's Ferry, still further inflamed the citizens. A graduate of West Point, who had seen service in the Seminole War in Florida,[33] he rode to town carrying his shot-gun, and was shot in the neck and instantly killed. According to one narrative, he was in the act of firing on two of the raiders when a bullet from them struck him; it was also related that he was killed while talking to a traveller who had strayed in from one of the delayed Baltimore and Ohio trains.[34] In any event, his death added greatly to the excitement of the Harper's Ferrians. But it was the shooting of the mayor of the town, Fontaine Beckham, which roused the citizens of Harper's Ferry to the highest pitch of indignation. Mr. Beckham, the agent of the Baltimore and Ohio Railroad at Harper's Ferry for the twenty-five years since its opening, had been a magistrate in Jefferson County for an even longer period. Sincerely attached to his helper, Hayward, and much agitated by his death, which occurred about four o'clock, Mayor Beckham, in his extreme nervousness, several times ventured out on the railroad in order to observe what was going on, though warned not to do so. From the engine house it looked as if he were trying to get a favorable position from which to shoot. To this Mr. John Thomas Allstadt testifies, for he was near Edwin Coppoc when the latter fired: [35]

"Now Mr. Beckham went behind the water tank and began peering around its corner, as it might be to take aim. 'If he keeps on peeking, I'm going to shoot,' said Coppoc, from his seat in the doorway. I stood close by him. Mr. Beckham peeked again and Coppoc fired, but missed. 'Don't fire, man, for God's sake! they'll shoot in here and kill us all,' shrieked the prisoners from behind. Some were laughing, others overwhelmed with fear. But Coppoc was already firing again. This shot killed Beckham. Undoubtedly he would not have been fired upon but for his equivocal appearance. Coppoc fired no more from the watch-house; in fact, no one remained in sight. But Brown's son, Oliver, sitting in the partly open engine-house door, spied someone peeping over the stone wall of the trestle in the act of sighting a gun. Young Brown instantly took aim; but even as he was in the act of firing, the other's shot struck him — a mortal wound that gave horrible pain."

The unarmed mayor died instantly, and his death was all that was needed to incite the now half-drunken and uncontrolled crowd around the Wager House to the worst killing of the day. William Thompson, with the wounded Stevens, was now a captive in the hotel. Mad with the desire to revenge Beckham's death,* the mob, headed by George W. Chambers, the saloon-keeper, and Harry Hunter, of Charlestown, attempted to make way with him in the hotel itself. A brief respite was secured to Thompson by a Miss Christine Fouke, who begged that his life be spared, from the mixed motive, as she afterwards explained, of a desire to have the law take its course and to save the house from becoming the scene of an outrage![36] What happened then was narrated by Harry Hunter during John Brown's trial, in answer to a question from his father, Andrew Hunter, the special prosecutor on behalf of the State:

"After Mr. Beckham, who was my grand-uncle, was shot, I was much exasperated, and started with Mr. Chambers to the room where the second Thompson was confined, with the purpose of shooting him. We found several persons in the room, and had leveled our guns at him, when Mrs. Fouke's sister threw herself before him, and begged us to leave him to the laws. We then caught hold of him, and dragged him out by the throat, he saying: 'Though you may take my life, 80,000,000 † will arise up to avenge me, and carry out my purpose of giving liberty to the slaves.' We carried him out to the bridge, and two of us, leveling our guns in this moment of wild exasperation, fired, and before he fell, a dozen or more balls were buried in him; we then threw his body off the trestlework, and returned to the bridge to bring out the prisoner Stevens, and serve him in the same way; we found him suffering from his wounds, and probably dying; we concluded to spare him, and start after others, and shoot all we could find. I had just seen my loved uncle and best friend I ever had, shot down by those villainous Abolitionists, and felt justified in shooting any that I could find; I felt it my duty, and I have no regrets."[37]

William Thompson was shot by Chambers and Hunter with their revolvers at his head, and thrust through the open space between the roadway and the side of the bridge. As he lay

---

* Mr. Beckham's friendliness to the negro appears from the fact that at the time of his death he was aiding one, Isaac Gilbert, to purchase the freedom of his wife and three children. As if foreseeing a sudden death, the mayor had made a will insuring the freedom of these four slaves, whom he had purchased in order to facilitate their liberation. See Will Book No. 16, p. 142, Jefferson County Court Records, Charlestown, West Virginia.

† Other reports quote Thompson as having said "80,000."

in the shallow water below, he, too, was riddled with bullets. The body, says a local historian, "could be seen for a day or two after, lying at the bottom of the river, with his ghastly face still exhibiting his fearful death agony." [38] Making all due allowance for the naturally intense indignation aroused by the killing of so universally beloved a man as Mayor Beckham, and for the horrors of the day, the killing of Thompson was none the less a disgrace to the State of Virginia. It loses nothing of its barbarity with the lapse of years. It is a pleasure, however, to record that the best public sentiment of Harper's Ferry and Charlestown has always condemned the act. This crime must also in part be offset by Brua's readiness to risk his life on behalf of Stevens, and by other highminded acts on the part of the citizens. Yet it remains in striking contrast to the kindliness and courtesy with which John Brown treated his prisoners, in keeping with the dictates of the Chatham Constitution and with his own character. This generous treatment was freely acknowledged by his prisoners, one of whom, J. E. P. Daingerfield, declined to attend John Brown's execution, because "he had made me a prisoner, but had spared my life and that of other gentlemen in his power; and when his sons were shot down beside him, almost any other man similarly situated would have exacted life for life." [39]

Just after Mr. Beckham's death, there arrived, to add to the excitement, a sturdy Martinsburg company, composed largely of employees of the Baltimore and Ohio Railroad. Headed by Captain E. G. Alburtis, they very nearly ended the conflict, for they boldly marched through the armory yard from the rear, thus cutting off Brown's only remaining avenue of escape, and engaged the raiders at close range, driving them into the engine house, during which manœuvre the company lost eight of its men by wounds. "During the fight," Captain Alburtis narrated afterwards,

"we found in the room adjoining the engine-house some thirty or forty prisoners who had been captured and confined by the outlaws. The windows were broken open by our party, and these men escaped. The whole of the outlaws were now driven into the enginehouse, and owing to the great number of wounded requiring our care, and not being supported by the other companies as we expected, we were obliged to return. Had the other companies come up, we could have taken the engine-house then. Immediately after we drew off, there was a flag of truce sent out to propose terms, which were that they should be permitted to retire across the river with their arms, and, I think, proceed as far as some lock on the canal, there to release their prisoners. These terms were not acceded to, and having understood that the United States marines and a number of troops from Baltimore were on their way, nothing further was done except to establish guards all around to prevent the desperadoes from escaping. We had a small piece of cannon, which we proposed to bring to bear on the engine-house, but were directed not to do so on account of endangering the prisoners."[40]

These captives were later a convenient excuse to explain the militia's shortcomings. Immediately after the arrival of the Martinsburg company, other troops began to pour in. Itself, like the second Charlestown company, organized on the spur of the moment, the Martinsburg organization was followed by two Shepherdstown, Virginia, militia companies, the Hamtramck Guards and the Shepherdstown Troop, which, however, accomplished but little. At dusk three companies from Frederick, Maryland, appeared; they were the first uniformed troops to report.[41] They, too, added to the noise and confusion of the streets, but were of little or no avail. For all practical purposes, John Brown and his handful of men had beaten off the several hundred armed citizens and militia who had come to capture him, living or dead. Later in the evening a Winchester company arrived, as did five Baltimore militia companies, which did not enter the town from Sandy Hook until morning.[42] Governor Wise and Company F of Richmond arrived five hours after the engine house was taken.

The record of the tragedies of the 17th of October at Harper's Ferry is not complete with the violent deaths of Beckham and William Thompson. On the Shenandoah, John Brown's outposts in the rifle works were slain or captured at about the same hour that the arsenal garrison was finally driven into the engine house. Kagi's early morning requests that the town be evacuated having met with no consideration at John Brown's hands, he and his men, hungry, isolated and menaced by more and more armed men, continued to obey orders and stick to their posts in true soldierly fashion. But

HARPER'S FERRY: THE FIGHTING AT THE ENGINE-HOUSE

the energetic Dr. Starry was mindful of their exposed and isolated position, and the opportunity it offered.

"I organized a party," he testified afterwards, "about half-past two or three o'clock, and sent them over there with directions to commence the fight as soon as they got near enough; that party was under the command of a young man named Irwin. He went over, and at the first fire Kagi, and the others who were with him in Hall's [the Rifle] Works, went out the back way towards the Winchester railroad, climbed out on the railroad and into the Shenandoah River. They were met on the opposite side by a party who were there and driven back. . . ."

Mr. A. R. Boteler, the Congressman from the Harper's Ferry district, was an eye-witness of what happened. The three raiders made for a large flat rock near the middle of the stream. Before reaching it, Kagi "fell and died in the water, apparently without a struggle;" Lewis Sheridan Leary was mortally wounded, and John A. Copeland was captured by a Harper's Ferrian, James H. Holt by name, who waded out to him as Schoppert had to Leeman. But Holt's gun, like Copeland's rifle, failed to go off because of its having become wet. Copeland surrendered as Holt, clubbing his gun, was about to knock him down. As soon as Copeland was brought to the bank, there were cries of: "Lynch him!" Fortunately, Dr. Starry rode up as the citizens, now near the armory wall with their prisoner, were tying their handkerchiefs together that they might hang the trembling negro. But Dr. Starry was not of the bloodthirsty kind. To his credit, and that of Harper's Ferry, he shielded Copeland by getting him into a corner and covering him with the horse who had carried his master so faithfully all day. In a little while a policeman arrived, and, Dr. Starry still holding back the crowd, Copeland was taken off to a safe place, thus escaping William Thompson's fate. Leary, the wounded negro, was in no wise molested, dying late the following night.[43]

Two men alone, of those of the Provisional Army who remained in the town after the Maryland bridge was taken by the Jefferson Guards, escaped from the Ferry, — Albert Hazlett and Osborn P. Anderson. The latter, the colored raider from Canada, subsequently wrote a misleading and exaggerated account of their escape from the armory, in which he states that they remained at their posts until the final capture of Tuesday. This is, however, incredible. It is not possible that they could have gone scot-free in daylight, when Lee's marines were everywhere on guard and the town swarmed with excited militia. In all probability they left their posts in the arsenal about nightfall on Monday, when everybody was watching the armory yard and the engine house. According to Anderson, they first went along the Shenandoah and climbed the hill just out of town, where they lay concealed for three hours; then, returning into the town along the river, they found an old boat and crossed in it to the Maryland side. If this, too, seems incredible, their escape by whatever means was miraculous, for they did reach the Kennedy Farm, and from there found their way into Pennsylvania, where Hazlett was finally captured. Of the rear-guard on the Maryland side, John E. Cook alone ventured back to the Ferry bridge, late in the afternoon of Monday. He had been on guard in the school-house to which Tidd and Owen Brown were moving arms, and had conversed quite freely with the schoolmaster, explaining the purposes of the attack and the views of the raiders.[44] He distinctly heard the firing, but not until four o'clock, when a second wagon-load of arms was brought to the school-house, did he feel free to leave. To acquaintances along the road he openly admitted his connection with the raiders. When opposite the Ferry, he scaled the mountain in order to get a view of what was going on, and beheld his comrades cooped up in the engine house with the citizens firing on them. As, he confessed after his capture,

"I saw that our party were completely surrounded, and as I saw a body of men on High Street firing down upon them — they were about half a mile distant from me — I thought I would draw their firing upon myself; I therefore raised my rifle and took the best aim I could and fired. It had the desired effect, for the very instant the party returned it. Several shots were exchanged. The last one they fired cut a small limb I had hold of just below my hand, and gave me a fall of about fifteen feet by which I was severely bruised and my flesh somewhat lacerated."

He then descended to the canal and returned to the school-house, where he rejoined the rear-guard, now comprising Owen Brown, Barclay Coppoc, Meriam, Tidd, and several of the

HIGH TREASON IN VIRGINIA

negroes liberated and armed. All of the latter left the raiders before the coming night passed.

With the disappearance of Cook, the withdrawal of Alburtis and the coming of night, the active hostilities of the day ceased. In loose fashion the militia picketed the engine house. A citizen, Samuel Strider by name, tied a handkerchief to his umbrella and delivered a summons to surrender,[45] to which John Brown replied by the following note:

Capt. John Brown answers:
In consideration of all my men, whether living or dead, or wounded, being soon safely in and delivered up to me at this point with all their arms and amunition, we will then take our prisoners and cross the Potomac bridge, a little beyond which we will set them at liberty; after which we can negotiate about the Government property as may be best. Also we require the delivery of our horse and harness at the hotel.

JOHN BROWN.

To this Colonel Baylor answered briefly that he could not accept the terms proposed; that under no conditions would he consent to a removal of the citizens across the river.[46] When the Frederick companies arrived, one of the captains, Sinn by name, went close up to the engine-house. Being hailed from there, he promptly entered, conversing at length with John Brown, who was then, as during the entire fight, wearing the sword of Frederick the Great. To Captain Sinn Brown again stated his terms, complaining also that his men when bearing flags of truce had been shot down like dogs. To this Captain Sinn replied that men who took up arms that way must expect to be shot down like dogs. John Brown's answer was that he knew what he had to undergo before he came there, "he had weighed the responsibility and should not shrink from it." He had had full possession of the town and could have massacred all the inhabitants had he thought proper to do so; hence he believed himself entitled to some terms. He insisted that he and his followers had killed no unarmed men. When told that Beckham was without any weapon when killed, he expressed deep regret. They then parted. Captain Sinn, who seems to have been a soldier of a fine type, recorded his disgust with conditions among the citizens.[47] Many of them were hopelessly intoxicated, only a few of them were under any discipline or control, all of them had guns, and some, according to Captain Sinn and others, were firing their guns in the air all night, whooping and yelling, and generally behaving as if the enemy were to be exorcised by noise and bravado. Entering the Wager House, the chivalrous Sinn found some young men taunting the gravely wounded Stevens and pointing their revolvers at him, but without in the least causing him to flinch. It was not the first time that day that death had thus approached Stevens, but it was the last, for Sinn drove the men out, saying: "If this man could stand on his feet with a pistol in his hand, you would all jump out of the window."* But Captain Sinn did not weary of well-doing here; he induced the surgeon of his command, a Dr. Taylor, of Frederick, to staunch the wounds of Watson Brown, in the engine house. The surgeon did so and promised to return early in the morning,[48] but by that time the engine-house was stormed and his patient, *in extremis*, beyond all surgical aid. This was a curious episode in what was a unique American tragedy; where else have men killed, then met and conversed with one another and aided the wounded, and then killed again?

With the withdrawal of Captain Sinn and Dr. Taylor, the engine house composed itself for the night. Prisoners and raiders lay down on the brick floor to get such rest as they could; the morrow, they all knew, would seal the raiders' fate. The doors, shut and barred, did not keep out the yelling of the drunken soldiery. But within all was dark; the liberators had no light; it was intensely cold.

"In the quiet of the night," the younger Allstadt remembers, "young Oliver Brown died. He had begged again and again to be shot, in the agony of his wound, but his father had replied to him, 'Oh you will get over it,' and, 'If you must die, die like a man.' Now John Brown talked, from time to time, with my father and with Colonel Washington, but I did not hear what was said. Oliver Brown lay quietly over in a corner. His father called to him, after a time. No answer. 'I guess he is dead,' said Brown."[49]

* Later, during the trial, Captain Sinn showed an equally fine spirit in going to Charlestown on a summons from John Brown to testify in his behalf, "so that Northern men would have no opportunity to say that Southern men were unwilling to appear as witnesses on behalf of one whose principles they abhorred."

JOHN H. KAGI

A. D. STEVENS

OLIVER BROWN

WATSON BROWN

VICTIMS OF HARPER'S FERRY

Near his brother, Watson lay quietly breathing his young life away. Stewart Taylor, the young Canadian, shot like Oliver in the doorway of the engine house, lay dead near-by. There were left alive and unwounded but five men, the commander-in-chief, Edwin Coppoc, J. G. Anderson, Dauphin Thompson and Shields Green. John Brown himself, though plainly anxious to have his terms accepted, betrayed no trepidation whatever. Although now over forty hours without sleep, he sought no rest. "Men, are you awake?" he asked from time to time in the stillness of the night. John E. P. Daingerfield remembered a talk with John Brown that night, in which he told him that the raiders were committing treason against the State and the United States. "Two of his men, hearing the conversation, said to their leader, 'Are we committing treason against our country by being here?' Brown answered, 'Certainly.' Both declared, 'If that is so, we don't want to fight any more. We thought we came to liberate the slaves and did not know that that was committing treason.'" At the break of dawn, these two young men, Dauphin Thompson and Jeremiah G. Anderson, gave up their lives on the bayonets of the marines.[50]

For representatives of the Federal Government had appeared on the scene; as the raiders learned from the friendly Captain Sinn, the United States marines had arrived and had supplanted the loose oversight of the militia with the sharp patrolling and guarding of regular soldiers. The news of the raid had stirred official Washington to prompt action early in the day. President Buchanan telegraphed at 1.30 to the president of the Baltimore and Ohio Railroad that three companies of artillery had been sent from Fort Monroe, and that he had accepted the services of Captain Ritchie's militia company at Fredericksburg, Maryland.[51] After sending the despatch, he also ordered to Harper's Ferry the only United States force in Washington, — a small company of marines at the navy yard, commanded by Lieutenant Israel Green. Mr. Buchanan's despatch did not satisfy the alarmed Mr. Garrett, who replied that his agents reported no less than seven hundred blacks and whites in possession of the Harper's Ferry arsenal. "It is a moment full of peril," he added.[52]

The raid now brought to the front two officers, both temporarily in Washington, who were soon to write their names large upon the pages of history. Since the raid on Harper's Ferry itself was to be in its every aspect a prologue to 1861, it was eminently fitting that the most conspicuous military rôles should fall to Brevet-Colonel Robert E. Lee, then lieutenant-colonel of the Second United States Cavalry, and to First Lieutenant J. E. B. Stuart, of the First Cavalry, to whom many students of military history assign first place among American cavalry generals. Their subsequent careers in the Confederate Army make it singularly suggestive that they should have been the ones to end John Brown's attack upon slavery, since it was in defence of slavery that they were so soon to draw their swords against the very government at whose behest they went to Harper's Ferry. Both officers attended a conference at the White House with the President and the Secretary of War, Mr. Floyd, and both set out that afternoon for Harper's Ferry, Lee to command all the troops, under his brevet commission, and Stuart to act as his aide.[53] They overtook the marines at Sandy Hook, a mile and a half from Harper's Ferry, at eleven o'clock that night, and marched them at once to the armory. Here the marines were so disposed about the engine house that no one could escape during the night. Lee then made all his preparations to attack at daylight, thus adopting John Brown's own policy of going at once to close quarters. "But for the fear of sacrificing the lives of some of the gentlemen held by them as prisoners in a midnight assault," Colonel Lee afterwards reported, "I should have ordered the attack at once."

What happened next, Lieutenant Stuart later described in these words:

"Within two hours of that time [midnight], say by two A. M., Colonel Lee communicated to me his determination to demand a surrender of the whole party at first dawn, and in case of refusal, which he expected, he would have ready a few picked men, who were at a signal to take the place at once with the bayonet. He chose to demand a surrender before attacking, because he wanted every chance to save the prisoners unhurt, and to attack with bayonets for the same reason." . . .[54] "I, too, had a part to perform, which prevented me in a measure from participating in the very brief onset made so gallantly by Green and Russell, well backed by their men. I was deputed by Col. Lee to read to the leader, then called *Smith*,

HIGH TREASON IN VIRGINIA 451

a demand to surrender immediately; and I was instructed to leave the door after his refusal, which was expected, and wave my cap; at which signal the storming party was to advance, batter open the doors, and capture the insurgents at the point of the bayonet. Col. Lee cautioned the stormers particularly to discriminate between the insurgents and their prisoners. I approached the door in the presence of perhaps 2000 spectators, and told *Mr. Smith* that I had a communication for him from Col. Lee. He opened the door about four inches, and placed his body against the crack, with a cocked carbine in his hand: hence his remark after his capture that he could have wiped me out like a mosquito. The parley was a long one. He presented his propositions in every possible shape, and with admirable tact; but all amounted to this: that the only condition upon which he would surrender was that he and his party should be allowed to escape. Some of his prisoners begged me to ask Col. Lee to come and see him. I told them he would never accede to any terms but those he had offered; and so soon as I could tear myself away from their importunities, I left the door and waved my cap, and Col. Lee's plan was carried out. When *Smith* first came to the door, I recognized old *Osawatomie Brown*, who had given us so much trouble in Kansas. No one present but myself could have performed that service. I got his bowie knife from his person and have it yet." [55]

The demand submitted to John Brown by Lieutenant Stuart read as follows: [56]

HEADQUARTERS HARPER'S FERRY,
October 18, 1859.

Colonel Lee, United States army, commanding the troops sent by the President of the United States to suppress the insurrection at this place, demands the surrender of the persons in the armory buildings.

If they will peaceably surrender themselves and restore the pillaged property, they shall be kept in safety to await the orders of the President. Colonel Lee represents to them, in all frankness, that it is impossible for them to escape; that the armory is surrounded on all sides by troops; and that if he is compelled to take them by force he cannot answer for their safety.

R. E. LEE.
Colonel Commanding United States Troops.

Even this letter failed to induce John Brown to surrender, and his decision thus taken caused three deaths within fifteen minutes, two of them of his own men, in the blind and purposeless struggle against overwhelming numbers. "My object was, with a view to saving our citizens, to have as short an interval as possible between the summons and attack,"

Colonel Lee reported officially; and the whole proceeding was marked by the despatch and efficiency characteristic of well-disciplined regular troops. Colonel Lee, who was in civilian clothes, stood on a slight elevation, about forty feet away, and supervised the whole undertaking. In the early morning hours he had offered the honor of storming the engine house to the volunteer soldiery,[57] but this was declined by Colonel Shriver, of the Frederick, Maryland, troops, who seems at this time to have been more in control than the senior Virginia Colonel, Baylor, who had superseded Colonel John T. Gibson. Colonel Shriver said that he had only come to help the people of Harper's Ferry. "These men of mine have wives and children at home. I will not expose them to such risks. You are paid for doing this kind of work."[58] Colonel Baylor also declined the honor, afterwards assigning the same reason.[59] But the "mercenaries," as Colonel Baylor called the marines, looked at the matter in a different light. When Colonel Lee turned to Lieutenant Israel Green and asked him whether he wished the honor of "taking those men out," Lieutenant Green at once, with soldierly courtesy, took off his hat and thanked Colonel Lee simply and sincerely.[60] He then picked a storming detail of twelve men, with a reserve of a similar number, and gave them the most careful instructions. At sunrise, when Lieutenant Stuart gave his signal, Green, with the greatest *sang-froid*, ordered the attack to begin. Neither he nor his men had been under fire before, but it made no difference in their bearing. Lieutenant Green himself was armed only with a light dress sword which he had picked up as he hastily left his quarters, ignorant of the duty for which he and his men were ordered out.[61] Near him, as a volunteer, stood a senior in rank, one of his own corps, Major W. W. Russell, who, as a paymaster and staff officer, could not take active command. Major Russell carried nothing but a rattan cane, yet he risked his life with *nonchalance*.[62]

Three marines, armed with sledge-hammers, began battering at the heavy doors of the engine-house, with slight success. A heavy ladder lay near by. Perceiving that, Lieutenant Green ordered his men to use it as a battering-ram. The door was broken in at the second blow. Up to this time, the few shots fired from within the engine house had struck

THE STORMING OF THE ENGINE-HOUSE

HIGH TREASON IN VIRGINIA

no one of the storming party. Within, said Colonel Washington, in this supreme moment, John Brown "was the coolest and firmest man I ever saw in defying danger and death. With one son dead by his side, and another shot through, he felt the pulse of his dying son with one hand and held his rifle with the other, and commanded his men with the utmost composure, encouraging them to be firm and to sell their lives as dearly as they could."[63] "The entrance," recorded Lieutenant Green, in after years,

"was a ragged hole low down in the right hand door, the door being splintered and cracked some distance upward. I instantly stepped from my position in front of the stone abutment and entered the opening made by the ladder. At the time I did not stop to think of it, but upon reflection I should say that Brown had just emptied his carbine at the point broken by the ladder, and so I passed in safely. Getting to my feet, I ran to the right of the engine, which stood behind the door, passed quickly to the rear of the house, and came up between the two engines. The first person I saw was Colonel Lewis Washington, who was standing near the hose-cart, at the front of the engine-house. On one knee, a few feet to the left, knelt a man with a carbine in his hand, just pulling the lever to reload."[64]

Colonel Washington greeted Green, whom he knew, calmly, and pointed Brown out to him, saying, "This is Osawatomie." What happened then was variously related by the several witnesses and by Lieutenant Green himself. It would seem as though Green sprang at Brown, lunging at him with his light sword and bringing him to his knees. The sword bent double in striking Brown's belt or a bone; taking the bent weapon in both hands, Lieutenant Green showered blows upon Brown's head, which laid him flat, brought the blood, and seemed to the onlookers as if they must reach the skull.[65] But fortunately for Brown and for his "greatest or principal object," the weapon was too light to inflict a mortal wound. All unawares, Lieutenant Green, by failing to buckle on his regulation sabre, had done a profound service to the cause that John Brown had at heart, and that Green, later a Confederate officer, though born in the North, hated. Men have carved their way to kingdoms by the stoutness of their swords, but here was one who by the flimsiness of his blade permitted his enemy to live to thrill half a nation by his spoken and written word.

At the time, however, it seemed as if Brown had perished as did Jeremiah Anderson and Dauphin Thompson. As the marines followed their lieutenant through the aperture, a shot rang out, and the first man, Private Luke Quin, went down, with a mortal wound. The next marine behind him was gravely wounded in the face. Jumping over their fallen comrades, the other marines were in no spirit to be gentle. "They came rushing in," said their officer,

"like tigers, as a storming assault is not a play-day sport. They bayoneted one man skulking under the engine, and pinned another fellow up against the rear wall, both being instantly killed.* I ordered the men to spill no more blood. The other insurgents were at once taken under arrest, and the contest ended. The whole fight had not lasted over three minutes."

As for the eleven prisoners, they were, recorded Lieutenant Green, "the sorriest lot of people I ever saw. They had been without food for over sixty hours, in constant dread of being shot, and were huddled up in the corner where lay the body of Brown's son and one or two others of the insurgents who had been killed." The dead, dying and badly wounded raiders were then carried out and laid on the grass in the armory yard. Of John Brown's force of twenty-two, he himself, his second in command, Stevens, two negroes, Copeland and Green, and Edwin Coppoc were in the enemy's hands. Watson Brown lived twenty hours after being taken from the engine-house; the bodies of nine others lay in front of their fort or scattered about the town. The remainder, seven in number, were already well started on their way toward Pennsylvania. Colonel Lee saw to it that the captured survivors were protected and treated with kindliness and consideration.[66] For Watson Brown, too, there was a good Samaritan, also a Southerner, C. W. Tayleure, a reporter of a Baltimore newspaper, who wrote to John Brown, Jr., just twenty years after the event, this touching story of Watson Brown's death: [67]

* According to other statements, Anderson did not die for some time after his removal from the engine house. Both Thompson and Anderson seem to have cried out as the marines came in that they surrendered.

"I am a South Carolinian, and at the time of the raid was very deeply imbued with the political prejudices of my State; but the serenity, calm courage, and devotion to duty which your father and his followers then manifested impressed me very profoundly. It is impossible not to feel respect for men who offer up their lives in support of their convictions, and the earnestness of my respect I put upon record in a Baltimore paper the day succeeding the event. I gave your brother a cup of water to quench his thirst (this was at about 7.30 on the morning of the capture) and improvised a couch for him out of a bench, with a pair of overalls for a pillow. I remember how he looked, — singularly handsome, even through the grime of his all-day struggles, and the intense suffering which he must have endured. He was very calm, and of a tone and look very gentle. The look with which he searched my very heart I can never forget. One sentence of our conversation will give you the keynote to the whole. I asked him, 'What brought you here?' He replied, very patiently, 'Duty, sir.' After a pause, I again asked: 'Is it then your idea of duty to shoot men down upon their own hearth-stones for defending their rights?' He answered: 'I am dying; I cannot discuss the question; I did my duty as I saw it.' This conversation occurred in the compartment of the engine-house adjoining that in which the defence had been made, and was listened to by young Coppoc with perfect equanimity, and by Shields Green with uncontrollable terror."

John Brown himself was carried to the office of the paymaster of the armory and there given medical attention, it soon appearing that his wounds were far less serious than at first supposed. But the end of the Provisional Army had come: John Brown's armed blow at slavery was spent.

"And they are themselves mistaken who take him to be a madman. He is a bundle of the best nerves I ever saw cut and thrust and bleeding and in bonds. He is a man of clear head, of courage, fortitude and simple ingenuousness. He is cool, collected and indomitable, and it is but just to him to say that he was humane to his prisoners as attested to me by Colonel Washington and Mr. Mills, and he inspired me with great trust in his integrity as a man of truth. He is a fanatic, vain and garrulous, but firm, truthful and intelligent. His men, too, who survive, except the free negroes with him, are like him."

Thus spoke Henry A. Wise, Governor of Virginia, on his return to Richmond from his visit to Harper's Ferry.[68] The interview with Brown upon which he predicated this opinion took place shortly after the Governor's arrival, at about one in the afternoon, in the paymaster's office, where A. D. Stevens had been carried to lie alongside of his leader. There have been few more dramatic scenes in American history; few upon which the shadows of coming events were more ominously cast. The two wounded prisoners, their hair clotted and tangled, their faces, hands and clothing powder-stained and blood-smeared, lay upon what the reporter of the New York *Herald*, who preserved for posterity this interview, called their "miserable shakedowns, covered with some old bedding." Near them stood Robert E. Lee, J. E. B. Stuart, Senator J. M. Mason, Governor Wise, Congressman Vallandigham, of Ohio, Colonel Lewis Washington, Andrew Hunter, and Congressman Charles James Faulkner, of Virginia, — nearly all destined soon to play important rôles, the first four in the Confederacy that was to come into being.

The courteous Colonel Lee began the interview by saying that he would exclude all visitors from the room if the wounded men were annoyed or pained thereby. To this John Brown answered that he was "glad to make himself and his motives clearly understood."

"He converses freely, fluently and cheerfully, without the slightest manifestation of fear or uneasiness, evidently weighing well his words, and possessing a good command of language. His manner is courteous and affable, while he appears to be making a favorable impression upon his auditory, which during most of the day yesterday averaged about ten or a dozen men,"

wrote the *Herald* representative. A reporter of the Baltimore *American* who was also present at the interview declared that during the conversation "no sign of weakness was exhibited by John Brown." [69]

In the midst of enemies, whose home he had invaded; wounded and a prisoner, surrounded by a small army of officials, and a more desperate army of angry men; with the gallows staring him full in the face, he lay on the floor, and, in reply to every question, gave answers that betokened the spirit that animated him. The language of Gov. Wise well expresses his boldness when he said 'He is the gamest man I ever saw.'"

From the long *Herald* interview, lasting fully three hours, the following are excerpts: [70]

Mr. Mason. — Can you tell us, at least, who furnished the money for your expedition?

Mr. Brown. — I furnished most of it myself. I cannot implicate others. It is by my own folly that I have been taken. I could easily have saved myself from it had I exercised my own better judgment, rather than yielded to my feelings.

Mr. Mason. — You mean if you had escaped immediately?

Mr. Brown. — No; I had the means to make myself secure without any escape, but I allowed myself to be surrounded by a force by being too tardy.

Mr. Mason. — Tardy in getting away?

Mr. Brown. — I should have gone away, but I had thirty-odd prisoners, whose wives and daughters were in tears for their safety, and I felt for them. Besides, I wanted to allay the fears of those who believed we came here to burn and kill. For this reason I allowed the train to cross the bridge, and gave them full liberty to pass on. I did it only to spare the feelings of those passengers and their families, and to allay the apprehensions that you had got here in your vicinity a band of men who had no regard for life and property, nor any feelings of humanity.

Mr. Mason. — But you killed some people passing along the streets quietly.

Mr. Brown. — Well, sir, if there was anything of that kind done, it was without my knowledge. Your own citizens, who were my prisoners, will tell you that every possible means were taken to prevent it. I did not allow my men to fire, nor even to return a fire, when there was danger of killing those we regarded as innocent persons, if I could help it. They will tell you that we allowed ourselves to be fired at repeatedly and did not return it.

A Bystander. — That is not so. You killed an unarmed man at the corner of the house over there (at the water-tank) and another besides.

Mr. Brown. — See here, my friend, it is useless to dispute or contradict the report of your own neighbors who were my prisoners.

Mr. Mason. — If you would tell us who sent you here — who provided the means — that would be information of some value.

Mr. Brown. — I will answer freely and faithfully about what concerns myself — I will answer anything I can with honor, but not about others.

Mr. Vallandigham (Member of Congress from Ohio, who had just entered). — Mr. Brown, who sent you here?

Mr. Brown. — No man sent me here; it was my own prompting and that of my Maker, or that of the devil, whichever you please to ascribe it to. I acknowledge no man in human form.

. . . .

Mr. Mason. — How many are engaged with you in this movement? I ask these questions for our own safety.

Mr. Brown. — Any questions that I can honorably answer I will, not otherwise. So far as I am myself concerned, I have told everything truthfully. I value my word, sir.

Mr. Mason. — What was your object in coming?

Mr. Brown. — We came to free the slaves, and only that.

A Young Man (in the uniform of a volunteer company). — How many men in all had you?

Mr. Brown. — I came to Virginia with eighteen men only, besides myself.

Volunteer. — What in the world did you suppose you could do here in Virginia with that amount of men?

Mr. Brown. — Young man, I don't wish to discuss that question here.

Volunteer. — You could not do anything.

Mr. Brown. — Well, perhaps your ideas and mine on military subjects would differ materially.

Mr. Mason. — How do you justify your acts?

Mr. Brown. — I think, my friend, you are guilty of a great wrong against God and humanity — I say it without wishing to be offensive — and it would be perfectly right in any one to interfere with you so far as to free those you wilfully and wickedly hold in bondage. I do not say this insultingly.

Mr. Mason. — I understand that.

Mr. Brown. — I think I did right, and that others will do right to interfere with you at any time and all times. I hold that the Golden Rule, "Do unto others as you would that others should do unto you," applies to all who would help others to gain their liberty.

Lieut. Stuart. — But you don't believe in the Bible.

Mr. Brown. — Certainly I do.

. . . .

Mr. Mason. — Did you consider this a military organization, in this paper [the Constitution]? I have not yet read it.

Mr. Brown. — I did in some sense. I wish you would give that paper close attention.

Mr. Mason. — You considered yourself the Commander-in-Chief of these "provisional" military forces.

Mr. Brown. — I was chosen agreeably to the ordinance of a certain document, commander-in-chief of that force.

Mr. Mason. — What wages did you offer?

Mr. Brown. — None.

Lieut. Stuart. — "The wages of sin is death."

Mr. Brown. — I would not have made such a remark to you, if you had been a prisoner and wounded in my hands.

A Bystander. — Did you not promise a negro in Gettysburg twenty dollars a month?

Mr. Brown. — I did not.

. . . .

Mr. Vallandigham. — When in Cleveland, did you attend the Fugitive Slave Law Convention there?

HIGH TREASON IN VIRGINIA

Mr. Brown. — No. I was there about the time of the sitting of the court to try the Oberlin rescuers. I spoke there publicly on that subject. I spoke on the Fugitive Slave law and my own rescue. Of course, so far as I had any influence at all, I was disposed to justify the Oberlin people for rescuing the slave, because I have myself forcibly taken slaves from bondage. I was concerned in taking eleven slaves from Missouri to Canada last winter. I think I spoke in Cleveland before the Convention. I do not know that I had any conversation with any of the Oberlin rescuers. I was sick part of the time I was in Ohio, with the ague. I was part of the time in Ashtabula County.

. . . .

A Bystander. — Did you go out to Kansas under the auspices of the Emigrant Aid Society?

Mr. Brown. — No, sir; I went out under the auspices of John Brown and nobody else.

Mr. Vallandigham. — Will you answer this: Did you talk with Mr. Giddings about your expedition here?

Mr. Brown. — No, I won't answer that; because a denial of it I would not make, and to make any affirmation of it I should be a great dunce.

Mr. Vallandigham. — Have you had any correspondence with parties at the North on the subject of this movement?

Mr. Brown. — I have had correspondence.

A Bystander. — Do you consider this a religious movement?

Mr. Brown. — It is, in my opinion, the greatest service a man can render to God.

Bystander. — Do you consider yourself an instrument in the hands of Providence?

Mr. Brown. — I do.

Bystander. — Upon what principle do you justify your acts?

Mr. Brown. — Upon the golden rule. I pity the poor in bondage that have none to help them; that is why I am here; not to gratify any personal animosity, revenge or vindictive spirit. It is my sympathy with the oppressed and the wronged, that are as good as you and as precious in the sight of God.

Bystander. — Certainly. But why take the slaves against their will?

Mr. Brown. — I never did.

Bystander. — You did in one instance, at least.

Stevens, the wounded prisoner, here said, in a firm, clear voice: "You are right. In one case, I know the negro wanted to go back."

. . . .

Mr. Vallandigham (to Mr. Brown). — Who are your advisers in this movement?

Mr. Brown. — I cannot answer that. I have numerous sympathizers throughout the entire North.

Mr. Vallandigham. — In northern Ohio?

Mr. Brown. — No more there than anywhere else; in all the free states.

Mr. Vallandigham. — But you are not personally acquainted in southern Ohio?

Mr. Brown. — Not very much.

Mr. Vallandigham (to Stevens). — Were you at the Convention last June?

Stevens. — I was.

Mr. Vallandigham (to Brown). You made a speech there?

Mr. Brown. — I did.

A Bystander. — Did you ever live in Washington city?

Mr. Brown. — I did not. I want you to understand, gentlemen — and [to the reporter of the *Herald*] you may report that — I want you to understand that I respect the rights of the poorest and weakest of colored people, oppressed by the slave system, just as much as I do those of the most wealthy and powerful. That is the idea that has moved me, and that alone. We expect no reward, except the satisfaction of endeavoring to do for those in distress and greatly oppressed, as we would be done by. The cry of distress of the oppressed is my reason, and the only thing that prompted me to come here.

A Bystander. — Why did you do it secretly?

Mr. Brown. — Because I thought that necessary to success; no other reason.

Bystander. — And you think that honorable? Have you read Gerrit Smith's last letter?

Mr. Brown. — What letter do you mean?

Bystander. — The New York *Herald* of yesterday, in speaking of this affair, mentions a letter in this way: "Apropos of this exciting news, we recollect a very significant passage in one of Gerrit Smith's letters, published a month or two ago, in which he speaks of the folly of attempting to strike the shackles off the slaves by the force of moral suasion or legal agitation, and predicts that the next movement made in the direction of negro emancipation would be an insurrection in the South."

Mr. Brown. — I have not seen the New York *Herald* for some days past; but I presume, from your remark about the gist of the letter, that I should concur with it. I agree with Mr. Smith that moral suasion is hopeless. I don't think the people of the slave States will ever consider the subject of slavery in its true light till some other argument is resorted to than moral suasion.

Mr. Vallandigham. — Did you expect a general rising of the slaves in case of your success?

Mr. Brown. — No, sir; nor did I wish it. I expected to gather them up from time to time and set them free.

Mr. Vallandigham. — Did you expect to hold possession here till then?

Mr. Brown. — Well, probably I had quite a different idea. I do

HIGH TREASON IN VIRGINIA

not know that I ought to reveal my plans. I am here a prisoner and wounded, because I foolishly allowed myself to be so. You overrate your strength in supposing I could have been taken if I had not allowed it. I was too tardy after commencing the open attack — in delaying my movements through Monday night, and up to that time I was attacked by the government troops. It was all occasioned by my desire to spare the feelings of my prisoners and their families and the community at large. I had no knowledge of the shooting of the negro [Hayward].

Mr. Vallandigham. — What time did you commence your organization in Canada?

Mr. Brown. — That occurred about two years ago, if I remember right. It was, I think, in 1858.

Mr. Vallandigham. — Who was the Secretary?

Mr. Brown. — That I would not tell if I recollected, but I do not recollect. I think the officers were elected in May, 1858. I may answer incorrectly, but not intentionally. My head is a little confused by wounds, and my memory obscure on dates, etc.

Dr. Biggs. — Were you in the party at Dr. Kennedy's house?

Mr. Brown. — I was at the head of that party. I occupied the house to mature my plans. I have not been in Baltimore to purchase caps.

Dr. Biggs. — What was the number of men at Kennedy's?

Mr. Brown. — I decline to answer that.

Dr. Biggs. — Who lanced that woman's neck on the hill?

Mr. Brown. — I did. I have sometimes practised in surgery when I thought it a matter of humanity and necessity, and there was no one else to do it, but I have not studied surgery.

Dr. Biggs. — It was done very well and scientifically. They have been very clever to the neighbors, I have been told, and we had no reason to suspect them except that we could not understand their movements. They were represented as eight or nine persons; on Friday there were thirteen.

Mr. Brown. — There were more than that.

. . . .

Reporter of the Herald. — I do not wish to annoy you; but if you have anything further you would like to say I will report it.

Mr. Brown. — I have nothing to say, only that I claim to be here in carrying out a measure I believe perfectly justifiable, and not to act the part of an incendiary or ruffian, but to aid those suffering great wrong. I wish to say, furthermore, that you had better — all you people at the South — prepare yourselves for a settlement of that question that must come up for settlement sooner than you are prepared for it. The sooner you are prepared the better. You may dispose of me very easily; I am nearly disposed of now; but this question is still to be settled — this negro question I mean — the end of that is not yet. These wounds were inflicted upon me — both sabre cuts on my head and bayonet stabs in the different parts of my body — some minutes after I had ceased fighting and had consented to a surrender, for the benefit of others, not for my own. [This statement was vehemently denied all around.]* I believe the major [meaning Lieutenant J. E. B. Stuart, of the United States Cavalry]† would not have been alive; I could have killed him just as easy as a mosquito when he came in, but I supposed he came in only to receive our surrender. There had been loud and long calls of "surrender" from us — as loud as men could yell — but in the confusion and excitement I suppose we were not heard. I do not think the major, or any one, meant to butcher us after we had surrendered.

An officer here stated that the orders to the marines were not to shoot anybody; but when they were fired upon by Brown's men and one of them killed, they were obliged to return the compliment.

Mr. Brown insisted that the marines fired first.‡

An Officer. — Why did not you surrender before the attack?

Mr. Brown. — I did not think it was my duty or interest to do so. We assured the prisoners that we did not wish to harm them, and that they should be set at liberty. I exercised my best judgment, not believing the people would wantonly sacrifice their own fellow-citizens, when we offered to let them go on condition of being allowed to change our position about a quarter of a mile. The prisoners agreed by vote among themselves to pass across the bridge with us. We wanted them only as a sort of guaranty of our own safety; that we should not be fired into. We took them in the first place as hostages and to keep them from doing any harm. We did kill some men in defending ourselves, but I saw no one fire except directly in self-defence. Our orders were strict not to harm any one not in arms against us.

Q. — Brown, suppose you had every nigger in the United States, what would you do with them?

A. — Set them free.

Q. — Your intention was to carry them off and free them?

A. — Not at all.

A Bystander. — To set them free would sacrifice the life of every man in this community.

---

* This portion of the interview is evidently erroneous. John Brown could hardly have maintained that he was struck down after surrendering, in view of the shooting of the two marines who entered the engine house after Lieutenant Green; moreover, in his testimony during his trial he twice stated that he never asked for quarter. It is true, however, that as the marines came in, two of the raiders, Thompson and Anderson, surrendered and there were shouts of: "One man surrenders." If John Brown had meant to surrender, the time to do so was when Lieutenant Stuart asked him to; not two minutes thereafter, when the marines came in under fire.

† This is evidently a confusion of Lieutenants Stuart and Green and Major Russell.

‡ This statement is erroneous; the marines fired no shots whatever.

Mr. Brown. — I do not think so.

Bystander. — I know it. I think you are fanatical.

Mr. Brown. — And I think you are fanatical. "Whom the gods would destroy they first make mad," and you are mad.

Q. — Was it your only object to free the negroes?

A. — Absolutely our only object.

Q. — But you demanded and took Colonel Washington's silver and watch?

A. — Yes; we intended freely to appropriate the property of slaveholders to carry out our object. It was for that, and only that, and with no design to enrich ourselves with any plunder whatever.

According to a later report in the *Herald*, Governor Wise, on his return to Richmond, said somebody in the crowd applied to Brown the epithet "robber," and that Brown retorted, "You [alluding to the slaveholders] are the robbers." And it was in this connection that he said, "If you have your opinions about me, I have my opinions about you." At this time the Governor remarked to him, "Mr. Brown, the silver of your hair is reddened by the blood of crime, and it is meet that you should eschew these hard allusions and think upon eternity. . . ."

Brown replied by saying:

"Governor, I have, from all appearances, not more than fifteen or twenty years the start of you in the journey to that eternity of which you kindly warn me; and whether my tenure here shall be fifteen months, or fifteen days, or fifteen hours, I am equally prepared to go. There is an eternity behind and an eternity before, and the little speck in the centre, however long, is but comparatively a minute. The difference between your tenure and mine is trifling and I want to therefore tell you to be prepared; I am prepared. You all [referring to slaveholders] have a heavy responsibility, and it behooves you to prepare more than it does me." [71]

There was a passage in Governor Wise's speech on his arrival in Richmond which gave great offence to the military, for it voiced freely and frankly his own bitterness of spirit that it was left to United States marines to capture nineteen raiders upon Virginia soil. In it, he spoke thus:

"On Monday night the gallant and noble Virginia Colonel, Robert Lee, worthy of any service on earth, arrived with his regular corps of marines. He waited only for light. Then tendered the assault, in State pride, to the Virginia volunteers who were there. Their feelings for the prisoners made them decline the risk of slaying their own friends, and Lee could not delay a moment to retake the arsenal, punish the impudent invaders and release the prisoners at the necessary risk of their own lives. His gallantry was mortified that the task was so easy. . . . With mortification and chagrin inexpressible, he picked twelve marines and took the engine-house in ten minutes, with the loss of one marine killed and one wounded, without hurting a hair of one of the prisoners. And now I say to you that I would have given my right arm to its shoulder for that feat to have been performed by the volunteers of Virginia on Monday before the marines arrived there. But there was no cowardice or panic on the part of the inhabitants who were made prisoners, or on the part of the volunteers who first reached the scene. . . ."

The matter did not end here. Governor Wise's son, O. Jennings Wise, who gave his life for the Confederacy two years later, after a brief career of undoubted bravery, preferred charges against Colonel Robert W. Baylor, the colonel of militia cavalry who had assumed command of all the State forces on the afternoon of Monday. At Colonel Baylor's request, a court of inquiry was held in June, 1860, but it failed to touch upon the real point at issue, — Colonel Baylor's behavior on October 17, 1859.[72] Fearing that this would be the case, Jennings Wise, on its assembling, wrote to the court, which apparently ignored his letter, that Colonel Baylor illegally assumed command "contrary to his grade and the nature of his commission," acted without orders, was guilty of cowardice in not storming the engine house, and of "unofficerlike conduct" in assigning a "false, cowardly and insulting reason for not leading the attack on the engine house when the service was offered to him by Colonel Lee: towit . . . that it was a duty which belonged to the *mercenaries* of the regular service — meaning the marines — who were paid for it;" and finally for using "violent and ungentlemanly language about his commander-in-chief [Governor Wise]."[73]

A member of the Shepherdstown militia, the Hamtramck Guards, charged in the local newspaper that his company was permitted to stand idle in the streets from the time of the Martinsburg company's attack, when one platoon fired a few rounds at the engine-house, until late in the evening, because of the captain's inability to obtain orders from Colonel Baylor.[74] The only commands given during the evening, he

HIGH TREASON IN VIRGINIA

related, "were from a set of drunken fellows whooping and bellowing like a pack of maddened bulls, evidently too drunk, many of them, to hold their guns." He also charged that the wounded of the Martinsburg company were shot not by the raiders but by their own men. There is intrinsic evidence of the accuracy of much of this letter; it is certainly true that, wherever the fault lay, no effective use whatever was made of the Hamtramck Guards after their one attack upon the engine house. From the adjoining houses they could have poured in a deadly fire.

The truth seems to be that, as might have been expected with a practically paper militia, the hastily called-out Virginia soldiery were quite unequal to the task set, by reason of the utter inability of their officers to control and direct them and to keep them sober. Throughout the entire conflict, there were but two really aggressive movements,— the taking of the bridge by the Jefferson Guards, and the charge of the Martinsburg company. Had Colonel Baylor been capable of aggressive leadership, the discredit to the Virginia arms would never have taken place. But there was no concerted action, and but little intelligent direction, at any time of the day, after the taking of the bridge. On the other hand, the militia companies, like those so hastily organized, were inadequately armed and equipped, and the presence of the prisoners with the enemy was a happy excuse to cover the delays and hesitations of the afternoon. For this, the commanding officer, Colonel Baylor, must naturally be held responsible. It was the old story, so soon to be repeated on many battlefields, of excellent military material ineffective through lack of discipline and vigorous leadership.

For all of Governor Wise's admiration of John Brown as a man, he did not hesitate to describe him and his men as "murderers, *traitors*, robbers, insurrectionists," and "wanton, malicious, unprovoked felons." [75] Yet just a year and a half later, April 16, 1861, Henry A. Wise, then out of office and with no more legal authority for his acts than had John Brown, actively conspired with Captain — later General — J. D. Imboden, General Kenton Harper and the superintendent, Alfred W. Barbour, and through them captured the Harper's Ferry arsenal precisely as had John Brown, save that there was no loss of life.[76] But the blow was none the less directly aimed at the Federal Government. The undertaking of this act of treason was a compelling reason for the passage of the Virginia Ordinance of Secession on April 17, 1861. Governor Wise dramatically announced to the Secession convention that "armed forces are now moving upon Harper's Ferry to capture the arms there in the Arsenal for the public defence, and there will be a fight or a foot-race between volunteers of Virginia and Federal troops before the sun sets this day."[77] On June 1, this same Henry A. Wise, whose abhorrence of John Brown's acts had been so profound, in a speech at Richmond urged his neighbors to: "Get a spear — a lance. Take a lesson from John Brown, manufacture your blades from old iron, even though it be the tires of your cart-wheels."[78] Forgetful, too, of his panegyric of his Yankee captive's bravery and coolness, he assured his auditors that: "Your true-blooded Yankee will never stand still in the presence of cold steel." In so scant a space of time as a year and a half had the erstwhile Governor, by a singular revolution of the wheel of fate, himself come to occupy the position of a rebel against the established political order.

CHAPTER XIII

GUILTY BEFORE THE LAW

WITH the capture of John Brown an accomplished fact, the military were free to take account of what had happened, and to endeavor to ascertain precisely what this attack upon the peaceful town meant.¹ In the morning, a Maryland militia company, the Baltimore Greys, under command of Lieut.-Col. S. S. Mills, of the Fifty-third Maryland Regiment, visited the school-house, took the arms there deposited, and acquired some of John Brown's papers, many of which were later regained in Baltimore, after considerable trouble.² Lieutenant Stuart and a detachment of the marines were then sent, early in the afternoon, to the Kennedy Farm, to bring back to the arsenal the property of the raiders. They did not, however, arrive until John Brown's dwelling, so recently the home of high hopes and philanthropic ambitions, had been ransacked by curious neighbors. It was characteristic of John Brown that he had left at the Farm, undestroyed, all his correspondence bearing on his preparations and his plans, and that belonging to his men as well.* Had he succeeded, therefore, in gaining the hills and beginning his guerrilla raids, his enemy would have been in full possession of his purposes and of the names of his confederates in the North. The Baltimore troops found Colonel Washington's wagon and its scattered horses, with which some of the weapons were taken to the armory. Lieutenant Stuart found at the Farm most of the pikes, which were speedily distributed as souvenirs, and for months thereafter were hawked about with so ready a sale as to lead to the manufacture of spurious ones.³ Every one who aided in mov-

* Hugh Forbes wrote to the editor of the *Herald* on October 27, 1859: "When I transmitted to Capt. Brown copies of all my correspondence with his friends, I never dreamed that the most terrible engine of destruction which he would carry with him in his campaign would be a carpet-bag loaded with 400 letters, to be turned against his friends, of whom the journals assert that more than forty-seven are already compromised."

ing the rifles and revolvers likewise helped himself to some as legitimate spoils of war.

Of Cook, the only one of the escaped raiders of whose existence the victors at first knew, there was naturally no sign. He, with Owen Brown, Tidd, Meriam and Barclay Coppoc, had spent the night of Monday in the bushes near the cabin of the Kennedy Farm. Here they lay until early morning, when the last one of the negroes whom they had armed and freed, deserted them and set them at three o'clock to climbing the mountain as fast as their load of arms and other impedimenta permitted.[4] This negro's conduct was characteristic of all of the slaves impressed by John Brown. They followed the orders of the raiders and obeyed them to the extent of carrying, for a time, arms or pikes, and doing guard-duty. When, however, it came to firing in the engine house, or to accompanying those who had escaped, they refused in the one case to attack the slaveholders, and in the other they chose to slip away and return to their masters with tales of being kept against their will, rather than to risk their lives or make any effort to escape.[5] The great uprising among the blacks upon which John Brown counted so confidently never came to pass; the thousands of reinforcements he looked for appeared not at all. There was not one who joined of his own accord; of those that did go with Brown, a negro hired by Colonel Washington from a neighbor was found drowned in the river, where some thought he was driven by citizens in an attempt to run away, while others held that he was shot by Cook.[6] No satisfactory explanation of his death was ever given. Mr. Allstadt's negro, Phil, who at Brown's orders had broken loopholes in the engine-house walls for the raiders to fire through, was taken to the jail at Charlestown, where he died of pneumonia, complicated by very great fear.[7] Otherwise, the negro population was unaffected by the raid, and its imperturbability, when once established, went far toward reassuring the South.

Outraged as they were by the attack on their homes, the Harper's Ferrians and the whole South breathed again when they realized that the negroes themselves had not risen in the excitement Brown created. "And this is the only consolation I have to offer you in this disgrace," said Governor Wise in his Richmond speech, "that the faithful slaves refused to take up

GUILTY BEFORE THE LAW

arms against their masters; and those who were taken by force from their happy homes deserted their liberators as soon as they could dare to make the attempt. Not a slave around was found faithless." Senator Mason likewise rejoiced at this. "On the part of the negroes," he stated in a signed résumé of his own investigation of the raid issued to the press immediately thereafter,[8] "it is certain that the only emotion evinced by them was of alarm and terror, and their only refuge sought at their masters' homes." The negro who deserted Cook's party, in the early morning hours of Tuesday, went down to the Ferry and informed the authorities that Cook was there in the mountain,[9] just as Cook's party had foreseen that he would. A vigorous, organized pursuit would doubtless have run Cook to earth at once; but they being ignorant of how many of the raiders were at large, nothing was done by either the Maryland or Virginia military.

The scenes of Tuesday evening at Harper's Ferry were fortunately recorded by an able Northern witness, Joseph G. Rosengarten, a director of the Pennsylvania Railroad,[10] who strayed by accident into Harper's Ferry during the riot, and, being near Captain Turner when he was killed, was promptly marched off to spend the night in the Charlestown jail as a suspect. Being released the next day through the intercession of Governor Wise, he returned to Harper's Ferry in time to see the immediate aftermath of the raid. Of it he records:

"Night soon came, and it was made hideous by the drunken noise and turmoil of the crowd in the village; matters were made worse, too, by the Governor's orders to impress all the horses; and the decent, sober men trudged home rather out of humor with their patriotic sacrifice; while the tipsy and pot-valiant militia fought and squabbled with each other, and only ceased that sport to pursue and hunt down some fugitive negroes and one or two half-maddened drunken fellows who, in their frenzy proclaimed themselves John Brown's men. Tired out at last, the Governor took refuge in the Wager House; — for an hour or two, he had stood on the porch haranguing an impatient crowd as 'Sons of Virginia!' Within doors the scene was stranger still. Huddled together . . . the Governor and his staff at a table with tallow candles guttering in the darkness, the Richmond Grays lying around the floor in picturesque and (then) novel pursuit of soft planks, a motley audience was gathered together to hear the papers captured at John Brown's house — the Kennedy Farm on Maryland Heights — read out with the Governor's running comments. The purpose of all this was plain enough. It was meant to serve as proof of a knowledge and instigation of the raid by prominent persons and party-leaders in the North. The most innocent notes and letters, commonplace newspaper paragraphs and printed cuttings, were distorted and twisted by the reading and by the talking into clear instructions and positive plots."

Wednesday morning there took place the transfer of the prisoners by train to Charlestown. They were well guarded by Lieutenant Israel Green and some of his men, and were in the joint charge of the sheriff of Jefferson County and the United States marshal of the Western District of Virginia. Governor Wise, Senator Mason and other prominent men accompanied them.[11] The removal to the train occurred under circumstances which thoroughly warranted the using of the marines as a guard, instead of a local militia company. Stevens and Brown had to be taken to the station in a wagon; Shields Green and Coppoc walked between files of soldiers and were followed by hundreds of highly excited men. As the procession reached the train, the mob gathered menacingly, crying, "Lynch them! Lynch them!" Governor Wise called out, "Oh, it would be cowardly to do so now!" The crowd then fell back, and the prisoners were safely placed on the train.[12] Most of the militia had already returned to their homes, and with but one company on duty after the departure of the prisoners,[13] the town rapidly quieted down, and Colonel Lee felt free to move about as he pleased.

When, therefore, news came at nine o'clock that evening from the village of Pleasant Valley, Maryland, that a body of men at sunset had descended from the mountains, attacked the house of a settler and massacred him, his wife and children, Lee, accompanied by Lieutenants Green and Stuart, hastened with twenty-five marines to the outraged hamlet, four or five miles away, only to find everything quiet and the massacred family sound asleep.[14] He returned with his party in plenty of time to embark with all the marines shortly after midnight upon the train for Washington. Here Colonel Lee handed in a written report to the Secretary of War, in ignorance, however, of the fact that just twenty-four hours before his visit there, five escaping raiders had descended from the

GUILTY BEFORE THE LAW 471

mountains into Pleasant Valley, and had heard cries of alarm which made them wrongfully believe that they were discovered. After incredible hardships, all but Cook of this party of five safely reached the North.[15] Of the other raiders who got away from Harper's Ferry, Hazlett was taken and Anderson escaped. Had Cook and Hazlett not exposed themselves because of hunger, they, too, would have reached safety. Tidd reported afterward in person to Thomas Wentworth Higginson, that his experiences while escaping had convinced him that "twenty-five men in the mountains of Virginia could paralyze the whole business of the South, and nobody could take them." It was the best guerrilla country in the world, in his opinion, — all crags and laurel-bushes. There was no attempt, he pointed out, to pursue him and his comrades in the mountains; the man-hunters invariably kept to the roads. Their inability to travel directly made the fugitives cover one hundred and twenty miles in going to Chambersburg, only forty-five miles away as the bird flies, and they were gravely handicapped by Meriam's weakness and inability to go more than a mile or so without resting.

When John Brown was lodged in the Charlestown jail, he had every reason for thanksgiving that his life had been spared. Not that he was under any illusion as to the precariousness of his position; he realized perfectly that the sands of time had nearly run out for him, and that his captors were certain to make every effort to take his life by due process of law. He was quick to perceive, as were his friends in the North, what rare good fortune it had been that Lieutenant Green's blade was so ineffective, for, had John Brown fallen in the engine house, the whole raid must needs have been a few days' wonder and then have been forgotten. Deprived of their leader, the fate of Stevens, Shields Green and Edwin Coppoc could only have mildly interested the country. Unknown marauders, they must have perished with but few voices of sympathy raised in their behalf. Thanks to the chief's survival, and to the discovery of his friendship with prominent Abolitionists and Republicans in high political positions, the Harper's Ferry *émeute* assumed at once national proportions. The Democratic pro-slavery press of the North lost no time in seizing upon the raid to discredit the "Black Republicans" of all degrees. In their columns, John Brown's deeds were, if anything, magnified, in order to let the country understand just how culpable were Senator Seward, Congressman Giddings, Horace Greeley, Gerrit Smith and many others. The New York *Herald* was particularly violent in its attacks on Smith and Seward; the latter was the "arch agitator who is responsible for this insurrection," whom it wished to see hanged in place of Brown.[16] Him it characterized as one "rendered daring, reckless and an abolition monomaniac by the scenes of violence and blood through which he had passed." "He has met," the *Herald* declared, "with the fate which he courted; but his death and the punishment of all his criminal associates will be as a feather in the balance against the mischievous consequences which will probably follow from the rekindling of the slavery excitement in the South." [17]

The Republican press was at first inclined to discredit the whole episode, or to dismiss it as the work of a madman. In this the *Tribune* took the lead, saying on Tuesday that the extraordinary happening in Harper's Ferry was attributed to negroes and Abolitionists. "But, as negroes are not abundant in that part of Virginia, while no Abolitionists were ever known to peep in that quarter, we believe the nature of the affair must be grossly misapprehended." The next day it spoke of the raid thus: "The whole affair seems the work of a madman, but John Brown has so often looked death serenely in the face that what seems madness to others doubtless wore a different aspect to him." The Cleveland *Leader* sought to minimize the whole affair in this wise: "But for the loss of life attending the foray of the crazy Brown among the Virginians, the whole thing would be positively ridiculous, and it is fast becoming so even with the frightened chivalry themselves. The eccentric Governor Wise, as reported by telegraph, has so far recovered from his fright under the backing of Virginia, Maryland and United States troops, that he has ventured to pitch into the Harper's Ferry cowards in rather sharper than his usual sarcastic style." [18] The Hartford *Evening Press* considered Brown a poor, demented old man; the calamity, it believed, would never have occurred had there been no lawless and criminal invasion of Kansas.[19] To the St. Louis *Evening News* the raid was the freak of madmen, ending in humiliating

GUILTY BEFORE THE LAW

discomfiture.[20] To the Topeka, Kansas, *Tribune* the foray seemed like "the wild scheme of a bad man who, seeking for personal distinction (not fame) and, perhaps, plunder, was ready to endanger the lives of thousands, perhaps even the existence of the State; for, had he succeeded, had he distributed the arms he possessed in the armory, what hand, what mind could have guided the wild mass his mind had crazed and his hand had clothed with the instruments of death?"[21] The Atchison City, Kansas, *Freedom's Champion* recognized that "this madman has met a tragic end at last. An insane effort to accomplish what none but a madman would attempt, has resulted as any one but a madman would have foreseen, in death, to all who were engaged in it."[22]

The politically independent *Liberator*, mouthpiece of the most radical, but at the same time the non-resistant wing of the Abolitionists, who were ever counselling the negroes not to rise in revolt or to use force to right their wrongs, thus commented on the first news from Harper's Ferry:

"The particulars of a misguided, wild, and apparently insane, though disinterested and well intended effort by insurrection to emancipate the slaves in Virginia, under the leadership of Capt. John, alias 'Ottawatomie' Brown, may be found on our third page. Our views of war and bloodshed, even in the best of causes, are too well known to need repeating here; but let no one who glories in the revolutionary struggle of 1776, deny the right of the slaves to imitate the example of our fathers."[23]

In its next issue it described the comments of the leading Democratic and Republican newspapers as characterized "by an equal mixture of ferocity and cowardice." Gradually, however, the Republican press came to see in the affray just retribution for the South's policy of violence in Kansas, and a perfectly inevitable protest against the wickedness of slavery. The opportunity to make a martyr of John Brown, to let him typify the protest of increasing hundreds of thousands against human bondage, they soon made use of to the fullest extent. John Brown's own attitude, his nobility of spirit and readiness for his sacrifice, were of enormous aid. The political opportunity his martyrdom offered was not neglected. "Already the Black Republican press has commenced to apologize for him," said the Portage, Ohio, *Weekly Sentinel* of October 26.

"They say that exasperated by wrongs done him in Kansas he was driven to madness. They say he reasoned thus, 'that the slave drivers tried to put down Freedom in Kansas by force of arms and he would try to put down Slavery in Virginia by the same means.' Thus is the 'irrepressible conflict' of Seward and Smith and Giddings, and the Black Republican party, carried out practically by a bold, bad, desperate man. Who is responsible for this? Not Brown, for he is mad; but they, who by their countenance and pecuniary aid have induced him thus to resort to arms to carry out their political schemes, must answer to the country and the world for this fearfully significant outbreak."

The New York *Abend-Zeitung* declared that:

"Brown and his companions made themselves MARTYRS OF A CAUSE IN ITSELF noble; and, although the mode in which they sought to advance it was not adapted to the end proposed, we still cannot refuse our respect for the self-sacrificing zeal with which they offered up their lives for it. WE HAVE NO REPROOF TO OFFER BROWN, EXCEPT this, that the way in which he set to work hindered rather than forwarded his plans."[24]

The South itself was compelled to admiration by Brown's manly bearing under fire and in adversity, as had been Governor Wise and the other eye-witnesses at Harper's Ferry.* Its leaders had, heretofore, been on the offensive; theirs was the successful war with Mexico; theirs the Fugitive Slave Law, the attempt to conquer Kansas; theirs the control of the Federal Government, which they bent to their will. Here now was the North deliberately invading their soil and assailing their sacred institution, and though it filled them with horror and anger, at least they had to admit that besides its daring, its reckless folly, the raid did not lack a certain consistency. No longer could they taunt the Abolition North with lacking the courage of its opinions; no longer could they say that the New England lover of the negro was too fond of his skin to risk it in the South. It was a cry of anxious rage that went up. Would

---

* Describing John Brown's appearance as he lay wounded before him, Governor Wise once said that he likened his attitude to nothing but "a broken-winged hawk lying upon his back, with fearless eye, and talons set for further fight if need be." — John S. Wise, *The End of an Era*, p. 132.

GUILTY BEFORE THE LAW

the very news of the raid put the word "insurrection" into the minds of the millions held in bondage from Harper's Ferry to the Gulf? How many imitators of John Brown would appear, to seek revenge for his failure? Then, as the South discovered the North's readiness to lionize, even in some quarters to deify Brown, its anger increased. To them he was a fanatic who sought not only to steal cherished property, but to establish anarchy, to reënact the Nat Turner horrors, to make the terrible scenes of the Haytian negro revolt insignificant beside the atrocities he would set on foot.* That such a man could be likened to the Saviour, and be considered a direct instrument of the Almighty, was maddening far beyond the actual outrage. The killing of Beckham and other unoffending citizens was surely murder, plain and simple. To applaud it, to describe it as an act especially pleasing to the Deity, was to argue one's self morally defective, of a criminal spirit, and so bitterly hostile to the injured and innocent people of the South as to make more than one person come to John Brown's views that the issue between the two sections had passed beyond the possibility of peaceable settlement. Mr. William Hand Browne has recently well characterized the Southern attitude in the following passage:

"But the atrocious attempt of John Brown at Harper's Ferry came like a fire bell in the night. The attempt itself might have been considered merely the deed of a few fanatical desperadoes, but for the universal uproar of enthusiastic approbation that burst out at the North. Doubtless there were many who abhorred the idea of midnight massacre; but their voices were drowned in what seemed to be a universal chorus of applause, mingled with regrets that the assassins had not succeeded in their purpose. The South could not be blamed for supposing that the North had passed from the stage of political antagonism to that of furious personal hate." [25] †

Said the Richmond *Enquirer* of October 25, 1859:

---

* "Nothing," declared the London *Times* of November 2, 1859, "but sickening and bootless slaughter could come of it [the raid]. First the slaughter of white families by their slaves, and then the bloody revenge of the exasperated masters." It correctly observed, however, that "the state of society which causes such a scheme to be formed and carried out is not the less threatening."

† "The conviction became common in the South that John Brown differed from the majority of Northerners merely in the boldness and desperation of his methods." — Frederic Bancroft, *Life of William H. Seward*, pp. 497–498.

"The Harper's Ferry invasion has advanced the cause of Disunion more than any other event that has happened since the formation of the Government; it has rallied to that standard men who formerly looked upon it with horror; it has revived with tenfold strength the desires of a Southern Confederacy. The, heretofore, most determined friends of the Union may now be heard saying, 'if under the form of a Confederacy, our peace is disturbed, our State invaded, its peaceful citizens cruelly murdered, and all the horrors of servile war forced upon us, by those who should be our warmest friends; if the form of a Confederacy is observed, but the spirit violated, *and the people of the North sustain the outrage*, then let disunion come.'"

This same newspaper noted with satisfaction that what it called the conservative, that is, the pro-slavery press of the North, "evinces a determination to make the moral of the Harper's Ferry invasion an effective weapon to rally all men not fanatics against that party whose leaders have been implicated directly with the midnight murder of Virginia citizens and the destruction of government property." But the attempt to use the acts of extreme Abolitionists to make capital against them was an old political game. Southern politicians had long been indulging in it, yet the cause of the anti-slavery men had steadily progressed. In this case, too, the John Brown raid, though it appeared at first a severe injury to the Republicans, did them little harm. The November elections were favorable to the new party, even though their vote fell off in certain places. Horace Greeley correctly foresaw that the ultimate effect of the raid would be beneficial. "It will drive the slave power to new outrages," he wrote. "It presses on the 'irrepressible conflict,' and I think the end of slavery in Virginia and the Union is ten years nearer than it seemed a few weeks ago."[26] Indeed, the raid revealed to many besides John Brown that there was to be a bloody conflict on a far greater scale; and no student of this period can fail to be impressed by the prevision of coming events given to hundreds, if not thousands, on both sides.

When the iron door of his cell had been slammed behind John Brown, the State authorities discovered that a trial speedy enough to satisfy the anger of Virginia was, by chance, a possibility. The Grand Jury was in session, and the semi-annual term of the Circuit Court, over which Judge Richard

GUILTY BEFORE THE LAW

Parker, of Winchester, presided, had begun. The Virginia statutes then required that "when an indictment is found against a person for felony, in a court wherein he may be tried, the accused, if in custody, shall, unless good cause be shown for a continuance, be arraigned and tried in the same term."[27] Nothing, it was felt, could so quickly allay the excitement among the whites and blacks alike as to send these men to the gallows. If this law were not obeyed, and the case were continued, there could be no trial until the following April; during these six months the State would be in a ferment and some militia would have to be under arms. There arose, however, the question of jurisdiction. Should John Brown be turned over to the United States? Some of his offences had been committed on United States property, and the Federal courts could, therefore, take cognizance of them. Here was an opportunity to place the United States Government in the position of prosecutor of these Abolitionists, of which, it seems to-day, Governor Wise should have availed himself for strategic reasons. To embroil the Federal Government might well have seemed most tempting to the slave-power. But Governor Wise and his associates, exceedingly shrewd politicians, finally decided otherwise. The Federal courts, it must be remembered, were not then as important as to-day; the nearest Federal prison was at some distance, and Wise had no desire to have it said that the State of Virginia was forced to hide behind the skirts of the Federal Government, and to obtain its help to punish those who violated her soil and killed her citizens.[28]

None the less, Governor Wise vacillated for some time, particularly when it came to trying Brown's companions. Thus on November 7 he telegraphed to Andrew Hunter: "You had better try Cooke and turn Stephens [Stevens] over to the United States Court. Do that definitely."[29] His and Hunter's position at this time is explained by a letter of Hunter's, dated five days earlier:

"I have seen your letter to Gov. Willard and am considering the suggestion as to transferring one of the prisoners to the Federal authorities. It strikes me very favorably but I have not yet conferred with the Judge, and as neither of the murders, that is, as to the death of the victims, except the Marine, occurred on the Government property, one must consider carefully how far the prisoner transferred can be certainly convicted in the Federal Court, particularly Cooke, who is the only white prisoner we have left except Stephens. Our State Court, of course, has no power to summon Forbes from N. York . . . and this renders it the more important to send one of the scoundrels to Uncle Sam, in order to get at the greater villains implicated who are still out of our reach."[30]

On November 7, Hunter announced in court, amid a great sensation, that Stevens would be given up to the United States; that Virginia was now after "higher and wickeder game."[31] Yet in December the hunt for the greater prey was abandoned. When, on December 15, President Buchanan inquired by telegraph whether Stevens had been turned over to the United States, Andrew Hunter replied: "Stephens has not been delivered to the authorities of the United States. Undetermined as yet whether he will be tried here."[32]

On hearing of this query from the President, Governor Wise, on December 18, exactly reversed his position of six weeks earlier, in this message to Andrew Hunter:

"In reply to yours of the 15th I say definitively that Stephens ought not to be handed over to the Federal authorities for trial. . . . I hope you informed the President of the status of his case before the court. I am convinced that there is a political design in trying now to have him tried before the Federal courts. He will not be delivered up with my consent."[33]

We have no means of knowing what the political conspiracy was which Governor Wise then thought he scented. But the chief reason for the change of policy in regard to Stevens's trial was the appointment, on December 14, of a committee of investigation of the United States Senate, consisting of three pro-slavery Senators and two from the North, headed by Senator Mason, of Virginia. As this committee was avowedly appointed to strike at the "higher and wickeder" villains, the special reason for having one trial in a United States court — the examining of the Northern friends and backers of Brown, and of the Republican leaders — had disappeared.[34] Hunter and Wise found it easy to show that Stevens had not actually been turned over to the Federal authorities, though his trial in November in Judge Parker's court had been interrupted for that express purpose. Against this unjust and

GUILTY BEFORE THE LAW

hurtful vacillation with Stevens, his counsel argued and protested in vain.[35] He was tried and sentenced to death in Charlestown.

John Brown was put on trial for his life before Judge Richard Parker,[36] in the court-house at Charlestown, on October 25, one week after his capture. That so brief an interval only should have elapsed between crime and trial created an unfavorable impression in the North. In the excitement of the hour, high-minded men and women forgot that, through John Brown's agency, Beckham, Turner, Boerley and Hayward had been killed without warning; they complained that Virginia was mercilessly and inhumanly rushing him to the gallows; that his being done to death was a foregone conclusion; and finally that Virginia had gone mad with fright. Fear there undoubtedly was at Charlestown and Richmond that this was but the beginning of extensive hostilities between North and South; the letters which now began to pour in on Governor Wise convinced him, as will be seen later, that there was a widespread conspiracy, of which the raid was only a part. To him it made no difference that John Brown's wounds were not yet healed, for they were at worst superficial. But that they were still unhealed, intensified the feeling of outrage in the North. That John Brown heard his arraignment, lying on a cot at the bar, deeply stirred Northern newspaper-readers, as did the fact that Stevens had to be carried into court. Lydia Maria Child wrote to Governor Wise that she did not know of a single person who would have approved of the raid, if he had been apprised of John Brown's intention in advance. "But," she added, "I and thousands of others feel a natural impulse of sympathy for the brave and suffering man. . . . He needs a mother and sister to dress his wounds, and speak soothingly to him. Will you allow me to perform that mission of humanity?"[37] To this Governor Wise responded that he knew of no reason why she should not minister to John Brown, for he would permit no woman to be insulted, even if she came to minister to "one who whetted knives of butchery for our mothers, sisters, daughters, and babes."[38]*

---

* "Do not allow Mrs. Child to visit B. He does not wish it because the infuriated populace will have new suspicions aroused & great excitement and injurious results are certain. He *is comfortable*. Has all his wants supplied kindly,

The Lawrence, Kansas, *Republican* voiced the sentiments of many Northerners in saying:

"We defy an instance to be shown in a civilized community where a prisoner has been forced to trial for his life, when so disabled by sickness or ghastly wounds as to be unable even to sit up during the proceedings, and compelled to be carried to the judgment hall upon a litter. . . . Such a proceeding shames the name of justice, and only finds a congenial place amid the records of the bloody Inquisition."

It was no answer to this, the *Republican* thought, to say that the Virginia public was too wrought up to admit of delay. That there was intense popular excitement was the best of reasons why delay should have been granted, that the trial might proceed with due calm and deliberation. "And what a comment upon the state of society engendered by slavery is it that the peace and safety of a community of twenty thousand population is endangered by the prisoned, bolted and barred presence of a sick and wounded old man." [39]

Even the New York *Herald* had to admit the obvious signs of haste in dooming the prisoners. Horace Greeley, in the *Tribune*, at first wrote on October 25:

"As the Grand Jury of Jefferson County . . . is already in session, the trial of Brown and his confederates may be expected to take place at once, unless delay should be granted to prepare for trial, or a change of venue to some less excited county should be asked for. Neither of these is probable. The prisoners in fact have no defence, and their case will probably be speedily disposed of. We trust the whole proceeding may partake of the same spirit of decency, propriety, and respect for the law, and the rights of the prisoners, which characterizes the charge given by the presiding Judge to the Grand Jury."

Later, however, the *Tribune* felt that the trial was unfair because, among other reasons, Brown was not allowed the time and opportunity to make a full and complete defence

and is not sick enough to be nursed. He *don't* want *women* there to unman his heroic determination to maintain a firm and consistent composure. KEEP MRS. CHILD *away at all hazards. Brown* and *associates* will certainly be lynched if she goes there. This ought to be shown to Mr. Andrew and others, but no *public exhibition.*" — Thus wrote George H. Hoyt, John Brown's lawyer, to J. W. Le Barnes. (Original in the *Kansas Historical Society Collections.*) Mrs. Child did not go to Virginia.

to the multifarious charges brought against him.[40] The Boston *Transcript* went so far as to say: "Whatever may be his guilt or folly, a man convicted under such circumstances, and, especially, a man *executed* after such a trial, will be the most terrible fruit that slavery has ever borne, and will excite the execration of the whole civilized world."[41] To an observer of the protracted criminal trials in this country to-day, it seems odd that any one should have objected to a prompt trial for Brown. But public sentiment was far too aroused on both sides to permit of calm judgments. The spectacle of the gray-haired prisoner sentenced while lying on his couch, when combined with the belief that the trial was an unfair one by reason of haste, made John Brown a martyr in the eyes of the North.

Tactically, from the point of view of slavery, it would seem that Governor Wise erred in not suggesting a delay, unless it be believed that he, who had bombastically threatened secession in 1854 in the event of the election of an Abolitionist President,[42] was as anxious to see John Brown's acts embroil the States as he was ready to utilize Brown's imprisonment as an excuse for training the militia of Virginia for the impending conflict. In 1888, nearly thirty years after the raid, when the heat of the hour had long since passed away, Judge Parker reviewed the trial of his most distinguished criminal in these words:

"Frequent misrepresentations have been made respecting it. For example, it has been said that the trial was indecently conducted, and so hurried through as virtually to deny to the accused an opportunity to make his defense. I submit, with all deference, that censures of this character can only have proceeded from ignorance of what really transpired on that occasion. It is my principle — I may say my only purpose in this paper, to show how groundless were all such charges, and to set forth, in a plain narrative, the spirit and temper in which the trial was conducted; that there was no denial to the accused of any presumption, benefit or right to which he was entitled; that no bias against him was exhibited by the jury or the Court; that he was defended by learned and zealous counsel, who, without let or interruption, were granted all the time they were pleased to consume in the examination of witnesses, in discussing the various questions of law and fact, which arose during the trial, in excepting to every opinion of the Court wherein they supposed there might be an error, and in arguing before the Jury every matter which they deemed important or beneficial to the defense; in a word, to show that John Brown had a fair and impartial trial, just such as should be granted to all persons so unfortunate as to be accused of crime." [43]

Judge Parker's own bearing throughout the trial, and his eminently judicial spirit, have never been questioned. He was bravely ready at all times to take his stand without regard to the violent feelings of his neighbors, and his word as to the trial is, as a whole, to be accepted. It is to be regretted, however, that he did not give the additional time to Brown's counsel for which the prisoner pleaded; had he done so, it must have mitigated many of the Northern criticisms of the procedure.

These were not all from irresponsible sources. So good a lawyer, so just and public-spirited a man as John A. Andrew, for instance, felt indignant at what seemed to him the undue haste of the trial. He testified before the Senate inquiry into the raid that,

"such speed and hurried action . . . as to render it probable that there was to be no sufficient opportunity to make a full and complete defense . . . struck my mind, and the minds of various other gentlemen whom I met with . . . as being a judicial outrage. . . . It was wholly unlike anything I had ever known or heard in my practice as a lawyer. When some persons had been indicted for kidnapping, in Massachusetts, last September, the court gave Gen. Cushing, their counsel, two or three months after their arraignment before he was required even to file a plea." [44]

But Mr. Andrew was probably ignorant of the Virginia statute governing the case, already quoted. After this lapse of time it is plain that the authorities had ample justification in this statute, and in the popular excitement, in expediting the trial; that the outcome of a deferred trial would have been the same is also obvious. It certainly cannot be successfully maintained that substantial injustice was done to John Brown by the celerity of his conviction. When all was said and done, and the trial finished, John Brown expressed his opinion in the following words: "I feel entirely satisfied with the treatment I have received on my trial. Considering all the circumstances, it has been more generous than I expected." [45] It remains to add the testimony of Daniel W. Voor-

GUILTY BEFORE THE LAW

hees, the great Indiana lawyer and orator, who later became United States Senator from that State. Mr. Voorhees was present at John Brown's trial, having been summoned by Governor Willard, Cook's brother-in-law, to defend his relative. Of the court procedure he had, in later years, this to say:

"If justly represented by the pen of the historian, it will pass into history as the most temperate and conservative judicial tribunal convened, when all the surrounding circumstances are considered. With perfect calmness, forbearing patience and undisturbed adherence to the law, as known and decided throughout generations, that court arises upon my mind with increased and increasing claims to the respect and veneration of the American people and of the world. Nothing was yielded to outside excitement or popular frenzy." [46]

The question of counsel for John Brown early presented itself. There being no Northern lawyers on hand, in accordance with universal custom, Charles B. Harding, attorney for the State, asked at the first examination that the Magistrates' court assign counsel for the prisoners.[47] Charles J. Faulkner and Lawson Botts were designated. Mr. Faulkner asked to be relieved, because he resented the criticisms by the prisoner of his and Mr. Botts's appointment. Having helped to end the raid by force, he had, moreover, freely expressed his opinion of the raiders and their deserts, besides which, he had important professional engagements elsewhere. Mr. Faulkner's serving through the preliminary examination was insisted on; after that he withdrew, to bear public witness in the next month that he had never in the course of his professional career "witnessed an examination which was entered upon and conducted with more deliberation and decorum and with a more sacred regard to all the requirements, which the humane system of our criminal laws throws around the life and liberty of the accused, than was extended to those wicked disturbers of our peace." [48]

Mr. Botts felt it his duty to carry on the case, and Thomas C. Green, mayor of Charlestown, was appointed by the court to take Mr. Faulkner's place. Both of these counsel were able lawyers of standing, Mr. Botts being thirty-six years old and Mr. Green in his thirty-ninth year. The latter was afterwards for fourteen years a distinguished judge of the West Virginia Supreme Court of Appeals, while Mr. Botts gave his life for the Confederacy at the second Bull Run. There can be no doubt that in Messrs. Green and Botts,[49] John Brown had assigned to him far abler counsel than would have been given to the ordinary malefactor.

His friends in the North had not forgotten him, however. On the day the news of the raid was received, John W. Le Barnes, of Boston, engaged, at his own expense, a young lawyer of Athol, Massachusetts, George H. Hoyt, and asked him to go to Harper's Ferry ostensibly as counsel to John Brown, but really as a spy, to see if it would be possible to rescue the prisoners. Mr. Hoyt's instructions were,

"first, to watch and be able to report proceedings, to see and talk with Brown, and be able to communicate with his friends anything Brown might want to say; and second, to send me [Le Barnes] an accurate and detailed account of the military situation at Charlestown, the number and distribution of troops, the location and defences of the jail, and nature of the approaches to the town and jail, the opportunities for a sudden attack, and the means of retreat, with the location and situation of the room in which Brown is confined, and all other particulars that might enable friends to consult as to some plan of attempt at rescue."

Le Barnes chose Hoyt because, although twenty-one years of age, he looked not over nineteen, and was physically of fragile appearance. His very youth and evident lack of worldly experience would, Le Barnes thought, make it impossible for any one to suspect him of ulterior motives, if he appeared at Charlestown. Dr. Samuel G. Howe, when consulted by both men, doubted the wisdom of the scheme; but Le Barnes persisting and giving him seventy-five dollars, Hoyt set forth,[50] little dreaming that upon his frail shoulders would shortly rest the burden of the whole defence of John Brown. His inexperience told against him in Charlestown. He had not been there an hour before his very youth had aroused the suspicions of Andrew Hunter, the special prosecutor of the State of Virginia. Knowing full well that Massachusetts had no need to rely on callow striplings when skilled legal talent was in order, he shrewdly inferred that something else was in the wind, and, but for Judge Parker's magnanimity,

GUILTY BEFORE THE LAW   485

would have excluded Hoyt from participation in Brown's trial as incompetent to practise in the courts of Virginia. "A beardless boy came in last night as Brown's counsel," reported Hunter to Governor Wise on October 28. "I think he is a spy. There are divers other strangers here. . . . They are watched closely."[51] But the watch set upon the "beardless boy" was not close enough to prevent his communicating freely with the client to whom he had so unexpectedly attached himself, and he wasted no time in acquainting Brown with the real purpose of his unannounced arrival.[52]

Brown's legal advisers were called upon to joust with two prosecutors for the State. One of these was the regular commonwealth's attorney, Charles Harding, whose notorious dissipation made it impossible for the State really to entrust to him the prosecution of so important a case. Usually intoxicated, he knew but little of what was going on behind the scenes, Governor Wise giving his directions for the conduct of affairs to Andrew Hunter, and completely ignoring the commonwealth's attorney. To Hunter, Harding was a "pestiferous little prosecutor,"[53] whom he longed to have out of the way. "When Harding began to speak, if you shut your eyes and listened, for the first few minutes you would think Patrick Henry had returned to earth; after that he dwindled away into ineptitudes,"—is the recollection of one who knew him well.[54] During the trial he frequently fell asleep as the result of his libations. Of a different type was Andrew Hunter, a man of distinguished bearing, a vigorous Southern personality, handsome face and undoubted ability. Deeply impressed with the importance of the trial, he prosecuted John Brown with marked aggressiveness, yielding no point and fighting every moment, often with some bombast, but without, said Mr. Voorhees, "a single tone of malevolence or exasperation."[55] Mr. Hunter sincerely felt that, in view of the public temper, no time was to be lost; he wanted Brown condemned and executed within ten days. "The Judge," Mr. Hunter wrote to Governor Wise, "is for observing all the judicial decencies; so am I, but at double quick time. . . . Stephens will hardly be fit for trial. He will probably die of his wounds if we don't hang him promptly."[56]

With Charlestown all agog and crowded with newspapermen, militia and armed citizens, John Brown and his four fellow prisoners, Coppoc, Stevens, Copeland and Green, took, on October 25, the first of their short pilgrimages from the jail to the court-house diagonally opposite, which they were to make historic. Its venerable air, the distinctively Southern character of its architecture, made it then, as now, an impressive structure. A gaping mob watched in silence as, between two lines of militia, the Yankee prisoners took their way. For John Brown and Stevens, though carried later, on this occasion walked the brief distance, the former with head erect and defiant bearing. "His confinement has not at all tamed the daring of his spirit; his height, as he stood erect, appeared to be full six feet; his figure rather slender and wiry," — so telegraphed the *Herald* correspondent.[57] Brown's eyes were swollen; the marks of bruises and contusions were plain enough. Stevens's terrible wounds were so evident, and his inability to walk unsupported so pitiful, that, anxious as the crowd was for these men's blood, there was not a hostile demonstration as they entered the crowded, down-at-the-heel court-room, reeking with tobacco smoke and looking as if it were familiar with every kind of being save the scrub-woman. John Brown, manacled to Coppoc, found no trace of pity in the faces of the crowd he beheld, nor in those of the eight magistrates forming the court of examination to which the prisoners were now presented by the sheriff.

"Sundry witnesses," so read the minutes, "were examined, and the Court being unanimously of opinion that the Prisoners are Guilty of the offence with which they stand charged, it is ordered and considered by the Court that they be sent on to the Circuit Court of this County for trial according to Law."[58] Behind this brief record lies one of the dramatic incidents of the trial, for when the court, before assigning to the prisoners Messrs. Faulkner and Botts, asked whether they had counsel, John Brown of Osawatomie rose feebly from his seat and, with his usual vigor of utterance, his undaunted courage and indomitable spirit, thus addressed, not the court but his countrymen, amid the most profound silence and attention of all who heard:

THE PRISON, GUARD-HOUSE, AND COURT-HOUSE, CHARLESTOWN, WEST VIRGINIA
(The Prison is on the extreme left)

"Virginians, I did not ask for any quarter at the time I was taken. I did not ask to have my life spared. The Governor of the State of Virginia tendered me his assurance that I should have a fair trial; but, under no circumstances whatever will I be able to have a fair trial. If you seek my blood, you can have it at any moment, without this mockery of a trial. I have had no counsel; I have not been able to advise with any one. I know nothing about the feelings of my fellow prisoners, and am utterly unable to attend in any way to my own defence. My memory don't serve me: my health is insufficient, although improving. There are mitigating circumstances that I would urge in our favor, if a fair trial is to be allowed us: but if we are to be forced with a mere form — a trial for execution — you might spare yourselves that trouble. I am ready for my fate. I do not ask a trial. I beg for no mockery of a trial — no insult — nothing but that which conscience gives, or cowardice would drive you to practise. I ask again to be excused from the mockery of a trial. I do not even know what the special design of this examination is. I do not know what is to be the benefit of it to the Commonwealth. I have now little further to ask, other than that I may not be foolishly insulted only as cowardly barbarians insult those who fall into their power."[59]

When asked if he would accept Messrs. Faulkner and Botts as counsel, he replied: "I wish for counsel if I am to have a trial, but if I am to have nothing but the mockery of a trial, as I said, I do not care anything about counsel — it is unnecessary to trouble any gentleman with that duty."[60] He declined to say whether he would or would not accept the counsel offered, but Stevens chose them, and they were duly assigned, in the face of John Brown's assertion that he had sent for some persons in the North whose names he could not then recall. He was but little interested when the witnesses, Colonel Washington and seven others, testified to their knowledge of the raid. Still less was he moved when the presiding justice, Colonel Braxton Davenport, announced the decision of the court. His bearing was as impressive as before when, again manacled, he and his fellow prisoners left the dingy court-room with its five or six hundred spectators, and took their way back to the jail. That same afternoon their comrade Cook was arrested in Pennsylvania, thanks to the reward offered by Virginia.[61]

The next move in the judicial machinery was the process of indictment. At two o'clock the examining magistrates reported their conclusions. Judge Parker at once charged the

Grand Jury ably and dispassionately, and having heard from excellent authority of a deliberate plot to lynch the prisoners, he added to his charge a warning against any such conduct, which, he declared, would be disgraceful to the State and nothing else than murder, for which its perpetrators might themselves incur the extreme penalty of the law. Thereafter no talk of lynching was heard, and Judge Parker was deservedly congratulated far and wide for his high-minded and courageous stand. The Grand Jury then retired with the State's witnesses. Before it were rehearsed anew their oft-told stories, and adjournment time came before they were finished. At noon on the next day, Wednesday, the Grand Jury reported its true bill against each of the prisoners on three counts — treason to the commonwealth, conspiring with slaves to commit treason, and murder; they being "evil-minded and traitorous persons," "not having the fear of God before their eyes, but being moved and seduced by the false and malignant counsel of other evil and traitorous persons and the instigations of the devil,"[62] — so runs the indictment.

Those instigated by the Evil One were soon brought into court, — Stevens on a mattress, making, because of his difficulty in breathing, the impression of a dying man. Captain Avis, the jailer, when ordered to bring Brown into court, found him in bed and unwilling to arise. "He was accordingly carried into the court-room on a cot," wrote the *Tribune* correspondent. "The prisoner lay most of the time with his eyes closed, and the counterpane drawn close up to his chin. He is evidently not much injured, but is determined to resist the pushing of his trial, by all the means in his power."[63] It was at this time that John Brown arose and made an unavailing plea for delay to Judge Parker:

"I do not intend to detain the court, but barely wish to say, as I have been promised a fair trial, that I am not now in circumstances that enable me to attend a trial, owing to the state of my health. I have a severe wound in the back, or rather in one kidney, which enfeebles me very much. But I am doing well, and I only ask for a very short delay of my trial, and I think I may be able to listen to it; and I merely ask this that, as the saying is 'the devil may have his dues,' no more. I wish to say further that my hearing is impaired and rendered indistinct in consequence of wounds I have about my

GUILTY BEFORE THE LAW

head. I cannot hear distinctly at all; I could not hear what the Court has said this morning. I would be glad to hear what is said on my trial, and am now doing better than I could expect to be under the circumstances. A very short delay would be all I would ask. I do not presume to ask more than a very short delay, so that I may in some degree recover, and be able at least to listen to my trial, and hear what questions are asked of the citizens, and what their answers are. If that could be allowed me, I should be very much obliged." [64]

Judge Parker, dignified and firm, with a singularly stern countenance in marked contrast to his mild and quiet manner, insisted on the arraignment being read before passing upon John Brown's appeal. Both the wounded prisoners were compelled to stand during this solemn performance, Stevens being held up by two bailiffs. Thereupon, both Mr. Hunter and Mr. Harding having opposed the motion for delay, and the jail physician, a Dr. Mason, having testified that John Brown's wounds had affected neither his hearing nor his mind, nor seriously disabled him, the judge refused to postpone his trial. As each of the prisoners had pleaded not guilty and elected to be tried separately, the State had chosen to try the Commander-in-Chief of the defeated Provisional Army first, and the rest of the afternoon was given to choosing the jury. Twenty-four men duly qualified to act as jurors were then selected from a large panel, after being asked the usual question whether they had formed any opinion about the guilt of the prisoners which would disqualify them from giving the offenders a fair trial. Of these twenty-four, John Brown, through his counsel, exercised his right to challenge peremptorily eight; from the remaining sixteen the final twelve were then chosen by lot, and the court adjourned until the next day, after solemnly adjuring the twelve to discuss the case with no one.[65] It is, of course, impossible to believe that the twelve men chosen had not formed any opinion about the case. There were no men in Jefferson County who had not prejudged Brown, and if ever a motion for a change of venue to another county was in order, it was in this case. But his Southern counsel did not attempt it.

On Thursday, when court opened, Mr. Botts surprised prisoner and prosecution alike by reading a telegram from Akron, Ohio, alleging insanity in John Brown's family. Of the plea of insanity which this suggested, John Brown promptly declined to avail himself, as will appear later. But, his counsel having again urged delay, the vigilant prosecutors again opposed, and the judge once more decided that he could see no proper cause for postponement. The indictment being read, the attorneys for the State and Mr. Botts made their opening addresses. It was due to the prisoner, said his chivalrous counsel, to state that he believed himself to be actuated by the highest and noblest feelings that ever coursed through a human breast, and that his instructions were to destroy neither life nor property. Mr. Hunter confined himself to a definition of treason, told of a previous murder in the arsenal grounds for which the murderer was tried and executed, not by the United States but by Virginia, and wound up by begging for a fair and impartial consideration of the case, "without fear or favor. . . . I ask only that the penalty be visited on the prisoner which the law denounces, which reason denounces, which our safety requires, and which the laws of God and man approve." [66] Thereupon began the examination of witnesses.

It was the next morning, Friday, that the "beardless boy" from Boston walked into the court-room and asked to be made an additional counsel for Brown. The astonishment was profound; it increased when Hoyt expressed the wish not to take part in the case at present, and when he was unable to prove that he was actually a member of the Massachusetts Bar, as the suspicious Mr. Hunter asked him to demonstrate. But the just judge was not inclined to quibble. Visiting lawyers from the North were already, as the *Tribune* reported, eulogizing his method of presiding, and were "profuse in praises of his candor and integrity." [67] It was enough for the judge that Mr. Green remembered that his partner had seen letters speaking of Hoyt as a full-fledged attorney. Thereupon the oath was administered [68] and the examination of witnesses continued. By this time the prisoner was taking more interest in his defence. He had drawn up the following suggestions for his counsel:

"We gave to numerous prisoners perfect liberty.
"*Get all their names.*
"We allowed numerous other prisoners to visit their families, to quiet their fears.

"*Get all their names.*

"We allowed the conductor to pass his train over the bridge with all his passengers, I myself crossing the bridge with him, and assuring all the passengers of their perfect safety.

"*Get that conductor's name, and the names of the passengers, so far as may be.*

"We treated all our prisoners with the utmost kindness and humanity.

"*Get all their names, so far as may be.*

"Our orders, from the first and throughout, were, that no unarmed person should be injured, under any circumstances whatever.

"*Prove that by* ALL *the prisoners.*

"We committed no destruction or waste of property.

"*Prove that.*" [69]

The prosecution having rested on Friday afternoon, the defence began. Messrs. Botts and Green followed John Brown's suggestion, and essayed to prove, apparently with a view to mitigating the offence charged, the kindness with which Brown treated his prisoners. This drew from Andrew Hunter the caustic and truthful comment that testimony to Brown's forbearance in not shooting other citizens had no more to do with the case than had the dead languages.

Only on one occasion during the trial did John Brown show emotion. He "cried out" for details, so read the reports, when Harry Hunter narrated the revolting story of William Thompson's slaughter on the Harper's Ferry bridge. It became Andrew Hunter's painful duty to listen to his son's open and unabashed tale of how he and George W. Chambers shot down Thompson, when the latter was unarmed and pleading for his life. It is to the father's credit that he bade his son conceal nothing; but it is doubtful if any father ever listened to a more cold-blooded recital of deliberate killing by his offspring. Yet the audience listened apparently unmoved, while John Brown groaned. Shortly afterward, when the names of several witnesses were called with no response, John Brown excitedly rose to his feet and spoke thus to the keen-eyed judge on the dais above him:

"May it please the Court:—I discover that notwithstanding all the assurances I have received of a fair trial, nothing like a fair trial is to be given me, as it would seem. I gave the names, as soon as I could get them, of the persons I wished to have called as witnesses, and was assured that they would be subpœnaed. I wrote down a memorandum to that effect, saying where those parties were; but it appears that they have not been subpœnaed as far as I can learn; and now I ask, if I am to have anything at all deserving the name and shadow of a fair trial, that this proceeding be deferred until tomorrow morning; for I have no counsel, as I before stated, in whom I feel that I can rely, but I am in hopes counsel may arrive who will attend to seeing that I get the witnesses who are necessary for my defence. I am myself unable to attend to it. I have given all the attention I possibly could to it, but am unable to see or know about them, and can't even find out their names; and I have nobody to do any errands, for my money was all taken when I was sacked and stabbed, and I have not a dime. I had two hundred and fifty or sixty dollars in gold and silver taken from my pocket, and now I have no possible means of getting anybody to go my errands for me, and I have not had all the witnesses subpœnaed. They are not within reach, and are not here. I ask at least until tomorrow morning to have something done, if anything is designed; if not, I am ready for anything that may come up."[70]

"When, upon finding that his witnesses were absent," reported the *Herald's* correspondent,

"Brown rose and denounced his counsel, declaring he had no confidence in them, the indignation of the citizens scarcely knew bounds. He was stigmatized as an ungrateful villain, and some declared he deserved hanging for that act alone. His counsel, Messrs. Botts and Green, had certainly performed the ungrateful task imposed upon them by the Court in an able, faithful and conscientious manner; and only the evening before Brown had told Mr. Botts that he was doing for him even more than he had promised."[71]

No sooner had Brown finished this speech than Mr. Hoyt sprang to his feet, adding greatly to the stir in the court-room, and asking that the case be postponed, because Judge Tilden from Ohio was coming and due that night to aid in the defence. He, himself, was unable to go on alone with Brown's case, for he had but just come from Boston, travelling night and day, had had no time to read the indictment, and was wholly ignorant of the criminal code of Virginia. After asserting that they had done everything possible for their client, Mr. Botts and Mr. Green announced that they could no longer act in behalf of the prisoner, since he had declared that he had no confidence in them. Judge Parker at once replied that he would not compel them to stay in the case, and that he therefore granted Mr. Hoyt's request and adjourned the trial until the next morning

GUILTY BEFORE THE LAW

at ten. Thus, to his utter amazement and inward consternation, the "beardless boy," the spy sent to survey the ground, found himself charged with the sole responsibility for the conduct of a case of which he knew little or nothing, under a code and procedure with which he was entirely unfamiliar, and this in a trial which the hostile New York *Herald* had four days before characterized as the most notable in the last half-century "in point of national importance." The trial of Aaron Burr had excited less intense feeling; the *Herald* even felt that the life and death of the whole Republic was involved. The situation in which the inexperienced Mr. Hoyt now found himself might have tried the soul of a veteran and skilled practitioner; it undoubtedly blanched his beardless cheeks. But it is to his everlasting credit that he bent manfully to his task.

Mr. Botts put his notes, his office and his services at Hoyt's command, and sat up with him the greater part of the night.[72] When Judge Parker took his seat on the bench the next morning, there was reinforcement for Brown's inexperienced counsel, — not Judge Tilden, as had been expected, but Samuel Chilton, of Washington, and Hiram Griswold, of Cleveland. Mr. Chilton's arrival was due to John A. Andrew, of Boston, who first asked Judge Montgomery Blair, of Washington, to act as Brown's defender, guaranteeing him adequate compensation. Judge Blair being unwilling to appear, Mr. Andrew agreed to his substitution of Mr. Chilton.[73] John Brown himself had written to Judge Daniel R. Tilden, of Cleveland, and Judge Thomas Russell, of Boston, asking them to become his legal advisers. Judge Russell came in person, but not until the day of sentence; Judge Tilden sent Mr. Griswold in his place. To Tilden and Russell, John Brown wrote that, without such counsel, "neither the facts in our case can come before the world; nor can *we* have the benefit of such facts (as might be considered mitigating in the view of others) upon our trial. . . . Do not send an ultra Abolitionist." [74]

Both Chilton and Griswold asked for a delay of a few hours, in order that they might be better equipped for their tasks, but the inexorable judge ordered the trial to proceed. The prisoner had had able counsel and ample defence; he had chosen to make a change, for which the responsibility was on his own shoulders. If this were the only case before the court, he would at once grant the request; but the nearness of the end of the term, and the other cases to be disposed of, necessitated prompt action, in justice to the prisoners and to the State. Mr. Hoyt then resumed the defence along the same lines as Messrs. Botts and Green, hoping to prove through those witnesses who had been prisoners in the engine house the absence of any malicious intent. John Brown himself now took a hand in examining the witnesses from his cot, without objection from any one to this unusual procedure.

In the afternoon session, a new policy was adopted, Mr. Chilton submitting a motion that the prosecution be compelled to elect one count of the indictment and abandon the others. His argument, supported by a couple of hastily gathered citations, was that different descriptions of treason could not be united in the same indictment, as was the case there. That it was a grave hardship upon the prisoner to defend himself at one and the same time against three such distinct charges as murder, treason and inciting slaves to rebel, Mr. Chilton also pointed out. The judge, after hearing spirited replies from Hunter and Harding, ruled that, as the trial had been begun under the indictment, it must continue; that the only remedy now was to move an arrest of judgment at its conclusion. "The very fact that the offence can be charged in different counts, varying the language and circumstances, is based upon the idea that distinct offences may be charged in the same indictment," ruled Judge Parker. "The prisoners are to be tried on the various counts as if they were various transactions. There is no legal objection against charging various crimes in the same indictment. The practice has been to put a party upon election where the prisoner would be embarrassed in his defence; but that is not the law." * In this contention Judge Parker was later upheld by the full bench of the Virginia Court of Appeals.[75]

---

* The decision of Judge Parker is in accord with the law of New York State to-day, which holds that where the same acts constitute different crimes, they may be set out in the indictment in different counts. Thus an indictment may unite burglary in the third degree, petit larceny and receiving stolen property. See People vs. Stock, 21 Misc. 147; People vs. Wilson, 151 N. Y. 403. In People vs. Austin, 1 Park Criminal Reports, 154, it was held that "the right of election is confined to cases where the indictment contains charges which are actually distinct and grew out of different transactions."

This argument was the crucial point in the trial of John Brown. The court now pressed the lawyers to argue the case at once. John Brown's counsel protested, Hoyt because he had worked the previous night until he fell unconscious from exhaustion, and had had but ten hours sleep in the last five days and nights. Mr. Hunter battled, of course, against any delay, and the court, taking a position which would seem strange indeed in a modern murder trial, — that the jurors, having been in the box three days, were entitled to early release, — ordered the prosecution to begin their summing up. Mr. Harding did so by dwelling on the absurdity of John Brown's claim that he should have been treated according to the rules of warfare, when he was merely in command of a band of murderers and thieves. The court then adjourned over Sunday, to Andrew Hunter's vexation, for he had insisted that the trial be concluded that night. At the time and later, Hunter accused John Brown — the "crafty old fiend," he called him — of feigning illness on this day to gain time.[76] When the court had reassembled on Saturday afternoon, word came from the jail, according to Hunter,

"that Brown was too sick to appear that evening. I suspected the ruse, and at once suggested to the court to have the jail physician summoned to examine whether he was too sick and to report. This was done, and the physician, who was Dr. Mason, promptly reported that he was not too sick and that he was feigning. On my motion the court directed him to be brought into court on a cot. . . . The trial went on to a certain extent, but every effort was made to protract it. I resisted it, but at last, late in the evening, the Judge called me up and said he thought we had better agree, to avoid all further cavil at our proceedings, to let the case be adjourned over until Monday, which was done. Brown did not require to be carried back to jail that evening; he walked back. After the adjournment was procured, he was well enough to walk."[77]

On Sunday, Hoyt reported to his employer, Le Barnes, that Mr. Chilton and Mr. Griswold had been closeted with John Brown for three or four hours, that,

"Brown is well pleased with what has transpired; is perfectly satisfied, and more than all the rest, seems to be inspired with a truly noble Resignation." "I confess," Hoyt continues, "I did not know which most to admire, the thorough honor and admirable qualities of the brave old border soldier, or the uncontaminated simplicity of the man. My friend John Brown is an astonishing character. The people about here, while determined to have him die for his alleged offences, generally concede and applaud the conscientiousness, the honor, and the supreme bravery of the man." [78]

On Monday, Mr. Griswold and Mr. Chilton argued at length and as ably as it was possible under the circumstances, and at half-past one Mr. Hunter concluded the case by saying to the jury, "Administer it [justice] according to your law — acquit the prisoner if you can; but if justice requires you by your verdict to take his life, stand by that column [of justice] uprightly, but strongly, and let retributive justice, if he is guilty, send him before that Maker who will settle the question forever and ever."

Three-quarters of an hour later, the jury filed back into court to answer the question whether the prisoner at the bar was guilty or not guilty. Of all the men in that stifling courtroom, — and the crowd not only filled every inch of space around the prisoner, but jammed the wide entrance-hall and even stood on the entrance-steps in the hope of catching a word from within, — the least moved was John Brown, as indomitable and iron-willed as ever in his life. When, in reply to the clerk of the court, the foreman answered "Aye" to the question whether John Brown was guilty of treason, and conspiring and advising with slaves and others to rebel, and murder in the first degree, that leader of men said not a word. Turning, he readjusted the covers of his pallet and stretched himself upon it as if he had no interest in the proceedings. Indeed, if he had expressed any interest, it would doubtless have been jubilation. For by then John Brown had dreamed his dream and seen his vision. There had come to him, as by a revelation, the knowledge that through the portals of death alone lay the way to the success denied in life. His eagle eye had pierced the veil of the future; it was as if it had been given to him to see tramping over the hills of Virginia those blue-coated hosts to whom, two years later, John Brown was neither lunatic, nor fanatic, nor murderer. He had become, in his own words, "fully persuaded that I am worth inconceivably more to *hang* than for any other purpose," [79] and the longer he lay in his prison cell and wore his chains, the more ready was he for the sacrifice and the atonement. His only

GUILTY BEFORE THE LAW

fear had been that all the effect of his work would be undone by a pronunciamento that he was insane.

It is to the credit of the Charlestown crowd and of Virginia that not a single sound of elation or of triumph assailed the dignity of the court, when the jury sealed Brown's doom. In solemn silence the crowd heard Mr. Chilton make his formal motion for an arrest of judgment because of errors in the indictment and in the verdict, and it filed out equally silent when Judge Parker, owing to the exhaustion of the counsel on both sides, ordered the motion to stand over until the next day. The judge lost, however, not a moment in beginning the trial of Edwin Coppoc, for a jury was sworn that afternoon.

On November 1 the argument on the motion was heard, John Brown again lying on his cot, though now fully able to walk. Judge Parker reserved his decision, but only for twenty-four hours. For on November 2 came the final act in the court-room. Judge Parker afterward wrote:

"I went into court at the usual early hour with an opinion I had prepared the preceding night, in which I had at length stated the reasons for over-ruling the objections which Brown's counsel had made to judgment being rendered, intending to pronounce it so soon as the court was opened; but a jury for the trial of Coppoc . . . were in their seats, and as the same objections, or some of them, might be made in this case as had been presented in that of Brown, I refrained from reading the opinion. I did this because by the Virginia practice a jury in a criminal case were held to be judges of the law as well as triers of facts, and I would do nothing to prejudice this their right. For this reason I did not overrule Brown's motion in arrest until late on the day, after a verdict was rendered in the case of Coppoc." [80]

Again there was a thrill in the crowded court-room, when the clerk asked John Brown whether he had anything to say why sentence should not be pronounced upon him. And well the crowd might be stirred, for what it was now to hear from the lips of the man for whose life it thirsted must forever remain on the list of great American speeches,[81] an utterance worthy not merely of the man who voiced it, but of the mighty cause of human freedom for which he struck so powerful a blow. Drawing himself up to his full stature, with flashing eagle eyes and calm, clear and distinct tones, John

Brown again addressed, not the men who surrounded him, but the whole body of his countrymen, North, South, East and West:*

"I have, may it please the Court, a few words to say.

"In the first place, I deny everything but what I have all along admitted: of a design on my part to free slaves. I intended certainly to have made a clean thing of that matter, as I did last winter, when I went into Missouri and there took slaves without the snapping of a gun on either side,† moving them through the country, and finally leaving them in Canada. I designed to have done the same thing again on a larger scale. That was all I intended. I never did intend murder, or treason, or the destruction of property, or to excite or incite slaves to rebellion, or to make insurrection.

"I have another objection, and that is that it is unjust that I should suffer such a penalty. Had I interfered in the manner which I admit, and which I admit has been fairly proved — for I admire the truthfulness and candor of the greater portion of the witnesses who have testified in this case — had I so interfered in behalf of the rich, the powerful, the intelligent, the so-called great, or in behalf of any of their friends, either father, mother, brother, sister, wife or children, or any of that class, and suffered and sacrificed what I have in this interference, it would have been all right. Every man in this Court would have deemed it an act worthy of reward rather than punishment.

"This Court acknowledges, too, as I suppose, the validity of the law of God. I see a book kissed, which I suppose to be the Bible, or at least the New Testament, which teaches me that all things whatsoever I would that men should do to me, I should do even so to them. It teaches me, further, to remember them that are in bonds as bound with them. I endeavored to act up to that instruction. I say I am yet too young to understand that God is any respecter of persons. I believe that to have interfered as I have done, as I have always freely admitted I have done, in behalf of His despised poor, I did no wrong, but right. Now, if it is deemed necessary that I should forfeit my life for the furtherance of the ends of justice, and mingle my blood further with the blood of my children

---

* An eye-witness, Judge Thomas Russell, wrote in the Boston *Traveller*, November 5, 1859, that John Brown "delivered the remarkable speech which you have just read, speaking with perfect calmness of voice and mildness of manner, winning the respect of all for his courage and firmness. His self-possession was wonderful, because his sentence, at this time, was unexpected, and his remarks were entirely unprepared."

† This statement is hard to understand in view of Stevens's killing of Cruise. Brown may have intended to speak here only of that party of raiders that he himself commanded.

GUILTY BEFORE THE LAW

and with the blood of millions in this slave country whose rights are disregarded by wicked, cruel, and unjust enactments, I say, let it be done.

"Let me say one word further. I feel entirely satisfied with the treatment I have received on my trial. Considering all the circumstances, it has been more generous than I expected. But I feel no consciousness of guilt. I have stated from the first what was my intention, and what was not. I never had any design against the liberty of any person, nor any disposition to commit treason or incite slaves to rebel or make any general insurrection. I never encouraged any man to do so, but always discouraged any idea of that kind.

"Let me say, also, in regard to the statements made by some of those who were connected with me, I hear it has been stated by some of them that I have induced them to join me. But the contrary is true. I do not say this to injure them, but as regretting their weakness. Not one but joined me of his own accord, and the greater part at their own expense. A number of them I never saw, and never had a word of conversation with, till the day they came to me, and that was for the purpose I have stated.

"Now, I have done."[82]

With all solemnity, Judge Parker then pronounced the sentence of death, and fixed Friday, the 2d of December, as the date of execution, specifying that the hanging should be public, and recording his belief that no reasonable doubt could exist as to John Brown's guilt. But, in allowing him a whole month more of life, the judge gave him that opportunity to influence public opinion in the North in his favor, of which he so admirably availed himself. It was a bitter disappointment to Hunter that Judge Parker permitted the condemned man to live so long. Indeed, one of the leading men in the county, when informed in advance by Mr. Parker that he would give John Brown thirty days prior to his execution, declared that then there would be a grave tumult in the courtroom; that the people "would tear Brown to pieces before he could be taken from the building." This somewhat disturbed the judge, who notified the jailer, Captain Avis, what to expect, but declined to let soldiers into the court-room; for he could not get over the jurist's righteous repugnance to seeing "armed men in a court of justice." When the sentence was pronounced, there was again perfect order in the court-room; one man clapped his hands, but was promptly suppressed, the citizens expressing due regret, afterward, at this breach of decorum. The judge then ordered all present to retain their seats until the prisoner was removed. There was prompt obedience, and John Brown reached his cell unharmed, without even hearing a taunt.[83] In view of the public fears and excitement, such self-control does great credit to this deeply stirred Virginia community.

With John Brown sentenced to be hanged, Governor Wise became immediately the recipient of much individual and journalistic advice as to what course he should pursue. The Joint Committee of the Virginia General Assembly reported, the following January, that,

"a great many letters were received by the Governor from citizens of Northern states, urging him to pardon the offenders, or to commute this punishment. Some of them were written in a spirit of menace, threatening his life and that of members of his family. . . . Others gave notice of the purpose of resolute bands of desperadoes to fire the principal towns and cities of Virginia. . . . Others appealed to his clemency, to his magnanimity, and to his hopes of future political promotion as . . . motives for his intervention in behalf of the convicted felons. Another class (and among these were letters from men of national reputation) besought him to pardon them on the ground of public policy."[84]

But even in the South there were two voices, those that were for execution of the sentence, and those that wished mercy to be shown. "Like the neighboring population, we go in for a summary vengeance," said the Savannah *Republican*. "A terrible example should be made, that will stand out as a beacon-light in all time to come."[85] "Virginia and the South are ready to face all the consequences of the execution of old Brown and his confederates," wrote the Richmond *Whig:*

"Though it convert the whole Northern people, without an exception, into furious, armed abolition invaders, yet *old Brown will be hung!* That is the stern and irreversible decree, not only of the authorities of Virginia, but of the PEOPLE of Virginia, without a dissenting voice. And, therefore, Virginia, and the people of Virginia, will treat with the contempt they deserve, all the *craven appeals* of Northern men in behalf of old Brown's pardon. *The miserable old traitor and murderer belongs to the gallows*, and the gallows *will* have its own."[86]

GUILTY BEFORE THE LAW

These sentiments were shared in the North by the New York *Observer*, the organ of the Presbyterians, and the *Herald*, of course, could see no reason why the law should not claim its victims.

But there were other voices in both sections. Thus the New York *Journal of Commerce*, rabidly pro-slavery and bitter in its denunciations of Brown, thought that:

"To hang a fanatic is to make a martyr of him and fledge another brood of the same sort. Better send these creatures to the penitentiary, and so make of them miserable felons. In the present state of the country, the latter course is, no doubt, the wisest; and if those men in Virginia who desire to apply the Lynch code to the helpless wretches now awaiting trial, reflect for a moment, they will perceive the folly of such a course. They would not only disgrace their State, but place another weapon in the hands of their enemies. The murder of Joe Smith did not check Mormonism, but rather gave it a new impetus; nor would the hanging of scores of Abolitionists have any better effect. Monsters are hydra-headed, and decapitation only quickens vitality, and power of reproduction." [87]

The *Liberator*, which was the particular abomination of the *Journal of Commerce*, was for once of the same opinion. "It will be a terribly losing day for all Slavedom," wrote Mr. Garrison, "when John Brown and his associates are brought to the gallows." [88] From the Berryville, Virginia, *Clarke Journal* came this wise warning:

"As a Christian people we are bound to respect the motives of the sincere and conscientious, however mistaken. We do not care to weaken our position by shedding the blood of such and giving them no time for repentance, if we can free ourselves from their annoyance by their confinement, as we would confine a mad dog. But blood for blood has been shed — more blood on their side than on ours. It is now only a question of policy as to the further proceeding. Will it do more good to go on shedding blood while we can find any to shed, or to stop now and confine the rest for life? Our judgment is — and we are bound to give it, if every subscriber stops his paper, as we have been threatened to some extent — in favor of the latter. More good can be done, as a pure question of policy, by staying the effusion of blood. Now, if this be treason, make the most of it. We will be as ready to die for a conviction as John Brown. As a pure question of policy, we have most to gain by a moderate, placable, conservative course. . . . But now the deed is done, and blood has been shed in return, and a few are fugitives and outcasts on the earth, and the rest are in chains and dungeons. How much more can a generous, magnanimous people ask? *How will it appear in the eyes of* the world, the unfavoring world to slavery, *to ask more — even to the last drop of their blood?* We must remember that but a small part of the Christian and civilized world are on our side in regard to Slavery." [89]

A Kentucky newspaper, the Frankfort *Yeoman*, held similar views:

"If old John Brown is executed, there will be thousands to dip their handkerchiefs in his blood; relics of the martyr will be paraded throughout the North . . . and Governor Wise would be compared to Julian the Apostate or to Graham of Claverhouse. . . . If a European despot . . . can strike the chains from thousand of captives . . . think of the shame that must rest upon the commonwealth of Virginia . . . if her security demands and receives the blood of one old brave bad man." [90]

Among the thousands of other letters prophesying, threatening, imploring or arguing for John Brown's life, none was more interesting than that from Fernando Wood, the notorious New York politician, soon to be chosen for the third time mayor of the city in which he wrote:

"Your proceedings and conduct thus far in the matter of the conspiracy at Harper's Ferry meets with general approval, and elicits commendation from your enemies. The firmness and moderation which has characterized your course cannot be too highly applauded and *today* you stand higher than any other man in the Union. Now, my friend, dare you do a bold thing and temper 'justice with Mercy'? Have you nerve enough to send Brown to the States Prison instead of hanging him? Brown is looked upon here as the mere crazy or foolhardy emissary of other men. Circumstances create a sympathy for him even with the most ultra friends of the South. I am of this latter class, as by recent speeches you may have observed. No southern man could go further than myself in behalf of southern rights, but yet were I the Governor of Virginia, Brown should not be hung, though Seward should be if I could catch him. And in such a course my conduct would be governed by sound policy. The South will gain by showing that it can be magnanimous to a fanatic in its power. We who fight its battles can gain largely by pointing to such an instance of 'chivalry.'" [91]

Governor Wise's reply is so characteristic of the man, and states so clearly the reasons which actuated him in refusing

GUILTY BEFORE THE LAW

to urge clemency or mitigation of sentence upon the Legislature, — which alone had the power to so act in treason cases, although the Governor's language conveys a different impression, — that it merits consideration here:

RICHMOND VA Nov. 4th, 1859.

MY DEAR SIR, — I have duly received and weighed every word of your letter. I give it all credit for good motive and good morals, and as suggesting what perhaps is good policy. Now, listen to me, for my mind is inflexibly made up.

Had I reached Harpers Ferry before these men were captured (and I would have reached there in time, had I been forwarded as I ought to have been from Washington & the relay house), I would have proclaimed martial law, have stormed them in the quickest possible time, have given them no quarter, and if any had survived, I would have tried and executed them under sentence of Court Martial. But I was too late. The prisoners were captives, and I then determined to protect them to the uttermost of my power, and I did protect them with my own person. I escorted them to prison and placed around them such a force as to overawe Lynch-law. Every comfort was given them by my orders. And they have been scrupulously afforded a fair and speedy trial, with every opportunity of defence for crimes, which were openly perpetrated before the eyes of hundreds and as openly confessed. They could escape conviction only by technical exceptions, and the chances for these they had to a greater degree by the expedition of prosecution. And the crimes deliberately done by them are of the deepest and darkest kind which can be committed against our people. Brown, the chief leader, has been legally and fairly tried and convicted and admits the humanity of his treatment as a prisoner, the truth of the indictment and the truthfulness of the witnesses against him. He has been allowed excess of counsel, and the freedom of speech beyond any prisoner known to me in our trials. It was impossible not to convict him. He is sentenced to be hung; — that is the sentence of a mild code humanely adjudged and requires no duty from me except to see that it be executed. I have to sign no death warrant. If the Executive interposes at all, it is to pardon. And to pardon him I have received petitions, prayers, threats, from almost every free State in the Union. From honest patriotic men like yourself, many of them, I am warned that hanging will make him a Martyr. Ah! — Will it? — Why? — The obvious answer to that question shows me above anything the necessity for hanging him. You ask: — "Have you nerve enough to send Brown to States Prison for life instead of hanging him?" — Yes, if I did n't think he ought to be hung and that I would be inexcusable for mitigating his punishment. I could do it without flinching, without a quiver of a muscle against a universal clamor for his life. But was it ever known before that it would be impolitic for a state to execute her laws against the highest crimes without bringing down upon herself the vengeance of a public sentiment outside of her limits and hostile to her laws? — Is it so that it is wisely said to her that she had better spare a murderer, a robber, a traitor, because public sentiment elsewhere will glorify an insurrectionist with Martyrdom? If so it is time to do execution upon him and all like him. And I therefore say to you firmly that I have precisely the nerve enough to let him be executed with the certainty of his condemnation. He shall be executed as the law sentences him, and his body shall be delivered over to surgeons, and await the resurrection without a grave in our soil. I have shown him all the mercy which humanity can claim.

Yours truly
HENRY A. WISE.[92]

HON. F. WOOD.

This last threat Governor Wise thought better of later on.* But his purpose not to interfere with the court's decree, or to use his influence with the Legislature, was not to be changed. Two days after his answer to Fernando Wood, he wrote to Andrew Hunter, at Charlestown: "I wish you to understand, confidentially, that I will not reprieve or pardon one man *now* after the letters I have rec'd from the North."[93] After Brown's death, in a message to the Legislature of December 5, 1859, Governor Wise officially put on paper more elaborate reasons for his position.[94] He admitted in this message, however, as to the raid, that,

"causes and influences lie behind it more potent far than the little band of desperadoes who were sent ahead to kindle the sparks of a

---

* Among the letters received by Governor Wise was one from Dr. Lewis A. Sayre, of New York, suggesting dissection as part of the punishment; and the following ghoulish note from a Virginia professor to Andrew Hunter is worthy of preservation: —

RICHMOND, Nov. 1, 1859. DEAR SIR, — We desire, if Brown and his coadjutors are executed, to add their heads to the collection in our museum. If the transference of the bodies will not exceed a cost of five dollars each, we should also be glad to have them. This request will, of course, not interfere with any clemency which it may be found desirable to extend to those convicted. Attention to this request will confer a great favor.

A. E. PETICOLAS, M. D.
Prof Anat at Med.
College of Va.

These two letters are respectively in the Tatham Collection and in the Massachusetts Historical Society.

GUILTY BEFORE THE LAW

general conflagration. . . . Indeed, if the miserable convicts were the only conspirators against our peace and safety, we might have forgiven their offences and constrained them only by the grace of pardon. But an entire social and sectional sympathy has incited their crimes and now rises in rebellion and insurrection, to the height of sustaining and justifying their enormity."

Obviously, if the "miserable convicts" were merely the petty tools of a great and monstrous "rebellion and insurrection," the Governor's flight of rhetoric to Fernando Wood was uncalled for; it was then perfectly proper for Virginia to take cognizance in her actions of public sentiment elsewhere, and to be guided by her interpretation of it in her punishment of those Abolition "tools." It has never been considered impolitic for a State to have due regard for outside sentiment when that was, as Governor Wise insisted in the case of Virginia, menacing its very existence.

As to the appeal to his magnanimity, the Governor said in this message: "I know of no magnanimity which is so inhumane, . . . which would turn felons like these, proud and defiant in their guilt, loose again on a border already torn by a fanatical and sectional strife which threatens the liberties of the white even more than it does the bondage of the black race." Then there was the question of making a martyr of Brown. To this the Governor's reply was:

"To hang would be no more martyrdom than to incarcerate the fanatic. The sympathy would have asked on and on for liberation, and to nurse and soothe him whilst life lasted, in prison. His state of health would have been heralded weekly, as from a palace, visitors would have come affectedly reverent, to see the *shorn* felon at hard labor, the work of his hands would have been sought as holy relics, and his parti-colored dress would have become, perhaps, a uniform for the next band of marauders." *

* Mr. F. E. Spinner, of Worcester, used to tell of one occasion when Governor Wise and Senator Mason heard Thaddeus Stevens, the Pennsylvania Congressman, endorse Governor Wise's action. At the Relay House, the Southerners took seats opposite Mr. Spinner and Congressman Stevens. As the former related it: "They said things that displeased us. I said to Mr. Stevens that it was a pity that Brown had not been sentenced to prison for life, instead of being made a martyr by hanging. Mr. Stevens had evidently longed for an opportunity to give the two eminent Virginia statesmen a shot in return, and turned to me and said in a loud voice: 'No, sir, he ought to have been hung for attempting to capture Virginia with a dozen white men, five negroes and an old cow.' 'Why, sir,' he said, 'he ought to have taken at least *thirty men to have conquered Virginia.*'"

A pertinent answer to this is that there was such a thing possible as solitary confinement, and that not every jail permits the recording of its prisoners' health or doings, or their being the object of pilgrimage. In brief, the Governor's logic is not convincing. After the lapse of fifty years, it still appears bad tactics and policy to have made a martyr of John Brown, save on the theory that secession and war were inevitable and might as well be hastened.* Nothing could so have solidified Northern sentiment just at that moment as John Brown on the scaffold; nor made men in that section who had, heretofore, refused to take sides, search their hearts and decide whether they were for or against human bondage. From that time, no one could get away from the slavery and, soon, the secession issue, try as he might. It is idle, of course, to expect that Governor Wise should have foreseen the John Brown song. Yet, afterwards, when leading his gallant troops against their conquerors from the North, the Governor might sometimes have wished that his enemies were not profiting so much by the mighty battle hymn in regard to John Brown's soul. For it sent them, thrilling and inspired, to many a battlefield, as ready to die for freedom as had been the man whose name was on their lips.

There was still one more reason for clemency urged on Brown's behalf — his alleged insanity. The despatch received on the second day of his trial by his counsel, Lawson Botts, read thus:

Akron, Ohio, Thursday,
Oct. 27, 1859.

To C. J. Faulkner and Lawson Botts:

John Brown, leader of the insurrection at Harper's Ferry, and several of his family, have resided in this county many years. Insanity is hereditary in that family. His mother's sister died with it, and a daughter of that sister has been two years in a lunatic asylum. A son and daughter of his mother's brother have also been confined in the lunatic asylum, and another son of that brother is now insane and under close restraint. These facts can be conclusively proven

---

* John Sherman, when Secretary of State, wrote December 27, 1897, to the Rev. Elijah B. Jones at Owatomia, Minn.: "It would have been wiser to have kept him [John Brown] in confinement, rather than to execute him as was done for his Virginia raid." This is the view of Judge Roger A. Pryor, a bellicose Virginia Congressman at the time of John Brown's raid, later a gallant Confederate soldier, and long an eminent New York jurist.

GUILTY BEFORE THE LAW

by witnesses residing here, who will doubtless attend the trial if desired.

A. H. LEWIS.[95]

Mr. Lewis was vouched for by the Akron telegraph operator who sent the message. On receiving it, Mr. Botts and Mr. Green, his associate, read it to Brown, who at once absolutely declined to avail himself of this possible means of escape from the hangman. Not even to save his life would he consent to have the sacrifices already made minimized, and his entire twenty years' war upon slavery written down as the mere mania of a lunatic. He informed his counsel that there was no insanity on his father's side, but admitted that there were repeated instances of mental derangement on his mother's side, that his first wife was similarly afflicted, and two of her sons (John Brown, Jr., and Frederick) at times. Some of the statements in the telegram he knew to be correct; others were new to him. Mr. Botts informed the court of John Brown's refusal to avail himself of the plea of insanity, and of his ignorance that any effort was being made in Ohio along these lines until the despatch was read to him. As Mr. Botts concluded his statement, the prisoner, raising himself up on his couch, said:

"I will add, if the Court will allow me, that I look upon it as a miserable artifice and pretext of those who ought to take a different course in regard to me, if they took any at all, and I view it with contempt more than otherwise. As I remarked to Mr. Green, insane persons, so far as my experience goes, have but little ability to judge of their own sanity; and if I am insane, of course I should think I know more than all the rest of the world. But I do not think so. I am perfectly unconscious of insanity, and I reject, so far as I am capable, any attempt to interfere in my behalf on that score."[96]

The matter did not, however, rest here. On November 7, Mr. Griswold, of Brown's counsel, wrote to the Governor, enclosing a petition and affidavit from one Thompson, affirming the charge of insanity, and added:

"Whether any further effort will be made to obtain Brown's pardon, or a commutation of his sentence on the ground of insanity, I do not know, I am in communication with no person on this subject.

But I avail myself of this occasion to say that my conviction is that, on questions connected with slavery and the liberation of the slave, he is insane." [97]

Governor Wise responded that a plea of insanity could be filed at any time before conviction or sentence,[98] and wrote an admirable letter to Dr. Stribling, Superintendent of the Lunatic Asylum of Staunton, Virginia, ordering him to proceed to Charlestown and examine the prisoner, saying: "If the prisoner is insane he ought to be cured, and if not insane the fact ought to be vouched in the most reliable form, now that it is questioned under oath and by counsel since conviction." [99]

Unfortunately, the impetuous Governor countermanded these instructions, and the letter was never sent. This was a genuine misfortune, for the word of so eminent an alienist would have done much to answer the question which has puzzled men and will continue to puzzle some, as long as the story of John Brown is told. On the 23d of November, Governor Wise received in Washington, from George H. Hoyt himself, nineteen affidavits that, on the advice of Montgomery Blair, had been collected by him in Ohio.[100] The good friends and relatives there were not willing that Brown should go to the scaffold if they could prevent it. To save him, they gladly laid bare some sad family secrets. These affidavits varied, so far as John Brown himself was concerned, from statements that he was occasionally insane, of an "unbalanced mind," a monomaniac, to outright assertions that he had been clearly insane for the previous twenty-four years. But on the family record they all agreed. These generous admissions of nearest of kin proved that, aside from other cases of less serious derangement, Brown's grandmother on the maternal side, after lingering six years in hopeless insanity, had died insane; that of his grandmother's children, Brown's uncles and aunts, two sons and two daughters were intermittently insane, while a third daughter had died hopelessly lunatic; that Brown's only sister, her daughter and one of his brothers were at intervals deranged; and that of six first cousins, two were occasionally mad, two had been discharged from the state lunatic asylum after repeated commitments, while two more were at the time in close restraint, one of these being a hopeless

GUILTY BEFORE THE LAW

case. This is a fearful record, and one surely grave enough to have warranted the employing of alienists to make certain that Justice, in her blindness, did not execute an irresponsible man.

But the Governor failed to act. It was then too late for the issue to be raised legally, for there was no procedure by which the question of sanity could be raised after the sentence had been confirmed by the Court of Appeals. Governor Wise had, moreover, personally reached a decision on the point, after repeatedly seeing and conversing with the prisoner to whom he owes so much of his fame. "As well as I can know the state of mind of any one," the Governor declared to the Virginia Legislature,

"I know that he was sane, and remarkably sane, if quick and clear perception, if assumed rational premises and consecutive reasoning from them, if cautious tact in avoiding disclosures and in covering conclusions and inferences, if memory and conception and practical common sense, and if composure and self-possession are evidence of a sound state of mind. He was more sane than his prompters and promoters, and concealed well the secret which made him seem to do an act of mad impulse, by leaving him without his backers at Harper's Ferry; but he did not conceal his contempt for the cowardice which did not back him better than with a plea of insanity, which he spurned to put in at his trial at Charlestown."

No historian of John Brown can fail to take note of the facts in the affidavits, and to scrutinize the life of his subject in the light thus cast upon his inheritance from one line of his progenitors. If it could be roundly declared that he was partially or wholly deranged, it would be easy to explain away those of his acts which at times baffle an interpreter of this remarkable personality, — the Pottawatomie murders, for instance. But this cannot be done. Governor Wise was correct in his estimate of John Brown's mentality; the final proof is the extraordinary series of letters written by him in jail after his doom was pronounced. No lunatic ever penned such elevated and high-minded, and such consistent epistles. If to be devoted to one idea, or to a single cause, is to be a monomaniac, then the world owes much of its progress toward individual and racial freedom to lunacy of this variety. If John Brown was insane on the subject of slavery, so were

Lucretia Mott and Lydia Maria Child, while Garrison and Phillips and Horace Greeley should never have been allowed to go at large. That their methods of advancing their joint cause differed from John Brown's violent ones, in no wise argues that he went beyond the bounds of sound reason in his efforts for freedom for the blacks. If John Brown was the victim of an *idée fixe*, so was Martin Luther, and so were all the martyrs to freedom of faith. But, examining his record day by day, weighing all the actions of a life of great activity, and reading the hundreds of letters from his pen which have survived to this hour, the conclusion is inevitable that, however bad his judgment at times, however wild the planless assault on Harper's Ferry, John Brown himself had escaped the family taint, — and this despite the kindly affidavits of those who wished to save him from the gallows. Moreover, while lunatics have often for a time imposed their will upon weaker intellects, persuaded them that fancied wrongs were real, and nerved them to acts of violence, John Brown lived too long and too intimately with many men to have been able to mislead them always. The paranoiac invariably betrays himself at last. But the man who sacrifices business prospects, a quiet orderly life, his family's happiness, and the lives of himself and his children, in a crusade which the world has since declared to have been righteous as to its object, cannot, because of his devotion to that purpose, be adjudged a maniac — else asylums for the insane have played too small a part in the world's history. Dr. Starry, the gallant physician of Harper's Ferry, said, years after the raid, that such devotion as Brown's followers had for him he, Dr. Starry, had never beheld before or since. "They perfectly worshipped the ground the old fellow trod on." [101] The hard-headed, able Americans, like Stevens, Kagi, Cook and Gill, who lived with John Brown month in and month out and were ready to die with him, worshipped no lunatic.

CHAPTER XIV

BY MAN SHALL HIS BLOOD BE SHED

MANY of them veterans of a hundred frontier roils or dangerous anti-slavery undertakings, it was not to be expected that John Brown's friends and supporters would see him go to his death at the hands of the assaulted Virginians without lifting a finger in his behalf. No sooner was he safely in jail in Charlestown, and his recovery from his wounds certain, than plotting for a rescue began. To the Kansas Free State fighters, capture by Border Ruffian forces or incarceration in a Southern prison did not imply that they were beyond hope of escape. At the hour of Brown's raid, Dr. John Doy, who had been rescued from the St. Joseph, Missouri, jail just in time to avoid serving five years in the penitentiary at Jefferson, was touring the North and lecturing on slavery as he had found it. What Kansans had done, Kansans could do again, and Massachusetts men, too.

The first to move were John W. Le Barnes and Thomas Wentworth Higginson. The latter's interest was to have been expected, because of his militant record. Other clergymen might feel scruples about taking up arms when wearing the garb of the church and teaching the doctrines of the Prince of Peace, but Mr. Higginson had none. He sympathized not at all with the Garrison school of non-resistant Abolitionists, and he had unbounded physical and moral courage. For instance, on May 26, 1854, Mr. Higginson and a sturdy negro were the first of the men who broke down the door of the Boston court-house, in a brave but vain attempt to save Anthony Burns, a fugitive slave, from being returned to slavery. Mr. Higginson, unarmed as he was, attacked the policemen and deputies within the jail. As he did so, a shot rang out and one of the deputies fell dead, — the first Massachusetts man to lose his life in the contest over slavery.[1]

As already related, Mr. Le Barnes engaged George H. Hoyt to go to Harper's Ferry, ostensibly as counsel, but really as a spy, to see if the prison could be stormed and Brown and his fellow prisoners set free. As soon as Hoyt had obtained access to John Brown, he revealed to him the plan of rescue then under way in Massachusetts, and urged him to coöperate to the fullest extent. But in the tone of command which had never permitted debate on the plains of Kansas, John Brown made it clear to Hoyt that he would lend himself to no scheme of rescue. That same night, October 28, Hoyt wrote to his employer that Brown "positively refused his consent to any such plan;"[2] and what he said to Hoyt, the prisoner repeated on the day of his sentence to Judge Thomas Russell, of Boston, and Mrs. Russell, and later on to his old Free State friend, S. C. Pomeroy, subsequently Senator from Kansas.[3] The chimney in Brown's prison-room was enormous; two men could easily have got up or down it. Jurist as he was, Judge Russell looked at it and groaned: "Two good Yankees could get these men out and away *so* easily!" But Brown was "calm and at peace;" his words "measured and quiet;" the longings of his visitors kindled no response in kind.[4] Besides his vision of what his death would mean to his cause, he felt under moral obligation to his jailer, Captain John Avis, for many kindnesses received. To him he had already given his pledge not to attempt to escape.[5]

His positive prohibition, conveyed through Hoyt, did not, however, check the ardor of his friends. Le Barnes, F. B. Sanborn, James Redpath, R. J. Hinton and T. W. Higginson kept up their plotting until November 28, Higginson vainly hoping that, since Brown's sentence had not been commuted, he might change his mind about desiring aid.[6] Even a second and more emphatic warning from Hoyt failed to deter them. Writing on October 30 to Le Barnes, the young lawyer said:

"*There is no chance* of his. [Brown's] ultimate escape; there is nothing but the most unmitigated failure, & the saddest consequences which it is possible to conjure, to ensue upon an attempt at *rescue*. The county all around is guarded by armed patrols & a large body of troops are constantly under arms. If you hear anything about such an attempt, for Heaven's sake do not *fail to restrain the enterprise.*"[7]

In his ardor for a rescue, Mr. Higginson bethought himself of the grief-stricken family at North Elba, and decided to induce Mrs. Brown to visit her husband and urge him to give his consent to an attempt to free him. This he was successful in doing.[8] Mrs. Brown left North Elba in his company on November 2, and went direct to Boston, where funds were found to forward her to Harper's Ferry by way of Philadelphia, from which place she was escorted to Baltimore by J. Miller McKim, a leading Philadelphia Abolitionist.[9] As soon, however, as Brown learned that his wife was on the way, he telegraphed to Mr. Higginson through George Sennott[10] not to let her come.* She was finally reached by telegram at Baltimore, on the morning of November 8, just as she was about to take a Harper's Ferry train,[11] and there ended this effort to move from his purpose a man who was as impregnable as Gibraltar when his mind was made up. Whether Brown had received an inkling of his wife's real purpose is not clear. He wrote thus to Mr. Higginson, in explanation of Mr. Sennott's telegram, on the 9th of November:

> If my wife were to come here just now it would *only tend* to distract *her mind* TEN FOLD; and would only add to my affliction; and *can not possibly* do me *any good*. It will also use up the scanty means she has to supply Bread & cheap but comfortable clothing, fuel, &c for herself & children through *the winter*. DO PERSUADE her to remain *at home* for a time (at least) till she can learn further from me. She will receive a thousand times the consolation AT HOME that she can possibly find elsewhere. I have just *written her* there & will write her CONSTANTLY. Her presence *here* would deepen my affliction a thousand fold. I beg of her to be *calm* and *submissive*; & not to go *wild* on my account. I lack *for nothing* & was feeling quite cheerful before I heard she talked of *coming on* — I ask her to *compose her mind* & to remain *quiet* till the last of *this month;* out of pity to me. I can certainly judge better in the matter than *any one* ELSE. My warmest thanks to yourself and *all other* kind friends.
>
> God bless you all. Please *send this line* to *my afflicted wife* by first possible conveyance.
>   Your Friend in truth
>   JOHN BROWN.[12]

George L. Stearns, of Boston, was the first to turn to Kansas for aid. He wrote immediately after the raid to Charles Jennison and James Stewart, two of the boldest "jayhawkers" in Kansas, urging them to help Brown escape, and author-

---

* Mr. Sennott's message read: "Mr. Brown says for God's sake don't let Mrs. Brown come. Send her word by telegraph wherever she is."

izing them to draw on him for funds if there was anything they could do.[13] They do not seem to have acted. Captain James Montgomery and Silas C. Soulé, who had played an important part in the rescue of Dr. John Doy, are erroneously believed to have come East promptly and looked over the field. But, as Soulé did not meet Montgomery until he presented a letter of introduction from James H. Lane on December 27, it is obvious that they could not have been East together in November. It is certain that women figured in the Kansas plans, as well as in the Massachusetts one. A Miss Mary Partridge, of a fighting Free State family of Linn County, whose brother George was killed at Osawatomie while fighting under Brown, was selected to visit him in his cell at Charlestown, to convey information of the plans if it could be given to the captive in no other way. Miss Partridge was to throw her arms around Brown's neck and, while embracing him most affectionately, was to get into his mouth a billet giving the plan of campaign and the time of the attempt. Miss Partridge was ready and willing to go to Virginia, but Brown's attitude and the physical and financial difficulties in the way relieved her of the necessity of venturing to Harper's Ferry.[14]

To Lysander Spooner, an active Abolitionist of Boston, belongs the credit of devising, early in November, an audacious scheme of retaliation upon the South for the sentencing to death of John Brown, which, had it been carried into execution, would, as Higginson put it at the time, have terrified the South as much as the Harper's Ferry affair.[15] It was nothing less than a plan to kidnap Governor Wise some evening in Richmond; to carry him aboard a sea-going tug, and hold him either on the high seas, or in some secret Northern place, as hostage for the safety of Brown. That so buccaneering a scheme, worthy of the imagination of a Marryat or a Cooper, should have been seriously considered by sober-minded Boston men of the middle of the nineteenth century, shows clearly how rapidly the "irrepressible conflict" was approaching. Their passionate hatred of slavery had led them to sanction Brown's armed attack upon it; their disappointment and grief over his failure and capture made no scheme of revenge too wild for their consideration. They

BY MAN SHALL HIS BLOOD BE SHED

actually planned, in time of profound peace, to steal by night into the capitol of a friendly State and carry off its Chief Executive; and there is good reason to believe that dauntless spirits like those of Le Barnes and Higginson would have set the undertaking afoot, had it been possible to raise the large sum of money necessary. They were willing to imitate Brown and "carry the war into Africa;" if the government was not ready to begin war on the South for the freedom of the slaves, there was no hesitation on their part. Looking back on it now, Mr. Higginson says truly that "it seems almost incredible that any condition of things should have turned honest American men into conscientious law-breakers."[16] Only a few people were able, in the heat of the moment, to realize that this lawless spirit was as clear an indication of the impending upheaval as were those acts of lawlessness like the Boston Tea-Party and the burning of the schooner Gaspee, which preceded the Revolution.

Spooner first broached the Wise plot to Le Barnes in Boston.[17] Recourse was had, before the middle of November, to Higginson, who, having been for some years a stockholder in a yacht, the Flirt, kept in commission to aid incoming fugitive slaves and circumvent slave-catchers,[18] was not without sympathy for a maritime adventure. Spooner was able to report to him within a week that Le Barnes had discovered a reliable man "who will undertake to find the men, a pilot, and a boat, for the Richmond expedition, if the necessary money can be had. . . . Will you not come down at once, and help to move men here to furnish the money. . . . We can do nothing without you. Do not fail to come."[19] By November 22, Le Barnes wrote[20] that he had no doubt that the arrangements could be made, "it is the *money* that is uncertain." His agent was in the shipping business and could furnish the tug and crew needed without causing comment, particularly if it were offered for sale at Richmond, because tugs were just then in great demand there. Other details he set forth as follows:

"Tug will cost $5000 to $7000, to steam 15 to 18 knots an hour. There is only one gunboat on the station, (whether in the *Bay* or not, is not precisely known.) But this makes only 13 knots; & there is nothing else as fast in those waters. The pilot knows all the rivers of that region thoroughly. The expedition would cost ten to fifteen thousand dollars. $10,000 wd be necessary to start with, with more, (say proceeds of sale of boat) promised in case of success. This, if it were necessary to hire hands. If the men volunteered, the expenses, aside from the security of the boat would not exceed $2000."

But Le Barnes declared that he would not go himself, and did not "wish any of our men led into it," although if a safe agreement could be reached with "*professional* men," he would make the arrangements. With money the thing could be done, but the money was the rub. Where could it be had? He himself had been to see "W. P." [Wendell Phillips], who was in favor, "if our men will go." "W. I." [Bowditch] would contribute to the project if it was undertaken, but "H. I." [Bowditch] was opposed. Le Barnes himself was impressed with the fact that "*success* would be *brilliant — defeat* fatally inglorious." He had, moreover, doubts as to whether the successful kidnapping of Wise would save John Brown. It was, after all, the judge who issued the warrant of death and saw to its execution, not the Governor. Still, if nothing else could be done, he was for attempting the scheme.[21] Gradually, however, the hopelessness of raising the money became patent, and upon this obstacle the scheme was wrecked. Le Barnes was one of the last to give it up; but gradually he devoted himself to the alternative plan of a deliberate overland invasion of Charlestown. This he was personally quite willing to join.[22]

Some German-born lovers of liberty in New York, who had fought tyranny in their native land, were brought together in a meeting on November 22,[23] and agreed to take part in an attack on the prison. In a short time, "a hundred or more" men were reported to the Boston conspirators as ready to go as a reinforcement to the Ohioans who, so rumor said, were preparing to move on Charlestown under John Brown, Jr. But if it should prove that there were no Ohio men ready to lead, only "from 15 to 20 or 25" were prepared to follow Le Barnes, Hinton and the Kansas leaders.[24] By Sunday, November 27, the plan was to rendezvous some distance from Charlestown, to make a cross-country rush on that town, and, after freeing the prisoners, to seize the horses of the cavalry companies and escape. The attack was to be either on Wednesday, November 30, or on December 2, the day of the execution, "at the hour," and Le Barnes reported from New York that the men were confident of success, "strange as it may seem to us."[25] Dr. Howe suggested that they be armed with "Orsini" bombs and hand-grenades, in lieu of artillery. With these weapons he felt sure they would terrify the Virginia chivalry on guard in Charlestown.[26]

Again it became a question merely of funds. The rescuers wanted one hundred dollars apiece, and an agreement that the survivors would be provided for in places of safety, and that the families of all would be taken care of. For this purpose, fifteen hundred or two thousand dollars was needed by Tuesday morning the 29th, and five hundred or a thousand dollars the day after. Le Barnes demanded also that a definite promise be sent on the following day.[27] James Redpath had been previously selected to go to Ohio to ascertain just what was on foot there. But he had delayed his departure, and on the day Le Barnes wrote this ultimatum in regard to funds, and added, "It is for you in Boston to say 'go' or 'stay,'" George H. Hoyt, fresh from his achievements as Brown's counsel, arrived in Boston from the Western Reserve. He reported that nothing whatever was on foot in Ohio. The next day, discouraged by Hoyt's news, for he had counted on Ohio's stirring, and being unable to raise the needed funds, Sanborn in Boston gave up the undertaking and wired to Le Barnes to return. This the latter did after telegraphing to Higginson, "Object abandoned." Sanborn wrote with a heavy heart to that militant clergyman: "So I suppose we must give up all hope of saving our old friend."[28]

It must not be thought that the Virginia authorities were without a belief that there was plotting going on. In his message to the Legislature after the execution, Governor Wise said: "I did not remove the prisoners further into the interior, because I was determined to show no apprehension of a rescue; and if the jail of Jefferson had been on the line of the State, they would have been kept there, to show that they could be kept anywhere chosen in our limits."[29] But for all this bravado after the execution, there is plenty of evidence, besides the extraordinary assembling of troops around Brown's scaffold, to show Wise's anxiety and that of Andrew Hunter. Every mail brought to them or to John Brown, whose letters they carefully examined and withheld if they saw fit, warnings, some more or less fantastic, of an expedition or plan. Many were anonymous, others signed by Southern sympathizers in the North, and still others were plainly written for the sole purpose of alarming and deceiving Governor Wise and the military.[30] From Zanesville, Ohio, "T. A. B." wrote that he had seen "between 30 & 36 men, all armed with Colts Six Shooters & a Species of home made Bowie knife, well calculated to do Exicution," who were to cross the Ohio near "Cisterville" with two hundred and seventy others and arrive at Harper's Ferry December 1. "Harrisburg" wrote from Harrisburg, Pennsylvania, of a force of armed men who were to leave there in time to free Brown on the day of execution. The United States marshal at Cleveland forwarded a letter from North Bloomfield, Ohio, which reported that John Brown, Jr., had boasted that "9000 desperate men" were in readiness, and that his father would not be hanged. "Henry" wrote from Boston to Brown, in an easily read cipher, that "twenty of them left this morning and thirty-three start Thursday. They will bring you with them or die." Philadelphia reported five thousand men armed with "Pike's rifles" and four cannon, and New York twenty-five hundred men who were to attack Charlestown on December 1, — a little late, apparently, because, on the day before, eight thousand desperate men from Detroit, sworn to rescue Brown or die, and more than "armed to the teeth," were to fire ten shots a minute at the jail guards from their new-style carbines.

Some of these missives Hunter endorsed, "Contemptible nonsense," others he marked, "Consider." To John Brown himself the threatening letters caused nothing but annoyance. "He protests against them," reported the special correspondent of the Richmond *Despatch* on November 11, "and feels unwilling to believe that they proceed from his own friends." To the correspondent of the *Tribune* he thus expressed himself on November 4: "I do not know that I ought to encourage any attempt to save my life. I am not sure that it would not be better for me to die at this time." * He told one of his

* Henry Ward Beecher had said five days before: "Let no man pray that Brown

guards, not long before his execution, that his friends would surely have attempted his rescue in the first few weeks, had they known how small a guard was on duty, but that he hoped and trusted no effort would then be made.[31] But Governor Wise actually thought it advisable to turn over to the military a well-written letter from Lewisburg, Union County, Pennsylvania, telling of the organization of "The Noble Sons of Liberty," numbering about five hundred and led by "Capt. James Smelly, alias Limber Jim, the ultra-abolitionist." Its members were to drop into Charlestown and adjacent places by ones and twos, and then on a given signal storm the jail. This was one of the letters that led to the extending of the pickets well outside of the town. Some of the sentries were a full mile from their quarters, and it took an hour and forty minutes to post the guard.[32] Under Mr. Hunter's advice, the old Southern system of mounted patrols was established in every precinct of the county.[33]

Before that took place, however, there had been a bad scare at Harper's Ferry, on October 26, the superintendent of the arsenal having received "reliable information" that an attempt at rescue might be made at night by parties from New York and Pennsylvania. President Garrett, of the Baltimore and Ohio Railroad, was not willing to run any risks, and himself called out a company of Maryland militia, the United Guards of Frederick, who reached Harper's Ferry fifteen strong that evening, with a promise that the rest of the company would arrive in the morning. "There is a strong guard on duty," reported that evening to Mr. Garrett his Master of Transportation, W. P. Smith, "and I am ordered to 'halt' at all points as I move about in the storm and darkness." But he added: "The feeling of uncertain dread is very strong, and there surely ought to be full and well-organized reliance [reserve?] to restore confidence."[34] That the Charlestown authorities were ready to take extreme measures appears from a despatch of Colonel J. Lucius Davis, a West Point graduate, with a long, flowing beard and of otherwise curious appear-

be spared. Let Virginia make him a martyr. Now, he has only blundered. His soul was noble; his work miserable. But a cord and a gibbet would redeem all that, and round up Brown's failure with a heroic success." See New York *Herald* of October 31 and November 22. When John Brown read this, he wrote opposite it the single word "good."

ance, who was the immediate commander of the troops. Telegraphing to the Secretary of the Commonwealth November 2, Colonel Davis said: "We are ready for them. If attack be made, the prisoners will be shot by the inside guards."[35]

To add to the nervousness of the authorities, there occurred in the neighborhood of Charlestown a number of fires, all of them doubtless accidental. They continued through November, instances being the burning of the barn and stock-yards of Mr. Walter Shirley, three miles from Charlestown, loss four thousand dollars, and also those of George H. Tate and John Burns, all three of whom had been on the jury that decided Brown's fate.[36] Judge Lucas's haystack, burned about this time, was but one of many that lit up the heavens. A shot fired under his window, another night, led to the belief that the judge had been marked for assassination, and induced the mayor, Thomas C. Green, on November 12, to order the removal from Charlestown of all strangers who could not give a satisfactory account of themselves. Among those forced to leave on that day were George H. Hoyt, who was, however, ready to go, as he had finished his legal work for Brown, and a representative of *Frank Leslie's Illustrated Paper*, who was charged with the grave offence of being a correspondent of the New York *Tribune*.[37] But the fires continued to be recorded in almost every issue of the Richmond papers from November 12 on. The resultant dread and nervousness of the citizens were intensified by repeated false alarms, some of them given for drill purposes by Colonel Davis, until the cry of wolf no longer excited people.[38]*

But the return home of an excited native of Charlestown, for some time previously a resident of Kansas, with a report that five hundred Kansans were planning a rescue and were already on their way, did thoroughly frighten the town. This man, a certain Smith Crane, told terrible tales of the band of desperadoes who, in Kansas, always had rescued Brown, and would again, and reported overhearing a conversation in Bellair, Ohio, — whence he had just come, — in which conspirators had detailed their plans to come in force and

---

* Colonel Davis reported on November 19 that "the majority [of citizens] think the recent fires made by local spy companies forming everywhere," — which illustrates clearly the panic then prevailing. — Telegram to Governor Wise. — Original in Mr. Edwin Tatham's collection.

BY MAN SHALL HIS BLOOD BE SHED

rescue the prisoner. Curiously enough, Andrew Hunter received the next day a telegram from Marshal Johnson, of Cleveland, saying that a thousand men were arming there. The coincidence seemed to confirm Crane's stories, and created much alarm for the time being. Mr. Hunter himself was convinced of their truth.[39]

That all of this had its effect on Governor Wise's nerves appears clearly in his letter of November 16 to Andrew Hunter, which has only recently been brought to light:

RICHMOND, V^A, Nov. 16th, 1859.

MY DEAR SIR, — Information from every quarter leads to the conviction that there is an organized plan to harrass our whole slave-border at every point. *Day* is the *very* time to commit arson with the best chance ag^t detection. No light shines, nor smoke shows in daylight before the flame is off & up past putting out. The rascal too escapes best by day; he sees best whether he is not seen, and best how to avoid persons pursuing. I tell you those Devils are trained in all the Indian arts of predatory war. They come, *one by one, two by two,* in *open day,* and make you stare that the thing be *attempted* as it was *done*. But on the *days* of execution what is to become of the borders? Have you tho't of that? 5 or 10,000 people flock into Chastown & leave homesteads *unguarded!* When then but most burnings to take place? To prevent this you must get all your papers in Jeff: Berk: & Fred^k & Morgan & Hamp: to beg the people to stay at home & keep guard. Again a promiscuous crowd of women & children would hinder troops terribly if an emeute of rescue be made; and if our own people will only shoulder arms that day & keep thus distinct from strangers the guards may be prompt to arrest & punish any attempt. I have ordered 200 minie muskets to be sent to Charlestown at once with fixed amt^n and the Col^s of Berkely, Jeff: & Fred: to order regt^s to be ready at a moment. I shall order 400 men under arms. Then, ought there to be more than one day of execution? Judge P. ought to have thought of this, but he did n't. If C^t Appl^s dont decide before 2nd Decr I'll hang Brown. If they do & sustain sentence will it not be best to postpone his ext^n with the rest. He ought to be hung between two negroes & there ought n't to be two days of excitement. Again it gives Legislature the opportunity of uniting with Executive in hanging Brown. Another question. Ought *I to be there?* It might possibly be necessary in order to proc: M. law. Say to Col. Davis that I have ordered him to act as Commissary Genl for all the troops in Jefferson and he must remain & act until we are through. The Gov^t may pay out of contingent fund & I gave M^r. Brown the forms of U. S. army t'other day, shall of course call on Genl Assembly for an appropriation the first week. The guards must be kept up until 16th Decr. Watch Harper's Ferry people. Watch, I say, and I *thought* watch when there. Gerritt Smith is a stark madman, no doubt! Gods, what a moral, what a lesson. Whom the Gods wish to make mad they first set to setting others to destroying. . . .

Yrs. truly
HENRY A. WISE.[40]

A. HUNTER, ESQ.

Another outbreak of fear at Harper's Ferry, two days after Governor Wise wrote this letter, led him hastily to call out four hundred men in Richmond and Petersburg, and go with them in person, on November 20, to that place and to Charlestown, which, in great excitement, were momentarily "expecting from one to two hundred armed men from the West to rescue Brown." "Send me 500 men armed and equipped, instanter. A large body are approaching from Wheeling, armed with pikes and revolvers. Pardon haste" — telegraphed Colonel J. Lucius Davis to Governor Wise. But this was too much for that excitable official, who replied: "Be cautious. Commit no mistake to-night. Men will march to-morrow morning."[41]

One hundred and fifty more soldiers reached Harper's Ferry with cannon on November 21, but they were destined to stay only a short time, for the impulsive Governor ordered them back that night. The railroad men were at a loss to know why the Governor had called out so many men, but thought he "must be in possession of information — we have not — to justify him." All except one company were on their way back again by the 22d. Four days later, Governor Wise began the concentration of troops for the execution, and with it came the end of what may truthfully be called the reign of terror in Charlestown and Harper's Ferry.[42]

Andrew Hunter's state of mind was considerably less feverish, but he afterwards admitted his genuine alarm lest the none too strong jail be attempted, and urged every possible precaution as the day of execution approached, — even to the extent of being ready to tear up the railroad tracks.[43] Eight days in advance of the event upon which the interest of the nation was concentrated, Governor Wise sent the following orders to Major-General William B. Taliaferro, then the commander of the troops in succession to Colonel Davis, after promising more soldiers:

BY MAN SHALL HIS BLOOD BE SHED 523

". . . keep full guard on the line of frontier from Martinsburg to Harper's Ferry, on the day of 2d Dec. Warn the inhabitants to arm and keep guard and patrol on that day and for days beforehand. These orders are necessary to prevent seizure of hostages. Warn the inhabitants to stay away and especially to keep the women and children at home. Prevent all strangers, and especially all parties of strangers from proceeding to Charlestown on 2nd Decr. To this end station a guard at Harper's Ferry sufficient to control crowds on the cars from East and West. Let mounted men, except one or two companies, remain on guard at the outposts, and keep one or two for the purpose of keeping the crowd clear of the outer line of military on the day of execution. Form two concentric squares around the gallows, and have strong guard at the jail and for escort to execution. Let no crowd be near enough to the prisoner to hear any speech he may attempt. Allow no more visitors to be admitted into the jail."[44]

Greater precautions could hardly have been taken had a grave state of war existed, with a menacing and active enemy.

Not content with the militia forces which he could and did assemble, including the cadets from the Virginia Military Institute at Lexington, Virginia, one of whose commanders was Professor T. J. Jackson, later famous as "Stonewall" Jackson, Governor Wise induced President Buchanan again to send Colonel Robert E. Lee to Harper's Ferry. He arrived there on November 30, and under his command were 264 artillerymen from Fort Monroe, to guard the bridges and town until after the execution. In his appeal to the President, on November 25, to keep the peace between the States, Governor Wise stated that he had information "specific enough to be reliable" which convinced him that "an attempt will be made to rescue the prisoners, and if that fails, then to seize citizens of this State as hostages and victims in case of execution." He himself had called out one thousand militia, and if necessary he would "call out the whole available force of the State to carry into effect the sentence of our laws on the 2d and 16th proximo." He added that "places in Maryland, Ohio and Pennsylvania have been occupied as depots and rendezvous by these desperadoes, unobstructed by guards or otherwise to invade this State, and we are kept in continual apprehension of outrages from fire and rapine on our borders."[45] How unfounded in fact these allegations were, now appears clearly. The most careful search fails to reveal, in

Ohio or elsewhere, any proof that there were actual conspiracies of would-be rescuers, save those elsewhere described. In insisting that desperadoes had actually occupied rendezvous in three States, Governor Wise was merely taking counsel of his fears, and of his largely anonymous informants. Nevertheless, he sent copies of his letter to the Governors of those States, and by arming and showing his great anxiety, he betrayed to his, for the greater part unknown, correspondents that they had accomplished their end,—the terrifying of the great State of Virginia.

Naturally, President Buchanan, while willing to send Colonel Lee to guard United States property at Harper's Ferry, characterized Governor Wise's beliefs as "almost incredible," and pointed out that he had no right or power to keep peace between the States as suggested. Governor Hicks, of Maryland, was skeptical, but ready to take some civil and military measures to coöperate. Governor Packer, of Pennsylvania, correctly characterized the information received by Governor Wise as "utterly and entirely without foundation," and reminded him sharply that Pennsylvania had done and would do her duty. Salmon P. Chase, Governor of Ohio, replied that he had heard nothing of any desperadoes assembling in Ohio until he received Governor Wise's letter. In answer to Wise's threats that Virginia troops might have to pursue rescuers into Ohio, Governor Chase gave to Governor Wise the information that the laws of the United States prescribed the mode in which persons charged with crime escaping into Ohio might be demanded and surrendered; and he added that Ohio under no circumstances would consent to the invasion of her territory by armed bodies from other States.[46]

Hunter and Wise did not cease their emergency preparations, after making their military arrangements. Through the former, the Baltimore and Ohio Railroad was induced to take the most elaborate precautions. A canny Boston Yankee, Josiah Perham, had asked the railroad for reduced rates for one or two thousand sight-seers, to whom he wished to show Brown on the scaffold, and then the sights of Washington at the time of the opening of Congress. He asserted that he had moved two hundred thousand people in the nine previous years without accident and without complaint that

BY MAN SHALL HIS BLOOD BE SHED

"any of them did not behave well." But under Hunter's advice the Baltimore and Ohio declined to profit by this opportunity to make money, on account of the "peculiar relation of the criminals to a portion of the Eastern community and the great liability to at least an unpleasant excitement on the occasion," — so Mr. Perham was informed. All excursions or movements of any number of people as a body were forbidden. Local passenger traffic from the adjoining towns to Harper's Ferry and Charlestown was practically suspended on the day before the execution, no tickets being sold save to persons well known to the agents. Every intending passenger was urged to travel on another day, as every one insufficiently provided with a pass faced "arrest and imprisonment on attempting to stop at Martinsburg or Harper's Ferry." [47] As Mr. Hunter avers that four Congressmen who were desirous of seeing Brown hanged, and were escorted by a well-known citizen of Harper's Ferry, were nevertheless jailed on suspicion as soon as they reached Charlestown, this warning to travellers was plainly well worth obeying. [48] Even innocent passengers were liable to arrest and removal from trains, as in the case of three Baltimoreans arrested at Martinsburg on November 29. From as far west as Wheeling, no one could go east on December 1 or 2 without a certificate of good character from a station agent, and not more than sixty certificates could be issued. Conductors were ordered to telegraph in detail about their trains to W. P. Smith, the Master of Transportation. That official even asked aid in New York, for he excitedly telegraphed, as late as November 30, to J. P. Jackson, Vice-President of the New Jersey Railroad Company, begging for news: [49]

"Great alarm exists here from expectations of large forces of desperadoes from North, East and West, to attempt rescue of Virginia prisoners. Will you favor us by promptly despatching any information you may have respecting parties who may be of this character taking your trains for the South, and also advise us personally if any unusual party of unknown men start for this direction."

In brief, there was voluntary enforcement of martial law, and the whole countryside behaved as if in a state of siege. When the execution came, there was not the slightest disturbance of the peace of any kind, either at Charlestown or on any part of Governor Wise's embattled frontier.

Not unnaturally, that Executive was severely criticised for his military display and its costliness. Part of the Virginia and Maryland press denounced it as unnecessary, and credited it to Wise's alleged desire to make political capital out of the raid.[50] But a study of contemporary reports of conditions at Charlestown, and of the Virginia press, makes it plain that Wise would have been justified in calling out a strong military force, had he not been himself so convinced that hordes of desperadoes were about to descend upon his State. He owed it to the citizens of Charlestown not merely to safeguard the prisoners, but also to protect the town from the bloodshed of even an unsuccessful attempt at a rescue. There was, moreover, extraordinary popular excitement throughout the Union, and if this were in itself not excuse enough, the weakness of the South's "peculiar institution" would have furnished it. The Free State men in Kansas had not only made slavery impossible in their Territory, but had endangered it in Missouri by their raids into the State, and their helping hand to any slave who came over the border in search of freedom. From the Southern point of view, it would seem to have been good policy to show the power of the sovereign State of Virginia to defend her own when attacked, and to punish those who violated her laws. Certainly, Mr. Hunter, in his article in the New Orleans *Times-Democrat* of September 5, 1887, reviewing the raid and Brown's trial, makes out a strong case for the force employed. The report of the Legislature's special committee, headed by Alexander H. H. Stuart, unreservedly sustained Governor Wise, in the following language:

"The testimony before the committee amply vindicates the conduct of the Executive in assembling a strong military force at the scene of excitement; and the promptness and energy with which he discharged his duty, merit, and doubtless will receive the commendation of the Legislature and people of the State."[51]

It must be admitted, of course, that Wise still had political ambitions, although his term as Governor was about expiring: for a few months later, he was willing to have his name presented to the National Democratic Convention at Charleston, South Carolina, provided the Virginia State delegation were a unit for his nomination.[52] But in his treatment of the military situation, the politician disappears behind the Governor. His bombastic and excitable way of dealing with it was due to his fears, and also to his nature. His biographer, Barton H. Wise, a relative, has characterized him as "largely a creature of impulse," of a "remarkably mercurial" temperament, with a "temper exceptionally excitable and his bump of combativeness developed in an extraordinary degree."[53] That Hunter and the Governor realized that the State would profit largely by the drill and experience the troops obtained at Charlestown, Mr. Hunter admits in these words:

"From facts disclosed in the trials, from the intercepted correspondence of Brown and his followers, and from other sources, a new view of the case was opened to us in respect to the political significance of this movement of John Brown; we began to see that all it meant was not on the surface. My views were from time to time conveyed to Governor Wise, and before the trials both he and I became convinced, that this Brown raid was the beginning of a great conflict between the North and the South on the subject of slavery, and had better be regarded accordingly. This furnishes an additional explanation of the reason Governor Wise assembled so large a military volunteer force at Charlestown and the neighboring points. It was not alone for the protection of the jail and the repelling of parties who were known to be organizing with the view of rescuing Brown and the prisoners, but it was for the purpose of preparing for coming events."

To General Taliaferro, the commander-in-chief at Charlestown, it was apparent that the Governor had another motive besides protecting the prisoners, in assembling so many troops, for immediately after John Brown's execution he thus questioned the Governor by telegraph: "Shall I send home the First Regiment Virginia Volunteers? Which companies beside do you wish to retire? What are your views with regard to sending more troops here? Do you design a school of instruction? There is no absolute need for half we have."[54] Thus far Governor Wise may properly be accused of having allowed ulterior motives to influence his handling of the Charlestown situation, but no further. It is, moreover, certain that his disposition of the troops and the other precautions taken made a rescue practically impossible, or possible only after severe loss of life. There are to-day survivors of those stirring days at Charlestown, who believe that if a determined attempt had been made, by means of a feint a mile or two from the town, the rawness of the militia and the generally panicky state of the town would have made the storming of the jail possible. But among the hundreds of troops who were steadily in camp throughout November, and those that came to reinforce them, there were some experienced officers and trustworthy men. As Le Barnes wrote to Higginson, the real leaders of those who wished to rescue John Brown could see no hope of success, even were the means needed at their disposal. And as to the cost to Virginia of the military display, it hardly exceeded the amount appropriated at that same time for new arms and ammunition by the Legislature of South Carolina with a view to the existing state of its relations to the Union.

While the Virginia authorities were thus guarding John Brown in order to prevent a rescue, the "higher and wickeder game," namely, the chief accessories before the fact to his raid, whom Andrew Hunter and Governor Wise were so anxious to stalk until the Mason Committee was decided on, were by no means all at ease in their Massachusetts or New York preserves. When the raid turned out to be not another slave liberation like that in Missouri, but a drama with the whole nation as audience, there was something akin to trepidation among the self-appointed committee which had made John Brown's raid possible. Its members were plainly unaware that to support a forcible attack upon a system, however iniquitous, in a country founded on the principle that differences of opinion must be settled by the ballot, carries with it both heavy responsibilities and grave personal danger. Few of them had believed Brown's plans feasible; none had apparently asked themselves how far they would be compromised in the eyes of the law when John Brown failed. The result was disastrous to some of them, though none of the leaders went to jail or were otherwise punished for conspiring with John Brown. The conduct of a few illustrates clearly how good men of high principles and excellent motives may flinch gravely when they suddenly find their future reputa-

BY MAN SHALL HIS BLOOD BE SHED

tions, and perhaps even their lives, at stake in a grave and unexpected crisis.

Of the men who, as we have already seen in the previous chapters, knew most about John Brown's plans and principally aided him, — Sanborn, Howe, Stearns, Gerrit Smith, Parker and Higginson, — the Boston and Worcester clergymen alone stand out as being entirely ready to take the consequences, whatever they might be. Theodore Parker was in Europe on a futile search for health, when Harper's Ferry was attacked; but he bore his testimony manfully: "Of course, I was not astonished to hear that an attempt had been made to free the slaves in a certain part of Virginia. . . . Such 'insurrections' will continue as long as Slavery lasts, and will increase, both in frequency and in power, just as the people become intelligent and moral. . . . It is a good Anti-Slavery picture on the Virginia shield: a man standing on a tyrant and chopping his head off with a sword; only I would paint the sword-holder *black* and the tyrant *white*, to show the *immediate application* of the principle."[55] As for Mr. Higginson, he stood his ground in Worcester, where all the world might find him. He wisely reasoned from information sent him from Washington as to Senator Mason's plans, "that no one who leaves the country will be pursued, and no one who stands his ground will be molested. I think the reason why Phillips & I have not been summoned is that it was well understood that we were not going to Canada. Mason does not wish to have John Brown heartily defended before the committee & the country — nor does he wish to cause an *émeute*, either in Massachusetts or Washington. He wishes simply to say that he tried for evidence & it was refused him. If his witnesses go to Canada or Europe, he is freed from all responsibility."[56] The event wholly bore Mr. Higginson out, but the others were not of his opinion at any time.

There was an early exodus of them to Canada. Frederick Douglass left Rochester for the shelter of the British flag as early as October 19, or the day after Brown was captured, and was soon on his way to England.[57] Mr. Sanborn was only a day behind, departing from Concord on October 20, to return, however, by the 26th.[58] From Portland, Mr. Sanborn thus jocularly notified Mr. Higginson of his departure:

PORTLAND, Oct. 21st, 1859.

DEAR FRIEND: According to advice of good friends and my own deliberate judgment I am going to try change of air for my old complaint. By this means it is thought that others will benefit as well as I; whether my absence will be long or short will depend on circumstances. Yours of the 19th was rec'd yesterday before I left home. Should you have occasion to write me again I have a friend in *Quebec* named *Frederick Stanley* to whom you can write.

Burn this.

Yours ever.[59]

The reason for the hasty move was John A. Andrew's opinion that the conspirators might be suddenly and secretly arrested and hurried out of the State. Mr. Sanborn believed, too, that it was "very important that the really small extent of our movement should be concealed, and its reach and character exaggerated. . . ."[60] After a more careful study of the question, Mr. Andrew advised George L. Stearns and Dr. Howe that he could find nothing for which they could be tried in Massachusetts or "carried to any other state."[61] Nevertheless, Stearns and Howe were on the way to Canada by October 25, remaining outside of the jurisdiction of the United States until after the execution of the crusader they had helped to send into Virginia.[62] Later, on December 12, Mr. Andrew wrote to Senator Fessenden, of Maine:

"I am confident that there are some half dozen men who ought not to testify *anywhere*, and who never will, with my consent as counsel, or otherwise, do so. Not that they knew, or foreknew Harper's Ferry; — but, that their relations with Brown were such & their knowledge of his movements & intentions, as a 'practical abolitionist,' aiding the escape of slaves by force, — even at the risk of armed encounter, — that they could not without personal danger say anything. Nor could they be known as having those relations, without giving some color to the charge that Republicans co-operate in such movements."[63]

Mr. Stearns "escaped from Dr. Howe" — so his son records — on the fatal December 2. He was never as worried as Dr. Howe, whom he found much agitated the first time they met after the raid.

Unfortunately, Dr. Howe let his anxieties control him. He issued on November 14 a card dated in Boston, although he was still absent, in which he made the following inexplicable statements:

"Rumor has mingled my name with the events at Harper's Ferry. So long as it rested on such absurdities as letters written *to* me by Col. Forbes, or others, it was too idle for notice. But when complicity is distinctly charged by one of the parties engaged [John E. Cook], my friends beseech me to define my position; and I consent the less reluctantly, because I divest myself of what, in time, might be considered an honor, and I want no undeserved ones. As regards Mr. Cook . . . I never saw him . . . never even heard of him until since the outbreak at Harper's Ferry. That event was unforeseen and unexpected by me; nor does all my previous knowledge of John Brown enable me to reconcile it with his characteristic prudence and his reluctance to shed blood, or excite servile insurrection. It is still, to me, a mystery, and a marvel. As to the heroic man who planned and led that forlorn hope, my relations with him in former times were such as no man ought to be afraid or ashamed to avow. If ever my testimony as to his high qualities can be of use to him or his, it shall be forthcoming at the fitting time and place. But neither this nor any other testimony shall be extorted for unrighteous purposes, if I can help it."

Dr. Howe then explained that there were certain "deadly instruments" among the statutes of the Union under which "we of the North may be forced to uphold and defend the barbarous system of Human Slavery," because a "dishonest Judge in the remotest South" could through a marshal cause the arrest of any citizen and have him brought before the court. He concluded as follows:

"I am told by high legal authority that Massachusetts is so trammelled by the bonds of the Union, that, as matters now stand, she cannot, or dare not protect her citizens from such forcible extradition; and that each one must protect himself as best he may. Upon that hint I shall act; preferring to forego anything rather than the right to free thought and free speech." [64]

In view of Dr. Howe's having known of the raid from February 26, 1858, when Mr. Sanborn informed him of all Brown's plans except the precise location at Harper's Ferry,[65] the statements above can be defended only on the theory that it is proper to misrepresent when one finds one's self in an uncomfortable or dangerous position. This sad attitude of a man at all other times a brave and high-minded philanthropist and a rarely useful servant of humanity, brought forth a vigorous reproach from Mr. Higginson.[66] In his indignation of the moment he notified Mr. Sanborn that he regarded Dr. Howe's card as anything but honorable.[67]

For three months Dr. Howe could not find time to reply to Mr. Higginson. On February 16 he attempted to justify his course, writing as to the card of November 14:

". . . I was not very decided in the belief of its expediency. It was done, however, in consequence of an opinion which I held, and hold, that everything which could be honestly done to show that John Brown was not the Agent, or even the ally of others, but an individual acting upon his own responsibility, would increase the chances of escape for him and his companions. I believed, and I believe, that every manifestation at that time of public sympathy for him and his acts, lessened the chances of his escape, whether by rescue or otherwise. . . . Of course, there were other considerations, but this was the leading one. . . . You say that it was skilfully written; but you seem to imply that honorable men, who knew all the facts, would disapprove it. But, my friend, it was *simply* written and not intended to carry a false impression. It was submitted to an honorable man who knew all that I knew about John Brown's movements, and a great deal more, and he approved it,* before its publication." [68]

As for his last interview with John Brown, Dr. Howe reiterated that "he [Brown] did not then reveal to me his destination, or his purpose. We *had no conversation about* his future *plans*. His appearance at 'Harper's Ferry' was to me not only unexpected but quite astonishing. The original plan as I understood it was quite different from this one; & even that I supposed was abandoned." Dr. Howe averred that the last fifty dollars he had sent to Brown when he was at the Kennedy Farm, were given to show his sympathy and "without cognizance of his purpose." [69] When Dr. Howe finally appeared before the Mason Committee, he made every effort to baffle the inquirers. For instance, he tried to make them believe that the last fifty dollars he gave went toward the purchase of the Thompson farm for Brown. Fortunately for him and the other conspirators, the Mason Committee was not only easily led astray, but, as Mr. Sanborn has well said, its questions

---

* This was presumably John A. Andrew; if this excellent man and lawyer advised Dr. Howe's course, he must also share the responsibility.

BY MAN SHALL HIS BLOOD BE SHED 533

were "so unskilfully framed that they [the witnesses] could, without literal falsehood, answer as they did." [70] Mr. Sanborn was of a different mind from Mr. Higginson as to Dr. Howe's card.[71] His reasoning, however, only aroused Mr. Higginson anew, and led him to ask on November 17, 1859: "Is there no such thing as *honor* among confederates?"[72] Making all due allowances for the heat of the moment as expressed in Colonel Higginson's letter, it does not seem even at this date that his reasoning was far wrong.

Mr. Sanborn has lately set forth in detail his own movements and the reasons therefor. By the 19th of November, 1859, he had decided "to pursue my usual occupation or any that I may take up, whatever summons or other process may be issued; shall resist arrest by force, shall refuse to sue a writ of *habeas corpus* — but, if arrested, shall consent to be rescued only by force. It is possible the anxiety of friends may induce me to modify this course, but I think not."[73] Early in January, 1860, he received a summons from the Mason Committee. Like John Brown, Jr., he refused to go to Washington because there was no assurance of his personal safety, — he might be seized in passing through Maryland. When, for this reason, Mr. Sanborn offered to testify in Massachusetts, Senator Mason wrote that he would be personally responsible for Mr. Sanborn's safety. To this the latter replied that as Senator Sumner had been brutally assaulted in the Senate, he could hardly rely on Senator Mason's offer of protection. Says Mr. Sanborn:

"Upon the receipt of this missive, Mason reported me to the Senate as a contumacious witness, and my arrest was voted, February 16, 1860, as that of John Brown, Jr., and James Redpath was. A few of the Southern Senators, seeing that my attitude about State Rights was quite similar to theirs, voted against my arrest, and began to send me their political speeches. Not choosing to be seized before I was quite ready, I retired to Canada, in the latter part of February, taking North Elba in my northward route, in order to see the Brown family, and to make arrangements for two of Brown's daughters, Anne and Sarah, to enter my school, as they did, in March."[74]

On the night of April 3, 1860, peaceful Concord was aroused by one of the dramatic incidents of its history. Five men, headed by a Boston constable, Silas Carleton, arrested Sanborn in his home. The outcries of his sister, his own struggles, the ringing of the alarm-bells, the rallying to his support of his neighbors, saved him from being carried off. His counsel was quickly at his side and hurried at once to Judge Rockwood Hoar, a near-by neighbor, who on hearing the tumult had quietly begun to fill out the "proper blank for the great writ of personal replevin." It was in the hands of a deputy sheriff within ten minutes. When he demanded Mr. Sanborn's surrender of Carleton's men, they refused to give him up, — only to have him taken from them by a hastily formed but most zealous *posse comitatus*. The Supreme Court quickly decided the next day that his arrest by the emissaries of the Senate was without warrant of law, and Mr. Sanborn returned to Concord a hero to his townspeople. He protested to the Senate and began suit against Carleton and his men, and thereafter he remained in peace.

Mr. Stearns appeared before the Mason Committee on February 24, 1860, and his testimony is as interesting as it is historically valuable. He, too, denied any pre-knowledge of the raid except as a plan to "relieve slaves" by force. But he was obviously unafraid. When Senator Mason asked, the three-hour examination being over, and all the members of the committee but himself having left the room: "Don't your conscience trouble you for sending those rifles to Kansas to shoot our innocent people?" Mr. Stearns replied: "Self-defence. You began the game. You sent Buford and his company with arms before we sent any from Massachusetts."[75] Senator Mason later remarked to Mr. Stearns: "I think when you go to that lower place, the Old Fellow will question you rather hard about this matter and you will have to take it." "Before that time comes," retorted Mr. Stearns wittily, "I think he will have about two hundred years of Slavery to investigate, and before he gets through that, will say, we have had enough of this business — better let the rest go."[76] Senator Mason laughed and left the room. Asked, in the course of the formal examination, if he disapproved of the raid at Harper's Ferry, Mr. Stearns responded: "I should have disapproved of it if I had known of it; but I have since changed my opinion; I believe John Brown to be the representative man of this century, as Washington was of the last — the Harper's Ferry affair, and

BY MAN SHALL HIS BLOOD BE SHED   535

the capacity shown by the Italians for self-government, the great events of this age. One will free Europe and the other America."[77] Mr. Stearns returned to Boston to render valuable service to his State in the Civil War, and retained, as long as he lived, the respect and regard of the community in which he dwelt.

Upon Gerrit Smith the news of the raid had as deplorable an effect as upon Dr. Howe. His biographer, O. B. Frothingham, states that a high medical authority had declared Gerrit Smith to have reached the stage of insanity known as "exaltation of mind" early in 1859;[78] that in the fall of 1859 he ate and slept little and was exhausted without knowing it. When the Harper's Ferry attack became public, it had an astounding influence upon Mr. Smith. The outcries against him as an accessory, in the pro-slavery press and by his political enemies, the rumor that the Virginia authorities were about to requisition the Governor of New York for his extradition, and the bloody and futile character of the raid itself, all reduced him to a state of terror. He saw crumbling before him the high social and political position he had won, — Mr. Smith had been candidate for the governorship of New York in 1858. A reporter of the New York *Herald* found him, on October 30, nervously agitated, "as though some great fear were constantly before his imagination," and repeating again and again that he was going to be indicted. Edwin Morton, Mr. Sanborn's classmate, who had been cognizant of the Brown plot as a member of Gerrit Smith's household, promptly fled to England,[79] and Colonel Charles D. Miller, Mr. Smith's son-in-law, was sent to Ohio and to Boston to obtain or destroy all of Mr. Smith's letters to the confederates, lest they be used against him.[80] "After struggling for several days," wrote Mr. Frothingham, "he went down under a troop of hallucinations." On November 7 he was removed to the Utica Asylum for the Insane, whose superintendent, Dr. Gray, is said to have declared that a delay of even forty-eight hours would have been fatal, so great was the "physical prostration of the patient."

If this were the whole story, it would be easy to pass over Mr. Smith's case with an expression of unbounded sympathy and a regret that he, too, had failed properly to weigh the consequences of committing himself to John Brown's schemes.

Unfortunately, after his return from his brief stay in the asylum (on December 29), he concealed or denied the extent of his knowledge and complicity in the raid. Mr. Frothingham has put the case as charitably as possible:

"On emerging from the mental obscuration at Utica, the whole scheme or tissue of schemes had vanished and become visionary. . . . It was a dream, a mass of recollections tumultuous and indistinct. Then cool reflection came in. The practical objections to the enterprise, which had flitted across his mind before, settled down heavily upon it. The ill-judged nature of the plan in its details and in its general scope forced itself upon his consideration, and made him wish he had never been privy to it. The wish was father to a thought, the thought to a purpose. His old horror of blood, his old disbelief in violence as a means of redressing wrong, resumed its sway over his feelings. The man of business repelled the association with the visionary and tried to persuade himself that he had taken no part in operations that were so easily disconcerted. He set himself to the task of making the shadowy recollections more shadowy still, and reducing his terms of alliance with the audacious conspirator to sentiments of personal sympathy and admiration." [81]

This led him to deny, even as late as 1867, that he gave money to John Brown with the purpose of aiding his insurrection.[82] Mr. Frothingham was unable to defend him or to exculpate him on the ground of insanity, and Mr. Sanborn, in his recently published account of this episode, — long withheld out of consideration for the family, — makes it as clear as have the earlier chapters of this narrative, that Gerrit Smith was, like Sanborn, Howe and the others, cognizant of every detail of the raid save the place of its beginning. Indeed, in a letter to the chairman of the Jerry Rescue Committee, dated August 27, 1859, Mr. Smith had foreshadowed the raid by writing: "For insurrection then we may look any year, any month, any day. A terrible remedy for a terrible wrong! But come it must unless anticipated by repentance and the putting away of the terrible wrong." [83]

However great the perturbation of his Northern associates, no prisoner in Virginia's history up to that time had displayed greater serenity of spirit than did John Brown himself behind his cell doors in Charlestown. It was a revelation to the Virginians. Here was a man sore in body, who ought to be sore in spirit, two of whose sons had been killed

BY MAN SHALL HIS BLOOD BE SHED

at his side, whose own death was not far away. More than that, the object of a lifetime had wholly miscarried. Propriety and precedent prescribed a cast-down prisoner, chagrined, humiliated, despairing. Instead, the miscreant in the custody of Sheriff Campbell proved a man of unquenchable spirit, of most equable temperament, and of unswerving courage, who apparently believed himself the conqueror, even with the light chains upon his ankles which he wore for the first few days. He wrote but the truth as to his own spirit and composure in his first letter from the jail to his family at North Elba:

CHARLESTOWN, JEFFERSON CO, VA.
31st Oct.

MY DEAR WIFE, & CHILDREN EVERY ONE

I suppose you have learned before this by the newspapers that Two weeks ago today we were fighting for our lives at Harpers ferry: that during the fight Watson was mortally wounded; Oliver killed, Wm Thompson killed, & Dauphin slightly wounded. That on the following day I was taken prisoner immediately after which I received several Sabre-cuts in my head; & Bayonet stabs in my body. As nearly as I can learn Watson died of his wound on Wednesday the 2d or on Thursday the 3d day after I was taken.

Dauphin was killed when I was taken; & Anderson I suppose also. I have since been tried, & found guilty of Treason, etc; and of murder in the first degree. I have not yet received my sentence. No others of the company with whom you were acquainted were, so far as *I can learn*, either killed or taken. Under all these terrible calamities; I feel quite cheerful in the assurance that God reigns; & will overrule all for his glory; & the best possible good. I feel *no* consciousness of *guilt* in the matter: nor even mortifycation on account of my imprisonment; & irons; & I feel perfectly sure that very soon no member of my family will feel any possible disposition to "blush on my account." Already dear friends at a distance with kindest sympathy are cheering me with the assurance that *posterity* at least will do me justice. I shall commend you all together, with my beloved; but bereaved daughters in law, to their sympathies which I do not doubt will reach you.

I also commend you all to Him "whose mercy endureth forever:" to the God of my *fathers* "whose I am; & whom I serve." "He will never leave you nor forsake you," unless you forsake Him. Finally my dearly beloved be of good comfort. Be sure to remember *& to follow my advice* & my example too; so far as it has been consistent with the holy religion of Jesus Christ in which I remain a most firm, & humble believer. Never forget the poor nor think anything you bestow on them to be lost, to you even though they may be as *black* as Ebedmelch the Ethiopean eunuch who cared for Jeremiah in the pit of the dungeon; or as *black* as the one to whom Phillip preached Christ. Be sure to entertain strangers, for thereby some have — "Remember them that are in bonds as bound with them." I am in charge of a jailor *like* the one who took charge of "Paul & Silas;" & you may rest assured that both *kind hearts* & *kind faces* are more or less about me; whilst thousands are thirsting for my blood. "These *light* afflictions which are but *for a moment* shall work out for us a *far more exceeding & eternal* weight of Glory." I hope to be able to write to you again. My wounds are doing well. Copy this, & send it to your sorrow stricken brothers, Ruth; to comfort them. Write me a few words in regard to the welfare of all. God Allmighty bless you all: & "make you joyful in the midst of all your tribulations." Write to John Brown Charlestown Jefferson Co, Va, care of Capt John Avis.

    Your Affectionate Husband, & Father,
                  JOHN BROWN

P S Yesterday Nov 2d I was sentenced to be hanged on Decem 2d next. Do not grieve on my account. I am still quite cheerful. God bless you all.
       Yours ever
                J BROWN [84]

In their generous permission to John Brown to write freely to all whom he wished to address, his captors were unwittingly allowing him to use a — for them — far more dangerous weapon than the Sharp's rifle they had taken from him at Harper's Ferry. As a wielder of arms, John Brown inspires no enthusiasm; not even the flaming sword of Gideon in his hands lifts him above the ordinary run of those who battled in their day for a great cause. For all his years of dreaming that he might become another Schamyl, or Toussaint L'Ouverture, or the Mountain Marion of a new war of liberation, he was anything but a general. In his knapsack was no field-marshal's baton; where he thought there might be one, lay instead an humble pen to bring him glory. For when he was stripped of his liberty, of the arms in which he exulted, the great power of the spirit within was revealed to him. The letters which now daily went forth to friends and relatives, and speedily found their way into print, found their way also to the hearts of all who sympathized with him, and of many who abhorred his methods, or who had heretofore steeled themselves against him. Some idea of their power may be gathered from the fact that Sheriff Campbell was compelled many times to wipe

BY MAN SHALL HIS BLOOD BE SHED

the tears from his eyes when, as a matter of duty, he read over his captive's epistles.[85] The innate nobility of the man, his essential unselfishness and his readiness for the supreme sacrifice, all heightened the impending tragedy, and brought to many the conviction that, misguided as he was, here was another martyr whose blood was to be the seed, not of his church, but of his creed. Some of these moving products of his pen may well find a place here:

CHARLESTOWN, JEFFERSON COUNTY, VA., Nov. 1, 1859.

MY DEAR FRIEND E. B. OF R. I.: Your most cheering letter of the 27th of Oct. is received, and may the Lord reward you a thousand fold for the kind feeling you express toward me; but more especially for your fidelity to the "poor that cry, and those that have no help." For this I am a prisoner in bonds. It is solely my own fault, in a military point of view, that we met with our disaster — I mean that I mingled with our prisoners and so far sympathized with them and their families that I neglected my duty *in other* respects. But God's will, not mine, be done.

You know that Christ once armed Peter. So also in my case, I think he put a sword into my hand, and there continued it, so long as he saw best, and then kindly took it from me. I mean when I first went to Kansas. I wish you could know with what cheerfulness I am now wielding the "Sword of the Spirit" on the right hand and on the left. I bless God that it proves "mighty to the pulling down of strongholds." I always loved my Quaker friends, and I commend to their kind regard my poor, bereaved widowed wife, and my daughters and daughters-in-law, whose husbands fell at my side. One is a mother and the other likely to become so soon. They, as well as my own sorrow-stricken daughter[s], are left very poor, and have much greater need of sympathy than I, who, through Infinite Grace and the kindness of strangers, am "joyful in all my tribulations."

Dear sister, write them at North Elba, Essex Co., N. Y., to comfort their sad hearts. Direct to Mary A. Brown, wife of John Brown. There is also another — a widow, wife of Thompson, who fell with my poor boys in the affair at Harper's Ferry, at the same place.

I do not feel conscious of guilt in taking up arms; and had it been in behalf of the rich and powerful, the intelligent, the great — as men count greatness — of those who form enactments to suit themselves and corrupt others, or some of their friends, that I interfered, suffered, sacrificed, and fell, it would have been doing very well. But enough of this.

These light afflictions which endure for a moment, shall work out for me *a far more exceeding and eternal weight of glory*. I would be very grateful for another letter from you. My wounds are healing.

Farewell. God will surely attend to his own cause in the best possible way and time, and he will not forget the work of his own hands.
Your friend,

JOHN BROWN.[86]

To his wife he wrote thus on November 10:

CHARLESTOWN JEFFERSON CO. VA. 10th Nov. 1859.
MY DEAR DEVOTED WIFE

I have just learned from Mr. Hoyt of Boston that he saw you with dear kind friends in Philadelphia on your return trip you had so far made in the expectation of again seeing me in this world of "sin & sorrow." I need not tell you that I had a great desire to see you again: but that many strong objections exist in my mind against it. I have before alluded to them in what I have said in my other letters (which I hope you will soon get) & will not now repeat them; as it is exceedingly laborious for me to write at all. I am under renewed obligation to you my ever faithful & beloved wife, for heeding what may be my last but earnest request. I have before given you a very brief statement of the fall of our dear sons; & other friends. Full particulars relating to our disaster; I cannot now give: & may never give *probably.* I am greatly comforted by learning of the kindness already shown you; & allow me *humbly* to repeat the language of a far greater man & better sinner than I. "I have been young; & now am old: yet have I not seen the righteous forsaken nor his seed begging bread." I will here say that the sacrifizes *you;* & I, have been called to make in behalf of the *cause we love* the *cause of God; & of humanity:* do not seem to me as at all too great. I have been *whiped* as the saying *is;* but am sure I can recover all the lost capital occasioned by that disaster; by only hanging a few moments by the neck; & I feel quite determined to make the utmost possible out of a defeat. I am dayly & hourly striving to gather up what little I may from the wreck. I mean to write you as *much & as often* as I have Strength (or may be permitted to write.) "Be of good cheer:" in the world we must have tribulation: but the *cords* that have bound *you* as well as I; to earth: have been many of them severed already. Let us with sincere gratitude receive all that "our Father in Heaven" may send us; for "he doeth all things well." *You* must kiss our dear children and grandchildren for me. May the "God of my fathers" be the God, & father of all — "To him be everlasting praise." "Although the fig tree shall not blossom: neither shall fruit be in the vines: the labour of the olive shall fail, and the fields shall yield no meat: the flock shall be cut off from the fold, and there shall be no herd in the stalls: yet *I will rejoice* in the Lord, I will joy in the God of my salvation." I want dear Ruth; or *Anne;* to send copies (when they can) to their deeply afflicted brothers, of all I write. I cannot muster strength to write them all. If after Virginia has applied the finishing stroke to the picture already made

BY MAN SHALL HIS BLOOD BE SHED

of me (in order to *"establish Justice"*) you can afford to meet the expence & trouble of coming on here to gather up the bones of our beloved sons, & of your husband; and the people here will suffer you to do so; I should be entirely willing. I have just received a most welcome letter from a dear old friend of my youth; Rev. H. L. Vail of Litchfield Connecticut. Will you get some kind friend to copy this letter to you & send him very plain as all the acknowledgement I have *now* strength to make him; & the other kind friends he mentions. I cannot write my friends as I would do; if I had strength. Will you answer to Jeremiah in the same way *for the present* a letter I have received from him? Write me wont you? God bless you all
 Your affectionate Husband
 JOHN BROWN.[87]

He had previously adjured his wife and children to remember, all,

"that *Jesus of Nazareth* suffered a most excruciating death on the cross as a fellon; under the most agravating circumstances. Think also of the prophets, & Apostles, & Christians of former days; who went through *greater* tribulations than you & I; & be reconciled. May God Allmighty 'comfort all your hearts and soon wipe away all tears from your eyes.' To him be endless praise. Think *too* of the crushed Millions who 'have no comforters.' *I charge you all never* (in your trials) *to forget* the griefs of 'the poor that cry; & of those that have none to help them.'"[88]

On the 16th of November he thus expressed himself as to the education of his daughters:

"Now let me say a word about the effort to educate our daughters. I am no longer able to provide means to help towards that object, and it therefore becomes me not to dictate in the matter. I shall gratefully submit the direction of the whole thing to those whose generosity may lead them to undertake in their behalf, while I give *anew* a little expression of my own choice respecting it. You, my wife, *perfectly well* know that I have always expressed a decided preference for a very *plain but perfectly practical* education for both *sons and daughters*. I do not mean an education so very miserable as that *you* and *I* received in early life; nor as some of our children enjoyed. When I say plain but practical, I mean enough of the learning of the schools to enable them to transact the common business of life, comfortably and respectably, together with that thorough training to good business habits which best prepares both men and women to be *useful though poor*, and to meet the *stern* Realities of life with a *good* grace. You well know that I always claimed that the *music* of the broom, washtub, needle, spindle, loom, axe, scythe, hoe, flail, etc., should first be learned, at all events, and that of the piano, etc., afterwards. I put them in that order as most conducive to health of body and mind; and for the obvious reason, that after a life of some *experience and of much observation*, I have found *ten women* as well as *ten men* who have made their mark in life *Right*, whose early training was of that *plain*, *practical* kind, to *one* who had a more popular and fashionable *early* training. But enough of that."

To this he added:

"Now, in regard to your coming here; If you feel sure that you can endure the trials and the shock, which will be *unavoidable* (if you come), I should be most glad to see you *once more;* but when I think of your being insulted on the road, and perhaps *while here*, and of only seeing your wretchedness made complete, I *shrink* from it. Your composure and fortitude of mind may be *quite equal to it all;* but I am in *dreadful* doubt of it. *If you do come*, defer your journey till about the 27th or 28th of this month. The scenes which you will have to pass through on coming here will be *anything but those* you now pass, with tender, kind-hearted friends, and kind faces to meet you everywhere. *Do consider the matter well* before you make the *plunge*. I think I had better say *no more* on this *most painful* subject. My health improves a little; my mind is very tranquil, I may say joyous, and I continue to receive every kind attention that I have any possible need of." [89]

To a sympathizer in West Newton, Massachusetts, Brown wrote as follows:

CHARLESTOWN, JEFFERSON CO, 15th Nov. 1859.

GEORGE ADAMS ESQR.

MY DEAR SIR

Your most kind communication of the 5th inst was received by me in due time. You request a few lines from me: which I cannot deny you: though much at a loss what to write. Your kind mention of *some* things in my conduct here which you approve; is very comforting indeed to my mind: yet I am conscious that you do me more than justice. I do certainly feel that through divine grace *I have endeavoured* to be "faithful in a very few things;" mingling with even those much of imperfection. I am certainly unworthy even to "suffer affliction with the *people of God;*" yet, in Infinite grace he has *thus* honored me. May the *same grace* enable me to serve him in *"new obedience"* through my little remainder of this life; and to rejoice in him forever. I cannot feel that God will suffer even the poorest service we may any of us render him or his cause to be lost; or in vain. I do feel "dear Brother;" that I am wonderfully "strengthened from on high." May I use that strength in "showing *his strength* unto this generation," and his power to every one that is to come. I am most grateful for your assurance that

(Facsimile)

Charlestown, Jefferson Co, Va. 15.th Nov. 1859.

George Adams Esqr

My Dear Sir

Your most kind communication of the 5.th inst was received by me in due time. You request a few lines from me: which I cannot deny you; though much at a loss what to write. Your kind mention of some things in my conduct here which you approve; is very comforting indeed to my mind: yet I am conscious that you do me more than justice. I do certainly feel that through divine grace I have endeavoured to be "faithful in a very few things"; mingling with even those much of imperfection. I am certainly unworthy to suffer affliction with the "people of God"; yet in Infinite grace he has thus honored me. May the same grace enable me to serve him in "new obedience" through my little remainder of this life; & to rejoice in him forever. I cannot feel that God will suffer even the poorest service we may any of us render him or his cause to be lost, or in vain. I do feel dear "Brother"; that I am wonderfully "strengthened from on high." May I use that strength in "showing his strength unto this generation". & his power to

~~to~~ every one that is to come. I am most grateful for your assurance that my poor shattered "heart broken family will not be forgotten". I have long tried to commend them to the "God of my Fathers". I have many opportunities for faithful plain dealing with the more powerful, influential, & inteligent class; in this region: which I trust are not entirely missimproved. I humbly trust that I firmly believe that "God reigns"; & I think I can truly say "Let the Earth rejoice" May God take care of his own cause; & of his own great name; as well as of them who love their neighbours.

    Farewell   Your in truth
                      John Brown

George Adams Esqr.
West Newton
Mass

my poor shattered heart-broken "family *will not* be forgotten." I have long tried to commend them to "the God of my Fathers." I have *many* opportunities for *faithful plain dealing;* with the more powerful, influential, and inteligent class; in this region: which I trust are not entirely misimproved. I *humbly trust that I* firmly believe that "God reigns;" and I think I can truly say "Let the Earth *rejoice*."

May God take care of his *own cause; and of his own great name:* as well as of them who love their neighbours.
        Farewell
                Your[s] in truth
                  JOHN BROWN [90]

In a letter to a kinsman, Luther Humphrey, dated November 19, occur these passages:

"Your kind letter of the 12th inst. is now before me. So far as my knowledge goes as to our mutual kindred; I suppose *I am the first* since the landing of Peter Brown from the Mayflower that has *either been sentenced to imprisonment;* or to the Gallows. But my dear old friend; let not that fact *alone* grieve you. You cannot have forgotten *how; & where* our Grand Father Capt (John Brown:) fell in 1776; & *that he too;* might have perished on the Scaffold had circumstances been but *very little* different. *The fact* that a man dies under the hand of an executioner (or otherwise) has but little to do with his true character; as I suppose: John Rogers perished at the stake a *great & good* man as I suppose: but *his being so*, does *not prove* that any other man who has died in the same way was *good:* or *otherwise.* Whether I have any reason to 'be of good cheer' (or not) in view of my end; I can assure you that *I feel so;* & that I am totally *blinded* if I do not realy *experience* that *strengthening;* & *consolation* you so faithfully implore in my behalf. God of *our Fathers* reward your fidelity. I neither feel *mortified, degraded, nor in the least ashamed* of my imprisonment, my chain, or my near prospect *of death by hanging.* I feel assured 'that not one hair shall fall from my head without my heavenly Father.' I also feel that I have *long been* endeavoring to hold exactly 'such a *fast* as God has chosen.' See the passage in Isaiah which you have quoted. No part of my life has been more hapily spent; than that I have spent here; & I humbly *trust* that no part has been spent to better purpose. I *would not* say this *boastingly*, but 'thanks be unto God who giveth us the victory; *through Infinite grace*.'" [91]

And, finally, to his staunch friend, Thomas Wentworth Higginson, he wrote on November 22:

DEAR SIR

I write you a few lines to express to you my deep feeling of gratitude for your journey to visit & comfort my family as well as myself

in different ways & at different times; since my imprisonment here.
Truly you have proved yourself to be "a friend in need;" & *I feel
my many obligations for all your kind attentions, none the less;* for
my wishing my Wife *not* to come on when she first set out. I would
it were in my power to make *to all* my kind friends; some *other
acknowledgements* than a mere tender of *our & my* thanks. I can
assure *all:* Mrs. Stearns, my young friend Hoyt; & many others I
have been unable to write to as yet; that I *certainly do not forget;*
their love, & kindness. *God Allmighty* bless; & save them *all;* &
grant *them to see;* a fulfilment of all their reasonable desires. . . .
I am getting much better of my wounds; but am *yet rather lame.*
Am very cheerful *& trust* I may continue so "to the end."

  My love to all   Yours for *God* &
  dear friends.   *the right;*
                  JOHN BROWN [92]

As he lay in jail at Charlestown, so vividly did the press portray John Brown in his prison background that those in the North who were moved by his speeches in court and his letters could fairly hear the clanking of his chains, could behold him on his bed of suffering, and later could see him toiling with his pen. The reporting was detailed and faithful. From it the public learned that in Captain John Avis he had a kind and considerate jailer; that by the 2d of November all his wounds were healed, save one cut on the back of his head;[93] that he welcomed and greeted his visitors cordially, even Captain Sinn and his militiamen from Frederick, who were permitted to enter the jail at the end of October and stare at the prisoners as if they were caged animals. They were amazed at John Brown's composure and contentment as he told them of his admiration for the picked company of Virginia riflemen he had been thrown with in the War of 1812, and expressed his regret that circumstances prevented his seeing Captain Sinn's men on parade.[94] Only one visitor did John Brown render really uncomfortable. He was a Methodist clergyman, Norval Wilson, who, after calling on Brown with others of his cloth, proposed a prayer. "Mr. Wilson," asked Brown, "do you believe in slavery?" Mr. Wilson replied, "I do, under the present circumstances." "Then," said Brown with great earnestness, "I do not want your prayers. I don't want the prayers of any man that believes in slavery. You can pray to your Father that heareth in secret."[95] In a similar spirit he wrote to the Rev. Mr. McFarland, of Wooster, Ohio:

"You may wonder, are there no ministers of the gospel here? I answer, No. There are no ministers of *Christ* here. These ministers who profess to be Christian, and hold slaves or advocate slavery, I cannot abide them. My knees will not bend in prayer with them while their hands are stained with the blood of souls." [96]

To the local newspaper editors who called, he was frank and cordial, answering freely every question which did not "involve others" and that was "consistent with honor." When asked by the Charlestown *Independent Democrat* if he were ready to meet death under the law, his reply was: "Am entirely ready so far as I know," and, "I feel no shame on account of my doom. Jesus of Nazareth was doomed in like manner. Why should not I be?" [97]

The first of several friendly visitors from the North were Judge and Mrs. Russell. The latter remembers to this day how calm, rugged and comfortable Brown looked on the day the court fixed the bounds of his life. "Oh, my dear," he exclaimed to Mrs. Russell, "this is no place for you." But she found that there was some woman's work to do, for she had the captive's coat cleaned, and repaired it with her skilful hands, while her husband, as they conversed, was ever looking at the wide chimney in the room and praying that John Brown might be spirited away to freedom by that ample channel.[98] To the judge the prisoner reiterated his assertion, often made in those prison days, that he was not personally concerned in the Pottawatomie murders, — an assertion which misled Judge Russell into saying, on John Brown's word, that the latter had "nothing to do" with the killing; and Wendell Phillips into announcing publicly in Cooper Union that Brown was not at Pottawatomie — "not within twenty-five miles of the spot." [99]

"Have you objections," the Russells heard John Brown say to Captain Avis, in calm, unmoved tone, "to my writing to my wife and telling her that I am to be hanged on the second of December?" "At last," says Mrs. Russell, "we had to take our leave. I kissed him, weeping. His mouth trembled, ever so little, but he only said: 'Now, go.'" And back to their hotel the Russells went in tears, marvelling at the utter absence in their doomed friend of self-commiseration, or of anything suggesting a quarrel with fate. Just as they reached Boston, Mrs. Brown was starting for Harper's Ferry. There the Russells gave her the reassuring news of her husband's comfort and happiness, and told her that he would not walk out of jail then if its doors were thrown open, — so indebted to Captain Avis did he feel.[100]

If John Brown did not let his wife join him at that time, he did receive a visit from Mrs. Rebecca Spring, of Perth Amboy, New Jersey, who exclaimed to her husband, "I must go and help them," the instant she heard that there were wounded Abolitionists in prison at Harper's Ferry. "We have talked against slavery all these years; and now somebody has done something. These men have risked their lives; I must go," she said. And go she did, to tell John Brown, when she reached his cell, by permission of Judge Parker, that "it is better to die for a great idea than of a fever," and to learn from his lips that no spirit of revenge had actuated the raid. Mrs. Spring, too, ministered unto John Brown and his cellmate Stevens, the latter handsome and impressive despite his terrible wounds, and bearing his sufferings with grim and silent fortitude, expecting to die, but never once complaining.[101] *

To study Brown as he sat at his cell-desk, Edwin A. Brackett, a sculptor, of Boston, came, — thanks to Mrs. G. L. Stearns's generosity, — and sketched him from the door of the cell, as the first step toward the familiar idealized bust.[102] Later came an old friend of the Pennsylvania days, M. B. Lowry, to bid his instructor in tanning farewell.[103] Samuel C. Pomeroy, the friend from Kansas, and later its Senator, was greeted with, "In prison ye came unto me," when he entered Brown's cell to ask, "You remember the rescue of John Doy. Do you want your friends to attempt it?" But Brown only repeated, "I am worth now infinitely more to die than to live."[104] It was Henry Clay Pate, however, the conquered at Black Jack, who most vividly called up the Kansas days to Brown. Their meeting was not cordial. Captain Pate came to gloat over his ensnared conqueror, and Captain Brown of Osawatomie declared frankly that he had met many men possessed of more courage than Captain Pate, ex-Border Ruffian. To which Captain Pate responded by charging Brown with all kinds of villainy, particularly theft.[105]

* Mrs. Spring now lives in Los Angeles, having nearly reached the century mark.

BY MAN SHALL HIS BLOOD BE SHED

When, in response to the panic fears of his commanders at Charlestown, Governor Wise reached there on November 20, with four hundred soldiers, the little Virginia town had assumed all the appearance of a beleaguered city. The troops were quartered in the churches, schools and in the court-house. The very graveyards were invaded for washing and cooking purposes when the militia were not parading or playing "fox and hounds" in the streets.[106] Extraordinary were some of the military make-ups worn by the cavaliers. "Among many corps, each military gentleman selected his own uniform; and, while all seemed affected with a contempt for their citizen clothes, rarely more than two agreed in the selection of the color of their military dress."[107] But these men in buckram, as well as Governor Wise, were more desirous of seeing John Brown than of seeing even the charming women of Charlestown; and to his cell they were admitted in squads of ten and fifteen, save when the Governor himself was closeted with him.[108] It is an interesting fact that, much as the Virginians abhorred John Brown's actions, they respected his word. When he certified that a suspect brought before him had been a Border Ruffian and not a Free State man, the prisoner was instantly set free without question.[109] So Governor Wise talked once more with the State prisoner, with absolute confidence in his veracity and integrity. This interview Governor Wise himself has described:

"I visited John Brown but once after his incarceration to await his trial. I especially desired to ascertain whether he had any communication to make to me other than he had already made. He repeated mostly the same information, expressed his personal regard and respect for me, thanked me for my kindness in protecting him from all violence and in providing for his comfort. He complained of some disease of the kidneys, and I tendered him the best aid of physician and surgeon, which he declined, for the reason that he was accustomed to an habitual treatment, which he had already provided for himself. He talked with me freely and I offered to be the depositary of any confidential request consistent with my honor and duty; and when we parted he cordially gave me his blessing, wishing me every return for the attentions to him as a prisoner."[110]

While Governor Wise was with him, Brown corrected an obvious conflict between his statements as to his real object, after his capture (that it was not to carry off the slaves and free them), and his declaration in court, on being sentenced, that his sole object was to run the slaves off as he had done in Missouri. The next day he sent for Andrew Hunter, and after a talk with him, addressed to him the following note:

> CHARLESTOWN, JEFFERSON COUNTY, VA.,
> November 22, 1859.
>
> DEAR SIR: I have just had my attention called to a seeming conflict between the statement I at first made to Governor Wise and that which I made at the time I received my sentence, regarding my intentions respecting the slaves we took *about the Ferry*. There need be no such conflict, and a few words of explanation will, I think, be quite sufficient. I had given Governor Wise a *full and particular* account of that, and when called in court to say whether I had anything further to urge, I was taken wholly by surprise, as I did not expect my sentence before the others. In the hurry of the moment, I forgot much that I had before *intended to say*, and did *not* consider the full bearing of what *I then said*. I intended to convey this idea, that it was my object to place the slaves in a condition to defend their liberties, if they would, *without any bloodshed, but not* that I intended *to run them out of the slave States*. I was not *aware* of any such apparent conflict until my attention *was called* to it, and I do not suppose that a man in *my then circumstances* should be *superhuman* in respect to the *exact purport* of every word he might utter. What I said to Governor Wise was spoken with all the deliberation I was master of, *and was intended for truth;* and what I said in court was *equally intended for truth*, but required a more full explanation *than I then gave*. Please make such use of this as you think calculated to correct any *wrong* impressions I may have given.
>
> Very respectfully, yours,
>
> JOHN BROWN
>
> ANDREW HUNTER, ESQ., Present.[111] *

The suffering wife of the prisoner had not returned to North Elba, after being stopped at Baltimore on her way to her husband. It seemed best to those friends who now came to her aid to keep her where she could leave for Harper's Ferry at a moment's notice. So, heavy of heart, she went first to Mr.

---

* Andrew Hunter always declined to believe Brown's explanation that he was taken by surprise in court. It is interesting to note, however, that Dr. John D. Starry stated to a correspondent of the *Tribune* in May, 1884, that it was not true that John Brown had prevaricated after his capture; that he was a man of excitable temperament prone to error in excitement, but that when over his excitability "he was as exact as could be." See New York *Semi-Weekly Tribune*, May 27, 1884.

BY MAN SHALL HIS BLOOD BE SHED

William Still's home at Philadelphia, whence, with Mrs. Spring just from John Brown's cell, she went to Eagleswood, Mrs. Spring's Perth Amboy home. Here she received every attention, but it was deemed wise to have her return to Philadelphia on November 16, with Mr. McKim, with whom, and with Lucretia Mott, she spent the remaining weeks of her husband's life, quite content to abide by her husband's decision that it was unwise for her to go to his side.[112] On the 21st, with Mr. McKim's aid, she composed a touching letter to Governor Wise, begging for the "mortal remains of my husband and his sons" for decent and tender interment among their kindred.[113] Of his reply Governor Wise made two drafts, — the first even more creditable to him than the one sent, for in it he wrote: "If duty and law permitted, you should have the lives of your husband and sons instead of their mortal remains;" and that his feelings as a man "yearned toward her as a wife and a mother, a woman afflicted." The letter Mrs. Brown received contained these characteristic paragraphs:

"I am happy, Madam, that you seem to have the wisdom and virtue to appreciate my position of duty. Would to God that 'public considerations could avert his doom,' for The Omniscient knows that I take not the slightest pleasure in the execution of any whom the laws condemn. May He have mercy on the erring and the afflicted.

"Enclosed is an order to Major Genl. Wm. B. Taliaferro, in command at Charlestown, Va. to deliver to your order the mortal remains of your husband 'when all shall be over;' to be delivered to your agent at Harper's Ferry; and if you attend the reception in person, to guard you sacredly in your solemn mission.

"With tenderness and truth, I am,
"Very respectfully your humble servant,
HENRY A. WISE."[114]

On the 30th, Mrs. Brown, in response to the letter already quoted, was at Harper's Ferry, accompanied by Mr. and Mrs. McKim and Hector Tyndale, a rising young lawyer of Philadelphia. Governor Wise ordered by telegraph that she, alone, be permitted to visit her husband the next day, on condition of returning to Harper's Ferry that evening and awaiting there the delivery of his body.[115] A sergeant and eight men of the Fauquier Cavalry escorted her carriage on the long, dreary ride to Charlestown on December 1, and a

militia captain sat beside her.[116] At half-past three o'clock
they were in Charlestown, and a few minutes later began
that tragic last interview between husband and wife which
so deeply stirred the onlooking North. But, as was to be expected
from two such self-controlled characters as John and
Mary Brown, they in nowise gave way to their grief, save for
a minute or two as they met. Mrs. Brown had had her moment
of uncontrollable anguish in Philadelphia, when Governor
Wise's letter came to her with its final assurance that
there was no hope for her husband's life.[117] Now husband
and wife sat down to their final communion, — primarily to
discuss his will, her future, the education of their children.
When the coming event was touched upon, and her courage
began to fail, he assured her that while it would be pleasant
to live longer, he was content to go, for, after all, go he must
sooner or later.

When, however, it became evening and John Brown heard
that they must part soon, he begged that she be permitted
to pass the night with him. But the commanding general,
Taliaferro, had no option in the face of the Governor's explicit
instructions. It was the only time in all his confinement
that this great prisoner gave way to anger or passion. It
availed him not; and when the parting came, both husband
and wife "exhibited a composure, either feigned or real, that
was truly surprising." In Captain Avis's room Mrs. Brown's
tears came freely, and with her husband's last blessing ringing
in her ears, she began the long, dark ride back to her waiting
friends in Harper's Ferry.[118] They were practically prisoners,
these kind souls, for when they first went out to walk the
streets, a bullet whistled in the air, to Hector Tyndale's especial
annoyance. For he little dreamed that twenty-six months
later, on February 7, 1862, to him would fall the military duty,
while major of the Twenty-eighth Pennsylvania Infantry, of
burning nearly all of Harper's Ferry, save John Brown's fort.
So quickly did time then bring its revenges!

With his wife gone, John Brown, whose will had been drawn
for him by Andrew Hunter,[119] devoted himself for a time to
his last letters and to a brief but calm sleep. He had already
sent a final letter to his family, and, among half a dozen other
last farewells, this note:

BY MAN SHALL HIS BLOOD BE SHED

CHARLESTOWN, JEFFERSON CO VA. 29th Nov. 1859.

MRS GEORGE L STEARNS
   Boston Mass
MY DEAR FRIEND
   No letter I have received since my imprisonment here, has given me more satisfaction, or comfort; than yours of the 8th inst. I am quite cheerful: & was never more happy. Have only time [to] write you a word. May God forever reward you & *all yours. My love to All* who love their neighbours. I have asked to be *spared* from having any *mock; or hypocritical prayers made over me*, when I am publicly *murdered:* & that my only *religious attendants* be poor *little, dirty, ragged, bare headed, & barefooted Slave boys;* & *Girls;* led by some old grey headed Slave Mother.

Farewell. Farewell.
Your Friend
JOHN BROWN [120]

The letter to his family read in part thus:

CHARLESTOWN, PRISON, JEFFERSON CO, VA.
30th Nov 1859

MY DEARLY BELOVED WIFE, SONS: & DAUGHTERS, EVERYONE
   As I now begin what is probably the last letter I shall ever write to any of you; I conclude to write you all at the same time. . . . I am waiting the hour of my public *murder* with great composure of mind, & cheerfulness: feeling the strongest assurance that in no other possible way could I be used to so much advance the cause of God; & of humanity: & that nothing that either I or all my family have sacrificed or suffered: *will be lost.* The reflection that a *wise & merciful, as well as just & holy God:* rules not only the affairs of *this world;* but of all worlds; is a rock to set our feet upon; under all circumstances: *even* those more severely *trying ones:* into which our own follies; & rongs have placed us. I have now no doubt but that our seeming *disaster:* will ultimately result in the most *glorious success.* So my dear *shattered & broken* family be of good cheer; & believe & trust in God; *"with all your heart & with all your soul;"* for "*he* doeth *All things well."* Do not feel ashamed on my account; nor *for one moment* despair of the cause; or grow *weary of well doing.* I bless God; I never felt stronger confidence in the certain and near approach of a *bright Morning;* & a *glorious day;* than I have felt; & do now feel; since my confinement here. I am endeavouring to "return" like a "poor Prodigal" *as I am*, to my Father: against whom I have *always* sined: *in the hope;* that he may kindly, & forgivingly "meet me: though *a verry great way off*." Oh my dear Wife & Children would "to God" you could know how I have been "travelling in birth for you" *all:* that no one of you "may fail of the grace of God, through Jesus Christ:" that no one of you may be blind to the truth: & glorious "light of *his* word," in which Life;

& Immortality; are brought to light. I beseech you *every one* to make the bible your *dayly & Nightly study;* with a *childlike honest, candid, teachable spirit:* out of love and respect for your Husband; & Father: & I beseech *the God* of *my Fathers;* to open all your eyes to a discovery of *the truth.* You *cannot imagine* how much *you* may *soon need* the consolations of the Christian religion.

Circumstances like my own; for more than a month past; convince me beyound *all doubt:* of our great *need:* of something more to rest our hopes on; than merely our own vague theories framed up, while our *prejudices* are excited; *or* our *vanity* worked up to its highest pitch. Oh do not trust your eternal all uppon the boisterous Ocean, without *even* a *Helm;* or *Compass* to *aid* you in steering. I do *not ask any* of you; to throw *away your reason:* I only *ask* you, to make a candid & sober *use of your reason:* My dear younger children will you listen to the last poor admonition of one who can only love you? Oh be determined at once to give your whole hearts to God; & let *nothing* shake; or alter; that resolution. You need have no fear *of regreting it.* Do not be vain; and thoughtless: but *sober minded.* And let me entreat you all to love *the whole remnant* of our once great family: "with a pure *heart fervently.*" Try to *build again:* your broken walls: & to make *the utmost* of every *stone* that is left. Nothing can so tend to make life a blessing as the consciousness that you *love: & are beloved:* & "love ye the stranger" *still.* It is ground of the utmost comfort to *my mind:* to know that so many of you as have had *the opportunity;* have given full proof of your fidelity to the great family of man. Be faithful until death. From the exercise of habitual love to man: *it cannot* be very *hard:* to *learn to love* his *maker.* I must *yet* insert a reason for my firm belief in the Divine inspiration of the Bible: notwithstanding I am (perhaps naturally) skeptical: (certainly not, credulous.) I wish you all to consider *it most thoroughly;* when you read the blessed book; & see whether you *can not* discover such evidence yourselves. It is the purity of *heart, feeling, or motive:* as well as *word, & action* which is everywhere insisted on; that distinguish it from *all other teachings;* that *commends* it to *my conscience:* whether *my heart* be "willing, & obedient" *or not.* The inducements that it holds out; are another reason *of my conviction* of its *truth: & genuineness:* that I cannot here *omit;* in this my *last argument* for the Bible. *Eternal life;* is that my soul *is "panting after"* this moment. I mention this; as reason for endeavouring to leave a valuable copy of the Bible to be carefully *preserved* in remembrance of *me:* to so many of my posterity; *instead* of some other things of equal *cost.*

I beseech you all to live in habitual contentment with verry *moderate* circumstances: & gains, of worldly store: & most earnestly to teach this: to your *children; & Childrens Children;* after you: by *example: as well;* as precept. Be determined to know by experience as *soon as may be:* whether bible instruction is of *Divine origin* or not; *which says;* "*Owe no man anything but* to love one another."

BY MAN SHALL HIS BLOOD BE SHED

John Rogers wrote to his children, "Abhor the arrant whore of Rome." John Brown writes to his children to abhor with *undiing hatred*, also: that "sum of all vilainies;" Slavery. *Remember* that "he that is *slow* to *anger* is *better* than the mighty: and he that ruleth his spirit; than he that taketh a city." Remember also: *that* "they that be *wise* shall *shine*: and they that *turn* many to *righteousness*: as the stars forever; & ever." And now dearly beloved Farewell, To God & the word of his grace I comme[n]d you all.
    Your Affectionate Husband & Father
                JOHN BROWN [121]

The last night was quickly over; with the coming of the dawn men were stirring, for this day was to see a "judicial murder" which, more than any other in the country's history, thrilled it from ocean to ocean. He who was to pay the penalty was early at his Bible, in which, before bestowing it upon a confectioner who had been kind to him, he had marked the passages which had most influenced his life.[122] Then there was still another letter to be written to his wife:

           CHARLESTOWN, JEFFERSON CO, VA.
              2d Decem, 1859

MY DEAR WIFE
 I have time to enclose the within: *& the above:* which I forgot yesterday: & to bid you another Farewell: "be of good cheer" and God Allmighty bless, save, comfort, guide, & keep; you, to "the end."
    Your Affectionate Husband
        JOHN BROWN.

The enclosures read thus:

"To be inscribed on the old family Monument at North Elba.
"Oliver Brown born   1839 was killed at Harpers ferry Va Nov 17th 1859.
"Watson Brown, born   1835 was wounded at Harpers ferry Nov 17th and died Nov 19th 1859.
"(My Wife can) supply *blank* dates to above
"John Brown born May 9th 1800 was executed at Charlestown, Va, December 2d 1859."

"Charlestown, Jefferson Co, Va, 2d Decem. 1859. It is my desire that my Wife have all my personal property *not previously disposed of by me; & the entire use* of all my landed property during her natural life; & that after her death the proceeds of such land be equally divided between all my then living Children: & that what would be a Childs share be given to the Children of each of *my Two sons*; who *fell* at *Harpers ferry*; Va: & that a Childs share be *divided among* the children of any of my *now living* Children who *may die before* their Mother (my present much beloved Wife.) No *formal* will: can be of use when my expressed wishes; are made known to my *dutiful;* and dearly beloved family.

JOHN BROWN" [123] *

And while he was thus using his pen, the prison guards who should have hated were moving automatically, silently, with bowed heads, lest the tears so near to welling up should overflow. The majesty of death had now laid its spell upon them, as the dominating personality of the man they guarded had won from them a regard they wished not to bestow. To each quivering guard John Brown now gave a book; to his trusty jailer his silver watch.[124] Then, after a few minutes alone on his knees in prayer, it was "God bless you, my men," and "May we all meet in Heaven," to those who had followed him even to the verge of the grave — save two. To John E. Cook he was reproachful because of some phrases in Cook's confession which seemed to his leader untruthful and misleading. To Hazlett he said not a word, for neither he nor any of the other raiders would admit that this was one of their chosen company, in the vain hope thus to cheat the scaffold of his young life.[125]

And then John Brown stood on the porch of the jail, the last long journey begun, with lieutenants and guards by his side. No little slave-child was held up for the benison of his lips, for none but soldiery was near and the street was full of marching men. "I had no idea that Governor Wise considered my execution so important," burst from his lips.[126] But even in that supreme moment the race for which his life was forfeit was not forgotten. For, as he left his cell, he handed to one who stood near this final, wonderfully prophetic and imperishable message to the "million hearts" of his countrymen, which, as Wendell Phillips said, had been "melted by that old Puritan soul:"

"I John Brown am now quite *certain* that the crimes of this *guilty land: will* never be purged *away;* but with Blood. I had *as I now think: vainly* flattered myself that without *very much* bloodshed; it might be done." [127]

* He had already determined, with absolute equanimity of spirit, the kind of coffin in which he was to be buried. For his other wills, see Appendix.

Charlestown, Va, 2, December, 1859.

I, John Brown am now quite certain that the crimes of this guilty, land; will never be purged away; but with Blood. I had as I now think: vainly flattered myself that without very much bloodshed; it might be done.

JOHN BROWN'S LAST PROPHECY

BY MAN SHALL HIS BLOOD BE SHED

To this true prophet on the brink of eternity it now appears that nothing was concealed on that last morning. Must he not again have read the onrushing future as he surveyed the troops massed about the scaffold on that clear and warm and beautiful December day? For behind his gibbet stood "Stonewall" Jackson, some of whose young artillerymen, in the cadet red and gray of the Virginia Military Institute, were, within three years' time, while still tender lads, to offer up their lives in defence of the very valley upon whose beauties they now gazed; Jackson himself was to give his life's blood to purge the nation of its crimes; and through the loss of his high-spirited and gifted son then in the ranks of the Richmond company, Governor Wise was soon to know what John Brown, the father, had suffered in the engine house at Harper's Ferry. There, on a snow-white horse, rode to and fro Captain Turner Ashby, of knightly bearing and superb horsemanship, destined, less than three years later, to die a general of Confederate cavalry.[128] And in the closed ranks stood now, shoulder to shoulder, the colonels and generals of many a veteran legion-to-be, whose blood was soon to besprinkle Virginia from end to end. Here was forecast, too, the cruelest blood-letting of all the long and ghastly line; for, in a Richmond company, rifle on shoulder, stood the sinister figure of J. Wilkes Booth,[129] than whom no single American ever dealt a wickeder blow to his country. If John Brown's prophetic sight wandered across the hills to the scene of his brief Virginia battle, it must have beheld his generous captor, Robert E. Lee, again in military charge of Harper's Ferry, wholly unwitting that upon his shoulders was soon to rest the fate of a dozen confederated States. And if the prisoner's spiritual glance carried thus far, it must also have found its way through the flimsy walls of the Wager House, into a room where waited a little group around a heart-broken woman with "hands locked, eyes streaming, hearts uplifted in prayer," waiting for the hour to strike which should tell them that John Brown was beyond the reach of enemies and friends alike.[130]

His visions did not, however, prevent his drinking in the rare charm of the landscape. "This *is* a beautiful country. I never had the pleasure of seeing it before," fell from his lips,[131] as he came upon the field, seated on his coffin, in a wagon drawn by two white horses, and preceded by three companies of infantry. There were fifteen hundred soldiers present to see that this one old man was hanged. But, watch him as they might, they could detect no sign of flinching. With alacrity the despised Abolitionist climbed down from the wagon and ascended the scaffold to take one last, longing glance at the Blue Ridge Mountains which had to him spelled liberty for the enslaved these many long years. With cheerfulness he shook the hands of those near him and bade others adieu. Not when the cap was drawn over his head, his arms pinioned at the elbows, the noose slipped around his neck, was there a single waver. Even in all the unpicturesqueness of his ill-fitting suit and trousers and loose carpet-slippers, John Brown was a wonderfully dignified and impressive figure on the scaffold, because of the serenity and calmness of his spirit. The solemnity of it all moved every one, from the boyish cadets to the oldest soldiers. The most deeply religious man among the troops, "Stonewall" Jackson, was shaken like the rest, and "sent up a fervent petition" to Heaven that John Brown might be saved. Awful was the thought, to him, that this man about to die "might receive the sentence 'Depart, ye wicked, into the everlasting fire.'" [132] But no such thought was in the mind of John Brown. His soul was bent on high, facing in confidence the future. While the three companies that had been his escort deployed slowly into place, he stood erect as a soldier of the Lord. As if to test his courage to the end, they were a long twelve minutes filing into place, while John Brown showed Virginia how a brave man could die.

"The sheriff asked him," writes Colonel J. T. L. Preston, who stood hard by, "if he should give him a private signal, before the fatal moment. He replied in a voice that sounded to me unnaturally natural — so composed was its tone and so distinct its articulation — that 'it did not matter to him, if only they would not keep him too long waiting.'" But the little-drilled troops took forever, it seemed, in moving into place, — not, as was alleged in the North, to try the prisoner's nerves, but because the exact formation had been ordained in advance and there was no one thoughtful or daring enough to give the signal before it was complete. But come the word

BY MAN SHALL HIS BLOOD BE SHED

did at last. A single blow of the hatchet in the sheriff's hand and,

"the man of strong and bloody hand, of fierce passions, of iron will, of wonderful vicissitudes, — the terrible partisan of Kansas — the capturer of the United States Arsenal at Harper's Ferry — the would-be Catiline of the South — the demigod of the Abolitionists — the man execrated and lauded — damned and prayed for . . . John Brown, was hanging between heaven and earth."[133]

The painful silence that followed was broken by Colonel Preston's solemnly declaring: "So perish all such enemies of Virginia! All such enemies of the Union! All such foes of the human race!" It was said without a shade of animosity, without a note of exultation; but the blind man was not he who swung from the rope above. For his eyes had seen, long before his light had failed, the coming of the blue-clad masses of the North who were to make a mockery of Colonel Preston's words and strike down the destroying tyranny of slavery, to free Virginia from the most fateful of self-imposed bonds. As the troops now solemnly tramped away, with all decorum and without any demonstrations, in far-off Albany they were firing one hundred guns as the dirge of the martyr.[134] And meanwhile, John Brown's soul was marching on, and all in the North who had a conscience and a heart knew that John A. Andrew voiced the truth when he declared that "whether the enterprise of John Brown and his associates in Virginia was wise or foolish, right or wrong; I only know that, whether the enterprise itself was the one or the other, John Brown himself is right."[135]

CHAPTER XV

YET SHALL HE LIVE

"There need be no tears for him, for few men die so happily, so satisfied with time, place and circumstance as did he," wrote Samuel Bowles in the Springfield *Republican*, the day when John Brown's body had hung for thirty-seven minutes on the scaffold. Perhaps at the very hour when he penned this editorial, only forty-four days after John Brown left Harper's Ferry in chains, yet about to shake the nation to its depths, Brown's lifeless body was taken back to the scene of his raid and delivered to his wife, — not, however, until Hector Tyndale had insisted on the opening of the coffin to make sure that no other body had been substituted, as some had insinuated would be the case.[1] But the Virginians had done more than keep faith; they had furnished, by order of General Taliaferro, a body-guard of fifteen civilians, who volunteered to see that no harm befell the body in its simple pine coffin during its brief trip from Charlestown to Harper's Ferry, on a special train of two cars.[2] The very courtesy and humanity of this action revealed the impossibility of making of this execution the ignominious hanging of a wicked criminal. The Virginians were willing, too, that Mrs. Brown should take with her the bodies of Oliver and Watson Brown; but the latter's remains had been taken to the Winchester Medical College for preservation as an anatomical specimen, and Mrs. Brown felt herself unequal to the task of identifying the body of Oliver.[3] His remains, with those of the eight other raiders who died in Harper's Ferry, were buried in two large boxes by James Mansfield, to whom the county gave five dollars for his services. Almost at the water's edge of the Shenandoah, in an unmarked grave, he interred them, wrapping them first in the blanket-shawls they had worn over their shoulders as they went to their death in Harper's Ferry.[4] Here they lay while the hosts in Blue and Gray marched and fought over them.*

* Until 1899, when, with Mansfield's aid, the bodies were moved to North Elba by Dr. Thomas Featherstonhaugh, of Washington, and others interested, and

YET SHALL HE LIVE

All was quiet enough at Harper's Ferry when the funeral party started for Philadelphia, but the North at that hour was ringing with the news and echoing with protests. At Ravenna, Ohio, at seven o'clock there was a meeting of sympathy, to which were invited all "who hate oppression and all its vengeful, savage barbarities and who sympathize with the devoted Martyrs of Liberty." [5] In Cleveland, Melodeon Hall was draped in mourning for a meeting attended by fourteen hundred persons; and as the train bearing Brown's body moved on toward Baltimore, this gathering solemnly resolved that his execution "for a conscientious observance of the law of brotherhood as inculcated by Jesus Christ, and the law of freedom as taught by Thomas Jefferson," proved that "the State of Virginia under the lead of Henry A. Wise" was a "contemptible caricature of the Old Dominion in the days of George Washington. . . ." [6] In Philadelphia they had not waited as long; a public prayer meeting was held at the hour of the execution, only, however, to be broken up by a number of Southern medical students, with whom the public openly sympathized.[7] In New York, Rochester, Syracuse, Fitchburg, Concord (Massachusetts), Plymouth, New Bedford, Concord (New Hampshire), and Manchester, meetings were held, and in many places the bells were tolled.

But it was in Boston that the excitement reached its height. Motions to adjourn in honor of Brown were defeated in both houses of the Massachusetts Legislature, — by only three votes in the Senate, while in the House the vote stood 141 to 6.[8] That night, however, Tremont Temple was filled to the doors by one of the greatest meetings of the many notable ones it had sheltered. When the doors were opened, men and women were swept in, some without touching their feet to the ground. The meeting, held under the auspices of the American Anti-slavery Society, was presided over by Samuel E.

---

reinterred by the side of their commander with those of Stevens and Hazlett, Watson Brown's body having previously been brought there. The changed opinion of their country appears from the fact that whereas Dauphin Thompson and Jeremiah G. Anderson were killed by United States marines in 1859, United States infantrymen of the Twenty-sixth Regiment fired a salute over their graves and those of their associates at North Elba in 1899. The Rev. Joshua Young, who read the service over John Brown's body in 1859, again officiated; Bishop Henry C. Potter also took part in the ceremonies.

Sewall. Among the many placards which decorated the hall was one bearing these words of Lafayette: "I never would have drawn my sword in the cause of America, if I could have conceived that thereby I was helping to found a nation of slaves." William Lloyd Garrison declared that the meeting was called to witness John Brown's resurrection, and read Brown's address to the court when sentenced. He said in the course of his speech:

"Nevertheless, I am a non-resistant, and I not only desire, but have labored unremittingly to effect, the peaceful abolition of slavery, by an appeal to the reason and conscience of the slaveholder; yet, as a peace man — an 'ultra' peace man — I am prepared to say: 'Success to every slave insurrection at the South, and in every slave country.' And I do not see how I compromise or stain my peace profession in making that declaration. . . . Rather than see men wearing their chains in a cowardly and servile spirit, I would, as an advocate of peace, much rather see them breaking the head of the tyrant with their chains. Give me, as a non-resistant, Bunker Hill, and Lexington, and Concord, rather than the cowardice and servility of a Southern slave-plantation."[9]

The size and enthusiasm of this meeting were the more remarkable because there had been, just two weeks earlier, on November 19, a gathering in the same place in aid of John Brown's family. Ralph Waldo Emerson, the Rev. Jacob M. Manning, Wendell Phillips and John A. Andrew spoke, the last named also presiding and thereby apparently endangering his political future. It was on this occasion that he uttered his famous sentiment about John Brown's being right, and declared that the conflict between freedom and slavery was as irresistible as that between right and wrong. Wendell Phillips's oratory was at its best, for to his deep feeling about slavery itself was added all the chivalry of his generous, high-spirited, yet aristocratic nature. Said Emerson:

"It is easy to see what a favorite he [John Brown] will be with history, which plays such pranks with temporary reputations. Nothing can resist the sympathy which all elevated minds must feel with Brown, and through them the whole civilized world; and, if he must suffer, he must drag official gentlemen into an immortality most undesirable, and of which they have already some disagreeable forebodings."[10]

YET SHALL HE LIVE 561

Not often is it given to a condemned man to have the opinion of posterity thus interpreted to him by such great souls as Andrew, Phillips and Emerson, whose words, penetrating as they did to the prisoner of Charlestown, must have strengthened his already wonderful composure.

When the train which bore John Brown's body and its guardians arrived at Philadelphia, about one o'clock on the day after the execution, it was met by a reception committee headed by Dr. William H. Furness, who, with Hector Tyndale, led Mrs. Brown away.[11] But the excitement in the great crowd on all sides of the station was so intense that it was not safe to take the body to the undertaker's, as had been planned. An empty hearse driven hastily away dispersed a part of the crowd as effectually as a platoon of police, and then the coffin was placed in a furniture car and carried to the Walnut Street wharf, whence it was taken by boat to New York on its way to North Elba.[12] Thither Wendell Phillips and J. Miller McKim escorted the body, as well as Mrs. Brown; at every town at which they tarried, Troy, Rutland, Vergennes and Westport, bells tolled and the citizens appeared, to express their sympathy to Mrs. Brown.[13] At Elizabethtown, the last resting-place for a night, a guard of honor watched the coffin in the court-house until dawn. Thence over almost impassable roads for the twenty-five miles to North Elba, which John Brown had himself so often covered on foot, with the elements against him, the funeral party journeyed, all day of Wednesday, December 7. The next day, in the early afternoon, they laid all that was mortal of John Brown in a grave by the great boulder near his still unfinished house, — the huge stone being then, as to-day, the best possible monument to the native ruggedness and steadfastness of his character. Near-by, the towering White Face Mountain rises in all its grandeur, and well beyond, the tallest peak in the Adirondacks stands sentinel over the grave.

The women of his family, with Salmon Brown, the sole son who dared be present, and Henry Thompson, were the chief mourners.[14] Four widows were there, Mrs. Brown and the wives of Oliver and Watson Brown — Oliver's soon to die with the infant its father had not lived to see — and of William Thompson. The Rev. Joshua Young had come from his pulpit in Burlington, Vermont, to read from the Scriptures and to pray at the grave, for which service he was promptly deprived of his church. Mr. McKim once more bore his testimony, and then, in the place of William Lloyd Garrison, whose absence from Boston prevented his receiving in time the invitation to attend and speak, Wendell Phillips, the matchless orator of the Abolition cause, addressed the little gathering in the crowded house. Said he of John Brown:

"Marvellous old man! . . . He has abolished slavery in Virginia. You may say this is too much. Our neighbors are the last men we know. The hours that pass us are the ones we appreciate the least. Men walked Boston streets, when night fell on Bunker's Hill, and pitied Warren, saying, 'Foolish man! Thrown away his life! Why did n't he measure his means better?' Now we see him standing colossal on that blood-stained sod, and severing that day the tie which bound Boston to Great Britain. That night George III ceased to rule in New England. History will date Virginia Emancipation from Harper's Ferry. True, the slave is still there. So, when the tempest uproots a pine on your hills, it looks green for months — a year or two. Still, it is timber, not a tree. John Brown has loosened the roots of the slave system; it only breathes, — it does not live, — hereafter."

And as the coffin was lowered, members of a neighboring colored family, that of Lyman Epps, sang some of the hymns for which he had cared, and John Brown was at rest among the negroes he had labored for, near the women of his family who had toiled and suffered anguish for him and his cause, in the shadow of the great mountains he had loved.

But the meetings of sympathy and grief did not stop with the funeral. They went on for one reason or another, — the raising of funds for the family was one, — and soon there were gatherings of protest and denunciation by pro-slavery sympathizers. The great Cooper Union meeting in New York, addressed by Wendell Phillips, on December 15, was interrupted throughout by men sent there by denunciations of it in the *Herald*. On the same day, an anti-slavery convention in Philadelphia devoted itself to the Charlestown martyr.[15] A week earlier, a large Union meeting in Faneuil Hall, in Boston, had repudiated the raid, acclaimed the Union, and boldly asserted the right of Virginia to her peculiar institution.

THE NORTH ELBA FARMHOUSE

JOHN BROWN'S GRAVE

An ex-Governor of the State, Levi Lincoln, presided, and the names of four other ex-Governors and some of the best known men in Boston were on the list of vice-presidents.[16] The Union meeting in New York, on December 19, adopted a resolution denouncing "all acts or inflammatory appeals which intend or tend to make this Union less perfect, or to jeopard or disturb its domestic tranquillity, or to mar the spirit of harmony, compromise and concession upon which the Union was formed by our fathers. . . ." Another resolution read: "That we regard the recent outrage at Harper's Ferry as a crime — not only against the State of Virginia, but against the Union itself. . . . That, in our opinion, the subject of slavery has been too long mingled with party politics." Among the speakers were Charles O'Conor, ex-Governor Washington Hunt, John A. Dix, Professor Ormsby M. Mitchel, later a distinguished Northern general, and the Rev. Dr. George W. Bethune. Mayor Daniel F. Tieman was in the chair. There were three overflow meetings in the street.[17] Similar meetings were held in many another town and city, of those who wanted to preserve the Union of the States by keeping silent on the slavery question, and the New York Democracy was bitter in its denunciations of the "Northern Abolitionists," who now stood convicted of having "long contemplated a war of races," and of having, as the Brown raid revealed, "slowly and deliberately" plotted to that end.[18] Individuals of prominence, too, went on record in those days. Emerson, in his ignorance of Pottawatomie, had spoken of Brown before his execution as "that new saint, than whom none purer or more brave was ever led by love of men into conflict and death, — the new saint awaiting his martyrdom, and who, if he shall suffer, will make the gallows glorious like the cross." Thoreau felt similarly. Longfellow wrote in his diary on the day of the hanging: "This will be a great day in our history; the date of a new Revolution, — quite as much needed as the old one. Even now as I write, they are leading old John Brown to execution in Virginia for attempting to rescue slaves! This is sowing the wind to reap the whirlwind, which will come soon." [19]

George William Curtis felt that John Brown was "not buried but planted. He will spring up a hundred-fold. I do not wonder at the solemn pomp of his death. They would have none but a Southern-made rope to hang him, but that rope had two ends — one around the neck of a man, the other around the system [of slavery]." [20] "Let the American State hang his body and the American Church damn his soul. Still, the blessing of such as are ready to perish will fall on him, and the universal justice of the Infinitely Perfect God will make him welcome home. The road to heaven is as short from the gallows as from the throne," wrote Theodore Parker.[21] "The day before yesterday old Brown was executed," wrote Francis Lieber to a friend. "He died like a man and Virginia fretted like an old woman. . . . The deed was irrational, but it will be historical. Virginia has come out of it damaged, I think. She has forced upon mankind the idea that slavery must be, in her own opinion, but a rickety thing. . . ." [22]

The politicians, too, were quick to give their opinions. Abraham Lincoln, at Troy, Kansas, on December 2, 1859, remarked: "Old John Brown has been executed for treason against a State. We cannot object, even though he agreed with us in thinking slavery wrong. That cannot excuse violence, bloodshed and treason. It could avail him nothing that he might think himself right." [23] On February 27, 1860, speaking more at length in Cooper Union, he declared:

"John Brown's effort was peculiar. It was not a slave insurrection. It was an attempt by white men to get up a revolt among slaves, in which the slaves refused to participate. In fact, it was so absurd that the slaves, with all their ignorance, saw plainly enough it could not succeed. That affair, in its philosophy, corresponds with the many attempts, related in history, at the assassination of kings and emperors. An enthusiast broods over the oppression of a people till he fancies himself commissioned by Heaven to liberate them. He ventures the attempt, which ends in little else than his own execution. Orsini's attempt on Louis Napoleon, and John Brown's attempt at Harper's Ferry were in their philosophy precisely the same." [24]

Lincoln's great rival for the Republican nomination for the Presidency, William H. Seward, did not mince matters. All good citizens, he said, would agree "that this attempt to execute an unlawful purpose in Virginia by invasion, involving servile war, was an act of sedition and treason, and criminal in just the extent that it affected the public peace and was destructive of human happiness and life." But, besides lamenting the deaths of innocent citizens, "slain from an ambush and by surprise," Mr. Seward felt that the executions of the offenders themselves might be thought pitiable, "although necessary and just, because they acted under delirium, which blinded their judgments to the real nature of their criminal enterprise." [25] In Massachusetts, Edward Everett and Caleb Cushing voiced their protests and painted the horrors of servile insurrections, in the Boston Union meeting of December 8, in which Cushing called attention, in vain, to Brown's blood guilt on the Pottawatomie. Public opinion in the North was in no mood to believe ill of John Brown, and even in the South his previous record made far less impression than did the manner of his dying. None the less, both Everett and Cushing roundly denounced the lawlessness of the raid, and the latter did not hesitate to insinuate that Phillips, Garrison, Parker and the other anti-slavery leaders were as insane as Gerrit Smith.

Stephen A. Douglas, the author of the vicious Kansas-Nebraska act, but for which there would probably have been no raid on Harper's Ferry, who was then nearing the premature ending of his remarkable career, touched upon Brown's taking horses belonging to citizens of Missouri. Naturally, he beheld in Brown a "notorious man who has recently suffered death for his crimes," [26] and he was glad to saddle upon the Republican party the responsibility for those crimes. As for the Southerners themselves, the attitude of their leaders is easily conceivable. In Jefferson Davis's eyes, John Brown deservedly "suffered a felon's death," for he came "to incite slaves to murder helpless women and children." [27] Robert Toombs was fiery enough to suit even Governor Wise, for in the Senate, in the following January, he thus talked of civil war:

"Never permit this Federal government to pass into the hands of the black Republican party. It has already declared war against you and your institutions. It every day commits acts of war against you: it has already compelled you to arm for your defence. . . . Defend yourselves! The enemy is at your door, wait not to meet him at your hearthstone; meet him at the doorsill, and drive him from the

Temple of Liberty, or pull down its pillars and involve him in a common ruin." [28]

In the course of an excited debate in the Virginia House of Delegates, five days after John Brown's death, General James L. Kemper, one of the most talented and influential members of the Legislature, was almost as bloodthirsty: "All Virginia . . . should stand forth as one man and say to fanaticism, in her own language, whenever you advance a hostile foot upon our soil, we will welcome you with bloody hands and to hospitable graves." [29]

A similar vein was that of a State Senator of Mississippi, Brown by name, to the Legislature of his State:

"I have said of Mr. Seward and his followers, that they are our enemies and *we are theirs*. He has declared that there is an 'irrepressible conflict' between us. So there is! He and his followers have declared war upon us, and I am for fighting it out to the bitter end. It is clear that one or the other must go to the wall, and the sooner the better." [30]

In the view of Senator Mason, of Virginia:

"John Brown's invasion was condemned [in the North] only because it failed. But in view of the sympathy for him in the North and the persistent efforts of the sectional party there to interfere with the rights of the South, it was not at all strange that the Southern States should deem it proper to arm themselves and prepare for any contingency that might arise." [31]

In his annual message to Congress, President Buchanan took the unusual view that while many feared that the Harper's Ferry outbreak was but a symptom of an "incurable disease in the public mind," it was in his opinion likely to be altogether a blessing in its after effects. He informed the country of his belief that:

"the events at Harper's Ferry, by causing the people to pause and reflect upon the possible peril to their cherished institutions, will be the means, under Providence, of allaying the existing excitement and preventing further outbreaks of a similar character. They will resolve that the Constitution and the Union shall not be endangered by rash counsels, knowing that should 'the silver cord be loosed or the golden bowl be broken . . . at the fountain,' human power could never reunite the scattered and hostile fragments."

The Joint Committee of the General Assembly of Virginia, which investigated the raid, held a different opinion when it reported, on January 26, 1860; for it felt that as long as the Republican party

"maintains its present sectional organization, and inculcates its present doctrines, the South can expect nothing less than a succession of such traitorous attempts to subvert its institutions and to incite its slaves to rapine and murder. The crimes of John Brown were neither more nor less than practical illustrations of the doctrines of the leaders of the Republican party. The very existence of such a party is an offence to the whole South."

The Committee offered a resolution that Virginia should put its militia on a war-service basis, and then, without violating the Federal Constitution, achieve its commercial independence of the North by establishing its own manufactures and promoting direct trade with foreign countries.[32] Only nine days earlier, the General Assembly had listened to an address of O. G. Memminger, special commissioner from South Carolina to urge Virginia to join the conference of Southern States which South Carolina was calling, to consider and act upon the grave situation created by the "increasing violence in new and alarming forms" of the attacks upon slavery. "Every village bell," he said, "which tolled its solemn note at the execution of Brown, proclaims to the South the approbation of that village of insurrection and servile war." Harper's Ferry, he declared, "proved that the North and South are standing in battle array."[33] Similar sentiments were voiced by Governor Gist, of South Carolina, in his annual message to the Legislature. For him the Rubicon had been crossed.[34]

In marked contrast to this, the utterance of one Northern Governor, Samuel J. Kirkwood, of Iowa, may be cited in this connection, since it was an accurate interpretation of the opinions of the bulk of the plain people of the Middle West:

"I cannot wonder at the most unfortunate and bloody occurrence at Harper's Ferry. But while we may not wonder at it, we must condemn it. It was an act of war — of war against brothers, and in that a greater crime than the invaders of Cuba and Nicaragua were guilty of; relieved to some extent of its guilt in the minds of many, by the fact that the blow was struck for freedom, and not for slavery. . . . While the great mass of our people utterly condemn the act of John Brown, they feel and they express admiration and sympathy for the disinterestedness of purpose by which they believe he was governed, and for the unflinching courage and calm cheerfulness with which he met the consequences of his failure."

But even this was not allowed to pass uncriticised by the Democratic minority in the Iowa Legislature, fifty-eight members of which voted that such sentiments were out of place in a gubernatorial message, and quite "demagogic." [35]

As for the newspapers, North and South, they took sides about as they had prior to the execution. Curiously enough, some in the South turned on their friend the New York *Herald*, because it printed so many Abolitionist speeches and documents, the reprinting of which, it was felt, would do much harm. A collapsing economic system, slavery was more than ever afraid of free speech, as was shortly to be shown by its treatment of a powerful tract, 'The Impending Crisis,' from the pen of Hinton Rowan Helper, a poor white of Southern birth and breeding. Newspapers like the Richmond *Enquirer*, Charleston, South Carolina, *Mercury*, and the Baltimore *Patriot*, put remarkably little faith in the action taken by the various Northern anti-Brown meetings, which they suspected of being planned to appease the South for the moment. The *Patriot* believed that there was no sincerity and a great deal of political time-serving in the resolutions passed, favorable as they were to the South.[36] The *Enquirer* was pleased with the words, but demanded "acts, acts." It sympathized with the remark of the London *Times* that "the first thing that strikes us is that the North did nothing until Brown was executed, and then it began to talk." [37] The Baltimore *Sun* [38] found in the pro-Brown outbursts proof, hitherto lacking, that Brown was really a "representative man" of the North. "That the South can afford to live under a Government, the majority of whose subjects or citizens regard John Brown as a martyr and a Christian hero, rather than a murderer and robber, and act up to those sentiments, or countenance others in so doing, is a preposterous idea, as will be comprehended by all the North ere the end of the next session of Congress. . . ." Naturally, newspapers of this stripe could only denounce as treason the editorial utterance of the Cleveland

YET SHALL HE LIVE

Daily Herald,[39] entitled "Hung be the Heavens with Black," which declared that "The gloom upon all hearts is too deep for words. Slavery drives John Brown to madness and then hangs him for that insanity. What a spectacle in a Christian community! — What a solemn day for this Christian nation!" But they found fresh comfort in the Portage, Ohio, *Sentinel*, published in John Brown's old home, which rejoiced in his proper penalty for his many crimes, for "his whole life . . . has been that of a lawbreaker."[40] Thus were Northern communities of a sudden clearly cleaved by the actions of twenty-two men in a Southern State.

But nowhere were there abler editorials on the Southern side than appeared in the Baltimore *American*, which sincerely hoped that the death of John Brown would end the "confusion, excitement and parade" among the Virginians, which, it felt bound to say, had not "presented them in a very favorable aspect to the country." Uttering "a word of caution to those who are inclined to attach importance to the fact that Brown met his fate with perfect calmness," the *American* rightly declared that in itself this proved nothing. "Pirates," it said, "have died as resolutely as martyrs. . . . If the firmness displayed by John Brown proves anything, the composure of a Thug, dying by the cord with which he had strangled so many victims, proves just as much."[41] Not unnaturally, the Southern press absolutely failed to comprehend such a point of view as that of Victor Hugo, perhaps the greatest man of letters in Europe, in whose far-reaching opinion: "In killing Brown, the Southern States have committed a crime which will take its place among the calamities of history. The rupture of the Union will fatally follow the assassination of Brown. As to John Brown, he was an apostle and a hero. The gibbet has only increased his glory and made him a martyr."[42] For his epitaph Victor Hugo suggested, "Pro Christo sicut Christus."

The Baltimore *American's* hope, that Virginia might settle down after John Brown's execution, came to naught as long as Brown's followers were yet to be disposed of. The trials of Edwin Coppoc, Shields Green, John Copeland, Jr., and John E. Cook followed in that order, and by November 9 they were all sentenced to die on December 16, their trials being in all essentials repetitions of Brown's, without the dramatic features, George Sennott, of Boston, making a splendid legal fight for them. His contention that a negro could not be convicted of treason in Virginia was agreed to by Andrew Hunter and the court, and Green and Copeland were convicted on the other charges. In Cook's behalf, the eloquent Daniel W. Voorhees, of Indiana, later United States Senator from that State, made a plea which is said to have reduced the court-room to tears — but in vain.[43] In Edwin Coppoc's behalf, Governor Wise appeared before the Senate and House Committees for Courts of Justice in Richmond, and stated his readiness to have Coppoc's sentence commuted to imprisonment for life.[44] This action justly won for the impulsive and high-spirited Governor not a little praise from both North and South, and the unfortunate Quaker youth might possibly have escaped the scaffold, had there not most inopportunely appeared in the New York *Tribune* a letter from Coppoc to Mrs. John Brown, telling of the death of Watson and Oliver Brown, in which he spoke of the Harper's Ferrians as "the enemy." At once the Senate Committee took sides against Coppoc, and the Governor's intercession became of no avail. This might, however, have been the case had the letter not appeared, for while it was alleged in some quarters that Coppoc had shot no one, it was clearly brought out before the Senate Committee that his rifle was responsible for Mayor Beckham's death. Coppoc denied having written the letter, but it is believed that he signed it after it had been written for him by Cook.[45]

Naturally, the friends of John Brown in the North watched the fate of his associates with all devotion, hoping against hope for the prisoners' lives, and eager to do anything to aid them. The failure of their efforts to rescue John Brown from death on the scaffold only increased the determination of his three militant friends, Thomas Wentworth Higginson, John W. Le Barnes and Richard J. Hinton, to cheat the Virginia hangman of some of his victims. But before they could do else than begin to plot, four more raiders, John E. Cook, Edwin Coppoc, Shields Green and John Copeland, Jr., were executed on a single day, December 16. As if to intensify the bitterness and disappointment of their Northern allies, Cook and Cop-

YET SHALL HE LIVE

poc all but escaped, the night before their deaths. Despite the watchfulness of Andrew Hunter and the military commanders in Charlestown, one of the men enrolled for service in the prison guards soon after the raid was Charles Lenhart, the Kansas Free State fighter, whose sole motive for this service was a desire to succor the raiders.[46] It was easy for him to get into touch with them, and from him Cook and Coppoc learned that on the night of December 14, 1859, he would be on duty at the angle of the prison wall most favorable for an escape. They had borrowed a knife from a prison guard and "forgotten" to return it; taken a screw out of the bedstead, and obtained a knife-blade from Shields Green. With these slight implements they had worked a whole week and made an aperture in the wall which they were able to conceal during the day. With the knife-blade they made teeth in the knife, and with this roughly improvised saw cut off their shackles. Their cell being on the first floor, there was a drop of not over five feet to the prison yard. Once there, only a fifteen-foot brick wall was between them and freedom.

On the appointed night, Lenhart was on guard and everything in readiness. But anxiously as he walked his post those long wintry hours, not a sound came to his longing ears before the arrival of his relief sent him back to his quarters. A fatal consideration for his brother-in-law, the then Governor Willard, of Indiana, and his sister Mrs. Willard, who were in town to bid him farewell, but were to leave the next day, induced Cook to postpone the attempt lest the escape reflect upon them.[47] He was generous enough to urge Coppoc to go alone, but Coppoc was not of that stuff. Not even the thought of his grief-stricken Quaker mother in the quiet village of Springdale, to which his brother Barclay had now safely returned, would induce him to abandon his comrade. On July 25 of the same year, Barclay Coppoc had said to his mother, after getting a letter from John Brown: "We are going to start for Ohio to-day." "Ohio!" said his mother, "I believe you are going with old Brown. When you get the halters around your necks, will you think of me?"[48] The halter was fairly around Edwin's neck now, but nothing could induce him to deprive Cook of his chance for life by going out alone.

On the next night, Coppoc removed his chains and crawled out first, Cook following. To their joy they found no one in the prison yard. Fortunately, the timbers of the scaffold upon which Brown had perished, and upon which they were to die, were still in the yard, and gave them an easy means of arriving at the top of the wall. Alas for their high hopes! A loyal soldier of Virginia stood where Lenhart was to have been, and the instant Cook appeared upon the wall, the guard shot at him.[49] Both men tried to jump down, but the sentry threatened to bayonet them if they did, and so, sadly enough, they walked back into the jail and delivered themselves up to the astonished Captain Avis and his guards. Their stay in their cell thereafter was short — a brief twelve hours. At half-past twelve of the next day they left it forever, calm, cool and collected, to show, as did the negroes Green and Copeland, that Brown's men could die like himself, "with the most unflinching firmness," as the Associated Press told the story.

With these deaths there remained alive at Charlestown only Aaron Dwight Stevens and Albert Hazlett, of Brown's little band. The latter went by the name of William H. Harrison, the *nom de guerre* of Richard J. Hinton, which Hazlett had assumed when arrested at Newville, Pennsylvania. Under it he had illegally been extradited to Virginia, there being no proof produced that he had ever been in that State, or was in any way connected with the Harper's Ferry raid. In jail, as already told, his comrades refused to recognize him or call him else than Harrison. "Hazlett," says Mrs. Annie Brown Adams, "was a really good, kind-hearted man, with little or no education. He had always lived among the roughest kind of people, and was the least accustomed to polite living of any of them, but he was brave and manly in every respect."[50] As for Stevens, with his superb physique, fine face and beautiful voice, and reputation for matchless physical courage, the young men of Charlestown thronged to see him, to hear him sing, or to talk of his belief in spiritualism. Women easily fell under the sway of his charms, and a young woman from Ohio, Jennie Dunbar, went to Richmond in vain, just before his execution in March, to beg for his life of Governor Letcher,[51] who had succeeded Governor Wise on January 1, 1860. No one who met Stevens failed to remember him, uneducated

YET SHALL HE LIVE

though he was, and since boyhood an adventurer. His personality was a special incentive to those who plotted for his release.

Before the hanging of Cook and Coppoc, Richard J. Hinton telegraphed to Leavenworth in an endeavor to get hold once more of Captain James Montgomery, of Kansas. He was restless on December 13 that no answer had come. "Count me in for one, Stephens and Haslitt *must* be saved," he wrote to Mr. Higginson on that date, and urged that something be done without regard to Montgomery.[52] But Higginson, knowing Montgomery's reputation as a Free State leader, insisted on his coming East to take the leadership in their rescue plan. The two did not meet personally until the rescuers had assembled at Harrisburg. Then Higginson was delighted with the Kansan, and wrote to his wife on February 17, 1860, that Montgomery "is one of the most charming men I ever saw . . . and a man to follow anywhere. He was at first reluctant to come, but now his soul is in it. Says the obstacles sound much greater than they are."[53]

The reason for Montgomery's reluctance in coming was, as he himself wrote to Higginson on February 1, from Mound City, Kansas, "the strong possibility that my services will be needed nearer home. One of our citizens has been shot down and another carried off by a mob from Missouri." Between his duty to his family, his duty to his creditors, and his duty to the cause, he had spent a sleepless night, and then decided to send some one else East in his place. Before this letter was penned, Mr. Higginson had started R. J. Hinton on January 11, 1860, for Kansas, to plead with Montgomery personally.[54] This Hinton did at Moneka, early in February, with such success that Montgomery agreed to leave for the East at once, and, instead of mailing his letter of declination to Mr. Higginson, handed it to him at Harrisburg.[55] It was addressed to the "Rev. Theo. Brown," and signed by "Henry Martin;" but when they met, Higginson was going by the name of Charles P. Carter, while Captain Montgomery was always referred to in the letters that passed between the conspirators as the "master machinist."[56]

Before they actually met in Harrisburg, on February 16, much preliminary work was done. Besides contributing liberally of his own means, Higginson obtained permission from John Brown's widow to use part of the funds placed in his hands for the benefit of the Brown family, in his endeavor to save Hazlett and Stevens.[57] The young publishers of Redpath's hastily written and printed life of Brown, William W. Thayer and Charles Eldridge, were enlisted in the cause and contributed eight hundred dollars, partly an outright gift, partly as a loan, Thayer taking four hundred and thirty-one dollars in a bag to Harrisburg and spending, *en route*, a sleepless night at the Astor House in New York, lest he be robbed by an unknown room-mate. Wendell Phillips promised one hundred dollars, and E. A. Brackett, the sculptor, two hundred dollars. Colonel D. R. Anthony, of Leavenworth, contributed three hundred dollars to Hinton and Montgomery. All in all, $1721 were disbursed in the undertaking, and no one regretted the expenditure then or at any time.[58]

Mr. Higginson at once saw the desirability of getting in touch with those of Brown's men who had escaped from Harper's Ferry, because of the invaluable knowledge attained by them in their recent and perilous escape through the mountains. He soon succeeded in finding Charles Plummer Tidd, then in hiding in Ohio, and learned from him that he was anxious to aid the expedition. But Tidd wrote on January 20 that it would be impossible for him "to act openly in the Southern part of this State [Ohio] or in Virginia. I am too well known, and at this season of the year I think it a great undertaking to camp out." He would be willing to go in the spring, but as it became evident that Stevens and Hazlett would not be alive in the spring unless rescued, — they were both sentenced to death on February 14, 1860, — Tidd came to Boston in February to counsel with Higginson and Thayer and Eldridge. He then again stated his belief that the plan of rescue conceived by Higginson, of an overland dash to Charlestown through the mountains, was impracticable owing to the cold. To camp without fires was impossible; to camp with them was to court discovery and capture.[59]

For the moment, however, Higginson refused to be discouraged by the unquestionable truth of this statement, and continued his planning with unabated enthusiasm. John W. Le Barnes had, meanwhile, returned to New York to reënlist for the new undertaking the group of German revolutionists of 1848 who had expressed a willingness to join in the effort to save Brown from the gallows. It was through the editor of the *Staats-Zeitung*, Oswald Ottendorfer, and Friedrich Kapp, one of the foremost of the German refugees, that Le Barnes had got into touch with this group and obtained the adherence of their leader, Colonel Richard Metternich, who subsequently died in the cause of freedom in the Union army. Metternich asserted that he had a dozen or more men ready to go, and their terms as to themselves, and their families in case of accident, were moderate. But doubts having arisen as to the genuineness of their enthusiasm in the cause, Hinton was hurried to New York on his return from Kansas, to see each of them personally,—"to cinch the Teutons,"[60] as Higginson put it. Their willingness to start was never actually tested. Le Barnes and Hinton saw to it that they were armed "with the tools necessary, large and small," that is, rifles and revolvers. Rockets and ammunition were also purchased in New York, and Mr. Higginson had attended to the obtaining of "tools" for the others of the band, most of which were borrowed in Boston. One box of rifles was sent to New York in care of Oliver Johnson, editor of the *Anti-Slavery Standard*, and one box of revolvers to Le Barnes, who was to bring them in his trunk if summoned to Harrisburg; but he was urged to be careful of them, as they were to be "returned if not wanted."[61]

There was no difficulty in getting men together in Kansas under Montgomery's leadership, and no question as to their loyalty and enthusiasm, with or without pay. Naturally, the men who had safely delivered Dr. John Doy from the St. Joseph, Missouri, jail were the first thought of. Silas Soulé, Joseph Gardner, J. A. Pike and S. J. Willis were selected from their number.[62] Willis, being in Troy, New York, first heard of the undertaking through a letter from Hinton. He at once wrote to Higginson, in the spirit characteristic of all the Kansans, "I am now on call," and assured him that the entering of Missouri's strongest prison and taking therefrom his friend and neighbor Dr. Doy "are among the most pleasing incidents of a somewhat eventful life." From Linn County came John Brown's close friend, Augustus Wattles, together with Henry Carpenter and Henry C. Seaman. Henry Seaman's brother Benjamin was summoned from his home in Iowa, and Benjamin Rice from Bourbon County, Kansas. Augustus Wattles went on ahead.[63]

Captain Montgomery, signing himself "Henry Martin," telegraphed to Mr. Higginson from Leavenworth, on February 10, 1860, "I have got eight machines. Leave St. Joseph thirteenth," "machines" being the code word for "men."[64] Curiously enough, at that moment Mr. Higginson seems to have felt that the proper time for the venture had passed. According to his own memorandum on the telegram, he answered, "Too late — send back machines and come here yourself. T. B. [Theodore Brown]." But the answer cannot have reached Montgomery, for five days later, a telegram from J. H. Reed [Hinton] in Pittsburg announced the arrival there of "eight machines awaiting transfer."[65] After two days more, the "machines" were safely transferred to Harrisburg in the guise of cattlemen looking for bargains. Those from Linn County had had a thrilling adventure in crossing the Missouri River to St. Joseph at night, in an overloaded skiff, but experienced no difficulty in passing through that Southern city. The three Doy rescuers, Gardner, Pike and Soulé, naturally gave St. Joseph a wide berth, and the two parties do not seem to have met until Pittsburg was reached.[66] The eight "machines" reported there could only have been Montgomery, Rice, Pike, Gardner, Soulé, Carpenter and the two Seamans, for Wattles had gone ahead, and Willis was still in Troy.

At Harrisburg, Montgomery speedily found Higginson, who had taken up his abode with Dr. William W. Rutherford, an Abolitionist and a "tower of strength," and probably the only man in Harrisburg who was entrusted with the secret.[67] The problem which confronted Montgomery and Higginson, as they sat down to it in the Doctor's parlor, Higginson put on a bit of paper he has carefully preserved. It reads as follows:[68]

This is what involved —
1. Traverse a mountainous country miles at 10 miles a night, carrying arms ammunition & blankets & provisions for a week — with certain necessity of turning round and retreating the instant of discovery, & of such discovery causing death to our friends: and

this in a country daily traversed by hunters. Also the certainty of retreat or detection in case of a tracking snow wh. may come *any time*. Being out 5 nights at mildest, possibly 10. Includ'g crossing Potomac, a rapid stream where there may be no ford or boats.

2. Charge on a build'g defended by 2 sentinels outside & 25 men inside a wall 14 ft. high. Several men inside prison besides, & a determined jailer. Certainty of rousing town & impossibility of having more than 15 men.

3. Retreat with prisoners & wounded probably after daylight — & No. 1. repeated.

T. W. HIGGINSON.

Montgomery, as Higginson at once reported to his wife and to Le Barnes on the same day, February 17, was not dismayed by this apparently hopeless and impossible undertaking, but insisted that he must first scout over the country by himself. For that purpose he needed a whole week, for he must take his time and do it thoroughly. "He [Montgomery]," wrote the Worcester clergyman, "has excellent suggestions which I cannot give — if undertaken at all it can be done at one dash, not taking long. But he says & I agree that an unsuccessful attempt to introduce the machinery would re-act very unfavorably and nothing must be done without a fair prospect of success." [69]

Bad luck pursued the conspirators from the beginning. Tidd was to arrive from Massachusetts that (Friday) night, but was compelled to postpone his coming until the following Monday or Tuesday. Before their arrival, the heavens proved in league with their enemies, for a heavy fall of snow made their hearts sick as they gazed upon it on reaching Harrisburg. The next day it again snowed heavily, "further depressing the hopes of our machinist," as Higginson reported.[70] He himself left on Monday for Chicago, to do some lecturing there and at Yellow Springs,[71] returning just in time to receive Montgomery's report of a daring venture he had made.

True to his Kansas reputation, he had gone with but one comrade, Soulé, straight to the portals of Charlestown, risking not only the elements, but discovery at the hands of the Virginia patrols, with which the roads teemed. He travelled openly, and relied, with success, upon that Southern accent which was his by right of his Kentucky birth and ancestry.

Soulé played the jovial Irishman to perfection, and, leaving Montgomery, entered Charlestown apparently in such a state of intoxication, that to his unutterable delight, he was speedily locked up in the very jail with the men he had come to rescue. He as skilfully obtained an interview with Stevens and Hazlett, and informed them of the undertaking on hand. Deeply moved, both declared a rescue impossible, for if most of the troops had left, and civil rule had been established after the executions of December 16, there was still a constant guard of eighty men. Troops were, moreover, on call in all the surrounding towns and could arrive in two or three hours. The loss of life would certainly be heavy. Their kind jailer, Captain Avis, they knew would fight to the last. They did not wish liberty at the cost of his life and those of some of the rescuers. Hazlett sent personal messages of farewell to Hinton before the interview concluded. Soulé was then haled before a justice of the peace, listened gravely enough to a lecture on the evils of intemperance, and doubtless on the especial danger of getting drunk in a town under semi-military control. Discharged, he promptly made his way back to Harrisburg.[72]

There, too, came Montgomery and also Gardner, who, being of Pennsylvania-Dutch birth, had been allowed to try the "underground" Quaker routes, with but ill success; for, according to Hinton, he was threatened with exposure by some to whom he had entrusted his secret, and compelled to return.[73] It was perhaps owing to Gardner's indiscretions that Governor Letcher again got word that there was a conspiracy afoot, but warnings had already been given him. For, on January 26, he wrote to Andrew Hunter:

"If from the information you receive, you shall be satisfied that a rescue will be attempted, inform me at once, either by telegraph or otherwise. I have made my arrangements to have all the necessary troops upon the grounds at the earliest practicable moment — and in a very few hours, after I shall be notified that they are required."[74]

In the second-rate Drover's Tavern in Harrisburg, in which the comrades of Montgomery, Soulé and Gardner had awaited their return, a council of war was held. Soulé made his report of Stevens's and Hazlett's wishes. Mr. Higginson declares that he never knew what effect, if any, this attitude of the prisoners had upon Montgomery's mind.[75] That he had already made it up was speedily clear. He had found the entire countryside between Charlestown and Harrisburg on the alert, and easily discovered that the pretence of a hunting-party would not hold good at that time of year. Finally, the continuing heavy snows made rapid movements impossible, and great suffering certain. The elements were the deciding factors, and Montgomery reluctantly submitted to their decree. Higginson, who presided at the conference, asserts that he consented reluctantly to the abandonment of the enterprise upon which he had built high hopes. Thayer's recollection, thirty-three years after, was that the clergyman's eloquent insistence that fifteen or twenty lives ought not to be sacrificed in a hopeless attempt to save one or two, carried the day.[76] Certain it is that the other Kansans gave up the expedition with the greatest reluctance. They had come East to die, if need be, in order to rescue their comrades of Free State days. But their readiness to sacrifice themselves was in vain. Montgomery remained firm, and the opposition of their chosen leader could not be disregarded. To the great disappointment of Hinton and Le Barnes, who were still in New York with Metternich and his Teutons, awaiting the word, Stevens and Hazlett were now left to their fate. The twenty-one men who were ready to take their lives in their hands and go — one less in number than the men who went to Kennedy Farm — dispersed to their homes or took up their normal occupations. Most of the Kansans returned direct to their Territory.

Lest it be thought that these men were not of the fighting blood that is willing to risk all against great odds, it must be recorded that the majority took up arms as soon as the Union was openly attacked. Higginson became colonel of the First South Carolina, the first regiment of blacks raised for the Union army, while Montgomery's military record as colonel of three regiments has already been given. Le Barnes was a lieutenant in a German company of the Second Massachusetts, while Tidd died as Sergeant Charles Plummer of the Twenty-first Massachusetts, and Colonel Metternich is known to have fallen for the Union in Texas. Hinton became a captain in the Second Kansas Colored Volunteers, and H. C. Seaman, Gardner, Pike, Rice and Willis served in various capacities from sergeant to captain, the first three being of the latter rank in Kansas regiments at the expiration of their service.[77] The willingness of the party to risk death was well proved. Higginson in after years went over the ground between Harrisburg and Charlestown only to convince himself that the decision reached by Montgomery was the proper one. An attempt would have failed utterly. While ready at that time to risk all, it is plain that Higginson realized how desperate the undertaking was to be; for once, when it appeared that the Germans might not materialize, he wrote to his wife that this meant "another chance on your side," — that is, another faint prospect that he might return to her alive. When this fiery apostle of liberty finally reached his home safe and sound, his first entry in his note-book after getting to Worcester on March 1, 1860, was the famous message in Dickens's 'A Tale of Two Cities' — "Recalled to Life."[78] Fifteen days later, Stevens and Hazlett perished on the scaffold; Stevens certain of a return to earth in spirit form, while Hazlett, rejoicing in the news that his body was to be "taken from this land of chains," added, "my death will do more than if I had lived."[79]

To add to the political excitement of the winter of 1859–60, and to keep John Brown before the public, two events contributed besides the trials and executions in Charlestown. These were the meetings of the Mason Investigating Committee of the United States Senate, to which references have already been made, and the contest in the House of Representatives over the Speakership. The Mason Committee's sessions began on December 16, 1859, and ended on June 14, 1860. The next day, Senator Mason presented a majority report signed by himself, Senator Jefferson Davis, of Mississippi, and Senator G. N. Fitch, of Indiana. The minority of the committee, Senators Jacob Collamer, of Vermont, and James R. Doolittle, of Wisconsin, also presented a short report. In it the minority expressed no sympathy with John Brown or his purpose; indeed, their chief effort seemed to be to offset any political effect the majority report might have in connecting

Northern Abolitionists or prominent Republicans with John Brown and his men. Hence they reached the extraordinary conclusion that there was no evidence that any other citizens than those at Harper's Ferry were accessory to the outbreak, or had "any suspicion of its existence or design" before the explosion. They also recorded their belief that no evidence was presented of any conspiracy or design, by any one, to rescue John Brown and his associates from prison. The raid the minority believed to be "but an offshoot from the extensive outrages and lawlessness in Kansas." It was astonishing to them that, "in a country like ours . . . there should still be found large bodies of men laboring under the infatuation that any good object can be effected by lawlessness and violence. . . . It can, in its nature, beget nothing but resistance, retaliation, insecurity and disaster." Said Messrs. Collamer and Doolittle: "Ages might not produce another John Brown, or so fortuitously supply him with such materials." The fatal termination of the raid had, they thought, furnished "assurance against the most distant possibility of its repetition," and they inveighed against the example of lawlessness furnished by the slave-power in its aggressions on neighboring nations, the armed invasions of Kansas, and the "merciless breaches of our laws against the African slave trade, 'unwhipt of justice.'"

As for the majority report, viewed after fifty years, it is disappointingly ineffective from the slavery point of view, when it is considered that such able men as Jefferson Davis and J. M. Mason constructed it. Their narrative of what happened at Harper's Ferry is succinct and accurate, and tells the facts without any attempt at coloring. As for their opinions, the majority dwelt upon Brown's desire to "incite insurrection" among the slaves, and declared that "it was owing alone to the loyalty and well-affected disposition of the slaves that he did not succeed in creating a servile war, with its necessary attendants of rapine and murder of all sexes, ages and conditions." The Committee, being "not disposed to draw harsh, or perhaps uncharitable conclusions," commented severely on the way Kansas arms were turned over to Brown after they had been denied to him by the Kansas National Committee. "The expedition, so atrocious in its character, would have been arrested, had even ordinary care been taken on the part of the Massachusetts Committee to ascertain whether Brown was truthful in his professions." The report contains next a severe attack upon Congressman Giddings for his doctrine of a "higher law," the law of nature, which, superior to any statute law, gave to each soul the right to live, to enjoy happiness, and to be free. Quoting also from the testimony of Dr. Howe and Mr. Stearns, the majority of the Committee felt that "with such elements at work, unchecked by law and not rebuked but encouraged by public opinion, with money freely contributed and placed in irresponsible hands, it may easily be seen how this expedition to excite servile war in one of the States of the Union was got up, and it may equally be seen how like expeditions may certainly be anticipated in future wherever desperadoes offer themselves to carry them into execution." The majority report admitted that John Brown's reticence was such that "it does not appear that he intrusted even his immediate followers with his plans, fully, even after they were ripe for execution."

Finally, Messrs. Davis, Mason and Fitch could suggest no legislation which would be adequate to prevent like occurrences in the future. The invasion to them "was simply the act of lawless ruffians under the sanction of no public or political authority," with the aid of money and firearms contributed by citizens of other States "under circumstances that must continue to jeopard the safety and peace of the Southern States, and against which Congress has no power to legislate." If the several States would not, for the sake of policy or a desire for peace, guard by legislation against the raid's recurrence, the Committee could "find no guarantee elsewhere for the security of peace between the States of the Union." Its only definite recommendation was that military guards be kept at armories and arsenals. It reported that four persons, John Brown, Jr., James Redpath, Frank B. Sanborn and Thaddeus Hyatt, having failed to appear before the Committee, warrants had been issued for their arrest. Of these, Mr. Hyatt alone was taken into custody. He languished for three months in the jail of the District of Columbia, refusing to testify for the sake of the principle involved, and was finally released by the Senate on June 16, 1860,[80] the day that Senator Mason laid the findings of his Committee before the Senate.

The two reports attracted little attention when finally printed, for by that time the excitement engendered by the raid and the contest between North and South over the Speakership had burned itself out. The actual findings were so mild and had been so thoroughly discounted, and the progress of political events had gone so far beyond the raid, that this final story of it, valuable as were and are the testimonies that accompanied the reports, became merely one of the many events now rapidly leading up to the secession of the Southern States. The *Liberator* noticed the reports only to say that the Mason Committee mountain had labored and brought forth a mouse.[81] The *Herald*, like many other newspapers, did not deem them worthy of editorial comment. This did not mean, however, that John Brown was already forgotten. His name appeared constantly in the press all through the year 1860; the raising of a fund for his family and the surviving raiders, the publication of the first biography of him by James Redpath, the reunion of his family and friends at the grave at North Elba on July 4, 1860, — all these attracted attention to the victim of the Charlestown gallows, and to his men.

In the Speakership fight in Congress — dramatic in the extreme — John Brown's name was often mentioned and his acts denounced by the representatives of the South and many from the North. This contest lasted from the Monday following John Brown's execution, December 5, to February 1.[82] The election would undoubtedly have gone to John Sherman, of Ohio, had it not appeared that he had endorsed Hinton Rowan Helper's book, 'The Impending Crisis of the South: How to Meet it,' which had infuriated the South about as much as 'Uncle Tom's Cabin,' — if anything more so, for Helper was a North Carolina poor white, who wrote with all the intensity of feeling of his class, for whom the aristocratic system of slavery held out hopes of nothing but a steady degeneration, materially and socially. Helper was no friend to the slave, but he demanded the abolition of slavery, the expulsion of the negroes, and the destruction of the oligarchical despotism which slavery had made possible. The arguments voiced against his book were chiefly abuse of the writer, rather than an attempt to controvert his facts and statistics, which were, indeed, unanswerable. But Mr. Sherman's endorsement of Helper's book, and John Brown's raid and death, had brought Congressmen's passions to the boiling point, and there was a tremendous outburst of feeling. Personal altercations and bitter disputes were of frequent occurrence, and two members were arrested and placed under heavy bonds to keep the peace. Men freed their minds on the whole slavery question in a debate that did much to help on the work of popular education John Brown had so stimulated. Speaking of the vote in the Massachusetts Legislature on the motion to adjourn out of sympathy for John Brown's death, Senator Iverson declared that Southerners "stand on the brink of a volcano," and that the Republican disclaimers of responsibility for Brown's raid were "not worth the paper on which they are printed."[83] "Do you suppose that we intend to bow our necks to the yoke; that we intend to submit to the domination of our enemies?" asked Senator C. C. Clay, of Alabama; "that we intend to sit here as hostages for the good behavior of our conquered people — a people under your Republican administration not sovereigns but subjects?"[84] Besides the Southern leaders who were eager for a break-up of the Union, a number of Southern representatives for the first time talked secession, and they found themselves heartily applauded and supported by many influential newspapers, which acclaimed also the message sent to the Legislature by Governor Perry, of Florida.[85] In this he said:

"What else then have we to expect while the Union continues, but the repetition, no one can say when, where, how often, or with what bloody issues, of attempts like that lately thwarted in Virginia? Florida as the youngest and least populous of the Southern Sovereignties, can only follow in action the lead of her sisters. . . . I believe that her voice should be heard in ' tones not loud but deep,' in favor of an eternal separation from those whose wickedness and fanaticism forbid us longer to live with them in peace and safety."

For months it was impossible to supply the demand for Helper's book, even though it was forbidden in the South, — the latter fact a notice that its cherished economic conditions must not be subjected to criticism or debate. Men were even imprisoned for circulating it, as if its falsehoods — if such they were — would not render it innocuous; and the North retorted that the South dared not let the truth spread abroad. Not even Sherman's explanation that he had endorsed the book by proxy, without reading it, could save him. He was finally defeated, and Pennington, of New Jersey, chosen in his stead. The Union meetings in the North, engineered generally by well-to-do merchants and others who had a pecuniary interest in peace and pacific trade with the South, added to the general feeling that the country was in the throes of a great crisis. Late in April came the Charleston convention of the Democrats, with the resultant splitting up of the party along Southern and Northern lines, and adjournment without nominations to Baltimore on June 18. Then Douglas was chosen by the Northern faction to run against Lincoln, who had meanwhile been nominated by the Republicans.

There was but one issue in the campaign, and that was slavery and the future attitude of the Federal Government toward it. Within a trifle over six months after John Brown's death, the nation was practically divided into two camps, though hundreds of thousands did not realize how far the contest had gone, and hoped and believed like Lincoln that, even if he were elected, some way might be found of avoiding the "irrepressible conflict" and averting a national disaster. But all through the campaign, threats of disruption were rife; South Carolina let the world know that she was ready to leave the Union if the Republican party should be victorious. On November 6, 1860, Abraham Lincoln was chosen President of the United States. On July 18, 1861, eight months later, Colonel Fletcher Webster's regiment, the Twelfth Massachusetts, marched through the streets of Boston singing the John Brown song, which four of its members had just improvised.[86] Its men, too, were bound to Virginia with arms in their hands, but their movements, in contrast to John Brown's, were open and above board; they marched under the laws of war, duly commissioned by their government and known of all men. Theirs, too, were the cheers and plaudits of the crowds as they sang their great song through the streets of Boston and New York, until in Baltimore they chanted it with grim defiance of the silent hostility on every side.

Now, fifty years later, it is possible to take an unbiased view of John Brown and his achievements, even if opinions as to his true character and moral worth diverge almost as violently as in 1859. There are those in the twentieth century, appointed to teach history in high places, who are so blind as to see in John Brown only the murderer of the Pottawatomie, a "horse-thief and midnight assassin." Still others behold in him not merely a sainted martyr of the most elevated character, but the liberator of Kansas, and the man who, unaided, struck their chains from the limbs of more than three million human beings. These writers would leave nothing to be credited to Abraham Lincoln, nothing to the devoted band of uncompromising Abolitionists who, for thirty years prior to Harper's Ferry, had gone up and down the North denouncing slavery in its every form, stirring the public conscience and preparing the popular mind for what was to come. The truth lies between these two extremes. Were men who have powerfully moulded their time to be judged solely by their errors, however grievous, all history would wear a different aspect. In Virginia, John Brown atoned for Pottawatomie by the nobility of his philosophy and his sublime devotion to principle, even to the gallows. As inexorable a fate as ever dominated a Greek tragedy guided this life. He walked always as one blindfolded. Something compelled him to attack slavery by force of arms, and to that impulse he yielded, reckoning not at all as to the outcome, and making not the slightest effort to plan beyond the first blow. Without foresight, strategy or generalship, he entered the Harper's Ferry trap confident that all was for the best, to be marvellously preserved from the sabre which, had it gone home, must have rendered barren his entire life, his sacrifice and his devotion.

When Brown assailed slavery in Virginia, the outlook for Abolition was never so hopeful. The "irrepressible conflict" was never so irrepressible, and he who believes there would have been no forcible abolition of slavery had there been no John Brown, is singularly short-sighted. The South was on the brink of a volcano the day before the blow at Harper's

Ferry, as it was the day after, because slavery was intolerable morally and economically. It was bound to be overthrown because, in the long run, truth and righteousness prevail. Helper's book was written before John Brown struck, and the facts it contained, as to the social and economic injury to the South from its system of unpaid labor, lost and gained nothing by the bloodshed at the Harper's Ferry arsenal or the deaths on the Charlestown scaffold. The secession movement was too far under way for any peaceable solution; the minds of too many Southern leaders besides Governor Wise were thoroughly committed to it even before the raid. "The truth is," wrote Alexander Stephens on November 30, 1860, "our leaders and public men . . . do not desire to continue it [the Union] on any terms. They do not wish any redress of wrongs, they are disunionists *per se* and avail themselves of present circumstances to press their object." [87] This feeling and that sense of personal hostility which, as Senator Iverson remarked in the following month, kept the Northern Senators on their side of the Senate "sullen and gloomy" while "we sit on our side with portentous scowls. . . . We are enemies as much as if we were hostile States," [88] — all this was not the outgrowth of a year's excitement, nor did it begin in the John Brown raid. There was seething bitterness when the Kansas-Nebraska act was passed. There were two hostile camps when Sumner was struck down and one side of the Senate mourned, while the other exulted.

In 1859, the public recognized in John Brown a fanatic, but one of those fanatics who, by their readiness to sacrifice their lives, are forever advancing the world. Plenty exclaimed, like George Hoadley: "Poor old John Brown, God sanctify his death to our good, and give us a little of his courage, piety and self-sacrificing spirit, with more brains!" [89] They saw that he had no personal ambition; they felt that he was brave, kind, honest, truth-telling and God-revering. The nature of the conflict before the country was thereby revealed to them, and the revelation advanced the conflict immeasurably, just as it stirred the slave-power to new aggressions. It was like the lightning from the sky that lights up the darkness of the coming storm, so that men may for a fraction of a second take measure of its progress. So even across the water it illuminated the heavens to Victor Hugo and let him look so far into the future that he wrote:

"The gaze of Europe is fixed at this moment on America. . . . The hangman of Brown — let us speak plainly — the hangman of Brown will be neither District-Attorney Hunter, nor Judge Parker, nor Governor Wise, nor the little State of Virginia, but — you shudder to think it and to give it utterance — the whole great American Republic. . . . It will open a latent fissure that will finally split the Union asunder. The punishment of John Brown may consolidate slavery in Virginia, but it will certainly shatter the American Democracy. You preserve your shame but you kill your glory."

It was to Victor Hugo, too, the "assassination of Deliverance by Liberty." [90]

But the true Deliverance came with John Brown behind the bars at Charlestown, when there was suddenly revealed to him how inferior a weapon was the sword he had leaned upon from the time he had abandoned the pursuits of peace for his warfare on slavery. Not often in history is there recorded such a rise to spiritual greatness of one whose hands were so stained with blood, whose judgment was ever so faulty, whose public career was so brief. John Brown is and must remain a great and lasting figure in American history. Not, however, because he strove to undo one wrong by committing another; not because he took human lives in a vain effort to end the sacrifice of other lives and souls entailed by slavery. Judged by the ordinary legal and moral standards, John Brown's life was forfeit after Harper's Ferry. The methods by which he essayed to achieve reforms are never to be justified until two wrongs make a right. It was the weapon of the spirit by which he finally conquered. In its power lies not only the secret of his influence, and his immortality, but the finest ethical teachings of a life which, for all its faults, inculcates many an enduring lesson, and will forever make its appeal to the imagination. His brief, yet everlasting, prison life is the clearest condemnation of his violent methods both in Kansas and in Virginia. For the Abolitionists, it will be remembered, he had had nothing but contempt. Theirs were "but words, words;" yet it was by words, and words, embodying his moral principles, the theological teachings he valued so highly, the doctrines of the Saviour, who knew no distinction of race, creed or color, and by the beauty of his own peace of spirit in the face of death, that he stirred his Northern countrymen to their depths and won the respect even of the citizens of the South. It was in jail that he discovered, too, how those very words of the Abolition preachers he had despised had prepared and watered the soil so that his own seed now fell upon fertile fields, took root, and sprouted like the magic plants of children's fables.

Thus it came about that when the men of the North, within an amazingly brief space of time, found themselves, to their astonishment, likewise compelled to go South with arms in their hands, it was not the story of bloody Pottawatomie, nor of the battle at Osawatomie, that thrilled them, nor even of the dauntless lion at bay in the engine house. It was the man on the scaffold sacrificing, not taking life, who inspired. The song that regiment after regiment sang at Charlestown dealt not with John Brown's feeble sword, but with his soul. It was the heroic qualities of his spirit that awed them, his wonderful readiness to die with joy and in peace, as so many of them were about to die for the nation and the freedom of another race. They, too, were giving up all that was dear to them, their wives, their children, the prospect of happy homes and long, useful lives, to march and suffer; to see their brothers, yea their sons, fall by their side; even to receive upon their own bodies the sabres of their enemies. Theirs, too, was the ennobling experience of self-sacrifice. How great, then, must have been their inspiration, to feel that he who was the first in America to die for a treason which became as if overnight the highest form of devotion to an inspired cause, was marching on in the realms above!

And so, wherever there is battling against injustice and oppression, the Charlestown gallows that became a cross will help men to live and die. The story of John Brown will ever confront the spirit of despotism, when men are struggling to throw off the shackles of social or political or physical slavery. His own country, while admitting his mistakes without undue palliation or excuse, will forever acknowledge the divine that was in him by the side of what was human and faulty, and blind and wrong. It will cherish the memory of the prisoner of Charlestown in 1859 as at once a sacred, a solemn and an inspiring American heritage.

NOTES

CHAPTER I

THE MOULDING OF THE MAN

1. The original is in the possession of the Stearns family at Medford, Mass.
2. *Recollections of an Old Settler*, by Christian Cackler, Hudson, Ohio, 1870, pp. 20–21.
3. Ibid., p. 29.
4. John Brown to George B. Gill and others, Chatham, Canada West, May 18, 1858, printed in Davenport, Iowa, *Gazette*, Feb. 27, 1878.
5. *The Autobiography of Nathaniel Southgate Shaler*, Boston, 1909, p. 3.
6. For these and subsequent facts relating to the Brown ancestry, the author is indebted to George E. Bowman, Esq., Secretary of and Editor for the Massachusetts Society of Mayflower Descendants, who settled the question of the Windsor Peter Brown's family in *The Mayflower Descendant* for January, 1903, vol. 5, no. 1, pp. 29–37; to the Librarian of the New England Historical and Genealogical Society, Mr. William P. Greenlaw, who is also satisfied, after a search of the records, that Peter Brown of the Mayflower left no male issue, and to Mrs. Mary Lovering Holman, who, at the author's request, worked out a complete genealogy of the Brown and Mills family as far back as the Windsor connections.
7. The extracts here given are from the original MS. in the possession of Mrs. S. C. Davis, Kalamazoo, Mich.
8. Owen Brown to John Brown, Hudson, Ohio, March 27, 1856. — Original in the collections of the Kansas State Historical Society, Topeka, Kansas.
9. From the original MS. in the possession of Miss Mary E. Thompson, Pasadena, Cal.
10. Owen Brown was also credited with a rich vein of humor, intensified by a habit of stuttering and a keen perception of the ridiculous. The following bit of his philosophy of marriage, not heretofore recorded and now in the possession of Miss Mary E. Thompson, he sent to his granddaughter, Ruth Brown Thompson, shortly after her marriage, when he was himself eighty years of age: "There is much said about womens wrights in these days and it is tru they have there wrights and what are they but the love and care of a faithful Husband, with a share in all his honours joys and comforts of every kind, if he has good Company she must be a shearer if he has no company she must be his good company. If hir Husband is in trouble and affliction she must be afflicted and sympathise with him and make them as lite as posable. Sometimes Men bring troubles on themselves, in such cases Men or Women want there comforters and had not ought to be deprived while at some time we see it quite the reverce. I was once in company with a woman and asked about another Cupple, how they got along. She said they jest rubed along. I told hir I was indebted to hir for the way she had expressed it, this is the case of very many Husbands and wives, they jest rub along and the wheals of time never go chearfull and clean but are always rubing."
11. *Reminiscences of Hudson*, Supplement to the Hudson *Independent*, reprinted as a pamphlet, Hudson, Ohio, 1899.
12. From the MS. records of the Trustees of Oberlin College, Oberlin, Ohio.

13. For these anecdotes see, for example, *Historical Collections of Ohio*, by Henry Howe, Columbus, 1891, vol. 3, pp. 331–333, article written by M. C. Read, of Hudson, Ohio, a member of the faculty of Western Reserve College; see also statement of Charles P. Read to Dr. F. C. Waite, Hudson, Dec. 25, 1908, in possession of the author; also Christian Cackler's pamphlet.

14. *Life and Letters of John Brown*, by Frank B. Sanborn, Boston, 1885, pp. 38–39.

15. Statement of Dr. Francis Bacon, New Haven, Conn., Feb. 13, 1908, to K. Mayo; 'John Brown,' by Leonard Woolsey Bacon, *New Englander and Yale Review*, April, 1886, pp. 289–302.

16. From MS. of Mrs. Ruth Brown Thompson, in possession of her daughter. The Rev. H. L. Vaill, of Litchfield, Conn., fixed the year of John Brown's attendance at Morris Academy as 1817. See letter of L. W. Bacon to the Editor of the New York *Independent*, reprinted in the *Liberator* of Dec. 2, 1859. In his letter to his men from Chatham, May 18, 1858, John Brown states that he was travelling "between the sea-side and Ohio" in the spring of 1817. See Davenport *Gazette*, Feb. 27, 1878.

17. *John Brown and His Men*, by R. J. Hinton, New York, 1894, p. 13; letter of William H. Hallock in Hartford *Press*, Nov. 11, 1859.

18. Mrs. Ruth Brown Thompson's MS.

19. As narrated by Mrs. Danley Hobart, Levi Blakeslee's daughter, Cleveland, Dec. 31, 1908, to Miss Katherine Mayo, and in Mrs. Ruth Brown Thompson's MS.

20. California *Christian Advocate*, July 18, 1894.

21. Statement of Mrs. Annie Brown Adams, Petrolia, Cal., Oct. 2, 1908; of Benjamin Kent Waite, Columbus, Ohio, Dec. 26, 1908; and of Mrs. Nelson Waite and Mrs. Henry Pettingill, Hudson, Dec. 1908; all to K. Mayo. The last three witnesses state that both of Dianthe Lusk's sisters died mentally infirm.

22. Sanborn, pp. 33–34.

23. Statement of Jason Brown, Akron, Dec. 28, 1908, to K. Mayo. The other facts in regard to Brown's attitude toward his children are largely drawn from the manuscript of Mrs. Thompson; from the statements of four of the surviving children, Miss Sarah Brown, Jason Brown, Salmon Brown and Annie Brown Adams; and from the statements of the following neighbors familiar with the Brown family life: Alfred Hawkes, Mrs. Sherman Thompson, Mrs. Danley Hobart, Charles Lusk, Mrs. Charles P. Brown, R. M. Sanford, Miss Annie Perkins, Mrs. Charles Perkins, Col. George T. Perkins, R. W. Thompson, Mrs. Nelson Waite, Mrs. Henry Pettingill and Mrs. Porter Hall, all in December, 1908; and of James Foreman, see Note 25 below.

24. Statement of Jason Brown, Dec. 13 and 14, 1908, confirmed by Mrs. Thompson.

25. MS. letter of James Foreman, Youngsville, Warren Co., Pa., Dec. 28, 1859, to James Redpath, now in Hinton Papers, in the Kansas Historical Society.

26. Ibid.

27. An article entitled 'An Abolitionist,' by Edward Erf, in the Pittsburg *Post* of May 28, 1899, gives briefly the main facts of Brown's life in Richmond; other details are from the Foreman letter, from the MS. narrative of George B. Delamater, a copy of which is in Miss Thompson's possession, and from the records of the Post Office Department at Washington.

28. According to the Bible of Mrs. Julia Pitkin, Dianthe Lusk's sister, the latter was born January 12, 1801, and was therefore in her thirty-second year

NOTES

at the time of her death. Jason Brown vividly recalls being summoned, with his brothers, by their father to stand by the bedside of their dying mother, and recalls also the admonition she gave them.

29. The recollections of Miss Sarah Brown, Saratoga, Cal., have been largely drawn upon for this characterization of Mary Day Brown.

30. See interview with John Brown, Jr., in the Cleveland *Press*, May 3, 1895; Henry L. Kellogg's report of Owen Brown's version of the incident, in the *Christian Cynosure* of March 31, 1887; interview of Mrs. John Brown in the Kansas City *Journal* of April 8, 1881; the story is also confirmed by Henry Thompson's statement, Aug. 27, 1908, by Miss Brown's statement of Sept. 16, 1908, and by that of George B. Gill, Attica, Kansas, Nov. 12, 1908, all to K. Mayo.

31. From a facsimile of the original in the Kent, Ohio, *Courier*, Sept. 14, 1906.

32. For the facts as to Brown's business and real estate transactions, see the Kent *Courier* of Sept. 14, 1906, the statements in it being furnished by the late Marvin Kent; also *Fifty Years and Over of Akron and Summit County*, by ex-Sheriff Samuel A. Lane, Akron, 1892, p. 385 et seq.; also statement of Mr. William S. Kent, son of Marvin Kent, Kent, Ohio, Dec. 23 and 24, 1908, to K. Mayo.

33. On pages 87–89 of Sanborn's *Life* there is an able review by John Brown, Jr., of his father's business mistakes, from which this excerpt is taken.

34. He and his wife sold, on Sept. 17, 1838, a lot of land in Franklin township for $3500. The deed is in Miss Sarah Brown's possession.

35. Original in possession of Mrs. Ellen Brown Fablinger, Campbell, Cal.

36. See his first note-book, now preserved in Boston Public Library.

37. Original in possession of Miss Sarah Brown, Saratoga, Cal.

38. Sanborn, pp. 55–56.

39. From the original in the possession of George D. Smith, 48 Wall Street, New York City.

40. Sanborn, p. 56.

41. The narrative of John Brown's negotiations with the Trustees of Oberlin is drawn from the official records, and from the correspondence in the case in the Treasurer's Office of Oberlin College, Oberlin, Ohio; the letter of April 27, 1840, will be found in Sanborn, p. 134.

42. From the original court inventory of Sept. 28, 1842, in possession of Miss Sarah Brown.

43. John Brown to John Brown, Jr., Richfield, Jan. 11, 1844, Sanborn, pp. 59–60 (edited by Mr. Sanborn).

44. Original in possession of Miss Sarah Brown.

45. 'The Last Days of Old John Brown,' by Lou V. Chapin, *Overland Monthly*, April, 1899, pp. 322–332.

46. Statement of Mrs. William A. Hall to W. P. Garrison, April 18, 1895; statement of Mrs. Charles Perkins, Akron, Ohio, Dec. 12, 1908, to K. Mayo.

47. Summaries of all these various cases were kindly obtained for the author by Mr. W. D. Jenkins, Clerk of the Courts, Ravenna, Ohio.

48. It is entitled Heman Oviatt *versus* John Brown, Daniel C. Gaylord, Amos Chamberlain, Tertius Wadsworth, Joseph Wells and others, Supreme Court of Ohio, January term, 1846, and is reported at length in 14 Ohio Reports, 286.

49. There is a mass of evidence in regard to Brown's refusal to give up the farm to Chamberlain. The author has examined, besides John Brown, Jr.'s story of the trouble (Sanborn, pp. 86–87), Gen. N. Eggleston's charges printed in the Rockford, Ill., *Journal-Herald* of Nov. 3, 1883, and John Brown, Jr.'s answer to them in the Topeka *Capital* of Dec. 22, 1883; also statements of Jason Brown,

made in Akron, Dec. 1908, and of R. W. Thompson and R. M. Sanford, of Hudson, near neighbors of Brown's, made at Hudson, Dec. 20, 1908, to K. Mayo; Mrs. Sherman Thompson, of Hudson, a daughter of Mr. Chamberlain, kindly furnished the view of the case taken by the Chamberlain family; the pamphlet of Christian Cackler, already referred to, gives his unfavorable opinion on pp. 36–37.

50. The original of this letter is in the possession of the author.

CHAPTER II

"HIS GREATEST OR PRINCIPAL OBJECT"

1. Sanborn, pp. 40–41 (edited).
2. See, for a careful analysis of this whole question in the light of Brown's first memorandum-book, *The Preludes of Harper's Ferry*, a pamphlet by Wendell Phillips Garrison, comprising two papers contributed to the *Andover Review* in December, 1890, and January, 1891. Upon this the author has freely drawn.
3. Sanborn, p. 61 (edited).
4. See letter of F. B. Sanborn, Dec. 22, 1890, in the *Nation* of Dec. 25, 1890, which includes the one from John Brown, Jr., here quoted.
5. John Brown, Jr.'s affidavit in the Gerrit Smith case was given at Sandusky, Ohio, July 19, 1867. A copy of the original is in the author's possession; cf. Sanborn, p. 39.
6. From Miss Thompson's copy of the Delamater MS.
7. Quoted in James Freeman Clarke's *Anti-Slavery Days*, New York, 1884, pp. 155–156.
8. *Life and Times of Frederick Douglass*, by Himself, Hartford, Conn., 1882, pp. 309–314.
9. F. B. Sanborn (MS.) to W. P. Garrison, Concord, Dec. 5, 1890.
10. Sanborn, p. 134.
11. Statement of Miss Sarah Brown, Saratoga, Cal., Sept. 16, 1908, to K. Mayo.
12. For the garbled version, see the account of Daniel B. Hadley in *McClure's Magazine*, Jan. 1898, pp. 278–282. Mrs. Annie Brown Adams states (Oct. 2, 1908) that the man Ruggles, who committed the assault, did so when Brown lay helpless from fever in his ox-cart. John Brown's children know nothing of his alleged non-resistant views.
13. Hinton's *John Brown*, p. 585. "The Branded Hand" was the sobriquet of Jonathan Walker, sea captain, of Harwich, Mass., who was captured on his vessel by a United States ship, when smuggling slaves to a free port, imprisoned, pilloried and branded on the hand for the offence. The Rev. Elijah P. Lovejoy, of Alton, Ill., was the editor of an anti-slavery religious paper, the *Observer*. Three times his presses were destroyed by a mob determined to stop his utterances. In defending a fourth press, Nov. 7, 1837, he was murdered. The Rev. Charles T. Torrey suffered imprisonment for his attempts to run off negroes from the border States, and died in prison.
14. Hinton's *John Brown*, pp. 587–588.
15. From the original in the possession of Mrs. Ellen Brown Fablinger.
16. Statements of Henry Myers and Daniel Woodruff Myers to K. Mayo, Hudson, Ohio, Dec. 11, 1908.
17. Sanborn, p. 191.
18. Statement of Mrs. Adams, Petrolia, Cal., Oct. 2, 1908, to K. Mayo; also

letter of same to R. J. Hinton, Petrolia, June 7, 1894, Hinton Papers, Kansas Historical Society.

19. Cf. Sanborn, p. 133. Thomas Thomas personally asserted this to Mr. Sanborn.

20. "Did I ever tell you that Father changed his plan several times and finally adopted the old original one?" — Mrs. Adams to R. J. Hinton, June 7, 1894, as above.

21. See, for instance, *Cheerful Yesterdays*, by Thomas Wentworth Higginson, Boston, 1898, pp. 222–223; also Sanborn, p. 525.

22. Agnes Brown to J. H. Holmes, Portland, Oregon, Oct. 15, 1902, setting forth her father's (Salmon Brown's) views. — Copy in possession of author.

23. *Life of Frederick Douglass*, pp. 309–310. The author has consulted George A. Graves, a neighbor of Brown's, and other residents of Springfield for facts as to this period of Brown's life.

24. *Life of Frederick Douglass*, p. 311.

25. Related by Salmon Brown, Portland, Oregon, Oct. 13, 1908, to K. Mayo.

26. Sanborn, p. 63.

27. The original letter-book was kindly loaned to the author by Mrs. Ellen Brown Fablinger, of Campbell, Cal.

28. Perkins & Brown to Messrs. Crafts & Still, Springfield, July 11, 1846, Letter-Book No. 1, p. 31.

29. Letter-Book No. 1, p. 70.

30. Perkins & Brown to Hamilton Gay, ibid., p. 116.

31. The same to Friend Benjamin W. Ladd, Springfield, Dec. 14, 1846, Letter-Book No. 1, p. 158.

32. Cleveland, Ohio, *Weekly Herald*, March 17, 1847.

33. When John Brown was in jail in Charlestown, Aaron Erickson, a wool-merchant and a highly esteemed pioneer in Rochester, N. Y., wrote to Gov. Wise of his belief in Brown's insanity, because of the latter's "delusion that wool had never been properly graded." Mr. Erickson also alleged that Brown was not skilful in testing wools, and that his whole "defiance of the plainest and simplest laws of commerce," which led to his business collapse, could be charged only to an unbalanced mind. The original Erickson letter is in the possession of Mr. Edwin Tatham, of New York.

34. See Sanborn, pp. 67–68.

35. Sanborn, p. 72 (edited).

36. Originals in possession of Miss Sarah Brown.

37. Original in possession of Mrs. John Brown, Jr., Put-in-Bay, Ohio.

38. Ibid.

39. This figure has been frequently said to be $70,000. The estimate here given seems about correct to Col. George T. Perkins, the son of Simon Perkins (letter of July 22, 1908, to the author).

40. Original in possession of Mrs. John Brown, Jr.

41. Original in possession of Mrs. John Brown, Jr., as is that of the letter next quoted.

42. Statement of Miss Anna Perkins, daughter of Simon Perkins, Akron, Ohio, Dec. 12, 1908, to K. Mayo; Miss Perkins also says that her father "never questioned John Brown's exact probity."

43. John Brown to his "Wife and Children every one, Ingersol, Canada West, 16th April, 1858." — Original in possession of Alfred A. Sprague, of Chicago.

44. John Brown to Simon Perkins, Troy, 26th Jan. 1852. — Original in the Higginson Collection, Boston Public Library.

45. Sanborn, pp. 79–80.
46. John Brown to his son John, Feb. 24, 1854, Sanborn, pp. 156–157.
47. From the original, dated April 3, 1854, in the possession of Mrs. John Brown, Jr.
48. Mrs. Ruth Brown Thompson's MS., in possession of Miss Thompson.
49. Printed in full in the *Liberator* of Feb. 3, 1860.
50. Springfield *Republican*, article on 'John Brown's Fugitives,' June 12, 1909.
51. Original in possession of Alfred A. Sprague, of Chicago.
52. Original in possession of Charles P. Brown, Akron, Ohio.
53. To John Brown, Jr., Akron, Aug. 26, 1853. — Sanborn, pp. 45–51.
54. *Gerrit Smith*, by O. B. Frothingham, 1st, or suppressed edition, New York, 1878, pp. 102–107 et seq.
55. Ibid., pp. 235–236.
56. New York *Tribune*, Nov. 5, 1852.
57. Mrs. Ruth Brown Thompson's MS. John Brown to Simeon Perkins, Springfield, Mass., May 24, 1859. — Original in possession of Mr. Hull Platt, Wallingford, Pa.
58. Transactions Essex County, N. Y., Agricultural Society, 1850, p. 229; *The Life, Trial and Conviction* of Capt. John Brown, New York, R. M. DeWitt, Publisher, 1859, pp. 9–10.
59. From copy in the Library of Harvard University.
60. Ibid.
61. Statement of Annie Brown Adams to the author, April, 1909.
62. Mrs. Ruth Brown Thompson's MS.
63. 'How We Met John Brown,' by Richard Henry Dana, Jr., in the *Atlantic Monthly* for July, 1871, pp. 1–9.
64. John Brown to his son, John Brown, Jr., Vernon, Oneida County, N. Y., March 24, 1851. — Original in possession of Mrs. John Brown, Jr. Further evidence of John Brown's unsettled life at this period appears in his letter to his father, dated "Steamer United States, Lake Champlain, 23rd May, 1850." — Original in possession of Mrs. S. C. Davis, Kalamazoo, Mich.
65. John Brown to Ruth and Henry Thompson, Akron, Feb. 13, 1855. — Original in Haverford College Library, Haverford, Pa.
66. Original in the Byron Reed Collection, Omaha Public Library, as is also the original of the letter of Aug. 24, 1854, previously mentioned in text.
67. MS. statement of Gerrit Smith, Jan. 3, 1874, property of Mr. Sanborn.
68. Statement of Annie Brown Adams to the author.

CHAPTER III

IN THE WAKE OF THE WAR CLOUD

1. Sanborn, p. 191.
2. *A brief history of John Brown*, etc. By one who knows (John Brown). MS. Dreer Collection, Pennsylvania Historical Society.
3. Statement of Jason Brown, Dec. 13 and 14, 1908, to K. Mayo, at Sherbondy, Ohio; John Brown, Jr., in Cleveland *Leader*, Nov. 29, 1883.
4. Cf., for instance, Gen. D. R. Atchison, of Missouri, in the *Platte Argus*, cited in Robinson's *Kansas Conflict*, p. 94: "If abolitionism under its present auspices, is established in Kansas, there will be constant strife and bloodshed between Kansas and Missouri. Negro stealing will be a principle and a voca-

NOTES

tion. It will be the policy of philanthropic knaves, until they force the slaveholder to abandon Missouri; nor will it be long until it is done. . . . If Kansas is abolitionized, all men who love peace and quiet will leave us, and all emigration to Missouri from the slave states will cease." Senator Alfred Iverson, of Georgia, said in a speech at Columbus, Ga., reported in the *Savannah Georgian* of Nov. 2, 1855: "If Slavery gives way in Kansas, Missouri will be surrounded on three sides by non-slaveholding States, and the institution must give way there; it will also be in peril in the Indian Territory lying south of Kansas; it will then only remain for the Abolitionists to extend their influence to Western Texas, and the great object of their ambition will be attained. The South will then be reduced to a hopeless minority in the Union; her institutions will be confined to the narrow limits they at present occupy, and their overthrow will only be a question of time." See also speech of Congressman Felix K. Zollicoffer, Appendix to the *Congressional Globe*, 33d Congress, 1st session, vol. xxxv, p. 584; address by citizens of western Missouri to the people of the United States, after Lexington, Mo., convention, N. Y. *Tribune*, Sept. 25, 1855; letter of Atchison to Committee of Battle of King's Mountain Celebration, N. Y. *Tribune*, Nov. 2, 1855.

5. James Ford Rhodes, *History of the United States*, New York, 1904, vol. 1, pp. 475 and 489; Louis A. Reese, *The Admission of Kansas into the Union* (MS.).

6. Statement of Jason Brown, Dec. 13 and 14, 1908.

7. Salmon Brown to John Brown, Brownsville, K. T., May 21, 1855. — Original in possession of Miss Sarah Brown.

8. John Brown, Jr., in Cleveland *Leader*, Nov. 29, 1883.

9. Letter of John Brown, Jr., Brownsville, K. T., dated May 20, 24, and 26, to John Brown. — Original in Dreer Collection, Pennsylvania Historical Society.

10. *A brief history of John Brown*, etc.

11. John Brown to John W. Cook, of Walcottville, Conn., from Akron, Ohio, 13th Feb., 1855. — Original in Torrington, Conn., Public Library.

12. *Frederick Douglass: The Colored Orator*, by Frederic May Holland, New York, 1891, p. 247.

13. John Brown to his wife and children, Syracuse, June 28, 1855. — Copy in possession of Miss Sarah Brown. The "old British army officer" mentioned in this letter was Capt. Charles Stuart (sometimes erroneously called "Stewart"). See *Life of William Lloyd Garrison*, by his Children, Boston, 1894, vol. 1, p. 262, and vol. 3, p. 418; Sanborn, p. 194.

14. John Brown, Akron, Ohio, Aug. 15, 1855, to his wife and children. — Original in possession of Mrs. Ellen Brown Fablinger. Jason Brown, in his statement of Dec. 28, 1908, confirms Sheriff Lane's recollection of Brown's method of raising arms in Akron.

15. John Brown to his wife and children, Aug. 23, 1855. — Original in possession of Alfred A. Sprague, of Chicago.

16. John Brown, Jr., to John Brown, June 22, 1855. — Original in Kansas Historical Society.

17. Original in Dreer Collection, Pennsylvania Historical Society.

18. John Brown to John Brown, Jr., Aug. 9, 1858, from copy of the letter in possession of Miss Mary E. Thompson, Pasadena, Cal.

19. Statement of Henry Thompson, Pasadena, Cal., August, 1908, to K. Mayo.

20. John Brown to his wife and children, Osawatomie, K. T., Oct. 13 and Nov. 2, 1855, — originals in Kansas Historical Society; also letter of Nov. 23, 1855, in possession of Miss Sarah Brown. The distress of the family is again described by Jason Brown, Osawatomie, Jan. 23, 1856, to his grandfather. — Original in possession of Mrs. S. L. Clark, Berea, Ky.

21. Mrs. John Brown, Jr., to Mrs. John Brown, Osawatomie, K. T., Sept. 16, 1855, now in possession of the writer of the letter.
22. Letter of Nov. 2, 1855, as above.
23. Letter of Nov. 23, 1855, as above.
24. Mrs. John Brown Jr.'s letter of Sept. 16, 1855.
25. Statement of Jason Brown at Sherbondy, Ohio, Dec. 28, 1908, to K. Mayo.
26. Ibid.
27. Statement of Salmon Brown, Portland, Oregon, Oct. 11–13, 1908, to K. Mayo.
28. Kansas *Free State*, Lawrence, July 2, 1855; *Herald of Freedom*, Lawrence, Kansas, Aug. 8, 1857, chapter 10 of 'A Complete History of Kansas;' G. W. Martin, *The First Two Years of Kansas*, Topeka, 1907, p. 14.
29. Henry Thompson to Ruth Brown Thompson, May 18, 1856. — Original in possession of Miss Mary E. Thompson.
30. *Herald of Freedom*, cited in A. T. Andreas, *History of the State of Kansas*, Chicago, 1883, p. 108; also see Andreas, p. 110, for list of members of the first Free State Executive Committee.
31. *Statutes of the Territory of Kansas*, Shawnee M. L. School, 1855. Mrs. Charles Robinson says that the Free State settlers interpreted the Black Laws to mean that it was a prison offence to have in their homes the Declaration of Independence. — Sara T. L. Robinson, *Kansas: its Interior and Exterior Life*, Boston, 1856, p. 116.
32. D. W. Wilder's *Annals of Kansas*, Topeka, 1875, p. 57.
33. Letter of John Brown, Jr., to Mrs. John Brown, Sept. 15 and 21, 1855. — Original in possession of Mrs. John Brown, Jr. At the convention in Lawrence, Aug. 15, 1855, held to ratify the acts of the meetings of the past two days, according to the *Herald of Freedom* of Aug. 18, 1855, "Frederick Brown, of Mill Creek, one of the five Browns alluded to in the State convention of Radical Abolitionists at Syracuse, New York, was in favor of military organization for the purpose of resisting invasion and aggression." — See Andreas, p. 108.
34. Letter of Mrs. John Brown, Jr., Sept. 16, 1855, now in her possession.
35. Thomas H. Webb's Scrap-Book, vol. 5, p. 157, in the Kansas Historical Society.
36. John Brown to John W. Cook, Akron, Ohio, Feb. 13, 1855; to John Teesdale, of Des Moines, March, 1859, printed March 16, 1895, in the New York *Evening Sun*; statement of Henry Thompson, Aug. 1908.
37. Letter of Mrs. John Brown, Jr., to Mrs. John Brown, Osawatomie, Jan. 6, 1856. — Original in possession of Miss Brown.
38. Letter of Henry Thompson to Ruth Brown Thompson, Oct. 19, 1855, — original in possession of Miss Thompson; statement of Henry Thompson, Aug. 1908.
39. Reese MS.; Census of Kansas, Jan. and Feb. 1855, completed March 8, 1855.
40. Report of the Majority of the Special Committee Appointed to Investigate the Troubles in Kansas. Report No. 200, House of Representatives, 34th Congress, 1st session, Washington, 1856; hereinafter called the Howard Report. See also Charles Sumner's speech of May 19, 1856, 'The Crime Against Kansas,' Appendix to the *Congressional Globe*, vol. xli, 34th Congress, 1st session, 1855–56, p. 529.
41. Majority Report of Howard Committee, p. 8.
42. Reported in Platte *Argus*, cited in T. N. Holloway's *History of Kansas*, Lafayette, Ind., 1868, p. 135; also in N. Y. *Tribune*, Dec. 2, 1854.

NOTES

43. See letter of the *Tribune's* Washington correspondent, J. D. Pike, in issue of Feb. 13, 1855: "The bowie-knife Missourians will elect the Legislature of Kansas as they elected its delegate;" also correspondence of Cleveland *Herald* and Philadelphia *Ledger*, quoted in New York *Tribune*, Dec. 9, 1854.
44. Howard Report, p. 4.
45. Ibid., pp. 5–6.
46. Reese MS.; Andreas, p. 94; Howard Report, p. 79 et seq.
47. Howard Report, p. 8; Reese MS.; Andreas, p. 94.
48. Kansas *Herald*, April 6, 1855, cited in Andreas, p. 97.
49. St. Louis *Pilot*, cited in N. Y. *Tribune*, Dec. 9, 1854; see also views of Washington *Sentinel*, cited in *Tribune*, Jan. 18, 1855.
50. Washington letters of J. A. Pike in the N. Y. *Tribune* of Feb. 5, 6 and 10, 1855; Rhodes, vol. 2, p. 81. *The Liberator* stated on April 13, 1855, after the second election: "Beyond doubt the fate of Kansas is sealed."
51. New York *Tribune*, Dec. 9 and 25, 1854.
52. Andreas, p. 85; Richard Cordley, *History of Lawrence*, Lawrence, Kansas, 1895, p. 6.
53. Cited in Andreas, p. 83.
54. Cited in Andreas, p. 89; see also address of Citizens' Committee of Lexington, Mo., convention, New York *Tribune*, Sept. 25, 1855.
55. See, for instance, *Squatter Sovereign*, Feb. 20, 1856; *Kickapoo Pioneer*, Jan. 18, 1856; R. H. Williams, *With the Border Ruffians*, New York, 1907, p. 85; see also Webb's Scrap-Book, vol. 15, p. 83, Kansas Historical Society; and files of all pro-slavery papers from Sept. 1854, on; see also (Memoir of Samuel Walker) *Kansas Historical Society Collections*, vol. 6, pp. 251–255.
56. Webb's Scrap-Book, vol. 14, p. 35.
57. W. A. Phillips, *Conquest of Kansas*, Boston, 1856, pp. 28–30.
58. T. H. Gladstone, *The Englishman in Kansas*, New York, 1857, p. 41.
59. Sara T. L. Robinson's *Kansas*, pp. 15 and 19–20; see also graphic picture of Atchison's Missourians at Doniphan City, in the N. Y. *Tribune* of April 21, 1855; also N. Y. *Tribune* of April 30, 1855; and *Kansas Historical Society Collections*, vol. 5, p. 79; also N. Y. *Tribune* of April 12 and 17, 1855.
60. For these newspaper quotations, see *Kansas Historical Society Collections*, vol. 7, pp. 29 and 30.
61. Statement of Gen. G. W. Deitzler, in Charles Robinson's *Kansas Conflict*, Lawrence, 1898, pp. 123–124; Howard Report, pp. 84–85, 1157. It is interesting to note that Charles Sumner, in his great speech of May 19, 1856, thus denied the activity of the Emigrant Aid Society: "For it has supplied no arms of any kind to anybody. It is not true that the Company has encouraged any fanatical oppression of the people of Missouri, for it has consulted order, peace, forbearance;" see also Robinson, pp. 123–124; also Howard Report, pp. 86 and 1157.
62. See Reeder's testimony, Howard Report; also Executive Minutes of Gov. Reeder, *Kansas Historical Society Publications*, vol. 1, pp. 59–60.
63. Andreas, p. 94.
64. Howard Report, p. 9 et seq.
65. Sara T. L. Robinson's *Kansas*, p. 27; Howard Report, p. 1010; see also Boonville, Mo., handbill on the "Coming Election," dated March 13, cited in N. Y. *Tribune* of April 6, 1855.
66. Andreas, p. 90; Holloway, pp. 122–123. The Self-Defensive Association, having committed numerous outrages, was compelled to disband, after being denounced by a mass-meeting of one hundred and seventy-four citizens of Weston, held Sept. 1, 1854. See Holloway, p. 127.

NOTES

67. Howard Report, pp. 81–82; see also Andreas, p. 90; Holloway, pp. 124–125.
68. Howard Report, p. 30.
69. Ibid., pp. 35 and 936.
70. Cordley's *Lawrence*, p. 38; Andreas, p. 102. "We understand and believe," said the St. Louis *News* on May 12, 1855, "that David R. Atchison is at the bottom of all the troubles that have afflicted Kansas, and is the chief instigator of the meetings, mobs and cabals, threats and excitement, which threaten to plunge the border into a wild fratricidal strife."
71. Webb's Scrap-Book, vol. 4, p. 3; *Kansas Historical Society Collections*, vol. 7, pp. 30–34.
72. Webb's Scrap-Book, vol. 3, p. 158; N. Y. *Tribune*, April 23 and May 9, 1855; Holloway, p. 156.
73. Webb's Scrap-Book, vol. 3, p. 213; see N. Y. *Tribune*, April 23 and 26, 1855. The St. Louis *Democrat*, April 21, 1855, was one of a number of papers to approve the destruction of the Parkville *Luminary*. The Platte, Mo., *Argus* said: "The 'freedom of the press' is not for traitors and incendiaries;" see Robinson, p. 131.
74. See article in the *Western Reporter*, April 21, 1856, condemning Blue Lodges and the emigration from Missouri into Kansas; also the article 'The Passing of Slavery in Western Missouri,' by John G. Haskell, *Kansas Historical Society Collections*, vol. 7, pp. 28–39; also the amusing testimony of Thos. Thorpe, of Platte County, Missouri, in Phillips's *Conquest of Kansas*, pp. 91–97.
75. July 6, 1855, was the date of Gov. Reeder's veto. For the message in full, see Journal of the House of Representatives of the Territory of Kansas, 1855, p. 29. A similar veto message will be found in full in the N. Y. *Tribune* for July 31, 1855; see also Andreas, p. 103.
76. Journal of the Council of the Territory of Kansas, 1855, July 30, Appendix, pp. 1 and 2.
77. Reeder's Testimony, Howard Report, pp. 944–945. For memorial for removal of Gov. Reeder, see *Kansas Historical Society Collections*, vol. 5, pp. 200–204. For the official letter removing Reeder, see 34th Congress, 1st session, Sen. Ex. Doc. No. 23.
78. Rhodes, vol. 2, p. 86.
79. Cf. Holloway, pp. 170–171; N. Y. *Tribune*, Aug. 25, 1855.
80. Journal of the House of Representatives of Kansas Territory, 1855.
81. Cordley, p. 33; Robinson, p. 121.
82. Andreas, p. 107; Reese MS.
83. Andreas, p. 106; Holloway, p. 178; Cordley, p. 34.
84. Cordley, p. 35; Andreas, p. 106; Holloway, p. 178.
85. Robinson, p. 143; Andreas, p. 106; *James Henry Lane*, by W. E. Connelley, Topeka, 1899, p. 47.
86. Holloway, p. 179; Andreas, pp. 106–107.
87. This summary of the two conventions of Aug. 14 and 15 is drawn from the accounts of Andreas, Robinson, Holloway, Reese, the N. Y. *Tribune*, and contemporary Kansas newspapers.
88. Minutes of the Big Springs Convention, a pamphlet in the Kansas Historical Society; see also Andreas, pp. 108–109.
89. Cited in Robinson, pp. 172–173; see also Robinson, pp. 140–142, for a criticism of the Garrisonian attitude toward the Robinsonian policy in Kansas.
90. Horace Greeley, editorial in N. Y. *Tribune* of Sept. 21, 1855.
91. Reese MS.; Andreas, pp. 111–112.

NOTES

92. Reese MS.; Andreas, p. 112.
93. Cf. Rhodes, vol. 2, p. 101; Reese MS.
94. Andreas, p. 109; N. Y. *Tribune*, Sept. 21, 1855; Wilder's *Annals*, p. 61.
95. Andreas, p. 110. John Brown, Jr., was also a member of the Executive Committee appointed by the Lawrence convention of Aug. 14-15, 1855, but this was not a delegate convention. — Wilder, p. 55.
96. Reese MS.
97. Ibid.; also John Brown, Jr., in *Kansas Historical Society Publications*, vol. I, p. 272.
98. Howard Report, pp. 44-45.
99. Andreas, p. 111; Wilder, p. 67.
100. Andreas, p. 122; Rhodes, vol. 2, pp. 126, 201.
101. Howard Report, p. 53; Andreas, pp. 111-112.
102. Howard Report, pp. 53-54.
103. N. Y. *Tribune*, Nov. 26, 1855; Wilder, p. 70; Andreas, p. 114; Phillips, pp. 148-149.
104. *Kansas Historical Society Collections*, vol. 5, p. 74: "From the spring and summer of 1854 to the establishment of a legitimate territorial government by the success of the free-state men and actual settlers in the election of 1857 and 1858, the territory was practically without law and legal machinery, aside from the territorial judges and marshal appointed by the president." — W. H. T. Wakefield. See also Howard Report, p. 1026, testimony of D. J. Johnson. Mr. A. H. Case, of Topeka, long a leader of the Kansas bar, with a large practice in criminal cases, testifies that it was some time after his arrival in July, 1858, before any one was prosecuted for murder, "although they were prosecuted for stealing cattle." — Statement of Aug. 16, 1908, in Topeka, Kansas, to K. Mayo.
105. Howard Report, p. 64.
106. Webb's Scrap-Book, vol. 2, pp. 59, 155; Martin, *First Two Years of Kansas*, p. 11; Howard Report, pp. 1162-1163.
107. Andreas, p. 99; Leavenworth *Herald*, May 4, 1855; Howard Report, pp. 965-970.
108. For story of McCrea's trial and escape, see N. Y. *Tribune*, Oct. 2, 6, 8, and 17, 1855; also Sara T. L. Robinson's *Kansas*, pp. 104-105, 112-113, 126-127; also Howard Report, pp. 967-968, 970; also Andreas, p. 425. For Chief Justice Lecompte's defence of himself, see *Kansas Historical Society Collections*, vol. 8, pp. 389-405.
109. Howard Report, p. 1026, testimony of D. J. Johnson.
110. Howard Report, testimony of R. R. Rees, pp. 970-972.
111. Personal Recollections of Pardee Butler, N. Y. *Tribune*, May 19, 1856, Aug. 30, 1855; Phillips, pp. 145-147; Howard Report, pp. 960-963.
112. Phillips, p. 145; *Squatter Sovereign*, Aug. 7, 1855, cited in N. Y. *Tribune*, Aug. 23, 1855; Howard Report, pp. 960-962.
113. N. Y. *Tribune*, Nov. 3, 1855.
114. To Mrs. John Brown, Osawatomie, K. T., Oct. 13 and 14, 1855. — Original in possession of Kansas Historical Society.

CHAPTER IV

THE CAPTAIN OF THE LIBERTY GUARDS

1. Mrs. Jason Brown to Mrs. John Brown, Osawatomie, November 25, 1855, — original in possession of Miss Brown; letter of John Brown, Jr., in the Cleveland *Leader*, November 29, 1883.
2. Letter of John Brown to wife and children, Brownsville, November 30, 1855, — original in possession of Mrs. Ellen Brown Fablinger; also letter of December 16 from the same to the same, — original in Kansas Historical Society; John Brown to his father, Brownsville, November 9, 1855, — original in possession of Mrs. S. L. Clark.
3. Phillips, *Conquest of Kansas*, pp. 141–144; N. Y. *Tribune*, November 13, 20, 1855; Holloway, pp. 208–209; John H. Gihon, *Geary and Kansas*, Philadelphia, 1857, pp. 47–48. For another version of this affair, attributing the killing of Collins to one Lynch, see N. Y. *Tribune*, February 16, 1856.
4. For the killing of Dow and the arrest and rescue of Branson, see letter of S. N. Wood to Augustus Wattles, August 29, 1857, quoted in Robinson's *Kansas Conflict*, pp. 184–186; Howard Report, pp. 59–60, 1040 et seq.; Mrs. Robinson, p. 105 et seq. For Coleman's narrative, see G. Douglas Brewerton, *The War in Kansas*, New York, 1856, p. 223 et seq.; N. Y. *Tribune*, Dec. 31, 1855.
5. N. Y. *Tribune*, December 8, 1855; Robinson, pp. 188–189; Mrs. Robinson, pp. 109–111.
6. Testimony of L. A. Prather, Howard Report, p. 1065 et seq.; Mrs. Robinson, p. 109; Phillips, pp. 162–163.
7. Executive Minutes of Gov. Shannon, *Kansas Historical Society Publications*, vol. 1, p. 98.
8. Shannon to Franklin Pierce, November 28, 1855, *Kansas Historical Society Publications*, vol. 1, p. 101; Shannon to Richardson and to Strickler, ibid., pp. 99–100.
9. Affidavit of Hargis (otherwise Hargus or Hargous) in regard to the burning. See *Kansas Historical Society Collections*, vol. 5, pp. 244–245; see also Howard Report, pp. 60, 1044, 1051, 1059, 1064, 1107; also, Brewerton, p. 150.
10. *Kansas Historical Society Publications*, vol. 1, pp. 99–100, Shannon to Major-General W. P. Richardson and General H. J. Strickler, November 27, 1855.
11. Executive Minutes, *Kansas Historical Society Publications*, vol. 1, p. 102; Brewerton, p. 164.
12. Brewerton, p. 166.
13. Brewerton, p. 164; Rhodes, vol. 2, p. 105; Charles Robinson placed the number of Kansas residents enrolled in the pro-slavery forces at fifty, Howard Report, p. 1072; Phillips, p. 185, estimated it as never exceeding seventy-five or eighty; Sheriff Jones gave it as "not more than 150 or 200." See also Howard Report, testimony of James F. Legate, p. 1095; Andreas says: "There were some fifty pro-slavery residents — the Kickapoo Rangers, in the command."
14. Telegram to St. Louis *Republican* dated Kansas, Thursday, December 6, 1855, quoted in N. Y. *Tribune*, December 10.
15. N. Y. *Tribune*, December 12, 1855; Andreas, p. 117; see also Kickapoo City *Pioneer*, November 28, 1855: "To Arms! To Arms! The Enemy is in the Field. Up, Citizens. Up, Pro-slavery Men. Up, Southerners. Up, Law and Order Men!"

NOTES

16. Howard Report, p. 1096.
17. Howard Report, testimony of J. M. Winchell, pp. 1088 and 1090; ibid., testimony of James S. Legate, p. 1095; ibid., testimony of Gov. Shannon, p. 1109; Cordley, p. 54; Gihon, p. 58; Andreas, p. 118; Rhodes, vol. 2, p. 105.
18. See Missouri *Democrat*, cited in N. Y. *Tribune* of December 31, 1855.
19. Andreas, p. 119; Phillips, pp. 171–172, 181; Cordley, p. 56.
20. Howard Report, pp. 60 and 1129–1131.
21. Cordley, pp. 52, 59–61; Phillips, pp. 174–176; Holloway, p. 219; Andreas, p. 118.
22. John Brown to wife and children, Osawatomie, K. T., December 16, 1855, — original in possession of Kansas Historical Society; see also letter of S. L. Adair, Osawatomie, Dec. 9, 1855, to Owen Brown in Hudson, — original in possession of Mrs. S. C. Davis, Kalamazoo, Mich.
23. Howard Report, p. 62.
24. Dreer Collection, Pennsylvania Historical Society.
25. Original certificate of service, in possession of Mrs. John Brown, Jr.; see also Andreas, p. 121.
26. Letter of R. G. Elliott to K. Mayo, Lawrence, August 6, 1908.
27. James F. Legate, in the Leavenworth *Weekly Press*, October 23, 1879; John Brown Scrap-Book, vol. 1, Kansas Historical Society.
28. Ibid.; see also statement of George Leis, Lawrence, Nov. 30, 1909, for the author.
29. John Brown to Orson Day, Brown's Station, December 14, 1855, from copy in J. H. Holmes Papers in possession of the author.
30. For the varying accounts of the meeting and the speeches, see Phillips, p. 222; letter of R. G. Elliott to Miss Mayo; statement of Jason Brown, December 13 and 14, 1908; letter of Salmon Brown to J. H. Holmes, Portland, Oregon, July 8, 1901; statement of Salmon Brown, Portland, Oregon, October 11, 1908; *Reminiscences of Old John Brown*, by G. W. Brown, M. D., Rockford, Ill., 1880, p. 8; statement of E. A. Coleman, Sanborn, p. 220; *Herald of Freedom*, October 10, 1857.
31. Statement of Jason Brown, Dec. 13 and 14, 1908, confirmed by Salmon Brown; G. W. Brown, *Reminiscences of Old John Brown*, p. 8.
32. Robinson, pp. 207, 217.
33. R. G. Elliott. In a statement of July 27, 1908, at Lawrence, Kansas, to K. Mayo, Mr. Elliott says: "The people would never have submitted to the Shannon treaty had they understood its nature. It is also believed that if John Brown's policy of attack had been followed, it would have been very bad for the Free State cause."
34. Andreas, p. 119; Phillips, p. 225; Robinson, p. 204. For Shannon's Explanation, see *Kansas Historical Society Collections*, vol. 5, p. 248.
35. Phillips, p. 227; Howard Report, pp. 62, 1126; N. Y. *Tribune*, December 29, 1855; L. Spring, *Magazine of Western History*, vol. 9, p. 80; for Jones's statement, see Report on Kansas Claims, signed by E. Hoogland, H. J. Adams and S. A. Kingman, a committee of the Kansas Legislature, p. 62. This long report was published in Report No. 104, House of Representatives, 36th Congress, 2d session, Washington, 1861.
36. Phillips, pp. 226–227.
37. Ibid., p. 228.
38. For Shannon's letter and the authority given Robinson and Lane, see Brewerton, pp. 197–201; see also Governor Shannon's Explanation, *Kansas Historical Society Collections*, vol. 5, pp. 247–249.

NOTES

39. Howard Report contains eight testimonies; see also Gihon, pp. 65-70; Mrs. Robinson, pp. 144-146 and 160-163; Brewerton, pp. 137, 306, 329, for statements of Barber's widow and other relatives; Phillips, p. 211 et seq.
40. James F. Legate, Leavenworth *Weekly Press*, October 23, 1879.
41. John Brown to Orson Day, December 14, 1855.
42. Letter to wife and children from "Westpoint," Mo., January 1, 1856. — Original in possession of Mrs. Ellen Brown Fablinger.
43. Mrs. John Brown, Jr., to Mrs. John Brown, Osawatomie, Jan. 6, 1856, — original in possession of Miss Brown; Henry Thompson to Ruth Brown Thompson, Brown's Station, K. T., January 6, 1856, — original in possession of Miss Mary E. Thompson. Frederick Brown was the nominee of the meeting, but at the request of the chairman, John Brown, who urged that the elder brother would make a better representative, having greater knowledge of such matters, the vote was given to John Brown, Jr., — statement of Henry Thompson, September, 1908.
44. Mrs. John Brown, Jr., to Mrs. John Brown, Osawatomie, January 6, 1856.
45. Ibid.; John Brown to wife and children, Osawatomie, Feb. 1, 1856, — original in Kansas Historical Society; letter to his father, Brownsville, Nov. 9, 1855, — original in possession of Mrs. S. L. Clark, Berea, Ky.; letter of Jason Brown to his grandfather, Owen Brown, Osawatomie, Jan. 23, 1856, — original in possession of Mrs. S. L. Clark.
46. Mrs. Robinson, pp. 171-174; Gihon, pp. 71-72; *Kansas Historical Society Collections*, vol. 7, p. 525; Howard Report, many testimonies; and p. 63 et seq.; Charles Robinson, p. 222; Andreas, pp. 124, 426; Phillips, pp. 240-246.
47. Quoted in Andreas, p. 125.
48. Quoted in Wilder, p. 91.
49. Quoted in Andreas, p. 125; Webb's Scrap-Book; *Kansas Historical Society Collections*, vol. 8, p. 19; also in N. Y. *Tribune* of February 2, 1856.
50. Mrs. Robinson, p. 167; Howard Report, p. 969; *Kansas Historical Society Collections*, vol. 7, p. 525.
51. Andreas, p. 124; Holloway, pp. 275-276.
52. Andreas, p. 125; Holloway, p. 278.
53. Letter of Henry Thompson to Ruth Brown Thompson, January 26, 1856. — Original in possession of Miss Thompson.
54. Now first published. — Original in possession of Miss Kate Giddings, Jefferson, Ohio.
55. John Brown to his father, Owen Brown, Osawatomie, January 19, 1856. — Original in possession of Mrs. S. C. Davis.
56. Jason Brown to his grandfather, Osawatomie, Jan. 23, 1856. — Original in possession of Mrs. S. L. Clark; also to Orson Day, February 21, 1856.
57. Original in Kansas Historical Society. See Sanborn, p. 224.
58. Andreas, p. 125; Executive Minutes of the Territory of Kansas, *Kansas Historical Society Publications*, vol. 1, p. 104.
59. Reese's MS.; St. Louis *Democrat*, quoted in N. Y. *Tribune* of March 27, 1856; *Kansas Historical Society Collections*, vol. 6, p. 298.
60. John Brown to wife and children, Osawatomie, March 6, 1856. — Original in possession of Tuskegee Institute, Tuskegee, Alabama.
61. Letter of H. H. Williams to C. A. Foster, Foster MS., in Kansas Historical Society; for John Brown, Jr.'s own account of the proceedings of this Legislature, and of his part therein, see his letter to his grandparents, Brown's Station, Osawatomie, without date, — original in possession of Mrs. S. L. Clark.
62. Miscellaneous Documents, No. 82, House of Representatives, 34th Congress, 1st session.

NOTES

63. Kansas *Tribune*, March 5 and 12, 1856; see also letter of John Brown, Jr., to his grandparents, above cited.
64. Letter of Mrs. John Brown, Jr., to Ruth Brown Thompson, Brown's Station, April 8, 1856. — Original in possession of Miss Thompson.
65. Letter of Henry Thompson to his wife, Brown's Station, March 23, 1856. — Original in possession of Miss Thompson.
66. Henry Thompson to his wife, April 16, 1856. — Original in possession of Miss Thompson.
67. Henry Thompson to his wife, May, 1856. — Original in possession of Miss Thompson.
68. This account of the Settlers' Meeting has been drawn from the letter of S. L. Adair to J. H. Holmes, Osawatomie, July 9, 1894; statements by Henry Thompson, August and September, 1908; the speech of Martin White, which will be found in the Leavenworth, Kansas, *Journal* of March 12, 1857; also 'The Settlers' Meeting and Protest of April 16, 1856, in Osawatomie,' by O. C. Brown, a participant, Adams, N. Y., October, 1895, a MS. now in the O. C. Brown Papers, Kansas Historical Society.
69. The resolutions as given here are taken from the Kansas *Free State*, published in Lawrence, May 5, 1856.
70. Statement of Salmon Brown, October 11, 1908.
71. From a copy of the original, taken by James H. Holmes.
72. 'The Settlement of Lane and Vicinity,' MS. by James Hanway, in Hanway Miscellanies, vol. 4, Kansas Historical Society. "I was in sight but in the background when our committee served the resolutions on the Judge. He made no reply. There was a little side-work done to intimidate that Jury in a secret way on our part that never got out to the public." — Salmon Brown to J. H. Holmes, Portland, January 28, 1903, — original in possession of the author.
73. Statement of Salmon Brown, October, 11, 1908; MS. of John Brown entitled 'An Idea of Things in Kansas,' in possession of the Kansas Historical Society; statement of Jason Brown, December 13–14, 1908; statement of Henry Thompson, August, 1908.
74. See 'The Buford Expedition to Kansas,' by Walter L. Fleming, *American Historical Review* for October, 1900; see also N. Y. *Tribune*, May 5 and 10, 1856; Mrs. Robinson, pp. 216–217.
75. N. Y. *Tribune*, May 13, 1856.
76. Fleming, *American Historical Review*, October, 1900.
77. N. Y. *Tribune*, May 2, 1856.
78. See, for instance, Greeley's editorial of March 7, 1856.
79. N. Y. *Tribune*, May 5, 1856. An example of the recruiting that went on at this time in the South is afforded by a circular now in the possession of the author dated June 12, 1856:

"TO ALL TRUE
SOUTHERN MEN!!"

Shall Kansas be surrendered to the Abolitionists?
 Shall we sit down in idleness and permit our enemies to wall up Southern institutions, and thus endanger our existence as a people? We have the ability to prevent it — Do we lack the *patriotism*?
 Massachusetts says we must be driven out. Her Legislature has just appropriated $20,000 to effect this purpose, and her people propose to raise immediately by private efforts $100,000 more. These people are engaged in the business of fanaticism and treason. Will Alabamians be less liberal in maintaining

their substantial, vital rights under the Constitution? — Shall we turn our backs on the brave Missourians who stretch out their hands to us for help in a common cause? If we intend to do anything now is the time. This is a living, pressing issue. Is it possible that we are dead to its importance? Southern Freemen must be true to themselves. We know there are men among us who discourage this great movement to save the South, by predictions of failure and inability to succeed. Down with such men. Turn from them as our worst enemies and let all true men unite in crushing out this spirit of submission to abolition aggression and willingness to surrender Southern Rights without a struggle.

Messrs. BAKER & JOHNSTON,

Who have been aiding in emigrating Southern men to Kansas, have just returned for the purpose of raising more men and money. H. D. CLAYTON, ESQ., AND DR. JOSEPH JONES, will accompany and assist them in this enterprise. They are prepared to give reliable and valuable information, and for these purposes will meet and address the people at the following times and places.

The meetings were to be held throughout July at twenty-four places, among them Tuskegee and Mount Meigs, where are now located industrial schools for the freed negroes.

80. N. Y. *Tribune*, March 3, 1856.
81. N. Y. *Tribune*, Jan. 19, 1856.
82. The best accounts of Sheriff Jones's activity in Lawrence and his wounding are to be found in Andreas; Mrs. Robinson; the official report of Lieut. James McIntosh, *Kansas Historical Society Collections*, vol. 4, pp. 418–419; the N. Y. *Tribune;* and Phillips; see also *Kansas Historical Society Collections*, vol. 4, p. 410. For pro-slavery side see H. C. Pate's letter to St. Louis *Republican*, dated April 14, 1856, 9 P. M.; also *Kansas Historical Society Collections*, vol. 4, pp. 414–416; Shannon to Pierce. The *Life of Gen. J. H. Lane*, by John Speer, Garden City, Kansas, 1897, pp. 77–80, is also of value.
83. Sworn testimony of three members of Jones's posse, April 28, 1856; *Kansas Historical Society Collections*, vol. 4, p. 410.
84. See letters of Frank B. Swift and B. W. Woodward, of Lawrence, in the *Western Home Journal* of Lawrence, November 20, 1879; also letter of Philip W. Woodward to F. G. Adams from Leavenworth, September 18, 1897. Woodward, a room-mate of Filer at the time of the shooting, loaned him his revolver. Filer returned it later, saying that he had shot Jones. Not unnaturally, Filer subsequently denied this. He soon left Kansas and returned to New York. Lenhart died during the Civil War as first lieutenant of the Second Indian Regiment of the Federal army.
85. N. Y. *Tribune*, May 8, 1856; Mrs. Robinson, pp. 201–202; Andreas, p. 126.
86. Mrs. Robinson, p. 210; N. Y. *Tribune*, May 13; Phillips, p. 258; N. Y. *Evening Post*, May 13, 1856.

"Such a state of things as this maddens men and throws them back upon their own resources for redress. And it is dreadful to see how all the evil passions rise and rage at the recital of these terrible outrages so near home. Children catch fire and give vent to the undisguised feelings of their souls in words which under other circumstances would seem terrible. O, the depth of revenge in the human heart when the powers that should execute justice not only connive at the wrong, but abet and help it on, and screen the offender. May Heaven grant us deliverance soon." — S. L. Adair, Osawatomie, May 16, 1856, to Owen Brown in Hudson, — original in possession of Mrs. S. C. Davis, Kalamazoo, Mich.

NOTES

87. N. Y. *Tribune*, May 15, 1856.
88. For Butler's own story, see N. Y. *Tribune*, May 19, 1856; see also Gihon, p. 75 et seq.; Phillips, p. 259 et seq.
89. *Kansas Historical Society Collections*, vol. 4, p. 157; vol. 5, pp. 81–82; Gihon, pp. 82–83; Mrs. Robinson, p. 238; Phillips, p. 286; N. Y. *Tribune*, June 5, 1856.
90. Lexington *Express*, May 20, 1859; Missouri *Republican*, June 26, 1856: Hinton, pp. 78–80; Gihon, p. 83; Phillips, pp. 286–287. Stewart was formerly of Bushford, Allegany County, N. Y. See N. Y. *Evening Post*, June 9, 1856.
91. Andreas, pp. 127–128; Rhodes, vol. 2, p. 156; N. Y. *Tribune*, May 19, 1856; Charles Robinson, p. 234 et seq.; for 'Letter from a Grand Juror,' see N. Y. *Tribune*, June 9, 1856.
92. Mrs. Robinson, p. 267 et seq.; Charles Robinson, pp. 237–239.
93. Reeder's Diary, *Kansas Historical Society Publications*, vol. 1, p. 13 et seq.
94. Memorial to the President from Inhabitants of Kansas, *Kansas Historical Society Collections*, vol. 4, p. 392.
95. *Kansas Historical Society Collections*, vol. 4, p. 394; Andreas, p. 128; Cordley, p. 93; Phillips, p. 276; Holloway, p. 317.
96. Phillips, p. 278; Holloway, p. 319; Andreas, pp. 128–129; *Kansas Historical Society Collections*, vol. 4, p. 394.
97. Andreas, p. 129; Holloway, p. 329; Phillips, pp. 289–290; Gihon, p. 82; N. Y. *Tribune*, June 4, 1856; W M. Paxton, *Annals of Platte County, Mo.*, Kansas City, 1897, pp. 212–214.
98. Rhodes, vol. 2, p. 158.
99. *Kansas Historical Society Collections*, vol. 4, pp. 397–399; Andreas, pp. 129–130; Mrs. Robinson, p. 238.
100. The author's story of the Lawrence raid is drawn from the following sources: Memorial to the President from Inhabitants of Kansas, *Kansas Historical Society Collections*, vol. 4, p. 392 et seq.; Mrs. Robinson, pp. 240–248; Phillips, pp. 289–309; Gihon, pp. 83–86; Holloway, pp. 329–338; Cordley, pp. 99–103; Andreas, p. 130; N. Y. *Tribune*, May 29, 30, June 2, 3, 4, 7, 9, 13, 19, 20; St. Louis *Democrat*, May 27, 1856. For a statement of some of the brutalities committed by the Border Ruffians, see R. H. Williams's *With the Border Ruffians*, the story of an Englishman who served under Atchison at the taking of Lawrence, pp. 83–86; see also testimony of John A. Perry before the Congressional Committee, N. Y. *Tribune*, July 26, 1856. Details of the needless looting and destruction of property are sworn to by many witnesses in the Report on Kansas Claims already referred to. This is a store-house of valuable information as to the property loss inflicted on both sides from November 1, 1855, to December 1, 1856.
101. Statement of Robert G. Elliott, July 27, 1908; Phillips, p. 299; James F. Legate, *Kansas Memorial*, p. 63.
102. Andreas, p. 130; Phillips, p. 299; Holloway, pp. 336–337.
103. *Kansas Historical Society Collections*, vol. 4, p. 401; Phillips, pp. 296–297; N. Y. *Tribune*, June 2; Holloway, p. 333.
104. Eli Thayer, *History of the Kansas Crusade*, New York, 1889, p. 211.
105. Horace Greeley, N. Y. *Tribune*, May 21, 1856.

CHAPTER V

MURDER ON THE POTTAWATOMIE

Besides the personal narratives of two of the participants in the Pottawatomie murders, Henry Thompson and Salmon Brown, the author has been fortunate in finding three members of the Grant family alive to give their testimony, and has consulted in addition no less than fifty-six narratives of early settlers, including those of H. H. Williams, James Blood, August Bondi, John Speer, John T. Grant, James Hanway, O. C. Brown, Martin White, H. C. Pate and others who had a more or less intimate knowledge of conditions as they existed at the time of the murders. Jason Brown's story, that of John Brown, Jr., Townsley's statements and the testimonies in the Oliver minority report of the Howard Committee have also been drawn upon, as well as contemporary newspaper publications, besides all the lives of Brown and histories of Kansas. It is believed that the narrative here given is the first complete story of the crime.

1. Sanborn, pp. 236–237.
2. John Brown, Jr., in the Cleveland *Leader*, November 29, 1883.
3. Letter of Henry H. Williams, July 20, 1856, in N. Y. *Tribune* of August 20, 1856. Cf. also, narrative of Captain Samuel Anderson, a member of the company, in the Hyatt Papers, Kansas Historical Society.
4. John Brown, Jr., Cleveland *Leader*, Nov. 29, 1883.
5. H. H. Williams, N. Y. *Tribune*, Aug. 20, 1856; James Hanway, of Capt. John Brown, Jr.'s company, in Lawrence *Daily Journal*, November 27, 1879.
6. John Brown, Jr., Cleveland *Leader*, Nov. 29, 1883; H. H. Williams, N. Y. *Tribune*, Aug. 20, 1856; C. A. Foster, a member of the Pottawatomie Rifles, to F. G. Adams, April 15, 1895, Foster MS., in Kansas Historical Society.
7. Letter of Jason Brown, Osawatomie, June 28, 1856, to the family at North Elba, — original in possession of Miss Thompson, used here for the first time; official report of Second Lieut. John R. Church, First U. S. Cavalry, May 26, 1856, *Kansas Historical Society Collections*, vol. 4, p. 421. Lieut. Church dwells upon the fact that the presence of the Free State companies had frightened away two families. One of these was undoubtedly that whose slaves were freed by John Brown, Jr.
8. John Brown, Jr., Cleveland *Leader*, Nov. 29, 1883; Jason Brown's statement of December 13–14, 1908; statement of Salmon Brown, October 11, 1908.
9. Jason Brown to F. G. Adams, April 2, 1884, at College Hill, Topeka, in Kansas Historical Society; statement of Jason Brown, December 13, 1908.
10. Statement of December 13, 1908.
11. Martin Van Buren Jackson to W. E. Connelley, November 6, 1900, in Mr. Connelley's possession.
12. Statement of October 11, 1908. In a letter to Eli Thayer, dated Fort Scott, August 4, 1879, George A. Crawford states that John Brown, in Brown's camp at Trading Post, Linn County, Kansas, early in January, 1859, speaking to him of the Pottawatomie killings, said that "the death of those pro-slavery men had been determined upon at a meeting of free-state settlers the day before — that he was present at the meeting and, I think, presided, and that the executioners were then and there appointed." — Original in G. W. Brown Papers, in Kansas Historical Society.
13. *Kansas Historical Society Collections*, vol. 8, p. 279; Bondi's MS. narrative, in Kansas Historical Society.

NOTES

14. Hanway to Hinton, December 5, 1859.— Original in Hinton Papers, Kansas Historical Society.

15. Besides Salmon Brown, the following testify to the cheering that greeted the departure of the little company: Jason Brown, John Brown, Jr., and James Hanway. See Hanway to Redpath, March 12, 1860, quoted in Andreas, p. 604.

16. It is only fair to state that J. G. Grant testifies that H. H. Williams urged George Grant to keep out of the expedition because "something rash" was going to be done. Statement of J. G. Grant, San Francisco, Oct. 7, 1908, to K. Mayo.

17. Confession of Townsley, written out by Attorney Hutchings on December 4, 1879, and published in the Lawrence *Daily Journal*, December 10, 1879. Other confessions of Townsley, varying slightly from the above, have also been drawn upon. Johnson Clarke's version of Townsley's confession is in the *United States Biographical Dictionary*, Kansas volume, 1879, p. 526; a third version is in Andreas, pp. 603–604, this having been made Aug. 3, 1882.

18. John Brown, Jr., in Cleveland *Press*, May 3, 1895; statement of Jason Brown, December 13, 1908. "Gen." Bierce's title came from a northern Ohio secret society, the "Grand Eagles," organized to attack the Canadian Government. The arms given by Bierce to John Brown had belonged to this society, and included artillery broadswords that bore either on hilt or blade the device of an eagle, and which were the identical weapons used in the Pottawatomie killings. See Jason Brown's statement of December 28, 1908; Western Reserve Historical Society Tracts, vol. 2, pp. 4–5; for Bierce's own statement of his gift of arms to John Brown, see address delivered at Akron, Ohio, on 'The Execution of John Brown,' Columbus, 1865.

19. John Brown, Jr., and Jason Brown.

20. Statement of George Grant, San José, Cal., September 25, 1908, to K. Mayo.

21. Statement of Dr. W. B. Fuller to J. H. Holmes, December 7, 1903, in possession of author.

22. James H. Hanway to R. J. Hinton, December 5, 1859, Hinton Papers, Kansas Historical Society.

23. See 'Old John Brown,' by Capt. J. M. Anthony, Leavenworth *Weekly Times*, February 14, 1884.

24. Colonel James Blood, Lawrence, November 29, 1879, to G. W. Brown, published in Leavenworth *Weekly Press*, December 4, 1879. Neither Salmon Brown nor Henry Thompson can remember this meeting with Colonel Blood. But as Colonel Blood gave his testimony with unswerving precision on several occasions, and made his original statement before the appearance of Townsley's confession, the author is of the opinion that it must be accepted as correct, particularly in view of the accuracy of his detailed description of the party he met.

25. Townsley, December 6, 1879.

26. Statement of Henry Thompson, August and September, 1908.

27. Statement of Mrs. B. F. Jackson, Topeka, Kansas, August, 1908, to K. Mayo. But Henry Sherman's character was not so black as to keep the Commissioners on Kansas Claims from awarding $1035 damages to the administrator of his estate for cattle taken illegally by John Brown and others (Report, vol. 3, Part 2, pp. 1184–1190).

28. Letter of Maggie Moore and Mahala Doyle to A. A. Lawrence, Chattanooga, May 26, 1885, in the Massachusetts Historical Society Library.

29. Joint interview of G. W. and Henry Grant, given in Lawrence *Journal* office, December 4, 1879, and published the next day.

30. John Brown, Jr., Cleveland *Leader*, November 29, 1883; statement of

Henry Thompson, August, 1908; statement of Salmon Brown, October, 1908; statement of Jason Brown, December 13, 1908; E. A. Coleman, in *The Kansas Memorial*, a report of the Old Settlers' Meeting at Bismarck, Grove, Kansas, Charles S. Gleed, Editor, Kansas City, Mo., 1880, pp. 196–197.

31. *John Brown as viewed by Henry Clay Pate*, New York, 1859 (pamphlet).
32. Martin White, Speech in the Kansas House of Representatives, reported in the Leavenworth *Journal*, March 12, 1857.
33. Oliver Minority Report to the Howard Committee Report, pp. 105–106.
34. Statement of Salmon Brown, October, 1908.
35. Ibid.; also statement of Jason Brown, December, 1908.
36. Howard Report Appendix, *ex parte* testimony, p. 1193.
37. Ibid., pp. 1194–1195.
38. Ibid., pp. 1197–1198.
39. Ibid., pp. 1195–1197.
40. *Virginia Magazine of History and Biography*, July, 1902, pp. 31–32.
41. Statement of Jason Brown to K. Mayo; also his statement to F. G. Adams, Topeka, April 2, 1884.
42. Jason Brown to K. Mayo, December, 1908.
43. Jason Brown; Salmon Brown.
44. Statement of J. G. Grant, San Francisco, October 7, 1908, to K. Mayo.
45. Reprinted in Overbrook (Kansas) *Citizen*, June 25, 1908, from Watertown (New York) *Reformer* of 1856.
46. O. C. Brown Papers, Kansas Historical Society.
47. H. L. Jones to F. G. Adams, January 20, 1879, in Kansas Historical Society.
48. George Thompson, Twin Mound, Kansas, July 30, 1894, in J. H. Holmes Papers, Kansas Historical Society.
49. Also found in Andreas, p. 132.
50. Shannon to Pierce, Lecompton, May 31, 1856, *Kansas Historical Society Collections*, vol. 4, pp. 414–418.
51. Lawrence *Journal*, December 11, 1879.
52. *Correspondence of John Sedgwick, Major-General*, privately printed for C. and E. B. Stoeckel, 1903, vol. 2, pp. 8–9. Governor Robinson testified that Major Sedgwick was not only very kind to the Free State prisoners at Leavenworth, but a warm sympathizer with their cause. Major Sedgwick was, of course, misled, in one respect: there was no mutilation of the Pottawatomie victims.
53. Original in Hanway Papers, Kansas Historical Society.
54. MS. by James Hanway, in Kansas Historical Society. At the meeting of the Anti-Slavery Society in Lawrence, Dec. 19, 1859 (reported in the New York *Herald* of Jan. 2, 1860), Governor Robinson said: "It made no difference whether he [Brown] raised his hand or otherwise; [at Pottawatomie] he was present, aiding and advising to it, and did not attempt to stop the bloodshed, and is, of course, responsible, though justifiable, according to his understanding of affairs." Robinson also stated in this meeting that he himself thought the murders justifiable at the time. The Anti-Slavery Society, after the discussion, voted that the murders were not unjustifiable, and that they were performed "from the sad necessity . . . to defend the lives and liberties of the settlers in that region."
55. T. W. Higginson, *Cheerful Yesterdays*, pp. 207–208. The Rev. E. Nute wrote from Boston to R. J. Hinton, June 4, 1893, that he was in Boston at the time of the murders; that he returned soon after, and heard nothing but expressions of satisfaction concerning them. — Hinton Papers, Kansas Historical Society.

NOTES

56. John B. Manes, son of Poindexter Manes, in the Garnet, Kan., *Plaindealer*, January 9, 1880, in Kansas Historical Society; S. J. Shively, 'The Pottawatomie Massacre,' in *Kansas Historical Society Collections*, vol. 8, p. 179; Andreas, p. 603.
57. Martin's *The First Two Years of Kansas*, p. 19.
58. Capt. J. M. Anthony, in Leavenworth *Weekly Times*, February 14, 1884; James F. Legate, in Topeka *Weekly Capital*, February 28, 1884; Hinton, p. 87.
59. Statement of Mrs. John Brown, Jr., Put-in Bay, November, 1908, to K. Mayo.
60. Original in possession of Miss Mary E. Thompson.
61. Statement of Mrs. Mary E. Brown, San José, California, to K. Mayo, September 24, 1908.
62. Statement of Mrs. B. F. Jackson, Topeka, August, 1908, to K. Mayo.
63. See, for instance, Gihon, pp. 75, 85, 91, 98.
64. Mrs. Robinson, p. 328. In a later statement, in possession of the author, Mrs. Robinson affirms, however, that her charge above mentioned was made only on the authority of a rumor circulated by Redpath, which was later entirely discredited.
65. Statement of George Grant, San José, Cal., September 25, 1908. It is to be noted, in this connection, that J. G. Grant, his brother, stated, on Oct. 7, 1908, in San Francisco, to Miss Mayo: "Prior to Pottawatomie, no violence had been committed in our region on either side. The Free State men had, however, a general sense of danger from the continued threats from Missouri, and from depredations elsewhere rife." According to John T. Grant (see his letter to Rev. L. W. Spring, in Spring's 'John Brown,' Proceedings Massachusetts Historical Society, March, 1900), Henry Sherman told Mrs. J. T. Grant that Morse and Weiner had been ordered to leave for giving ammunition to the Pottawatomie Rifles.
66. Col. James Blood, in Topeka *Weekly Capital* and *Farmers' Journal*, January 1, 1884.
67. Mrs. Mary E. Brown; George W. Grant, statements of September, 1908.
68. J. H. Holmes papers, in possession of the author.
69. M. V. B. Jackson to W. E. Connelley, Emporia, Kansas, November 6, 1900. — Original in possession of Mr. Connelley.
70. Garnett, Kan., *Plaindealer*, January 9, 1880.
71. Mr. Adair's son, Charles S. Adair, is also of the opinion that this list was submitted. In a long and interesting letter, written in May, 1856, to his "Bro. and Sis. Hand," the elder Adair tells the story of the massacre and says that some of the murdered men "had made threats, had threatened the lives of Free State men, and acted most outrageously for some time past," but makes no mention of an Index Expurgatorius of the Free State men. The original letter is in possession of Mrs. S. C. Davis, Kalamazoo, Mich.
72. *The Kansas Memorial*, p. 196.
73. Statement of Col. Edward Anderson to K. Mayo, Boston, January 10, 1908; see also letter, quoting Brown, of George A. Crawford to Eli Thayer, Fort Scott, Kan., Aug. 4, 1879, in G. W. Brown Papers, in Kansas Historical Society.
74. John Speer, in Topeka *Commonwealth*, January 30, 1886.
75. F. G. Adams to R. J. Hinton, October 25, 1883, in Kansas Historical Society.
76. The original of the Pomeroy letter is in the possession of the author.
77. Wilder's *Annals*, p. 99.
78. Howard Report, p. 107.

79. Samuel Walker to Judge James Hanway, Lawrence, February 8, 1875, Hanway Papers, in Kansas Historical Society.

80. F. B. Sanborn's open letter to Mr. Winthrop, in Boston *Transcript*, December 6, 1884.

81. This charge of John Brown, Jr., is in the Topeka *Commonwealth* of February 16, 1884. For ex-Governor Robinson's reply and the continuation of the controversy, see Topeka *Commonwealth* of 1884.

82. Statement of Henry Thompson in J. H. Holmes Papers.

83. T. W. Higginson, *Cheerful Yesterdays*, p. 208.

84. Judge Thomas Russell to C. A. Foster, Hinton Papers, Kansas Historical Society.

85. *Recollections of Forty Years*, by John Sherman, New York, 1896, p. 100.

86. Rhodes, vol. 2, p. 78.

87. For the Hamilton murders, see Andreas, pp. 1104-1105; William P. Tomlinson, *Kansas in 1858;* New York, 1859, pp. 61-76.

88. *Massachusetts Historical Society Proceedings*, 2d Series, vol. 1, Boston, June, 1884.

89. "The truth is that the Pottawatomie massacre was so at variance with the whole course and policy of the Free-State party in Kansas up to that time, that its horrible details were not credited in the East. . . . The testimony of impartial observers was that the proslavery men were lawless and aggressive, and the Free-State settlers submissive, industrious, and anxious for liberty and order. Their previous good character prevented the country from believing that the killing done in their name by one of their number was an unprovoked massacre." — Rhodes, vol. 2, pp. 199-200.

90. In justice to Mr. Salmon Brown and to the reader, it is only fair that there should be appended to the discussion of the Pottawatomie tragedy the following letter, particularly as it has been printed in an altered and misleading form which conveys the denial, not found in its original, that John Brown was present at the Pottawatomie murders. It will be seen from this letter that Salmon Brown does not deny that his father was present, but evades a direct statement, as did his father. The letter was written in a period of great stress and anxiety, subsequent to the execution of John Brown, when it did not seem advisable to let the real facts come out. The original of this letter is in the possession of the family of the late Dr. Joshua Young, of Winchester, Mass.

REV JOSHUA YOUNG.   NORTH ELBA, N. Y. Dec. 27th '59.
DEAR SIR: —

Your letter to my mother was received to-night. You wished me to give you the facts in regard to the Pottawatomie execution or murder, and whether my Father was a participator in the ACT. I was one of his company at the time of the *homicides* and was never away from him one hour at a time after we took up arms in Kansas. *Therefore I say positively that he was not a participator in the deed.*

Although I should think none the less of him if he had been for it was the grandest thing that was ever done in Kansas. It was all that saved the territory from being run over with drunken land pirates from the Southern States. That was the first act in the history of our country that proved to the demon of Slavery that there was as much room to give blows as to take them it was done to save life and to strike terror through there wicked ranks. I should like to write you more about it but I have not time now. We all feel very grateful to you for your kindness to us.

             Yours Respectfully

                       SALMON BROWN.

CHAPTER VI

CLOSE QUARTERS AT BLACK JACK

1. Rhodes, vol. 2, pp. 198–200.
2. For a strong expression of Mr. Garrison's opinion as to the Kansas policies of Beecher and Theodore Parker, see the *Liberator*, vol. 26, p. 42.
3. Pro-Slavery Circular, in *Squatter Sovereign*, July 15, 1856.
4. Shannon to Pierce, *Kansas Historical Society Collections*, vol. 4, p. 416.
5. W. H. Coffin, 'The Settlement of the Friends in Kansas,' *Kansas Historical Society Collections*, vol. 7, pp. 337–338.
6. N. Y. *Tribune*, June 17, 1856.
7. Mrs. Sara T. L. Robinson, on pp. 273–274 of her book, describes her approach to the Territory on June 3 from the East. Rumors of war increased as the Border was neared. Inflammatory extras depicting the Pottawatomie murders in lurid terms, and inciting to revenge and reprisal, were current in western Missouri, and the excited people were everywhere preparing to respond. "'Murder is the watchword and midnight deed,' said one journal, 'of a scattered and scouting band of abolitionists. . . . Men peaceable and quiet, cannot travel on the public roads of Kansas. . . . No Southerner dare venture alone and unarmed.'"
8. Correspondence N. Y. *Tribune* from Fort Scott, June 4, printed July 1, 1856.
9. Mrs. Robinson, in the Wichita (Kansas) *Eagle*, December 12, 1878.
10. Reprinted in the St. Louis *Republican*, June 14, 1856; see also John Sherman, *Recollections of Forty Years*, p. 100.
11. Statement of Jason Brown to K. Mayo, December 13, 1908.
12. William Hutchinson ("Randolph") to the N. Y. *Times*, from Lawrence, June 23, 1856; in Hutchinson Scrap-Book, Kansas Historical Society.
13. N. Y. *Tribune*, July 2, 1856.
14. Statement of Jason Brown as above. The original official notes of this examination of John Brown, Jr., Jason Brown and their fellow prisoners, before the U. S. Commissioner, Edward Hoogland, are in possession of Mr. M. W. Blackman, Cleveland, Ohio.
15. From an unpublished MS. of Owen Brown, in the possession of Miss Mary E. Thompson.
16. Bondi, in *Kansas Historical Society Collections*, vol. 8, pp. 282–283.
17. James Redpath, *The Public Life of Captain John Brown*, Boston, 1860, pp. 112–114.
18. Bondi's narrative; also Owen Brown's story.
19. *Rebellion Records*, Series 1, vol. 36, p. 778, report of P. H. Sheridan, Major-General commanding; also, report of General Custer, ibid., p. 818; see also *University of Virginia*, New York, 1904, vol. 2, p. 54. Pate thus challenged Horace Greeley for impugning his bravery: "If you doubt that I will fight you can have a chance to try me in any way you want to, at any time you want to. My address for the present is, 89, Guy's National, Washington, D. C., and for the future, Lecompton, Kansas Territory, until further notice;" also statement of Major Thomas S. Taliaferro, Richmond, April 23, 1909, to K. Mayo.
20. Owen Brown, in the Springfield *Republican*, January 14, 1889.
21. *John Brown as viewed by H. Clay Pate.*
22. Quoted in Sanborn, p. 239.
23. *John Brown*, by H. Clay Pate.
24. John Brown to his family, June, 1856, Sanborn, p. 240.

25. John Brown several times wrote out the list of those who took part in the engagement. The following, from the original in the Kansas Historical Society, is the roster as he wrote it: —

Saml T Shore, Capt. Silas More. David Hendricks (Horse Guard). Hiram McAllister. Mr. Parmely (wounded) Silvester Harris. O A Carpenter (wounded). Augustus Shore. Mr. Townsley of Pottowatomie. Wm B Hayden. John McWhinney. Montgomery Shore. Elkanah Timmons. T. Weiner. A. Bondy. Hugh McWhinney. Charles Keiser Elizur Hill. Wm Davis. Mr. Cochran of Pottowatomie. Henry Thompson (dangerously wounded) Elias Basinger. Owen Brown. Fredk. Brown (horse guard) Salmon Brown (wound & cripled.) Oliver Brown.

JOHN BROWN.

List of names of men wounded in the battle of Palmyra or Black Jack: also of Eight volunteers who maintained their position during that fight: & to whom the surrender was made June 2d 1856.

O A Carpenter } wounded badly; Thompson dangerously
Henry Thompson

Mr Parmely } wounded slightly in nose also in Arm so that he had to leave the ground

Charles Keiser
Elizur Hill
Wm David
Hugh McWhinney
Mr. Cochran of Pottawatomie
Salmon Brown (accidentally wounded after the fight & liable to remain a cripple)
Oliver Brown

Names of all who either fought or guarded the Horses during the fight at Palmyra June 2d 1856 will be found on the other side

Respectfully submitted by

JOHN BROWN

Mess. Whitman }
    Eldridge }
    & others }

26. Annual Report of the Secretary of War, Exec. Doc. No. 1, 34th Congress, 3d session, House of Representatives, pp. 44–45.

27. *Correspondence of John Sedgwick, Major-General*, vol. 2, pp. 7–8.

28. For this raid the authorities are August Bondi, MS. narrative (hitherto unpublished) in the Kansas Historical Society Library; testimony of J. D. Pennypacker, one of Pate's men, in the *Richmond Despatch* of November 19, 1859; the lengthy testimony of J. M. Bernard in the Report on Kansas Claims, vol. 3, Part 1, pp. 842–862, where are also the sworn statements of six other witnesses; letter of J. M. Bernard in the Missouri *Republican*, quoted in the N. Y. *Tribune* of June 20, 1856. The same incident is referred to in the Oliver Minority Report, p. 108, but the date is erroneously given as May 27 and 28. Bernard was awarded $9,524.91 on May 6, 1859, for the damage inflicted by Brown's men.

29. That it was Col. Preston, and not one Fain, or Marshal Donaldson, as variously stated, appears from Gov. Shannon's letter of June 4, 1856, to Col. Sumner, *Kansas Historical Society Publications*, vol. 1, p. 122; and from a letter of J. Bernard to Missouri *Republican*, written at Westport, Monday, June 9, 1856.

30. Statements of Salmon Brown and Henry Thompson of October 11, 1908,

NOTES

and August 22, 1908, respectively; also letter of J. Bernard as above, quoted in the N. Y. *Tribune* of June 20. The story is variously told by different chroniclers.

31. Gov. Shannon to the President, Lecompton, June 17, 1856, *Kansas Historical Society Collections*, vol. 4, pp. 386–387.

32. Correspondence of Gov. Shannon, *Kansas Historical Society Collections*, vol. 4, p. 414.

33. Proclamation of Gov. Shannon, Annual Report of the Secretary of War for 1856, pp. 47–48; see also Executive Minutes of Gov. Shannon, *Kansas Historical Society Publications*, vol. 1, p. 121.

34. *Kansas Historical Society Collections*, vol. 4, p. 421.

35. Andreas, pp. 132–133; N. Y. *Tribune*, June 16, 1856.

36. Bondi MSS., Kansas Historical Society.

37. Andreas, p. 134; O. C. Brown's letter of June 24, 1856, Kansas Historical Society; Mrs. Robinson, p. 278; Phillips, pp. 374–375; N. Y. *Tribune* of June 14 and June 17, 1856.

38. Gihon, p. 90; Phillips, pp. 364–369; Mrs. Robinson, p. 283; N. Y. *Tribune*, June 26 and 27, 1856; *Herald of Freedom*, May 16, 1857; Holloway, p. 361.

39. Report of Secretary of War for 1856, p. 49.

40. Phillips, p. 380.

41. Report of Lieut. McIntosh to acting Governor Woodson, *Kansas Historical Society Collections*, vol. 4, p. 391.

42. Original in Kansas Historical Society.

43. Mrs. Robinson, p. 283; Phillips, p. 380; see also N. Y. *Tribune*, July 8, for statement of robberies; report on Kansas Claims, vol. 3, Part 1, pp. 206–207.

44. N. Y. *Tribune*, June 19; Mrs. Robinson, pp. 284–285.

45. N. Y. *Tribune*, June 26 and 27; Mrs. Robinson, p. 298.

46. Gihon, p. 91; N. Y. *Tribune*, June 1, 3 and 11.

47. Phillips, p. 389.

48. Gladstone, p. 281; Gihon, p. 93; Cordley, p. 113; Mrs. Robinson, p. 324; 'Life of Samuel Walker,' *Kansas Historical Society Collections*, vol. 6, pp. 268–269: Andreas, p. 142.

49. Cordley, pp. 105–107; statement of Jason Brown, Dec. 13 and 14, 1908; Andreas, pp. 320 and 427; Mrs. Robinson, p. 328; N. Y. *Tribune*, Sept. 8 and 9, 1856.

50. Andreas, p. 133.

51. For instances of Free State thefts of horses owned by pro-slavery men, see *Kansas Historical Society Collections*, vol. 10, p. 645. The Oliver Minority Report, pp. 1199–1205, gives many instances of robberies of pro-slavery stores and houses immediately after the Pottawatomie murders. The long report of the Commissioners of Kansas, already referred to, should also be studied in this connection.

52. Quoted in N. Y. *Tribune* of June 18, 1856.

53. Ibid.

54. *Squatter Sovereign*, July 15, 1856.

55. Proclamation of acting Governor Woodson, Annual Report of the Secretary of War for 1856, pp. 57–58.

56. See Report of Secretary of War for 1856, pp. 26, 56, 61; Shannon to Sumner, June 23, Executive Minutes, *Kansas Historical Society Publications*, vol. 1, p. 123. For a sample of the rejoicing of pro-slavery papers when Sumner was relieved, see Richmond *Enquirer* of September 5, 1856.

57. Secretary of War's Report for 1856, p. 69.

58. Gen. Edwin Vose Sumner, born in Boston, January 30, 1797, entered the army in 1819 as second lieutenant of infantry. He served in the Black Hawk

War, and led the cavalry charge at Cerro Gordo, Mexico, in April, 1847; was Governor of New Mexico, 1851–53; he died at Syracuse, N. Y., March 21, 1863, as a brigadier-general in the regular army and major-general of volunteers, from disease resulting from the Fredericksburg campaign, in which he commanded a division. He had the respect of the army as an able and gallant soldier, especially in Indian warfare. In a letter dated "Camp of U. S. Cavalry, near Lecompton, July 7, 1856," addressed to Col. Sumner and bearing also the signatures of Geo. W. Smith, Gaius Jenkins, John Brown, Jr., Henry H. Williams and Geo. W. Deitzler, Charles Robinson wrote as follows:

"Whatever judgment the people of Kansas or the country may pass upon the conduct of the administrator of Government, or I should rather say, administrator of *outrage*, in Kansas, all parties must concede to you, personally, the character of an honorable, impartial, high-minded and efficient officer; notwithstanding, in the discharge of your official duty, your superiors incur the censure of persons of all shades of political faith." — See N. Y. *Tribune*, July 24, 1856.

59. The correspondence of Shannon, Woodson and Sumner, and between Jefferson Davis and Sumner, and the proclamation of acting Governor Woodson, will be found in the Annual Report of the Secretary of War for 1856. See also *Kansas Historical Society Collections*, vol. 4; and vol. 9, pp. 360–363.

60. Philadelphia *North American*, quoted in the Mobile *Daily Tribune* of August 1, 1856; Mrs. Robinson, pp. 309–315; Phillips, pp. 392–406; N. Y. *Tribune*, July 10 and 19, 1856; letter of James Redpath, dated Topeka, July 4, in the Milwaukee *Sentinel* of July 17, 1856.

61. Statements of Salmon Brown and Henry Thompson; letter of S. L. Adair to T. H. Hand and Stephen Davis and families, Osawatomie, July 17, 1856.— Original in possession of Mrs. S. C. Davis.

62. Quoted in W. A. Phillips's article, in *Atlantic Monthly* for December, 1879.

63. Original in possession of Mrs. John Brown, Jr.

64. John Brown, Jr., to Jason Brown, dated Camp U. S. Cavalry, near Lecompton, Kansas, July 30, 1856; S. L. Adair, Osawatomie, July 17, 1856, wrote to T. H. Hand and Stephen Davis and families as follows: "Bro. J. B. and unmarried sons expect to leave the territory immediately. They are known as fighting men and are a terror to Mo." — Original in possession of Mrs. S. C. Davis.

65. Statement of Salmon Brown, Oct. 11, 1908.

66. MS. diary of Samuel J. Reader, Topeka, Kansas, in his possession.

67. Record of Court-Martial of Private A. D. Stevens, Company F, First Dragoons, May, 1855, in office of Judge-Advocate-General, War Department, Washington; also letter of Judge-Advocate-General G. B. Davis, U. S. Army, November 23, 1908, to author.

68. Statement of Henry Thompson, August, 1908, and of Salmon Brown, October, 1908; the story of Samuel Walker, *Kansas Historical Society Collections*, vol. 6, pp. 267–268, also treats of John Brown's movements at this juncture. The invalids were taken in an ox-wagon as far as Tabor, Iowa, where Owen was especially kindly received and remained until he had fully recuperated, when he returned to Kansas. The progress homeward of Oliver Brown, Henry Thompson and Salmon Brown, together with William Thompson, a brother of Henry, whom they met on their way out and dissuaded from entering Kansas, is thus described by Salmon Brown: "We other four bought a double buggy and harness from the Oberlin people on credit, at Tabor, drove to Iowa City, sold the horses, sent back the money to pay for the wagon and all four went home. The horses for the double buggy we came by thus: we heard, on the way through Nebraska, that some pro-slavery men were after us. Oliver, who was always a dare-devil, and William

NOTES

Thompson ambushed these men, deliberately turning aside for that purpose. The men, ordered off their horses, took it for a regular hold-up in force, and surrendered their animals. Oliver and William immediately jumped on and lit out for Tabor. It was these horses that took us across Iowa." The need of converting pro-slavery animals into good anti-slavery stock was thus urgent with the Brown sons in peaceful, placid Nebraska as it had been in bleeding Kansas.

CHAPTER VII

THE FOE IN THE FIELD

1. Andreas, p. 138; T. W. Higginson and other correspondents, in the N. Y. *Tribune* of July 7, 1856; N. Y. *Tribune*, July 14, 1856; statement of Thomas W. Bicknell, Providence, R. I., Jan. 24, 1908, to K. Mayo; the *Squatter Sovereign* of July 1, 1856, under the caption of "More Arms Captured!" made this pro-slavery comment, characteristic of the view of the Border Ruffian press: "On the way up the river they were boasting of what they would do, should any one attempt to molest them. . . . When they arrived at the *Political Quarantine* the whole party of seventy-eight, all of them 'armed to the teeth,' surrendered to a company of twenty Border Ruffians. . . . If this is the material we have to encounter in Kansas we have but little to fear of the result. Fifty thousand such 'cattle' could not subdue the Spartan band now in possession of Kansas."

2. Andreas, pp. 138–139; Holloway, pp. 363–364; N. Y. *Tribune*, July 9, 15 and 17, 1856.

3. Andreas, pp. 136–137; Chicago *Daily Tribune*, June 2, 1856; John Speer's *Lane*, pp. 101–107.

4. *The Republican Party*, edited by John D. Long, p. 47. (No place of publication given.)

5. James Ford Rhodes, in the *Atlantic Monthly*, May, 1909.

6. *Congressional Globe*, 34th Congress, 1st session, vol. xli, pp. 1009–1013.

7. *Congressional Globe*, 34th Congress, 1st session, vol. xli, p. 869.

8. *Congressional Globe*, 34th Congress, 1st session, vol. xl, p. 1873, for action of the House against Whitfield and Reeder.

9. *Congressional Globe*, 34th Congress, 1st session, vol. xxxix, p. 1541.

10. For a more detailed narrative of the struggle over Kansas, see Rhodes, vol. 2, pp. 201–202.

11. See N. Y. *Tribune*, Jan. 27, 1857, for report of Horace White, Assistant Secretary of the Committee.

12. For Samuel Walker's story of this ride, see *Kansas Historical Society Collections*, vol. 6, pp. 267–268.

13. Walker to Hanway, from Lawrence, Feb. 18, 1875; Hanway Papers, Kansas Historical Society.

14. Andreas, p. 142; Bondi MSS.; Charles R. Tuttle, *History of Kansas*, Madison, Wis., 1876, p. 358; J. H. Holmes's testimony, N. Y. *Tribune*, Aug. 21, 1856.

15. Bondi MSS., Part 3, Kansas Historical Society.

16. Printed in the *Missouri Democrat* of Aug. 27, 1856, and reprinted in the N. Y. *Tribune* of Sept. 8, 1856; *Squatter Sovereign*, Aug. 26, 1856; see also Leavenworth City *Journal*, Aug. 17, 1856; *Missouri Republican*, Aug. 23, 1856.

17. Bondi MSS.

18. Original in possession of Miss Thompson.

19. See their manifesto in the *Squatter Sovereign* of Aug. 26, 1856.

20. "Randolph's" letters of Aug. 29 and Sept. 7, 1856, in the N. Y. *Times*.
21. Article entitled 'Old John Brown,' in John Brown Scrap-Book No. 3, Kansas Historical Society.
22. Statement of Ezra Robinson at Paola, Kansas, Oct. 3, 1908, to the author.
23. Statement of Mrs. Mary Grant Brown, San José, Cal., Sept. 24, 1908, to K. Mayo. Ephraim Coy testifies similarly to a panic of the Border Ruffians on hearing that John Brown was coming with six hundred rifles and a thousand men. See MS. entitled 'Kansas Experiences of Ephraim Coy,' Hyatt Papers, Kansas Historical Society.
24. Statement of R. G. Elliott, July 27, 1908, to K. Mayo.
25. Quoted in N. Y. *Tribune* of Aug. 25, 1856.
26. Statement of. Major James B. Abbott, *Kansas Historical Society Collections*, vols. 1-2, p. 221. This cannon is now in the Kansas Historical Society.
27. *Kansas Historical Society Collections*, vols. 1-2, pp. 218-219.
28. Holloway, p. 379.
29. Letter to the Editor of the Mobile *Tribune*, reprinted in N. Y. *Tribune*, Aug. 23, 1856.
30. Andreas, pp. 142-143; Cordley, p. 115; Holloway, p. 379; Mrs. Robinson, pp. 324-325; N. Y. *Tribune*, Aug. 25 and 29, 1856.
31. The best account of the Fort Titus affair is to be found in Capt. Samuel Walker's narrative already referred to, in the *Kansas Historical Society Collections*, vol. 6, pp. 269-273. Captain Shombre was a member of James H. Lane's party, and had therefore but just arrived in the Territory; see also Cordley, pp. 115-120; Speer's *Lane*, p. 115; and Andreas, pp. 142-143.
32. Statement of Luke F. Parsons to the author, Salina, Kansas, Oct. 7, 1908.
33. Statement of Jason Brown, Dec. 13 and 14, 1908.
34. John Brown, Jr., to John Brown, Aug. 11, 1856. — Original in the possession of Mrs. John Brown, Jr.
35. *Kansas Historical Society Publications*, vol. 1, p. 131.
36. N. Y. *Tribune*, Aug. 29, 1856; Andreas, p. 143.
37. Andreas, p. 143. Tribute to Shannon, by B. F. Simpson, *Kansas Historical Society Publications*, vol. 1, pp. 87-91.
38. Andreas, p. 143; Executive Minutes, *Kansas Historical Society Publications*, vol. 1, p. 131; *Kansas Historical Society Collections*, vol. 4, p. 403.
39. Letter of Jan. 14, 1860, of Martin White, in Bates County, Mo., *Standard*, Jan., 1860; Bondi; J. H. Holmes to Gov. Geary, Oct. 2, 1856, in Executive Papers of 1856, in Kansas Historical Society. In an appeal to the public printed in the *Squatter Sovereign* of Aug. 26, 1856, and signed by Atchison, Russell, Boone and Stringfellow, the following appears: "On the 13th inst., a party numbering some fifty attacked the house of Mr. White in Lykins Co., and drove him into Missouri, robbing him of everything. He is a Free State man, but sustains the laws, and was attacked for attempting to procure the arrest of the murderers of Wilkinson."
40. See *Kansas Historical Society Collections*, vol. 4, p. 737, letter of Gov. Geary to Williams and Heiskell; joint letter of Totten and Wilson to acting Governor Woodson, same volume, p. 743; statement of C. S. Adair, Osawatomie, Oct. 2, 1908, to the author; statement of J. G. Grant, San Francisco, Oct. 7, 1908, to K. Mayo; Andreas, p. 605; letter of Daniel Woodson to Lewis Cass, Lecompton, March 31, 1857, in the Executive Minutes of 1857, in Kansas Historical Society.
41. From John Brown's *Memorandum-Book* No. 2. — Original in Boston Public Library.

NOTES

42. Statement of C. G. Allen to James Redpath, undated, Hinton Papers, Kansas Historical Society.

43. This narrative of South Middle Creek is drawn from the statements of Capt. Cline, Holmes, Bondi, George Grant, Thomas Bedoe, C. G. Allen, all in the Kansas Historical Society except Capt. Cline's, which is in the *Tribune* of Sept. 17, 1856; also the sworn statements of Thomas Rice, James N. Gibson, R. W. Wood, Benjamin F. Brantley, R. E. Noel, J. H. Little and William Rogers (from whom Brown's men stole horses and other property), all in the Report on Kansas Claims, vol. 3, Part 2. A confirmatory letter of S. L. Adair of Aug. 13, 1856, to his "Bro & Sis. Davis" is in the possession of Mrs. S. C. Davis at Kalamazoo, Mich.

44. *John Brown the Hero*, by J. W. Winkley, M. D., Boston, 1905, pp. 71–72.

45. Ibid., pp. 79–81; Holmes testimony, Hyatt Papers, Kansas Historical Society.

46. Bedoe's testimony, Hyatt Papers, Kansas Historical Society. See Report of H. J. Strickler on the claims of the citizens of Kansas Territory, House Misc. Doc. No. 43, 35th Congress, 2d session, 1859, p. 17, for petition of Thomas H. Brown, of Linn County, containing list of property, clothing, household gear and live stock taken from him and his brother [Capt.] John E. Brown, by John Brown of Osawatomie, on this raid. Similar statements of losses inflicted by Brown's men are in the Report of the Commissioners on Kansas Claims.

47. Bondi; 'Old John Brown,' by Capt. J. M. Anthony, Leavenworth *Weekly Times*, Feb. 14, 1884; statement of Jason Brown, Dec. 13 and 14, 1908.

48. J. H. Holmes. MS. story of his experiences at Osawatomie, in possession of the author.

49. Letter of A. G. Hawes to J. H. Holmes, San Francisco, Feb. 26, 1895, in possession of the author; the same to F. G. Adams, San Francisco, Aug. 13, 1889, Kansas Historical Society; the Rev. S. L. Adair to Mrs. S. C. Davis, Osawatomie, Aug. 29, 1856, in possession of Mrs. Davis.

50. The following sources have been consulted, among others, in the preparation of the story of the battle of Osawatomie: Narratives of Bartow Darrach, N. Y. *Evening Post*, Sept. 15, 1856; George Grant, J. G. Grant, August Bondi, James H. Holmes, Thomas Bedoe, Joseph R. Morey, J. M. Anthony, Mary Fuller, O. C. Brown, Luke F. Parsons, Alexander G. Hawes, Charles S. Adair, Robert Reynolds, James J. Holbrook, Robert W. Wood, Thomas Roberts, Spencer K. Brown, George Cutter, Nelson J. Roscoe, Morgan Cronkhite, Dr. John Doy; contemporary letters of the Rev. and Mrs. S. L. Adair, Dr. W. W. Updegraff, Jason Brown, Capt. James B. Cline, George B. Gill, James Hanway, Lydia S. Hall, Mrs. S. A. Stevens, C. G. Allen, Sperry Dye, Samuel Anderson, George Cutter, Mary E. Jackson, William Chesnut and John Brown; on the pro-slavery side, the Rev. Martin White, Gen. J. W. Reid, Capt. Jernigan, James Chiles, Congrave Jackson, Capt. G. M. B. Maughas, W. Limerick (in the Weekly *Missouri Statesman* for Sept. 5, 1856), the Missouri *Republican*, the Missouri *Statesman*, the Leavenworth *Herald*, the Jefferson *Enquirer*, the St. Louis *Morning Herald*, the St. Louis *Evening News;* anti-slavery newspapers: the N. Y. *Tribune*, the *Liberator*, the New York *Evening Post*, the St. Louis *Democrat;* also official report of Gen. P. F. Smith and Gov. Geary, and of acting Gov. Woodson, *Kansas Historical Society Collections*, vol. 4; also statements and letters of Mrs. Emma Adair Remington and Mr. C. S. Adair, of Osawatomie, to the author. A particularly valuable story of the conflict is the joint letter of the Rev. and Mrs. Adair, under date of Aug. 29 and Sept. 2, 1856, to Mrs. S. C. Davis, in whose possession

the original now is, as is Mr. Adair's letter to Mrs. Hand, Osawatomie, Sept. 2, 1856, which well supplements the narrative.

51. Quoted in Leavenworth *Journal*, March 12, 1857.
52. N. Y. *Tribune*, Sept. 17, 1856.
53. Statement of Ezra Robinson to the author at Paola, Kansas, Oct. 3, 1908.
54. Missouri *Weekly Statesman*, Sept. 5, 1856; St. Louis *Daily Democrat*, Sept. 8, 1856.
55. *St. Louis Intelligencer*, Sept. 6, 1856, copied from Glasgow *Times* of Sept. 4, 1856.
56. Original in Kansas Historical Society.
57. Original in possession of Francis J. Garrison, Lexington, Mass.
58. Original manuscript in possession of Mrs. B. W. Woodward, Lawrence, Kansas.
59. Statement of Joseph H. Morey, a prisoner, in the Rochester (N. Y.) *Daily Democrat* of Sept. 12, 1856; see also testimony of Robert Reynolds, in Report on Kansas Claims, vol. 3, Part 2, pp. 1101–1103.
60. See *Spencer Kellogg Brown, his Life in Kansas and Death as a Spy*, edited by George Gardner Smith, New York, 1903.
61. Report of Secretary of War for 1856, pp. 90–92.
62. Ibid., pp. 29–31.
63. Walker's Narrative, *Kansas Historical Society Collections*. vol. 6, pp. 273–274; Report of the Secretary of War for 1856, pp. 101–103.
64. Report of the Secretary of War for 1856, p. 102.
65. Statement of Henry Reisner, Topeka, July 22, 1908, to K. Mayo.
66. Statements of Holmes, Parsons and Jason Brown.
67. Letter of Aaron D. Stevens, signed "Charles Whipple, Col. 1st Regiment Kansas Volunteers," to his brother, Aug. 28, 1856; Headquarters 2d Regiment, Kansas Volunteers. — Original in possession of Dr. Henry B. Stevens, Boston.
68. J. B. Donaldson, U. S. Marshal, to Gov. Geary, Lecompton, Sept. 25, 1856, Executive Correspondence, Kansas Historical Society. Facts about Col. Harvey's horse-thefts are scattered throughout vol. 3, Part 1, of the Report on Kansas Claims.
69. C. F. Gilman to Col. A. G. Boone, of Westport, Council Grove, Sept. 16, 1856. Executive Correspondence, Kansas Historical Society.
70. "Randolph" to the N. Y. *Times*, Lawrence, Sept. 10, 1856.
71. These documents will be found in the Report of the Secretary of War for 1856, and in *Kansas Historical Society Collections*, vol. 4, pp. 522–527.
72. For the Hickory Point fight, see report of Capt. T. J. Wood, 1st U. S. Cavalry, to Lieut.-Col. P. St. G. Cooke, Sept. 16, 1856, in Report of the Secretary of War, pp. 123–126; Andreas, pp. 149 and 501–502; Speer's *Lane*, pp. 123–124; MS. Journal of Samuel J. Reader, of Topeka, Kansas; Gihon, p. 140 et seq.; Gov. Geary to Secretary Marcy, Lecompton, Sept. 16, 1856, *Kansas Historical Society Collections*, vol. 4, p. 535 et seq.; Holloway, pp. 401–402; Report on Kansas Claims, vol. 3, Part 1, pp. 287–289.
73. Lieut.-Col. Cooke to Major F. J. Porter, Lecompton, Sept. 13, 1856, in report of Secretary of War for 1856, pp. 113–114.
74. Ibid., pp. 121–122, Lieut.-Col. Cooke to Major F. J. Porter, Sept. 16, 1856.
75. Original in Kansas Historical Society.
76. Statement of Major James Burnett Abbott to F. G. Adams, Abbott Papers, Kansas Historical Society; Capt. Joseph Cracklin in Lawrence *Daily Tribune*, April 18, 1881; John Speer, Lawrence *Journal*, Jan. 22, 1880; Robinson, *Kansas Conflict*, pp. 324–328; Nathaniel Parker, in *Hyatt Journal of Investigation*, Dec.

NOTES

5, 1856; statement of Col. O. E. Leonard to K. Mayo, Lawrence, Kan., July 28, 1908; H. Miles Moore, Topeka *Capital*, Oct. 10, 1897; Andreas, p. 150; Hinton, pp. 46–52; Sanborn, pp. 333–336; statement of George Leis, Lawrence, Nov. 29, 1909, for the author; Hinton, in an otherwise inaccurate letter, dated Dec. 13, 1859, to the Boston *Traveller*, and reprinted in the *Tribune* of Dec. 8, 1859, affirmed that John Brown was asked on Sept. 13, 1856, "by *all* the prominent citizens, to take charge of the defence."

77. Hinton, pp. 49–50. Hinton wrote to W. E. Connelley, June 9, 1900, that the account given of Brown's speech "is accurate. I took it down in shorthand. I am a stenographer. I was by his side. It was published in one of my letters to the Boston *Traveller*."

78. Executive Minutes of Gov. Geary, *Kansas Historical Society Collections*, vol. 4, pp. 571 and 629–631; Robinson, p. 339; Andreas, pp. 151–153; Holloway, pp. 408–409; Gihon, pp. 166–181; Report on Kansas Claims, vol. 3, Part 2, pp. 1377–1380.

79. Secretary of War's Report for 1856, pp. 142–143, Lieut.-Col. Cooke to Major F. J. Porter, Oct. 10, 1856.

80. Ibid., p. 146.

81. Charleston, S. C., *Standard*, letter signed "Ingomar," dated Lecompton, September 5, 1856, quoted in N. Y. *Tribune* of September 29.

82. Letter of John Brown, Jr., July 30, 1856, to Jason Brown. — Original in possession of Mrs. Thompson.

83. John Brown to his family. Tabor, Iowa, October 11, 1856. — Original in the possession of Mrs. John Brown, Jr. John Brown wrote to his brothers Frederick and Jeremiah, Tabor, Iowa, 11th October, 1856: "I left Kansas both on business and to recover my health, being so unwell that I had to be brought here on a bed in a wagon. There is just now a kind of dead calm of the elements there. I expect to go back should the trouble continue and my health admit. Am getting better fast, and hope to see you soon." — Original in the possession of Mrs. S. L. Clark.

84. MS. lecture entitled 'John Brown the Liberator,' by James H. Holmes, in possession of the author.

85. Report of the Secretary of War for 1856, pp. 139–140.

86. Another narrow escape of John Brown has been described for the author by Mrs. Emma Wattles Morse in these words: "One evening in, I think, early September, 1856, Captain Brown left my father, Mr. Wattles's house, then in Douglas County, going southward on a trip to Miami and Linn Counties. He learned on the road a little after midnight, that a company of dragoons was on the way to arrest him, so he returned to my father's just after daylight. Late in the afternoon Lieut. (now General) Eugene A. Carr, First Cavalry, arrived at the Wattles house and asked Brown's whereabouts. On learning of his departure the night before, the soldiers sat down and were served with all the melons they would eat. As Brown lay on the floor of the attic, whither he had gone to sleep, he could look down between the roof boards and the top log of the wall, hearing every word, seeing every movement, with his two loaded Colt's revolvers in his hands. The soldiers rode away in disgust, certain, however, that their fellow-troopers in the south would catch Brown."

87. From a copy in A. A. Lawrence's letter-book, in the possession of Mrs. Frederic Cunningham, Longwood, Mass.

88. Original in Kansas Historical Society.

89. See Topeka *Commonwealth* for December 12, 1883, and February 16, 1884; the Hiawatha *World* for December 27, 1883; the Lawrence, Kansas, *Herald*, January 2, 1884.

90. Dated Lecompton, March 12, 1857; see *Kansas Historical Society Collections*, vol. 4, p. 739.

91. Report of Commissioners of Kansas Territory, July, 1857, in Report of Committees, 36th Congress, 2d session, vol. 3, Part 1, p. 92.

92. See, for example, speech of Gerrit Smith at Buffalo, July 10, 1856, in *Liberator*, vol. 26, p. 125.

93. For instance, the Weston, Platte Co., Mo., *Reporter* (pro-slavery), on April 21, 1856, said: "Experience has shown that most of the emigrants from slave states have become free state men in Kansas." It was stated in a debate before the Georgia Legislature in 1856 that out of 89 men transported from Tennessee to Kansas, 80 proved false and voted against the South. See Newark, Georgia, *Mercury*, March 3, 1856. See also Fleming's 'Buford Expedition,' *American Historical Review*, October, 1900, p. 48.

CHAPTER VIII

NEW FRIENDS FOR OLD VISIONS

1. For the story of Tabor, see *Early Settlement and Growth of Western Iowa*, by Rev. John Todd, Des Moines, 1906, which contains his reminiscences; also, *John Brown Among the Quakers*, by Irving B. Richman, Des Moines, 1894, pp. 15–18.

2. Todd's *Early Settlement of Western Iowa*, pp. 121–122.

3. Both Mr. White's letter and that of Mr. Webster are in the Kansas Historical Society.

4. Statement of Salmon Brown for the author.

5. Watson Brown to his mother, brothers and sisters, St. Charles, Iowa, October 30, 1856. — Original in Kansas Historical Society.

6. F. B. Sanborn, Boston, January 5, 1857, to Thomas Wentworth Higginson. — Original in Higginson Collection, Boston Public Library.

7. *William Lloyd Garrison*, by his Children, vol. 3, pp. 487–488.

8. *Life and Correspondence of Theodore Parker*, by John Weiss, New York, 1864, vol. 2, p. 161.

9. Report of the Mason Investigating Committee of the United States Senate, 36th Congress, 1st session, p. 227, Washington, June, 1860.

10. *Life and Public Service of George Luther Stearns*, by Frank Preston Stearns, Philadelphia, 1907, pp. 133–134.

11. *Life of Amos A. Lawrence*, by his son, William Lawrence, Boston, 1888, p. 124.

12. Ibid., p. 125.

13. *A Yankee in Canada*, by Henry D. Thoreau, Boston, 1866, pp. 156–157; also in Thoreau's *Miscellanies*, Boston, 1893, pp. 202–203.

14. *Life of George Luther Stearns*, p. 132.

15. Letter of George L. Stearns, Chairman of State Committee, January 8, 1857. — Copy of original in possession of the Stearns family.

16. George L. Stearns to John Brown, April 15, 1857, in Mason Report, p. 229.

17. Letter of G. L. Stearns to H. B. Hurd, Boston, September 30, 1856, in Sanborn, p. 368.

18. Mason Report, pp. 247–248.

19. Sanborn, p. 348.

NOTES

20. H. B. Hurd, Chicago, March 19, 1860, to George L. Stearns. — Original in Stearns Papers, Kansas Historical Society.

21. Memorandum of H. B. Hurd for Captain John Brown. — Original in Kansas Historical Society.

22. Mason Report, p. 249.

23. Original in Kansas Historical Society. See Appendix.

24. The correspondence between Horace White and John Brown is all in the possession of the Kansas Historical Society.

25. Original in Kansas Historical Society.

26. Statement of Annie Brown Adams; see also Hinton, p. 144.

27. John Brown to Augustus Wattles, Boston, February 16, 1857 (from a copy in the Holmes Papers).

28. This question and others were reported by Redpath. See pp. 182–184 of his *Life of Brown*.

29. Letter of September 22, 1856, of Charles H. Branscomb, from Boston, to John Brown. — Original in Kansas Historical Society.

30. John Brown to A. A. Lawrence, New Haven, March 19, 1857,—original in possession of Mrs. Frederic Cunningham, Longwood, Mass.; testimony of W. H. D. Callender, Mason Report, p. 114.

31. John Brown to his wife and children, Springfield, March 12, 1857. — Original in Kansas Historical Society.

32. A. A. Lawrence to John Brown, Boston, February 19, 1857; G. L. Stearns to John Brown, Boston, April 15, 1857. — Originals of both in Stearns Papers.

33. John Brown to P. T. Jackson (letter and draft), Springfield, Mass., April 21, 1857; H. Sterns to P. T. Jackson of same date. — Both originals in the P. T. Jackson Papers, Massachusetts Historical Society.

34. N. Y. *Tribune*, March 4, 1857.

35. John Brown to A. A. Lawrence, March 19, 1857, — original in possession of Mrs. Frederic Cunningham; to his brother, Jeremiah Brown, Springfield, April 1, 1857, — original in possession of Mrs. S. L. Clark.

36. A. A. Lawrence to John Brown, Boston, March 20, 1857; Lawrence letter-book, in possession of Mrs. Cunningham.

37. G. L. Stearns Papers.

38. John Brown to G. L. Stearns, Vergennes, Vt., May 13, 1857. — Original in Stearns Papers.

39. Report of F. B. Sanborn to G. L. Stearns and others, August 25, 1857. — Original in Stearns Papers.

40. Original in Kansas Historical Society; see the Worcester *Daily Spy* of March 24 and 25, 1857, for Brown's visit to Worcester.

41. Francis Wayland to F. B. Sanborn, Sanborn, p. 381.

42. *A Memoir of Ralph Waldo Emerson*, by James Elliot Cabot, Boston, 1887, vol. 2, p. 596.

43. Address delivered in Tremont Temple, Boston, Saturday, November 18, 1859, in Redpath's *Echoes of Harper's Ferry*, Boston, 1860, pp. 67–71; Emerson's *Miscellanies*, Boston, 1904, p. 268.

44. See letter of Eli Thayer, April 4, 1857. — Original in Kansas Historical Society, where will be found further correspondence covering these points. See also letter of John Brown to Eli Thayer, Springfield, April 16, 1857. — Original in possession of W. K. Bixby, St. Louis, Mo.

45. Sanborn, p. 387.

46. John Brown to ex-Governor Reeder, Springfield, April 1, 1857. — Original in possession of F. G. Logan, Chicago.

NOTES

47. John Brown to his wife, Springfield, March 31, 1857. — Original in possession of Mrs. Ellen Brown Fablinger.

48. See Blair's testimony for the story of the pikes, in Mason Report, pp. 121–129. The originals of Blair's letters to John Brown are to be found in the Kansas Historical Society.

49. This account of Brown's relations with Forbes is drawn from Sanborn, Hinton, Redpath; the testimonies of Wilson, Seward, Howe and Realf before the Mason Committee; the reports of Joseph Bryant to John Brown, now in the Kansas Historical Society; the N. Y. *Tribune;* and from Forbes's own story in the N. Y. *Herald* of October 27, 1859; see also John Brown's letter, Cleveland, Ohio, June 22, 1857, to H. Forbes, demanding repayment of the $600, — original in Dreer Collection, Pennsylvania Historical Society.

50. Gerrit Smith to Thaddeus Hyatt, Peterboro, July 25, 1857. — Original in Hyatt Papers, Kansas Historical Society.

51. Jason Brown to John Brown, Akron, Ohio, April 3, 1857. — Original in possession of Miss Sarah Brown.

52. John Brown to Eli Thayer, Springfield, Mass., April 16, 1857. — Original in possession of W. K. Bixby, St. Louis. See also letter to his brother, Jeremiah Brown, West Newton, Mass., April 15, 1857. — Original in possession of Mrs. S. L. Clark.

53. Statement of Mrs. Thomas Russell, Jamaica Plain, Mass., January 11, 1908, to Miss K. Mayo.

54. Original in possession of Stearns family.

55. The complete correspondence relating to this matter is to be found in the Stearns Papers, in possession of the Stearns family, and in the Kansas Historical Society.

56. John Brown to G. L. Stearns, Albany, April 28, 1857. — Original in Library of Congress.

57. Sanborn, p. 406.

58. John Brown to G. L. Stearns, Vergennes, Vt., May 13, 1857. — Original in possession of the Stearns family.

59. Mason Report, p. 220. There was a real Nelson Hawkins, a brother-in-law of Mrs. Jason Brown.

60. John Brown, Jr., to John Brown, Lindenville, Ohio, April 23, 1857. — Original in possession of Miss Thompson.

61. G. L. Stearns to Mrs. Abby Hopper Gibbons, Boston, May 18, 1857. — Original in Stearns Papers.

62. Testimony of G. L. Stearns, Mason Report, pp. 227–228.

63. John Brown to F. B. Sanborn, Tabor, August 13, 1857, Sanborn, pp. 412–414.

64. John Brown to His Wife and Children, Hudson, Ohio, May 27, 1857. — Original in possession of Mrs. Ellen Brown Fablinger.

65. Mason Report, p. 221.

66. From a copy in the Stearns Papers.

67. Ibid.

68. See letter of Caleb Calkins, Peterboro, June 20, 1857, — original in possession of Miss Brown; John Brown's *Memorandum-Book*, Boston Public Library.

69. Letter of Leonard Bacon to Governor Wise, New Haven, November 14, 1859. — Original in Dreer Collection. Mr. Bacon erroneously places the date of the celebration in July, 1857. It actually took place June 24, 1857

70. Tabor, July 6, 1857; from copy in the possession of the Stearns family.

71. Brown to Sanborn, Tabor, August 13, 1857, Sanborn, pp. 412–414.

NOTES

72. Rhodes, vol. 2, p. 239.
73. This résumé of Gov. Walker's service, and the following account of the political events in Kansas during Brown's absence from the Territory, are drawn from Rhodes, Andreas, Holloway, Robinson's *Kansas Conflict*, Gihon, Wilder, the manuscript history of Louis A. Reese, and the publications of the Kansas Historical Society.
74. The originals of these letters of August 8 and 10 to Mr. Stearns are in the possession of the Stearns family.
75. These quotations from the *Duty of the Soldier* are taken from Augustus Wattles's copy, bearing John Brown's manuscript annotations, in the possession of the author.
76. Sanborn, p. 422; A. B. Hart, *Life of Salmon Portland Chase*, Boston, 1899, p. 174.
77. Gerrit Smith to Thaddeus Hyatt, Peterboro, September 12, 1857. — Original in Hyatt Papers, Kansas Historical Society.
78. Redpath, p. 197; Todd's *Reminiscences*, p. 156.
79. Hugh Forbes to Charles Sumner, December 27, 1857. — Original in Sumner Correspondence in Harvard University Library.
80. Todd's *Reminiscences*, pp. 154–155.
81. Statement of Rev. H. D. King, Kinsman, Ohio, January 4–5, 1909, to K. Mayo.
82. Original in Kansas Historical Society.
83. Letter of Rev. John Todd, May 25, 1892, cited in Richman's *John Brown Among the Quakers*, pp. 16–17; John Brown to F. B. Sanborn, August 13, 1857, Sanborn, p. 413.
84. Original in possession of Miss Sarah Brown.
85. Original in Kansas Historical Society.
86. Original in Kansas Historical Society.
87. From copy in possession of the Stearns family.
88. James Redpath to Captain Brown, Falls City, Nebraska, September 20, 1857, from a copy in the Stearns Papers.
89. See Higginson's *Cheerful Yesterdays*, pp. 204–205. Both he and Samuel F. Tappan were made brigadier-generals.
90. Original in Kansas Historical Society.
91. John Brown to F. B. Sanborn, Tabor, October 1, 1857, Sanborn, p. 401.
92. From copy of original in Kansas Historical Society.
93. This is the October 1 letter referred to above.
94. From the same letter.
95. Original in possession of Mrs. Remington, Osawatomie, Kansas.
96. F. B. Sanborn to T. W. Higginson, Boston, September 11, 1857. — Original in T. W. Higginson Papers, Kansas Historical Society.
97. Compare with this opinion of Sanborn, Hinton's assertion, in his *Life*, p. 136, that Brown was a "Unionist of Unionists, a Loyalist of Loyalists."
98. E. B. Whitman to G. L. Stearns, Lawrence, October 25, 1857. — Original in Stearns Papers.
99. Original in Kansas Historical Society.
100. E. B. Whitman to G. L. Stearns, Lawrence, February 20, 1858. — Original in Stearns Papers.
101. W. A. Johnson, *History of Anderson County, Kansas*, Garnett (Kansas), 1877, p. 110; Holloway, p. 508.
102. Original in Stearns Papers.
103. Original in possession of Mrs. Remington.

104. Stearns to E. B. Whitman. — Original in Colonel E. B. Whitman Papers, in possession of E. B. Whitman, Boston.
105. Letter of R. G. Elliott to K. Mayo, Lawrence, August 6, 1908; also, *Kansas Historical Society Collections*, vol. 10, p. 187.
106. See pamphlet entitled *Confession of John E. Cook*, brother-in-law of Governor A. P. Willard, of Indiana, and one of the participants in the Harper's Ferry Invasion. Published for the benefit of Samuel C. Young, Charlestown, 1859.

CHAPTER IX

A CONVENTION AND A POSTPONEMENT

1. *Confession of John E. Cook*, p. 6.
2. Kagi was twenty-three, Cook twenty-eight, Realf twenty-three, Stevens twenty-seven, Parsons twenty-five, Leeman eighteen, Tidd twenty-three, Moffet thirty, Owen Brown thirty-three, and Stewart Taylor twenty-two.
3. Statement of L. F. Parsons, Salina, Kan., October 7, 1908, to the author.
4. Ibid.
5. Statement of George B. Gill to R. J. Hinton, Hinton Papers, Kansas Historical Society.
6. Those from which these and subsequent quotations are drawn are, first, extracts from December 21 to February 17, in the Richmond *Daily Whig* of October 29, 1859; second, from August 25 to December 8, quoted in the N. Y. *Times;* third, from March 13 to March 28, in the Dreer Collection, Pennsylvania Historical Society.
7. Richman, *John Brown Among the Quakers*, pp. 12–13. Annie Brown Adams declares the Townsend incident apocryphal.
8. John Brown's *Memorandum-Book* No. 2, entries of December 30, 1857, and January 11, 1858, in Boston Public Library.
9. Letter to Dr. Howe, May 14, 1858, published in the New York *Herald* of October 27, 1859.
10. Statement of Luke F. Parsons to Redpath and Hinton, Osawatomie, December, 1859, in Hinton Papers, Kansas Historical Society.
11. Richman, pp. 26–27.
12. Ibid., pp. 28–29.
13. Statement of L. F. Parsons to the author, October, 1908.
14. Richman, p. 23.
15. John Brown's *Memorandum Book* No. 2, entry for January 28, 1858.
16. See letter of Owen Brown, of February 28, 1858, — copy in possession of Miss Thompson; also letter of Jason Brown, January 29, 1858, — original in possession of Miss Sarah Brown.
17. Frederick Douglass, *Life and Times*, p. 353.
18. Testimony of Senator Wilson before Mason Committee, Mason Report, p. 140 et seq.
19. Testimony of William H. Seward, Mason Report, p. 253.
20. Forbes to Dr. Howe, April 19, 1858, published in N. Y. *Herald* of October 29, 1859.
21. John Brown to John Brown, Jr., Sanborn, pp. 432–433; *Memorandum-Book*, entry of February 9.
22. John Brown to F. B. Sanborn, Rochester, February 17, 1858. — Original in Higginson Collection.

NOTES

23. Original in possession of Miss Thompson.
24. John Brown to T. W. Higginson, Rochester, February 2, 1858. — Original in the Higginson Collection, Boston Public Library.
25. Frothingham's *Gerrit Smith*, first edition, p. 237.
26. John Brown to wife and children, Peterboro, February 24, 1858. — Original in possession of Mrs. Ellen Brown Fablinger.
27. See Sanborn's *Life*, and especially in vol. 1 of his *Recollections of Seventy Years*, Boston, 1909, the chapter entitled 'Aftermath of the John Brown Foray,' where the relations of Mr. Smith to the enterprise are set forth in greater detail than ever before. See also first edition of O. B. Frothingham's *Gerrit Smith;* the later editions were altered by taking out unfavorable statements.
28. Sanborn, *Recollections*, vol. 1, p. 147.
29. Sanborn, p. 444 (in facsimile).
30. See *Memorandum-Book* No. 2 for confirmatory evidence of Brown's movements during this period.
31. *Memorandum-Book* No. 2; Sanborn, *Life*, p. 451; Hinton, p. 169.
32. Sanborn, pp. 450–451; see also letter of John Brown, Jr., in reply to his father, Lindenville, Ashtabula, February 13, 1858. — Original in possession of Miss Brown.
33. Henry Thompson, Salmon Brown, Annie Brown Adams and Miss Sarah Brown all share this feeling, and have so stated to the author.
34. Letter of January 30, 1858, as above.
35. Henry Thompson to John Brown, North Elba, April 21, 1858. — Original in possession of Miss Brown.
36. John Weiss, *Life of Parker*, vol. 2, p. 164.
37. Sanborn, p. 449.
38. Sanborn, p. 443.
39. Original in Higginson Collection, Boston Public Library.
40. See telegram of George L. Stearns to T. W. Higginson, Boston, March 18, 1858, and letter of F. B. Sanborn to the same, Boston, March 21, 1858, — both originals in T. W. Higginson Collection.
41. *Cheerful Yesterdays*, p. 219.
42. James Freeman Clarke's *Anti-Slavery Days*, pp. 153–154.
43. Sanborn, p. 451.
44. *Memorandum-Book* No. 2, and letter of John Brown to his son John, April 8, 1858, Sanborn, p. 452.
45. 'John Brown in Canada,' by James C. Hamilton, *Canadian Magazine*, December, 1894; *The Underground Railroad*, by William H. Siebert, New York, 1898, pp. 221–222.
46. J. C. Hamilton, 'John Brown in Canada,' as above cited.
47. *Life and Public Services of Martin R. Delany*, by Frank A. Rollins, Boston, 1868, pp. 85–90.
48. Mrs. E. S. Butler, in the *Midland Monthly*, November, 1898.
49. Owen Brown to his father, Springdale, February 28, 1858. — Copy in possession of Miss Thompson.
50. Letter of Moses and Charlotte Varney, pp. 96–98 of Appendix to Message I, Documents relative to the Harper's Ferry Invasion, printed by the State of Virginia, 1859.
51. The original of this letter is in the possession of Dr. Henry B. Stevens, of Boston. Leeman's letters are in the Hinton Papers, Kansas Historical Society.
52. Testimony of Richard Realf before Mason Committee, Mason Report, p. 95; narrative of George B. Gill. Hinton Papers.

53. Richman, pp. 32–33.
54. Ibid., p. 36.
55. This narrative of the Chatham proceedings is based on the Journal of the two conventions published in the Appendix to Message I, by the State of Virginia; on Realf's testimony before the Mason Committee; on Cook's *Confession;* and on 'John Brown in Canada,' by J. C. Hamilton.

The thirty-four colored men actually in attendance were, besides Munroe, Osborn P. Anderson, Richardson, Delany, and J. H. Harris, Stephen Ditten, James Smith, Charles Smith, Isaac Hobbar, Thomas Hickerson, John Connel, George Akin, Elias Chitman, Robert Newman, J. B. Shadd, Simon Fisher, John A. Thomas, Robert Van Vruken, Thomas W. Stringer, Thomas M. Kinnard, Thomas F. Cary, Robinson Alexander, James W. Purnell, J. C. Grant, J. G. Reynolds, A. J. Smith, James M. Jones, M. F. Bailey, W. Lambert, S. Hunton, Job J. Jackson, Alfred Whipper, James M. Bell and Alfred L. Ellsworth.

56. Realf's testimony, Mason Report, pp. 96–98.
57. As printed in the Appendix to Message I, Documents relative to the Harper's Ferry Invasion, Virginia State Papers.
58. *John Brown*, by Dr. Hermann von Holst, Boston, 1889, edited by Frank Preston Stearns, pp. 109–111. "To judge by the provisions of this extraordinary document [the Constitution], the conduct of a revolution never fell into hands more utterly unable to direct it. It would seem that Mr. Brown and his friends had no conception of any manner of carrying on public business. . . ."—*London Times*, November 4, 1859.
59. Hinton, pp. 180–181.
60. Sanborn, p. 456.
61. Ibid.
62. John Brown to his son Owen and others of his men, Chatham, May 18, 1858. — Originally printed in Davenport, Iowa, *Gazette*, February 27, 1878.
63. From the same to the same, May 21, 1858, in Davenport *Gazette*, February 27, 1878.
64. See letter of Richard Realf to John Brown, Cleveland, May 31, 1858, — original in Kansas Historical Society; also letter of L. F. Parsons to Leeman, Cleveland, May 16, 1858, — original in possession of Miss Brown.
65. Richard Realf to John Brown, as above.
66. *Memorandum-Book* No. 2; Realf testimony, Mason Report; telegram of Sanborn to Higginson, Boston, May 31, 1858,—original in Higginson Collection. It is stated by Sanborn, Hinton, Chadwick and others that Brown met Stearns in New York on or about May 20. This is erroneous, as the two letters from Chatham of May 18 and May 21 prove. He could not then leave Chatham, for lack of funds; and had he done so, he would have had no reason for returning, as his work in Canada was done. Had he made such a costly flying trip to New York, it must have appeared in his correspondence or his memorandum-book.
67. Original in Higginson Collection, Boston Public Library.
68. Ibid.
69. Mason Report, p. 177.
70. Copy in Stearns Papers.
71. Original in Higginson Collection.
72. Sanborn, p. 466.
73. Ibid., p. 465.
74. *The Causes of the Civil War*, Rear Admiral F. E. Chadwick, New York, 1906, pp. 75–76.
75. Sanborn, p. 350.

NOTES

76. For the movements of the arms, see letter of John Brown, Jr., to his father, Lindenville, Ohio, May 1, 1858,—original in possession of Miss Brown; also statements of Mrs. E. A. Fobes and of Mr. and Mrs. J. B. Noxon, Wayne, Ohio, of Mrs. Fred Blakeslee, Ashtabula, Ohio, of Charles D. Ainger, Andover, Ohio, in January, 1909, all to K. Mayo; statements of Miss Rebecca Dean, Jefferson, Ohio, July 9, 1897, and of Mrs. Edwin King, Dunkirk, N. Y., June 22, 1897, to Mrs. E. L. Mark, of Cambridge, Mass., both in possession of the author; see also Sanborn, p. 494

77. Sanborn, p. 471.

78. Statement of Gill, Hinton, p. 733; Kagi to "Friend Addie" [L. F. Parsons], Moneka, Kansas, August 13, 1858,—original in Mr. Parsons's possession.

79. For this dispersing of the men, see Gill's narrative, in Hinton, p. 734; statement of Luke F. Parsons to author; his letter of May 26, 1858, to George B. Gill, in Hinton Papers; and various letters of the conspirators to each other.

80. Owen Brown to John Brown, Akron, July 12, 1858. — Original in possession of Mrs. Brown.

81. Statement to author, Salina, Kansas, October 7, 1908.

82. Letter to Hinton, in Hinton Papers, Kansas Historical Society, marked "1878 or 1879."

83. Redpath's *John Brown*, pp. 199–200. Hinton and Redpath were in error in this statement, as will be seen later. The actual date of Brown's arrival was Saturday, June 26, 1858. The special correspondent of the N. Y. *Tribune*, writing from Lawrence, Kansas, June 27, 1858, said: "Our 'warrior of the Lord and of Gideon' — the renowned Old Brown — has just arrived in Lawrence. He leaves to-morrow morning to visit Capt. Montgomery." — N. Y. *Tribune*, July 8, 1858.

CHAPTER X

SHUBEL MORGAN, WARDEN OF THE MARCHES

1. These figures are taken from Reese's MS. history, *The Admission of Kansas*, Mr. Reese having made a most accurate re-study of all the returns of the various elections.

2. Cf. Rhodes, vol. 2, p. 301.

3. The author has been fortunate in having at his disposal, besides the accounts of the Hamilton Massacre in Andreas, pp. 1104–1105, and Tomlinson's *Kansas in 1858* (chapter v), the narrative of Elias Snyder, son of the blacksmith, as told to the author at the scene of the massacre, which Mr. Snyder was the first to reach after the crime. Other narratives are those of Ed R. Smith, *Kansas Historical Society Collections*, vol. 6, pp. 365–370; of B. L. Read, Linn Co. Scrap-Book, Kansas Historical Society; and of the N. Y. *Tribune* of May 28, and June 2 and 7, 1858. Not until October 30, 1863, was any one punished for this crime. Then William Griffith was hanged, with William Hairgrove, a survivor, as executioner.

4. See Tomlinson, pp. 81–84.

5. N. Y. *Evening Post*, June 4, 1858; letter signed G. W. N.

6. Statement of Mrs. J. C. Burnett, Topeka, August 3, 1908, to K. Mayo.

7. Statement of Mrs. Emma Wattles Morse, Mound City, Kansas, to the author, October 2, 1908.

8. Andreas, p. 1104.

9. See Andreas, p. 1107; for Montgomery's shocking vandalism in the Civil

War, see *The Story of a Brave Black Regiment* (the 54th Massachusetts Infantry), by Luis F. Emilio, Boston, 1894, pp. 41–44.

10. Capt. George T. Anderson, First U. S. Cavalry, resigned June 11, 1858, *Official Army Register* for 1859, p. 37.

11. Andreas, pp. 1102–1103.

12. Governor Denver to Lewis Cass, Secretary of State, Lecompton, June 23, 1858, *Kansas Historical Society Collections*, vol. 5, pp. 531–535; also his letter of June 7, ibid., pp. 528–530. See also letter of Governor Denver to the N. Y. *Tribune* of October 15, 1858, describing Montgomery's and other Free State men's lawless acts, and reviewing the whole disorder.

13. Printed in the N. Y. *Tribune* of April 23, 1858.

14. Redpath, pp. 200–201.

15. Original in Higginson Collection, Boston Public Library, here printed for the first time.

16. Sanborn, p. 473.

17. Elias Snyder, statement to W. E. Connelley, October 18, 1907, and to the author, October 2, 1908, at the scene of the Hamilton Massacre, on the Snyder claim.

18. Original in Higginson Collection, Boston Public Library.

19. From the copy made by John Brown, Jr., now in possession of Miss Thompson.

20. See letter of A. Wattles, dated Moneka, November 4, 1859, in *Missouri Republican*, November 26, 1859. Two of Brown's sons, Jason and John, Jr., opposed this plan, in letters of October 10, 1858, and August 24, 1858, whose originals are now respectively in the possession of Miss Brown and of Miss Thompson. John Brown, Jr., wrote: "But many a man has committed his greatest blunder when attempting to write a book."

21. See letter of Kagi to his sister, Moneka, August 13, 1858: "Since I wrote you from Lawrence, I have been busily engaged in fortifying along the State line, to prevent further inroads from Missouri;" in the Hinton Papers, Kansas Historical Society; see also George B. Gill's MS. marked "1860 or '61," in the Hinton Papers, Kansas Historical Society.

22. Statement of Register J. G. Wood, of the U. S. Land Office, Topeka, July 5, 1908; see also letter of George W. Martin, in the Topeka *Capital* of September 17, 1905; interview of Ed R. Smith in the Mound City *Republic*, September 22, 1905; letter of the same in the Topeka *Capital*, August 31, 1905; also George B. Gill's MS. referred to above, for Kagi's statement that negotiations of purchase were begun between Brown and Snyder.

23. From an article by W. A. Mitchell, entitled 'Historic Linn,' in La Cygne, Kansas, *Journal*, June 7, 1895.

24. See Sanborn, p. 366; also narrative of William Hutchinson, *Kansas Historical Society Collections*, vol. 7, p. 397.

25. Captain Eli Snyder to James H. Holmes, at Osawatomie, in 1894, original in possession of the author.

26. James Hanway to R. J. Hinton, December 5, 1859, Hinton Papers, Kansas Historical Society.

27. Statement of Charles S. Adair to James H. Holmes, May 11, 1904, original in possession of the author; also letter of the same to the author, January 27, 1909.

28. Original in possession of Mrs. G. A. Miller, Hudson, Ohio.

29. Statement of Mrs. J. B. Remington to the author, at Osawatomie, October 2, 1908.

NOTES 631

30. Kagi to his sister, Lawrence, September 23, 1858. — Original in Hinton Papers, Kansas Historical Society.
31. These two letters are in the possession of Mrs. Ellen Brown Fablinger.
32. Mason Report, Conway testimony, pp. 204–208; see also Martin F. Conway's letter to the editor of the *Herald of Freedom*, quoted in the White Cloud *Kansas Chief*, of December, 1859.
33. Original in Kansas Historical Society.
34. Sanborn, p. 465.
35. Mason Report, p. 206.
36. Sanborn, p. 465; the original of the receipt for the goods is in the hands of E. B. Whitman, of Boston.
37. This letter, also, is in the possession of Mr. Whitman the younger.
38. Original in Kansas Historical Society.
39. Sanborn, p. 465.
40. Mason Report, pp. 69–70.
41. Mrs. George Plumb, widow of Senator Plumb, to William Allen White, November, 1909. Brown went to see Messrs. Stores and Eckbridge, of Emporia.
42. Kagi, in the N. Y. *Tribune*, November 11, 1858. This statement of Kagi's should be compared with the following mistaken editorial comment of the *Tribune* of October 21, 1859: "Even after the partisan war had been appeased in other parts of the Territory, it was kept up in Southern Kansas, and Brown had an actual part in it. He began on the principle of defence — he now acted on that of revenge."
43. See letter of Kagi in Lawrence, Kansas, *Republican*, December 9, 1858; Gill MS., Hinton Papers, Kansas Historical Society.
44. Gill MS., cited above.
45. Originals in possession of Mrs. Ellen Brown Fablinger.
46. Statements of Mrs. Emma Wattles Morse and of Mrs. Sarah Wattles Hiatt, to the author, at Mound City, Kansas, October 2, 1908.
47. Mr. Gill's statement of November 12, 1908, at Attica, Kansas, to K. Mayo.
48. Theodosius Botkin, *Kansas Historical Society Collections*, vol. 7, p. 440; Gill MS., Kansas Historical Society.
49. See Executive Minutes for 1858, *Kansas Historical Society Collections*, vol. 5, p. 547.
50. Governor S. Medary to President James Buchanan, January 31, 1859, *Kansas Historical Society Collections*, vol. 5, p. 602.
51. A. J. Weaver to acting Governor Walsh, Paris, November 26, 1858, *Kansas Historical Society Collections*, vol. 5, p. 551.
52. Lawrence *Republican*, December 23, 1858.
53. Sheriff C. M. M'Daniel to acting Governor Walsh, Paris, December 3, 1858, *Kansas Historical Society Collections*, vol. 5, pp. 551–552.
54. J. W. Weaver to acting Governor Walsh, November 15, 1858, *Kansas Historical Society Collections*, vol. 5, p. 548.
55. Original in possession of Mrs. Ellen Brown Fablinger.
56. See N. Y. *Tribune*, December 29, 1858, for letter from Moneka, Kansas, of December 8; also Kagi's account in the Lawrence *Republican* of December 23, 1858.
57. Another treaty, drafted by John Brown, and in his handwriting, which does not seem to have been published heretofore, is in the possession of the Wattles family, also bearing date of January 1, 1859, and carrying the signature of several persons. It reads thus:

The undersigned have this day entered into the following pledge or agreement (viz) That hereafter we will not either as a company, or companies; or as individuals; be concerned or in any way connected with the robbing plundering or in any other way molesting of any person, or persons; whose case shall not have been thoroughly examined & decided upon (by a regularly chosen committee of discreet members) as one requireing attention; or punishment. And we further agree to hold as enemies of the community & of this organization all & every unprincipled person; or persons who shall *for the sake of plunder* disturb any inhabitant of the territory of the adjoining State; & to deal with them accordingly. And we hereby further agree to make an equal distribution of all property captured by any company of the members to the company making such capture & to insist upon the observance of this rule by all the members.

KANSAS 1st Jany 1859.

58. Andreas, p. 1070; Hinton, p. 218; Holloway, pp. 542–543; Report of Samuel Walker, Deputy U. S. Marshal, to Governor Medary, Kanwaka, January 3, 1859, *Kansas Historical Society Collections*, vol. 5, pp. 577–578; see also other correspondence in *Kansas Historical Society Collections*, vol. 5, p. 561 et seq.; N. Y. *Tribune*, January 8, 1859.

59. T. F. Robley, *History of Bourbon County*, Fort Scott, 1894, p. 128 et seq.; C. W. Goodman, *Memoirs and Recollections of the Early Days of Fort Scott*, Fort Scott, 1899, p. 79; James Hanway, in Lawrence *Daily Tribune*, May 30, 1881; Andreas, p. 1070.

60. Andreas, p. 1070.

61. It was at this period that Brown was first intimately thrown with two of his future followers, Albert Hazlett and Jeremiah Anderson. On the day of the Fort Scott raid he was at Wimsett farm, the rendezvous; near by lived Anderson's brother, with whom Brown then spent a few days. — G. B. Gill, Milan, Kansas, May 10, 1893, to R. J. Hinton, Hinton Papers, Kansas Historical Society.

62. Governor Medary to President James Buchanan, Lecompton, December 28, 1858, *Kansas Historical Society Collections*, vol. 5, pp. 565–566; ibid., pp. 580–581 et seq.

63. Narrative of George B. Gill, Hinton Papers, Kansas Historical Society.

64. 'John Brown's Raids,' by Burr Joyce, in the St. Louis *Globe-Democrat* for April 15, 1888.

65. Ibid.; see also St. Louis *Missouri Democrat* of December 30, 1858, for proslavery account of losses. This is indubitably an exaggeration.

66. Statement of Mrs. Annie Brown Adams to K. Mayo, Petrolia, Cal., October 2, 1908.

67. Article of Burr Joyce as aforesaid.

68. George B. Gill to R. J. Hinton, Milan, Kansas, May 10, 1893, Hinton Papers, Kansas Historical Society.

69. Harrisonville, Mo., *Democrat*, quoted in *Kansas Herald*, Leavenworth City, January 8, 1859.

70. Wyandotte *Western Argus*, January 15, 1859.

71. Lawrence *Republican*, January 6, 1859; Kansas *Herald*, Leavenworth, January 29, 1859; George A. Crawford to James Buchanan, President, *Kansas Historical Society Collections*, vol. 5, pp. 579–580. The *Herald of Freedom*, of course, did not lose the opportunity to assail Brown. It declared on January 22, 1859, after condemning Brown and Montgomery: "If the people of Missouri should raise an army and march over into Linn county and wipe the perpetrators of those wrongs from ex˘ ˙ence, all of us woulc̣ join in denouncing the outrage, and yet such transactions as those Brown rejoices over are inaugurating a state of things

which can only be seen through a river of blood. . . . Brown should be arrested and set to work on the public improvements at Jefferson City, Mo., until he is restored to reason, and unless we mistake such will be the case, *unless he hangs for murder.* . . ." Again, a few days later, February 2, 1859, it said: "'Old Brown' and a portion of his piratical band have escaped into Nebraska, no doubt on their way East. On their arrival they will make a demand upon the charitable for contributions to pay for their expenses while engaged in robbing the people of Kansas. We do wish *Gerrit Smith* could know Brown as he is. If so, instead of lending him further pecuniary assistance, he would exert all his energies to send him to an Insane Asylum."

72. *Herald of Freedom*, January 15, 1859.
73. Osawatomie letter of December 27, 1859, in the *Missouri Democrat* for January 5, 1859.
74. Governor Medary to the Kansas Legislature, House Journal, 1859, p. 44.
75. Mrs. Emma Wattles Morse, in the N. Y. *Tribune*, reprinted in the *Linn County Republic*, Mound City, Kansas, May 28, 1897.
76. Rev. S. L. Adair to James Hanway, Osawatomie, Kansas, February 2, 1878, Hanway Papers, Kansas Historical Society.
77. MS. of William H. Ambrose, entitled 'The Concealment of the Twelve on the Pottawatomie;' see also letter, with map, of James Hanway, to F. G. Adams, Lane, Kansas, February, 1878, both in Kansas Historical Society.
78. *Kansas Historical Society Collections*, vol. 7, pp. 398–399.
79. John Brown to James Montgomery, Turkey Creek, January 2, 1859, Montgomery Papers, Kansas Historical Society; here utilized for the first time.
80. Letter signed "Marcus," Moneka, Kansas, January 22, 1859, in Lawrence *Republican*, February 3, 1859; see also letter from Moneka, January 24, 1859, in the same issue.
81. Original in George W. Brown Papers, Kansas Historical Society. In his letter of March, 1859, to John Teesdale, Brown positively denied that he had been asked to leave Kansas. This letter was printed in the New York *Evening Sun* of March 16, 1895.
82. Mason Report, p. 223.
83. See article of Mrs. Emma Wattles Morse.
84. From an original draft, in Brown's handwriting, in the Kansas Historical Society.
85. The "atrocity" of Brown's raid, painted in the richest colors, was described to Buchanan by Lieut. J. P. Jones, of the Second United States Artillery, who had frequently traversed southern Kansas for Governor Denver, whose aide he had been. Lieutenant Jones, who was new to the army, could always see the Free State mote and never the Pro-Slavery beam; Hamilton's massacre, according to him, took place in a fair and honorable combat! See Lieut. J. P. Jones and B. J. Newsom to Governor Denver, Lecompton, June 3, 1858, *Kansas Historical Society Collections*, vol. 5, pp. 526–538; Lieut. J. P. Jones to President James Buchanan, Washington, D. C., January 9, 1859, *Kansas Historical Society Collections*, vol. 5, pp. 585–587.
86. Governor Medary to the Kansas Legislature, January 11, 1859, House Journal, 1859, p. 44 et seq.
87. Kansas House Journal, 1859, p. 57 et seq., and p. 64.
88. Reprinted in the N. Y. *Tribune* of January 29, 1859.
89. N. Y. *Tribune*, January 29, 1859, Lawrence correspondence.
90. Governor Medary to President Buchanan, Lawrence, February 2, 1859, *Kansas Historical Society Collections*, vol. 5, p. 602. Montgomery was at the time

in extreme poverty, and the rank and pay of a colonel of volunteers were very welcome when he was entrusted, thirty months later, with the raising of the Third Kansas Infantry, to aid in the defence of the Union.

91. N. Y. *Tribune*, January 28, 1859.

92. See letter of Gerrit Smith to Sanborn, Peterboro, January 22, 1859, Sanborn, p. 483.

93. *Kansas Historical Society Collections*, vol. 5, pp. 603–604; *Herald of Freedom*, February 19, 1859.

94. Original in possession of Mrs. Ellen Brown Fablinger.

95. Statement of George B. Gill to Hinton.

96. Samuel F. Tappan, Washington, D. C., December 19, 1907, to the author. To Brown's disappointment, he received here a letter from Martin F. Conway, advising him that he need not expect further aid from E. B. Whitman.

97. *Narrative of John Doy*, [by Himself], Boston, 1860, pp. 23–27, 123 and 130–132.

98. Gill says that he left Grover's, "riding a fine stallion which Brown had given Hazlett a forty-acre land warrant for. The land warrant Gerrit Smith had sent Brown, and the stallion Hazlett had picked up down in Missouri. Brown afterward sold it at auction in Cleveland."

99. MS. statement of Olive Owen, Topeka, 1904, in Kansas Historical Society.

100. There is some confusion of dates at this point, but those here given seem accurate. They, like the following narrative of the 'Battle of the Spurs,' have been deduced from the story of William F. Creitz, of Holton, Kansas, to James Redpath, December 17, 1859, Hinton Papers, Kansas Historical Society; 'The Battle of the Spurs,' by L. L. Kiene, *Kansas Historical Society Collections*, vol. 8, pp. 443–449; letter of G. M. Seaman, same volume, pp. 448–449; statement by William Graham, of Sabetha, Kansas, to W. E. Connelley, January, 1901; articles in N. Y. *Tribune*, February 12, 1859; Lawrence *Republican*, February 10, 1859; Atchison *Freedom's Champion*, February 12, 1859; letter of John H. Kagi to William A. Phillips, Tabor, Iowa, February 7, 1859; letter of William Hutchinson to the N. Y. *Times*, February 4, 1859; see also quotations in the Cleveland *Plain Dealer* of March 2, 1859, from the *Nebraska City News* and the Daily St. Joseph *Gazette;* and the *Missouri Democrat* of February 5 and 8, 1859.

101. Governor S. Medary to James Buchanan, President, January 31 and February 2, 1859, *Kansas Historical Society Collections*, vol. 5, p. 602.

102. Ibid., p. 601.

103. L. L. Kiene, in *Kansas Historical Society Collections*, vol. 8, p. 447.

104. St. Louis *Missouri Democrat*, February 8, 1859.

105. Quoted in the Lawrence *Republican*, February 10, 1859.

106. B. F. Gue, *History of Iowa*, New York, 1903, vol. 1, p. 381; Gill's narrative in Hinton, p. 225.

107. Original in possession of Mrs. Ellen Brown Fablinger.

108. Statement of Rev. H. D. King, Kinsman, Ohio, January 4 and 5, 1909, to K. Mayo.

109. 'John Brown's Last Visit to Tabor,' by Prof. J. E. Todd, *Annals of Iowa*, Third Series, vol. 3, p. 458 et seq., April to July, 1898.

110. George Gill MS. of "1860 or '61," Hinton Papers, Kansas Historical Society.

111. From the copy in the possession of Miss Mary Thompson.

112. Statement of Rev. H. D. King; and *Reminiscences* of Rev. John Todd, pp. 159–161.

113. To show how little this taking of the horses affected strong anti-slavery

men in the East, it is worth recording that John A. Andrew, on February 9, 1860, made the following statement before the Mason Committee: "I had heard it frequently said that sometimes during the controversy between free-State men and the pro-slavery men, they were accustomed, when they prevailed against each other, to treat their horses as fairly the spoils of war. I am quite confident that I had heard this statement made in connection with Captain Brown, but I did not regard him singular in that respect, and I always believed and do now believe that the free-State men were acting defensively in substantially all that was done by them in Kansas." — Mason Report, p. 192.

114. This itinerary is given by Gill in Hinton, pp. 226–227.

115. This letter was republished without exact date in N. Y. *Evening Sun* of March 16, 1895.

116. At another time Brown justified the Missouri raid by asserting that the Denver truce had been broken; that it was in accordance with his settled policy; that it was intended as a "descriminating blow" at slavery; that "it was calculated to lessen the value of slaves;" and finally that "it was (over and above all other motives) right." See *Startling Incidents and Developments of Osawatomy Brown's Insurrectory and Treasonable Movements at Harper's Ferry, Virginia*, by A Citizen of Harper's Ferry, Baltimore, 1859.

117. *Men and Events of Forty Years*, by Josiah Busnell Grinnell, Boston, 1891, p. 210 et seq.

118. From the original, in possession of the Kansas Historical Society.

119. This narrative of the attempt to capture Brown is taken from the *History of Johnson County*, Iowa City, Iowa, 1883, pp. 471–474.

120. This letter is reprinted in Bulletin for May, 1900, of Boston Public Library.

121. Gill MS. of "1860 or '61."

122. L. R. Witherell, in Davenport, Iowa, *Gazette* of March 13, 1878; Mrs. E. S. Butler, 'A Woman's Recollections of John Brown's Stay in Springdale,' *Midland Monthly*, November, 1898, p. 576; Narcissa Macy Smith, 'Reminiscences of John Brown,' *Midland Monthly*, September, 1895, pp. 231–236.

123. E. H. Gregg to J. H. Holmes, Kansas City, Mo., December 22, 1895. Mr. Gregg was an employee of Keith's Mill.

124. Iowa City *Republican*, Leaflet No. 11, November 17, 1880.

125. Grinnell, p. 216.

126. Major Allan Pinkerton's paper read at meeting in honor of Mrs. John Brown; and paper by John Jones read at the same time, both in Chicago *Times*, September 1, 1882; also H. O. Waggoner, in Spokane, Wash., *Review* of September 2, 1892; also Kagi to Tidd, Detroit, March 13, 1859, in Document No 1, Appendix to [Gov. Wise's] Message 1, to Virginia Legislature, December, 1859 (referred to hereinafter as Document No. 1); Hinton, pp. 227–228.

127. N. Y. *Tribune*, March 17, 1859; letter of Kagi to Tidd, Detroit, March 13, 1859, Document No. 1, p. 113.

CHAPTER XI

THE EVE OF THE TRAGEDY

1. Mrs. Amanda M. Sturtevant to James Redpath, Cleveland, April 17, 1860, Hinton Papers, Kansas Historical Society; Mrs. Sturtevant, in Cleveland Weekly *Plain Dealer*, November 9, 1859; J. W. Schuckers, in Cleveland *Leader* for April

29, 1894; Kagi to Tidd, Detroit, March 13, 1859; Document No. 1, pp. 113–114.

2. Cleveland *Leader* of March 21, 1859.

3. Cleveland Daily *Plain Dealer*, March 22, 1859, and Weekly *Plain Dealer*, March 30, 1859.

4. J. W. Schuckers, as above.

5. Hinton, p. 233.

6. J. W. Schuckers; Annie Brown Adams to the author.

7. J. W. Schuckers.

8. John Brown to wife and children, Ashtabula, Ohio, March 25, 1859. — Original in possession of Miss Brown.

9. See N. Y. *Tribune*, October 31, 1859, and Ashtabula *Sentinel*, November 15, 1859, giving the speech of J. R. Giddings in Philadelphia on Friday, October 28, 1859; also statement of Mrs. Mary Curtis Giddings, Jefferson, Ohio, January 2, 1909, to K. Mayo.

10. Letter of Mrs. Amanda M. Sturtevant to Redpath; statement of Mrs. J. H. Scott, Oberlin, Ohio, December 9, 1908, to K. Mayo; J. H. Kagi, Cleveland, Ohio, April 4, 1859, to Thaddeus Hyatt, — original in possession of Dr. Thaddeus Hyatt, Brooklyn, N. Y.; Kagi to H. Thompson, Cleveland, April 21, 1859, — original in possession of Miss Thompson.

11. John Brown to wife and children, Kingsville, Ohio, April 7, 1859. — Original in Byron Reed Collection, in Omaha Public Library.

12. Frothingham's *Gerrit Smith*, first edition, p. 237.

13. John Brown to Kagi, Westport, April 16, 1859, Document No. 1, p. 135; Owen Brown to John Brown, Akron, May 2, 1859, — original in possession of Mrs. John Brown, Jr.

14. John Brown to John Henrie (Kagi), North Elba, April 25, 1859. — Original in Dreer Collection, Pennsylvania Historical Society.

15. John Brown's *Memorandum-Book* No. 2, Boston Public Library.

16. Sanborn, p. 467.

17. This correspondence between Sanborn and Higginson is in the Higginson Collection, Boston Public Library.

18. Higginson to John Brown, Brattleboro, Vt., May 1, 1859, Higginson Collection, Boston Public Library.

19. T. W. Higginson, *Cheerful Yesterdays*, pp. 222–223.

20. Sanborn, p. 523.

21. Document No. 1, p. 134.

22. Original in possession of Mrs. Ellen Brown Fablinger.

23. Brown to wife and children, Boston, May 13, 1859. — Original in Byron Reed Collection, Omaha Public Library.

24. *Memorandum-Book* No. 2.

25. A. Bronson Alcott, MS. statement in Mrs. G. L. Stearns's *Emancipation Evening Album*, in possession of Stearns's family.

26. *John Murray Forbes*, Letters and Recollections, edited by his daughter, Sarah Forbes Hughes, Boston, 1899, vol. 1, pp. 179–182.

27. Mason Report, p. 144.

28. *Life of A. A. Lawrence*, p. 130.

29. Mason Report, p. 192.

30. Ibid., testimony of Henry Wilson, pp. 144–145.

31. Ibid., pp. 124–127, testimony of Charles Blair.

32. Original in Dreer Collection, **Pennsylvania Historical Society.**

33. Sanborn, p. 523.

NOTES

34. This portion of the diary will be found in the N. Y. *Herald*, October 25, 1859; see also letter of Oliver Brown to his wife, West Andover, Ohio, June 18, 1859, — original in possession of Miss Brown.

35. John Brown to wife and children, Akron, June 23, 1859. — Original in possession of Miss Thompson. (Much altered in Sanborn's *Life*, p. 526.)

36. Statement of Miss Fannie Dean, Jefferson, Ohio, January 2, 1909, to K. Mayo, and of John Brown, Jr., in Cleveland *Press*, May 3, 1895. Statements of Alfred Hawkes, Jefferson, Ohio, January 2, 1909, Mr. and Mrs. J. B. Noxon, Wayne, Ohio, January 3, 1909, and Charles Garlick, Jefferson, January 2, 1909, all to K. Mayo; also E. C. Lampson, 'The Black String Band,' Cleveland *Plain Dealer*, October 8, 1899.

37. Original in Dreer Collection.

38. Oliver Brown to his wife, Bedford Springs, Pa., June 26, 1859, — original in possession of Miss Brown; I. Smith (John Brown) to John Henrie (Kagi), Bedford, Pa., June 27, 1859, — original in Dreer Collection.

39. Original in Dreer Collection.

40. Sanborn, p. 527.

41. Mason Report, p. 5.

42. See the Unseld testimony, Mason Report, pp. 1-6, for details of the move to Kennedy Farm.

43. Statement of Patrick Higgins to the author, Sandy Hook, Maryland, April, 1908; Unseld, Mason Report, pp. 1-6.

44. Annie Brown Adams to Hinton, Petrolia, Cal., February 15, 1893. — Original in Hinton Papers, Kansas Historical Society.

45. Original in possession of Miss Brown; also Brown's diary, N. Y. *Herald*, October 25, 1859.

46. Letter of Mary A. "Smith" to "Isaac Smith," North Elba, June 29, 1859. — Original in Dreer Collection.

47. Mason Report, p. 4; Isaac Smith (John Brown) to his family, Chambersburg, July 22, 1859, — original in possession of Mrs. Ellen Brown Fablinger; narrative of Annie Brown Adams, in possession of the author.

48. F. B. Sanborn, *Memoirs of John Brown*, Concord, 1878, p. 73.

49. Original in Dreer Collection.

50. Statement of Annie Brown Adams to the author; see also Hinton's *John Brown*, p. 246.

51. I. Smith and Sons (John Brown) to John Henrie, Harper's Ferry, Va., July 12, 1859. — Original in Dreer Collection.

52. Letter of C. W. Moffet, Document No. 1, pp. 110-111.

53. John Brown, Jr., to his father, Lindenville, Ohio, May 1, 1858. — Original in possession of Miss Brown.

54. Original in Dreer Collection.

55. John Smith (John Brown, Jr.) to J. Henrie (Kagi), West Andover, July 27, 1859, Document No. 1, pp. 136-137; the same to the same, August 7, 1859. — Original in Dreer Collection.

56. J. Henrie to Messrs. I. Smith and Sons, Chambersburg, August 11, 1859. — Original in Dreer Collection.

57. John Brown to John Brown, Jr., Chambersburg, August, 1859, printed in N. Y. *Herald*, October 25, 1859.

58. Statement of Annie Brown Adams to the author.

59. Annie Brown Adams to Hinton, Petrolia, February 15, 1893, as above.

60. *Virginia Free Press*, Charlestown, W. Va., April 5, 1860; statement of

Mrs. Virginia Kennedy Cook Johnston, Chicago, November 23, 1908, and of Mr. Cleon Moore, Charlestown, April, 1909, to K. Mayo.

61. William H. Leeman, Harper's Ferry, October 2, 1859, to his mother. — Original in Hinton Papers, Kansas Historical Society.
62. Original in Dreer Collection.
63. Letter of August 6, 1859. — Original in Dreer Collection.
64. Original in possession of Mrs. John Brown, Jr.
65. Mason Report, testimony of Secretary John B. Floyd, pp. 250–252.
66. Statement of David J. Gue, New York, November, 1907, to K. Mayo; see also *History of Iowa*, by Benjamin F. Gue, vol. 2, pp. 26–30.
67. Sanborn to Higginson, August 24, September 4 and 14, 1859. — Originals in Higginson Collection, Boston Public Library.
68. Document No. 1, p. 145.
69. *Life and Times of Frederick Douglass*, pp. 354–358. For Douglass's contemporaneous statement, see his letter from Canada West, October 31, 1859, to the editor of the Rochester *Democrat and American*, reprinted in the *Liberator* of November 11, 1859.
70. Document No. 1, p. 140.
71. Oliver Brown to John Brown, North Elba, April 21, 1858.—Original in possession of Miss Brown; statement of Annie Brown Adams, Petrolia, Cal., October 2 and 3, 1908, to K. Mayo.
72. Document No. 1, pp. 137–138; see also letter of the same to the same, West Andover, September 27, 1859, in N. Y. *Herald*, October 25, 1859.
73. John Brown to John Henrie (Kagi), Washington County, Maryland, August 11, 1859.—Original in Dreer Collection.
74. From the narrative of Owen Brown, written at his dictation by Mrs. Ruth Brown Thompson, — in possession of Miss Thompson.
75. *A Voice from Harper's Ferry*, by Osborn P. Anderson, Boston, 1861, p. 23.
76. Harriet Newby's pathetic letters to her husband are in Document No. 1, pp. 116–117.
77. Letters of Watson Brown to Isabel, his wife, Chambersburg, September 8 and October 14, "Home," September 28, and a fourth, undated, — from copies in possession of Miss Brown.
78. Isabel Brown to Watson Brown, North Elba, September 14, 1859.—Original in Dreer Collection.
79. Original in Dreer Collection.
80. Statement of Annie Brown Adams to the author.
81. Quoted by Annie Brown Adams to the author.
82. John Brown to wife and children, Chambersburg, October 1, 1859, Sanborn, p. 550.
83. Statement of Annie Brown Adams to author.
84. 'John Brown and His Friends,' by F. B. Sanborn, *Atlantic Monthly*, July, 1872.
85. Quoted by F. B. Sanborn in 'The Virginia Campaign of John Brown,' *Atlantic Monthly*, December, 1875.
86. Letter of Francis J. Meriam to Wendell Phillips Garrison, Rutland, Vt., September 22, 1858. — Original in possession of the author.
87. *Abraham Lincoln and Men of War Times*, by A. K. McClure, Philadelphia, 1892, p. 309.
88. *Confession of John E. Cook.*
89. Original in possession of Miss Brown.

NOTES

90. From the copy by John Brown, Jr., in the Higginson Collection, Boston Public Library.

91. Ibid.

92. Statement of Salmon Brown, at Portland, Oregon, October 12, 1908, to K. Mayo.

CHAPTER XII

HIGH TREASON IN VIRGINIA

1. For an account of the last day at Kennedy Farm and the march to Harper's Ferry, see O. P. Anderson, *A Voice from Harper's Ferry*, pp. 28–32; the story of the parting of the Coppocs is from Mrs. Annie Brown Adams's recollections of O. P. Anderson's verbal account; see also, on this point, *John Brown's Men*, by Thomas Featherstonhaugh, Harrisburg, 1899, p. 12.

2. N. Y. *Herald*, November 1, 1859; Doc. No. XXXI, Report of the Joint Committee of the General Assembly of Virginia on the Harper's Ferry Outrages, January 26, 1860, p. 4.

3. Thomas Jefferson, *Notes on the State of Virginia*, London, 1787, pp. 27–28.

4. New York *Tribune*, November 24, 1856.

5. Josephus, Jr., *Annals of Harper's Ferry*, Hagerstown, Md., 1869, pp. 17–18; New York *Herald*, October 19, 1859; *Life, Trial and Conviction of Captain John Brown*, New York, 1859, p. 76.

6. N. Y. *Tribune*, November 24, 1856.

7. Testimony of Daniel Whelan, Mason Report, p. 22.

8. O. P. Anderson, *A Voice*, pp. 26 and 33.

9. For Col. Washington's narrative of his capture, see Mason Report, pp. 29–40, and *Life, Trial and Execution of Captain John Brown*, pp. 39–40, 71 and 72; see also O. P. Anderson, pp. 33–35.

10. O. P. Anderson, p. 35.

11. Statement of John Thomas Allstadt, Kearneysville, W. Va., April 15, 1909, to K. Mayo.

12. Mason Report, p. 34.

13. Statement of Patrick Higgins, Sandy Hook, Md., January, 1908, to the author; *Annals of Harper's Ferry*, p. 18; statement of W. W. Throckmorton, N. Y. *Herald*, October 24, 1859; testimony of Conductor Phelps, *Life, Trial and Conviction of Captain John Brown*, p. 69. (The *Life, Trial and Conviction of Captain John Brown* differs but slightly from the *Life, Trial and Execution of Captain John Brown*. Both were pamphlets of 108 pages, published by Robert W. DeWitt, New York, 1859.)

14. For the story of the stopping of the train and of the shooting of Hayward, see Phelps's testimony; see also statements of C. W. Armstrong, a passenger, N. Y. *Herald*, October 19, and of W. W. Throckmorton, N. Y. *Herald*, October 24; also testimony of Dr. J. D. Starry, Mason Report, pp. 23–24; for Hayward's character, see Starry's testimony; also that of Col. Washington, Mason Report, p. 39. Hayward's body was escorted to the grave by the Morgan Continentals, under Major R. B. Washington, with two other militia companies. A militia band led the procession, in which were the mayor and many officers and white citizens, who listened reverently to the reading of the burial service by an old negro preacher.

15. *Confession of John E. Cook*, p. 11.

16. Phelps testimony, *Life, Trial and Conviction of Captain John Brown*, p. 69.

17. For the despatch and its sequels, see Document Y, *Correspondence Relating*

to the Insurrection at Harper's Ferry, Annapolis, 1860, p. 1 et seq. (published by the Maryland Legislature), hereinafter referred to as Document Y.

18. Dr. Starry's testimony in full is given in the Mason Report.

19. Report of Col. John Thomas Gibson, commanding the 55th Regiment Virginia Militia, Harper's Ferry, October 18, 1859, to Governor Wise, Document No. 1, Virginia State Papers, pp. 61–62; speech of Governor Wise in Richmond, October 21, N. Y. Herald, October 26, 1859; also statement of Mr. Cleon Moore to the author, January, 1908.

20. Report of Col. Gibson; article entitled 'The Jefferson Guards,' Virginia Free Press, October 27, 1859.

21. Statement of W. W. Throckmorton, clerk of the Wager House, N. Y. Herald, October 24, 1859; testimony of Col. Washington, Mason Report, p. 40; statements of J. T. Allstadt, Kearneysville, April 15, 1909, and of Miss Annie Miller, Charlestown, March 20, 1908, both to K. Mayo.

22. Testimony of Terence Byrne, Mason Report, pp. 13–21; Confession of John E. Cook.

23. See testimony of Armistead Ball, Life, Trial and Conviction of Captain John Brown, p. 73; testimony of Joseph A. Brewer [Brua], ibid., p. 75; testimony of Reason Cross, ibid., p. 76; testimony of John P. Da[i]ngerfield, ibid., p. 79.

24. Charlestown Virginia Free Press, October 27 and November 3, 1859; testimony of Benjamin T. Bell, Life, Trial and Execution of Captain John Brown, p. 74.

25. Col. Gibson's Report; Col. Baylor's Report, Document No. 1, pp. 63–64; 'The Jefferson Guards,' Virginia Free Press, October 27, 1859.

26. Statement of Col. Richard B. Washington, Charlestown, March 26, 1908, to K. Mayo; Annals of Harper's Ferry, p. 34; statement of Patrick Higgins to the author. The shooting of Newby has been ascribed to other hands, though all narratives agree as to the place whence the shot came.

27. Statement of Patrick Higgins to the author, January, 1908; this incident was reported in the Frederick, Md., Herald, cited in the Liberator, November 11, 1859; see Richmond Despatch, October 25, 1859.

28. Cross's testimony, Life, Trial and Execution of Captain John Brown, p. 76.

29. For the mission and the wounding of Stevens and of Watson Brown, see testimony of A. M. Kitzmiller, Life, Trial and Execution of Captain John Brown, p. 75; testimony of James Beller, ibid., p. 75; of John P. Daingerfield, ibid., p. 79; and of Major Mills, ibid., p. 80; also letter of George Sennott, Stevens's counsel, in the N. Y. Tribune, November 29, 1859.

30. Testimony of Joseph A. Brewer [Brua], Life, Trial and Execution of Captain John Brown, p. 75.

31. Schoppert's affidavit is in the possession of Mr. Braxton Davenport Gibson, of Charlestown, who vouches for his father's, Colonel Gibson's, endorsement of Schoppert's statement; for the riddling of Leeman's body, see Baltimore Sun, October 19, 1859; also statement of Mr. E. B. Chambers, Harper's Ferry, March 24, 1908, to K. Mayo; also statement of eye-witness in the Frederick, Md., Herald, quoted in the Liberator of Nov. 11, 1859; for Leeman's attempt to escape, and his movements precedent thereto, see Annals of Harper's Ferry, by Joseph Barry (a later edition), Martinsburg, W. Va., 1872.

32. Statement of John Brown, Charlestown Independent Democrat, November 22, 1859; letter of 'An Observer,' Shepherdstown, Va., Register, October 29, 1859; statement of Mr. and Mrs. Alfred Burton, Charlestown, April 14, 1909, to K. Mayo.

33. George W. Turner was graduated from West Point, July 1, 1831, becoming

NOTES 641

a second lieutenant in the 1st Artillery. He resigned June 30, 1836, and became a farmer in Rippon, Jefferson County. His sister lost her reason on hearing of her brother's death, and died soon after of shock and grief.

34. J. G. Rosengarten, 'John Brown's Raid,' *Atlantic Monthly*, June, 1865.
35. Statement of John Thomas Allstadt, April 15, 1909, to K. Mayo.
36. Letter of Miss Christine Fouke, Harper's Ferry, November 27, 1859, to the St. Louis *Republican* of December 2, 1859.
37. N. Y. *Tribune*, October 29, 1859; for a more detailed report of Mr. Hunter's testimony, see N. Y. *Herald*, October 31, 1859; *Virginia Free Press*, October 27, 1859.
38. Annals of Harper's Ferry, p. 25; see also N. Y. *Herald*, October 19, 1859.
39. John E. P. Daingerfield, 'John Brown at Harper's Ferry,' *Century*, June, 1885, p. 267.
40. Statement of Capt. Ephraim G. Alburtis, N. Y. *Herald*, October 24, 1859; telegram of W. P. Smith to L. M. Cole, Harper's Ferry, October 18, Document Y, p. 17; telegram of same to J. W. Garrett, Monocacy, October 18, ibid., p. 23; Alexander R. Boteler, 'Recollections of the John Brown Raid,' *Century*, July, 1883, p. 407; report of Col. Baylor; Baltimore *Despatch* of October 18, quoted in N. Y. *Tribune* of October 19, 1859.
41. Statement of W. S. Downer, N. Y. *Herald*, October 24, 1859.
42. Report of Col. Robert E. Lee, as printed in Mason Report, p. 40; Reports of Cols. Gibson and Baylor.
43. For the story of the fight at the Rifle Works, see Mason Report, p. 27; Mr. Boteler's narrative in his *Century* article above cited; Copeland's account of the whole affair is given in his letter of December 10, 1859, to Addison W. Halbert, — original in Department of Archives and History, Richmond, Virginia; N. Y. *Tribune*, October 19, 1859; narrative of D. H. Strother, *Harper's Weekly*, November 5, 1859.
44. Testimony of Lind F. Currie, Mason Report, pp. 54–59; *Confession of John E. Cook*. Cf. 'Owen Brown's Escape from Harper's Ferry,' by Ralph Keeler, *Atlantic Monthly*, March, 1874.
45. Boteler's narrative; affidavit of G. A. Schoppert.
46. For John Brown's proposal and Col. Baylor's reply, see the official report of the latter.
47. Capt. Sinn's narrative is found in his testimony at Brown's trial, for the "manly and truthful" character of which John Brown afterward thanked him. See N. Y. *Tribune*, October 31, 1859.
48. Statement of Col. Washington, *Life, Trial and Execution of Captain John Brown*, p. 40.
49. Statement of John Thomas Allstadt, April 15, 1909. Testimonies conflict as to the hour of Oliver Brown's death, some averring that he died within fifteen minutes after sustaining his mortal wound.
50. John E. P. Daingerfield, *Century*, June, 1885; statement of John Brown, N. Y. *Herald*, October 22, 1859; letter of Edwin Coppoc, November 22, 1859, quoted by Hinton, p. 488; letter of John Brown to wife and children, Charlestown, 31st Oct. 1859, — original in possession of Miss Brown.
51. Document Y, p. 10.
52. Ibid., p. 14.
53. Gen. J. E. B. Stuart, as quoted by John Esten Cook in the St. Joseph, Mo., *Herald*, September 2, 1879; Col. Lee's official report to the Adjutant-General, Mason Report, p. 41.
54. Given in *Life and Letters of Robert Edward Lee, Soldier and Man*, by the Rev. J. William Jones, New York, 1906, p. 105.

NOTES

55. From Stuart's letter to his mother, Fort Riley, January, 1860, given in *Life and Campaigns of J. E. B. Stuart*, by H. B. McClellan, Boston, 1885, pp. 28–30.
56. Col. Lee's Report.
57. See speech of Gov. Wise, Richmond, October 21, 1859.
58. Statement of Col. and Mrs. John A. Tompkins, Baltimore, Feb. 24, 1908, to K. Mayo. Mrs. Tompkins is a daughter of Col. Shriver.
59. Letter of O. Jennings Wise to Col. J. T. Gibson, Richmond, June 5, 1860. — Original in possession of Mr. Braxton Davenport Gibson, Charlestown, W. Va.
60. Affidavit of G. A. Schoppert.
61. Israel Green entered the Marine Corps of the United States Navy with the rank of second lieutenant on March 3, 1847, and was dismissed May 18, 1861, because he resigned to go South. Although a Vermonter, he joined the Confederate Marine Corps with the rank of major and adjutant, on its organization, March 16, 1861, serving throughout the war in that position. He died in Mitchell, South Dakota, on May 26, 1909, in his 86th year.
62. "Major Russell had been requested by the Secretary of the Navy to accompany the marines, but, being a paymaster, could exercise no command; yet it was his corps." — Letter of Lieut. J. E. B. Stuart to his mother, Fort Riley, Jan. 1860.

"Major Russell was a charming and cultivated man of great coolness, and then about thirty-five years old. He jumped through the door with Green, unarmed, carrying in his hand only a little rattan switch." — Statement of Col. John A. Tompkins, Baltimore, Feb. 24, 1908, to K. Mayo.

"Major Russell, of marines, headed them in person, unarmed. I never saw so thrilling a scene." — W. P. Smith (Master of Transportation, B. and O. Railroad) to J. W. Garrett, Harper's Ferry, Oct. 18, 1859, Document Y, p. 21.

Major W. W. Russell became second lieutenant of Marines, April 5, 1843, first lieutenant, Nov. 18, 1847, and later paymaster with rank of major. He died Oct. 31, 1862.

63. Quoted by Governor Wise in his speech at Richmond, October 21, 1859.
64. 'The Capture of John Brown,' by Israel Green, *North American Review*, Dec. 1885, pp. 564–569.
65. Ibid., p. 566; John E. P. Daingerfield, in the *Century*, June, 1885; 'John Brown's Raid,' narrative of master armorer Ben. Mills, Louisville *Courier-Journal*, July 9, 1881; statement of John Thomas Allstadt.
66. Colonel Lee's Report; Col. Lee's despatch to the Secretary of War, Document Y, p. 22; N. Y. *Herald*, October 21, 1859.
67. Letter of C. W. Tayleure to John Brown, Jr., June 15, 1879, a copy of which is in the Maryland Historical Society's Library.
68. Governor Wise, speech of October 21, 1859.
69. Baltimore *American*, quoted in N. Y. *Tribune*, October 22, 1859.
70. N. Y. *Herald*, October 21, 1859.
71. N. Y. *Herald*, November 1, 1859.
72. The Court of Enquiry met June 4, at Charlestown. See entry of June 28, 1860, Executive Journal, Library of the Secretary of the Commonwealth, Richmond. The Court remained in session six days. See also Charlestown *Independent Democrat*, June 19, 1860; the *Virginia Free Press*, June 21, 1860, gives a full account of the proceedings.
73. O. Jennings Wise to Col. J. T. Gibson, Richmond, June 5, 1860. — Original in possession of Mr. Braxton Davenport Gibson.

NOTES 643

74. Shepherdstown, Va., *Register*, October 29, 1859.
75. Message of Gov. Wise to the Virginia Legislature, December 5, 1859, Document No. 1, December, 1859, Journal of the House of Delegates.
76. *Life of Henry A. Wise*, by Barton H. Wise, New York, 1899, pp. 274-277.
77. Ibid., p. 278.
78. Ibid., p. 283.

CHAPTER XIII

GUILTY BEFORE THE LAW

1. For the movements of the troops on the 18th, see Col. Lee's official report of October 19; Lieutenant Stuart's letter to his mother, Fort Riley, Jan. 1860; Col. R. W. Baylor's official report, *Herald*, Oct. 19, 1859; testimony of John C. Unseld, Mason Report, pp. 7-12.
2. Gov. Wise to J. W. Garrett, Washington, 20th Oct., Document Y, pp. 28-29; W. P. Smith to J. T. Crow, Baltimore, Oct. 25, ibid., p. 31; W. P. Smith to A. Hunter, Baltimore, October 25, ibid., pp. 31-32; W. P. Smith to Gov. Wise, Baltimore, Oct. 25, ibid., pp. 32-33; testimony of Andrew Hunter, Mason Report, p. 65.
3. Richmond *Despatch*, Nov. 27, 1859.
4. *Confession of John E. Cook*; 'Owen Brown's Escape from Harper's Ferry,' by Ralph Keeler; Notes of conversation with C. P. Tidd, by T. W. Higginson, Feb. 10, 1860, — original in Higginson Collection, Boston Public Library.
5. Notes of conversation with C. P. Tidd, by T. W. Higginson, Feb. 10, 1860; testimony of Colonel Washington, Mason Report, p. 39; see also testimony of John P. Da[i]ngerfield, *Life, Trial and Conviction*, p. 79, and testimony of John H. Allstadt, ibid., pp. 73-74.
6. Testimony of Colonel Washington, Mason Report, pp. 39-40; speech of Gov. Wise of Oct. 19, 1859.
7. Testimony of John H. Allstadt, Mason Report, pp. 42-44; *Virginia Free Press*, Nov. 3, 1859.
8. N. Y. *Herald*, Oct. 26, 1859.
9. N. Y. *Herald*, Oct. 19, 1859. The man belonged to Mr. Allstadt, — statement of John Thomas Allstadt of April 15, 1909, to K. Mayo.
10. *Atlantic Monthly*, June, 1865.
11. Official Report of Colonel Lee; N. Y. *Tribune*, October 20; N. Y. *Herald*, October 21, 1859.
12. Speech of Gov. Wise of October 19, 1859; Andrew Hunter, in New Orleans *Times-Democrat*, Sept. 5, 1887; N. Y. *Herald*, Oct. 20, 1859; Redpath, pp. 286-287.
13. Official report of Col. Baylor.
14. Official reports of Col. Lee and of Col. Baylor; letter of Lieut. J. E. B. Stuart to his mother, Fort Riley, Jan. 1860.
15. The adventures of the five refugees will be found in 'Owen Brown's Escape from Harper's Ferry,' by Ralph Keeler; *Confession of John E. Cook*; Notes of conversation with C. P. Tidd, by T. W. Higginson, Feb. 10, 1860, in Higginson Collection; O. P. Anderson, *A Voice from Harper's Ferry*. Important letters relating to the escape of the survivors, and the efforts set on foot by J. Miller McKim, William W. Rutherford, of Harrisburg, Redpath and others, to aid their flight, are to be found in the J. M. McKim Correspondence, Cornell University Library.
16. N. Y. *Herald*, Oct. 20, 1859.

17. N. Y. *Herald*, Oct. 19, 1859.
18. Cleveland *Weekly Leader*, Oct. 26, 1859.
19. Oct. 20, 1859.
20. Oct. 22, 1859.
21. Oct. 22, 1859.
22. Oct. 22, 1859.
23. *Liberator*, October 21, 1859.
24. Cited in the N. Y. *Anzeiger des Westens*, Oct. 23, 1859.
25. *Maryland. The History of a Palatinate*, by William Hand Browne, Boston, 1904, pp. 349-351.
26. Greeley to Schuyler Colfax, *Life of Schuyler Colfax*, by O. J. Hollister, New York, 1886, p. 150.
27. Chapter CCVIII SS2 of Code of Virginia, published in 1849 pursuant to an Act of the General Assembly of Virginia, passed August 15, 1847.
28. See Message of Governor Wise to the House of Delegates, Dec. 1859, Document No. 1. Caleb Cushing, speaking in the Union Meeting in Faneuil Hall, Boston, Dec. 8, 1859, mentioned a decision once handed down by himself that the arsenal of Harper's Ferry was in the exclusive jurisdiction of the United States; but, continuing, he showed that John Brown, besides those offences done within the armory grounds, committed in the exclusive jurisdiction of the Commonwealth of Virginia, burglary, robbery, incitement to sedition, treason and murder. Reported in the New York *Herald*, Dec. 9, 1859.
29. Original in possession of Mr. Edwin Tatham.
30. Letter of Andrew Hunter to Governor Wise, Charlestown, Nov. 2, 1859, — Original in Department of Archives and History, Richmond.
31. N. Y. *Tribune*, Nov. 10, 1859.
32. Quoted by Andrew Hunter in a letter to Governor Wise, Winchester, Dec. 15, 1859. — Original in the possession of Mr. Edwin Tatham.
33. Original in the possession of Mr. Edwin Tatham.
34. Correspondence from Richmond of Dec. 8, in N. Y. *Herald*, Dec. 11, 1859.
35. Richmond *Enquirer*, Feb. 7, 1860.
36. Judge Richard Parker died in Winchester, Va., Nov. 10, 1893, in his eighty-fourth year. He was a son of Judge Richard E. Parker, of the Virginia Court of Appeals, and graduated in law at the University of Virginia. In 1849 he was Representative in the 34th Congress, and in 1851 became Circuit Court Judge. During the "reconstruction," he was forced to retire from the bench by the military authorities, and then opened a law school in Winchester. Until a few years before his death he was in active practice, and was always one of the leading lawyers of the State.
37. Lydia Maria Child to Governor Wise, Wayland, Oct. 26, 1859, in *Correspondence between Lydia Maria Child, Gov. Wise and Mrs. Mason of Virginia*, New York, 1860 (pamphlet), pp. 1-2; *Letters of Lydia Maria Child*, Boston, 1883, p. 104.
38. Ibid., pp. 4-6; ibid., p. 106.
39. Nov. 17, 1859.
40. N. Y. *Tribune*, Oct. 31, 1859.
41. Quoted in the *Liberator*, Nov. 4, 1859.
42. Letter of Gov. Wise to the Philadelphia *Press*, quoted in the *Liberator*, Sept. 26, 1856.
43. St. Louis *Globe-Democrat*, April 8, 1888.
44. Mason Report, p. 187.

NOTES

45. *Life, Trial and Conviction*, p. 95; see also letter of Judge Russell signed "T.," Boston *Traveller*, Nov. 5, 1859.

46. D. W. Voorhees, United States Senate, Jan. 7, 1889, to Miss Florence Hunter. — Original in possession of Miss Hunter, Charlestown, W. Va.

47. The entire proceedings of the Court of Examination and of the Circuit Court in the trial of Brown, with testimony, speeches and rulings, are best reported in the New York *Herald*. The story of the trial here given has been drawn from the pamphlet *Life, Trial and Execution of Captain John Brown*, New York, 1859, and from a careful comparison of the accounts of the *Tribune, Herald, Liberator* and other contemporary papers, Northern and Southern, after an examination of the official minutes of the trial, at Charlestown. Gen. Marcus J. Wright's two magazine articles, *The Trial of John Brown, its Impartiality and Decorum Vindicated*, Southern Historical Society Papers, vol. 16, 357-366, and *The Trial and Execution of John Brown*, American Historical Association Papers, vol. 4, pp. 437-452, have also been examined.

48. Charles James Faulkner to M. W. Cluskey, Boydville, Nov. 5, 1859, quoted from Washington *States and Union*, by Richmond *Enquirer*, Nov. 25, 1859.

49. Lawson Botts was a son of Gen. Thomas H. Botts, of Virginia, grandson of Benjamin Botts, counsel for Aaron Burr, and was, on his mother's side, of the family of General Washington. In the Confederate army he was quickly promoted for distinguished gallantry, and held the rank of Colonel of the Second Virginia Regiment, when mortally wounded on the field, Aug. 28, 1862. Thomas C. Green served as a private in his friend's command. After the war he returned to his profession, was appointed to the bench in 1875, and served as judge in the West Virginia Supreme Court of Appeals until 1889, in which year he died.

50. For the above quotation and account of the despatch of Hoyt to Charlestown, see Hinton's *John Brown and His Men*, pp. 365-366.

51. Andrew Hunter to Governor Wise, Calendar of Virginia State Papers, vol. 11, p. 87.

52. Hinton, p. 366.

53. Letter of Andrew Hunter to Henry A. Wise, Charlestown, Nov. 8, 1859. — Original in the possession of Mr. Edwin Tatham. A man of fine natural parts and of a classical training, Charles Harding was now a physical wreck. At the outbreak of the war, however, he shouldered a musket and, despite his years, went into the Confederate ranks, serving with devotion. Left unrelieved on outpost guard all one stormy winter night, by oversight, he died the next day from pneumonia.

54. Statement of Mr. Cleon Moore, Charlestown, April 15, 1909, to K. Mayo.

55. Letter of D. W. Voorhees to Miss Florence Hunter, Jan. 7, 1889. Andrew Hunter was born in Berkeley County, Virginia, March 22, 1804, graduated at Hampden-Sidney College in 1822, and soon began the practice of law in Harper's Ferry, removing to Charlestown in 1825. He served in the Legislature of Virginia before and during the Civil War. His Charlestown home was destroyed by his cousin, Gen. David Hunter, of the Union Army, in 1864. He died in Charlestown, November, 22, 1888.

56. Andrew Hunter to Gov. Wise, Charlestown, Oct. 22. — Original in Executive Papers, Department of Archives and History, Richmond, Va.

57. N. Y. *Herald*, October 28, 1859.

58. Order Book No. 12, p. 428, Court Records of Jefferson County, Charlestown, W. Va.

59. N. Y. *Herald*, October 26, 1859.

60. Ibid.

61. For the arrest of Cook, see circumstantial letters dated Chambersburg, Pa., Oct. 26 and Oct. 29, in the N. Y. *Tribune* of Oct. 29 and Nov. 4, 1859.
62. *Life, Trial and Execution*, pp. 59–61; N. Y. *Herald*, Oct. 30, 1859.
63. N. Y. *Tribune*, Oct. 28, 1859.
64. N. Y. *Herald*, Oct. 27, 1859.
65. Common Law Orders No. 6, p. 281, Court Records of Jefferson County.
66. N. Y. *Herald*, Oct. 28, 1859; *Life, Trial and Execution*, p. 68.
67. N. Y. *Tribune*, Nov. 5, 1859.
68. Common Law Orders No. 6, p. 283, Court Records of Jefferson County.
69. Redpath's *John Brown*, p. 325.
70. N. Y. *Herald*, Oct. 29, 1859.
71. N. Y. *Herald*, Nov. 1, 1859; see also Richmond *Despatch*, Nov. 1, 1859.
72. N. Y. *Tribune*, Oct. 29, 1859.

73. Letter of Wendell Phillips to T. W. Higginson, Oct. 26, 1859, — original in Higginson Collection; of George Sennott to Thaddeus Hyatt, Boston, Dec. 31, 1859, — original in possession of Dr. Thaddeus Hyatt, Brooklyn, N. Y.; testimony of John A. Andrew and of Samuel Chilton, Mason Report, pp. 186–188 and 137–140; Washington *Star*, Nov. 2, 1859. On Nov. 2, Samuel E. Sewall, Dr. Howe, Ralph Waldo Emerson and T. W. Higginson sent out a printed circular appealing for contributions for the defence of Brown and his companions, and offering to act as a committee to receive and apply them. Originals of the circular are preserved in the McKim and the Higginson Collections.

74. Brown's letters to Judges Tilden and Russell were identical. The first will be found in the N. Y. *Tribune*, Oct. 29. The original of the second is in the Kansas Historical Society. Judge Tilden's reply, dated Cleveland, Oct. 27, stating that he was himself unable to serve, but that he was sending Messrs. Griswold and [Albert Gallatin] Riddle, is in the possession of Miss Brown. Mr. Riddle decided, however, because of reluctance to appear with Griswold, not to undertake the case. For this in after years he expressed lasting regret. See *Personal Recollections of War Times*, by Albert Gallatin Riddle, New York, 1895, p. 3.

75. N. Y. *Herald*, Nov. 21, 1859. William Green, of Richmond, a distinguished member of the Virginia bar, was employed to assist Mr. Chilton in presenting Brown's case to the Court of Appeals. Mr. Green's copy of the brief to the Court of Appeals, with his manuscript summary, in his own hand, of the finding of the full bench, is in possession of Miss Sarah Brown.

76. Letter of Andrew Hunter, Charlestown, Oct. 25, 1859, to Gov. Wise, Calendar of Virginia State Papers, vol. 11, p. 87.

77. 'John Brown's Raid,' by Andrew Hunter, New Orleans *Times-Democrat*, Sept. 5, 1887.

78. Letter of George H. Hoyt, Charlestown, Oct. 30, 1859, to J. W. Le Barnes. — Original in Hinton Papers, Kansas Historical Society.

79. Letter of John Brown to his brother Jeremiah, Charlestown, Nov. 12, 1859, *The John Brown Invasion*, Boston, 1860, p. 49.

80. In St. Louis *Globe-Democrat*, April 8, 1888.

81. "His brief speech at Gettysburg will not easily be surpassed by words on any recorded occasion. This and one other American speech, that of John Brown to the court that tried him, and a part of Kossuth's speech at Birmingham, can only be compared with each other, and with no fourth," — said Ralph Waldo Emerson, at the funeral services for Abraham Lincoln, held in Concord, April 19, 1865.

"I'm *so* sorry not to exult with you with joy unutterable over Brown's perfect words. Has anything like it been said in this land or age, so *brave, wise, considerate*

NOTES 647

all round. Slavery & Freedom brought face to face standing opposite; the one all one black wrong, the other white as an angel," wrote W. H. Furness to J. M. McKim, Nov. 3, 1859. — Original in J. M. McKim Papers, Cornell University Library.

82. N. Y. *Herald*, Nov. 3, 1859.

83. Judge Parker in the St. Louis *Globe-Democrat*, April 8, 1888. "Sentence was pronounced and was received in perfect silence, except a slight demonstration of applause from one excited man, whom the Judge instantly ordered into custody. It illustrates the character of the people, that several officials and members of the bar hastened to inform us that this man was not a citizen of the county." — Letter of Judge Thomas Russell, from Charlestown, in Boston *Traveller*, Nov. 5, 1859.

84. Doc. No. XXXI, of the Virginia General Assembly, January 26, 1860.

85. Quoted in the *Liberator*, Nov. 11, 1859.

86. Quoted in the *Liberator*, Nov. 18, 1859.

87. Quoted in the *Liberator*, Nov. 4, 1859.

88. *Liberator*, Oct. 28, 1859.

89. Berryville, Va., *Clarke Journal*, Nov. 11, 1859.

90. Quoted in the *National Anti-Slavery Standard*, Nov. 26, 1859.

91. Original in Dreer Collection.

92. Original in Dreer Collection.

93. Original in the Massachusetts Historical Society. Among those who wrote to Gov. Wise in behalf of clemency was a certain Ellwood Fisher, who feared that if the "obscure whites and negroes" in captivity after Brown's death were hanged, it would be a waiver by Virginia of her "imputations" against the real offenders, the anti-slavery and Black Republican party of the North. — Richmond, Dec. 14, 1859. — Original in Department of Archives and History, Richmond.

94. Document No. 1, Dec. 1859, Journal of the House of Delegates.

95. N. Y. *Herald*, Oct. 28, 1859; *Life, Trial and Execution*, p. 64.

96. N. Y. *Herald*, Oct. 28, 1859.

97. Original in the possession of Mr. Edwin Tatham.

98. See the Governor's autograph endorsement on the above.

99. Original in the possession of Mr. Edwin Tatham.

100. "Blair thinks a demonstration of Brown's insanity might please Wise. He says he has seen something in the Richmond *Enquirer* — probably the st. [statement] he exhibited to Andrew — which looks like an invitation." Hoyt to Le Barnes, Washington, Nov. 14, 1859. — Original in Kansas Historical Society. "Mr. Hoyt ... is now in the city for the purpose of getting affidavits of the acquaintances of Brown as to his sanity. A large number of affidavits have been prepared at Akron, Hudson, Cleveland, etc., and they are made by men of the first respectability, who have known Brown for many years intimately; there is no difference of opinion among them as to the monomania of Brown upon the subject of slavery." Cleveland (Daily) *Leader*, Nov. 18, 1859. The originals of all the affidavits are in the possession of Mr. Edwin Tatham. Hoyt submitted the affidavits, accompanied by a letter to Gov. Wise written in Chilton's name. For this letter, see *Liberator*, Dec. 2, 1859; for a letter by Chilton, denying any hand in the matter and stating his position concerning it, see *National Intelligencer*, Dec. 13, 1859.

101. New York *Semi-Weekly Tribune*, May 27, 1884.

CHAPTER XIV

BY MAN SHALL HIS BLOOD BE SHED

1. T. W. Higginson, *Cheerful Yesterdays*, pp. 147–159.
2. Letter of J. W. Le Barnes to R. J. Hinton. See Hinton's *John Brown and His Men*, p. 366. Hoyt's original sketch of the jail, showing arrangement of cells and stations of guards, as drawn for and remitted to the New England confederates, is now in the Hinton Papers, Kansas Historical Society.
3. S. C. Pomeroy in the *Christian Cynosure*, March 31, 1887.
4. Statement of Mrs. Russell, Jamaica Plain, Mass., Jan. 11, 1908, to K. Mayo.
5. Letter of T. W. Higginson, Worcester, Nov. 4, 1859, to the family of John Brown at North Elba.—Original in possession of Miss Brown.
6. Ibid.
7. Original in Hinton Papers, Kansas Historical Society; see also letter of George H. Hoyt, undated, to "Mr. Tomlinson."—Original in J. M. McKim Papers, Cornell University Library.
8. *Cheerful Yesterdays*, pp. 226–228.
9. J. M. McKim, Philadelphia, Nov. 8, 1859, to T. W. Higginson.—Original in Higginson Collection, Boston Public Library. J. M. McKim's correspondence relating to Mrs. Brown's movements during the month of November is preserved in the Cornell University Library; see also *Life and Letters of Peter and Susan Lesley*, edited by Mary Lesley Ames, New York, 1909, pp. 377–380.
10. Telegram of George Sennott, received in Worcester, Nov. 5, to T. W. Higginson.—Original in Higginson Collection.
11. J. M. McKim to T. W. Higginson, Nov. 8, 1859,—original in Higginson Collection; see also letter of T. W. Higginson to J. M. McKim, Worcester, Nov. 5, 1859,—original in Cornell University Library.
12. Copied in letter of S. G. Howe to T. W. Higginson, Nov. 9, 1859,—original in Higginson Collection; letter of T. W. Higginson to J. M. McKim, Worcester, Nov. 10, 1859,—original in Cornell University Library.
13. *Life of G. L. Stearns*, by F. P. Stearns, p. 187.
14. Reminiscences of James Hanway, Topeka *Commonwealth*, Jan. 31, 1878. This is erroneous as to dates, but is otherwise vouched for by R. J. Hinton, who engineered the Kansas effort to rescue Stevens and Hazlett. S. C. Adair, nephew of John Brown, confirms the story concerning Mary Partridge, in his statement of Oct. 2, 1908, to the author.
15. Memorandum of T. W. Higginson attached to Le Barnes's letter of Nov. 15, 1859, to Higginson.—Original in Higginson Collection.
16. *Cheerful Yesterdays*, p. 166.
17. Le Barnes to T. W. Higginson, Nov. 14 and 15, 1859.—Original in Higginson Collection.
18. *Cheerful Yesterdays*, p. 165.
19. Lysander Spooner to T. W. Higginson, Nov. 20, 1859.—Original in Higginson Collection.
20. Le Barnes to Higginson, Nov. 22, 1859.—Original in Higginson Collection.
21. Ibid.
22. Ibid.
23. Ibid.

NOTES 649

24. Le Barnes, Nov. 27, from New York, to Higginson.— Original in Higginson Collection.
25. Ibid.
26. Ibid.
27. Ibid.
28. Sanborn to Higginson, Nov. 28, 1859.— Original in Higginson Collection.
29. Message of Wise to Legislature of Virginia, Dec. 5, 1859.
30. The character of these letters is well summarized in the report of the Joint Committee of the Legislature of Virginia, Jan. 26, 1860. Many of them have been reprinted in the Richmond *Times* of Dec. 22, 1901, and in the *Virginia Magazine of History and Biography*, April, 1902, to July, 1903. Those cited here are to be found therein, save the one from Lewisburg, which is in the possession of Braxton Davenport Gibson, of Charlestown, West Virginia.
31. Webb Scrap-Book, vol. 17, p. 157, Kansas Historical Society; see also N. Y. *Herald*, Dec. 4 and 17, 1859.
32. Richmond *Despatch*, Nov. 24, 1859.
33. See 'John Brown's Raid,' by Andrew Hunter, New Orleans *Times-Democrat*, Sept. 5, 1887.
34. See Document Y, pp. 31–38.
35. Original in possession of Mr. Edwin Tatham.
36. Richmond *Enquirer*, Nov. 21 and 25, 1859.
37. Richmond *Despatch*, Nov. 15, 1859. For Hoyt's own account of his expulsion, see his letter to the N. Y. *Tribune* of Nov. 17, 1859. Sennott, however, in a letter signed as "Counsel for Brown and A. D. Stevens," in the Philadelphia *Press* of Nov. 16, 1859, denied that Brown's counsel was advised to leave Charlestown.
38. Statement of Cleon Moore, a member of the Charlestown militia company, Charlestown, March 20, 1908, to the author.
39. Ibid., and Charlestown despatch in Baltimore *American* of Nov. 22, 1859.
40. Printed in the *Proceedings* of the Massachusetts Historical Society, May, 1907.
41. Harper's Ferry, Nov. 19, 1859.— Originals of both in Mr. Edwin Tatham's collection.
42. Document Y, pp. 41–50.
43. 'John Brown's Raid,' by Andrew Hunter, New Orleans *Times-Democrat*, Sept. 5, 1887.
44. Gov. Wise's copy of original order of Nov. 24, 1859, in Department of Archives and History, Richmond.
45. Document No. 1, p. 51.
46. Ibid., pp. 52–60.
47. Document Y, p. 62.
48. Mr. Hunter, in New Orleans *Times-Democrat*, Sept. 5, 1887.
49. Document Y, p. 62.
50. See, for example, quotation from Charlestown *Spirit of Jefferson*, in Richmond *Enquirer* of Dec. 13, 1859, and the *Enquirer's* editorial of that date; Baltimore *Exchange* of Dec. 9; also *Life of Henry A. Wise*, by Barton H. Wise, p. 255. Later, in a speech at the State Whig Convention of 1860, John Minor Botts ridiculed Gov. Wise and his "men in buckram," calling him the "unepauletted hero of the Osawatomie war." "Whatever John Brown left undone against the peace and prosperity of Virginia," declared Mr. Botts, "has been most effectually carried out by his executor, the late Governor of Virginia." From *Four Years Under Marse Robert*, by Major Robert Stiles, New York, 1904, p. 32.

51. Document No. XXXI, Virginia State Papers, p. 6.
52. *Life of Henry A. Wise*, by Barton H. Wise, pp. 263–264.
53. Ibid., p. 405.
54. Major-Gen. William B. Taliaferro to Governor Wise, Charlestown, Dec. 2, 1859. — Original in possession of Mr. Edwin Tatham.
55. *John Brown's Expedition*, Reviewed in a Letter from Rev. Theodore Parker, at Rome, to Francis Jackson, Boston. Boston, 1860 (pamphlet), p. 7.
56. Higginson to Sanborn, Worcester, Feb. 3, 1860. — Original in Higginson Collection, Boston Public Library. This letter never was sent.
57. *Life and Times of Frederick Douglass*, by Himself, p. 343 et seq. and p. 358; see also Douglass's self-justification in his paper, the *North Star*, of Nov. 4, 1859.
58. Sanborn, *Recollections of Seventy Years*, vol. 1, pp. 188 and 200.
59. Original in Higginson Collection.
60. Sanborn, *Recollections of Seventy Years*, vol. 1, p. 188.
61. J. A. Andrew to G. L. Stearns, Oct. 21, 1859. — Original in G. L. Stearns Papers.
62. *Life of George L. Stearns*, by F. P. Stearns, pp. 188 and 198.
63. John A. Andrew to Hon. William Pitt Fessenden, Boston, Dec. 12, 1859. — Original in possession of the author.
64. See N. Y. *Tribune*, Nov. 16, 1859.
65. *Recollections of Seventy Years*, pp. 228–230; see also Sanborn's *Life and Letters of John Brown*, pp. 438 and 447.
66. See a first draft of a letter dated Nov. 15, 1859, now in the Higginson Collection, for an emphatic statement of Mr. Higginson's feeling at that time about Dr. Howe's conduct.
67. See letter of Higginson to Sanborn, Worcester, Nov. 15, 1859; also letter of Sanborn to Higginson, Concord, Nov. 17, 1859. — Both originals in Higginson Collection.
68. S. G. Howe to T. W. Higginson, Boston, Feb. 16, 1860. — Original in Higginson Collection.
69. Ibid.
70. See F. B. Sanborn's letter to the N. Y. *Evening Post*, dated March 15, 1878, quoted in *Recollections of Seventy Years*, p. 230.
71. F. B. Sanborn to T. W. Higginson, Concord, Nov. 17, 1859. — Original in Higginson Collection.
72. A first draft of this letter is also in the Higginson Collection.
73. Sanborn, *Recollections of Seventy Years*, p. 250. For the original of the letter here cited, see F. B. Sanborn to T. W. Higginson, Concord, Nov. 19, 1859, in Higginson Collection. In *Recollections of Seventy Years*, Mr. Sanborn recounts circumstantially his experiences in this connection. Other related matter will be found in the Higginson Collection, and also in Mr. Sanborn's letters to Charles Sumner in the month of April, 1860. — Originals in Sumner Correspondence, Library of Harvard University.
74. Sanborn, *Recollections*, pp. 206–207.
75. See letter of G. L. Stearns to S. G. Howe, Philadelphia, Feb. 27, 1860. — Original in G. L. Stearns Papers.
76. Ibid.
77. Mason Report, p. 242.
78. Frothingham's *Gerrit Smith* (suppressed edition), p. 244.
79. See letter of Sanborn to Higginson of Nov. 17, 1859. — Original in Higginson Collection. Cf. *Recollections of Seventy Years*, p. 196; see also Sanborn's *Life and Letters of John Brown*, p. 438, and Frothingham's *Gerrit Smith*, pp. 242–243.

NOTES 651

80. Testimony of John Brown, Jr., taken before a United States Commissioner in the case of Gerrit Smith *vs.* the [Chicago] *Tribune* Company, at Sandusky, Ohio, July 19, 1867, — Mr. Horace White's copy of this, in the handwriting of the stenographer who took the notes, is in the author's possession; Sanborn's *Recollections,* pp. 196–197.

81. Frothingham's *Gerrit Smith* (suppressed edition), p. 249.

82. Gerrit Smith's Manifesto, ibid., pp. 253–255.

83. Ibid., p. 241. The editor of the Chicago *Tribune* in 1867, Mr. Horace White, a man of highest integrity and judicial temperament, when his paper was sued for libel by Gerrit Smith for asserting that the latter feigned insanity in order to escape the consequences of the raid, made an investigation of his own, taking the testimony of John Brown, Jr., and Frederick Douglass, and became fully convinced that the assertion was true. The *Tribune* retracted its charge, but Mr. White remains of the same opinion.

84. Original in possession of Miss Brown.

Well might the words written by another anti-slavery worker, when confined in a Southern prison for attacking slavery, have been penned of John Brown at this time:

> "High walls and huge the BODY may confine,
> And iron gates obstruct the prisoner's gaze,
> And massive bolts may baffle his design,
> And vigilant keepers watch his devious ways;
> Yet scorns the immortal MIND this base control!
> No chains can bind it, and no cell enclose:
> Swifter than light, it flies from pole to pole,
> And, in a flash, from earth to heaven it goes!"

From a sonnet, 'Freedom of the Mind,' by William Lloyd Garrison. — *Life of William Lloyd Garrison,* vol. I, p. 179.

85. Col. William Fellows, a jail guard, in N. Y. *Sun,* Feb. 13, 1898.

86. *The John Brown Invasion,* pp. 47–48.

87. Original in Dreer Collection.

88. John Brown to "Wife & Children *every one*," Charlestown, Nov. 8, 1859.— Original in possession of Mrs. Clara Endicott Debuchy, Boston, Mass.

89. From copy in possession of Miss Brown.

90. From the original in the possession of Theodore Parker Adams, Plymouth, Mass.

91. John Brown to Rev. Luther Humphrey. — Original in possession of Messrs. D. R. and William G. Taylor, Cleveland, Ohio.

92. Original in Higginson Collection.

93. N. Y. *Tribune,* Nov. 5, 1859.

94. N. Y. *Herald,* Oct. 31, 1859.

95. From MS. of the late Rev. George V. Leech, who was present at this interview. — Original in possession of Mrs. George V. Leech, Washington D. C.

96. Letter of Nov. 23, 1859; Redpath's *Life,* p. 359.

97. See issue of *Independent Democrat* of Nov. 22, 1859.

98. Statement of Mrs. Russell, Jan. 11, 1908, to K. Mayo.

99. See letter of Thomas Russell to C. A. Foster, Plymouth, Mass. — Original in Hinton Papers, Kansas Historical Society; Mr. Phillips's speech will be found in the N. Y. *Herald* of Dec. 16, 1859.

100. T. W. Higginson to the family at North Elba, Worcester, Nov. 4, 1859. — Original in possession of Miss Brown.

101. Mrs. Spring's MS. narrative is in the possession of the author.

102. Statement of E. A. Brackett to K. Mayo, Winchester, Jan. 13, 1908; for Hoyt's letter, and a *Liberator* editorial, relating to this bust, see the *Liberator*, Jan. 6, 1860.

103. See letter of M. B. Lowry in the *True American*, Nov. 26, 1859; *A Tribute of Gratitude to the Hon. M. B. Lowry*, Philadelphia, 1869 (pamphlet), p. 31; letter of Gov. Wise to B. F. Sloan, Richmond, Dec. 10, 1859, — original in Dreer Collection; letter of M. B. Lowry to Mrs. John Brown, Erie, Pa., Dec. 3, 1859, — original in possession of Miss Brown.

104. See S. C. Pomeroy's letter in the *Christian Cynosure* of March 31, 1887.

105. Richmond *Enquirer*, Nov. 29, 1859, quoting correspondence of Baltimore *American*; *John Brown*, by Henry Clay Pate.

106. Telegram of Col. Davis to Gov. Wise, Nov. 19, 1859, — original in possession of Mr. Edwin Tatham; N. Y. *Herald*, Nov. 22, 23 and Dec. 3; N. Y. *Tribune*, Nov. 30; Richmond *Enquirer*, Nov. 25 and 29, 1859, citing correspondence of Baltimore *American*.

107. *The Two Rebellions, or Treason Unmasked*, by a Virginian, Richmond, 1865, p. 97.

108. Richmond *Daily Despatch*, Nov. 24, 1859. "A member of a volunteer company who visited Old Brown some days ago, was put under arrest and sent home under an escort for having observed to Brown that he would like to have the pleasure of putting a rope around his neck." — N. Y. *Herald*, Dec. 4, 1859.

109. See Cooper Union speech of Wendell Phillips, reported in N. Y. *Herald*, Dec. 16, 1859.

110. *Henry A. Wise*, by Barton H. Wise, pp. 249–250.

111. Mason Report, pp. 67–68. A MS. copy of the letter, now in the Dreer Collection, bears the following endorsement in Gov. Wise's hand: "This was prepared from a promise made to me after a statement made in presence of Brig. Genl. William C. Scott of Powhatan. H. A. WISE."

112. J. M. McKim to T. W. Higginson, Philadelphia, Nov. 8 and 11, 1859, — original in Higginson Collection; T. W. Higginson to Mrs. John Brown, Worcester, Nov. 13, 1859, — original in possession of Miss Brown; J. M. McKim to John Brown, Philadelphia, Nov. 22, 1859, — original in possession of Miss Brown.

113. Mary D. Brown to the Hon. H. A. Wise, Philadelphia, Nov. 21, 1859, — original in Dreer Collection; J. M. McKim to T. W. Higginson, Philadelphia, Nov. 23, 1859, — original in Higginson Collection.

114. The originals of both letters of Gov. Wise to Mrs. Brown are in the Dreer Collection.

115. See draft of telegram in Gov. Wise's hand, endorsed on telegram of Gen. Taliaferro, Charlestown, Nov. 30, 1859. — Original in Dreer Collection.

116. Richmond *Enquirer*, Dec. 6, 1859, citing correspondence of Baltimore *American*.

117. See letter of J. M. McKim, unsigned, dated Nov. 28, in *National Anti-Slavery Standard*, Dec. 3, 1859.

118. For accounts of the meeting, see N. Y. *Tribune* and N. Y. *Herald* of Dec. 3 and 5, 1859.

119. Testimony of Andrew Hunter, Mason Report, p. 67; see also 'John Brown's Raid,' by Andrew Hunter, New Orleans *Times-Democrat*, Sept. 5, 1887. This will, dated Dec. 2, 1859, is recorded in Will Book No. 16, p. 143, of Jefferson County Court Records.

120. Original in the George L. Stearns Papers, Medford, Mass.

121. Original in Dreer Collection.

NOTES 653

122. The passages marked are thus given in the N. Y. *Illustrated News* of Dec. 10, 1859:
"Genesis XV, 13, 14; XL, 11, 12, 13, 55, 56, 57; L, 15 to 21. Exodus I, all; II, 3, 4, 11 to 15; III, 7, 12 to 22; V, 13 to 23; VI, 4 and 5; XV, 1 to 13; XVIII, 9 to 11; XXI, 5 to 10, 15, 26 to 34; XXII, 21 to 24; XXIII, 1 to 9. Leviticus XXIV, 13, 15, 18, 33 to 37; XXV, 8 to 17, 35 to 55; XXVI, 13, 35, 36. Deuteronomy I, 17; X, 17 to 19; XV, 12 to 19; XVI, 11 to 14; XXI, 10 to 14; XXIII, 15 to 17; XXIV, 7, 14 to 18, 22. Job XXIV, 17 to 19; XXIX, 12 to 14; XXXI, 13 to 16, 38 to 40. Proverbs XIV, 20 to 22, 31; XXII, 16, 22, 23. Ecclesiastes IV, 1, 2; III, 16, 17; V, 8, 9; VII, 7. Isaiah IX, 13 to 17; XXXIII, 15; XLII, 7; XLIX, 24 to 26; LII, 5; LIV, 14; LXI, 3 to 8; LXIV, 3 to 15; LXI, 1, 2. Jeremiah II, 8, 34, 35; V, 13, 14, 25 to 31; VI, 13 to 17; VII, 1 to 9; VIII, 10 to 12; IX, 1 to 10, 23, 24; XII, 1 to 4. Matthew V, 16 to 44; VII, 16 to 19; IX, 13; XII, 7; XXIII, 14, 23, 29 to 35; XXV, 44 to 46. Revelations XVIII, 13." This Bible, originally presented to John H. Blessing, of Charlestown, is now in the possession of Mr. Frank G. Logan, of Chicago.

123. The original of this letter, with its enclosures, is in the Dreer Collection.

124. Col. William Fellows, in N. Y. *Sun* of Feb. 13, 1898.

125. N. Y. *Tribune* and N. Y. *Herald*, Dec. 3, 1859; Dr. Starry's 'Recollections, in Semi-Weekly *Tribune*, May 27, 1884.

126. Col. William Fellows, in N. Y. *Sun* of Feb. 13, 1898.

127. Original in possession of Mr. Frank G. Logan, of Chicago.

128. General Turner Ashby was born in Rose Hill, Fauquier County, Virginia, in 1824. A planter and a local politician, at the outbreak of the war he raised a regiment, the Seventh Virginia Cavalry, and became its lieutenant-colonel. He was killed in action near Harrisburg, Virginia, June 6, 1862.

129. See Richmond *Enquirer*, Nov. 29, 1859.

130. See letter of J. M. McKim to Mrs. John Brown, Philadelphia, Dec. 2, 1860. — Original in possession of Miss Brown.

131. Statement of Mr. Cleon Moore, Charlestown, March 20, 1908, to K. Mayo; N. Y. *Herald* and N. Y. *Tribune*, Dec. 3, 1859.

132. *Memoirs of Stonewall Jackson*, by his widow, Mary Anna Jackson, Louisville, 1895, p. 131.

133. For Col. Preston's detailed account of the execution, dated Charlestown Dec. 2, 1859, see *Life and Letters of Margaret Junkin Preston*, by Elizabeth Preston Allan, Boston, 1903, pp. 111–117; see also Gen. T. J. Jackson's narrative, in the volume cited above; Murat Halstead's recollections were published in the *Independent*, Dec. 1, 1898; Mr. Andrew Hunter's article in the New Orleans *Times-Democrat* is important here. The author has also consulted, among other sources, aside from local and metropolitan press accounts, the Military Order-Book of the John Brown Raid, Department of Archives, Richmond; Doc. No. XXVIII, Virginia State Papers; military orders in the possession of Mr. Braxton Davenport Gibson, of Charlestown; the affidavit of John Avis (see Appendix), in possession of Rev. Dr. Abner Hopkins, of Charlestown; and the statements of Col. Chew, Mr. Cleon Moore and Mr. L. P. Starry, Charlestown, March, 1908, of Mr. Charles P. Conklyn, Charlestown, April 9, 1909, of Mayor Philip A. Welford, Richmond, April 21, 1909, and of Mr. Jacob Tutwiler, Harper's Ferry, April 14, 1909, all eye-witnesses of the execution, all to K. Mayo.

134. N. Y. *Herald*, Dec. 3, 1859.

135. *Life of John A. Andrew*, by Henry Greenleaf Pearson, Boston, 1904, vol. I, p. 100.

CHAPTER XV

YET SHALL HE LIVE

1. *A Memoir of Hector Tyndale*, Philadelphia, 1882, p. 8; letter of Major T. J. Jackson to his wife, Charlestown, Dec. 2, 1859, cited in *Memoirs of Stonewall Jackson*.
2. Order of Gen. William B. Taliaferro to Andrew E. Kennedy, N. Y. *Herald*, Dec. 5, 1859; Order No. 55, Special Order-Book of the John Brown Raid, Department of Archives and History, Richmond.
3. N. Y. *Herald*, Dec. 6, 1859; see also letter of Alfred M. Barbour, Superintendent of the arsenal, to J. Miller McKim, Harper's Ferry, Dec. 8, 1859, — original in J. M. McKim Collection, Cornell University.
4. Thomas Featherstonhaugh, 'Burial of John Brown's Followers,' *New England Magazine*, April, 1901.
5. Broadside announcement, dated Ravenna, Friday morning, Dec. 2, 1859, in Department of Archives and History, Richmond, Va.
6. See *A Tribute of Respect Commemorative of the Worth and Sacrifice of John Brown of Ossawatomie*, Cleveland, 1859, a pamphlet containing an account of the Cleveland meeting.
7. *Historical Address* delivered 12th of January, 1908, by Horace Howard Furness, Philadelphia, 1908, p. 16; see also *Life and Letters of Peter and Susan Lesley*, p. 379.
8. *Liberator*, Dec. 9, 1859.
9. N. Y. *Herald*, Dec. 5, 1859; *Liberator*, Dec. 9, 1859. Less than two months later, at another meeting, Mr. Garrison said: "The sympathy and admiration now so widely felt for him [John Brown] prove how marvelous has been the change effected in public opinion during thirty years of moral agitation — a change so great, indeed, that whereas, ten years since, there were thousands who could not endure my lightest word of rebuke to the South, they can now easily swallow John Brown whole, and his rifle into the bargain. In firing his gun, he has merely told us what time of day it is. It is high noon, thank God!" — *Liberator*, Feb. 3, 1860.
10. *Herald*, Nov. 20, 1859; *Liberator*, Nov. 25, 1859; *The John Brown Invasion*, pp. 96–110.
11. Horace Howard Furness, *Historical Address* of Jan. 12, 1908, p. 18.
12. N. Y. *Herald*, Dec. 5, 1859.
13. This story of the trip to North Elba with the body is drawn from the N. Y. *Herald*, Dec. 5 and 6; *The John Brown Invasion*, pp. 70–79; and the letter of D. Turner to Dr. Joshua Young, Salem, Jan. 29, 1899, — original in possession of Dr. Young's family, Winchester, Mass.
14. N. Y. *Tribune*, Dec. 12, 1859; *The John Brown Invasion*, pp. 72–79; 'The Funeral of John Brown,' by Rev. Joshua Young, *New England Magazine*, April, 1904.
15. N. Y. *Herald*, Dec. 1859.
16. Boston *Courier* Report of the Union Meeting in Faneuil Hall, Thursday, Dec. 8, 1859; Boston, 1859 (pamphlet).
17. N. Y. *Herald*, Dec. 20, 1859.
18. *Rise and Progress of the Bloody Outbreak at Harper's Ferry* published by the New York Democratic Vigilant Association, New York, 1859 (pamphlet), p. 4.

NOTES 655

19. Cabot's *Emerson*, p. 597; *Life of Henry W. Longfellow*, by Samuel Longfellow, vol. 2, p. 347.
20. Lecture delivered in Worcester, Mass., Dec. 12, reported in Ashtabula, Ohio, *Sentinel*, Dec. 15, 1859.
21. Letter from Theodore Parker at Rome to Francis Jackson, Boston, Nov. 24, 1859; John W. Chadwick's *Theodore Parker*, Boston, 1900, p. 366.
22. Letter of Dec. 4, 1859, to Dr. Henry Drisler, *Life and Letters of Francis Lieber*, edited by Thomas S. Perry, Boston, 1882, pp. 307-308.
23. As reported at the time by Dr. Wilder; see Topeka, Kansas, *Capital*, October, 25, 1908.
24. New York *Herald*, Feb. 28, 1860.
25. *Works of William H. Seward*, Boston, 1884, vol. 4, p. 636.
26. *Congressional Globe*, 36th Congress, 1st session, vol. 50, pp. 553-554.
27. Ibid., p. 61.
28. Delivered Jan. 24, 1860. Cited in Pleasant A. Stovall's *Robert Toombs*, New York, 1892, pp. 169-174.
29. N. Y. *Herald*, Dec. 10, 1859.
30. *Liberator*, Dec. 16, 1859.
31. N. Y. *Herald*, Dec. 15, 1859.
32. Doc. No. XXXI; report of the Joint Committee of the General Assembly of Virginia on the Harper's Ferry Outrages, Jan. 26, 1860.
33. Virginia State Papers, Doc. No. LVIII.
34. *Liberator*, Dec. 16, 1859.
35. Benjamin F. Shambaugh, *Messages and Proclamations of the Governors of Iowa*, Iowa City, 1903, vol. 2, pp. 240-241; for the Minority Protest, see Senate and House Journal of the 8th General Assembly of Iowa.
36. Quoted in the *Liberator*, Dec. 16, 1859.
37. Richmond *Enquirer*, Jan. 17, 1860.
38. Nov. 28, 1859.
39. Dec. 2, 1859.
40. *Weekly Portage Sentinel*, Dec. 7, 1859.
41. Dec. 3 and 7, 1859.
42. *John Brown*, par Victor Hugo, Paris, 1861.
43. Hon. Daniel W. Voorhees. . . . *Speech delivered at Charlestown, Virginia, Nov. 8, 1859*. . . . Tallahassee, Fla. 1860 (pamphlet).
44. N. Y. *Herald*, Dec. 16, 1859.
45. The Coppoc letter is in the N. Y. *Tribune* of Dec. 12, 1859. See also letter of Thomas Winn, Springdale, Iowa, 1st mo. 13, 1860, to Mary A. Brown, — original in possession of Miss Brown; statement of Mrs. Annie Brown Adams, Petrolia, Oct. 2 and 3, 1908.
46. Charles Lenhart, an Iowan, a printer by trade, had led a company of fourteen men in numerous attacks upon the Border Ruffians, making a name for himself as a Free State leader second only to those of Capt. Montgomery and John Brown. He easily found employment in a printing-office in Charlestown, and, professing profound hatred for all Abolitionists, was readily enlisted as a guard. He remained in Charlestown until after the execution of Stevens and Hazlett, when he returned to Kansas. He died in March, 1863, when a first lieutenant in Col. William A. Phillips's Third Regiment of the Indian Brigade. See letter to Leavenworth, Kansas, *Conservative*, May, 1863, by Richard J. Hinton; also Hinton's *John Brown*, pp. 396-397.
47. Confession of Cook and Coppoc on the morning of their execution, Hinton, pp. 402-403; see also N. Y. *Tribune*, Dec. 17, 1859.

48. Richman's *John Brown*, p. 49.
49. Confession of Cook and Coppoc.
50. Statement of Annie Brown Adams, Petrolia, Oct. 2, 1908; an important letter in the extradition proceedings in the case of Hazlett is in the J. Miller McKim Collection, Cornell University Library, signed "C" and dated Carlisle, Nov. 1, 1859; see also *John Brown's Raid*, a pamphlet by W. J. Shearer, comprising a lecture delivered Jan. 17, 1905, at Carlisle, Pa.
51. MS. narrative of Jennie Dunbar Garcelon, October, 1908, in possession of the author; Miss Dunbar's letter to Redpath, Cherry Valley, Ohio, May 7, 1860, — copy in possession of the author; Mrs. Spring's MS. narrative, in possession of the author; see also MS. material in the Kansas Historical Society.
52. Hinton to Higginson, Dec. 13, 1859. — Original in Higginson Collection.
53. T. W. Higginson to his wife, Feb. 17, 1860. — Original in Higginson Collection.
54. Le Barnes to Higginson, Boston, Jan. 11, 1860. — Original in Higginson Collection.
55. See Reminiscences of James Hanway in Topeka *Commonwealth*, Jan. 31, 1878, in Hinton Papers, Kansas Historical Society, and Hinton's letter of April 29, 1894, appended thereto; see also Hinton's *John Brown*, p. 521.
56. James Montgomery (Henry Martin) to T. W. Higginson (Rev. Theo. Brown), — original in T. W. Higginson Collection; *Kansas Historical Society Collections*, vol. 8, p. 215.
57. T. W. Higginson, *Cheerful Yesterdays*, p. 230; letter of Annie Brown, North Elba, Jan. 11, 1860, to T. W. Higginson. — Original in Higginson Collection.
58. W. W. Thayer, Indianapolis, Nov. 15, 1894, to R. J. Hinton, — original in Hinton Papers, Kansas Historical Society; see also interview of Thayer in Weekly *Indiana State Journal*, Indianapolis, Aug. 23, 1893; also *Kansas Historical Society Collections*, vol. 8, p. 215, and Hinton, p. 526, and Hinton Collections.
59. T. W. Higginson's pencilled memorandum of conversation with C. P. Tidd, Feb. 10, 1860, and letter of C. P. Tidd to T. W. Higginson, Jan. 20, 1860. — Originals in Higginson Collection.
60. For the negotiations with the Germans, see Hinton Papers, in Kansas Historical Society, published in vol. 8 of the *Collections*; also letter of Hinton to Higginson, Feb. 18, 1860, in Higginson Collection; Hinton's *John Brown*, p. 525.
61. Higginson in Worcester to Le Barnes in New York, Feb. 15 and 16, 1860. — Original in Hinton Papers, Kansas Historical Society; Hinton, p. 525.
62. O. E. Morse, 'Attempted Rescue of John Brown,' in *Kansas Historical Society Collections*, vol. 8, p. 215. Like Hanway, Col. D. R. Anthony, J. A. Pike and others, Mr. Morse proves the fallibility of the human mind by insisting that the Kansans under Montgomery went East to rescue John Brown, not Stevens and Hazlett. The weight of evidence is clearly on the other side, because of R. J. Hinton's denial of Hanway's statement, and the contemporary letters written by Col. Higginson from Harrisburg to his wife, the preservation of which was a most valuable service to history on Col. Higginson's part. The testimony of W. W. Thayer is also on the side of the later expedition. Curiously enough, J. W. Le Barnes, who, with Hinton and Montgomery, had more to do with the efforts to save Stevens and Hazlett than any one else, and many of whose contemporary letters telling of the plot are preserved, assured Hinton on June 30, 1894, "I never knew anything about the Stevens and Hazlett plan." These lapses of memory will suggest to the reader the difficulty of reconciling the recollections of men contemporary with Brown which has repeatedly confronted the writer.
63. *Kansas Historical Society Collections*, vol. 8, pp. 215-216.

NOTES

64. See original telegram in Higginson Collection.
65. See original telegram in Higginson Collection.
66. *Kansas Historical Society Collections*, vol. 8, pp. 216, 219, 222, 225.
67. Hinton, p. 524; T. W. Higginson, *Cheerful Yesterdays*, p. 232.
68. Original memorandum in Higginson Collection.
69. T. W. Higginson to his wife, Feb. 17, 1860. — Original in Higginson Collection.
70. T. W. Higginson to J. W. Le Barnes, Feb. 17, 1860. — Original in Hinton Papers, Kansas Historical Society.
71. T. W. Higginson to his wife, Harrisburg, Feb. 19, 1860. — Original in Higginson Collection.
72. T. W. Higginson, *Cheerful Yesterdays*, p. 233; Hinton, pp. 501–502; O. E. Morse, in *Kansas Historical Society Collections*, vol. 8, p. 218.
73. Hinton, p. 524.
74. John Letcher to Andrew Hunter, Richmond, Va., Jan. 26, 1860. — Original in Department of Archives and History, Richmond.
75. *Cheerful Yesterdays*, p. 234; W. W. Thayer, in Indianapolis, Ind., *State Journal*, Aug. 23, 1893.
76. Thayer, as above.
77. *Kansas Historical Society Collections*, vol. 8, p. 220; *Cheerful Yesterdays*, p. 231; R. J. Hinton, *The Rebel Invasion of Missouri and Kansas*, Chicago, 1865, pp. 65–66.
78. *Cheerful Yesterdays*, p. 234.
79. Hinton, *John Brown and His Men*, p. 526; Hazlett to Mrs. Rebecca Spring, March 15, 1860. — Original in possession of the author.
80. Aside from that in correlated biographies and in the contemporary press, interesting material regarding the Hyatt case will be found in the letters of John A. Andrew, Horace Greeley, G. L. Stearns, S. E. Sewall and others, to Charles Sumner, in the Sumner Correspondence, Library of Harvard University; see also the letter and scrap-book of Thaddeus Hyatt, kept during his imprisonment and now in possession of his son, Dr. Thaddeus Hyatt, of Brooklyn.
81. June 22, 1860.
82. An admirable outline of the contest for the Speakership is to be found in Rhodes, vol. 2, pp. 418–426.
83. *Congressional Globe*, 36th Congress, 1st session, vol. 50, pp. 29–30.
84. Ibid., p. 124.
85. Quoted in the *Liberator*, Dec. 23, 1859. On Nov. 20, 1859, the N. Y. *Herald* printed the following from its Richmond correspondent: "Every seventy-five men out of a hundred in this community are in favor of disunion at this moment. I have not spoken to a man for four weeks past upon that subject who was not ready to take grounds in favor of a Southern confederacy. A hint from Governor Wise favoring such a project would be followed by a substantial declaration in approval of it in Virginia and the whole South."
86. 'The John Brown Song,' by J. H. Jenkins, N. Y. *Evening Post*, Nov. 27, 1909.
87. Johnston and Browne, *Life of Alexander H. Stephens*, Philadelphia, 1878, p. 367.
88. *Congressional Globe*, vol. 54, Part 1, 36th Congress, 2d session, p. 12.
89. George Hoadley to Salmon P. Chase, Cincinnati, Dec. 3, 1859. — Original in Salmon P. Chase Correspondence, MSS. Department, Library of Congress.
90. "L'Assassinat de la Délivrance par la Liberté" John Brown, par Victor Hugo, Paris, 1861, p. 5.

APPENDIX

A

SAMBO'S MISTAKES

The original document, as written by John Brown, is preserved in the Maryland Historical Society and reads thus: —

CHAP 1ST

Sambo's Mistakes   For the Rams Horn
Mess Editors Notwithstanding I may have committed a few mistakes in the course of a long life like others of my colored brethren yet you will perceive at a glance that I have always been remarkable for a seasonable discovery of my errors and quick perception of the true course. I propose to give you a few illustrations in this and the following chapters. For instance when I was a boy I learned to read but instead of giving my attention to sacred & profane history by which I might have become acquainted with the true character of God & of man learned the true course for individuals, societies, & nations to pursue stored my mind with an endless variety of rational and practical ideas, profited by the experience of millions of others of all ages, fitted myself for the most important stations in life, & fortified my mind with the best & wisest resolutions, & noblest sentiments, & motives, I have spent my whole life devouring silly novels & other miserable trash such as most of newspapers of the day & other popular writings are filled with, thereby unfitting myself for the realities of life & acquiring a taste for nonsense & low wit, so that I have no rellish for sober truth, useful knowledge or practical wisdom. By this means I have passed through life without proffit to myself or others, a mere blank on which nothing worth peruseing is written. But I can see in a twink where I missed it. Another error into which I fell in early life was the notion that chewing & smoking tobacco would make a man of me but little inferior to some of the whites. The money I spent in this way would with the interest of it have enabled me to have relieved a great many sufferers supplyed me with a well selected interesting library, & pa[i]d for a good farm for the support & comfort of my old age; whereas I have now neith[er] books, clothing, the satisfaction of having benefited others nor wher to lay my hoary head. But I can see in a moment where I missed it. Another of the few errors of my life is that I have joined the Free Masons Odd Fellows Sons of Temperance, & a score of other secret societies instead of seeking the company of intelligent

wise & good men from whom I might have learned much that would be interesting, instructive, & useful & have in that way squandered a great amount of most precious time, & money enough sometimes in a single year which if I had then put the same out on interest and kept it so would have kept me always above board given me character, & influence amongst men, or have enabled me to pursue some respectable calling, so that I might employ others to their benefit & improvement, but as it is I have always been poor, in debt, & now obliged to travel about in search of employment as a hostler shoeblack & fiddler. But I retain all my quickness of perception I can see readily where I missed it.

Chap 2d
Sambos Mistakes.

Another error of my riper years has been that when any meeting of colored people has been called in order to consider of any important matter of general interest I have been so eager to display my spouting talents & so tenacious of some trifling theory or other that I have adopted that I have generally lost all sight of the business in hand consumed the time disputing about things of no moment & thereby defeated entirely many important measures calculated to promote the general welfare; but I am happy to say I can see in a minute where I missed it. Another small error of my life (for I never committed great blunders) has been that I never would (for the sake of union in the furtherance of the most vital interests of our race) yield any minor point of difference. In this way I have always had to act with but a few, or more frequently alone & could accomplish nothing worth living for, but I have one comfort, I can see in a minute where I missed it. Another little fault which I have committed is that if in anything another man has failed of coming up to my standard, notwithstanding he might possess many of the most valuable traits & be most admirably adapted to fill some one important post, I would reject him entirely, injure his influence, oppose his measures, and even glory in his defeats while his intentions were good, & his plans well laid. But I have the great satisfaction of being able to say without fear of contradiction that I can see *verry quick* where *I* missed it.

To be continued

Chap 3d
Sambos Mistakes.

Another small mistake which I have made is that I could never bring myself to practise any present self denial although my theories have been excellent. For instance I have bought expensive gay clothing, nice Canes, Watches, Safety Chains, Finger-rings, Breast Pins & many other things of a like nature, thinking I might by that means distinguish myself from the vulgar, as some of the better class of whites do. I have always been of the foremost in getting up

APPENDIX 661

expensive parties, & running after fashionable amusements, and have indulged my appetite freely whenever I had the means (& even with borro[w]ed means) have patronized the dealers in Nuts, Candy, etc., freely & have sometimes bought good suppers & was always a regular customer at Livery stables. By these & many other means I have been unable to benefit my suffering Brethren, & am now but poorly able to keep my own Soul & boddy together; but do not think me thoughtless or dull of apprehention, for I can see at once where I missed it.

Another trifling error of my life has been that I have always expected to secure the favour of the whites by tamely submitting to every species of indignity contempt & wrong, insted of nobly resisting their brutal aggressions from principle & taking my place as a man & assuming the responsibilities of a man a citizen, a husband, a father, a brother, a neighbour, a friend as God required of every one (if his neighbour will allow him to do it;) but I find that I get for all my submission about the same reward that the Southern Slaveocrats render to the Dough-faced Statesmen of the North for being bribed & browbeat, & fooled & cheated, as the Whigs & Democrats love to be, & think themselves highly honored if they may be allowed to lick up the spittle of a Southerner. I say I get the same reward. But I am uncomm[on] quick sighted I can see in a minute where I missed it. Another little blunder which I made *is*, that while I have always been a most zealous Abolitionist I have been constantly at war with my friends about certain religious tenets. I was first a Presbyterian, but I could never think of acting with my Quaker friends for they were the rankest heretiks & the Baptists would be in the water, & the Methodists denied the doctrine of Election, etc. & later years since becoming enlightened by Garrison, Abby Kelley and other really benevolent persons I have been spending all my force on my friends who love the Sabbath, & have felt that all was at stake on that point just as it has proved to be of late in France in the abolition of Slavery in their colonies. Now I cannot doubt, Mess Editors, notwithstanding I have been unsuccessful, that you will allow me full credit for my *peculiar* quick-sightedness. I can see in one second where I missed it.

B

JOHN BROWN'S COVENANT FOR THE ENLISTMENT OF HIS VOLUNTEER-REGULAR COMPANY. August, 1856

KANSAS TERRITORY, A. D. 1856

1. *The Covenant.*

We whose names are found on these & the next following pages do hereby enlist ourselves to serve in the Free State cause under John

Brown as commander during the full period of time affixed to our names respectively: and we severally pledge our word and sacred honor to said Commander; and to each other, that during the time for which we have enlisted we will faithfully and punctually perform our duty (in such capacity or place as may be assigned to us by a Majority of all the votes of those associated with us or of the companies to which we may belong as the case may be) as a regular volunteer force for the maintenance of the rights and liberties of the Free State citizens of Kansas: and we further agree that as individuals we will conform to the *by Laws of this association &* that *we will insist* on their regular and punctual *enforcement* as a first and last duty; and in short that we will observe and maintain a strict an[d] thorough military discipline at all times untill our term of service expires.

Names, date of enlistment, and term of service on next Pages. Term of service omitted for want of room (principally for the War.)

2. *Names and date of enlistment.*

Aug. 22. Wm. Partridge (imprisoned), John Salathiel, S. Z. Brown, John Goodell, L. F. Parsons, N. B. Phelps, Wm. B. Harris.
Aug. 23. Jason Brown (son of commander; imprisoned.)
Aug. 24. J. Benjamin (imprisoned)
Aug. 25. Cyrus Tator, R. Reynolds (imprisoned), Noah Fraze (1st Lieut.), Wm. Miller, John P. Glenn, Wm. Quick, M. D. Lane, Amos Alderman, August Bondie, Charles Kaiser (murdered Aug. 30), Freeman Austin (aged 57 years), Samuel Hauser, John W. Foy, Jas. H. Holmes (Capt).
Aug. 26. Geo. Partridge (killed Aug. 30), Wm. A. Sears.
Aug. 27. S. H. Wright.
Aug. 29. B. Darrach (Surgeon), Saml. Farrar.
Sept. 8. Timothy Kelley, Jas. Andrews.
Sept. 9. W. H. Leman, Charles Oliver, D. H. Hurd.
Sept. 15. Wm. F. Harris.
Sept. 16. Saml. Geer (Commissary).

3. *Bylaws of the Free-State regular Volunteers of Kansas enlisted under the command of John Brown.*

Article 1st. Those who agree to be governed by the following articles & whose names are appended will be known as the Kansas regulars.

Article 2d. Every officer connected with this organization (except the Commander already named) shall be elected by a majority of the members *if* above a Captain; & if a Captain or under a Captain, by a majority of the company to which they belong.

Article 3d. All vacancies shall be filled by vote of the majority of members; or companies as the case may be: & all members shall be alike eligible to the highest office.

APPENDIX 663

Article 4th. All trials of officers or of privates for misconduct shall be by a jury of Twelve chosen by a majority of members of company or companies as the case may be. each Company shall try its own members.

Article 5th. All valuable property taken by honorable warfare from the enemy, shall be held as the property of the whole company or companies as the case may be equally, without distinction; to be used for the common benefit, or be placed in the hands of responsible agents for sale: the proceeds to be divided as nearly equally amongst the company or *companies* capturing it as may be. except that no person shall be entitled to any dividend from property taken * before he entered the service; and any person guilty of desertion, or convicted of gross violations of his obligations to those with whom he should act, whether officer or private, shall forfeit his interest in all dividends made after such misconduct has occurred.

Article 6th. All property captured shall be delivered to the receiver of the force or company, as the case may be; whose duty it shall be to make a full inventory of the same (assisted by such person, or persons as may be chosen for that purpose), a copy of which shall be made into the books of this organization and held subject to examination by any member, on all suitable occasions.

Article 7th. The Receiver shall give his receipts in a book for that purpose for all moneys & other property of the Regulars placed in his hands and keep an inventory of the same and make copy as provided in Article VI.

Article 8th. Captured articles when used for the benefit of the members shall be receipted for by the Commissary the same as moneyes placed in his hands. the receivers to hold said receipts.

Article 9th. A disorderly retreat shall not be suffered at any time and every officer and private, be, and is by this article fully empowered to prevent the same by force if need be, & any attempt at leaving the ground be and during a fight is hereby declared disorderly, unless the consent or direction of the officer then in command have authorized the same.

Article 10th. A disorderly attack or charge shall not be suffered at any time.

Article 11th. When in camp a thorough watch both regular and picket shall be maintained both by day and by night, and visitors shall not be suffered to pass or repass without leave from the Captain of the Guard and under common or ordinary circumstances it is expected that the Officers will cheerfully share this service with the privates for examples sake.

Article 12th. Keeping up fires or lights after dark, or firing of guns pistols or caps, or boisterous talking while in camp shall not be allowed except for fires and lights when unavoidable.

* As far as the word "taken," the document is written in John Brown's hand, as is Article 23; the remainder is in another chirography.

Article 13th. When in camp neither officers nor privates shall be allowed to leave without consent of the Officer then in command.

Article 14th. All uncivil, ungentlemanly, profane, vulgar talk or conversation shall be discountenanced.

Article 15th. All acts of petty theft needless waste of property of the members or of citizens is hereby declared disorderly, together with all uncivil and unkind treatment of citizens or of prisoners.

Article 16th. In all cases of capturing property, a sufficient number of men shall be detailed to take charge of the same, all others shall keep in their position.

Article 17th. It shall at all times be the duty of the Quarter master to select ground for encampment subject however to the approbation of the commanding officer.

Article 18th. The Commissary shall give receipts in a book for that purpose, for all moneys provisions, and stores put into his hands.

Article 19th. The Officers of Companies shall see that the arms of the same *are in constant good order* and a neglect of this duty shall be deemed disorderly.

Article 20th. No person after having first surrendered himself a prisoner shall be put to death or subjected to corporeal punishment, without first having had the benefit of an impartial trial.

Article 21st. A wagon master and an assistant shall be chosen for each Company whose duty it shall be to take a general oversight and care of the teams, wagons, harness and all other articles of property pertaining thereto: and who shall both be exempt from serving on guard.

Article 22d. The ordinary use, or introduction into the camp of any intoxicating liquors, as a beverage: is hereby declared disorderly.

Article 23d. A majority of Two thirds of all the Members may at any time alter or amend the foregoing articles.

Most of John Brown's recruits had served with the Lawrence Stubbs, among them Luke F. Parsons. W. H. Leeman, whose name appears on the list, stuck to his new commander until his death at Harper's Ferry.

C

JOHN BROWN'S REQUISITION UPON THE NATIONAL KANSAS COMMITTEE FOR AN OUTFIT FOR HIS PROPOSED COMPANY. January, 1857

"Memorandum of articles wanted as an Outfit for Fifty Volunteers to serve under my direction during the Kansas war: or for such specified time as they may each enlist for: together with estimated cost of same delivered in Lawrence or Topeka." — John Brown MSS. Original in Kansas Historical Society.

APPENDIX 665

2	substantial (but not heavy) baggage Waggons with good covers	$200.00
4	good serviceable waggon Horses	400.
2	sets strong plain Harness	50.
100	good Heavy Blankets say @ 2. or 2.50	200.
8	Substantial larg sized Tents	100.
8	large Camp Kettles	12.
50	Tin Basons	5.
50	Iron Spoons	2.
4	plain strong Saddles & Bridles	80.
4	Picket Ropes & Pins	3.
8	Wooden Pails	2.
8	Axes & Helves	12.
8	Frying Pans (large size)	8.
8	Large sized Coffee Pots	10.
8	do do Spiders or bake Ovens	10.
8	do do Tin Pans	6.
12	Spades & Shovels	18.
6	Mattocks	6.
2	Weeks provisions for Men & Horses	150.
	Fund for Horse hire & feed, loss & damage of same	500.
		$1774.

D

JOHN BROWN'S PEACE AGREEMENT

Peace Agreement drafted by John Brown and presented to the meeting at Sugar Mound, Linn County, Kansas, by Captain Montgomery for John Brown.— From the Lawrence *Republican*, December 16, 1858.

Agreement.

The citizens of Linn County, assembled in mass meeting at Mound City, being greatly desirous of securing a permanent peace to the people of the Territory generally, and to those along the border of Missouri in particular, have this day entered into the following agreement and understanding, for our future guidance and action, viz:

Article 1. All criminal processes, against any and all Free-State men, for any action of theirs previous to this date, growing out of difficulties heretofore existing between the Free-State and Pro-Slavery parties, shall be forever discontinued and quashed.

Art. 2. All Free-State men held in confinement for any charges against them, on account of former difficulties, between the Free State and Pro-Slavery parties, to be immediately released and discharged.

Art. 3. All Pro-Slavery men, *known* to have been actively and criminally engaged in the former political difficulties of the Territory, and who have been forcibly expelled, shall be compelled to remain away, as a punishment for their oft repeated and aggravated crimes.

Art. 4. No troops, marshal or other officers of the General Government, shall be either sent or called in to enforce or serve criminal processes against any Free-State man or men, on account of troubles heretofore existing, for any act prior to this date.

Art. 5. All parties shall hereafter in *good faith* discontinue, and thoroughly discountenance acts of *robbery, theft or violence* against others, on account of their *political differences.*

The following recommendation was unanimously agreed to by the meeting: "That we earnestly recommend that all those who have recently taken money or other property from *peaceable* citizens within this county, immediately restore the same to their property owners." The meeting then adjourned peaceably.

A variation of this agreement less offensive to the Pro-Slavery men than Articles 2 and 3 of the above form is also preserved; it was drawn late in December in order to obtain the signatures of men of all parties. It begins: "We the citizens of Kansas and Missouri," and bears date of January 1. This will be found in William Hutchinson's letter in the New York *Times* of January 18, 1859, from Mapleton, Kansas, January 3.

E

SHUBEL MORGAN'S COMPANY

Articles of Agreement of Shubel Morgan's Company, drawn up in July, 1858, in Kagi's writing. — Original in Kansas Historical Society.

We the undersigned, members of Shubel Morgan's Company, hereby agree to be governed by the following Rules: —

I. A gentlemanly and respectful deportment shall at all times and places be maintained toward all persons; and all profane or indecent language shall be avoided in all cases.

II. No intoxicating drinks shall be used as a beverage by any member, or be suffered in camp for such purpose.

III. No member shall leave camp without leave of the commander.

IV. All property captured in any manner shall be subjected to an equal distribution among the members.

V. All acts of petty or other thefts shall be promptly and properly punished, and restitution made as far as possible.

VI. All members shall, so far as able, contribute equally to all necessary labor in or out of camp.

APPENDIX 667

VII. All prisoners who shall properly demean themselves shall be treated with kindness and respect, and shall be punished for crime only after trial and conviction, being allowed a hearing in defence.

VIII. Implicit obedience shall be yielded to all proper orders of the commander or other superior officers.

IX. All arms, ammunition, etc., not strictly private property, shall ever be held subject to, and delivered up on, the order of the commander.

Names	Date, 1858
Shubel Morgan	July 12
C. P. Tidd	" "
J. H. Kagi	" "
A. Wattles	" "
Saml Stevenson	" "
J. Montgomery	" "
T. Homyer	" "
Simon Snyder	" 14
E. W. Snyder	" 15
Elias J. Snyder	" "
John H. Snyder	" "
Adam Bishop	" "
William Hairgrove	" "
John Mikel	" "
Wm. Partridge	" "

F

JOHN BROWN'S WILLS

While in the hospitable home of Judge Thomas Russell, near Boston, on April 13, 1858, John Brown signed a will, that he might duly protect those who had placed funds and other property in his possession for particular purposes. It is still preserved in the G. L. Stearns papers, and reads thus:

"I, John Brown of North Elba, New York, intending to visit Kansas, and knowing the uncertainty of life, make my last will as follows: I give and bequeath all trust funds and personal property for the aid of the Free-State cause in Kansas now in my hands or in the hands of W. H. D. Callender of Hartford, Conn. to George L. Stearns of Medford, Mass., Samuel Cabot, Jr. of Boston, Mass. and William H Russell of New Haven, Conn., to them and the survivor or survivors, and their assigns forever, in trust that they will administer said funds and other property including all now collected by me or in my behalf, for the aid of the free-state cause in Kansas, leaving the manner of so doing entirely to their discretion."

APPENDIX

Another will dated one day later, is also extant, in the papers of Judge Thomas Russell, Jamaica Plain, Mass. This is signed by but one witness, the one above cited having three. While differently phrased, the documents are alike in substance.

Another will, written in prison on the day before his execution, was as follows:

CHARLESTOWN, JEFFERSON CO, VA. 1st December 1859

I give to my Son John Brown Jr my Surveyors Compass & other surveyors articles if found also my old Granite Monument now at North Elba, N. Y. to receive upon its Two sides a further inscription as I will hereafter direct. Said Stone monument however to remain at North Elba, so long as *any of my children or my wife:* may remain there; as residents.

I give to my Son Jason Brown my Silver Watch with my name egraved on iner case.

I give to my Son Owen Brown my double Spry or opera Glass & my Rifle Gun (if found) presented to me at Worcester Mass It is Globe sighted & new. I give also to the same Son Fifty Dollars in cash to be paid him from the proceeds of my Fathers Estate in consideration of his terible sufferings in Kansas: & his cripled condition from his childhood.

I give to my Son Salmon Brown Fifty Dollars in cash to be paid him from my Fathers Estate, as an offset to the first Two cases above named.

I give to my Daughter Ruth Thompson my large old Bible containing family record.

I give each of my sons and to each of my *other* daughters in Law; as good a coppy of the Bible as can be purchased at some Book store in New York or Boston at a cost of Five Dollars each; in Cash to be paid out of the proceeds of my Fathers Estate.

I give to each of my Grand Children that may be living when my Fathers Estate is settled: as good a copy of the Bible as can be purchased (as above) at a cost of $3, Three Dollars each

All the Bibles to be purchased at one and the same time for Cash on best terms.

I desire to have $50, Fifty Dollars *each* paid out of the final proceeds of my Fathers Estate: to the following named persons. To wit to Allen Hammond, Esqr of Rockville Tolland Co, Connecticut, *or* to George Kellogg Esqr: former Agent of the New England Company at that place: *for the use; & benefit of that Company.* Also Fifty Dollars to Silas Havens formerly of Irvinsburg, Summit Co, Ohio, if he can be found. Also Fifty Dollars to a man formerly of Stark Co, Ohio, at Canton who sued my Father in his lifetime Through Judge Humphrey & Mr. Upson of Akron to be paid by J. R. Brown to the man in person if can be found His name I cannot remember My father made a compromise with the man by turning out House & Lot at Monroeville. I desire that any remaining balance that may become my due from my Fathers Estate may be paid in equal

APPENDIX 669

amounts to my Wife & to each of my Children; & to the Widows of Watson & Oliver Brown by my brother Jeremiah R. Brown of Hudson Ohio
JOHN BROWN*
Witnes
JOHN AVIS

Endorsed,
"Copy to be sent to Jeremiah R. Brown."

THE WILL OF DECEMBER 2, 1859

[Will Book No. 16, Page 143, Jefferson Co. West Virginia Court Records, Charlestown.]

John Brown's Will & Codicil

I, John Brown, a prisoner now in the prison of Charlestown, Jefferson County, Virginia, do hereby make and ordain this as my true last Will and Testament. I will and direct that all my property, being personal property, which is scattered about in the States of Virginia and Maryland, should be carefully gathered up by my Executor hereinafter appointed and disposed of to the best advantage, and the proceeds thereof paid over to my beloved wife, Mary A. Brown. Many of these articles are not of a war like character, and I trust as to such and all other property that I may be entitled to that my rights and the rights of my family may be respected: And lastly, I hereby appoint Sheriff James W. Campbell, Executor of this my true last Will, hereby revoking all others.

Witness my hand and seal this 2nd day of December 1859
JOHN BROWN (Seal)

Signed, sealed and declared to be
the true last Will of John
Brown, in our presence, who
attested the same at his request,
in his presence and in the presence of
each other.
JOHN AVIS
ANDREW HUNTER

Codicil. I wish my friends, James W. Campbell, Sheriff, and John Avis, Jailer, as a return for their kindness, each to have a Sharp-rifle of those belonging to me, or if no rifle can be had, then each a pistol.

Witness my hand and seal this 2nd day of December 1859
JOHN BROWN (Seal)

Signed, sealed and declared to be
a codicil to the last Will and testament
of John Brown, in our presence, who attested
the same at his request in his presence, and
in the presence of each other.
ANDREW HUNTER,
JOHN AVIS.

* Every word of this, except Avis's signature, in John Brown's own hand.

VIRGINIA, JEFFERSON COUNTY, *Scr.;* In the County Court, Decr. Term, 1859.

At a Court held for the said County on the 19th day of December, 1859, the foregoing last Will and Testament and Codicil thereto, of John Brown deceased, approved in open Court by the oaths of John Avis, and Andrew Hunter subscribing witnesses thereto, and ordered to be recorded.

Teste T. A. MOORE, Clerk.

G

JOHN AVIS'S AFFIDAVIT AS TO HIS ASSOCIATION WITH JOHN BROWN

(From Original owned by Rev. Abner C. Hopkins, D. D., Charlestown, W. Va.)

I, John Avis, a Justice of the Peace of the County of Jefferson, State of West Virginia, under oath do solemnly declare that I was Deputy Sheriff and Jailor of Jefferson County, Virginia, in 1859 during the whole time that Captain John Brown was in prison & on trial for his conduct in what is familiarly known as the Harper's Ferry Raid; that I was with him daily during the whole period; that the personal relations between him and me were of the most pleasant character; that Sheriff James W. Campbell & I escorted him from his cell the morning of his execution one on either side of him; that Sheriff Campbell & I rode with Captain Brown in a wagon from the jail to the scaffold one on either side; that I heard every word that Captain Brown spoke from the time he left the jail till his death; that Sheriff Campbell (now deceased) and I were the only persons with him on the scaffold.

I have this day read, in the early part of chapter 8 of a book styled 'The Manliness of Christ,' by Thomas Hughes, Q. C., New York: American Book Exchange, Tribune Building, 1880, the following paragraph, to wit: —

"Now I freely admit that there is no recorded end of a life that I know of more entirely brave and manly than the one of Captain John Brown, of which we know every minutest detail, as it happened in the full glare of our northern life not twenty years ago. About that I think there could scarcely be disagreement anywhere. The very men who allowed him to lie in his bloody clothes till the day of his execution, & then hanged him, recognize this. 'You are a game man, Capt. Brown,' the Southern Sheriff said in the wagon. 'Yes,' he answered, 'I was so brought up. It was one of my Mother's lessons. From infancy I have not suffered from physical fear. I have suffered a thousand times more from bashfulness;' and then he kissed a negro child in its mother's arms, and walked cheerfully on to the scaffold, thankful that he was 'allowed to die for a cause and not merely to pay the debt of nature as all must.'"

Respecting the statements contained in the above paragraph quoted from the book above mentioned, I solemnly declare: —

First, that Captain John Brown was not "allowed to lie in his

APPENDIX 671

bloody clothes till the day of his execution," but that he was furnished with a change of clothing as promptly as prisoners in such condition usually are; that he was allowed all the clothing he desired; and that his washing was done at his will without any cost to himself. As an officer charged with his custody, I saw that he was at all times & by all persons treated kindly, properly and respectfully. I have no recollection that there was ever any attempt made to humiliate or maltreat him. Captain Brown took many occasions to thank me for my kindness to him and spoke of it to many persons including his wife. In further proof of the kindness he received at my hands I will state that Captain Brown in his last written will & testament bequeathed to me his Sharpe's Rifle and a pistol. Furthermore, on the night before the execution Captain Brown and his wife, upon my invitation, took supper with me and my family at our table in our residence which was a part of the jail building.

2. I have no recollection that the Sheriff said to Captain Brown, "You are a game man," and received the reply quoted in the above paragraph, or that any similar remarks were made by either parties. I am sure that neither these remarks nor any like them were made at the time. The only remarks made by Captain Brown between his cell and the scaffold were commonplace remarks about the beauty of the country and the weather.

3. The statement that "he kissed a negro child in his mother's arms" is wholly incorrect. Nothing of the sort occurred. Nothing of the sort could have occurred, for his hands, as usual in such cases, were confined behind him before he left the jail; he was between Sheriff Campbell and me, and a guard of soldiers surrounded him, and allowed no person to come between them and the prisoner, from the jail to the scaffold, except his escorts.

4. Respecting the statement that he "walked cheerfully to the scaffold," I will say that I did not think his bearing on the scaffold was conspicuous for its heroism, yet not cowardly.

5. Whether he was "thankful that he was allowed to die for a cause and not merely to pay the debt of nature as all must," or not, I cannot say what was in his heart; but if this clause means, as the quotation marks would indicate, that Captain Brown used any such language or said anything on the subject, it is entirely incorrect. Captain Brown said nothing like it. The only thing that he did say at or on the scaffold was to take leave of us & then just about the time the noose was adjusted he said to me: "Be quick."

(*Signed*) JOHN AVIS

CHARLESTOWN, WEST VIRGINIA,
April 25, 1882.

STATE OF WEST VIRGINIA, COUNTY OF JEFFERSON SS:

I, Cleon Moore, a notary public in and for the County of Jefferson, State aforesaid, hereby certify that John Avis whose name is signed to the foregoing affidavit this day personally appeared before me in my county aforesaid and made oath that the statements contained in said affidavit are true to the best of his knowledge and belief.

Given under my hand and notarial seal at Charlestown, West Virginia, this 25th day of April, 1882.

CLEON MOORE
Notary Public

H

A CHRONOLOGY OF JOHN BROWN'S MOVEMENTS, FROM HIS DEPARTURE FOR KANSAS TO HIS DEATH, DECEMBER 2, 1859

1855

August	13.	Left North Elba with Henry Thompson for Kansas.
	15.	At Akron, Ohio.
		At Hudson, Ohio.
	18.	At Cleveland, Ohio.
	19.	At Detroit.
	20.	Arrived at Chicago.
	23.	Left Chicago for Kansas with his one-horse wagon, and *en route* to Osawatomie until October 6.
October	7.	Arrived at Osawatomie and the Brown claims.
December	6.	Left Osawatomie for the defence of Lawrence.
	7–12.	At Lawrence.
	14.	At the Brown claims near Osawatomie.

1856

January	1.	At West Point, Missouri.
	4.	Back at Osawatomie.
7 and	8.	Returned to Missouri for provisions.
	31.	Returned to Osawatomie from a third trip to Missouri.
Feb. 1–April	15.	In Osawatomie and vicinity.
April	16.	Attended Osawatomie settlers' meeting to resolve against the "bogus law" taxes.
	21.	Attended Judge Cato's court near Lane.
May	22.	Left Osawatomie for relief of Lawrence.
	23.	Left camp of Pottawatomie Rifles and camped one mile above Dutch Henry's Crossing.
	24.	In camp all day; Pottawatomie killings at night.
	25.	About noon left camp, rejoining John Brown, Jr., at Ottawa Jones's, near midnight.
	26.	Left the Pottawatomie Rifles and spent night at Jason Brown's cabin.
	27–31.	In a secluded camp on Ottawa Creek.
June	1.	Moved to Prairie City; searched till late for Pate's command.
	2.	Battle of Black Jack.

June	3–4.	Encamped with prisoners at Middle Ottawa Creek.
	5.	Brown's men disbanded by Colonel E. V. Sumner, First U. S. Cavalry, Major Sedgwick, Lieutenant J. E. B. Stuart.
June 5–July	1.	Hidden in thickets of Middle Ottawa Creek in vicinity of Palmyra.
July	2.	At Lawrence; camping at night one mile southwest of Big Springs.
	3.	Arrived in the early morning on outskirts of Topeka.
	4.	In camp on Willets farm, on Shunganung Creek near Topeka.
	4–22.	Whereabouts unknown.
	23.	Probably left Topeka for Nebraska.
August	3–4.	Met S. J. Reeder on his way to Nemaha Falls, N. T.
	7.	At Nemaha Falls.
	9.	Left Nebraska City.
	10.	Arrived at Topeka.
	10–16.	Whereabouts in doubt.
	17.	At Lawrence on arrival of Walker's prisoners from Fort Titus.
	20.	(About) Reached Osawatomie.
	24.	Brown's and Cline's companies in camp at Sugar Creek, Linn County.
	25.	Searched for a pro-slavery force.
	26.	Encounter with Cline's company; raid on Captain J. E. Brown.
	27.	Raiding.
	28.	Returned to Osawatomie with 150 head of cattle.
	29.	Moved his camp one mile from Osawatomie.
	30.	Battle of Osawatomie.
August 31 –September 6.		In camp at Hauser farm, two and one-half miles from Osawatomie.
September	7.	Arrived in Lawrence with Luke F. Parsons.
	8–14.	In Lawrence.
	15–22.	At Augustus Wattles's home near Lawrence, "with his sons and sons' wives."
October	1.	At Osawatomie, according to his letter of October 11, 1856.
	5.	Narrowly escaped capture by Lieut.-Colonel Cooke near Nebraska City.
	10.	At Tabor, Iowa.
	18.	(About) Left Tabor by stage for Chicago.
	25–26.	At Chicago.
	27.	(About) Started back to Tabor in pursuit of his sons Salmon and Watson.

December	1.	Again in Chicago; left soon to visit Ohio relatives; then went to Albany, Rochester and Peterboro.
	27.	At Frederick Douglass's in Rochester.

1857

January	4–22.	At Boston.
	23–26.	In New York at meeting of National Kansas Committee.
January 27 –February 16.		Visited Rochester, Peterboro and North Elba, and returned to Boston.
February	16–18.	Boston.
	19.	Springfield, Mass.
March	1.	Collinsville, Conn.; first meeting with Blair to contract for pikes.
	4.	Brown's Appeal to Friends of Freedom appeared in New York *Tribune*.
	6.	At Hartford, Conn., and Springfield, Mass.
	9–11.	Canton and Collinsville, Conn.
	12.	Passed this night with R. W. Emerson at Concord.
	13.	At Medford with George L. Stearns and family.
	19.	At New Haven, Conn.
	21–26.	At Worcester (also brief trip to Springfield).
	26–28.	Visiting ex-Governor Reeder at Easton, Pa., with Sanborn and Conway.
	30.	Contracted with Blair at Collinsville for pikes.
Mar. 31–April 2.		At Springfield, Mass.
April	6–15.	In Boston and West Newton; visiting Judge and Mrs. Russell.
	16–20.	In Springfield and vicinity.
	23.	In New Haven, Conn.
	25.	In Springfield, Mass.
	27.	In Troy, New York.
	28.	In Albany, New York.
April 30–May	12.	At North Elba.
May	13.	Left Vergennes, Vermont, for **Kansas**.
	14.	At Canastota, New York.
	15.	At Peterboro, New York.
	21.	At Wayne, Ohio.
	22.	At Cleveland, Ohio.
	23.	At Akron, Ohio.
May 27–June	12.	At Hudson, Ohio; disabled by **sickness**.
June	16.	In Milwaukee, Wisconsin.
	22.	Parted from Gerrit Smith in Chicago.
	24.	At Tallmadge, Ohio.
	29.	Left Cleveland for Iowa.

APPENDIX 675

July	5–6.	Iowa City.
July 7–Aug.	6.	Crossing Iowa.
Aug. 7–Nov.	1.	At Tabor.
November	2.	Left Tabor, parting from Forbes at Nebraska City.
	5.	Arrived at Whitman's farm near Lawrence.
	6.	In consultation with Cook.
	14–16.	At Topeka, with Cook, Realf, Parsons, and Stevens.
	17.	Left Topeka.
	18.	*En route* to Nebraska City.
	22.	(About) Arrived at Tabor, Iowa.
December	4.	Left Tabor for Springdale.
	25.	Passed Marengo, Iowa.
	28 or 29.	Arrived at Springdale.

1858

January	15.	Left Springdale for East.
	21.	At Lindenville, Ohio.
Jan. 28–Feb.	17.	At Frederick Douglass's in Rochester.
February	18–24.	At Peterboro.
Feb. 26–Mar.	3.	With Mr. and Mrs. J. N. Gloucester at Brooklyn.
March	4–7.	At Boston.
	8.	Left Boston for Philadelphia.
	9–16.	At Philadelphia.
	18.	At New Haven, Conn.
	19.	Left New Haven for New York.
	23.	Arrived at North Elba.
Mar. 23–April	1.	At North Elba.
April	2.	At Peterboro.
	3.	Left Peterboro for Rochester.
	4–7.	At Rochester.
	8–12.	At St. Catherine's, Canada.
	13.	In Canada West.
	14.	At St. Catherine's.
	16.	At Ingersoll, Canada West.
	17–24.	In Canada West.
	25.	Passed through Chicago; arrived in Springdale.
	26.	At Springdale.
	27.	Left Springdale at 11.45 A. M.
	28.	Arrived at Chicago.
	29.	Reached Detroit and Chatham, Canada.
April 30–May	29.	At Chatham.
May 8 and	9.	Two conventions met.
	29.	Left Chatham.
	31.	Arrived at Boston.
June	1–3.	At Boston.

APPENDIX

June
- 3. Left Boston for Kansas, via North Elba and Ohio.
- 5. (About) At North Elba.
- 20. Left Cleveland with Tidd and Kagi.
- 22. At Chicago.
- 26. Reached Lawrence, Kansas.
- 27–28. At Lawrence.
- 28. Left Lawrence for southern Kansas.

July
- 1. On the Snyder Claim for a four weeks' stay.
- 9. Visited James Montgomery's cabin.
- 23. Ill of ague.

August
- 3–9. At Augustus Wattles's home near Moneka, Kansas.
- 15. (About) Taken to Rev. Mr. Adair's, at Osawatomie, ill of fever.

September
- 23. In Lawrence.

October
- 7. At Ottumwa, Kansas.
- 11. At Osawatomie.
- 15–16. At Lawrence.
- 22–25. At Osawatomie.

Oct. 30–Nov.
- 1. At Augustus Wattles's.

November.
- Building the Montgomery fort during this month.
- 13. Marched with Montgomery to Paris, Kansas.

December
- 1. Left Snyder Claim with George Gill for Osawatomie.
- 2. Attempt of Captain Weaver and Sheriff McDaniel to capture Brown at Snyder Claim; the latter arrived at Osawatomie.
- 3. At Osawatomie.
- 5. Returned to Montgomery's fort with George Gill.
- 6. Drafted agreement presented to peace meeting at Sugar Mound by Montgomery.
- 16. At Sugar Creek during Montgomery's attack on Fort Scott.
- 16–18. At Wimsett Farm of Jeremiah G. Anderson's brother.
- 20. The raid into Missouri.
- 21. Camped all day in a deep ravine.
- 22. Reached Augustus Wattles's house.
- 22–30. At Wattles's or in the neighborhood, ready to repel invasion from Missouri.
- 30–31. At Wattles's with William Hutchinson.

1859

January
- 1. Went into camp on Turkey Creek.
- 2. Wrote Montgomery asking him to be ready to fight.

APPENDIX 677

January	3.	(About) Visited by George A. Crawford, agent for the Governor and President Buchanan.
	7.	Wrote his "Parallels" at Augustus Wattles's.
	8.	Left Wattles's for the last time.
	10–20.	At Osawatomie.
	20.	With George Gill left Garnett, Kansas, for Lawrence, with the fugitive slaves.
	24.	Reached Major J. B. Abbott's, near Lawrence.
	25.	Left Lawrence going North with the slaves.
	28.	At Holton.
	29.	At Straight or Spring Creek.
	30.	Resting at Spring Creek.
	31.	"Battle of the Spurs;" reached Sabetha.
February	1.	Brown's last day in Kansas. Crossed Nemeha River; entered Nebraska.
	4.	Crossed the Missouri River at Nebraska City.
	5–11.	At Tabor.
	11.	Left Tabor to cross Iowa.
	12.	At Toole's.
	13.	At Lewis Mills's house.
	14.	At Porter's Tavern, Grove City.
	15.	At Dalmanutha.
	16.	At Mr. Murray's, Aurora.
	17.	At Mr. James J. Jordan's.
	18.	Passed through Des Moines; at Mr. Hawley's.
	19.	At Dickerson's.
	20.	Reached Grinnell.
	21–22.	At Grinnell.
	24.	Passed through Iowa City.
	25.	Arrived at Springdale.
Feb. 25–Mar.	9.	At Springdale.
March	9.	Left Springdale for West Liberty.
	10.	Left West Liberty by train for Chicago.
	11.	Arrived at Chicago.
	12.	Arrived at Detroit; saw his slaves ferried over to Windsor.
	12–14.	At Detroit.
	15–24.	At Cleveland.
	25.	In Ashtabula Co., Ohio.
	26.	At Jefferson, Ohio.
	27.	Lectured at Jefferson, Ohio.
	28.	At Cleveland.
April	7.	At Kingsville, Ohio.
	10.	At Rochester.
	11–13.	At Peterboro.
	14.	Left Peterboro for North Elba.
	16.	At Westport, New York.
April 19–May	5.	At North Elba.

May	7.	With F. B. Sanborn at Concord.
	8.	Spoke in Concord Town Hall.
	9.	At Concord and Boston.
May 10–June	2.	At Boston.
June	3.	Left Boston; arrived in Collinsville, Conn.
	4.	Reached New York.
	5–6.	In New York.
	7.	At Troy.
	9.	At Keene, New York.
	10.	At Westport.
	16.	(Probably) Left North Elba for last time.
	18.	At West Andover, Ohio.
	19.	Left West Andover.
	23.	Akron, Ohio, and Pittsburg, Pa.
	23–27.	Bedford Springs, Bedford Co., Pa.
	27–28.	At Chambersburg.
	30.	Left Chambersburg; spent night at Hagerstown, Md.
July	3.	At Sandy Hook, Md. (Harper's Ferry).
	12.	(About) Moved to Kennedy Farm.
August	16–21.	At Chambersburg with Frederick Douglass.
September	27.	At Chambersburg, *en route* to Philadelphia.
	30.	On his way back through Harrisburg.
October	1.	At Chambersburg.
	8.	At Chambersburg.
	16.	(Sunday) Raid began.
	17.	In battle at Harper's Ferry.
	18.	Captured at daybreak.
	19.	Taken to Charlestown jail.
	25.	Trial begun.
November	2.	Sentenced.
December	2.	Executed.

I

JOHN BROWN'S MEN-AT-ARMS

John Brown's band consisted of twenty-one men besides himself, sixteen of whom were white and five colored. Most of the whites he commissioned as officers in his army; according to the best obtainable printed list, Stevens, Cook, Brown's three sons, — Oliver, Owen and Watson, — and Tidd were captains. But this is incomplete. There is conflicting testimony as to whether Hazlett was a captain or a lieutenant. Cook states that only two lieutenants were commissioned, Edwin Coppoc and Dauphin Thompson. Colonel Lee in his official report rates Hazlett, Edwin Coppoc, and Leeman as lieutenants. A captain's commission was found on Leeman's body. Probably William Thompson and J. G. Anderson were also captains. The white private soldiers were Stewart Taylor, Barclay Coppoc, and F. J. Meriam. The colored were Shields Green, Lewis Sheridan Leary, John A. Copeland, Jr., Osborn Perry Anderson, and Dangerfield Newby. The eldest of the band after Brown was Newby, aged forty-four; Owen Brown came next, at thirty-five; all the others were under thirty. Oliver Brown, Barclay Coppoc, and Leeman were not yet twenty-one. The average age of the twenty-one followers was twenty-five years and five months. Only one was of foreign birth; nearly all were of old American stock. Sketches of their lives follow.

John Henry Kagi was the best educated of all the raiders, but was largely self-taught. Many admirably written letters survive as the productions of his pen, in the New York *Tribune*, the New York *Evening Post*, and the *National Era*. He was, moreover, an able man of business, besides being an excellent debater and speaker. He was an expert stenographer and a total abstainer. His father was the respected village blacksmith in Bristolville, Ohio, whose family was of Swiss descent, the name being originally Kägy. John A. Kagi was born at Bristolville, March 15, 1835; and was killed October 17, 1859. In 1854-55 he taught school at Hawkinstown, Virginia, where he obtained a personal knowledge of slavery. This resulted in such abolition manifestations on his part, that he was compelled to leave for Ohio under a pledge never to return to Hawkinstown. Kagi then went to Nebraska City, Nebraska, where he was admitted to the bar. He next entered Kansas with one of General James H. Lane's parties. He enlisted in A. D. Stevens's ("Colonel Whipple's") Second Kansas Militia, and was captured in 1856 by United States troops. Kagi was imprisoned first at Lecompton and then at Tecumseh, but was finally liberated. He was assaulted and severely injured by Judge Elmore, the pro-slavery judge, who struck him over the head with a gold-headed cane, on January 31, 1857. Kagi drew his revolver and shot the Judge in the groin. Elmore then fired three times and shot Kagi over the heart, the bullet being stopped by a memorandum-book. Kagi was long in recovering from his wounds. After a visit to his Ohio home he returned to Kansas and joined John Brown. When in Chambersburg as agent for the raiders, he boarded with Mrs. Mary Rittner.

Aaron Dwight Stevens, in many ways the most interesting and attractive of the personalities gathered around him by John Brown, ran away from home at the age of sixteen, in 1847, and enlisted in a Massachusetts volunteer regiment, in which he served in Mexico during the Mexican War. Later, he enlisted in Company F of the First United States Dragoons, and was tried for "mutiny, engaging in a drunken riot, and assaulting Major George A. H. Blake of his regiment," at Taos, New Mexico, in May, 1855. Stevens was sentenced to death, but this was commuted by President Pierce to imprisonment for three years at hard labor at Fort Leavenworth, from which post he escaped and joined the Free State forces. In these he became colonel of the Second Kansas Militia, under the name of Whipple. Thereafter his story is so intertwined with that of John Brown as to need no retelling here. Stevens came of old Puritan stock, his great-grandfather having been a captain in the Revolutionary army. He was a man of superb bravery and of wonderful physique; he was well over six feet, was blessed with a great sense of humor, and was sustained at the end by his belief in spiritualism. George B. Gill wrote of him in 1860: "Stevens — how gloriously he sang! His was the noblest soul I ever knew. Though owing to his rash, hasty way, I often found occasion to quarrel with him, more so than with any of the others, and though I liked Kagi better than any man I ever knew, our temperaments being adapted to each other, yet I can truly say that Stevens was the most noble man that I ever knew." George H. Hoyt, Brown's counsel, in a letter to J. W. Le Barnes, October 31, 1859, thus recorded his first impression of Stevens at Harper's Ferry: "Stevens is in the same cell with Brown. I have frequent talks with him. He's in a most pitiable condition physically, his wounds being of the most painful and dangerous character. He has now four balls in his body, two of these being about the head and neck. He bears his sufferings with grim and silent fortitude, never complaining and absolutely without hope. He is a splendid looking young fellow. Such black and penetrating eyes! Such an expansive brow! Such a grand chest and limbs! He was the best, and in fact the only man Brown had who was a good soldier, besides being reliable otherwise." Stevens was executed March 16, 1860.

John E. Cook, who could successfully have escaped had he not, against the advice of his comrades, been reckless in his search for food, was born in the summer of 1830, in Haddam, Connecticut. He was of a well-to-do family, and studied law in Brooklyn and New York. He went to Kansas in 1855. His movements from the time of his first meeting with Brown, just after the battle of Black Jack, in June, 1856, until after his capture, are set forth in his "Confession" made while in jail (published at Charlestown as a pamphlet in the middle of November, 1859, for the benefit of Samuel C. Young, who was crippled for life in the fighting at Harper's Ferry). For this confession Cook was severely censured at the time by the friends of Brown; he was even called the "Judas" of the raid. But the document, when examined to-day, obviously contains only facts which are of great historical value, and whose promulgation at the time in no wise injured the case of his fellow raiders. Had it not been made, the result of the trial would have been the same. Cook preceded John Brown to the Harper's Ferry neighborhood by more than a year, there sometimes teaching school, and again living as

APPENDIX 681

a lock-tender, while in the registration of his marriage to Mary V. Kennedy, of Harper's Ferry, April 18, 1859, he was described as a book-agent. He was captured eight miles from Chambersburg, Pennsylvania, October 25, 1859, and hanged on December 16. He was a remarkably fine shot, and had seen much fighting in Kansas. He was reckless, impulsive, indiscreet, but genial, generous and brave.

Charles Plummer Tidd, known as Charles Plummer, died of fever, on the transport Northerner, as a first sergeant of the Twenty-first Massachusetts Volunteers, on February 8, 1862, with the roar of the battle of Roanoke Island in his ears. This he had particularly wished to take part in, for ex-Governor Henry A. Wise was in command of the Confederates, his son, O. Jennings Wise, being killed in the engagement. Tidd had enlisted July 19, 1861, as a private. He was born in Palermo, Maine, in 1834, and changed his name after the raid in order to avoid possible arrest and trial as a Harper's Ferry raider — a precaution of greater importance when he entered the army. He emigrated to Kansas with the party of Dr. Calvin Cutter, of Worcester, in 1856. He joined John Brown's party at Tabor, in 1857, and thereafter, in Canada and elsewhere, was one of Brown's closest associates, returning to Kansas in 1858 as a follower of "Shubel Morgan." He took part in the raid into Missouri. After his escape from Virginia, he visited Massachusetts, Pennsylvania, Ohio, and Canada, and was freely consulted in the plans for rescue of Stevens and Hazlett. "Tidd," writes Mrs. Annie Brown Adams, "had not much education, but good common sense. After the raid he began to study, and tried to repair his deficiencies. He was by no means handsome. He had a quick temper, but was kind-hearted. His rages soon passed and then he tried all he could to repair damages. He was a fine singer and of strong family affections." His grave is No. 40 in the New Berne, N. C., National Cemetery.

Jeremiah Goldsmith Anderson was born April 17, 1833, in Indiana, and was therefore in his twenty-seventh year when killed at Harper's Ferry. He was the son of John Anderson, and was the grandson of slaveholders; his maternal grandfather, Colonel Jacob Westfall, of Tygert Valley, Virginia, was a soldier in the Revolutionary War; he went to school at Galesburg, Illinois, and Kossuth, Iowa; was a peddler, farmer, and employee of a saw-mill, before emigrating to Kansas in August, 1857, where he settled on the Little Osage, Bourbon County, a mile from Fort Bain. He was twice arrested by pro-slaveryites, and for ten weeks imprisoned at Fort Scott; he then became a lieutenant of Captain Montgomery, and was with him in the attack on Captain Anderson's troop of the First U. S. Cavalry. He also witnessed the murder on his own doorstep of a Mr. Denton by Border Ruffians. He was with John Brown on the slave raid into Missouri, and thereafter followed Brown's fortunes. Writing

July 5, 1859, of his determination to continue to fight for freedom, he said: "Millions of fellow-beings require it of us; their cries for help go out to the universe daily and hourly. Whose duty is it to help them? Is it yours? Is it mine? It is every man's, but how few there are to help. But there are a few who dare to answer this call, and dare to answer it in a manner that will make this land of liberty and equality shake to the centre."

Albert Hazlett was born in Pennsylvania, September 21, 1837, and was executed March 16, 1860. George B. Gill says: "I was acquainted with Hazlett well enough in Kansas, yet after all knew but little of him. He was with Montgomery considerably, and was with Stevens on the raid in which Cruise was killed. He was a good-sized, fine-looking fellow, overflowing with good nature and social feelings. . . . Brown got acquainted with him just before leaving Kansas." Before the raid he worked on his brother's farm in western Pennsylvania, joining the others at Kennedy Farm in the early part of September, 1859. To Mrs. Rebecca Spring he wrote on March 15, 1860, the eve of his execution, "Your letter gave me great comfort to know that my body would be taken from this land of chains. . . . I am willing to die in the cause of liberty, if I had ten thousand lives I would willingly lay them all down for the same cause." He was arrested in Carlisle, Pennsylvania, under the name of William Harrison, on October 22, extradited to Virginia, tried and sentenced at the spring term of the Court, and hanged on March 16, 1860.

Edwin Coppoc, brother of Barclay, was captured with Brown in the engine house, tried immediately after him, sentenced on November 2, and hung with Cook on December 16, 1859. The father of the Coppocs died when Edwin was six, the latter having been born June 30, 1835. For nine years thereafter Edwin lived with John Butler, a farmer, near Salem, Ohio, removing then with his mother to Springdale, Iowa. This place he left in the spring of 1858, to become a settler in Kansas. He took no part in the Territorial troubles, and returned to Springdale in the autumn of 1858, when he became acquainted with Brown. He always bore an excellent reputation as an honest, brave, straightforward, well-behaved man, and his death was particularly lamented by many friends. An exemplary prisoner, there were many Southerners who hoped for his pardon. He was buried first in Winona [later in Salem, Ohio], after a public funeral, attended by the entire town. In jail he regretted his situation, wrote his mother of his sorrow that he must die a dishonorable death, and explained that he had not understood what the full consequences of the raid would be. He died with absolute fortitude.

Barclay Coppoc was born at Salem, Ohio, January 4, 1839, and

APPENDIX 683

had not attained his majority at the time of the raid. He escaped from Harper's Ferry, but only to meet a tragic fate in that he was killed by the fall of a train into the Platte River from a trestle forty feet high, the supports of which had been burned away by Confederates. Coppoc was then a first lieutenant in the Third Kansas Infantry, Colonel Montgomery's regiment, having received his commission July 24, 1861. Barclay Coppoc went straight to Iowa after his escape from Harper's Ferry, whither Virginia agents followed to attempt his arrest. He went back to Kansas in 1860, helped to run off some Missouri slaves, and nearly lost his life in a second undertaking of this kind. The accident which ended his life took place at night; he survived his injuries until the next day, September 3, 1861. He was buried at Leavenworth, Kansas. He was in Kansas for a time in the fall of 1856.

William Thompson, son of Roswell Thompson, was born in August, 1833, and was killed October 17, 1859. He married Mary Ann Brown, a neighbor, but no relation of the Brown family. He had no hesitation as to where his duty lay when the call came to help free the slaves. He started for Kansas in 1856, but turned back on meeting the Brown sons, who returned to North Elba in the fall of that year. He was full of fun and good nature, and bore himself unflinchingly when face to face with death. Both William Thompson and his brother Dauphin went to Harper's Ferry without being urged and purely from a sense of right and duty to a great cause.

Dauphin Osgood Thompson, brother of William and also a neighbor of the Browns at North Elba, was born April 17, 1838, and was killed in the engine house on October 18, 1859. He was the brother of William Thompson, who also fell, and of Henry Thompson. Their sister Isabella married Watson Brown. Dauphin Thompson was a handsome, inexperienced, country boy, "more like a girl than a warrior," and "diffident and quiet."

Oliver Brown, the youngest son of John Brown to reach manhood, was born March 9, 1839, at Franklin, Ohio. He went to Kansas in 1855 with his father, returning to North Elba in October, 1856. For a time in 1857 he was at work in Connecticut. He married Martha E. Brewster, April 7, 1858, when but nineteen years old, and died at Harper's Ferry, October 18, 1859, in his twenty-first year. His girl-wife and her baby died early in 1860. "Oliver developed rather slowly," says Miss Sarah Brown. "In his earlier teens he was always pre-occupied, absent-minded, — always reading, and then it was impossible to catch his attention. But in his last few years he came out very fast. His awkwardness left him. He read every solid book that he could find, and was especially fond of Theodore Parker's writings, as was his father. Had Oliver lived, and not killed himself by over-study, he would have made his mark. By his exertions the sale of liquor was stopped at North Elba."

John Anthony Copeland, Jr., a free colored man, was born at Raleigh, North Carolina, August 15, 1834, and executed at Charlestown, December 16, 1859. His parents removed to Oberlin, Ohio, in 1842. He was for some time a student in the preparatory department of Oberlin College, and was enlisted for John Brown in September, 1859, by Lewis Sheridan Leary, his uncle, who was at that time also residing at Oberlin. He was one of the thirty-seven men concerned in the famous Oberlin rescue of a fugitive slave, John Price, for which he was for some time imprisoned at Cleveland. "Copeland," Judge Parker stated in his story of the trials (St. Louis *Globe Democrat*, April 8, 1888), "was the prisoner who impressed me best. He was a free negro. He had been educated, and there was a dignity about him that I could not help liking. He was always manly." Andrew Hunter at the same time was quoted as saying: "Copeland was the cleverest of all the prisoners . . . and behaved better than any of them. If I had had the power and could have concluded to pardon any man among them, he was the man I would have picked out." On November 26, from his cell in Charlestown, Copeland sent a letter to his parents, now in the possession of his sister, Miss Mary Copeland, of Oberlin, Ohio, of which the following is an extract:

"DEAR PARENTS, — my fate as far as man can seal it is sealed, but let this not occassion you any misery for remember the cause in which I was engaged, remember that it was a 'Holy Cause,' one in which men who in every point of vew better than I am have suffered and died, remember that if I must die I die in trying to liberate a few of my poor and oppress people from my condition of serveatud which God in his Holy Writ has hurled his most bitter denunciations against and in which men who were by the color of their faces removed from the direct injurious affect, have already lost their lives and still more remain to meet the same fate which has been by man decided that I must meet."

Stewart Taylor, the only one of the raiders not of American birth, was but twenty-three when killed, having been born October 29, 1836, at Uxbridge, Canada. Of American descent, and a wagonmaker by trade, he went to Iowa in 1853, where in 1858 he became acquainted with John Brown through George B. Gill. He is described as being "heart and soul in the anti-slavery cause. An excellent debater and very fond of studying history. He stayed at home, in Canada, for the winter of 1858–59, and then went to Chicago, thence to Bloomington, Illinois, and thence to Harper's Ferry. He was a very good phonographer [stenographer], rapid and accurate. He was overcome with distress when, getting out of communication with the John Brown movement, he thought for a time that he was

APPENDIX 685

to be left out."—Letter of Jacob L. Taylor, Pine Orchard, Canada West, April 23, 1860, to Richard J. Hinton,—in Hinton Papers, Kansas Historical Society. Taylor was a spiritualist.

William H. Leeman, born March 20, 1839, and killed on October 17, 1859, the youngest of the raiders, had early left home, being of a rather wild disposition. Owen Brown found him hard to control at Springdale. Mrs. Annie Brown Adams writes of him: "He was only a boy. He smoked a good deal and drank sometimes; but perhaps people would not think that so very wicked now. He was very handsome and very attractive." Educated in the public schools of Saco and Hallowell, Maine, he worked in a shoe-factory in Haverhill, Massachusetts, at the age of fourteen. In 1856 he entered Kansas with the second Massachusetts colony of that year, and became a member of John Brown's "Volunteer Regulars" September 9, 1856. He fought well at Osawatomie, when but seventeen years old. George B. Gill says of him that he had "a good intellect with great ingenuity."

Osborn Perry Anderson, colored, survived the raid to die of consumption at Washington, D. C., December 13, 1872. Born July 27, 1830, at West Fallowfield, Pennsylvania, he was in his thirtieth year at the time of the raid, of which and of his escape he left a record in 'A Voice from Harper's Ferry,' which contains, however, many erroneous statements. He learned the printing trade in Canada, where he met John Brown in 1858. After his escape he returned to Canada. During the Civil War, in 1864, he enlisted, became a noncommissioned officer, and was mustered out at the close of the war in Washington.

Francis Jackson Meriam was born November 17, 1837, at Framingham, Massachusetts, and died suddenly November 28, 1865, in New York City, after having served in the army as a captain in the Third South Carolina Colored Infantry. Erratic and unbalanced, he was forever urging wild schemes upon his superiors, and often attempting them. In an engagement under Grant he was severely wounded in the leg. Early in the war he married Minerva Caldwell, of Galena, Illinois. He was in Boston, coming from Canada, on the day of John Brown's execution, but was finally induced by friends to go back to Canada. Mr. Sanborn has characterized Meriam as of "little judgment and in feeble health," but "generous, brave and devoted."

Lewis Sheridan Leary, colored, left a wife and a six months old child at Oberlin, to go to Harper's Ferry. The latter was subsequently educated by James Redpath and Wendell Phillips; the widow, now Mrs. Mary Leary Langston, is still a resident of Lawrence, Kansas. Leary was descended from an Irishman, Jeremiah

APPENDIX

O'Leary, who fought in the Revolution under General Nathanael Greene, and married a woman of mixed blood, partly negro, partly of that Croatan Indian stock of North Carolina, which is believed by some to be lineally descended from the "lost colonists" left by John White on Roanoke Island in 1587. Leary, like his father, was a saddler and harness-maker. In 1857 he went to Oberlin to live, marrying there, and making the acquaintance of John Brown in Cleveland. He survived his terrible wounds for eight hours, during which he was well treated and able to send messages to his family. He is reported as saying: "I am ready to die." His wife was in ignorance of his object when he left home. Leary was born at Fayetteville, North Carolina, March 17, 1835, and was therefore in his twenty-fifth year when killed.

Owen Brown, born November 4, 1824, at Hudson, Ohio, was John Brown's third son, and his stalwart, reliable lieutenant both in Kansas and at Harper's Ferry. It was due largely to his unfaltering determination and great physical strength that the little group of survivors of which he was the leader reached safe havens. After the war he was for some time a grape-grower in Ohio, in association with two of his brothers. Thence he removed to California, where he died, January 9, 1891, in his mountain home, "Brown's Peak," near Pasadena, poor in worldly goods, but with the respect and regard of his neighbors. A marble monument marks his mountain-side grave. He never married. He was, like all the Browns, original in expression and in thought, and not without considerable humor. He was the only one of the five men who escaped from the raid who did not enter the Union army, and he was the last of the raiders to die.

Watson Brown, born at Franklin, Ohio, October 7, 1835, married Isabella M. Thompson in September, 1856, and died of his wounds at Harper's Ferry on October 18, 1859. He was: "Tall and rather fair, with finely knit frame, athletic and active." Of little education, he was a man of marked ability and sterling character, who bore well the family responsibilities which fell to him when all the other men of the clan went to Kansas. His son lived only to his fifth year; his widow later married her husband's cousin, Salmon Brown.

Dangerfield Newby, colored, was born a slave in 1815, in Fauquier County, Virginia. His father, a Scotchman, freed his mulatto children. Newby's wife, from whom he received the touching letters given in the text, was the slave of Jesse Jennings, of Warington, Virginia. She and her children were "sold South" after the raid, but it is said that she subsequently lived in Ohio. The shot that gave to Newby his death-wound cut his throat from ear to ear, the missile being a six-inch spike in lieu of a bullet. Newby was six feet two inches tall, a splendid physical specimen, of light color.

APPENDIX

Shields Green, colored, otherwise known as "Emperor," was born a slave. After the death of his wife, he escaped on a sailing vessel from Charleston, South Carolina, leaving a little son in slavery. He eventually found his way to Rochester, New York, three years after his escape and after a sojourn in Canada. Here he became acquainted with Frederick Douglass, and through him with John Brown, and here he lived as a servant and a clothes-cleaner. He went with Douglass to Chambersburg to meet John Brown, and went on with Brown when Douglass turned back. Several reliable prisoners in the engine house testified to Shields Green's cowardice during the fight. He endeavored to avoid arrest by palming himself off as one of the slaves impressed by Brown. O. P. Anderson, however, speaks of Green's bravery, and declares that Green could have escaped with him, but that the former slave protested that he would go back "to de ole man," even if there was no chance of escape. Owen Brown had a poor opinion of Green's staunchness, after his experience in bringing him down from Chambersburg to the Kennedy Farm. Green's age is said to have been twenty-three years. He was a full-blooded negro.

BIBLIOGRAPHY

I. MANUSCRIPT COLLECTIONS

The Kansas State Historical Society Archives contain one volume of letters and manuscripts written by John Brown or members of his family. They contain also a large set of scrap-books devoted exclusively to John Brown history, and a bequest of the late Col. R. J. Hinton comprises a mass of letters and other manuscript material collected by him when writing his 'John Brown and His Men.' The manuscript executive minutes of the early governors of Kansas, and vast masses of manuscript papers of many Kansas pioneers, make them a prime field of interest for any student of John Brown.

In the Historical Society of Pennsylvania is the Dreer Manuscript Collection, containing letters and papers of Brown and letters and official documents written by and sent to the Virginia authorities at the time of the raid, as well as a volume of the correspondence of President Buchanan. Most of the matter relating to the raid was taken from the State House at Richmond and brought North by Federal soldiers and by Dreer himself. In the collection of Mr. Edwin Tatham of New York City are similar letters and documents which supplement the Dreer collection in a remarkable way. His valuable possessions also bear upon the relation of the State of Virginia to the raid.

Two volumes of John Brown's diaries or note-books, the gift of the late Wendell Phillips Garrison, are in the Boston Public Library, which also owns the priceless Thomas Wentworth Higginson Collection of manuscripts and letters written by John Brown and his New England allies concerning his enterprises. The Public Library at Torrington, Connecticut, the Public Library at Omaha, Nebraska, in its Byron Reed collection of manuscripts, Oberlin College, Ohio, and Haverford College, Pennsylvania, are also possessors of Brown documents. No student of John Brown's life can afford to overlook the collections of the Massachusetts Historical Society, particularly the John Brown papers of the late A. A. Lawrence, or the papers of the late George L. Stearns, some of which are owned by the Kansas Historical Society and some in the possession of the Stearns family, who also own John Brown's autobiography. As will be seen from the Notes, many indispensable letters are in the possession of the various members of the Brown family. In the author's collection are a number of the James H. Holmes papers relating to John Brown, and many valuable papers of the late Col. R. J. Hinton regarding John Brown and Richard Realf. The original Mason Report papers and correspondence are in the Senate archives.

II. BIOGRAPHIES

(Chronologically arranged)

REDPATH, JAMES. — The Public Life of Captain John Brown. — Boston: Thayer and Eldridge. 1860. Pp. 408.
WEBB, RICHARD D. — Life and Letters of Captain John Brown. — London: Smith Elder & Co. 1861. Pp. 453.
SANBORN, FRANKLIN BENJAMIN. — The Life and Letters of John Brown. — Boston: Roberts Bros. 1885. Pp. 645.

HINTON, RICHARD J. — John Brown and his Men. With some Account of the Roads they Travelled to Reach Harper's Ferry. — New York: Funk & Wagnalls Co. 1894. Pp. 752.
CHAMBERLIN, JOSEPH EDGAR. — John Brown. — Boston: Small, Maynard & Company. 1899. Pp. 138.
CONNELLEY, WILLIAM ELSEY. — John Brown. — Topeka, Kansas: Crane & Company. 1900. Pp. 426.
NEWTON, JOHN. — Captain John Brown of Harper's Ferry. — London: T. Fisher Unwin. 1902. Pp. 288.
DU BOIS, W. E. B. — John Brown. — Philadelphia: George W. Jacobs & Company. 1909. Pp. 406.
VILLARD, OSWALD GARRISON. — John Brown, 1800–1859. A Biography Fifty Years After. —Boston and New York: Houghton Mifflin Company. 1910. Pp. 738.

III. MAGAZINE AND OTHER ARTICLES

ADAMS, S. H. — John Brown. Tabor, Iowa, College Monthly. May, 1894.
ALLABEN, A. E. — John Brown as a Popular Hero. Magazine of Western History. November, 1893.
APPLETON, W. S. — John Brown and the Destruction of Slavery. Massachusetts Historical Society Proceedings. Second Series, vol. 14. 1901.
ATKINSON, ELEANOR. — The Soul of John Brown. American Magazine. October, 1909.
BACON, LEONARD, D. D. — The Moral of Harper's Ferry. The New Englander. November, 1859.
BACON, LEONARD WOOLSEY. — John Brown. New Englander and Yale Review. April, 1886. (Review of Sanborn's Life and Letters of John Brown.)
BAUMGARTNER, J. HAMPTON. — Fifty Years after John Brown. Book of the Royal Blue. Published by the Baltimore & Ohio R. R. Co., Baltimore. December, 1909.
BEALE, JAMES. — A Famous War Song. Paper read before the United Service Club, Philadelphia. Printed by the Author. (No date.)
BETZ, I. H. — An Hour with John Brown. The Pennsylvania German. October, 1909.
BOTELER, ALEXANDER R. — Recollections of the John Brown Raid, with comment by F. B. Sanborn. The Century. July, 1883.
BOWMAN, GEORGE E. — Peter Browne's Children. The Mayflower Descendant. January, 1902.
—— —— The Settlement of Peter Browne's Estate. The Mayflower Descendant, January, 1903.
BROWN. — The John Brown Letters: Found in the Virginia State Library in 1901. Virginia Magazine of History and Biography, vols. 9–11. 1901–1903.
BROWN'S FUGITIVES, JOHN. — Anonymous article in Springfield Republican. June 12, 1909.
BROWN, OWEN. — A Letter. Atlantic Monthly. July, 1874.
BUTLER, MRS. E. S. — A Woman's Recollections of John Brown's Stay in Springdale. Midland Monthly. November, 1898.
CHAMBERS, JENNIE. — What a School-Girl saw of John Brown's Raid. Harper's Monthly. January, 1902.
CHAPIN, LOU V. — The Last Days of Old John Brown. Overland Monthly. April, 1899.

BIBLIOGRAPHY 691

CLEMENS, WILL M. — John Brown, the American Reformer. Peterson Magazine. January–August, 1898.
COOKE, G. W. — Brown and Garrison. The American, vol. 11. October, 1885–April, 1886. [Philadelphia].
COPPOC, EDWIN. — [Article on; anonymous] Iowa Historical Records. April, 1895.
COPPOC, REV. J. L. — John Brown and His Cause. Midland Monthly. September, 1895.
COTTERELL, GEORGE. — Sanborn's Life and Letters of John Brown. Brown's Character Estimated. The Academy, London. February 20, 1886.
COURTENAY, AUSTEN M. — The Actual John Brown. Chautauquan. January, 1897.
DAINGERFIELD, JOHN E. P. — John Brown at Harper's Ferry. The Century. June, 1885.
DANA, RICHARD HENRY, JR. — How We Met John Brown. Atlantic Monthly. July, 1871.
DAY, W. G. — John Brown's Invasion of Virginia. Southern Magazine. October, 1873.
EMERY, INA CAPITOLA. — The Hero of Harper's Ferry. Nickell Magazine. June, 1897.
ERB, EDWARD. — An Abolitionist. Pittsburg Post. May 28, 1899.
EWING, THOMAS. — The Struggle for Freedom in Kansas. Cosmopolitan Magazine. May, 1894.
"F., M. H." — The Wife of Capt. John Brown of Osawatomie; a Brave Life. Overland Monthly. October, 1885.
FEATHERSTONHAUGH, THOMAS, M. D. — A Bibliography of John Brown. — Baltimore: The Friedenwald Company. 1897. Pp. 9. Reprint from Publications of the Southern History Association. July, 1897.
—— —— John Brown's Men . . . with a Supplementary Bibliography of John Brown. — Harrisburg, Pa.: Harrisburg Publishing Company. 1899. Pp. 28. Reprinted from Publications of Southern History Association. October, 1899.
—— —— The Final Burial of the Followers of John Brown. New England Magazine. April, 1901.
FELLOWS, COL. WILLIAM. — Saw John Brown Hanged. New York Sun. February 13, 1898.
FLEMING, WALTER L. — The Buford Expedition to Kansas. American Historical Review. October, 1900.
FORSTER, W. E. — Harper's Ferry and "Old Captain Brown." Macmillan's. February, 1860.
GREEN, ISRAEL. — The Capture of John Brown. North American Review. December, 1885.
GRIFFIS, REV. WILLIAM ELIOT. —Refutation of Several Romances about the Execution of John Brown. Southern Historical Society Papers, vol. 13. Richmond, 1885.
GUE, B. F. — John Brown and his Iowa Friends. Midland Monthly. February and March, 1897.
HADLEY, DANIEL B. — Reminiscences of John Brown. McClure's. January, 1898.
HALSTEAD, MURAT. — The Tragedy of John Brown. The Independent. December 1, 1898.
HAMILTON, JAMES CLELAND. — John Brown in Canada. Canadian Magazine. December, 1894.
HARRIS, RANSOM LANGDON. — John Brown and His Followers in Iowa. Midland Monthly. October, 1894.

HASSARD, J. R. G. — The Apology for John Brown. Catholic World. January, 1886.
HAWES, ALEXANDER G. — In Kansas with John Brown. The Californian. July, 1881.
HILL, FREDERICK TREVOR. — Decisive Battles of the Law; The Commonwealth vs. John Brown. Harper's Monthly. July, 1906.
HINTON, RICHARD J. — John Brown and His Men. Frank Leslie's Popular Magazine. June, 1889.
——— ——— Old John Brown and the Men of Harper's Ferry. Time [London]. July, 1890.
HUHNER, LEON. — Some Jewish Associates of John Brown. Magazine of History. September and October, 1908.
HUNTER, ANDREW. — John Brown's Raid. New Orleans Times-Democrat. September 5, 1887.
——— ——— John Brown's Raid. Southern History Association Publications, vol. 1. 1897.
INGALLS, JOHN J. — John Brown's Place in History. North American Review. February, 1894.
ISELY, W. H. — The Sharp's Rifle Episode in Kansas. American Historical Review. April, 1907.
JOYCE, BURR. — John Brown's Raids. St. Louis Globe-Democrat. April 15, 1888.
KEELER, RALPH. — Owen Brown's Escape from Harper's Ferry. Atlantic Monthly. March, 1874.
KEIM, A. R. — John Brown in Richardson County [Nebraska]. — Nebraska State Historical Society Transactions, vol. 2. 1887.
KEITH, JOHN. — John Brown as a Poet. Magazine of Western History. May, 1889.
KIMBALL, GEORGE. — Origin of the John Brown Song. New England Magazine. New Series, vol. 1. December, 1889.
LAMBERTON, JOHN PORTER. — John Brown. — Lippincott's. 1888.
LAMPSON, E. C. — The Black-String Bands. Cleveland Plain-Dealer. October 8, 1899.
LAWRENCE, SAMUEL. — Three Letters. . . . I. John Brown. Old Residents' Historical Association, vol. 1. Lowell, Massachusetts. 1873.
LEE, FRANCIS W. — Letter, giving history of inscription on boulder on the North Elba Farm. Garden and Forest. March 11, 1896.
LEECH, REV. S. V. — The Raid of John Brown into Virginia. The Athenæum of West Virginia University. April 14, 1900.
LEWIS, WALTER. Life of Capt. John Brown. The Academy [London]. February 20, 1886.
LLOYD, FREDERICK. — John Brown among the Pedee Quakers. Annals State Historical Society, Iowa, vol. 4. April–October, 1866.
MCCLELLAN, KATHERINE ELIZABETH. — A Hero's Grave in the Adirondacks. — Saranac Lake, New York: Published by the Author. 1896. Pp. 20.
MCKIM, J. MILLER. — Mrs. Brown and Her Family. National Anti-Slavery Standard. December 3, 1859.
MACLEAN, J. P., Ph. D. — The Shaker Community of Warren County. Ohio Archæological and Historical Society Publications, vol. 10. Columbus. 1901.
MARSHALL, G. A. — Another John Brown Song. The Independent. July 21, 1910.
[THE] MOCK AUCTION. — Hudibras Redivivus. A Review of Osawattomie Sold. A Satire. Southern Literary Messenger. June, 1860.

BIBLIOGRAPHY 693

Morse, J. T., Jr. — Review of F. B. Sanborn's Life and Letters of John Brown. Atlantic Monthly. February, 1886.
Morse, Sidney H. — Editorial Commemoration of the 9th Anniversary of Brown's Execution. The Radical. December, 1868.
Nichols, May E. — John Brown and His Adirondack Grave and Home. National Magazine. July, 1903.
Norton, C. E. — Review of Redpath's "Public Life of Captain John Brown." Atlantic Monthly. March, 1860.
Parker, Judge Richard. — John Brown's Trial. St. Louis Globe-Democrat. April 8, 1888.
Phillips, William A. — Three Interviews with John Brown. Atlantic Monthly. December, 1879.
—— —— Lights and Shadows of Kansas History. Magazine of Western History. May, 1890.
Poindexter, P. — The Capture and Execution of John Brown. Lippincott's. January, 1889.
Robinson's "The Kansas Conflict." Reviewed in the Nation, June 30, 1892.
Rockwell, Joel Clark. — How I Captured John Brown. (A grossly erroneous narrative.) Independent. Vol. 62.
Rosengarten, J. G. — John Brown's Raid. Atlantic Monthly. June, 1865.
Sanborn, F. B. — John Brown in Massachusetts. Atlantic Monthly. April, 1872.
—— —— John Brown and His Friends. Atlantic Monthly. July, 1872.
—— —— The Virginia Campaign of John Brown. Atlantic Monthly. December, 1875.
—— —— A Concord Note Book. The Critic. October, 1895.
—— —— New Hampshire Biography and Autobiography. — Concord, New Hampshire. July, 1905.
—— —— Gerrit Smith and John Brown. The Critic. October, 1905.
—— —— The Real John Brown. Sunday Magazine. July 29, 1906.
—— —— The Early History of Kansas, 1854–1861. Proceedings of Massachusetts Historical Society. February, 1907.
Sanborn's Life and Letters of John Brown. Reviewed in the Nation, October 15, 1885; in The Dial, October, 1885; in the (London) Academy, February 20, 1886; in the Atlantic Monthly, February, 1886.
Scott, Mary A. — Across Country in a Van. Midland Monthly. March, 1897.
Shackleton, Robert, Jr. — John Brown's Raid and its Localities. National Magazine. April, 1893.
—— —— What Support did John Brown Rely Upon? Magazine of American History. April, 1893.
Shaw, Albert. — John Brown in the Adirondacks. Review of Reviews. September, 1896.
Sheldon, Charles M. — God's Angry Men. (Poem.) The Independent. July 21, 1910.
Shoup, Samantha Whipple. — The John Brown Song. The Independent. July 21, 1910.
Small, Charles H. — The Last Letter of John Brown. New England Magazine. July, 1899.
Smith, Narcissa Macy. — Reminiscences of John Brown. Midland Monthly. September, 1895.
Spring, Leverett W. — John Brown at Dutch Henry's Crossing. Lippincott's. January, 1883.
—— —— Catching Old John Brown. Overland Monthly. June, 1883.

Spring, Leverett W. — John Brown and the Destruction of Slavery. Proceedings of the Massachusetts Historical Society. March, 1900.
Stearns, Frank P. — John Brown and his Eastern Friends. New England Magazine. July, 1910.
Stimson, John Ward. — An Overlooked American Shelley [Richard Realf]. The Arena. July, 1903.
Thayer, William [Hardy]. — The Black Strings of 1859. Weekly Indiana State Journal. August 23, 1893. [Interview.]
Todd, J. E. — John Brown's Last Visit to Tabor. Annals of Iowa. April–July, 1898.
Utter, David N. — John Brown of Osawattomie. North American Review. November, 1883.
—— Review of Sanborn's Life of John Brown. The Dial. October, 1885.
Vallandigham, E. N. — John Brown — Modern Hebrew Prophet. Putnam's Magazine. December, 1909.
Van Rensselaer, M. G. — Protest against erecting a Monument on the Adirondack Farm. Garden and Forest. January 29, 1896.
Villard, Oswald Garrison. — How Patrick Higgins met John Brown. Harper's Weekly. June 26, 1909.
Washington, B. C. — The Trial of John Brown. The Green Bag. April, 1899.
Wayland, John W. — One of John Brown's Men [John H. Kagi]. The Pennsylvania German. October, 1909.
Weeks, Stephen B., Ph. D. — The Lost Colony of Roanoke: its Fate and Survival. [In relation to L. S. Leary]. Papers of the American Historical Society. October, 1891.
Wells, John D. — The Scars of War in the Shenandoah. Metropolitan Magazine. August, 1898.
Williams, Harold Parker. — Brookline in the Anti-Slavery Movement. Brookline Historical Society Publications, no. 11. 1900.
Willson, Seelye A. — Owen Brown's Escape from Harper's Ferry. Magazine of Western History. February, 1889.
Witherell, L. R. — Old John Brown. A series of articles in the Davenport (Iowa) Gazette of February and March, 1878.
Wright, Harry Andrew. — John Brown in Springfield. New England Magazine. May, 1894.
Wright, General Marcus J. — The Trial and Execution of John Brown. Papers of the American Historical Association. October, 1890.
—— The Trial of John Brown, its Impartiality and Decorum Vindicated Southern Historical Society Papers, vol. 16.
Young, George W. — Story of John Brown's Capture. [An interview.] The Confederate Veteran. February, 1907.
Young, Rev. Joshua, D. D. — The Funeral of John Brown. New England Magazine. April, 1904.
X. V. B. — John Brown at Akron. Kansas Magazine. Topeka. October, 1873.

IV. AUTHORITIES ON THE KANSAS PERIOD

Adams, F. G., Letter-book of. MSS. In Kansas State Historical Society Library.
Andreas, A. T. — History of the State of Kansas. — Chicago. 1883. Pp. 1616.
Atchison, D. R., Russell, William H., Anderson, Jos. C., Boone, A. G., Stringfellow, B. F., Buford, J. — The Voice of Kansas. Let the South Respond. De Bow's Commercial Review. August, 1856.

BIBLIOGRAPHY 695

BAILEY, JUDGE L. D. — Border Ruffian Troubles in Kansas. Some Newspaper Articles written for the Garden City Sentinel and Kansas Cultivator. . . . Edited by Charles R. Green. — Lyndon, Kansas. July, 1899. Pp. 101.

BLACKMAR, FRANK W. — Charles Robinson. The First Free-State Governor of Kansas. — Topeka: Crane & Co. 1900. Pp. 115.

BREWERTON, G. DOUGLAS. — The War in Kansas. — New York: Derby and Jackson. 1856. Pp. 400.

BRIGGS, C. W. — The Reign of Terror in Kansas. — Boston. 1856.

BROWN, G. W. — The Rescue of Kansas from Slavery, with False Claims Corrected. — Rockford, Ill.: The Author. 1902. Pp. 160.

—— —— Reminiscences of Old John Brown. . . . — Rockford, Ill.: Abraham E. Smith. 1880. Pp. 80.

—— —— Reminiscences of Gov. R. J. Walker. — Rockford, Ill.: Printed and Published by the Author. 1902. Pp. 204.

BROWN, SPENCER KELLOGG. — His Life in Kansas and his Death as a Spy, 1842–1863, as disclosed in his diary. Edited by George Gardner Smith. — New York: D. Appleton & Co. 1903. Pp. 380.

COLT, MRS. MIRIAM DAVIS. — Went to Kansas. . . . — Watertown: L. Ingalls & Co. 1862. Pp. 294.

CONNELLEY, WILLIAM ELSEY. — An Appeal to the Record. — Topeka, Kansas: Published by the author. Pp. 130.

—— —— James Henry Lane. — Topeka: Crane & Company. 1899. Pp. 126.

CORDLEY, REV. RICHARD, D. D. — History of Lawrence, Kansas. — Lawrence, Kansas: E. F. Caldwell. 1895. Pp. 269.

DOY, JOHN, OF LAWRENCE, KANSAS, Narrative of. — New York: Thomas Halman. 1860. Pp. 132.

ELLIOTT, R. G. — Foot-Notes on Kansas History. — Lawrence, Kansas. 1906. Pp. 30. Pamphlet.

GIHON, JOHN H. — Geary and Kansas. — Phila.: J. H. C. Whiting. 1857. Pp. 348.

GLADSTONE, THOMAS H. — Kansas; or Squatter Life and Border Warfare in the Far West. — London: G. Routledge & Co. 1857. Pp. 295.

GOODLANDER, C. W. — Memoirs and Recollections of the Early Days of Fort Scott. — Fort Scott, Kansas. 1899. Pp. 79.

HIGGINSON, THOMAS WENTWORTH. — A Ride Through Kansas. — Pamphlet privately printed. 1857. Pp. 24.

HOLLOWAY, J. N. — History of Kansas. . . . — Lafayette, Ind.: James, Emmons & Co. 1868. Pp. 584.

HOWARD REPORT. — Report of the Special Committee appointed to Investigate the Troubles in Kansas. . . . — 34th Congress, 1st Session. Report No. 200. — Washington: Cornelius Wendell. 1856. Pp. 1206.

HUGHES, THOMAS. — A Sketch of the History of the United States, by J. M. Ludlow, to which is added "The Struggle for Kansas," by Thomas Hughes. — London: Macmillan & Co. 1862. Pp. 404.

JOHNSON, OLIVER. — The Abolitionists Vindicated, in a Review of Eli Thayer's Paper on the N. E. Emigrant Aid Company. — Worcester: F. P. Rice. 1887,

JOHNSON, W. A. — History of Anderson County, Kansas. — Garnett, Kansas: Kauffman & Iler. 1877. Pp. 289.

KANSAS. — Report of Commissioners of Kansas Territory. Printed in Reports of Committees of House of Representatives, 36th Congress, 2d session. Part I, vols. 2 and 3. — March 2, 1861. Washington, 1861.

KANSAS. — [An] Illustrated Historical Atlas of Miami County, Kansas. — Philadelphia: Edwards Brothers. 1878. Pp. 60.

Kansas. — History of the New England Emigrant Aid Company. . . . — Boston: John Wilson and Son. 1862. Pp. 33.
Kansas. — The Kansas Memorial. . . . Charles S. Gleed, Editor. — Kansas City, Mo.: Ramsey, Millett & Hudson. 1880. Pp. 261.
Kansas. — Kansas State Historical Society Publications and Collections. 10 vols.
Kansas. Minutes of the Big Springs Convention. No place. 1855.
Kansas. — The Statutes of the Territory of Kansas. . . . — Shawnee M. L. School, Kansas: John T. Brady, Public Printer. 1855. Pp. 1509.
Kansas. — U. S. Biographical Dictionary, Kansas Volume. — Chicago and Kansas City: S. Lewis & Co. 1879. Pp. 883.
Kansas State Papers. — Executive Papers, 1855–1859. — Kansas State Historical Society Archives. MSS.
—— —— —— Records of the Adjutant-General. State House, Topeka.
Martin, George W. — The First Two Years of Kansas. . . . — Topeka, Kansas: State Printing Office. 1907. Pp. 30.
Missouri. — History of Clay and Platte Counties, Missouri. (No author.) — St. Louis: National Historical Company. 1885. Pp. 1121.
Paxton, W. M. — Annals of Platte County, Missouri. — Kansas City, Mo.: Hudson-Kimberly Publishing Company. 1897. Pp. 1182.
Phillips, William A. — The Conquest of Kansas by Missouri and Her Allies. — Boston: Phillips, Sampson & Co. 1856. Pp. 414.
Reese, Louis A. — History of the Admission of Kansas as a State. MSS.
Robinson, Charles. — The Kansas Conflict. — Lawrence, Kansas: Journal Publishing Company. 1898. Pp. 487.
Robinson, Sara T. L. — Kansas: its Interior and Exterior Life. . . . — Boston: Crosby, Nichols and Company. 1856. Pp. 366.
Robley, T. F. History of Bourbon County, Kansas, to the Close of 1865. Fort Scott, Kansas: Published by the Author. 1894. Pp. 210.
Ropes, Hannah Anderson. — Six Months in Kansas, by a Lady. — Boston: John P. Jewett & Co. 1856. Pp. 231.
Smith, Samuel C. — Kansas and the Emigrant Aid Co.; Reply to "T. W. H." in Boston *Advertiser*. 1903. Pp. 35.
Speer, John. — Life of Gen. James H. Lane. — Garden City, Kansas: John Speer, Printer. 1897. Pp. 352.
—— —— Perversions of History. — Archives of the Kansas Historical Society. MSS.
Spring, Leverett W. — Kansas, The Prelude to the War for the Union. — Boston: Houghton, Mifflin & Company. 1885. Pp. 334.
Sumner, Charles. The Crime against Kansas. Speech in the Senate of the United States, May 19–20, 1856. Washington: Buell & Blanchard. 1856. Pp. 32.
Thayer, Eli. — A History of the Kansas Crusade. . . . — New York: Harper & Brother. 1889. Pp. 294.
Three Years on the Kansas Border, by a Clergyman. — New York and Auburn: Miller, Orton & Mulligan. 1856. Pp. 240.
Tomlinson, William P. — Kansas in Eighteen Fifty-Eight. — New York: H. Dayton. 1859. Pp. 304.
Tuttle, Charles R. — History of Kansas. — Madison, Wisconsin, and Lawrence, Kansas: Interstate Book Company. 1876. Pp. 708.
War, Secretary of. — Official Report for 1856. Exec. Doc. No. 1, 34th Congress, 3d Session, House of Representatives.
Webb, Thomas H. — Information for Kansas Immigrants. — Boston: Alfred Mudge. 1855. Pp. 24.

BIBLIOGRAPHY

WEBB, THOMAS H. — Scrap-Books of Kansas happenings. In Kansas Historical Society Library.
WILDER, DANIEL W. — The Annals of Kansas. — Topeka, Kansas: George W. Martin. 1875. Pp. 691.
WILLIAMS, R. H. — With the Border Ruffians . . . edited by E. W. Williams. — New York: E. P. Dutton & Company. 1907. Pp. 478.
WILSON, HENRY. — State of Affairs in Kansas. Speech of Henry Wilson in the Senate February 18, 1856. Washington: Republican Association of the District of Columbia. 1856. Pp. 15.
WINKLEY, J. W. John Brown the Hero. — Boston: James K. West Company. 1905. Pp. 126.
WOOD, MARGARET L. — Memorial of Samuel N. Wood. — Kansas City: Hudson-Kimberly Publishing Company. 1892. Pp. 284.

V. BOOKS, PAMPHLETS AND DOCUMENTS RELATING PARTICULARLY TO THE HARPER'S FERRY RAID

ADAM, L. — La Question Américaine. — Nancy. 1861. Pp. 72.
ANDERSON, OSBORN P. — A Voice from Harper's Ferry. . . . — Boston: The Author. 1861. Pp. 72.
L'ANGLE-BEAUMANOIR, RAOUL DE. — La Correspondance de Harper's Ferry. — Paris: M. de Brunkhoff. 1886. Pp. 271.
ANTI-ABOLITION TRACT, NO. 3. — The Abolition Conspiracy to Destroy the Union. — New York: Van Evrie, Horton & Co. 1863.
ANTI-SLAVERY HISTORY of the John Brown Year, being the Twenty-Seventh Annual Report of the American Anti-Slavery Society. — New York: American Anti-Slavery Society. 1861. Pp. 337.
ANTI-SLAVERY TRACT, No. 7. NEW SERIES. — Testimonies of Capt. John Brown at Harper's Ferry. . . . — New York: The American Anti-Slavery Society. 1860. Pp. 16.
ARBELLI, H. P. — John Brown, ou Le Pendu de Victor Hugo. — Bordeaux: Durand. 1861. Pp. 8.
AVEY, ELIJAH. — The Capture and Execution of John Brown, a Tale of Martyrdom. . . . — Chicago: The Hyde Park Bindery. 1906. Pp. 144.
BAGBY, G. W. — 1860–1880. John Brown and William Mahone. A Historical parallel foreshadowing civil trouble. — Richmond, Va.: C. F. Johnston. 1880. Pp. 23.
BARKER, JOSEPH. — Slavery and Civil War, or The Harper's Ferry Insurrection. With a Review of Discourses on the Subject by Rev. W. H. Furness, Hon. J. R. Giddings, and Wendell Phillips, Esqre. — (Philadelphia. 1860?)
BOTTS, JOHN MINOR. — Interesting and Important Correspondence between Opposition Members of the Legislature of Virginia and Hon. John Minor Botts, January 17, 1860. — Washington: Lem. Towers. 1860. Pp. 16.
BRANDT, ISAAC. — History of John Brown. — Des Moines: Watters-Talbott Printing Company. 1895. Pp. 26.
BROWN, CAPT. JOHN, The Life, Trial, and Conviction of. — New York: Robert M. DeWitt. 1859. Pp. 108.
——— The Life, Trial, and Execution of. — New York: Robert M. DeWitt. 1859. Pp. 108.
CHANNING, WILLIAM ELLERY. — John Brown, and the Heroes of Harper's Ferry. — Boston: Cupples, Upham & Company. 1886. Pp. 143.

BIBLIOGRAPHY

CHANNING, WILLIAM ELLERY.— The Burial of John Brown.— Boston: 1860. Pp. 8.
CHAWNER, ROBERT. — The Life of John Brown. (In verse.) — Washington, D. C.: Published by the author. 1896. Pp. 16.
CHEVALIER, HENRI EMILE, ET PHARAON F. — Un Drame Esclavagiste. Prologue de la Sécession Americaine. . . . — Paris: Charlieu et Huillery. 1864. Pp. 60.
CHILD, LYDIA MARIA, Correspondence between, and Governor Wise and Mrs. Mason, of Virginia. — Boston: American Anti-Slavery Society. 1860. Pp. 28.
COOK, JOHN E., CONFESSIONS OF, Brother-in-Law of Governor A. P. Willard, of Indiana. . . . Published for the Benefit of Samuel C. Young, a Non-Slaveholder, who is Permanently Disabled by a Wound Received in Defense of Southern Institutions. — Charlestown: D. Smith Eichelberger. 1859. Pp. 16.
DREW, THOMAS. — The John Brown Invasion: an Authentic History of the Harper's Ferry Tragedy. — Boston: J. Campbell. 1860. Pp. 112.
FANATICISM AND ITS RESULTS: Fact *versus* Fancies. — By a Southerner. — Baltimore: Joseph Robinson. 1860. Pp. 36.
FERNAND, JACQUES. — John Brown et ses amis Stephens, Copp, Green et Coplands Morts pour l'Affranchissement des Noirs. — Paris: C. Vanier. 1861. Pp. 15. (Verse.)
FOUQUIER, A. — John Brown, l'Abolitioniste. — Paris: Lainé et Havard. 1861. Pp. 16.
GARRISON, WENDELL PHILLIPS. — The Preludes of Harper's Ferry. — From Andover Review of December, 1890, and January, 1891, privately printed as a pamphlet. 1891.
[GARRISON, WILLIAM LLOYD]. — The New "Reign of Terror" in the Slave-holding States 1859-1860. — New York: American Anti-Slavery Society. 1860. Pp. 144.
—— —— A Fresh Catalogue of Southern Outrages upon Northern Citizens. — New York: American Anti-Slavery Society. 1860. Pp. 72.
GLASGOW, J. EWING. — The Harper's Ferry Insurrection. — Edinburgh: Myles MacPhail. 1860. Pp. 47.
GROVE, S. E. — Souvenir and Guide-Book of Harper's Ferry, Antietam and South Mountain Battlefields. — Hagerstown, Maryland. 1905. Pp. 102.
HARPER'S FERRY, Rise and Progress of the Bloody Outbreak at. — Published by direction of the New York Democratic Vigilant Association. New York. 1859.
HOVENDEN. — Last Moments of John Brown. Painted by Thomas Hovenden, M. A., 1884. Etched by Thomas Hovenden, M. A., 1885. (A brief sketch of the subject of the painting, and opinions of the press concerning the painting.) — Philadelphia: G. Gebbie. 1885. Pp. 16.
HUGO, VICTOR. — John Brown. — Paris: E. Dentu. 1861. Pp. 8.
—— —— Letter from General C. F. Henningsen in reply to the letter of. — New York: Davies and Kent. 1860. Pp. 32.
HUGO, VICTOR, AND STEPHENS, MRS. ANN S. — Victor Hugo's letter on John Brown with Mrs. Ann S. Stephens's Reply. — New York: Irwin P. Beadle & Co. 1860. Pp. 24.
INSURRECTION AT HARPER'S FERRY, THE, and a Faithful History of Know Nothingism and Black Republicanism and their Proposed Union under the Irrepressible Conflict Doctrine of Seward and his Allies, North and South. — Baltimore. 1859. Pp. 12.
JOHN BROWN RAID, THE, Special Order Book of. MSS. — Virginia State Library, Department of Archives and History.
JOSEPHUS, JUNIOR (JOSEPH BARRY). — The Annals of Harper's Ferry. — Martinsburg, West Virginia. 1872. Pp. 126.

BIBLIOGRAPHY 699

KAPP, F. — Die erste politische Hinrichtung in den vereinigten Staaten, John Brown. Demokratische Studien. — Hamburg. 1860–1861. Vol. 1.
LEECH, REV. SAMUEL VANDERLIP. — The Raid of John Brown at Harper's Ferry as I Saw It. — Washington: Published by the Author. 1909. Pp. 24.
LOGAN, FRANK G. — The Logan Emancipation Cabinet of Letters and Relics of John Brown and Abraham Lincoln. Reprinted from Chicago Tribune. — Chicago. 1892. Pp. 40.
LUCIENNES, VICTOR. — Le Gibet de John Brown. — Paris: Castel. 1861. Pp. 8. (Poem.)
MACDONALD. — The Two Rebellions; or, Treason Unmasked. By a Virginian. — Richmond: Smith, Bailey & Co. 1865. Pp. 144.
MARQUAND, HENRI. — John Brown. — Paris: Dentu. 1860. Pp. 246.
MARYLAND STATE PAPERS. — Correspondence Relating to the Insurrection at Harper's Ferry, 17th October, 1859. (Document Y.) — Annapolis; B. H. Richardson. 1860. Pp. 79.
MASON REPORT. — Report of the Select Committee of the Senate appointed to inquire into the late invasion and seizure of the public property at Harper's Ferry. — Rep. Com. No. 278, 36th Congress, 1st Session.
MOORE, CLEON. — John Brown's Attack on Harper's Ferry. — Point Pleasant, West Virginia: Mrs. Livia Simpson Poffenbarger, Editor and Publisher. 1904. Pp. 22.
[MOORE, WM. H.] — Startling Incidents & Developments of Osawotomy Brown's Insurrectory and Treasonable Movements at Harper's Ferry, Virginia, October 17th, 1859. By a Citizen of Harper's Ferry. — Baltimore: John W. Woods, Printer. 1859. Pp. 72.
PARKER, REV. THEODORE. — John Brown's Expedition Reviewed in a Letter from Rev. Theodore Parker at Rome to Francis Jackson, Boston. — Boston: The Fraternity. 1860. Pp. 19.
PATE, H. CLAY. — John Brown as Viewed by H. Clay Pate. — New York: Published by the Author. 1859. Pp. 48.
PRICE, WILLIAM THOMPSON. — "Old John Brown of Harper's Ferry;" a drama in five acts. — (New York? 1895?) Pp. 8.
PROWE, A. — John Osawatomie Brown, der Negerheiland. Festschrift zur ersten säkular Feier der Vereinigten Staaten von Nord Amerika. — Braunschweig: W. Bracke, Jr. 1876. Pp. 148.
REDPATH, JAMES. — Echoes of Harper's Ferry. — Boston: Thayer & Eldridge. 1860. Pp. 513.
REPORT: A FULL AND AUTHENTIC REPORT of the Famous Case of The People, upon the relation of John Brown, praying for a writ of habeas corpus to release his soul from the custody of Lucifer Diavolo, Respondent. Pp. 8.
RICHMAN, IRVING B. — John Brown Among the Quakers. — Des Moines: Historical Department of Iowa. 1894. Pp. 239.
ROBINSON, WILLIAM S. — "Warrington" Pen-Portraits. — Boston: Edited and Published by Mrs. W. S. Robinson. 1887. Pp. 587.
SANBORN, F. B. — Memoirs of John Brown, written for Rev. Samuel Orcutt's History of Torrington, Ct. . . . with Memorial verses, by William Ellery Channing. — Concord, Massachusetts. January, 1878. Pp. 107.
SCHILLING, JOHN L. — The Three Emancipators. — Bellaire, Ohio. 1892. Pp. 59.
——— The Story of John Brown's Raid and Capture and the Founding of Historic Harper's Ferry. — Toledo, Ohio. 1895. Pp. 12.
SWAYZE, MRS. J. C. — Ossawatomie Brown, or the Insurrection at Harper's Ferry. A Drama in Three Acts. New York: Samuel French. 1859.

TODD, REV. JOHN. — Reminiscences, or Early Settlement and Growth of Western Iowa. — Des Moines: Historical Department of Iowa. 1906.
TRIALS; REMARKABLE TRIALS OF ALL COUNTRIES, with the Evidence and Speeches of Counsel. — New York: S. S. Peloubet & Co. 1882. Pp. 436.
VALENTINE, MANN S. — The Mock Auction. Ossawatomie Sold. — Richmond: J. W. Randolph. 1860. Pp. 261.
VESINIER, PIERRE. — Le Martyr de la Liberté des negres, ou John Brown Le Christ des Noirs. — Berlin: Jules Abelsdorff. 1864. Pp. 403.
VILLEROI, B. DE. — Subscription for the Erection of a Monument to the Memory of the Brave and Unfortunate John Brown. — Philadelphia: Jones & Thacher. 1867. Pp. 8.
VIRGINIA STATE PAPERS. — Address of the Hon. C. G. Memminger, Special Commissioner from the State of South Carolina, before the Assembled Authorities of the State of Virginia. — Doc. No. LV II. January 19, 1860. Pp. 43.
—— —— Calendar of Virginia State Papers, vol. 11.
—— —— Court of Appeals of Virginia. Commonwealth vs. Brown. — Richmond. 1859. Pp. 16.
—— —— Document No. 1. Appendix to Message 1. Documents Relative to the Harper's Ferry Invasion. — Richmond. December, 1859.
—— —— Document No. 1. Appendix to Message 2. — Richmond. December, 1859.
—— —— Report of the Superintendent of the Virginia Military Institute to the Board of Visitors. Doc. No. XXVIII. January 20, 1860.
—— —— Communication from the Governor of Virginia enclosing letters from the Governor of Ohio, relative to requisitions for fugitives from justice. Doc. No. LIX. March 14, 1860.
—— —— Report of the Joint Committee of the General Assembly of Virginia on the Harper's Ferry Outrages. Doc. No. XXXI. January 26, 1860. Pp. 24.
—— —— Executive's Letter Book, 1856–1860. — Virginia State Library, Department of Archives and History.
—— —— Journal of the House of Delegates of Virginia. 1859–1860.
VIRGINIA STATE PUBLICATIONS. — List of Field Officers, Regiments and Battalions in the Confederate States Army. 1861–1865.
VON HOLST, DR. HERMANN. — John Brown. Edited by Frank Preston Stearns. — Boston: Cupples and Hurd. 1889. Pp. 232.
WILLIAMS, EDWARD W. — The Views and Meditations of John Brown. — Washington: The Author. 1893. Pp. 16.
WILLIAMS, JAMES, late United States Minister to Turkey. — Letters on Slavery from the Old World; written during the Canvass for the Presidency of the United States in 1860. To which are added a Letter to Lord Brougham on the John Brown Raid. — Nashville, Tenn.: Southern Methodist Publishing House. 1861. Pp. 321.
WRIGHT, HENRY C. — The Natick Resolution. — Boston. 1859. Pp. 36.
ZITTLE, CAPT. JOHN H. — A Correct History of the John Brown Invasion. Edited and published by his widow. — Hagerstown, Maryland. 1905. Pp. 259.

VI. REPORTS OF IMPORTANT MEETINGS DEALING WITH THE RAID AND EXECUTION

AMERICAN SLAVERY. — Demonstration in favor of Dr. Cheever, in Scotland. Letter of Sympathy from Distinguished Clergymen and other Gentlemen.

BIBLIOGRAPHY 701

Speeches at Meetings in Edinburgh and Glasgow. — New York: John A. Gray. 1860. Pp. 17.

THE MARTYRDOM OF JOHN BROWN. — The Proceedings of a Public Meeting Held in London on the 2nd December, 1863, to Commemorate the Fourth Anniversary of John Brown's Death. — London: Emancipation Society. 1864. Pp. 23.

SPEECHES OF HON. A. C. BARSTOW, Rev. George T. Day, Rev. A. Woodbury. Hon. Thomas Davis, and Resolutions Adopted at a Meeting of Citizens held in Providence, R. I. . . . on the Occasion of the Execution of John Brown. — Providence: Amsbury & Co. 1860. Pp. 32.

BOSTON COURIER Report of the Union Meeting in Faneuil Hall, Thursday, December 8, 1859. — Boston: Published by Clark, Fellows & Company. 1859. Pp. 32.

GREAT UNION MEETING. — Philadelphia, December 7, 1859. — Philadelphia: Cressy and Marks. 1859. Pp. 59.

REPORT of the Public Meeting held in Tremont Temple, Boston, December 2, 1859, on the Occasion of the Execution of John Brown. — See The Liberator (Boston) for December 9 and 16, 1859.

REPORT of the Union Meeting held in Brewster's Hall, New Haven. . . . December 14, 1859. — New Haven: Printed by Thomas J. Stafford. 1860. Pp. 52.

A TRIBUTE of Respect Commemorative of the Worth and Sacrifice of John Brown. . . . It being a full Report of . . . a meeting held in the Melodeon. . . . — Cleveland: Published for the Benefit of the Widows and Families of the Revolutionists of Harper's Ferry. 1859. Pp. 62.

THE REPUBLIC AND ITS CRISES. — Speeches of Hon. Edward Everett, at the Boston Union Meeting, December 8, 1858, and of ex-Gov. Thos. H. Seymour and Professor Samuel Eliot, of Trinity College, at the Hartford Union Meeting, December 14, 1859. —January, 1860. Pp. 28.

OFFICIAL REPORTS of the Great Union Meeting in the New York Academy of Music, December 19, 1859. — New York: Davies & Kent. 1859. Pp. 176.

VII. IMPORTANT SPEECHES AND ADDRESSES ON JOHN BROWN AS SEPARATELY PUBLISHED

ANDERSON, BENNING, PRESTON. — Addresses delivered before the Virginia State Convention by Hon. Fulton Anderson, Commissioner from Mississippi, Hon. Henry L. Benning, Commissioner from Georgia, and Hon. John S. Preston, Commissioner from South Carolina, February, 1861. — Richmond: Wyatt M. Elliott, Printer. 1861. Pp. 64.

ANDREW, JOHN A. — Speeches of, at Hingham and Boston, together with his Testimony before the Harper's Ferry Committee of the Senate. . . . — Boston. 1860. Pp. 16.

BARKER, JOSEPH. — Address: Slavery and Civil War, or the Harper's Ferry Insurrection, with a Review of Discourses on the Subject by Rev. W. H. Furness, Hon. J. R. Giddings, and Wendell Phillips, Esq. — Phila. 1860.

BEECHER, HENRY WARD. — Patriotic Address; Edited by John R. Howard. — New York: Fords, Howard and Hulbert. 1889. Pp. 857.

BIERCE, GEN. L. V. — Address delivered at Akron, Ohio, on the Evening of the Execution of John Brown. . . . — Columbus, Ohio. 1865. Pp. 11.

CLARKE, DR. JAMES FREEMAN. An Address before the Massachusetts Historical Society on John Brown. — Massachusetts Historical Society Proceedings, June, 1884.

DOUGLASS, FREDERICK. — John Brown: An address . . . at the Fourteenth Anniversary of Storer College. — Dover, N. H. 1881. Pp. 28.

FURNESS, HORACE HOWARD. — Historical Address delivered in Connection with the Installation of the Reverend Charles E. St. John as Minister of the First Unitarian Church of Philadelphia. . . . — Phila. 1908. Pp. 20.

HALL (N.). The Iniquity (Brown's execution); — The Man (Brown), the Deed, the Event (two addresses).— Boston. 1859.

LAWRENCE, AMOS A. — An Address before the Massachusetts Historical Society. Massachusetts Historical Society Proceedings. May, 1884.

RAMEAU, S. — Oration on John Brown. — Aux Payes. 1860. Pp. 7.

ROE, ALFRED S. — John Brown: a Retrospect. — Worcester. Pp. 25. (A eulogy read before the Worcester Society of Antiquities, December, 1884.)

ROSS, ALEXANDER MILTON. — Speech, delivered October 21, 1864, at the Annual Meeting of the Society for the Abolition of Human Slavery held in Montreal. — Montreal: John Lovell. 1864. Pp. 8.

SHEARER, W. J. — John Brown's Raid. An address delivered at the Hamilton Library (Carlisle, Pa.), January 17, 1905. — Pamphlet. Pp. 12.

SWINTON, JOHN. — Old Ossawattomie Brown. Speech . . . delivered in Turn Theatre, New York, December 2, 1881. Pp. 11.

TRUMBULL, LYMAN. — Remarks of Hon. Lyman Trumbull, of Illinois, on Seizure of Arsenals at Harper's Ferry, Virginia, and Liberty, Missouri. . . . Delivered in the U. S. Senate, December 6, 7, and 8, 1859. — Washington: Buell and Blanchard. 1859. Pp. 16.

VOORHEES, HON. DANIEL W. — Speech delivered at Charlestown, Virginia: November 8, 1859, upon the trial of John E. Cook. — Tallahassee: Printed by Dyke and Carlisle. 1860. Pp. 28.

—— —— Addresses of Hon. Daniel W. Voorhees, of Indiana; comprising his Argument delivered at Charlestown, Virginia, November 8, 1859, upon the Trial of John E. Cook, for Treason and Murder. — Richmond, Virginia: West & Johnson. 1861. Pp. 55.

WADE, BENJAMIN FRANKLIN. — The Invasion of Harper's Ferry. Speech delivered in the United States Senate, December 14, 1859. — Washington: Buell & Blanchard. 1859. Pp. 8.

VIII. SOME TYPICAL SERMONS

AMES, REV. CHARLES GORDON. — The Death of John Brown. . . . Delivered at Bloomington, Ill., December 4, 1859. Reprinted in 1909. Pp. 38.

CHEEVER, REV. GEORGE BARRELL. — "The Curse of God against Political Atheism." — Boston: Walker, Wise & Co. 1859. Pp. 24.

CLARKE, REV. JAMES FREEMAN. Causes and Consequences of the Affair at Harper's Ferry. A Sermon preached in the Indiana Place Chapel on Sunday morning, November 6, 1859. — Boston: Walker, Wise & Co. 1859. Pp. 14.

COLVER, REV. NATHANIEL, D. D. — The Harper's Ferry Tragedy: a symptom of disease in the heart of the nation. . . . — Cincinnati. 1860. Pp. 16.

FURNESS, W. H. — Put up thy Sword. A Discourse delivered before Theodore Parker's Society at the Music Hall, Boston, Sunday, March 11, 1860. Boston: R. F. Walcutt. 1860. Pp. 23.

GREGORY, REV. JOHN. — The Life and Character of John Brown. . . . — Pittsburgh: A. A. Anderson. 1860. Pp. 16.

GULLIVER, REV. J. P. — The Lioness and Her Whelps. A Sermon on Slavery. Preached in the Broadway Congregational Church, Norwich, Connecticut, December 18, 1859. — Norwich: Manning, Perry & Co. 1860. Pp. 12.

BIBLIOGRAPHY 703

HALL, NATHANIEL. — Two Sermons on Slavery and its Hero-Victim. — Boston: John Wilson & Son. 1859. Pp. 37.
NEWHALL, REV. FALES HENRY. — A Funeral Discourse occasioned by the Death of John Brown of Osawatomie. . . . — Boston: J. M. Hewes. 1859. Pp. 22.
PATTON, REV. W. W. — The Execution of John Brown . . . Delivered . . . December 4, 1859. — Chicago: Church, Goodman & Cushing. 1859. Pp. 14.
RICE, REV. DANIEL. — Harper's Ferry and Its Lesson. — Lafayette, Ind.: Luse & Wilson. 1860. Pp. 18.
TAFT, REV. S. H. — Discourse on the Character and Death of John Brown, delivered at Martensburgh, New York, December 12, 1859. . . . — Des Moines: Carter & Hussey. 1872.
TOWER, REV. PHILO. — Slavery Unmasked and the Invasion of Kansas. — Rochester. 1856.
TUFTS, REV. SAMUEL N. — Slavery and the Death of John Brown. Preached in Auburn Hall, Auburn, December 11, 1859. — Lewiston. 1859. Pp. 20.
WHEELOCK, REV. EDWIN M. — A Sermon for the Times. Preached at Music Hall, Boston, Sunday, November 27, 1859. — Boston: The Fraternity. 1859.
YOUNG, JOSHUA. — Man Better than a Sheep: A Sermon preached Thanksgiving Day, November 24, 1859. — Burlington, N. H.: E. A. Fuller. 1859. Pp. 22.

IX. BIOGRAPHIES, AUTOBIOGRAPHIES, AND REMINISCENCES OF CORRELATED OR IMPORTANT PERSONAGES

ANDREW, JOHN A., The Life of. — By Henry Greenleaf Pearson. — Boston: Houghton, Mifflin & Co. 1904. 2 vols.
ASHBY, GENERAL TURNER, Memoirs of, and his Compeers. — By Rev. James B. Avirett. — Baltimore: Selby and Dulaney. 1867. Pp. 408.
BOWDITCH, HENRY INGERSOLL, Life and Correspondence of. — By Vincent Y. Bowditch. — Boston: Houghton, Mifflin & Co. 1902. 2 vols.
BOWLES, SAMUEL, Life and Times of. — By George S. Merriam. — New York: The Century Company. 1885. 2 vols.
BUCHANAN, JAMES (President). Mr. Buchanan's Administration on the Eve of the Rebellion. — New York: D. Appleton & Co. 1866. Pp. 296.
CHASE, SALMON P. — By Albert Bushnell Hart. — Boston: Houghton, Mifflin & Co. 1899. Pp. 465.
———— Correspondence of. — MSS. in Library of Congress.
CHILD, LYDIA MARIA, Letters of. — Introduction by J. G. Whittier. Appendix by Wendell Phillips. — Boston: Houghton, Mifflin & Co. 1883. Pp. 280.
CLARKE, DR. JAMES FREEMAN. — Anti-Slavery Days. — New York: J. W. Lovell Co. 1883. Pp. 224.
COLEMAN, LUCY N. — Reminiscences. — Buffalo: H. L. Green. 1891. Pp. 86.
COLFAX, SCHUYLER, Life of. — By O. J. Hollister. — New York: Funk and Wagnalls. 1886. Pp. 535.
CONWAY, MONCURE D. — Autobiography, Memories and Experiences. — Boston: Houghton, Mifflin & Co. 1904. 2 vols.
DELANEY, MARTIN R., Life and Public Services of. — By Frank A. Rollins. Boston. 1868.
DOUGLASS, FREDERICK, Life and Times of. (By Himself.) — Hartford: Park Publishing Company. 1882. Pp. 564.
———— the Colored Orator. — By Frederic May Holland. — New York: Funk and Wagnalls. 1891. Pp. 423.

BIBLIOGRAPHY

EMERSON, RALPH WALDO, A Memoir. — By James Elliot Cabot. — Boston: Houghton, Mifflin & Co. 1888. 2 vols.
—— —— Miscellanies. — Boston: Houghton, Mifflin & Co. 1888. Pp. 425.
EVERETT, EDWARD. — Orations and Speeches. — Boston: Little, Brown & Co. 1868. 4 vols.
O'FERRALL, CHARLES T. — Forty Years of Active Service. — New York and Washington: The Neale Publishing Co. 1904.
FORBES, JOHN MURRAY, Letters and Recollections of. Edited by his daughter, Sarah Forbes Hughes. — Boston: Houghton, Mifflin & Co. 1899. 2 vols.
GARRISON, WILLIAM LLOYD. The Story of His Life Told by His Children. — New York: The Century Company, 1885–89. Boston: Houghton, Mifflin & Co. 1894. 4 vols.
—— —— Correspondence of. MSS. Boston Public Library.
GRANT, U. S. — Personal Memoirs. — New York: C. L. Webster & Co. 1885. 2 vols.
GRINNELL, JOSIAH BUSNELL. — Men and Events of Forty Years. — Boston: D. Lathrop Company. 1891. Pp. 426.
HIGGINSON, THOMAS WENTWORTH. — Cheerful Yesterdays. — Boston: Houghton, Mifflin & Co. 1898. Pp. 374.
—— —— Contemporaries. (A chapter entitled: "Capt. Brown — A Visit to his Household in 1859.") — Boston: Houghton, Mifflin & Co. 1899.
HOWE, JULIA WARD. — Reminiscences. — Boston: Houghton, Mifflin & Co. 1899. Pp. 465.
HOWE, SAMUEL GRIDLEY, Letters and Journals of. Edited by his daughter, Laura E. Richards. — Boston: Dana Estes & Co. 1908–1909. 2 vols.
HOWE, DR. SAMUEL G., Memoir of. — By Julia Ward Howe. — Boston: Howe Memorial Committee. 1866. Pp. 127.
HOWE, DR. S. G., the Philanthropist. — By F. B. Sanborn. — New York: Funk and Wagnalls. 1891. Pp. 370.
JACKSON, STONEWALL, Memoirs of. — By his widow, Mary Anna Jackson. — Louisville: The Prentice Press. 1895. Pp. 647.
JACKSON, THOMAS J. (Stonewall Jackson), Life and Letters of. — By his wife, Mary Anna Jackson. — New York: Harper and Brothers. 1892. Pp. 479.
JACKSON, LIEUTENANT-GENERAL THOMAS J., Life and Campaigns of. — By R. L. Dabney, D. D. — New York: Blelock and Company. 1866. Pp. 742.
JOHNSON, DR. WILLIAM HENRY, Autobiography of. Albany, N. Y.: The Argus Printing Co. 1900.
LAWRENCE, AMOS A., Life of. — By his son, William Lawrence. — Boston: Houghton, Mifflin & Co. 1888. Pp. 289.
—— —— MSS. in Massachusetts Historical Society.
LEE, GENERAL ROBERT E., Recollections and Letters of. — By his son, Captain Robert E. Lee. — New York: Doubleday, Page & Co. 1904. Pp. 461.
LEE, ROBERT EDWARD, Soldier and Man, Life and Letters of. — By Rev. J. William Jones, D. D. — New York: Neale Publishing Co. 1906. Pp. 486.
LESLEY, PETER AND SUSAN, Life and Letters of. — Edited by their daughter, Mary Lesley Ames. — New York: G. P. Putnam's Sons. 1909. 2 vols.
LIEBER, FRANCIS, Life and Letters of. — Edited by Thomas Sergeant Perry. — Boston: J. R. Osgood. 1882. 2 vols.
LINCOLN, ABRAHAM, Speeches of. — L. E. Chittenden, compiler. — New York: Dodd, Mead & Co. 1895.
—— —— The True. — By William Elroy Curtis. — Philadelphia: J. B. Lippincott. 1903.
—— —— By John G. Nicolay and John Hay. — New York: The Century Company. 1890. 10 vols.

BIBLIOGRAPHY

LONGFELLOW, HENRY WADSWORTH, Life of. — Edited by Samuel Longfellow. Boston: Houghton, Mifflin & Co. 1891. 3 vols.
LONGFELLOW, SAMUEL, Memoir and Letters of. — Edited by Joseph May. — Boston: Houghton, Mifflin & Co. 1894. Pp. 307.
LOWRY, HON. M. B., A Tribute of Gratitude to. — Philadelphia: Jas. B. Rodgers Co., Printers. 1869. Pp. 36.
MCCLURE, COLONEL ALEXANDER K. — Recollections of Half a Century. — Salem, Massachusetts. 1902. Pp. 502.
—— —— Lincoln and Men of War Times. — Philadelphia: The Times Publishing Company. 1892. Pp. 496.
MCKIM, SARAH A. In Memoriam. — By Wendell Phillips Garrison. — New York: De Vinne Press, Privately Printed. 1891. Pp. 23.
MASON, JAMES M., Public Life and Diplomatic Correspondence of, with some personal history. — By his daughter. — Roanoke, Virginia: The Stone Company. 1903. Pp. 603.
MAY, SAMUEL J. — Some Recollections of our Anti-Slavery Conflict. — Boston: Fields, Osgood & Co. 1869. Pp. 408.
MORLEY, HON. JOHN LOTHROP, Memoir of. — By Oliver Wendell Holmes. — Massachusetts Historical Society Proceedings. December, 1878.
MOTT, JAMES AND LUCRETIA, Life and Letters of. — Edited by Anna Davis Hallowell. — Boston: Houghton, Mifflin & Co. 1884. Pp. 566.
PARKER, THEODORE, Preacher and Reformer. — By John White Chadwick. — Boston: Houghton, Mifflin & Co. 1900. Pp. 422.
—— —— Life of. — By O. B. Frothingham. — Boston: J. R. Osgood & Co. 1874.
—— —— Life and Correspondence of. — By John Weiss. — New York: D. Appleton & Company. 1864. 2 vols.
PHILLIPS, WENDELL, the Agitator. — By Carlos Martyn. — New York: Funk and Wagnalls. 1890. Pp. 600.
—— —— Orator and Agitator. — By Lorenzo Sears. — New York: Doubleday, Page Co. 1909. Pp. 379.
—— —— Speeches, Lectures and Letters. — Boston: James Redpath. 1863.
—— —— Speeches, Lectures and Letters. Second Series. — Boston: Lee and Shepard. 1891. Pp. 476.
PILLSBURY, PARKER. — Acts of the Anti-Slavery Apostles. — Boston: Cupples, Upham & Co. 1883.
PRESTON, MARGARET JUNKIN, Life and Letters of. — By Elizabeth Preston Allan. — Boston: Houghton, Mifflin & Co. 1903. Pp. 378.
REALF, RICHARD. — Richard Realf's Free-State Poems. Edited by Col. Richard J. Hinton. — Topeka: Crane & Company. 1900. Pp. 135.
—— —— Poems by. With a Memoir by Richard J. Hinton. — New York: Funk and Wagnalls Co. 1898. Pp. 232.
RIDDLE, ALBERT GALLATIN. — Recollections of War Times. — New York: G. P. Putnam's Sons. 1895. Pp. 380.
ROBINSON, CHARLES, the First Governor of Kansas, A Chapter in the Life of. — By Frank W. Blackmar. — American Historical Association, Annual Report. 1894.
—— —— Life of. — By Frank W. Blackmar. — Topeka: Crane & Co. 1902. Pp. 438.
ROSS, ALEXANDER MILTON. — Recollections and Experiences of an Abolitionist. — Toronto: Roswell & Hutchinson. 1875. Pp. 224.
RUSSELL, ADDISON PEALE. — Characteristics. — Boston: Houghton, Mifflin & Co. 1884. Pp. 362.

BIBLIOGRAPHY

SANBORN, F. B. — Recollections of Seventy Years. — Boston: Richard G. Badger. 1909. 2 vols.
SEDGWICK, JOHN, MAJOR-GENERAL, Correspondence of. — De Vinne Press. Printed for Carl and Ellen Battelle Stoeckel. 1903. 2 vols.
SEWALL, SAMUEL E., A Memoir. — By Nina Moore Tiffany. — Boston: Houghton, Mifflin & Co. 1898. Pp. 175.
SEWALL, SAMUEL E., and ANDREW, JOHN A. — Argument on behalf of Thaddeus Hyatt. (Pamphlet.) Pp. 20.
SEWARD, FRED. W. — Seward at Washington, 1846–1861. — New York: Derby and Miller. 1891. Pp. 446.
SEWARD, WILLIAM H., The Works of. — Edited by George E. Baker. — Boston: Houghton, Mifflin & Co. 1884. 5 vols.
—— —— Life of. — By Frederic Bancroft. — New York: Harper and Brothers. 1900. 2 vols.
—— —— By T. K. Lothrop. — Boston: Houghton, Mifflin & Co. 1895.
SHERMAN, JOHN. — Recollections of Forty Years in the House, Senate and Cabinet. — New York: The Werner Company. 1906. Pp. 949.
SMITH, GERRIT. — A Biography. By Octavius Brooks Frothingham. — New York: G. P. Putnam's Sons. First Edition. 1878. Pp. 381.
—— —— Memorandum relative to Gerrit Smith's Intercourse with Captain John Brown. — Peterboro, August 15, 1867. Pp. 8.
SMITH, GERRIT *vs.* N. Y. Democratic Vigilant Association. Important Libel Suits. Reprinted from Syracuse Journal. — Syracuse, 1860. Pamphlet.
STEARNS, GEORGE LUTHER, The Life and Public Services of. — By Frank Preston Stearns. — Philadelphia: J. B. Lippincott Company. 1907. Pp. 402.
STEPHENS, ALEXANDER H., Life of. — By R. M. Johnston and William Hand Browne. — Philadelphia: J. B. Lippincott Company. 1878.
STUART, J. E. B., Life and Campaigns of. — By H. B. McClellan. — Boston: Houghton, Mifflin & Co. 1885. Pp. 468.
SUMNER, CHARLES, Correspondence of. — MSS. Library of Harvard University.
—— —— Memoir and Letters of. By Edward L. Pierce. — Boston: 1877. 4 vols.
THOREAU, HENRY D. — A Yankee in Canada, with Anti-Slavery and Reform Papers. — Boston: Ticknor & Fields. 1861. Pp. 286.
TOOMBS, ROBERT. — By Pleasant A. Stovall. — New York: Cassell Publishing Co. 1892.
TRUMBULL, LYMAN, Life of. — By Horace White. MSS.
TUBMAN, HARRIET. The Moses of Her People. — By Sarah H. Bradford. — New York: J. J. Little & Co. 1901. Pp. 171.
TYNDALE, GENERAL HECTOR, Memoir of. — By John McLaughlin. — Philadelphia. 1882. Pp. 118.
VALLANDIGHAM, CLEMENT LAIRD. — Speeches, Arguments, Addresses and Letters. — New York: J. Walter & Company. 1864. Pp. 580.
WEED, THURLOW, Autobiography of. Edited by his daughter, Harriet A. Weed (Vol. 1). — Memoir of Thurlow Weed. By his grandson, Thurlow Weed Barnes (Vol. 2). — Boston: Houghton, Mifflin & Co. 1884.
WISE, HENRY A. — Seven Decades of the Union. — Philadelphia: J. B. Lippincott & Co. 1872. Pp. 320.
—— —— OF VIRGINIA. — By his grandson, the late Barton H. Wise. — New York: The Macmillan Company. 1899. Pp. 434.
WISE, JOHN S. — The End of an Era. — Boston: Houghton, Mifflin & Co. 1899. Pp. 474.

X. LOCAL AND GENERAL HISTORIES WITH SPECIAL REFERENCES TO JOHN BROWN AND HIS MEN

ASHTABULA COUNTY, O., HISTORY OF. — Philadelphia: Williams Bros. 1878. Pp. 256.
BOTTS, JOHN MINOR. — The Great Rebellion. — New York: Harper & Brothers. 1866. Pp. 402.
BROWNE, WILLIAM HAND. — Maryland, the History of a Palatinate. — Boston: Houghton, Mifflin & Co. 1904. Pp. 381.
BURGESS, JOHN WILLIAM. — Civil War and the Constitution, 1859-1865. — New York: Charles Scribner's Sons. 1901. 2 vols.
—————— The Middle Period, 1817-1858. — New York: Charles Scribner's Sons. 1897. Pp. 542.
BYERS, S. H. M. — Iowa in War Times. — Des Moines: W. D. Condit & Co. 1888. Pp. 615.
CACKLER, CHRISTIAN. — Recollections of an Old Settler. — Ravenna, Ohio: Samuel D. Harris, Ravenna Democrat Office. 1874. Pp. 38.
CASWELL, LILLEY B. — Athol, Massachusetts, Past and Present. — Athol: The Author. 1899. Pp. 448.
CHADWICK, FRENCH ENSOR. — Causes of the Civil War. — New York: Harper & Brothers. 1906. Pp. 372.
COFFIN, CHARLES C. — The Drum Beat of the Nation. — New York: Harper & Brothers. 1888.
CONNECTICUT. — Memorial History of Hartford County, Connecticut. — Edited by J. Hammond Trumbull. — Boston: Edward L. Osgood. 1886. 2 vols.
—————— Record of Connecticut Men in the Military and Naval Service during the War of the Revolution, 1775-1783. Edited by Henry P. Johnston, A. M., under the authority of the Adjutant-General of Connecticut. — Hartford. 1889.
COX, S. S. — Three Decades of Federal Legislation. — Providence: J. A. and R. A. Reid. 1884. Pp. 726.
DEVENS, R. M. — Our First Century. — Springfield, Massachusetts: C. A. Nichols & Co. 1876.
DRAPER, JOHN W. — The Civil War in America. — New York: Harper & Brothers. 1867.
EMILIO, LUIS F. — History of the Fifty-fourth Regiment of Massachusetts Volunteer Infantry, 1863-1865. — Boston: The Boston Book Company. 1894.
EVANS, CLEMENT A. — Confederate Military History. Edited by General Clement A. Evans. — Atlanta. 1899. 12 vols.
ELSON, WILLIAM HENRY. — History of the United States of America. — New York: The Macmillan Company. 1904. Pp. 911.
FOWLER, WILLIAM CHAUNCEY. — The Sectional Controversy. — New York. 1862. Pp. 269.
GREELEY, HORACE. — The American Conflict. — Hartford: O. D. Case & Company. 1864. 2 vols.
GREELEY, HORACE, AND CLEVELAND, JOHN F. — Political Text-Book for 1860. — New York: The Tribune Association. 1860. Pp. 254.
GREEN, MASON A. — Springfield, 1636-1886. History of Town and City. — Springfield: C. A. Nichols & Co. 1888. Pp. 644.
GUE, B. F. — History of Iowa. — New York: The Century History Company. 1903. 4 vols.
HELPER, HINTON ROWAN. — The Impending Crisis of the South: How to Meet it. — New York: A. B. Burdick. 1860. Pp. 420.

HERBERT, GEORGE B. — Popular History of the Civil War. — Lupton, N. Y. 1884.
HINTON, RICHARD J. — Rebel Invasion of Missouri and Kansas and the Campaign of the Army of the Border against General Sterling Price. — Chicago: Church and Goodman. 1865. Pp. 351.
HORTON, R. G. — A Youth's History of the Great Civil War in the United States. — New York: Van Evrie, Horton & Co. 1866. Pp. 384.
HOWE, HENRY. — Historical Collections of Ohio. — Columbus, Ohio: Henry Howe & Son. 1891. 3 vols.
HUME, J. F. — The Abolitionists. — New York: G. P. Putnam's Sons. 1905.
HUMPHREYS, FREDERICK. — The Humphreys Family in America, Part II. September, 1883. — New York: Humphreys Print. 1883.
IOWA, ANNALS OF. — Des Moines, Iowa: Historical Department of Iowa.
—— History of Cedar County. — Chicago: Western Historical Company. 1878. Pp. 728.
—— History of Johnson County. — Iowa City. 1883. Pp. 966.
—— Historical Record. State Historical Society. Iowa City.
JEFFERSON COUNTY, WEST VIRGINIA. — Records; MSS. Common Law Order Books, Nos. 6 and 12; Will Book, No. 16.
JOHNSON, ROSSITER. — Camp-Fire and Battlefield. — New York: Knight and Brown. 1894.
—— Short History of the War of Secession, 1861–1865. — Boston: Houghton, Mifflin & Co. 1889.
JORDAN, DAVID STARR. — The Innumerable Company. — San Francisco: The Whitaker and Ray Company. 1896. Pp. 294.
—— —— Imperial Democracy. — New York: D. Appleton & Co. 1899.
KEIFER, JOSEPH WARREN. — Slavery and Four Years of the War. — New York: G. P. Putnam's Sons. 1900.
KETTELL, THOMAS P. — History of the Great Rebellion. — New York: N. C. Miller. 1862.
LANE, SAMUEL A. — Fifty Years and Over of Akron and Summit County. — Akron: Beacon Job Department. 1892. Pp. 1167.
LEE, GUY CARLETON. — True History of the Civil War. — Philadelphia: J. B. Lippincott Co. 1903.
LEONARD, D. R. — The Story of Oberlin. — Boston: The Pilgrim Press. 1898.
LEVASINIER, F. E. — Reflexions sur l'Esclavage. — New York: S. Hallet. 1860.
MCMASTER, JOHN BACH. — History of the People of the United States from the Revolution to the Civil War. — New York: D. Appleton & Co. 7 vols.
MASSACHUSETTS. — Record of the Massachusetts Volunteers, 1861–1865. — Published by the Adjutant-General: Boston. 1870.
MERRIAM, GEORGE S. — The Negro and the Nation. — New York: Henry Holt & Company. 1906. Pp. 436.
MONROE, JAMES. — Oberlin Thursday Lectures, Addresses and Essays. — Oberlin, Ohio: Edward J. Goodrich. 1897. Pp. 373.
NICOLAY, J. G. — Outbreak of the Rebellion. — New York: Charles Scribner's Sons. 1881.
NORRIS, J. E. — History of the Lower Shenandoah Valley. — Chicago: A. Warner & Company. 1890. Pp. 812.
OHIO, HISTORY OF PORTAGE COUNTY. — Chicago: Warner, Beers & Company. 1885.
—— History of Summit County. — Chicago: Baskin & Battey. 1881.
—— Hudson, Reminiscences of. Supplement to the Hudson Independent. Reprinted as pamphlet, Hudson, Ohio, 1899.

BIBLIOGRAPHY 709

ORCUTT, REV. SAMUEL. — History of Torrington, Connecticut. — Albany: S. Munsell. 1878. Pp. 817.
POLLARD, EDWARD A. — The First Year of the War. — Richmond: West & Johnston. 1862. Pp. 389.
QUINT, ALONZO H. — The Potomac and the Rapidan. — Boston: Crosby and Nichols. 1864. Pp. 407.
REBELLION RECORD, THE. — A Diary of American Events. Edited by Frank Moore. — New York: G. P. Putnam. 1864–1866. 11 vols. Vol. 1.
RHODES, JAMES FORD. — History of the United States. — New York: The Macmillan Company. 1904. 6 vols.
RICHARDSON, ALBERT D. — Beyond the Mississippi, 1857–1867. — Hartford: American Publishing Company. 1867. Pp. 572.
SANDERS, LLOYD C. — Celebrities of the Century. — London: Cassell & Company.
SCHARF, J. THOMAS. — History of the Confederate Navy. — New York: Rogers and Sherwood. 1887. Pp. 874.
SCHOTT, W. W. — History of Orange County, Virginia. — Richmond: Everett Waddey Company. 1907. Pp. 292.
SCHOULER, JAMES. — History of the United States of America. — New York: Dodd, Mead & Company. 1891. 5 vols.
SHAMBAUGH, BENJ. F. — Messages and Proclamations of the Governors of Iowa (vol. 2). — Iowa City. 1903. 8 vols.
SIEBERT, WILBUR H. — The Underground Railway. — New York: The Macmillan Company. 1898. Pp. 478.
SMITH, H. A. — One Hundred Famous Americans. — New York: George Routledge & Sons. 1886.
STILES, ROBERT. — Four Years under Marse Robert. — New York: Neale Publishing Company. 1904. Pp. 368.
STILL, WILLIAM. — The Underground Railroad. — Philadelphia: People's Publishing Company. 1872. Pp. 780.
TRUMBULL, H. CLAY. — War Memories of a Chaplain, by H. Clay Trumbull, formerly Chaplain of the Tenth Regiment Connecticut Volunteers. — New York: Charles Scribner's Sons. 1898. Pp. 421.
VICTOR, ORVILLE JAMES. — History of American Conspiracies. — New York: James D. Torrey. 1863. Pp. 579.
VIRGINIA, UNIVERSITY OF. — New York: Lewis Publishing Co. 1904. 2 vols.
WALCOTT, CHARLES FOLSOM. — History of the Twenty-First Regiment Massachusetts Volunteers in the War for the Preservation of the Union. — Boston: Houghton, Mifflin & Co. 1882. Pp. 502.
WAR OF THE REBELLION. — Official Records of the Union and Confederate Armies.
WIGHAM, ELIZA. — The Anti-Slavery Cause in America and its Martyrs. — London. 1863.
WILLIAMS, GEORGE W. — History of the Negro Race in America from 1619 to 1880. — New York: G. P. Putnam's Sons. 1883. 2 vols.
WILLIAMS, JAMES. — Letters on Slavery from the Old World. — Nashville: Southern Methodist Publishing House. 1861. Pp. 321.
WILSON, HENRY. — History of the Rise and Fall of the Slave Trade in America. — Boston: J. R. Osgood & Company. 1872–1874. 2 vols.
WILSON, WOODROW. — A History of the American People. — New York: Harper and Brothers. 1902. 5 vols.
WITHROW, W. H. — The Underground Railroad. — Proceedings and Transactions of the Royal Society of Canada, 2d Series. Vol. 8 (1902).

INDEX

The letters noted in the Index include all those which are quoted, whether in whole or in part, in the text. In some cases the names of the persons to whom the letters were addressed are found only in the Notes. The Index contains also references to some of the more important matters of interest embodied in the Notes; but no attempt has been made to index the Notes and Appendix as text. The capital letter B refers always to the subject of the book.

Abbott, James Burnett, reinforces B at Black Jack, 208; attacks Franklin, 212; in command of defence of Lawrence, 258; 380.
Abolition, outlook for, never so hopeful as at time of Harper's Ferry raid, 586.
Abolitionism, Owen Brown's conversion to, 14; charge of, disavowed by Big Springs Convention, 104.
Abolitionists, causes of B's later disgust with, 45; B's first contact with those of New England, 49, 50; radical, disappointed by platform of Big Springs Convention, 103; militant, reap harvest in sack of Lawrence, 188; charged with responsibility for Pottawatomie murders, 191; difference between their view and B's of the slavery issue, 336; in their view slavery was the sum of human wickedness, 384; Southern view of their wishes, 436. See Radical Political Abolitionists.
Abolitionists in Kansas, in 1854 and 1855. See Free State men.
Adair, Charles S., warns Osawatomie of approach of Border Ruffians, 243; 175.
Adair, Mrs. Florilla, half-sister of B, 82, 166, 196. Wife of
Adair, Rev. Samuel Lyle, settles at Osawatomie, Kansas, 79; quoted concerning meeting of settlers at Osawatomie, 104, 135; gives shelter to Jason and John, Jr., after Pottawatomie, 166; refuses to receive Owen, 167; later, approves B's action, 167; receives slaves freed by B in Missouri raid, 372; 82, 128, 179, 196, 210, 239, 242, 293, 304, 308, 358, 398. *Letters to* Owen Brown, 606 n. 86, S. C. and Mrs. Davis, 253 n., James Hanway, 372; *from* B, 136, 303, 306.
Adams, Annie (Brown), daughter of B, first heard of proposed raid in 1854, 54, 55, 56; joins B at Kennedy Farm, 405; her recollections of the life there, 416-420; sent away from Harper's Ferry, 420; enters Sanborn's school, 533; quoted, concerning Hazlett, 572, and Tidd, 681; as to other matters, 78, 81 n., 408, 421, 422, 424, 594 n. 12, 595 n. 20.
Adams, F. G., 181.
Adams, George, letter from B, 542.
Adams, John Quincy, Pres. of U. S., 23.
Adamson, Mr., 239.
Æsop's Fables, 16.
Akron (Ohio), B's operations at, in 1855, 85; 27, 34.
Alabama, pro-slavery men from, in Kansas, 137, 138.
Albany Journal, quoted, 138, 139.
Alburtis, Capt. E. G., of the Martinsburg company, quoted concerning fight at Harper's Ferry, 443, 444; 447.
Alcott, Amos Bronson, impressions of B in 1859, 398.
Alderman, Amos D., 121.
Alderman, Henry, 121.
Allan, Elizabeth Preston, *Life and Letters of Margaret Junkin Preston,* quoted, 556.

Allegheny Mountains, B's first thought of, as future scene of his operations, 48.
Allen, C. G., 236.
Allen, Ethan, and Co., 282.
Allstadt, John H., taken prisoner by B's men, 431, 432, 437, 439.
Allstadt, John Thomas, taken prisoner by B's men, 432; quoted concerning killing of Mayor Beckham, 441; and the wounding, 441, and death, 448, of Oliver Brown.
American Anti-Slavery Society, 559.
Anderson, Col. Edward, 179.
Anderson, Capt. G. T., 351.
Anderson, Jeremiah Goldsmith, killed in engine-house, 449, 454 and n.; sketch of, 681, 682; 400, 402, 407, 419, 462 n., 558 n.
Anderson, Osborn Perry (colored), elected "member of Congress" at Chatham Convention, 333; quoted, 420; receives George Washington's sword from Col. Washington, 431; his escape, 445, 471; his incredible account of his escape and Hazlett's, in *A Voice from Harper's Ferry,* 445, 446, 685; sketch of, 685; 331, 413, 415, 419, 439, 537.
Anderson, Samuel, 175.
Andreas, A. T., *History of the State of Kansas,* quoted, 117, 212, 350, 602 n. 13.
Andrew, John A., his impressions of and sympathy with B, 400; criticises undue haste of B's trial, 482; retains Chilton to defend B, 493; quoted, 557; before the Mason Committee, 634 n. 113; 479 n., 560, 561. *Letters to* W. P. Fessenden, 530, Dr. S. G. Howe, 532 n. And see Pearson, Henry G.
Anthony, Col. D. R., 574.
Anthony, Capt. J. M., his *Old John Brown,* quoted, 154.
Anti-Slavery doctrines, disavowed by both Free State conventions in autumn of 1855, 104, 105.
Anti-Slavery meetings, attended by B, 49.
Anti-Slavery party, depressed by result of first election in Kansas, 95; designs of, as represented by pro-slavery leaders, 97.
Anti-Slavery Standard, 575.
Arabia, river steamer, 225.
Archibald, Eben, 380.
Army Appropriation Bill, 1856, 227.
Arny, William F. M., 276, 277, 361.
Arrest of judgment, motion for, in B's case, argued and denied, 497.
Arsenal, at Harper's Ferry, 428, 429, 430.
Ashby, Capt. Turner, 555, 683 n. 128.
Atchison, David R., pro-slavery leader in Kansas, urges Missourians to vote in Kansas election, 94; his speech at Weston, 94, 97; urges Missourians to invade Kansas, 117; and the Lawrence treaty of peace, 124; commands Platte County Riflemen, 144; leaves Border Ruffians to attack Free State Hotel, 145; pro-slavery circular of, 156; commands forces marching on Osawatomie, 240; disbandment of his forces a fatal blow to hopes of Mis-

INDEX

sourians, 260; quoted, 596 n. 4; 130, 179, 192, 225, 229, 230, 250, 257.
Atchison Freedom's Champion, on the Harper's Ferry raid, 473.
Atlantic Monthly, 221, 304 n., 349, 362.
Austin, Freeman, captain of Osawatomie Company, 229, 244, 245, 246, 250.
Avery, Dr., 233.
Avis, Capt. John, B's kind and considerate jailer at Charlestown, 488, 544; B pledged not to attempt to escape, 512; his affidavit as to his relations with B, 670, 671; 439, 499, 545, 546, 571, 578.
Ayres, name of two Missouri raiders, 368.

B., E., of Rhode Island, letter from B, 539.
B., T. A., letter to Gov. Wise, 518.
Babb, Edmund, suspected of writing "Floyd letter," 411.
Babcock, Mr., 233.
Bacon, Rev. Dr. Leonard, schoolmate of B, 17; interview with B at Tallmadge, Ohio, 293.
Bacon, Rev. Leonard W., his *John Brown*, 592 n. 15.
Baker, Mr., outrage on, 172.
Baillie, John A., 214.
Ball, A. M., master-machinist of B. & O. R. R., taken prisoner at Harper's Ferry, 439.
Baltimore, sends five militia companies to Harper's Ferry, 444.
Baltimore American, quoted, 569.
Baltimore Convention (1860), 585.
Baltimore Greys, 467.
Baltimore Patriot, quoted, 568.
Baltimore Sun, 417, 568.
Baltimore and Ohio R. R., train of, held up by B's men, 432, 433; employees of, in Martinsburg Company, 443; and the precautions taken for execution of B, 524, 525.
Bancroft, Frederic, his *Life of W. H. Seward*, quoted, 475 n.
Barber, Gen., 189.
Barber, Thos. W., murdered by Clark, 118, 180, 330, 352; his the only life lost in the "Wakarusa War," 126; rival claimants to the honor of having killed him, 126.
Barbour, Alfred W., 465.
Barnes, William, letters from B, 276, 283.
Bates County (Mo.) Standard, letter from Rev. Martin White, 242.
Battle of the Spurs, the, 381-383; authorities for account of, 634 n. 100.
Baumer, Mr., 388.
Baxter, Richard, his *Saint's Rest*, 16.
Baylor, Col. Robert W., at Harper's Ferry, 447, 452, 465; charges preferred against, 464; court of inquiry, 464.
Beckham, Fontaine, Mayor of Harper's Ferry, killed by Edwin Coppoc, 441; fierce indignation of citizens, 441, 442; a friend to the negro, 442 n.; 447, 479, 570.
Beecher, Henry Ward, 188, 191, 518 n.
"Beecher's Bibles," Sharp's rifles so-called, 188, 306.
Bell, James M., colored, 330.
Benjamin, Jacob, 151, 152, 178, 240, 247.
Bernard, J., on the Pottawatomie murders, 190.
Bernard, J. M., his store pillaged, by B's orders, 210.
Berryville (Va.) Clarke Journal, quoted, 501.
Bertram, John, 281.
Bethune, Dr. George W., 563.
Bickerton, Capt. Thomas, concerning the second attack on Franklin, 230, 234; 232, 256.
Bierce, Gen. Lucius V., 85, 153.
Big Springs Convention (Free State), Sept. 5, 1855, 91; nominates A. H. Reeder for Congress, 103; its platform disappointing to radical Abolitionists, 103, 104; favors exclusion from Kansas of all negroes, and denounces attempts to interfere with slaves and slavery; 104; disavows charge of abolitionism, 104; denounced by Charles Stearns, 104; its cowardliness fails to mollify hostile Missourians, 104; entitled to a measure of credit, 105; but attempts to face both ways, 105; creates Territorial Executive Committee, 106.
Biggs, Dr., 461.
Black Jack, a spring on the Sante Fe trail, fight at, 200 seqq.; described by B and by H. C. Pate, 202-207; Pate's article in N. Y. *Tribune*, 204; crucial moment of, 207; list of participants on B's side, 614 n. 25; authorities for narrative of, 614 n. 28.
Black Laws of Shawnee Legislature, 91, 92, 101; no genuine attempt to enforce, 101; effect of, in north and east, 101.
Blair, Charles, contracts to make pikes for B, 283, 284, 400, 401; his delay in delivering them, 284; the procedure of "a canny Yankee," 284, 285.
Blair, Montgomery, 493, 508.
Blake, Major G. A. H., 224.
Blakesley, Levi, adopted brother of B, 2, 14, 17.
"Bleeding Kansas," direct relation of, to Harper's Ferry and the Civil War, 201.
Blessing, John H., B gives his Bible to, 553.
Blood, James, quoted concerning Pottawatomie affair, 154; 175, 176, 232.
Blue Lodges, in Kansas election, 98.
Blunt, John, 168.
Boerley, Thomas, shot by B's raiders, 435, 437, 479.
Boice, Capt., 247.
Bolivar Heights, 428, 429, 431, 435, 437.
Bondi, August, his story of B's camp on Ottawa Creek, 198, 199; his store burned and cattle stolen, 200; concerning the outrages committed by pro-slavery men, 212, and the "lifting" of Dutch Henry's horses, 235; 151, 152, 155, 175, 177, 178, 202, 210, 211, 229, 234, 236, 240, 247.
Boone, Col., 189.
Boonville (Mo.) Observer, quoted, 99, 216.
Booth, John Wilkes, 555.
Border Ruffians, eastern settlers' opinion of, 96; described by W. A. Phillips, 96, 97; and by T. H. Gladstone and Sara T. L. Robinson, 97; misrepresentations of their leaders, 97; destroy Free State Hotel, 145, 146; lawless character of, 171; not guilty of assaults on women, 173, 174; threats of violence common among, 178, 179; elated by sack of Lawrence, 181; believed thoroughly in justice of their cause, 186; causes of their bitterness against Free State men, 186; under Rev. M. White, arrest Jason Brown, 194; Jason's story of their treatment of himself and John Brown, Jr., 194 seqq.; bent on rescuing Pate, are headed off by Col. Sumner, 209; blockade Missouri River against Lane's Free State men, 225; put to flight by Cline's company on South Middle Creek, 237; their raid on Osawatomie, 240 seqq.; destroy the settlement, 246; losses in Osawatomie fight, 248, 249; no worse than "Kansas Ruffians" in summer of 1856, 264; in the Marais des Cygnes massacre, 348 seqq.; at Fort Scott, 352; 93, 130. See also Alabama, Georgia, Missourians as Kansas Militia, Pro-slavery men, etc., and South Carolina.
Border Times, 193.
Boston, great meeting in Tremont Temple on day of B's execution, 559, 560.
Boston Transcript, quoted, 481.
Boston Traveller, 498 n.
Boteler, A. R., concerning death of Kagi and Leary, 445.
Botts, Capt., 439.
Botts, John Minor, quoted, 649 n. 50.
Botts, Lawson, assigned as counsel for B, 483.

484; opening address of, 490; denounced by B, and withdraws from defence, 492; assists Hoyt, 493; sketch of, 645 n. 49; 486, 487, 489, 491, 507. *Letter from* A. H. Lewis, 506.
Bowditch, Henry I., 516.
Bowditch, William I., 516.
Bowen, Dr. Jesse, consignee of B's revolvers, 289; and B's escape from arrest in Iowa City, 388. *Letter from* B, 388.
Bowles, Samuel, quoted, 558.
Bowman, George E., 591 n. 6.
Brackett, Edwin A., sketches B in jail, 546; 574.
"Branded Hand, The," sobriquet of Jonathan Walker, 51, 594 n. 13.
Branson, Jacob, arrest and rescue of (1855), 113, 114, 129, 140, 380.
Brennen, Francis, 121.
Brewster, Martha E. See Brown, Mrs. Martha E.
Brockett, Lieut., Pate's lieutenant at Black Jack, 202, 206, 207; declines to take part in Marais des Cygnes massacre, 348; clerk in Land Office at Fort Scott, 352; quoted by Crawford, 374.
Brooks, Preston, assault on Charles Sumner, 154, 327.
Brown, Col. (pro-slavery), 240.
Brown, Dr. (pro-slavery), at public meeting in Tabor, 385.
Brown, Mr., State Senator of Mississippi (pro-slavery), quoted, 566.
Brown, Agnes, daughter of Salmon, 595 n. 22.
Brown, Amelia, daughter of B, death of, 3*.
Brown, Annie, daughter of B. See Adams, Mrs. Annie (Brown).
Brown, Austin, son of Jason, death of, 81.
Brown, Mrs. Dianthe (Lusk), first wife of B, her character and disposition, 6, 7, 18; her marriage to B, 18; mother of seven children, 19; her lineage, 19; insanity in her family, 19, 592 n. 21; mental derangement, 19, 507; her death, 19, 24, 592 n. 28; 22, 23.
Brown, Ellen, infant daughter of B, death of, 67.
Brown, Ellen, daughter of B. See Fablinger, Mrs. Ellen (Brown).
Brown, Frederick, uncle of B, his children, 12; 18, 37.
Brown, Frederick, brother of B, birth of, 13. *Letter from* B, 43.
Brown, Frederick, infant son of B, death of, 24.
Brown, Frederick, son of B, third sergeant of Liberty Guards, 121; and the claim-jumper, 130; on B's surveying tour, 133; in the Pottawatomie party, 153; keeps his hands unstained at Pottawatomie, 165, 166; and the alleged assault on Mary Grant, 173; at Black Jack, 203; his appearance there decisive, 207, 208; his reasons for returning to Kansas with B, 224; his last parting with B, 239; murdered by Rev. Martin White (Aug. 1856), 241, 242, 357; mental derangement of, 507; 19, 76, 81, 83, 91, 120, 121, 159, 160, 162, 198, 210, 222, 247, 278, 598 n. 33.
Brown, Frederick, son of Watson, 415, 416.
Brown, George Washington, indicted for treason, 142; B's opinion of his *Herald of Freedom*, 354.
Brown, Mrs. Isabella (Thompson), wife of Watson, 422, 561. *Letters from* Watson Brown, 415, 416.
Brown, Jason, son of B, in Springfield office of Perkins and Brown, 59; goes to Kansas, 75, 76; his "shanty" at Osawatomie, 89; and the Indians, 90; ignorant of real purpose of Pottawatomie expedition, 153; horrified by the murders, remonstrates with B, 165; questions Frederick, 165, 166; returns to Osawatomie with John, Jr., 166; taken in by the Adairs, 166; and the alleged assault on Mary Grant,

173; arrested by Border Ruffians under Rev. Martin White, 194; his story of their treatment of John, Jr. and himself, 194 seqq.; taken to Lecompton and released, 197; joins his **father's company**, 197; goes to Iowa with B, 261, 262; with B in Chicago, 269; declines to join B at Harper's Ferry, 413; quoted, concerning B's temperance principles, 21, the Browns' migratory habit, 28 n., the first news of Pottawatomie murders, 151, B's parting company with John, Jr. at Prairie City, 151, B and burning Osawatomie, 248; 19, 39, 44, 45, 46, 81, 91, 112, 118, 148, 179, 207, 210, 223, 245, 246, 247, 253, 287, 343, 397. *Letters to* Mary Anne Brown, 172, 173, Ruth (Brown) Thompson, 229.
Brown, Mrs. Jason, 173, 197, 223. *Letter to* Mary Anne Brown, 112.
Brown, Jeremiah, brother of B, 270.
Brown, John, great-great-grandfather of B, 10.
Brown, John, great-grandfather of B, 10.
Brown, John, grandfather of B, a revolutionary soldier, 1, 10, 278, 543; children of, 11.
Brown, John, uncle of B, 12.
Brown, John, of Osawatomie.
EARLY YEARS. — Birth (Torrington, Conn., May 9, 1800), 1, 13; early years and character described by himself in letter to Henry L. Stearns, 1-7; descent, 1, 10, 15; moved to Ohio (1805), 2; in school of adversity, 2; addicted to lying in boyhood, 3; effect on, of war of 1812, 4; interest in slavery question first aroused, 4; taste for reading,4, 5; desire to excel, 5; an early convert to Christianity, 5; familiar with the Bible, 6; his trading instincts, 6; vanity fed by success in business, 6; marries Dianthe Lusk, 6, 18; liking for domestic animals and for shepherd's calling, 7; accustomed to adversity, 8; character, as moulded by his early training, 9; resemblance to his father, 11; "a representative of the best type of old New England citizenship," 15; influence of ancestry on, 15; the first American hanged for treason, 15; boyhood, 16; an excellent Bible-teacher, 16; the Bible his favorite book, 16; range of reading, 16; schooling in Ohio, Connecticut, and Massachusetts, 16, 17; thinks of entering ministry, 17; returns to Ohio and tanning, 17; an excellent cook, 17; opposition to slavery confirmed, 17, 18; kindness of heart, 18; genuineness of his Christian principles, 18; a domestic despot, 19, 36; his children devoted to him, 19; his early severity to them, 19, 592 n. 23; his tenderness and devotion in later years, 19, 20; requires strict observance of the Sabbath, 20; his intense religious training of his sons results in a reaction, 21; views on temperance, 21; early marrie l life of, described by James Foreman, 21-23; debate with Methodist minister, 22; moves to Richmond, Penn. (1825), 23; his value to that new settlement, 23; postmaster of Randolph, Penn., 23; his connection with school and church work there, 24; marries his second wife, Mary Anne Day, 24, 25; organizes an independent Congregational Church, 25; mail-carrier, 25; an "Adams man" in politics, 25; unabated interest in fugitive slaves, 25; Free Masonry and the murder of Morgan, 26; moves to Franklin Mills, Ohio (1835), 26; in financial distress, 26; contractor for canal construction, 27; unsuccessful land speculations, 27; interested in Franklin Land Co., 27; insolvency due to failure of real-estate ventures, 28; his integrity unjustly questioned, 28; his business misfortunes explained, 28, 29, 593 n. 32, 33; returns to Hudson, Ohio (1837), 29; breeds race-horses, 29; first visit to New York, 29; beginning of his career as "John Brown, shepherd," 29; uses

714　　　　　　　　　　INDEX　　　　　　　　[John Brown

money placed in his hands by New England Woolen Co. for purchase of sheep, 30; his distressing circumstances, 30; negotiations with trustees of Oberlin College, concerning purchase of land in Virginia, come to nothing through his vacillation, 31–33; shepherd for Capt. Oviatt, 33; moves to Richfield, Ohio (1842), 33; loses four young children, 34; goes through bankruptcy, 34; success in raising cattle and sheep, 34; moves to Akron, Ohio (1844), 34; in partnership with Simon Perkins, Jr. in sheep-raising, 34, 35; involved in extensive litigation, 36, 37; suit of Western Reserve Bank and its complications, 37–39; his conduct in this litigation open to criticism, 38; quarrel with A. P. Chamberlain, 39–41, 593 n. 49.

GENSIS OF HIS GREAT PLAN.— When did the forcible overthrow of slavery become " his greatest or principal object "? 42 seqq.; no documentary evidence of special interest in slavery until 1834, 43; plans school for negroes, 44; requires his children to swear to do their utmost to abolish slavery (1839?), 45, 46; Gen. Carrington's anecdote of, 47; confides his plan to Frederick Douglass, 47, 48; idea of using force probably not conceived until after 1840, 48; gradual evolution of his plan, 48, 49; removes to Springfield, Mass. (1846), 49; in touch with militant Boston Abolitionists, 49; early acquaintance with the *Liberator*, 49; approves of Greeley's doctrine of opposing slavery with Sharp's rifles, but not of the Garrisonian policy of non-resistance, 49; his *Sambo's Mistakes*, 50, 659–661; policy of armed resistance clearly developed in 1851, 50, 51; founds U. S. League of Gileadites, 50; his *Words of Advice* to them, 50, 51, 52; strives to band negroes together to resist slave-catchers, 51; obtains signatures of 44 negroes to his " agreement " and resolutions, 52, which contain direct counsel to resist officers of the law with force, and to " shoot to kill," 53; his memorandum-book, no. 2, 53; confides details of Virginia plan to Woodruff and others in 1854 or 1855, 54; tries to secure Woodruff's cooperation, 54; Harper's Ferry design probably revealed to others as early, 54, 55, but may have been conceived much earlier, 55; his plan and his object probably varied from year to year, 55, 56; hopes to help Southern leaders to secede, and his reason therefor, 56; his main motive to come to close quarters with slavery, 56.

WOOL-MERCHANT.— Establishes headquarters at Springfield for sale of Perkins and Brown's wool, 57; his home and mode of life in Springfield, described by Fred'k Douglass, 57; his personal appearance and characteristics at that period, 57, 58; interested in export of wool, 59, 61; not fitted for the business, 60, 61; trip to Europe (1849), 61; on the continent, 61, 62; ill-success of trip, 62, 63; relations with Simon Perkins, 64, 65; litigation with Warren, 65, and with Burlington Mills Co., 66; close of his career as a wool-merchant, 66; continues in farming and sheep-raising with Perkins, till 1854, with some success, 66, 67; deaths of infant children, 67; residence in Springfield, 67; controversy with Sunderland the hypnotist, 67, 68; attends Zion Methodist Church, 68; disturbed by his sons' religious backsliding, 68–70; his wish to help negroes inspires his plan to move to Adirondacks, 70; visits North Elba, 71; beginning of his friendship with Gerrit Smith, 71; removes family to North Elba (1849), 72; hires farm there, 72; wins prize at cattle fair, 72; his counsel to the negroes, 72; defends them against white residents of North Elba, 73; described by R. H. Dana, Jr., 74; urges North Elba negroes to resist Fugitive Slave Law, 75; commands his children to resist attempts to enforce it, 75; leaves for Akron, 75; continues farming and sheep-raising there four years, 75; second removal to North Elba (June, 1855), 76; buys three farms there, 72, 76; his restlessness leaves him no peace, and he turns toward Kansas, 76, 596 n. 64.

FIRST DAYS IN KANSAS. — Metamorphosis into Capt. John Brown of Osawatomie, 77, 78; a natural leader, 77; his straightforward unselfishness, 78; parting words to his family on leaving for Kansas, 78; receives letters from John, Jr. in Kansas, reciting conditions and appealing for arms, 82, 83; their effect on him, 84, 85; leaves North Elba again (Aug. 1855), 85, 86; attends anti-slavery convention at Syracuse, 85; money raised for him, 85; ships firearms to Cleveland, 85; holds meetings and receives contributions at Akron and elsewhere in Ohio, 85; in Chicago, 86; journey thence described, 87; what he saw in Missouri, 87; his meeting with a Missourian, 88; joins sons at Osawatomie (Oct. 7, 1855), 88; his destitute condition, 88; finds the settlement in distress, 88; his purpose not to settle in Kansas, but to fight along the Kansas-Missouri line, 93; believes in " meddling directly with the peculiar institution," 93; prepared to take property or lives of Border Ruffians, 93; effect upon him of crimes of Missourians in Kansas, 111; goes armed to election of Free State delegate, 111; describes relief of Lawrence by Free State men and end of " Wakarusa War," 118–120; muster-roll of his company, the Liberty Guards, 121; is called captain, 121; his part in events at Lawrence slurred over by himself, 122; R. G. Elliott concerning, 122; impression of age produced by him, 122; James F. Legate concerning, 122; his view of the treaty of Lawrence, 123, 124, 127; declares himself an Abolitionist and offers to attack Border Ruffian camp, 123; talk with Legate about slavery, 124; returns, with sons, to Brown's Station, 126, 127; visits Missouri, 127; chairman of Osawatomie convention to nominate state officers, 127; position won by him in Kansas, 127; in Missouri again, 128; his surveying tour, 133; Henry Thompson's regard for him, 134; at settlers' meeting at Osawatomie, 134; words attributed to him by Rev. Martin White, 134; Judge Cato's court, 135, 136; his knowledge of surveying turned to account, 137.

POTTAWATOMIE. — His brief report of the Pottawatomie murders, 148; question of his criminality in the business still subject of dispute in Kansas, 148; place in history depends on view taken of his conduct in that business, 148; leaves camp of John, Jr.'s company at Prairie City, 151; his action determined by complaints of Weiner, 151; his plan revealed to a council of some of John, Jr.'s company, 152; preparations for the expedition, 153; " tired of caution," 153; his manner on the journey, 154; plan disclosed to Townsley, 155; proposes to strike at night, 155, 157; his influence over his sons, 158; the killing of the Doyles, 158–161; none of them killed by his hand, 159; the killing of Wilkinson, 161, and of William Sherman, 162–164; recognized by Harris, 163; satisfied at last, 164; did he intend to kill Judge Wilson? 165; meets Jason Brown and talks with him, 165; hue and cry after, 166; opinions of Free State men concerning his action, 167–169; Charles Robinson concerning, 169, 170; views of James Hanway and T. W. Higginson, 170; possible justification of his act discussed, 170 seqq.; not recalled to Pottawatomie because Free State women were in danger, 172, 173; had not heard of attack on Morse, 175; was he warned of threats by an unidentified " messenger"? 175, 176; his conduct inconsistent with " messenger " theory, 176; probable grounds of his determination, 176; probably impelled largely by general body of threats against Free State settlers, 177, 178; why, then, did he start for Lawrence? 178, 179; his own statements of his reasons for the murders, 179, 180; E. A. Coleman's and Col. Anderson's reports of his words, 179; logical result of this plea, 179; other excuses offered for his crime, 180, 181; said to have been divinely inspired, 181; his action a failure as a peace measure, but successful as a war measure, 181, 182; was he obeying orders of Free State leaders? 182-184; S. C. Pomeroy on this point, 182, 183; not in Lawrence May 21, as alleged by Pomeroy, 183; likened by C. Robinson to the Saviour, 184; never claimed to have acted under orders, 184; said to have stated that victims were tried by jury, 184; believed a conflict inevitable, 185; killed his men in the honest belief that he was a faithful servant of Kansas and the Lord, 185; his motives wholly unselfish, 185; his aim to free a race, 185; his act no more excusable than similar acts of Border Ruffians, 186; absurdity of likening him to Grant, etc., 187; always disingenuous about the murders, 187; ethically the Pottawatomie crime cannot be successfully palliated or excused, 187, 188, 612 n. 90.

BLACK JACK TO OSAWATOMIE. — Prowls about camp where Jason and John, Jr. were prisoners, hoping to rescue them, 196; at Jason's claim, 197; thence to Ottawa Creek, 198; meets and eludes U. S. troops, 198; camp on Ottawa Creek described by Bondi and Redpath, 198-200; preparing "a handful of young men for the work of laying the foundations of a free commonwealth," 199; hears of camp of Missourians at Black Jack, 200; J. E. B. Stuart and H. C. Pate, 201; starts with Prairie City Rifles for Pate's camp at Black Jack, 201, 202; accused of violating flag of truce, 203, 205, 206; describes battle of Black Jack in letter to his family, 203, and in N. Y. Tribune, 204-207; his and Shore's written agreement with Pate, 207; releases Pate's prisoners, 208; his views of Free State men, 208; his camp broken up, prisoners released, and men dispersed, by Col. Sumner, 209; orders pillaging of Bernard's stores, 209, 210; thinks raiding for supplies justified, 210; in hiding, 210, 211, 220; reign of terror at Osawatomie due to Pottawatomie murders, 213, 215; resumes activity in July (1856), 220; in Lawrence en route to Topeka, 220; ride to Topeka described by W. A. Phillips, 221; his view of affairs in Kansas, 221; censures both parties, 221; his sociological views, 221; slavery " the sum of all villainies," 222; at the Willets farm near Topeka, 222; leaves Topeka neighborhood, 222-224; members of his party, 222; his contest with his son Oliver, 223; S. J. Reader's impressions of him, 223, 224; first meeting with Aaron D. Stevens, 224; turns back at Nebraska City, 224; starts with Walker and Lane for Lawrence, 228; at Topeka again, 228; Walker deemed him insane, 228; talk with Walker on Pottawatomie murders and responsibility therefor, 228; and with John, Jr., 228, 229 and n.; in Lawrence, 229; the " old terrifier," 230; probably not at capture of " Forts " Stanwood and Titus, 232; demands extreme penalty against prisoners taken at Titus, 233; his renewed activity after exchange of prisoners, 235 and n.; 1 Osawatomie, 235; his plans, according to Bondi, 235; his concern for good mounts for his men, 235; begins to organize his " volunteer-regular " force, 236; the covenant drawn up by him, 236, 661-664; his plan for meeting the enemy, 236; marches south into Linn County, 236; speech to his company, 236; his company and Cline's nearly fight each other, 237; speech to his prisoners, 237, 238; raids pro-slavery settlement at Sugar Creek, 238; returns to Osawatomie with 150 cattle, 238; camps at Crane's ranch, 238; his activity, 238, 239; described by J. H. Holmes, 239; urged by Lane to return to Lawrence, 239; last parting with his son Frederick, 239; anticipation of attack on Osawatomie, 240; warned of Reid's approach, 243; his part in the battle, 244 seqq.; tactical disadvantage of his position, 245; his forces retreat into the river, 245; his linen duster, etc., 245, 246; report of his death, 247; makes no attempt to rally his force, 247; " I will carry the war into Africa," 248; exaggerates pro-slavery losses, 248, 249; his newspaper account of the fight, 249; his arrival in Lawrence (Sept. 7, 1856), described by H. Reisner, 253; movements in the interim, 253; offered and declines command of expedition against Leavenworth, 254; remains with John, Jr., 254, 255; his share in defence of Lawrence, 258, 259; his reasons for deciding to leave Kansas for the East, 261; at Tabor, Iowa, 261, 267; narrowly escapes arrest, 261, 621 n. 86; Jason Brown's narrative of the journey, 261; controversy concerning his private meeting with C. Robinson, 263; condition of affairs in Kansas when he left, 264; his then status in the country's eyes, 266; uncompromising hostility to slavery his chief claim to a place in history, 266.

IN THE EAST. — Tabor, a congenial haven, 267; chooses it as headquarters of his " volunteer-regular " force, 268; unjustly denounces Gov. Geary, 268; his plans for war on slavery, 268; in Chicago, 268, 269; returns to Tabor, at request of Kansas Nat. Com., 269, 270; to Chicago and North Elba, with his son Watson, 270; quoted concerning defeat of Frémont by Buchanan, 270 n.; in Boston early in 1857, 271; meets F. B. Sanborn, Theo. Parker, William Lloyd Garrison, and others, 271; Sanborn's and Garrison's impressions, 271, 272; first visit to G. L. Stearns, 272; his view of Free State leaders in Kansas, 272; A. A. Lawrence's impressions of, 273; Thoreau's impressions of, 273, 274; his connection with Pottawatomie murders never known to Stearns, and not thoroughly to other Boston friends, 274; his Virginia plans not then made known to them, 274, 275; Massachusetts State Kansas Com. votes to furnish rifles and money, 274; controversy concerning the rifles, 275; at meeting of Kansas Nat. Com., 275, 276; $5000 voted to him for *defensive* measures, 276; charges National Com. with bad faith, 276; his requisition for supplies, 276, 277, 664; visits Peterboro, N. Y., and North Elba, 277; again in Boston, 277; wandering restlessly through New England and New York, 277, 278; speech before committee of Mass. Legislature, 278; trying to raise money for his volunteer-regulars, 278 seqq.; at Canton, Conn., 278; contributions received, 278 seqq.; his appeal in N. Y. *Tribune*, 279; assured by Lawrence that his family shall be taken care of, 280; $1000 raised to purchase homestead for family, 280; urges collection of subscriptions, 281; purchase of Thompson land in No. Elba consummated,

281; makes addresses in Worcester, March, 1857, 281; his plans stated, 281; Dr. F. Wayland and R. W. Emerson on his oratory, 281, 282; slim results of Worcester meetings, 282; in Easton, Penn., with ex-Gov. Reeder, 282; learns of his sons' decision to fight no more, 282; financial progress unsatisfactory, 283; expected in Kansas, 283; makes contract for pikes with C. Blair, 283, 284; for what purpose were they ordered? 284, 285; delay in delivery due to lack of funds, 284; first acquaintance with Hugh Forbes, 285; attracted by him and confides plans to him, 285, 286; an unfortunate alliance, 286; his suspicions soon aroused, 286; "helped" by Gerrit Smith, 287; threatened with arrest, 287; with Judge Russell in Boston, 288; his "farewell to the Plymouth Rocks," etc., 288; G. L. Stearns buys revolvers for him, 289; at Albany, N. Y., and Vergennes, Vt., 290; assumes nom de guerre of Nelson Hawkins, 290; John, Jr. fears for his safety in Kansas, 291; leaves for Kansas with considerable supplies, 291, 292; Stearns's confidence in him, 292; reduced to distress before reaching his destination, 292; stages of his retarded journey, 292-294; nom de guerre of James Smith, 292; at Tallmadge, O., semi-centennial, 293; his memorandum-book quoted, 293, 294; in Iowa City, 294; learns that Pottawatomie indictments are nol-pros'd, 294; in Tabor, Aug. 7, 1857, 294; his close friends, at Grasshopper Falls Convention, oppose taking part in election of delegate to Congress, 296; their defeat helped turn his mind to his contemplated raid against slavery, 297; applies to G. L. Stearns for money, 297; his addendum to Forbes's *Duty of a Soldier*, 298; sends copies to Wattles and others, with appeals for aid, 298; Forbes's usefulness of brief duration, 298; table-talk recalled by Rev. H. D. King, 299; in his mind, slavery the one wrong, 299; disagreement with Forbes, 299; leaves Tabor, Nov. 2, 1857, 299; reasons for delay, 299 seqq.; appointed "brigadier-general" by Lane, 301; Jamison's mission, 301; his immediate plans confided to Sanborn, 302; financial condition, 302; apparent lack of determination at this time, 302, 303; defended by Sanborn in letter to Higginson, 303; "the best disunion champion you can find," 303, 304; aided with money by E. B. Whitman, and the Adairs, 304; goes to Lawrence, Kansas, 304, and disappears after two days, 304, 305; stet nominis umbra, 305; in Topeka, 305; not content with policy of Free State leaders to accept existing territorial government, 307; the Free State secret society, 307; enrolls first recruits for Harper's Ferry, 307, 308; J. E. Cook concerning his recruiting operations, 308; his ultimate destination first made known to his men, 308; his vacillation at an end, 308, 309; henceforth all his energies bent upon "troubling Israel" in Virginia, 309; his men not pleased with Virginia plan, 310; has words with Cook, 310; his magnetism prevails, 310; travels across Iowa (Dec. 1857), 311, 312; at Springdale, 312; anecdote of, and J. Townsend, 312; his diary quoted, 312; discloses details of his plan, 313 seqq.; first mention of Harper's Ferry, Jan. 15, 1858, 313; differences with Forbes, 313; his Virginia plan divulged by Forbes, 313, 314; "The Well-Matured Plan," 314; Forbes's plan the more practical, 314; efforts to dissuade him, 316; with F. Douglass in Rochester, 317; unpleasant relations with Forbes, 317 seqq.; dictates disingenuous letter from John, Jr. to Forbes, 318; tries to arrange meeting at Gerrit Smith's, 319; confides his plan to Smith, 420; reads to Smith and Sanborn his constitution for governing the territory he might redeem from slavery, 321; his will prevails, 321, 322; discloses his plan to the Gloucesters and other negroes in Brooklyn and Phila., 323; tries to enlist new recruits, 323; disappointed by H. Thompson's refusal, 323, 324; in Boston, 324; asks Theo. Parker to prepare addresses to U. S. troops and to citizens generally, 324, 325; concern for his men's reading, 325; method of raising funds for him, 325; Higginson's characterization, 326; Senator Sumner's coat, 327; in various parts of N. Y., 327; in St. Catherine's, Canada, 327; and Harriet Tubman, 327; his stay in Canada a reconnoissance, 328; Dr. Delaney, 328; returns to Springdale for his "sheep," 328; new recruits, 328; Springdale to Chatham, Canada, via Chicago, 329, 330; vain attempts to keep his men from writing indiscreet letters, 330; speech to the Chatham Convention, 331, 332; his "Provisional Constitution," etc., 332, 333; chosen commander-in-chief, 333; the constitution considered as a revelation of his character and philosophy, 334 seqq.; some provisions suggest insanity, 334, 335; difference between his views and those of the Abolitionists, 336; Chatham Convention exhausts his funds, 336, 337; needs of his men, 337; in Boston again, 338; consents to temporary shelving of Virginia plan, 339, 340; his opinion of his "backers," as reported by Higginson, 340; receives some money and arms, 340, 341; attitude of Boston group at this time (spring of 1858) the first sign of the effort to evade responsibility, 342.

KANSAS AGAIN; THE MISSOURI RAID. — In North Elba and Cleveland, en route to Kansas, 343; loses five of his men by postponement of his plan, 344; in Lawrence in disguise, June 25, 1858, 345; assumes name of Shubel Morgan 345; attracted by exploits of James Montgomery, 352; in touch with Montgomery, 353; prepares "Articles of Agreement for Shubel Morgan's Company," 353; describes condition of affairs in southeastern Kansas, 354, 355; his opinion of the *Herald of Freedom*, 354; interesting personal disclosures in letter to John, Jr. 355; directs him to collect material for "A Brief History of John Brown, otherwise (old B)," etc., 356; builds "Fort Snyder," 356; did he acquire title to Snyder's claim? 356, 357; tries to obtain revolvers sent by National Kansas Com., 357; refuses to take revenge on Martin White, 357, 358; ill at the Adairs', Aug.–Sept., 1858, 358; in Lawrence, 359; need of funds supplied in part by notes sent by G. L. Stearns, 359, 360; signs as agent for National Kansas Com., 360; his authority denied by H. B. Hurd, 360; a pardonable error of judgment, 360, 361; his view of the slavery question, according to W. A. Phillips, 362; prophesies war, 362; his whereabouts in Oct. (1858), 362, 363; state of his health, 363; the Wattles family's recollection of him, 363; with Montgomery in his raid on Paris, Kans., 364; Acting-Gov. Walsh urges offer of reward for his apprehension, 364; plot to capture, 364; drafts a peace agreement, which is adopted at meeting of Free Soilers and pro-slaverymen, 365, 366, 665, 666; joins Montgomery in attack on Fort Scott, 366; his dislike of serving under another keeps him from taking an active part, 366; wrongfully charged by Robinson and others with responsibility for Fort Scott affair, 367; why Montgomery assumed leadership, 367; the Missouri raid (Dec. 1858), 367 seqq.; due to the story told by Jim Daniels, 367; his companions in the raid, 368; slaves not the only property taken.

368, 369; Pres. Buchanan and the Governor of Missouri offer reward for his arrest, 371; returns to Kansas with freed slaves, 371, 372; prepares to repel counter-invasion, 373; in camp on Turkey Creek, 373; at Osawatomie, 374; interview with G. A. Crawford, 374, 375; his "Parallels" published in N. Y. *Tribune*, 375, 376; denounced by Gov. Medary and censured by Kansas Legislature, 376, 377; his presence in Kansas the cause of excitement and strife, 378; effect of Missouri raid on his Virginia plans, 378; his friends not fully informed as to the trifling results of his last visit to Kansas, 378, 379; peace restored there as soon as he had gone, 379; leaves Osawatomie Jan. 20, 1859, 379; reticence in letters to his family, 379; travels north through Kansas with freed slaves, 379-383; case of Dr. Doy, 380; finances recruited at Lawrence, 380; pursued, 381; the "Battle of the Spurs," and his escape, 381-383; the terror of his name, 382; leaves Kansas for the last time, Feb. 2, 1859, 383; receives a cool welcome at Tabor, 384; requests church there to offer thanksgiving for himself and his freed slaves, 384; addresses public meeting, 385; Dr. Brown of St. Joseph, 385; disgusted with timid resolutions of Tabor meeting, 385; from Tabor to Springdale, 386, 387; at J. B. Grinnell's, 386; " coals of fire " message to backsliders in Tabor, 387; leaves Springdale, 387, 389; attempt to arrest him, 388; his claim on the arms remaining at Tabor, 388, 389; journeys with freed slaves to Chicago, Detroit, and Canada line, 389, 390; lectures in Cleveland (March), 391; his person and lecture described by " Artemus Ward," 391-393; his account of his doings in Kansas and the Missouri raid, 392, 393, 635 n. 116; remark about " fence stakes," 393; Cleveland *Leader's* report of the lecture, 393; his " converted " cattle, 393; his contempt for the U. S. authorities, 393; reward offered for his capture, 393, 394; lectures in Jefferson, O., 394; reticent with Giddings, 394; with Gerrit Smith at Peterboro, N. Y., 395; ill at No. Elba, 395; at Concord, Mass., with Sanborn, 395, 396; everything ready for the great blow, 396; meetings with secret committee in Boston, 397; address in Concord (May, 1859), 398; A. B. Alcott's impressions, 398; and John M. Forbes's, 398, 399; conversation with Senator Wilson as to Missouri raid, 399; A. A. Lawrence's diary quoted as to him, 400; meets Gov. Andrew, 400; last public appearance in the North, 400; leaves Boston, June 3, 400; negotiations with Blair on pikes, 400, 401; again at No. Elba for the last time, 401; with John, Jr. at West Andover, O., 401.

HARPER'S FERRY. — Preparing for attack on Virginia, without mentioning his real plan, 402; in Ohio and Penn., 402; leaves Penn. for "the seat of war," June 30, 1859, 402; at Hagerstown (Md.), 402, 403; in quarters at Sandy Hook near Harper's Ferry, July 3, 403; reconnoitring in Maryland, 403; looking for land to buy, 403; rents Kennedy Farm and moves thither, 403, 404; desires to have women on hand to avert suspicion, 405; joined by daughter Annie, and daughter-in-law (Oliver's wife) 405; short of funds again, 406; arms forwarded by John, Jr., 406, 407; his success endangered by inquisitiveness of neighbors and indiscretion of his men, 408; dreads Cook's loquacity, 408; disturbed by defection of Gill and Carpenter, 409; his plan denounced to Sec'y of War Floyd, by anonymous correspondent, 410; story of the anonymous letter and its purpose, 411, 412; financial difficulties solved by F. J. Meriam and others,

412, 421; his plan disapproved by F. Douglass, 412, 413; his chagrin at Douglass's defection, 413; other disappointments, 413; members of the "Provisional Government" assembled at Kennedy Farm, 414, 415; their confidence in him, 416; Mrs. Annie Brown Adams's description of life at the farm, 416-420; sends the women away, 420; frequent absences from the farm during the summer, 420; assigns Meriam to duty of guarding arms left at the farm, 421; imminence of the attack foreshadowed in his letters to Kagi and John, Jr., 422, 423; last obstacle to attack removed by Meriam, 423; his previous delay discussed, 424; was the raid unduly delayed or unduly hastened? 424.

Leaves Kennedy Farm for the Ferry, Oct. 16, 426; disposition of his forces, 426, 427; he alone had faith in his purpose, 427; no plan of campaign beyond seizing the town, 427, 438; seemed bent on violating every military principle, 427; had no well-defined purpose in attacking Harper's Ferry except to begin his revolution in a spectacular way, 427; attack on arsenal, etc., described in detail, 429 seqq.; his remark to the first prisoner, 430; Geo. Washington's sword and pistol, 431; speech to Col. L. Washington, 432; his orders as to avoiding bloodshed violated at the outset, 433; first alarm given prematurely for that reason, 434; fails to allow for the spirit of the people, 434; his men take many prisoners, 437; urged by Kagi to leave Harper's Ferry, 438; why did he not escape while there was time? 438; soon put on the defensive, 438; cut off from his men in the rifle works and the arsenal, 439; at bay in the fire-engine house, 439, 440; kindly treatment of his prisoners, 443; last avenue of escape cut off, 443; surrounded in engine house by increasing numbers of troops, 444; his reply to a summons to surrender, 447; interview with Capt. Sinn, 448; " I have weighed the responsibility and shall not shrink from it," 447; death of Oliver Brown, 448; but five men alive and unwounded, 449; betrays no trepidation, 449; two of the five refuse to fight more, 449; Lieut. Stuart, for Col. Lee, demands his surrender, 450, 451; his refusal and its result, 451; engine house stormed by Lieut. Green, 452 seqq.; his bravery at the supreme moment, 453; attacked and wounded by Lieut. Green, 453; his escape from death due to lightness of Green's sword, 453, 454; not seriously wounded, 455; Gov. Wise quoted concerning him, 455; his " interview " with Gov. Wise and others immediately after his capture, as reported in N. Y. *Herald*, 456-463; circumstances of his surrender, 461, 462 and notes; colloquy with Gov. Wise, 463; his act compared with Wise's conduct in 1861, 465, 466; his correspondence left at Kennedy Farm, 467; portions of it read to the crowd after the raid, 469, 470; removed to jail in Charlestown, 470; his survival fortunate for the cause he had at heart, 471; his act discussed in Democratic and Republican press, 471 seqq.; gradual change of attitude of latter toward the raid, 473, 474; southern opinion concerning B, 474-476; possibility of a speedy trial, 476, 477; question of jurisdiction raised, 477; before the magistrates, 479, 486; was his trial unduly hastened? 479-482; in court on a couch, 479, 480, 481, 488; question of counsel, 483-485; the prosecuting attorneys, 485; committed for trial, 486; his speech on that occasion, 487; indicted by Grand Jury, Oct. 26, for treason to Virginia, 488; appeals for delay on account of wounds, 488, 489; the trial jury empanelled, 489; suggestion of insanity in his family, 489, 506-510,

718 INDEX [John Brown

595 n. 33, 647 n. 100; declines to avail himself of insanity plea, 490, 507; his suggestions to his counsel, 490, 491; renewed appeal for delay because of absence of witnesses, 491, 492; denounces his counsel, 492; correspondence with Judges Tilden and Russell, 493; takes a hand in examining witnesses, 494; accused by Hunter of feigning illness, 495; Hoyt quoted concerning B's character and bearing, 495, 496; found guilty of treason, 496; how he received the verdict, 496; his vision of the future, 496; "I am worth inconceivably more to hang than for any other purpose," 496, 546; his great speech to the court before sentence, 498, 499; sentenced to be hanged publicly on Dec. 2, 1859, 499; delay of execution affords opportunity to influence public opinion in the North, 499; diversity of opinion concerning execution of sentence, 500 seqq.; Gov. Wise declines to interfere with sentence, 503, 504; question of commutation of sentence discussed, 506; plots to rescue, 511 seqq.; declines to lend himself to any scheme of rescue, 512; his pledge to Capt. Avis, 512; forbids his wife to visit him, 513; anonymous letters to, relating to plans of rescue, and their effect, 518; precautions taken for his execution, 522 seqq.; predicament and attitude of his Northern supporters, 528 seqq.; Dr. Howe's card concerning the raid, 531-533; B's bearing after judgment, 536, 537; permission to write freely a dangerous weapon in his hands, 538; tremendous power and influence of his letters from the jail, 538, 539; detailed reports of his life in jail spread through the country, 544 seqq.; conversation with Rev. Norval Wilson, 544; his visitors, 545-548; visited by H. C. Pate, 546; and by Gov. Wise, 547, 548; universal confidence in his veracity and integrity, 547; writes to A. Hunter, 548; his real object, 548; last interview with his wife, 550; last injunctions to his family, 551-553; gives his Bible to J. H. Blessing, 553; his various wills, 553, 667-670; emotion of his guards, 554; the journey to the scaffold, 554 seqq.; prophetic message to his countrymen, 554; on the scaffold, 556; his execution, 557, 653 n. 13; his body delivered to his wife and taken to No. Elba, 559, 561; and there buried, 561, 562; views of prominent men North and South concerning him and his raid, 562 seqq.; and of representative newspapers, 568, 569; Victor Hugo quoted concerning him, 569, 588; report of the minority of the Mason committee, 580, 581; and of the majority, 581, 582; his name involved in speakership contest, 583, 584; divergent views of B and his achievements fifty years after, 586; the truth lies between the extreme views, 586; a fanatic, but one of those fanatics who, by their readiness to sacrifice their lives, are forever advancing the world, 587; brave, kind, honest, truth-telling, God-revering, 588 : his rise to spiritual greatness after his sentence, 588; a great and lasting figure in American history, 588; the lesson of his life, 588, 589.
Chronology of his movements, Aug. 1855 to his death, 672-678; details as to his "men-at-arms" at Harper's Ferry, 678-687.
LETTERS TO Rev. S. L. Adair, 136, 303, 306, Geo. Adams, 542, E. B., 539, Wm. Barnes, 276, 283, Jesse Bowen, 388, Ellen Brown, 398, Frederick Brown, 43, John Brown, Jr., 34, 61, 62, 63, 64, 66, 67, 70, 79, 86 and n., 343, 353, 354-356, 358, 407, 409, 422, 423, Mary Anne Brown,[1] 29, 30, 35, 64,

89, 118-120, 127, 128, 132, 148, 203, 248, 278, 282, 292, 299, 320, 337, 358, 365, 383, 395, 398, 404, 409, 422, 537, 540, 541, 542, 551, 553, Levi Burnell, 32, 33, Amos P. Chamberlain, 40, Lydia Maria Child, 249, his children, 69, John W. Cook, 85, J. T. Cox, 361, Orson Day, 123, 127, J. R. Giddings, 131, G. B. Gill, 337, T. W. Higginson, 320, 513, 543, W. A. Hodges, 72, L. Humphrey, 543, A. Hunter, 548, J. H. Kagi, 397, 402, 406, 408, Geo. Kellogg, 31, Zenas Kent, 26, J. H. Lane, 301, A. A. Lawrence, 279, Rev. Mr. McFarland, 545, Theo. Parker, 324, S. Perkins, 59, F. B. Sanborn, 294, 302, 319, 320, 322, 353, 354, Geo. L. Stearns, 281, 305, 320, Mrs. Stearns, 551, H. L. Stearns, 1-7, John Teesdale, 93, 386, Eli Thayer, 287, Ruth B. Thompson, 324, Aug. Wattles, 290, 292.
LETTERS FROM John Brown, Jr., 82, 83, 229 n., 290, Mahala Doyle, 164, T. W. Higginson, 338, 397, J. H. Holmes, 300, J. H. Lane, 300, 301, 304, A. A. Lawrence, 280, C. Robinson, 262, 263, H. Stratton, 235 n., Aug. Wattles, 30, Horace White, 269.
Brown, John, autobiography of, 43, 86, 87.
Brown, John, children of, general characteristics, 21.
Brown, John, Jr., oldest son of B, quoted concerning B and the Free Masons, 26; his conflicting statements as to date of B's requiring his family to swear to fight slavery, 46; in Springfield office of Perkins and Brown, 59; goes to Kansas, 75, 76; his narrative of the expedition, in the Cleveland *Leader* (1883), 81, 82; describes conditions in Kansas and recommends arming anti-slaverymen there, 83, 84; his "shanty" at Osawatomie, 89; and the Indians, 90; vice-president of Free State convention at Lawrence, 91; member of first Territorial Executive Com., 91; defies penal code of Shawnee Legislature, 92; at Free State convention, 102; at convention of radical Free State men, 103; nominated for Territorial legislature, 127, and elected, 130; incident of the claim-jumper, 130; attends session of Legislature, 132, 133; on committee to memorialize Congress for admission of Kansas to statehood, 133; other legislative service of, 133; on B's surveying tour, 136; in Judge Cato's court, 136; his article in the Cleveland *Leader* (1883), quoted, 149, 152, 153; and the Pottawatomie murders, 149 seqq.; camps at Prairie City, en route to relief of Lawrence, 149, 150; camp broken up by U. S. cavalry, 150; deposed from command by company, for freeing two slaves, 150; another reason for his deposition, 151; vainly opposes return of slaves to their masters,151; returns to camp after the murders, 165; his feeling concerning them, 166; returns to Osawatomie with "Pottawatomies," 166; taken in by the Adairs, 166; his distress deprives him of reason, 166, 167; affirms the reality of the unidentified "messenger," 175; charges Robinson with urging his father to other killings, 184; arrested, 193; maltreated by Border Ruffians after arrest, 194 seqq.; driven on foot from Paola to Osawatomie, 195; his condition of mind and body, 195, 196; treatment of, causes indignation in North, 197; taken to Lecompton and held in custody on charge of high treason, 197; Capt. Walker's testimony concerning him and B, 228, 229; released September 10, 1856, 254, 255; goes to Iowa with B, 261; controversy with Gov. Robinson, 263; with B, in Chicago, 269; disturbed by B's proposed return to Kansas, 290; his views of the situation there, 291; with B in Philadelphia, 323; entrusted with forwarding of arms to Chambersburg, Pa., 406, 407; his

---

[1] Most of these letters were written to Mrs. Brown and such of the children as were with her: "My dear wife and children every one."

INDEX 719

mental condition, 406, 413, 414; effect of his aberration, 414; has ill-success in obtaining recruits, 414; warned by Kagi and B of imminence of attack on Harper's Ferry, 422, 423; his extraordinary statements, 423; his mental derangement, 507; reviews his father's business mistakes, 593 n. 33; 19, 28, 36, 39, 56, 81, 86, 106, 112, 118, 120, 121, 148, 178, 198, 207, 210, 233, 249, 262, 277, 343, 396, 397, 401, 402, 424, 516, 518, 533, 582, 601 n. 95. *Letters to* B, 82, 83, 222, 290, Jason Brown, 222, Mary Anne Brown, 92, Hugh Forbes, 318, J. H. Kagi, 413, F. B. Sanborn, 45; *from B*, 34, 66, 67, 86 and n., 353, 354-356, 358, 407, 409, C. W. Tayleure, 454, 455.
Brown, John Carter, 280.
Brown, Capt. John E., commands pro-slavery force at Sugar Creek, 238.
Brown, Mrs. John E., 238.
Brown, Mrs. Martha E. (Brewster), wife of Oliver, starts for Harper's Ferry, 405; sent away, with her sister-in-law, 420; 417, 418, 419, 422, 561.
Brown, Mrs. Mary Anne (Day), second wife of B, 24; mother of thirteen children, 25; her sacrifices for the cause to which B gave his life, 25; described by R. H. Dana, Jr., 74; B appeals to A. A. Lawrence in behalf of, 280; unwilling to join B at Harper's Ferry, 405; urged by T. W. Higginson, starts to visit B after sentence, in order to obtain his consent to rescue, 513; is turned back by B, 513; writes to Gov. Wise, 549; at Harper's Ferry, 549; last interview with B, 550; B's body delivered to, 558; 36, 43, 45, 46, 53, 76, 88, 277, 545, 546, 548, 555, 560, 570, 574. *Letters from* B, 128, 148, 248, 278, 282, 299, 320, 337, 358, 365, 383, 398, 404, 409, 422, 537, 540, 541, 542, 551, 553, Mrs. Jason Brown, 112, Mrs. John Brown, Jr., 127, Gov. H. A. Wise, 549.
Brown, Mrs. Mary E. (Grant). See Grant, Mary E.
Brown, Rev. Nathan, 15.
Brown, O. C., founder of Osawatomie, reproves Pottawatomie murderers, 167; quoted, concerning the reign of terror in Osawatomie, 214, and the power of B's name, 230; his safe robbed, 246.
Brown, Old Man, name often applied to B. See Brown, John, of Osawatomie.
Brown, Oliver, son of B, goes to Kansas, 76; incident of the claim-jumper, 130; on B's surveying tour, 133; in the Pottawatomie party, 153; his hands unstained, 158; his contest with B, 223; starts for Harper's Ferry with B, 402; mortally wounded, 441; his death, 448; sketch of, 683, 684; 81 n., 86, 112, 118, 160, 198, 210, 222, 404, 405, 419, 420, 422, 432, 438, 439, 441, 537, 553, 558, 570.
Brown, Owen, father of B, descent of, 1; in the War of 1812, 4; quoted concerning his mother, 11; stood well with everybody, 11; in one locality in Ohio 51 years, 12; marries Ruth Mills, 12; early married life of, at Canton, Norfolk and Torrington, Conn., and Hudson, Ohio, 13; describes conditions in Ohio, 13; marries (2) Sallie Root, and (3) Lucy Hinsdale, 14; how he became an Abolitionist, 14; an agent of the Underground Railroad 14; ceases to support Western Reserve College, 15; trustee of Oberlin College, 15; loses heavily in B's insolvency, 28; an early subscriber to the *Liberator*, 49; his philosophy of marriage, 591 n. 10; his autobiography (MS.) quoted, 11, 12-14; 30, 31, 43, 507. *Letter to* B, 11.
Brown, Owen, son of B, goes to Kansas, 76, 81; in B's Pottawatomie party, 153; personally concerned in Doyle murders, 160; and the murder of Sherman, 162, 163, 164; denied shelter by Adair, 167; goes to Iowa with B, 261; leaves Tabor for Kansas with B, 299; elected "Treasurer" at Chatham convention, 333; starts for Harper's Ferry with B, 402; left on guard at Kennedy Farm, 426; escapes, 471; sketch of, 686; his diary, quoted, 311, 312, 315, 316; 19, 39, 45, 46, 72, 75, 83, 120, 121, 165, 197, 198, 202, 208, 220, 222, 262, 270, 294, 298, 302, 308, 329, 330, 343, 344, 397, 402, 406, 407, 414, 415, 416, 418, 421, 424, 437, 446, 468.
Brown, Peter, of Windsor, Conn., ancestor of B, not the Mayflower Peter, 10, 591 n. 6.
Brown, Peter, of the Mayflower, 10, 543.
Brown, Capt. Reese P., killed at Leavenworth, 129, 133, 180, 352.
Brown, Ruth, daughter of B. See Thompson, Mrs. Ruth (Brown).
Brown, Mrs. Ruth (Mills), mother of B, 3, 12; death of (1808), 3, 13; descent of, 15; insanity in family of, 507.
Brown, Mrs. Sallie (Root), stepmother of B, 3, 16.
Brown, Salmon, brother of B, 12, 14.
Brown, Salmon, son of B, goes to Kansas, 76; in Judge Cato's court, 135, 136; concerning B's surveying tour, 137; concerning the Pottawatomie plan, 151, 152; in the Pottawatomie party, 153; reports effect of news of assault on Sumner, 154; as to the time chosen for murders, 155; as to Townsley and Weiner, 157, 158; as to attack on Doyles, 159 seqq.; personally concerned in latter, 160; as to murders of Wilkinson and W. Sherman, 162, 164; denies that Judge Wilson was on proscribed list, 165; denies that there was a "messenger," 175; or that Pottawatomie victims were "tried" by jury, 184; accidentally wounded after Black Jack, 203, 210; describes contest between B and Oliver, 223; second visit to Kansas, 269, 270; declines to join B at Harper's Ferry, 413; his reasons for declining, 424; as to B's peculiarities, 424; as to "retreat" from Kansas in 1856, 616 n. 68; 20, 24, 54, 56, 72, 81 and n., 83, 91, 120, 121, 128, 149, 168 n., 173, 177, 183, 198, 202, 222, 405, 561. *Letter to* B, 82, Rev. Joshua Young, 612, n. 90.
Brown, Sarah, daughter of B, and the plan to attack Harper's Ferry, 55; quoted, concerning Watson Brown, 683; 405, 533.
Brown, Spencer Kellogg, 244, 246, 250.
Brown, Rev. Theodore, alias of T. W. Higginson, 573, 576.
Brown, Watson, son of B, not personally concerned in Pottawatomie murders, 159; his first journey to Kansas, 269, 270; turns back at Tabor, and goes with B to North Elba, 270; starts for Harper's Ferry, 405; mortally wounded carrying flag of truce, 439; his death described by C. W. Tayleure, 454, 455; sketch of, 686; 20, 58, 72, 76, 407, 409, 414, 419, 448, 449, 537, 553, 558 and n., 570. *Letters to* Mrs. Isabella Brown, 415, 416; *from* Mrs. Wealthy Brown, 92.
Brown, Mrs. Wealthy, wife of John Jr., describes conditions at Osawatomie, 88; 118. *Letters to* John Jr., 172, Mary Anne Brown, 88, 89, 127, Watson Brown, 92.
"**Brown and Thompson's addition to Franklin Village,**" 27, 28.
Brown settlement, near Osawatomie, various names of, 112.
Brown's Station, temporary name of Brown settlement, 112.
Browne, Charles F. See Ward, Artemus.
Browne, William Hand, his *Maryland, the History of a Palatinate,* quoted, 475.
Brownsville, temporary name of Brown settlement, 82, 112.

720 INDEX

Brua, Joseph A., 438, 439, 440, 443.
Brussels, visited by B, 62.
Bryant, Joseph, and Hugh Forbes, 286; 293.
Buchanan, James, Pres. of U. S., and Gov. Walker, 295; offers reward for capture of B, 371; notified by Garrett, of Harper's Ferry raid, 434; orders artillery and marines thither, 449, and Robert E. Lee and J. E. B. Stuart, 450; message to Congress in Dec., 1859, 566; 374, 381, 478, 523, 524.
" Buckskin," 233.
Buffum, David C., murdered, 260.
Buford, Major Jefferson, in command of Border Ruffians in Kansas, 137, 138; his pro-slavery circular, 216; appeals for aid, 231; 144, 146, 150, 192.
Bunyan, John, the *Pilgrim's Progress* familiar to B, 16.
Burlington (Iowa) Gazette, denounces Pottawatomie murders, 191.
Burlington Mills Co., suit against Perkins and Brown, 66.
Burnell, Levi, treasurer of Oberlin College, 32. *Letters from B*, 32, 33.
Burns, Anthony, fugitive slave, 384, 511.
Burns, Col. James N., disputes Major Clarke's claim to have murdered Barber, 126.
Burns, John, 520.
Butler, Rev. Pardee, maltreated by pro-slavery men, 110; stripped and "cottoned," 141.
Buxton, Canada, 327.
Byrne, Terence, captured by B's raiders, 437, 439.

Cabot, James Elliot, *A Memoir of Ralph Waldo Emerson*, quoted, 282.
Cabot, Dr. Samuel, Jr., 271, 275, 325.
Cackler, Christian, the *Recollections of an Old Settler*, quoted, 9.
Calais (France), visited by B, 61.
Calhoun, John, 296, 307.
California, rush of gold-seekers to, 80.
Callender, W. H. D., 278, 279, 286.
Campbell, Bishop, 59.
Campbell, John F., murdered by Hamilton and his men, 348, 375.
Campbell, Sheriff, 537, 538, 539, 556.
Canterbury (Conn.), suppression of schools for negroes in, 45.
Canton (Conn.), 278, 279.
Cantrall, Mr., murder of, 181, 213; mock trial of, by court-martial, 213.
Carleton, Silas, 533, 534.
Carpenter, Henry, defection of, 409; 576.
Carpenter, Howard, 198.
Carpenter, O. A., guides B's Pottawatomie party to Ottawa Creek, 198; 210.
Carr, a settler, 239, 242.
Carr, Lieut. Eugene A., 621 n. 86.
Carrington, Gen. Henry B., quoted, 47.
Carruth, James H., 167.
Carter, Mr., murder of, 214.
Carter, Charles P., alias of T. W. Higginson, 573.
Carter, T. W., agent of Mass. Arms Co., 289.
Case, A. H., quoted, 601 n. 104.
Cass, Lewis, Sec'y of State, letters from Gov. Denver, 351, Acting-Gov. Walsh, 364.
Castele, A., 168.
Cato, Judge Sterling G., holds court at Sherman settlement, 135, 136; issues warrants for arrest of the Browns, 135; 137, 195, 254, 260.
Central Committee for Kansas, 275.
Chadwick, Rear-Adm. French E., *The Causes of the Civil War*, quoted, 341.
Chamberlain, Amos P., and the title to Westlands, 38 seqq.; B's quarrel with, 39–41, 593 n. 49. *Letter from B*, 40.
Chambers, George W., shoots A. D. Stevens,

439; and the killing of W. Thompson, 442; 491.
Chambersburg (Penn.), Kagi's headquarters at, 406, 407.
Chapin, Messrs., 278.
Chapin, Lou V., *Last Days of Old John Brown*, quoted, 36.
Charleston Convention, 1860, 585.
Charleston Courier, quoted, 97.
Charleston Independent Democrat, B quoted in, 545.
Charleston Mercury, quoted, 97, 568.
Charles Town (West Va.), 429. And see Charlestown.
Charlestown (Va.), news of raid carried to, by Dr. Starry, 436; dread of a slave rising, 436; militia and other volunteers turn out, 436; B and others lodged in jail, 470; trial of B, 486 seqq.; reception of verdict, 497; self-control of people after sentence, 499, 500; proposed attack on, 516 seqq.; rescue scares, 519, 520; numerous fires, 520; end of reign of terror, 522; preparations for execution, 522 seqq.
" Charley." See Kaiser, Charles.
Chase, Salmon P., Gov. of Ohio, 271 and n., 298, 524.
Chatham (Canada), convention of B's followers there, 330 seqq.; really two conventions, 331; 327, 328.
Chatham Convention, proceedings of, 330 seqq.; oath of secrecy imposed, 333; " Provisional Constitution " adopted, 333; second convention called under new constitution, 333; officers elected at, 333; list of colored men in attendance, 628 n. 55.
Chicago Tribune, 46, 352.
Child, D. Lee, 293.
Child, Lydia Maria, her proposed visit to B, 479 n.; 510. *Letter to Gov. Wise*, 479.
Chilton, Samuel, retained by John A. Andrew to defend B, 493; prays that government be required to elect on which count they will proceed, 494, 495; argues for defence, 496; motion in arrest of judgment, 497.
Chippewa Indians, 9.
Church Anti-Slavery Society, B at meeting in Boston, 400.
Church, Lieut. John R., breaks up John Brown, Jr.'s camp, 150.
Claim-Jumper, a, expulsion of, by minute-men, 130.
Clark, Malcolm, killed by C. McCrea, 109, 110.
Clark, Rev. Wm. C., assault on, 111.
Clarke, Major Geo. E., *soi-disant* murderer of Barber, 126, 352.
Clarke, James Freeman, *Anti-Slavery Days*, Gen. Carrington quoted in, 47; his characterization of B, 186, 187; 213, 326, 327.
Clarke, Wm. Penn, 388, 390.
Clay, C. C., quoted, 585.
Cleveland (Ohio), public sentiment in, 394.
Cleveland Herald, quoted, 569.
Cleveland Leader, John Brown, Jr.'s statement in (1883), 81, 82, 149; announces B's lecture, March 18, 1859, 391; its report of the lecture, 393; and the raid, 472.
Cleveland Plain Dealer, " Artemus Ward's " description of B and Kagi in, 391, 392; and of B's lecture, 392, 393.
Cline, Capt. James B., his company marches south from Osawatomie with B, 236: meets pro-slavery force at South Middle Creek and puts it to flight, 237; accidental collision with B's company, 237; in battle of Osawatomie, 244; 238, 239, 249.
Cochrane, Benjamin, 200, 293.
Cochren, Benjamin L., 121.
Coffee, Gen., and Col. Sumner, 209.
Coffin, W. H. *The Settlement of the Friends in Kansas*, 192.

INDEX 721

Coine, W. W., 121.
Colby, Deputy Marshal, 381.
Coleman, E. A., reports B's words justifying Pottawatomie murders, 179.
Coleman, Franklin N., murderer of C. Dow, 113; political consequences of his act, 113 seqq.; suspected of shooting Stewart, 142.
Coleman, William, 343.
Collamer, Jacob, U. S. Senator from Vermont, of minority of Mason Committee, 580.
Collins, Samuel, shot by P. Laughlin, 112, 113, 180.
Collinsville (Conn.), 278, 279.
Collis, Daniel W., 121.
Columbia (Mo.) Statesman, 99.
Colpetzer, William, murdered by Hamilton's gang, 348, 375.
Colt, Mrs. M. D., *Went to Kansas*, 89 n.
Concord (Mass.), B's address at, in May, 1859, 398; arrest of F. B. Sanborn at, 533, 534.
Congress of the U. S., and the Lecompton Constitution, 347; passes the English compromise, 347.
Conkling, Rev. Mr., 68.
Contempt of court, extraordinary charge of, made by Sheriff Jones, 140.
Conway, Martin F., Free State leader, 101, 103, 106, 272, 277, 282, 293, 296, 359, 360.
Cook, Gen. Joe, alias of J. H. Lane, 225, 231, 235 n., 252.
Cook, John E., B's first recruit for Harper's Ferry, 307, 308, 680; his confession, 308, 680; describes B's recruiting operations, 308; has words with B about Virginia plan, 310, 311; corresponds with friends in Springdale, 330; his indiscretion, 338; sent to Harper's Ferry to reconnoitre, in June, 1858, 344; locktender there, 408; his perilous loquacity, 408; with the rear-guard, 446, 447; arrested in Penn., 487; convicted and sentenced, 569, 570; executed, after almost escaping, 570–572; sketch of, 680, 681; 142, 215, 216, 315, 329, 412, 415, 419, 426, 427, 429, 431, 435, 437, 468, 469, 471, 477, 478, 483, 510, 531, 554.
Cook, John W., letter from B, 84.
Cooke, Lt.-Col. Philip St. George, reports as to changed conditions in Kansas, 213, 214; declines to obey Woodson's order to invest Topeka, 250, 251; and Lane and Walker's demonstration against Lecompton, 252; his good advice to them rejected, 252; escorts Gov. Geary to Lawrence, 257; with Gov. Geary averts threatened attack on Lawrence, 259; narrowly misses arresting B, 261; 211, 217, 258, 260.
Cooper Union, New York, great meeting in, 562.
Copeland, John Anthony, Jr., in the Harper's Ferry party, 415, 421, 431; captured, 445; saved from being lynched by Dr. Starry, 445; convicted and sentenced, 569, 570; executed, 570; sketch of, 684; 454, 486, 572.
Coppoc, Barclay, joins B at Springdale, 328, 3 9; in Harper's Ferry party, 414, 420, 421; left on guard at Kennedy Farm, 426; final escape of, 471; sketch of, 682, 683; 446, 468, 571.
Coppoc, Edwin, joins B at Springdale, 328, 329; in Harper's Ferry party, 414, 421, 426, 430, 441, 449; kills Mayor Beckham, 441; made prisoner in engine house, 454; trial of, 497; convicted and sentenced, 569, 570; commutation of sentence prevented by his letter to Mrs. Brown, 570; executed after almost escaping, 570–572; sketch of, 682; 470, 471, 486.
Coppoc, Mrs., mother of Barclay and Edwin, 329, 571.
Cox, J. T., letter from B, 361.
Cracklin, Capt. Jos., in command of defence of Lawrence, 258.

Craft, Ellen, 384.
Crafts and Still, letter from Perkins and Brown, 59.
Crane, Smith, and his tale of rescuers from Kansas, 520, 521.
Cransdell, Archie, shoots Dutch Henry Sherman, 236.
Crawford, Geo. A., his interview with B in Jan. 1859, 374, 375; 370. *Letters to* Eli Thayer, 374, 608 n. 12.
Cromwell, Oliver, life of, one of the books which influenced B, 16.
Cross, Mr., taken prisoner by the raiders, 439.
Cruise, David, murdered by A. D. Stevens in Missouri raid, 369; great excitement caused by his death, 370.
Curtis, Geo. William, quoted, 563, 564.
Cushing, Caleb, on the law of B's case, 644 n. 28; 565.
Cutter, George, a Free State settler, 239, 242; seriously wounded, 243.
Cyrus, negro boy, 75.

Daingerfield, J. E. P., paymaster's clerk of the armory at Harper's Ferry, 439, 443; his conversation with B, 443.
Dana, Richard H., Jr., *How we met John Brown*, quoted, 74; entertained by B at No. Elba, 74; his description of B, his family, and his home, 74.
Daniels, Jim, slave, whose appeal led to B's Missouri raid, 367, 368, 376.
Davenport, Col. Braxton, presiding justice at preliminary hearing in case of B and others, 487.
David, William, 293.
Davis, Henry, Border Ruffian, killed by Lucius Kibbey, 109.
Davis, Jefferson, as Sec'y of War, censures Col. Sumner, 217; and Col. Sumner, 217, 218, 219; instructions to Gen. Smith, 251; as U. S. Senator from Miss., quoted, 565; joins in report of majority of Mason Committee, 580; 130. *Letter to* Col. Sumner, 218.
Davis, Col. J. Lucius, quoted, 519, 520 and n.; 521, 522.
Davis, S. C., letter from S. L. Adair, 253 n.
Davis, Mrs. S. C., quoted, 270 n.
Day, Charles, father of B's second wife, 24.
Day, Horace H., 178.
Day, Mary Anne, married to B (1833), 24, 25. See Brown, Mary Anne (Day). Sister of
Day, Orson, 71, 148, 178. *Letters from* B, 123, 127.
Dayton, Oscar V., secretary of settlers' meeting at Osawatomie, 135.
Deitzler, Geo. W., indicted for treason, 142; arrested, 145; 98.
Delahay, Mark W., Free Soil candidate for delegate in Congress, 129.
Delamater, Geo. B., 24, 46.
Delany, Dr. Martin R., colored, 328, 331, 333.
Democratic pro-slavery press, and the Pottawatomie murders, 191; and the Harper's Ferry raid, 471, 472.
Democrats, Northern, vote for Kansas-Nebraska Act, 80.
Denver, James Wilson, Acting-Gov. and Gov. of Kansas, adjusts troubles growing out of Marais des Cygnes massacre, 349, 350; hostile to Montgomery, 351; his peace compact substantially renewed by Sugar Mound Convention, 366; 346, 364, 376. *Letter to* Secretary Cass, 351.
Des Moines (Iowa), 387.
Dix, John A., 569.
Donaldson, J. B., U. S. marshal, his proclamation to law-abiding citizens, 143; is sent first to pro-slavery strongholds, 143; his forces composed of Border Ruffians, 144, 145; 144 n., 180, 185, 211, 252, 254.

Doniphan (Kansas), scene of murder of Saml. Collins, 112.
Doolittle, James R., U. S. Senator from Wisconsin, of minority of Mason Com., 580.
Douglas, Stephen A., U. S. Senator from Illinois, favors Kansas-Nebraska Act, 80; and the Toombs bill, 227; opposed to Lecompton Constitution, 306, 347; quoted, 365; nominated for President, 585.
Douglass, Frederick, his *Life and Times of Frederick Douglass*, quoted, 47, 48, 57, 58; describes B's home in Springfield, Mass., and his personal aspect, 57, 58; urges contributions for B, at Syracuse convention, 85; B's first confidant as to his Virginia plan, 317; B visits him early in 1858, 317; gives money to Forbes, 317; B's disappointment with him, 323; feeling of B's family toward him, 323, 627 n. 33; at final conference with B disapproves plan of raid, 412, 413; withdraws his support from B, 413; leaves the country after the raid, 529; 67, 269, 390, 398.
Dow, Charles, shot by F. N. Coleman, 113, 180.
Doy, Dr. John, captured with his liberated slaves, and rescued, 380; 511, 514, 546, 575.
Doyle, Mr., husband of Mahala, and father of Drury, John, and William; murder of, 159 seqq.
Doyle, Drury, murder of, 159 seqq.
Doyle, John, quoted concerning Doyle murders, 160; 164.
Doyle, Mrs. Mahala, describes murder of her husband and sons, 158 seqq.; Salmon Brown concerning, 159; 156, 190, 195. *Letter to* B, 164.
Doyle, William, murder of, 159 seqq.
Doyle family, on Pottawatomie Creek, character of, 156; attack on, 158–161; John Doyle and Townsley concerning mutilation of their bodies, 160, 161; alleged intimidation by, 172; and the Morse case, 174; said by some to have deserved their fate, 180.
Dunbar, Jennie (Mrs. Garcelon), 572.
Duncan, L. A., 388.
Dutch Henry. See Sherman, Henry.
Dutch Henry's Crossing, 151, 155, 157.
Duty of the Soldier, The, by Hugh Forbes, 297, 298; disapproved by Sanborn and Theodore Parker, 298.

Eastin, Brig.-Gen. Lucien J., publishes call to arms against Free State men, 116; Woodson's letter to him denounced as forgery, 116.
Easton (Kansas), Leavenworth election held at (Jan. 1856), 128.
Edwards, Rev. Jona., his works owned by B, 16.
Eldredge, Col., 260.
Eldridge, Charles, 574.
Elections Committee of House of Representatives reports against Whitfield and in favor of Reeder as delegate, 226.
Elgin Association, a colony for escaped slaves, 327.
Eliot, George, *Adam Bede,* 326.
Elliott, R. G., quoted, 122, 230, 307.
Ellsworth, Alfred M., elected member of Congress, at Chatham Convention, 333.
Elmore, Rush, Justice of Kansas Terr., upholds legality of Shawnee Legislature, 100; 377, 378.
Emerson, Ralph Waldo, meets B, 273; quoted, 282, 560, 563; as to B's speech before sentence, 646 n 81; 561.
Emigrant Aid Societies, New England, recruits of, in Kansas, 95, 96; 98, 265.
Emigrant Aid Society, ships Sharp's rifles to C. Robinson, 98; saw-mill of, at Osawatomie spared by Border Ruffians, 246; 146, 227.
English bill, The, a compromise measure passed by Congress, 347; a pro-slavery victory, 347; a bribe to Kansas to accept Lecompton Constitution, 347.
Epps, Lyman, colored neighbor of B at No. Elba, 55, 562.
Erickson, Aaron, concerning B's insanity, 595 n. 33.
Ervin, Dr., 369.
Everett, Edward, 565.
Executive Committee. See Free State Executive Committee and Territorial Executive Committee.

Fablinger, Mrs. Ellen (Brown), daughter of B, 405. *Letter from* B, 398.
Fain, U. S. Deputy Marshal, at Free State Hotel, 145; makes arrests in Lawrence, 145.
Fairfield, temporary name of Brown settlement near Osawatomie, 112.
Faneuil Hall, Union meeting in, 562, 563, 565.
Faulkner, Charles J., assigned as counsel for B, and declines, 483; his opinion of the trial, 483; 456, 486, 487. *Letter to* M. W. Cluskey, 483; *from* A. H. Lewis, 506.
Fauquier Cavalry, 549.
Fayette, Mr., a colored preacher, 45, 46.
Featherstonhaugh, Dr. Thomas, 558 n.
Fessenden, Wm. Pitt, letter from John A. Andrew, 530.
Field, David Dudley, 230.
Filer, James N., shoots Sheriff Jones, 140.
Fisher, Ellwood, letter to Gov. Wise, 47 n. 93.
Fitch, G. N., U. S. Senator from Indiana, joins in majority report of Mason Com., 580.
Flanders farm at No. Elba, hired by B, 72.
Flirt (yacht), 515.
Floyd, John B., Sec'y of War, anonymous letter to, denouncing B's plan, 410; discredits the warning, 410; publishes the letter after the raid, 411; 450, 470. And see " Floyd letter."
"**Floyd letter,**" authorship and motive of, 411. And see Gue, David J.
Fobes, E. Alexander, 343, 406.
Forbes, Hugh, B's first acquaintance with, 285; his antecedents and character, 285; becomes instructor of B's " volunteer-regular " company, 286; his *Manual of the Patriotic Volunteer,* 286, 298, 313; B becomes suspicious of him, 286; money raised by him, 287; his *The Duty of the Soldier,* 297, 298; his usefulness to B of brief duration, 298; disagreement with B as to future operations, 299; denounces the " Humanitarians," 299; his differences with B, 313, 314; his own plan, 314; abuses B and his supporters, 317 seqq.; his blackmailing operations, 317, 318; postponement of B's plan caused by his threats, etc., 338, 339; quoted, 467 n.; authorities for story of B's relations with him, 624 n. 49; 291, 293, 302, 304, 337, 338, 340, 343, 396, 478, 531. *Letters to* S. G. Howe, 313, 318; *from* John Brown Jr., 318.
Forbes, John M., his impressions of B, 398, 399.
Foreman, James, recollections of B's early life, 21–23, 25; does not mention B's project of abolishing slavery, 46, 47. *Letter to* James Redpath, 21–23.
Fort Scott (Kansas), young men of, form a watch-guard, 192, 193; attempt to burn, 349, 351; " the only place in Kansas where the Border Ruffians now (April, 1858) show their teeth," 352; attacked by Montgomery, 366; evil effects of attack on, 366, 367.
Foster, Abby Kelley, 50 and n.
Foster, Daniel, 293.
Fouke, Christine, 442.
Fowler, O. S., phrenologist, on B, 20.
Frank Leslie's Illustrated Paper, 520.
Frankfort (Ky.) *Yeoman,* quoted, 502.
Franklin (Kansas), attacked by Major Abbott, 212; second Free State attack on, 230, 231.

INDEX 723

Franklin, Benjamin, influence of his writings on B, 16, 50.
Franklin Land Co., 27.
Franklin Mills (Ohio), 26 seqq.
Frazee, Mr., 292, 293.
Frederick (Md.), militia of, at Harper's Ferry, 444.
Frederick the Great, sword reputed to have been given by him to Geo. Washington, 431, worn by B throughout the fight, 447.
Free Soil. See Free State.
Free State cause, helped on by Lawrence outrages, 146; lost a great moral advantage by Pottawatomie murders, 187, 188; prejudiced by Montgomery's attack on Fort Scott, 366, 367.
Free State Central Committee, 304.
Free State Convention, at Lawrence, resolutions of, 91; in Topeka, in 1857, 295, 296.
Free State election of Aug. 9, 1857, 296.
Free State emigrants, in Lane's "caravan," 225; Missouri River closed against, 225; go from Chicago to Kansas via Iowa and Nebraska, 225; forwarded by National Kansas Com., 227.
Free State Executive Committee, appointed by Topeka Convention, 108.
Free State Hotel at Lawrence, meetings at, 123, 124; its demolition recommended by U. S. Grand Jury, 143; demolished, 145, 146.
Free State leaders, the claim that B was carrying out their orders in Pottawatomie exploit, 180, 182.
Free State Legislature, election of members of, 128; assembles, elects U. S. senators, memorializes Congress for admission of Kansas, and is dispersed by Sumner's troops, 132; only fifteen members sign memorial to Congress, 133.
Free State men, code of punishments for, enacted by Shawnee Legislature, 91; early drift of affairs in Kansas adverse to, 94; fewer in numbers at first than *bona-fide* Missouri settlers, 95; elected to Kansas Legislature and ousted by pro-slavery majority, 99; decide to repudiate Shawnee Legislature, 101–103; their policy, to call a constitutional convention, 101, 102; of divers opinions, 101; classed as moderates and radicals, 102; jealousies among, 102; six conventions of, June 8 to Aug. 14, 1855, 102, 103; conflict of opinion between radicals and moderates, 102; two conventions on same day, distinction between, 103; two constitutional conventions called, 103; forced to abandon platform of Big Springs Convention, 104; hold Topeka Constitutional Convention, 105; abstain from voting for delegate in election ordered by Shawnee Legislature, 106; elect Reeder at election ordered by Big Springs Convention, 106; appointment of Howard Com. a triumph for them, 107; duality of management among, 107; enraged by McCrea-Clark murder, 109; rescue of Branson by, 113, 114; answer to appeal for help from Lawrence, 118; B's description of the relief expedition, 118–120; denounced by Pres. Pierce in special message to Congress, 130; several indicted for treason after Pottawatomie, 142, 143; their attitude toward the murders, 167, 168, 169, 170; no law for them in Kansas, 180, 181; some of the indicted men arrested, 192; others banished, 192; out, under arms, after the murders, 197; Pate's prisoners released by B, 208; after Black Jack fight, 208; attack and sack Franklin, 212; their robberies treated as lawful acts of war by Northern press, 212; less guilty than pro-slavery men in respect of crimes of violence, 215; aggressive guerrilla warfare carried on by, 215, 216, 229 seqq.; drive out pro-slavery settlement at New Georgia, 229; second attack on Franklin, 230, 231; enraged by murder of Major Hoyt, 231; attack "Fort" Saunders, 231; real fighting at "Fort" Titus, 231; Lt.-Col. Cooke's good advice, 252; movement against Leavenworth, 253, 254; offer command to B, then to Col. Harvey, 254; large number in confinement, 256; Capt. Wood's "haul" checks their lawlessness, 256; from Iowa, including S. C. Pomeroy, arrested, 260; losses between Nov. 1855 and Dec. 1856, 264; indictments on Pottawatomie score nol pros'd, 294; pouring into Kansas in 1857, 295; decline to take part in election of delegates to Constitutional Convention, June, 1857, 296; vote at Free State election in Aug. shows their preponderance in Kansas, 296; vote at Grasshopper Falls to take part in election of delegate, 296; predominance of peace party among, 296; victorious in election of Territorial Legislature and delegate, Oct. 1857, 306; decide to work under existing government, 307; and the Marais des Cygnes massacre, 348, 349; in southeastern Kansas, 352; in joint meeting with pro-slavery men, adopt B's peace agreement, 366.
Free State movement, great gains of, in 1855, 108.
Free State party, divided counsels of, in first territorial election, 95; defeated in second territorial election, 98 seqq.; vote of, cast for Delahay as delegate and C. Robinson for governor, Jan. 1856, 129; blamed for incident in Judge Cato's court, 137, and for Pottawatomie murders, 190; its position and prospects in June, 1858, 346 seqq.; refrains from voting at first election on Lecompton Constitution, 346; at second election secures rejection of the constitution, 346.
Free State settlers, reports of threats against those near Osawatomie, not spread by any one man, 177; general threats against, probably B's impelling motive in Pottawatomie murders, 177, 178; some deed of violence thought by some necessary to rouse them, 180; their previous good reputation of value to them in the crisis, 191, 192; criticised by Democrats, 226.
Fremont, John C., 220, 265.
Fremont-Buchanan campaign of 1856, Kansas a leading issue in, 226.
Frothingham, Octavius B., his *Life of Gerrit Smith*, quoted, 535, 536; 627 n. 27.
Fugit (or Fugert), Mr., murders Wm. Hoppe on a wager, 215; tried and acquitted, 215; 352.
Fugitive Slave Law, 50, 74, 75.
Fuller, Abram, 381.
Fuller, Bain, 153.
Fuller, W. B., 246.
Fulton (Mo.) Telegraph, 99.
Furness, Wm. H., 560; quoted as to B's speech before sentence, 646 n. 81.

Galt House, Harper's Ferry, 429, 439, 440.
Garcelon, Mrs. Jennie Dunbar. See Dunbar, Jennie.
Gardner, Joseph, 575, 576, 578, 580.
Garnett, Rev. H. H., colored, 323.
Garrett, John W., Pres. B. & O. R. R., acts on news of hold-up of train, 434; 449, 519.
Garrison, David, murder of, 181, 210, 242, 243.
Garrison, Wendell P. *The Preludes of Harper's Ferry*, 46 and n., 594 n. 2.
Garrison, Wendell P. and Francis J., their *William Lloyd Garrison* quoted, 272.
Garrison, William Lloyd, his first meeting with B, and his impressions, 271, 272; quoted, 500, 654 n. 9; at Tremont Temple meeting, 560; his sonnet, *Freedom of the Mind*, 651 n. 84; 50, 139, 191, 510, 562, 565.

724 INDEX

Garrisonian doctrine of non-resistance, not acceptable to B, 49.
Gaston, Geo. B., 267.
Gaston, Mrs. Geo. B., quoted, concerning conditions in Tabor, 267, 268.
Gay, Hamilton, letter from Perkins and Brown, 59.
Gay, William, murder of, 181, 215.
Gaylord, Daniel C., 37, 38, 41.
Geary, John W., succeeds Shannon as Gov. of Kansas (Sept., 1856), 234; his arrival ushers in a better era, 255; issues address and proclamations, 255; orders disbandment of pro-slavery militia and organization of a new body, 255; equally severe on pro-slavery murderers and Free State marauders, 255; more and more favorable to Free State cause, 255; in Lawrence, with U. S. troops under Cooke, 256, 257; averts pro-slavery attack there, 259; unjustly denounced by B, 268; resigns, 294; his administration, 294; leaves Kansas a Free State man, 294; 254, 263, 264, 277.
Georgia, pro-slavery men from, in Kansas, 137, 138.
Gibbons family, 327.
Gibson, Col. John T., 438, 440, 452.
Giddings, Joshua R., attacked in majority report of Mason Com., 582; 394, 398, 459, 472, 474. *Letter to* B, 134; *from* B, 131.
Giddings, Mrs. Joshua R., 394.
Gihon, Mr., 173.
Gilbert, Isaac, 442 n.
Gileadites, U. S. league of, organized in Springfield (1851), 50; B's "Words of Advice" for, 50, 51, 52; object of, 51; agreement and resolutions of, 52, 53; 55, 75.
Gill, Geo. B., elected "Sec'y of the Treasury" at Chatham Convention, 333; and Jim Daniels's story, 367, 368; in Missouri raid, 368; quoted, 363, 364, 379, 382, 389, 680, 682; final parting from B, 390 n.; his defection, 409; 328, 330, 344, 353, 364, 370, 380, 381, 385, 386, 413, 414, 424, 510. *Letters from* B, 337.
Gill, Dr. H. C., 316. *Letter from* R. Realf, 330.
Gilman, Charles F., quoted, 254.
Gilpatrick, Rufus, elected judge of Squatters' Court as "Old Brown," 168, 175, 358.
Gist, Gov., of So. Carolina, 567.
Gladstone, Thomas H., *The Englishman in Kansas*, quoted, 97; 179.
Glasgow (Mo.) Times, 99.
Gloucester, J. N., colored, B discloses his plans to, 323.
Gloucester, Mrs. J. N., colored, 323, 412.
Golding, R., 168.
Goodin, Joel K., Sec'y of Territorial Exec. Com., 106, and of Free State Exec. Com., 108.
Gordon, William, 247.
Graham, Dr., 208.
Graham, Mr., quoted as to B's last day in Kansas, 383.
Grand Jury, Federal, indicts Free State men for treason without hearing witnesses, 142; recommends abatement of Free State newspapers as nuisances, 143, and demolition of Free State Hotel, 143.
Grant, Charles, son of John T. Grant, 173.
Grant, Geo. W., son of John T. Grant, and the case of Morse, 174, 175; not the mysterious messenger, 175; quoted, 245; 153, 156, 169.
Grant, Henry C., son of John T. Grant, 156, 169.
Grant, J. G., son of John T. Grant, 167, 175.
Grant, John T., condemns Pottawatomie raid, 167; 169, 172, 173.
Grant, Mrs. John T., 173.
Grant, Mary E., daughter of John T. Grant, alleged assault of W. Sherman on, 172, 173, 175, 177; quoted, 230.
Grasshopper Falls Convention, 296.

Gray, Dr., 535.
Greeley, Horace, quoted as to G. Smith, 71, 72; quoted, 95, 104, 126, 147, 476, 480; challenged by H. C. Pate, 613 n. 19; 49, 138, 139, 188, 230, 287, 472, 510. *Letter to* S. Colfax, 476.
Green, Lieut. Israel, commands marines at Harper's Ferry, 440, 450; leads attack on engine house, 452-454; his *Capture of John Brown*, quoted, 453; sketch of, 642 n. 61; 462 n., 470.
Green, Shields, colored, decides to go with B, despite advice of F. Douglass, 412, 413; in Harper's Ferry party, 414, 418, 421, 431, 449; made prisoner in engine house, 454; convicted and sentenced, 569, 570; executed, 570; sketch of, 687; 470, 471, 486, 571, 572.
Green, Thomas C., mayor of Charlestown, assigned as counsel for B, 483, 484; denounced by B and withdraws, 492; sketch of, 645 n. 49; 490, 491, 507, 520.
Green, William, employed as counsel for B before the Court of Appeals, 646 n. 75.
Greenlaw, Wm. P., 591 n. 6.
Gregg, E. H., letter to J. H. Holmes, 389.
Grinnell, Josiah B., his warm welcome of B, 386, 387; 390.
Griswold, Hiram, sent by D. R. Tilden to assist in B's defence, 493, 495; argues for defence, 496; lays evidence of B's insanity before Gov. Wise, 507, 508.
Grover, Capt. Joel, at "Fort" Titus, 231.
Grover, Mr., 380.
Grow, Galusha A., his bill for admission of Kansas under Topeka Constitution passed by House of Representatives, 226.
Gue, Benjamin F., 411.
Gue, David J., author of Floyd letter, 411; his motive in writing it, 411, 412.

Hadley, Daniel B., 594 n. 12.
Hadsall, C. C., and the sale of Eli Snyder's claim at Moneka, 356, 357.
Hagerstown (Md.), 402, 403.
Haine, Deputy Sheriff, 215.
Hairgrove, Asa, 348, 354, 375.
Hale, John P., U. S. Senator from New Hampshire, 339.
Hall, Amos, murdered by Charles A. Hamilton and his men, 348, 375.
Hall, Austin, 348, 375.
Haller, William, kills J. T. Lyle, 295.
Hallock, Rev. Jeremiah, 12.
Hallock, Rev. Moses, 17.
Hallock, William H., quoted, 17.
Hamburg, visited by B, 61.
Hamilton, Charles A., Border Ruffian, bloody deed of, 186, 187, 348, 349, 375; motive for his crime, 349; authorities for the story of, 629 n. 3.
Hammond, Col. C. G., 390.
Hamtramck Guards, at Harper's Ferry, 444, 464, 465.
Hannibal (Mo.) Messenger, 99.
Hanway, James, *The Settlement of Lane and Vicinity*, quoted, 136; in *Kansas Monthly*, 153; condemns Pottawatomie murders, 167; but later approves, 167, 170; 175, 358. *Letter to* R. J. Hinton, 358; *from* S. Walker, 228, 229.
Harding, Charles B., State's attorney, character of, 485, 645 n. 53; sums up for prosecution, 495; 483, 489, 494.
Harper, Gen. Kenton, 465.
Harper's Ferry, B's plan to seize arsenal disclosed to Col. Woodruff in 1854 or 1855, 54; but may have been conceived much earlier, 55; details of plan discussed, 313; B arrives at, July 3, 1859, 403; details of attack on, 426 seqq.; B moves his force from Kennedy Farm to, 426, 427; place ill-chosen for an attack on slavery, 427, 428; the arsenal, 428, 429, 430;

INDEX 725

description of the town, 428, 429; unfavorable strategic position, 429; approaches to, unsuspecting of invasion, 430; rush of militia to, 444; conduct of citizens of, 447, 448.
Harper's Ferry Raid, assumes national proportions only because of B's survival, 471, 472; Southern opinion concerning, 474–476; its real significance, 476.
Harris, James, his story of the murder of W. Sherman, 162–164.
Harris, James H., colored, 331, 413.
"Harrisburg," letter to Gov. Wise so signed, 518.
Harrison, Jeremiah, 121.
Harrison, William H., alias of R. J. Hinton and of A. Hazlett, 572.
Harrisonville (Mo.) Democrat, quoted, 370.
Hartford (Conn.), 278.
Hartford Evening Press and the raid, 472.
Harvey, James A., commands abortive expedition against Leavenworth, 254; captures proslavery force at Hickory Point, 256; many of his men taken prisoners by Capt. Wood, 256; 233, 252, 253.
Hawes, Alexander G., 239, 245, 247.
Hawkins, Nelson, *nom de guerre* adopted by B, in 1857, 290, 325 and n., 339.
Hayden, Lewis, and F. J. Merriam, 421.
Haymaker, Mr., 27.
Haynau, Mr. See Haine.
Hayward, Shephard, colored, shot to death by B's raiders, 433, 434; 441, 461, 479.
Hazlett, Albert, in Harper's Ferry party, 414, 419, 420, 430, 439; his escape, 445, 446; captured in Penn., 446; ignored by B and the other prisoners in the hope of saving his life, 554, 572; attempts to save him after B's execution, 573 seqq.; executed, 580; sketch of, 682; 368, 369, 471, 554, 558 n.
Heiskell, Gen., 189, 257.
Helper, Hinton Rowan, his *Impending Crisis*, 568, 583, 584, 585, 587.
"Henry," letter to B, 518.
Herald of Freedom, 91, 143, 231, 354, 371, 632 n. 71.
Hicklan (or Hicklin), Harvey G., Jim Daniels's temporary master, 368; his account of B's Missouri raid, 368.
Hickory Point, pro-slavery force at, threatened by Lane and captured by Harvey, 256.
Hicks, Gov., of Maryland, 524.
Higgins, Patrick, first man wounded at Harper's Ferry, 432 and n.
Higginson, Thomas Wentworth, his *Cheerful Yesterdays* quoted, 170, 326, 397, 579, 580, 595 n. 21; on Lane's eloquence, 226; anger at delay in autumn of 1857, 303; his characterization of B, 326; his memorandum on postponement of Virginia plan, 340; disinclined to aid B in May, 1859, 397; his feeling on hearing of Harper's Ferry raid, 397; one of the first to move for rescue of B, 511; his temperament and principles, 511; appeals to Mrs. Brown to induce B to consent to rescue, 512, 513; Mr. Spooner's plan to kidnap Gov. Wise, 515; after the failure at Harper's Ferry, 529; reproaches Dr. Howe, 532; his part in attempts to save Stevens and Hazlett, 573 seqq.; his aliases, 573; 324, 421, 471, 514, 515, 517, 570. *Letters to* B, 338, 397, Dr. Howe, 533, F. B. Sanborn, 529; *from* B, 320, 513, 543, Dr. Howe, 532, F. B. Sanborn, 303, 325, 326, 339, 396, 530.
Higginson, Mrs. T. W., 573, 577, 581.
Hill, Mr., 214, 292.
Hinckley, Alexis, 413.
Hinsdale, Abel, 29.
Hinton, R. J., his *John Brown and his Men*, quoted, 17, 484, 625 n. 97; his journal, quoted, 258; and the attempt to save Stevens and Hazlett, 572 seqq.; 175, 308, 336, 352, 413, 414, 424, 512, 516, 570.
Hoadley, George, letter to S. P. Chase, 587.
Hoar, E. Rockwood, 396, 534.
Hobart, Mrs. Danley, quoted, 18.
Hodges, Willis H., coöperates with B in assisting negroes at No. Elba, 73. *Letter from* B, 72.
Holbrook, James J., 3d Lieut. of Liberty Guards, 121.
Holland, F. M., *Frederick Douglass: the Colored Orator*, quoted, 85.
Holman, Mrs. Mary L., 591 n. 6.
Holmes, James H., 234, 236, 238, 239, 240, 243, 245, 247, 261, 290, 293. *Letter to* B, 300.
Holmes, Mrs., 172.
Holt, J. H., captures Copeland, 445.
Hopkins, Mr., murder of, 215.
Hoppe, Wm., murder of, 181, 215, 352.
Hopper family, 327.
House of Representatives (U. S.), votes to admit neither Whitfield nor Reeder as delegate, 226; passes Grow bill for admission of Kansas, under Topeka Const., 226; and rejects Toombs bill, 227; attaches Free State rider to Army Appropriation bill, which fails of passage, 227; Speakership contest in 1859–60, 583, 585.
Howard Committee of House of Representatives, appointed in March, 1856, to investigate Kansas situation, 94 and n., 100, 116, 117, 141, 143, 183; decision of, on election of Territorial delegate, 106, 107 and n.; reports of, 107, 109, 120, 226; their value, and effect on public opinion, 107.
Howard, William A., chairman of Howard Committee, 94 n.; and John Sherman, report of, quoted, 120.
Howe, Dr. Samuel G., accused of duplicity and prevarication by Adm. Chadwick, 341; and the proposed attack on Charlestown, 517; goes to Canada after the raid, 530; his self-exculpatory card, 531; his attitude discussed, 531–533; attacked by Higginson, 532; before the Mason Com., 532; 271, 324, 325, 326, 340, 397, 399, 484, 582. *Letters to* T. W. Higginson, 532, Henry Wilson, 341; *from* H. Forbes, 313, T. W. Higginson, 533, Henry Wilson, 339.
Hoyt, David S., murder of, 181, 215, 231.
Hoyt, George H., retained by Le Barnes to defend B, 484; his instructions, 484; his youth arouses A. Hunter's suspicions, 484, 485; his first appearance in court, 490; allowed to act as counsel, 490; asks for delay, 492; becomes sole counsel, 493; reinforced by Chilton and Griswold, 493; proceeds with defence, 494, 495; submits affidavits concerning B's insanity to Gov. Wise, 508; tells B of plan to rescue him, 512; forced to leave Charlestown, 520; quoted, concerning Stevens, 680; 517, 540, 544. *Letters to* J. W. Le Barnes, 479 n., 495, 512.
Hudson (Ohio), 9.
Huffmaster, Mrs., an inquisitive neighbor of Kennedy Farm, 417, 418, 419.
Hughes, Mrs. Sarah F., her *John Murray Forbes* quoted, 398, 399.
Hugo, Victor, his *John Brown* quoted, 569, 588.
"Humanitarians, The," H. Forbes's name for B's friends in Mass., 299.
Humphrey, Rev. Heman, 15.
Humphrey, Rev. Luther, 15. *Letter from* B, 543.
Hunnewell, James, 302.
Hunt, Washington, 563.
Hunter, Andrew, special prosecutor to try B., 442; suspicious of Hoyt's youth, 484, 485; his character and ability, 485; his conduct of the prosecution, 485; opening address to jury, 490; and his son's story of the shooting of Wm. Thompson, 491; accuses B of feigning

illness to gain time, 495; his *John Brown's Raid* quoted, 495, 522, 525, 527; his closing argument, 496; and the rescue scares, 521, 522; makes B's will, 550; sketch of, 645 n. 55; 456, 491, 494, 499, 524, 525, 526, 527, 548 and n., 570, 571, 588. *Letters to* Gov. Wise, 477; *from* B, 548, Gov. Letcher, 578, Dr. Peticolas, 504 n., Gov. Wise, 478, 504, 521. Father of
Hunter, Harry, describes killing of Wm. Thompson by himself and Chambers, 442, 491.
Hurd, H. B., Sec'y of National Kansas Com., denies B's authority to sign as agent, 360; 275, 276. *Letters to* G. L. Stearns, 275, E. B. Whitman, 360.
Hutchings, John, 175.
Hutchinson, William, 307, 373, 374. *Letter to* Mrs. Hutchinson, 373.
Hyatt, Thaddeus, *Journal of Investigations in Kansas*, 89 n.; Pres. of National Kansas Com., 227; arrested and released, 582, 583; 235, 287, 298.

Imboden, Gen. J. D., 465.
Independence (Mo.) *Messenger*, 99.
Indians, near Hudson, Ohio, 9, 13; in Osawatomie neighborhood, 89, 90.
Ingersoll (Canada), 328.
Insanity, suggested plea of, in B's family, 489, 490; the whole question discussed, 508–510.
Iowa, Historical Dept. of, 384.
Iowans, in B's force in Kansas, 236.
Irrepressible Conflict, The, imminence of, indicated by Mr. Spooner's plan to kidnap Gov. Wise, 514; 527, 586.
Irving, Washington, his *Life of Washington*, 325.
Isaacks, A. J., U. S. Dist. Att'y for Kansas, upholds legality of Shawnee Legislature, 100.
Iverson, Lieut., 196.
Iverson, Alfred, U. S. Senator from Georgia, 584, 587, 596 n. 4.

Jackson, Andrew, President of the U. S., 14.
Jackson, Mrs B. F., quoted, 155; 173.
Jackson, Congrave, and Maughas, G. B. M., their report of the fight at Osawatomie, 247.
Jackson, Francis, 420.
Jackson, J. P., 525.
Jackson, M. V. B., 151, 178.
Jackson, Patrick T., 271, 274.
Jackson, Prof. T. J. ("Stonewall"), 523, 555, 556.
Jacobs, Judge, befriends Jason Brown, 194, 195.
Jamison, "Quartermaster General," 301.
"Jayhawkers," 350, 513.
Jefferson, Thomas, President of the U. S., his *Notes on the State of Virginia* quoted, 428; 559.
Jefferson, Thomas, B's colored driver, 72.
Jefferson City Inquirer, 99, 189.
Jefferson Guards, turn out at Charlestown, 436; well led, 437; 438, 465.
Jenkins, Gaius, indicted for treason, 142, and arrested, 145.
Jennison, Charles, Free State leader of an armed band, and a raider 187, 366; in Missouri raid, 368; 513.
Jerry Rescue Committee, 536.
John Brown Song, The, 506, 585.
Johnson, Oliver, 575.
Johnston, Lt.-Col. Joseph E., at Lawrence, in command of U. S. troops, 257, 259, 260.
Jones, Rev. Elijah B., letter from John Sherman, 506 n.
Jones, H. L., describes feeling of Free State men as to Pottawatomie murders, 167, 168.
Jones, John, shooting of, 141, 142, 180.
Jones, John, colored, 390.
Jones, Lieut. J. P., 633 n. 85.

Jones, John T. ("Ottawa"), his house destroyed, 253 and n.; 154, 165, 195, 196, 207, 277.
Jones, Mrs. John T., 253.
Jones, Jonas, 276, 277, 293, 299, 388.
Jones, Samuel J., Sheriff, and the rescue of Branson, 113, 114; appeals to Gov. Shannon, 114; blamed in report of Howard Com., 120; his alleged language, 120; correspondence with Robinson and Lane, 129; declares treaty of Lawrence violated by Free State men, 130; again in Lawrence, 139; arrests S. N. Wood, 140; resisted, brings U. S. troops to Lawrence, 140; wholesale arrests by, 140; wounded by J. N. Filer, 140; his death announced by pro-slavery papers, 140; shooting of, unfortunate for people of Lawrence, 140, 141; at burning of Free State Hotel, 146; 124, 145, 179, 180, 185, 190.
Joyce, Burr, his *John Brown's Raids*, quoted, 368, 369.
Jurisdiction, question of, as between State and Federal Courts in matter of the raid, 477, 478.

Kagi, John Henry, approves B's Harper's Ferry plan when first broached, 313; secretary of Chatham Convention, 331; elected "Secretary of War" at Chatham Convention, 333; quoted, 364, 365; in Missouri raid, 368; attempt to arrest, 388; stationed at Chambersburg, Penn., 406, 407; "a melancholy brigand" according to A. Ward, 392; urges B to leave Harper's Ferry, 438; his steadfast conduct and death, 444, 445; sketch of, 679; 254, 308 and n., 315, 330, 337, 343, 344, 353, 357, 358, 359, 360, 362, 363, 366, 374, 375, 379, 386, 387, 390, 391, 393, 394, 395, 397, 401, 402, 412, 417, 419, 420, 427, 429, 431, 510. *Letters to* John Brown, Jr., 422, N. Y. *Tribune*, 362, 363, his sister, 358; *from* B, 397, 402, 406, 408, John Brown, Jr., 413.
Kaiser, Charles, murdered, 250; 199, 200, 246.
Kansas, evil days in, 54; objects of colonization in, 80; its natural characteristics, 80; the slavery issue in, 80; conditions in, as seen by John Brown, Jr., 83; hardships of settlers in, during winter of 1855–1856, 89 and n.; rival parties in, 94; first election in, decided by fraudulent votes of Missourians, 94; H. Greeley concerning prospects in, 95; New Englanders sent to, by Emigrant Aid Societies, 95; second election in, 98 seqq.; first Territorial legislature, elected in 1855, solidly pro-slavery, 99; effect of that election on sentiment at the North and in Missouri, 99, 100; meeting of first legislature at Pawnee, and later at Shawnee, 100; its voters in favor of excluding all negroes, 105; two elections for delegate to Congress, Oct. 1855, 106; two hostile governments in, 107; Constitution framed by Topeka Convention ratified by people, 107; claimed to be an organized free state, 107; invaded by Missourians posing as Kansas militia, 115, 116; Free State Legislature memorializes Congress for admission under Topeka Const., 133; pro-slavery men from other states in, 137, 138; colonists from New England in, 138; fears of Free State sympathizers of rush of settlers from Southern States, 139; Marshal Donaldson's proclamation to law-abiding citizens, 143; rush of colonists to, after Lawrence outrages, 146, 147; nation's attention centred on, as result of Lawrence raid, 147; Pottawatomie murders the most prolific subject of discussion in its history, 148; conditions in 1856 as bearing on resort to extra-legal methods, 171 seqq.; seething with lawlessness, 211; in Frémont-Buchanan campaign, 226; and the Howard Com. report, 226; discussions on, in Congress,

INDEX 727

226; Grow bill, for admission under Topeka Const., passed by House of Representatives, 226; Toombs bill, for taking census in, etc., 227; minor warfare in (Aug. 1856), 234 seqq.; situation intensified by B's defeat, and burning of Osawatomie, 250 seqq.; Gov. Geary's arrival ushers in a better era, 255; last organized Missourian invasion of, 257 seqq.; peace prevails in Nov. 1856, 260; destruction of life and property between Nov. 1855, and Dec. 1856, 264; effect of climate and soil on political views of settlers, 265; no one man decided its fate, 265, 266; Mass. Legislature asked to appropriate money for Free State cause in, 277; fate of, as concerned in B's plans, 284; Gov. Walker's administration, 294, 295; 1857 a year of quiet and progress, 295; Free State and pro-slavery conventions in that year, 295, 296; Free State victory in election of Oct. 1857, 306; peace-party in ascendant in autumn of 1857, 306, 307; success at polls more effective than "Beecher's Bibles," 306, 307; policy of Free State leaders, 307; causes of freedom and prosperity of, 307; in June, 1858, 346 seqq.; Lecompton Const. — with slavery — adopted at fraudulent election, 346; rejected at second election, 346; state officers chosen, 346; bribe offered to, by Congress, in English bill, 347; Lecompton Const. finally rejected, 347; renewal of lawlessness in S. E. counties, 348; B's description of conditions in those counties in July and Aug. 1858, 354; Legislature of, and B's Missouri raid, 377; B's presence in 1858 a cause of excitement and strife, 378; peace restored when he had left the Territory, 379; legislative act of amnesty for certain crimes, 379; enjoys peace and quiet thereafter until the Civil War, 379. And see Free State, Lawrence, Lecompton Constitution, Pottawatomie Creek, Pro-slavery, Shawnee Legislature, Topeka Constitutional Convention.

Kansas-Nebraska Act (1854), 75, 79, 80, 587.
Kansas Free State, 122, 143.
Kansas Historical Society, collections of, 174.
"Kansas Legion," 112, 113.
Kansas militia, Atchison's army poses as, 250; organization of, ordered by Pres. Pierce, 251; disbanded by order of Gov. Geary, 255; new organization of, to be mustered into service of U. S., 255.
Kansas Pioneer, accessory before the fact to murder of Reese P. Brown, 129.
"Kansas Ruffians," compared with Border Ruffians, 264.
Kansas Weekly Herald, quoted concerning pro-slavery triumph in 1854, 95, 157, 169, 190.
Kapp, Friedrich, 575.
Kellogg, George, agent of New England Woolen Co., 30. *Letter from* B, 31.
Kelly, J. W. B., thrashed for holding abolition views, 110.
Kemper, Gen. James L., quoted, 566.
Kennedy, Dr., B rents farm of, near Harper's Ferry, 403.
Kennedy, Mary V., married to John E. Cook, 408, 681.
Kennedy Farm, rented by B, description of, 404; B's force of 21 men-at-arms at, in Aug. 1859, 414, 415; daily life at, described by Mrs. Annie Brown Adams, 416-420; all B's correspondence left there, 467.
Kent (Ohio), 27.
Kent, Marvin, quoted as to B's character, 28; 27, 58.
Kent, Zenas, B's partner at Franklin Mills, 27, 28. *Letter from,* 26.
Kibbey, Lucius, his killing of Davis not a political crime, 109.
Kickapoo Rangers, 129, 144, 223, 260.

Kiene, Llewellyn L., describes the "Battle of the Spurs," 381, 382.
Kilbourne, Mr., 196.
King, Charles, 230.
King, Rev. H. D., recalls B's table-talk, 298, 299; and B's request for a thanksgiving service at Tabor, 384, 385.
King Brothers, arms stored in their ware-rooms, 343.
Kinnaird, Thomas M., 333.
Kirkwood, Samuel J., Gov. of Iowa, quoted, 567, 568.
Kitzmiller, A. M., temporarily in charge of arsenal at Harper's Ferry, 435, 439.
Ladd, Benj. W., letter from Perkins and Brown, 60.
Lafayette, Marquis de, pistol presented to Geo. Washington by, 431.
Lane, James H., chairman of a convention in Lawrence, 103; joins Free Soilers, 103; chairman of Topeka Const. Conv., 105; at Big Springs Conv., 106; early attitude on negro question, 106; chairman of Free State Exec. Com., 108; rival of C. Robinson, 108; refused leave to act as counsel for McCrea, 109; addresses meeting at Lawrence after treaty of peace, 123; addresses meeting of pro-slavery captains at Franklin, 124; authorized by Shannon to preserve peace at Lawrence, 125; elected provisionally U. S. Senator by Free State Legislature, 132; indicted for treason, 142; escapes arrest, 143; said to have inspired B's Pottawatomie expedition, 183, 184; his Free State "caravan," 223; at Nebraska City with his caravan, 225; assumes alias of Cook, 225; speech at Chicago, 225, 226; his eloquence described by T. W. Higginson, 226; leaves Nebraska City for Lawrence with B and S. Walker, 228; reaches Lawrence alone, 228; with S. Walker makes demonstration against Lecompton and effects release of prisoners, 252; returns to Lawrence, 252; message from, recalls expedition against Leavenworth, 254; leaves for Nebraska on Geary's arrival, 256; projected siege of pro-slavery men at Hickory Point abandoned, 256; again in Kansas, 291; presides over Topeka Conventions, June and July, 1857, 295, 296; desires B's presence in Kansas, 300; appoints B "brigadier-general," 301; and B's Missouri raid, 370, 371; 121, 129, 140, 229, 231, 233, 235 n., 239, 255, 262, 265, 266, 296, 297, 302, 306, 346, 514. *Letters to* B, 300, 301, 304; *from* B, 300, 301.
Lane, Samuel A., testifies in 1898 as to B's movements *en route* to Kansas in 1855, 85; his *Fifty Years and over of Akron and Summit County,* 593 n. 32; 597 n. 14.
Larue, John, his slaves liberated by B in Missouri raid, 369.
Larue, John B., 369.
Laughlin, Patrick, shoots S. Collins, 112, 113.
Law-and-Order Party, formed by pro-slavery men, 108; address concerning Pottawatomie murders, 192; meeting of protest, 192; appoints vigilance committee, 192; 212.
Lawrence (Kansas), Free State convention at, 91; radical meeting at, Aug. 1855, 91; conventions of Free Soilers at, June to Aug., 1855, 102, 103; the rescue of Branson by citizens of, and its consequences, 113 seqq.; Committee of Safety formed, 113, 114; threatened by pro-slavery forces, 114; number of troops assembled against, 116; appeals to all Free State men to come to her rescue, 118; operations for relief of, 118-120; end of siege of, 120; open-air meetings, 123; terms of treaty, 123; treaty of, accepted by both parties, 124; protection of, intrusted to Lane and Robin-

728　INDEX

son by stratagem, 125; treaty of, an ill-fated pact, 126; invasion of, characterized in report of Howard Com., 120; citizens of, condemn shooting of Jones, to no effect, 140, 141; pro-slavery appeals for her destruction, 141; movement of force under Donaldson against, 144, 145; committee of citizens offer submission, and surrender their arms, 145; helplessness of her citizens, 146; destruction of newspaper offices and Free State Hotel, 146; sack of, 180, described by S. C. Pomeroy, 182; sources for story of sack of, 607 n. 100; threatened by pro-slavery force, 257 seqq.; R. J. Hinton concerning conditions at, 258; fortifications of, 258; defence of, in hands of Maj. Abbott and Capt. Cracklin, 258; attack on, averted by Gov. Geary and Lt.-Col. Cooke, 259.
Lawrence, Amos A., first impressions of B, 273; calls him the "Miles Standish of Kansas," 273; his admiration for B cools, 400; his diary quoted, 400; 279, 281, 291. *Letter to* B, 280; *from* B, 279.
Lawrence, Wm. R., 280.
Lawrence Republican, 364, 365, 370, 480.
Lawrence "Stubbs," J. B. Abbott's company, reinforces B at Black Jack, 208.
Le Barnes, J. W., retains G. H. Hoyt to defend B, 484; among the first to plan rescue of B, 511; and the Spooner plan to kidnap Wise, 515 seqq.; and the proposed attack on Charlestown, 516, 517; and the attempt to save Stevens and Hazlett, 574; 512, 515, 528, 570. *Letter to* T. W. Higginson, 515; *from* G. H. Hoyt, 479 n., 495, 512.
Leary, Lewis Sheridan, in B's Harper's Ferry party, 415, 421, 431; his death, 445; sketch of, 685.
Leather Manufacturers' Bank of New York, 37.
Leavenworth, vote of, not counted in vote ratifying Topeka Const., 107, 108; public meeting at, applauds outrage on W. Phillips, 110; disturbances at, in Jan. 1856, 128, 129; pro-slavery mayor prohibits election under Topeka Const., 128; election adjourned to Easton, 128; murder of Reese P. Brown, 129; news of Pottawatomie murders at, 192; Free State expedition against, under Harvey, 254, recalled by Lane, 254.
Leavenworth Herald, 110, 116, 129, 230, 370.
Leavenworth Times, "Battle of the Spurs" described in, 382, 383.
Leavitt, Rev. Joshua, introduces Hugh Forbes to B, 285; 318.
Lecompte, S. D., Chief Justice of Kansas Territory, upholds legality of Shawnee Legislature, 100; and the trial of McCrea for the murder of Clark, 109; his pro-slavery charge to Grand Jury after Pottawatomie, 142; his novel definition of constructive treason, 142.
Lecompton Constitution, slavery question, how affected by, 346; two elections on adoption of, 346; election of officers under, 346; in Congress, 347; rejected at election of Aug. 2, 1858, 347; 296, 306, 351.
Lecompton Constitutional Convention, in pro-slavery hands, 296; 306, 307.
Lecompton Union, and the Pottawatomie murders, 190.
Lee, Col. Robert E., sent to Harper's Ferry to command all the forces there, 450; prepares to attack at daylight, 450; his orders as detailed by Stuart, 450, 451; execution of his plan, 451 seqq.; at the interview following B's capture, 456 seqq.; 463, 464; in Harper's Ferry for execution of B, 523; 470, 555.
Leeman, William H., indiscreet letter to his mother, 408; circumstances of his death, 440; sketch of, 685; 308, 311, 329, 330, 337, 343, 344, 414, 419, 437.

Legate, James F., 126, 175.
Lenhart, Charles, wrongfully suspected of shooting Sheriff Jones, 140; attempts to effect escape of Cook and Coppoc, 571, 572; sketch of, 655 n. 46; 142, 215, 216, 414.
Leonard, O. E., 232.
Letcher, John, Gov. of Virginia, 572; warned of attempt to rescue Stevens and Hazlett, 578. *Letter to* A. Hunter, 578.
Lewis, A. H., despatch to Faulkner and Botts, 505.
Lexington (Mo.) Express, 117, 189.
Liberator, The, B's acquaintance with, 49; ignores Pottawatomie murders, 191; and the raid, 473; 501, 583, 599 n. 50.
Liberty (Mo.), arms stolen from U. S. armory there by Missourians invading Kansas, 117.
Liberty Guards, B's company of Kansas militia so-called, 121; muster-roll, 121; their length of service, 121, 122.
Liberty Platform, 96.
Lieber, Francis, letter to Dr. H. Drisler, 564.
Limerick, W., quoted, 240, 241. *Letter to* Gen. Shields, 240.
Lincoln, Abraham, quoted, 564; nominated for President, and elected, 585.
Lincoln, Levi, ex-Gov. of Mass., 563.
Little, J. H., killed in attack on Fort Scott, 366.
Lodge, John E., 280.
Loguen, J. W., colored, 323, 327, 328.
London, B's visit to, 61, 63.
London Times, 475 n., 568.
Longfellow, H. W., his diary quoted, 563.
Longstreet, James, Lieut.-Gen., myth concerning, 224 n.
Loudon Heights, 428, 429.
Lovejoy, Elijah P., 51, 594 n. 13.
Lowry, Grosvenor P., 140.
Lowry, M. B., visits B in jail, 546.
Lucas, Judge, 520.
"Limber Jim," 519.
Lusk, Mrs. Amos, B's mother-in-law and housekeeper, 18.
Lusk, Dianthe. See Brown, Dianthe (Lusk).
Lusk, Milton, B's brother-in-law, 19.
Luther, Martin, 510.
Lyle, James T., killed by Haller, 295.
Lynch law, when justifiably resorted to, 171, 181.

McClellan, Geo. B., report on the armies of Europe, 325.
McClellan, H. B., *Life and Campaigns of J. E. B. Stuart* quoted, 450, 451.
McClure, Alex. K., 421.
McClure's Magazine, 594 n. 12.
McCrea, Cole, charged with murder of Clark, 109; treatment of, by Chief Justice Lecompte, 109; indicted and escapes, 109, 110.
McCrea-Clark homicide, of marked political significance, 109.
McDaniel, Sheriff, 349, 364, 365.
McDow, W. C., 168.
McFarland, Rev. Mr., letter from B, 544, 545.
McIlvaine, Messrs., 137.
McIntosh, Lieut. James, supports Sheriff Jones with U. S. troops, 140; concerning disorders in Kansas, 214; 197.
McKim, J. Miller, 513, 549, 561, 562.
Mace, J. N., shooting of, 141.
Manes, John B., 178.
Manes, Poindexter, 172.
Manning, Rev. Jacob M., 560.
Mansfield, James, 558 and n.
"Manual of the Patriotic Volunteer," translation by H. Forbes, 286, 298.
Marais des Cygnes, 149, 196, 229, 235, 236, 239, 244, 247, 249.
Marais des Cygnes Massacre, 186, 187, 354, 355, 375. And see Hamilton, Charles A.
"Marais du Cygne, Le," by J. G. Whittier, 349.

INDEX 729

Marais des Cygnes River, 198.
Marcy, W. L., Sec'y of State, 255.
"Marion Rifles," 149, 150.
Martin, Henry, alias of Montgomery, 573, 576.
Martin, Hugh, 369.
Martinsburg company, at Harper's Ferry, 443; cuts off B's only avenue of escape, 443.
Maryland Heights, 428, 429.
Mason, Dr., jail-physician, 489, 495.
Mason, J. M., U. S. Senator from Virginia, his questions to B in the interview following his capture, 457 seqq.; quoted, 469; chairman of investigating committee of U. S. Senate, 478; and F. B. Sanborn, 533; and G. L. Stearns, 534; presents majority report of his committee, 580; 456, 470, 505 n., 529, 566.
Mason Committee, F. B. Sanborn's testimony before, 533; and G. L. Stearns's, 534, 535; its sessions, 580; reports of majority, 580, 581–583, and minority, 580, 581; 182, 331, 342, 359, 399, 409.
Massachusetts and the Anthony Burns case, 384.
Massachusetts Arms Co., sells revolvers to G. L. Stearns, for B, 289; 341.
Massachusetts Kansas Committee, votes to give B 200 rifles previously sent to Tabor, Iowa, 274, 275; controversy as to arms and money, 341–343; accused of duplicity, 341; its defence, 342; its affairs confused with those of National Kansas Com., 360, 361; 227, 271, 279, 289, 317, 339, 340, 359.
Massachusetts Legislature, urged to appropriate $100,000 for Free State cause in Kansas, 277; B before Committee on Federal Relations, 277; refuses appropriation, 278.
Massasoit House, Chicago, color-line drawn at, 329.
Massasoit House, Springfield, B a welcome visitor at, 278; 282, 284.
Maughas, G. B. M. See Jackson, Congrave.
Maxson, William, 312, 315, 316, 328.
May, Samuel J., 85.
Mayflower Company, 1, 19.
Medary, Gov. Samuel, prejudiced against Free State leaders by Montgomery's attack on Fort Scott, 366, 367; applies for U. S. troops, and for arms for Kansas militia, 367; his action on B's Missouri raid, 376, 377; 364, 370, 371, 374, 378, 379, 381.
Memminger, O. G., quoted, 567.
Memorandum Book, No. 2, B's (in Boston Public Library), quoted, 53.
Mendenhall, Richard, 134.
Meriam, Francis J., joins B at Chambersburg, and supplies him with funds, 412, 420, 421; his character and antecedents, 421; at Harper's Ferry, 421; left to guard arms at Kennedy Farm, 421, 426; his arrival removes last obstacle to making attack, 423; his final escape, 471; sketch of, 685; 415, 446, 468.
"Meridezene." See Marais des Cygnes.
Messenger, the, who brought news to "Pottawatomies'" camp of threats against Free State settlers, his identity, or actuality, disputed, 175, 176; probably non-existent, 176, 177.
Metternich, Col. Richard, 575, 579.
Meulen, Peter Wouter van der, maternal ancestor of B, 15.
Mexican War, 59, 79.
Middle West, difficulties of pioneering in, in early 19th century, 8, 9.
Miller, Col. C. D., G. Smith's son-in-law, 535.
Mills, Benj., master-armorer at Harper's Ferry, a prisoner, 439, 455.
Mills, Rev. Gideon, B's maternal great-grandfather, 15.
Mills, Lieut. Gideon, B's maternal grandfather, 15.
Mills, Lucius, 220, 222, 223.
Mills, Owen, 30.
Mills, Peter, son of Peter van der Meulen, and B's maternal great-great-grandfather, 15.
Mills, Ruth, descent of, 15; marries Owen Brown, 12. And see Brown, Ruth (Mills).
Mills, Ruth (Humphrey), B's maternal grandmother, 15.
Mills, Lt.-Col. S. S., 467.
Mina, Spanish leader of guerrillas, 53.
Missouri, crucial position of, 80; her relation to Kansas controversy, 83; effect of Kansas election of 1855 on soberer elements, 99; B's raid into, 367 seqq.; its deplorable results, 370 seqq.; governor offers reward for B's arrest, 371.
Missouri Compromise, repeal of, 79.
Missouri Democrat, 99, 382.
Missouri River, blockaded by Missourians against Lane's Free State force, 225.
Missourians, armed, at Osawatomie, 90; fraudulent votes cast by, in Kansas election of 1854, 94; and New England emigrants to Kansas, 96; their preparations for the second election in Kansas, 98, and easy triumph, 98, 99; posing as Kansas militia, 115, 116, 123, 124; refrain from voting in election under Topeka Const., except in Leavenworth, 128; in camp at Black Jack, 200; raided at Franklin, 212; large force invades Kansas, 257 seqq.; their threatened attack on Lawrence averted by Geary and Cooke, 259; disbandment of Atchison's army a fatal blow to their hopes, 261.
Mitchel, Prof. Ormsby M., 563.
Mitchell, Col. R. R., 349, 365.
Mitchell, W. A., his Historic Linn quoted, 356, 357.
Mobile Tribune, 231.
Moffet, Charles W., suspected of writing "Floyd letter," 411; 308, 330, 344, 406, 409.
Moneka (Kansas), B at, 353, 354.
Monroe, S., alias used by B in 1859, 402.
Montgomery, James, one of the most interesting figures of the border warfare, 350; his Civil War record, 350, 351; his exploits in Kansas, 351; a border chieftain after B's own heart, 352; in touch with B, 353; attempted assassination of, 363; his raid on Paris, Kansas, 364; the plot to capture him and B, 365; at Sugar Mound meeting, 365, 366; attacks Fort Scott, in violation of agreement adopted by that meeting, 366; his reason for assuming leadership of this exploit, 367; reward offered for his arrest, 371; writes to Lawrence Republican, 377; surrenders, 377; speaks in church at Lawrence, 377; his efforts for peace, 378; T. W. Higginson concerning, 573; interested in attempt to save Stevens and Hazlett, 573 seqq.; his daring venture in that cause, 577, 578; 179, 180, 187, 349, 362, 370, 373, 374, 375, 376, 377, 379, 514.
Montgomery, Mrs. James, 350.
Moore, Mr., a preacher, 201, 202, 208.
Moore, Eli, murderer, 352.
Morey, Joseph H, 246.
Morgan, Shubel, alias assumed by B on his last visit to Kansas, 345, 352 seqq.; articles of agreement and roster of his company, 666, 667.
Morgan, William, murder of, 26.
Morse, Mr., ill-treated by Wilkinson, Doyles, and Sherman, 174, 175.
Morse, Mrs. Emma Wattles, describes B's return after Missouri raid, 371, 372; describes one of his narrow escapes, 621 n. 86.
Morse, O. E., his Attempted Rescue of John Brown, 656 n. 62.
Morton, Edwin, 320, 322, 535.
Mott, Lucretia, 50 n., 510, 549.

Munroe, Rev. W. C., colored, president of Chatham Convention, 331.
Myers, Henry, 54.
Myers, Mrs. Henry, 54.

Napoleon I, life of, among books which influenced B, 16, 325.
Napoleon III, 564.
National Democratic Party in Kansas, abortive attempt to form, 102.
National Kansas Committee, organized at Buffalo, 227; work of, 227; meeting in New York, Jan. 24, 1857, 275; controversy concerning rifles, 275; votes B $5000 for defensive measures, 276; charged by B with bad faith, 276; its affairs confused with those of Mass. Kansas Com., 360, 361; B's requisition on, for outfit for volunteer-regulars, 664 seqq.; 269, 294, 298, 317, 342, 357, 359, 360, 388, 389, 581.
National Republican Party, organized at Pittsburg, 132; 147.
Nebraska City, Lane's caravan at, 225.
Negroes, B's plan for their education, 44; denounced by B in *Sambo's Mistakes* for their " supineness " in face of wrong, 50; B founds U. S. League of Gileadites in their interest, 50, 51; signatures of, to B's agreement and resolutions, 52; B's counsel to those in No. Elba, 72; assisted by B, 73; their settlement at No. Elba not a success, 73; advised by B to resist Fugitive Slave Law, 75; in Canada, 327, 328; in B's party at Chatham, 330, 331; significance of Chatham Convention to, 333, 334; no uprising among them induced by B's Harper's Ferry raid, 468, 469; B's negro followers could not be convicted of treason, 570.
Negroes, free, two conventions of Free State party in Kansas vote to exclude, 104, 105; excluded by popular vote, 105.
New England, recognizes distinction between " butchery " and " killing," 264, 265.
New England Emigration Society, 101, 227.
New England Woolen Co., and B's misuse of money advanced, 30.
New Englanders in Kansas, epithets applied to, 96.
New Georgia, pro-slavery settlement at, broken up, 229.
New Haven, suppression of schools for negroes in, 45; colony from, in Kansas, 138; 278.
New Lucy, steamboat, 81.
New Orleans Bee, 14.
New York, law of, concerning indictments like B's, 494 n.
New York Abend-Zeitung, 474.
New York City, union meeting in, 563.
New York Evening Post, 350.
New York Herald, report of " interview " between B, Gov. Wise, and others, in issue of Oct. 21, 1859, 456-463; H. Forbes in, 467; attacks Gerrit Smith and Seward, 472; quoted, 492, 493, 535; 125, 480, 486, 501, 518 n., 568, 583.
New York Independent, 285, 318.
New York Journal of Commerce, quoted, 501.
New York Observer, 501.
New York Times, quoted concerning maltreatment of Jason Brown and John, Jr. as prisoners, 196; concerning release of John, Jr., 254, 255; 230, 373.
New York Tribune, aimed at by penal code of Shawnee Legislature, 92; Black Jack affair discussed in, 202; publishes B's account of Black Jack affair, 204-207; quoted, 378, 488; and the attack on Harper's Ferry, 472; mistaken editorial comment of, 631 n. 42; 49, 93, 95, 96, 123, 126, 129, 137, 138, 139, 172, 174, 175, 179, 192, 197, 199, 213, 220, 234, 235, 244, 285, 287, 480, 490, 518, 520, 548 n., 570.

Newby, Dangerfield, in B's Harper's Ferry party, 415, 419; killed by R. B. Washington, 439; the first of the raiders to die, 439; his body treated with shocking indignity, 439; sketch of, 686.
Nicolay and Hay, *Life of Lincoln*, 326.
" Noble Sons of Liberty, The," 519.
North, ignorance in, of demoralization and lawlessness of Free State men, 265; opinion in, unfavorably affected by B's speedy trial, 479, 480; predicament of B's supporters in, after the failure at Harper's Ferry, 528 seqq.; outburst of feeling in, after B's execution, 559.
North Elba, negro settlement in Adirondacks, 67; visited by B, 71; B's first settlement at, 72; settlers displeased by arrival of negroes, 73; why negro settlement there was not a success, 73; B's second home at, 76.
Northern press, attitude of, toward raids committed by Free State men and by pro-slavery men in Kansas, 212; ignores Free State outrages, 264.
Nute, Rev. Ephraim, 215, 255.

Oberlin College, Owen Brown a supporter and trustee of, 15; B's negotiations with trustees of, concerning purchase of real estate in Virginia, 31-33.
O'Conor, Charles, 563.
Ohio, early settlement, 8, 9; wild animals in, 9.
Ohio and Pennsylvania Canal, 27.
" Old Osawatomie Brown," name by which B was known after battle of Osawatomie, 244.
Oliver, Mordecai, member of Congress from Missouri, on Howard Com., 94 n.; quoted concerning A. Wilkinson, 156; charges Free State leaders with inspiring B's Pottawatomie expedition, 183, 184; files report of minority of Howard Com., 226; 161, 191.
Orsini, his attempt on Louis Napoleon compared by A. Lincoln to B's raid, 564.
Osawatomie, Rev. S. L. Adair settles at, 79; B's sons settle at, 81; B arrives at, 88; condition of Brown settlement, in freezing weather, 88; first brigade of Kansas volunteers enrolled at, 121; election of Jan. 1856, 130; settlers' meeting, 134, 135; public meeting at, condemns Pottawatomie murders, 168, 169; no killings and but five definite pro-slavery offences in neighborhood prior to those murders, 171, 172; pillaged by Whitfield's men, 212, 213; " reign of terror " in, 214; B and Free State men at, Aug. 29, 1856, 239, 240; attack on, 241; destroyed after battle, 246; sources for story of the battle, 619 n. 50.
Osawkee, raided by A. D. Stevens, 254.
Ottawa Indians, 9, 133.
Ottawa Jones. See Jones, J. T.
Ottendorfer, Oswald, 575.
Oviatt, Heman, 27, 28, 33, 37-39.
Oviatt, Orson M., 17.
Owen, Mr., 380.

Packer, William F., Gov. of Pennsylvania, 524
Painter, John H., 312, 316, 389.
Palmyra, Battle of, B's name for Black Jack fight, 204.
Paola (Kansas), 193, 194.
" Parallels ": the Marais des Cygnes massacre, contrasted with B's Missouri raid, by B, 375, 376.
Paris (France), B's visit to, 61.
Paris (Kansas), raided by B and Montgomery, 364.
Paris (Mo.) Mercury, 99.
Parker, Laben, murder of, 215.
Parker, Nathaniel, 253.
Parker, Judge Richard, presides at trial of B and other raiders, 476, 479 seqq.; reviews the trial in 1888 (St. Louis *Globe-Democrat*), 481,

INDEX 731

482; his impartiality and judicial spirit, 482; charges grand jury, 488; denies B's request for delay, 489; refuses to delay trial on account of change of counsel, 493, 494; denies motion to require prosecution to elect, 494 and n.; his decisions upheld by Court of Appeals, 494; denies motion for arrest of judgment, 497; pronounces sentence of death, 499; sketch of, 644 n. 36; 484, 485, 490, 492, 521, 546, 588.

Parker, Rev. Theodore, his attitude toward B, 272; his *John Brown's Expedition*, quoted, 529; after the failure at Harper's Ferry, 529; quoted, 564; 269, 271, 273, 274, 289, 298, 320, 324, 326, 339, 340, 397, 565. *Letters to* B, 325, F. Jackson, 564; *from* B, 324.

Parkville (Mo.) *Luminary*, destroyed by pro-slavery mob, 99, 100.

Parrott, Marcus J., elected delegate to Congress in Oct. 1857, 306.

Parsons, Luke F., in battle of Osawatomie. 243 seqq.; 232, 250, 253, 308, 313, 314, 315, 330, 343, 344, 409.

Partridge, George W., killed in the river, 245; 196, 237, 239, 514.

Partridge, Mary, and the plot to rescue B, 514.

Partridge, William, 121, 358.

Pate, Henry C., his *John Brown as viewed by Henry Clay Pate*, quoted concerning Pottawatomie murders, 156; and concerning Black Jack, 202, 203; in *Missouri Republican*, 189; goes to assist U. S. marshal to arrest murderers, 193; his earlier and later history, 201; in camp at Black Jack, 202; B's story of the " battle " with him, 202, 203; claims to have been taken prisoner by treachery, 203; his story in N. Y. *Tribune*, 203; why he resorted to a flag of truce, 203, 204, 205; his story reviewed by B in the *Tribune*, 204–207; his written agreement with B and Capt. Shore, 207; his later account of the battle, after the Harper's Ferry raid, 207; his captivity and release, 208; visits B in jail, 546; his challenge to Horace Greeley, 613 n. 19; 200, 211, 212, 283.

Pawnee Legislature. See Shawnee Legislature.

Peabody, S. E., 281.

Pearson, Henry G., his *Life of John A. Andrew*, quoted, 557.

Pennington, William, of New Jersey, chosen Speaker of the House over John Sherman, 585.

Perham, Josiah, 524, 525.

Perkins, Anna, daughter of Simon, quoted, 65, 595 n. 42.

Perkins, George T., son of Simon, letter to author, 64.

Perkins, Simon, Jr. partner of B in sheep-raising (1844), 34, 35, 39, 41; B's admiration of him, 64; his generous treatment of B, 64, 65; further business relations with B, 66, 67.

Perkins and Brown, office of, in Springfield, 57; business of, 58, 59; exporting wool, 59; troubles with manufacturers, 60; ill-success of B's trip to Europe, 61 seqq.; increasing difficulties and final failure, 64, 65; law-suits by and against, 64, 65, 75; their creditors, 64; 75. *Letters to* Crafts and Still, 59, Hamilton Gay, 59, B. W. Ladd, 60.

Perkins Hill, 35.

Perry, Gov. of Florida, his message to the legislature, 584.

Peticolas, Dr. A. E., letter to A. Hunter, 504 n.

Phelps, B. and O. conductor, 432, 433, 434.

Phil (Allstadt's negro), 468.

Philadelphia, B's body at, 561; anti-slavery convention at, 562.

Philadelphia *North American*, quoted concerning dispersal of Topeka Free State Legislature, 220.

Phillips, Wendell, his address at B's grave, 562; 271, 281, 330, 510, 516, 545, 554, 560, 561, 563, 565, 574.

Phillips, William, friend of C. McCrea, tarred and feathered, 110; murdered at Leavenworth, 252; 123, 124, 125, 129, 179, 181.

Phillips, W. A., his *Conquest of Kansas*, quoted, 96, 97, 602 n. 13; concerning pro-slavery outrages, 214; starts for Topeka with B, 220; describes the journey in *Atlantic Monthly*, 221; 293, 296, 304 n., 352, 362.

" Pickles," with B in Missouri raid, 368.

Pickman, W. D., 281.

Pierce, Franklin, President of U. S., special message concerning Shawnee Legislature, and acts of Free State men, 130; proclamation in favor of pro-slavery men, 130, 131; Gov. Shannon reports fight at Black Jack to, 211; his despatches to Shannon, 211; makes Col. Sumner a scapegoat, 217; calls Congress in special session (Aug. 1856), 227; removes Gov. Shannon from office, 234; failure of his administration to support Gov. Geary causes Geary's resignation, 294; 93, 115, 117, 132, 134, 135, 138, 139, 144 n., 169, 209, 233.

Pike, J. A., 575, 576, 580.

Pike, J. D., quoted, 599 n. 43.

Pinkerton, A., and B's party of freed slaves, 390.

Platte County *Argus*, quoted, 96.

Platte County Riflemen, commanded by Atchison in movement on Lawrence, 144.

Pleasant Valley (Md.), false alarm at, 470, 471.

Plummer, Charles, alias of C. P. Tidd, 579.

Plutarch's Lives, 16, 325.

Pomeroy, S. C., concerning Pottawatomie murders, 182; inaccuracies in his letter, 183; arrested on entering Kansas, 260; visits B in jail, 546; 119, 272, 512. *Letter to* Rebecca B Spring, 182.

Pomeroy Guards, 149, 150.

Portage (O.) *Sentinel*, 473, 474, 569.

Post, Zina, 41.

Pottawatomie Creek, murders on, May 24–25, 1856, 148 seqq.; first reported to Free State companies, 151; attitude of Free State men toward, 167, 168; possible justification of, discussed, 170 seqq.; not due to meeting at Dutch Henry's, 177; were they a peace measure? 180; called a just act of retaliation for sack of Lawrence, etc., 180; not both a peace and a war measure, 181; did not put an end to Border Ruffian violence, 181; successful as a war measure, 181, 182; defended by S. C. Pomeroy, 182, 183; victims not tried by jury, 184, 185; deprived Free State cause of a great moral advantage, 187, 188; ethically and morally without excuse or palliation, 187, 188; sensational announcement of, by Missouri journals, 189; persons under arrest for, 189; press comments on, 190, 191; not mentioned by *Liberator*, 191; reported to Pres. Pierce by Shannon, 192; news of, posted in Leavenworth, 192; meeting of Law-and-Order party concerning, 192; Whitfield's men take revenge for, at Osawatomie, 212, 213; country not " at peace " after, 213; in Oliver's report of minority of Howard Com., 226; did not injure Free State cause in the North, 226; little known about them in Boston at time of B's first visit, 274; B's connection with them never known to G. L. Stearns, 274; what of other Boston friends? 274; B's connection with them, 545; authorities for story of, 608 headnote. And see Doyle family, Wilkinson, and Sherman, Dutch Bill.

" Pottawatomies," John Brown, Jr.'s company, 149, 150; revulsion of feeling among, after the murders, 166.

Potter, Rt. Rev. H. C., 558 n.

Powers, Theo. P., 244.

732 INDEX

Prairie City Rifles, B's force at Black Jack so-called, 201.
Press, North and South, comments of, on B and the raid, 568, 569.
Preston, Col. J. T. L., 556, 557. And see Allen, Elizabeth Preston.
Preston, Wm. J., deputy U. S. marshal, afraid to serve warrants, 210.
Price, C. H., chairman of public meeting at Osawatomie, 168, 169.
Price, Hiram, 390.
Pro-slavery Congressmen, effect of their action, to unify Free State determination, 139.
Pro-slavery leaders, of Missouri, contemptuous of Free State movement, 108; meet at Franklin after treaty of peace, 124; and Border Ruffian invasion of Kansas under Buford, 138; exultation over Lawrence burnings, 146; ascribe all virtues to Pottawatomie victims, 156, 157.
Pro-slavery men, unseated in Kansas, 99; divers outrages perpetrated by, 110, 111 and n.; Weiner's complaints of their outrages responsible for B's Pottawatomie plan, 151, 152; names of certain men selected by H. H. Williams for death, 152; offences committed by, in Osawatomie region prior to murders, 171, 172; raided by Free State men at Franklin, 212; W. A. Phillips, concerning outrages committed by, 214; more guilty than Free State men in respect to crimes of violence, 215; attitude of non-slaveholders among, 216; plunder Quaker mission, 235; in force in neighborhood of B's company, 237; attacked by Cline, and put to flight, 237; raid Osawatomie, 240 seqq.; deny charges of outrages, 264; control Lecompton Const. Conv., 296; joint meeting with Free State men adopts B's peace agreement, 366; attempt to check B's journey with freed slaves, 381 seqq., 388.
Pro-slavery outrages in Kansas in summer of 1856, 214, 215.
Pro-slavery party, in Kansas, early triumphs of, 94, 95; its hatred of Gov. Reeder the true reason of his dismissal, 100; its duty according to Stringfellow, 101; Law-and-Order party formed by, 108; homicides by, 112, 113; and the rescue of Branson, 113, 114; forces raised by, to besiege Lawrence, 114 seqq.; Pres. Pierce's proclamation in support of, 130, 131; finds in Pottawatomie murders an answer to Northern criticisms of sack of Lawrence, 188; turns against Gov. Walker, 295; and the vicissitudes of the Lecompton Const., 346 seqq.; passage of English bill by Congress a victory for, 347; finally defeated in election of Aug. 2, 1858, 347, 348.
Pro-slavery press, attitude of, concerning Pottawatomie murders, 189-191.
Pro-slavery settlements in Linn and Bourbon counties threatened by B, 235.
"Provisional Constitution and Ordinances for the People of the U. S.," drawn up by B., 332 seqq.; preamble of, 334; provisions of, discussed, 334, 335; some parts suggest insanity, 334, 335; extraordinary provisions concerning treaty-making, 335; Article 46, 336.
Provisional Constitutional Convention at Chatham, 331 seqq. And see Chatham Convention.
Pryor, Judge Roger A., 506 n.

Quaker Mission, plundered by pro-slavery men, 235.
Quin, Luke, marine, killed in engine house, 454.

Radical Political Abolitionists, hold convention at Syracuse, 85.
Ram's Horn, *Sambo's Mistakes* published in, 50.

Randolph, Penn., B postmaster at, 43.
Ravenna (Ohio), 27, 36, 37.
Reader, Samuel J., his impressions of B, 223, 224.
Realf, Richard, his report of B's speech to Chatham Convention, 331, 332; elected " Sec'y of State " at that convention, 333; suspected of writing " Floyd letter," 411; 308, 310, 311, 312, 315, 316, 329, 337, 338, 343, 344, 413. *Letter to* B, 294, H. C. Gill, 330.
Recruiting of settlers for Kansas, 137 seqq.
Redpath, James, his *Public Life of Captain John Brown*, quoted, 63, 199, 345; describes B's camp on Ottawa Creek, 199, 200; his book hastily written, 574; 139, 174, 179, 296, 301, 352, 421, 517, 533, 582, 583. *Letter from* James Foreman, 21-23.
Reed, Rev. B. L., 348, 375.
Reed, J. H., alias of R. J. Hinton, 576.
Reeder, Andrew H., first territorial governor of Kansas, orders second election (1855), 98; unseats pro-slavery men elected to legislature, 99; declares first Territorial legislature illegal, 100; his contention denied by judges, 100; dismissed by Pres. Pierce, ostensibly for speculation in Indian lands, 100; becomes leader of Free Soilers, 100; regarded in East as martyr to abolition cause, 100; leaves Kansas in disguise (1856), 101, 143; elected delegate to Congress by Free State votes, 106; his election ignored by Shannon, 106, and declared illegal by Howard Com., 107 n.; elected provisionally U. S. Senator by Free State Legislature, 132; indicted for treason, 142; his election as delegate confirmed by Committee on Elections, but denied by House, 226; declines B's invitation to return to Kansas and assume leadership of Free State party, 282; 140, 190, 294.
Reese, Louis A. *The Admission of Kansas* (MSS.), 629 n. 1.
Reid, Gen. John W., in attack on Osawatomie, 240 seqq.; denies that there was a battle, 246; protests in vain against destruction of Osawatomie by his men, 246; his report of the affair, 246, 247; 257.
Reisner, Henry, describes B's arrival at Lawrence, Sept. 7, 1856, 253.
Republican National Convention (the first), and Kansas, 226.
Republican Press, and the Pottawatomie murders, 191; and Harper's Ferry, 472-474.
Rescue, plans of Le Barnes and others, 511 seqq.; frowned upon by B, 512.
Reynolds, Ephraim, Sergeant of Liberty Guards, 121.
Reynolds, Robert, 246.
Rhodes, James Ford, his *History of the U. S.*, 191, 294, 612 n. 89.
Rice, Benjamin, 366, 576, 580.
Richardson, Richard, a runaway slave, 308, 316; discriminated against in Chicago, 329; 330, 337, 338, 344, 413.
Richardson, Gen. W. P., and the " Wakarusa War," 114, 116; 192.
Richman, Irving B., his *John Brown among the Quakers*, 316.
Richmond (Penn.), 23 seqq., 43.
Richmond (Va.) sends militia to Harper's Ferry, 444.
Richmond Despatch, quoted, 518.
Richmond Enquirer, quoted, 475, 476, 568.
Richmond Grays, 469.
Richmond Whig, quoted, 500.
Riddle, Albert G., his *Personal Recollections of War Times*, 646 n. 74.
Ripley (Va.), 31, 48.
Ritchie, Capt. John, reinforces B near Topeka (Jan. 1859), 381 seqq.; 449.

INDEX 733

Robertson, Richard. See Richardson, Richard.
Robinson, Charles, Free Soil leader, obtains rifles from Emigrant Aid Society, 98; chairman of Com. on Resolutions in Free State Convention of Aug. 14-15, 1856, 102; in second convention of Aug. 15, 103; chairman of Territorial Exec. Com., 106; addresses meeting at Lawrence after treaty of peace, 123, and pro-slavery meeting at Franklin, 124; invites Shannon and Jones to peace gathering, 124; his ruse and its result, 125, 126; Free Soil candidate for governor, 129; his inaugural address, 132; Kansas member of Nat. Republican Com., 132; at indignation meeting for shooting of Mace, 141; indicted for treason, 142; and for avoiding arrest on indictment not yet found, 142, 143; in confinements four months, 143; his house burned, 146; quoted concerning Pottawatomie murders, 169, 170; said to have inspired the murders, 183, 184; denies all complicity in them, 184; likens B to Jesus, and later denounces him, 184; his *Kansas Conflict*, 232 n., 596 n. 4; and Gov. Shannon, 234; favorably impressed by Gov. Geary, 257; significance of his letters as bearing on the question who saved Kansas 262; controversy with John Brown, Jr., concerning interview with B, 263; at Topeka Convention, 296; 101, 108, 122, 140, 150, 190, 191, 255, 265, 266, 271, 272, 297, 307, 346, 367. *Letters to B*, 262, 263.
Robinson, Michael, murdered by Hamilton's gang, 348, 375.
Robinson, Mrs. Sara T. L., wife of Charles, her *Kansas: its Interior and Exterior Life*, 89 n., 97, 98, 142; concerning assaults on women, 173, 174; 179, 192, 598 n. 31, 611, n. 64, 613 n. 7.
Rollin's Ancient History, 16.
Ropes, Hannah Anderson, her *Six Months in Kansas*, 89 n.
Rosengarten, Joseph G., his account of the aftermath of the raid, 469, 470.
Ross, Patrick, murdered by Hamilton's gang, 348.
Rosser, Col. P. H., 240.
Root, Dr. J. P., conductor of Nat. Kansas Com. "train" to Tabor, 269, 270. *Letter from J. D. Webster*, 269.
Rotch, W. J., 281.
Rowan, Captain, 436, 438.
Russell, G. R., 325.
Russell, Judge Thomas, B in hiding at his house in Boston, 288; quoted concerning B's speech before sentence, 498 n.; visits B in jail, 545; quoted, 647 n. 83; 271, 493, 512.
Russell, Mrs. Thomas, 288, 512, 545.
Russell, Maj. W. W., a volunteer in Lieut. Green's storming party, 452 seqq.; sketch of, 642 n. 62; 450, 462 n.
Rutherford, Dr. W. W., 576.

St. Joseph, Mo., city attorney of, a fraudulent voter in Kansas, 94.
St. Louis Evening News, quoted as to affairs in Kansas, 216; as to the raid, 472.
St. Louis Intelligencer, 99, 117.
St. Louis Missouri-Democrat, 199, 371.
St. Louis Missouri-Republican, 83, 156, 189, 190, 191, 193, 201.
St. Louis Morning Herald and the Pottawatomie murders, 191; 247.
St. Louis Pilot, 95.
Sacs and Foxes, in Kansas, 90.
Sambo's Mistakes, 50; quoted in full, 659-661.
Sanborn, Franklin Benjamin, B's first meeting with, 271; his first impressions of B, 271; introduces B to other friends of the cause, 271; and sale of Thompson farm to B, 281; defends B against blame for delay, 303; with B at Gerrit Smith's, 321, 322; agrees with Smith to support B, 322; B visits him in May, 1859, 395; his faithful labors in the cause, 395, 396; his statement as to the conspirators' knowledge of B's plans, 397; after the failure at Harper's Ferry, 529, 530; his opinion of Dr. Howe's card, 533; his account of his own movements, 533; arrested, 533, 534; his *Life and Letters of John Brown*, quoted, 28, 29, 46, 341, 361; his *Recollections of Seventy Years*, quoted, 321, 530, 533, 627 n. 27; his *John Brown and his Friends*, and *Virginia Campaign of John Brown*, quoted, 421; 184, 275, 277, 282, 284, 298, 299, 305, 319, 320, 324, 325, 330, 336, 338, 340, 342, 399, 421, 512, 517, 536, 582. *Letters to T. W. Higginson*, 271, 303, 325, 326, 339, 396, 530; *from B*, 322, 353, 354. *John Brown, Jr.*, 45.
Sanborn, Miss, 534.
Saunders, "Fort," near Lawrence, attacked by Free State men, 231.
Savannah Republican, quoted, 500.
Sayre, Dr. Lewis A., 504 n.
Scadsall, C. C. See Hadsall, C. C.
Schoppert, G. A., and the killing of Leeman, 440.
Scott, Sir Walter, 326.
Seaman, Benjamin, 576.
Seaman, Henry C., 576, 580.
Secession issue, as affected by B's execution, 506.
Secession movement, too far advanced before the raid for peaceable solution, 587.
Sedgwick, Major John, quoted concerning Lawrence raid and Pottawatomie murders, 169; concerning dispersal of B's force after the battle of Black Jack, 209; 197, 212, 217, 232, 234.
Self-Defensive Association, in Platte Co., Mo., proceedings of, 98; compelled to disband, 599 n. 66.
Senate of U. S., passes Toombs bill, but rejects Grow bill, 227; appoints committee to investigate raid, 478. *And see* Grow, G. A., and Toombs, Robert.
Seneca Indians, 9.
Sennott, George, 513, 570.
Severns, Charles, 372.
Sewall, S. E., 559, 560.
Seward, W. H., and H. Forbes, 318; attacked by *N. Y. Herald*, 472; quoted, 564, 565; 339, 474, 502, 566.
Shaler, Nathaniel S., autobiography, quoted, 10.
Shannon, Wilson, second Territorial Governor of Kansas, his character, 103; ignores Reeder's action as delegate, 106; and the Coleman-Dow murder and rescue of Branson, 114 seqq.; orders out militia against Lawrence, 114; his duplicity, 115; addresses meeting at Lawrence after treaty of peace, 123, and pro-slavery meeting at Franklin, 124; deceived by Robinson, gives him and Lane authority to preserve peace, 125; his letter to the *N. Y. Herald*, 125; blamed by pro-slavery men, 126; U. S. troops in Kansas put under his orders, 131; returns to Kansas, 132; refuses to send troops to protect citizens of Lawrence, 144; reports to Pres. Pierce as to effect of Pottawatomie murders, 169, 192; reports Black Jack affair to same, 211; his difficulties, 211; his proclamation, 211; makes requisition for U. S. troops, 211; Col. Sumner and the dispersal of the Free State legislature, 217-220; effects release of Titus and other prisoners, and resigns governorship, 233, 234; his farewell speech to citizens of Lawrence, 234; his resignation not accepted, 234; removed by Pres. Pierce, 234; his later residence in Lawrence, 234; 92, 108, 130, 133, 209. *Letter to Col. Sumner*, 218.

734 INDEX

Sharp's rifles, doctrine of opposing slavery with, commended by N. Y. *Tribune*, 49; shipped to Robinson as "Revised Statutes" and "books," 98; supplied by Mass. Kans. Com., controversy about, 275; story of transfer of, to B, in spring of 1858, 340 seqq.

Shawnee Legislature, denounced by Free State Convention, 91; code of punishments for Free State men, enacted by, 91, 92; meeting and organization (at Pawnee), 100; declared illegal by Gov. Reeder, 100; petitions Pres. Pierce to remove Reeder, 100; acts of, 101; no genuine attempt made to enforce "Black Laws," 101; attacked by successive Free State conventions, 102, 103; denounced by Big Springs Convention, 104; declared a legal body by Pres. Pierce, 130; defied by settlers' meeting at Osawatomie, 134, 135; its laws declared effective by Judge Lecompte, 142; resistance to its laws declared to be high treason, 142; 131, 136, 156.

Shawnee Mission, sessions of pro-slavery legislature held at. See Shawnee Legislature.

Shelby, Col. Joseph, 225.

Shepherdstown Troop at Harper's Ferry, 444.

Sheridan, Mrs., 308.

Sherman, Dutch Bill, murder of, 162–164; Harris's story of the murder, 162–164; and Mary Grant, 172, 173, 177; and the Morse case, 174; 151, 155, 182.

Sherman, Dutch Henry, his horses taken by B, 235; murdered by Cransdell, 236; and Ottawa Jones, 253 and n.; 135, 156, 162, 163, 212.

Sherman, Dutch Pete, 155.

Sherman, John, member of Congress from Ohio, on Howard Com., 94 n.; and W. A. Howard, report of, quoted, 120; his indorsement of Helper's book causes his defeat in Speakership contest, Dec. 1859, 583, 584, 585; 184, 227. *Letter to* Rev. E. B. Jones (1897), 506 n.

Sherman, William. See Sherman, Dutch Bill.

Shermans, pro-slavery settlement of, on Pottawatomie Creek, 135; their unsavory reputation, 155, 156; alleged intimidation by, 172; 180.

Shields, Gen., letter from W. Limerick, 240.

Shirley, Walter, 520.

Shore, Samuel T., captain of Osawatomie company, 150; in Black Jack fight, 202 seqq.; many of his men quit, 202, 204; and return after the battle, 208; killed at "Fort" Titus, 231, 232; 200, 240.

Shriver, Col., 452.

Silsbee, Benj. H., 281.

Silsbee, John H., 281.

Sinn, Capt., his interview with B in the engine house, 447; disgusted with conduct of citizens, 447, 448; protects Stevens, 448; his fine spirit, 448 and n.; visits B in jail, 544.

Slave States, their political supremacy endangered by the carving of new states out of western territory, 80.

Slaveholders, B's object at one time to terrorize, 56; to be held as hostages according to B's plan, 332.

Slavery, B's first personal knowledge of, 4; his second experience with, 17, 18; hatred of, in his family, 21; its forcible overthrow his "greatest and principal object," 42 seqq.; gradual evolution of his plan to abolish, 48 seqq.; to relieve pro-slavery pressure there, 56; B's main purpose to come to close quarters with, 56; and the Kansas-Nebraska Act, 79; to be fastened on Kansas, 83; opposition to, made a disqualification for holding office by Shawnee Legislature, 91; mere belief in its illegality a grave crime, 92; its existence dependent on its fate in Kansas, according to pro-slavery leaders, 97; the one issue in Kansas, according to Stringfellow, 101; opposition to, disavowed by Big Springs Convention, 104; tendency of, to induce lawless action, 171; B's plan to attack it in Virginia divulged to his recruits, 308; all his recruits bitterly hostile to, 310; characterized in "Provisional Constitution," 334; and the Lecompton Const., 346; Abolitionist view of, 384; its fear of free speech, 568; the sole issue in campaign of 1860, 585; would have been abolished had B never lived, 586, 587; intolerable morally and economically, 587.

Slavery issue, B's views on, 362; impossible to be put aside after B's execution, 506.

Slaves, severe penalty for encouraging disaffection among, enacted by Shawnee Legislature, 91, 92; two freed by J. Brown, Jr., 150, 151; small number in Kansas, 295; part assigned to them in B's Virginia plan, and in Forbes's plan, 314, 332; a fugitive, in Canada, 327, 328; freed by B in Missouri raid, 368, 369, 372, 373; more carefully guarded after Missouri raid, 378; B's journey to Canada with his freed slaves, 379–390; Northern sentiment concerning fugitives, 384; fears of general insurrection aroused by news of Harper's Ferry, 436; conduct of those impressed by B there, 468.

"Smelly, Capt. James," 519.

Smith, A. L., and the "Floyd letter," 411, 412.

Smith, Geo. W., commanding first brigade of Kansas Volunteers, 121; indicted for treason, 142, and arrested, 145; elected Gov. of Kansas under Lecompton Const., 346.

Smith, Gerrit, his suit against Chicago *Tribune*, 46; offers land to negroes, 71; becomes B's warm friend, 71; his earnest opposition to slavery, 71; described by Greeley, 71, 72; gives money to B and to Forbes, 287; approves of Forbes's tract, 298; his affection for B, 320; B's plans made known to and approved by him, 320; agrees with Sanborn to support B, 322; rejoices in result of B's Missouri raid, 379; B's last visit to, 395; his public approval of B's course contrasted with his later attitude, 395; after the raid, 535, 536; his insanity, 535; his quick recovery and subsequent denial of complicity in, or knowledge of, the raid, 536; 84, 85, 269, 272, 277, 281, 291, 293, 319, 327, 330, 333, 339, 340, 396, 460, 472, 474, 522, 565.

Smith, I., alias assumed by B in 1859, 402, 404.

"Smith, I., and Sons," B, Oliver and Owen so known at Chambersburg, 402, 409.

Smith, Dr. J. V. C., 96.

Smith, James, one of B's *noms de guerre*, 292.

Smith, Judge, 255.

Smith, Owen, alias of Owen Brown, 416.

Smith, Gen. Persifor T., succeeds Col. Sumner in Kansas, 217; his instructions from J. Davis, Sec'y of War, 251; condemns acts of Reid's force, 251; 260.

Smith, Rev. Stephen, 323.

Smith, W. P., master of transportation of B. & O. R. R., Conductor Phelps's dispatch to, 433, 434; is incredulous, 434; 519, 525.

Snyder, Charles, 348, 375.

Snyder, Eli, headquarters of B's party with, 353; the disputed title to his claim, 356, 357; tells of B's encounter with Rev. M. White, 357; 348, 354.

Snyder, Elias, 348.

Soulé, Silas C., 514, 575, 576, 577, 578.

South, the, not a colonizing section, 265; attitude toward B, 474–476; division of opinion in, concerning B's fate after sentence, 500.

South Carolina, pro-slavery men from, in Kansas, 137, 138; attitude of, 585.

INDEX

South Middle Creek, fight at, 237.
Spartacus, 362.
Speakership contest, in House of Representatives in 1859-1860, 583, 585.
Speer, John, 181.
Spinner, F. E., 505 n.
Spooner, Lysander, and his scheme to kidnap Gov. Wise, 514 seqq.
Spring, Rebecca B., visits B in jail, 546 and n.; 549. *Letter from* S. C. Pomeroy, 182.
Springdale (Iowa), B and his party at, 312; their life there, 314 seqq.; B and his party of freed slaves at, 387; 328, 329.
Springdale "Legislature," a mock body, 315.
Springfield (Mass.), B's residence at, 48, 49, 67; 278.
Springfield Republican, 558.
Squatter Sovereign, quoted, 93, 110, 129, 131, 141, 178, 617 n. 1, 618 n. 39; and the Pottawatomie murders, 190.
Squatter Sovereignty Idea, all of Kansas's misfortunes due to, 347.
Squatters' Court, judge of, called "Old Brown," 305.
Staats-Zeitung, 575.
"Standish, Miles, of Kansas," B so called by A. A. Lawrence, 400.
Stanton, Frederick P., Sec'y of State of Kansas under Gov. Walker, removed by Pres. Buchanan, 295; acting governor, 306, 346.
Star of the West (steamer), 142, 225.
Starry, Dr. John D., the "Paul Revere of Harper's Ferry," 434, 435; rides about, giving the alarm, 435; quoted as to progress of events, 435, 436, and concerning Kagi's death, 445; saves Copeland from being lynched, 445; quoted, 510; 548 n.
Startling Incidents and Developments of Osawatomie Brown's Insurrectory and Treasonable Movements at Harper's Ferry, Virginia, 635 n. 116.
Stearns, Charles, denounces Big Springs Convention in *Kansas Free State,* 104.
Stearns, Frank P., his *Life and Public Services of George Luther Stearns,* quoted, 272, 274.
Stearns, George Luther, B's first visit to, 272; never knew of B's connection with Pottawatomie murders, 274; buys revolvers for B, 288, 289; his confidence in B and large generosity to the cause, 292; advises contest at polls and only defensive fighting, 306, 307; treachery to B's policy in the home of its friends, 307; controversy over notes sent to B, 359-361; turns to Kansas for aid in effecting B's escape, 513; goes to Canada after raid, 530; his testimony before Mason Com., 534, 535; 7, 271, 279, 280, 281, 291, 297, 319, 320, 324, 325, 326, 333, 338, 339, 340, 341, 342, 343, 396, 397, 399, 582. *Letters to* B, 339, E. B. Whitman, 306; *from* B, 305, E. B. Whitman, 304.
Stearns, Mrs. G. L., Alcott's statement in her *Emancipation Evening Album,* quoted, 398; 544, 546.
Stearns, Henry L., letter from B, 1-7.
Stephens, Alex. H., quoted, 587.
Sterns, Henry, 279.
Stevens, Aaron Dwight, his first meeting with B, 224; why he used an alias, 224; raids Osawkee, 254; his men arrested by Marshal Donaldson, 254; kills David Cruise in Missouri raid, 369, 370; "a born crank," 419; shot by G. W. Chambers while carrying flag of truce, 439, 440; protected by Capt. Sinn, 454; made prisoner in engine house, 454; his pitiable condition at his trial, 486; his personality, 572, 573; attempts to save him after B's execution, 572 seqq.; executed, 586; sketch of, 679, 680; 256, 308, 312, 315, 329, 330, 343, 344, 353, 363, 364, 366, 368, 379, 381, 382, 385, 389, 390, 414, 420, 421, 427, 429, 431, 432, 442, 456, 459, 460, 470, 471, 477, 478, 479, 485, 487, 488, 489, 510, 545, 558 n. *Letter to* his brother, 254.
Stevens, "Thad.," anecdote of, 505 n.
Stewart, Capt., 217.
Stewart, Maj.-Gen. Geo. H., Maryland Volunteers, notified by Garrett of B's raid, 434.
Stewart, James, 513.
Stewart, John, shot by Border Ruffians, 142, 180.
Still, John, 239.
Still, William, 323, 549.
Stilwell, W. E., murdered by Hamilton's gang, 348, 375.
Stocqueler, J. H., his *Life of Field-Marshal the Duke of Wellington,* 53.
Stow, Joshua, 37.
Stratton, H., letter to B, 235 n.
Stribbling, Dr., 508.
Strickler, Adj.-Gen. H. J., and the "Wakarusa War," 114, 116.
Strider, Samuel, summons B to surrender, 447.
Stringfellow, B. F., 92, 94, 144, 145, 192, 216, 229, 230, 257.
Stringfellow, Gen. J. H., Speaker of Kansas Territorial House of Representatives, 92, 93, 94, 101, 124, 144, 145.
Stuart, Alex. H. H., 526.
Stuart, Charles, 85, 322.
Stuart, Lieut. J. E. B., sent to Harper's Ferry, 450; describes disposition made and parley with "Smith" (B), 450, 451; text of his summons to B, 451; 201, 209, 456, 458, 462 and n., 467, 470.
"Stubbs," 258. See "Lawrence Stubbs."
Sturtevant, Mrs. C. M., 391.
Stulz, Capt., 233.
Sugar Mound meeting of Free State and proslavery men, adopts B's peace agreement, 366.
Sultan (steamer), 225.
Sumner, Charles, effect on Pottawatomie party of news of Brooks's assault on, 154; his "Crime against Kansas" speech, 188, 599 n. 61; his only meeting with B, 327; Brooks's assault on, 587.
Sumner, Col. Edwin V., under Gov. Shannon's orders, 132; his troops disperse Free State legislature, 132, 217-220; releases Pate and his men, 208; disperses B's band and heads off Border Ruffians under Whitfield and Coffee, 209; criticised by pro-slavery men for not arresting B, 210; and Deputy-Marshal Preston, 210; and Whitfield's breach of faith, 213; on furlough, 217; in disfavor with Pierce administration, 217; slighted by Jefferson Davis, 217, 219; made a scapegoat by Pres. Pierce, 217, 219; his speech to the legislature, 219; career and character of, 615 n. 58; 115, 144, 145, 206, 226, 381. *Letter to* Acting-Gov. Woodson, 218; *from* Jefferson Davis, 218, Gov. Shannon, 218.
Sunderland, La Roy, hypnotist, B's controversy with, described by himself, 67, 68.

Tabor (Iowa), a colony of Ohioans, an important station on Underground Railroad, 267; conditions in, in autumn of 1856, as described by Mrs. Gaston, 267, 268; B arrives at, with only $25, 292, 294; intensely "Abolition," and loyal to B, 302; conditions at, in Feb. 1859, 383, 384; public opinion disapproves of some aspects of Missouri raid, 384; B coolly welcomed, 384; public meeting, and resolutions passed thereat, 385; fear of pro-slavery attacks, 386. And see Todd, Rev. John.
Taliaferro, Maj.-Gen. W. B., Gov. Wise's instruction to, 523; 522, 527, 549, 550, 558.
Tallmadge (Ohio), semi-centennial, 293.

Tappan, Lewis, 85.
Tappan, Samuel F., resists arrest, 140; assistant clerk of Topeka Free State Legislature, 219; 380.
Tate, Geo. H., 520.
Tayleure, C. W., letter to John Brown, Jr., 454, 455.
Taylor, Dr., 448.
Taylor, Jacob L., quoted concerning Stewart Taylor, 684, 685.
Taylor, Stewart, in B's Harper's Ferry party, 414, 419, 424; death of, 449; sketch of, 684, 685; 328, 330, 343, 344.
Teesdale, John, editor of Des Moines *Register*, 386; *Letter from B*, 386.
Territorial Executive Committee, created by Big Springs Convention, 106; report of, 132; 91, 304.
Tessaun, half-breed Indian, 383.
Texas, annexation of, 79.
Thayer, Eli, his *History of the Kansas Crusade*, quoted, 146; B's host in Worcester, Mass., 281; contributes weapons, 282; 265, 287, 289. *Letter from* G. A. Crawford, 374.
Thayer, Wm. W., 574, 579.
Thomas, H. K., 246.
Thomas, John A., colored, 338.
Thomas, Thomas, 55.
Thompson, Dauphin Osgood, in B's Harper's Ferry party, 414, 419, 420; death of, in engine house, 449, 454 and n.; sketch of, 683; 462 n., 537, 558 n.
Thompson, George, first condemns, then approves Pottawatomie murders, 168.
Thompson, Henry, marries B's daughter Ruth, 76; goes to Kansas, 76; *en route* to Kansas with B, 86; anecdote of B told by, 88; and the claim-jumper, 130; on B's surveying tour, 133; his regard for B, 134; in B's Pottawatomie party, 153; Wilkinson and Sherman killed by Wiener and him, 162, 164; denies that Judge Wilson was on prescribed list, 165; charges Robinson with urging B to further killings, 184; denies that Pottawatomie victims were tried by jury, 184; wounded at Black Jack, 203, 208; quoted, 224; declines to reënlist for Virginia expedition, 323, 324; declines to join B at Harper's Ferry, 413; 81 n., 112, 118, 127, 135, 136, 149, 155, 159, 160, 198, 202, 210, 220, 222, 561. *Letters to* Mrs. Ruth (Brown) Thompson, 133.
Thompson, Isabella, sister of Dauphin O., Henry, and William, marries Watson Brown. See Brown, Mrs. Isabella (Thompson).
Thompson, Mrs. Ruth (Brown), B's daughter, wife of Henry Thompson, quoted, 16, 73, 74, 75; her carelessness causes a sister's death, 35; 19, 20, 36, 76, 591 n. 10. *Letters from* Jason Brown, 229, B, 324, Henry Thompson, 133.
Thompson, Seth, 41.
Thompson, William, in B's Harper's Ferry party, 414, 419, 437; taken prisoner, 439; killing of, by Harry Hunter and Chambers, described by H. H., 442 and n., 491; his death a disgrace to Virginia and condemned by best public sentiment, 443; sketch of, 683; 537.
Thompson, Mrs. Wm., 561.
Thompson brothers, sell land at No. Elba to B, 281.
Thompson, Mr., B's partner in real-estate speculations in 1835, 27.
Thomson, Rev. Mr., and his runaway slave, 14.
Thoreau, Henry D., his *Plea for Captain John Brown*, quoted, 273, 274, 563.
Three Years on the Kansas Border, 89 n.
Tidd, Charles P., in B's Harper's Ferry party, 414, 416, 417, 426, 427, 431, 446, 468; final escape of, 471; sketch of, 681; 303, 306, 308, 311, 329, 330, 343, 344, 353, 357, 363, 368, 379, 406, 468, 574, 577.

Tieman, Dan'l F., Mayor of New York, 563.
Tilden, Judge Daniel R., 492, 493.
Timbucto. See North Elba.
Titus, "Fort," captured, after severe fighting, by Free State men under Captain S. Walker, 231, 232.
Titus, Col. H. T., captured with his "fort" by Free State men, 231, 232; owed his life to S. Walker, 232, 233; finally released by Gov. Shannon, 233, 234; 352.
Todd, Rev. John, his action on B's request for thanksgiving service at Tabor, 384, 385; 267, 270, 274, 299, 386.
Toole's, a station on Underground Railroad, 386.
Toombs, Robert, U. S. Senator from Georgia, his bill for taking census as basis for election of a new constitutional convention, passed by Senate, and rejected by House, 227; speech in Senate, 565, 566; 191, 226.
Topeka, Free State conventions in (1857), 295, 296.
Topeka Constitution, ratified by the people, 107, 127; its adoption angers pro-slavery party, 108; election under, 128; 132.
Topeka Constitutional Convention (Oct. 23, 1855), favors exclusion of free negroes, as well as slaves, but submits question to the people, 105; constitution framed by, 107, and ratified by popular vote, 107, 127; 131, 184.
Topeka Free State Legislature, dispersed by Col. Sumner, 217-220; meetings of, in 1857, 295; 227, 346, 347.
Topeka *Tribune*, 473.
Torrey, Rev. Charles T., 51, 594 n. 13.
Torrington (Conn.), B's birthplace, 1.
Toussaint l'Ouverture, 331.
Townsend, James, of the "Traveller's Rest," 312, 316.
Townsley, James, and the Pottawatomie expedition, 151, 152, 153, 154, 155; tries to dissuade B, 157; and the Doyle murders, 158 seqq.; concerning the murders of Wilkinson and Sherman, 162; at Black Jack, 208; 165, 166, 167, 175, 177, 178, 184, 198.
Tracy, John F., 390.
Traveller's Rest, Springdale, 312, 316.
Tremont Temple (Boston), great meeting in, on day of B's execution, 559, 560.
Tribute of Respect, A, commemorative of the Worth and Sacrifice of John Brown of Osawatomie, quoted, 559.
Trimble, Governor of Ohio, 18.
Trowbridge, Colonel, 388.
Truth, Sojourner, 48.
Tubman, Harriet, colored, "the Moses of her people," 327, 396.
Tucker, Captain, 233.
Turner, Capt. Geo. W., slave-holder, effect of killing of, 440, 441; sketch of, 640 n. 33; 469, 479.
Turner, James, with Pate at Black Jack, 205.
Tyndale, Hector, 549, 550, 558, 561.

Uncle Tom's Cabin, 583.
Underground Railroad, Owen Brown, senior, an agent of, 14; 43, 267, 367, 386, 412.
United States Artillery, ordered to Harper's Ferry, 449.
United States marines at Harper's Ferry, 449, 450; storm engine house, 452-454.
United States troops, criticised by Atchison and others, 216, and by Free State writers, 217; reinforcements sent to Kansas, 251; ordered to Lawrence (Sept. 1856), 257.
Unseld, John, C., B's conversation with, 403; 404.
Updegraff, Captain, of Marion Rifles, 150.
Updegraff, H. Harrison, 121.
Updegraff, Dr. Wm. W., lieut. of Liberty Guards, 121, 240, 243, 245, 293.

INDEX   737

Vaill, Rev. H. L., 541, 592 n. 16.
Vallandigham, C. L., 456, 457, 458, 459, 460, 461.
Vandaman, S. V., 168.
Varney, Moses, and the "Floyd letter," 411, 412; 316.
Vigilance Committee of 52, of Kansas, 304.
Virginia General Assembly, report of Joint Investigating Com. of, 500, 567.
Virginia militia, behavior of, at Harper's Ferry, 464, 465.
Volunteer-regulars, B's covenant for enlistment of, 661 seqq.
Von Holst, Hermann, his *John Brown*, 334, 335.
Voorhees, Dan'l W., quoted as to B's trial, 483; defends John E. Cook, 570. *Letter to* Florence Hunter, 485.

Wadsworth, Frederick, 27.
Wadsworth, Tertius, 37.
Wager House, Harper's Ferry, scenes in, after the raid, 469, 470; 429, 437, 438, 440, 441, 442, 448.
Wakarusa Company, at Franklin, 212.
Wakarusa River, 116.
"Wakarusa War," end of, 126.
Wakefield, W. H. T., quoted, as to conditions in Kansas, 1854 to 1858, 601 n. 104.
Walker, Jona., alias "The Branded Hand," 594 n. 13.
Walker, Robert J., becomes governor of Kansas, 294; his previous career, 294; is opposed by pro-slavery party and Pres. Buchanan, and resigns, 295; and the election for delegate to Congress, 296; guarantees free election, 296; 306.
Walker, Capt. Samuel, memoir of, 89 n.; maltreated, as a Yankee, 111 n.; statements of, concerning Robinson's and Lane's connection with Pottawatomie murders, 184; rides from Nebraska City Kansasward with B and Lane, 228; deems B to have been then insane, 228; his talk with B concerning the murders, 228; as to correspondence between B and John Brown, Jr., 228, 229; commands Free State forces at "Fort" Titus, 231, 232; saves Titus's life after his surrender, 232, 233; his description of scene at Lawrence, 252. *Letters to* James Hanway, 184, 228, 229.
Walker Tariff, the, 59.
Walsh, Hugh S., acting-governor of Kansas, 364. *Letter to* Lewis Cass, 364.
"Ward, Artemus," his description of B in March, 1859, 392; and of Kagi, 392; his report of B's lecture in Cleveland, 392, 393.
Warren, Mr., creditor of Perkins and Brown, litigation with, 65, 66.
Wascott, Laura, 315.
Washington, George, Pres. of U. S., Harper's Ferry arsenal established during his term, 428; his Lafayette pistol and Frederick the Great sword, 431.
Washington, Col. Lewis W., and the historic sword and pistol, 431; compelled to deliver the sword to a negro, 431; made prisoner, 431; quoted as to B's bearing during siege of engine house, 453; 437, 438, 448, 455, 456, 463, 467, 468, 487.
Washington, Richard B., 439.
Waterloo, visited by B, 62.
Waters, R. P., 281.
Watertown (N. Y.) *Reformer*, 167.
Watson, Henry, colored, 412.
Wattles, Augustus, 277, 298, 353, 356, 358, 363, 371, 373, 375, 398, 575, 576. *Letters to* B, 293, 300; *from* B, 290, 292.
Wattles, Mrs. Aug., 371.
Wattles, J. O., 372.
Wayland, Francis, on B's oratory, 281, 282. *Letter to* F. B. Sanborn, 281.

Weaver, Capt. A. J., 364, 365.
Webster, Col. Fletcher, 585.
Weiner, Theodore, complains to B of ill-treatment by pro-slavery men, 151; in B's Pottawatomie party, 153–154; Salmon Brown's description of, 157, 158; Wilkinson and Sherman killed by Thompson and, 162, 164; not concerned in Sherman murder, according to Townsley, 162; was he the mysterious messenger? 175; and Orson Day, 178; his store plundered, 200; 155, 159, 177, 198, 210, 211.
Weiss, John, his *Life and Correspondence of Theodore Parker* quoted, 272.
"Well-matured Plan, The," 314.
Wellington, Duke of, Stocqueler's life of, 53.
Wells, Joseph, 37.
Western Despatch, and the Pottawatomie murders, 189.
Western Reporter, 99.
Western Reserve Bank, suit of, against Brown and others, 37–39.
Western Reserve College, denies admission to a colored man, 15.
Westfall, Dr., 200.
Westlands, B's curious manipulation of, in Western Reserve Bank litigation, 38–41.
Westport (Mo.) Border Times, its sensational announcement of news of Pottawatomie murders, 189; appeals to South for men and money, 189.
Wetmore brothers, 37.
Wharton, Lieutenant, 217.
Whedan, B., 13.
Whelan, Daniel, second prisoner taken at Harper's Ferry, 430.
Whipple, Charles, alias of Stevens, 224, 365. And see Stevens, Aaron Dwight.
White, Horace, and G. Smith's feigned insanity, 651 n. 83; 275, 276, 277, 357. *Letter to* B, 269.
White, Rev. Martin, represents Border Ruffians at settlers' meeting, 134; his report thereof to Shawnee Legislature, 134; as to A. Wilkinson, 156; leader of band that arrested Jason Brown, 194 seqq.; his house raided by Free State men, 234; kills Fred'k Brown, 241; his own version of the killing, 241, 242; B declines to take revenge on him, 357, 358; 90, 269, 270. *Letter to* Bates County *Standard*, 242.
Whiteman, John S., 163, 164.
Whitfield, Gen. J. W., pro-slavery candidate for governor of Kansas, elected by fraudulent votes, 94; elected delegate to Congress at election ordered by Shawnee Legislature, 106; seated by the House and ousted after report of Howard Com., 106, 107 and n.; and Col. Sumner, 208, 209; his men pillage Osawatomie, 212, 213; his election as delegate denied by Elections Com., and by the House, 226; 95, 211, 257. *Letter to* editor of *Border Times*, 193.
Whitman, Edmund B., B at his house in Kansas, 304; vexed at B's disappearance, 304; 255, 277, 294, 305, 307, 359. *Letter to* G. L. Stearns, 304; *from* H. B. Hurd, 360, G. L. Stearns, 304.
Whittier, John G., his *Le Marais du Cygne*, 349.
Wilberforce Institute, 327.
Wilder, D. W., his *Annals of Kansas*, 92; 183.
Wilkinson, Allen, member of Shawnee Legislature, his character from both sides, 156, 157; his murder by Thompson and Weiner described by his wife, 161, 162; and the Morse case, 174; 173, 180, 182, 192.
Wilkinson, Mrs. Allen, quoted, 156, 157, 161, 162.
Willard, A. P., Gov. of Indiana, 477, 483, 571.
Willard, Mrs. A. P., 571.

INDEX

Williams, Henry H., lieutenant of Liberty Guards, 121; member of Free State Legislature, 133; lieutenant in John Brown Jr.'s company, 149; his story of Pottawatomie, 149 seqq.; deposes John, Jr. from command, 150; declared by Salmon Brown to have led in the council that decided on necessity of Pottawatomie massacre, and to have prepared list of men to be killed, 152; secretary of public meeting at Osawatomie, 168; his attitude toward Pottawatomie expedition, 168 and n., 169; his claim to have been the mysterious messenger, 175; 166, 177. *Letter to C. A. Foster*, 133.
Williams, J. M. S., 280.
Williams, R. H., his *With the Border Ruffians*, 607 n. 100.
Williams, William, 249.
Williams, William, the first prisoner at Harper's Ferry, 429, 430, 432.
Willis, S. J., 575, 576, 580.
Wilson, George, Probate Judge, was he on B's proscribed list? 165.
Wilson, Henry, U. S. Senator from Mass., conversation with B, 399; 317, 318, 340, 342. *Letter to S. G. Howe*, 339; *from S. G. Howe*, 341.
Wilson, Rev. Norval, visits B in jail, 544.
Winchester Company, at Harper's Ferry, 444.
Winkley, Dr. J. W., his *John Brown the Hero*, quoted, 237, 238.
Wise, Barton H., his *Life of Henry A. Wise*, quoted, 466, 527, 547.
Wise, Henry A., Gov. of Virginia, notified by Garrett of attack on Harper's Ferry, 434; at Harper's Ferry, 444; quoted concerning B, 455; his "interview" with B, 455 seqq.; colloquy with B, 463; speech concerning behavior of Virginia militia, 463, 464; his later characterization of B, in light of his own capture of the same arsenal, 465, 466; quoted, 468, 469; after the raid, 469, 470; and the question of jurisdiction, 477, 478; receives much contradictory advice as to his course, 500 seqq.; declines to interfere with sentence, 503, 504; his message to the legislature, 504, 505, 517; weakness of his logic, 506; the question of B's insanity, 507–509; L. Spooner's scheme to kidnap, 514; warned of plots of rescue, 518; warning letters received by him, 519; effect of rescue scares on him, 521; calls out troops, 522; appeals to Pres. Buchanan, 523; his unfounded fears of a rescue, 524; criticized for excessive precautions taken, 526; sustained by legislative committee, 526; his conduct discussed, 526, 527; possible ulterior views in display of force at Charlestown, 526, 527; at Charlestown, 546; visits B in jail, 547, 548; and Mrs. Brown, 549, 550; in favor of leniency to E. Coppoc, 570; John Minor Botts quoted concerning 649 n. 50; 164, 293, 472, 474 and n., 479, 481, 485, 505 n., 528, 554, 559, 565, 572, 587, 588. *Letters to Mrs. Mary A. Brown*, 549, A. Hunter, 478, 504, 521, F. Wood, 503; *from Lydia M. Child*, 479, F. Wood, 502.
Wise, John S., his *End of an Era*, quoted, 474 n.
Wise, O. Jennings, prefers charges against Col. R. W. Baylor for inefficiency at Harper's Ferry, 464. *Letter to Col. J. T. Gibson*, 464.
Witherspoon, Rev. John, his works read by B, 16.
Wood, A. P., pursues B and his band of freed slaves, 381.
Wood, Fernando, urges that B be not hanged, 502. *Letter to Gov. Wise*, 502; *from Gov. Wise*, 503.
Wood, R. W., sergeant in Liberty Guards, 121.
Wood, Sam'l N., leader of rescuers of Jacob Branson, 113; arrested by Sheriff Jones, and escapes, 140; indicted for treason, 142; 132.
Wood, Capt. Thos. J., his cruelty to John Brown, Jr., 195, 196; searches vainly for B after Pottawatomie, 196; later, a distinguished Northern general, 197; captures many of Col. Harvey's force after fight at Hickory Point, 256; 210.
Woodruff, Col. Daniel, B tries to obtain his co-operation in his Virginia project, 54, 55.
Woodson, Dan'l, Sec'y of Kansas Territory, his alleged letter to Gen. Eastin denounced as forgery, 116; acting-governor of Kansas, 217; Col. Sumner and the dispersal of the Free State Legislature, 217–220; his proclamation, 218, 250, not enforced against Atchison's and Reid's force, 250; orders Cooke to invest Topeka, 250, 251; 252, 257. *Letter from Col. E. V. Sumner*, 218.
Wool-growing, effect of Walker tariff on, 59; Perkins and Brown's operations in, 59 seqq.
"Words of Advice" for the Gileadites, 50, 52.
Workman, Samuel, 387.
Wooster (Ohio), Bank of, sues B, 37.
Wright, S. H., 293.
Wyandotte City Western Argus, quoted, 370.

Yankees, frowned upon, merely as such, in Kansas, 111.
Yelton, John, brings warning of attack on Osawatomie, 240; 121, 246.
Young, Rev. Joshua, 558 n., 561, 562.

Zion Methodist Church, in Springfield, Mass., attended by B, 68.

NOTE. This index was compiled for the author by Mr. George B. Ives of the Riverside Press, to whom the author makes special acknowledgment for his skill and thoroughness.